India

a travel survival kit

**Geoff Crowther
Prakash A Raj
Tony Wheeler
Hugh Finlay
Bryn Thomas**

India – a travel survival kit

5th edition

Published by

Lonely Planet Publications
Head Office: PO Box 617, Hawthorn, Vic 3122, Australia
Branches: PO Box 2001A, Berkeley, CA 94702, USA
             12 Barley Mow Passage, Chiswick, London W4 4PH, UK

Printed by
Colorcraft Ltd, Hong Kong

Photographs by

Michelle Coxall (MC)	Geoff Crowther (GC)	Greg Elms (GE)	Hugh Finlay (HF)
Faith Harper (FH)	Joost Hoetjes (JH)	Mal Holliday (MH)	Richard I'Anson (RI)
Hilarie Kavanagh (HK)	John Preston (JP)	Bryn Thomas (BT)	Jane Thomas (JT)
Paul Tracey (PT)	Gary Weare (GW)	Paul Wentford (PW)	Tony Wheeler (TW)

Front cover: Palace of the Winds, Jaipur, Rajasthan, The Photographic Library of Australia Pty Ltd (HK)
Back cover: Taj Mahal (PW)

First Published
October 1981

This Edition
July 1993

Although the authors and publisher have tried to make the information as accurate as possible, they accept no responsibility for any loss, injury or inconvenience sustained by any person using this book.

National Library of Australia Cataloguing in Publication Data

Finlay, Hugh
India: a travel survival kit.

5th ed.
Includes index.
ISBN 0 86442 179 6.

1. India – Guidebooks. I. Crowther, Geoff, 1944- . II. Thomas, Bryn, 1959- .
III. Title. (Series: Lonely Planet travel survival kit).

915.40452

Geoff Crowther

Born in Yorkshire, England, Geoff started his travelling days as a teenage hitchhiker in search of the miraculous. After many short trips around Europe and two years in Asia and Africa, Geoff became involved with the London alternative information centre BIT in the late '60s. With Lonely Planet, which he joined in 1977, Geoff has written or collaborated on guides to Africa, South America, Malaysia, Brunei, Taiwan, Korea, East Africa, Kenya, Morocco, Algeria and Tunisia.

Geoff, Hyung Pun and their son Ashley currently live in a solar-powered, shingle-roofed, pole-and-beam bushman's paradise along with their goats in a house which they built over many years in the rainforests of northern New South Wales, Australia. When not travelling, Geoff continues building, landscaping, pursuing noxious weeds, playing guitar and brewing elderberry wine.

Prakash A Raj

Prakash was born in Nepal and studied for two years in Varanasi where he learnt to speak fluent Hindi. He spent five years at university in the USA and a year in the Netherlands. He travelled extensively in Europe and returned to Nepal where he worked on the Kathmandu English-language daily as a journalist and also for the Nepalese government's planning agency. Prakash has also worked for the OECD in Paris, the UN secretariat in New York and is now working for the UNHCR in Asia. Prakash has written several books about Nepal and his life there in both English and Nepali.

Tony Wheeler

Tony was born in England but grew up in Pakistan, the Bahamas and the USA. He returned to England to do a degree in engineering at Warwick University, worked as an automotive design engineer, returned to university to complete an MBA in London, then dropped out on the Asian overland trail with his wife Maureen.

Eventually settling in Australia they've been travelling, writing and publishing guidebooks ever since, having set up Lonely Planet Publications in the mid-1970s. Travel for the Wheelers is considerably enlivened by their daughter Tashi and their son Kieran.

Hugh Finlay

After a failed career in engineering, Hugh set off around Australia in the mid '70s, working at everything from parking cars to diamond prospecting in outback South Australia. He spent three years travelling on three continents, all financed by Arab petrobucks earned working on an irrigation project in Saudi Arabia. He finally descended from the ozone in 1985 and joined Lonely Planet soon after.

Hugh has also written Lonely Planet's guide to Jordan & Syria, with Geoff has written guides to North Africa and Kenya, and has also worked on LP's guides to Australia and Malaysia, Singapore & Brunei.

Bryn Thomas

Born in Zimbabwe, where he grew up on a farm, Bryn contracted an incurable case of wanderlust during camping holidays by the Indian Ocean in Mozambique.

An anthropology degree at Durham University in England earned him a job polishing the leaves of pot plants in London. He has also worked as a ski-lift operator in Colorado, encyclopaedia seller in South Dakota and English teacher in Cairo, Singapore and Tokyo. Travel on four continents has included a 2500-km Andean cycling trip and five visits to India.

Bryn's first guide, the *Trans-Siberian Handbook*, was short listed for the Thomas Cook Guidebook of the Year awards. He is currently working on the new LP guide to Britain.

This Book

When the first edition of this book emerged in 1981 it was the biggest, most complicated and most expensive project we'd tackled at Lonely Planet. It began with an exploratory trip to south India by Tony and Maureen to see what information would be needed. The following year Geoff, Prakash Raj, Tony and Maureen returned to India and spent a combined total of about a year of more-or-less nonstop travel. Succeeding editions were researched by Tony, Prakash, Geoff, and Hugh Finlay.

The first edition exceeded all our hopes and expectations: it instantly became our best-selling guide. In Britain it won the Thomas Cook Guidebook of the Year award and in India it became the most popular guide to the country – a book used even by Indians to explore their own country. It has continued to be one of Lonely Planet's most popular and successful guides.

This Edition

For this fifth edition of *India – a travel survival kit*, we once again returned and comprehensively covered the country from one end to the other. Hugh covered Goa, Rajasthan, Gujarat, Haryana, New Delhi and Himachal Pradesh; Geoff roamed the south, Sikkim and North-Eastern Region; while Bryn Thomas covered the rest, including a foray to Kashmir and Ladakh. Hugh also handled the final integration of the three writers' material and completed much of the additional desk research.

In addition, most of the maps for the book were completely redrawn, with topography being added to the province maps and colour country maps being produced for the first time. Overall this edition features an enhanced use of colour photographs. The authors also put a lot of effort into researching unusual and interesting aspects of Indian life and culture.

Apart from the three writers, thanks must also go to a number of additional contributors including Britons Ken Twyford and Gerald Smewing, on whose information the motorcycling section is largely based, ditto for American Ann Sorrel and the cycling section, to Mark Carter who wrote the 'gricing' section about India's wonderful railway steam engines, and to Murray D Bruce & Constance S Leap Bruce for their contribution to the Fauna & Flora section.

Last, but by no means least, thanks to the many, many travellers who took the time to write in and give us their opinions on what was good, bad or indifferent about the previous editions. We've taken all suggestions on board, and tried to accommodate as many as possible. A list of all your names is included on pages 1091 to 1096.

Acknowledgements

From Geoff Geoff would like to specially thank several people who made this particular trip either enjoyable and interesting and/or who helped in various ways, consciously or otherwise, by contributing factual information or increasing his appreciation of Indian culture as well as his appreciation of what motivates Westerners to visit India.

Bob Bathie of Burringbar, Australia, my travelling companion, for his freshness of vision, his tolerance of what would drive others to distraction, his assistance, and his rejection of bullshit of any kind from whatever source. May you one day swap your hybrid nationality for membership of the Sioux Nation!

Luis & Nandita de Souza and their respective parents of Panjim, Goa, India, for their enduring friendship, matchless hospitality and for looking after Bob while he 'waited for money' (which never arrived!).

Ms Tsering Dolma of Gangtok, India, receptionist at the Hotel Tibet, and Mr Kunzang Chewong Denzongpa, also of Gangtok, both of whom in their separate ways made our stay in the Sikkimese capital so pleasant.

Jan King and Tom Harriman of Sebastopol, California, USA, those inveterate travellers who had been writing to me for years but whom I'd never met until I finally bumped into them quite by chance in Gangtok. Many thanks for the information on western Sikkim.

Jeremy Smith of Calcutta, India, for being a good friend and introducing us to the social life of inner Calcutta.

Susan Mathews and Ravi Shankar, students, of Bangalore, India, for their good humour and insight on being young and unestablished in contemporary India.

Gail Fairbanks of Nova Scotia, Canada, for her companionship and disregard of ageism in the search for the miraculous.

Harry Gröber of Munich, Germany, for his sardonic humour and savoir-faire 'beyond the Black Stump' in Karnataka and in the beverage halls of central Bombay. May you never have to face another luke-warm Kingfisher.

And to all my so-called buddies who never got it together to even write a postcard despite being provided with a fistful of forwarding addresses.

From Hugh Hugh would again like to thank Abhijeet and Smita Roy for their help and hospitality in Bombay.

From Bryn Bryn would like to thank Jane Thomas and Katie Lorimer for being such tolerant travelling companions (most of the time) and for their numerous helpful insights, especially into matters culinary and alcoholic. Thanks also to all the other travellers I met along the way, particularly Eddie Austin, Mary Jack (for testing the health services in Ladakh), Jo Brooks, Julie Leslie, Dean Park, Kathy (in the Abdul Khalique, Calcutta) and Chris Jenney (in Khan's, Bayswater).

Of those living and working in India, I'd like to thank Gajendra Kumar in Varanasi, Nils Finn Munch-Petersen in Port Blair, Bob Wright in Calcutta, James Young at Kanha, Mani Ria Chhetri at the Darjeeling Youth Hostel, Kabir Saxena in Bodhgaya, Col and Mrs Nagu in Narsinghpur, Raju Singh in Raipur, Rigzin Jura in Leh and Bubu in Puri. To the driver of the blue Ambassador from Daman & Diu, last seen under the bonnet by the roadside in the middle of Madhya Pradesh – thanks for getting us that far.

Thanks also from all of the authors to editors Michelle Coxall and Greg Alford, and designers Jane Hart, Tamsin Wilson, Rachel Black and Ann Jeffree for all their help on this edition.

From the Publisher
This book was edited by Michelle Coxall and Greg Alford. Mapping, design, illustration and layout was coordinated by Jane Hart, with assistance from Tamsin Wilson, Rachel Black and Ann Jeffree. Artiste extraordinaire Tamsin Wilson drew the majority of the illustrations, before fleeing to the wilds of New South Wales for well-deserved R&R. For proofing and final checking, thanks to Sharan Kaur, Simone Calderwood, Kristin Odijk and Sue Mitra. Vicki Beale checked the final artwork, and Chris Lee Ack assisted

Jane Hart with valuable technical input during Jane's production of the colour country maps. Indexing was done by Sharon Wertheim. Special thanks to James Lyon for luring Jane and Michelle out from under their desks with promises of chocolate when the pressure was on.

Thanks also to the aptly named Richard Everist, LP's Nepal researcher and writer, for extra info on border crossings; to Carolyn Miller from our US office and Andrea Webster from our UK office for help with air fares and tours to India from their corners of the world. The cartoons were drawn by LP's resident Charlie Manson lookalike, Peter Morris; climate charts were adapted by our ineffable computer wizard, Dan Levin.

For supplying valuable additional information and advice, LP would also like to thank: David Bradley (Latrobe University, Melbourne) for information on travel permits, and travel in Sikkim and West Bengal; G S Sachdev at the Government of India Tourist Office, Sydney; Faith Harper (Yelgun, NSW) for information about and photos of Kathakali dancing; Dayasankar and Selvi for assistance with the Tamil language section; Asha & Mario Lobo for Goa information.

Finally, we'd like to thank the authors for completing a big job with a minimum of fuss: to Bryn ('guru') Thomas, for a splendid first effort; to Hugh ('Hubert') Finlay for patiently dealing with reams of nitpicking editorial queries and coordinating the whole project; and, of course, the legendary Geoff Crowther (for whom no nickname is sufficient) – hope the arm's better Geoff!

Warning & Request

Things change – prices go up, schedules change, good places go bad and bad places go bankrupt – nothing stays the same. So if you find things better or worse, recently opened or long since closed, please write and tell us and help make the next edition better.

Your letters will be used to help update future editions and, where possible, important changes will also be included in a Stop Press section in reprints.

We greatly appreciate all information that is sent to us by travellers. Back at Lonely Planet we employ a hard-working readers' letters team to sort through the many letters we receive. The best ones will be rewarded with a free copy of the next edition or another Lonely Planet guide if you prefer. We give away lots of books, but, unfortunately, not every letter/postcard receives one.

Contents

Map Legend

BOUNDARIES

▬ ▪ ▬ ▪ ▬ ▪ ▬	........International Boundary
▬ ▪▪ ▬ ▪▪ ▬	................Internal Boundary
++++++++++++	....National Park or Reserve
▬ ▬ ▬ ▬ ▬ ▬	.........................The Equator
....	.........................The Tropics

SYMBOLS

◉	NATIONAL	.......................National Capital
●	PROVINCIAL	........Provincial or State Capital
●	Major	.............................Major Town
●	Minor	.............................Minor Town
■		.........................Places to Stay
▼		............................Places to Eat
⊠		................................Post Office
✈		....Airport
i		.....................Tourist Information
⊖		.............Bus Station or Terminal
66		............Highway Route Number
✚		......................................Hospital
✳		....Lookout
🛆		...................................Lighthouse
⋈		...................................Shipwreck
▲		.........................Camping Area
⊓		.............................Picnic Area
⌂		...........................Hut or Chalet
▲		..........................Mountain or Hill
⊢⊣		.........................Railway Station
═		................................Road Bridge
+++++		.............................Railway Bridge
⇒ ⇐		..............................Road Tunnel
⊶⟩ ⟨⊶		...........................Railway Tunnel
⁀⁀⁀⁀		....................Escarpment or Cliff
‿		....Pass
⊓⊔⊓		.............Ancient or Historic Wall

ROUTES

▬▬▬▬	.......Major Road or Highway
▬ ▬ ▬ ▬	.........Unsealed Major Road
▬▬▬▬	........................Sealed Road
▬ ▬ ▬ ▬	.....Unsealed Road or Track
════	.............................City Street
+++++++++	...................................Railway
●━◉━●	...................................Subway
▬▬▬▬	...........................Walking Track
▬ ▬ ▬ ▬	................................Ferry Route
+|+|+|+|+	........Cable Car or Chair Lift

HYDROGRAPHIC FEATURES

〰	.....................River or Creek
⌒ ⌒ ⌒	..............Intermittent Stream
⬭ ⬭	........Lake, Intermittent Lake
〜	..........................Coast Line
〜	....................................Spring
〜 #	..............................Waterfall
⊥⊥ ⊥⊥ ⊥⊥	..................................Swamp
▓▓▓	................Salt Lake or Reef
▨▨▨	..................................Glacier

OTHER FEATURES

▒▒▒	Park, Garden or National Park
⊠	........................Built Up Area
▨	... Market or Pedestrian Mall
⊠	.........Plaza or Town Square
+++++	..............................Cemetery

Note: not all symbols displayed above appear in this book

Introduction

India, it is often said, is not a country but a continent. From north to south and east to west, the people are different, the languages are different, the customs are different, the country is different. There are few countries on earth with the enormous variety that India has to offer. It's a place that somehow gets into your blood. Love it or hate it you can never ignore India. It's not an easy country to handle, and more than a few visitors are only too happy to finally get on an aircraft and fly away. Yet a year later they'll be hankering to get back.

It all comes back to that amazing variety – India is as vast as it is crowded, as luxurious as it is squalid. The plains are as flat and featureless as the Himalaya are high and spectacular, the food as terrible as it can be magnificent, the transport as exhilarating as it can be boring and uncomfortable. Nothing is ever quite the way you expect it to be.

India is far from the easiest country in the world to travel around. It can be hard going, the poverty will get you down, Indian bureaucracy would try the patience of even a Hindu saint, and the most experienced travellers find themselves at the end of their tempers at some point in India. Yet it's all worth it.

Very briefly, India is a triangle with the top formed by the mighty Himalayan mountain chain. Here you will find the intriguing Tibetan region of Ladakh and the astonishingly beautiful Himalayan areas of Kashmir, Himachal Pradesh, the Garhwal of Uttar Pradesh and the Darjeeling and Sikkim regions. South of this is the flat Ganges basin with the colourful and comparatively affluent Punjab to the north-west, the capital city New Delhi and important tourist attractions like Agra (with the Taj Mahal), Khajuraho, Varanasi and the holy Ganges. This plain reaches the sea at the northern end of the Bay of Bengal where you find teeming Calcutta, a city which seems to sum up all of India's enormous problems.

South of this northern plain the Deccan plateau rises. Here you will find cities that mirror the rise and fall of the Hindu and Muslim kingdoms, and the modern metropolis that their successors, the British, built at Bombay. India's story is one of many different kingdoms competing with each other, and this is never more clear than in places like Bijapur, Mandu, Golconda and other centres in central India. Finally, there is the steamy south where Muslim influence reached only fleetingly. Here Hinduism was least altered by outside influences and is at its most exuberant. The temple towns of the south are quite unlike those of the north and are superbly colourful.

Basically India is what you make of it and what you want it to be. If you want to see temples, there are temples in profusion with enough styles and types to confuse anybody. If it's history you want India has plenty of it; the forts, abandoned cities, ruins, battlefields and monuments all have their tales to tell. If you simply want to lie on the beach there are

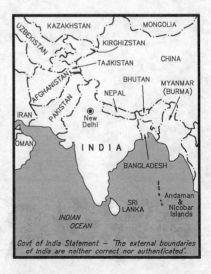

Govt of India Statement – 'The external boundaries of India are neither correct nor authenticated'.

enough of those to satisfy the most avid sun worshipper. If walking and the open air is your thing then head for the trekking routes of the Himalaya, some of which are as wild and deserted as you could ask for. If you simply want to meet the real India you'll come face to face with it all the time – a trip on Indian trains and buses may not always be fun, but it certainly is an experience. India is not a place you simply and clinically 'see'; it's a total experience, an assault on the senses, a place you'll never forget.

A	B
C	D

A (JP)
B (GE)
C (RI)
D (RI)

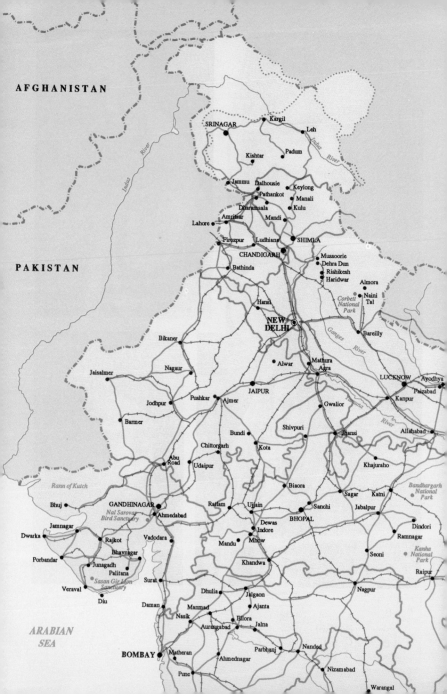

NORTHERN
INDIA

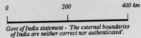

0   200   400 km

*Govt of India statement - 'The external boundaries
of India are neither correct nor authenticated'.*

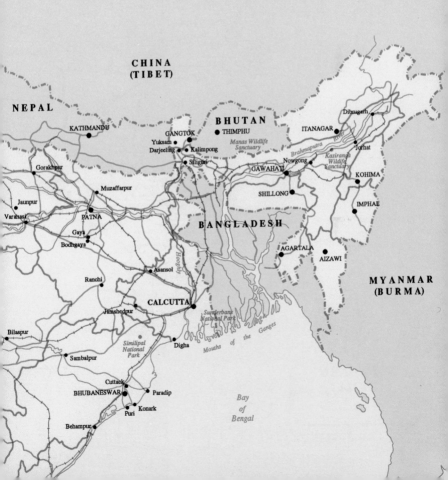

**CHINA
(TIBET)**

NEPAL

KATHMANDU

Gorakhpur

Jaunpur

Varanasi

Muzaffarpur

PATNA

Gaya

Bodhgaya

Ranchi

Bilaspur

Jamshedpur

Sambalpur

*Similipal
National
Park*

Cuttack

BHUBANESWAR

Behampur

Puri

Konark

Paradip

Digha

Mouths of the Ganges

*Sunderbans
National Park*

CALCUTTA

Asansol

Hooghly

BANGLADESH

GANGTOK

Yuksam

Darjeeling

Kalimpong

Siliguri

BHUTAN

THIMPHU

*Manas Wildlife
Sanctuary*

GAWAHATI

SHILLONG

AGARTALA

AIZAWI

ITANAGAR

Dibrugarh

Jorhat

Nowgong

Brahmaputra

*Kaziranga
Wildlife
Sanctuary*

KOHIMA

IMPHAL

**MYANMAR
(BURMA)**

*Bay
of
Bengal*

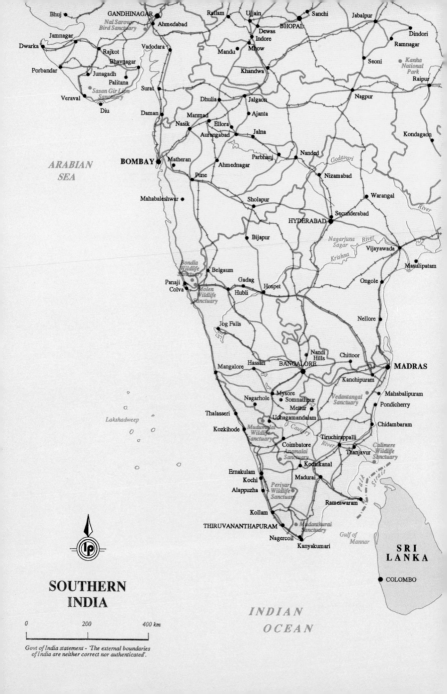

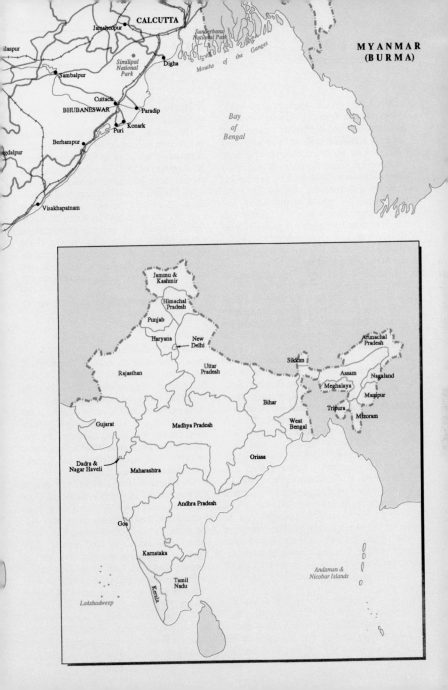

Facts about the Country

India is one of the few countries in the world today in which the social and religious structures which define its identity remain intact and have continued to do so for at least 4000 years despite invasions, famines, religious persecutions, political upheavals and many other cataclysms. To describe it as a land of contrasts is to state the obvious. There are many countries which would qualify for such a description in terms of the different ethnic groups, languages, religions, geography and traditions which make up the whole, but few can match the vast scale and diversity to be found in India.

Change is inevitably taking place as modern technology reaches further and further into the fabric of society, yet essentially village India remains much the same as it has for thousands of years. So resilient is its social and religious institutions and, at the same time, so static, that it has either absorbed or thrown off all attempts to radically change or destroy them. Even in the fast-paced modern cities like Bombay, Bangalore and Delhi, what appears to be a complete change of attitude and lifestyle is only the surface gloss. Underneath, the age-old verities, loyalties and obligations still rule people's lives.

There is possibly no other country where religion is so inextricably intertwined with every aspect of life. Coming to understand it can be a long process littered with pitfalls, particularly for those educated in the Western liberal tradition with its basis in logic. For those people, 'Indian logic' can often seem bizarre, convoluted and even exasperating. Yet, in its own way, it encompasses a unique cosmology which is both holistic and coherent as well as being fascinating.

It's well to remember that India was the birthplace of two of the world's great religions (Hinduism and Buddhism) and one of its smallest (Jainism). It's also home to one of the world's few remaining communities of Parsis, adherents of the faith of Zoroastrianism.

The modern state itself is a relatively recent creation born out of a people's desire to throw off the yoke of colonialism. Even the mightiest of India's ancient civilisations did not encompass all of modern India, and today it is still as much a country of diversities as of unities. You may hear it said that there are many Indias. In terms of ethnic origin, language and geographical location, that is undoubtedly true and it sometimes bedevils efforts at creating a national consciousness. Yet, ever since Independence, India has remained the world's largest democracy.

All these factors combine to ensure India's historical importance.

HISTORY
Indus Valley Civilisation
India's first major civilisation flourished for 1000 years from around 2500 BC along the Indus River valley in what is now Pakistan. Its great cities were Mohenjodaro and Harappa, where a civilisation of great complexity developed. The major city sites were only discovered during this century but other, lesser cities have been subsequently unearthed at sites like Lothal, near Ahmedabad in India.

The origins of Hinduism can be traced all the way back to this early civilisation. Here the society was ruled by priests rather than by kings and it was they who interceded with the gods, dictated social modes and determined such issues as land tenure. Clay figurines suggesting worship of a Mother Goddess (later personified as Kali) and a male, three-faced god sitting in the attitude of a yogi attended by four animals (the prehistoric Siva) as well as black stone pillars (phallic worship associated with Siva) have all been found there. Even at this time, certain animals were regarded as sacred, the most prominent being the humped bull (later,

Siva's mount). The traditional Hindu fear of pollution and the need for ritual washing is also reflected in the intricate system of drains found at Harappa. There is even evidence of an organised system of garbage collection!

Comparatively little is known about the development and eventual demise of this civilisation. Their script has still not been deciphered, nor is it known why such an advanced civilisation collapsed so quickly following invasion by the Aryans.

Early Invasions & the Rise of Religions

The Aryan invaders swept south from central Asia between 1500 and 200 BC until they controlled the whole of northern India as far as the Vindhya belt of hills, in the process pushing the original inhabitants (the Dravidians) further south. The invaders brought with them their nature gods, among whom the ones of fire and battle were predominant, as well as their cattle-raising and meat-eating traditions.

Yet, even by the 8th century BC, the priestly caste had succeeded in reasserting its supremacy and the nature gods were displaced or absorbed into the concept of a universal soul (Brahman) to which the *atman* (individual soul) was identical. These events are recorded in the literature of the time as the victory of Brahma over Indra (formerly the goddess of food and the law but later of thunder and battle). Indra supposedly led a bizarre double life, being a woman for one phase of the moon and then changing overnight and being a man for the next phase. It was also during this period of transition that the Hindu sacred scriptures, the *Vedas*, were written (1500-1200 BC).

The social order which reflected the assimilation of the Aryans and the supremacy of the priests became consolidated in the caste system, which survives to this day despite efforts by the central government to enhance the status of those at the bottom of the pile. Control over this social order was maintained by extremely strict rules designed to secure the position of the Brahmins (priests). Elaborate taboos were established concerning marriage, diet, travel, modes of eating and drinking and social intercourse. Within the system, each caste adopted its own unique set of rules with which to assert its superiority over those considered to be inferior. Anyone disregarding the rules would be outcast and driven away. Yet the priests could not have it all their own way. Despite the strictures concerning respect for the priests and for all animal life, the meat-eating traditions of the Aryans had to be accommodated. It's essentially from these times that the vague division between the meat-eating north and vegetarian south stems.

During the period when the Aryans were consolidating their hold on northern India, the heartland narrowly missed two other invasions from the West. The first was by the Persian king, Darius (521-486 BC), who annexed the Punjab and Sind to his empire but went no further. Not long afterwards, Alexander the Great reached India in his epic march from Greece during 326 BC, but his troops refused to march further than the Beas River, the easternmost extent of the Persian Empire he had conquered, and he turned back without extending his power into India itself. The most lasting reminder of his appearance in the East was the development of Gandharan art, that intriguing mixture of Grecian artistic ideals with the new religious beliefs of Buddhism.

Buddhism itself arose around 500 BC contemporaneously with Jainism and presented Brahmanical Hinduism with its greatest challenge. The appeal of both of these cosmologies was that they rejected the *Vedas* and condemned caste, though, unlike the Buddhists, the Jains never denied their Hindu heritage and their faith never made any converts beyond India.

Buddhism, however, drove a radical swathe through the spiritual and social body of Hinduism and enjoyed spectacular growth after Ashoka embraced it and declared it the state religion. Nevertheless, it gradually lost touch with the general population and faded as Hinduism underwent a revival between 200 and 800 AD based on devotion to a personal god represented today by sects based on Rama and Krishna *(avatars,* or manifestations, of Vishnu). Yet such was the appeal of the greatest of India's spiritual teachers that the Buddha could not be simply sidelined and forgotten but had to be incorporated into the Hindu pantheon as yet another of the avatars of Vishnu. It was a prime example of the way in which Hinduism has absorbed spiritual competitors and heretical ideologies.

The Mauryas & Ashoka

Two centuries before Alexander made his long march east, an Indian kingdom had started to develop in the north of India. It expanded into the vacuum created by Alexander's departure when Chandragupta Maurya's empire came to power in 321 BC. From its capital at the site of present-day Patna, the Mauryan Empire eventually spread across northern India. The Mauryas set up a very rigid and well-organised empire with a huge standing army paid for directly by the emperor, as well as an efficient bureaucracy which kept tabs on everyone for the collection of taxes, tithes and agricultural produce. There were heavy penalties for those who evaded taxes and an extensive system of spies, yet corruption was rife and life for the ordinary peasant remained unrelentingly harsh.

Under Emperor Ashoka, one of the classic figures of Indian history, the empire reached its peak and in 262 BC he was converted to Buddhism. Throughout his kingdom he left pillars and rock-carved edicts which delineate to this day the enormous span of his empire. Ashokan edicts and pillars can be seen in Delhi, Gujarat, Orissa, Sarnath in Uttar Pradesh, and at Sanchi in Madhya Pradesh.

Ashoka also sent missions abroad; in Sri Lanka his name is revered since he sent his brother as a missionary to carry Buddhism to that land. The development of art and sculpture also flourished during his rule, and his standard, which topped many of his pillars, is now the seal of the modern state of India. Under Ashoka the Mauryan Empire controlled more of India than probably any

Famous figure of yakshi maiden, Sanchi (BT)

subsequent ruler prior to the Moghuls or the British. Following his death in 232 BC the empire rapidly disintegrated and finally collapsed in 184 BC.

An Interlude, then the Guptas

A number of empires rose and fell following the collapse of the Mauryas. The successors to Alexander's kingdoms in the north-west expanded their power into the Punjab and this later developed into the Gandharan kingdom. In the south-east and east the Andhras or Telugus expanded inland from the coast, while the Mauryan Empire was directly replaced by the Sungas, who ruled from 184 to 70 BC. During this period many more Buddhist structures were completed and the great cave temples of central India were commenced. This was the period of the 'lesser vehicle' or Hinayana Buddhism, in which the Buddha could never be directly shown but was alluded to through symbols such as stupas, footprints, trees or elephants.

Although this form of Buddhism probably continued until about 400 AD, it was already being supplanted by 100 AD by the 'greater vehicle' or Mahayana Buddhism.

In 319 AD Chandragupta II founded the Gupta Empire, the first phase of which became known as the Imperial Guptas. His successors extended their power over northern India, first from Patna and later from other capitals in north India, such as Ayodhya. The Imperial Guptas gave way to the later Guptas in 455 AD but the Gupta period continued to 606 AD. The arts flourished during this period, with some of the finest work being done at Ajanta, Ellora, Sanchi and Sarnath. Poetry and literature also experienced a golden age. Towards the end of the Gupta period, however, Buddhism and Jainism both began to decline and Hinduism began to rise in popularity once more.

The invasions of the White Huns signalled the end of this era of history, although at first they were repelled by the Guptas. They had earlier driven the Gandharas from the northwest region, close to Peshawar, into Kashmir. North India broke up into a number of separate Hindu kingdoms and was not really unified again until the coming of the Muslims.

Meanwhile in the South

A continuing theme of Indian history has been that events in one part of the country do not necessarily affect those in another. The kingdoms that rose and fell in the north of the country generally had no influence or connection with those in the south. While Buddhism and, to a lesser extent, Jainism were displacing Hinduism in the centre and north of India, Hinduism continued to flourish in the south.

The south's prosperity was based upon its long-established trading links with other civilisations. The Egyptians and later the Romans both traded by sea with the south of India and, later still, strong links were formed with South-East Asia. For a time Buddhism and later Hinduism flourished in the Indonesian islands and the people of the region looked towards India as their cultural mentor. The *Ramayana*, that most famous of Hindu epics, is today told and retold in various forms in many South-East Asian countries. Today, only the island of Bali remains Hindu and though it's clearly recognisable as such, its isolation from the heartland of Hinduism has resulted in considerable modification.

Other outside influences which came to the south of India in this period included St Thomas the Apostle who is said to have arrived in Kerala in 52 AD. To this day there is a strong Christian influence in the region.

Great empires that rose in the south included the Cholas, Pandyas, Cheras, Chalukyas and Pallavas. The Chalukyas ruled mainly over the Deccan region of central India, although at times their power extended further north. With a capital at Badami in Karnataka, they ruled from 550 to 753 AD before falling to the Rashtrakutas – only to rise again in 972 and continue their rule through to 1190. Further south, the Pallavas pioneered Dravidian architecture with its exuberant, almost baroque, style. They also carried Indian culture to Java in Indonesia, Thailand and Cambodia.

In 850 AD the Cholas rose to power and gradually superseded the Pallavas. They too were great builders, as their temple at Thanjavur indicates. They also carried their power overseas and, under the reign of Raja Raja (985-1014 AD), controlled almost the whole of southern India, the Deccan, Sri Lanka and parts of the Malay peninsula and the Sumatran-based Srivijaya kingdom.

First Muslim Invasions

While the Hindu kingdoms ruled in the south and Buddhism was fading in the north, Muslim power was creeping towards India from the Middle East. In less than a century after the death of the Prophet Mohammed, there were raids into the Sind and even to Gujarat by Arabs carrying, as Mohammed had recommended, the Koran and the sword.

Muslim power first made itself strongly felt on the subcontinent with the raids of Mahmud of Ghazni. Today Ghazni is just a grubby little town between Kabul and Kandahar in Afghanistan, but from 1001 AD Mahmud conducted raids on virtually an annual basis. His army would descend upon India, destroying infidel temples and carrying off everything of value that could be moved. In 1033, after his death, one of his successors actually took Varanasi; but in 1038 the Seljuk Turks, also expanding eastwards, took Ghazni and the raids into India soon ceased.

These early visits were no more than banditry and it was not until 1192 that Muslim power arrived on a permanent basis. In that year Mohammed of Ghori, who had been expanding his powers across the Punjab, broke into India and took Ajmer. The following year his general Qutb-ud-din took Varanasi and then Delhi and, after Mohammed of Ghori was killed in 1206, he became the first of the Sultans of Delhi. Within 20 years they had brought the whole of the Ganges basin under their control, but the Sultans of Delhi were never consistent in their powers. With each new ruler the kingdom grew or shrank depending on personal abilities.

In 1297, Ala-ud-din Khilji pushed the borders south into Gujarat; his general subsequently moved further south, but could not maintain the extension. In 1338, Mohammed Tughlaq decided to move his capital south from Delhi to Daulatabad, near Aurangabad in Maharashtra, but having marched most of Delhi's population south, eventually had to return north. Soon after, the Bahmani Kingdom arose here and the Delhi Sultanate began to retreat north, only to be further weakened when Timur (Tamerlane) made a devastating raid from Samarkand into India in 1398. From then on the power of this Muslim kingdom steadily contracted, until it was supplanted by another Muslim kingdom, that of the Moghuls.

The Muslims were a somewhat different breed of invader. Unlike previous arrivals, they retained their own identity and the contempt which they heaped on their infidel subjects prevented their absorption into the prevailing Hindu religious and social systems. Nevertheless, Hinduism survived and Islam was to find India relatively infertile ground for conversion, so that by the 20th century, after 800 years of Muslim domination, only 25% of the population had converted to Islam.

The Muslims, too, could not rule without Hindu assistance so that many Hindus had to be inducted into the bureaucracy. This resulted in the development of a common language, Urdu, which is a combination of Persian vocabulary and Hindi grammar using Perso-Arabic script. It remains the language of large parts of northern India and of Pakistan.

Meanwhile in the South (again)

Once again events in the south of India took a different path than in the north. Just as the Aryan invasions never reached the south, so the early Muslim invasions failed to permanently affect events there. Between 1000 and 1300 AD the Hoysala Empire, with centres at Belur, Halebid and Somnathpur, was at its peak but fell to a predatory raid by Mohammed Tughlaq in 1328, and then to the combined opposition of other Hindu kingdoms.

Two other great kingdoms developed in the north of modern-day Karnataka – one Muslim and one Hindu. With its beautiful capital at Hampi, the Hindu kingdom of Vijayanagar was founded in 1336. It was probably the strongest Hindu kingdom in India during the time the Muslim Sultans of Delhi were dominating the north of the country. Meanwhile, the Bahmani Muslim kingdom also developed, but in 1489 it split into five separate kingdoms at Berar, Ahmednagar, Bijapur, Golconda and Ahmedabad. In 1520 Vijayanagar took Bijapur, but in 1565 the kingdom's Muslim opponents combined to destroy Vijayanagar in the epic Battle of Talikota. Later the Bahmani kingdoms were to fall to the Moghuls.

The Moghuls

Only Ashoka is as giant a figure in Indian history as the Moghul emperors. These

Jain temples, Khajuraho (BT)

larger-than-life individuals ushered in another golden age of building, arts and literature and spread their control over India to an extent rivalled only by Ashoka and the British. Their rise to power was rapid but their decline was equally quick. There were only six great Moghuls; after Aurangzeb the rest were emperors in name only.

The Moghuls did more than simply rule, however, they had a passion for building which resulted in some of the greatest buildings in India – Shah Jahan's magnificent Taj Mahal ranks as one of the wonders of the world. Art and literature also flourished under the Moghuls and the magnificence of their court stunned early European visitors.

The six great Moghuls and their reigns were:

Babur	1527-1530
Humayun	1530-1556
Akbar	1556-1605
Jehangir	1605-1627
Shah Jahan	1627-1658
Aurangzeb	1658-1707

Emperor Shah Jahan

Babur, a descendant of both Timur and Genghis Khan, marched into the Punjab from his capital at Kabul in Afghanistan in 1525 and defeated the Sultan of Delhi at Panipat. This initial success did not totally destroy opposition to the Moghuls, and in 1540 the Moghul Empire came to an abrupt but temporary end when Sher Shah defeated Humayun, the second great Moghul. For 15 years Humayun lived in exile until he was able to return and regain his throne. By 1560 Akbar, his son and successor, who had come to the throne aged only 14, was able to claim effective and complete control of his empire.

Akbar was probably the greatest of the Moghuls, for he not only had the military ability required of a ruler in that time, but he was also a man of culture and wisdom with a sense of fairness. He saw, as previous Muslim rulers had not, that the number of Hindus in India was too great to simply subjugate them. Instead he integrated them into his empire and made use of many Hindu advisers, generals and administrators. Akbar

also had a deep interest in religious matters and spent many hours in discussion with religious experts of all persuasions, including Christians and Parsis. He eventually formulated a religion which combined the best points of all those he had studied.

Jehangir followed Akbar and maintained his father's toleration of other religions but took advantage of the stability of the empire to spend most of his time in his beloved Kashmir, eventually dying while en route there. His tomb is at Lahore in Pakistan. Shah Jahan, however, who secured his position as emperor by executing all male collateral relatives, stuck much more to Agra and Delhi, and during his reign some of the most vivid and permanent reminders of the Moghuls' glory were constructed. Best known, of course, is the Taj Mahal, but that was only one of Shah Jahan's many magnificent buildings. Indeed some say that it was his passion for building that led to his downfall and that his son, Aurangzeb, deposed his father in part to put a halt to his architectural extravagances. Shah Jahan also ditched Akbar's policy of religious tolerance in favour of a return to Islamic fundamentalism; yet it was during his reign that the British were granted their trading post at Madras in 1639.

The last of the great Moghuls, Aurangzeb, devoted his resources to extending the empire's boundaries, but it was the punitive taxes which he levied on his subjects to pay for his military exploits and his religious zealotry that eventually secured his downfall. It was also during his reign that the empire began to rapidly rot from the inside as luxury and easy living corroded the mettle and moral fibre of the nobles and military commanders. His austere and puritanical beliefs led him to destroy many Hindu temples and erect mosques on their sites, alienating the very people who were such an important part of his bureaucracy.

It didn't take long for revolts to break out on all sides and, with his death in 1707, the Moghul Empire's fortunes rapidly declined. There were Moghul 'emperors' right up to the time of the Indian Mutiny, when the

Taj Mahal, Agra (HF)

British exiled the last one and executed his sons, but they were emperors without an empire. In sharp contrast to the magnificent tombs of his Moghul predecessors, Aurangzeb's tomb is a simple affair at Rauza, near Aurangabad.

The successor states which followed on from the Moghul Empire did, in some cases, continue for a while. In the south, the viceroyalty in Hyderabad became one of the British-tolerated princely states and survived right through to Independence. The nawabs of Oudh in north India ruled eccentrically, flamboyantly and badly until 1854 when the British 'retired' the last nawab. In Bengal, the Moghuls unwisely clashed with the British far earlier, and their rule was terminated by the Battle of Plassey in 1757.

The Rajputs & the Marathas

Moghul power was not simply supplanted by another, greater power. It fell through a series of factors and to a number of other rulers. Not least of these were the Marathas. Throughout the Muslim period in the north of India there were still strong Hindu powers, most notably the Rajputs. Centred in Rajasthan, the Rajputs were a warrior caste with a strong and almost fanatical belief in the dictates of chivalry both in battle and in the conduct of state affairs. Their place in Indian history is much like that of the knights of medieval Europe. The Rajputs opposed every foreign incursion into their territory, but were never united or sufficiently organised to be able to deal with superior forces on a long-term basis. Not only that, but when not battling foreign oppression they squandered their energies fighting each other. This eventually led to them becoming vassal states of the Moghul Empire, but their prowess in battle was well recognised, and some of the best military men in the emperors' armies were Rajputs.

The Marathas first rose to prominence with Shivaji, who took over his father's kingdom and between 1646 and 1680 performed feats of arms and heroism all over central India. Tales of his larger-than-life exploits are popular with wandering storytellers in small villages. He is a particular hero in Maharashtra, where many of his wildest exploits took place, but is also revered for two other things: as a lower-caste Sudra he showed that great leaders do not have to be Kshatriyas (soldiers or administrators), and he demonstrated great abilities in confronting the Moghuls. At one time Shivaji was even captured by the Moghuls and taken back to Agra but, naturally, he managed to escape and continue his adventures.

Shivaji's son was captured, blinded and executed by Aurangzeb. His grandson was not made of the same sturdy stuff, but the Maratha Empire continued under the Peshwas, hereditary government ministers who became the real rulers. They gradually took over more and more of the weakening Moghul Empire's powers, first by supplying troops and then by actually taking control of Moghul land.

When Nadir Shah from Persia sacked Delhi in 1739, the declining Moghuls were even further weakened, but the expansion of Maratha power came to an abrupt halt in 1761 at Panipat. There, where Babur had won the battle that established the Moghul Empire over 200 years earlier, the Marathas were defeated by Ahmad Shah Durani from Afghanistan. Their expansion to the west halted, they nevertheless consolidated their control over central India and their region known as Malwa. Soon, however, they were to fall to India's final great imperial power, the British.

Expansion of British Power

The British were not the first European power to arrive in India, nor were they the last to leave – both those honours go to the Portuguese. In 1498, Vasco da Gama arrived on the coast of modern-day Kerala, having sailed around the Cape of Good Hope. Pioneering this route gave the Portuguese a century of uninterrupted monopoly over Indian and Far Eastern trade with Europe. In 1510 they captured Goa, the Indian enclave they controlled right through to 1961, 14 years after the British had left. So rich was

Goa during its heyday that it was rated as the Lisbon of the East. In the long term, however, the Portuguese simply did not have the resources to hold onto a worldwide empire and they were quickly eclipsed by the arrival of the British, French and Dutch.

In 1612, the British made their first permanent inroad into India when they established a trading post at Surat in Gujarat. In 1600, Queen Elizabeth I had granted a charter to a London trading company giving them a monopoly on British trade with India. For 250 years British power was exercised in India not by the government but by the East India Company which developed from this initial charter. British trading posts were established on the other coast at Madras in 1640, at Bombay in 1668 and at Calcutta in 1690.

The British and Portuguese were not the only Europeans in India. The Danes and Dutch also had trading posts, and in 1672 the French established themselves at Pondicherry, an enclave that they, like the Portuguese in Goa, would hold even after the British had finally departed.

The stage was set for over a century of rivalry and violent contest between the British and French for control of Indian trade. In 1746 the French took Madras only to hand it back in 1749. In subsequent years there was to be much intrigue between the imperial powers. If the British were involved in a struggle with one local ruler they could be certain the French would be backing him with arms, men or expertise. In 1756 Siraj-ud-daula, the Nawab of Bengal, attacked Calcutta and outraged Britain with the 'black hole of Calcutta' incident. A year later Robert Clive retook Calcutta and in the Battle of Plassey defeated Siraj-ud-daula and his French supporters, thus not only extending British power but also curtailing French influence. The victory ushered in a long period of unbridled profiteering by members of the East India Company until its powers were taken over by the British Government in the 19th century.

India at this time was in a state of flux due to the power vacuum created by the disintegration of the Moghul Empire. The Marathas were the only real Indian power to step into this gap and they were more a group of local kingdoms who sometimes cooperated, sometimes did not, than a power in their own right. In the south, where Moghul influence had never been so great, the picture was confused by the strong British-French rivalries, with one ruler consistently played off against another.

This was never clearer than in the series of Mysore Wars with that irritation to British power, Tipu Sultan. In the 4th Mysore War in 1789-99, Tipu was killed at Srirangapatnam and British power took another step forward, French influence another step back. The long-running British struggle with the Marathas was finally concluded in 1803, which left only the Punjab outside British control. Even that fell to the British in 1849 after the two Sikh Wars.

It was during this time that the borders of Nepal were delineated following a brief series of battles between the British and the Gurkhas in 1814. The Gurkhas were initially victorious but, two years later, were forced to sue for peace as the British marched on Kathmandu. As part of the price for peace, the Nepalese were forced to cede the provinces of Kumaon and Shimla, but mutual respect for each others' military prowess prevented Nepal's incorporation into the Indian Empire and led to the establishment of the Gurkha regiments of the British Army.

British India

By the early 19th century India was effectively under British control. In part this takeover had come about because of the vacuum left by the demise of the Moghuls, but the British also followed the rules Akbar had laid down so successfully. To them India was principally a place to make money, and the Indians' culture, beliefs and religions were left strictly alone. Indeed it was said the British didn't give a damn what religious beliefs a person held so long as they made a good cup of tea. Furthermore, the British had a disciplined, efficient army and astute political advisers. They followed the policy of

divide and rule with great success and negotiated distinctly one-sided treaties giving them the right to intervene in local states if they were inefficiently run; 'inefficient' could be and was defined as the British saw fit.

Even under the British, India remained a patchwork of states, many of them nominally independent but actually under strong British influence. This policy of maintaining 'princely states' governed by maharajas, nawabs (and a host of other titles) continued right through to Independence and was to cause a number of problems at that time. The British interest in trade and profit resulted in expansion of iron and coal mining; the development of tea, coffee and cotton growing; the construction of the basis of today's vast Indian railways network; the commencement of irrigation projects which have today revolutionised agriculture; and other important and worthwhile developments.

In the sphere of government and law, Britain gave India a well-developed and smoothly functioning government and civil service structure. The fearsome love of bureaucracy which India also inherited from Britain may be a down side of that, but overall the country reached Independence with a better organised, more efficient and less corrupt administrative system than most ex-colonial countries.

There was, however, a price to pay for this: colonies are not established for altruistic reasons. Cheap textiles from the new manufacturing industry of Britain flooded into India, virtually crippling the local cottage industries. On one hand the British outlawed

Victoria Memorial, Calcutta (TW)

sati, the Hindu custom of burning the wife on her husband's funeral pyre, but on the other hand they encouraged the system of *zamindars*. These absentee landlords eased the burden of administrative and tax collection for the British, but contributed to an impoverished and landless peasantry in parts of India – a problem which in Bihar and West Bengal is still chronic today.

The British also established English as the local language of administration. While this may have been useful in a country with so many different languages and still fulfils a very important function in nationwide communication even today, it did keep the new rulers, to varying degrees, at arm's length from the Indians.

The Indian Mutiny

In 1857, less than half a century after Britain had taken firm control of India, they had their first serious setback. To this day the causes of the 'Indian Mutiny' are hard to unravel – it's even hard to define if it really was the 'War of Independence' by which it is referred to in India, or merely a mutiny. The causes were an administration which had been run down and other more specific cases. The dismissal of local rulers, inefficient and unpopular as they might have been, proved to be a flash point in certain areas, but the main single cause was bullet lubricant. A rumour, quite possibly true, leaked out that a new type of bullet issued to the troops, many of whom were Muslim, was greased with pig fat. A similar rumour developed that the bullets were actually greased with cow fat. Pigs, of course, are unclean to Muslims, and cows are holy to Hindus.

The British were slow to deny these rumours and even slower to prove that either they were incorrect or that changes had been made. The result was a loosely coordinated mutiny of the Indian battalions of the Bengal Army. Of the 74 battalions, seven (one of them Gurkhas) remained loyal, 20 were disarmed and the other 47 mutinied. The Mutiny first broke out at Meerut, close to Delhi, and soon spread across north India. There were massacres and acts of senseless cruelty on both sides, long sieges, decisive victories and protracted struggles, but in the end the Mutiny died out rather than came to a conclusive finish. It never spread beyond the north of India, and although there were brilliant self-made leaders on the Indian side, there was never any real coordination or common aim.

Post-Mutiny

The British made two moves with the conclusion of the Mutiny. First, they wisely decided not to look for scapegoats or to exact official revenge, although revenge and looting had certainly taken place on an unofficial level. Second, the East India Company was wound up and administration of the country was belatedly handed over to the British government. The remainder of the century was the peak period for the empire on which 'the sun never set' and in which India was one of its brightest stars.

Two parallel developments during the latter part of the 19th century gradually paved the way for the independent India of today. First, the British slowly began to hand over power and bring more people into the decision-making processes. Democratic systems began to be implemented in India although the British government retained overall control. In the civil service higher and higher posts were opened up for Indians and not simply retained for colonial administrators.

At the same time Hinduism began to go through another of its periodic phases of resurgence and adjustment. During the Moghul and early British periods it had gradually lost much of its mass appeal, if only because of the demise of its once-great Hindu kingdoms and their conquest by Muslim and, later, Christian invaders. It was clearly time to drag the religion back into the present and re-establish its relevance for the common people. The main protagonists of this were reformers like Ram Mohan Roy, Ramakrishna and Swami Vivekananda who pushed through sweeping changes in Hindu society and paved the way for the Hindu beliefs of today, beliefs which have enormous appeal to modern Western society. Other reformers, such as Sri Aurobindo, attempted to meld Hindu philosophy with the rapidly emerging precepts of modern science.

It was largely as a result of their efforts that hybrid spiritual groups based on Hinduism and a variety of pre-Christian Western mysticism also made their appearance in the early part of the 20th century. Societies like the Theosophical Society of Annie Besant and her guru, Krishnamurti, date from this period. Even Aleister Crowley owed a debt to these popularisers of Hindu philosophy and mysticism.

Road to Independence

With the turn of the century, opposition to British rule began to take on a new light. The 'Congress' which had been established to give India a degree of self-rule now began to push for the real thing. Outside the Congress, more hot-blooded individuals pressed for independence by more violent means. Eventually the British mapped out a path towards independence similar to that pursued in Canada and Australia. However, WW I shelved these plans plus the events in Turkey, a Muslim country, alienated many Indian Muslims. After the war the struggle was on in earnest and its leader was Mahatma Gandhi.

In 1915, Mohandas Gandhi returned from South Africa, where he had practised as a lawyer and devoted himself to fighting the racial discrimination which the country's many Indian settlers had to face. In India he soon turned his abilities to the question of independence, particularly after the infamous massacre at Amritsar in 1919 when a British army contingent opened fire on an unarmed crowd of protesters. Gandhi, who subsequently became known as Mahatma, the 'great soul', adopted a policy of passive resistance, or *satyagraha*, to British rule. The central pillar of his achievement was to broaden the scope of the independence struggle from the middle classes to the peasants and villagers. He led movements against the

Mahatma Gandhi

iniquitous salt tax and boycotts of British textiles, and for his efforts was jailed on a number of occasions.

Not everyone involved in the struggle agreed with or followed Gandhi's policy of noncooperation and nonviolence, yet the Congress Party and Mahatma Gandhi remained in the forefront and by the time WW II was concluded independence was inevitable. The war had dealt a deathblow to colonialism and the myth of European superiority, and Britain no longer had the power or the desire to maintain a vast empire. Within India, however, a major problem had developed: the large Muslim minority had realised that an independent India would also be a Hindu-dominated India, and that despite Gandhi's fair-minded and even-handed approach, others in the Congress Party would not be so willing to share power.

Independence

The July 1945 Labour Party victory in the British elections brought to power leaders of a different political persuasion than had previously ruled and it was they who realised that a search for a solution to the Indian problem was imperative.

Nevertheless, elections within India itself revealed an ominous development, namely, the alarming growth of communalism. The country was obviously divided along purely religious lines with the Muslim League, led by Muhammad Ali Jinnah, speaking for the overwhelming majority of Muslims, and the Congress Party, led by Jawaharlal Nehru, commanding the Hindu population. Mahatma Gandhi remained the father figure for Congress, but without an official role and, as events were to prove, his political influence was slipping.

'I will have India divided, or India destroyed', were Jinnah's words. This uncompromising demand with Congress' desire for an independent greater-India, and Jinnah's egotistical bid for power over a separate nation, proved to be the biggest stumbling block to the British grant of independence, but with each passing day the prospects for intercommunal strife and bloodshed increased. In early 1946, a British mission failed to bring the two sides together and the country slid increasingly towards civil war. A 'Direct Action Day', called by the Muslim League in August 1946, led to a slaughter of Hindus in Calcutta followed by reprisals against Muslims. Attempts to make the two sides see reason had no effect and in February 1947 the British government made a momentous decision. The current viceroy, Lord Wavell, would be replaced by Lord Louis Mountbatten and independence would come by June 1948.

Already the Punjab region of northern India was in a state of chaos and the Bengal region in the east was close to it. The new viceroy made a last-ditch attempt to convince the rival factions that a united India was a more sensible proposition, but they – Jinnah in particular – remained intransigent and the reluctant decision was made to divide the country. Only Gandhi stood firmly against the division, preferring the possibility of a civil war to the chaos he so rightly expected.

As in so many other parts of the world, neatly slicing the country in two proved to be an impossible task. Although some areas were clearly Hindu or Muslim, others had very evenly mixed populations, and still others remained isolated 'islands' of Muslims surrounded by Hindu regions no matter how the country was divided. The patent impossibility of attempting to divide all the Muslims from all the Hindus is illustrated by the fact that after Partition India was still the third-largest Muslim country in the world – only Indonesia and Pakistan had greater populations of Muslims. Even today India has a greater Muslim population than any of the Arab countries, or Turkey or Iran.

Worse, the two overwhelmingly Muslim regions were on the exact opposite sides of the country – Pakistan would inevitably have an eastern and western half divided by a hostile India. The instability of this arrangement was self-evident, but it took 25 years before the predestined split came and East Pakistan became Bangladesh.

Other problems showed up only after independence was achieved. Pakistan was painfully short of the administrators and clerical workers with which India was so well endowed; these were occupations simply not followed by many Muslims. Many other occupations, such as moneylenders, were purely Hindu callings and the unfortunate untouchables did the dirty work not only for higher-caste Hindus but also for the Muslims. The Sikhs, too, would find their 'homeland' split in half.

Mountbatten decided to follow a breakneck pace to independence and announced that it would come on 14 August 1947. Historians have wondered ever since if much bloodshed might not have been averted if the impetuous and egotistical Mountbatten had not decided on such a hasty process.

Once the decision had been made to divide the country, there were countless administrative decisions to be made, the most important being the actual location of the dividing line. Since a locally adjudicated dividing line was certain to bring recriminations from either side and take forever to settle, an independent British referee was given the odious task of drawing the line, knowing that its effects would be disastrous for countless people. The most difficult decisions had to be made in Bengal and the Punjab. In Bengal, Calcutta, with its Hindu majority, port facilities and jute mills, was divided from East Bengal, which had a Muslim majority, and jute production as its major industry, yet not a single jute mill for its processing, or a suitable port for its export.

The problem was far worse in the Punjab, where intercommunal antagonisms were already running at fever pitch. Here one of the most fertile and affluent regions of the country had large percentages of Muslims (55%) and Hindus (30%), and a substantial number of India's Sikhs. The Punjab contained all the ingredients for an epic disaster and, with the announcement of the dividing line only days after Independence, the resulting bloodshed was even worse than expected. Huge exchanges of population took place as Muslims moved to Pakistan and Hindus and Sikhs to India.

The dividing line cut neatly between the Punjab's two major cities – Lahore and Amritsar. Prior to Independence Lahore's total population of 1.2 million included approximately 500,000 Hindus and 100,000 Sikhs. When the dust had finally settled, Lahore had a Hindu and Sikh population of only 1000.

For months the greatest exodus in human history took place east and west across the Punjab. Trainloads of Muslims, fleeing westward, would be held up and slaughtered by Hindu and Sikh mobs. Hindus and Sikhs fleeing to the east would suffer the same fate. The army force sent to maintain order proved totally inadequate and at times all too ready to join the partisan carnage. By the time the Punjab chaos had run its course, over 10 million people had changed sides and even the most conservative estimates calculate that 250,000 people had been slaughtered. The figure may well have been over half a million. An additional million people changed sides in Bengal, mainly Hindus since few Muslims migrated from West Bengal to East Pakistan.

The outright division of the Punjab was not to be the only excuse for carnage. Throughout the British era India had retained many 'princely states', and incorporating these into independent India and Pakistan proved to be a considerable headache. Guarantees of a substantial measure of Independence convinced most of them to opt for inclusion into the new countries, but at the time of Independence there were still three holdouts.

One was Kashmir, predominantly Muslim but with a Hindu maharaja. In October 1948 the maharaja had still not opted for India or Pakistan and a ragtag Pathan (Pakistani) army crossed the border from Pakistan, intent on racing to Srinagar and annexing Kashmir without provoking a real India-Pakistan conflict. Unfortunately for the Pakistanis, the Pathans had been inspired to mount their invasion by the promise of plunder, and they did so much plundering on the way that India had time to rush troops to Srinagar and prevent the town's capture. The indecisive maharaja finally opted for India, provoking the first, although brief, India-Pakistan war.

The UN was eventually persuaded to step in and keep the two sides apart but the issue of Kashmir has remained a central cause for disagreement and conflict between the two countries ever since. With its overwhelming Muslim majority and its geographic links to Pakistan, many people were inclined to support Pakistan's claims to the region. But, by then, Kashmir had become a *cause célèbre* in the Congress Party and, despite a promised plebiscite, India has consistently evaded holding such a vote. To this day, India and Pakistan are divided in this region by a demarcation line (known as the Line of Actual Control) yet neither side agrees that this constitutes the official border.

The final stages of Independence had one last tragedy to be played out. On 30 January 1948, Gandhi, deeply disheartened by Partition and the subsequent bloodshed, was assassinated by a Hindu fanatic.

Independent India

Since Independence, India has made enormous strides but faced enormous problems. The mere fact that India has not, like so many Third World countries, succumbed to dictatorships, military rule or wholesale foreign invasion is a testament to the basic strength of the country's government and institutions. Economically it has made major steps forward in improving agricultural output, and its industries have expanded to the stage where India is one of the world's top 10 industrial powers.

Jawaharlal Nehru, India's first prime minister, tried to follow a strict policy of nonalignment and was universally recognised as one of the major leaders of the Nonaligned Movement, along with Tito (of Yugoslavia) and Soekarno (of Indonesia). Yet, despite maintaining generally cordial relations with its former coloniser and electing to join the Commonwealth, India moved towards the former USSR – partially because of conflicts with China and partially because of US support for arch-enemy Pakistan. There were also further clashes with Pakistan in 1965 and 1971, one over the

Jawaharlal Nehru

intractable Kashmir dispute and the other over Bangladesh.

A border war was also fought with China in 1962 in the North-East Frontier Agency (NEFA; now referred to as the North-Eastern Region or NER) and Ladakh which resulted in the loss of Aksai Chin (Ladakh) and smaller areas in the NEFA. India continues to dispute sovereignty over these areas but, over the last few years, there has been a *rapprochement* between the two countries.

These outside events drew attention away from India's often serious internal problems. As in any Third World country, population growth holds the potential for ultimate disaster. India weathered the first energy crisis of the early '70s remarkably well and no better advertisement could be found for the green revolution.

Indira's India

Politically, India's major problem since Independence has been the personality cult that has developed with its leaders. There have only been three real prime ministers of stature – Nehru, his daughter Indira Gandhi (no relation to the Mahatma) and her son Rajiv Gandhi. Having won election in 1966, Indira Gandhi faced serious opposition and unrest in 1975 which she countered by declaring a state of emergency, a situation which in many other countries might quickly have become a dictatorship.

During the 'emergency' a mixed bag of good and bad policies were followed. Freed of many parliamentary constraints, Indira Gandhi was able to control inflation remarkably well, boost the economy and decisively increase efficiency. On the negative side, political opponents often found themselves behind bars, India's judicial system was turned into a puppet theatre, the press was fettered and there was more than a hint of personal aggrandisement, particularly in relation to her son, Sanjay Gandhi. His disastrous programme of virtually forced sterilisations, in particular, caused much anger.

Despite murmurings of discontent, Indira decided that the people were behind her and in 1977 called a general election to give credence to her emergency powers. Sanjay had counselled against holding the election and his opinion proved to be a wise one, because Indira and her Congress Party were bundled out of power in favour of the hastily assembled Janata Peoples' Party.

Janata, however, was a device with only one function and that was to defeat Indira Gandhi and her partially renamed Congress Party (Indira). Once it had won, however, it quickly became obvious that it had no other cohesive policies and its leader, Moraji Desai, seemed more interested in protecting cows, banning alcohol and getting his daily glass of urine than coming to grips with the country's problems. With inflation soaring, unrest rising and the economy faltering, nobody was surprised when Janata fell apart in late 1979 and the 1980 election brought Indira back to power with a larger majority than ever.

India in the '80s

Mrs Gandhi's political touch seemed to have faded as she grappled unsuccessfully with communal unrest in several areas, violent attacks on untouchables, numerous cases of police brutality and corruption, and the upheavals in the north-east and the Punjab. Then her son and political heir, the none-too-popular Sanjay, was killed in a light aircraft accident, and in 1984 Mrs Gandhi herself was assassinated by her Sikh bodyguards, clearly in reprisal for her earlier, and somewhat ill-considered, decision to send in the Indian Army to flush out armed Sikh radicals from the Golden Temple in Amritsar, the Sikh holy-of-holies.

What the radicals were demanding was a separate Sikh state to be named Khalistan. Regardless of the viability of such a landlocked state adjacent to a hostile Pakistan and what would have been a none-too-friendly India, her decision to desecrate the Sikhs' holiest temple was a disaster which led to large-scale riots, big problems in the army (in which Sikhs form a significant part of the officer corps), and a seemingly intrac-

Indira Gandhi

table legacy of hate and distrust in the Punjab which has defied solution ever since.

Meanwhile, Indira's son, Rajiv, an Indian Airlines pilot until his younger brother's death, quickly become the next heir to the throne, and was soon swept into power with an overwhelming majority and enormous popular support.

Despite his former lack of interest in politics, Rajiv Gandhi brought new and pragmatic policies to the country. Foreign investment and the use of modern technology were encouraged, import restrictions eased and many new industries were set up. They undoubtedly benefited the middle classes and provided many jobs for those who had been displaced from the land and migrated to the cities in search of work, but whether these policies were necessarily in the long-term best interests of India is open to question. They certainly projected India into the 1990s in many ways and out of its partially self-induced isolationism and pro-

Chinese fishing nets, Fort Cochin, Kerala (MH)

tectionist attitude in terms of world trade, but they didn't stimulate the rural sector particularly.

Furthermore, his administration continually failed to quell unrest in the Punjab or Kashmir. It was also during his tenure in power that the Indian armed forces became bogged down in the turmoil in neighbouring Sri Lanka caused by Tamil secessionists in that country demanding an independent state. Support for the Sri Lankan Tamils was clearly being supplied by their mainland brethren, and police activities in Tamil Nadu state aimed at rooting out sympathisers and curtailing the flow of arms and equipment made Rajiv a marked man.

There was also the Bofors scandal which continued to dog his administration. This concerned alleged bribes paid to various members of the government to secure acceptance of the contract for supply and construction of the Swedish heavy artillery gun which the army was interested in acquiring. It was even alleged that Rajiv, or at least his Italian wife, Sonia, were recipients of such bribes. The affair has never been satisfactorily exposed and has even threatened to bring down the current administration which is headed by Narasimha Rao. As recently as 1992, the Minister of External Affairs, Mahavsingh Solanski, was forced to resign following what appeared to be an attempt to induce Swiss lawyers to abandon their investigation of certain bank accounts in that country which were suspected of holding the alleged bribes. It's unlikely the truth will ever emerge but it smells badly of a determined cover-up by people in high places.

Following the November 1989 elections, Rajiv Gandhi's Congress Party, although the largest single party in Parliament, was unable to form a government in its own right. As a result, a new National Front Government, made up of five parties including the Hindu fundamentalist Bharatiya Janata Party, headed by V P Singh (a former cabinet minister under Rajiv Gandhi) were to form the next government. Like the previous attempt to cobble together a government of national unity from minority parties with radically different viewpoints, it didn't last long and fresh elections had to be announced.

During the election campaign, disaster struck. While on a campaign tour of Tamil Nadu, Rajiv Gandhi, many of his aides and a number of bystanders were blown to smithereens by a bomb carried by a supporter of the Tamil Tigers (who was herself killed in the blast). The assassination had clearly been planned in advance and a massive police crackdown subsequently resulted in a shootout with mainland leaders and the arrest of several others. Meanwhile, the septuagenarian Narasimha Rao assumed the leadership of the Congress Party and led it to victory at the polls. There were attempts, after the assassination, to induce Rajiv's wife Sonia to assume the leadership but she made it clear she had little interest in doing so.

India Today

Although no political heavyweight in many senses, Narasimha Rao has displayed remarkable savvy in surviving and deflecting the often acrimonious and sometimes scurrilous accusations of the opposition, particularly in respect of the Bofors affair. Nevertheless, it has become clear that he supported Rajiv's determination to drag India (kicking and screaming, if necessary) into the economic realities of the 1990s, particularly after the collapse of the Soviet Union, India's long-term ally and aid supplier.

After years of languishing behind tariff barriers and a somewhat unrealistic currency exchange rate for the rupee, the economy was given an enormous boost in 1992 when the finance minister, Manmohan Singh, made the momentous step of partially floating the rupee against a basket of 'hard' currencies and legalising the import of gold by nonresident Indians. He also announced a number of price hikes in unprofitable state-controlled industries – in particular, the railways. It certainly didn't endear him to lower-paid urban workers, especially commuters, but it definitely made black-marketeering and the corruption associated with it less attractive. Diplomatic initiatives were also launched with a view to improving relations with Western countries.

On the other hand, Rao has inherited a number of intractable problems which have already tested the mettle of his government.

Although elections were finally held under difficult circumstances in the Punjab, and Congress secured power at state level, the elections were boycotted by the Sikh opposition parties, and Khalistani militants threatened to shoot anyone who voted. The resulting turnout was extremely low. It remains to be seen whether the state government can establish some degree of credibility given such a limited franchise. Meanwhile the unpredictable carnage in that state continues with up to 20 people per day losing their lives in shoot-outs.

The Kashmir issue again moved onto centre stage during 1991 and 1992 with demonstrations on both sides of the Line of Actual Control and an alarming increase in Jammu & Kashmir Liberation Front (JKLF) guerrilla activities in the Vale of Kashmir. Pakistan was almost certainly involved in encouraging, funding and supplying arms to the militants on the Indian side of the 'border' (which, of course, is denied) but reports suggest that the over-zealous activities of the Indian Army are also partially responsible for the upsurge in militancy. Mutual suspicions, however, brought India and Pakistan to the brink of war yet again in early 1992. It was averted in the nick of time following a meeting between the leaders of the two countries in Switzerland and Pakistani Army intervention in preventing Kashmiri radicals from attempting to cross the Line of Actual Control.

On the other hand, Pakistan's support of the Kashmiri militants, both on its side of the 'border' (known as Azad Kashmir) and in the Vale itself, have rebounded. By early 1992, Kashmiri militants and their supporters on both sides were demanding nothing short of independence from both India and Pakistan. This new demand is anathema to both India and Pakistan but with the examples of the former USSR and Yugoslavia, and the events

in Afghanistan fresh in everyone's mind, anything could happen.

Another problem which Rao faces is the long-running conflict in many of the states of the North-Eastern Region. For many years, a number of these states – particularly Nagaland and Assam – have been under central government control, though there have been periods when a state assembly was able to function. The biggest threat to the government is the United Liberation Front of Assam (ULFA) which accuses the government of exploiting the resources of Assam (particularly oil) yet neglecting its development. Its guerrilla forces were able to restrict the movements of the armed forces for many years until a massive army operation ('Operation Rhino') in 1992 forced them to the negotiating table. The talks, however, were inconclusive and the conflict simmers on. A resolution to the conflict in Nagaland is as far away as it ever was.

Other secessionist movements have surfaced in Bihar/West Bengal ('Jharkhand') and in the Darjeeling district of West Bengal ('Gorkhaland'), though the latter owes much to the political opportunism of its leader, Ghising.

Bihar's problems stem from the days of the British with their encouragement of the zamindar system. At one time, it may have been a convenient and efficient (though exploitative and iniquitous) way of collecting taxes and maintaining what the ruling powers decided was acceptable 'law and order', but it has been transformed into what is essentially the Indian Mafia. Just about everyone in this state from politicians to police officers and bureaucrats operates on bribes and, failing that, violence or murder. Anyone who is game enough to stick their neck out and criticise those with power, money or influence is on dangerous ground. This has been going on for years yet no-one at central government level has ever considered seriously addressing the problem.

Perhaps Rao's biggest headache though is the rising tide of communalism – that potentially explosive conflict between different religious groups, particularly between

Did you know?

In a country as large and diverse as India, where the weird and the wonderful are even more weird and wonderful than anywhere else, it comes as no surprise that the country holds many world records – although some of them are of dubious worth!

Obviously with its vast population, a number of records relate to crowds and people: the largest recorded assembly of people was an estimated 15 million at the Kumbh Mela at Allahabad in 1989; a similar number attended the funeral of the Tamil Nadu Chief Minister in 1969; the largest single employer in the world is Indian Railways with 1,624,121 people on the payroll; the South Point High School in Calcutta has the largest enrolment with 12,350 regular students; and in the world's largest democracy the 1989 Lok Sabha elections produced a few records when 304,126,600 people voted for the 291 parties contesting the 543 seats at over 593,000 polling stations across the country!

India also has its fair share of biggest, longest and highest: Hero Cycles in Punjab are the world's largest manufacturer: in 1989 they built no less than 2,936,073 clunkers; the longest railway platform in the world (833 metres) is at Kharagpur in West Bengal; the State Bank of India has the most branches, with 12,203 across the country; the wettest place on earth is also in India, at Cherrapunji in Meghalaya which in one 12-month period copped a massive 26.46 metres; and pop star Lata Mangeshkar holds the record for the greatest number of recordings, with over 30,000 songs recorded in 20 Indian languages.

The bizarre and downright silly? Yes, India has them too. Indians hold the records for nonstop talking (360 hours), balancing on one foot (34 hours), clapping (58 hours, nine minutes), nonstop chanting (10,040 days and still rising), continuous typewriting (123 hours), standing still (over 17 years!), crawling (1,400 km), nonstop solo singing (262 hours), whistling (45 hours, 20 minutes), and walking with a full milk-bottle balanced on the head (65 km).

India also has the tree with the largest canopy – a banyan tree in the Calcutta Botanical Gardens covers 1.2 hectares; the highest bridge in the world (5600 metres) is found on the Manali to Leh road; and, not surprisingly, the Howrah Bridge in Calcutta is the world's busiest – every day it carries 57,000 vehicles and innumerable pedestrians; while the Qutab Minar in Delhi, at 72.5 metres, is the tallest free-standing stone tower.

Indian disasters, both natural and otherwise, also feature in the record books. No-one could forget Bhopal, where 4000 people died and at least 200,000 others were injured, but in 1888, 246 people were killed in a hailstorm, while a dam which burst its banks in Gujarat killed at least 5000 in 1979.

Lastly, a record that's hardly likely to be challenged is that held by a Pune man who in 1966 won a court case which had been filed by his ancestor 761 years earlier – the Indian bureaucracy in full swing! ∎

Howrah Bridge, Calcutta (TW)

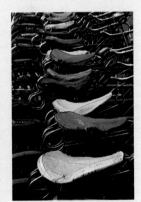

Bikes, Kolhapur (HF)

Hindus and Muslims. 'Ayodhya' is the current call to arms. This small town in central Uttar Pradesh is revered by Hindus as the birthplace of Rama and many Hindu temples stand here, yet, during Moghul times, the emperors razed several of the temples and constructed mosques on the same sites.

It's claimed that one of these mosques, the Babri Masjid, stands on the site of what was previously the Rama Temple. Fundamentalists among the Hindus agitated for the mosque to be demolished and a new Rama Temple built in its place. Just about everyone who stood to gain political capital out of this issue jumped into the fray, but particularly the Bharatiya Janata Party (BJP), which controlled the UP state government, and its paramilitary organisation, the Rashtriya Swayamsevak Sangh (RSS). The BJP is staunchly Hindu revivalist and it's quite clear that they are prepared to push this issue regardless of the outcome. As a consequence, hardly a day went by in 1992 without newspaper reports of confrontations or riots, the effects reverberating around the country. Finally, in December 1992, the mosque was destroyed by Hindus, leading almost immediately to rioting in various cities and over 200 deaths.

Though this issue doesn't affect foreign visitors (apart from the inconveniences suffered during strikes), it is one which the Rao government must urgently address before attitudes become entrenched. India can ill afford such major inter-religious strife.

The above problems aside, it's worth remembering that of all the people in the world who live in what we know as democratic societies, nearly 50% of them are Indians and, as 1977 indicated, it's a democratic society with teeth. Furthermore, India, despite its population problems, rural poverty, corruption at government and bureaucratic levels, and political opportunism, manages to do several things which neither the former USSR or China – or many other countries – can manage.

Among the list of pluses is that it can feed its own people without importing food, it can turn out hi-tech products virtually without outside assistance, it has a free and highly critical press, you can go where you like (except in a few sensitive border regions where permits are required) and hassles by security and customs officials are either nonexistent or minimal. Where can you find that elsewhere in Asia?

GEOGRAPHY

India has a total area of 3,287,263 sq km. The north of the country is decisively bordered by the long sweep of the Himalaya, the highest mountains on earth. They run from the south-east to the north-west, separating India from China. Bhutan in the east and Nepal in the centre actually lie along the Himalaya, as does Darjeeling, the northern part of Uttar Pradesh, Himachal Pradesh and Jammu & Kashmir.

The Himalaya are not a single mountain range but a series of ranges with beautiful valleys wedged between them. The Kulu Valley in Himachal Pradesh and the Vale of Kashmir in Jammu & Kashmir are both Himalayan valleys, as is the Kathmandu Valley in Nepal. Kanchenjunga (8598 metres) is the highest mountain in India although until Sikkim (and Kanchenjunga) were absorbed into India that honour went to Nanda Devi (7817 metres). Beyond the Himalaya stretches the high, dry and barren Tibetan plateau; in Ladakh a small part of this plateau actually lies within India's boundaries.

Mt Kanchenjunga, Sikkim (RI)

Campsite at Humpet, in the Kanital Valley, Kashmir (GW)

The final southern range of the Himalaya, the Siwalik Hills, ends abruptly in the great northern plains of India. In complete contrast to the soaring mountain peaks, the northern plain is oppressively flat and slopes so gradually that all the way from Delhi to the Bay of Bengal it drops only 200 metres. The mighty Ganges River, which has its source in the Himalaya, drains a large part of the northern plain and is the major river of India. The Brahmaputra, flowing down from the north-east of the country, is the other major river of the north. In the north-west the Indus River starts out flowing through Ladakh in India but soon dives off into Pakistani territory and is the most important river of that nation.

South of the northern plains the land rises up into the high plateau known as the Deccan. The Deccan plateau is bordered on both sides by ranges of hills which parallel the coast to the east and west. The Western Ghats are higher and have a wider coastal strip than the Eastern Ghats. The two ranges meet in the extreme south in the Nilgiri Hills.

The southern hill stations are in these hills – Matheran and Mahabaleshwar near Bombay in the Western Ghats, Ooty and Kodaikanal in the extreme south in the Nilgiri Hills. The major rivers of the south are the Godavari and the Krishna. Both rise on the eastern slope of the Western Ghats and flow across the Deccan into the sea on the east coast.

The eastern boundary of India is also defined by ranges of hills, foothills of the Himalaya, which separate the country from Myanmar (Burma). In this north-eastern region India bends almost entirely around Bangladesh, a low-lying country at the delta of the Ganges and Brahmaputra, and almost meets the sea on the eastern side.

On the western side, India is separated from Pakistan by three distinct regions. In the north, in the disputed area of Kashmir, the Himalaya forms the boundary between the two countries. The Himalaya drop down to the plains of the Punjab, which then merge into the Great Thar Desert. In the western part of Rajasthan this is an area of great natural beauty and extreme barrenness.

Tiger Hill dawn, Darjeeling (RI)

Finally, the Indian state of Gujarat is separated from the Sind in Pakistan by the unusual marshland known as the Rann of Kutch. In the dry season the Rann dries out, leaving isolated salt islands on an expansive plain; in the wet season it floods over to become a vast inland sea.

CLIMATE

India is so vast that the climatic conditions in the far north have little relation to that of the extreme south. While the heat is building up to breaking point on the plains, the people of Ladakh will still be waiting for the snow to melt on the high passes. Basically India has a three-season year – the hot, the wet and the cool.

The Hot

The heat starts to build up on the plains of India from around February, and by April or May it becomes unbearable. In central India temperatures of 45°C and above are commonplace. It's dry and dusty and everything is seen through a haze. From the air the country looks parched and barren, but usually all you can see below is a blanket of hazy brown from all the dust in the atmosphere. Later in May the first signs of the monsoon are seen – short sharp rainstorms, violent electric storms, and dust storms that turn day into night and cover everything with a film of dust. The heat towards the end of the hot season is like a hammer blow; you feel listless and tired and tempers are short. It's said to be the time of year when murders and suicides take place!

The hot season is the time to leave the plains, which are at their worst, and retreat to the hills. Kashmir and the Kulu Valley come into their own, and all the Himalayan hill stations are at their best. The hill stations further south – Mt Abu in Rajasthan, Matheran in Maharashtra, Ooty and Kodaikanal in Tamil Nadu – are generally not high enough to be really cool but they are better than being down at sea level. By early June the snow on the passes into Ladakh should be melted and the roads will be open. This is the best trekking season in northern India.

The Wet

When the monsoon finally arrives it's a great relief. As the chart indicates, it doesn't simply arrive in one day. After a period of advance warning the rain comes in steadily, starting around 1 June in the extreme south and sweeping north to cover the whole country by early July. The monsoon doesn't really cool things off; at first you simply trade the hot, dry, dusty weather for hot, humid, muddy conditions. Even so it's a great relief, not least for farmers who now have the busiest time of year ahead of them as they prepare their fields for planting.

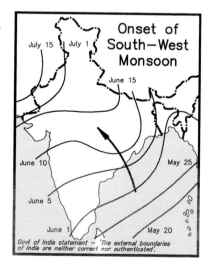

Onset of South–West Monsoon

July 15   July 1
June 15
June 10   May 25
June 5
June 1   May 20

Govt of India statement – 'The external boundaries of India are neither correct nor authenticated'.

During the monsoon it doesn't simply rain solidly all day every day; it certainly rains every day but the water tends to come down in buckets for a while and then the sun comes out and it's quite pleasant.

Some places are at their best during the monsoon – like Rajasthan with its many palaces on lakes. In Nepal, the monsoon is a very bad time to trek, yet in the north-west Indian Himalayan regions it is a good time to trek. In Nepal, the trekking season commences when the monsoon finishes, but the regions of Himachal Pradesh, Kashmir and Ladakh in India are further north and the weather is too cold for trekking.

Although the monsoon brings life to India it also brings its share of death. Every year there are many destructive floods and thousands of people are made homeless. Rivers rise and sweep away road and railway lines and many flight schedules are disrupted. Travel can definitely be more difficult during the monsoon.

The Cool

Finally around October the monsoon ends, and this is probably the best time of year in India. Everything is still green and lush but you don't get rained on daily. The temperatures are delightful, not too hot and not too cool. The air is clear in the Himalaya, and the mountains are clearly visible, at least early in the day. As the cool rolls on it actually becomes cold at night in the north. Delhi and other northern cities become quite crisp at night in December and January.

In the far north it's more than just a little chilly, it's downright cold. Snow does bring India's small skiing industry into its own, however, so a few places in the far north, such as the Kulu Valley, have a winter season too. In the far south, where it never really gets less than hot, the temperatures do become comfortably warm rather than hot. Then around February the temperatures start to climb again and before you know it you're back in the hot weather.

Some Regional Variations

As in Sri Lanka, the south-east coast is also

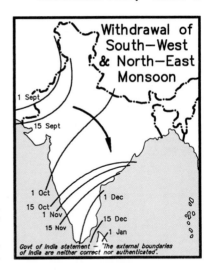

Withdrawal of South—West & North—East Monsoon

1 Sept
15 Sept
1 Oct
15 Oct
1 Nov
15 Nov
1 Dec
15 Dec
1 Jan

Govt of India statement – 'The external boundaries of India are neither correct nor authenticated'.

affected by the short north-east monsoon which brings rain from mid-October to the end of December. The usual monsoon comes from the south-west. It can get surprisingly wet during the north-east monsoon.

It's easy to forget just how cold it can get in the far north. Even along the Ganges you'll need a sweater or jacket at night, and in the mountains the snow will be up to your neck. Basically the best time to visit India is November through February, except for the northern Himalayan region where April through July is the best time.

The table shows average minimum and maximum temperatures (in °C) and rainfall (in mm) for the main cities in India.

Seasons

English	Hindi	Period
Spring	Vasanta	mid-March to mid-May
The Hot	Grishma	mid-May to mid-July
The Wet	Varsha	early-July to mid-September
Autumn	Sharada	mid-September to mid-November
Winter	Hemanta	mid-November to mid-January
The Cool	Shishira	mid-January to mid-March

Average Temperatures & Rainfall

		Jan	Feb	Mar	Apr	May	Jun	Jul	Aug	Sep	Oct	Nov	Dec
Agra	min °C	7	10	16	22	27	30	27	26	24	19	12	8
	max °C	22	26	32	38	42	41	35	33	33	33	30	24
	rain mm	16	9	11	5	10	60	210	263	152	24	2	4
Bangalore	min °C	15	17	19	21	21	20	19	19	19	19	17	15
	max °C	27	30	32	32	33	29	27	27	28	28	26	26
	rain mm	3	10	6	46	117	80	117	147	143	185	54	16
Bombay	min °C	19	20	23	25	27	26	25	25	25	25	23	21
	max °C	29	30	31	32	33	32	30	30	30	32	32	31
	rain mm	2	1	–	3	16	520	710	439	297	88	21	2
Calcutta	min °C	14	17	22	25	27	27	26	26	26	24	18	14
	max °C	27	30	34	36	36	34	32	32	32	32	30	27
	rain mm	14	24	27	43	121	259	301	306	290	160	35	3
Darjeeling	min °C	3	4	8	11	13	15	15	15	15	12	7	4
	max °C	9	11	15	18	19	19	20	20	20	19	15	12
	rain mm	22	27	52	109	187	522	713	573	419	116	14	5
Delhi	min °C	7	10	15	21	27	29	27	26	25	19	12	8
	max °C	21	24	30	36	41	40	35	34	34	33	30	23
	rain mm	25	22	17	7	8	65	211	173	150	31	1	5
Goa	min °C	19	20	23	25	27	25	24	24	24	23	22	21
	max °C	31	32	32	33	33	31	29	29	29	31	33	33
	rain mm	2	–	4	17	18	500	892	341	277	122	20	37
Jaipur	min °C	8	11	15	21	26	27	26	24	23	18	12	9
	max °C	22	25	31	37	41	39	34	32	33	33	29	24
	rain mm	14	8	9	4	10	54	193	239	90	19	3	4
Jaisalmer	min °C	8	11	17	21	26	27	27	26	25	20	13	9
	max °C	24	28	32	38	42	41	38	36	36	36	31	26
	rain mm	2	1	3	2	5	7	90	86	14	1	5	2
Jodhpur	min °C	9	12	17	22	27	29	27	25	24	20	14	11
	max °C	25	28	33	38	42	40	36	33	35	36	31	27
	rain mm	7	5	2	2	6	31	122	145	47	7	3	1
Kochi	min °C	23	24	26	26	26	24	24	24	24	24	24	24
	max °C	31	31	31	31	31	29	28	28	28	29	30	30
	rain mm	10	34	50	140	364	756	572	386	235	333	184	37
Leh	min °C	-14	-12	-6	-1	3	7	10	10	5	-1	-7	-11
	max °C	-3	1	6	12	17	21	25	24	21	14	8	2
	rain mm	12	9	12	7	7	4	16	20	12	7	3	8
Lucknow	min °C	9	11	16	22	27	28	27	26	23	20	13	9
	max °C	23	26	33	38	41	39	34	33	33	33	29	25
	rain mm	24	17	9	6	12	94	299	302	182	40	1	6

		Jan	Feb	Mar	Apr	May	Jun	Jul	Aug	Sep	Oct	Nov	Dec
Madras	min °C	20	21	24	26	28	28	26	26	25	25	23	21
	max °C	29	31	33	35	38	37	35	35	34	32	29	28
	rain mm	24	7	15	25	52	53	84	124	118	267	309	139
Mysore	min °C	16	18	20	21	21	20	20	20	19	20	18	17
	max °C	28	31	34	34	33	29	27	28	29	28	27	27
	rain mm	3	6	12	68	156	61	72	80	116	180	67	15
Shimla	min °C	2	4	7	15	15	17	16	15	14	10	7	4
	max °C	9	10	14	19	23	24	21	20	20	18	15	11
	rain mm	66	50	61	38	54	147	420	385	195	45	7	24
Srinagar	min °C	-2	-1	4	7	11	14	18	18	13	6	0	-2
	max °C	4	8	13	19	25	29	31	30	28	23	16	9
	rain mm	73	72	100	78	63	30	61	63	32	29	18	36
Thiruvanan-thapuram	min °C	22	23	24	25	25	24	23	23	23	23	23	22
	max °C	31	32	33	32	32	29	29	29	30	30	30	31
	rain mm	20	20	44	122	249	331	215	164	123	271	207	73
Udaipur	min °C	8	10	15	20	25	25	24	23	22	19	11	8
	max °C	24	28	32	36	38	36	31	29	31	32	29	26
	rain mm	9	4	3	3	5	87	197	207	120	16	6	3
Udhagaman-dalam (Ooty)	min °C	5	6	8	10	11	11	11	11	10	10	8	6
	max °C	20	21	22	22	22	18	10	17	18	19	19	20
	rain mm	26	12	30	109	173	139	177	128	110	213	127	59
Varanasi	min °C	9	11	17	22	27	28	26	26	25	21	13	9
	max °C	23	27	33	39	41	39	33	32	32	32	29	25
	rain mm	23	8	14	1	8	102	346	240	261	38	15	2

Flooded street, Calcutta (RI)

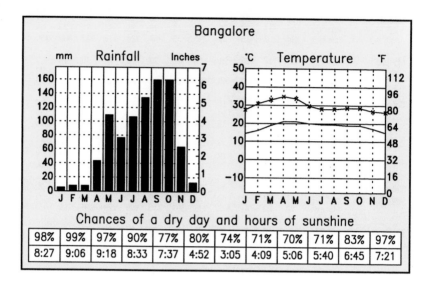

Bangalore

98%	99%	97%	90%	77%	80%	74%	71%	70%	71%	83%	97%
8:27	9:06	9:18	8:33	7:37	4:52	3:05	4:09	5:06	5:40	6:45	7:21

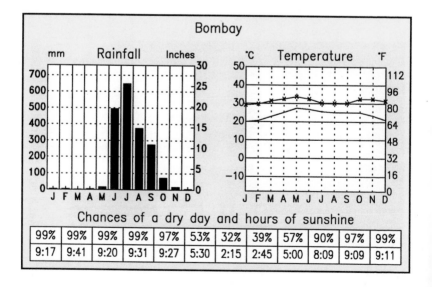

Bombay

99%	99%	99%	99%	97%	53%	32%	39%	57%	90%	97%	99%
9:17	9:41	9:20	9:31	9:27	5:30	2:15	2:45	5:00	8:09	9:09	9:11

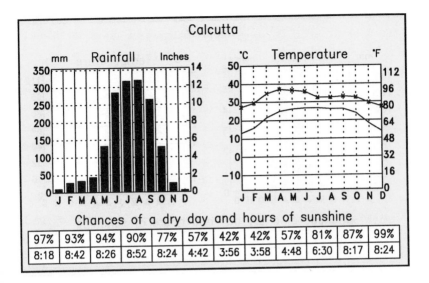

Calcutta

97%	93%	94%	90%	77%	57%	42%	42%	57%	81%	87%	99%
8:18	8:42	8:26	8:52	8:24	4:42	3:56	3:58	4:48	6:30	8:17	8:24

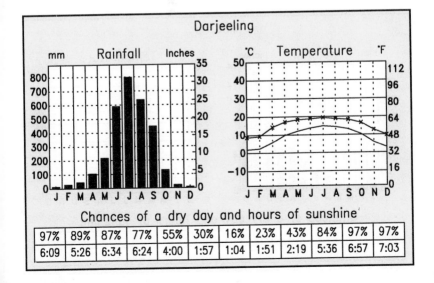

Darjeeling

97%	89%	87%	77%	55%	30%	16%	23%	43%	84%	97%	97%
6:09	5:26	6:34	6:24	4:00	1:57	1:04	1:51	2:19	5:36	6:57	7:03

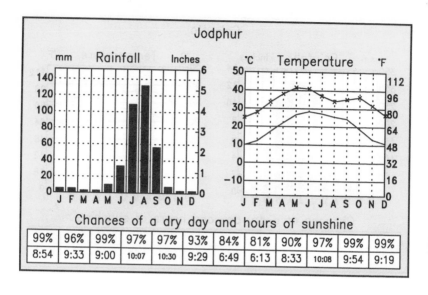

Jodphur

Rainfall (mm / Inches)

Temperature (°C / °F)

Chances of a dry day and hours of sunshine

J	F	M	A	M	J	J	A	S	O	N	D
99%	96%	99%	97%	97%	93%	84%	81%	90%	97%	99%	99%
8:54	9:33	9:00	10:07	10:30	9:29	6:49	6:13	8:33	10:08	9:54	9:19

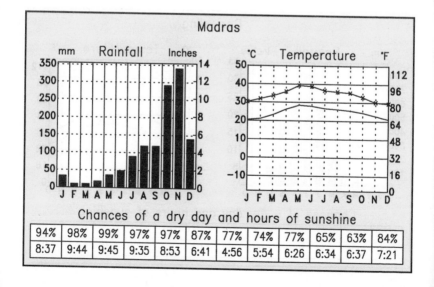

Madras

Rainfall (mm / Inches)

Temperature (°C / °F)

Chances of a dry day and hours of sunshine

J	F	M	A	M	J	J	A	S	O	N	D
94%	98%	99%	97%	97%	87%	77%	74%	77%	65%	63%	84%
8:37	9:44	9:45	9:35	8:53	6:41	4:56	5:54	6:26	6:34	6:37	7:21

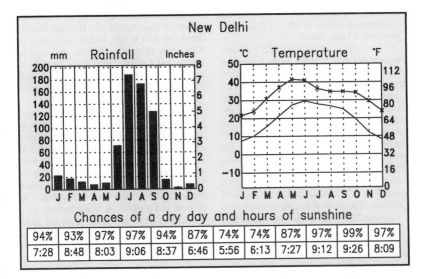

New Delhi

Rainfall — mm / Inches

	J	F	M	A	M	J	J	A	S	O	N	D

Temperature — °C / °F

Chances of a dry day and hours of sunshine

94%	93%	97%	97%	94%	87%	74%	74%	87%	97%	99%	97%
7:28	8:48	8:03	9:06	8:37	6:46	5:56	6:13	7:27	9:12	9:26	8:09

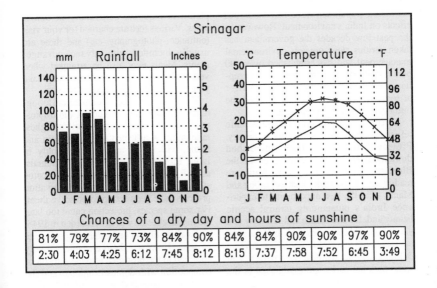

Srinagar

Rainfall — mm / Inches

Temperature — °C / °F

Chances of a dry day and hours of sunshine

81%	79%	77%	73%	84%	90%	84%	84%	90%	90%	97%	90%
2:30	4:03	4:25	6:12	7:45	8:12	8:15	7:37	7:58	7:52	6:45	3:49

FLORA & FAUNA

The following description of India's flora and fauna was written by Murray D Bruce & Constance S Leap Bruce.

The concept of forest and wildlife conservation is not new to India. Here, since time immemorial, wildlife has enjoyed a privileged position of protection through religious ideals and sentiment. Early Indian literature, including the Hindu epics, the Buddhist Jatakas, the Panchatantra and the Jain strictures, teach nonviolence and respect for even lowly animal forms. Many of the gods are associated with certain animals: Brahma with the deer, Vishnu, the lion and cobra; Siva, the bull, and Ganesh, the eternal symbol of wisdom, is half man and half elephant. The earliest known conservation laws come from India in the 3rd century BC, when Emperor Ashoka wrote the Fifth Pillar Edict, forbidding the slaughter of certain wildlife and the burning of forests.

Unfortunately, during the recent turbulent history of India, much of this tradition has been lost. Extensive hunting by the British and Indian rajas, large-scale clearing of forests for agriculture, availability of guns, poaching, strong pesticides and the ever-increasing population have had disastrous effects on India's environment. However, in the past few decades the government has taken serious steps towards environmental management and has established over 100 parks, sanctuaries and reserves. But, corruption in the local management of Project Tiger at some reserves has severely reduced the initial success of that programme.

A visit to one or more of these wildlife refuges is a must on any traveller's itinerary. Protected areas have been established throughout India, and many, such as the Bharatpur Bird Sanctuary near Agra, are readily accessible. Parks such as Corbett and Manas offer the best opportunity to experience India's outstanding natural scenic beauty and, for abundance and visibility of a variety of wildlife, parks such as Kaziranga compare with some of those in East Africa.

Many of the wildlife sanctuaries, and some national parks, are established in the former private hunting reserves of the British and Indian aristocracy. Often the parks are renowned for one particular creature, such as the Asian lion in Gir, Indian rhinoceros in Kaziranga, elephant in Periyar, and tiger in Kanha and Corbett; other areas have been established to preserve unique habitats such as lowland tropical rainforest or the mangrove forest of the Sunderbans.

Some parks offer modern-style guest houses with electricity, while in others only dak-style bungalows are available. Facilities usually include van and jeep rides, and at some you can take an elephant ride or boat trip to approach wildlife more discreetly. In addition, watchtowers and hides are often available and provide good opportunities to observe and photograph wildlife close up.

National parks and other protected areas in India are administered at the state level and are often promoted as part of each state's tourist attractions. To encourage more visitors, accommodation, road systems, transport and other facilities continue to be developed and upgraded. Whenever possible, book in advance for transport and accommodation through the local tourist offices or state departments, and check if a permit is required, particularly in border areas. Various fees are charged for your visit (entrance, photography, etc) and these are usually included with advance arrangements. Meals may also be arranged when you book, but in some cases you must take your food and have it prepared for you.

The diversity of India's climate and topography, varying from arid desert and tropical rainforest to some of the world's highest mountains, is reflected in its rich flora and fauna, with many species found only in India. More than 500 species of mammals, as well as the tiger, elephant and rhinoceros still exist in India and many conservation projects have been set up to preserve them. For some species, protection came too late; the Indian cheetah was last recorded in 1948.

A variety of deer and antelope species can be seen. However, these are now virtually confined to the protected areas as a result of competition with domestic animals and the

Spotted deer (BT)

storks, cranes, pelicans and others, are seen not only in parks but at numerous special waterbird sanctuaries. These sanctuaries contain large breeding colonies, and are also of great importance for the countless numbers of migrating birds which visit India annually.

Among the other wildlife are over 500 species of reptiles and amphibians, including the magnificent king cobra, other large snakes such as pythons, and crocodiles, large freshwater tortoises and monitor lizards. Then there are the 30,000 insect species, including large and colourful butterflies.

The vegetation, from dry desert scrub to alpine meadow, comprises some 15,000 species of plants recorded to date.

Geographically, India is divided into three main regions, each with many subregions and distinctive altitudinal climatic variations. From these regions, 23 important national parks, wildlife sanctuaries and reserves are listed. These and other reserves are included in more detail in the relevant chapters.

National Parks & Wildlife Sanctuaries

Northern India This is a region of extremes ranging from the snow-bound peaks and deep valleys of the Himalaya to flat plains and tropical lowlands.

Dachigam Wildlife Sanctuary (Kashmir)

This sanctuary is in a very scenic valley with a large meandering river. The surrounding mountainsides contain the rare Kashmir stag (hangul), as well as black and brown bears. A trek to the upper reaches, where you can camp, offers spectacular vistas. There you may also see the musk deer, a small species widely hunted for the male's musk gland, considered valuable in treating impotence and a major export to Europe's perfumeries. The sanctuary is 22 km by road from Srinagar and is certainly worth a visit (if Kashmir is open). The best time is from June to July.

Valley of Flowers National Park (Uttar Pradesh) This 'garden on top of the world'

effects of their diseases. They include the graceful Indian gazelle (chinkara); the Indian antelope (blackbuck); the diminutive four-horned antelope (chowsingha); the large and ungainly looking blue bull (nilgai), which is capable of great speed; the rare swamp deer (barasingha); the sambar, India's largest deer; the beautiful spotted deer (chital), usually seen in herds; the larger barking deer (muntjac); and the tiny mouse deer (chevrotain).

Also seen are wild buffalo, massive Indian bison (gaur), shaggy sloth bear, striped hyena, wild pig, jackal, Indian fox, wolf (although much more local in range now), and Indian wild dog (dhole), resembling a giant fox but found in packs in forests. Amongst the smaller mammals are the mongooses, renowned as snake killers, and giant squirrels.

Cats include leopard, panther, the short-tailed jungle cat, and the beautiful leopard cat. Various monkeys can be seen, with the rhesus macaque, bonnet macaque (in the south only), and long-tailed common langur as the most likely.

With over 2000 species and varieties of birds, few countries can compete with India. The diverse birdlife of the forests includes large hornbills, serpent eagles and fishing owls, as well as the elegant national bird, the peacock. Waterbirds, such as herons, ibises, is in the north of Uttar Pradesh near Badrinath, at an elevation of 3500 metres. The famous Valley of Flowers is a national park and, when in bloom, an unforgettable experience. Unfortunately it has suffered intense tourist pressure and is periodically closed. The best time is from June to August.

Gangetic Plain Some of the most famous parks in Asia are in this region. It contains the flat, alluvial plains of the Indus, Ganges and Brahmaputra rivers – an immense tract of level land stretching from sea to sea and separating the Himalayan region from the southern peninsula proper. Climate varies greatly, from the arid, sandy deserts of Rajasthan and Gujarat, with temperatures up to 50°C, to the cool highlands of Assam, where annual rainfall can exceed 15 *metres*, perhaps the wettest place on earth.

Corbett National Park (Uttar Pradesh) This is the most famous park for the tiger, now rare throughout India but saved from extinction by India's initially successful Project Tiger. Despite its fame, Corbett is not the best place to see tigers – Kanha in Madhya Pradesh and Ranthambhor in Rajasthan are both better.

Other wildlife includes chital and hog deer, elephant, leopard, sloth bear and muntjac. There are numerous watchtowers, but only daylight photography is allowed. The park has magnificent scenery, from sal forest (giant, teak-like hardwood trees) to extensive river plains. The Ramganga River offers tranquil settings and good fishing. It's a bit touristy, but worth a visit. The best time is from November to May.

Hazaribagh Wildlife Sanctuary (Bihar) This is an area of rolling, forested hills with large herds of deer, notably sambar but also nilgai and chital, as well as tiger and leopard. The best time is from February to March.

Palamau Game Preserve (Bihar) Palamau is smaller than Hazaribagh, but has good concentrations of wildlife including tiger, leopard, elephant, gaur, sambar, chital, nilgai

and muntjac, as well as rhesus macaque, common langur and (rarely) wolf. It is 150 km south of Ranchi, with bungalows at Betla. The best time is from February to March.

Sunderbans Wildlife Sanctuary (West Bengal) These extensive mangrove forests of the Ganges Delta are an important haven for tiger. The reserve is south-east of Calcutta, bordering Bangladesh. The area protects the largest area of mangroves in India. Unfortunately there's no way you'll see a tiger here unless you're being eaten by one! The reserve extends into Bangladesh. Because of the problem of savage tigers, the park guards won't take you into the narrow channels where you might see one of these big cats. There's great birdlife here, though.

Other wildlife includes the fishing cat, which can be seen looking for fish at the water's edge. The only access is by chartered boat (Sunderbans Launch Association, Calcutta). It's best from February to March.

Jaldhapara Wildlife Sanctuary (West Bengal) The tropical forests extending from South-East Asia end around here, and if you don't go further east, this is your chance to see the Indian rhinoceros, elephant and other wildlife. The area protects 100 sq km of lush forest and grasslands, cut by the wide Torsa River. It is 224 km from Darjeeling, via Siliguri and Jalpaiguri (nearest railhead, Hashimara). There's a rest house at Jaldhapara. The park is best from March to May.

Manas Wildlife Sanctuary (Assam) This lovely area is formed from the watershed of the Manas, Hakua and Beki rivers and borders with Bhutan. The bungalows at Mothanguri, on the banks of the Manas, offer views of jungle-clad hills. Established trails enter nearby forests and follow the river-banks. Try to arrange a boat cruise. Besides tiger, the grassland is home to wild buffalo, elephant, sambar, swamp deer and other wildlife; the rare and beautiful golden langur may be seen on the Bhutan side of the Manas. The best time is from January to March.

Kaziranga National Park (Assam) This is the most famous place to see the one-horned Indian rhinoceros, hunted almost to extinction for its prize as big game and for the Chinese apothecary trade. The park is dominated by tall (up to six metres) grasslands and swampy areas (*jheels*). The first sighting of a rhinoceros is always impressive and awesome, as they can reach a height of over two metres and weigh more than two tonnes. Despite the prehistoric appearance, rhinos are incredibly agile and fast. Spotting them in the tall grass may be difficult. Watch for egrets and other birds who use the rhino's armoured back as a perch, and also listen for the 'churring' sound of a large animal moving through the grass. Best viewing may be by the jheels, where they bathe. The best time is from February to March.

Sariska & Sawai Madhopur Wildlife Sanctuaries (Rajasthan) Both of these areas provide good opportunities to see the wildlife of the Indian plains. Sariska is notable for night viewing and its nilgai herds. Sawai Madhopur (or Ranthambhor) is smaller, which can make seeing animals easier, and it has a lake with crocodiles. It is on the Delhi to Bombay railway line, and is 160 km south of Jaipur by road. The best time is from February to June (Sariska), and November to May (Sawai Madhopur). It may be difficult to see tigers at Ranthambhor, though; *BBC World* magazine (Jan/Feb '93) revealed that corrupt officials have allowed illegal poaching to rapidly deplete the tiger population.

Keoladeo Ghana Bird Sanctuary (Rajasthan) This is the best known and most touristy bird sanctuary (usually just called Bharatpur). It features large numbers of breeding waterbirds and thousands of migrating birds from Siberia and China, including herons, storks, cranes and geese. The network of crossroads and tracks through the sanctuary can increase opportunities to see the birds, deer and other wildlife. It is also on the Delhi to Bombay railway line. It's best from September to February.

Gir National Park (Gujarat) Famous for the last surviving Asian lions (around 284), Gir also supports a large variety of other wildlife, notably the chowsingha. This forested oasis in the desert contains Lake Kamaleshwar, complete with crocodiles. The lake and other watering holes are good places to spot animals. The best time is from January to May. The park is closed during the monsoon.

Asian lion, Gir Lion Sanctuary (HF)

Velavadar National Park (Gujarat) This park, 65 km north of Bhavnagar, protects the rich grasslands in the delta region on the west side of the Gulf of Khambhat (Cambay). The main attraction is a large concentration of the beautiful blackbuck. There is a park lodge available for visitors. The best time is from October to June.

Little Rann of Kutch Wildlife Sanctuary (Gujarat) This sanctuary was designated for the protection of the desert region of northwest Gujarat, especially the outer rim and a narrow belt of adjacent land. A variety of desert life can be found here, notably the surviving herds of the Indian wild ass (khur). Also in residence at this sanctuary are wolf and caracal (a large, pale cat with tufted ears). Access is difficult, but can be arranged at Bhuj. The best time to visit is from October to June.

Shivpuri National Park (Madhya Pradesh) This picturesque park close to Gwalior has open forests surrounding a lake. There are good opportunities for photographing various deer, including chinkara, chowsingha and nilgai. It is also home to tiger and leopard. The best time to visit is from February to May.

Kanha National Park (Madhya Pradesh)
Kanha is one of India's most spectacular and exciting parks for both variety and numbers of wildlife, and is well worth a visit. Originally proposed to protect a unique type of swamp deer (barasingha), it is also an important area for tiger. There are large herds of chital, plus blackbuck, gaur, leopard and hyena. The best time is from November to March.

Bandhavgarh National Park (Madhya Pradesh)
Smaller and less touristy than Kanha, Bandhavgarh's setting is impressive, with an old fort on the cliffs above the plains. November to March is the best time to come and view the wildlife here. Although the park is not part of Project Tiger, tiger are occasionally seen.

Similipal Tiger Reserve (Orissa)
This reserve is a vast and beautiful area protecting India's largest region of sal forest, with magnificent scenery and a variety of wildlife, including tiger, elephant, leopard, sambar, chital, muntjac and chevrotain. The best time is from November to June.

Tiger (BT)

Elephant, Kanha National Park (BT)

Southern India Southern India is the location of the Deccan peninsula, which takes the form of a triangular plateau, ranging in altitude from 300 to 900 metres, intersected with rivers, scattered peaks and hill ranges, including the Western and Eastern Ghats. The Ghats form a natural barrier to the monsoons and have created areas of great humidity and rainfall, as on the Malabar Coast where lush lowland tropical rainforest still occurs, with drier regions on the mountains' leeward sides.

Krishnagiri Upavan National Park (Maharashtra)
This park, formerly known as Borivilli, protects an important and scenic area close to Bombay and other attractions. Amongst the smaller types of wildlife to be seen are a variety of waterbirds. The best time is from October to June.

Taroba National Park (Maharashtra)
This is a large park featuring mixed teak forests and a lake, with night viewing available to see its large wildlife populations which include tiger, leopard, gaur, nilgai, sambar and chital. It is 45 km from Chandrapur, south-west from Kanha National Park. You can arrange to stay in the park. The best time is from March to May.

Periyar Wildlife Sanctuary (Kerala)
Periyar is a large and scenic park formed by the watershed of a reservoir developed around a large, artificial lake. It is famous for the large elephant population which can

easily be seen as you travel by boat on the lake.

Other wildlife sometimes seen from the boat are the gaur, Indian wild dog and nilgiri langur, as well as otters, large tortoises, and a rich birdlife, including flights of hornbills. Along the water's edge you may see the flashing, brilliant hues of several kinds of kingfisher, perhaps even a fishing owl. The best time is from February to May.

Jawahar National Park There was a recent proposal to merge Bandipur and Nagarhole national parks (Karnataka), Mudumulai Wildlife Sanctuary (Tamil Nadu), and Wynaad Wildlife Sanctuary (Kerala).

Situated at the junction of the Western Ghats, the Nilgiri Hills and the Deccan plateau, the merging of these contiguous areas would protect the largest elephant population in India, as well as one of the most extensive forested areas in the south. The mixed, diverse forests and their terrain also protect a large variety of other wildlife, including many rare species such as leopard, gaur, sambar, chital, muntjac, chevrotain, bonnet macaque and giant squirrels.

The very rich birdlife includes many spectacular species such as hornbills, barbets, trogons, parakeets, racquet-tailed drongos and streamer-tailed Asian paradise flycatchers. The two most popular areas are Bandipur and Mudumulai. This area should not be missed if you visit the south. The best time is from January to June.

GOVERNMENT

India has a parliamentary system of government with certain similarities to the US government. There are two houses – a lower house known as the Lok Sabha (House of the People) and an upper house known as the Rajya Sabha (Council of States). The lower house has 544 members, all but two elected on a population basis (the other two are nominated to represent the Anglo-Indian community) while the upper has 244 members. Of the 544 seats, 125 are reserved for the Scheduled Castes & Tribes. (See the Population & People section later in this chapter for details on these people.)

As in the British House of Commons or the Australian House of Representatives, the lower house can be dissolved but the upper house, unlike Britain's or Australia's, cannot. Elections for the Lok Sabha have to be held every five years, if the government doesn't call for one earlier than that.

There are also state governments with legislative assemblies known as Vidhan Sabha. The two national houses and the various state houses elect the Indian president who is a figurehead – the prime minister wields the real power.

There is a strict division between the activities handled by the states and by the national government. The police force, education, agriculture and industry are reserved for the state governments. Certain other areas are jointly administered by the two levels of government.

The central government also has the controversial right to assume power in any state if the situation in that state is deemed to be unmanageable. Known as President's Rule, it has been enforced in recent years, either because the law and order situation has got out of hand – notably in Punjab from 1985 to 1992, Kashmir in 1990 and in Assam in 1991 – or because there is a political stalemate – such as occurred in Goa, Tamil Nadu, Pondicherry, Haryana and Meghalaya, also in 1991, and Nagaland in 1992. Of these states, only Meghalaya and Nagaland are still under central rule.

All Indians over the age of 18 have the right to vote.

The current government, headed by P V Narasimha Rao, is a minority government, as Rao's Congress (I) party failed to win an absolute majority in the 1991 elections. The party breakdown of the Lok Sabha seats is: Congress (I) 226, BJP 119, Janata Dal 55, Telugu Desam 13, CPI (M) 35, CPI 13, Independents & Others 47.

The radical Hindu nationalist party, the BJP, has made great gains in the last couple of elections. It is now the main opposition party and actually holds power in Gujarat. It also held Uttar Pradesh until the destruction of the Babri Mosque in Ayodhya led to the dissolution of that state's government.

National Flag & Anthem

The national flag is known as the tricolour. It features three horizontal bands of colour – from top to bottom orange, white and dark green. The *charkha* wheel in the centre of the flag symbolises the *khadi* spinning wheel, which, through its association with Mahatma Gandhi, became a powerful image during the struggle for independence.

The words of the national anthem are taken from a poem by Rabindranath Tagore:

Jana-gana-mana-adhinayaka jaya he
Bharat-bhagya-vidhata
Punjaba-Sindhu-Gujarata-Maratha
Dravida-Utkala-Banga
Vindhya-Himachala-Yamuna-Ganga
Uchchhala-Jaladhi-taranga
Tava Subha name jage, Tava subha asisa mage,
Gahe tava jaya-gatha.
Jana-gana-mangala-dayaka, jaya he
Bharata-bhagya-vidhata
Jaya he, jaya he, jaya he
Jaya jaya jaya, jaya he.

The Indian flag - the tricolour

Tagore's English translation is as follows:

Thou art the ruler of the minds of all people,
Dispenser of India's destiny.
Thy name rouses the hearts of the Punjab,
Sind, Gujarat and Maratha.
Of the Dravid and Orissa and Bengal.
It echoes in the hills of the Vindhyas and Himalayas,
Mingles in the music of the Jamuna and the Ganges,
And is chanted by the waves of the Indian Sea.
They pray for the blessings and sing thy praise,
The saving of all people waits in thy hand,
Thou dispenser of India's destiny,
Victory, victory, victory to thee.

ECONOMY

Although India is a predominantly agricultural country, it is also one of the world's major industrial powers with important heavy industries, such as iron, steel and textiles. It has a large manufacturing base and is now gaining a reputation for computer software development.

Agriculture

The agriculture sector, for so long the mainstay of the Indian economy, now accounts for only about 30% of GDP, yet still employs over 50% of the population. For some years after Independence India depended on foreign aid to meet its food needs, but in the last 30 years production has risen steadily, mainly due to the much larger areas that have been brought under irrigation and the increasing use of high-yield seeds, fertilisers

Rabindranath Tagore

Women in rice field, Hampi, Karnataka (JT)

and pesticides. The country now has large grain stockpiles and is a net exporter of food grains.

The main crops are rice (annual yield of 75 million tonnes) and wheat (55 million tonnes), but it's the cash crops such as cotton, tea and coffee which are the export winners. India is the world's largest producer of tea with an annual production of around 700 million kg, of which over 200 million tonnes is exported. Virtually all the Indian tea is grown in the states of Assam, West Bengal, Kerala and Tamil Nadu.

India also has nearly 200 million cattle which in the rural economy are vitally important – pulling the farmer's cart to market or ploughing the fields. Their religious protection probably first developed as a means of protecting them during droughts or famine when the cows might have been killed off and subsequently been hard to replace. There is also some dairy production. In the cities cows are an involuntary arm of the garbage disposal department and, when not roaming the streets munching on card-board, can be seen rummaging through the concrete bins where waste vegetable matter is tipped.

Industry

For many years India's industrial sector was strictly controlled by the central government, but the level of central intervention has decreased markedly over the past decade. Coupled with easing of foreign investment and technology restrictions, it is hoped that industry can become much more competitive internationally. The partial floating of the rupee in March 1992 also made it much easier for domestic firms to import foreign technology and spare parts.

Currently the vast majority of industries are hopelessly inefficient, use outdated technology and equipment, produce inferior goods unsuitable for export, are often dangerous places to work, and are polluting the environment at an incredible rate. Despite these problems, the country has a huge industrial base with output growing at around 6% per year. Virtually everything you

Pottery from Jaisalmer (RI)

come across in Indian shops is made locally, which is quite an amazing achievement given that the country had very little industrial diversity at Independence.

Textiles account for around 25% of exports, while engineering goods, marine products, and chemicals are all important exports. The major import is oil and petroleum products, accounting for around 25% of imports.

POPULATION & PEOPLE

India has the second-largest population in the world, exceeded only by that of China. In 1961 it had 439 million; in 1971 it had 547 million and by 1981 the population had reached 687 million. In 1991 the figure was 843 million. Despite extensive birth control programmes it is still growing far too rapidly for comfort – around 2.5% per year.

Yet, despite India's many large cities, the country is still overwhelmingly rural. It is estimated that about 230 million of the total population live in urban areas, but with increasing industrialisation the shift from village to city continues to grow.

The Indian people are not a homogeneous group. It is quite easy to tell the difference between the shorter Bengalis of the east, the taller and lighter-skinned people of the centre and north, the Kashmiris with their distinctly central Asian appearance, the Tibetan people of Ladakh, Sikkim and the north of Himachal Pradesh, and the dark-skinned Tamils of the south. Despite these regional variations, the government has managed to successfully establish an 'Indian' ethos and national consciousness.

Although India is overwhelmingly Hindu, there are large minorities of other religions. These include 75 million Muslims, making India one of the largest Muslim countries in the world, much larger than any of the Arab Middle East nations. Christians number about 16 million, Sikhs 13 million, Buddhists five million and Jains three million. About 7% of the population is classified as 'tribal'. They are found scattered throughout the country although there are concentrations of them in the north-east corner of the country as well as in Bihar, Orissa, Madhya Pradesh and Andhra Pradesh.

The literacy rate is 53% nationally, up from 44% in 1981. Men are generally more literate than women – 64% to 39% respectively. The literacy rate varies hugely from

Typical street chaos, Jaipur, Rajasthan (HF)

state to state – Kerala boasts 91% literacy, while in Uttar Pradesh it's 42%. Amongst the Scheduled Castes & Tribes, the literacy rates are abysmal – 28% among men and 9% among women.

The average per capita income is Rs 2830 per annum, or less than Rs 8 per day. For comparison, taxi drivers earn about Rs 7000, teachers about Rs 15,000, bank clerks Rs 25,000, and engineers Rs 35,000. In the government, the head of a small government department receives about Rs 50,000, the prime minister receives a paltry Rs 27,000 (plus perks), while the president gets Rs 240,000 and a Supreme Court judge Rs 108,000.

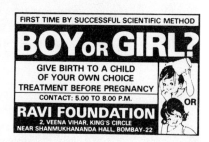

India's Million-Plus Cities

Nearly 30% of India's people live in urban areas, and the country has 20 cities with populations of more than one million. In order, they are:

City	Million people
Bombay	12.6
Calcutta	10.9
Delhi	8.4
Madras	5.4
Hyderabad	4.3
Bangalore	4.1
Ahmedabad	3.3
Pune	2.4
Kanpur	2.1
Lucknow	1.7
Nagpur	1.6
Surat, Jaipur	1.5
Indore	1.2
Coimbatore, Vadodara, Patna, Madurai	1.1
Bhopal, Varanasi	1.0

Birth Control

India's attempts at birth control have been varied. In the early '70s India had a birth control blitz with slogans and posters appearing all over the country, and the famous 'transistor radio in exchange for sterilisation' campaign. More sinister was the brief campaign of the emergency era when squads of sterilisers terrorised half the country and people were afraid to go out after dark. That overkill campaign probably put the birth control programme in India back by years.

It wasn't until the mid '80s that population control was once again a government priority – Rajiv Gandhi mounted an ambitious project, with the target of 1.3 billion Indians by the year 2050.

Although there has been some success at slowing the rate of increase the picture is far from promising. Many experts feel that the solution to the population increase problem in India is to educate the women, particularly in the rural communities. Literate and educated women are much better equipped to understand the need for limiting the size of families and the population as a whole. Decreasing the mortality rate among small children is also seen as a significant factor in reducing the desire for large families. So long as children are a source of security in old age and so long as male heirs are so avidly desired, it is difficult to successfully limit the population growth.

Although educating women is an important part of the programme, the emphasis is

Ladakhi, base of Konke La (RI)

once again on sterilisation, with women the main target. It seems men are unwilling to volunteer for a vasectomy. Women, on the other hand, are better able to see the advantages of not constantly having small children to raise.

In regional areas, social workers are recruited to find 'volunteers' for the operation. As an incentive they are paid a small fee for every person encouraged to go through with it. There is also a small financial incentive offered to people who undergo sterilisation.

Another part of the family planning drive involves widespread use of the media – particularly TV. The two-child family is portrayed as the ideal, and the use of contraceptives, especially condoms, is encouraged – you'll see large billboard ads for condoms such as the Kama Sutra brand.

Castes

The caste system is one of India's more confusing mysteries – how it came about, how it has managed to survive for so long and how much harm it causes are all topics of discussion for visitors to India. Its origins are lost in the mists of time but basically it seems to have been developed by the Brahmins or priest class in order to make their own superior position more permanent. Later it was probably extended by the invading Aryans who felt themselves superior to the indigenous pre-Aryan Indians. Eventually the caste system became formalised into four distinct classes, each with rules of conduct and behaviour.

At the top are the Brahmins who are the priests and the arbiters of what is right and wrong in matters of religion and caste. Next come the Kshatriyas, who are soldiers and administrators. The Vaisyas are the artisan and commercial class, and finally the Sudras are the farmers and the peasant class. These four castes are said to have come from Brahma's mouth (Brahmins), arms (Kshatriyas), thighs (Vaisyas) and feet (Sudras).

Beneath the four main castes is a fifth group, the untouchables. These people, members of the so-called Scheduled Castes, literally have no caste. They perform the most menial and degrading jobs. At one time, if a high-caste Hindu used the same temple as an untouchable, was touched by one, or even had an untouchable's shadow cast across them, they were polluted and had to go through a rigorous series of rituals to be cleansed.

Today the caste system has been much weakened but it still has considerable power, particularly amongst the less educated people. Gandhi put great effort into bringing the untouchables into society, including renaming them the 'Harijans' or 'Children of God'. But an untouchable by any other name...Recently the word Harijan has lost favour, and the use of it in official business has actually been banned in Madhya Pradesh. The term the members of these groups themselves prefer is Dalit, meaning Oppressed or Downtrodden.

It must be remembered that being born into a certain caste does not limit you strictly to one occupation or position in life, just as being black in the USA does not mean you are poverty stricken and live in Harlem. Many Brahmins are poor peasants, for example, and hundreds of years ago the great Maratha leader Shivaji was a Sudra. None of the later Marathas, who controlled much of India after the demise of the Moghuls, were Brahmins. Nevertheless you can generalise that the better-off Indians will be higher caste and that the 'sweeper' you see desultorily cleaning the toilet in your hotel will be a Dalit. In fact when Indian Airlines appointed its first Dalit flight attendant it was front-page news in Indian newspapers.

How can you tell which caste a Hindu belongs to? Well, if you know that their job is a menial one such as cleaning streets or in some way defiling, such as working with leather, they are a Dalit. But for most Hindus you can't really tell which caste they belong to. However, if you see a man with his shirt off and he has the sacred thread looped round one shoulder he belongs to one of the higher castes, but then Parsis also wear a sacred thread. Of course the Sikhs, Muslims and Christians do not have caste.

In many ways the caste system also functions as an enormous unofficial trade union with strict rules to avoid demarcation disputes. Each caste has many subdivisions so that the servant who polishes the brass cannot, due to their caste, also polish silver. Many of the old caste rules have been considerably relaxed, although less educated or more isolated Hindus may still avoid having a lower-caste person prepare their food for fears of becoming polluted. Better educated people are demonstrably none too worried about shaking hands with a caste-less Westerner though! Nor does the thought of going overseas, and thus losing caste completely, carry too much weight these days. Often, quite the opposite, particularly if they return with a degree from an overseas university, and even better with an MBA from Harvard, Yale or the LSE!

The caste system still produces enormous burdens for India, however. During the last few years there have been frequent outbreaks of violence towards members of the Scheduled Castes and so-called Backward classes ('tribals' and those who are poor and/or poorly educated for reasons other than caste). In an effort to improve the lot of these people, the government reserves huge numbers of public sector jobs, parliamentary seats and university places for them. At present, 22.5% of civil service posts are reserved for members of the Scheduled Tribes (STs) and Scheduled Castes (SCs), 27% for members of the so-called Socially & Educationally Backward Classes (SEBCs) and a further 10% for other Backward sections not already covered, including upper-caste poor. The result is that with nearly 60% of the jobs reserved, many well-educated people are missing out on jobs which they would easily get on merit. In 1991 there were serious protests against the raising of the quotas. These protests were most violent in Gujarat, Uttar Pradesh, Delhi and Harayana, and at least 100 people died or were seriously injured in self-immolation incidents.

It's interesting to compare these problems with the situation in the USA where, during the desegregation era, many Blacks experienced great difficulties in being allowed into 'all-White' schools and restaurants. Going far back into Western history, it's equally important to remember that the medieval ideal of heaven was developed in part to keep the peasants in their place – behave yourself, work hard, put up with your lot and you'll go to heaven. Probably caste developed in a similar fashion – your life may be pretty miserable but that's your *karma*; behave yourself and you may be born into a better one next time around.

Tribals

For most people it comes as a surprise to learn that more than 50 million Indians belong to tribal communities as distinct from the great mass of Hindu caste society. These Adivasi, as they are known in India, have origins which precede the Vedic Aryans and even the Dravidians of the south. For thousands of years they have lived more or less undisturbed in the hills and densely wooded regions which were regarded as unattractive by the peasantry of more dynamic populations. Many still speak tribal languages not understood by the politically dominant people, and they follow archaic customs foreign to both Hindus and Muslims alike.

Although there was obviously some contact between the tribals and the Hindu villagers of the open plains in some areas, this rarely led to friction since there was little or no competition for resources and land. All this changed dramatically when improved communications opened up previously inaccessible tribal areas, and rapid growth of the Indian population led to pressure on the land's resources. In the space of just over 40 years the vast majority of tribal people have been dispossessed of their ancestral land and turned into impoverished labourers exploited by all and sundry. The only region where this has not taken place and where tribals continue to manage their own affairs is in Arunachal Pradesh, in the extreme north-east of India. Only here can it be said that the tribes have benefited from contact with modern civilisation and are managing to hold their own.

Elsewhere in India, and especially in Madhya Pradesh, Andhra Pradesh, and Bihar, a shocking tale of exploitation, dispossession and widespread hunger has unfolded with the connivance and even encouragement of officialdom. It's a record which the government would prefer to forget about and which it vehemently denies. Instead, it points to the millions of rupees which it says have been sunk into schemes to improve the condition of the aborigines. Undoubtedly some of this has actually got through but much of it has disappeared in various corruption scams.

It's unlikely that any genuine effort will be made to improve the lot of the tribals in peninsular India, given the pressure for land. What is far more likely is that the erosion of their cultures and traditions will continue until they eventually 'disappear' as distinct tribes.

Sun Temple, Konark (BT)

ARTS
Painting, Sculpture & Architecture

Indian art and sculpture is basically religious in its themes and developments, and appreciation requires at least some knowledge of its religious background. The earliest Indian artefacts are found in the Indus Valley cities in modern-day Pakistan. Pieces are mainly small items of sculpture and it was not until the Mauryan era that India's first major artistic period flowered. This classical school of Buddhist art reached its peak during the reign of Ashoka. The superb sculpture of this period can be seen at its best at Sanchi. The Sungas, who followed the Mauryas, continued their artistic traditions.

When this empire ended the Gandharan period came into its own in the north-west. Close to Peshawar, in today's Pakistan, the Gandharan period combined Buddhism with a strong Greek influence from the descendants of Alexander the Great's invading army. During this period the Buddha began to be represented directly in human form

rather than by symbols such as the footprint or the stupa.

Meanwhile in India proper another school began to develop at Mathura, between Agra and Delhi. Here the religious influence was also Buddhist but was beginning to be altered by the revival of Brahmanism, the forerunner of Hinduism. It was in this school that the tradition of sculpturing *yakshis*, those well-endowed heavenly damsels, began.

During the Gupta period from 320-600 AD, Indian art went through a golden age, and the Buddha images developed their present-day form – even today in Buddhist countries the attitudes, clothing and hand positions have scarcely altered. This was, however, also the end of Buddhist art in India, for Hinduism began to reassert itself. At the same time as the Guptas were bringing Buddhist art to its final zenith in the north, a strongly Hindu tradition was developing in the south. Both schools of art produced metal cast sculptures by the lost wax method, as well as larger sculptures in stone.

The following 1000 years saw a slow but steady development through to the exuberant medieval period of Indian Hindu art. This development can be studied at the caves of Ajanta and Ellora, where there are some of the oldest wall paintings in India, and the sculpture can be traced from the older, stiff and unmoving Buddhist sculptures through to the dynamic and dramatic Hindu figures.

These reached their culmination in the period when sculpture became an integral part of architecture; it is impossible to tell where building ends and sculpture begins. Some of the finest examples of this era can be seen in the Hoysala temples of Karnataka, the elaborate Sun Temple at Konark and the Chandelas' temples at Khajuraho. In all of these the architecture competes valiantly with the artwork, which manages to combine high quality with quite awesome quantity. An interesting common element is the highly detailed erotic scenes. The heavenly maidens of an earlier period have blossomed into scenes, positions and possibilities that leave little to the imagination. Art of this period was not purely a representation of gods and goddesses. Every aspect of human life appeared in the sculptures and obviously in India sex was considered a fairly important aspect!

The arrival of the Muslims with their hatred of other religions and 'idols' caused enormous damage to India's artistic relics. The early invaders' art was chiefly confined to paintings, but with the Moghuls, Indian art went through yet another golden period. Best known of the art forms they encouraged was the miniature painting. These delightfully detailed and brightly coloured paintings showed the events and activities of the Moghuls in their magnificent palaces. Other paintings included portraits, or studies of wildlife and plants.

At the same time there was a massive revival of folk art; some of these developments embraced the Moghul miniature concepts but combined them with Indian religious arts. The popular Rajasthan or Mewar schools often included scenes from Krishna's life and escapades – Krishna is usually painted blue. Interestingly, this school followed the Persian-influenced Moghul school in its miniaturised and highly detailed approach, but made no use of the Persian-developed sense of perspective, and works are generally almost two dimensional.

In the north of India – at Jammu, Basohli and Kangra – the Pahari miniatures followed the Moghul school in having a definite sense of perspective, but in their often religious themes were closer to the Rajasthan school. The Basohli paintings are very dark and use much gold colouring, while the Pahari paintings are often pale and delicate.

The Moghuls' greatest achievements were, however, in the architectural field; it is chiefly for their magnificent buildings that they are remembered. After the Moghuls there has not been another major artistic period of purely Indian background. During the British period art became imitative of

Miniature painting (TW)

Western trends and ideals. Although there was much British painting in India it is interesting primarily as an historical record rather than as art itself.

Music

Indian music is most unlike the concept of music in the West. It is very difficult for a Westerner to appreciate it without a lengthy introduction and much time spent in listening.

The two main forms of Indian music are the southern Carnatic and the northern Hindustani traditions. The basic difficulty is that there is no harmony in the Western sense. The music has two basic elements, the *tala* and the *raga*. Tala is the rhythm and is characterised by the number of beats. *Teental* is a tala of 16 beats. The audience follows the tala by clapping at the appropriate beat which in teental is at one, five and 13. There is no clap at the beat of nine since that is the *khali* or 'empty section' indicated by a wave of the hand.

Just as tala is the rhythm, so is raga the melody; just as there are a number of basic talas so there are many set ragas. The classical Indian music group consists of three musicians who provide the drone, the melody and the rhythm – in other words a background drone, a tala and a raga. The musicians are basically soloists – the concept of an orchestra of Indian musicians is impossible since there is not the harmony that a Western orchestra provides – each musician selects their own tala and raga. The players then zoom off in their chosen directions, as dictated by the tala and the raga selected, and, to the audience's delight, meet every once in a while before again diverging.

Yehudi Menuhin, who has devoted much time and energy to understanding Indian music, suggests that it is much like Indian society: a group of individuals not working together but every once in a while meeting at some common point. Western music is analogous to Western democratic societies, a group of individuals (the orchestra) who each surrender part of their freedom to the harmony of the whole.

Although Indian classical music has one of the longest continuous histories of any musical form, the music had never, until quite recently, been recorded in any written notation. Furthermore, within the basic framework set by the tala and the raga, the musicians improvise – providing variations on the basic melody and rhythm.

Best known of the Indian instruments are the *sitar* and the *tabla*. The sitar is the large stringed instrument popularised by Ravi Shankar in the West – and which more than a few Westerners have discovered is more than just slightly difficult to tune. This is the instrument with which the soloist plays the raga. Other stringed instruments are the *sarod* (which is plucked) or the *sarangi* (which is played with a bow). The tabla, a twin drum rather like a Western bongo, provides the tala. The drone, which runs on two basic notes, is provided by the oboe-like *shehnai* or the *tampura*.

Dance

Indian dancing relates back to Siva's role as Nataraj, Lord of the Dance. Lord Siva's first wife was Sati and when her father, who disliked Siva, insulted him Sati committed suicide in a sacrifice by fire that later took her name. Outraged, Siva killed his father-in-law and danced the Tandava – the Dance of Destruction. Later Sati reincarnated as Parvati, married Siva again and danced the Lasya. Thus the Tandava became the male form of dance, the Lasya the female form. Dancing was a part of the religious temple rituals and the dancers were known as *devadasis*. Their dances retold stories from the *Ramayana* or the *Mahabharata*.

Temple dancing is no longer practised but classical Indian dancing is still based on its religious background. Indian dance is divided into *nritta* – the rhythmic elements, *nritya* – the combination of rhythm with expression, and *natya* – the dramatic element. Nritya is usually expressed through eye, hand and facial movements and with nritta makes up the usual dance programmes. To appreciate natya, dance drama, you have

Hunting Music in India

Years and years ago, back in the '60s, I first heard Indian music. It got me in its spell and last year I finally made my passage to India, with the LP in hand and the idea to buy a sitar in mind.

Music cassettes are always a good buy. Most cassette stands sell many songs from Bombay movies. When you ask for classical or folk music the offer usually consists of a variety of music of moderate quality. A very good place to look for music is around temples – religion and music are inseparable in India. *Bhakti* or devotional music is what you hear on the street at festivals. A ringing tabla and sweet voices build a very Indian atmosphere indeed.

The best city for classical music is without doubt Varanasi. Music is a living part of the town. I walked into a music shop, intending to pass a little time, and spent several days there. Sur Sangam is run by Shibu and Gudda, who offer a rich variety of classical music, beautiful instruments and, most importantly, patience and love of music. In my days there I learned more about music than I had in all the years before. If you come to Varanasi and have some interest in Indian music, this really is the place to visit. It is here you will meet many musicians and music lovers. Sur Sangam is right in the centre of Varanasi, two minutes walk from the main ghat.

Buying a sitar is easy in India; finding a good one is something else. The price of the instrument is not the problem – for US$40 you can get a lookalike in a handicraft shop. If you want an instrument to play, you can find real masterpieces for around US$250. Add another US$150 for a good carrying case. I ended up with two sitars. In Varanasi I bought a beautiful piece at Sur Sangam. The instrument has everything you would expect: a beautiful buzzing sound, very elaborate decorations and more. If you cannot make it to Varanasi, go to Rikhi Ram at the Marina Arcade, Connaught Circus, New Delhi. His instruments are of a very good quality as well, although they are more expensive and the decorations are not as elaborate.

Playing the sitar is not as difficult as I feared it would be, but you really need experience on something like a guitar. A good bookshop will offer a variety of books on playing and on music. In Varanasi there are several possibilities for lessons. Ask at Sur Sangam.

Enjoy your stay, keep your ears and mind open, *namaste.*

Peter van Ooijen – Netherlands

Musicians (HF)

to understand and appreciate Indian legends and mythology.

Dance is divided into four basic forms known as Bharat Natyam, Kathakali, Kathak and Manipuri. Bharat Natyam is further sub-divided into three other classical forms. One of the most popular, it originated in the great temples of the south and usually tells of events in Krishna's life. Bharat Natyam dancers are usually women and, like the sculptures they take their positions from, always dance bent-kneed, never standing upright, and use a huge repertoire of hand movements. Orissi, Mohini Attam and Kuchipudi are variations of Bharat Natyam which take their names from the places where they originated.

Kathakali, the second major dance form, originated in Kerala and is exclusively danced by men. It tells of epic battles of gods and demons and is as dynamic and dramatic as Bharat Natyam is austere and expressive. Kathakali dancing is noted for the elaborate make-up and painted masks which the dancers wear. They even use special eye-drops to turn their eyes a bloodshot red!

Manipuri dances come, as the name indicates, from the Manipur region in the north-east. These are folk dances and the message is made through body and arm movements. The women dancers wear hooped skirts and conical caps which are extremely picturesque.

The final classical dance type is Kathak, which originated in the north and at first was very similar to the Bharat Natyam school. Persian and Muslim influences later altered the dance from a temple ritual to a courtly entertainment. The dances are performed straight-legged and there are intricately choreographed foot movements to be followed. The ankle bells which dancers wear must be adeptly controlled and the costumes and themes are often similar to those in Moghul miniature paintings.

There are many opportunities to see classical Indian dancing while you are in India. The major hotels often put on performances to which outsiders as well as hotel guests are welcome.

Film

The Indian film industry is the largest in the world in purely volume terms – in 1990, a massive 948 films were registered for classification with the censorship board! There are more than 12,000 cinemas across the country, and at least five times as many 'video halls'. The vast proportion of what is produced are your average 'masala movies' – cheap melodramas based on three vital ingredients: romance, violence and music. Most are dreadful, but it's cheap escapism for the masses, a chance to dream.

However, for all the dross churned out, India has produced some wonderful films from brilliant directors, foremost among them being Satyajit Ray. Ray first came onto the scene in the '50s when his film *Pather Panchali* gained international recognition. For the next 40 years Ray turned out consistently excellent work, and in 1992, shortly before he died, he was awarded an Oscar, which was presented to him at his bedside in

Kathakali dancer (FH)

Film billboards (TW)

Calcutta where he was seriously ill. His best films include *Pather Panchali, Apur Sansar, Ashani Sanket* and *Jana Aranya.*

Shot on the streets of Bombay is the excellent film *Salaam Bombay* by Meera Nair. It concentrates on the plight of the street children in Bombay, and won the Golden Camera Prize at Cannes in 1989.

Other notable Indian directors include Mrinal Sen, Rotwik Ghatak, Shaji N Karuns, Adoor and Aravindan.

See the section called Foreign Films in the Facts for the Visitor chapter for details on films about India which have been made in the West.

CULTURE
Marriage
One place where the caste system is still well entrenched is the choosing of marriage partners. You only need to read a few of the 'matrimonial' advertisements which appear in many places, including the national newspapers, to realise that marriage across the

'caste bar', even among wealthy, well-educated or higher caste people, is basically not on. The majority of marriages are still arranged by the parents, although 'love marriages' are becoming more common, particularly in the big cities.

When a couple are choosing a partner for their son or daughter, a number of factors are taken into consideration: caste of course is pre-eminent, but other considerations are beauty and physical flaws – the matrimonial ads can seem brutally frank in this regard – and a horoscope for the would-be partner is often called for. Many potential matches are rejected simply because the astrological signs are not propitious. The financial status of the prospective partner's family is also taken into account.

Another facet of marriage is the pernicious dowry. A dowry was originally a gift to the bride from her parents, so she would have something of her own and would in turn be able to provide a dowry to her own daughters. These days, however, the dowry is a

LIFE-companion for 28 year old, good-looking boy, well-settled in decent job, suffering from sexual disorder, i.e., acute premature ejaculation. Girl should either be suffering from same disease or is not interested in sex otherwise.

Intermediate, wheatish complexioned, healthy and emotional after motor-cycle accident, can freely move about limping on one leg, fully recoverable after operation (doctor's opinion), own business (machinery parts) in lakhs, transactions in lakhs with local State Bank, through Govt Deptts, after accident, himself can start and drive own motor cycle, belonging to small and happy prosperous family, father gazetted officer and all relatives class one officers, handsome youth, wants beautiful, smart bride. Boy will bear himself, all expenses of both sides. Punjabi, smart, beautiful girl, desiring inter-caste marriage, welcome. No sub-caste Kayasth bar within Kayasth. Early court marriage. Girl can also correspond herself.

Looking for a partner?

matter of status for the bride's family – the bigger the dowry and grander the ceremony, the greater the prestige to the family.

Although the practice is officially outlawed, a dowry is still expected in the majority of cases. For poorer families the marriage can become a huge financial burden. Many men have to borrow the money, either for their daughter's dowry or to stage a lavish ceremony and feast (or both), usually at outrageous rates of interest. The end result is that for the rest of their lives they are indebted to the feared moneylenders, or become bonded labourers.

The amount of an expected dowry varies, but it is never small. The main determining factor is the level of education and social standing of the young man; a dowry of at least US$20,000 would be expected from the family of a young woman hoping to marry a graduate of a foreign university, a doctor or other highly paid professional. A 'Green Card' (American residence card) is also highly desirable, and the holder of one can command a high price.

Another deplorable side of the dowry system is the practice of 'bride burning'. It's amazing how often women are burned to death in kitchen fires, usually from 'spilt' kerosene. The majority of these cases, however, are either suicides – desperate women who could no longer cope with the pressure from their parents-in-law for dowry payments – or outright murders by in-laws who want their son to remarry someone who is better able to provide a sizeable dowry.

The official age for marriage is 18 years, but this is widely ignored – 8% of girls aged between 10 and 14 are married, and nearly 50% of females aged between 15 and 19 are married, although the average age for marriage is 18.3 for women and 23.3 for men. Virginity is also of vital importance, and it is often listed among the woman's attributes in the matrimonial columns.

Indian Clothing

Many travellers start wearing Indian clothes while in India – after all, much of it is a lot more appropriate to India's climate than jeans and T-shirts. The best known Indian clothing is the *sari*. It is also the one piece of clothing which is very difficult for Western women to carry off properly. This supremely graceful attire is simply one length of material, a bit over a metre in width and five to nine metres long (usually around six metres long). It's worn without any pins, buttons or fastenings to hold it in place so in part its graceful appearance is a necessity. The tightly fitted, short blouse worn under a sari is a *choli*. The final length of the sari, which

Rajasthani women (RI)

is draped over the wearer's shoulder, is known as the *pallav* or *palloo*.

There are a number of variations in types of saris and styles of wearing them, but there are also other styles of women's costume in India. Kashmiri and Sikh women wear pyjama-like trousers drawn tightly in at the waist and the ankles. Over these trousers, known as *salwars*, they wear a long, loose tunic known as a *kameez*. This attire is comfortable and 'respectable'. A *churidhar* is similar to the salwar but tighter fitting at the hips. Over this goes a collarless or mandarin-collar *kurta* – an item of clothing just as popular in the West, where it is worn by men as much as women, as in India.

Although the overwhelming majority of Indian women wear traditional costume, many Indian men wear quite conventional Western clothing. Indeed a large proportion of India's consumer advertising appears to be devoted to 'suitings & shirtings' – the material made for tailor-made, Western-style business suits and shirts. You can easily get

a suit made to measure, although the styling is likely to be somewhat dated. The collarless jackets, known as 'Nehru jackets', are a popular buy among travellers. These khadi (homespun cloth) coats are best bought at the government khadi emporiums found in the major cities.

The traditional *lungi* originated in the south and today is worn by women as well as men. It's simply a short length of material worn around the thighs rather like a sarong. The lungi can be rolled up but should be lowered when sitting down or when entering someone's home or a temple. A *dhoti* is like a longer lungi but with a length of material pulled up between the legs, effective but a long way from elegant! A dhoti is a more formal piece of attire than a lungi, however. Pyjama-like trousers, worn by countryfolk, are known as *lenga*. Regular striped pyjamas are casual and comfortable but they're looked upon as a labourer's outfit; not something to wear to a fancy restaurant or to somebody's home.

Festival clothing (RI)

Zanskari woman, Ladakh (HF)

There are many religious and regional variations, such as the brightly mirrored Rajasthani skirts and their equally colourful tie-dye materials. In Ladakh the women wear superbly picturesque Tibetan costumes with high 'top hats'. The men wear long dressing-gown-like coats. Muslim women, of course, wear much more staid and all-covering attire than their Hindu sisters. More traditional Muslim women wear the all-enveloping, tent-like *burkha*.

Sport

Indians follow a variety of sports including field hockey, soccer and cricket. In hockey they are one of the world's leaders with several Olympic golds to their credit. Soccer has a keen following in a number of big cities, particularly Calcutta, where it is a major sport.

India's national sport (obsession almost) has to be cricket. There's something about a game with as many idiosyncrasies and peculiarities as cricket which simply has to appeal to the Indian temperament. During the cricket season, if an international side is touring India and there is a test match on, you'll see crowds outside the many shops which have a TV, and people walking down the street with a pocket radio pressed to their ears. Test matches with Pakistan have a particularly strong following as the rivalry is intense. One thing you can count on is that most Indians will know the names of the entire touring cricket team and, if you come from the same country but don't know their names, then you may well be regarded as mentally retarded. On the other hand, if you do have an interest in cricket, it can be a great way to start up conversations.

RELIGION

India has a positive kaleidoscope of religions. There is probably more diversity of religions and sects in India than anywhere else on earth. Apart from having nearly all the world's great religions represented, India was the birthplace of Hinduism and Buddhism, an important home to Zoroastrianism, one of the world's oldest religions, and home to Jainism, an ancient religion unique to India.

Hinduism

India's major religion, Hinduism, is practised by approximately 80% of the population, over 670 million people. Only in Nepal, the Indonesian island of Bali, the Indian Ocean island of Mauritius and possibly Fiji, do Hindus also predominate, but it is the largest religion in Asia in terms of number of adherents. Despite its colourful appearance it is actually one of the oldest extant religions with firm roots extending back to beyond 1000 BC.

The Indus Valley civilisation developed a religion which shows a close relationship to Hinduism in many ways. Later, it further developed through the combined religious practices of the southern Dravidians and the Aryan invaders who arrived in the north of India around 1500 BC. Around 1000 BC, the Vedic scriptures were introduced and gave the first loose framework to the religion.

Hinduism today has a number of holy books, the most important being the four *Vedas* (Divine Knowledge) which are the foundation of Hindu philosophy. The *Upanishads* are contained within the *Vedas* and delve into the metaphysical nature of the universe and soul. The *Mahabharata* (Great War of the Bharatas) is an epic poem containing over 220,000 lines. It describes the battles between the Kauravas and Pandavas, who were descendants of the Lunar race. In it is the story of Rama, and it is probable that the most famous Hindu epic, the *Ramayana*, was based on this. The *Ramayana* is highly revered by Hindus, perhaps because a verse in the introduction says 'He who reads and repeats this holy life-giving *Ramayana* is liberated from all his sins and exalted with all his posterity to the highest heaven'. The *Bhagavad Gita* is a famous episode of the *Mahabharata* where Krishna relates his philosophies to Arjuna.

Nandi Bull, Mysore (MC)

Basically the religion postulates that we will all go through a series of rebirths or reincarnations that eventually lead to *moksha*, the spiritual salvation which frees one from the cycle of rebirths. With each rebirth you can move closer to or further from eventual moksha; the deciding factor is your karma, which is literally a law of cause and effect. Bad actions during your life result in bad karma, which ends in a lower reincarnation. Conversely, if your deeds and actions have been good you will reincarnate on a higher level and be a step closer to eventual freedom from rebirth.

Dharma or the natural law defines the total social, ethical and spiritual harmony of your life. There are three categories of dharma, the first being the eternal harmony which involves the whole universe. The second category is the dharma that controls castes and the relations between castes. The third dharma is the moral code which an individual should follow.

The Hindu religion has three basic practices. They are *puja* or worship, the cremation of the dead, and the rules and regulations of the caste system. There are four main castes: the Brahmin, or priest caste; the Kshatriyas, or soldiers and governors; the Vaisyas, or tradespeople and farmers; and the Sudras or menial workers and artisans. These basic castes are then subdivided into a great number of lesser divisions. Beneath all the castes are the Dalits (formerly known as Harijans), or untouchables, the lowest caste-less class for whom all the most menial and degrading tasks are reserved.

Westerners have trouble understanding Hinduism principally because of its vast pantheon of gods. In fact you can look upon all these different gods simply as pictorial representations of the many attributes of a god. The one omnipresent god usually has three physical representations. Brahma is the creator, Vishnu is the preserver and Siva is the destroyer and reproducer. All three gods are usually shown with four arms, but Brahma has the added advantage of four heads to represent his all-seeing presence.

The four *Vedas* are supposed to have emanated from his mouths.

Each god has an associated animal known as the 'vehicle' on which they ride, as well as a consort with certain attributes and abilities. Generally each god also holds a symbol; you can often pick out which god is represented by the vehicle or symbol. Brahma's consort is Sarasvati, the goddess of learning. She rides upon a white swan and holds the stringed musical instrument known as a *veena*.

Vishnu, the preserver, is usually shown in one of the physical forms in which he has visited earth. In all, Vishnu has paid nine visits and on his 10th he is expected as a Kalki, riding a horse. On earlier visits he appeared in animal form, as in his boar or man-lion (Narsingh) incarnations, but on visit seven he appeared as Rama, regarded as the personification of the ideal man and the hero of the *Ramayana*. Rama also managed to provide a number of secondary gods including his helpful ally Hanuman, the monkey god. Hanuman's faithful nature is illustrated by the representation of him often found guarding fort or palace entrances. Naturally incarnations can also have consorts and Rama's lady was Sita.

On visit eight Vishnu came as Krishna, who was brought up with peasants and thus became a great favourite of the working classes. Krishna is renowned for his exploits with the *gopis* or shepherdesses and his consorts are Radha the head of the gopis, Rukmani and Satyabhama. Krishna is often blue in colour and plays a flute. Vishnu's last incarnation was on visit nine, as the Buddha. This was probably a ploy to bring the Buddhist splinter group back into the Hindu fold.

When Vishnu appears as Vishnu, rather than one of his incarnations, he sits on a couch made from the coils of a serpent and in his hands he holds two symbols, the conch shell and the discus. Vishnu's vehicle is the half-man half-eagle known as the Garuda. The Garuda is a firm do-gooder and has a deep dislike of snakes – Indonesia's national airline is named after the Garuda. His consort is the beautiful Lakshmi (Laxmi) who came from the sea and is the goddess of wealth and prosperity.

Siva's creative role is phallically symbolised by his representation as the frequently worshipped lingam. Siva rides on the bull Nandi and his matted hair is said to have Ganga, the goddess of the river Ganges, in it. He is supposed to live in the Himalaya and devote much time to smoking dope. He has the third eye in the middle of his forehead and carries a trident. Siva is also known as Nataraj, the cosmic dancer whose dance shook the cosmos and created the world. Siva's consort is Parvati, the beautiful. She, however, has a dark side when she appears as Durga, the terrible. In this role she holds weapons in her 10 hands and rides a tiger. As Kali, the fiercest of the gods, she demands sacrifices and wears a garland of skulls. Kali usually handles the destructive side of Siva's personality.

Siva and Parvati have two children.

Chamunda, manifestation of the goddess Durga (TW)

Ganesh (GE)

Ganesh is the elephant-headed god of prosperity and wisdom, and is probably the most popular of all the gods. Ganesh obtained his elephant head due to his father's notorious temper. Coming back from a long trip, Siva discovered Parvati in her room with a young man. Not pausing to think that their son might have grown up a little during his absence, Siva lopped his head off! He was then forced by Parvati to bring his son back to life but could only do so by giving him the head of the first living thing he saw – which happened to be an elephant. Ganesh's vehicle is a rat. Siva and Parvati's other son is Kartikkaya, the god of war.

A variety of lesser gods and goddesses also crowd the scene. Most temples are dedicated to one or other of the gods, but curiously there are very few Brahma temples – perhaps just two or three in all of India. Most Hindus profess to be either Vaishnavaites (followers of Vishnu) or Shaivites (followers of Siva). The cow is, of course, the holy animal of Hinduism.

Hinduism is not a proselytising religion since you cannot be converted. You're either born a Hindu or you are not; you can never become one. Similarly, once you are a Hindu you cannot change your caste – you're born into it and are stuck with it for the rest of that lifetime. Nevertheless Hinduism has a great attraction to many Westerners and India's 'export gurus' are many and successful.

A *guru* is not so much a teacher as a spiritual guide, somebody who by example or simply by their presence indicates what path you should follow. In a spiritual search one always needs a guru. A *sadhu* is an individual on a spiritual search. They're an easily recognised group, usually wandering around half-naked, smeared in dust with their hair and beard matted. Sadhus following Siva will sometimes carry his symbol, the trident. A sadhu is often someone who has decided that his business and family life have reached their natural conclusions and that it is time to throw everything aside and go out on a spiritual search. He may previously have been the village postman, or a businessman. Sadhus perform various feats

Sadhus on pilgrimage, Pahalgam, Jammu & Kashmir (GE)

of self-mortification and wander all over India, occasionally coming together in great pilgrimages and other religious gatherings. Many sadhus are, of course, simply beggars following a more sophisticated approach to gathering in the paise, but others are completely genuine in their search.

Entry Prohibited One clear contrast to the general Indian mood of tolerance is the way Westerners are not allowed into some Hindu temples. This chiefly applies to the temples in Orissa and Varanasi, and to some temples in the south, particularly in Kerala. It's in complete contrast to Jain and Buddhist temples or Muslim mosques, where you are almost always allowed to wander at will. These regulations have been relaxed over the years and today there are far fewer places where an outright ban applies. It's worth noting that it took Mahatma Gandhi to open many temples, even to some Hindus.

Untouchables were banned from entering temples earlier this century.

An irritation is that in many cases the national or state tourist boards expound at length about the glories of these places, and yet never mention, even in the smallest print, that if you're a Westerner you may not be allowed into various parts of the temples, or in some, even across the threshold. The Orissa publicists are particularly guilty of this. In Tamil Nadu, where there are many wonderful temples, attitudes are fairly relaxed and, at most places, you can explore all but the inner sanctum. If you're appropriately dressed and sufficiently respectful you may even be invited in there.

Buddhism

Although there are only about five million Buddhists in India, the religion is of great importance because it had its birth here and there are many reminders of its historic role. Strictly speaking Buddhism is not a religion, since it is not centred on a god, but a system of philosophy and a code of morality.

Buddhism was founded in northern India about 500 BC when Siddhartha Gautama, born a prince, achieved enlightenment. Gautama Buddha was not the first Buddha but the fourth, and is not expected to be the last 'enlightened one'. Buddhists believe that the achievement of enlightenment is the goal of every being so eventually we will all reach Buddhahood.

The Buddha never wrote down his dharma or teachings, and a schism later developed so that today there are two major Buddhist schools. The Theravada (Doctrine of the Elders) or Hinayana (Small Vehicle) holds that the path to *nirvana*, the eventual aim of all Buddhists, is an individual pursuit. In contrast, the Mahayana (Large Vehicle) school holds that the combined belief of its followers will eventually be great enough to encompass all of humanity and bear it to salvation. To some the less austere and ascetic Mahayana school is a 'soft option'. Today it is chiefly practised in Vietnam, Japan and China, while the Hinayana school is followed in Sri Lanka, Myanmar (Burma),

Cambodia and Thailand. There are other, sometimes more esoteric, divisions of Buddhism such as the Hindu-Tantric Buddhism of Tibet which you can see in Ladakh and other parts of north India.

The Buddha renounced his material life to search for enlightenment but, unlike other prophets, found that starvation did not lead to discovery. Therefore he developed his rule of the 'middle way', moderation in everything. The Buddha taught that all life is suffering but that suffering comes from our sensual desires and the illusion that they are important. By following the 'eight-fold path' these desires will be extinguished and a state of nirvana, where we are free from their delusions, will be reached. Following this process requires going through a series of rebirths until the goal is eventually reached and no more rebirths into the world of suffering are necessary. The path that takes you through this cycle of births is karma, but this is not simply fate. Karma is a law of cause

Buddha, Bodhgaya (TW)

and effect; your actions in one life determine the role you will play and what you will have to go through in your next life.

In India, Buddhism developed rapidly when it was embraced by the great Emperor Ashoka. As his empire extended over much of India, so was Buddhism carried forth. He also sent out missions to other lands to preach the Buddha's word, and his own son is said to have carried Buddhism to Sri Lanka. Later, however, Buddhism began to contract in India because it had never really taken a hold on the great mass of people. As Hinduism revived, Buddhism in India was gradually reabsorbed into the older religion. Today Buddha, to Hindus, is another incarnation of Vishnu. At its peak, however, Buddhism was responsible for magnificent structures erected wherever it held sway. The earlier Theravada form of Buddhism did not believe in the representation of the Buddha in human form. His presence was always alluded to in Buddhist art or architecture through symbols such as the bo tree, under which he was sitting when he attained enlightenment, the elephant, which his mother dreamed of before he was born, or the wheel of life. Today, however, even Theravada Buddhists produce Buddha images.

Islam

Muslims, followers of the Islamic religion, are India's largest religious minority. They number about 75 million in all, over 10% of the country's population. This makes India one of the largest Islamic nations in the world. India has had two Muslim presidents, several cabinet ministers and state chief ministers since Independence. Islam is the most recent and most widespread of the Asian religions; it predominates from the Mediterranean across to India and is the major religion east of India in Bangladesh, Malaysia and Indonesia.

The religion's founder, the prophet Mohammed, was born in 570 AD at Mecca, now part of Saudi Arabia. He had his first revelation from Allah (God) in 610 and this and later visions were compiled into the

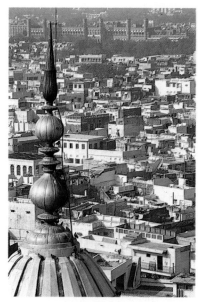

Jami Masjid, New Delhi (TW)

continents. The Arabs, who first propagated the faith, developed a reputation as being ruthless opponents but reasonable masters, so people often found it advisable to surrender to them. In this way the Muslims swept aside the crumbling Byzantine Empire, whose people felt no desire to support their distant Christian emperor.

Islam only travelled west for 100 years before being pushed back at Poitiers, France, in 732, but it continued east for centuries. It regenerated the Persian Empire, which was then declining from its protracted struggles with Byzantium, and in 711, the same year the Arabs landed in Spain, they sent dhows up the Indus River into India. This was more a casual raid than a full-scale invasion, but in the 12th century all of north India fell into Muslim hands. Eventually the Moghul Empire controlled most of the subcontinent. From here it was spread by Indian traders into South-East Asia.

At an early stage Islam suffered a fundamental split that remains to this day. The third caliph, successor to Mohammed, was murdered and followed by Ali, the prophet's son-in-law, in 656. Ali was assassinated in 661 by the governor of Syria, who set himself up as caliph in preference to the descendants of Ali. Most Muslims today are Sunnites, followers of the succession from the caliph, while the others are Shias or Shi'ites who follow the descendants of Ali.

Despite its initial vigour, Islam eventually became inertial and unchanging though it remains to be seen what effect the fanatical fundamentalism of Shi'ite Iran will have on the religion worldwide. In India itself, despite Islam's long period of control over the centuries, it never managed to make great inroads into Hindu society and religion. Converts to Islam were principally made from the lowest castes, with the result that at Partition Pakistan found itself with a shortage of the educated clerical workers and government officials with which India is so liberally endowed. Although it did not make great numbers of converts, the visible effects of Muslim influence in India are strong in architecture, art and food.

Muslim holy book, the Koran. As his purpose in life was revealed to him, Mohammed began to preach against the idolatry for which Mecca was then the centre. Muslims are strictly monotheistic and believe that to search for God through images is a sin. Muslim teachings correspond closely with the Old Testament of the Bible, and Moses and Jesus are both accepted as Muslim prophets, although Jesus is not the son of God.

Eventually Mohammed's attacks on local business caused him and his followers to be run out of town in 622. They fled to Medina, the 'city of the prophet', and by 630 were strong enough to march back into Mecca and take over. Although Mohammed died in 632, most of Arabia had been converted to Islam within two decades.

The Muslim faith was more than a religion; it called on its followers to spread the word – if necessary by the sword. In succeeding centuries Islam was to expand over three

Converts to Islam have only to announce that 'There is no God but Allah and Mohammed is his prophet' and they become Muslims. Friday is the Muslim holy day and the main mosque in each town is known as the Jami Masjid or Friday Mosque. One of the aims of every Muslim is to make the pilgrimage *(haj)* to Mecca and become a *hajji*.

Sikhism

The Sikhs in India number 13 million and are predominantly located in the Punjab, although they are found all over India. They are the most visible of the Indian religious groups because of the five symbols introduced by Guru Gobind Singh so that Sikh men could easily recognise each other. They are known as the five *kakkars* and are: *kesh* – uncut hair; *kangha* – the wooden or ivory comb; *kachha* – shorts; *kara* – the steel bracelet; and *kirpan* – the sword. Because of their kesha, Sikh men wear their hair tied up in a bun and hidden by a long turban. Wearing kachha and carrying a kirpan came about because of the Sikhs' military tradition – they didn't want to be tripping over a long dhoti or be caught without a weapon. Normally the sword is simply represented by a tiny image set in the comb. The steel bracelet has the useful secondary function of making a good bottle opener. With his beard, turban and upright, military bearing, the 'noble' Sikh is hard to miss!

The Sikh religion was founded by Guru Nanak, who was born in 1469. It was originally intended to bring together the best of the Hindu and Islamic religions. Its basic tenets are similar to those of Hinduism with the important modification that the Sikhs are opposed to caste distinctions and pilgrimages to rivers. They are not, however, opposed to pilgrimages to holy sites.

They worship at temples known as *gurdwaras*, baptise their children, when they are old enough to understand the religion, in a ceremony known as *pahul*, and cremate their dead. The holy book of the Sikhs is the *Granth Sahib* which contains the works of the 10 Sikh gurus together with Hindu and Muslim writings. The last guru died in 1708.

In the 16th century, Guru Gobind Singh introduced military overtones into the religion in an attempt to halt the persecution the Sikhs were then suffering. A brotherhood, known as the *khalsa* was formed, and entry into it was conditional on a person undergoing baptism *(amrit)*. From that time the majority of Sikhs have borne the surname Singh which means Lion (although just because a person has the surname Singh, doesn't mean they are necessarily a Sikh; many Rajputs also have this surname).

Sikhs believe in one god and are opposed to idol worship. They practise tolerance and love of others, and their belief in hospitality extends to offering shelter to anyone who comes to their gurdwaras. Because of their get-on-with-it attitude to life they are one of the better-off groups in Indian society. They have a well-known reputation for mechanical aptitude and specialise in handling

Golden Temple, Amritsar (GE)

machinery of every type, from jumbo jets to auto-rickshaws.

At present, the Punjab region of India is torn by strife due to a minority of Sikhs demanding greater autonomy for the Punjab, or even an independent state to be called Khalistan. A solution to these problems is still not in sight. Foreigners can travel freely in Punjab without permits, but the situation is still volatile and outbreaks of violence (mainly hit-and-run shootings) are still quite common.

Jainism

The Jain religion is contemporaneous with Buddhism and bears many similarities to it. It was founded around 500 BC by Mahavira, the 24th and last of the Jain prophets, known as *tirthankars* or Finders of the Path. The Jains now number only about 3.2 million and are found all over India, but predominantly in the west and south-west. They believe that the universe is infinite and was not created by a deity. They also believe in reincarnation and eventual spiritual salvation, or moksha, through following the path of the tirthankars. One factor in the search for salvation is *ahimsa*, or reverence for all life and the avoidance of injury to all living things. Due to this belief Jains are strict vegetarians and some monks actually cover their mouths with a piece of cloth in order to avoid the risk of accidentally swallowing an insect.

The Jains are divided into two sects, the Shvetambara and the Digambara. The Digambaras are the more austere sect and their name literally means Sky Clad since, as a sign of their contempt for material possessions, they do not even wear clothes. Not surprisingly Digambaras are generally monks who confine their nudity to the monasteries! The famous Sravanabelagola shrine in Karnataka state, south India, is a Digambara temple.

Jain temples are noted for the large number of similar buildings which are often erected at one place – such as the Palitana group in Gujarat. Their temples also have many columns, no two of which are ever identical. The Jains tend to be commercially

Jain temples atop Girnar Hill, Junagadh, Gujarat (HF)

successful and have an influence disproportionate to their actual numbers. Their temples are often extremely well kept. There are many Jains in Rajasthan, Gujarat and Bombay.

Zoroastrianism

This is one of the oldest religions on earth and was founded in Persia by the prophet Zarathustra (Zoroaster) in the 6th or 7th century BC. He was born in Mazar-i-Sharif in what is now Afghanistan. At one time Zoroastrianism stretched all the way from India to the Mediterranean but today is found only around Shiraz in Iran, Karachi in Pakistan, and Bombay in India. The followers of Zoroastrianism are known as Parsis since they originally fled to India to escape persecution in Persia.

Zoroastrianism was one of the first religions to postulate an omnipotent and invisible god. Their scripture is the *Zend-Avesta*, which describes the continual conflict between the forces of good and evil. Their god is Ahura Mazda, the god of light, who is symbolised by fire. Humanity ensures the victory of good over evil by following the principles of *humata* or good thoughts, *hukta* or good words and *huvarshta* or good deeds.

Parsis worship in fire temples and wear a *sadra* or sacred shirt and a *kasti* or sacred thread. Children first wear these sacred items in a ceremony known as Navjote. Flames burn eternally in their fire temples but fire is worshipped as a symbol of God, not for itself. Because Parsis believe in the purity of elements they will not cremate or bury their dead since it would pollute the fire, earth, air or water. Instead they leave the bodies in 'Towers of Silence' where they are soon cleaned off by vultures.

Although there are only about 85,000 Parsis, concentrated in Bombay, they are very successful in commerce and industry, and have become notable philanthropists. Parsis have influence far greater than their numbers would indicate and have often acted as a channel of communication between India and Pakistan when the two countries were at loggerheads. Because of the strict requirements that a Parsi must only marry another Parsi and children must have two Parsi parents to be Parsis, their numbers are gradually declining.

Christianity & Judaism

India has around 16 million Christians. There have been Christian communities in Kerala as long as Christianity has been in Europe, for St Thomas the Apostle is supposed to have arrived here in 54 AD. The Portuguese, who unlike the English were as enthusiastic about spreading their brand of Christianity as making money from trade, left a large Christian community in Goa. Generally though, Christianity has not had great success in India, if success is counted in number of converts. The first round of Indian converts to Christianity were generally those from the ruling classes and after that the converts were mainly from the lower castes.

There are, however, two small states (Mizoram and Nagaland) where Christians form a majority of the population. A quarter of the population of Kerala and a third of Goa are also Christian.

There are small Jewish communities in a number of cities, but the Jews of Kochi (Cochin) in Kerala are of interest because a group claims to have arrived here in 587 BC.

LANGUAGE

There is no 'Indian' language, which is part of the reason why English is still widely spoken over 40 years after the British left India, and it's still the official language of the judiciary. The country is divided into a great number of local languages and in many cases the state boundaries have been drawn on linguistic lines. In all there are 15 languages recognised by the constitution, and these fall into two groups: Indic or Indo-Aryan, and Dravidian. Additionally, there are over 700 minor languages and dialects. The scope for misunderstanding can be easily appreciated!

The Indic languages are a branch of the Indo-European group of languages (of which English is also a member), and were the language of the central Asian peoples who invaded what is now India. The Dravidian languages are native to south India, although they have been influenced by Sanskrit and Hindi.

Most of the languages have their own script, and these are used along with English. In some states, such as Gujarat, you'll hardly see a word of English whereas in Himachal Pradesh virtually everything is in English. For a sample of the different scripts, look at a Rs 5 or larger banknote where 13 languages are represented. From the top they are: Assamese, Bengali, Gujarati, Kannada, Kashmiri, Malayalam, Hindi (Devanagari), Oriya, Punjabi, Rajasthani, Tamil, Telugu and Urdu.

Major efforts have been made to promote Hindi as the national language of India and to gradually phase out English. A stumbling block to this plan is that while Hindi is the predominant language in the north, it bears little relation to the Dravidian languages of the south; and in the south very few people speak Hindi. It is from the south, particularly the state of Tamil Nadu, that the most vocal opposition to the adoption of Hindi comes, along with the strongest support for the retention of English.

For many educated Indians, English is virtually their first language, and for a great number of Indians who speak more than one language it will be their second language.

The 15 main languages in India are:

Hindi The most important Indian language, although it is only spoken as a mother tongue by about 20% of the population – mainly in the area known as the Hindi-belt, the cow-belt or Bimaru – Bihar, Madhya Pradesh, Rajasthan and Uttar Pradesh. This Indic language is the official language of the government, as well as of the states already mentioned, plus Haryana and Himachal Pradesh.

Assamese State language of Assam, and spoken by nearly 60% of that state's population. Dates back to the 13th century.

Bengali Spoken by nearly 200 million people (mostly in what is now Bangladesh), and the state language of West Bengal. Developed as a language in the 13th century.

Gujarati State language of Gujarat, Indic.

Kannada State language of Karnataka, spoken by about 65% of that state's population.

Kashmiri Kashmiri speakers account for about 55% of the population of Jammu & Kashmir. It is an Indic language written in the Perso-Arabic script.

Malayalam A Dravidian language, it is the state language of Kerala.

Marathi An Indic language dating back to around the 13th century, Marathi is the state language of Maharashtra.

Oriya Another Indic language, it is the state language of Orissa where it is spoken by 87% of the population.

Punjabi Also Indic, it is the state language of Punjab. Although based on the same script as Hindi (Devanagari), it is written in a 16th-century script, known as Gurumukhi, which was created by the Sikh guru, Guru Angad.

Sanskrit One of the oldest languages in the world, and the language of classical India. All the *Vedas* and classical literature such as the *Mahabharata* and the *Ramayana* were written in this Indic language.

Sindhi A significant number of Sindhi speakers are found in what is now Pakistan, although the greater number are in India. In Pakistan the language is written in a Perso-Arabic script, while in India it uses the Devanagari script.

Tamil An ancient Dravidian language at least 2000 years old, and the state language of Tamil Nadu. It is spoken by at least 65 million people.

Telugu The Dravidian language spoken by the largest number of people, it is the state language of Andhra Pradesh.

Urdu Urdu is the state language of Jammu & Kashmir. Along with Hindi it evolved in early Delhi. While Hindi was largely adopted by the Hindu population, the Muslims embraced Urdu, and so the latter is written in the Perso-Arabic script and includes many Persian words.

Recently there have been moves to have Konkani, a language spoken by many in the Goa area, Manipuri and Nepali (Gorkhali) recognised under the constitution. ■

Thus it is very easy to get around India with English – after all, many Indians have to speak English to each other if they wish to communicate. Nevertheless it's always nice to know at least a little of the local language.

Hindi

See LP's *Hindi/Urdu Phrasebook* for a comprehensive list of Hindi words and phrases.

big	*bara*
small	*chhota*
today	*aaj*
day	*din*
night	*rat*
week	*haftah*
month	*mahina*
year	*sal*
medicine	*davai*
yes/no	*han/nahin*
hello, goodbye	*namaste*
excuse me	*maf kijiye*
please	*meharbani se*
ice	*baraf*

egg	*anda*
fruit	*phal*
vegetables	*sabzi*
sugar	*chini*
butter	*makkhan*
rice	*chaval*
water	*pani*
tea	*chai*
coffee	*kafi*
milk	*dudh*

Do you speak English?
Kya ap angrezi samajhte hun?
I don't understand.
Meri samajh men nahin aya.
Where is a hotel?
Hotal kahan hai?
How far is...?
...kitne dur hai?
How do I get to...?
...kojane ke liye kaise jana parega?
How much?
Kitne paise? Kitne hai?
This is expensive.
Yeh bahut mehnga hai.
Show me the menu.
Mujhe minu dikhayee.
The bill please.
Bill de dijiyee.
What is your name?
Apka shubh nam kya hai?
What is the time?
Kitne baje hain?
Come here.
Idhar aaiyee.
How are you?
Ap kaise hain?
Very well, thank you.
Bahut achche shukriya.

Beware of *acha*, that all-purpose word for 'OK'. It can also mean 'OK, I understand what you mean, but it isn't OK'. As in 'Have you got a room available?' to which the answer *'acha'* means 'I understand you want a room but I haven't got one'.

'Please Don't Pluck The Flowers' (BT)

Tamil

Although Hindi is promoted as the 'official' language of India, it won't get you very far in the south, where Tamil reigns supreme (although English is also widely spoken). Tamil is a much more difficult language to master and the pronunciation is not easy.

big	*periyadhu*
small	*siriyadhu*
today	*indru*
day	*pagal*
night	*iravu/rathiri*
week	*vaaram*
month	*maadham*
year	*aandu*
medicine	*marundhu*
yes/no	*aamam/illai*
hello	*vanakkam*
goodbye	*sendru varugiren*
excuse me	*mannithu kollungal*
please	*dhayavu seidhu*
ice	*panikkatti*
egg	*muttai*
fruit	*pazhlam*
vegetables	*kaaikari*
sugar	*sarkarai/seeni*
butter	*vennai*
rice	*saadham/soru*
water	*thanner*
tea	*thenneer*
coffee	*kapi*
milk	*paal*

A	B
C	D
	E

A (HF)
B (BT)
C (BT)
D (HF)
E (HF)

Do you speak English?
Neengal aangilam pesuveergala?
I don't understand.
Yenakku puriyavillai.
Where is there a hotel?
Hotel yenge irrukindradhu?
How far is...?
Yevallavu dhooram...?
How do I get to...?
Naan yeppadi selvadhu...?
How much?
Yevvalvu?
This is expensive.
Idhu vilai adhigam.
Show me the menu.
Saapatu patiyalai kamiungal.
The bill please.
Vilai rasidhai kodungal.
What is your name?
Ungal peyar yenna?
What is the time?
Ippoludhu mani yevalavu?
Come here.
Inge vaangal.
How are you?
Neengal nalama?
Very well, thank you.
Nandri, nandraga irukkindren.

Numbers

Whereas we count in tens, hundreds, thousands, millions and billions, the Indian numbering system goes tens, hundreds, thousands, hundred thousands, ten millions. A hundred thousand is a *lakh* and 10 million is a *crore*.

These two words are almost always used in place of their English equivalent. Thus you will see 10 lakh rather than one million and one crore rather than 10 million. Furthermore, the numerals are generally written that way too – thus three hundred thousand appears as 3,00,000 not 300,000, and ten million, five hundred thousand would appear numerically as 1,05,00,000 (one crore, five lakh) not 10,500,000. If you say something costs five crore or is worth 10 lakh it always means 'of rupees'.

When counting from 10 to 100 in Hindi, there is no standard formula for compiling

numbers – they are all different! Here we've just given you enough to go on with!

	Hindi	Tamil
1	ek	onru
2	do	irandu
3	tin	moonru
4	char	naangu
5	panch	ainthu
6	chhe	aaru
7	sat	ezhu
8	ath	ettu
9	nau	onpathu
10	das	pathu
11	gyarah	padhinondru
12	barah	pannirendu
13	terah	padhimundru
14	choda	padhinaangu
15	pandrah	padhinainthu
16	solah	padhinaaru
17	satrah	padhinezhu
18	aththarah	padhinettu
19	unnis	patthonpathu
20	bis	irubadhu
21	ikkis	irubadhiondru
22	bais	irubadhirandu
23	teis	irubadhimoonru
24	chobis	irubadhinaangu
25	pachis	irubadhiainthu
26	chhabis	irubadhiaaru
27	sattais	irubadhiezhu
28	aththais	irubadhiettu
29	unnattis	irubadhionpathu
30	tis	muppathu
35	paintis	muppathiainthu
40	chalis	narpathu
45	paintalis	narpathiainthu
50	pachas	aimbathu
55	pachpan	aimbathiainthu
60	sath	arubathu
65	painsath	arubathiainthu
70	sattar	ezhbathu
75	pachhattar	ezhubathiainthu
80	assi	enbathu
85	pachasi	enabathiainthu
90	nabbe	thonoru
95	pachanabbe	thonootriainthu
100	so	nooru
200	do so	irunooru
300	tin so	munooru
1000	ek hazar	aayiram
2000	do hazar	irandaayiram
100,000	lakh	lacham
10,000,000	crore	kodi

Top: Woman from Pushkar, Rajasthan (RI)
Bottom: Heave ho! Kovalam, Kerala (MH)

Phrasebooks

Lonely Planet has the subcontinent well covered, with phrasebooks for Hindi/Urdu, Nepali and Sinhala.

There are also many phrasebooks and teach-yourself books available in India for Hindi and the other major languages, if you want to learn more of the language. Some of them are typically and amusingly Indian. A section on a visit to the doctor in one phrasebook, for example, included the following useful series of phrases for the traveller, the first of which is quite unlikely in India!

I suffer from severe constipation.
I am feeling a bit out of sorts today.
The patient is sinking fast.
He has much run down.

The patient is in a precarious condition.
Cholera has broken out in the city.
He is dying by inches.

Some more examples can be found in *Hindi Made Easy* (Sitaram P Bhat, 1983 reprint) which includes the following handy phrases:

I want to shoot a tiger.
Your breast-plate is dirty.
One hundred sepoys were killed.
Should an enemy attack you in front and rear at the same time, what will you do?

For a quirky account of Indian-English, get hold of *Hanklyn-Janklin: A Stranger's Rumble-Tumble Guide to Some Words, Customs and Quiddities Indian and Indo-British* by Nigel B Hankin (Banyan Books).

Facts for the Visitor

VISAS, PERMITS & EMBASSIES

Virtually everybody needs a visa to visit India. The application is (in theory) straightforward and the visas are usually issued with a minimum of fuss.

Tourist visas are valid for six months, but this is usually six months *from the date of issue of the visa*, not the date you enter India. This means that if you enter India five months after the visa was issued, it will be valid only for one more month, not the full six months. If you enter India the day after it was issued, you can stay for the full six months.

Occasionally six-month visas are valid from the date of entry into India, and it also happens that one-month tourist visas are issued, and these are also valid from the date of entry. It seems to depend on where you apply for the visa. Just make sure you know exactly what conditions apply to the visa you have.

Tourist visas are usually multiple-entry, but it's worth specifically requesting this if you intend hopping across to Nepal, just in case they give you a single-entry.

The cost of the visa varies enormously, from reasonable to extortionate, depending on your nationality. Currently Brits are supposed to pay UK£8, while hapless Aussies get slugged for A$41 (and this only recently came down from A$70!). Most other nationalities are somewhere between these two extremes.

If your passport hasn't come back in a couple of weeks, get on to the embassy or consulate and find out what is going on. If you have not submitted enough money, or there is some other hitch, chances are they'll just sit on it until you contact them, rather than contacting you to let you know there's a problem. In fact, getting your visa will probably be your first encounter with the morass of Indian bureaucracy and, although generally your application will go through smoothly, we consistently receive more complaints about problems, delays, extra costs and unfair actions over visas for India than for any other country.

Andrea at our UK office supplied the following exasperated memoir:

When I was in Bangkok, I applied for my Indian visa. I was not travelling direct from Thailand to India; I was going to stop in Nepal and planned to travel overland into India.

At the Indian Embassy in Bangkok I had to queue for two hours to get a form to fill in for the visa. I was informed it would take two weeks for the visa to come through, so I decided to go to Chiang Mai and apply to the Indian Consulate there, to avoid waiting around in Bangkok.

In Chiang Mai, the Indian Consulate told me that a British citizen had to have a letter from the British Consulate certifying that they were actually British! This letter cost 250 baht (UK£5.50) and is a waste of time and money.

Next I had to take the letter and completed visa application form back to the Indian Consulate. They told me that they have to send a telex to the Indian Embassy in London to ask if you are 'clear' to apply for a visa. This telex takes two weeks and costs 700 baht (UK£16). Finally, after two weeks, if you are 'clear' you may proceed with your application. A multiple-entry visa for a one-month stay (valid for three months from date of issue) costs 350 baht (UK£8). A visa for up to 6 months costs 750 baht.

In all, it cost me a lot of extra money; I had to budget for an extra two weeks in Thailand. When I finally had my visa I was told that I could have had my clearance telex forwarded to the Indian Embassy in Nepal, where my visa could have been completed.

Finally, due to restricted time I decided to fly into Varanasi from Nepal. On arrival at the airport I was informed at the exchange booth that they only accepted pounds sterling cash or Barclays travellers' cheques. They would not accept any other travellers' cheques or a credit card advance. If I had not met a girl on the flight who had some Indian currency I would have been stuck.

It seems that the best thing to do is either apply well in advance in your own country and go straight to India once your visa comes through, or apply in a country near India where you don't mind hanging around for a few weeks waiting for the visa to arrive.

Indian Embassies

India's embassies and consulates include:

Australia
3-5 Moonah Place, Yarralumla, ACT 2600 (☎ (06) 273-3999)
153 Walker St, North Sydney, NSW 2060 (☎ (02) 955-7055)
238 Bell St, Coburg, Vic 3058 (☎ (03) 350-4684)

Bangladesh
120 Road 2, Dhanmodi Residential Area H, Dhaka (☎ (2) 50-3606)

Canada
10 Springfield Rd, Ottawa K1M 1C9 (☎ (613) 744-3751)

Denmark
Vangehusvej 15, 2100 Copenhagen (☎ (1) 3118-2888)

Egypt
5 Aziz Ababa St, Zamalek, Cairo (☎ (2) 341-3051)

France
15 rue Alfred Dehodencq, 75016 Paris (☎ (1) 4520-3930)

Germany
Adenaverallee 262, 5300 Bonn (☎ (228) 54-050)

Italy
Via XX Settembre 5, 00187 Rome (☎ (6) 46-4642)

Japan
2-11 Kudan Minami 2-Chome, Chiyoda-ku, Tokyo (☎ (3) 262-2391)

Jordan
1st Circle, Jebel Amman, Amman (☎ (6) 62-2098)

Kenya
Jeevan Bharati Bldg, Harambee Ave, Nairobi (☎ (2) 22-566)

Malaysia
20th floor, West Block, Wisma Selangor Dredging, 142-C Jalan Ampang, Kuala Lumpur (☎ (3) 261-7000)

Myanmar (Burma)
545-547 Merchant St, Yangon (Rangoon) (☎ (1) 82-550)

Nepal
Lainchaur, GPO Box 292, Kathmandu (☎ 41-0900)

Netherlands
Buitenrustweg 2, The Hague (☎ (70) 346-9771)

New Zealand
180 Molesworth St, Princess Towers, Wellington (☎ (4) 73-6390)

Pakistan
G-5 Diplomatic Enclave, Islamabad (☎ (51) 81-4371)
India House, 3 Fatima Jinnah Rd, Karachi (☎ (21) 52-2275)

Singapore
India House, 31 Grange Rd (☎ 737-6777)

Sri Lanka
36-38 Galla Rd, Colombo 3 (☎ (1) 21-605)

Switzerland
Effingerstrasse 45, CH-3008 Berne (☎ (31) 26-3111)

Syria
40/46 Adnan Malki St, Yassin Nouwelati Bldg, Damascus (☎ (11) 71-9580)

Tanzania
11th Floor, NIC Investment House, Samora Ave, Dar es Salaam (☎ (51) 20-295)

Thailand
46 Soi 23 (Prasarnmitr), Sukhumvit Rd, Bangkok (☎ (2) 258-0300)
113 Bumruangrat Rd, Chiang Mai 50000 (☎ (53) 24-3066)

UK
India House, Aldwych, London WC2B 4NA (☎ (071) 836-0990)
82 New St, Birmingham B2 4BA (☎ (21) 643-0366)

USA
2107 Massachusetts Ave NW, Washington DC 20008 (☎ (202) 939-7000)
3 East 64th St, New York, NY 10021-7097 (☎ (212) 879-7800)
540 Arguello Blvd, San Francisco, CA 9418 (☎ (415) 668-0662)

Visa Extensions

If your stay in India is going to take you beyond the 180 days from the date of issue of your visa, *regardless of your date of entry into India*, you're going to have to set aside a few days to extend your visa.

As with the cost of the visa itself, the cost of an extension also varies. Some official sources say that it is free, yet we have had reports from travellers who've had to pay up to Rs 625. Three-month extensions are routinely given, and four photos are required.

If you stay beyond four months you are also supposed to get an income tax clearance before you leave. See the Tax Clearance Certificates section further on for details.

Foreigners' Registration Offices

Visa extensions and permits for Sikkim, the Andaman & Nicobar Islands and Lakshadweep are issued by the Foreigners' Registration Offices. The main offices include:

Bombay
  Special Branch II, Annexe 2, Office of the Commissioner of Police (Greater Bombay), Dadabhoy Naoroji Rd (☎ 26-8111)
Calcutta
  237 Acharya J C Bose Rd (☎ 47-3301)
Darjeeling
  Laden La Rd
Madras
  9 Village Rd (☎ 47-8210)
New Delhi
  1st floor, Hans Bhavan, Tilak Bridge (☎ 331-9489)

Visas can also be extended in all state and district capitals at the office of the Superintendent of Police.

Tax Clearance Certificates

If you stay in India for more than 120 days you need a 'tax clearance certificate' to leave the country. This supposedly proves that your time in India was financed with your own money, not by working in India or by selling things or playing the black market.

Basically all you have to do is find the Foreign Section of the Income Tax Department in Delhi, Calcutta, Madras or Bombay and turn up with your passport, visa extension form, any other similar paperwork and a handful of bank exchange receipts (to show you really have been changing foreign currency into rupees officially). You fill in a form and wait for anything from 10 minutes to a couple of hours. You're then given your tax clearance certificate and away you go. We've never yet heard from anyone who has actually been asked for this document on departure.

Special Permits

Even with a visa you are not allowed everywhere in India. Certain places require special additional permits. These are covered in the appropriate sections in the main text, but briefly they are:

Andaman Islands If you are arriving at these islands by ship, you need a permit in advance; the shipping company won't let you board without one. For those arriving by plane, permits are issued on arrival in Port Blair. The permits are obtainable from an embassy or consulate abroad or from the Ministry of Home Affairs in New Delhi. The application to these places must be made at least six weeks in advance, although they recommend you allow 12 weeks. In Madras, however, you can get a permit in just three days.

Bhutan Although Bhutan is an independent country, India has firm control over foreign policy and most other things. Applications to visit Bhutan must be made through the Director of Tourism, Ministry of Finance, Tachichho Dzong, Thimpu, Bhutan; or through the Bhutan Foreign Mission (☎ 60-9217), Chandra Gupta Marg, New Delhi 110021, India; or through the Bhutanese mission in New York. And don't hold your breath – unless you have high-up Indian connections or a personal friend in the Bhutanese aristocracy, you needn't expect to get a permit. Very few permits are issued for overland travel. The only way around these restrictions is to book an organised tour, and these don't come cheap.

Lakshadweep A permit for these islands west and south-west of Kerala state is problematic. Only one island is currently open to foreigners. See the Lakshadweep section at the end of the Kerala chapter for full details.

North-Eastern Region You must have a permit for these remote north-eastern states, and you are restricted in where you may go. Furthermore, don't hold your breath when applying as they can take months to come through, if at all. It helps if you have a reference from an Indian who has political elbow.

Basically, the only states it's worth trying to get a permit for are Assam and Meghalaya but even these can become off limits to foreigners at a moment's notice. Currently, the office in Calcutta which deals with Meghalaya can only issue permits on the spot for a minimum of four people travelling together. Individuals have to obtain clearance from New Delhi, which must be done in person. Permits allow transit through western Assam up to Gawahati, but you are not supposed to stay overnight there. Assam was briefly opened up in early 1992 – and was just as quickly closed off again.

The other north-eastern states are totally closed to foreigners at present, although Arunachal Pradesh is trying to get permission from the central government to open for foreign tourists. Applications for permits should be made through Arunachal House in Calcutta.

Sikkim Permits are issued either while you wait or within two or three hours (depending on where you apply for them) – see the Sikkim chapter for full details.

Other Visas

If you're heading to other places near India the visa situation is as follows.

Myanmar (Burma) The embassy in New Delhi is fast and efficient and issues two-week visas. There is *no* Burmese consulate in Calcutta, although there is one in Kathmandu and in Dhaka, Bangladesh.

Nepal The Nepalese Embassy in New Delhi is on Barakhamba Rd, quite close to Connaught Place, not out at Chanakyapuri like most other embassies. It is open from 10 am to 1 pm Monday to Friday. Single-entry, 30-day visas take 24 hours and cost Rs 570. A 14-day visa is available on arrival in Nepal for US$20, and can be extended, but doing so involves rather a lot of form filling and queueing – it's better to have a visa in advance if possible. There is also a consulate in Calcutta.

Sri Lanka Most Western nationalities do not need a visa to visit Sri Lanka, but there are diplomatic offices in New Delhi, Bombay and Madras.

Thailand There are Thai embassies in New Delhi and Calcutta. One-month visas cost about US$10 and are issued in 24 hours. They can be extended in Thailand. If you are

flying into and out of Thailand and don't intend to stay more than 15 days, a visa is not required, but you cannot extend your period of stay.

Foreign Embassies in India

Most foreign diplomatic missions are in the nation's capital, Delhi, but there are also quite a few consulates in the other major cities of Bombay, Calcutta and Madras. See the relevant cities for listings.

DOCUMENTS

You must have a passport; it's the most basic travel document. In fact you should have your passport with you all the time. We had a letter from two Australians who spent four days in jail during the Pushkar cattle fair because they'd left their passports for safe-keeping in Jaipur. Two of the four days were spent while a friend returned to Jaipur and collected the passports for them! Another traveller who was comprehensively ripped off on a day trip to Gwalior had fortunately left his passport in Agra. The police, however, were more upset about the passport left behind than the theft! The fact had he been carrying it with him, he would not now have it to show to the police, made no difference at all!

A health certificate, while not necessary in India, may well be required for onward travel. Student cards are virtually useless these days – many student concessions have either been eliminated or replaced by 'youth fares' or similar age concessions. Similarly, a Youth Hostel card is not generally required for India's many hostels, but you do pay slightly less at official youth hostels with one.

There is not much opportunity to get behind the wheel in India, but if you do intend to drive then get an International Driving Permit from your local national motoring organisation. These days motorcycles are more readily available for hire, particularly in Goa, and an International Permit is useful if you rent one. An International Permit can also be used for other identification purposes, such as plain old bicycle hire.

It's worth having a batch of passport photos for visa applications and other uses. If you run out, Indian photo studios will do excellent portraits at pleasantly low prices.

CUSTOMS

The usual duty-free regulations apply for India; that is, one bottle of whiskey and 200 cigarettes. If you bring in more than US$10,000 in cash and/or travellers' cheques you are supposed to fill in a currency declaration form.

You're allowed to bring in all sorts of Western technological wonders, but big items, such as video cameras, are likely to be entered on a 'Tourist Baggage Re-Export' form to ensure you take them out with you when you go. It's not necessary to declare still-cameras even if you have more than one.

MONEY

The rupee (Rs) is divided into 100 paise (p). There are coins of five, 10, 20, 25 and 50 paise, Rs 1, 2 and 5 (rare), and notes of Rs 1, 2, 5, 10, 20, 50, 100 and 500.

Encashment Certificates

You are not allowed to bring Indian currency into the country or take it out of the country. You are allowed to bring in unlimited amounts of foreign currency or travellers' cheques, but you are supposed to declare anything over US$10,000 on arrival.

All money is supposed to be changed at official banks or moneychangers, and you are supposed to be given an encashment certificate for each transaction. In practice, some people surreptitiously bring rupees into the country with them – they can be bought at a useful discount price in places like Singapore or Bangkok. Indian rupees can be brought in fairly openly from Nepal and again you can get a slightly better rate there.

Banks will usually give you an encashment certificate, but occasionally they don't bother. Some charge between Rs 10 and Rs 20 for them; most of the time they're free. It is worth getting them for several reasons: firstly, you will need one for any re-exchange when you depart India.

Secondly, certain purchases, such as airline tickets and accommodation at most middle-range hotels, must be paid for either with foreign currency or with rupees accompanied by sufficient certificates to account for the ticket price or the accommodation. This is actually a complete waste of time since some little note will be scrawled on the form to the effect that it was sighted when you paid for something. When you buy something else somebody else can quite easily scrawl a similar little note on another corner of the same form!

The third reason for saving encashment certificates is that if you stay in India longer than four months, you have to get an income tax clearance. This requires production of a handful of encashment certificates to prove you've been changing money all along and not earning money locally.

Banknotes

Indian currency notes circulate far longer than in the West and the small notes in particular become very tatty – some should carry a government health warning! A note can have holes right through it (most do in fact, as they are bundled together with staples when new) and be quite acceptable but if it's slightly torn at the top or bottom on the crease line then it's no good and you'll have trouble spending it. Even a missing corner makes a bill unacceptable. The answer to this is to simply accept it philosophically or think of clever uses. Use it for tips or for official purposes. I'd love to pay the Rs 300 departure tax with 300 totally disreputable Rs 1 notes – although someone who did just that wrote to say he had some trouble getting them to accept it! Some banks have special counters where torn notes will be exchanged for good ones, but who wants to visit banks more than necessary? ■

Currency

In major cities you can change most foreign currencies or travellers' cheques – Australian dollars, Deutschmarks, yen or whatever – but out of town it's best to stick to US dollars or pounds sterling. Thomas Cook and American Express are both popular travellers' cheques, and these two companies have a number of branches in India.

Although it's usually not a problem to change travellers' cheques, it's best to stick to the well-known brands – American Express, Visa, Thomas Cook, Citibank and Barclays – as more obscure ones may cause problems. It also happens occasionally that a bank won't accept American Express cheques, and for this reason it's worth carrying more than one flavour.

Outside the main cities, the State Bank of India is usually the place to change money, although occasionally they'll direct you to another bank, such as the Bank of India, the Punjab National Bank or the Bank of Baroda.

Many people make the mistake of bringing too many small-denomination cheques. Although many middle-range hotels now demand payment in foreign currency, unless you are moving rapidly from country to country you only need a handful of small denominations for end-of-stay conversions. In between, change as much as you feel happy carrying. This applies particularly in India where changing money can take time – especially in the smaller towns. You can also spend a lot of time finding a bank which will change money. The answer is to change money as infrequently as possible and to change it only in big banks in big cities.

Exchange Rates

A$1	=	Rs 22
C$1	=	Rs 25
DM1	=	Rs 19
FFr1	=	Rs 5.5
Jap Y100	=	Rs 26
Nep Rs100	=	Rs 62
NZ$1	=	Rs 17
US$1	=	Rs 31
UK£1	=	Rs 46

In the 1992 budget, the rupee was made a partially convertible currency, mainly in an effort to bring the money circulating in the black economy into the legitimate economy. As a result, when you change money in a bank, the rupee equivalent will be calculated on the basis of 40% at the official Reserve Bank of India rate (around Rs 25.82 to the US dollar) and 60% at the prevailing free market rate on any particular day (around Rs 30).

Initially, this partial floating of the rupee had the effect of wiping out the currency black market. Once the situation had stabilised, however, street dealers were once again at work offering conversion rates between Rs 30 and Rs 33 to the US dollar (ie between Rs 2 and Rs 5 above the bank rate). US$100 bills fetch the best rates.

On the other hand, you must remember that changing money unofficially is still illegal, you are open to rip-offs, and there's the moral question that your hard currency is then not available to the government to help it purchase much needed foreign goods, medicines or technology.

Airline tickets (both domestic and international) must be paid for either directly with foreign currency (cash or travellers' cheques) or with a specific bank exchange form. You will need to bring proof of your air booking to the bank in order to obtain the exchange form, which you can then bring back to the agency with whom you booked your flight, together with the required amount of cash, in order to purchase and collect your ticket.

Credit Cards

Credit cards are widely accepted in India, particularly Diners Club, MasterCard, American Express and Visa. Card acceptability can vary depending on how fast the credit card company is paying their bills.

All bills paid with an international credit card are billed to your account at the same rate as travellers' cheques at a bank in India (ie 40% at the Reserve Bank of India rate and 60% at the free market rate).

With American Express you can use your

card to obtain dollar or sterling travellers' cheques, or get cash rupees locally from an Amex office, but you must have a personal cheque to cover the amount, although counter cheques are available if you ask for them. Similarly, you can obtain rupees on a Visa card at any Bank of Baroda branch.

All state governments in India levy various taxes on middle and top-end hotel accommodation and restaurants, the most significant being what is called luxury/expenditure tax (between 15% and 20%). You will cop this if you pay in rupees but it will not be charged if you pay by credit card (or hard currency). Unless otherwise stated, the accommodation prices quoted in this book do not include taxes.

Transferring Money

Don't run out of money in India unless you have a credit card against which you can draw travellers' cheques or cash. Having money transferred through the banking system is very time-consuming, frustrating and a minefield of bureaucracy even with the best will in the world. Even transferred by cable it can take weeks, and by mail it can take forever. Banks have a reputation for not telling people when money has arrived – better in their balance than your pocket seems to be the idea.

If you must have money sent to you in India, specify the bank, the branch and the address you want it sent to; get it sent by telex or cable (never by mail), and then keep your fingers crossed. Preferably send it to a foreign bank since they are much more efficient when it comes to overseas transactions than Indian banks. Overseas banks with branches in India include Bank of America, Chartered Bank, Banque Nationale de Paris, Citibank and, particularly, ANZ Grindlays which has many branches in smaller cities as well as in the major cities. Amex and Thomas Cook are also efficient organisations to transfer money through.

Costs

It is virtually impossible to say what travelling around India will cost you. It depends on where you stay, what you eat, how you travel and how fast you travel. Two people travelling at exactly the same standard can spend vastly different amounts on a daily basis if one travels twice as fast as the other. A week lying on the beach at Goa watching the waves roll in brings daily costs down very rapidly.

Whatever budget you decide to travel on, you can be assured that you'll be getting a whole lot more for your money than in most other countries – it's fantastic value.

From top to bottom: if you stay in luxury hotels, fly everywhere, and see a lot of India in a very short trip, you can spend a lot of money. India has plenty of hotels at US$50 or more a day and some where a room can cost US$100 plus – more than what most Indians earn in a year. At the other extreme, if you scrimp and save, stay in dormitories or the cheapest hotels, always travel 2nd class on trains, and learn to exist on dhal and rice, you can see India on less than US$7 a day.

Most travellers will probably be looking for something between these extremes. If so, you'll stay in reasonable hotels with the sort of standard provided by the tourist bungalows in many states – a clean but straightforward room with fan cooling and bathroom. You'll eat in regular restaurants but occasionally splash out on a fancy meal when you're in a big town. If you mix your travel, you'll try 2nd class most of the time, and opt for 1st class only if you're travelling on a long overnight trip. You'll take autorickshaws rather than always looking for a bus. In that case India could cost you something like US$15 to US$25 a day on average. It totally depends on what you're looking for.

As everywhere in Asia, you get pretty much what you pay for, and many times it's worth paying a little more for the experience. That old-fashioned Raj-style luxury is part of India's charm and sometimes it's foolish not to lay out the money and enjoy it.

Tipping

In most Asian countries tipping is virtually unknown, but India is an exception to that rule – although tipping has a rather different role in India than in the West. The term *baksheesh*, which encompasses tipping and a lot more besides, aptly describes the concept in India. You 'tip' not so much for good service, but to get things done. A 'tip' to a station porter will ensure you a seat when the train is packed out to the very limit.

Judicious baksheesh will open closed doors, find missing letters and perform other small miracles. Tipping is not necessary for taxis nor for cheaper restaurants, but if you're going to be using something repeatedly, an initial tip will ensure the standards are kept up – this may explain why the service is slower every time in your hotel restaurant for example. Keep things in perspective though. Demands for baksheesh can quickly become never-ending. Ask yourself if it's really necessary or desirable before shelling out.

In tourist restaurants or hotels, where service is usually tacked on in any case, the normal 10% figure usually applies. In smaller places, where tipping is optional, you need only tip a few rupees, not a percentage of the bill. Hotel porters usually get about Rs 1 per bag; other possible tipping levels are Rs 1 to Rs 2 for bike-watching, Rs 10 for train conductors or station porters performing miracles for you, and Rs 5 to Rs 15 for extra services from hotel staff.

Many Westerners find this aspect of Indian travel the most trying – the constant demands for baksheesh and the expectations that because you're a foreigner, you'll tip. However, from an Indian perspective, baksheesh is an integral part of the system – it wasn't invented simply to extract money from tourists. Take some time to observe how Indians (even those who are obviously not excessively wealthy) deal with baksheesh situations; they always give something, it's expected and accepted by both sides.

Although you may not consider yourself well off, think of how an Indian who earns Rs 500 a month sees you. Foreigners who spend their whole time trying to fight the system, instead of rolling with it philo-sophically, inevitably find themselves constantly involved in vitriolic and unpleasant arguments with people over what is, in the end, a pittance. No-one would be naive enough to suggest that all demands for baksheesh are justified, or that the amount demanded is always reasonable, but if you can accept the fact that this is how things work here, and tip fairly, chances are you'll find that things are a whole lot easier.

When you have given a tip it's always interesting to watch the reaction – call it the 'price-you-paid indicator'. There are three standard responses:

1. Eyes light up, ear-to-ear grin, profound expressions of undying friendship and goodwill – you paid too much.
2. Expressionless 'figure of eight' waggle of the head and eyes down – you paid about the right amount.
3. Genuine wide-eyed amazement, abuse, general surliness, protestations of poverty – you probably didn't give enough.

WHAT TO BRING

The usual travellers' rule applies – bring as little as possible. It's much better to have to get something you've left behind than find you have too much and need to get rid of it. In the south of India you can count on short-sleeves weather year round, but in the north it gets cool enough to require a sweater or light jacket in the evenings during the winter. In the far north it will get down to freezing and you will need all the warm-weather gear you can muster.

Remember that clothes are easily and cheaply purchased in India. You can buy things off the peg or have clothes made to measure in the small tailor shops found throughout the country. In the big cities there are plenty of the Indian fashions so popular in the West, and the prices often approximate in rupees what they cost in dollars back home! One item of clothing to have made as soon as possible is a pair of lightweight pyjama-style trousers. You'll find them far cooler and more comfortable than jeans and they'll only cost a few rupees.

Modesty rates highly in India, as in most Asian countries. Although men wearing shorts is accepted as a Western eccentricity, women should dress more discreetly. Even for men, however, wearing shorts or going shirtless in a more formal situation is definitely impolite. A reasonable clothes list would include:

- underwear and swimming gear
- one pair of cotton trousers
- one pair of shorts
- a few T-shirts or short-sleeved shirts
- sweater for cold nights
- one pair of sneakers or shoes plus socks
- sandals and/or thongs
- lightweight jacket or raincoat
- a set of 'dress up' clothes

Other useful items include washing gear, medical and sewing kits, sunglasses and a padlock. A length of clothesline and a handful of clothes pegs are also worth considering if you're going to do your own laundry. A number of travellers have sug-gested taking small gifts such as ballpoint pens (very popular), combs, sweets, etc for people, especially children, who have been friendly or helpful. Another item to consider is an umbrella – invaluable in the monsoon. See the section called Miscellaneous Items for more details.

Sleeping Bag

A sleeping bag can be a hassle to carry, but can serve as something to sleep in (and avoid unsavoury looking hotel bedding), a cushion on hard train seats, a seat for long waits on railway platforms or a bed top-cover (since cheaper hotels rarely give you one).

If you're trekking in the north then a sleeping bag will be an absolute necessity. Unlike in Nepal, it is not easy to hire trekking gear in India. A sheet sleeping bag, like those required by youth hostels in the West, can be very useful, particularly if you don't trust the hotel's sheets. Mosquito nets are also rare, so your own sheet or sheet sleeping bag will also help to keep mosquitoes at bay.

Some travellers find that a plastic sheet is

Dhobi-Wallahs

When you travel in India there's hardly any need for more than one change of clothes. Every day there will be a knock on your door and the laundry boy will collect all those dusty, sweaty clothes you wore yesterday, and every evening those same clothes will reappear -- washed and ironed with more loving care than any washing-powder-ad mum ever lavished upon anything. And all for a few rupees per item. But what happened to your clothes between their departure and their like-new return?

Well, they certainly did not get anywhere near a washing machine. First of all they're collected and taken to the *dhobi ghat*. A ghat is a place with water, a dhobi is a washerperson, so the dhobi ghat is where the dhobis ply their trade and wash clothes. In big cities, dhobi ghats will be huge places with hundreds of dhobis doing their thing with thousands of articles of clothing.

Then the clothes are separated – all the white shirts are washed together, all the grey trousers, all the red skirts, all the blue jeans. By now, if this was the West, your clothes would either be hopelessly lost or you'd need a computer to keep track of them all. Your clothes are soaked in soapy water for a few hours, following which the dirt is literally beaten out of them. No multiprogrammed miracle of technology can wash as clean as a determined dhobi, although admittedly after a few visits to the Indian laundry your clothes do begin to look distinctly thinner. Buttons also tend to get shattered, so bring some spares. Zips sometimes fare likewise.

Once clean, the clothes are strung out on miles of clothesline to quickly dry in the Indian sun. They're then taken to the ironing sheds where hundreds of ironers wielding primitive irons press your jeans like they've never been pressed before. Not just your jeans – your socks, your T-shirts, even your underwear will come back with knife-edge creases. Then the Indian miracle takes place. Out of the thousands upon thousands of items washed that day, somehow your very own brown socks, blue jeans, yellow T-shirt and red underwear all find their way back together and head for your hotel room. A system of marking clothes, known only to the dhobis, is the real reason behind this feat. They say criminals have been tracked down simply by those telltale 'dhobi marks'. ■

useful for a number of reasons, including to bedbug-proof unhealthy looking beds. Others have recommended an inflatable pillow as a useful accessory. These are widely available for Rs 30.

Toilet Paper

Toilet paper is a necessity if you can't adapt to the Indian method of a jug of water and your left hand. It is widely available throughout the country in all but the smallest towns. Quality varies enormously, and it's generally not that cheap, so if you find some good stuff it might be worth stocking up with a spare or two.

Toiletries

Soap, toothpaste and other toiletries are readily available. A sink plug is worth having since few cheaper hotels have plugs. A nailbrush can be very useful. For women, tampons are not that easy to find in India. Except in 'strange, varied, toxic-shock-inducing forms', wrote one woman.

Men can safely leave their shaving gear at home. One of the pleasures of Indian travel is a shave in a barber shop every few days. With AIDS becoming more widespread in India, however, choose a barber's shop that looks clean, avoid roadside barbers, and make sure that a fresh blade is used. For just a few rupees you'll get the full treatment – lathering, followed by a shave, then the process is repeated, and finally there's the hot, damp towel and sometimes talcum powder. If you're not quick you'll find that before you know it you're also in for a scalp massage followed by a dangerous twisting of the neck – leave that sort of caper to the experts.

How to Carry It

Where to put all this gear? Well, for budget travellers the backpack is still the best carrying container. You can make it a bit more thief proof by sewing on tabs so you can padlock it shut. A modern variation on the backpack is the travel pack – a backpack with a flap which zips over the shoulder straps to turn it into a soft bag. It looks more presentable that way and is also less prone to damage – the major problem with backpacks. Some airlines will no longer accept responsibility for damage or theft from backpacks.

An alternative is a large, soft, zip bag with a wide shoulder strap. It's not so easy to carry for distances, but it is rather more thief proof and less damage prone. Suitcases are only for jet-setters!

Lots of plastic bags will keep your gear in some sort of order and will also be invaluable for keeping things dry during the wet season.

Miscellaneous Items

It's amazing how many things you wish you had with you when you're in India. One of the most useful for budget travellers is a padlock. In fact a padlock is a virtual necessity. Many cheaper hotels (in fact most of them) have doors locked by a latch and padlock. You'll find having your own sturdy lock on the door instead of the flimsy thing the hotel supplies does wonders for your peace of mind. Other uses are legion. You can lock a pack onto a railway luggage rack at night, for example. It may not make it thief proof, but it helps. You can buy a reasonable lock in India for Rs 25 to Rs 50.

A universal sink plug is also useful as sinks never have them. Ever tried to wash your underwear in a sink without a plug? A knife (preferably Swiss Army) finds a whole field of uses, in particular for peeling fruit. Some travellers rhapsodise about the usefulness of a miniature electric element to boil water in a cup. A sarong is a handy item. It can be used as a bed sheet, an item of clothing, an emergency towel, something to lie on at the beach, and a pillow on trains!

Insect repellent can also be extremely useful. Electric mosquito zappers are widely available. Power cuts are common in India ('load shedding' as it is euphemistically known) and there's little street lighting at night so a torch (flashlight) and candles can be useful. A small rubber wedge door-stop was one suggestion; it helps keep doors both open and closed. Bring along your spectacle prescription if you're short-sighted. Should you lose or damage your glasses a new pair can be made very cheaply, although the quality may be suspect. Earplugs are useful for light sleepers, and even heavier sleepers can have difficulty shutting out the din in some hotels.

Hot-weather survival requires another book of rules in India. First of all a sun hat is essential. Stepping out into the sun in the hot season is like using your head as a blacksmith's anvil. You don't just feel the sun, it reaches out and hits you. Secondly, a water bottle should always be by your side; and thirdly, if you're not drinking mineral water, have water purification tablets. You'll also need something with long sleeves, particularly if you're going to ride a bicycle very far. High-factor sun block cream is becoming more widely available, especially at beach resorts, but it's *expensive*!

TOURIST OFFICES
Local Tourist Offices
Within India the tourist office story is somewhat blurred by the overlap between the national (Indian Tourist Development Corporation – ITDC) and state tourist offices. As well as the national tourist office, each state maintains its own tourist office and this can lead to some confusion. In some cities the national office is much larger than the state one, or the state one is virtually nonexistent. ITDC offices include:

Agra
  191 The Mall (☎ 36-3377)
Aurangabad
  Krishna Vilas, Station Rd (☎ 24-817)
Bangalore
  KFC Building, 48 Church St (☎ 57-9517)
Bombay
  123 Maharishi Karve Rd, Churchgate (☎ 29-1585)
Calcutta
  4 Shakespeare Sarani (☎ 22-1402)
Jaipur
  Rajasthan State Hotel (☎ 72-200)
Khajuraho
  Near Western Group Temples (☎ 2047)
Kochi (Cochin)
  Willingdon Island (☎ 34-0352)
Madras
  154 Mount Rd (☎ 86-9685)

New Delhi
  88 Janpath (☎ 332-0005)
Panaji (Goa)
  Communidade Bldg, Church Square (☎ 3412)
Patna
  Tourist Bhavan, Beer Chand Patel Path (☎ 26-721)
Shillong
  Tirot Singh Syiem Rd, Police Bazaar (☎ 25-632)
Varanasi
  15B The Mall (☎ 43-744)

The state tourist offices vary widely in their efficiency and usefulness. Some of them are very good, some completely hopeless. In many states the tourism ministry also runs a chain of tourist bungalows which generally offer good accommodation at very reasonable prices. State tourist offices will usually be in the tourist bungalows (where there is one).

The confusion and overlap between the national and state tourist offices often causes wasteful duplication. Both offices produce a brochure on place A, neither produces anything on place B. More confusion arises with the division between the Government of India tourist office and the Indian Tourism Development Corporation (ITDC). The latter is more an actual 'doing' organisation than a 'telling' one. The ITDC will actually operate the tour bus on the tour for which the tourist office sells tickets. The ITDC also runs a series of hotels and travellers' lodges around the country under the Ashok name. States may also have a tourist transport operation equivalent to the national ITDC, so in some cities you can have a national and a state tourist operator as well as a national and a state tourist office!

Foreign Reps
The Government of India Department of Tourism maintains a string of tourist offices in other countries where you can get brochures, leaflets and some information about India. The tourist office leaflets and brochures are often very high in their informational quality and worth getting hold of. On the other hand, some of the foreign offices are not always as useful for obtaining

information as those within the country. There are also smaller 'promotion offices' in Osaka (Japan) and in Dallas, Miami, San Francisco and Washington DC (USA).

Australia
    Level 1, 17 Castlereagh St, Sydney NSW 2000 (☎ (02) 232-1600)
Canada
    60 Bloor St West, Suite No 1003, Toronto, Ontario M4W 3B8 (☎ (416) 962-6279)
France
    8 Blvd de la Madeleine, 75009 Paris (☎ 42-65-83-86)
Germany
    Kaiserstrasse 77-III, D-6000 Frankfurt-am-Main-1 (☎ 23-5423)
Italy
    Via Albricci 9, 20122 Milan (☎ 80-4952)
Japan
    Pearl Bldg, 9-18 Ginza, 7-Chome, Chuo ku, Tokyo 104 (☎ 571-5062)
Malaysia
    Wisma HLA, Lot 203 Jalan Raja Chulan, 50200 Kuala Lumpur (☎ 242-5285)
Netherlands
    Rokin 9-15, 1012 KK Amsterdam (☎ 20-8991)
Sweden
    Sveavagen 9-11, S-III 57, Stockholm 11157 (☎ (08) 21-5081)
Switzerland
    1-3 rue de Chantepoulet, 1201 Geneva (☎ (022) 732-1813)
Thailand
    Kentucky Fried Chicken Bldg, 3rd floor, 62/5 Thaniya Rd, Bangkok 10500 (☎ 235-2585)
UK
    7 Cork St, London W1X 2AB (☎ (081) 734-6613)
USA
    30 Rockefeller Plaza, 15 North Mezzanine, New York NY 10112 (☎ (212) 586-4901)
    3550 Wilshire Blvd, Suite 204, Los Angeles CA 90010 (☎ (213) 380-8855)

BUSINESS HOURS

Indian shops, offices and post offices are not early starters. Generally shops are open from 10 am to 5 pm Monday to Saturday. Some government offices open on alternate Saturdays and some commercial offices are open on Saturday morning. Post offices are open 10 am to 5 pm weekdays, and on Saturday morning. Main city offices may be open longer hours, such as 8 am to 6 pm in Delhi.

Banks are open for business between 10 am and 2 pm on weekdays and until noon on Saturday. Shops and offices are usually closed on Sunday.

HOLIDAYS & FESTIVALS

Due to its religious and regional variations India has a great number of holidays and festivals. Most of them follow the Indian lunar calendar and therefore change from year to year according to the Gregorian calendar, particularly the Muslim holidays and festivals, which are listed at the end of this section.

Apart from the holidays and festivals celebrated nationally there are many local and regional events. In the following lists, public holidays are marked with the initials 'PH'.

The Indian lunar months and their Gregorian equivalents are as follows:

Chaitra	March-April
Vaishaka	April-May
Jyaistha	May-June
Asadha	June-July
Sravana	July-August
Bhadra	August-September
Asvina	September-October
Kartika	October-November
Aghan	November-December
Pausa	December-January
Magha	January-February
Phalguna	February-March

January

Makar Sankranti This Hindu festival, marking the change of season when the sun is supposed to move to its northern home and the days get longer and the nights get shorter, is celebrated predominantly in Andhra Pradesh and amongst the Tamil people of the south in Tamil Nadu. It falls sometime in the middle of January.

Pongal This is a Tamil festival to mark the end of the harvest season. It is observed on the first day of the Tamil month of Thai, which is in the middle of January. The festivities last four days and include such activities as the boiling-over of a pot of *pongal* (a mixture of rice, sugar, dhal and milk), symbolic of prosperity and abundance. On the third day cattle are washed, decorated and even painted, and then fed the pongal.

Vasant Panchami The most notable feature of this spring festival, held on the 5th of Magha, is that many people wear yellow clothes. In some places, however, especially in West Bengal, Saraswati, the goddess of learning, is honoured.

Books, musical instruments and other objects related to the arts are placed in front of the goddess to receive her blessing.

Kite Festival This colourful festival is celebrated in Ahmedabad (Gujarat) each year, and an international competition is held.

Republic Day Republic Day on 26 January celebrates the anniversary of India's establishment as a republic in 1950; there are activities in all the state capitals but most spectacularly in New Delhi, where there is an enormously colourful military parade. (PH)

Beating the Retreat As part of the Republic Day celebrations, three days later a Beating of the Retreat ceremony takes place outside Rashtrapati Bhavan, the residence of the Indian president, in New Delhi.

February-March

Sivaratri This day of fasting is dedicated to Lord Siva – his followers believe that it was on this day he danced the *tandav*. Processions to the temples are followed by the chanting of mantras and anointing of lingams.

Holi This is one of the most exuberant Hindu festivals, with people marking the end of winter by throwing coloured water and red powder at one another – don't wear good clothes on this day! On the night before Holi, bonfires are built to symbolise the destruction of the evil demon Holika. It's mainly a northern festival; in the south, where there is no real winter to end, it takes place only in certain places.

In Maharashtra this festival is known as *Rangapanchami* and is celebrated with dancing and singing. (PH)

March

Gangaur This Rajasthani festival honours Siva and Parvati. The Rajasthani women are at their most colourful, and can be seen dancing, praying and singing near any Siva idol.

March-April

Mahavir Jayanti This major Jain festival marks the birth of Mahavira, the founder of Jainism. (PH)

Ramanavami In temples all over India the birth of Rama, an incarnation of Vishnu, is celebrated on this day. In the week leading up to Ramanavami, the *Ramayana* is widely read and performed. (PH)

Good Friday This Christian holiday is also celebrated in India. (PH)

April-May

Baisakhi This Sikh festival commemorates the day that Guru Gobind Singh founded the Khalsa, the Sikh brotherhood, which adopted the 'five kakkars' as part of their code of behaviour. The *Granth Sahib* is read right through at Gurdwaras, and then is put in a procession. Feasting and dancing follow in the evening.

May-June

Buddha Jayanti The Buddha's birth, enlightenment and attainment of nirvana are all celebrated on this day. The Buddha is supposed to have gone through each of these experiences on the same day but in different years. (PH)

June-July

Rath Yatra (Car Festival) Lord Jagannath's great temple chariot makes its stately journey from his temple in Puri, Orissa during this festival. Similar but far more grandiose festivals take place in other locations, particularly in the Dravidian south. Lord Jagannath is one of Krishna's names (Krishna being the eighth incarnation of Vishnu). The main procession in Puri celebrates Krishna's journey to Mathura to visit his aunt for a week! The images of his brother (Balarama) and sister (Subhadra) are paraded with him.

Teej Another Rajasthani festival, this one celebrates the onset of the monsoon. Idols of the goddess Parvati are paraded through the streets, amid much singing and dancing.

July-August

Naag Panchami This festival is dedicated to Ananta, the serpent upon whose coils Vishnu rested between universes. Offerings are made to snake images, and snake charmers do a roaring trade. Snakes are supposed to have power over the monsoon rainfall and keep evil from homes.

Raksha Bandhan (Narial Purnima) On the full-moon day of the Hindu month of Sravana, girls fix amulets known as *rakhis* to their brothers' wrists to protect them in the coming year. The brothers give their sisters gifts. Some people also worship the Vedic sea-god deity, Varuna, on this day. Coconuts are thrown into the sea.

Janmashtami The anniversary of Krishna's birth is celebrated with happy abandon – in tune with Krishna's own mischievous moods. Although it is a national holiday, Agra, Bombay and Mathura (his birthplace) are the main centres. Devotees fast all day until midnight. (PH)

Independence Day This holiday on 15 August celebrates the anniversary of India's independence from Britain in 1947. The prime minister delivers an address from the ramparts of Delhi's Red Fort. (PH)

August-September

Ganesh Chaturthi This festival, held on the fourth day of the Hindu month Bhadra, is dedicated to the popular elephant-headed god Ganesh. It is widely celebrated all over India, but with particular enthusiasm in Maharashtra. In every village, shrines are erected and a clay Ganesh idol is installed. Firecrackers are let off at all hours. Each family also buys a clay idol, and on the day of the festival it is brought into the house where it is kept and worshipped for a specified period before being ceremoniously immersed in a river, tank or the sea. As Ganesh is the god of wisdom and prosperity, Ganesh Chaturthi is considered to be the most auspicious day of the year. It is considered unlucky to look at the moon on this day.

Shravan Purnima After a day-long fast, high-caste Hindus replace the sacred thread which they always wear looped over their left shoulder.

Pateti This is the day on which Parsis celebrate their new year. A week later *Khordad Sal* celebrates the birth of Zarathustra.

Onam Harvest Festival During this Keralan harvest festival, the famous snake boat races are held at Alappuzha (Alleppey).

September

Dussehra This is the most popular of all the Indian festivals and takes place over 10 days, beginning on the first day of the Hindu month of Asvina. It celebrates Durga's victory over the buffalo-headed demon Mahishasura. In many places it culminates with the burning of huge images of the demon king Ravana and his accomplices in effigy, and this is symbolic of the triumph of good over evil. In Delhi it is known as Ram Lila (Life-story of Rama) and there are re-enactments of the *Ramayana* and fireworks. In Mysore and Ahmedabad there are great processions. In West Bengal the festival is known as *Durga Puja*; in Gujarat it's *Navratri* (Festival of Nine Nights). In Kulu, in the north, the festival takes place a little later than elsewhere. It is a delightful time when the Kulu Valley shows why it is known as the 'Valley of the Gods'. (PH – two days)

October

Gandhi Jayanti This is a solemn celebration of Gandhi's birthday on 2 October with prayer meetings at the Raj Ghat in Delhi where he was cremated. (PH)

November

Diwali (or *Deepavali*) This is the happiest festival of the Hindu calendar, celebrated on the 15th day of Kartika. At night countless oil lamps are lit to show Rama the way home from his period of exile. Today the festival is also dedicated to Lakshmi (particularly in Bombay) and to Kali in Calcutta. In all, the festival lasts five days. On the first day, houses are thoroughly cleaned and doorsteps are decorated with intricate *rangolis* (chalk designs). Day two is dedicated to Krishna's victory over Narakasura, a legendary tyrant. In the south, new clothes are worn on this day following a pre-dawn oil bath. Day three is spent in worshipping Lakshmi, the goddess of fortune. Traditionally, this is the beginning of the new financial year for companies. Day four commemorates the visit of the friendly (but uppity) demon Bali whom Vishnu put in his place. On the fifth day men visit their sisters to have a *tikka* put on their forehead.

Diwali has also become the 'festival of sweets' and families give and receive sweets. This has become as much a part of the tradition as the lighting of oil-lamps and firecrackers. Diwali is also celebrated by the Jains as their New Year's Day. (PH)

Govardhana Puja This is a Hindu festival dedicated to that holiest of animals, the cow. (PH)

Pushkar Camel Fair This incredibly colourful camel and cattle fair in Rajasthan includes camel races amongst other events

Nanak Jayanti The birthday of Guru Nanak, the

Camel at Pushkar Camel Fair, Rajasthan

founder of the Sikh religion, is celebrated with prayer readings and processions, particularly in Amritsar and Patna. (PH)

December

Feast of St Francis Xavier On 3 December this festival and the feast of Our Lady of the Immaculate Conception are two of the most important festivals in Goa.

Christmas Day A holiday in India. (PH)

Muslim Holidays

The dates of the Muslim festivals are not fixed, as they fall about 11 days earlier each year.

Ramadan
The most important Muslim festival is a 30-day dawn-to-dusk fast. It was during this month that the prophet Mohammed had the Koran revealed to him in Mecca.

In Muslim countries this can be a difficult time for travellers since restaurants are closed and tempers tend to run short. Fortunately, despite India's large Muslim minority, it causes few difficulties for visitors. Ramadan starts around 12 February 1994, 1 February 1995 and 21 January 1996.

Id-ul-Fitr
This day celebrates the end of Ramadan. (PH)

Id-ul-Zuhara
This is a Muslim festival commemorating Abraham's attempt to sacrifice his son. It is celebrated with prayers and feasts. (PH)

Muharram
Muharram is a 10-day festival commemorating the martyrdom of Mohammed's grandson, Imam Hussain. (PH)

POST & TELECOMMUNICATIONS
Post

The Indian postal and poste restante services are generally excellent. Expected letters almost always are there and letters you send almost invariably reach their destination, although they take up to three weeks. American Express, in its major city locations, offers an alternative to the poste restante system.

Have letters addressed to you with your surname in capitals and, underlined, the poste restante, GPO, and the city in question. Many 'lost' letters are simply misfiled under given (Christian) names, so always check under both your names.

You can often buy stamps at good hotels, saving a lot of queueing in crowded post offices.

Postal Rates Aerogrammes cost Rs 6.50, postcards Rs 6, airmail letters Rs 11.

Posting Parcels Most people discover how to do this the hard way, in which case it'll take half a day. Go about it this way, which can still take up to an hour:

(1) Take the parcel to a tailor and tell him you'd like it stitched up in cheap linen and the seams sealed with sealing wax. The wax has to be pressed with a seal which cannot be duplicated (if all else fails a foreign coin will serve). At some larger post offices this stitching service is offered either outside or inside the office. Negotiate the price first.

Festival Calendar

Festival	Place	1993	1994	1995
Pongal	Tamil Nadu	13-15 Jan	13-15 Jan	13-15 Jan
Republic Day	New Delhi	26 Jan	26 Jan	26 Jan
Basant Panchami	All over	Jan/Feb	Jan/Feb	Jan/Feb
Holi	All over	7-8 Mar	26-27 Mar	15-16 Mar
Good Friday	All over	9 April	1 April	14 April
Car Festival	Puri	21 Jun	Jun/Jul	Jun/Jul
Teej	Jaipur	22-23 Jul	10-11 Aug	30-31 Jul
Diwali	All over	12-13 Oct	1-2 Nov	22-23 Nov
Durga Puja	Calcutta	21-24 Oct	10-13 Oct	30 Sep-3 Oct
Dussehra	All over	24 Oct	13 Oct	3 Oct
Camel Fair	Pushkar	26-29 Nov	15-18 Nov	4-7 Nov

(2) Go to the post office with your parcel and ask for the necessary customs declaration forms. Fill them in and glue one to the parcel. The other will be stitched onto it. Write your passport number, nationality and the words 'bona fide tourist' across the top of both forms. To avoid excise duty at the delivery end it's best to specify that the contents are a 'gift'. Be careful with how much you declare the contents to be worth. If you specify over Rs 1000, your parcel will not be accepted without a bank clearance certificate. You can imagine the hassles involved in getting one of these so always state the value as less than Rs 1000.

(3) Have the parcel weighed and franked at the parcel counter.

If you are just sending books or printed matter, these can go by bookpost, which is considerably cheaper than parcel post, but the package must be wrapped a certain way: make sure that the package can either be opened for inspection along the way, or else is just wrapped in brown paper or cardboard and tied with string, with the two ends

exposed so that the contents are visible. No customs declaration form is necessary for such parcels.

Be cautious with places which offer to mail things to your home address after you have bought them. Government emporiums are usually OK, but although most people who buy things from other places get them eventually, some items never turn up (were they ever sent?) or what turns up isn't what they bought.

Sending parcels in the other direction (to you in India) is an extremely hit-and-miss affair. Don't count on anything bigger than a letter getting to you. And don't count on a letter getting to you if there's anything worthwhile inside it.

Telephone & Fax

The telephone system in India has undergone massive change in the last few years. Most places are now hooked up to the STD (long-distance)/ISD network, and so making local, interstate and international calls is simplicity itself from even the smallest town.

Everywhere you'll come across private STD/ISD call booths with direct interstate and international dialling. These phones are usually found in shops or other businesses, but are well signposted with large 'STD/ISD' signs advertising the service. A digital meter lets you keep an eye on what the call is costing, and gives you a printout at the end. You then just pay the shopowner – quick, painless and a far cry from the not so distant past when a night spent at a telegraph office waiting for a line was not unusual. Direct international calls from these phones cost Rs 50 per minute, regardless of where you are calling.

Also available is the Home Country Direct service, which gives you access to the international operator in your home country. You can then make reverse charge (collect) or credit card calls. It is currently available to eight countries, but more places should be added soon. You may also have trouble convincing the owner of the telephone you are using that they are not going to get charged for the call. The countries and numbers to dial are:

Canada	000167
Italy	0003917
Japan	0008117
Netherlands	0003117
Singapore	0006617
Spain	0003417
USA	000117
UK	0004417

Many of the STD/ISD booths also have a fax machine for public use.

The Indian government has set up modern, 24-hour communications centres in the four main cities, and these can be handy. The government company which runs these centres is VSN Ltd (Videsh Sanchar Nigam), and the addresses are:

Bombay
  Videsh Sanchar Bhavan, Mahatma Gandhi Rd, Bombay 400 001 (☎ (022) 204-2728; fax (022) 95-4321)
Calcutta
  Poddar Court, 18 Ravindra Sarani, Calcutta 700 001 (☎ (033) 26-6264; fax (033) 95-4321)
Madras
  Videsh Sanchar Bhavan, Swami Sivananda Salai, Madras 600 002 (☎ (044) 56-6740; fax (044) 95-4321)
New Delhi
  Videsh Sanchar Bhavan, Bangla Sahib Rd, New Delhi 110001 (☎ (011) 35-0289; fax (011) 95-4321)

There are also similar government exchanges in some other state capitals but they are generally only open between 8 am and 8 pm daily (not 24 hours).

Telex

Domestic and international telex services in India are good, reasonably priced and not heavily used like the telephone services. Telex is a good way to reconfirm flights, as you have evidence of having done so. The bigger hotels will sometimes let you use their telex (for a price).

TIME

India is 5½ hours ahead of GMT, 4½ hours behind Australian Eastern Standard Time and 10½ hours ahead of American Eastern Standard Time.

ELECTRICITY

The electric current is 230-240 volts AC, 50 cycles. Electricity is widely available in India but breakdowns and blackouts are not uncommon. Sockets are of the two round-pin variety.

You can buy small immersion elements, perfect for boiling water for tea or coffee, for Rs 30. For about Rs 70 you can buy electric mosquito zappers. These are the type that take chemical tablets which melt and give off deadly vapours (deadly for the mosquito, that is). There are many different brands and they are widely available – they come with quaint names such as Good Knight.

BOOKS & MAPS

India is a great place for reading – there's plenty to read about, there's plenty of time to read on those never-ending bus or train trips, and when you get to the big cities you'll find plenty of bookshops where you can purchase the reading matter.

India is one of the world's largest publishers of books in English. After the USA and the UK, it's up there with Canada or Australia as a major English-language publisher. You'll find a great number of interesting books on India by Indian publishers, which are generally not available in the West.

Indian publishers also do cheap reprints of Western bestsellers at prices far below Western levels. A meaty Leon Uris or Arthur Hailey novel, ideal for an interminable train ride, will often cost less than US$3. Compare that with your local bookshop prices. The favourite Western author is probably P G Wodehouse – 'Jeeves must be considered another incarnation of Vishnu', was one explanation.

Recently published British and American books also reach Indian bookshops remarkably fast and with very low markups. If a bestseller in Europe or America has major appeal for India they'll often rush out a paperback in India to forestall possible pirates. The novel *City of Joy* (a European bestseller about Calcutta) was out in paperback in India before the hardback had even reached Australia.

The suggested books that follow are only a few interesting ones that should be readily available. Of course there are many more now long out of print which you may still find in some shops. There are also many beautiful coffee-table books on India – ideal for whetting the appetite or for conjuring up the magic of India after your return. India has spawned an equally large number of cookery books – if you want to get into curry and all those spices you'll have no trouble finding plenty of instructions. Indian art has also generated a great number of interesting books of all types. So, too, have politics, economics and environmental issues.

Novels

Plenty of authors have taken the opportunity of setting their novels in a country as colourful as India. Rudyard Kipling, with books like *Kim* and *Plain Tales from the Hills*, is the Victorian English interpreter of India *par excellence*. In *A Passage .to India*, E M Forster perfectly captures that collision of incomprehension between the English and the Indians. A very readable book.

Much more recent but again following that curious question of why the English and Indians, so dissimilar in many ways, were so similar in others, is Ruth Prawer Jhabwala's *Heat & Dust*. The contemporary narrator of the tale also describes the backpacker's India in a flawless fashion. Other books by this author are equally impressive.

Probably the most widely acclaimed Indian novel in recent times was Salman Rushdie's *Midnight's Children*, which won the Booker Prize. It tells of the children who were born, like modern India itself, at the stroke of midnight on that August night in 1947 and how the life of one particular 'midnight's child' is inextricably intertwined with events in India itself. Rushdie's follow-up, *Shame*, was set in modern Pakistan. His

sardonic treatment of the post-Independence rulers of India and Pakistan in these two novels upset quite a few overinflated egos. His most recent, *The Satanic Verses*, inflamed Muslim passions to the limit and resulted in Iran's now-deceased Ayatollah Khomeini pronouncing a death sentence on him. The book is banned in India.

Vikram Seth's epic 1366-page novel about post-Independence India, *A Suitable Boy*, is set to become a classic. Seth was given an advance of UK£500,000 for this novel.

Paul Scott's *The Raj Quartet* and *Staying On* are other important novels set in India. The big 'bestseller' Indian novel of recent years was the monster tome *Far Pavilions* by M M Kaye. Women's magazine romance in some ways, but it has some interesting angles on India.

Nectar in a Sieve by Kamala Markandaya is an interesting account of a woman's life in rural India. See the Calcutta chapter for more on *City of Joy*, the 1986 bestseller in Europe and India which has recently been made into a popular film.

Kushwant Singh is one of India's most published contemporary authors and journalists, although he seems to have as many detractors as fans. His most recent offering is simply titled *Delhi* (Penguin India, 1990). This novel spans a 600-year time frame and brings to life various periods in Delhi's history through the eyes of poets, princes and emperors. It is ingeniously spiced with short dividing chapters describing the author's peripatetic affair with a *hijda* (hermaphrodite) whore and his own age-induced and overindulgent activities which play havoc with his libido. As the author states: 'History provided me with the skeleton. I covered it with flesh and injected blood and a lot of seminal fluid into it'. A lively and essential read!

Kushwant Singh has also written the harrowing *Train to Pakistan* on the holocaust of Partition, the humorous *India – An Introduction*, and a collection of short stories, published in hardback, some of which are superb.

Also extremely well known and highly

regarded are the books of R K Naryan. Many were set in the fictional town of Malgudi, and offer unique glimpses and insights into Indian village life. They're excellent reading. His most well-known works include: *Swami & His Friends*, *The Financial Expert*, *The Guide*, *Waiting for the Mahatma* and *Malgudi Days*.

If you prefer pulp in the form of Dallas-type financial double-dealing, adultery and sex in the boardroom amongst the Bombay stock market elite, try Shobha De's series of upmarket Mills & Boon novels. The latest was *Sisters*.

General Interest

John Keay's *Into India* (John Murray, London, 1973) is a fine general introduction to travelling in India. One traveller's observations and perceptions of life in India today provide an illuminating idea of what it's really like.

Paul Theroux's best-selling railway odyssey *The Great Railway Bazaar* takes you up and down India by train (and across most of the rest of Asia) and turns the whole world into a railway carriage. Engrossing, like most such books, as much for its insights into the author as for those into the people he meets. *Slow Boats to China* by Gavin Young follows much the same path but this time by boat. *Slowly Down the Ganges* by Eric Newby is another boat-trip tale; this one borders, at times, on sheer masochism!

Karma Kola by Gita Mehta is accurately subtitled 'the marketing of the mystic east'. It amusingly and cynically describes the unavoidable and hilarious collision between India looking to the West for technology and modern methods, and the West descending upon India in search of wisdom and enlightenment.

India File by Trevor Fishlock (Indian paperback by Rupa, New Delhi, 1984) is a very readable collection of articles on India by the *Times* correspondent. The chapter on sex in India is often hilarious.

Ved Mehta has written a number of interesting personal views of India. *Walking the Indian Streets* (Penguin paperback) is a slim and highly readable account of the culture shock he went through on returning to India after a long period abroad. *Portrait of India* is by the same author.

Ronald Segal's *The Crisis of India* (Penguin, London, 1965) is written by a South African Indian on the theme that spirituality is not always more important than a full stomach. *The Gunny Sack* by M G Vassanji explores a similar theme, this time from the point of view of a group of Gujarati families who migrated to East Africa in Raj times but retain their connections with India. It's a good read and has been dubbed 'Africa's answer to Midnight's Children' by certain literary critics.

Third Class Ticket by Heather Wood is an interesting account of the culture shock experienced by a group of Bengali villagers as they explore the country for the first time. *Unveiling India* (Penguin) by Anees Jung is a contemporary documentary on women in India. *An Indian Attachment* by Sarah Lloyd is an interesting recent account of an Englishwoman's life in small villages in Punjab and Uttar Pradesh.

Chasing the Monsoon by Alexander Frater (Penguin India, 1990) is an Englishman's account of, as the title suggests, a journey north from Kovalam in Kerala all the way to the wettest place on earth (Cherrapunji in Meghalaya), all the while following the onset of the monsoon as it moves north across the country. It's a fascinating insight into the significance of the monsoon, and its affect on people.

Goddess in the Stones by Norman Lewis is an interesting account of the author's travels through Bihar and the tribal villages of Orissa.

Finally, no survey of personal insights into India can ignore V S Naipaul's two controversial books *An Area of Darkness* and *India – A Wounded Civilisation*. Born in Trinidad but of Indian descent, Naipaul tells in the first book of how India, unseen and unvisited, haunted him and of the impact upon him when he eventually made the pilgrimage to the motherland. You may well find that much of this book rings very true with your own experiences while in India. In the second book he writes of India's unsuccessful search for a new purpose and meaning for its civilisation.

History

If you want a thorough introduction to Indian history then look for the Pelican two-volume *A History of India*. In volume one Romila Thapar follows Indian history from 1000 BC to the coming of the Moghuls in the 16th century AD. Volume two by Percival Spear follows the rise and fall of the Moghuls through to India since Independence. At times both volumes are a little dry, but if you want a reasonably detailed history in a handy paperback format they're worth having. More cumbersome, but offering more detail, is the 900-page paperback *Oxford History of India* by Vincent Smith (OUP, Rs 140).

The Wonder that was India by A L Basham gives detailed descriptions of the Indian civilisations, origins of the caste system and social customs. and detailed information on Hinduism, Buddhism and other religions in India. It is also very informative about art and architecture. It has a wealth of background material on ancient India without being overly academic.

Christopher Hibbert's *The Great Mutiny – India 1857* (Penguin, London, 1980) is a single-volume description of the often lurid events of the Mutiny. This readable paperback is illustrated with contemporary photographs.

Plain Tales from the Raj, edited by Charles Allen (Futura paperback, London, 1976), is the delightful book derived from the equally delightful series of radio programmes of the same name. It consists of a series of interviews with people who took part in British India on both sides of the table. Extremely readable and full of fascinating little insights into life during the Raj era.

British historian Bamber Gascoigne's *The Moghuls* is an excellent combination of informed and interesting historical text and glossy pictures. Well worth the Rs 500 price tag.

The Nehrus & the Gandhis (Picador,

1988) by Tariq Ali is a very readable account of the history of these families and hence of India this century.

Freedom at Midnight is one of India's best-selling books. Its authors Larry Collins & Dominique Lapierre have written other equally popular modern histories, but you could hardly ask for a more enthralling series of events than those that led to India's independence in 1947. In India you can find *Freedom at Midnight* in a cheap Bell Books paperback (Vikas Publishing, Delhi, 1976).

Highness – the Maharajas of India by Ann Morrow (Grafton Books, 1986) provides an illuminating, if at times sycophantic, insight into the rarefied and extravagant lives of these Indian rulers during the days of the Raj and since Independence.

For a good insight into the country since Independence there is *From Raj to Rajiv – 40 Years of Indian Independence* (BBC Books UK, Universal Book Stall, Delhi, 1988). It is written by old India hand and BBC correspondent Mark Tully & Zareer Masani.

Two current-affairs books which are well worth reading are *Bhopal – the Lessons of a Tragedy* by Sanjoy Hazarika and *Riot after Riot – Reports on Caste & Communal Violence in India* by M J Akbar. Both are published by Penguin.

Finally, for those interested in the continuing and often shocking and sad story of India's treatment of its tribals, there is the scholarly *Tribes of India – the Struggle for Survival* by Christoph von Fürer-Haimendorf (Oxford University Press, 1982).

Two autobiographical books by one of India's most prominent contemporary writers, Nirad Choudhuri, *Autobiography of an Unknown Indian* and *Thy Hand, Great Anarch!: India 1921-1952*, are an excellent account of the history and culture of modern India.

Religion

If you want a better understanding of India's religions there are plenty of books available in India. The English series of Penguin paperbacks are amongst the best and are generally available in India. In particular, *Hinduism* by K M Sen (Penguin, London, 1961) is brief and to the point. If you want to read the Hindu holy books these are available in translations: *The Upanishads* (Penguin, London, 1965) and *The Bhagavad Gita* (Penguin, London, 1962). *Hindu Mythology*, edited by Wendy O'Flaherty (Penguin, London), is an interesting annotated collection of extracts from the Hindu holy books. Convenient if you don't want the whole thing.

A Classical Dictionary of Hindu Mythology & Religion by John Dowson (Rupa, New Delhi, 1987) is an Indian paperback reprint of an old English hardback. As the name suggests, it is in dictionary form and is one of the best sources for unravelling who's who in Hinduism. There's also *Indian Mythology* by Jan Knappert (Harper Collins, Delhi, 1992), a paperback encyclopedia.

Penguin also has a translation of the Koran. If you want to know more about Buddhism, *Buddhism* by Christmas Humphreys (Penguin, London, 1949) is an excellent introduction. *A Handbook of Living Religions* edited by John R Hinnewls (Pelican, London, 1985) provides a succinct and readable summary of all the various religions you will find in India, including Christianity and Judaism.

An excellent, detailed and dispassionate introduction to 16 of India's best known gurus and religious teachers is the recently published *Guru – the Search for Enlightenment* by John Mitchiner (Viking, 1991, Rs 150, available in India). It's essential reading for anyone interested in the relevance and contribution of Indian gurus to contemporary thought and experience.

Travel Guides

First published in 1859, the 22nd edition of *A Handbook for Travellers in India, Pakistan, Nepal, Bangladesh & Sri Lanka* (John Murray, London, 1975) is that rarest of animals, a Victorian travel guide. If you've got a deep interest in Indian architecture and

can afford the somewhat hefty price, then take along a copy of this immensely detailed guidebook. Unfortunately its system of following 'routes', in the manner of all good Victorian guidebooks, makes it somewhat difficult to locate things, but the effort is worth it. Along the way you'll find a lot of places where the British army made gallant stands, and more than a few statues of Queen Victoria – most of which have been replaced by statues of Mahatma Gandhi.

For relatively cheap but excellently produced photo-essays of the subcontinent, try Insight Guides' *Rajasthan* and *India* by APA Productions. They're both done by a team of experienced writers, many of them Indian, and while the text and photographs are generally excellent, the 'Guide in Brief' section at the back is of extremely limited use. The Nelles Guides' *Northern India* and *Southern India* (Nelles Verlag, 1990) are similar general guides with good photographs and text but skimpy hard information.

There are a great number of regional and local guidebooks published in India. Many of them are excellent value and describe certain sites (the Ajanta and Ellora Caves or Sanchi for example) in much greater detail than is possible in this book. The guides produced by the Archaeological Survey of India are particularly good. Many of the other guides have a most amusing way with English. Another good guide, this time on the painted *havelis* (merchant's mansions) of a small region in Rajasthan, is *The Guide to Painted Towns of Shekhawati* by Ilay Cooper which comes complete with street maps. It's available in the bookshops of Jaipur.

Books on wildlife are difficult to get, but birdwatchers may find the *Collins Handguide to the Birds of the Indian Subcontinent* useful. It doesn't cover all the birds by any means but it does have the best illustrations and text, and if you're not a very serious birdwatcher you will probably find it useful. Visitors to Kashmir and Sikkim can use *Birds of Nepal*, which includes notes on Kashmir and Sikkim. The Insight *Indian Wildlife* guide (APA, 1988) is available from major bookshops in India and is valuable if you're keenly interested in visiting national parks.

Railway buffs should enjoy *India by Rail* by Royston Ellis.

Other Lonely Planet Regional Guides

It's pleasing to be able to claim that for more information on India's neighbours and for travel beyond India, most of the best guides come from Lonely Planet! If you're heading north to Nepal then look for *Nepal – a travel survival kit* for complete information on this Himalayan nation. If you're planning on trekking in Nepal or simply want more information on trekking in general, look for *Trekking in the Nepal Himalaya* and *Trekking in the Indian Himalaya*. Or you can cross right over the Himalaya with our *Tibet – a travel survival kit* and *Karakoram Highway – a travel survival kit*.

There are Lonely Planet guides for other Indian neighbours. *Pakistan – a travel survival kit* is our guide to the 'unknown land of the Indus'. We also have a guide to India's other Muslim neighbour: *Bangladesh – a travel survival kit*. *Myanmar – a travel survival kit* covers that unpredictable country. If you're travelling to Sri Lanka then you need *Sri Lanka – a travel survival kit*, or for a visit to the Maldives and other islands there is also Lonely Planet's *Maldives & Islands of the East Indian Ocean – a travel survival kit*. Finally, if you want more information on the north-west of India then look for our comprehensive guide *Kashmir, Ladakh & Zanskar – a travel survival kit*.

If you're travelling further than India across Asia to Europe, then our book is *West Asia on a shoestring*. If it's further east you want then look for *South-East Asia on a shoestring*.

Also Recommended

Readers have recommended numerous other books such as *Eating the Indian Air* by John Morris; *The Gorgeous East* by Rupert Croft-Cooke; *Delhi is Far Away* and *The Grand Trunk Road* by John Wiles; and books by Jan & Rumer Godden. *A Princess Remembers* by Gayatri Devi is useful if you're going to Jaipur. Irish wanderer Dervla Murphy heads south in her book *On a Shoestring to Coorg*.

There are some wonderful Indian comic books dealing with Hindu mythology and Indian history. *An Indian Summer* by James Cameron (Penguin) is an autobiographical account of independence and south India.

Maps

The Lascelles 1:4,000,000 map of *India, Pakistan, Nepal, Bangladesh & Sri Lanka* is probably the most useful general map of India. It gives you plenty of detail on small towns and villages to help speed along those long bus or train trips. If it has any fault for the traveller, it is that it does not always include places of great interest but small population. The Bartholomews map is similar, and is widely available in India as well as overseas.

The Nelles Verlag series gives more detailed coverage, but you need to carry five maps to cover the whole country. They are excellent maps, but they're not cheap and you can't buy them in India.

Locally, the Government Map Office produces a series of maps covering all of India. In Delhi their office is opposite the tourist office on Janpath. It's upstairs, above the cafeteria beside the Central Cottage Industries Emporium. The maps are not all that useful since they will not allow production of anything at a reasonable scale which shows India's sea or land borders, and many of them date back to the 1970s. They do, however, have some good city maps. It is illegal to take any Survey of India map of larger than 1:250,000 scale out of the country.

The Government of India tourist office has a number of excellent giveaway city maps and also a reasonable all-India map. State tourist offices do not have much in the way of maps, but the Himachal Pradesh office has three excellent trekking maps which cover the trekking routes in that state.

FOREIGN FILMS

A number of foreign films have been made about India over the years. Keep your eyes open for a showing of Louis Malle's two-part film *Phantom India*. Running to about seven hours in all, this is a fascinating in-depth look at contemporary India. At times it's very self-indulgent and is now somewhat dated, but as an overall view it can't be beaten – it has been banned in India. The Australian ABC TV has produced two excellent documentary series on India, one titled *Journey into India*, the other *Journey into the Himalayas*. Both of them, but particularly the former, are worth seeing if you get a chance.

Of course the epic *Gandhi* was a major film, spawning a host of new and reprinted books on the Mahatma. *Heat & Dust* has also been made into an excellent film, as has *A Passage to India* and *Far Pavilions*. The film version of Lapierre's *City of Joy* was filmed in Calcutta in 1992 at a purpose-built slum. Directed by Roland Joffe (of *The Killing Fields*) with the principal character played by Patrick Swayze, it attracted a lot of flak from the West Bengal government which felt it was yet another condescending look at India's poor, but the critics, in general, felt otherwise.

For a discussion on the Indian film industry, see the relevant section under Arts in the Facts about the Country chapter.

MEDIA
Newspapers & Magazines

A number of daily English-language newspapers are printed in India. All of them are of the heavy news variety; none of them are tabloids (although there are weekly English tabloids). English-language dailies include the *Times of India*, the *Hindu*, the *Indian Express* and the *Statesman*; many feel the *Express* is the best of the bunch. The *Times* has its headquarters in Bombay and the *Statesman* in Calcutta, but there are many regional editions in both cases.

Forget about international coverage in Indian newspapers. You may get half a page of it, but that's it. The rest is all about Indian politics and economics, and is invariably strewn with a plethora of acronyms, the majority of which mean nothing to the uninitiated. One exception is the *Independent* which is published in Bombay and is an excellent quality broadsheet with good international coverage.

On the other hand, there's an excellent variety of meaty weekly magazines which cover a whole range of issues in depth and make good reading on long train rides as well as giving you an insight into contemporary India. Possibly *Frontline* is the best of the lot, but *India Today, The Week, Sunday* and the *Illustrated Weekly of India* are also very good. They're all available at bookshops, especially those at major railway stations. As with daily newspapers, however, you won't find much international news in them. What you will find are stories and photographs which, though interesting and of major regional importance, would never make the pages of Western daily newspapers. They're also interesting for the different slant which

they give to political and social issues of worldwide concern.

There are dozens of other Indian magazines written in English although many are of very limited interest to Western visitors – it takes a long time to build up an interest in Indian movie stars and their fanzines. Indian women's magazines, so alike yet so unlike their Western counterparts, are definitely worth looking at – *Femina* is probably the most well known. There's even an Indian 'male interest' magazine called *Debonair* with some fairly tame photographs of beautiful Indian women in various state's of undress.

In keeping with the Indian preoccupation with sport, there is an incredible proliferation of sports magazines, but apart from tennis and cricket, there is little about what's happening on the international scene.

Time and *Newsweek* are only available in the main cities, and anyway, once you've become used to Indian prices they seem very expensive! You can also find newspapers like the *Herald Tribune* and *Guardian* and magazines like *Der Spiegel* and its English, French and Italian clones in the major cities and at expensive hotels but, again, they're not cheap.

One thing you'll quickly find is that newspapers and magazines become public property on trains and buses. By your side you may have your virgin copy of a *Time* magazine which you have lashed out on to help pass the time on a long train journey, and are just waiting for the right moment to start reading it. If a fellow passenger spots it, you'll be expected to hand it over, and it will then circulate until you go and collect it. If this annoys you, keep any reading matter out of sight until you are ready to use it.

Radio & TV

The revolution in the TV network has been the introduction of cable TV. It's amazing to see satellite dishes (each costing around Rs 160,000), even in the remotest villages. The result is that the national broadcaster, Doordarshan, has lost viewers in droves, who now tune in to CNN, the BBC and

MTV! Star TV, broadcasting out of Hong Kong, gives a lot of coverage to international sporting events. For the sports-mad Indians it's been a huge success, particularly when an Indian cricket team is playing abroad!

Doordarshan still plods along with its dry, dull and generally dreadful programmes, while still insisting its viewers have not deserted it for the cable network. Occasionally there are some excellent cultural programmes on Doordarshan, but finding out exactly when something good is going to be screened is bloody near impossible – the TV programmes given in the daily papers just give the Hindi name of the show.

Most middle-range and all top-end hotels now have a colour TV in every room with a choice of cable or Doordarshan.

FILM & PHOTOGRAPHY

Colour print film is readily available in India, and developing and printing facilities are not hard to find in the major cities. They're usually cheap and the quality is usually (but not always) good. Kodak 100 colour print film costs around Rs 120 for a roll of 36. Developing costs are around Rs 25, plus Rs 3 per photo for printing.

If you're taking slides bring the film with you, and bring plenty – India is a photogenic country. Colour slide film can really only be found in the major cities. Colour slides can be developed in major centres, and the quality is usually good. Fujichrome slide film costs around Rs 200 for 36 exposures. Developing costs about Rs 85 with paper mounts, or Rs 130 with plastic mounts.

Kodachrome or other 'includes developing' film will have to be sent overseas. It's up to you whether you send it straight back or carry it back with you at the end of your trip. Film manufacturers warn that once exposed, film should be developed as quickly as possible; in practice the film seems to last, even in India's summer heat, without deterioration for months. But, if that's how long you're going to be carrying exposed film, consult a specialist photography handbook about ways of enhancing preservation.

There are plenty of camera shops which should be able to make minor repairs should you have any mechanical problems.

Photography itself presents some special problems in India. In the dry season the hazy atmosphere makes it difficult to get sharp shots or to get much contrast between what you are photographing and the background. Everything looks washed out and flat even with a polarising filter. In the mountains you should allow for the extreme clarity of the air and light intensity, and take care not to over-expose your shots. In general, photography is best done in the early morning and late afternoon.

Be careful what you photograph. India is touchy about places of military importance – this can include train stations, bridges, airports and any military installations. If in doubt, ask. In general most people are happy to be photographed, but care should be taken in pointing cameras at Muslim women. Again, if in doubt, ask.

HEALTH

Travel health depends on your predeparture preparations, your day-to-day health care while travelling and how you handle any medical problem or emergency that does develop. While the list of potential dangers can seem quite frightening, with a little luck, some basic precautions and adequate information, few travellers experience more than upset stomachs.

Travel Health Guides

There are a number of books on travel health:

Staying Healthy in Asia, Africa & Latin America, Moon Publications. Probably the best all-round guide to carry, as it's compact but very detailed and well organised.

Travellers' Health, Dr Richard Dawood, OUP. Comprehensive, easy to read, authoritative and also highly recommended, although it's rather large to lug around.

Where There is No Doctor, David Werner, Hesperian Foundation. A very detailed guide intended for someone, like a Peace Corps worker, going to work in an undeveloped country, rather than for the average traveller.

Travel with Children, Maureen Wheeler, Lonely Planet Publications. Includes basic advice on travel health for younger children.

Predeparture Preparations

Health Insurance A travel insurance policy to cover theft, loss and medical problems is a wise idea. There are a wide variety of policies and your travel agent will have recommendations (though not necessarily informed recommendations or personal experience). The international student travel policies handled by STA or other student travel organisations are usually good value. Some policies offer lower and higher medical expenses options but the higher one is chiefly for countries like the USA which have extremely high medical costs. Check the small print:

1. Some policies specifically exclude 'dangerous activities' which can include scuba diving, motorcycling, and even trekking. If such activities are on your agenda you don't want that sort of policy.
2. You may prefer a policy which pays doctors or hospitals direct rather than you having to pay on the spot and claim later. If you have to claim later make sure you keep all documentation. Some policies ask you to call back (reverse charges) to a centre in your home country where an immediate assessment of your problem is made.
3. Check if the policy covers ambulances or an emergency flight home. If you have to stretch out you will need two seats and somebody has to pay for them!

Medical Kit A small, straightforward medical kit is a wise thing to carry. A possible kit list includes:

1. Aspirin or Panadol – for pain or fever.
2. Antihistamine (such as Benadryl) – useful as a decongestant for colds, allergies, to ease the itch from insect bites or stings or to help prevent motion sickness.
3. Antibiotics – useful if you're travelling well off the beaten track, but they must be prescribed and you should carry the prescription with you.
4. Kaolin preparation (Pepto-Bismol), Imodium or Lomotil – for stomach upsets.
5. Rehydration mixture – for treatment of severe diarrhoea; this is particularly important if travelling with children.

6. Antiseptic, Mercurochrome and antibiotic powder or similar 'dry' spray – for cuts and grazes.
7. Calamine lotion – to ease irritation from bites or stings.
8. Bandages and Band-aids – for minor injuries.
9. Scissors, tweezers and a thermometer (note that mercury thermometers are prohibited by airlines).
10. Insect repellent, sunscreen, suntan lotion, chap stick and water purification tablets.

Ideally antibiotics should be administered only under medical supervision and should never be taken indiscriminately. Overuse of antibiotics can weaken your body's ability to deal with infections naturally and can reduce the drug's efficacy on a future occasion. Take only the recommended dose at the prescribed intervals and continue using the antibiotic for the prescribed period, even if the illness seems to be cured earlier. Antibiotics are quite specific to the infections they can treat; stop immediately if there are any serious reactions and don't use it at all if you are unsure if you have the correct one.

In India, if a medicine is available at all, it will generally be available over the counter and the price will be much cheaper than in the West. However, be careful when buying pharmaceutical drugs, particularly where the expiry date may have passed or correct storage conditions may not have been followed. It's possible that drugs which are no longer recommended or have even been banned in the West are still being dispensed in developing countries such as India.

Various so-called 'AIDS kits' are available in the UK and other Western countries, and these have all the gear necessary for blood transfusions and injections. If you are going to be in India for a long time and intend to get off the beaten track, they can be a good idea. In fact even in many places where there are plenty of tourists – such as Jaisalmer in Rajasthan – the medical facilities are extremely basic. Having your own sterile equipment could be worthwhile if you have an accident and are hospitalised. For such a kit to be useful for a blood transfusion, however, it needs to have the plastic tube which carries the blood from the bag or bottle, as well as the intravenous needle which actually goes into the arm – some kits have the latter but not the former.

Reports have reached Lonely Planet that some of the apparently safe 'disposable' syringes for sale in some chemists and markets are not properly sterilised. They look OK, but often they have been collected from hospital waste bins, superficially washed and then packed in plastic for sale to chemists and clinics. So to be sure, it's best to bring your own needles.

Health Preparations Make sure you're healthy before you start travelling. If you are embarking on a long trip ensure your teeth are OK; a visit to an Indian dentist, especially in a small village, is the last thing you'd want.

If you wear glasses take a spare pair and your prescription. Losing your glasses can be a real problem, although in the major cities replacements can be made quickly, cheaply and competently.

If you require a particular medication take an adequate supply, as it may not be available locally. Take the prescription, with the generic rather than the brand name (which may not be locally available), as it will make getting replacements easier. It's a wise idea to have the prescription with you to show you legally use the medication – it's surprising how often over-the-counter drugs from one place are illegal without a prescription or even banned in another.

Immunisations Vaccinations provide protection against diseases you might meet along the way. No immunisations are necessary for entry into India, but the further off the beaten track you go the more necessary it is to take precautions. Vaccination as an entry requirement is usually only enforced when you are coming from an infected area – yellow fever and cholera are the two most likely requirements. Nevertheless, all vaccinations should be recorded on an International Health Certificate, which is available from your physician or government health department.

Plan ahead for getting your vaccinations: some of them require an initial shot followed by a booster, while some vaccinations should not be given together. Most travellers from Western countries will have been immunised against various diseases during childhood but your doctor may still recommend booster shots against measles or polio. The period of protection offered by vaccinations differs widely and some are contraindicated if you are pregnant.

The possible list of vaccinations includes:

Smallpox Smallpox has now been wiped out worldwide, so immunisation is no longer necessary.

Cholera Protection is not very effective, only lasts six months and is contraindicated for pregnancy.

Tetanus & Diphtheria Boosters are necessary every 10 years and protection is highly recommended.

Typhoid Protection lasts for three years and is useful if you are travelling for long in rural areas. You may get some side effects such as pain at the injection site, fever, headache and a general unwell feeling.

Infectious Hepatitis (Hep A) Gamma globulin is not a vaccination but a ready-made antibody which has proven very successful in reducing the chances of hepatitis infection. Because it may interfere with the development of immunity, it should not be given until at least 10 days after administration of the last vaccine needed; it should also be given as close as possible to departure because of its relatively short-lived protection period of up to six months.

Basic Rules

Care in what you eat and drink is the most important health rule; stomach upsets are the most likely travel health problem but the majority of these upsets will be relatively minor. Don't become paranoid – trying the local food is part of the experience of travel after all.

Drinks

Bottled mineral water is available virtually everywhere, and most travellers drink this rather than risk what comes out of the tap. However, some so-called 'mineral' waters have recently come under investigation, and a couple of travellers have even

observed bottles of well-known brands being filled with tap water!

Take care with fruit juice, particularly if water may have been added, and with drinks which contain ice blocks. Milk should be treated with suspicion, as it is often unpasteurised. Boiled milk is fine if it is kept hygienically and yoghurt is always good. Tea or coffee should also be OK, since the water should have been boiled.

Water Purification The simplest way of purifying water is to boil it thoroughly. Technically this means boiling for 10 minutes, something which happens very rarely! Remember that at high altitude water boils at lower temperature, so germs are less likely to be killed.

Simple filtering will not remove all dangerous organisms, so if you cannot boil water it should be treated chemically. Chlorine tablets (Puritabs, Steritabs or other brand names) will kill many but not all pathogens. Iodine is very effective in purifying water and is available in tablet form (such as Potable Aqua), but follow the directions carefully and remember that too much iodine can be harmful.

If you can't find tablets, tincture of iodine (2%) or iodine crystals can be used. Two drops of tincture of iodine per litre or quart of clear water is the recommended dosage; the treated water should be left to stand for 30 minutes before drinking. Iodine loses its effectiveness if exposed to air or damp so keep it in a tightly sealed container. Flavoured powder will disguise the taste of treated water and is a good idea if you are travelling with children.

Food Salads and fruit should be washed with purified water or peeled where possible. Ice cream is usually OK if it is a reputable brand name, but beware of street vendors and of ice cream that has melted and been refrozen. Thoroughly cooked food is safest but not if it has been left to cool or if it has been reheated. Take great care with shellfish or fish and avoid undercooked meat. If a place looks clean and well run and if the vendor

Mineral Water

As in many other countries where tourists regard the local water supply as potentially if not actually lethal, you'll see an amazing number of tourists in India walking around clutching bottles of mineral water as if they were new-born babies. Sadly, the majority remain totally unaware of just what the contents of their precious bottle are and they're more than willing to part with up to twice what it would cost them to eat a thali in order to feel 'safe'.

'Safe' they will be, but, in the majority of cases, they certainly won't be drinking mineral water. What they will be drinking is water drawn from normal municipal supplies treated with ozone gas, ultraviolet rays or silver steriliser purveyed in PVC bottles (which themselves have been banned in many Western countries because of fears that the plastic is carcinogenic).

Currently, India has no standards to define what is and is not mineral water so manufacturers are at liberty to bottle what they like and call it mineral water. Yet, what is essentially a confidence trick remains unchallenged and the market is booming. In the summer of 1992 over four million bottles of the dubious stuff were sold, with Bisleri Acqua Minerale grabbing the lion's share. Lesser players include UB's Officer's Choice, Gangotri Minerals' Gangotri and Himalayan Minerals' Himalayan Bliss Gangajal. The latter contend that they sell the genuine article as does Pondicherry Agro-Industries with their product Pondichéry ('Natural Mineral Water with traces of Natural Silver') but Bisleri's producers make no such claims! A franchise owner for Bisleri's Acqua Minerale was recently quoted as saying, 'We bottle Bombay's municipal water, which is purified by silver sterilizer, ozone gas and ultraviolet rays'.

The only Indian mineral water which is internationally recognised as the genuine article is Mohan Meakin's Golden Eagle, sold, incidentally, in a glass bottle.

So next time you see a tourist slugging away on one of those 'mineral water' bottles, ask him or her whether it's the Delhi or the Bombay municipal water variety and enjoy the reaction. In the meantime, don't ask what is happening to the millions of empty PVC bottles. We'll leave that to your imagination or the ubiquitous crunch of plastic under your sandalled feet. ∎

---

also looks clean and healthy, then the food is probably safe. In general, places that are packed with travellers or locals will be fine, while empty restaurants are suspect.

Nutrition If your food is poor or limited in availability, if you're travelling hard and fast and therefore missing meals, or if you simply lose your appetite, you can soon start to lose weight and place your health at risk.

Make sure your diet is well balanced. Eggs, beans, lentils (dhal) and nuts are all safe ways to get protein. Fruit you can peel (bananas, oranges or mandarins for example) is always safe and a good source of vitamins. Try to eat plenty of grains (rice) and bread. Remember that although food is generally safer if it is cooked well, overcooked food loses much of its nutritional value. If your diet isn't well balanced or if your food intake is insufficient, it's a good idea to take vitamin and iron pills.

In hot weather make sure you drink enough – don't rely on feeling thirsty to indicate when you should drink. Not needing to urinate or very dark yellow urine is a danger sign. Always carry a water bottle with you on long trips. Excessive sweating can lead to loss of salt and therefore muscle cramping. Salt tablets are not a good idea as a preventative, but in places where salt is not used much, adding salt to food can help.

Everyday Health A normal body temperature is 98.6°F or 37°C; more than 2°C higher is a 'high' fever. A normal adult pulse rate is 60 to 80 beats per minute (children 80 to 100, babies 100 to 140). You should know how to take a temperature and a pulse rate. As a general rule the pulse increases about 20 beats per minute for each °C rise in fever.

Respiration (breathing) rate is also an indicator of illness. Count the number of breaths per minute: between 12 and 20 is normal for adults and older children (up to 30 for younger children, 40 for babies). People with a high fever or serious respiratory illness (like pneumonia) breathe more quickly than normal. More than 40 shallow breaths a minute usually means pneumonia.

Many health problems can be avoided by taking care of yourself. Wash your hands frequently – it's quite easy to contaminate your own food. Clean your teeth with purified water rather than straight from the tap. Avoid climatic extremes: keep out of the sun when it's hot, dress warmly when it's cold. Avoid potential diseases by dressing sensibly. You can get worm infections through walking barefoot or dangerous coral cuts by walking over coral without shoes. You can avoid insect bites by covering bare skin when insects are around, by screening windows or beds or by using insect repellents. Seek local advice: and in situations where there is no information, discretion is the better part of valour.

Medical Problems & Treatment

Potential medical problems can be broken down into several areas. First there are the climatic and geographical considerations – problems caused by extremes of temperature, altitude or motion. Then there are diseases and illnesses caused by insanitation, insect bites or stings, and animal or human contact. Simple cuts, bites or scratches can also cause problems.

Self-diagnosis and treatment can be risky, so wherever possible seek qualified help. Although we do give treatment dosages in this section, they are for emergency use only. Medical advice should be sought before administering any drugs.

An embassy or consulate can usually recommend a good place to go for such advice. So can five-star hotels, although they often recommend doctors with five-star prices.

(This is when that medical insurance really comes in useful!) In some places standards of medical attention are so low that for some ailments the best advice is to get on a plane and go somewhere else.

Climatic & Geographical Considerations

Sunburn In the desert or at high altitude you can get sunburnt surprisingly quickly, even through cloud. Use a sunscreen and take extra care to cover areas which don't normally see sun – eg, your feet. A hat provides added protection, and you should also use zinc cream or some other barrier cream for your nose and lips. Calamine lotion is good for mild sunburn.

Prickly Heat Prickly heat is an itchy rash caused by excessive perspiration trapped under the skin. It usually strikes people who have just arrived in a hot climate and whose pores have not yet opened sufficiently to cope with greater sweating. Keeping cool but bathing often, using a mild talcum powder or even resorting to air-conditioning may help until you acclimatise.

Heat Exhaustion Dehydration or salt deficiency can cause heat exhaustion. Take time to acclimatise to high temperatures and make sure you get sufficient liquids. Salt deficiency is characterised by fatigue, lethargy, headaches, giddiness and muscle cramps and in this case salt tablets may help. Vomiting or diarrhoea can deplete your liquid and salt levels. Anhydrotic heat exhaustion, caused by an inability to sweat, is quite rare. Unlike the other forms of heat exhaustion it is likely to strike people who have been in a hot climate for some time, rather than newcomers.

Heat Stroke This serious, sometimes fatal, condition can occur if the body's heat-regulating mechanism breaks down and the body temperature rises to dangerous levels. Long, continuous periods of exposure to high temperatures can leave you vulnerable to heat stroke. You should avoid excessive alcohol or strenuous activity when you first arrive in a hot climate.

The symptoms are feeling unwell, not sweating very much or at all and a high body temperature (39°C to 41°C). Where sweating has ceased the skin becomes flushed and red. Severe, throbbing headaches and lack of coordination will also occur, and the sufferer may be confused or aggressive. Eventually the victim will become delirious or convulse. Hospitalisation is essential, but meanwhile get patients out of the sun, remove their clothing, cover them with a wet sheet or towel and then fan continually.

Fungal Infections Hot weather fungal infections are most likely to occur on the scalp, between the toes or fingers (athlete's foot), in the groin (jock itch or crotch rot) and on the body (ringworm). You get ringworm (which is a fungal infection, not a worm) from infected animals or by walking on damp areas, like shower floors.

To prevent fungal infections wear loose, comfortable clothes, avoid artificial fibres, wash frequently and dry carefully. If you do get an infection, wash the infected area daily with a disinfectant or medicated soap and water, and rinse and dry well. Apply an antifungal powder like the widely available Tinaderm. Try to expose the infected area to air or sunlight as much as possible and wash all towels and underwear in hot water as well as changing them often.

Cold Too much cold is just as dangerous as too much heat, particularly if it leads to hypothermia. If you are trekking at high altitudes or simply taking a long bus trip over mountains, particularly at night, be prepared. Hypothermia occurs when the body loses heat faster than it can produce it and the core temperature of the body falls. It is surprisingly easy to progress from very cold to dangerously cold due to a combination of wind, wet clothing, fatigue and hunger, even if the air temperature is above freezing. It is best to dress in layers; silk, wool and some of the new artificial fibres are all good insulating materials. A hat is important, as a lot

of heat is lost through the head. A strong, waterproof outer layer is essential, as keeping dry is vital. Carry basic supplies, including food containing simple sugars to generate heat quickly and lots of fluid to drink.

Symptoms of hypothermia are exhaustion, numb skin (particularly toes and fingers), shivering, slurred speech, irrational or violent behaviour, lethargy, stumbling, dizzy spells, muscle cramps and violent bursts of energy. Irrationality may take the form of sufferers claiming they are warm and trying to take off their clothes.

To treat hypothermia, first get the patient out of the wind and/or rain, remove their clothing if its wet and replace it with dry, warm clothing. Give them hot liquids – not alcohol – and some high-kilojoule, easily digestible food. This should be enough for the early stages of hypothermia, but if it has gone further it may be necessary to place victims in warm sleeping bags and get in with them. Do not rub patients, place them near a fire or remove their wet clothes in the wind. If possible, place a sufferer in a warm (not hot) bath.

Altitude Sickness Acute Mountain Sickness or AMS occurs at high altitude and can be fatal. The lack of oxygen at high altitudes affects most people to some extent. Take it easy at first, increase your liquid intake and eat well. Even with acclimatisation you may still have trouble adjusting – headaches, nausea, dizziness, a dry cough, insomnia, breathlessness and loss of appetite are all signs to heed. If you reach a high altitude by trekking, acclimatisation takes place gradually and you are less likely to be affected than if you fly straight there.

Mild altitude problems will generally abate after a day or so but if the symptoms persist or become worse the only treatment is to descend – even 500 metres can help. Breathlessness, a dry, irritating cough (which may progress to the production of pink, frothy sputum), severe headache, loss of appetite, nausea, and sometimes vomiting are all danger signs. Increasing tiredness, confusion, and lack of coordination and balance are real danger signs. Any of these symptoms individually, even just a persistent headache, can be a warning.

There is no hard and fast rule as to how high is too high: AMS has been fatal at altitudes of 3000 metres, although 3500 to 4500 metres is the usual range. It is always wise to sleep at a lower altitude than the greatest height reached during the day.

Motion Sickness Eating lightly before and during a trip will reduce the chances of motion sickness. If you are prone to motion sickness try to find a place that minimises disturbance – near the wing on aircraft, close to midships on boats, near the centre on buses. Fresh air usually helps, reading or cigarette smoke doesn't. Commercial anti-motion-sickness preparations, which can cause drowsiness, have to be taken before the trip commences; when you're feeling sick it's too late. Ginger is a natural preventative and is available in capsule form.

Diseases of Insanitation

Diarrhoea A change of water, food or climate can all cause the runs; diarrhoea caused by contaminated food or water is more serious. Despite all your precautions you may still have a bout of mild travellers' diarrhoea but a few rushed toilet trips with no other symptoms is not indicative of a serious problem. Moderate diarrhoea, involving half-a-dozen loose movements in a day, is more of a nuisance.

Dehydration is the main danger with any diarrhoea, particularly for children, so fluid replenishment is the number one treatment. Weak black tea with a little sugar, soda water, or soft drinks allowed to go flat and diluted 50% with boiled water are all good. With severe diarrhoea a rehydrating solution is necessary to replace minerals and salts. These are available over the counter in India – Electral is one brand. You should stick to a bland diet as you recover.

Lomotil or Imodium can be used to bring relief from the symptoms, although they do not actually cure the problem. Imodium is

preferable for children. Only use these drugs if absolutely necessary – eg, if you *must* travel, but do not use them if the patient has a high fever or is severely dehydrated.

Antibiotics can be very useful in treating severe diarrhoea especially if it is accompanied by nausea, vomiting, stomach cramps or mild fever. Ampicillin, a broad spectrum penicillin, is usually recommended. Two capsules of 250 mg each taken four times a day is the recommended dose for an adult. Children aged between eight and 12 years should have half the adult dose; younger children should have half a capsule four times a day. Note that if the patient is allergic to penicillin, ampicillin should not be administered.

Three days of treatment should be sufficient and an improvement should occur within 24 hours.

Giardia This intestinal parasite is present in contaminated water. The symptoms are stomach cramps, nausea, a bloated stomach, watery, foul-smelling diarrhoea and frequent gas. Giardia can appear several weeks after you have been exposed to the parasite. The symptoms may disappear for a few days and then return; this can go on for several weeks. Metronidazole, known as Flagyl, is the recommended drug, but it should only be taken under medical supervision. Other antibiotics are of no use.

Dysentery This serious illness is caused by contaminated food or water and is characterised by severe diarrhoea, often with blood or mucus in the stool. There are two kinds of dysentery. Bacillary dysentery is characterised by a high fever and rapid development; headache, vomiting and stomach pains are also symptoms. It generally does not last longer than a week, but it is highly contagious.

Amoebic dysentery is more gradual in developing, has no fever or vomiting but is a more serious illness. It is not a self-limiting disease: it will persist until treated and can recur and cause long-term damage.

A stool test is necessary to diagnose which

kind of dysentery you have, so you should seek medical help urgently. In case of an emergency, note that tetracycline is the prescribed treatment for bacillary dysentery, metronidazole for amoebic dysentery.

With tetracycline, the recommended adult dosage is one 250 mg capsule four times a day. Children aged between eight and 12 years should have half the adult dose; the dosage for younger children is ⅓ the adult dose. It's important to remember that tetracycline should be given to young children only if it's absolutely necessary and only for a short period; pregnant women should not take it after the 4th month of pregnancy.

With metronidazole, the recommended adult dosage is one 750 mg to 800 mg capsule three times daily for five days. Children aged between eight and 12 years should have half the adult dose; the dosage for younger children is ⅓ the adult dose.

Cholera Cholera vaccination is not very effective. However, outbreaks of cholera do happen, and you should avoid such problem areas. The disease is characterised by a sudden onset of acute diarrhoea with 'rice water' stools, vomiting, muscular cramps, and extreme weakness. You need medical help – but treat for dehydration, which can be extreme, and if there is an appreciable delay in getting to hospital then begin taking tetracycline. See the Dysentery section for dosages and warnings.

Viral Gastroenteritis This is caused not by bacteria but, as the name suggests, by a virus. It is characterised by stomach cramps, diarrhoea, and sometimes by vomiting and/or a slight fever. All you can do is rest and drink lots of fluids.

Hepatitis Hepatitis A is the more common form of this disease and is spread by contaminated food or water. The first symptoms are fever, chills, headache, fatigue, feelings of weakness and aches and pains. This is followed by loss of appetite, nausea, vomiting, abdominal pain, dark urine, light-coloured faeces and jaundiced skin; the whites of the eyes may also turn yellow. In some cases there may just be a feeling of being unwell or tired, accompanied by loss of appetite, aches and pains and the jaundiced effect. You should seek medical advice, but in general there is not much you can do apart from resting, drinking lots of fluids, eating lightly and avoiding fatty foods. People who have had hepatitis must forego alcohol for six months after the illness, as hepatitis attacks the liver and it needs that amount of time to recover.

Hepatitis B, which used to be called serum hepatitis, is spread through sexual contact or through skin penetration – it could be transmitted via dirty needles or blood transfusions, for instance. Avoid having your ears or nose pierced, tattoos done or injections where you have doubts about the sanitary conditions. The symptoms and treatment of type B are much the same as for type A, but gamma globulin as a prophylactic is effective against type A only.

A variant of the B strain, called hepatitis C, now also exists. Transmission and symptoms are similar to hepatitis B, however, there is presently no vaccine against hepatitis C. It is not very common, though, and should not be of too much concern to travellers.

Typhoid Typhoid fever is another gut infection that travels the fecal-oral route – ie, contaminated water and food are responsible. Vaccination against typhoid is not totally effective and it is one of the most dangerous infections, so medical help must be sought.

In its early stages typhoid resembles many other illnesses: sufferers may feel like they have a bad cold or flu on the way, as early symptoms are a headache, a sore throat, and a fever which rises a little each day until it is around 40°C or more. The victim's pulse is often slow relative to the degree of fever present and gets slower as the fever rises – unlike a normal fever where the pulse increases. There may also be vomiting, diarrhoea or constipation.

In the second week the high fever and slow pulse continue and a few pink spots may appear on the body; trembling, delirium, weakness, weight loss and dehydration are other symptoms. If there are no further complications, the fever and other symptoms will slowly go during the third week. However you must get medical help before this because pneumonia (acute infection of the lungs) or peritonitis (burst appendix) are common complications, and because typhoid is very infectious.

The fever should be treated by keeping the victim cool and dehydration should also be watched for. Chloramphenicol is the recommended antibiotic but there are fewer side affects with ampicillin. The adult dosage is two 250 mg capsules, four times a day. Children aged between eight and 12 years should have half the adult dose; younger children should have ⅓ the adult dose.

Patients who are allergic to penicillin should not be given ampicillin.

Worms These parasites are most common in rural areas and a stool test when you return home is not a bad idea. They can be present on unwashed vegetables or in undercooked meat and you can pick them up through your skin by walking in bare feet. Infestations may not show up for some time, and although they are generally not serious, if left untreated they can cause severe health problems. A stool test is necessary to pinpoint the problem, and medication is often available over the counter.

Diseases Spread by People & Animals
Tetanus This potentially fatal disease is found in undeveloped tropical areas. It is difficult to treat but is preventable with immunisation. Tetanus occurs when a wound becomes infected by a germ which lives in the faeces of animals or people, so clean all cuts, punctures or animal bites. Tetanus is known as lockjaw, and the first symptom may be discomfort in swallowing, or stiffening of the jaw and neck; this is followed by painful convulsions of the jaw and whole body.

Rabies Rabies is caused by a bite or scratch

by an infected animal. Dogs are a noted carrier. Any bite, scratch or even lick from a mammal should be cleaned immediately and thoroughly. Scrub with soap and running water, and then clean with an alcohol solution. If there is any possibility that the animal is infected medical help should be sought immediately. Even if the animal is not rabid, all bites should be treated seriously, as they can become infected or can result in tetanus. A rabies vaccination is now available and should be considered if you are in a high-risk category – eg, if you intend to explore caves (bat bites could be dangerous) or work with animals.

Meningococcal Meningitis This disease is found in Nepal, although it could possibly be caught in India too.

Trekkers to rural areas should be particularly careful, as the disease is spread by close contact with people who carry it in their throats and noses, spread it through coughs and sneezes and may not be aware that they are carriers. Lodges in the hills where travellers spend the night are prime spots for the spread of infection.

This very serious disease attacks the brain and can be fatal. A scattered, blotchy rash, fever, severe headache, sensitivity to light and neck stiffness which prevents forward bending of the head are the first symptoms. Death can occur within a few hours, so immediate treatment is important.

Treatment is large doses of penicillin given intravenously, or, if that is not possible, intramuscularly (ie, in the buttocks). Vaccination offers good protection for over a year, but you should also check for reports of current epidemics.

Tuberculosis Although this disease is widespread, it is not a serious risk to travellers. Young children are more susceptible than adults and vaccination is a sensible precaution for children under 12 travelling in endemic areas. TB is commonly spread by coughing or by unpasteurised dairy products from infected cows. Milk that has been boiled is safe to drink; the souring of milk to make yoghurt or cheese also kills the bacilli.

Diphtheria Diphtheria can be a skin infection or a more dangerous throat infection. It is spread by contaminated dust contacting the skin or by the inhalation of infected cough or sneeze droplets. Frequent washing and keeping the skin dry will help prevent skin infection. A vaccination is available to prevent the throat infection.

Sexually Transmitted Diseases Sexual contact with an infected sexual partner spreads these diseases. While abstinence is the only 100% preventative, using condoms is also effective. Gonorrhoea and syphilis are the most common of these diseases; sores, blisters or rashes around the genitals, discharges or pain when urinating are common symptoms. Symptoms may be less marked or not observed at all in women. Syphilis symptoms eventually disappear completely but the disease continues and can cause severe problems in later years. The treatment of gonorrhoea and syphilis is by antibiotics.

There are numerous other sexually transmitted diseases, for most of which effective treatment is available. However, there is no cure for herpes and there is also currently no cure for AIDS. Despite official denials, the latter is not at all uncommon in India, and using condoms is the most effective preventative.

AIDS can be spread through infected blood transfusions; most developing countries cannot afford to screen blood for transfusions. It can also be spread by dirty needles – vaccinations, acupuncture and tattooing can be potentially as dangerous as intravenous drug use if the equipment is not clean. It's a good idea to bring your needles, as some 'disposable' needles for sale in pharmacies may have been resurrected from hospital waste bins and only superficially cleaned. If you don't have your own needles, sterilise a needle by immersion for several seconds in a flame.

The AIDS situation in India is quite serious; a recent article in *Navbharat Times*

estimated that 30% of the 100,000 prostitutes in Bombay are HIV positive. Further, a random survey of truck drivers revealed that 25% were HIV positive and most did not know anything about AIDS.

Insect-Borne Diseases

Malaria This serious disease is spread by mosquito bites. If you are travelling in endemic areas it is extremely important to take malarial prophylactics. Symptoms include headaches, fever, chills and sweating which may subside and recur. Without treatment malaria can develop more serious, potentially fatal effects.

Antimalarial drugs do not actually prevent the disease but suppress its symptoms. Chloroquine is the usual malarial prophylactic; a tablet is taken once a week for two weeks prior to arrival in the infected area and six weeks after you leave it. Unfortunately there is now a strain of malaria which is resistant to Chloroquine and so an alternative drug is necessary. Maloprim (weekly) or Proguanil (daily) can be used to supplement the Chloroquine. Better still is Lariam which is taken once a week and is effective against Chloroquine-resistant strains.

Chloroquine is quite safe for general use, side effects are minimal and it can be taken by pregnant women. Maloprim can have rare but serious side effects if the weekly dose is exceeded and some doctors recommend a checkup after six months of continuous use. Fansidar, once used as a Chloroquine alternative, is no longer recommended as a prophylactic, as it can have dangerous side effects, but it may still be recommended as a treatment for malaria. Chloroquine is also used for malaria treatment but in larger doses than for prophylaxis. Doxycycline is another antimalarial for use where chloroquine resistance is reported; it causes hypersensitivity to sunlight, so sunburn can be a problem.

Mosquitoes appear after dusk. Avoiding bites by covering bare skin and using an insect repellent will further reduce the risk of catching malaria. Insect screens on windows and mosquito nets on beds offer protection, as does burning a mosquito coil, or using one of the widely available electric mosquito zappers. Mosquitoes may be attracted by perfume, aftershave or certain colours – light coloured clothes are generally better than dark. The risk of infection is higher in rural areas and during the wet season.

Dengue Fever There is no prophylactic available for this mosquito-spread disease; the main preventative measure is to avoid mosquito bites. A sudden onset of fever, headaches and severe joint and muscle pains are the first signs before a rash starts on the trunk of the body and spreads to the limbs and face. After a further few days, the fever will subside and recovery will begin. Serious complications are not common.

Typhus Typhus is spread by ticks, mites or lice. It begins as a bad cold, followed by a fever, chills, headache, muscle pains and a body rash. There is often a large painful sore at the site of the bite and nearby lymph nodes are swollen and painful. Seek local advice on areas where ticks pose a danger and always check yourself carefully for ticks after walking in a danger area. A strong insect repellent can help, and serious walkers in tick areas should consider having their boots and trousers impregnated with benzyl benzoate and dibutylphthalate.

Cuts, Bites & Stings
Cuts & Scratches Skin punctures can easily become infected in hot climates and may take time to heal. Treat any cut with an antiseptic solution and Mercurochrome. Where possible avoid bandages and Band-aids, which can keep wounds wet. Coral cuts are notoriously slow to heal, as the coral injects a weak venom into the wound. Avoid coral cuts by wearing shoes when walking on reefs, and clean any cut thoroughly.

Bites & Stings Bee and wasp stings are usually painful rather than dangerous. Calamine lotion will give relief or ice packs will reduce the pain and swelling. There are some spiders with dangerous bites but antivenins

are usually available. Again, local advice is the best suggestion.

Snakes To minimise your chances of being bitten always wear boots, socks and long trousers when walking through undergrowth where snakes may be present. Don't put your hands into holes and crevices, and be careful when collecting firewood.

Snake bites do not cause instantaneous death and antivenins are usually available. Keep the victim calm and still, wrap the bitten limb tightly, as you would for a sprained ankle, and then attach a splint to immobilise it. Then seek medical help and, if possible, bring the dead snake along for identification. Don't attempt to catch the snake if there is even a remote possibility of being bitten again. Tourniquets and sucking out the poison are now comprehensively discredited.

Bedbugs & Lice Bedbugs live in various places, but particularly in dirty mattresses and bedding. Spots of blood on bedclothes or on the wall around the bed can be read as a suggestion to find another hotel. Bedbugs leave itchy bites in neat rows. Calamine lotion may help.

All lice cause itching and discomfort. They make themselves at home in your hair (head lice), your clothing (body lice) or in your pubic hair (crabs). You catch lice through direct contact with infected people or by sharing combs, clothing and the like. Powder or shampoo treatment will kill the lice and infected clothing should then be washed in very hot water.

Leeches & Ticks Leeches may be present in damp rainforest conditions; they attach themselves to your skin to suck your blood. Trekkers often get them on their legs or in their boots. Salt or a lighted cigarette end will make them fall off. Do not pull them off, as the bite is then more likely to become infected. An insect repellent may keep them away. Vaseline, alcohol or oil will persuade a tick to let go.

Women's Health

Gynaecological Problems Poor diet, lowered resistance due to the use of antibiotics for stomach upsets and even contraceptive pills can lead to vaginal infections when travelling in hot climates. Keeping the genital area clean, and wearing skirts or loose-fitting trousers and cotton underwear will help to prevent infections.

Yeast infections, characterised by a rash, itch and discharge, can be treated with a vinegar or even lemon-juice douche or with yoghurt. Nystatin suppositories are the usual medical prescription. Trichomonas is a more serious infection; symptoms are a discharge and a burning sensation when urinating. Male sexual partners must also be treated, and if a vinegar-water douche is not effective, medical attention should be sought. Flagyl is the prescribed drug.

Pregnancy Most miscarriages occur during the first three months of pregnancy, so this is the most risky time to travel. The last three months should also be spent within reasonable distance of good medical care, as quite serious problems can develop at this time. Pregnant women should avoid all unnecessary medication, but vaccinations and malarial prophylactics should still be taken where possible. Additional care should be taken to prevent illness and particular attention should be paid to diet and nutrition.

Hospitals

Although India does have a few excellent hospitals such as the Christian Medical College Hospital in Vellore, Tamil Nadu, the Breach Candy Hospital in Bombay and the All India Institute of Medical Sciences in Delhi, most Indian cities do not have the quality of medical care available in the West. Usually hospitals run by Western missionaries have better facilities than government hospitals where long waiting lines are common. Unless you have something very unusual, these Christian-run hospitals are the best places to head for in an emergency.

India also has many qualified doctors with their own private clinics which can be quite

good and, in some cases, as good as anything available anywhere in the world. The usual fee for a clinic visit is about Rs 50; Rs 100 for a specialist. Home calls usually cost Rs 80.

WOMEN TRAVELLERS

Foreign women travelling in India have always been viewed by Indian men as free and easy, based largely on what they believed to be true from watching cheap Western soapies. Women would get hassled, stared at, spied on in hotel rooms, and often groped, although the situation was rarely threatening.

In the last few years, however, the situation has become more difficult for women travellers, mainly because the 'sexual revolution' which swept the West 25 years ago has now hit India. Movies and magazines are much more explicit, and the widespread billboard advertisements for condoms often quote passages from the Kama Sutra and depict naked or seminaked women and men. The message getting through to the Indian male is that sex before and outside of marriage is less of a taboo than in the past, and so foreign women are seen as even more free and easy than ever before.

Close attention to standards of dress will go a long way to minimising problems for female travellers. The light cotton drawstring skirts that many foreign women pick up in India are really sari petticoats and to wear them in the street is rather like going out half dressed. Ways of blending into the Indian background include avoiding sleeveless blouses, skirts that are too short and, of course, the bra-less look. Remember that lungis are only acceptable wear for women in the state of Kerala.

Getting stared at is something which you'll have to get used to. Don't return male stares, as this will be considered a come-on; just ignore them. Dark glasses can help.

Getting involved in inane conversations with men is also considered a turn-on. Keep discussions down to a necessary minimum unless you're interested in getting hassled. If you get the uncomfortable feeling he's encroaching on your space, the chances are that he is. A firm request to keep away is usually enough. Firmly return any errant limbs, put some item of luggage in between you and if all else fails, find a new spot. You're also within your rights to tell him to shove off!

It must be said that the further you get from the heavily touristed areas, the fewer problems you'll encounter. The south is also generally more relaxed than the north.

Being a woman also has some advantages. There is often a special ladies' queue for train tickets or even a ladies' quota and ladies' compartments. One woman wrote that these ladies' carriages were often nearly empty – another said that they were full of screaming children. Special ladies' facilities are also sometimes found in cinemas and other places.

DANGERS & ANNOYANCES
Theft
Having things stolen is a problem in India, not so much because it's a theft-prone country – it isn't – but because you can become involved in a lot of hassles getting the items replaced. If your passport is stolen you may have a long trip back to an embassy to replace it. Travellers' cheques may be replaceable if stolen, but, of course, it's best to avoid theft in the first place. Always lock your room, preferably with your own padlock in cheaper hotels. Lock it at night as well; countless people have had things stolen from their rooms when they've actually been in them.

Never leave those most important valuables (passport, tickets, health certificates, money, travellers' cheques) in your room; they should be with you at all times. Either have a stout leather passport wallet on your belt, or a passport pouch under your shirt, or simply extra internal pockets in your clothing. On trains at night keep your gear near you; padlocking a bag to a luggage rack can be useful, and some of the newer trains have loops under the seats which you can chain things to. Never walk around with valuables casually slung over your shoulder. Take extra

care in crowded public transport. In Bombay, for example, pickpockets are adept at the 'razor on the back pocket or shoulder bag' technique.

Thieves are particularly prevalent on train routes where there are lots of tourists. The Delhi to Agra express service is notorious; and Delhi to Jaipur, Delhi to Calcutta, Delhi to Bombay, Jodhpur to Jaisalmer and Agra to Varanasi are other routes to take care on. Train departure time, when the confusion and crowds are at their worst, is the time to be most careful. Just as the train is about to leave, you are distracted by someone, while his or her accomplice is stealing your bag from by your feet. Airports are another place to be careful, especially when international arrivals take place in the middle of the night, when you are unlikely to be at your most alert.

From time to time there are also drugging episodes. Travellers would meet somebody on a train or bus or in a town, start talking and then be offered a cup of tea or something similar. Hours later they'd wake up with a headache and all their gear gone. The tea was full of sleeping pills. Don't accept drinks or food from strangers no matter how friendly they seem, particularly if you're on your own.

Beware also of your fellow travellers. Unhappily there are more than a few back-packers who make the money go further by helping themselves to other peoples'. At places like Goa be very careful with things on the beach – while you're in the water your camera or money can walk away very fast.

Remember that backpacks are very easy to rifle through. Don't leave valuables in them, especially during flights. Remember also that something may be of little or no value to a thief, but to lose it would be a real heartbreak to you – like film. Finally, a good travel insurance policy helps.

If you do have something stolen, you're going to have to report it to the police. You'll also need a statement proving you have done so if you want to claim on insurance. Unfortunately the police are generally less than helpful, and at times are downright unhelpful, unsympathetic and even disbelieving, implying that you are making a false claim in order to defraud the insurance company. It's also tempting to think that in some cases the police are actually operating in collusion with the thieves.

Insurance companies, despite their rosy promises of full protection and speedy settlement of claims, are just as disbelieving as the Indian police and will often attempt every devious trick in the book to avoid paying out on a baggage claim.

Stolen Travellers' Cheques If you're unlucky enough to have things stolen, some precautions can ease the pain. All travellers' cheques are replaceable but this does you little immediate good if you have to go home and apply to your bank. What you want is instant replacement. Furthermore, what do you do if you lose your cheques and money and have a day or more to travel to the replacement office? The answer is to keep an emergency cash-stash in a totally separate place. In that same place you should keep a record of the cheque serial numbers, proof of purchase slips and your passport number.

American Express make considerable noise about 'instant replacement' of their cheques but a lot of people find out, to their cost, that without a number of precautions 'instantly' can take longer than you think. If you don't have the receipt you were given when you bought the cheques, rapid replacement will be difficult. Obviously the receipt should be kept separate from the cheques, and a photocopy in yet another location doesn't hurt either. Chances are you'll be able to get a limited amount of funds on the spot, and the rest will be available when the bank has verified your initial purchase of the cheques. American Express have a 24-hour number in Delhi (☎ (011) 687-5050) which you must ring within 24 hours of the theft.

One traveller wrote that his travellers' cheques were stolen and he didn't discover the loss for a month. They had been left in his hotel room and the thief (presumably from the hotel) had neatly removed a few cheques from the centre of the book.

Explaining that sort of theft is really difficult and, of course, the thief has had plenty of time to dispose of them.

Drugs

For a long time India was a place where you could indulge in all sorts of illegal drugs (mostly grass and hashish) with relative ease – they were cheap, readily available and the risks were minimal. These days things have changed. Although dope is still widely available, the risks have certainly increased – currently there are a number of foreigners languishing in jail in Goa awaiting trial. Many claim they are innocent and that the drugs (in most cases an insignificant amount) were planted on them.

Nevertheless, in the Indian justice system it seems the burden of proof is on the accused, and proving one's innocence is virtually impossible. The police forces are often corrupt and will pay 'witnesses' to give evidence. If convicted, sentences are long (*minimum* of 10 years), even for minor offences, and there is no remission or parole for drug sentences.

So, if you partake in drugs, be aware of the risks and be discreet.

VOLUNTARY WORK

Numerous charities and international aid agencies have branches in India and, although they're mostly staffed by locals, there are some opportunities for foreigners. Though it may be possible to find temporary volunteer work when you are in India, you'll probably be of more use to the charity concerned if you write in advance and, if they need you, stay for long enough to be of help. A week on a hospital ward may go a little way towards salving your own conscience but you may actually do not much more than get in the way of the people who work there long-term.

Some areas of voluntary work seem to be more attractive to volunteers than others. One traveller commented that there was no difficulty getting foreign volunteers to help with the babies in the orphanage where he was working but few came forward to work with the severely mentally handicapped adults.

For information on specific charities in India contact the main branches in your own country. For long-term posts, the following organisations may be able to help or offer advice and further contacts:

Voluntary Service Overseas (VSO)
317 Putney Bridge Rd, London SW15 2PN, UK (☎ (081) 780-2266, fax (081) 780-1326)
International Voluntary Service (IVS)
St John's Church Centre, Edinburgh EH2 4BJ, UK (☎ (031) 229-7318)
Co-ordinating Committee for International Voluntary Service
c/o UNESCO, 1 rue Miollis, F-75015 Paris, France (☎ (01) 45-68-27-31)
Peace Corps of the USA
1990 K St NW, Washington DC 20526, USA (☎ (202) 606-3970, fax (202) 606-3110)
Council of International Programs (CIP)
1101 Wilson Blvd Ste 1708, Arlington VA 22209, USA (☎ (703) 527-1160)
Australian Volunteers Abroad: Overseas Service Bureau Programme
PO Box 350, Fitzroy Vic 3065, Australia (☎ (03) 419-1788, fax (03) 419-4280)

The Mahabodhi International Meditation Centre, PO Box 22, Leh, Ladakh, 194 101 (Jammu & Kashmir state) Himalaya, India, which operates a residential school for poor children, requires volunteers to assist with teaching and secretarial work. Contact the centre at the above address, or through their head office: 14 Kalidas Rd, Gandhinagar, Bangalore, 560 009 (☎ (91-812) 26-0684; fax (91-812) 26-0292).

Mother Teresa's Missionaries of Charity headquarters, the 'Mother House', is at 54A Lower Circular Rd in Calcutta. For information about volunteering, contact the London branch: International Committee of Co-Workers (☎ (081) 574-1892), Missionaries of Charity, 41 Villiers Rd, Southall, Middlesex, UK.

HIGHLIGHTS

India can offer almost anything you want, whether it's beaches, forts, amazing travel experiences, fantastic spectacles or even a search for yourself. Listed here are just a few

of those possibilities and where to start looking.

Beaches

People generally don't come all the way to India just to laze on a beach – but there are some superb beaches if you're in that mood. On the west coast, at the southern end of Kerala, there's Kovalam; further north, Goa has a whole collection of beautiful beaches complete with soft white sand, gentle lapping waves and swaying palms. If you find it a little overcommercialised these days then head for the tiny ex-Portuguese island of Diu off the southern coast of Saurashtra (Gujarat).

Over on the east coast you could try the beach at Mahabalipuram in Tamil Nadu. From the Shore Temple the beaches stretch north towards Madras and there are some fine places to stay. In Orissa the beach at Gopalpur-on-Sea is clean and quiet.

While they're not easily accessible, some of the beaches in the Andamans are straight out of a holiday brochure for the Caribbean – white coral sand, gin-clear water and multi-coloured fish and coral.

Beach	State	Page
Kovalam	Kerala	959
–	Goa	830
Diu	Gujarat	660
Mahabalipuram	Tamil Nadu	994
Konark	Orissa	512
Gopalpur-on-Sea	Orissa	513
–	Andaman Islands	1066

Faded Touches of the Raj

Although the British left India over 45 years ago, there are many places where you'd hardly know it. Of course much of India's government system, bureaucracy, communications, sports (the Indians are crazy over cricket) and media are British to the core, but you'll also find the British touch in more unusual, enjoyable and amusing ways.

Could anything be more British than the Dal Lake houseboats, all chintz and over-stuffed armchairs? Or the Residency at Lucknow where with stiff upper lip the

Hill Stations

Although they may take the credit for having popularised the concept of the hill station, the British cannot claim to have invented it. Back in Moghul times the emperors were retreating into the Himalaya to avoid the searing heat of mid-summer on the plains. Their favourite spot was Kashmir.

In the 19th century, British troops exploring the country discovered that the incidence of disease was much lower in the cooler hills. In 1819 a hospital was opened in Shimla and the first hill station was established. As the British presence in India grew, other hill stations were built and it became the custom to despatch women and children to them for the summer months. They eventually developed into temporary capitals, with all the machinery of government decamping to the hills in the summer. Darjeeling was Calcutta's summer capital, and Delhi's was Shimla.

The cooler climate was certainly healthier but it seemed to infect most foreign residents with severe cases of nostalgia and they soon made their hill stations into little corners of England, building bungalows with names like 'Earl's Court', 'Windamere' and 'Windsor Cottage'. During the summer season they were great social centres with balls, theatrical performances and an endless round of dinner parties. The main thoroughfare was almost always known as The Mall and closed to all but pedestrians – as long as they were not Indian.

Today, most hill stations have become holiday resorts for middle class Indian tourists. Although they are dilapidated shadows of the preserves of the elite which they once were, they're nonetheless great fun to visit. The journey there is usually interesting in itself – often by narrow-gauge railway (up to Shimla, Darjeeling or Matheran, for example). Some hill stations are built around a lake, as at Naini Tal and Kodaikanal, and most have superb views and good walks along the surrounding ridges. ■

British held out against those pesky mutineers in 1857. Or relax in true British style for afternoon tea at Glenary's Tea Rooms in Darjeeling and later retire for a preprandial cocktail in front of the roaring fire in the lounge of the Windamere Hotel to await the gong which summons you to dinner. Or stay in fading Edwardian splendour at the Hotel Metropole in Mysore, or the twee Home Counties rural atmosphere of the Woodlands Hotel in Udhagamandalam (Ooty). Even better is the Fernhill Palace Hotel, also in Ooty.

The Fairlawn Hotel in Calcutta has become something of a Raj-remnant disaster, but it's still worth a look. The Tollygunge Club in Calcutta is run by a Brit and is also a great place to stay.

Other particularly British institutions include Victoria Terminus Railway Station in Bombay, and the Lutyens-designed parliament buildings in Delhi. The Naini Tal Boat Club is an old British club with a lakeside ballroom which was once the preserve of only true-blue Brits (the famous British hunter, Jim Corbett, having been born in Naini Tal, was refused membership). The Gymkhana Club in Darjeeling still has its original snooker tables, Raj ghosts and cobwebs. Perhaps more nostalgic than all these is St Paul's Cathedral (Calcutta), which is stuffed with memorials to the Brits who didn't make it home, plus a Burne Jones stained glass window.

Sight	Place	Page
Victoria Memorial	Calcutta (West Bengal)	445
Fairlawn Hotel	Calcutta (West Bengal)	454
Tollygunge Club	Calcutta (West Bengal)	453
St Paul's Cathedral	Calcutta (West Bengal)	445
Glenary's Tea Rooms	Darjeeling (West Bengal)	483
Windamere Hotel	Darjeeling (West Bengal)	482
Gymkhana Club	Darjeeling (West Bengal)	479
Maharaja's Palace	Mysore (Karnataka)	863
Hotel Metropole	Mysore (Karnataka)	870
Lalitha Palace	Mysore (Karnataka)	870
Fernhill Palace	Udhagamandalam (Tamil Nadu)	1029
Woodlands Hotel	Udhagamandalam (Tamil Nadu)	1029

Houseboats	Dal Lake	
	(Kashmir)	304
Hotel Brijraj Bhawan	Kota (Rajasthan)	580
Victoria Terminus	Bombay	
	(Maharashtra)	776
Parliament Buildings	New Delhi	205
The Residency	Lucknow	
	(Uttar Pradesh)	389
Naini Tal Boat Club	Naini Tal	
	(Uttar Pradesh)	372

Freak Centres

India has been the ultimate goal of the on-the-road hippie dream for years and somehow the '60s still continues in India's kind climate. Goa has always been a great freak centre. The beaches are an attraction at any time of the year and every full moon is the occasion for a great gathering of the clans – but Christmas is its peak period when half the freaks in India seem to flock to its beaches. There are occasional 'purges' of the Goan beaches which shouldn't worry most people, but the purist die-hards have decided this is too uncool and have moved to more remote locations.

Further south at Kovalam the fine beaches

attract a steady clientele. The holy lake of Pushkar in Rajasthan has a smaller, semipermanent freak population. The technicolour Tibetan outlook on life (they've got a way with hotels and restaurants too) works well in Kathmandu so why not in India – you'll find Dharamsala and Manali, both in Himachal Pradesh, also have longer-term populations of visitors. Hampi, capital of the Vijayanagar kingdom, has only a small number of visitors but is definitely on the circuit. Finally, Puri (Orissa) and Mahabalipuram (Tamil Nadu) both have temples and beaches, a sure-fire combination.

Centre	State	Page
–	Goa	836
Pushkar	Rajasthan	573
Kovalam	Kerala	959
Dharamsala	Himachal Pradesh	262
Manali	Himachal Pradesh	277
Hampi	Karnataka	887
Puri	Orissa	503
Mahabalipuram	Tamil Nadu	993

Great Places to Stay

India has some superb hotels – it's also got a large number of bug-infested filthy dumps and a fair number of 'international class' hotels which are mediocre in standards and service but decidedly 1st class in price. But it's hard to think of a more enchanting hotel than the Lake Palace in Udaipur – it's far more than merely a palace; elegant, whimsical and romantic are all labels that can be applied to it. In fact all over Rajasthan there are palaces and forts owned by the former rulers of the princely states – or their nobles – and many of these have been turned into hotels and are excellent places to stay – Samode, Bharatpur, Mandawa, Jodhpur, Bikaner, Mt Abu and Jaipur all have palace-hotels.

Or in Kashmir (assuming it's safe), staying on a houseboat is one of the main reasons for going there; they come in all price ranges, from the rock-bottom 'doonga boats' to 'five-star' luxury complete with TV.

In Bombay the elegant Taj Mahal Intercontinental Hotel is probably the best in India – even if you don't stay there its air-conditioned lounge and strategic location are a magnet for everyone from backpackers on up.

Further south in the ex-princely state of Mysore (now Karnataka), are the Hotel Metropole and the Ashok Radisson Lalitha Palace Hotel at Mysore city. In Udhagamandalam, there's the Fernhill Palace Hotel.

There are some very fine tourist bungalows, run by the state government tourist offices, scattered around India. They're often in fine locations and usually great value.

Backpackers' favourites include the wonderful old Broadlands in Madras and the equally well-kept Z Hotel in Puri. In Kochi (Cochin) the Bolgatty Palace Hotel is an old Dutch Palace built in 1744 and later a British Residency – now a relatively cheap hotel. The Hotel Sheesh Mahal, in a wing of the Jehangir Mahal palace in Orchha, is definitely worth a visit.

The Tollygunge Club in Calcutta is still run by a Brit and is an amazing place to stay. The clubhouse was once the mansion at the centre of a large indigo plantation, now a championship golfcourse. Sitting by the swimming pool here, with a cold beer or an excellent club sandwich, it's hard to believe you're still in Calcutta. Tolly (as it's affectionately called) is now the playground of the city's elite.

Hotel	Place	Page
Lake Palace Hotel	Udaipur (Rajasthan)	597
Houseboats	Dal Lake (Kashmir)	304
Taj Mahal	Bombay	
Intercontinental	(Maharashtra)	758
Broadlands Hotel	Madras (Tamil Nadu)	975
Fernhill Palace Hotel	Udhagamandalam	
	(Tamil Nadu)	1029
Hotel Metropole	Mysore (Karnataka)	870
Lalitha Palace Hotel	Mysore (Karnataka)	870
Z Hotel	Puri (Orissa)	505
Bolgatty Palace Hotel	Kochi (Cochin;	
	Kerala)	937
Sheesh Mahal	Orchha (Madhya	
	Pradesh)	698
Bikaner House	Mt Abu (Rajasthan)	608
Tollygunge Club	Calcutta (West	
	Bengal)	453

Getting There is Half the Fun

A lot of travel in India can be indescribably dull, boring and uncomfortable. Trains take forever, buses fall apart and shake your fillings loose, even Indian Airlines sometimes manages to make your delay time far longer than your flying time.

Despite the hassles there are a fair number of trips where getting there is definitely half the fun. Trains, of course, are the key to Indian travel and elsewhere in this book you'll find a section on India's unique and wonderful old steam trains. The Darjeeling toy train, which winds back and forth on its long climb up to the hill station, is half the fun of visiting Darjeeling (though service is sometimes suspended). Other 'toy trains' include the run up to Matheran, just a couple of hours outside Bombay; the 'rack train' which makes the climb to Ooty from Mettupalayam in Tamil Nadu; and the narrow-gauge line which connects the hill-station of Shimla (Himachal Pradesh) with Kalka on the plains.

Then there is the delightful backwater trip through the waterways between Kollam

(Quilon) and Alappuzha (Alleppey) – not only is the trip fascinating, it's absurdly cheap. Indian buses are generally a refined form of torture but the two-day trip between Manali in Himachal Pradesh and Leh in Ladakh is too good to miss. The bus route from Darjeeling or Kalimpong to Gangtok in Sikkim is pretty good too, as is the climb up to Kodaikanal from Madurai in Tamil Nadu. Finally, there could hardly be a more spectacular flight in the world than the Srinagar to Leh route which crosses the full width (and height!) of the Himalaya.

Trip	State	Page
Siliguri to Darjeeling (toy train)	West Bengal	486
Neral to Matheran (toy train)	Maharashtra	776
Mettupalayam to Udhagamandalam (rack train)	Tamil Nadu	1030
Kalka to Shimla (toy train)	Himachal Pradesh	257
Alappuzha to Kollam (backwater trip)	Kerala	952
Manali to Leh (bus or jeep)	Himachal Pradesh/ Jammu & Kashmir	326
Darjeeling to Gangtok (bus or jeep)	West Bengal/Sikkim	525
Madurai to Kodai-kanal (bus)	Tamil Nadu	1041
Srinagar to Leh (air)	Jammu & Kashmir	325

Colourful Events

India is a country of festivals and there are a number of places and times that are not to be missed. They start with the Republic Day Festival in New Delhi each January – elephants, a procession and military might with Indian princely splendour.

Also early in the year is the Desert Festival in Jaisalmer, Rajasthan.

In June/July the great Car Festival (Rath Yatra) in Puri is another superb spectacle as the gigantic temple car of Lord Jagannath makes its annual journey, pulled by thousands of eager devotees.

In Kerala, one of the big events of the year is the Nehru Cup Snake Boat Races on the backwaters at Alappuzha (Alleppey) which take place on the second Saturday of August.

September/October is the time to head for the hills to see the delightful Festival of the Gods in Kulu. This is part of the Dussehra Festival, which is at its most spectacular in Mysore. November is the time for the huge and colourful Camel Festival at Pushkar in Rajasthan. Finally, at Christmas where else is there to be in India than Goa?

Festival	Place	Page
Republic Day Festival	New Delhi	101
Desert Festival	Jaisalmer (Rajasthan)	620
Car Festival	Puri (Orissa)	503
Snake Boat Races	Alappuzha (Kerala)	947
Dussehra	Mysore (Karnataka)	866
Festival of the Gods	Kulu (Himachal Pradesh)	273
Camel Fair	Pushkar (Rajasthan)	573
Christmas	Goa	823

Deserted Cities

There are a number of places in crowded India where great cities of the past have been deserted and left. Fatehpur Sikri, near Agra, is the most famous since Akbar founded, built and left this impressive centre in less than 20 years. Hampi, the centre of the Vijayanagar Empire, is equally impressive. Not too far from there are the ancient centres of Aihole and Badami. Some of the great forts that follow are also deserted cities.

Site	State	Page
Fatehpur Sikri	Uttar Pradesh	349
Hampi	Karnataka	887
Aihole & Badami	Karnataka	896

Great Forts

India has more than its share of great forts – many of them now deserted – to tell of its tumultuous history. The Red Fort in Delhi is one of the most impressive, but Agra Fort is an equally massive reminder of Moghul power at its height. A short distance south is the huge, impregnable-looking Gwalior Fort. The Rajputs in Rajasthan could build forts like nobody else and they've got them in all shapes and sizes and with every imaginable tale to tell. Chittorgarh Fort is tragic, Bundi and Kota forts are whimsical,

Jodhpur Fort is huge and high, Amber Fort simply beautiful, and Jaisalmer the essence of romance.

Way out west in Gujarat, there are the impressive forts of Junagadh and Bhuj built by the princely rulers of Saurashtra.

Further south there's Mandu, another fort impressive in its size and architecture but with a tragic tale to tell. Further south again at Daulatabad it's a tale of power, ambition and not all that much sense with another immense fort which was built and soon deserted. Important forts in the south include Bijapur and Golconda.

Naturally the European invaders had their forts too. You can see Portuguese forts in Goa, Bassein, Daman and Diu, the last being the most impressive. The British also built their share: Fort St George in Madras is open to the public and has a fascinating museum. Those built by the French, Dutch and Danes are, regrettably, largely in ruins.

Fort	State	Page
Red Fort	New Delhi	201
Agra	Uttar Pradesh	340
Chittorgarh	Rajasthan	586
Bundi	Rajasthan	582
Kota	Rajasthan	579
Jodhpur	Rajasthan	611
Amber	Rajasthan	558
Jaisalmer	Rajasthan	619
Junagadh	Gujarat	670
Bhuj	Gujarat	682
Daman	Gujarat	654
Diu	Gujarat	661
Mandu	Madhya Pradesh	729
Gwalior	Madhya Pradesh	690
Daulatabad	Maharashtra	798
Bassein	Maharashtra	770
Bijapur	Karnataka	899
Golconda, Hyderabad	Andhra Pradesh	910
Warangal	Andhra Pradesh	917
Chapora	Goa	845
Aguada	Goa	842
St George, Madras	Tamil Nadu	973

Where Gandhi Went

Following the success of the film *Gandhi* you might be interested in making a Gandhi trek round India, starting at Porbandar where he was born and Rajkot where he spent the early years of his life. After his period in

South Africa he returned to India and stayed in Bombay, a city he visited on numerous occasions. The massacre of 2000 peaceful protesters, one of the seminal events in the march to independence, took place in Amritsar. For many years Gandhi had his ashram at Sabarmati, across the river from Ahmedabad. In the 1930s Gandhi established the Sevagram Ashram in Wardha, and spent more than 15 years there. Today it is a museum.

The British interned him in the Aga Khan's Palace in Pune. Finally he was assassinated in the garden of the wealthy Birla family in New Delhi and his cremation took place at Raj Ghat. His ashes were scattered in the Narmada River at Jabalpur in Madhya Pradesh.

Sight	Place	Page
Kirti Mandir	Porbandar (Gujarat)	674
Kaba Gandhi	Rajkot (Gujarat)	679
Mani Bhavan	Bombay (Maharashtra)	751
Jallianwala Bagh	Amritsar (Punjab)	241
Sabarmati Ashram	Ahmedabad (Gujarat)	640
Sevagram Ashram	Wardha (Maharashtra)	806
Aga Khan's Palace	Pune (Maharashtra)	784
Raj Ghat	New Delhi	204
Jabalpur	Madhya Pradesh	733

Gurus & Religion

With India's great importance as a religious centre it's no wonder that so many people embark on some sort of spiritual quest here. There are all sorts of ashrams and all manner of gurus.

Rishikesh, in Uttar Pradesh, has been a guru centre ever since the Beatles went there with the Maharishi Mahesh Yogi; it's still popular today. Vrindaban near Mathura, which is between Delhi and Agra, is the centre for the Hare Krishna movement. Muktananda had his ashram at Ganeshpuri but since his death, there has been a bitter battle for the succession. The Theosophical Society and the Krishnamurti Foundation have their headquarters in Madras. Not far from there, in Pondicherry, is the ashram of Sri Aurobindo and its offshoot, Auroville.

ing increasing numbers of travellers. The Dalai Lama spends a month here over the winter and the Tibetans stay for most of the winter – it's quite a 'scene'. And finally, with the Dalai Lama living in Dharamsala, where better to study Tibetan Buddhism.

Movement	Place	Page
various	Rishikesh (Uttar Pradesh)	367
Krishna Consciousness	Vrindaban (Uttar Pradesh)	355
Poonjaji	Lucknow (Uttar Pradesh)	387
Theosophical Society	Madras (Tamil Nadu)	973
Krishnamurti Foundation	Madras (Tamil Nadu)	973
Ramana Maharishi	Tiruvannamalai (Tamil Nadu)	1000
Ramakrishna	Calcutta (West Bengal)	449
Sri Aurobindo	Pondicherry (Tamil Nadu)	1001
Sai Baba	Puttaparthi (Andhra Pradesh)	920
Raja Yoga	Mt Abu (Rajasthan)	603
Osho	Pune (Maharashtra)	781
Tibetan Buddhism	Dharamsala (Himachal Pradesh)	263
Buddhism	Bodhgaya (Bihar)	431

Poonjaji

The Ramakrishna Mission has centres all over India, although Calcutta is its headquarters.

Sai Baba is at Puttaparthi near Bangalore while Brahma Kumaris' Raja Yoga (Prajapita Brahma) is based in Mt Abu. One of the most famous is the Rajneesh ashram (now renamed the Osho ashram) at Pune. It still attracts devotees by the thousand. Since the death of Rajneesh, however, many former Rajneeshis have begun flocking to the ashram of Poonjaji at Lucknow. His rise to fame has been meteoric. Poonjaji himself is a disciple of Ramana Maharishi whose ashram is at Tiruvannamalai in Tamil Nadu.

There are plenty of other centres but one guru you won't find in India is the Divine Light Mission's Guru Maharaji. He's currently resident in the USA but does a lot of jet-setting around the world to preside over various festivals and gatherings.

At Bodhgaya in Bihar there's been a lot of monastery-building activity. The Root Institute is a Western-run place offering courses in Buddhism/meditation etc that are attract-

Holy Cities

Though India has plenty of holy cities, seven of them are of particular holiness. Some of them, like Varanasi, are obvious while some, like Dwarka, are relatively unknown outside India. Three of them are dedicated to Siva, three to Vishnu; Kanchipuram covers both gods. India's richest temple, however, is the Tirumala Temple in Andhra Pradesh.

Ayodhya, the birthplace of Rama, is currently a hot and contentious political issue between the Hindu fundamentalists and the Muslims which is being exploited for all it's worth by opportunist parliamentarians at both state and national level. Events there have more than once provoked riots, some of them nationwide.

Other particularly holy cities include Rameswaram and Kanyakumari in Tamil Nadu, Puri in Orissa and Badrinath in Uttar Pradesh. A pilgrimage to Badrinath, Puri,

Rameswaram and Dwarka covers the four corners (north, east, south and west) of India.

The Jains also have their holy cities, the most spectacular being Palitana in eastern Gujarat – a mountain-top fortress filled with hundreds of beautiful temples. Down south, Sravanabelagola in Karnataka, though only a village, would qualify for this distinction.

City	State	Page
Varanasi	Uttar Pradesh	400
Haridwar	Uttar Pradesh	364
Mathura	Uttar Pradesh	352
Ayodhya	Uttar Pradesh	399
Palitana	Gujarat	659
Dwarka	Gujarat	676
Ujjain	Madhya Pradesh	721
Tirumala	Andhra Pradesh	918
Sravanabelagola	Karnataka	878
Madurai	Tamil Nadu	1034
Kanchipuram	Tamil Nadu	990
Rameswaram	Tamil Nadu	1047
Kanyakumari	Tamil Nadu	1049

SUGGESTED ITINERARIES

With such a mind-boggling array of amazing things and places to see, it can be difficult deciding which ones to visit in the time you have available.

The following itineraries assume you have a month to spend in India. They take in the highlights of a region and hopefully will help you make the most of your time. They also assume that you don't want to spend the greater part of your time actually travelling between places – it seems many first-time visitors to India make the mistake of trying to see too much in too short a period of time, and end up tired and frustrated.

Delhi to Bombay via Rajasthan

Delhi – Agra – Bharatpur – Jaipur – Shekhawati – Bikaner – Jaisalmer – Jodhpur – Pushkar – Bundi – Chittorgarh – Udaipur – Aurangabad (Ajanta and Ellora caves) – Bombay.

This route gives you a taste of just about everything – Moghul architecture, including, of course, the Taj Mahal, wildlife, the desert, Hindu temples, hippie hangouts, Rajput exuberance, unusual Islamic archi-

tecture and the superb Buddhist paintings and sculptures of the Ajanta and Ellora caves. Bombay and Delhi are both cities where you could happily spend a week, although a couple of days in each is usually all there's time for. Travel is by bus and train, except for the Udaipur to Aurangabad leg which can be flown.

Delhi to Bombay via Rajasthan & Gujarat

Delhi – Agra – Jaipur – Pushkar – Jodhpur – Ranakhpur – Udaipur – Bhuj – Rajkot – Junagadh – Sasan Gir – Diu – Palitana – Ahmedabad – Bombay.

Gujarat offers the chance to get off the well-beaten tourist circuit and is well worth any time spent there. The route takes in not only Rajasthan but also the best of what Gujarat has to offer – the tribal cultures of the Rann of Kutch in the far west of the state, the fortified town of Junagadh with some fine buildings, a history as long as your arm and the magnificent Jain temples atop Girnar Hill, Sasan Gir – the last home of the Asian lion, Diu – the old Portuguese enclave with its excellent beaches, Palitana – another town with hills and Jain temples, and Ahmedabad – the busy city which has, among other things, the Gandhi Ashram. Travel is by bus and train.

Delhi to Bombay via Madhya Pradesh

Delhi – Jaipur – Agra – Varanasi – Khajuraho – Jhansi – Sanchi – Mandu – Aurangabad – Bombay.

Madhya Pradesh is another state that is largely untouristed but has enough places of interest to make a visit worthwhile. The Hindu temples at Khajuraho are of course the big attraction, but Sanchi and Mandu between them have fine examples of Buddhist, Hindu and Afghan architecture.

Varanasi, one of the holiest places in the country, Agra, with the incomparable Taj Mahal, and the caves of Ajanta and Ellora are other attractions on this route.

Delhi, Hill Stations & the Himalaya

Delhi – Dalhousie – Dharamsala – Shimla – Manali – Leh – (Srinagar) – Delhi.

Travel in this part of the country is generally by bus and, because of the terrain, is slow. This is a good route to follow if you're in India during the summer, when the heat on the plains becomes unbearable, and in fact the road from Manali to Leh is only open for a couple of months a year when the snow melts.

The hill stations of Shimla and Dalhousie hark back to an era that is rapidly being consigned to history; Dharamsala is a fascinating cultural centre, being the home of the exiled Tibetan leader His Holiness the Dalai Lama; Manali in the Kulu Valley is simply one of the most beautiful places in the country; while the two-day bus trip from there to Leh, high on the Tibetan Plateau, is incredibly rough but equally memorable – it's one of the highest motorable roads in the world. Leh is the capital of Ladakh and centre for another unique Himalayan culture. If troubled Kashmir has once again become stable, a visit to Srinagar and the houseboats on Dal Lake is mandatory; otherwise there are direct flights from Leh back to Delhi.

Trekkers and adventure seekers are well catered for at various places on this route. From Manali there are literally dozens of treks, ranging from a couple of days to a couple of weeks, into places such as the remote Zanskar Valley. Leh, too, is a centre for trekkers, and the Markha Valley is a popular trip. Trekking agencies in both Manali and Leh can arrange everything, or you can strike out on your own.

Delhi to Calcutta via Agra, Khajuraho & Kanha

Delhi – Jaipur – Agra – Jhansi – Khajuraho – Jabalpur – Kanha – Varanasi – Calcutta.

Starting from Delhi, this route gives you a taste of Rajasthan and includes the Taj Mahal. Jhansi is the station for the bus journey to the famous temples of Khajuraho, but it's worth stopping at Orchha, 18 km

from Jhansi, to see this well-preserved old city of palaces and temples. From Khajuraho, a three-hour bus journey brings you to Satna for trains to Jabalpur. A boat trip through the Marble Rocks is the main attraction here. Next stop is Kanha National Park where you can go game-viewing on elephant-back and the chances of seeing a tiger are very good, and then it's back to Jabalpur to pick up a train to the holy city of Varanasi. There are direct trains from here to Calcutta, one of the most fascinating cities in the country.

Flight-Pass Route

Delhi – Agra – Khajuraho – Varanasi – Bhubaneswar – Calcutta – Andaman & Nicobar Islands – Darjeeling (Bagdogra) – Delhi.

With a US$400 flight pass, distance becomes no object and you can visit as many places as you like, within three weeks. This suggested itinerary links a number of the more exotic and distant places as well as 'musts' like the Taj. From Delhi fly to Agra, on to Khajuraho the next day and continue to Varanasi two days later. Next stop is the temple city of Bhubaneswar before taking the flight to Calcutta. An early morning departure brings you to Port Blair, the capital of the Andaman & Nicobar Islands for four or five days at this rarely visited tropical paradise. On the day you leave, you may have watched the sun rise over the ocean but you'll see it set over the Himalaya in Darjeeling, after a change of planes in Calcutta.

Madras to Bombay via Tamil Nadu, Karnataka & Maharashtra

Madras – Kanchipuram – Mahabalipuram – Pondicherry – Kumbakonam – Thanjavur – Tiruchirappalli – Madurai – Kodaikanal – Udhagamandalam (Ooty) – Mysore – Bangalore – Belur/Halebid/Sravanabelagola – Hampi – Badami – Bijapur – Bombay.

This route could be called the Temples & Ancient Monuments Route of central and southern India. Nevertheless, it also takes in a small slice of modern India plus a popular travellers' beach resort, a glimpse of ex-French India along with Auroville, and several days in the mountains bordering Tamil Nadu and Kerala. Transport is by train and bus plus the use of a one-day tourist development corporation bus ex-Mysore or ex-Bangalore to the temple towns of Belur, Halebid and Sravanabelagola.

Madras to Bombay via Tamil Nadu, Kerala, Karnataka & Maharashtra

Madras – Mahabalipuram – Pondicherry – Thanjavur – Tiruchirappalli – Madurai – Kanyakumari – Thiruvananthapuram – Kovalam Beach – Kollam – Alappuzha – Kochi – Coimbatore – Udhagamandalam – Mysore – Bangalore – Hampi – Bijapur – Bombay.

This route, a variation of the above, gives you a much broader perspective of southern India and takes you through the tropical paradise of Kerala with its beaches, backwaters, Kathakali dance-dramas and historical Indo-European associations. Yet it also includes some of the major temple complexes of Tamil Nadu, a hill station, the palaces of Mysore, the Vijayanagar ruins of Hampi and the Muslim splendour of Bijapur. Transport is by train, bus and boat. If time is getting short by the time you reach Bangalore, flights are available from there to Bombay.

ACCOMMODATION

India has a very wide range of accommodation possibilities apart from straightforward hotels.

Youth Hostels

Indian youth hostels are generally very cheap and sometimes in excellent condition with superb facilities. They are, however, often some distance from the town centres. You are not usually required to be a YHA member (as in other countries) to use the hostels, although your YHA card will generally get you a lower rate. The charge is typically Rs 15 for members, Rs 20 for non-

members. Nor do the usual rules about arrival and departure times, lights-out or not using the hostel during the day apply. A list of official hostels includes:

Andhra Pradesh
  Youth Hostel, near Secunderabad Sailing Club, Secunderabad
Delhi
  5 Nyaya Marg, Chanakyapuri (☎ 301-6285)
Goa
  Youth Hostel, Panaji (☎ 45-433)
Gujarat
  Youth Hostel, Sector 16, Gandhinagar
Himachal Pradesh
  Youth Hostel, Bus Stand, Dalhousie
Jammu & Kashmir
  Patnitop Youth Hostel, c/o Tourist Office, Kud (☎ 7)
Maharashtra
  Youth Hostel, Padampura, Station Rd, Aurangabad (☎ 3801)
Orissa
  Youth Hostel, Sea Beach, Puri (☎ 2424)
Rajasthan
  Youth Hostel, SMS Stadium, Bhagwandas Rd, Jaipur (☎ 67-576)
Tamil Nadu
  Youth Hostel, Indira Nagar, Madras (☎ 41-2882)
  Youth Hostel, Solaithandam Kuppam, Pondicherry
Uttar Pradesh
  Youth Hostel, Malli Tal near Ardwell Camp, The Mall, Naini Tal (☎ 2513)
  Mahatma Gandhi Rd, Agra
West Bengal
  Darjeeling Youth Hostel, 16 Dr Zakir Hussain Rd, Darjeeling (☎ 2290)

There are also some state government-operated youth hostels. In Tamil Nadu, for example, there are state hostels in Mahabalipuram, Madras, Rameswaram, Kanyakumari, Kodaikanal, Mudumalai and Ooty.

Government Accommodation

Back in the days of the British Raj, a whole string of government-run accommodation units were set up with labels like Rest Houses, Dak Bungalows, Circuit Houses, PWD (Public Works Department) Bungalows, Forest Rest Houses and so on. Today most of these are reserved for government officials, although in some places they may still be available for tourists, if there is room.

In an approximate pecking order the dak bungalows are the most basic; they often have no electricity and only essential equipment in out-of-the-way places. Rest houses are next up and at the top of the tree comes the circuit houses, which are strictly for travelling VIPs.

Tourist Bungalows

Usually run by the state government, tourist bungalows often serve as replacements for the older government-run accommodation units. Tourist bungalows are generally excellent value, although they vary enormously in facilities and level of service offered.

They often have dorm beds as well as rooms – typical prices are around Rs 20 to Rs 40 for a dorm bed, and Rs 100 to Rs 250 for a double room. The rooms have a fan, two beds and bathroom; more expensive air-conditioned rooms are often also available. Generally there's a restaurant or 'dining hall' and often a bar. Particularly good tourist bungalows can be found in Tamil Nadu (where they are known as Hotel Tamil Nadu), in Karnataka (Hotel Mayura) and in Rajasthan, although almost every state has some towns where the tourist bungalow is definitely the best place to stay. Their biggest drawback is that, in common with state-run companies virtually anywhere, the staff may be less than 100% motivated – in some cases they are downright lazy and rude – and maintenance is not what it might be.

In tourist bungalows, as in many other government-run institutions in India, such as the railways, you will find a curiously Indian institution: the 'complaints book'. In this you can write your complaints and periodically someone higher up the chain of command comes along, reads the terrible tales and the tourist bungalow manager gets his knuckles rapped. In disputes or other arguments, calling for the complaints book is the angry customer's final weapon. In many places the complaints book can provide interesting and amusing reading.

Railway Retiring Rooms

These are just like regular hotels or dormitories except they are at the railway stations. To stay here you are generally supposed to have a railway ticket or Indrail Pass. The rooms are, of course, extremely convenient

Arriving after midnight, we found the railway retiring rooms full, so we laid out our sleeping-bags on the deserted platform. It had been a long hard journey and we fell asleep immediately. We woke to find the station crowded and a waiter standing over us enquiring as to what we'd like for breakfast. We said we'd come to the refreshment room in a few minutes, but no, he insisted that we stay put and he'd bring us breakfast in bed. Ten minutes later he reappeared with trays laden with cornflakes, eggs, toast and coffee and stood by as we breakfasted under the feet of the early morning commuters!

A brilliant start to the day apart from the fact that the cornflakes had been fried in ghee!

Chris Jenney (UK)

if you have an early train departure, although they can be noisy if it is a busy station. They are often very cheap and in some places they are also excellent value. Some stations have retiring rooms of definite Raj pretensions, with huge rooms and enough furniture to do up a flat or apartment back home. They are usually excellent value, if a little institutional in feel, and are let on a 24-hour basis.

Railway Waiting Rooms

For emergency accommodation when all else fails or when you just need a few hours of shut-eye before your train departs at 2 am, waiting rooms are a free place to rest your weary head. The trick is to rest it in the comfortable 1st-class waiting room and not the crowded 2nd-class one. Officially you need a 1st-class ticket to be allowed to use the 1st-class room and its superior facilities. In practice, luck, a 2nd-class Indrail Pass or simply your foreign appearance may work. In other places your ticket will be checked.

Cheap Hotels

There are hotels all over India with conditions ranging from extremely drab and dismal (but with prices at rock bottom) up to quite reasonable in both standards and prices. Lazily swishing ceiling fans, mosquito nets on the beds, private toilets and bathrooms are all possibilities even in rooms which cost Rs 80 or less per night for a double.

Throughout India hotels are defined as 'Western' or 'Indian'. The differentiation is basically meaningless, although expensive hotels are always Western, cheap ones Indian. 'Indian' hotels will be more simply and economically furnished but the acid test is the toilet. 'Western' hotels have a sit-up-style toilet; 'Indian' ones usually (but not always) have the traditional Asian squat style. You can find modern, well-equipped, clean places with Indian toilets and dirty, dismal dumps with Western toilets. Some places even have the weird hybrid toilet, which is basically a Western toilet with foot-pads on the edge of the bowl!

Although prices are generally quoted in this book for singles and doubles, most hotels will put an extra bed in a room to make a triple for about an extra 25%. This is a considerable saving if there are more than two of you. In some smaller hotels it's often possible to bargain a little if you really want to. On the other hand these places will often put their prices up if there's a shortage of accommodation.

Many hotels, and not only the cheap ones, operate on a 24-hour system. This can be convenient if you check in at 8 pm, as it gives you until 8 pm the following day to check out. Conversely, if you arrive at 8 am one day it can be a nuisance to have to be on the streets again by 8 am the next day. There are, however, considerable regional variations. Some hotels maintain a noon checkout; hill stations often operate on a 9 am checkout. Ask what the checkout time is at your hotel. Most hotels offer a half-day rate if you want to stay a few extra hours. Enquire about this in advance if that's what you want.

Expensive Hotels

You won't find 'international standard' hotels throughout India. The big, air-conditioned, swimming-pool places are generally confined to the major tourist centres and the large cities. There are a number of big hotel chains in India. The Taj Group has some of India's flashiest hotels, including the luxurious Taj Mahal Intercontinental in Bombay, the romantic Rambagh Palace in Jaipur and the Lake Palace in Udaipur. Other interesting hotels are the Taj Coromandel in Madras, the Fort Aguada Beach Resort in Goa, and the Malabar Hotel in Kochi (Cochin). The Oberoi chain is, of course, well known outside India as well as within. Clarks is a small chain with popular hotels in Varanasi and Agra, amongst other places. The Welcomgroup (affiliated with Sheraton), the Ritz chain, and the Air India-associated Centaur hotels are other chains.

Other chains include the government-operated ITDC group which usually append the name 'Ashok' to their hotels. There's an Ashok hotel in virtually every town in India, so that test isn't foolproof, but the ITDC places include a number of smaller (but higher-standard) units in places like Sanchi or Konark where accommodation possibilities are limited. The ITDC has been under attack in India for some time about its overall inefficient operation, financial losses and poor standards in its hotels. In 1992 it decided to sell off a controlling share in a number of its hotels, thereby raising capital and at the same time allowing for improvement of the hotels by private commercial organisations.

Most expensive hotels operate on a noon checkout basis.

You may be able to negotiate a discount on air-con rooms in December and January since air-con often isn't necessary then.

Home Stays

Staying with an Indian family can be a real education. It's a change from dealing strictly with tourist-oriented people, and the differences and curiosities of everyday Indian life can be very interesting.

The only place where home-stay accommodation is organised on an official basis is in Rajasthan, and then only in the cities of Jaipur, Jodhpur and Udaipur. The cost is anything from Rs 50 upwards, depending on the level of facilities offered. The tourist offices in the three cities have comprehensive lists of the families offering this service. It's known as the Paying Guest Scheme and is administered by the Rajasthan Tourism Development Corporation.

Other Possibilities

There are YMCAs and YWCAs in many of the big cities – some of these are modern, well equipped and cost about the same as a middle-range hotel (but are still good value). There are also a few Salvation Army Hostels – in particular in Bombay, Calcutta and Madras. There are a few camping places around India, but travellers with their own vehicles can almost always find hotels with gardens where they can park and camp.

Free accommodation is available at some Sikh temples where there is a tradition of hospitality to visitors. It can be interesting to

try one, but please don't abuse this hospitality and spoil it for other travellers. At many pilgrimage sites there are *dharamsalas* and *choultries*, places which offer accommodation to pilgrims, and travellers are often welcome to use these. This particularly applies at isolated sites like Ranakpur in Rajasthan. The drawback here (especially with Jain choultries) is that no leather articles are allowed inside.

Taxes & Service Charges

Most state governments impose a variety of taxes on hotel accommodation. This is generally called expenditure tax or luxury tax and it varies from state to state. At most rock-bottom hotels you won't have to pay it. Once you get into the top end of budget places, and certainly for middle-range accommodation, you will have to pay it. As a general rule, you can assume that anything under Rs 100 will attract a 10% (sometimes just 5%) tax. Over Rs 200 will attract a 15% (sometimes 10%) tax, and over Rs 300 will attract 20% (sometimes 15%) tax. All luxury hotels attract a 20% loading. In addition to this there may also be a further 15% loading in luxury hotels taking the tax level to 35%. These taxes are always waived if you pay in foreign currency or by credit card.

Another common tax, which is additional to the above, is a service charge which is always pegged at 10%. In some hotels, this is only levied on food, room service and use of telephones, not on the accommodation costs. At others, it's levied on the total bill. If you're trying to keep costs down, don't sign up meals or room service to your room bill and keep telephone use to a minimum if you know that service charge is levied on the total bill.

Regarding these taxes, the other thing which varies a great deal is at what point they're levied in the calculation of your final bill. Some hotels add up accommodation, food and telephone charges, then levy luxury/expenditure tax and follow this up with an overall 10% service charge. Others levy the 10% service charge first on the total for accommodation, meals and telephone charges followed by the luxury/expenditure tax on the subtotal. Depending on which method they use, the final bill can vary quite significantly.

Hotel and restaurant bills paid by credit card will be billed to your account at the same rate which you get for travellers' cheques at a bank in India (ie 40% at Reserve Bank rate and 60% at the free market rate).

Rates quoted in this book are the basic rate only unless otherwise indicated. Taxes and service charges are extra.

Seasonal Variations

In popular tourist places (hill stations, beaches, Dal Lake, and the Delhi-Agra-Rajasthan triangle), hoteliers crank up their prices in the high season by a factor of two to three times the low-season price. This can make them very expensive, particularly where the increased room rates move accommodation costs from a lower to a higher tax bracket. Watch out for this.

The definition of the high and low seasons obviously varies depending on location. For the beaches and the Delhi-Agra-Rajasthan triangle it's basically a month before and two months after Christmas. In the hill stations and Kashmir, it's usually April to July when the lowlands are unbearably hot. In some locations and at some hotels, there are even higher rates for the brief Christmas/New Year period, or during major festivals such as Diwali.

Conversely, in the low season(s), prices at even normally expensive hotels can be surprisingly reasonable.

Touts

Hordes of accommodation touts operate in many towns in India – Agra, Jaipur and Varanasi in particular – and at any international airport terminal. Very often they are the rickshaw-wallahs who meet you at the bus or train station. The technique is simple – they take you to hotel A and rake off a commission for bringing you there rather than to hotel B. The problem with this procedure is that you may well end up not at the place you want to go to but at the place that

pays the best commission. Some very good cheap hotels simply refuse to pay the touts and you'll then hear lots of stories about the hotel you want being 'full', 'closed for repairs', 'no good anymore' or even 'flooded'. Nine chances out of 10 they will be just that – stories.

Touts do have a use though – if you arrive in a town when some big festival is on (or a cricket test match against England or Australia!), finding a place to stay can be very difficult. Hop in a rickshaw, tell the driver in what price range you want a hotel, and off you go. The driver will know which places have rooms available and unless the search is a long one you shouldn't have to pay the driver too much. Remember that the driver will be getting a commission from the hotel too!

FOOD

Despite the very fine meals that can be prepared in India, you'll often find food a great disappointment. In many smaller centres there is not a wide choice and you'll get bored with rice and dhal. When you're in larger cities where the food can be excellent, take advantage of it.

Contrary to popular belief, not all Hindus are officially vegetarians. Strict vegetarianism is confined more to the south, which has not had the meat-eating influence of the Aryan and later Muslim invasions, and also to the Gujarati community. For those who do eat meat, it is not always a pleasure to do so in India – the quality tends to be low (most chickens give the impression that they died from starvation) and the hygiene is not all that it might be. Beef, from the holy cow, is strictly taboo of course – and leads to interesting Indian dishes like the muttonburger. Where steak is available, it's usually buffalo and found only in Muslim restaurants. Pork is equally taboo to the Muslims and is generally only available in areas where there are significant Christian communities (such as Goa). If you're a non-vegetarian you'll end up eating a lot more vegetarian food in India.

Indian interpretations of Western cuisine can be pretty horrific; it's usually best to stick to Indian food. Meals served on trains are usually palatable and reasonably cheap. At most stops you will be besieged by food and drink sellers. Even in the middle of the night that raucous cry of 'Chai! Chai!' or 'Ah, coffeecoffeecoffee!' will inevitably break into your sleep. The sheer bedlam of an Indian station when a train is in is a part of India you never forget.

If, after some time in India, you do find the food is getting you down physically or psychologically, there are a couple of escapes. It is very easy for budget travellers to lose weight in India and feel lethargic and drained of energy. The answer is to increase your protein intake – eat more eggs, which are readily available. It also helps to eat more fruit and nuts, so buy bananas, mandarin oranges or peanuts, all easily found at stations or in the markets. Many travellers carry multivitamins with them. Another answer, if you're travelling on a budget, is to occasionally splash out on a meal in a fancy hotel or restaurant – compared to what you have been

---

Indian Menus

One of the delights of Indian menus is their amazing English. Start the morning, for example, with corn flaks, also useful for shooting down enemy aircraft. Or perhaps corn flex – Indian corn flakes are often so soggy they'll do just that.

Even before your corn-whatever you should have some tea, and what a variety of types of tea India can offer. You can try bed tea, milk tea, light tea, ready tea, mixed tea, tray tea, plain tea, half set tea and even (of course) full set tea. Eggs also offer unlimited possibilities: half-fried eggs, pouch eggs (or egg pooch), bolid eggs, scimbled eggs, skamal and egg tost, sliced omelettes, skerem boil eggs (interesting combination there), bread omelt, or simply aggs. Finally, you could finish off breakfast with that popular Scottish dish – pordge.

Soup before a meal – how about French onion soap? Or Scotch brath, mughutoni or perhaps start with a parn coactale. Follow that up with some amazing interpretations of Western dishes, like the restaurant that not only had Napoleon spaghetti but also Stalin spaghetti! Perhaps a seezling plator or vegetable augrotten sounds more like it? Or simply a light meal – well, why not have a sandwitch or a vegetable pup? Feeling strong – then try a carate salad, or a vegetable cutlass.

Chickens come in for some pretty amazing treatment too, with chicken buls, bum chicken, chicken cripes, chicken manure, chicken merrylens and possibly the all-time classic: chicken katan blueinside chess – no, I don't have any idea what it is either!

If you want a drink how about orange squish or that popular Indian soft drink Thumps Up.

Chinese dishes offer a whole new range of possibilities, including mashrooms and bamboo sooghts, spring rolos, American chopsy, Chinies snakes, vegetable chop off, vegetable nuddles, plane fried rice and park fried rice.

Finally for dessert you could try apple pai or banana panecake, or treat yourself to leeches & cream, or even semenolina pudding!

Travellers have sent in lots more menu suggestions since the first edition of this book. Like tired fruit juice (tinned you know), plane tost (the stuff they serve on Indian Airlines?), omlet & began, two eggs any shape, loose curds, curds bath, tomatoe stuff, scram bled eggs, chicken poodle soup, screambled eggs, banana frilters, pain-apple cream and chocolet padding. Or something even Colonel Sanders hasn't thought of yet – fried children. ∎

paying it may seem amazingly expensive, but try translating the price into what it would cost at home.

There are considerable regional variations from north to south, partly because of climatic conditions and partly because of historical influences. In the north, as already mentioned, much more meat is eaten and the cooking is often 'Moghul style' (often spelt 'Mughal' or 'Mughlai') which bears a closer relationship to food of the Middle East and central Asia. The emphasis is more on spices and less on chilli. In the north, grains and breads are eaten far more than rice.

In the south more rice is eaten, there is more vegetarian food, and the curries tend to be hotter – sometimes very hot. Another feature of southern vegetarian food is that you do not use eating utensils; food is always eaten with fingers (of the right hand only). Scooping up food that way takes a little practice but you soon become quite adept at it. It is said that eating this way allows you to get the 'feel' of the food, as important to south Indian cuisine as the aroma or arrangement are to other cooking styles. It also offers the added protection that you never need worry if the eating utensils have been properly washed.

In the most basic Indian restaurants and eating places, known as *dhabas* or *bhojanalyas*, the cooking is usually done right out front so you can see exactly what is going on and how it is done. Vegetables will be on the simmer all day and tend to be overcooked and mushy to Western tastes. In these basic places *dhal* is usually free but you pay for *chapatis, parathas, puris* or rice. *Sabzi* (vegetable preparations), dhal and a few chapatis make a passable meal for around Rs 10. If you order half-plates of the various dishes brewing out front you get half the quantity at half the price and get a little more variety. With chutneys and a small plate of onions, which come free, you can put together a reasonable vegetarian meal for Rs 20, or non-vegetarian for Rs 30. In railway station restaurants and other cheaper restaurants always check the prices and add up your bill. If it's incorrect, query it.

At the other end of the price scale there are many restaurants in India's five-star hotels that border on the luxurious and by Western standards are absurdly cheap. Paying US$10 to US$15 for a meal in India seems exorbitant after you've been there for a while, but check what a meal in your friendly local Hilton would cost you. Many of the international standard hotels, like the Oberoi Palace in Srinagar, the Malabar Hotel in Kochi (Cochin), the Taj Mahal Intercontinental in Bombay, the Connemara in Madras and the Umaid Bhawan Palace in Jodhpur offer all-you-can-eat buffet deals. One place to which *every* traveller used to go for a splurge was the Lake Palace in Udaipur where, for around US$10, you could treat yourself to a range of dishes in one of India's most luxurious settings – including a dance show and the boat fare. For budget travellers it made a very pleasant change from dhal and rice. However, the hotel is currently not open to nonresidents, but it's worth checking this out if you travel to Udaipur, as this may change.

Finally, a couple of hints on how to cope with curry. After a while in India you'll get used to even the fiercest curries and will find Western food surprisingly bland. If, however, you do find your mouth is on fire don't reach for water; in emergencies that hardly helps at all. Curd (*dahi*, yoghurt) or fruit do the job much more efficiently.

Curry & Spice

Believe it or not, there is no such thing as 'curry' in India. It's an English invention, an all-purpose term to cover the whole range of Indian food spicing. *Carhi*, incidentally, is a Gujarati dish, but never ask for it in Kumaon where it's a very rude word!

Although all Indian food is certainly not curry, this is the basis of Indian cuisine. Curry doesn't have to be hot enough to blow your head off, although it can do that if it's made that way. Curry most definitely is not something found in a packet of curry powder. Indian cooks have about 25 spices on their regular list and it is from these that they produce the curry flavour. Normally the spices are freshly ground in a mortar and pestle known as a *sil-vatta*. Spices are usually blended in certain combinations to produce *masalas* (mixes). *Garam masala* ('hot mix'), for example, is a combination of cloves, cinnamon, cardamom, coriander, cumin and peppercorns.

Popular spices include saffron, an expensive flavouring produced from the stamens of certain crocus flowers. This is used to give rice that yellow colouring and delicate fragrance. (It's an excellent buy in India, where a five-gram packet costs around Rs 100 – you'll pay about 10 times more at home.) Turmeric also has a colouring property, acts as a preservative and has a distinctive smell and taste. Chillies are ground, dried or added whole to supply the heat. They come in red and green varieties but the green ones are the hottest. Ginger is supposed to be good for the digestion, while many masalas contain coriander because it is said to cool the body. Strong and sweet cardamom is used in many desserts and in rich meat dishes. Other popular spices and flavourings include nutmeg, poppy seeds, caraway seeds, fenugreek, mace, garlic, cloves, bay leaves and curry leaves.

Breads & Grains

Rice is, of course, the basic Indian staple, but although it is eaten throughout the country, it's all-important only in the south. The best Indian rice, it is generally agreed, is found in the north where Basmati rice grows in the Dehra Dun Valley. It has long grains, is yellowish and has a slightly sweetish or '*bas*' smell. In the north (where wheat is the staple) rice is supplemented by a whole range of breads known as *rotis* or *chapatis*. In the Punjab a roti is called *phulka*. Western-style white sliced bread is widely available, and it's generally pretty good.

Indian breads are varied but always delicious. Simplest is the chapati/roti, which is simply a mixture of flour and water cooked on a hotplate known as a *tawa*. Direct heat blows them up but how well that works depends on the gluten content of the wheat. A *paratha* is also cooked on the hotplate but

ghee is used and the bread is rolled in a different way. There are also parathas that have been stuffed with peas or potato. Deepfried bread which puffs up is known as a *puri* in the north and a *luchi* in the east.

Found all over India, but originating from the south, are *dosas*. These are basically pancakes made from lentil flour. Curried vegetables wrapped inside a dosa makes it a *masala dosa* – a terrific snack meal. Bake the bread in a clay (tandoori) oven and you have *nan*. However you make them, Indian breads taste great.

Use your chapati or paratha to mop or scoop up your curry. An *idli* is a kind of rice dumpling, often served with a spicy curd sauce (*dahi idli*) or with spiced lentils and chutney. They're a popular breakfast dish. *Papadams* are crispy deep-fried lentil-flour wafers often served with *thalis* or other meals. An *uttapam* is like a dosa, but is made from a lentil and rice paste.

Outside the Delhi Jami Masjid you may see 'big' chapatis known as *rumali roti* (handkerchiefs). Note that Hindus use their tawa concavely, Muslims convexly!

Basic Dishes

Curries can be vegetable, meat (usually chicken or lamb) or fish, but they are always fried in ghee (clarified butter) or vegetable oil. North or south they will be accompanied by rice, but in the north you can also choose from the range of breads.

There are a number of dishes which aren't really curries but are close enough to them for Western tastes. *Vindaloos* have a vinegar marinade and tend to be hotter than most curries. Pork vindaloo is a favourite dish in Goa. *Kormas*, on the other hand, are rich, substantial dishes prepared by braising. There are both meat and vegetable kormas. *Navratan korma* is a very tasty dish using nuts, while a *malai kofta* is a rich, cream-based dish. *Dopiaza* literally means 'two onions' and is a type of korma which uses onions at two stages in its preparation.

Probably the most basic of Indian dishes is *dhal*, rather like a lentil soup. Dhal is almost always there, whether as an accompaniment to a curry or as a very basic meal in itself with chapatis or rice. In the very small rural towns dhal and rice is just about all there is on the menu. The favourite dhal of Bengal and Gujarat is yellow *arhar*; whereas in Punjab it is *black urad*; the common red lentils are called *moong*; *rajma* is the Heinz 57 varieties of dhal!

Other basic dishes include *mattar panir* – peas and cheese in gravy; *saag gosht* – spinach and meat; *alu dum* – potato curry; *palak panir* – spinach and cheese; and *alu chhole* – diced potatoes and spicy-sour chickpeas. Some other vegetables include *gobi* (cauliflower), *brinjal* (eggplant) and *mattar* (peas).

Tandoori & Biryani

Tandoori food is a northern speciality and refers to the clay oven in which the food is cooked after first being marinated in a complex mix of herbs and yoghurt. Tandoori chicken is a favourite. This food is not as hot as curry dishes and usually tastes terrific.

Biryani (again chicken is a popular biryani dish) is another northern Moghul dish. The meat is mixed with a deliciously flavoured, orange-coloured rice which is sometimes spiced with nuts or dried fruit. A Kashmiri biryani is basically fruit salad with rice.

A *pulao* is flavoured rice often with pulses and with or without meat. You will also find it in other Asian countries further west. Those who have the idea that Indian food is always curry and always fiery hot will be surprised by tandoori and biryani dishes.

Regional Specialities

Rogan josh is straightforward lamb curry, always popular in the north and in Kashmir where it originated. *Gushtaba*, pounded and spiced meatballs cooked in a yoghurt sauce, is another Kashmiri speciality. Still in the north, *chicken makhanwala* is a rich dish cooked in a butter sauce.

Many coastal areas have excellent seafood, including Bombay where the *pomfret*, a flounder-like fish, is popular; so is Bombay duck, which is not a duck at all but another fish dish. *Dhansaak* is a Parsi speciality found in Bombay – lamb or chicken cooked with curried lentils and steamed rice. Further south, Goa has excellent fish and prawns; in Kerala, Kochi (Cochin) is famous for its prawns.

Another indication of the influence of central Asian cooking styles on north Indian food is the popularity of kababs. You'll find them all across north India with a number of local variations and specialities. The two basic forms are *sikh* (skewered) or *shami* (wrapped). In Calcutta *kati kababs* are a local favourite. Another Bengali dish is *dahi maach* – curried fish in yoghurt sauce, flavoured with ginger and turmeric. Further south in Hyderabad you could try *haleen*, pounded wheat with a lightly spiced mutton gravy.

Lucknow is famous for its wide range of kebabs and for *dum pukht* – the 'art' of steam pressure cooking, in which meat and vegetables are cooked in a sealed clay pot.

Side Dishes

Indian food generally has a number of side dishes to go with the main meal. Probably the most popular is *dahi* – curd or yoghurt. It has the useful ability of instantly cooling a fiery curry – either blend it into the curry or, if it's too late, you can administer it straight to your mouth. Curd is often used in the cooking or as a dessert and appears in the popular drink *lassi*. *Raita* is another popular side dish consisting of curd mixed with cooked or raw vegetables, particularly cucumber (similar to Greek *tzatziki*) or tomato.

Sabzi is curried vegetables, and *began bharta* is puréed eggplant curry. *Mulligatawny* is a soup-like dish which is really just a milder, more liquid curry. It's a dish adopted into the English menu by the Raj. Chutney is pickled fruit or vegetables and is the standard relish for a curry.

Thalis

A *thali* is the all-purpose Indian vegetarian dish. Although it is basically a product of south India, you will find restaurants serving thalis or 'vegetarian plate meals' all over

India. Often the sign will simply announce 'Meals'. In addition, there are regional variations like the particularly sumptuous and sweet Gujarati thalis.

The name is taken from the 'thali' dish in which it is served. This consists of a metal plate with a number of small metal bowls known as *katoris* on it. Sometimes the small bowls will be replaced by simple indentations in the plate; in more basic places the 'plate' will be a big, fresh banana leaf. A thali consists of a variety of curry vegetable dishes, relishes, a couple of papadams, puris or dosas and a mountain of rice. A fancy thali may have a *pata*, a rolled leaf stuffed with fruit and nuts. There'll probably be a bowl of curd and possibly even a small dessert or pan.

Thalis are consistently tasty and good food value, but they have two other unbeatable plus points for the budget traveller – they're cheap and they're usually 100% filling. Thalis can be as little as Rs 8 and will rarely cost much more than Rs 25 at the very most, though Gujarati thalis are the exception and you'll consistently be paying Rs 25 to Rs 30 for these at reasonable restaurants. Most are 100% filling because they're normally 'all you can eat'. When your plate starts to look empty they come round, add another mountain of rice and refill the katoris. Thalis are eaten with fingers, although you may get a spoon for the curd or dhal. Always wash your hands before you eat one – a sink or other place to wash your hands is provided in a thali restaurant.

Snacks

Samosas are curried vegetables fried in a pastry triangle. They are very tasty and are found all over India. *Bhujias* or *pakoras* are bite-size pieces of vegetable dipped in chickpea flour batter and deep fried. Along with samosas they're the most popular snack food in the country.

Bhelpuri is a popular Bombay snack peddled across the city, and always found in holiday resort towns around the country. *Channa* is spiced chickpeas *(gram)* served with puris. *Sambhar* is a soup-like lentil and vegetable dish with a sour tamarind flavour. *Chat* is the general term for snacks, while *namkin* is the name for the various spiced nibbles that are sold prepackaged – although one waiter I encountered referred to them as 'bitings'.

Western Food

Sometimes Indian food simply becomes too much and you want to escape to something familiar and reassuring. It's not always easy, but railway station restaurants often have something palatable and close to the food 'back home'. The Indian-food blues are particularly prone to hit at breakfast time – somehow idlis never really feel like a breakfast. Fortunately that's the meal where you'll find an approximation to the West most easily obtained. All those wonderful Indian varieties of eggs can be had – half-fried, omelettes, you name it.

Toast and jam can almost always be found, and very often you can get cornflakes and hot

---

A really good place to eat, so we were told, was the tea house near the end of the street. Apparently it had no name but we'd recognise it by the tables in the garden. Sure enough, we found it and sat down in the well-tended garden. Service obviously wasn't a strong point at this restaurant as there was no-one about. Eventually a man appeared and asked us (rather curtly, we thought) what we wanted. We ordered dhal, chapatis and omelettes and he was gone for a very long time. When he came out again I said we had a train to catch so could he please hurry up. Without a reply he served the food and stomped off inside. Finishing the meal (which was none too good) I asked for the bill and he said 'Rs 100' which was rather high. I told him so and he took a deep breath, as if trying to keep his temper, and said: 'Sir, you are a very rude man! You enter my house, ask for food, complain about the delay when I have to send out my bearer to fetch it and then tell me I am robbing you!'

The restaurant, of course, was further down the street!

Chris Jenney (UK)

milk, although Indian cornflakes would definitely be rejects from Mr Kellogg's production line. The Scots must have visited India too, because porridge is often on the breakfast menu and is usually good.

That peculiar Raj-era term for a midmorning snack still lives – tiffin. Today tiffin means any sort of light meal or snack. One Western dish which Indians seem to have come 100% to terms with is chips (French fries). Unfortunately ordering chips is very much a hit and miss affair – sometimes they're excellent, and at other times truly dreadful. Some Indian cooks call potato chips 'Chinese potatoes', and 'finger chips' is also quite common.

Other Cuisines

Other Asian foods, apart from Indian, are often available. There's still a small Chinese population in India, particularly in Calcutta and Bombay. You can find Chinese food in the larger cities, and Bombay and Bangalore in particular have excellent Chinese food. In the north, where many Tibetans settled following the Chinese invasion of Tibet, you'll find Tibetan restaurants in places like Darjeeling, Dharamsala, Gangtok and Manali.

Desserts & Sweets

Indians have quite a sweet tooth and an amazing selection of desserts and sweets to satisfy it. The desserts are basically rice or milk based, and consist of various interesting things in sweet syrup or else sweet pastries. Most are horrendously sweet.

Kulfi is pistachio-flavoured ice cream and is widely available. You can, of course, also get Western-style ice cream all over India. The major brands, such as Vadelal, Go Cool, Kwality and Havmor, are healthy and very good. *Ras gullas* are another very popular Indian dessert; they're sweet little balls of cream cheese flavoured with rose water.

Gulub jamuns are a typical example of the small 'things' in syrup – they're fried and made from thickened boiled-down milk (known as *khoya*) and flavoured with cardamom and rose water. *Jalebis*, the orange-coloured squiggles with syrup inside, are made of flour coloured with saffron. *Ladu* are yellow coloured balls made from chickpea flour.

Barfi is also made from khoya and is available in flavours like coconut, pistachio, chocolate or almond. *Sandesh* is another milk sweet; it's a particular favourite in Calcutta. *Payasam* is a sweet southern drink made from coconut milk, mango pulp, cashews and spices. *Gajar ka halwa* is a translucent, vividly coloured sweet made from carrot, sweet spices and milk.

Many of the Indian sweets are covered in a thin layer of silver, as are some of the desserts. It's just that, silver beaten paper thin. Don't peel it off, it's quite edible. There are countless sweet shops with their goodies all lined up in glass showcases. Prices vary from Rs 40 to Rs 60 for a kg but you can order 50 or 100 grams at a time or simply ask

---

Salad & Indian Dressing

If 'salad' appears at all on an Indian menu, it generally means just a few raw vegetables. Since you can't trust a salad unless you've seen it being washed (which is unlikely) many travellers avoid it. A couple of keen salad-eaters I met had solved the problem by preparing their own. They bought tomatoes, cucumbers and onions at markets, and soaked them in a strong solution of iodine in their hotel room for half an hour. An essential piece of their travelling gear was a large plastic bowl for this purpose. No need for naked salad, for as they discovered, pure virgin olive oil is readily available in shops selling ayurvedic medicines. For a real treat they made their own fresh mayonnaise with a couple of egg yolks, half a cup of olive oil and a lot of patience. The oil must be added very slowly, only a few drops at a time, whilst the eggs are being beaten with a fork. ■

Bengali Sweet Maker

the milk the stallholder will split the coconut open and cut you a slice from the outer covering with which to scoop the flesh out.

Mangoes are delicious and are widespread in summer. Bananas are also found in many parts of India, particularly in the south; pineapples are found in Assam and Kerala as well as elsewhere. You don't see oranges all over the place (lots in Kerala though), but tangerines are widespread in central India, particularly during the hot season. You can go through an awful lot of them in a day.

Cooking Back Home
There are all sorts of books about Indian cooking should you want to continue after you leave India. *Indian Cookery* by Dharamjit Singh (Penguin, London, 1970) is a useful paperback introduction to the art. Premila Lal is one of the country's leading cookery writers, and her books are widely available. The problem is that ingredients are only given their local name, which makes many of the recipes impractical or impossible if you don't know exactly what is being called for. Charmaine Solomon's *Asian Cookbook* (Summit Books) is an excellent source, and includes not only Indian but also other Asian cuisines.

for a couple of pieces. These shops often sell curd, as well as sweet curd which makes a very pleasant dessert. Sweets include all sorts of unidentifiable goodies; try them and see.

Fruit
If your sweet tooth simply isn't sweet enough to cope with too many Indian desserts, you'll be able to fall back on India's wide variety of fruit. It varies all the way from tropical delights in the south to apples, apricots and other temperate-region fruits in the north. Some local specialities include cherries and strawberries in Kashmir, and apricots in Ladakh and Himachal Pradesh. Apples are found all over this north-western region but particularly in the Kulu Valley of Himachal Pradesh.

Melons are widespread in India, particularly watermelons, which are a fine thirst quencher when you're unsure about the water and fed up with soft drinks. Try to get the first slice before the flies discover it. Green coconuts are even better and there are coconut stalls on many city street corners, especially in the south. When you've drunk

Pan
An Indian meal should properly be finished with *pan* – the name given to the collection of spices and condiments chewed with betel nut. Found throughout eastern Asia, betel is a mildly intoxicating and addictive nut, but by itself it is quite inedible. After a meal you chew pan as a mild digestive.

Pan sellers have a whole collection of little trays, boxes and containers in which they mix either *sadha* 'plain' or *mitha* 'sweet' pans. The ingredients may include, apart from the betel nut itself, lime paste (the ash not the fruit), the powder known as *catachu*, various spices and even a dash of opium in a pricey pan. The whole concoction is folded up in a piece of edible leaf which you pop in your mouth and chew. When finished you spit the leftovers out and add another red blotch to the pavement. Over a long period

Pan

In India, as the red-stained walls and floors bear witness, the chewing of pan is something of a national obsession. Even the smallest village will have a pan-wallah, sitting cross-legged in front of a pile of pan leaves and tins of ingredients in a shop which is often not much more than a niche in a wall.

Although most pans cost around Rs 1 there are rumours of pan-wallahs who have become millionaires. In spite of reduced sales after the introduction of factory-prepared packets of pan masala, with low overheads and high turnover, the owners of some pan shops are undoubtedly very wealthy. At Prince Pan Centre, in Daryaganj in Delhi, the city's rich will pay up to Rs 100 for the best preparation.

Apart from the usual ingredients of lime, betel nut and catachu every pan-wallah has his or her secret recipe which may include tobacco, flower essences or even silver and gold leaf. Amongst the numerous varieties of pan is one subtly named *palang tor* ('bed breaker') that is sometimes given to the groom on his wedding night. Thought to contain rhino-horn and other traditional aphrodisiacs, its ingredients are more usually cocaine or opium, resulting in a performance that is likely to be an illusion to the groom and a disappointment to the bride. ■

of time, indulgence in pan will turn your teeth red-black and even addict you to the betel nut. Trying one occasionally won't do you any harm.

DRINKS

Nonalcoholic Drinks

Tea & Coffee Surprisingly, tea is not the all-purpose and all-important drink in India that it is in Iran and Afghanistan. What's worse, the Indians, for all the tea they grow, make some of the most hideously over-sweetened, murkily-milky excuses for that fine beverage that you'll ever see. It may go by the name of *chai*, just like in the rest of Asia, but what a letdown. Still, some people like it and it is cheap.

Better tea can be obtained if you ask for 'tray tea', which gives you the tea, the milk and the sugar separately and allows you to combine them as you see fit. Usually tea is 'mixed tea' or 'milk tea', which means it has been made by putting cold water, milk, sugar and tea into one pot and bringing the whole concoction to the boil, then letting it stew for a long time. The result can be imagined.

Tea is more popular in the north, while in the south coffee, which is generally good, is the number one drink. It's almost impossible to get a decent cup of coffee in the north. Even in an expensive restaurant instant coffee is almost always used. The branches of the Indian Coffee House are one of the few places in most towns with decent coffee.

Water In the big cities, the water is chlorinated and safe to drink, although if you've just arrived in India, the change from what you are used to drinking is in itself enough to bring on a mild dose of the shits.

Outside the cities you're on your own. Some travellers drink the water everywhere and never get sick, others are more careful and still get hit with a bug. Basically, you should not drink the water in small towns unless you know it has been boiled, and definitely avoid the street vendors' carts everywhere. Even in the better class of hotel and restaurant, the water is usually only filtered and not boiled. The local water filters remove solids and do nothing towards removing any bacteria. Water is generally safer in the dry season than in the monsoon when it really can be dangerous.

Water purifying tablets are available from pharmacies and camping shops in the West, but not in India. Most tablets, such as Puritabs, do not remove amoebic cysts (hepatitis, giardia, amoebic dysentery) but are sufficient to make tap water safe. Iodine solution or, more conveniently, tablets such as those made by Coghlans in the USA, do remove these amoebas and are necessary if you are trekking and will be drinking stream water. Either way, the purified water tastes pretty much like swimming-pool water!

Mineral Water Most travellers to India these days avoid tap water altogether and stick to mineral water. It is available virtually everywhere, and comes in one-litre plastic bottles. The price ranges from Rs 8 to Rs 30, with Rs 12 being about the average. Brand names include Bisleri, India King, Officer's Choice, Honeydew and Aqua Safe.

According to a report in the magazine *Sunday* (10-16 May 1992), most Indian-produced mineral water is not true mineral water at all. Some is just treated municipal water and much of it is sold in PVC containers, which are banned in Western countries. See the section called Drinks in the Health section earlier in this chapter.

Soft Drinks Soft drinks are a safe substitute for water although they tend to have a high sugar content. Coca-Cola got the boot from India a number of years back for not cooperating with the government, but both they and Pepsi Cola are back with a vengeance. There are many similar indigenous brands with names like Campa Cola, Thums Up, Limca, Gold Spot or Double Seven. By Asian standards they are pretty expensive at around Rs 5 to Rs 8 for a 190-ml bottle (more in restaurants). They're also sickly sweet.

Juices & Other Drinks One very pleasant escape from the sickly sweet soft drinks is apple juice, sold for Rs 3 per glass from the Himachal fruit stands found on many railway stations. Also good are the small Frooti cardboard boxes of mango, lemon and apple juice. For Rs 5 these are excellent, if a little sweet.

Coconut milk, straight from the young green coconut, is a popular drink, especially in the south. Another alternative to soft drinks is soda water – Bisleri, Spencer's and other brands are widely available. Not only does it come in a larger bottle, but it is also cheaper – generally around Rs 3.50. With soda water you can get excellent, and safe, lemon squash sodas.

Falooda is a popular drink made with milk, nuts, cream and vermicelli strands. Finally there's lassi, that oh so cool, refreshing and delicious iced curd (yoghurt) drink.

Alcohol
Alcohol is expensive – a bottle of Indian beer can cost anything from Rs 13 up to Rs 65 or more in a flashy hotel; Rs 20 to Rs 35 is the usual price range. In some states (like Goa and Pondicherry) it is very cheap, and in some (like Tamil Nadu) very expensive. Indian beers have delightful names like Golden Eagle, Rosy Pelican, Cannon Extra

Beer

India's climate being what it is, there are few travellers who don't relish a wee drop of the amber nectar at the end of a hot, dusty day or as an accompaniment to the setting sun at a beach cafe. There are a plethora of different brands, some of which are only brewed locally and others on a national basis.

In terms of taste, consistent quality, popularity and availability nationwide, the top five bottled beers would be Kingfisher, UB Export Lager, Kalyani Black Label, Black Knight and London Pilsner which average around 5% v/v. There are others which are usually only available locally but which are just as good such as Goa Pilsner Dry, Hamburg Pils, Khajuraho and Haywards. Draught beer (usually Kingfisher or London Pilsner) is also becoming more common in the big cities.

Beers which purport to be strong or even super strong (around 8% v/v) with dangerous names like Bullet, Hit and Knock Out are definitely in the 'hangovers installed and serviced' category and should be imbibed in moderation.

Since most beers are lagers, they should always be drunk as cold as possible. This is often not a fact appreciated by bar owners, so feel the bottle first before allowing the waiter to pop the top. Some beers, especially the stronger varieties, are totally unpalatable served in any way other than ice-cold.

Beer and other alcoholic drinks have always been regarded in India as luxury items and are frowned on by the Hindu and Muslim elites alike. As a result, they're heavily taxed by most state governments (except Pondicherry and Goa) making the price of a bottle of beer three to four times the price of a thali meal (Rs 30 to Rs 45 is the normal range).

Despite this disparity, brewing is a growth industry and bars proliferate except in Gujarat state where prohibition is still in force. Prohibition was a common feature in many states during the 1960s and its legacy survives (especially in Tamil Nadu) in the form of 'permit rooms' which are so dark you can't even see the drink in front of you. The overall impression is that you ought not to be involved in such nefarious activities as drinking beer. Other states have a much more enlightened attitude so bars are well lit, there's contemporary music playing and they're often the centre of social activity. They do, however, maintain licenced hours – commonly 11 am to 3 pm and 5 to 11 pm unless you're also eating.

Neither Pondicherry nor Goa have ever suffered from the approbation of rabid prohibitionists and it's there you'll find not only the cheapest beers (as low as Rs 13) but there are also no licenced hours – only the barperson's willingness to stay awake.

The majority of non-vegetarian restaurants these days also serve alcoholic drinks but you will never find them in vegetarian restaurants – they remain the preserve of those who eschew such impurities. ■

'Knock Out' beer (HF)

Strong, Bullet, Black Label, Knock Out, Kingfisher, Guru or Punjab. They're not too bad if you can find them cold, but most tend to be insipid. Avoid overindulgence or you'll wake up late in the morning feeling thoroughly disoriented with a thumping headache to boot. Preservatives (sulphur dioxide in the main) are lavishly used to combat the effects of climate on 'quality'.

Beer and other Indian interpretations of Western alcoholic drinks are known as IMFL – Indian Made Foreign Liquor. They include imitations of Scotch and brandy under a plethora of different brand names. The taste varies from hospital disinfectant to passable imitation Scotch. Always buy the best brand. Local drinks are known as Country Liquor and include *toddy*, a mildly alcoholic extract from the coconut palm flower, and *feni*, a distilled liquor produced from fermented cashew nuts or from coconuts. The two varieties taste quite different.

Arak is what the peasants (and bus drivers' best boys) drink to get blotto. It's a clear, distilled rice liquor and it creeps up on you without warning. Treat with caution and only ever drink it from a bottle produced in a government-controlled distillery. *Never, ever* drink it otherwise – hundreds of people die or are blinded every year in India as a result of drinking *arak* produced in illicit stills. You can assume it contains methyl alcohol (wood alcohol).

The only state in India which is 'dry' is Gujarat. You cannot buy beer or any other liquor here for love nor money, except at the most expensive hotels and even then you'll have to consume it in your room. Bars don't exist. The only way of satisfying that desperate, desert-like thirst is to visit one or both of the tiny enclaves of Daman or Diu where it flows freely. Gujaratis have discovered the same thing and flock there in the thousands at weekends.

THINGS TO BUY

India is packed with beautiful things to buy – you could easily load yourself up to the eyeballs with goodies you pick up around the country. The cardinal rule when purchasing handicrafts is to bargain and bargain hard. You can get a good idea of what is reasonable in quality and price by visiting the various state emporiums, particularly in New Delhi, and the Central Cottage Industries Emporiums which can be found in Delhi, Calcutta and Bombay. You can inspect items at these places from all over the country. Because prices are fixed, you will get an idea of how hard to bargain when you purchase similar items from regular dealers.

As with handicrafts in any country, don't buy until you have developed a little understanding and appreciation. Rushing in and buying the first thing you see will inevitably lead to later disappointment and a considerably reduced stash of travellers' cheques.

A Warning!

In touristy places, particularly places like Agra, Jaipur, Varanasi, and Calcutta, take extreme care with the commission merchants – these guys hang around waiting to pick you up and cart you off to their favourite dealers where whatever you pay will have a hefty margin built into it to pay their commission. Stories about 'my family's place', 'my brother's shop', 'special deal at my friend's place', are just stories and nothing more.

Whatever you might be told, if you are taken to a place, be it a hotel, craft shop, market or even restaurant, by a rickshaw driver or tout, the price you pay will be inflated. This can be by as much as 50%, so try to visit these places on your own. And don't underestimate the persistence of these guys. I heard of one desperately ill traveller who virtually collapsed into a cycle rickshaw in Agra and asked to be taken to a doctor – he ended up at a marble workshop, and the rickshaw driver insisted that, yes, indeed a doctor did work there! The high-pressure sales techniques of both the runners and the owners is the best in the world. Should you get up and leave without buying anything, the feigned anger is just that. Next time you turn up (if you do), it will be all smiles – and the prices will have dropped dramatically.

Another trap which many foreigners fall

into occurs when buying with a credit card. You may well be told that if you buy the goods, the merchant won't forward the credit slip for payment until you have received the goods, even if it is in three months time – this is total bullshit. No trader will be sending you as much as a postcard until he or she has received the money, in full, for the goods you are buying. What you'll find in fact is that within 48 hours of you signing the credit slip, the merchant has telexed the bank in Delhi and the money will have been credited to his or her account.

Also beware of any shop which takes your credit card out the back and comes back with the slip for you to sign. It has occurred that, while out of sight, the vendor will imprint a few more forms, forge your signature, and you'll be billed for items you haven't purchased. Get them to fill out the slip right in front of you.

If you believe any stories about buying anything in India to sell at a profit elsewhere, you'll simply be proving (once again) that old adage about separating fools from their money! Precious stones are a favourite for this game. They'll tell you that you can sell stones in Australia, Europe or the USA for several times the purchase price, and will even give you the (often imaginary!) addresses of dealers who will buy them. You'll also be shown written statements, supposedly from other travellers, documenting the money they have supposedly made – it's all a scam.

The stones you buy will be worth only a fraction of what you pay. Don't let greed cloud your judgement. It seems that with every edition of this book we make the warnings longer and more explicit, and yet we still get a steady trickle of letters from people with tales of woe, and they usually concern scams we specifically warn about!

While it is certainly a minority of traders who are actually involved in dishonest schemes, virtually all are involved in the commission racket, so you need to shop with care – take your time, be firm and bargain hard. Good luck!

Carpets

It may not surprise you that India produces and exports more hand-crafted carpets than Iran, but it probably is more of a surprise that some of them are of virtually equal quality. In Kashmir, where India's best carpets are produced, the carpet-making techniques and styles were brought from Persia even before the Moghul era. The art flourished under the Moghuls and today Kashmir is packed with small carpet producers. There are many carpet dealers in Delhi, Bombay, Calcutta, Madras and even Kovalam, as well as in Kashmir. Persian motifs have been much embellished on Kashmiri carpets, which come in a variety of sizes – three by five feet, four by six feet and so on. They are either made of pure wool, wool with a small percentage of silk to give a sheen (known as silk touch) or pure silk. The latter are more for decoration than hard wear. Expect to pay from Rs 5000 for a good quality four-by-six carpet and don't be surprised if the price is more than twice as high.

Other carpet-making areas include Badhoi and Mirzapur in Uttar Pradesh or Warangal and Eluru in Andhra Pradesh. In Kashmir and Rajasthan, the coarsely woven woollen *numdas* are made. These are more primitive and folksy than the fine carpets. Around the Himalaya and Uttar Pradesh *dhurries*, flat-weave cotton warp and weft rugs, are woven. In Kashmir *gabbas* are appliqué-like rugs. The many Tibetan refugees in India have brought their craft of making superbly colourful Tibetan rugs with them. A three-by-five Tibetan rug will be less than Rs 1000. Two of the best places to buy them are Darjeeling and Gangtok.

Unless you're an expert it is best to have expert advice or buy from a reputable dealer if you're spending large amounts of money on carpets. Check prices back home too; many Western carpet dealers sell at prices you would have difficulty matching even at the source.

Papier Mâché

This is probably the most characteristic Kashmiri craft. The basic papier-mâché article is made in a mould, then painted and polished in successive layers until the final intricate design is produced. Prices depend upon the complexity and quality of the painted design and the amount of gold leaf used. Items include bowls, cups, containers, jewel boxes, letter holders, tables, lamps, coasters, trays and so on. A cheap bowl might cost only Rs 25, a large, well-made item might approach Rs 1000.

Pottery
In Rajasthan interesting white-glazed pottery is made with hand-painted blue-flower designs – it's attractively simple. Terracotta images of the gods and children's toys are made in Bihar.

Metalwork
Copper and brass items are popular throughout India. Candle holders, trays, bowls, tankards and ashtrays are made in Bombay and other centres. In Rajasthan and Uttar Pradesh the brass is inlaid with exquisite designs in red, green and blue enamel. *Bidhri* is a craft of Andhra Pradesh and particularly Hyderabad, where silver is inlaid into gunmetal. Hookah pipes, lamp bases and jewellery boxes are made in this manner.

Jewellery
Many Indian women put most of their wealth into jewellery, so it is no wonder that so much of it is available. For Western tastes the heavy folk-art jewellery of Rajasthan has particular appeal. You'll find it all over the country, but particularly in Rajasthan. In the north you'll also find Tibetan jewellery, even chunkier and more folk-like than the Rajasthani variety.

If, on the other hand, you're looking for fine jewellery as opposed to folk jewellery, you may well find, as most of those who are *au fait* with *haute couture* do, that much of what is produced in India is way over the top. They simply don't know when to stop and certainly have no concept of elegant simplicity.

Leatherwork
Of course Indian leatherwork is not made from cow-hide but from buffalo-hide, camel or some other substitute. *Chappals*, those basic sandals found all over India, are the most popular purchase. In craft shops in Delhi you can find well-made leather bags, handbags and other items. Kashmiri leather shoes and boots, often of quite good quality, are widely found, along with coats and jackets of often abysmally low quality.

Textiles
This is still India's major industry and 40% of the total production is at the village level where it is known as khadi. There are government khadi emporiums (known as Khadi Gramodyog) around the country, and these are good places to buy handmade items of homespun cloth, such as the popular 'Nehru jackets' and the *kurta pajama*. Bedspreads, tablecloths, cushion covers or material for clothes are other popular khadi purchases.

There is an amazing variety of cloth styles, types and techniques around the country. In Gujarat and Rajasthan heavy material is embroidered with tiny mirrors and beads to produce the mirror-work used in everything from dresses to stuffed toys to wall hangings. Tie-dye work is also popular in Rajasthan and Kerala.

In Kashmir embroidered materials are made into shirts and dresses. Fine shawls and scarves of pashmina goats' wool are popular purchases in the Kulu Valley. Phulkari bedspreads or wall hangings come from the Punjab. Another place which is famous for its stunning embroidery work is Barmer, close to the Pakistani border and south-west of Jaisalmer in Rajasthan. Batik is a fairly recent introduction from Indonesia but already widespread; kalamkari cloth from Andhra Pradesh and Gujarat is an associated but far older craft.

Silks & Saris
Silk is cheap and the quality is often excellent. The 'silk capital' these days is

Kanchipuram in Tamil Nadu, although Varanasi is also popular, especially for silk saris.

If you are buying a silk sari, it helps to know a bit about both the silk and the sari. Saris are 5½ metres long, unless they have an attached blouse (choli), in which case they are six metres. Sari silk is graded and sold by weight – in grams per metres. Soft plain silk up to 60 grams per metre costs Rs 3.20 per gram; chiffon silk of 20 grams per metre is Rs 4.50 per gram, but you'll be lucky to find a sari of printed chiffon for less than Rs 600. A thin Kanchipuram silk sari weighs around 400 grams, a heavy sari around 600 grams. Pure gold jerri silk (the only one that doesn't blacken with time) costs Rs 12.50 per gram. A half-inch gold border weighs around 25 grams and is worth around Rs 320; a one-inch band, which weighs 35 grams, will cost about Rs 450. This must be added to the price of the silk.

Bronze Figures

In the south delightful small images of the gods are made by the age-old lost-wax process. A wax figure is made, a mould is formed around it and the wax is melted and poured out. The molten metal is poured in and when it's solidified the mould is broken open. Figures of Siva as dancing Nataraj are amongst the most popular.

Woodcarving

In the south, images of the gods are also carved out of sandalwood. Rosewood is used to carve animals – elephants in particular. Carved wooden furniture and other household items, either in natural finish or lacquered, are also made in various locations. In Kashmir intricately carved wooden screens, tables, jewellery boxes, trays and the like are carved from Indian walnut. They follow a similar pattern to that seen on the decorative trim of houseboats. Old temple carvings can be delightful.

Paintings

Reproductions of the beautiful old miniatures are painted in many places, but beware of paintings claimed to be antique – it's highly unlikely that they are. Also note that quality can vary widely; low prices often mean low quality and if you buy before you've had a chance to look at a lot of miniatures and develop some appreciation you'll inevitably find you bought unwisely. Udaipur (Rajasthan) has some good shops specialising in modern reproductions.

In Kerala, and, to a lesser extent, Tamil Nadu, you'll come across beautiful and incredibly vibrant miniature paintings on leaf skeletons enclosed on a printed card depicting domestic and rural scenes as well as gods and goddesses. They're a superb buy at between Rs 10 and Rs 20 depending on quality and how many you buy. Kovalam beach is the prime place to find them, though they're also marketed around Mahabalipuram (Tamil Nadu) these days.

Antiques

Articles over 100 years are not allowed to be exported from India without an export clearance certificate. If you have doubts about any item and think it could be defined as an antique, you can check with:

Bombay
    Superintending Archaeologist, Antiquities, Archaeological Survey of India, Sion Fort
Calcutta
    Superintending Archaeologist, Eastern Circle, Archaeological Survey of India, Narayani Bldg, Brabourne Rd
New Delhi
    Director, Antiquities, Archaeological Survey of India, Janpath
Madras
    Superintending Archaeologist, Southern Circle, Archaeological Survey of India, Fort St George
Srinagar
    Superintending Archaeologist, Frontier Circle, Archaeological Survey of India, Minto Bridge

Other Things to Buy

Marble inlay pieces from Agra are pleasant reminders of the beauty of the Taj. They come as either simple little pieces or larger items like jewellery boxes. Appliqué work is popular in many places, such as Orissa.

Indian musical instruments always have an attraction for travellers, although you don't see nearly as many backpackers lugging sitars or tablas around as you did 15 years ago. A more portable Indian music buy might be records or tapes. Certain Indian streets in major cities now resemble Taipei, Bangkok, Bali and Singapore in having street stalls and shops offering the full range of contemporary, '80s, '70s and even '60s Western music, though they're often pirated and on inferior tapes. You're looking at US$1.50 to US$2 per tape.

See the section under Music in Facts about the Country for details about purchasing musical instruments and tapes in India.

At the many Bata shoe shops in India, Western-style shoes are cheap and reasonably well made. The best quality men's shoes are about US$20 to US$25, far less than shoes of similar quality in London or New York.

THINGS TO SELL

All sorts of Western technological items are good things to sell in India, but cameras, tape

recorders and VCRs are as dead as a dodo in terms of making profit. The market is flooded with them. VCRs might well be entered into your passport to ensure they leave the country with you in any case. But there's always a good market, particularly in Calcutta, Delhi and Madras for your bottle of duty-free whisky.

Pocket calculators and watches are also a dead loss. Be very wary of the buying-to-sell-later game – most people buying things in India to sell elsewhere know what they are about and have spent a lot of time testing the market and establishing good relations with suppliers. Buying precious stones in Agra and Jaipur to sell in Nepal is a favourite game which is unlikely to return the average traveller any profit. We regularly get letters from unfortunate travellers who have been talked into buying precious stones which they are assured can be sold in the West for several times the purchase price. Inevitably it turns out the stones are worth a fraction of what was paid for them.

Getting There & Away

AIR

Buying a Plane Ticket

Your plane ticket will probably be the single most expensive item in your budget, and buying it can be an intimidating business. There is likely to be a multitude of airlines and travel agents hoping to separate you from your money, and it is always worth putting aside a few hours to research the current state of the market. Start early: some of the cheapest tickets have to be bought months in advance, and some popular flights sell out early. Talk to other recent travellers – they may be able to stop you making some of the same old mistakes. Look at the ads in newspapers and magazines, consult reference books and watch for special offers. Then phone around travel agents for bargains. (Airlines can supply information on routes and timetables; however, except at times of interairline war, they do not supply the cheapest tickets.) Find out the fare, the route, the duration of the journey and any restrictions on the ticket. (See Restrictions in the Air Travel Glossary in this chapter.) Then sit back and decide which is best for you.

You may discover that those impossibly cheap flights are 'fully booked, but we have another one that costs a bit more...' Or the flight is on an airline notorious for its poor safety standards and leaves you in the world's least favourite airport in mid-journey for 14 hours. Or they claim only to have the last two seats available for that country for the whole of July, which they will hold for you for a maximum of two hours. Don't panic – keep ringing around.

Use the fares quoted in this book as a guide only. They are approximate and based on the rates advertised by travel agents at the time of going to press. Quoted air fares do not necessarily constitute a recommendation for the carrier.

If you are travelling from the UK or the USA, you will probably find that the cheapest flights are being advertised by obscure bucket shops whose names haven't yet reached the telephone directory. Many such firms are honest and solvent, but there are a few rogues who will take your money and disappear, to reopen elsewhere a month or two later under a new name. If you feel suspicious about a firm, don't give them all the money at once – leave a deposit of 20% or so and pay the balance when you get the ticket. If they insist on cash in advance, go somewhere else. And once you have the ticket, ring the airline to confirm that you are actually booked on the flight.

You may decide to pay more than the rock-bottom fare by opting for the safety of a better-known travel agent. Firms such as STA, who have offices worldwide, Council Travel in the USA or Travel CUTS in Canada are not going to disappear overnight, leaving you clutching a receipt for a nonexistent ticket, but they do offer good prices to most destinations.

Once you have your ticket, write its number down, together with the flight number and other details, and keep the information somewhere separate. If the ticket is lost or stolen, this will help you get a replacement.

It's sensible to buy travel insurance as early as possible. If you buy it the week before you fly, you may find, for example, that you're not covered for delays to your flight caused by industrial action.

Air Travellers with Special Needs

If you have special needs of any sort – you've broken a leg, you're vegetarian, travelling in a wheelchair, taking the baby, terrified of flying – you should let the airline know as soon as possible so that they can make arrangements accordingly. You should remind them when you reconfirm your booking (at least 72 hours before departure) and again when you check in at the airport. It may also be worth ringing around the airlines before you make your booking to find out how they can handle your particular needs.

Airports and airlines can be surprisingly helpful, but they do need advance warning. Most international airports will provide escorts from check-in desk to plane where needed, and there should be ramps, lifts, accessible toilets and reachable phones. Aircraft toilets, on the other hand, are likely to present a problem; travellers should discuss this with the airline at an early stage and, if necessary, with their doctor.

Guide dogs for the blind will often have to travel in a specially pressurised baggage compartment with other animals, away from their owner, though smaller guide dogs may be admitted to the cabin. All guide dogs will be subject to the same quarantine laws (six months in isolation etc) as any other animal when entering or returning to countries currently free of rabies such as Britain or Australia. Deaf travellers can ask for airport and in-flight announcements to be written down for them.

Children under two travel for 10% of the standard fare (or free, on some airlines), as long as they don't occupy a seat. They don't get a baggage allowance either. 'Skycots' should be provided by the airline if requested in advance; these will take a child weighing up to about 10 kg. Children between two and 12 can usually occupy a seat for half to two-thirds of the full fare, and do get a baggage allowance. Push chairs can often be taken as hand luggage.

Round-the-World Fares

Round-the-World (RTW) fares are very competitive and are a popular way to travel to India. Basically there are two types – airline tickets and agent tickets. An airline RTW ticket usually means two or more airlines have joined together to market a ticket which takes you round the world on their combined routes. Within certain limitations of time and number of stopovers you can fly pretty well anywhere you choose using their combined routes so long as you keep moving in the same direction.

Compared to the full-fare tickets, which permit you to go anywhere you choose on any IATA airline so long as you do not exceed the 'maximum permitted mileage', these tickets are much less flexible. But they are also much cheaper.

Quite a few of these combined-airline RTW tickets go through India, including ones in combination with Air India which will allow you to make several stopovers within India. RTW tickets typically cost around A$2000 to A$3000, UK£1000 to UK£1750 and US$1250 to US$2500; tickets restricted to the northern hemisphere are cheaper

The other type of RTW ticket, the agent ticket, is a combination of cheap fares strung together by an enterprising travel agent. These can be cheaper than an airline RTW ticket but the choice of routes may not be so wide.

Cheap Tickets in India

Although you can get cheap tickets in Bombay and Calcutta, it is in Delhi that the real wheeling and dealing goes on. There are a number of 'bucket shops' around Connaught Place, but enquire with other travellers about their current trustworthiness! With most cheap tickets you will have to pay the full official fare through a bank – the agent gets you a bank form stating what the official fare is, you pay the bank and the bank pays the agent. You then receive a refund from the agent, but in rupees. Therefore, it is wise either to buy your ticket far enough ahead so that you can use those rupees up, or have plenty of bank exchange certificates in hand to change the rupees back. This also applies to credit card purchases.

Fares from Delhi to various European capitals cost between Rs 5000 to Rs 7000, a bit less from Bombay. The cheapest flights to Europe are with airlines like Aeroflot, LOT, Kuwait Airways, Syrian Arab Airways or Iraqi Airways. Delhi/Hong Kong/San Francisco costs around US$600.

Although Delhi is the best place for cheap tickets, many flights between Europe and South-East Asia or Australia pass through

Bombay; it's also the place for flights to East Africa. Furthermore, if you're heading east from India to Bangladesh, Myanmar or Thailand you'll probably find much better prices in Calcutta than in Delhi, even though there are fewer agents.

To/From Africa

There are plenty of flights between East Africa and Bombay due to the large Indian population in Kenya. Typical fares from Bombay to Nairobi are around US$440 return with either Ethiopian Airlines, Kenya Airways, Air India or Pakistan International Airlines (PIA; via Karachi).

Aeroflot operates a service between Delhi and Cairo (via Moscow).

To/From Australia & New Zealand

Advance-purchase return fares from the east coast of Australia to India range from A$1275 to A$1575 depending on the season and the destination in India. Fares are slightly cheaper to Madras and Calcutta than to Bombay or Delhi. From Australia fares are cheaper from Darwin or Perth than from the east coast. The low travel period is from March to September; peak is from October to February.

Tickets from Australia to London or other European capitals with an Indian stopover range from A$1930 to A$2390 return, again, depending on the season.

Return advance-purchase fares from New Zealand to India range from NZ$1821 to NZ$2171 depending on the season.

STA and Flight Centres International are major dealers in cheap air fares in both Australia and New Zealand. Check the travel agents' ads in the Yellow Pages and ring around.

To/From Bangladesh

Bangladesh Biman and Indian Airlines fly from Calcutta to Dhaka (US$43) and Chittagong (US$55) in Bangladesh. Many people use Biman from Calcutta through to Bangkok – partly because they're cheap and partly because they fly through Yangon (Rangoon) in Myanmar (Burma). Biman

should put you up overnight in Dhaka on this route but be careful – it appears they will only do so if your ticket is specifically endorsed that you are entitled to a room. If not, tough luck – you can either camp out overnight in the hot transit lounge or make your way into Dhaka on your own, pay for transport and accommodation, and get hit for departure tax the next day.

To/From Europe

Fares from continental Europe are mostly far more expensive than from London; see the To/From the UK section for comparison. At the rates listed below it's obviously much cheaper to go to London and buy a flight ticket from there.

From Amsterdam to Delhi/Bombay, return excursion fares are about DFL2400 (UK£900). To Calcutta, expect to pay around DFL2665 (UK£1000).

From Paris to Bombay/Delhi, return excursion fares range upwards from FFr7880 (UK£980; about ⅓ the standard return economy fare).

From Frankfurt to Bombay/Delhi, return excursion fares are around DM1950 (UK£820).

To/From Malaysia

Not many travellers fly between Malaysia and India because it is so much cheaper from Thailand, but there are flights between Penang and Madras. You can generally pick up one-way tickets for the Malaysian Airline System (MAS) flight from Penang travel agents for around M$680, which is rather cheaper than the regular fare.

To/From the Maldives

Thiruvananthapuram (Trivandrum)/Malé costs US$63. This is cheaper than flying to the Maldives from Colombo in Sri Lanka.

To/From Myanmar (Burma)

There are no land crossing points between Myanmar and India (or between Myanmar and any other country), so if you want to visit Myanmar your only choice is to fly there. Myanma Airways flies Calcutta/Yangon

(Rangoon); Bangladesh Biman flies Dhaka/ Yangon.

If you are coming from Bangkok via Myanmar, the one-way Bangkok-Yangon-Calcutta fare is around US$240 with Thai, or US$225 on Myanma Airways.

To/From Nepal

Royal Nepal Airlines Corporation (RNAC) and Indian Airlines share routes between India and Kathmandu. Both airlines give a 25% discount to those under 30 years of age on flights between Kathmandu and India; no student card is needed.

New Delhi is the main departure point for flights between India and Kathmandu. The daily one hour New Delhi to Kathmandu flight costs US$142.

Other cities in India with direct air connections with Kathmandu are Bombay (US$257), Calcutta (US$96) and Varanasi (US$71). The flight from Varanasi is the last leg of the popular New Delhi, Agra, Khajuraho, Varanasi, Kathmandu tourist flight.

If you want to see the mountains as you fly into Kathmandu from New Delhi or Varanasi, you must sit on the left side.

To/From Pakistan

Pakistan International Airlines (PIA) and Indian Airlines operate flights from Karachi to Delhi for US$67 and Lahore/Delhi for about US$128. Flights are also available between Karachi and Bombay.

To/From Singapore

Singapore is a great cheap-ticket centre and you can pick up Singapore/Delhi tickets for about S$1665 return.

To/From Sri Lanka

Far fewer travellers are continuing on to Sri Lanka from India due to the level of unrest and violence in the north of that unhappy country. In addition, because the ferry service is out of operation flying is now the only way to get there.

There are flights to and from Colombo (the capital of Sri Lanka) and Bombay,

Madras, Tiruchirappalli or Thiruvananthapuram (Trivandrum). Flights are most frequent on the Madras/Colombo route.

To/From Thailand

Bangkok is the most popular departure point from South-East Asia into Asia proper because of the cheap flights from there to Calcutta, Yangon (Rangoon) in Myanmar, Dhaka in Bangladesh or Kathmandu in Nepal. The popular Bangkok/Kathmandu flight is about US$250. You can make a stopover in Myanmar on this route and do a circuit of that fascinating country. Bangkok/ Calcutta via Myanmar is about US$225 to US$240.

To/From the UK

Various excursion fares are available from London to India, but you can get better prices through London's many cheap-ticket specialists or 'bucket shops'. Check the travel page ads in the *Times, Business Traveller* and the weekly 'what's on' magazines *City Limits* and *Time Out*; or check giveaway papers like *TNT*. Two reliable London bucket shops are Trailfinders (☎ (071) 938-3366), 46 Earls Court Rd, London W8; and STA (☎ (071) 937-9962), 74 Old Brompton Rd, London SW7 or 117 Euston Rd, London NW1.

Fares range from around UK£225 one way or UK£325 to UK£440 return, and depend very much on the carrier. The cheapest fares are usually with Middle Eastern or Eastern European airlines. You'll also find very competitive air fares to the subcontinent with Bangladesh Biman or Air Lanka. Thai International always seems to have competitive fares despite its high standards.

Some travel companies offer packages to Goa at competitive rates which include accommodation, breakfast, transfers and an Indrail Pass – check with travel agents and travel page ads in newspapers and magazines.

If you want to stop in India en route to Australia expect to pay around UK£500 to UK£600. You might find fares via Karachi

---

Air Travel Glossary

Apex Tickets Apex means Advance Purchase Excursion fare. It is a discounted ticket with restrictions. Usually, it must be paid for in advance, usually 21 days. Travel must be for a specified minimum period, normally 14 days, and you must return within a maximum period, usually 90 or 180 days. Stopovers are not allowed. There are penalties if you wish to change your route or departure dates. If you have to cancel or change an Apex ticket there are often heavy penalties involved; however, insurance can sometimes be taken out against these penalties.

Baggage Allowance This will be written on your ticket: usually one 20 kg item to go in the hold, plus one item of hand luggage.

Bucket Shop A travel agency specialising in discounted airline tickets. Airlines often offload drastically discounted tickets to bucket shops, as it's more profitable than flying with empty seats. Most bucket shops are reputable, but there is always the odd one who'll take your money and disappear. Be sure to check what you're buying.

Bumped Just because you have a confirmed seat doesn't mean you're going to get on the plane – see Overbooking.

Check In Airlines ask you to check in a certain time ahead of the flight departure (usually two hours on international flights). If you fail to check in on time and the flight is overbooked the airline can cancel your booking and give your seat to somebody else.

Confirmation Having an air ticket doesn't mean you have a seat until the agent has checked with the airline that your status is 'OK' or confirmed. Meanwhile you could just be on a waiting list.

Lost Tickets If you lose your airline ticket an airline will usually treat it like a travellers' cheque and, after enquiries, issue you with another one. Legally, however, an airline is entitled to treat it like cash and if you lose it then it's gone forever. This particularly applies to Indian Airlines, who will not accept responsibility for lost tickets. Take good care of your travel documents.

No Shows No shows are passengers who fail to show up for their flight. Full fare passengers who fail to turn up are sometimes entitled to travel on a later flight. The rest of us are penalised (see Apex Tickets).

(Pakistan) or Colombo (Sri Lanka) slightly cheaper than fares via India.

Most British travel agents are registered with ABTA (Association of British Travel Agents). If you have paid for your flight to an ABTA-registered agent who then goes out of business, ABTA will guarantee a refund or an alternative. Unregistered bucket shops are riskier but are also sometimes cheaper.

To/From the USA & Canada
The cheapest return air fares from the US west coast to India are around US$1200. Another way of getting there is to fly to Hong Kong and get a ticket from there. Tickets to Hong Kong cost about US$500 one way and just under US$800 return from San Francisco or Los Angeles; in Hong Kong you can find one-way tickets to Bombay for US$300 depending on the carrier. Alternatively, you can fly to Singapore for around US$535 one way, US$835 return or to Bangkok for US$535 one way, US$865 return.

From the east coast you can find return tickets to Bombay or Delhi for around US$1100. The cheapest one-way tickets will be around US$550 to US$600. An alternative way of getting to India from New York is to fly to London and buy a cheap fare from there.

Check the Sunday travel sections of papers like the *New York Times, San Francisco Chronicle/Examiner* or *Los Angeles Times* for cheap fares. Good budget travel agents include the student travel chains STA or CIEE. The magazine *Travel Unlimited* (PO Box 1058, Allston, Mass 02134) publishes details of the cheapest air fares and courier possibilities for destinations all over the world from the USA.

Open Jaw This is a return ticket where you fly out to one place but return from another. If available this can save you backtracking to your arrival point.

Overbooking Airlines hate to fly with empty seats and since every flight has some passengers who fail to show up (see No Shows) airlines often book more passengers than they have seats. Usually the excess passengers balance those who fail to show up but occasionally somebody gets bumped. If this happens guess who it is most likely to be? The passengers who check in late, of course.

Reconfirmation At least 72 hours prior to departure time of a flight you must contact the airline and 'reconfirm' that you intend to be on the flight. If you don't do this the airline can delete your name from the passenger list and you could lose your seat. You don't have to reconfirm if your stopover is less than 72 hours. It doesn't hurt to reconfirm more than once, just to make *absolutely* sure your seat is waiting for you!

Transferred Tickets Airline tickets cannot be transferred from one person to another. Travellers sometimes try to sell the return half of their ticket, but officials can ask you to prove that you are the person named on the ticket. This is unlikely to happen on domestic flights, but on an international flight, tickets may be compared with passports.

Travel Agencies Travel agencies vary widely and you should ensure you use one that suits your needs. Some simply handle tours while full-service agencies handle everything from tours and tickets to car rental and hotel bookings. A good one will do all these things and can save you a lot of money but if all you want is a ticket at the lowest possible price, then you really need an agency specialising in discounted tickets. A discounted ticket agency, however, may not be useful for other things, like hotel bookings.

Travel Periods Some officially discounted fares, Apex fares in particular, vary with the time of year. There is often a low (off-peak) season and a high (peak) season. Sometimes there's an intermediate or shoulder season as well. At peak times, when everyone wants to fly, not only will the officially discounted fares be higher, but so will unofficially discounted fares or there may simply be no discounted tickets available. Usually the fare depends on your outward flight – if you depart in the high season and return in the low season, you pay the high-season fare. ■

Fares from Canada are similar to the USA fares. From Vancouver the route is like that from the USA west coast, with the option of going via Hong Kong. From Toronto it is easier to travel via London.

The *Toronto Globe & Mail* and the *Vancouver Sun* carry travel agents' ads. The magazine *Great Expeditions* (PO Box 8000-411, Abbotsford BC V2S 6H1) is useful.

LAND

Drivers of cars and riders of motorbikes will need the vehicle's registration papers, liability insurance and an international drivers' permit in addition to their domestic licence. Beware: there are two kinds of international permit, one of which is needed mostly for former British colonies. You will also need a *carnet de passage en douane*, which is effectively a passport for the vehicle, and acts as

a temporary waiver of import duty. The carnet may also need to have listed any more expensive spares that you're planning to carry with you, such as a gearbox. This is necessary when travelling in many countries in Asia, Africa and Central and South America, and is designed to prevent car import rackets. Contact your local automobile association for details about all documentation.

Liability insurance is not available in advance for many out-of-the-way countries, but has to be bought when crossing the border. The cost and quality of such local insurance varies wildly, and you will find in some countries that you are effectively travelling uninsured.

Anyone who is planning to take their own vehicle with them needs to check in advance what spares and petrol are likely to be available. Lead-free is not on sale worldwide, and neither is every little part for your car.

Cycling is a cheap, convenient, healthy, environmentally sound and above all fun way of travelling. One note of caution: before you leave home, go over your bike with a fine-toothed comb and fill your repair kit with every imaginable spare. As with cars and motorbikes, you won't necessarily be able to buy that crucial gizmo for your machine when it breaks down somewhere in the back of beyond as the sun sets.

Bicycles can travel by air. You *can* take them to pieces and put them in a bike bag or box, but it's much easier simply to wheel your bike to the check-in desk, where it should be treated as a piece of baggage. You may have to remove the pedals and turn the handlebars sideways so that it takes up less space in the aircraft's hold; check all this with the airline well in advance, preferably before you pay for your ticket.

For more details on driving your own vehicle in India, see the Driving section in the Getting Around chapter.

To/From Bangladesh

Unfortunately most land entry and exit points are closed, so the choice is much more limited than a glance at the map would indicate. You do not need an exit permit to leave Bangladesh on the Calcutta route; you may need one on the Darjeeling route.

Calcutta to Dhaka The Calcutta to Dhaka route is the one used by the majority of land travellers. Stage one is a bus from Calcutta to Bangaon (two hours), the town closest to the border. From Bangaon it's about 10 km by rickshaw to the border at Haridaspur on the Indian side.

It's possible to change money at the border. Crossing the border takes an hour or two with the usual form filling and stamping. From the border it's about 10 minutes by rickshaw to Benapole on the Bangladesh side. If you leave Calcutta in the early afternoon you should be in Benopol (the Bangladeshi border town) in time for the bus departures between 6 and 8.30 pm. There are

no buses in the daytime between the border and Benopol.

Alternatively, you can take a Coaster (minibus) from the Bangladeshi border post to Jessore, from where you can proceed to Dhaka. The last 'direct' buses from Jessore leave around 1 to 2 pm.

From Benopol it's an eight or nine-hour bus trip to Dhaka, a distance of 291 km. The first leg of the trip, to Jessore, takes about 1½ hours; then it's an hour to a small ferry crossing. It only takes about 10 minutes to cross the river but the waiting, loading and unloading will occupy an hour or two. Another 1½ hours takes you to a larger ferry crossing at Aricha. Getting across the river takes a couple of hours; going to Dhaka this ferry takes about half an hour longer as the crossing is upstream. Finally it's another 1½ hours to Dhaka.

Coming from Dhaka it's wise to book your seat on the bus at least a day in advance. The buses that operate overnight between Dhaka and the border are direct. You can take a bus from 8 to 11 pm and arrive in Benapole at dawn.

From Darjeeling From Darjeeling to Siliguri, you can take the fast buses (three hours) or the slower but more picturesque toy train (about 10 hours). If you take the train, it is more convenient to get off at New Jalpaiguri than at the other two stations in Siliguri.

The trip from New Jalpaiguri takes two hours and costs Rs 7 by train to Haldibari, the Indian border checkpoint, but you have a little travelling yet before you reach Bangladesh. It's a seven-km walk along the disused railway line from Haldibari to the Bangladesh border point at Chiliharti! 'It's here you discover how much excess baggage you're carrying', wrote one traveller. You should be able to arrange for a rickshaw to carry you the first few km to the Bangladeshi border, however.

There's a train station at Chiliharti from where you can set off into Bangladesh. Bring some takas (the currency of Bangladesh) in with you. This is officially illegal but changing money in Chiliharti is virtually impossible. You should be able to change some at Haldibari.

To/From Europe

The classic way of getting to India has always been overland. Sadly the events in the Middle East and Afghanistan have turned the cross-Asian flow into a trickle. Afghanistan is still off limits but the trip through Turkey, Iran and into Pakistan is straightforward these days.

The Asia overland trip is certainly not the breeze it once was, but it is definitely possible. Many travellers combine travel to the subcontinent with the Middle East by flying from India or Pakistan to Amman in Jordan or one of the Gulf states. A number of the London-based overland companies operate their bus or truck trips across Asia on a regular basis. Check with Exodus, Encounter Overland, Top Deck or Hann Overland for more information.

For more detail on the Asian overland route see the Lonely Planet guides to Pakistan, Iran and Turkey.

To/From Nepal

There are direct buses from Delhi to Kathmandu, but these generally get bad reports from travellers. It's cheaper and more satisfactory to organise this trip yourself.

For more details of the land routes into Nepal see the Uttar Pradesh, Bihar and West Bengal sections in this book. The most popular routes are from Raxaul (near Muzaffarpur), Sunauli (near Gorakhpur), and Kakarbhitta (near Siliguri). If you are heading straight to Nepal from Delhi or elsewhere in western India then the Gorakhpur to Sunauli route is the most convenient. From Calcutta, Patna or most of eastern India, Raxaul to Birganj is the best entry point. (See, however, the warning in the Bihar chapter about immigration procedures at Birganj.) From Darjeeling it's easiest to go to Kakarbhitta.

To give an idea of costs, a 2nd-class rail ticket from Delhi to Gorakhpur costs US$4

and buses from Gorakhpur to the border and then on to Kathmandu cost another US$4.

There are other roads into Nepal from northern Bihar to the east of Birganj but they are rarely used by travellers. Furthermore, a couple of border crossings have recently been closed. One such is the crossing between Jogbani (near Purnia) and Biratnagar. Additionally, the narrow-gauge railway from Jaynagar (near Darbhanga) which crosses the border to Janakpur (an attractive Nepalese city famous as the birthplace of Sita) is also no longer open.

It is also possible to cross the border at Nepalganj, Dhangadi and Mahendranagar in the far west of Nepal. The entry at Mahendrenagar, just over the border from the northern Uttar Pradesh village of Banbassa, is the most interesting possibility. It may take a while for things to start operating smoothly, but when they do, this will present an interesting alternative route to/from Delhi. When the Mahendra Highway is finally completed (theoretically in mid-1993, but don't count on it) the route will be open all year, but until then it is a dry season-only proposition, and strictly for the hardy. Allow at least 13 hours for Delhi-Mahendrenagar, nine hours for Mahendrenagar-Nepalganj, and 16 hours for Nepalganj-Kathmandu. See under Banbassa in the Uttar Pradesh chapter for more details on this route.

To/From Pakistan

At present, due to the unstable political situation between India and Pakistan, there's only one border crossing open.

Amritsar to Lahore Due to the unrest in the Punjab the situation at this border crossing is liable to change. Presently, the crossing at Attari is open daily to all traffic. It may be worth checking the situation in the Punjab with the Home Ministry in New Delhi or the Indian Embassy in Islamabad, Pakistan, before you travel.

For the Lahore (Pakistan) to Amritsar (India) train you have to buy one ticket from Lahore to Attari, the Indian border town, and another from Attari to Amritsar. The train departs Lahore daily at 11.30 am and arrives in Amritsar at 3 pm after a couple of hours at the border passing through immigration and customs. Going the other way, you leave Amritsar at 9.30 am and arrive in Lahore at 1.30 pm. Pakistan immigration and customs are handled at Lahore station. Sometimes, however, border delays can make the trip much longer.

From Amritsar you cannot buy a ticket until the morning of departure and there are no seat reservations – arrive early and push. Moneychangers offer good rates for Pakistan rupees on the platform, but you cannot get Indian rupees coming the opposite way. Travellers have reported that whichever direction you're travelling, the exchange rate between Indian and Pakistan rupees is more advantageous to you on the Pakistan side of the border, but you can change Indian rupees to Pakistani rupees or vice versa at Wagah (the Pakistani border town) and in Amritsar – no matter what the Pakistanis may tell you!

Since the rail route opened far fewer travellers use the road. It's mainly of interest to people with vehicles or those on overland buses. By public transport the trip from Lahore entails taking a bus to the border at Wagah between Lahore and Amritsar, walking across the border and then taking another bus or taxi into Amritsar.

From Lahore, buses and minibuses depart from near the general bus station on Badami Bagh. The border opens at 9.15 am and closes at 3.30 pm. If you're stuck on the Pakistan side you can stay at the *PTDC Motel*, where there are dorm beds and double rooms.

To/From South-East Asia

In contrast to the difficulties of travelling overland in central Asia, the South-East Asian overland trip is still wide open and as popular as ever. From Australia the first step is to Indonesia – either Bali or Jakarta. Although most people fly from an east coast city or from Perth to Bali, there are also flights from Darwin and from Port Hedland in the north of Western Australia. The short-est route is the flight between Darwin and Kupang on the Indonesian island of Timor.

From Bali you head north through Java to Jakarta, from where you either travel by ship or fly to Singapore or continue north through Sumatra and then cross to Penang in Malaysia. After travelling around Malaysia you can fly from Penang to Madras in India or, more popularly, continue north to Thailand and eventually fly out from Bangkok to India, perhaps with a two-week stopover in Myanmar. Unfortunately, crossing by land from Myanmar to India (or indeed to any other country) is forbidden by the Myanmar government.

An interesting alternative route is to travel from Australia to Papua New Guinea and from there cross to Irian Jaya; then to Sulawesi in Indonesia. There are all sorts of travel variations possible in South-East Asia; the region is a delight to travel through, it's good value for money, the food is generally excellent and healthy, and all in all it's an area of the world not to be missed. For full details see the Lonely Planet guide *South-East Asia on a shoestring*.

SEA

The ferry service from Rameswaram, southern India, to Talaimannar in Sri Lanka is currently suspended due to the unrest in Sri Lanka. This was a favourite route for shipping arms and equipment to the Tamil guerrilla forces in the north of the country.

The shipping services between Africa and India only carry freight (including vehicles), not passengers.

The service between Penang and Madras is no longer operating.

TOURS

There are numerous foreign eco-travel and adventure travel companies which can provide unusual and interesting trips in addition to companies that provide more standard tours. There are too many to include them all; check newspapers and travel magazines for advertisements, and journals such as *Earth Journal* (USA) for listings. Companies that organise tours to various parts of India include the following:

Adventure Center
1311 63rd St, Suite 200, Emeryville, CA 94608, USA (☎ (800) 227-8747)

All Adventure Travel, Inc.
PO Box 4307, Boulder, CO 80306, USA (☎ (303) 440-7924)

Asian Pacific Adventures
826 S. Sierra Bonita Ave, Los Angeles, CA 90036 (☎ (800) 825-1680)

Encounter Overland
267 Old Brompton Rd, London SW5 9JA, UK (☎ (071) 370-6845)

Exodus Expeditions
9 Weir Rd, London SW12 OLT, UK (☎ (081) 673-0859)

Inner Asia Expeditions
2627 Lombard St, San Francisco, CA 94123, USA (☎ (415) 922-0448; fax (415) 346-5535)

New Experience Holidays
Lot 48, Wentworth Ave, Mt Nebo, Qld, 4520, Australia (☎ (07) 289-8163; fax (07) 289-8166)

Odyssey Tours
20 South Terrace, Clifton Hill, Melbourne, 3068, Australia (☎ (03) 489-2553)
3rd Floor, Raadhuisstraat 46, PO Box 11778, 1001 GT Amsterdam (☎ (020) 253-258)
(Odyssey also has offices in India; see the Goa chapter for details.)

Venturetreks
164 Parnell Rd (PO Box 37610), Parnell, Auckland, New Zealand (☎ (09)379-9855; fax (09) 377-0320)

World Expeditions
3rd Floor, 441 Kent St, Sydney, NSW, 2000, Australia (☎ (02) 264-3366; fax (02) 261-1974)

1st Floor, 393 Little Bourke St, Melbourne, Vic, 3000 (☎ (03) 670-8400; fax (03) 670-7474)

DEPARTURE TAX

For flights to neighbouring countries (Pakistan, Sri Lanka, Bangladesh, Nepal) the departure tax is Rs 100, but to other countries it's Rs 300.

This airport tax applies to everybody, even to babies who do not occupy a seat – in most countries airport tax applies only to seat occupants or adults. The method of collecting the tax varies but generally you have to pay it before you check in, so look out for an airport tax counter as you enter the check-in area.

INSURANCE

Regardless of how you plan to travel to India, it's worth taking out travel insurance. Work out what you need. You may not want to insure that grotty old army surplus backpack – but everyone should be covered for the worst possible case: an accident, for example, that will require hospital treatment and a flight home. It's a good idea to make a copy of your policy, in case the original is lost. If you are planning to travel for a long time, the insurance may seem very expensive – but if you can't afford it, you certainly won't be able to afford to deal with a medical emergency overseas.

Getting Around

AIR

India's major domestic airline, the government-run Indian Airlines, flies extensively throughout the nation and into neighbouring countries. Air India also operates domestic services, principally on the Bombay-Delhi, Bombay-Calcutta, Delhi-Calcutta and Bombay-Madras routes.

Vayudoot is India's second domestic airline, and it too is owned and run by the central government. It operates the twin-engined Dornier, Fokker F27 and Avro aircraft. Vayudoot flies to many small centres not covered by Indian Airlines, opening new possibilities for visitors with limited time.

One advantage of Vayudoot is that its flights are less crowded so it is often possible to get a booking only one day in advance. The major disadvantage is that its booking offices are not computerised, so getting a confirmed booking can be a major exercise. Fares on identical routes can also be a good deal more expensive than those offered by Indian Airlines.

In the last few years a number of small feeder airlines have started operating, such as Jagsan Airlines which flies out of Delhi to Chandigarh and Shimla, and Continental and East West, both of which operate out of Bombay.

Booking Flights

Indian Airlines has computerised booking at all but the smallest offices, so getting flight information and reservations is relatively simple – it's just getting to the head of the queue that takes the time. Nevertheless, all flights are heavily booked and you need to plan as far in advance as possible. Most flights also have a long waiting list, or 'chance list', and it's a good idea to stick your name on this, even if the list seems impossibly long. Strange things happen within the Indian Airlines computer system – 'full' flights suddenly are only half full, and spare seats appear after you've been told there's 'no chance' – so stick your name on that list just in case.

If you want to know what pre-computer air travel was like, however, Vayudoot can show you. Getting a seat on a Vayudoot flight is still fraught with the vicissitudes of chance. This situation is hampered by some of the Vayudoot agents who are either not kept up to date or don't make it their business to keep up with current flight schedules. Getting booked on a nonexistent flight is not impossible. Wherever possible, buy your ticket direct from a Vayudoot office.

The small, private operators are reasonably efficient.

Tickets

All Indian Airline tickets must be paid for with foreign currency or by credit card. Encashment certificates are not acceptable. Change, where appropriate, is given in rupees at the current bank rate (on the 40% official/60% free-market rate basis).

Infants up to two years old travel at 10% of the adult fare, but only one infant can travel at this fare per adult. Children two to 12 years old travel at 50% fare. There is no student reduction for overseas visitors but there is a youth fare for people 12 to 30 years old. This allows a 25% reduction.

There are heavy penalties for cancellations or no-shows, but only on the rupee tariff. Tickets bought with foreign currency are not subject to cancellation charges, but if you bought the ticket overseas a refund will not be given in India. Cancellations on tickets bought with a credit card in India will be refunded with a credit slip (credited to your account) but not cash. Alternatively, you can use the credit towards paying for a different flight.

Unlike almost every other airline in the world, Indian Airlines accepts no responsibility if you lose your tickets. They absolutely will not replace lost tickets, so treat them like cash, not travellers' cheques.

Fares

The accompanying chart details the main Indian Airlines and Vayudoot domestic routes and fares.

Indian Airlines also have a 21-day 'Discover India' fare which costs US$400. This allows unlimited travel on their domestic routes and can be reasonable value if you have limited time.

Indian Airlines also has a 21-day 'South India Excursion' which gives a 30% discount on selected routes in the south.

Check In

The check-in time depends on the type of aircraft. With Airbuses it's 75 minutes; for all other flights it's one hour. With all flights to and from Srinagar, an extra half hour is required.

Air India domestic flights leave from the international rather than the domestic terminals, and the check-in time is generally two hours, so make sure you know which carrier you are flying with. If you book an internal flight on the main trunk routes from overseas, chances are it will be with Air India – not many countries can justify the use of Jumbo jets on internal routes!

On some internal routes you are required to identify your checked-in baggage on the tarmac immediately prior to boarding. Don't forget to do this or it won't be loaded onto the plane. There's probably nowhere else in the world where you have to do this but it's an excellent security arrangement.

In Flight

Indian Airlines flights usually have a choice of vegetarian or non-vegetarian meals; unless you request otherwise, Westerners will always be assumed to be non-veg. The food is usually not very good in either case and Indian Airlines' flight attendants can be grumpy. All Indian Airlines flights are non-smoking.

Other minor Indian Airlines irritations are the complete lack of effort to keep you informed of delays, check-in counters that are rarely open as far ahead as the requested reporting time, and the snail's pace at which luggage is unloaded.

Offices

The Indian Airlines' office addresses are listed here with the distance from the office to the airport:

Agartala (12 km)
    Khosh Mahal Bldg, Central Rd (☎ 5470)
Agra (7 km)
    Hotel Clarks Shiraz, 54 Taj Rd (☎ 36-0153)
Ahmedabad (10 km)
    Airlines House, Lal Darwaja (☎ 35-3333)
Allahabad (12 km)
    18 Tashkant Marg, Auto Sales Bldg (☎ 60-2832)
Amritsar (11 km)
    48 The Mall (☎ 64-433)
Aurangabad (10 km)
    Dr Rajendra Prasad Marg (☎ 24-864)
Bagdogra (14 km)
    Hotel Sinclairs, Mallaguri, Siliguri (☎ 20-692)
Bangalore (13 km)
    Housing Board Bldg, Kempegowda Rd (☎ 21-1211)
Bhavnagar (8 km)
    Diwanpara Rd (☎ 27-144)
Bhopal (11 km)
    Bhadbhada Rd, TT Nagar (☎ 55-0480)
Bhubaneswar (4 km)
    Unit 1, Raj Path, Bapuji Nagar (☎ 40-0533)
Bhuj (6 km)
    Outside Waniawad Gate, Station Rd (☎ 20-204)
Bombay (26 km)
    Air India Bldg, 1st floor, Madam Cama Rd, Nariman Point (☎ 287-6161, 202-3031)
Calcutta (16 km)
    Airlines House, 39 Chittaranjan Ave (☎ 26-3135, 26-3390, 26-2548)
Chandigarh (11 km)
    SCO-186-187-188 Sector 17C (☎ 40-539)
Chittagong
    Hotel Agrabad (☎ 50-2814)
Coimbatore (11 km)
    Civil Aerodrome, Peelamedy (☎ 22-743)
Colombo, Sri Lanka (18 km)
    95 Sir Baron Jayatilaka Mawatha (☎ 23-136)
Dabolim, Goa (37 km)
    Dempo House, Campal, Panaji (☎ 4007)
Delhi (13 km)
    Malhotra Bldg, Connaught Place (☎ 331-0517)
    Barakhamba Rd (☎ 331-3732)
    Domestic Terminal (24 hours) (☎ 144, 141)
Dhaka, Bangladesh (7 km)
    Sharif Mansion, Motijheel (☎ 23-1687)

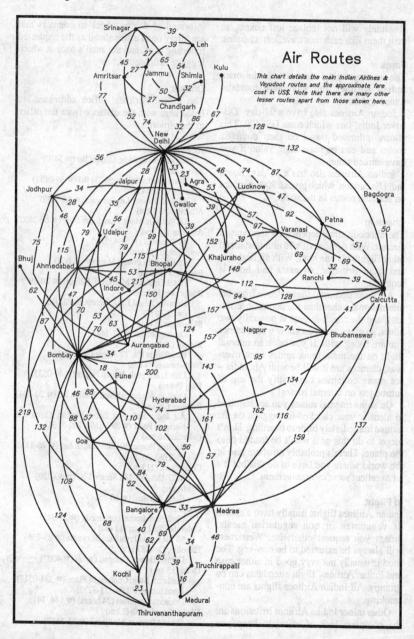

Air Routes

This chart details the main Indian Airlines & Vayudoot routes and the approximate fare cost in US$. Note that there are many other lesser routes apart from those shown here.

Dibrugarh (26 km)
CIWTC Bungalow, Assam Medical College Rd
(☎ 20-114)

Dimapur (5 km)
Dimapur-Imphal Rd (☎ 2875)

Gorakhpur (7 km)
Park Rd (☎ 33-6663)

Gawahati (22 km)
Paltan Bazar (☎ 23-128)

Gwalior (12 km)
Tansen Marg, Barrar (☎ 24-433)

Hyderabad (9 km)
Saifabad, near Legislative Assembly Bldg
(☎ 23-7237, 23-6902)

Imphal (7 km)
Mahatma Gandhi Rd (☎ 20-199)

Indore (9 km)
Dr R S Bhandari Marg (☎ 7069)

Jabalpur (15 km)
20, MIG Flats, Gobind Bhavan (☎ 22-178)

Jaipur (15 km)
Mundhara Bhavan, Ajmer Rd (☎ 70-624,
74-500)

Jammu (7 km)
Tourist Reception Centre, Veer Marg (☎ 42-735)

Jamnagar (10 km)
Indra Mahal, Bhind Bhanjan Rd (☎ 78-569)

Jodhpur (5 km)
Ratanada Rd (☎ 28-600)

Jorhat (6 km)
Tarajan Rd, Garhali (☎ 20-011)

Kabul, Afghanistan (7 km)
Chanrahi Malick, Asghar Desh (☎ 31-469)

Kanpur (13 km)
15/54A Civil Lines (☎ 21-1095)

Karachi, Pakistan (15 km)
Hotel Inter-Continental (c/o PIA) (☎ 51-1577)

Kathmandu, Nepal (8 km)
26 Durbar Marg (☎ 21-1987)

Keshod (8 km)
Rajmahal Plot, near the railway station (☎ 344)

Khajuraho (5 km)
Khajuraho Hotel (☎ 2035)

Kochi (Cochin) (6 km)
Durbar Hall Rd, Ernakulam (☎ 35-2065)

Kozikhode (Calicut)
Eroth Centre, Bank Rd (☎ 65-482)

Lahore, Pakistan (10 km)
Falletis Hotel, Eagerton Rd (☎ 21-1249)

Leh (8 km)
Ibex Guest House (☎ 276)

Lucknow (15 km)
Clarks Avadh, 5 Mahatma Gandhi Marg
(☎ 24-0927)

Madras (16 km)
19 Marshalls Rd, Egmore (☎ 47-7977)

Madurai (12 km)
Pandyan House, 7A West Veli St (☎ 22-795)

Malé, Maldives (3 km)
Beach Hotel (☎ 32-3003)

Mangalore (20 km)
Hotel Poonja International, KS Rao Rd
(☎ 21-300)

Mysore
Hotel Mayura Hoysala, 2 Jhansi Lakshmi Bai Rd
(☎ 21-486)

Nagpur (10 km)
242A Manohar Niwas, Rabindranath Tagore Rd,
Civil Lines (☎ 53-3962)

Patna (8 km)
South Gandhi Maidan (☎ 22-6433)

Porbandar (5 km)
Kamal Deep, Station Rd (☎ 20-057)

Port Blair (4 km)
Tagore Marg (☎ 21-108)

Pune (8 km)
15 Sadhu Vishwani Rd (☎ 66-1541)

Raipur (19 km)
LIC Bldg (☎ 28-707)

Rajkot (4 km)
Angel Chamber, Station Rd (☎ 27-916)

Ranchi (7 km)
Welfare Centre, Main Rd (☎ 21-841)

Silchar (25 km)
Red Cross Rd (☎ 20-072)

Srinagar (13 km)
Air Cargo Complex Bldg, Shervani Marg
(☎ 73-231)

Tezpur (18 km)
Jankin Rd (☎ 162)

Tiruchirappalli (8 km)
Southern Railway Employees Co-op Credit
Society Bldg, Dindigul Rd (☎ 42-233)

Tirupathi (15 km)
Hotel Vishnupriya, Ranigunta Rd (☎ 2369)

Thiruvananthapuram (Trivandrum) (7 km)
Mascot Hill Bldg, Museum Rd (☎ 66-370)

Udaipur (25 km)
LIC Bldg, outside Delhi Gate (☎ 24-433)

Vadodara (Baroda) (6 km)
University Rd, Fateh Ganj (☎ 32-9668)

Varanasi (22 km)
Mint House Motel, Vadunath Marg, Cantonment
(☎ 43-746)

Vijayawada (22 km)
Bunder Rd, Chanderamalipuram (☎ 72-218)

Visakhapatnam (14 km)
Jeevan Prakash, LIC Bldg Complex (☎ 64-665)

BUS

Travelling around India by train has such an
overpowering image – those up-and-down
mail trains, the sights, sounds and smells of
the stations, the romantic names and exotic
old steam engines – that people forget there

is also an extensive and well-developed bus system. In many cases it simply extends from the railway system, fanning out from railhead stations, or it goes where trains do not or cannot – to Kashmir for example.

There are, however, many places where buses offer a parallel service to the trains and in some cases a better or faster one. Where the only trains are on the narrower gauges it will often be much faster to take a bus – this includes the routes in northern Bihar and Uttar Pradesh to the Nepal border. Agra to Jaipur, Delhi to Jaipur, Delhi to Haridwar, and Bombay to Goa are examples of routes where buses are faster and more convenient than trains.

Types

Buses vary widely from state to state, although generally bus travel is crowded, cramped, slow and uncomfortable, especially in the north. In some states there is a choice of buses on the main routes – ordinary, express, semi-luxe, deluxe, and even deluxe air-con.

Ordinary buses generally have five seats across, although if there's only five people sitting in them consider yourself lucky! There's usually mounds of baggage in the aisles, chickens under seats and in some

more remote places there'll be people travelling 'upper class' (ie, on the roof) as well. These buses tend to be frustratingly slow, stopping frequently – often for seemingly no reason – and for long periods, and can take forever. They're certainly colourful and can be an interesting way to travel on short journeys. On longer trips you'll probably wish you'd stayed at home.

Express buses are a big improvement in that they stop far less often. They're still crowded, but at least you feel as though you're getting somewhere. The fare is usually a few rupees more than on an ordinary bus – well worth the extra.

Semi-luxe are also five seats across, but they have more padding and 'luxuries' such as tinted windows, and the buses stop infrequently. The fare is about 20% more than the ordinary fare, which discourages many of the locals who can only afford the cheapest mode of travel. The big difference between deluxe and semi-luxe is that deluxe buses have only four seats across and these will usually recline.

There is generally a state-operated bus company in each state, and in most places this is backed up by privately operated buses – although they may only operate on certain routes. Despite the extra speed buses often

All aboard!

offer, they become uncomfortable sooner than trains, and are less safe. If it's a long trip, particularly overnight, it's better opting for a train.

The thing that foreigners find hardest to cope with on the buses is the music. The Hindi pop music is usually played at maximum volume and seems to screech on and on without end. Requests to turn it down are usually greeted with amusement and complete disbelief. Just as bad are the video machines found on most deluxe buses. These generally screen macho garbage, also at full volume, for hours on end. If you're travelling overnight by bus, try to avoid video coaches.

Getting a Seat

If there are two of you, work out a bus-boarding plan where one of you can guard the gear while the other storms the bus in search of a seat. The other accepted method is to pass a newspaper or article of clothing through the open window and place it on an empty seat, or ask a passenger to do it for you. Having made your 'reservation' you can then board the bus after things have simmered down. This method rarely fails.

The big advantage of buses over trains is that they go more frequently and getting one involves comparatively little predeparture hassle. You can, however, often make advance reservations for a small additional fee, but this usually only applies to semi-luxe and deluxe services. Private buses should always be booked in advance.

At many bus stations there is a separate women's queue. You may not notice this because the relevant sign will not be in English and there may not be any women queueing. Usually the same ticket window will handle the male and the female queue, taking turn about. What this means is that women can usually go straight up to the front of the queue (ie straight up beside the front of the male queue) and get almost immediate service.

Baggage

Baggage is generally carried for free on the roof so it's an idea to take a few precautions.

Make sure it's tied on properly and that nobody dumps a tin trunk on top of your (relatively) fragile backpack. At times a tarpaulin will be tied across the baggage – make sure it covers your gear adequately.

Theft is sometimes a problem so keep an eye on your bags at chai stops. Having a large, heavy-duty bag into which your pack will fit can be a good idea, not only for bus travel but also for air travel.

If someone carries your bag onto the roof, expect to pay a few rupees for the service.

Toilet Stops

On long-distance bus trips chai stops can be far too frequent or, conversely, agonisingly infrequent. Long-distance trips can be a real hassle for women travellers – toilet facilities are generally inadequate to say the least.

TRAIN

The Indian Railways system is the world's fourth-largest with a route length of over 60,000 km. Every single day over 11,000 trains run, carrying over nine million passengers and connecting 7000 stations. It's also the world's largest single employer with a shade over 1.6 million employees!

The first step in coming to grips with Indian Railways is to get a timetable. *Trains at a Glance* (Rs 6) is a handy, 100-page guide covering all the main routes and trains. It is usually available at major railway stations, and sometimes on newsstands in the larger cities. If you can't find it, a regional timetable provides much the same information, including the more local train services and a pink section with timetables for the major mail and express trains (the fast ones) throughout the country.

There is also the 300-page *Indian Bradshaw* which covers every train service throughout the country. It's more detailed than most people need and it can be frustratingly difficult to find things, but for serious exploring it's invaluable. Published monthly, it's not widely available but you can usually find it at major city train stations. Thomas Cook's *Overseas Timetable* has good train timetables for India.

Gricing

For some travellers, India's rail system is more than just public transport: with its large number of working steam engines, train fanatics (otherwise known as gricers) find India irresistible.

Since the first railways appeared in India in the 19th century, locomotives of various designs have been imported from the UK and the USA, and of course a large number were actually built in India, initially using imported technology and designs.

Fortunately examples of most major designs have been preserved in the Rail Transport Museum in Delhi. Locomotives from all three gauges (broad, metre and narrow) have been beautifully restored, many in their original railway company colours. Amongst those on show is the oldest surviving engine in India, built in 1855, and a diminutive two-foot-gauge loco from Darjeeling, making a stark contrast beside a 234-ton Beyer Garratt locomotive.

The remaining 3000 or so broad-gauge steam locomotives in India are of only two basic and rather austere designs. The more attractive of the two is the distinctive semi-streamlined WP class introduced in 1947. The engine's of the WG class were originally built for heavy freight traffic, but as most of these duties are now worked by diesel and electric traction, the WGs have been allotted such menial tasks as shunting, local freight and slow passenger trains. There's plenty of room on the footplate of these broad-gauge giants and many of the crew are not averse to having you aboard; it's always worth asking.

The mainstays of the metre-gauge system are the post-war YP (passenger) and YG (freight) designs which are found everywhere. A large number were built in India, the last YG being made in 1972. A handful of the attractive YD and YB classes have managed to survive. The YDs still slog their way up the ghats east of Goa on local passenger trains, while the last few YBs are found on the Western Railway in Gujarat.

Other curiosities are the narrow-gauge lines: the rack railway to Ooty, which uses Swiss engines; the Darjeeling Himalayan Railway, arguably the most famous and most spectacular steam railway in the world; and the lines from Kalka to Shimla and from Neral (near Bombay) to Matheran. With the exception of the Darjeeling line, all these routes are now worked by diesels.

Although steam locomotives will be around in India well past the year 2000, the variety and colour that remain will certainly have disappeared before then. But before you point that camera, a word of warning. Indian authorities can go overboard when it comes to railway security, so try to ensure that no police or other officials are around. ■

Mark Carter

This 1906 CC class locomotive is on the line from Rupsa to Bangriposi.

The timetables indicate the km distance between major stations and a table in front shows the fares for distances from one km to 5000 km for the various train types. With this information it is very easy to calculate the fare between any two stations. The fares quoted in this guide are approximations of the fares on the faster trains. Travel times vary widely between trains and the times indicated are usually for the faster mail or express services. In any case Indian trains often suffer delays.

A factor to consider with Indian trains is that getting there may not always be half the fun but it is certainly 90% of the experience. Indian rail travel is unlike any other sort of travel in any other place on earth. At times it can be uncomfortable or incredibly frustrating (since the trains are not exactly fast) but an experience it certainly is. Money aside, if you simply want to get from A to B, fly. If getting from A to B is as much a part of India as what you see at both ends, then take the train.

During and shortly after the monsoon, rail services can be drastically affected by floods and high rivers, particularly in low-lying areas along the Ganges basin or where major rivers reach the sea, such as the coastal region of Andhra Pradesh.

Classes

There are generally two classes – 1st and 2nd – but there are a number of subtle variations on this basic distinction. For a start there is 1st class and 1st-class air-con. The air-con carriages only operate on the major trains and routes. The fare for 1st-class air-con is more than double normal 1st class. A slightly cheaper air-con alternative is the air-con sleeper, which costs about 25% more than 1st class. These carriages are a lot more common than 1st-class air-con, but are still only found on the major routes.

Between 1st and 2nd class there is another air-con option, the air-con chair car. As the name suggests, these are carriages with aircraft-type layback seats. Once again, these carriages are only found on the major routes, and only on day trains. The cost is about

double the 2nd-class fare, and 60% of the 1st-class fare. With a 1st-class Indrail Pass you can make use of air-con chair cars, which are often a better alternative.

Types

What you want is a mail or express train. What you do not want is a passenger train. No Indian train travels very fast, but at least the mail and express trains do keep travelling more of the time. Passenger trains spend a lot of time at a lot of stations, which quickly becomes very boring unless you have a keen interest in small-town stations. Passenger trains are usually 2nd class only; 2nd-class fares on passenger trains are less than on a mail or express train over the same route.

Air-con 'superfast' express services operate on certain main routes, and because of tighter scheduling and fewer stops they are much faster. A separate fare structure applies to them as meals are included. These trains are the *Rajdhani Express*, which operates between Delhi and Bombay and Delhi and Calcutta, and the *Shatabdi Express*, with separate services connecting Delhi with Kalka, Bhopal and Lucknow.

Gauge

There are three gauge types in India: broad, metre and narrow, and what you want nearly as much as a mail or express train is broad gauge. In broad gauge the rails are 1.676 metres apart; metre gauge is, as it says, one metre wide; narrow gauge is either 0.762 metres (two feet six inches) or 0.610 metres (two feet).

Broad gauge has a major advantage – it is much faster. The carriages are much the same between broad gauge and metre gauge, but on narrow gauge they are narrower and the accommodation less comfortable. In areas where there are no broad-gauge lines it may be worth taking a bus, which will often be faster. These areas include Rajasthan and the northern Bihar and Uttar Pradesh areas towards the Nepal border.

Life on Board

It's India for real on board the trains. In 2nd

class, unreserved travel can be a nightmare since the trains are often hopelessly crowded, and not only with people – Indians seem unable to travel without the kitchen sink and everything that goes with it. Combined with the crowds, the noise and the confusion there's the discomfort. Fans and lights have a habit of failing at prolonged stops when there's no air moving through the carriage, and toilets are often so dirty as to be unusable. Worst of all are the stops. Trains seem to stop often, interminably and for no apparent reason. Often it's because somebody has pulled the emergency stop cable because they are close to home – well, so it's said; some people deny this. Still, it's all part of life on the rails.

In 2nd-class reserved it's somewhat better since, in theory, only four people share each bench but there's inevitably the fifth, and sometimes even the sixth, person who gets the other four to bunch up so they can get at least part of their bottom on the seat. This normally doesn't happen in 1st class, where there are four people to a compartment.

Costs

Fares operate on a distance basis. The timetables indicate the distance in km between the stations and from this it is simple to calculate the cost between any two stations. If you have a ticket for at least 400 km you can break your journey at the rate of one day per 200 km so long as you travel at least 300 km on the first sector. This can save a lot of

hassle buying tickets and also, of course, results in a small saving.

The table below indicates fares for set distances.

Reservations

The cost of reservations is nominal – it's the time it takes which hurts, although even this is generally not too bad as computerised reservation becomes more widespread. At the moment it is limited to the major towns and cities only.

Reservations can be made up to six months in advance and the longer in advance you make them the better. Your reservation ticket will indicate which carriage and berth you have, and when the train arrives you will find a sheet of paper fixed to each carriage listing passenger names beside their appropriate berth number. Usually this information is also posted on notice boards on the platform. It is Indian rail efficiency at its best.

As at many bus stations, there are separate women's queues, usually with a sign saying Ladies' Queue. Usually the same ticket window handles the male and female queue, taking one at a time. This means that women can go to the front of the queue, next to the first male at the window, and get almost immediate service.

Reservation costs are Rs 20 in air-con class, Rs 10 in 1st class and air-con chair class, Rs 7 in a 2nd-class sleeper, and Rs 3 in 2nd-class sitting. There are very rarely any 2nd-class sitting compartments with reserva-

| **Indian Rail Fares** | | | | | |
km	1st-Class Air-Con	1st Class	Air-Con Chair	2nd-Class Express	2nd-Class Ordinary
50	Rs 144	Rs 63	Rs 44	Rs 12	Rs 9
100	Rs 231	Rs 97	Rs 60	Rs 22	Rs 14
200	Rs 350	Rs 156	Rs 95	Rs 42	Rs 24
300	Rs 490	Rs 218	Rs 134	Rs 57	Rs 33
400	Rs 627	Rs 279	Rs 163	Rs 73	Rs 40
500	Rs 741	Rs 327	Rs 194	Rs 87	Rs 46
1000	Rs 1212	Rs 534	Rs 295	Rs 143	Rs 67
1500	Rs 1640	Rs 717	Rs 398	Rs 177	Rs 84
2000	Rs 2030	Rs 881	Rs 481	Rs 201	Rs 101

tions. There are also some superfast express trains that require a supplementary charge.

If the train you want is fully booked, it's possible to get an RAC (reservation against cancellation) ticket. This entitles you to board the train and have seating accommodation. More importantly, it gives you preference over other passengers when a berth becomes available due to cancellations and no shows. This is different from a wait-listed ticket, as the latter does not give you the right to actually board the train. The booking clerk can tell you how many people are on the RAC list, and what your chances are of getting a confirmed berth.

If you've not had time to get a reservation or been unable to get one, it's worth just getting on the train in any reserved carriage. Although there's the risk of a Rs 50 fine for 'ticketless travel' (condemned as a 'social evil' on notices in trains and timetables), most TTEs (Travelling Ticket Examiners) are sympathetic. If there are spare seats they'll allot you one, and charge the normal fare plus an extra reservation fee. If all the seats are already reserved you'll simply be banished to the crush and confusion in the unreserved carriages. This trick only works for day travel. At night sleepers are generally booked out well in advance so if you can't get one then sitting up in 2nd class is your only choice.

If you plan your trip well ahead, you can avoid all the hassles by booking in advance from abroad. A good Indian travel agent will book and obtain tickets in advance and have them ready for you on arrival.

Refunds

Booked tickets are refundable but cancellation fees apply. If you present the ticket more than one day in advance, a fee of Rs 10 to Rs 30 applies, depending on the class. Up to six hours before you lose 25% of the ticket value; within six hours before departure and up to three hours after departure you lose 50%. Any later than that and you can keep the ticket as a souvenir.

Tickets for unreserved travel can be refunded up to three hours after the departure of the train, and the only penalty is a Rs 2 per passenger fee.

When presenting your ticket for a refund, you are officially entitled to go straight to the head of the queue, the rationale being that the berth or seat you are surrendering may be just the one required by the next person in the queue.

Sleepers

There are 2nd-class and 1st-class sleepers, although by Western standards even 1st class is not luxurious. Bedding is not supplied unless organised in advance. First-class sleepers are generally private compartments with two or four sleepers in them, sometimes with a toilet as well. Usually the sleeping berths fold up to make a sitting compartment during the day. First-class air-con sleepers are more luxurious, and more expensive, than regular 1st-class sleepers. Sleeping berths are only available between 9 pm and 6 am. On some 1st-class sleepers, two-tier sleepers and a few major 2nd-class sleepers, it is possible to hire a 'bed roll' for Rs 5 per night. These consist of linen, blankets and pillow, and are well worth it, but need to be booked with your ticket.

There is no additional sleeper charge in 1st class but there is one in 2nd class. The Rs 15 charge (up to Rs 25, depending on the distance) is on top of the sleeper reservation charge and is a once-only charge irrespective of the number of nights the trip lasts. For any sleeper reservation you must book at least several days ahead.

There is usually a board in each station indicating what is available or how long before the next free sleeper comes up on the various routes. At the major city stations this is usually computerised and TV screens give a continuous read-out. Once you've selected a particular train and date, you must fill in a sleeper reservation form. Do this before you get to the front of the queue. The forms are usually found in boxes around the reservation hall. The demand for 1st-class sleepers is generally far less than for 2nd class.

Runaway Luggage

I was taking the Jaipur to Jodhpur express, minding my own business in a 1st-class compartment occupied by a very pleasant Indian family. My backpack was padlocked and chained to the compartment's parcel shelf; for the first (and last!) time I'd taken my moneybelt off and put it in the locked pack because I was feeling rather hot and sweaty wearing it across the desert (the number of times I pulled out damp Rs 100 notes!). In true Indian fashion, the train stopped from time to time for anything from two to 20 minutes, to be besieged by hordes of chai, cold drink and snack sellers.

Halfway into the journey, I found my stocks of mineral water were low. Concerned about dehydration, I decided to replenish my supply at the next station. The Indian family assured me that it was to be a 10-minute stop, so I hopped off the train in search of mineral water. There was nothing for sale on the platform so I ran out of the station and tried a few stalls. I was greeted with blank stares which, I guess, meant: 'There's a tap over there – why do you want to pay for water in a bottle?' Little English was spoken and in the end, I settled for two cartons of mango fruit drink.

I'd been gone for about four minutes when I sprinted back to the station to find – you guessed it – only a stretch of empty track where my train should have been. I don't think I will ever forget the overwhelming sense of blind panic and desperation that came over me. This would have been bad enough in England...but in India! It was my worst nightmare realised, almost everything I had was on that train: backpack, clothes, camera, film, medical supplies, most of my money, and my moneybelt which had my passport and travellers' cheques. I was left with only the clothes I wore and around Rs 100 in change...oh, and two cartons of mango juice.

I raced madly up the platform, shouting at people and asking them where the train had gone. There was no sign of it along the track, and the vague wave one guy gave in the direction of the empty stretch of line confirmed that it had left without me.

After sprinting back to the stationmaster's office, I breathlessly tried to explain what had happened, only to find that he too spoke very little English and insisted that I write down whatever I wanted to say. It was the most frustrating half-hour of my life – playing with a pen and paper as my luggage steamed ever further into the dry, distant desert.

By this time I was really starting to lose my cool, and in true Indian fashion, the station staff seemed unperturbed by the whole scenario. I wandered around the office muttering a stream of invectives, thumping the walls and kicking the furniture in an effort not to go totally bananas – much to the amusement of a band of locals pressing at the door. In the middle of this desperate situation, the line that came flooding into my head was one from an English TV comedy, spoken by a hotel proprietor trying frantically to communicate with his Spanish waiter: 'Please try and understand before one of us dies!'

Several pieces of paper later, it became apparent that all I could hope for was that my luggage would be unloaded at Degana (a name eternally etched in my memory!), the next station about 45 km away and the last stop before Jodhpur. A hesitant call was duly put through to Degana, but it was hardly a confidence-inspiring effort. The line appeared to keep going dead and the phone was one of those 'wind-up' affairs! After an agonising half-hour wait, Degana replied confirming that my luggage was there.

Still not convinced that the luggage was safe, I decided to head off to Degana by road to collect my luggage rather than wait for it to return on the next train. There then followed a couple of sprints between the jeep taxi rank and the station in an effort to arrange the trip as quickly as possible; in the end I was stung Rs 250 for the two-hour journey. They're not daft, they know when there's a panic on.

At most major city stations there's usually a separate section or counter(s) in the booking hall (often called 'Tourist Cell'!) which deals with the tourist quota. Only foreigners and nonresident Indians are allowed to use this facility. Here you can make your reservations in relative comfort away from the madding crowds *but* you must pay in foreign currency (cash or travellers' cheques) and any change will be given in rupees.

Lastly, when deciding which train to take along any route, you may come up against that major source of bewilderment – the Indian custom of naming a train without indicating where it goes. On the timetable or

By this time I had my fan club, a group of 30 or so locals, following my every move, anxious to see what this eccentric Westerner would do next – more running around, more shouting and waving or more furniture thumping. They weren't disappointed as I made my way back to the mango juice stall and tried to explain I wanted 20 cartons to last me across the desert. The stallkeeper was amazed, and the locals loved the finale to the saga as the Western visitor leaped into a taxi jeep with two bulging carrier bags full of mango juice cartons. (I've gone off mango juice now.)

The ride seemed like an eternity, yet when I reached Degana all my luggage was there – intact! Not only had they removed it from the train (cutting the chain that secured the pack to the train in the process) but they'd taken all the contents out of the unlocked side and top pockets of the pack and put them into bags sealed with wax, to ensure that nobody could interfere with them. Everything had been carefully logged and held secure in a locked cupboard till I arrived – it was an amazing feat of organisation. I was given something to eat and drink – the station superintendent had a meal brought from his own home. I was given a chit stating what had happened and that I was to be allowed to continue my journey to Jodhpur on a different train but using the same ticket. I was safely deposited on the night train which arrived in Jodhpur at 5 am the next day. Was it all a dream I wondered when I woke up.

I offered the Degana crew some money for their trouble but they refused and insisted that all I should do is take some group photos and send them copies. I reckon they deserve medals – well done India!

Two important lessons I learnt from this experience were: never let go of the most important possessions – passport and money; and never lose sight of the train you are travelling in when stopped at a station. Both are painfully obvious 'golden rules' but it took my escapade to hammer them home to me. I'm left in no doubt that I was extraordinarily fortunate to get away with it all.

François Baker, UK

state-of-reservation board at a station you could, for example, see the *Brindavan Express* or the *Cholan Express*, etc. But where do they go to? It might be the train you want, but it might not. This is where your *Trains at a Glance* or *Indian Bradshaw* comes in. If you don't have one, you'll have to ask – and that's going to soak up time.

Tourist offices can usually help by suggesting the best trains but there isn't always a tourist office. It's something you'll just have to come to terms with.

Two-Tier vs Three-Tier

Second-class sleepers are of two sorts: two-tier and three-tier. Superficially the padded two-tier sleepers seem more comfortable than the hard wooden three-tier ones, although on broad-gauge routes three-tier sleepers are also padded. During the day the three-tier sleepers are folded up to make seats for six or eight. At night they are folded down, everybody has to bed down at the same time, and a guard ensures that nobody without a reservation gets into the carriage.

In the two-tier compartments there are still regular unreserved seats below the padded bunks, so people get on and off and it's noisier and more difficult to sleep. In any case the racket and noise from the chai-wallahs and other merchants operating at every station can make sleeping on Indian trains a hit-and-miss affair.

Getting a Space Despite Everything

If you want a sleeper and there are none left then it's time to try and break into the quotas. Ask the stationmaster, often a helpful man who speaks English, if there is a tourist quota, station quota or if there is a VIP quota. The latter is often a good last bet because VIPs rarely turn up to use their quotas.

If all that fails then you're going to be travelling unreserved and that can be no fun at all. To ease the pain get yourself some expert help. For, say, Rs 10 baksheesh you can get a porter who will absolutely ensure you get a seat. If it's a train starting from your station, the key to success is to be on the train before it arrives at the departure platform. Your porter will do just that so when it rolls up you simply stroll on board and take the seat he has warmed for you. If it's a through train then it can be a real free-for-all, and you can be certain he'll be better at it than you are – he'll also not be encumbered with baggage or backpacks.

Women can ask about the Ladies' Compartments which many trains seem to have and are often a refuge from the crowds in other compartments.

Left Luggage

Most stations have a left-luggage facility, quaintly called a Cloak Room, where back-packs can be left for Rs 1 per day. This is a very useful facility if you're visiting (but not staying in) a town, or if you want to find a place to stay, unencumbered by gear. The regulations state that any luggage left in a Cloak Room must be locked, although this is not strictly enforced.

Special Trains

A special 'Palace on Wheels' makes a regular circuit around Rajasthan – you not only travel by train, you stay in the 'fit for a maharaja' carriages. See the Rajasthan section for more details.

The English organisation Butterfield's Indian Railway Tours operates regular train tours of India using a special carriage in which you travel, eat and sleep. The carriage is hooked on to regular trains and is left on the sidings of various towns you visit. The accommodation facilities are basic but you cover a lot of India. Tours from 18 to 29 days are available, and prices start from UK£795. For more information contact Butterfield's Railway Tours (☎ (0262) 47-0230) Burton Fleming, Driffield, East Yorkshire, England, UK.

Indrail Passes

The very popular Indrail Passes permit unlimited travel on Indian trains for the period of their validity. The cost of the passes in US dollars is as follows:

Days	Air-Con	1st Class	2nd Class
7	220	110	55
15	270	135	65
21	330	165	75
30	410	205	90
60	600	300	135
90	800	400	175

Children aged five to 12 years pay half these fares. Indrail tickets can be bought overseas through travel agents or in India at certain major railway offices. Payment in India must be made in either US dollars or pounds sterling, cash or travellers' cheques. Indrail Passes cover all reservation and berth costs at night. They can be extended if you wish to keep on travelling. The main offices in India which handle Indrail Passes are:

Bombay
  Railway Tourist Guide, Western Railway, Churchgate
  Railway Tourist Guide, Centra¹ Railway, Victoria Terminus
Calcutta
  Railway Tourist Guide, Eastern Railway, Fairlie Place
  Central Reservation Office, South-Eastern Railway, Esplanade Mansion
Madras
  Central Reservation Office, Southern Railway, Madras Central
New Delhi
  Railway Tourist Guide, New Delhi Railway Station

They are also available from central reservation offices at Secunderabad-Hyderabad, Rameswaram, Bangalore, Vasco da Gama, Gorakhpur, Jaipur and Thiruvananthapuram (Trivandrum), as well as at certain 'recognised tourist agencies'.

SK Enterprises Ltd (☎ (081) 903-3411) is a UK company which specialises in Indrail Passes. They both sell the passes and can make reservations if given at least one month's notice. Their address is: 103 Wembley Park Drive, Wembley, Middlesex, HA9 8HG.

Is the Indrail Pass worth having? Well, yes and no. In purely financial terms it's probably not. Unless you're travelling very heavily, on the go nearly every day, it's virtually impossible to cover enough distance to make the pass worthwhile *if* you're looking at it on a purely cost basis. The shorter the length of the pass the less sense it makes cost-wise. The 1st-class passes are also far better value than the 2nd-class ones. Although there is an air-con Indrail Pass as well as a 1st-class one, you only find air-con carriages on certain main routes. You might find it disappointing to invest in an air-con pass and then find you travel by regular 1st class anyway.

That's the downside of Indrail Passes, but pure cost isn't all there is to it. First of all you never need to join the interminable queues to buy tickets. You already have your ticket, so if you're travelling unreserved you simply hop aboard. If you are travelling reserved then you still have to get a reservation, and that's where the second advantage comes in. There is always a tourist quota, a VIP quota, a stationmaster's quota and so on. Indrail Pass users report that when the train is 'full', production of their pass often results in another quota making a miraculous appearance.

Your Indrail Pass also allows you use of the station waiting rooms, often a peaceful haven in the 1st-class variety, and makes it easier to get into the retiring rooms. The main virtue of the Indrail Pass, however, is its ability to produce a seat or a sleeper when there isn't one. That can be worth far more than mere money, so overall, yes, an Indrail Pass can be a good buy, but convenience and simplicity (both very important features in India) are the plus points, not cost saving. In particular, short-term passes are not so worthwhile, especially the 2nd-class ones. If you're going to travel by Indrail then go the whole hog and get a 1st-class pass.

Other Considerations

In New Delhi, Bombay and Madras there are special tourist booking offices at the main stations. These are for any foreign tourists, not just Indrail Pass holders, and they make life much easier. The people at these offices are generally very knowledgeable, although you will be surprised how often you find other railway booking clerks who really know their stuff. They will often give you excellent advice and suggest connections and routes which can save you a lot of time and effort.

At other major stations with computerised reservation offices, such as Ahmedabad and Jaipur, one ticket window will deal with foreign tourists and other minorities. These windows are generally queue-free, so check to see if one exists.

As an alternative to an Indrail Pass or buying tickets as you go along, it's possible to buy a ticket from A to Z with all the stops along the way prebooked. It might take a bit of time sitting down and working it out at the start, but if your time is limited and you can fix your schedule fairly rigidly, this can be a good way to go.

DRIVING

Fewer people bring their own cars to India since the overland trip became so curtailed because of the problems in Afghanistan and Iraq. If you do decide to bring a car or motorcycle to India it must be brought in under a carnet, a customs document guaranteeing its removal at the end of your stay. Failing to do so will be very expensive.

Bringing your own motorcycle, on the other hand, is much more popular and you'll see quite a few Westerners touring the country on them.

Rental

Car rental in India is unlike that in the West since, with one exception (Hertz), self-drive hire is not allowed, so you're limited to hiring a car and driver. This tends to be a little expensive, not because of the chauffeur but because of the cost of the cars, fuel and upkeep – all very expensive in India by Western standards.

Basically a chauffeur-driven car is just a long-distance taxi. In some places they run fairly regularly such as Chandigarh to Manali or Jammu to Srinagar in the northwest, and Darjeeling to Gangtok and Siliguri to Gangtok in the north-east. It is also possible to hire jeeps for the two-day run from Manali to Leh in Ladakh.

Both Budget and Hertz (Bangalore, Bombay, Delhi, Faridabad, Goa, Hyderabad, Jaipur, Madras and Pune) maintain offices in the major cities, but where they don't, cars with drivers can usually be hired from the state tourist development corporation (at a tourist office). There's not a great deal of difference in terms of cost between renting from a private company or from a state tourist development corporation. Typical rates are:

City Use: Four hours – Rs 190 (40 km minimum) plus Rs 3.30 per extra km
Eight hours – Rs 375 (80 km minimum) plus Rs 3.30 per extra km
Intercity: Rs 625 (150 km minimum) plus Rs 50 for the driver, or Rs 4.10 per km plus Rs 75 for the driver plus Rs 100 for a night halt

The above rates include fuel. Rates for city use in Bombay are slightly higher.

Self-drive (Hertz only) costs Rs 475 per 24 hours (150 km minimum) plus Rs 2 per extra km. Fuel is in addition, and a deposit of Rs 1000 is payable (returnable if there's no damage whatsoever to the car – a scratch constitutes 'damage'). Again, rates for use in Bombay are slightly higher.

All the above price examples assume you'll be driving an Ambassador. The rates for hiring a Maruti are slightly less.

Buying a Car or Motorcycle

Buying a car is naturally expensive in India and not worth the effort unless you intend to stay for months. Buying a motorcycle, on the other hand, is becoming more popular with long-stays. See the Two-Wheeled Experiences section below for a detailed discussion on motorcycles.

Road Conditions

Because of the extreme congestion in the cities and the narrow bumpy roads in the country, driving is often a slow, stop-start process – hard on you, the car, and fuel economy. Service is so-so in India, parts and tyres not always easy to obtain, though there are plenty of puncture repair places. All in all driving is no great pleasure except in rural areas where there's little traffic.

People driving across India on the overland trip will most likely start either from Calcutta, Madras or Bombay. The route from Madras crosses the country to Bombay, then heads north to Delhi and out to Pakistan.

Road Safety

In India there are almost 100 road deaths daily – 35,000 or so a year – an astonishing total in relation to the number of vehicles on the road. In the USA, for instance, there are

43,000 road fatalities per year, but it also has more than 20 times the number of vehicles.

The reasons for the high death rate in India are numerous and many of them fairly obvious – starting with the congestion on the roads and the equal congestion in vehicles. When a bus runs off the road there are plenty of people stuffed inside to get injured, and it's unlikely too many of them will be able to escape in a hurry. One newspaper article recently stated that 'most accidents are caused by brake failure or the steering wheel getting free'!

Many of those killed are pedestrians involved in hit-and-run accidents. The propensity to disappear after the incident is not wholly surprising – lynch mobs can assemble remarkably quickly, even when the driver is not at fault!

Most accidents are caused by trucks, for on Indian roads might is right and trucks are the biggest, heaviest and mightiest. You either get out of their way or get run down. As with so many Indian vehicles they're likely to be grossly overloaded and not in the best of condition. Trucks are actually licensed and taxed to carry a load 25% more than the maximum recommended by the manufacturer. It's staggering to see the number of truck wrecks by the sides of the national highways, and these aren't old accidents, but ones which have obviously happened in the last 24 hours or so – if they haven't been killed, quite often the driver and crew will be sitting around, wondering what to do next.

The karma theory of driving also helps to push up the statistics – it's not so much the vehicle which collides with you as the events of your previous life which caused the accident.

If you are driving yourself, you need to be extremely vigilant at all times. At night there are unilluminated cars and ox carts, and in daytime there are fearless bicycle riders and hordes of pedestrians. Day and night there are the crazy truck drivers to contend with. Indeed, at night, it's best to avoid driving at all along any major trunk route unless you're prepared to get off the road completely every

Indian road signs

time a truck is coming in the opposite direction! The other thing you have to contend with at night is the eccentric way in which headlights are used – a combination of full beam and totally off (dipped beams are virtually unheard of). A loud horn definitely helps since the normal driving technique is to put your hand firmly on the horn, close your eyes and plough through regardless. Vehicles always have the right of way over pedestrians and bigger vehicles always have the right of way over smaller ones.

Indian Vehicles

The Indian vehicle manufacturing industry has gone through an explosion in the last decade, and the number of cars and motorcycles on the road has increased dramatically. The old totally Indian, Hindustan Ambassador, a copy of an early '50s British Morris Oxford, is still the everyday vehicle on the Indian roads but there are now several more modern ones. These include licence-manufactured Rover 2000s (for the Indian executive), Datsun-engined Fiat 124s and a version of the British Vauxhall – but the big story is the Maruti.

The Maruti is a locally assembled Japanese Suzuki minicar or minivan, put together in the abortive Sanjay Gandhi 'people's car' factory near New Delhi. They've swept the country and you now see them everywhere in surprisingly large numbers. Whether they will have the endurance of the old rock-solid (and rock-heavy), fuel guzzling Ambassador is a different question. Whether abandoning the old 'All Indian' policy in favour of assembly operations is a good idea is another moot point.

India's truck and bus industry was always a more important business, with companies like Tata and Ashok Leyland turning out sturdy trucks which you see all over India, and also in a number of other developing countries. Here too there has been a Japanese onslaught; modern Japanese trucks are starting to appear. All Japanese vehicle builders in India must have at least 50% Indian ownership. The name thus becomes an Indo-Japanese hybrid, so you get Maruti-Suzuki, Hindustan-Isuzu, Allwyn-Nissan, Swaraj-Mazda and Honda-Kinetic.

The active motorcycle and motor scooter industry has also experienced rapid growth. The motorcycles include the splendid Enfield India – a replica of the old British single-cylinder 350cc Royal Enfield Bullet of the '50s. Enthusiasts for the old British singles will be delighted to see these modern-day vintage bikes still being made. Motor scooters include Indian versions of both the Italian Lambretta and the Vespa. When production ceased in Italy, India bought the manufacturing plant from them lock, stock and barrel.

There is a variety of mopeds but the assembly of small Honda, Suzuki and Yamaha motorcycles is widespread and they are becoming as familiar a sight on the roads of India as in South-East Asia. The arrival of Japanese manufacturing companies in India has provided some insightful culture clashes. A *Time* magazine article a few years ago noted that Honda had found it impossible to instil the Japanese-style team spirit at the Hero-Honda plant near New Delhi. Workers didn't mind rubbing shoulders with the management – but not with the Dalits (untouchables), please. And despite having quality inspectors, unknown in Japanese plants where everybody is a quality inspector, the rejection rate at the end of the assembly line was 30% against 3% in Japan.

TWO-WHEELED EXPERIENCES

The following descriptions outline two different ways of travelling independently in India. The motorcycle section is based largely on information contributed by intrepid Britons Ken Twyford and Gerald Smewing, while the cycling information was originally from Ann Sorrel, with updates from various travellers.

India by Motorcycle

Travelling around India by motorcycle has become increasingly popular in recent years, and it certainly has its attractions – motoring along the backroads through small untouristed villages, picnics in the wilds, the freedom to go when and where you like – making it the ideal way to get to grips with the vastness that is India. You'll still get a sore bum, have difficult and frustrating conversations, get fed up with asking directions and receiving misleading answers, and get frequently lost, but you'll also have a wide range of adventures not available to the visitor who relies on public transport.

What to Bring An International Driving Licence is not mandatory, but is handy to have.

Helmets should definitely be brought with you. Although Indian helmets are cheap, it is often hard to find one that fits well, and the quality is suspect. You are not required by law to wear a helmet. If required, leathers, gloves, boots, waterproofs and other protective gear should also be brought from your home country.

A few small bags will be a lot easier to carry than one large rucksack.

Which Bike? The big decision to make is whether to buy new or secondhand. Obviously cost is the main factor, but remember that with a new bike you are less likely to get ripped off as the price is fixed, it will include free servicing and you know it will be reliable. Old bikes are obviously cheaper and you don't have to be a registered resident foreign national, but you are far more open to getting ripped-off, either by paying too much or getting a dud bike.

Everyone is likely to have their own preferences, and so there is no one bike which suits everybody. However, here is a rundown of what's readily available:

Mopeds These come with or without gears. As they are only 50cc capacity, they are really only useful around towns or for short distances.

Scooters There's the older design Bajaj and Vespa scooters, or the more modern Japanese designs by Honda-Kinetic and others. The older ones are 150cc while the Honda is 100cc and has no gears.

Scooters are inherently unstable creatures, largely due to the high centre of gravity and small wheels. On rough roads they're positively lethal.

On the plus side, they are economical to buy and run, are easy to ride, have a good

resale value, and most have built-in lockable storage.

100cc Motorcycles This is the area with the greatest choice. The four main Japanese companies – Honda, Suzuki, Kawasaki and Yamaha – all have 100cc, two-stroke machines, while Honda and Kawasaki also have four-stroke models.

There's little to differentiate between these bikes; all are light-weight, easy to ride, very economical and reliable, with good resale value. They are suitable for intercity travel on reasonable roads, but they should not be laden down with too much gear. Spares and servicing are readily available. The cost of a new bike of this type is about Rs 28,000, plus the costs of getting it on the road.

Another competitor in this market is the Rajdoot 175 XLT, based on a very old Polish model. It lacks power but is a cheap option, costing around Rs 6000 to Rs 10,000 less than the Japanese bikes.

The Enfield Fury is a modern machine with front disc brake. It's very unpopular, has a poor gearbox, spares are hard to come by and the resale value is low – avoid.

Bigger Bikes The Yezdi 250 Classic is a simple, cheap and basic bike. It's a rugged machine, and one which you often see in rural areas.

The Enfield Bullet is the classic machine and is the one most favoured among foreigners. Attractions are the traditional design, thumping engine sound, and the price, which is not much more than the new 100cc Japanese bikes. It's a wonderfully durable bike, is easy to maintain, economical to run, but mechanically they're a bit 'hit and miss', largely because of poorly engineered parts and inferior materials – valves and tappets are the main problem areas. Another drawback is the lack of an effective front brake – the small drum brake is totally inadequate for what is quite a heavy machine. The Bullet is also available in a 500cc single-cylinder version, but these are best avoided as spare parts are extremely rare and resale value is low. New price is around Rs 32,000, or Rs 35,000 for the 500cc model.

The Rajdoot 350 is a modern imported Yamaha 350cc. It's well engineered, fast and has good brakes. Disadvantages are that they are relatively uneconomical to run, and spares are hard to come by. They are best bought secondhand (Rs 10,000 to Rs 15,000), as a new one will set you back Rs 45,000. This bike is probably the best touring bike available, if you can ignore the aesthetic appeal of the Enfield.

Buying & Selling India does not have used-vehicle dealers, motorcycle magazines or weekend newspapers with pages of motorcycle classified advertisements. To purchase a secondhand machine one simply needs to enquire. A good place to start is with mechanics. They are likely to know somebody who is selling a bike.

To buy a new bike, you'll have to have a local address and be a resident foreign national. However, unless the dealer you are buying from is totally devoid of imagination and contacts, this presents few problems. When buying secondhand, all you need to do is give an address.

New bikes are generally purchased through a showroom. When buying second-hand it is best to engage the services of an 'autoconsultant'. These people act as go-betweens to bring buyers and sellers together. They will usually be able to show you a number of machines to suit your price bracket. These agents can be found by enquiring, or may sometimes advertise on their shop fronts.

For around Rs 500, which usually covers a bribe to officials, they will assist you in transferring the ownership papers through the bureaucracy. Without their help this could take a couple of weeks.

The overall appearance of the bike doesn't seem to affect the price greatly. Dents and scratches don't reduce the cost much, and added extras don't increase it by much.

When the time comes to sell the bike, don't appear too anxious to get rid of it, don't hang around in one town too long as word gets around the autoconsultants and the offers will get smaller as the days go by. If you get a reasonable offer, grab it. Regardless of which bike it is, you'll be told it's the 'least popular in India' and other such tales.

Ownership Papers A needless hint perhaps, but do not part with your money until you have the ownership papers, receipt and affidavit signed by a magistrate authorising the owner (as recorded in the ownership papers) to sell the machine. Not to mention the keys to the bike and the bike itself!

Each state has a different set of ownership transfer formalities. Get assistance from the agent you're buying the machine through or from one of the many 'attorneys' hanging around under tin roofs by the Motor Vehicles Office. They will charge you a fee of up to Rs 300, which will consist largely of a bribe to expedite matters.

Alternatively you could go to one of the many typing clerk services and request them to type out the necessary forms, handling the matter cheaply yourself – but with no guarantee of a quick result.

Check that your name has been recorded in the ownership book and stamped and signed by the department head. If you intend to sell your motorcycle in another state then you will need a 'No Objections Certificate'. This confirms your ownership and is issued by the Motor Vehicles Department in the state of purchase, so get it immediately when transferring ownership papers to your name. The standard form can be typed up for a few rupees, or more speedily and expensively through one of the many attorneys. This document is vital if you are going to sell the bike in another state.

Other Formalities As in most countries it is compulsory to have third-party insurance. The New India Assurance Company or the National Insurance Company are just two of a number of companies who can provide it. The cost is minimal by Western standards.

Road tax is paid when the bike is bought new. This is valid for the life of the machine and is transferred to the new owner when the bike changes hands.

On the Road It must be said that, given the general road conditions, motorcycling is a reasonably hazardous endeavour, and one best undertaken by experienced riders only – you don't want to discover on the Grand Trunk Road with a lunatic in a Tata truck bearing down on you that you don't know how to take evasive action! The hazards to be encountered range from families of pigs crossing the road to broken-down vehicles, left where they stopped, even if that is in the middle of the road.

Route finding can be very tricky. It's certainly much easier to jump on a bus and leave the navigating to someone who knows the way. The directions people give you can be very interesting. It is invariably a 'straight road', although if pressed the person might also reveal that the said straight road actually involves taking two right turns, three left turns and the odd fork or two. People generally seem to discount the fact that although the road appears to go straight across an intersection, and all the traffic is turning right, MG Rd in fact turns left. Pronunciation can also cause problems, particularly in country areas.

On the whole people are very welcoming, and curious about how you are coping with the traffic conditions.

Parking the bike and getting things stolen from it seems not to be a problem. The biggest annoyance is that people seem to treat parked motorcycles as public utilities – handy for sitting on, using the mirror to do the hair, fiddling with the switches – but they don't deliberately do any damage. You'll just have to turn all the switches off and readjust the mirrors when you get back on!

Run-ins with the law are not a major problem. The best policy is to give a smile and a friendly wave to any police officers, even if you are doing the opposite of what is signalled.

In the event of an accident, call the police straight away, and don't move anything until the police have seen exactly where and how

everything ended up. One foreigner reported spending three days in jail on suspicion of being involved in an accident, when all he'd done was taken a child to hospital from the scene of an accident.

Don't try to cover too much territory in one day. As such a high level of concentration is needed to survive, long days are tiring and dangerous. On the busy national highways expect to average 40 km/h without stops; on smaller roads, where driving conditions are worse, 10 km/h is not an unrealistic average. On the whole you can expect to cover between 100 km and 150 km in a day on good roads.

Night driving should be avoided at all costs. If you think driving in daylight is difficult enough, imagine what it's like at night when there's the added hazard of half the vehicles being inadequately lit (or not lit at all), not to mention the breakdowns in the middle of the road.

Putting the bike on a train for really long hauls can be a convenient option. You'll pay about as much as the 2nd-class passenger fare for the bike. It can be wrapped in straw for protection if you like, and this is done at the parcels office at the station, which is also where you pay for the bike. The petrol tank must be empty, and there should be a tag in an obvious place detailing name, destination, passport number, and train details.

Repairs & Maintenance Anyone who can handle a screwdriver and spanner in India can be called a mechanic or *mistri*, so be careful. If you have any mechanical knowledge it may be better to buy your own tools and learn how to do your own repairs. This will save a lot of arguments over prices.

Original spare parts bought from an 'Authorised Dealer' can be rather expensive compared to the copies available from your spare-parts wallah.

If you buy an older machine you would do well to check and tighten all nuts and bolts every few days. Indian roads and engine vibration tend to work things loose and constant checking could save you rupees and trouble. Check the engine and gearbox oil level regularly. With the quality of oil it is advisable to change it and clean the oil filter every couple of thousand km.

Punctures Chances are you'll be requiring the services of a puncture-wallah at least once a week. They are found everywhere, often in the most surprising places, but it's advisable to at least have tools sufficient to remove your own wheel and take it to the puncture-wallah (*punkucha wallah* in Hindi).

Fuel Petrol is expensive relative to the West and when compared to the cost of living in India – Rs 18 per litre – but diesel is much cheaper – around Rs 6.20 per litre. It is usually readily available in all larger towns and along the main roads so there is no need to carry spare fuel.

Should you run out, try flagging down a passing car (not a truck or bus since they use diesel) and beg for some. Most Indians are willing to let you have some if you have a hose or syphon and a container. Alternatively, hitch a truck ride to the nearest petrol station.

India by Bicycle

Every day millions of Indians pedal along the country's roads. If they can do it so can you. India offers an immense array of challenges for a long-distance bike tourer – there are high-altitude passes and rocky dirt tracks; smooth-surfaced, well-graded highways with roadside restaurants and lodges; coastal routes through coconut palms; and winding country roads through coffee plantations. Not to mention city streets with all manner of animal and human-powered carts and vehicles as well as the spectacle of the Asian bazaar. Hills, plains, plateaus, deserts – you name it, India's got it!

As elsewhere in the world, long-distance cycling is not for the faint of heart or weak of knee. You'll need physical endurance to cope with the roads and the climate, plus you'll face cultural challenges which I call 'the people factor'.

Books Before you set out, read some books on bicycle touring like *Bike Touring* by Raymond Bridge (Sierra Club, 1979), *Bike Tripping* by Tom Cuthbertson (10 Speed Press, 1972) or *The Bicycle Touring Book* by Tom & Glenda Wilhelm (Rodale Press, 1980). Cycling magazines in your own country will provide useful information and addresses of spare-parts suppliers which may be vital if you have to send for a part. They're also good places to look for a riding companion. For a real feel of the adventure of bike touring in strange places there's Dervla Murphy's classic *Full Tilt – From Ireland to India on a Bike* now available in paperback, or Lloyd Summer's *The Long Ride*. Look for *Riding the Mountains Down* for a more recent 'biking through India' adventure.

Using Your Own Bike Bringing your own lightweight touring bicycle will give you lots of mechanical advantages and make mountainous areas much more approachable, but it does have disadvantages. Your machine is likely to be a real curiosity and subject to much pushing, pulling and probing. If you can't tolerate people touching your quality bicycle don't bring it to India!

There are also technical problems, so have a working knowledge of your machine and bring any special tools with you. Bring a compact bike manual with lots of diagrams and pictures in case the worst happens and you need to get your rear derailleur or another strategic part remade – the right Indian mechanic/tinkerer can do wonders and illustrations help break down language barriers.

Either bring a good quality bicycle equipped with top-line touring components or a no-name 10-speed that you won't regret parting with when damaged, stolen or sold. Make sure it's a machine that you're comfortable with.

Spare Parts If you bring a bicycle to India, apart from all the normal tools and spares (plenty of spokes) bring a good wire cutter to cleanly cut brake and gear cables. Finding a suitable tool or chisel always seems difficult. Long, thin cables for derailleurs aren't available outside major cities so bring enough spares. Bike or moped brake cables bought in India have to be modified to fit brake levers correctly – I found a spoke nipple threaded through the cable is perfect. Be ready to make do and improvise. Roads don't have paved shoulders and are very dusty so take care to keep your chain lubricated.

Although India is theoretically metricated, tools and bike parts are 'standard' or 'English' measurement. Don't expect to find tyres for 700c rims, although 27 x 1¼ tyres are produced in India by Dunlop and Sawney. Indian cycle pumps cater to a tube valve different from the Presta and Schraeder valves common on bikes in the West. If you're travelling with Presta valves (most high-pressure 27 x 1¼ tubes) bring a Schraeder (car type) adapter. In India you can get the Indian pump adapter, which means you'll have an adapter on your adapter! But bring your own pump as well; most Indian pumps require two or three people to get air down the leaky cable.

In big cities Japanese tyres and parts (derailleurs, freewheels, chains) are available and pricey – but then so are postage costs, and transit time can be considerable. If you receive bike parts from abroad beware of exorbitant customs charges. Say you want the goods as 'in transit' to avoid these charges. They may list the parts in your passport!

There are a number of shops where you may locate parts. Try Metre Cycle, Kalba Devi Rd, Bombay or their branch in Thiruvananthapuram (Trivandrum); the cycle bazaar in the old city around Esplanade Rd, Delhi; Popular Cycle Importing Company on Popham's Broadway, Madras; and Nundy & Company, Bentinck St, Calcutta. Or locate the cycle market and ask around with your bike – someone will know which shop is likely to have things for your 'special' cycle. Beware of Taiwanese imitations and do watch out for old rubber

on tyres which may have been sitting collecting dust for years.

Luggage Your cycle luggage should be as strong, durable and waterproof as possible. I don't recommend a set with lots of zippers, as it makes pilfering of contents easier. As you'll be frequently removing luggage when taking your bike to your room, a set designed for easy removal from racks is a must and the fewer items the better. (*Never* leave your cycle in the lobby or outside – take it to bed with you!)

Think about a large-capacity handlebar bag and a rear pannier set. Front bags mean two more items to haul about. Richard Jones, PO Box 919, Fort Collins, Colorado 80522, USA makes a set of bike luggage that can be easily reassembled into a backpack. Just the thing when you want to park your bike and go by train or on a trek.

Theft If you're on an imported bike try to avoid losing your pump (and the water bottle from your frame) – they're popular items for theft because of their novelty, and their loss is very inconvenient. Don't leave anything on your bike that can be easily removed when it's unattended. Don't be paranoid about theft – outside the four big cities it would be well-nigh impossible for a thief to resell your bike as it'll stick out too much. And not many folk understand quick-release levers on wheels. Your bike is probably safer in India than in Western cities.

Buying a Bike in India Finding an Indian bike is no problem: every Indian town will have at least a couple of cycle shops. Shop around for prices and remember to bargain. Try to get a few extras – bell, stand, spare tube – thrown in. There are many different brands of Indian clunkers – Hero, Atlas, BSA, Raleigh, Bajaj, Avon – but they all follow the same basic, sturdy design. Recently a few mountain-bike lookalikes have come on the market, but they have no gears. Raleigh is considered the finest quality, followed by BSA which has a big line of models including some sporty jobs.

Hero and Atlas both claim to be the biggest seller. Basically look for the cheapest or the one with the snazziest plate label.

Once you've decided on the bike you have a choice of luggage carriers – mostly the rat-trap type varying in size, price and strength. There's a wide range of saddles available but all are equally bum-breaking. A stand is certainly a useful addition and a bell or airhorn is a necessity in India. An advantage of buying a new bike is that the brakes actually work. Centre-pull and side-pull brakes are also available but at extra cost and may actually make the bike more difficult to sell. The average Indian will prefer the standard model.

Spare Parts As there are so many repair 'shops' (some consist of a pump, box of tools, tube of rubber solution and water pan under a tree) there is no need to carry spare parts, especially as you'll only own the bike for a few weeks or months. Just take a roll of tube-patch rubber, a tube of Dunlop patch glue, two tyre irons and a wonderful 'universal' bike spanner for Indian bikes which will fit all the nuts. There are plenty of puncture-wallahs in all towns and villages who will patch tubes for a couple of rupees, so chances are you won't have to fix a puncture yourself anyway. Besides, Indian tyres are pretty heavy duty so with luck you won't get a flat.

Selling It Reselling the bike is no problem. Ask the proprietor of your lodge if they know anyone who is interested in buying a bike. Negotiate a price and do the deal personally or through the hotel. Most people will be only too willing to help you. Count on losing a couple of hundred rupees, depending on local prices. Retail bike stores are not usually interested in buying or selling second-hand bikes. A better bet would be a bike-hire shop, which may be interested in expanding its fleet.

On the Road The 'people factor' makes a bike ride in India both rewarding and frustrating. It is greatly reduced for those with

Indian bikes and can be decisive in opting not to bring a 10-speed sports bike. Mob scenes are likely to occur. A tea stop can cause a crowd of 50 men and boys to encircle you and your machine, who comment to one another about its operation – one points to the water-bottle saying 'petrol', another twists the shifter lever saying 'clutch', another squeezes a tyre saying 'tubeless' or 'airless', yet others nod knowingly as 'gear system', 'automatic' and 'racing bike' are mouthed. In some areas you'll even get 'disco bike'!

The worst scenario is stopping on a city street for a banana, looking up as you are pushing off to find rickshaws, cyclists and pedestrians all blocking your way! At times the crowd may be unruly – schoolboys especially. If the mob is too big just request a lathi-wielding policeman to come. The boys scatter pronto! Sometimes hostile boys may throw rocks. The best advice is to keep pedalling; don't turn around or stop, and don't leave your bike and chase them as this will only incite them further. Appeal to adults to discipline them. Children, especially boys seven to 13 years old, aren't disciplined and are dangerous in crowds. Avoid riding by a boys' school at recess.

Routes You can go anywhere on a bike that you would on trains and buses with the added pleasure of seeing all the places in between.

Try to avoid the major highways up north like NH1 through Haryana, and NH2 – the Grand Trunk (GT) between Delhi and Calcutta. They're plagued by speeding buses and trucks. Other national highways can be pleasant – often lonely country roads well marked with a stone every km. Learn some Hindi to translate signs, although at least one marker in five will be in English.

Distances If you've never cycled distances before, start with 20 to 40 km per day and build up as you gain stamina and confidence. Cycling long distances is 80% determination and 20% perspiration. Don't be ashamed to get off and push up steep hills either. For an eight-hour pedal a serious cyclist and interested tourist will average 125 to 150 km a day on undulating plains or 80 to 100 km in mountainous areas.

Accommodation There's no need to bring a tent, as cheap lodges are available almost everywhere and a tent pitched by the road would draw crowds. There's also no need to bring a stove and cooking kit (unless you cannot tolerate Indian food), as there are plenty of tea stalls and restaurants (called 'hotels'). When you want to eat ask for a 'hotel', when you want a room ask for a 'lodge'. On big highways stop at dhabas, the Indian version of a truck stop. The one with the most trucks parked in front has the best food (or serves alcohol). Dhabas have *charpoys* (string beds) to serve as tables and seats or as beds for weary cyclists. They're not recommended for single women riders and you should keep your cycle next to you throughout the night. There will be no bathroom or toilet facilities and plenty of road noise.

This is the best part of travelling on a bike – finding places to stay between the cities or important tourist places.

Directions Asking directions can be a real frustration. Approach people who look like they can speak English and aren't in a hurry. Always ask three or four different people just to be certain, using traffic police only as a last resort. Try to be patient; be careful about 'left' and 'right' and be prepared for instructions like 'go straight and turn here and there'!

Transporting your Bike Sometimes you may want to quit pedalling – for sports bikes, air travel is easy. With luck airline staff may not be familiar with procedures, so use this to your advantage. Tell them it doesn't need to be dismantled and you've never had to pay for it. Remove all luggage and accessories and let the tyres down a bit.

Bus travel with a bike varies from state to state. Generally it goes for free on the roof. If it's a sports bike stress that it's lightweight. Secure it well to the roof rack, check it's in a place where it won't get damaged and take all your luggage inside.

Train travel is more complex – pedal up to the railway station, buy a ticket and explain you want to book a cycle for the journey. You'll be directed to the luggage offices or officer where a triplicate form is prepared. Note down your bike's serial number and provide a good description of it. Again leave only the bike, not luggage or accessories. Your bike gets decorated with one copy of the form, usually pasted on the seat, you get another, and God only knows what happens to the third. Produce your copy of the form to claim the bicycle from the luggage van at your destination. If you change trains en route, *personally* ensure the cycle changes too!

Final Words Just how unusual is a cycle tourist in India? I'd venture to guess about 1000 foreign cyclists each year go on a month-long or more ride somewhere on the subcontinent. And the number is growing rapidly. Perhaps 5000 Indians do tours too – mostly young men and college students. 'Kashmir to Kanyakumari' or a pilgrimage to holy places are their most common goals. For your ego, newspaper attention is there for the asking.

If you're a serious cyclist or amateur racer and want to contact counterparts while in India there's the Cycle Federation of India; contact the Secretary, Yamun Velodrome, New Delhi. Last words of advice – make sure your rubber solution is gooey, all your winds are tailwinds and that you go straight and turn here and there.

The International Bicycle Fund (IBT; ☎ (206) 628-9314), 4887 Columbia Drive South, Seattle, Washington 98108-1919, USA, has two publications which may help you prepare for your cycling adventure. These are *Selecting and Preparing a Bike for Travel in Remote Areas* and *Flying With Your Bike*. Each is US$2 plus postage and handling (in the USA: US$1 for first item and US$.50 for each additional item; other countries: US$2 for first item and US$1 for each additional item).

The IBT are also happy to help prospective long-distance cyclists with information and advice.

HITCHING

Hitching is possible but not always easy. There are not that many private cars streaking across India so you are likely to be on board trucks. You are then stuck with the old quandaries of: 'Do they understand what I am doing?'; 'Should I be paying for this?'; 'Will the driver expect to be paid?'; 'Will they be unhappy if I don't offer to pay?'; 'Will they be unhappy if I offer or will they simply want too much?'. But it is possible.

However, it is a very bad idea for women to hitch. Remember India is a developing country with a patriarchal society far less sympathetic to rape victims than the West, and that's saying something. A woman in the cabin of a truck on a lonely road is perhaps tempting fate.

BOAT

Apart from ferries across rivers (of which there are many) the only real boating possibilities are the trips through the backwaters of Kerala – not to be missed (see the Kerala chapter for more details) and yacht cruises between Bombay and Goa. These latter trips are operated by Odyssey Tours – see the Goa chapter for details.

The only ferries connecting coastal ports are those from Calcutta and Madras to the Andaman Islands, and even these aren't all that regular. See Getting There & Away in the Port Blair section of the Andaman & Nicobar Islands chapter.

LOCAL TRANSPORT

Although there are comprehensive local bus networks in most major towns, unless you have time to familiarise yourself with the routes you're better off sticking to taxis, auto-rickshaws, cycle-rickshaws and hiring bicycles. The buses are often so hopelessly overcrowded that you can only really use them if you get on at the starting point – and get off at the terminus!

A basic ground rule applies to any form of transport where the fare is not ticketed or fixed (unlike a bus or train), or metered – agree on the fare beforehand. If you fail to do that you can expect enormous arguments and hassles when you get to your destination. And agree on the fare clearly – if there is more than one of you make sure it covers all of you. If you have baggage make sure there are no extra charges, or you may be asked for more at the end of the trip. If a driver refuses to use the meter, or insists on an extortionate rate, simply walk away – if he really wants the job the price will drop. If you can't agree on a reasonable fare, find another driver.

To/From the Airport

There are official buses, operated by the government, Indian Airlines or some local cooperative, to most airports in India. Where there aren't any, there will be taxis or auto-rickshaws. There are even some airports close enough to town to get to by cycle-rickshaw.

When arriving at an airport anywhere in India, make an effort to find out if there's a prepaid taxi booth inside the arrival hall. If there is, pay for one there. If you don't do this and simply walk outside to negotiate your own price, you'll invariably pay more. Taxi drivers are notorious for refusing to use the meter (where fitted) outside airport terminals.

Taxi

There are taxis in most towns in India, and most of them (certainly in the major cities) are metered. Getting a metered fare is rather a different situation. First of all the meter may be 'broken'. Threatening to get another taxi will usually fix it immediately, except during rush hours.

Secondly the meter will almost certainly be out of date. Fares are adjusted upwards so much faster and more frequently than meters are recalibrated that drivers almost always have 'fare adjustment cards' indicating what you should pay compared to what the meter indicates. This is, of course, wide open to abuse. You have no idea if you're being shown the right card or if the taxi's meter has actually been recalibrated and you're being shown the card anyway. In states where the numbers are written differently (such as Gujarat) it's not much use asking for the chart if you can't read it!

The only answer to all this is to try and get an idea of what the fare should be before departure (ask information desks at the airport or your hotel). You'll soon begin to develop a feel for what the meter says, what the cards say and what the two together should indicate.

Auto-Rickshaw
An auto-rickshaw is a noisy three-wheel device powered by a two-stroke motorcycle engine with a driver up front and seats for two (or sometimes more) passengers behind. They don't have doors (except in Goa) and have just a canvas top. They are also known as scooters or autos.

Although they are all made by Bajaj, it's amazing how the designs differ from town to town. Design seems to be unique to a particular town: in Chittorgarh in Rajasthan, for example, the auto-rickshaws are fitted with an extra seat facing backwards, and so they can carry four people (although they'll often carry eight or more!).

They're generally about half the price of a taxi, usually metered and follow the same ground rules as taxis.

Because of their size, auto-rickshaws are often faster than taxis for short trips and their drivers are decidedly nuttier – hair-raising near-misses are guaranteed and glancing-blow collisions are not infrequent; thrill-seekers will love it!

In busy towns you'll find that, when stopped at traffic lights, the height you are sitting at is the same as most bus and truck exhaust pipes – copping dirty great lungfuls of diesel fumes is part of the fun of auto-rickshaw travel. Also their small wheel size and rock-hard suspension makes them supremely uncomfortable; even the slightest bump will have you instantly airborne. The speed humps and huge potholes found everywhere are the bane of the rickshaw traveller – pity the poor drivers.

Tempo
Somewhat like a large auto-rickshaw, these ungainly looking three-wheel devices operate rather like minibuses or share-taxis along fixed routes. Unless you are spending large amounts of time in one city, it is generally impractical to try to find out what the routes are. You'll find it much easier and more convenient to go by auto-rickshaw.

Cycle-Rickshaw
This is effectively a three-wheeler bicycle with a seat for two passengers behind the rider. Although they no longer operate in most of the big cities except in the old part of Delhi and parts of Calcutta, you will find them in all the smaller towns, where they're the basic means of transport.

Fares must always be agreed on in advance. Avoid situations where the driver says something like: 'As you like'. He's punting on the fact that you are not well acquainted with correct fares and will overpay. Invariably no matter what you pay in situations like this, it will be deemed too little and an unpleasant situation often develops. This is especially the case in heavily touristed places, such as Agra and Jaipur. Always settle the price beforehand.

In the well-touristed places the riders are as talkative and opinionated as any New York cabby.

It's quite feasible to hire a rickshaw-wallah by time, not just for a straight trip. Hiring one for a day or even several days can make good sense.

Hassling over the fares is the biggest difficulty of cycle-rickshaw travel. They'll often go all out for a fare higher than it would cost you by taxi or auto-rickshaw. Nor does actually agreeing on a fare always make a difference; there is a greater possibility of a post-travel fare disagreement when you travel by cycle-rickshaw than by taxi or auto-rickshaw – metered or not.

Other Transport
In some places, tongas (horse-drawn two-wheelers) and victorias (horse-drawn

Cycle-Rickshaw

carriages) still operate. Calcutta has an extensive tramway network and India's first underground railway. Bombay, Delhi and Madras have suburban trains.

Once upon a time there used to be people-drawn rickshaws but today these only exist in Calcutta.

Bicycle

India is a country of bicycles – it's an ideal way of getting around the sights in a city or even for making longer trips – see the section on touring India by bicycle earlier in this chapter. Even in the smallest of towns there will be a shop which rents bicycles. They charge from around Rs 3 to Rs 5 per hour or Rs 10 to Rs 15 per day. In tourist areas (such as hill stations) and places where foreigners are common (like Pondicherry) you'll pay about double the normal rate. In some places they may be unwilling to hire to you since you are a stranger, but you can generally get around this by offering some sort of ID card as security, or by paying a deposit – usually Rs 300 to Rs 500. Check the time they enter in the log book before you pedal off.

If you should be so unfortunate as to get a puncture, you'll soon spot men sitting under trees with puncture-repair outfits at the ready – it'll cost just a couple of rupees to fix it.

If you're travelling with small children and would like to use bikes a lot, consider getting a bicycle seat made. If you find a shop making cane furniture they'll quickly make up a child's bicycle seat from a sketch. Get it made to fit on a standard-size rear carrier and it can be securely attached with a few lengths of cord..

TOURS

At almost any place of tourist interest in India, and quite a few places where there's not much tourist interest, there will be tours operated either by the Government of India tourist office, the state tourist office or the local transport company – sometimes by all three. These tours are usually excellent value, particularly in cities or places where the tourist sights are widespread. You probably could not even get around the sights in New Delhi on public transport as cheaply as you could on a half or full-day tour.

These tours are not strictly for Western tourists; you will almost always find yourself far outnumbered by local tourists, and in many places just a little off the beaten track you will often be the only Westerner on the bus. Despite this the tours are usually conducted in English – which is possibly the only common language for the middle-class Indian tourists in any case. These tours are an excellent place to meet Indians.

The big drawback is that many of them try to cram far too much into too short a period of time. A one-day tour which whisks you from Madras to Kanchipuram, Tirukalikundram, Mahabalipuram and back to Madras is not going to give you time for more than the most fleeting glimpse. If a tour looks too hectic, you're better off doing it yourself at a more appropriate pace or taking the tour simply to find out to which places you want to devote more time.

New Delhi

Population: 8.4 million
Area: 1485 sq km
People per sq km: 6139
Main Languages: Hindi, Urdu, Punjabi &
English

New Delhi is the capital of India and its
third-largest city. The city actually consists
of two parts. Delhi or 'Old' Delhi was the
capital of Muslim India between the 12th and
19th centuries. In Old Delhi you will find
many mosques, monuments and forts relating to India's Muslim history. The other
Delhi is New Delhi, the imperial city created
as the capital of India by the British. It is a
spacious, open city and contains many
embassies and government buildings.

In addition to its historic interest and role
as the government centre, New Delhi is a
major travel gateway. It is one of India's
busiest entrance points for overseas airlines,
the hub of the north Indian travel network,
and is on the overland route across Asia. The
city of New Delhi covers most of the Delhi
Union Territory, which is a federal district
similar to Washington DC, Canberra or
Brasilia.

HISTORY

Delhi has not always been the capital of India
but it has played an important role in Indian
history. The settlement of Indraprastha,
which featured in the epic *Mahabharata*
over 3000 years ago, was located approximately on the site of present-day New Delhi.
Over 2000 years ago, Pataliputra (near
modern-day Patna) was the capital of
Emperor Ashoka's kingdom. More recently,
the Moghul emperors made Agra the capital
through the 16th and 17th centuries. Under
the British, Calcutta was the capital until the
construction of New Delhi in 1911. Of
course, it is only comparatively recently that
India as we know it has been unified as one
country. Even at the height of their power the
Moghuls did not control the south of India,

Govt of India statement — 'The external boundaries
of India are neither correct nor authenticated'.

for example. But Delhi has always been an
important city or a capital of the northern
region of the subcontinent.

There have been at least eight cities
around modern Delhi. The first four were to
the south around the area where the Qutab
Minar stands. The earliest known Delhi was
called Indraprastha and was centred near
present-day Purana Qila. At the beginning of
the 12th century AD the last Hindu kingdom
of Delhi was ruled by the Tomara and
Chauthan dynasties and was also near the
Qutab Minar and Suran Kund, now in
Haryana.

This city was followed by Siri, constructed by Ala-ud-din near present-day
Hauz Khas in the 12th century. The third
Delhi was Tughlaqabad, now entirely in
ruins, which stood 10 km south-east of the
Qutab Minar. The fourth Delhi dates from
the 14th century and was also a creation of
the Tughlaqs. Known as Jahanpanah, it also
stood near the Qutab Minar.

The fifth Delhi, Ferozabad, was sited at Feroz Shah Kotla in present-day Old Delhi. Its ruins contain an Ashoka pillar, moved here from elsewhere, and traces of a mosque in which Tamerlane prayed during his attack on India.

Emperor Sher Shah created the sixth Delhi at Purana Qila, near India Gate in New Delhi today. Sher Shah was an Afghan ruler who defeated the Moghul Humayun and took control of Delhi. The Moghul emperor, Shah Jahan, constructed the seventh Delhi in the 17th century, thus shifting the Moghul capital from Agra to Delhi; his Shahjahan-abad roughly corresponds to Old Delhi today and is largely preserved. His Delhi included the Red Fort and the majestic Jami Masjid (a *masjid* is a mosque). Finally, the eighth Delhi, New Delhi, was constructed by the British – the move from Calcutta was announced in 1911 but construction was not completed and the city officially inaugurated until 1931.

Delhi has seen many invaders through the ages. Tamerlane plundered it in the 14th century; the Afghan Babur occupied it in the 16th century, and in 1739 the Persian emperor, Nadir Shah, sacked the city and carted the Kohinoor Diamond and the famous Peacock Throne off to Iran. The British captured Delhi in 1803, but during the Indian Mutiny of 1857 it was a centre of resistance against the British. Prior to Partition, Delhi had a very large Muslim population and Urdu was the main language. Now Hindu Punjabis have replaced many of the Muslims, and Hindi predominates.

ARCHITECTURE

The various periods of Delhi's history can be traced in the many historic buildings around the city. These can be roughly divided into early, middle and late-Pathan periods followed by early, middle and late-Moghul periods.

Early Pathan (1193-1320)

The Qutab Minar complex dates from this period, which was characterised by a combination of Hindu designs with those of the

Muslim invaders. Domes and arches were the chief imported elements.

Middle Pathan (1320-1414)

The Tughlaqabad buildings date from the beginning of this period. Later buildings include the Feroz Shah Kotla Mosque, the Hauz Khas Tomb, the Nizam-ud-din Mosque and the Khirki Mosque. At first, local stone and red sandstone were used; later, stone and mortar walls with plaster facing were employed. Characteristic design elements include sloping walls and high platforms for the mosques.

Late Pathan (1414-1556)

The Sayyid and Lodi tombs and the Purana Qila date from this period. The impressive domes and coloured marble or tile decorations are characteristic of this time.

Moghul (1556-1754)

During the early Moghul period, buildings were of red sandstone with marble details; Humayun's and Azam Khan's tombs are typical examples. During the middle period, much more use of marble was made, and buildings had bulbous domes and towering minarets. The Red Fort, the Jami Masjid and the Fatehpuri Mosque are all good examples, but the supreme building from this period is, of course, the Taj Mahal in Agra.

In the later Moghul period the style became over-elaborate; good examples of this decadent period are the Sunehri Mosque on Chandni Chowk in Old Delhi and the Safdarjang Tomb, probably the last notable Moghul building.

ORIENTATION

Delhi is a relatively easy city to find your way around although it is very spread out. The section of interest to visitors is on the west bank of the Yamuna River and is divided basically into two parts – Old Delhi and New Delhi. Desh Bandhu Gupta Rd and Asaf Ali Rd mark the boundary between the tightly packed streets of the old city and the spaciously planned areas of the new capital.

The 200-page *A to Z Road Guide for Delhi*

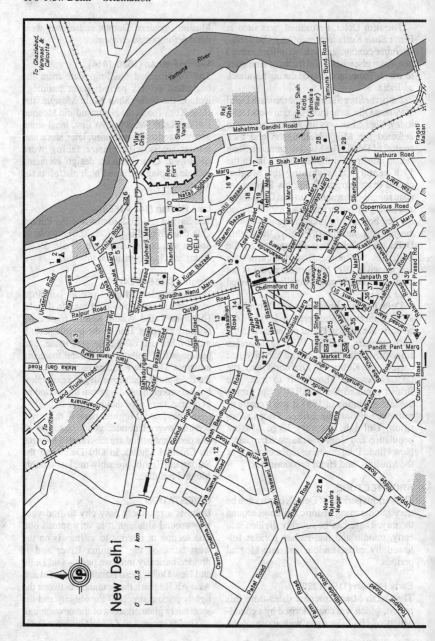

To Ghaziabad, Varanasi & Calcutta

Yamuna River

Feroz Shah Kotla (Ashoka's Pillar)

Yamuna Bund Road

Pragati Maidan

Raj Ghat

Shanti Vana

Mahatma Gandhi Road

Mathura Road

Vijay Ghat

Red Fort

Nataji Subhash Marg

B Shah Zafar Marg

Sikandra Road

Tilak Marg

Lothian Road

Chandni Chowk

Chilli Bazaar

Nehru Marg

Mirdard Marg

Kotla Marg

Dayal Upadhyaya Marg

Copernicus Road

Barakhamba Rd

Kasturba Gandhi Marg

OLD DELHI

Sitaram Bazaar

Asaf Ali Road

Jawaharlal Nehru Marg

Deen Dayal Upadhyaya Marg

Vivekanand Marg

Barakhamba Marg

Ferozeshah Road

Shradha Nand Marg

Qutab Road

Lal Kuan Bazaar

See Connaught Place Map

Janpath

Tolstoy Marg

Ashoka Road

Dr R P Road

Chelmsford Rd

Arakashan Road

Jhandewalan Marg

Main Bazaar

Panchkuin Marg

Parliament St

Bhagat Singh Marg

Sansad Marg

Pandit Pant Marg

Rajpur Road

Boulevard Road

Rani Jhansi Marg

Malka Gan Road

Bahadurgarh Road

Sadar Bazaar Road

Idgah Road

Desh Bandhu Gupta Road

Market Rd

Baba Kharak

Ramakrishna Ashram Marg

Mandir Marg

Talkatora Road

Church Road

To Amritsar

Grand Trunk Road

Roshanara

Guru Govind Singh Marg

Arya Samaj Road

Mandir Lane

Upper Ridge Road

Camp Cheetna Road

Ram Pyare Lal Khan Marg

Ridge Road

Sadhu Vaswani Marg

Stankar Road

New Rajendra Nagar

Patel Road

Todapur Road

Hillside Road

Pusa Road

New Delhi

0   0.5   1 km

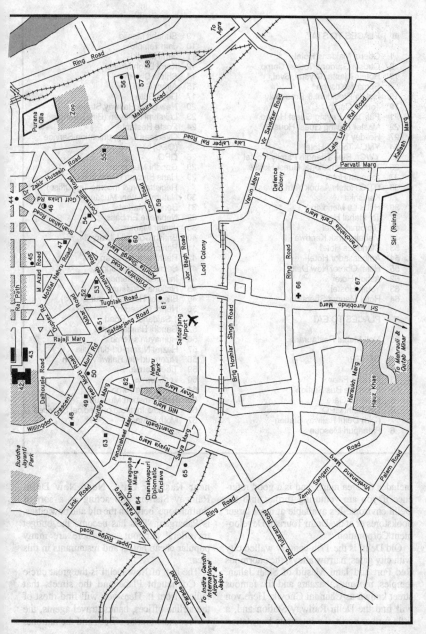

■ PLACES TO STAY

1	Oberoi Maidens Hotel
2	Qudsia Gardens Tourist Camp
13	Hotels Ajanta, Crystal, Syal, Soma & Krishna
18	Hotels President & Broadway
19	Tourist Camp
21	Puri Yatri Paying Guest House
22	Master Paying Guest House
27	Holiday Inn
34	YMCA Tourist Hotel
35	YWCA Blue Triangle Family Hostel
36	YWCA International Guest House
37	Janpath Hotel
38	ITDC Hotels Ashok Yatri Niwas & Kanishka
39	Hotel Le Meridien
47	Taj Mahal Hotel
48	Diplomat Hotel
49	Vishak Yurak Kendwa
53	Claridges Hotel
54	Ambassador Hotel
55	Hotel Oberoi New Delhi
62	Ashok Hotel
63	Youth Hostel
64	Hotel Maurya Sheraton

▼ PLACES TO EAT

| 16 | Moti Mahal Restaurant |

OTHER

3	Ashoka Pillar
4	Interstate Bus Station
5	Kashmir Gate
6	Old Delhi GPO
7	(Old) Delhi Railway Station
8	Fatehpuri Mosque

9	Sunehri Masjid
10	Jain Temple
11	Jami Masjid
12	Karol Bagh Market
14	Shiela Cinema
15	Ajmer Gate
17	Delhi Gate
20	New Delhi Railway Station
23	Lakshmi Narayan (Birla) Temple
24	Poste Restante
25	Overseas Communication Service (OSC)
26	GPO
28	Gandhi Memorial
29	Hans Bhavan (Foreigners' Registration & Income Tax Office)
30	Natural History Museum
31	Bengali Market
32	Nepalese Embassy
33	Jantar Mantar
40	British Council Library
41	Parliament Building
42	Rashtrapati Bhavan
43	Secretariat Buildings
44	India Gate Memorial
45	National Museum
46	Bikaner House (Jaipur Buses)
50	Nehru Museum
51	1 Safdarjang Road
52	Gandhi Balidan Stahl
56	Humayun's Tomb
57	Hazrat Nizam-ud-din Aulia
58	Nizam-ud-din Railway Station
59	Tibet House
60	Lodi Tombs
61	Safdarjang Tomb
65	Rail Transport Museum
66	All India Institute of Medical Services
67	Moth ki Masjid

includes 60 area maps, and is a good reference if you are venturing further into the Delhi environs. It's available at most larger bookstores or at the Delhi Tourism Development Corporation.

Old Delhi is the 17th-century walled city with city gates, narrow alleys, the enormous Red Fort and Jami Masjid of Shah Jahan, temples, mosques, bazaars and the famous street known as Chandni Chowk. Here you will find the Delhi Railway Station and, a little further north, the Interstate bus station near Kashmir Gate. Near New Delhi Railway Station, and acting as a sort of 'buffer zone' between the old and new cities, is Paharganj. This has become the budget travellers' hangout, and there are many popular cheap hotels and restaurants in this area.

The hub of New Delhi is the great circle of Connaught Place and the streets that radiate from it. Here you will find most of the airline offices, banks, travel agents, the various state tourist offices and the national one, more budget accommodation and several of the big hotels. The Regal Cinema, at the south side of the circle, and the Plaza Cinema, at the north, are two important Connaught Place landmarks and are very useful for telling taxi or auto-rickshaw drivers where you want to go.

Janpath, running off Connaught Place to the south, is one of the most important streets, with the Government of India tourist office, the Student Travel Information Centre in the Imperial Hotel and a number of other useful addresses.

New Delhi is a planned city of wide, tree-lined streets, parks and fountains. It can be further subdivided into the business and residential areas around Connaught Place and the government areas around Raj Path to the south. At the east end of Raj Path is the India Gate memorial and at the west end is Rashtrapati Bhavan, the residence of the Indian president.

South of the New Delhi government areas are Delhi's more expensive residential areas with names like Defence Colony, Lodi Colony, Greater Kailash and Basant Vihar. The Indira Gandhi International Airport is to the south-west of the city, and about halfway between the airport and Connaught Place is Chanakyapuri, the diplomatic enclave. Most of Delhi's embassies are concentrated in this modern area and there are several major hotels here.

INFORMATION
Tourist Offices

The Government of India tourist office (☎ 332-0005) at 88 Janpath is open from 9 am to 6 pm Monday to Friday, 9 am to 2 pm Saturday; closed Sunday. The office has a lot of information and brochures on destinations all over India, but none of it is on display – you have to know what you want and ask for it. They have a good giveaway map of Delhi and New Delhi, and can also assist you in finding accommodation.

In the arrivals hall at the international airport terminal there is a tourist counter (☎ 329-1213) open around the clock. Here, too, they can help you find accommodation

although, like many other Indian tourist offices, they may tell you the hotel you choose is 'full' and steer you somewhere else when actually your selected hotel is not full at all.

There is also a Delhi Tourism Corporation office (☎ 331-3637) in N Block, Connaught Place. They also have counters at New Delhi (☎ 35-0574), Delhi (☎ 251-1083) and Nizam-ud-din (☎ 61-1712) railway stations, as well as at the Interstate bus station (☎ 251-2181) at Kashmir Gate.

Most of the state governments have information centres in New Delhi, and the offices for Assam (☎ 34-3961), Bihar (☎ 31-1087), Gujarat (☎ 35-2107), Karnataka (☎ 34-3862), Maharashtra (☎ 34-5332), Orissa (☎ 34-4580) and Tamil Nadu (☎ 34-4651) are all on Baba Kharak Singh Marg.

The offices for Haryana (☎ 332-4911), Himachal Pradesh (☎ 332-5320), Rajasthan (☎ 332-2332), Uttar Pradesh (☎ 332-1068) and West Bengal (☎ 35-3840) are in the Chandralok Building at 36 Janpath.

Jammu & Kashmir (☎ 332-5373), Punjab (☎ 332-3055) and Madhya Pradesh (☎ 332-1187) have their offices in the Kanishka Shopping Centre between the Yatri Niwas and Kanishka hotels.

Others include: Andaman & Nicobar Islands (☎ 38-7015), F-105 Curzon Rd Hostel, Kasturba Gandhi Marg; Goa, Daman & Diu (☎ 462-9968), 18 Amrita Shergil Marg; and Sikkim, at Sikkim Bhavan, Chanakyapuri.

A monthly publication called *Genesis*, available for Rs 7 from many hotels and bookstands, gives information on what's happening in Delhi each month.

Money

The major offices of all the Indian and foreign banks operating in India can be found in New Delhi. As usual, some branches will change travellers' cheques, some won't. If you need to change money outside regular banking hours, the Ashok Hotel (not to be confused with the ITDC Hotel Ashok Yatri Niwas) has an efficient

24-hour service, but it means trekking out to Chanakyapuri.

American Express (☎ 332-7602) has its office in A Block, Connaught Place, and although it's usually crowded, service is very fast. You don't have to have Amex cheques to change money here. If you want to replace stolen or lost American Express travellers' cheques, you need a photocopy of the police report and one photo, as well as the proof-of-purchase slip and the numbers of the missing cheques. If you don't have the latter they will insist on telexing the place where you bought them before re-issuing. If you've had the lot stolen, Amex are empowered to give you limited funds while all this is going on. For lost or stolen cheques, they have a 24-hour number (687-5050) which you should contact as soon as possible.

There's a branch of Thomas Cook (☎ 332-8468) in the Imperial Hotel on Janpath. Other banks include Citibank (☎ 332-8989), Standard Chartered (☎ 31-0195), ANZ Grindlays (☎ 331-9643), Bank of America (☎ 331-5101), Banque Nationale de Paris (☎ 331-3883) and Hongkong Bank (☎ 331-4355).

Post & Telecommunications

There is a small post office at 9A Connaught Place but the GPO is on the traffic circle on Baba Kharak Singh Marg (Radial No 2), half a km south-west of Connaught Place. Poste restante mail can be collected nearby from the Foreign Post Office on Market Rd (officially renamed Bhai Vir Singh Marg). The poste restante office is around the back and up the stairs. Poste restante mail addressed simply to 'Delhi' will end up at the inconveniently situated Old Delhi post office, so ask your correspondents to specify 'New Delhi'. Some people also send mail to the tourist office on Janpath or the Student Travel Information Centre. Of course American Express have their clients' mail service.

There are plenty of the usual private long-distance/ISD call offices dotted around, or there's the Overseas Communications Service (OCS) office on Bangla Sahib Rd if you simply must deal with the bureaucracy.

For credit card and reverse charge (collect) calls there's the Home Country Direct service, available around the clock from Videsh Sanchar Bhavan, Bangla Sahib Rd, New Delhi, 110 001. This service is only available to the UK, USA, Japan and Italy.

The telephone area code for New Delhi is 011.

Foreign Embassies

Addresses of some of the foreign missions in Delhi include:

Afghanistan
  5/50-F Shantipath, Chanakyapuri (☎ 60-3331)
Australia
  1/50G Shantipath, Chanakyapuri (☎ 60-1336)
Bangladesh
  56 Ring Rd, Lajpat Nagar III (☎ 683-4668)
Bhutan
  Chandragupta Marg, Chanakyapuri (☎ 60-9217)
Canada
  7/8 Shantipath, Chanakyapuri (☎ 687-6500)
China
  50-D Shantipath, Chanakyapuri (☎ 60-0328)
Denmark
  11 Aurangzeb Rd (☎ 61-6273)
France
  2/50-E Shantipath, Chanakyapuri (☎ 60-4004)
Germany
  6/50-G Shantipath, Chanakyapuri (☎ 60-4861)
Indonesia
  50-A Chanakyapuri (☎ 60-2352)
Iran
  5 Barakhamba Rd (☎ 332-9600)
Iraq
  169 Jor Bagh Rd (☎ 61-8011)
Ireland
  13 Jor Bagh Rd (☎ 61-7435)
Italy
  13 Golf Links Rd (☎ 60-0071)
Japan
  50-G Shantipath, Chanakyapuri (☎ 687-6583)
Malaysia
  50-M Satya Marg, Chanakyapuri (☎ 60-1297)
Myanmar (Burma)
  3/50-F Nyaya Marg, Chanakyapuri (☎ 60-0251)
Nepal
  Barakhamba Rd (☎ 332-7361)
Netherlands
  6/50-F Shantipath, Chanakyapuri (☎ 688-4951)
New Zealand
  50 Nyaya Marg, Chanakyapuri (☎ 46-2254)
Pakistan
  2/50-G Shantipath, Chanakyapuri (☎ 60-0601)

Russia
    Shantipath, Chanakyapuri (☎ 60-6026)
Singapore
    61-E Chandragupta Marg, Chanakyapuri
    (☎ 60-4162)
Sri Lanka
    27 Kautilya Marg, Chanakyapuri (☎ 301-0201)
Sweden
    Nyaya Marg, Chanakyapuri (☎ 60-4961)
Syria
    28 Vasant Marg, Vasant Vihar (☎ 67-0233)
Thailand
    56-N Nyaya Marg, Chanakyapuri (☎ 60-5679)
UK
    50 Shantipath, Chanakyapuri (☎ 60-1371)
USA
    Shantipath, Chanakyapuri (☎ 60-0651)

See page 92 in the Facts for the Visitor chapter for more details on obtaining visas in New Delhi.

Visa Extensions & Other Permits Hans Bhavan, near the Tilak Bridge Railway Station, is where you'll find the Foreigners' Registration Office (☎ 331-9489). Come here to get visa extensions or permits for restricted areas such as Assam. It's as chaotic and confused as ever with no organisation or plan, but surprisingly, with a little push and shove, you can get visas renewed or permits issued remarkably quickly. Four photos are required for visa extensions; a photographer outside the building will do them on the spot for a small fee. The office is closed from 1 to 1.30 pm.

If you need a tax clearance certificate before departure, the Foreign Section of the Income Tax Department (☎ 331-7826) is around the corner from Hans Bhavan in the Central Revenue Building. Bring exchange certificates with you, though it's quite likely nobody will ask for your clearance certificate when you leave the country. The office is closed from 1 to 2 pm.

Libraries & Cultural Centres
The American Centre (☎ 331-6841) is at 24 Kasturba Gandhi Marg and is open from 9.30 am to 6 pm. It has an extensive range of books. The British Council Library (☎ 371-1401) is open from 9 am to 6 pm and is in the AIFACS Building, Rafi Marg. It's much better than its US equivalent but officially you have to join to get in. Other cultural centres include: Alliance Francaise (☎ 644-0128); Italy (☎ 644-9193), 38 Ring Rd; Japan (☎ 332-9838), 32 Ferozshah Rd; and Russia (☎ 332-9102), 24 Ferozshah Rd.

Sapru House on Barakhamba Rd is an institution devoted to the study of people of the world and has a good library. The India International Centre (☎ 61-9431), beside the Lodi Tombs, has lectures each week on art, economics and other contemporary issues by Indian and foreign experts.

Travel Agencies
Tripsout Travel at 72/7 Tolstoy Lane, behind the Government of India tourist office on Janpath, is popular, appears to be trustworthy and offers discounts which match (or beat) the many Connaught Place agencies. Lots of travellers use the place. In the Imperial Hotel, the Student Travel Information Centre (☎ 332-4788) is also used by many travellers and is the place to renew or obtain student cards, although their tickets are not usually as cheap as elsewhere. Aerotrek Travels (☎ 371-5966) in the Mercantile Building in E Block is reportedly reliable. Some of the ticket discounters around Connaught Place are real fly-by-night operations, so take care.

Outbound Travel (☎ 60-3902) at B-2/50 Safdarjang Enclave has been recommended as a reliable place to organise travel within India.

There are also a couple of agencies catering to budget travellers in Paharganj, and you'll be approached on the streets or in cafes.

For more upmarket travel arrangements, both within India and for foreign travel, there are a number of places, mostly around Connaught Place. These include: Cox & Kings (☎ 332-1028), Sita World Travels (☎ 331-1133), and the Travel Corporation of India (☎ 331-2570).

Bookshops
There are a number of excellent bookshops around Connaught Place – a good place to

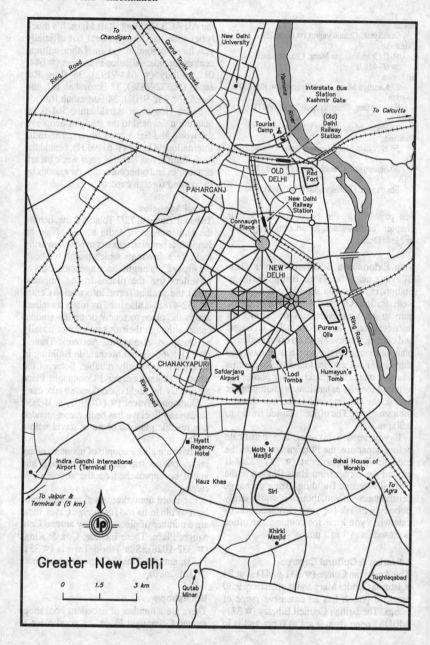

Greater New Delhi

0   1.5   3 km

look for interesting Indian books or to stock up with hefty paperbacks to while away those long train rides. Some of the better shops include: the New Book Depot at 18 B Block, Connaught Place; the English Book Depot; the Piccadilly Book Store; the Oxford Book Shop in N Block, Connaught Place, next to Air France; and Bookworm at 29B Radial Rd No 4, Connaught Place

There are plenty of pavement stalls at various places around Connaught Place, with the major concentration on Sansag Marg, just around the corner from the Regal Cinema. They have a good range of cheap paperbacks, and will often buy them back from you if they are returned in a reasonable condition.

Medical Services

If you need medical attention in Delhi, the East West Medical Centre (☎ 69-9229, 62-3738), 38 Golf Links Rd, has been recommended by many travellers, diplomats and other expatriates. It's well equipped and the staff know what they're doing. Charges are high by Indian standards, but if you want good treatment...

For 24-hour emergency service, try the All India Institute of Medical Sciences (☎ 66-1123) at Ansari Nagar. Other reliable places include the Dr Ram Manohar Lohia Hospital (☎ 34-5525), Baba Kharak Singh Marg; and the Ashlok Hospital (☎ 60-8407) at 25A Block AB, Safdarjang Enclave.

Ambulance service is available by phoning 102.

Film & Photography

The Delhi Photo Company, at 78 Janpath close to the tourist office, processes both print and slide film quickly, cheaply and competently.

OLD DELHI

The old walled city of Shahjahanabad stands to the west of the Red Fort and was at one time surrounded by a sturdy defensive wall, only fragments of which now exist. The **Kashmir Gate**, at the northern end of the walled city, was the scene for desperate

fighting when the British retook Delhi during the Mutiny. West of here, near Sabzi Mandi, is the British-erected **Mutiny Memorial** to the soldiers who lost their lives during the uprising. Near the monument is an **Ashoka pillar**, and like the one in Feroz Kotla, it was brought here by Feroz Shah Tughlaq.

Chandni Chowk

The main street of Old Delhi is the colourful shopping bazaar known as Chandni Chowk (Silver Street). It's hopelessly congested day and night, a very sharp contrast to the open, spacious streets of New Delhi. At the east (Red Fort) end of Chandni Chowk, and north of the Jami Masjid, there is a **Jain temple** with a small marble courtyard surrounded by a colonnade. Next to the Kotwali (police station) is the **Sunehri Masjid**. In 1739, Nadir Shah, the Persian invader who carried off the Peacock Throne when he sacked Delhi, stood on the roof of this mosque and watched while his soldiers conducted a bloody massacre of the Delhi inhabitants.

The west end of Chandni Chowk is marked by the **Fatehpuri Mosque** which was erected in 1650 by one of Shah Jahan's wives.

Red Fort

The red sandstone walls of Lal Qila, the Red Fort, extend for two km and vary in height from 18 metres on the river side to 33 metres on the city side. Shah Jahan started construction of the massive fort in 1638 and it was completed in 1648. He never completely moved his capital from Agra to his new city of Shahjahanabad in Delhi because he was deposed and imprisoned in Agra Fort by his son Aurangzeb.

The Red Fort dates from the very peak of Moghul power. When the emperor rode out on elephant-back into the streets of Old Delhi it was a display of pomp and power at its most magnificent. The Moghul reign from Delhi was a short one, however. Aurangzeb was the first and last great Moghul emperor to rule from here.

Today, the fort is typically Indian with

would-be guides leaping forth to offer their services as soon as you enter. It's still a calm haven of peace if you've just left the frantic streets of Old Delhi, however. The city noise and confusion are light-years away from the fort gardens and pavilions. The Yamuna River used to flow right by the eastern edge of the fort, and filled the 10-metre-deep moat. These days the river is over one km to the east and the moat remains empty. Entry to the fort is Rs 0.50, free on Fridays.

Lahore Gate The main gate to the fort takes its name from the fact that it faces towards Lahore, now in Pakistan. If one spot could be said to be the emotional and symbolic heart of the modern Indian nation, the Lahore Gate of the Red Fort is probably it. During the struggle for independence, one of the nationalists' declarations was that they would see the Indian flag flying over the Red Fort in Delhi. After independence, many important political speeches were given by Nehru and Indira Gandhi to the crowds amassed on the maidan outside, and on Independence Day (15 August) each year, the prime minister addresses a huge crowd.

You enter the fort here and immediately find yourself in a vaulted arcade, the Chatta Chowk (Covered Bazaar). The shops in this arcade used to sell the upmarket items that the royal household might fancy – silks, jewellery, gold. These days they cater to the tourist trade and the quality of the goods is certainly a little less, although some still carry a royal price tag! This arcade of shops was also known as the Meena Bazaar, the shopping centre for ladies of the court. On Thursdays the gates of the fort were closed to men, women staffed the shops and only women were allowed inside the citadel.

The arcade leads to the Naubat Khana, or Drum House, where musicians used to play for the emperor, and the arrival of princes and royalty was heralded from here. The open courtyard beyond it formerly had galleries along either side, but these were removed by the British Army when the fort was used as their headquarters. Other reminders of the British presence are the huge three-storey barrack blocks which lie to the north of this courtyard.

Diwan-i-Am The Hall of Public Audiences was where the emperor would sit to hear complaints or disputes from his subjects. His alcove in the wall was marble-panelled and set with precious stones, many of which were looted following the Mutiny. This elegant hall was restored as a result of a directive by Lord Curzon, the Viceroy of India between 1898 and 1905.

Diwan-i-Khas The Hall of Private Audiences, built of white marble, was the luxurious chamber where the emperor would hold private meetings. Centrepiece of the hall (until Nadir Shah carted it off to Iran in 1739) was the magnificent Peacock Throne. The solid gold throne had figures of peacocks standing behind it, their beautiful colours resulting from countless inlaid precious stones. Between them was the figure of a parrot carved out of a single emerald.

This masterpiece in precious metals, sapphires, rubies, emeralds and pearls was broken up, and the so-called Peacock Throne displayed in Tehran simply utilises various bits of the original. The marble pedestal on which the throne used to sit remains in place.

In 1760, the Marathas also removed the silver ceiling from the hall, so today it is a pale shadow of its former glory. Inscribed on the walls of the Diwan-i-Khas is that famous Persian couplet:

If there is a paradise on earth
it is this, it is this, it is this.

Royal Baths Next to the Diwan-i-Khas are the *hammams* or baths – three large rooms surmounted by domes, with a fountain in the centre – one of which was set up as a sauna! The floors used to be inlaid with *pietra dura* work, and the rooms were illuminated through panels of coloured glass in the roof. The baths are closed to the public.

Shahi Burj This modest, three-storey octagonal tower at the north-eastern edge of the fort was once Shah Jahan's private working area. From here water used to flow south through the Royal Baths, the Diwan-i-Khas, the Khas Mahal and the Rang Mahal. Like the baths, the tower is closed.

Moti Masjid Built in 1659 by Aurangzeb for his own personal use, the small and totally enclosed Pearl Mosque, made of marble, is next to the baths. One curious feature of the mosque is that its outer walls are oriented exactly to be in symmetry with the rest of the fort, while the inner walls are slightly askew, so that the mosque has the correct orientation with Mecca.

Other Features The **Khas Mahal**, south of the Diwan-i-Khas, was the emperor's private palace, divided into rooms for worship, sleeping and living.

The **Rang Mahal** pavilion or Palace of Colour, further south again, took its name from the painted interior, which is now gone. This was once the residence of the emperor's chief wife, and is where he ate. On the floor in the centre is a beautifully carved marble lotus, and the water flowing along the channel from the Shahi Burj used to end up here. Originally there was a fountain made of ivory in the centre.

There is a small Museum of Archaeology in the **Mumtaz Mahal**, still further south along the eastern wall. It's well worth a look, although most visitors seem to rush through the Red Fort, bypassing the museum.

The **Delhi Gate** to the south of the fort led to the Jami Masjid.

Gardens Between all the exquisite buildings were highly formal gardens, complete with fountains, pools and small pavilions. While the general outline and some of the pavilions are still in place, the gardens are not what they once were.

Sound & Light Show Each evening an interesting *Son et Lumière* show re-creates events of India's history, particularly those connected with the Red Fort. There are shows in English and Hindi, and tickets (Rs

10) are available from the fort. The English sessions are at 8.30 pm in winter and 9 pm in summer. It's well worth making the effort to see this show, but make sure you are well equipped with mosquito repellent.

Jami Masjid

The great mosque of Old Delhi is both the largest in India and the final architectural extravagance of Shah Jahan. Commenced in 1644, the mosque was not completed until 1658. It has three great gateways, four angle towers and two minarets standing 40 metres high and constructed of alternating vertical strips of red sandstone and white marble.

Broad flights of steps lead up to the imposing gateways. The eastern gateway was originally only opened for the emperor, and is now only open on Fridays and Muslim festival days. The general public can enter by either the north or south gate (Rs 5). Shoes should be removed and those people considered unsuitably dressed (bare legs for either men or women) can hire robes at the northern gate.

The courtyard of the mosque has a capacity of 25,000 people. For Rs 5 it's possible to climb the southern minaret, and the views in all directions are superb – Old Delhi, the Red Fort and the polluting factories beyond it across the river, and New Delhi to the south. You can also see one of the features that the architect Lutyens incorporated into his design of New Delhi – the Jami Masjid, Connaught Place and Sansad Bhavan (Parliament House) are in a direct line. There's also a fine view of the Red Fort from the east side of the mosque.

Coronation Durbar Site

This is a must for incurable Raj fans looking for their fix of nostalgia. It's north of Old Delhi and is best reached by auto-rickshaw. In open country stands a lone obelisk in a desolate field, and it was on this site that in 1877 and 1903 the durbars were enacted, and in 1911 that King George V was declared Emperor of India.

If you look closely you can still see the old

boy – a statue of him rises ghost-like out of the bushes nearby, where it was unceremoniously dumped after being removed from the canopy midway along Rajpath, between India Gate and Rashtrapati Bhavan. (The place where it was taken from remains empty. The statue of Gandhi that was meant to replace it was never installed, due to some petty disagreement.) Further inspection reveals other imperial dignitaries languishing in the scrub. These days this historic bit of spare ground is used for backyard cricket matches and is a place for young men to teach their girlfriends how to ride the family scooter.

FEROZ SHAH KOTLA

Erected by Feroz Shah Tughlaq in 1354, the ruins of Ferozabad, the fifth city of Delhi, can be found at Feroz Shah Kotla, between the old and new Delhis. In the fortress-palace is a 13-metre-high sandstone Ashoka pillar inscribed with Ashoka's edicts (and a later inscription). The remains of an old mosque and a fine well can also be seen in the area, but most of the ruins of Ferozabad were used for the construction of later cities.

RAJ GHAT

North-east of Feroz Shah Kotla, on the banks of the Yamuna, a simple square platform of black marble marks the spot where Mahatma Gandhi was cremated following his assassination in 1948. A commemorative ceremony takes place each Friday, the day he was killed.

Jawaharlal Nehru, the first Indian prime minister, was cremated just to the north at Shanti Vana (Forest of Peace) in 1964. His daughter, Indira Gandhi, who was killed in 1984, and grandsons Sanjay (1980) and Rajiv (1991) were also cremated in this vicinity.

The Raj Ghat area is now a beautiful park, complete with labelled trees planted by a mixed bag of notables including Queen Elizabeth II, Gough Whitlam, Dwight Eisenhower and Ho Chi Minh!

NEW DELHI
Connaught Place

At the northern end of New Delhi, Connaught Place is the business and tourist centre. It's a vast traffic circle with an architecturally uniform series of colonnaded buildings around the edge – mainly devoted to shops, airline offices and the like. It's spacious but busy, and you're continually approached by people willing to provide you with everything imaginable, from an airline ticket for Timbuktu to having your fortune read.

Jantar Mantar

Only a short stroll down Sansad Marg (Parliament St) from Connaught Place, this strange collection of salmon-coloured structures is one of Maharaja Jai Singh II's observatories. The ruler from Jaipur constructed this observatory in 1725 and it is dominated by a huge sundial known as the Prince of Dials. Other instruments plot the course of heavenly bodies and predict eclipses.

Lakshmi Narayan Temple

Due west of Connaught Place, this garish modern temple was erected by the industrialist Birla in 1938. It's dedicated to Lakshmi, the goddess of prosperity and good fortune, and is commonly known as Birla Mandir.

Rajpath

The Kingsway is another focus of Lutyens' New Delhi. It is immensely broad and is flanked on either side by ornamental ponds. At its eastern end lies the India Gate, while at the western end lies Rashtrapati Bhavan, now the president's residence, but built originally for the viceroy. It is flanked by the two large Secretariat buildings, and these three buildings sit upon a small rise, known as Raisina Hill.

The rise, and the approach road up to it (or, more precisely, the angle of the approach road up to it), were the cause of a trivial yet major dispute, known as the 'battle of the gradient', between Lutyens and his colleague, Herbert Baker. While Baker was charged with designing the Secretariat and parliament buildings, Lutyens made himself responsible for the viceregal residence and the India Gate. It was Lutyens' intention that the Residence should be slightly higher than the Secretariats and visible from a greater distance. Baker wanted all three buildings on the same level, so that the viceroy's residence would majestically come into view as one approached it up the rise. After numerous discussions, and referral to successive viceroys, Baker won, and the two men refused to talk to one another for some years.

India Gate

The 42-metre-high stone arch of triumph stands at the eastern end of the Rajpath. It bears the name of 85,000 Indian Army soldiers who died in the campaigns of WW I, the North-West Frontier operations of the same time and the 1919 Afghan fiasco.

Secretariat Buildings

The north and south Secretariat buildings lie either side of Rajpath on Raisina Hill. These imposing buildings, topped with *chhatris* (small domes), now house the ministries of Foreign Affairs and Finance respectively.

Rashtrapati Bhavan

The official residence of the President of India stands at the opposite end of the Rajpath from India Gate. Completed in 1929, the palace-like building is a blend of Moghul and Western architectural styles, the most obvious Indian feature being the huge copper dome. To the west of the building is a Moghul garden which occupies 130 hectares, and this is open to the public in February.

Prior to Independence this was the viceroy's residence. At the time of Mountbatten, India's last viceroy, the number of servants needed to maintain the 340 rooms and its extensive gardens was enormous. There were 418 gardeners alone, 50 of them boys whose sole job was to chase away birds!

Parliament House

Sansad Bhavan, the Indian parliament building, stands almost hidden and virtually unnoticed at the end of Sansad Marg, or Parliament St, just north of the Rajpath. The building is a circular colonnaded structure 171 metres in diameter. Its relative physical insignificance in the grand scheme of New Delhi shows how the focus of power has shifted from the viceroy's residence, which was given pride of place during the time of the British Raj when New Delhi was conceived.

Permits to visit the parliament and sit in the public gallery are available from the reception office on Raisina Rd, but you'll need a letter of introduction from your embassy.

MUSEUMS
National Museum

On Janpath just south of Rajpath, the National Museum has a good collection of Indian bronzes, terracotta and wood sculptures dating back to the Mauryan period (2nd-3rd century BC), exhibits from the Vijayanagar period in south India, miniature and mural paintings, and costumes of the various tribal peoples. The museum is definitely worth visiting and is open from 10 am to 5 pm daily; closed on Monday. The small entry fee varies through the week; it's free on Saturday and Sunday. There are film shows most days of the week.

Right next door is the Archaeological Survey of India office. Publications available here cover all the main sites in India. Many of these are not available at the particular sites themselves.

Nehru Museum

On Teen Murti Rd near Chanakyapuri, the residence of the first Indian prime minister, Teen Murti Bhavan, has been converted into a museum. Photographs and newspaper clippings on display give a fascinating insight into the history of the independence movement.

During the tourist season there is a Sound & Light show about his life and the independence movement. The museum is open from

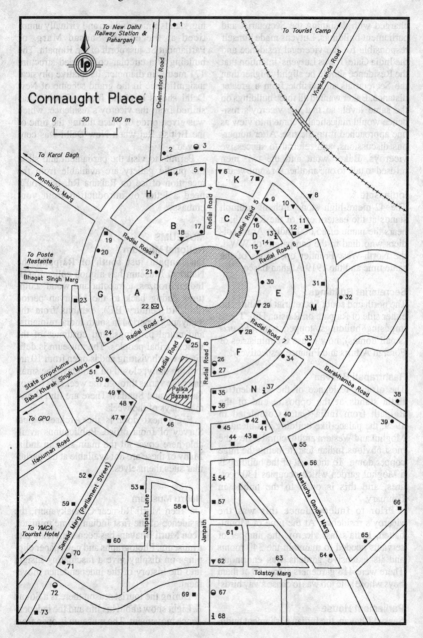

Connaught Place

To New Delhi Railway Station & Paharganj

To Tourist Camp

Chelmsford Road

Vivekananda Road

0   50   100 m

To Karol Bagh

Panchkuin Marg

To Poste Restante

Bhagat Singh Marg

To GPO

Hanuman Road

State Emporiums

Baba Kharak Singh Marg

To YMCA Tourist Hotel

Radial Road 4

Radial Road 5

Radial Road 6

Radial Road 3

Radial Road 2

Radial Road 1

Radial Road 8

Radial Road 7

H

B

K

C

L

D

G

A

E

M

F

N

Barakhamba Road

Kasturba Gandhi Marg

Sansad Marg (Parliament Street)

Janpath Lane

Janpath

Tolstoy Marg

Palika Bazaar

■ PLACES TO STAY

4	Hotel 55
7	York Hotel
11	Nirula's Hotel & Restaurant
12	Jukaso Inn
14	Hotel Palace Heights
19	Hotel Marina
23	Alka Hotel
31	Hotel Bright & Andhra Bank
35	Hotel Metro
41	Asia Guest House
43	Sunny Guest House
44	Ringo Guest House
53	Mrs Colaco's Guest House
57	Janpath Guest House
59	Park Hotel
60	Mr SC Jain's Guest House
66	Hotel Hans Plaza
69	Imperial Hotel, Thomas Cook & Student Travel Information Centre
73	YWCA International Guest House

▼ PLACES TO EAT

6	Chinar Restaurant
8	Kaka da Hotel
10	Delhi Durbar & Minar Restaurants
15	Embassy Restaurant
18	Volga Restaurant
28	The Host
29	United Coffee House
36	Nirula's & Wimpy
47	Kwality Restaurant & Pavement Bookstalls
48	El Arab Restaurant
49	Gaylord
62	Sona Rupa Restaurant & Royal Nepal Airlines

OTHER

1	Railway Booking Office
2	Cycle-Rickshaw Stand
3	Bus 620 to Youth Hostel & Chanakyapuri
5	Plaza Cinema
9	Libyan Arab Airlines
12	ITDC Tours Booking Office & Hotel Jukaso Inn
13	ITDC Booking Office
16	Odeon Cinema
17	Bookworm
20	Singapore Airlines, Gulf Air
21	Wenger's & American Express
22	Post Office
24	Malaysian & Royal Jordanian Airlines
25	Six-Seaters to Old Delhi
26	EATS Bus & Vayudoot
27	Indian Airlines
30	ANZ Grindlays Bank
32	Super Bazaar
33	Bank of Baroda
34	Aeroflot
37	Delhi Tourism Corporation Office
38	Indian Airlines & Emirates Air
39	Bank of America, Banque Nationale de Paris & Saudia Airlines
40	Hongkong Bank
42	Delhi Transport Corporation
45	Air France & Oxford Bookshop
46	Air India & Citibank
50	Regal Cinema
51	Khadi Gramodyog Bhavan
52	Standard Chartered Bank
54	Government of India Tourist Office & Delhi Photo Company
55	Pakistan International Airlines
56	American Centre
58	Central Cottage Industries Emporium, Map Sales Office & Bankura Cafe
61	Tripsout Travel
63	Cathay Pacific, Deutsche Bank & Qantas
64	Arian Afghan Airlines
65	KLM
67	Bus 505 to Qutab Minar
68	Haryana, Himachal Pradesh, Rajasthan, Uttar Pradesh & West Bengal Tourist Offices
70	Bus 620 to Youth Hostel & Chanakyapuri
71	Jantar Mantar
72	Bus 433 to Bahai Temple

from 10 am to 5 pm daily; closed on Monday. Admission is free.

Rail Transport Museum

This museum at Chanakyapuri will be of great interest to anyone who becomes fascinated by India's exotic collection of railway engines. The exhibit includes an 1855 steam engine, still in working order, and a large number of oddities such as the skull of an elephant that charged a mail train in 1894, and lost.

See the Gricing section in the Getting Around chapter for more details. The museum is open from 9.30 am to 5 pm (closed on Monday) and there's a small admission fee.

Tibet House

This small museum has a fascinating collection of ceremonial items brought out of Tibet when the Dalai Lama fled following the Chinese occupation. Downstairs is a shop selling a wide range of Tibetan handicrafts. There are often lecture/discussion sessions and there's also a nice little museum. It's in the Institutional Area, Lodi Rd, and hours are from 9.30 am to 1 pm and 2 to 5.30 pm. It's closed Sunday and admission is free.

International Dolls Museum

In Nehru House on Bahadur Shah Zafar Marg, this museum displays 6000 dolls from 85 countries. Over a third of them are from India and one exhibit comprises 500 dolls in the costumes worn all over India. The museum is open from 10 am to 5.30 pm daily; closed Mondays.

Crafts Museum

In the Aditi Pavilion at the Pragati Maidan Exhibition Grounds, Mathura Rd, this museum contains a collection of traditional Indian crafts in textiles, metal, wood and ceramics. The museum is part of a 'village life' complex where you can visit rural India without ever leaving Delhi. Opening hours are from 9.30 am to 4.30 pm; closed Sunday. Admission is free.

Gandhi Darshan

At Raj Ghat the Gandhi Darshan is a display of paintings and photos about the Mahatma's life and deeds. The Gandhi Smarak Sangrahalaya, also at Raj Ghat, has displays of some of Gandhi's personal possessions.

1 Safdarjang Rd

The former residence of Indira Gandhi has also been converted into a museum. On show are some of her personal effects, including the sari (complete with blood stains) she was wearing at the time of her assassination. A glass plaque in the garden, flanked constantly by two soldiers, marks where she actually fell.

Other Museums

The Museum of Natural History is opposite the Nepalese Embassy on Barakhamba Rd. Fronted by a large model dinosaur, it has a collection of fossils, stuffed animals and birds, and a 'hands on' discovery room for children. It's open from 10 am to 5 pm; closed Monday.

There is a National Philatelic Museum at Dak Tar Bhavan, Sardar Patel Square on Sansad Marg (Parliament St). It's closed on Saturday and Sunday. At Indira Gandhi International Airport there is an Air Force Museum open from 10 am to 1.30 pm; closed Tuesday.

PURANA QILA

Just south-east of India Gate and north of Humayun's Tomb and the Nizam-ud-din Railway Station is the old fort, Purana Qila. This is the supposed site of Indraprastha, the original city of Delhi. The Afghan ruler, Sher Shah, who briefly interrupted the Moghul Empire by defeating Humayun, built the fort during his reign from 1538-45, before Humayun regained control of India. The fort has massive walls and three large gateways.

Entering from the south gate you'll see the small octagonal red sandstone tower, the Sher Mandal, later used by Humayun as a library. It was while descending the stairs of this tower one day in 1556 that he slipped, fell and received injuries from which he later died. Just beyond it is the Qila-i-Kuhran Mosque, or Mosque of Sher Shah, which, unlike the fort itself, is in a fairly reasonable condition.

ZOO

The Delhi Zoo on the south side of the Purana Qila is not terribly good. The cages are poorly labelled and in winter many of the animals are kept inside. There is a white tiger though. The zoo is open from 8 am to 6 pm in summer, 9 am to 5 pm in winter; closed Friday. Entry is Rs 0.50.

HUMAYUN'S TOMB

Built in the mid-16th century by Haji Begum, wife of Humayun, the second Moghul emperor, this is an early example of Moghul architecture. The elements in its design – a squat building, lighted by high arched entrances, topped by a bulbous dome and surrounded by formal gardens – were to be refined over the years to the magnificence of the Taj Mahal in Agra. This earlier tomb is thus of great interest for its relation to the later Taj. Humayun's wife is also buried in the red-and-white sandstone, black-and-yellow marble tomb.

Other tombs in the garden include that of Humayun's barber and the Tomb of Isa Khan, a good example of Pathan (Afghan) architecture from the time of the Lodi dynasty. Entry to Humayun's Tomb is Rs 0.50, except on Friday when it is free. An excellent view can be obtained over the surrounding country from the terraces of the tomb.

HAZRAT NIZAM-UD-DIN AULIA

Across the road from Humayun's Tomb is the shrine of the Muslim saint, Nizam-ud-din Chishti, who died in 1325 aged 92. His shrine, with its large tank, is one of several interesting tombs here. The construction of Nizam-ud-din's tank caused a dispute between the saint and the constructor of Tughlaqabad, further to the south of Delhi – see Tughlaqabad, later in this section, for details.

Other tombs include the later grave of Jahanara, the daughter of Shah Jahan, who stayed with her father during his imprisonment by Aurangzeb in Agra's Red Fort. Amir Khusru, a renowned Urdu poet, also has his tomb here as does Azam Khan, a favourite of Humayun and his son Akbar. Azam Khan was murdered by Adham Khan in Agra. In turn Akbar had Adham Khan terminated and his grave is near the Qutab Minar.

The tomb of a modern Sufi saint, the Hazrat Inayat Khan, is also near here and every Friday evening just after sunset Qawali singers perform at it.

LODI TOMBS

About three km to the west of Humayun's tomb and adjoining the India International Centre are the Lodi Gardens. In these well-kept gardens are the tombs of the Sayyid and Lodi rulers. Mohammed Shah's Tomb (1450) is a prototype for the later Moghul-style Tomb of Humayun, a design which would eventually develop into the Taj Mahal. Other tombs include those of his predecessor Mubarak Shah (1433), Ibrahim Lodi (1526) and Sikander Lodi (1517). The Bara Gumbad Mosque is a fine example of its type of plaster decoration.

SAFDARJANG TOMB

Beside the small Safdarjang Airport, where Indira Gandhi's son Sanjay was killed in a light plane accident in 1980, is the Safdarjang Tomb. It was built in 1753-54 by the Nawab of Oudh for his father, Safdarjang, and is one of the last examples of Moghul architecture before the final remnants of the great empire collapsed. The tomb stands on a high terrace in an extensive garden. Entry is Rs 0.50; free on Friday.

HAUZ KHAS

Midway between Safdarjang and the Qutab Minar, this area was once the reservoir for the second city of Delhi, Siri, which lies slightly to the east. Interesting sights here include Feroz Shah's Tomb (1398), the remains of an ancient college, and the Moth ki Masjid, said to be the finest in the Lodi style. It was around this area that Timur defeated the forces of Mohammed Shah Tughlaq in 1398.

BAHAI HOUSE OF WORSHIP

Lying to the east of Hauz Khas is this relatively new building shaped like a lotus flower. It is set amongst pools and gardens, and adherents of any faith are free to visit the temple and pray or meditate silently according to their own religion. It looks particularly spectacular at dusk when it is floodlit.

Getting There & Away

Bus No 433 from opposite the Jantar Mantar

SAFDAR JANG TOMB   DELHI

on Sansad Marg near Connaught Place will bring you very close to the temple.

SWIMMING POOLS

The New Delhi Municipal Corporation has its pool at Nehru Park, near the Ashok Hotel in Chanakyapuri.

Most of the deluxe hotels have pools, and many allow nonresident use – for a fee, which can be anything from Rs 100 up to US$5! In the winter months many hotel pools are closed, which is hardly surprising given the weather. The pool at the Sheraton is heated and open year round.

ORGANISED TOURS

Delhi is very spread out, so taking a city tour makes a lot of sense. Even by public transport, getting from, say, the Red Fort to the Qutab Minar is comparatively expensive.

Two major organisations arrange Delhi tours – beware of agents offering cut-price (and sometimes inferior) tours. The ITDC (☎ 332-2336) has tours which include guides and a luxury coach. Their office is in L Block, Connaught Place, but their tours also start from the major hotels. Delhi Tourism (☎ 331-3637), a branch of the city

government, arranges similar tours and their office is in N Block.

A 4½-hour morning tour of New Delhi costs Rs 55 with ITDC. Starting at 8.30 am, the tour includes the Qutab Minar, Humayun's Tomb, India Gate, the Jantar Mantar and the Lakshmi Narayan Temple. The afternoon Old Delhi tour for Rs 45 covers the Red Fort, Jami Masjid, Raj Ghat, Shanti Vana and Feroz Shah Kotla. If you take both tours on the same day it costs Rs 90.

'Delhi by Evening' is a tour which takes in a number of sights, including the Sound & Light show at the Red Fort.

Tours further afield include ITDC day tours to Agra for Rs 90 or weekend tours to Hardwar and Rishikesh.

PLACES TO STAY
Places to Stay – bottom end

Camping If you want to camp there are several possibilities in Delhi. The *Tourist Camp* (☎ 327-8929) is one of the cheapest places to stay and is surprisingly popular. It's some distance from Connaught Place but is well served by buses. Most of the overland operators stay here and it's also the starting point for the direct buses to Kathmandu. Run by retired Indian Army officers, the camp is actually in Old Delhi, near Delhi Gate on Jawaharlal Nehru Marg, across from the J P Narayan Hospital (Irwin Hospital), only two km from Connaught Place. You can camp with your own tent, or there are basic rooms with shared bathrooms for Rs 60/90. They're nothing flash, but OK; this place generally gets good recommendations from travellers. There's a restaurant and a left-luggage room where you can leave your accumulated junk while you explore elsewhere.

There is a second camping site, the *Qudsia Gardens Tourist Camp* (☎ 252-3121), right across the road from the Interstate bus station. Camping here costs Rs 25 per person, or there are ordinary rooms for Rs 50/70, and deluxe doubles for Rs 125. It's convenient for an early morning bus departure, but little else.

Hotels Delhi is certainly no bargain when it comes to cheap hotels. You can easily pay Rs 80 for the most basic single room – a price that elsewhere in India will generally get you a reasonable double room with bath.

There are basically two areas for cheap accommodation in Delhi. The first is around Janpath at the southern side of Connaught Place in New Delhi. The second area, which these days is cheaper, more popular and has a greater range of places than Connaught Place, is Paharganj near New Delhi Railway Station – this is about midway between old and New Delhi.

There are also a number of rock-bottom hotels in Old Delhi itself. They're colourful but generally noisy and too far away from New Delhi's agents, offices, airlines and other facilities for most travellers, especially given Delhi's difficult public transport situation. Other possibilities are scattered around Delhi, such as the two popular tourist camps and the youth hostel in the Chanakyapuri diplomatic quarter.

Connaught Place & Janpath Area There are several cheap lodges or guest houses near the Government of India tourist office.

They're often small and cramped but you meet lots of fellow travellers; they're also conveniently central and there are often dormitories for shoestring travellers. Since many of these places are so popular, you may find that your first choice is full. If that's the case simply stay at one of the others until a room becomes available – it's unlikely you'll have to wait more than a day.

One of the most well-known places to stay is the *Ringo Guest House* (☎ 331-0605) at 17 Scindia House, down a small side street near the tourist office. This place has been a travellers' institution for many years, and it has its fair share of detractors. Nevertheless, it is still popular. Beds in crowded, 14-bed dorms are expensive at Rs 50; rooms with common bath are Rs 75/150 and with private bath it's Rs 175. You can also sleep on a charpoy on the roof for Rs 40. The rooms are very small but it's clean and the showers and toilets are well maintained. Meals are available in the rooftop courtyard, although at a higher price than in the nearby restaurants, and there are always plenty of other travellers to talk to.

Another place with similar prices is the *Sunny Guest House* (☎ 331-2909) at 152 Scindia House, a few doors further along the same side street. Dorm beds are Rs 50, singles/doubles with common bath are Rs 90/150, and for a double with attached bath you'll pay a hefty Rs 225. Again, the rooms are small but the atmosphere and location are what attracts so many people. The left-luggage facility is also expensive at Rs 5 per item per day. The somewhat spartan *Asia Guest House*, 14 Scindia House, has singles/doubles with bath but no window for Rs 130/160. Although gloomy, the rooms are a fair size and the place has central air-con.

Still on the east side of Janpath, the *Royal Guest House* (☎ 332-9485) is up four flights of gloomy steps at 44 Janpath, near Royal Nepal Airlines. The rooms are small and windowless, and the place is generally poorly maintained. Even by Delhi standards this place is way overpriced at Rs 150/200 for rooms with common bath, Rs 200/250 with bath and Rs 350/400 with bath and air-con.

On the west side of Janpath along Janpath Lane there's a couple of places which have been minor legends among travellers for well over a decade now. *Mrs Colaco's* (☎ 332-8758) at No 3 is the first one you'll come to. A charpoy in the reasonably roomy dormitory costs Rs 50, and there are good doubles for Rs 125 with common bath. There's a safe deposit for valuables, a laundry service and baggage storage. Round the corner, *Mr S C Jain's Guest House*, at 7 Pratap Singh Building also on Janpath Lane, is yet another legend. Extremely plain rooms with common bath cost Rs 120 to Rs 150, depending on the size. The big advantage of both these places is that they are in a quiet residential area.

Across on the north side of Connaught Place is the *Hotel Bright* (☎ 332-0444), 85 M Block Connaught Circus, opposite the Super Bazaar. There's definitely nothing bright about this place, but it would do in a pinch. The dark and somewhat grotty rooms cost Rs 118/192 with attached bath, and there are more expensive air-con rooms.

The *Hotel Palace Heights* (☎ 332-1419) in D Block, Connaught Place is a moderately priced place close to Nirula's. It's on the 3rd floor of an office building and has a huge verandah overlooking Connaught Place – great for breakfast or afternoon tea. Although the facilities are fairly primitive, it's a relaxed place with a small-town atmosphere. Rooms cost Rs 150/300 with bath, or there are double rooms with common bath for Rs 150.

Paharganj Area Directly opposite New Delhi Railway Station is the start of Main Bazaar, which stretches due west for about a km. Because of its proximity to the station it has become a major accommodation centre for Indians and foreigners alike. It has also become a crowded and bustling market selling virtually anything you'd care to name – from incense to washing machines. Walking along Main Bazaar at any time requires patience. There are any number of cheap hotels along this road, offering varying degrees of comfort and quality.

Many are very popular with budget travellers.

As you walk up Main Bazaar from the station, one of the first places you come to is the *Hotel Kanishta* (☎ 52-5365). It's not one of the more popular places as it's very close to the station and the accompanying noise of Qutab Rd. Air-cooled rooms with bath, TV and balcony cost Rs 175, and hot water is available by the bucket.

The next place is the *Kailash Guest House* (☎ 77-4993) at 4469. It's a modern, clean and quite friendly place, although many of the rooms face inwards and tend to be a bit stuffy; those with windows are fine. It's good value at Rs 75/105 with common bath, and Rs 140 for a double with attached bath. Hot water is available free by the bucket. The *Kiran Guest House* (☎ 52-6104) next door is virtually an identical twin to the Kailash, and prices are similar at Rs 75/125 with common bath, or Rs 150 with bath attached.

A little further along on the right is the *Hotel Bright* (☎ 752-5852) at 1089-90. It's one of the cheapest places in Paharganj, and one of the best for the money. Clean rooms around a small courtyard cost Rs 50/60 with common bath. There is, however, a charge of Rs 5 for a bucket of hot water and a further one-off charge of Rs 5 for a blanket, which you'll definitely need in winter. In summer, air-coolers are available for Rs 30.

Down a narrow alley to the right, not far beyond the Hotel Bright, is the modern *Hotel Namaskar* (☎ 572-1234), at 917 Chandiwalan. This is a very friendly place run by two brothers, and they go out of their way to make sure you are comfortable. All rooms have windows and attached bath, and there's a geyser on each floor so there's plenty of bucket hot water. There's filtered, cooled drinking water available, and luggage is stored free of charge. It's not the cheapest place, but is well worth the extra. Rooms cost Rs 125/150, and there are also rooms with three (Rs 250) and four (Rs 350) beds. A good place.

Moving further west along Main Bazaar, the next place is the funky old *Camran Lodge* (☎ 52-6053) at 1116. It's in an old

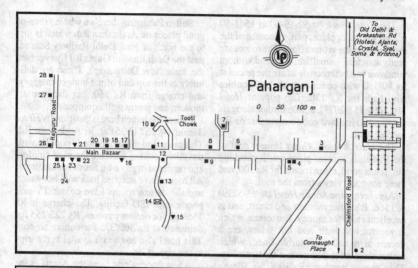

Paharganj

0   50   100 m

To
Old Delhi &
Arakashan Rd
(Hotels Ajanta,
Crystal, Syal,
Soma & Krishna)

To
Connaught
Place

PLACES TO STAY

3 Hotel Kanishta
4 Kailash Guest House
5 Kiran Guest House
6 Hotel Bright
7 Hotel Namaskar
8 Camran Lodge
9 Hotel Relaxo
10 Navrang Hotel
11 Hotel Payal
13 City Lodge
15 Golden Cafe
17 Hotel Vivek
18 Ankush Guest House
19 Anoop Hotel
20 Hotel Vishal &
    Hare Krishna Guest House
22 Kesri Hotel & Mehta Electricals
    (Bicycle rent)

24 Sapna Hotel
25 Hotel Satyam
26 Metropolis Tourist Home
27 Hotel Kelson
28 Chanakya Hotel

▼ PLACES TO EAT

16 Diamond Cafe
20 Appetite Restaurant &
    Lords Cafe
21 Madaan Cafe
23 Khosla Cafe

OTHER

1 New Delhi Railway Station
2 Railway Booking Office
12 Vegetable Market
14 Paharganj Post Office

building which is a bit of maze. The rooms are small and shabby, but cheap at Rs 50/80 with common bath, Rs 100 for a double with bath attached. Hot water by the bucket is free.

Just before the open vegie market area, a small lane off to the right leads to a small square known as Tooti Chowk. Just off to one

side is the *Navrang Hotel* (☎ 52-1965). It's somewhat dark and gloomy, a situation which is not helped by the dark grey paint job of the interior. It does have the advantage of being cheap, at Rs 50/60 with common bath, Rs 60/70 with bath attached. Bucket hot water costs Rs 5. There are better places around.

The *Hotel Vivek* (☎ 52-1948) at 1541-50 is a very popular place, partly because of the restaurant on the ground floor. The rooms are pretty standard – smallish, with and without windows and bathroom – as are the prices at Rs 80/110 with common bath, and doubles with bath for Rs 130. The popular *Hotel Vishal* (☎ 753-2079), a little further along, is similar, and has two good restaurants on the ground floor.

The *Hare Krishna Guest House*, next to the Vishal, is another place worth checking out. It has good, clean rooms for Rs 100, and there are good views from the roof.

· Also here is the *Anoop Hotel* (☎ 73-5219) at 1566. It's quite modern and clean, and is excellent value for money. The rooms, which have attached bath and hot water, are a decent size and are marble-lined, which makes them cool, although a bit tomb-like. They're well worth the Rs 100/150. There's also a few doubles with common bath for Rs 125. The biggest attraction of this place, however, is the rooftop terrace and snack bar. Checkout is based on the 24-hour system.

On Main Bazaar near Rajguru Rd, the *Sapna Hotel* (☎ 52-4066) is very basic and a bit tatty around the edges, but habitable and cheap at Rs 40/50 with common bath, and Rs 80 for a double with attached bath. Next door is the *Hotel Satyam* (☎ 73-1155), which is certainly a step up the scale, with clean rooms for Rs 100/150 with attached bath and hot water. The front rooms can be noisy, but that's true of all the places along Main Bazaar.

At the very top of the range is the *Metropolis Tourist Home* (☎ 753-5766) at 1634 Main Bazaar. This place has been completely renovated, and offers dorm beds with lockers in immaculate air-cooled, four-bed rooms for Rs 70, or there are doubles for Rs 250 with attached bath.

Also in this range is the *Hotel Kelson* (☎ 52-5811) on Rajguru Rd, just off Main Bazaar. It's a very clean and modern place, but the rooms are definitely on the small side, and are often without windows. However, it's not bad value at Rs 125/250, or Rs 225/350 with air-con.

Still in Paharganj there's a whole group of good places on Arakashan Rd, which is just to the north of New Delhi Railway Station, past the Desh Bandhu Gupta Rd flyover (see the main New Delhi map). These are definitely at the top end of the budget category, and charge from Rs 150, but they are all modern and pretty well equipped.

Pick of the bunch here is the friendly *Hotel Ajanta* (☎ 752-0925) at 36 Arakashan Rd. This clean and modern place is popular with travellers looking for a modicum of comfort and prepared to pay a bit above rock bottom. All rooms have attached bath with hot water, and the deluxe rooms have colour TV and phone with ISD facility. The charge is Rs 155/195 for ordinary rooms, Rs 225/265 for deluxe, and Rs 300/375 for deluxe air-con. This hotel also has a taxi available for trips to the airport, etc.

A few doors along from the Ajanta is the *Hotel Crystal* (☎ 753-5984) at 8501 Arakashan Rd (I defy you to find the logic in the numbering system!). The rooms are quite good, although the mock-brick wallpaper is a bit tacky. It's a bit cheaper than the Ajanta, charging Rs 125/175 with attached bath, and Rs 50 extra with TV. Almost next door is the *Hotel Syal* (☎ 51-0091) at 43 Arakashan Rd. It is similar to the Crystal, with rooms for Rs 150/175, or with TV for Rs 225/250. None of the rooms have air-cooling or air-con, which is a major inconvenience in summer.

The *Hotel Soma* (☎ 51-0551), close by at 33 Arakashan Rd, boasts a 'gay atmosphere'. The clean and modern rooms are a good size, and cost Rs 150/200, or Rs 200/250 with TV and Rs 350/400 with air-con. Also in this area is the *Krishna Hotel* (☎ 753-2033) at 45 Arakashan Rd. This place offers the standard facilities for Rs 150/200 with TV, attached bath and hot water, and Rs 225 for an air-cooled double room. It's good value.

The *Rail Yatri Niwas* (☎ 331-3484) on the Ajmer Gate side of New Delhi Railway Station has double rooms at Rs 150 with common bath, and Rs 175 with attached bath, but also has dorm beds for Rs 45. To stay there you have to arrive in Delhi by train and have the ticket to prove it.

Old Delhi At the west end of Chandni Chowk, around the Fatehpuri Mosque, there are a few basic hotels. These places are fine if you like the hustle and bustle, and don't mind being away from the business centre of Connaught Place.

The *Bharat Hotel* (☎ 23-5326) is on the opposite side of the road from the eastern gate of the mosque. It's an old rambling place with a few small courtyards and quite a bit of atmosphere. The rooms are a bit gloomy, and the 25-watt bulbs used to illuminate them certainly don't help. Nevertheless, it's cheap and cheerful, with rooms for Rs 50/80.

Just across the road from the southern gate of the Fatehpuri Mosque is the *Star Guest House* at 186 Katra Baryan. It's a more modern place than the Bharat, and is tolerably grubby. Rooms cost Rs 60/120 with common bath.

Other Places Out at Chanakyapuri is the *Vishwa Yuvak Kendra* or *International Youth Centre* (☎ 301-3631) on Circular Rd. The rooms are very good but not all that cheap, at Rs 161/196, but this does include breakfast. There's a cafeteria with good food at low prices. It's not a bad place to stay if you don't mind the 20-minute bus trip or shorter auto-rickshaw ride from Connaught Place. To get there take a No 620 bus from the Plaza Cinema in Connaught Place and get off near the Indonesian Embassy, or take a No 662 from the (Old) Delhi Railway Station and get off at the Ashok Hotel. It's right behind the Chinese Embassy and near the Chanakyapuri police station.

There is also a *Youth Hostel* (☎ 301-6285) in Chanakyapuri, at 5 Nyaya Marg. Dorm beds cost Rs 22 including breakfast. With the inconvenient location, and the fact that this place takes members only, it's a fairly unattractive proposition.

If all else fails there are railway *retiring rooms* at both railway stations (Old Delhi and New Delhi), with prices for both 24-hour and 12-hour periods. At the Old Delhi Railway Station the charges are Rs 25 for a dorm bed, and Rs 100 for a double room. At New Delhi it's Rs 45 in a dorm, Rs 100 in a

double and Rs 150 for a double with air-con. As you can imagine, they are noisy places and you deserve a medal if you can actually manage to get some sleep.

There are *retiring rooms* at both the domestic (Terminal I: (☎ 329-5126) and international (Terminal II: (☎ 545-2011) sections of the airport. You can use them if you have a confirmed departure within 24 hours, but you'll need to ring in advance as demand far outstrips supply. They cost Rs 175 for an air-con double at Terminal II; and Rs 40 for a dorm bed, Rs 175 for an ordinary double and Rs 250 for an air-con double at Terminal I. The tourist information officer at the desk at the airport may insist that the retiring rooms are 'full' and try to direct you to a hotel where the officer gets commission.

Places to Stay – middle

Connaught Place & Janpath Area There are several middle-range hotels around Janpath and Connaught Place. The *Janpath Guest House* (☎ 332-1935) is a few doors down from the tourist office at 82-84 Janpath. It's popular with travellers, reasonably well kept and clean, and the staff are friendly; the rooms, though, are claustrophobically small and most don't have a window to talk of. Singles/doubles cost Rs 180/200 with air-cooling, Rs 250/300 with air-con.

The *Hotel 55* (☎ 332-1244) at 55 H Block Connaught Circus is well designed with air-con throughout. Rooms with balcony and bath are Rs 375/595. The *Alka Hotel* (☎ 35-1796) is also centrally located at 16/90 Connaught Circus and has air-con singles/ doubles for Rs 395/700. As is typical of many places in this area, most of the rooms don't have windows. The *Hotel Metro* (☎ 331-3856) on N Block is better than initial impressions might indicate, with rooms at similar prices. The *York Hotel* (☎ 332-3769) in K Block is clean but fairly characterless, and the rooms cost Rs 395/650. In L Block the more modern *Jukaso Inn* (☎ 332-9694) has very small rooms, although at least most of them have windows. The charge here is Rs 399/700.

The ITDC *Ashok Yatri Niwas* (☎ 332-4511) is just 10 minutes walk from Connaught Place on Ashoka Rd at the intersection with Janpath. This huge (556 rooms) government-run hotel is a managerial disaster – if you really want to bash your head against a brick wall and go stark-raving mad with frustration, stay here; if your sanity is precious, don't even think about staying here. Simple matters such as check-in and out can easily take half an hour, the service is terrible – surly at best – the whole place is poorly maintained, bed linen is often threadbare, you may have to beg for a blanket and the lifts are hopelessly unreliable. All this can be yours for just Rs 312/426.

Just off Barakhamba Rd is the small, family-run *Roshan Villa Guest House* (☎ 331-1770) at 7 Babar Lane. To get there go down Barakhamba Rd from Connaught Place, turn left on Tolstoy Marg keeping to the left of the flyover, turn right onto Babar Rd, and take the second right again (this is Babar Lane). It's clean, quiet and well kept, although it's certainly not the friendly and relaxed place it once was. It's also overpriced, at Rs 250/280 with air-cooling but common bath, and Rs 450 with air-con.

Elsewhere There are two excellent private guest houses to the west of Connaught Place. The small inconvenience of being further from the heart of things is compensated for by the friendly and relaxed atmosphere you find at these places.

The first is the *Puri Yatri Paying Guest House* (☎ 752-5563) at 3/4 Rani Jhansi Rd, which is opposite the junction of Panchkuin Marg (Radial No 3) and Mandir Marg, about one km west of Connaught Place. It's calm, secure and moderately priced, and there's trees, lawn, and a small courtyard at the back. The good sized rooms, all with attached bath, are kept spotlessly clean and are great value at Rs 300/350, or Rs 350/400 for even larger rooms and Rs 450/500 with air-con. The owner is very friendly and helpful, and there's a car available for sightseeing.

The second place is further to the west, but

is still only a Rs 12 to Rs 15 auto-rickshaw ride from Connaught Place. The *Master Paying Guest House* (☎ 574-1089) is at R-500 New Rajendra Nagar. This small and friendly place is in a quiet area and the owner has worked hard to create a homelike atmosphere. It has large, airy and beautifully furnished double rooms for Rs 260/320 to Rs 300/380, and good meals are available.

North-east of Connaught Place is the *Hotel Broadway* (☎ 327-3821) on Asaf Ali Rd, not far from Delhi Gate, conveniently placed midway between Old and New Delhi. The rooms cost Rs 395/725, but it's on a very noisy road.

The *Hotel Ashoka Palace* (☎ 67-7308) is the cheapest hotel near the airport (three km from the domestic terminal, 13 km from the international). It's definitely nothing special, but you may be directed here from the airport by the tourist information desk or the taxi wallahs – the commission system is alive and well! For a shabby room with threadbare carpet and minimal facilities you'll be hit for Rs 750.

A better place for late flight arrivals is the *Classic Palace Hotel* in the Diplomatic Enclave at Chanakyapuri. It's quite clean and moderately priced at around Rs 500, and the Ex-Servicemen's Air Link Transport Service (EATS) bus will drop you there. (See the Getting Around section in this chapter for details on this service.)

The Ys There are three YMCA or YWCA places, all of which take either sex. The *YMCA Tourist Hotel* (☎ 374-6668) is very central, near the Regal Cinema on Jai Singh Rd and opposite the Jantar Mantar. It's excellent value with rooms having hot and cold water, and there are gardens, a swimming pool, lounge and a restaurant with Western, Indian and Mughlai cuisine. Despite what the touts may tell you if you arrive in Delhi late at night, the hotel is open 24 hours, and credit cards are accepted. The rooms cost Rs 210/350 with common bath, and Rs 380/650 with air-con and attached bath. There's also a temporary membership charge of Rs 10, valid for one month. It's good value for New Delhi.

The *YWCA International Guest House* (☎ 31-1561) at 10 Sansad Marg (Parliament St) has singles/doubles for Rs 250/450 (plus 10% service charge), and all rooms have bath and air-con. It's conveniently located near Connaught Place and has a restaurant, where a set breakfast costs Rs 35, and lunch or dinner is Rs 55.

There's a second, lesser known YWCA, the *YWCA Blue Triangle Family Hostel* (☎ 31-0202) on Ashoka Rd just off Sansad Marg (Parliament St). It's clean, well run and has a restaurant. Rates, including breakfast, range from Rs 160/225 up to Rs 210/350 with air-con and bathrooms. There's also a Rs 5 temporary membership fee and a 5% service charge. Again, this place is excellent value, and is only about a 10-minute walk from the heart of Connaught Place.

Places to Stay – top end

Many of the 'tourist class' hotels are at Chanakyapuri, the main location of the foreign embassies. This is about midway between the airport and the New Delhi city centre. There are, however, more places around the centre as well.

Moderately priced top-end hotels include *Nirula's Hotel* (☎ 332-2419) on L Block, Connaught Place, right beside the Nirula restaurants and snack bars. Singles/doubles range from Rs 500/800 in this small but good standard hotel.

The *Hotel Marina* (☎ 332-4568) on the outer circle of Connaught Place in G Block is surprisingly good inside; the outside is drab. The rooms, mostly with windows, are Rs 915/1030, and this includes a buffet breakfast (normally Rs 75).

Four-Star Unless otherwise stated, these four-star places do not have a swimming pool:

Ambassador Hotel (☎ 69-0391) is a small hotel at Sujan Singh Park, a short distance south of India Gate. There are just 75 rooms costing US$60/65. It has a noted vegetarian restaurant, coffee shop, bar, and in-house astrologer (!), and major credit cards are accepted.

Connaught Palace Hotel (☎ 34-4225) is due west of Connaught Place, on Bhagat Singh Marg. It offers restaurants, 24-hour room service and car rental. Rooms cost US$45/50.

Diplomat Hotel (☎ 301-0204), 9 Sadar Patel Marg, south-east of Rashtrapati Bhavan, is a smaller place with just 25 rooms, a restaurant and bar. All rooms have colour TV, phone and attached bath. The charge is US$40/53.

Hotel Hans Plaza (☎ 331-6868), Tolstoy Marg, is conveniently central but otherwise not very good value. Rooms are US$55/60.

Hotel Janpath (☎ 332-0070), beside the Imperial Hotel, is run by the ITDC with typically abysmal service. This large hotel has a good position on Janpath. Rooms start at Rs 950/1100.

Hotel Kanishka (☎ 332-4422) is another ITDC hotel. It's next to the disastrous Hotel Ashok Yatri Niwas, and fortunately is much better run. It is one of the few places in this class to have a swimming pool. The room rate is Rs 1350/1500.

Oberoi Maidens Hotel (☎ 252-5464), 7 Sham Nath Marg, is inconveniently located north of Old Delhi, but the building itself is a verandahed colonial relic and is very pleasant, as is the large garden. It also has a swimming pool. It's at the top of this range, with rooms at US$65/75.

Five-Star If you're looking for a little more luxury, try one of the following hotels:

Claridges Hotel (☎ 301-0211) at 12 Aurangzeb Rd is south of Rajpath in New Delhi. It's a very comfortable, older place, with four restaurants, a swimming pool and a travel agency. Singles/doubles start from US$70/78.

Imperial Hotel (☎ 332-5332) is conveniently situated on Janpath near the centre of the city. It's a pleasantly old-fashioned hotel with a big garden, and is surprisingly quiet given its central location. It's one of the cheaper top-end places, and represents good value for money at US$68/73.

Five-Star Deluxe Delhi's top-of-the-range hotels include:

Ashok Hotel (☎ 60-0121), 50B Chanakyapuri, is the 571-room flagship of the ITDC hotel fleet, although it has probably been privatised by now. It offers everything from restaurants, coffee shops, bars, discos, a travel agent, post office, bank, conference rooms and swimming pool to full air-conditioning, a baby-sitting service and evening music recitals. Singles/doubles cost US$108/115.

Park Hotel (☎ 35-2477) on Sansad Marg (Parliament St) is in a very central location only a block from Connaught Place. This hotel is brand new and has a swimming pool, bookshop, and a business centre. Rooms are US$76/84.

Centaur Hotel (☎ 545-2223) is on Gurgaon Rd, about two km from the international airport, and about five km from the domestic terminal. It's a big modern hotel with 376 rooms, swimming pool, health club, tennis courts, putting green, and a children's park. It also offers weekend package deals for Delhites who want to escape from the city for a weekend; however, with the bleak expanses of flat land all around it's hardly paradise, and the roar of planes overhead at all hours certainly doesn't add to the ambience. It is, however, the closest hotel to the airport. Room rates are US$73/84.

Holiday Inn (☎ 332-0101) is a brand new 500-room hotel which is very centrally located just off Barakhamba Rd, south-east of Connaught Place. It boasts every conceivable mod con, including an open-air swimming pool on a third-floor terrace, and it also has a floor of nonsmoking rooms. Standard single/double rooms cost US$150/160, and there are more expensive suites available.

Hyatt Regency (☎ 60-9911), with 535 rooms, is in the south of New Delhi, between Hauz Khas and Chanakyapuri. Facilities include a fitness centre, in-house movies, restaurants, bar and coffee shop. For all this you pay US$116 for a double room.

Hotel Le Meridien (☎ 371-0101) is another very modern place. This 538-room hotel has a swimming pool, restaurants, and 24-hour room service. The rates are US$110/120 for standard single/double rooms.

Hotel Oberoi New Delhi (☎ 36-3030) is south of New Delhi near the Purana Qila. This 350-room hotel is one of the best value luxury places. Services include a 24-hour business centre, travel desk, swimming pool and secretarial services. Rooms cost US$150/160.

Hotel Maurya Sheraton (☎ 301-0101) is between Connaught Place and Chanakyapuri on Sardar Patel Marg, the road to the airport. Apart from a high level of comfort, the hotel boasts two excellent restaurants, a solar-heated swimming pool (the only one in Delhi), and a disco. It has 500 rooms costing from US$130/145 up to US$205/220. Suites cost US$245 to US$600.

Taj Mahal Hotel (☎ 301-6162), at 1 Man Singh Rd, is a luxurious place that is fairly central but quiet. It has all the usual facilities including a swimming pool, photographer, restaurants and coffee shop, and even has telephones in the bathrooms! Singles/doubles start from US$160/175. The French restaurant here is expensive but excellent.

PLACES TO EAT

Delhi has an excellent array of places to eat – from a dhaba house with dishes for less than Rs 10 up to top-of-the-range restaurants where a meal for two can easily top Rs 1000!

Janpath & Connaught Place Area

There are many Indian-style fast-food places in this area. Their plus point is that they have good food at reasonable prices and are clean and healthy. A minus point for some of them is they have no place to sit – it's stand, eat and run. They serve Indian food (from samosas to dosas) and Western food (burgers to sandwiches). Ice-cream parlours have also hit Delhi with a vengeance.

Nirula's is probably the most popular and long running of these fast-food places and does a wide variety of excellent light snacks, both Indian and Western. They've also got good cold drinks, milk shakes and ice cream, or they will pack you a lunch box – ideal to take on train trips. The ice-cream parlour is amazingly busy, and is open from 10 am to midnight. The main Nirula's is on L Block on the outer circle, and there's a second snack bar on N Block where Janpath runs into the circle, and various other outlets dotted throughout suburban Delhi.

Next door to Nirula's L Block snack bar is an ice-cream parlour on one side and pizzas on the other. Above the ice-cream bar there's the fourth part of Nirula's, a sit-down restaurant called *Pot Pourri* with appetising food including a Rs 63 eat-all-you-like salad smorgasbord. They've also got pizzas (Rs 60), chilli con carne and a good range of soups and sweets. It's a good place for breakfast, served from 7.30 am; you can have an all-American breakfast of pancakes, eggs and bacon for Rs 37. It's a very pleasant place to eat and the service is good; all in all it's probably the number one place for a minor splurge. Also upstairs at Nirula's is the *Chinese Room*, with Chinese dishes in the Rs 60 to Rs 100 range, and a very congenial bar.

Opposite the main Nirula's is the *National Restaurant*, which is clean and has excellent non-vegetarian food and somewhat lower prices than Nirula's. The *Embassy* restaurant on D Block has excellent veg and non-veg food including korma and biryani. It's not too expensive and is popular among office workers.

On Janpath at N Block, opposite the underground bazaar, there is a small string of fast-food places including Nirula's. At the outer end is a branch (believe it or not) of the British *Wimpy* hamburger chain. Until Mac-Donalds is up and running, this is the closest you're going to get to a Big Mac (100% lamb!) in India. The burgers are fair imitations but, again, if you're used to Indian prices, spending Rs 50 on a burger and a shake seems like reckless extravagance.

In the same lane as the Ringo and Sunny guest houses, there are a number of basic eateries. *Don't Pass Me By* is a popular little place which caters to international tastes. Other places close by include the *Anand, New Light, Kalpana, Swaram* and *Vikram* restaurants.

Right across the street from Nirula's on the outer circle are a string of popular small dhaba places. The famous *Kake da Hotel* doesn't seem to have been discovered by Westerners at all. Despite having no atmosphere whatsoever, it is crowded most of the time. Try the excellent butter chicken, but note the warning sign that there will be 'no extra gravy'! A good place for an early breakfast in this area is the *Hotel Marina*, where for Rs 75 you can make unlimited attacks on the buffet spread.

Other places around Connaught Place include *Sona Rupa Restaurant* on Janpath with very good south Indian vegetarian food, and the *United Coffee House* on E Block, a pleasantly relaxed and popular place. Quite close by is the *Kovil*, an excellent south Indian vegetarian place with wonderful dosas from Rs 30 to Rs 50.

There's a good collection of cheap restaurants and food markets in Mohan Singh Place, on the same block as the Regal Cinema in Connaught Place. Look for fresh and dried fruits, curd, sweets and so on.

The fresh milk is excellent at *Keventers*, the small milk bar at the corner of Connaught Place and Radial Rd No 3, round the corner

from American Express. If you just want a cheap soft drink and somewhere cool to drink it, descend into the air-conditioned underground market between Janpath and Sansad Marg (Parliament St) at Connaught Place.

Moving up a price category, there are several restaurants worth considering on Sansad Marg and by the Regal Cinema. The *Kwality Restaurant* on Sansad Marg is spotlessly clean and very efficient but the food is only average. The menu is the almost standard non-vegetarian menu you'll find at restaurants all over India. Main courses are mainly in the Rs 30 to Rs 40 range. This is also a good place for non-Indian food if you want a break; you can have breakfast here for Rs 35.

El Arab Restaurant, right on the corner of Sansad Marg and the outer circle of Connaught Place, has an interesting Middle Eastern menu with most dishes in the Rs 45 to Rs 70 bracket and there's a buffet lunch or dinner. Underneath El Arab is *The Cellar*, where breakfast costs Rs 23 or main courses cost around Rs 35. Round the corner is the more expensive *Gaylord* with big mirrors, chandeliers and excellent Indian food. Also on Connaught Place you can find good vegetarian food at the *Volga Restaurant*; it's a little expensive but it's air-conditioned, and the food and service are excellent.

Another restaurant on Connaught Place is *The Host*, which serves excellent Indian and Chinese food. It's extremely popular with well-heeled Indians, but it ain't cheap – it wouldn't be hard to spend Rs 600 here on a meal and drinks for two!

In the Cottage Industries building on Janpath is the *Bankura Restaurant*. It makes a welcome retreat from the heat, and is popular with office workers at lunchtime.

Near the Bengali Market at the traffic circle where Tan Sen Marg meets Babar Rd, the neat and clean *Bengali Sweet House* is a good place for sweets or for a meal of the snacks known as chat. You could try cholaphatura (puffed rotis with a lentil dip), tikkas (fried stuffed potatoes), papri chat (sweet/hot wafers), or golguppas (hollow puffs you break open and use as a scoop for a peppery liquid accompaniment). They also do good masala dosas.

Finally there's one Delhi food place that should not be forgotten. *Wenger's* on Connaught Place is a cake shop with an awesome range of little cakes which they'll put in a cardboard box and tie up with a bow so you can self-consciously carry them back to your hotel room for private consumption.

Paharganj Area

In keeping with its role as a travellers' centre, Main Bazaar in Paharganj has a handful of cheap restaurants which cater almost exclusively to foreign travellers. They are all up towards the western end of Main Bazaar. The restaurant in the *Hotel Vivek*, the *Diamond Cafe* and *Lords Cafe* in the Hotel Vishal all have extensive menus and cheap food. The garlic steaks in Lords Cafe are pretty good at Rs 25, while the Diamond Cafe has a menu full of tortured English.

Next door to Lords Cafe and still in the Hotel Vishal building is the *Appetite Restaurant*. This place has similar food to the others, but is a bit more upmarket, and has some more sophisticated dishes. The pizzas here are popular, but what is even more popular is the fact that this place has cable TV – MTV and international sports broadcasts, especially cricket, draw big audiences.

Further along Main Bazaar are some very basic eating stalls with tables on the footpath. These are a popular place for chai, and for the really impecunious they offer cheap snack food.

Lastly there's the air-con *Metropolis Restaurant*, in the hotel of the same name just past Rajguru Rd. The food here is definitely more expensive than the other Main Bazaar cheapies, but it's worth the extra.

Old Delhi

In Old Delhi there are many places to eat at the west end of Chandni Chowk. The *Inderpuri Restaurant* has a good selection of vegetarian dishes, and *Giani* has good masala dosas. *Ghantewala*, near the Siganj Gurdwara on Chandni Chowk, is reputed to have some of the best Indian sweets in Delhi. An extremely cheap and good place to eat is *Sonis* in Chandni Chowk. It's upstairs in Nai Sarak (New Street). They have very good thalis. The stalls along the road in front of the Jami Masjid are very cheap. In the Interstate bus station the *ISBT Workers' Canteen* has good food at low prices, and Delhi Tourism's *Nagrik Restaurant* is also here.

At the other end of the price scale there are two well-known tandoori restaurants in Old Delhi. The *Tandoor* at the Hotel President on Asaf Ali Rd near the tourist camp is an excellent place with the usual two waiters-per-diner service and a sitar playing in the background. The tandoor kitchen can be seen through a glass panel.

Close by in the same street is the Hotel Broadway with its *Chor Bazaar (Thieves' Market)* restaurant. They've certainly put some effort into decorating this place with an eclectic mix of bits and pieces collected from various markets – a four-poster bed, an old sports car (now used as a salad bar), and an old cello. The food is good, although not outstanding, and main dishes range from Rs 40 to Rs 120.

Round the corner on Netaji Subhash Marg in Darayaganj, the famous old *Moti Mahal Restaurant* is noted for its tandoori dishes including murga musalam, but it seems to live more on reputation than actual ability these days. Quantities are large, however.

International Hotels

Many Delhi residents reckon that the best food to be found in the capital is at the large five-star hotels. At the Maurya Sheraton the *Bukhara* has many central Asian specialities, including tandoori cooking and dishes from the Peshawar region in north-west Pakistan. This is a place for big meat eaters and you can expect to pay around Rs 150 to Rs 250 for a main course. Another restaurant here is the *Dum Phukt*, named after a cuisine first invented by the nawabs of Avadh (Lucknow) around 300 years ago. It involves the dishes being covered by a pastry cap when cooked, so the food is cooked by steaming as much as anything else. It's quite distinctive and absolutely superb, and you'd be looking at around Rs 500 for two, plus drinks. The *Shatranj* cafe here does a good value buffet lunch, and the featured cuisine changes daily.

Claridges Hotel has a few unusual theme restaurants: the *Dhaba* offers 'rugged roadside' cuisine, and is set up like a typical roadside cafe; the *Jade Garden* serves Chinese food in a bamboo grove setting; *Pickwicks* offers Western food, and the decor is 19th-century England; while *Corbetts* gets its inspiration from Jim Corbett of man-eating tiger fame, and so has a hunting camp theme, complete with recorded jungle sounds. As might be expected, meat features prominently on the menu. All restaurants are moderately priced.

The *House of Ming* at the Taj Mahal Hotel is a popular Sichuan Chinese restaurant. The Hyatt also has a Sichuan Chinese restaurant, the *Pearls*.

Several cheaper hotels have noted vegetarian restaurants. Thalis at *Dasaprakash* in the Ambassador Hotel are good value. The Lodhi Hotel, in south Delhi, is noted for the vegetarian thalis at its *Woodlands Restaurant*. The old *Imperial Hotel* is great for an alfresco breakfast in the pleasant garden.

For Japanese food try the *Osaka Restaurant* in Hauz Khas, or the *Fujiya Restaurant* at 12/48 Malcha Marg in Chanakyapuri.

THINGS TO BUY

Good buys include silk products, precious stones, leather and woodwork, but the most important thing about Delhi is that you can find almost anything from anywhere in India. If this is your first stop in India, and you intend to buy something while you are here, then it's a chance to compare what is available from all over the country. If this is your last stop and there was something you missed elsewhere in your travels, Delhi provides a chance to find it.

Two good places to start are in New Delhi, near Connaught Place. The Central Cottage Industries Emporium is on Janpath, opposite the tourist office. In this large building you will find items from all over India, generally of good quality and reasonably priced. Whether it's woodcarvings, brasswork, paintings, clothes, textiles or furniture, you'll find it here. Along Baba Kharak Singh Marg, two streets round from Janpath, are the various State emporiums run by the state governments. Each displays and sells handicrafts from their state. There are many other shops around Connaught Place and Janpath. By the nearby Imperial Hotel there are a number of stalls and small shops run by Tibetan refugees and rapacious Kashmiris selling carpets, jewellery and many (often instant) antiques.

In Old Delhi, Chandni Chowk is the famous shopping street. Here you will find carpets and jewellery but you have to search the convoluted back alleys. In the narrow street called Cariba Kalan, perfumes are made as well.

Main Bazaar in Paharganj has a good range. You can find an interesting variety of perfumes, oils, soaps and incense at two places (both signposted), one near the Hotel Vivek and another near the Camran Lodge. Monday is the official weekly holiday for the shops in Main Bazaar, and many are closed on that day, although a surprising number remain open seven days a week. Sunday is a very busy day in Paharganj.

In recent years the Karol Bagh Market, two km west of Connaught Place along Panchkuin Marg (Radial Rd No 3), has become even more popular than Connaught Place or Main Bazaar.

Just south of the Purana Qila, beside Dr Zakir Hussain Rd and across from the Hotel Oberoi New Delhi, is the Sunder Nagar Market, a collection of shops selling antiques and brassware. The prices may be high but you'll find fascinating and high quality artefacts. Shops in the major international hotels often have very high quality items, at equally high prices.

GETTING THERE & AWAY

Delhi is a major international gateway to India; for details on arriving from overseas see the introductory Getting There & Away chapter. At certain times of the year international flights out of Delhi can be heavily booked so it's wise to make reservations as early as possible. This particularly applies to some of the heavily discounted airlines out of Europe – double-check your reservations and make sure you reconfirm your flight.

Delhi is also a major centre for domestic travel, with extensive bus, rail and air connections.

Air

Delhi's somewhat chaotic, confusing and tatty Palam Airport is now officially the Indira Gandhi International Airport. The domestic terminal is seven km from the centre, and the newer international terminal is a further nine km.

If you're arriving at New Delhi airport from overseas, there's a 24-hour State Bank foreign exchange counter in the arrivals hall, before you go through customs and immigration. Once you've left the arrivals hall you won't be allowed back in. The service is fast and efficient.

Many international flights to Delhi arrive and depart at terrible hours in the early morning. Take special care if this is your first foray into India and you arrive exhausted and jet-lagged. If you're leaving Delhi in the early hours of the morning, book a taxi the afternoon before. They'll be hard to find in the night. See the accommodation section for information about the retiring rooms at the airport.

When leaving Delhi with Air India (domestic or international flights) all baggage must be X-rayed and sealed, so do this at the machine just inside the departure hall before you queue to check in. For international flights the departure tax (Rs 300) must be paid at the State Bank counter in the departures hall, also before check-in.

Facilities at the international terminal include a dreadful snack bar, bookshop and bank. Once inside the departure lounge there's a few duty-free shops with the usual inflated prices, and another terrible snack bar where you have the privilege of paying in US dollars.

Delhi Transport Corporation buses connect the two terminals for Rs 10. There is also the free IAAI bus between the two terminals, although no-one seems willing to admit such a service exists. The EATS bus (see the New Delhi Getting Around section) will also transport you between the two terminals.

Domestic Airlines Indian Airlines has a number of offices. The Malhotra Building office (☎ 331-0517) in F Block is probably the most convenient. It is, however, fairly busy at most times, although there's a separate desk for foreign tourists, which speeds things up. It's open from 10 am to 5 pm daily except Saturday.

The Barakhamba Rd office (☎ 331-3732) handles Indian Airlines' international routes (Kabul, Colombo, Singapore, Kathmandu, Karachi, Lahore, Bangkok, Dhaka and Chittagong) as well as domestic flights. It's open from 10 am to 5 pm daily except Sunday.

There's yet another office in the PTI Building (☎ 371-9168) on Sansad Marg, open from 10 am to 5 pm daily except Sunday.

Out at the domestic terminal there's a 24-hour office (☎ 141, 144), and this can be a very quick place to make bookings, although it is of course a long way out there.

If you're lucky enough to be travelling Executive Class, you can check in by telephone on 329-5166. For prerecorded flight information, telephone 142 for arrivals, and 143 for departures.

The other main domestic carrier, Vayudoot, also has its office (☎ 331-2779) in the Malhotra Building, F Block, Connaught Place. It is open from 9 am to 8 pm daily.

Jagsan Airlines is a small operator running flights from Delhi to Kulu and Shimla. Their office (☎ 371-1069) is at 12E Vandava Building, 11 Tolstoy Marg. For reservations on East West flights to Bombay ring 375-5167.

Domestic Flights Indian Airlines flights depart from Delhi to all the major Indian centres. Check-in at the airport is two hours before departure. Note that if you have just arrived and have an onward connection to another city in India, it may be with Air India, the country's international carrier, rather than the domestic carrier, Indian Airlines. If that is the case, you must check in at the international terminal (Terminal II) rather than the domestic terminal. India must be one of the few countries in the world where they can fill 747s on domestic routes!

The destinations served from Delhi are: Agra (twice daily, US$23), Ahmedabad (daily, US$79), Amritsar (five times weekly (US$52), Bangalore (twice daily, US$182), Bombay (six direct flights daily, US$115), Calcutta (two flights daily, US$132), Chandigarh (four times weekly, US$32), Goa (daily, US$150), Hyderabad (twice daily, US$124), Jaipur (twice daily, US$28), Jammu (daily, US$74), Jodhpur (twice daily, US$56), Khajuraho (twice daily, US$53), Kochi (Cochin; daily, US$200), Leh (four times weekly, US$86), Lucknow (daily, US$46), Madras (two flights daily, US$162), Patna (three times weekly, US$87), Srinagar (twice daily, US$77), Thiruvananthapuram (Trivandrum; daily, US$219) Udaipur (twice daily, US$58) and Varanasi (twice daily, US$74).

Vayudoot has flights to: Chandigarh (daily, US$57), Dehra Dun (daily except Sunday, US$57), Dharamsala (three times weekly, US$120), Jammu (five times weekly, US$134), Kulu (daily, US$107), Lucknow (daily except Sunday, US$120) and Shimla (daily, US$95).

Jagsan Airlines operates flights to Kulu (daily except Thursday) and Shimla (three times weekly). East West has flights from Delhi to Bombay.

International Airlines Addresses of international airlines that fly to Delhi include the following:

Aeroflot
    Cozy Travels, BMC House, 1st floor, 1 N Block Connaught Place (☎ 331-2916)
Air France
    Scindia House, Connaught Place (☎ 331-0407)

Air India
    Jeevan Bharati Bldg, 124 Connaught Circus (☎ 331-1225)
Air Lanka
    Student Travel Information Centre, Imperial Hotel, Janpath (☎ 332-4789)
Alitalia
    19 Kasturba Gandhi Marg (☎ 331-1019)
British Airways
    DLF Bldg, Sansad Marg (Parliament St) (☎ 332-7428)
Iran Air
    Ashok Hotel, Chanakyapuri (☎ 60-4397)
Iraqi Airways
    Ansal Bhawan (☎ 331-8632)
Japan Airlines
    Chandralok Bldg, 36 Janpath (☎ 332-3409)
KLM
    Tolstoy Marg (☎ 331-5841)
Lot Polish Airlines
    G-55 Connaught Place (☎ 332-4308)
Lufthansa
    56 Janpath (☎ 332-3206)
Malaysian Airline System (MAS)
    G Block, Connaught Place (☎ 332-5786)
Pakistan International Airlines (PIA)
    Kailash Bldg, 26 Kasturba Gandhi Marg (☎ 331-6121)
Royal Nepal Airlines
    44 Janpath (☎ 332-0817)
SAS
    1 Block, Connaught Place (☎ 332-7503)
Syrian Arab Airlines
    GSA Delhi Express Travels, 13/90 Connaught Place (☎ 34-3218)
Thai International
    Amba Deep Bldg, Kasturba Gandhi Marg (☎ 332-3608)

International Flights The international routes served by Indian Airlines from Delhi include: Lahore (twice weekly, US$128), Karachi (twice weekly, US$67), Kabul (weekly, US$148) and Kathmandu (daily, US$142).

Bus
The large Interstate bus station is at Kashmir Gate, north of the (Old) Delhi Railway Station. Facilities here include 24-hour left-luggage, State Bank of India branch, post office, pharmacy, and Delhi Transport's Nagrik Restaurant. City buses depart from here to locations all around Delhi – ring

251-9083 for details. State government bus companies operating from here are:

Delhi Transport Corporation (☎ 251-8836) – bookings from 8 am to 8 pm.

Haryana Government Roadways (☎ 252-1262) – bookings from 6.15 am to 12.30 pm and 2 to 9.30 pm. Reservations can also be made at the Haryana Emporium from 10 am to 5 pm.

Himachal Pradesh Roadways (☎ 251-6725) – bookings from 7 am to 7 pm.

Punjab Roadways (☎ 251-7842) – bookings from 8 am to 8 pm.

Rajasthan Roadways (☎ 252-2246) – bookings from 7 am to 9 pm. Bookings can also be made at Bikaner House (☎ 38-3469) just south of Rajpath from 6 am to 7 pm.

Uttar Pradesh Roadways (☎ 251-8709) – bookings from 6 am to 9.30 pm.

Buses popular with travellers include the approximately hourly buses to Agra which cost Rs 44 semideluxe, or Rs 50 deluxe. The journey takes about five hours. There is also a frequent and fast service to Jaipur for Rs 60. Deluxe buses for Jaipur leave from Bikaner House, take five hours and cost Rs 98.

For the five-hour trip to Chandigarh, from where you can take a bus or the narrow-gauge train up to Shimla, the regular buses cost Rs 50. There are deluxe video buses for Rs 85 and even an air-con video bus. You can also get buses direct to Shimla (10 hours) for Rs 75; Dharamsala (13 hours), Rs 91; and there's a daily deluxe service to Manali (16 hours) for Rs 250. To northern Uttar Pradesh buses cost Rs 44 for Haridwar or Rs 46 for Dehra Dun.

Other destinations served by bus from Delhi include: Bharatpur, Bikaner, Jammu, Lucknow, Mussoorie, Naini Tal and Srinagar.

Around Paharganj and the other travellers's hangouts you'll probably see posters advertising direct buses to Kathmandu. These take around 36 hours and most travellers seem to find that it's cheaper, more comfortable and better value to do the trip by train to Gorakhpur (Uttar Pradesh), and then take the bus from there.

A number of travellers have also entered Nepal at the border crossing just east of the Northern Uttar Pradesh village of Banbassa. There are daily buses to this village from New Delhi. See the Uttar Pradesh chapter for more details.

Train

Delhi is an important rail centre and an excellent place to make bookings. There is a special foreign tourist booking office upstairs in New Delhi Station. This is the place to go if you want a tourist-quota allocation, are the holder of an Indrail Pass or want to buy an Indrail Pass. It gets very busy and crowded, and it can take up to an hour to get served. If you make bookings through here tickets must be paid for in foreign currency, and your change will be given in rupees.

The main ticket office is on Chelmsford Rd, between New Delhi Station and Connaught Place. This place is well organised, but incredibly busy. Take a numbered ticket from the counter as you enter the building, and then wait at the allotted window. Even with 50 computerised terminals, it can take up to an hour to get served. It's best to arrive first thing in the morning, or when it reopens after lunch. The office is open from 7.45 am to 1.50 pm and 2 to 9 pm Monday to Saturday. On Sundays it's open until 1.50 pm only.

Remember that there are two main stations in Delhi – Delhi Station in Old Delhi, and New Delhi Station at Paharganj. New Delhi is much closer to Connaught Place, and if you're departing from the Old Delhi Station you should allow adequate time to wind your way through the traffic snarls of Old Delhi. Between the Old Delhi and New Delhi stations you can take the No 6 bus for just Rs 1. There's also the Nizam-ud-din Station south of the New Delhi area where some trains start or finish. It's worth getting off here if you are staying in Chanakyapuri or elsewhere south of Connaught Place.

There are several special tourist trains operating from Delhi. The *Taj Express* is ideal for day trips to Agra, 199 km south. The train departs and returns to the New Delhi Station and takes three hours each way. The fare is Rs 42/156 in 2nd/1st class. The air-con *Shatabdi Express* is faster, leaves earlier (6.15 am) and costs Rs 200, which includes meals. This train continues on to Gwalior (Rs 255), Jhansi (Rs 300) and Bhopal (Rs 420).

The *Pink City Express* is a direct train from (Old) Delhi Station to Jaipur, departing at 6 am, arriving in Jaipur at 11am. The fare for the 308-km trip is Rs 63/224 in 2nd/1st class.

From Delhi it is 1588 km and 17 hours to Bombay, and the fare is Rs 181/751 in 2nd/1st. The *Rajdhani Express* is the fastest train; it's a special one-class train which costs Rs 580 in the air-con chair car, Rs 1170 in the air-con 1st-class sleeper. Fares include tea, dinner, coffee and breakfast on board. The *Rajdhani* also connects Delhi and Calcutta, 1446 km away, in 18 hours five times a week. The cost is Rs 590 in air-con chair car, Rs 1195 in air-con two-tier sleeper.

Some other important connections by mail or express train (with the time taken by the fastest connection) include:

	Time	1st class	2nd class
Amritsar	9 hours	Rs 301	Rs 91
Bangalore	40 hours	Rs 1065	Rs 225
Gorakhpur	13½ hours	Rs 472	Rs 124
Jammu Tawi	15 hours	Rs 310	Rs 87
Lucknow	8 hours	Rs 337	Rs 92
Madras	36 hours	Rs 961	Rs 210
Shimla	13½ hours	Rs 263	Rs 79
Thiruvanan-thapuram	52 hours	Rs 1274	Rs 255
Udaipur	15½ hours	Rs 446	Rs 118
Varanasi	13½ hours	Rs 463	Rs 123

GETTING AROUND

Distances around Delhi are large and the buses are generally hopelessly crowded. The alternative is a taxi, auto-rickshaw or bicycle.

To/From the Airport

Fortunately, airport-to-city and vice versa transport is relatively simple. EATS (the Ex-Servicemen's Air Link Transport Service; (☎ 331-6530) has a regular bus service between the airport and the Vayudoot office in Connaught Place. The fare is Rs 17 and they will drop you off or pick you up at most of the major hotels en route if you ask. There is also an EATS city-to-airport service which departs regularly from opposite the underground bazaar between 4 am and 11.30 pm. When leaving the international terminal, the counter for the EATS bus is just to the right before you exit the building.

There is also a regular Delhi Transport Corporation bus service that runs from the airport to New Delhi Railway Station and the Interstate bus station; it costs Rs 20 and there is a Rs 5 charge for luggage. At New Delhi Station it uses the Ajmer Gate side. There is also a public bus service to the airport (No 780) from the Super Bazaar at Connaught Place, but it can get very crowded.

Just outside the international terminal is a prepaid taxi booth, and a taxi to the centre costs Rs 110 when booked here. This is an excellent way to get into town if you're at all unsure of how things work. From Connaught Place to the airport you'll be asked for anything from Rs 120 upwards. Auto-rickshaws will run out to the airport too, although your teeth will be shaking by the time you get there! If you can find a driver willing to take you it should cost around Rs 60.

Bus

Avoid buses during the rush hours as the situation is hopeless. Whenever possible try to board (and leave) at a starting or finishing point, such as the Regal and Plaza cinemas in Connaught Place, as there is more chance of a seat and less chance of being trampled. There are some seats reserved for women on the left side of the bus. The Delhi Transport Corporation run the buses and you can get a route guide from their office in Scindia House, which is down a small side street off Janpath near the tourist office.

Useful buses include bus No 505 to the Qutab Minar from the Super Bazaar, or from Janpath opposite the Imperial Hotel. Bus No 101 runs between the Interstate bus station and Connaught Place. Bus No 620 or 630 will take you between Connaught Place (from opposite the Jantar Mantar) and Chanakyapuri. Bus Nos 101, 104 and 139 run between the Regal Cinema bus stand and the Red Fort. A short bus ride (like Connaught Place to Red Fort) is only about Rs 1.

Taxi & Auto-Rickshaw

All taxis and auto-rickshaws are metered but the meters are invariably out of date, allegedly 'not working' or the drivers will simply refuse to use them. It matters not a jot that they are legally required to do so. A threat to report them to the police results in little more than considerable mirth, so you will often have to negotiate a price before you set out. Naturally, this will always be more than it should be. There are exceptions; occasionally a driver will reset the meter without even a word from you. At places like New Delhi Station or the airport, where there are always plenty of police hanging around, you can generally rely on the meter being used because it's too easy to report a driver. Trips during the rush hour or middle-of-the-night journeys to the airport are the times when meters are least likely to be used.

At the end of a journey you will have to pay according to a scale of revised charges or simply a flat percentage increase. Some drivers display these cards in the cab, others consign them to the oily-rag compartment, still others feed them to the cows. So if you do come across a legible copy it's worth noting down a few of the conversions, paying what you think is the right price and leaving it at that. You may rest assured that no-one is going to be out of pocket, except yourself, despite hurt or angry protestations to the contrary.

Flagfall is Rs 3.50 in taxis and Rs 2.60 in auto-rickshaws. Connaught Place to the Red Fort should cost around Rs 35 by taxi or Rs 20 by auto-rickshaw, depending on the traffic. From 11 pm to 5 am there is a 25% surcharge in taxis.

There are also unusual 'four-seater' or 'six-seater' auto-rickshaws running fixed routes at fixed prices. From Connaught Place their starting point is Palika Bazaar and drivers chop their way through the traffic as far as the fountain in Chandni Chowk via the Red Fort in Old Delhi. They cost about Rs 2

per person and are good value, especially during rush hours.

Bicycle & Cycle-Rickshaw

Cycle rickshaws are banned from the Connaught Place area and New Delhi itself, but they can be handy for travelling between Connaught Place and Paharganj, and around Old Delhi.

As is so often the case, bicycle is an excellent way of getting around, especially in New Delhi where the roads are wide, in good condition and, by Indian standards, are virtually deserted. At the large traffic roundabouts you need to take a deep breath and plunge in, but otherwise the traffic is pretty orderly. All the sites of New Delhi are easily reached by bicycle, and even the Qutab Minar and the sites to the south are accessible if you don't mind a bit of exercise.

What is surprising is that there are so few places to hire bikes. In Paharganj, the only place seems to be Mehta Electricals in Main Bazaar next to the Kesri Hotel, near Rajguru Rd. The bikes are old but well maintained, and cost Rs 12 per day, with a Rs 300 deposit. As with many shops in Main Bazaar, this place is closed on Mondays. In New Delhi itself, ask around near the Bengali Market, or on Mohan Singh Place, near the Rivoli Cinema.

Around New Delhi

KHIRKI MASJID & JAHANPANAH

This interesting mosque with its four open courts dates from 1380. The nearby village of Khirki also takes its name from the mosque.

Close to the mosque are remains of the fourth city of Delhi, Jahanpanah, including the high Bijai Mandal platform and the Begumpur Mosque with its multiplicity of domes.

TUGHLAQABAD

The massively strong walls of Tughlaqabad, the third city of Delhi, are east of the Qutab

Minar. The walled city and fort with its 13 gateways was built by Ghiyas-ud-din Tughlaq and its construction involved a legendary quarrel with the saint Nizam-ud-din. When the Tughlaq ruler took the workers whom Nizam-ud-din wanted for work on his shrine, the saint cursed the king with the warning that his city would be inhabited only by Gujars (shepherds). Today that is indeed the situation.

The dispute between king and saint did not end with curse and countercurse. When the king prepared to take vengeance on the saint, Nizam-ud-din calmly told his followers (in a saying that is still current in India today) 'Delhi is a long way off'. Indeed it was, for the king was murdered on his way from Delhi in 1325.

The fort walls are constructed of massive blocks and outside the south wall of the city is an artificial lake with the king's tomb in its centre. A long causeway connects the tomb to the fort, both of which have walls that slope inward.

Getting There & Away

The easiest way to visit Tughlaqabad is to combine it with a visit to the Qutab Minar, and catch a bus from there.

QUTAB MINAR COMPLEX

The buildings in this complex, 15 km south of New Delhi, date from the onset of Muslim rule in India and are fine examples of early-Afghan architecture. The Qutab Minar itself is a soaring tower of victory which was started in 1193, immediately after the defeat of the last Hindu kingdom in Delhi. It is nearly 73 metres high and tapers from a 15-metre-diameter base to just 2½ metres at the top.

The tower has five distinct storeys, each marked by a projecting balcony. The first three storeys are made of red sandstone, the fourth and fifth of marble and sandstone. Although Qutab-ud-din began construction of the tower, he only got to the first storey. His successors completed it and, in 1368, Feroz Shah Tughlaq rebuilt the top storeys and added a cupola. An earthquake brought the cupola down in 1803 and an Englishman replaced it with another in 1829. However, that dome was deemed inappropriate and was removed some years later.

Today, this impressively ornate tower has a slight tilt, but otherwise has worn the centuries remarkably well. The tower is closed to visitors, and has been for some years after a stampede during a school trip led to a number of deaths.

Quwwat-ul-Islam Mosque

At the foot of the Qutab Minar stands the first mosque to be built in India, the Might of Islam Mosque. Qutab-ud-din began construction of the mosque in 1193, but it has had a number of additions and extensions over the centuries. The original mosque was built on the foundations of a Hindu temple, and an inscription over the east gate states that it was built with materials obtained from demolishing '27 idolatrous temples'. Many of the elements in the mosque's construction indicate their Hindu or Jain origins.

Altamish, Qutab-ud-din's son-in-law, surrounded the original small mosque with a cloistered court in 1210-20. Ala-ud-din added a court to the east and the magnificent

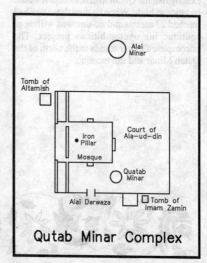

Qutab Minar Complex

Alai Darwaza gateway in 1300. Points of interest in and around the mosque include:

Iron Pillar

This seven-metre-high pillar stands in the courtyard of the mosque and has been there since long before the mosque's construction. A six-line Sanskrit inscription indicates that it was initially erected outside a Vishnu temple, possibly in Bihar, and was raised in memory of the Gupta King Chandragupta Vikramaditya, who ruled from 375 to 413 AD.

What the inscription does not tell is how it was made, for the iron in the pillar is of quite exceptional purity. Scientists have never discovered how this iron, which is of such purity that it has not rusted after 2000 years, could be cast with the technology of the time. It is said that if you can encircle the pillar with your hands whilst standing with your back to it, your wish will be fulfilled.

Alai Minar

At the same time Ala-ud-din made his additions to the mosque, he also conceived a far more ambitious construction programme. He would build a second tower of victory, exactly like the Qutab Minar, except it would be twice as high! When he died the tower had reached 27 metres and no-one was willing to continue his overambitious project. The uncompleted tower stands to the north of the Qutab Minar and the mosque.

Other Features

Ala-ud-din's Alai Darwaza gateway is the main entrance to the whole complex. It was built of red sandstone in 1310 and stands just south-east of the Qutab Minar. The tomb of Imam Zamin stands beside the gateway, while the tomb of Altamish, who died in 1235, is by the north-west corner of the mosque.

A short distance west of the enclosure is the Tomb of Adham Khan who, amongst other things, according to legend drove the beautiful Hindu singer Rupmati to suicide following the capture of Mandu (see Mandu in the Madhya Pradesh chapter). When Akbar became displeased with him he ended up being heaved off a terrace in the Agra Fort.

There are some summer palaces in the area and also the tombs of the last kings of Delhi, who succeeded the last Moghuls. An empty space between two of the tombs was intended for the last king of Delhi, who died in exile in Rangoon, Burma (Myanmar), in 1862, following his implication in the 1857 Indian Mutiny.

Getting There & Away

You can get out to the Qutab Minar on a No 505 bus from the Ajmer Gate side of New Delhi Railway Station, or from Janpath, opposite the Imperial Hotel.

Punjab & Haryana

The Punjab was probably the part of India which suffered the most destruction and damage at the time of Partition, yet today it is far and away the most affluent state in India. No natural resource or advantage gave the Punjabis this enviable position; it was sheer hard work.

Prior to Partition the Punjab extended across both sides of what is now the India-Pakistan border, and its capital Lahore is now the capital of the Pakistani state of Punjab. The population of the Punjab was split into a Muslim region and a Sikh and Hindu region by the grim logic of partition that sliced the region in two. As millions of Sikhs and Hindus fled eastward and equal numbers of Muslims fled west, there were innumerable atrocities and killings on both sides.

More recently Sikh political demands have wracked the state. In 1984, extremists occupied the Golden Temple in Amritsar and were only finally evicted after a bloody battle with the Indian army. The demands of the extremists are somewhat vague and difficult for outsiders to understand, and there are at least five different extremist organisations to complicate matters. The situation looks as insoluble as ever, but in 1992 there were fewer terrorist killings than in the previous year.

The major city in the Punjab is Amritsar, the holy city of the Sikhs, but it is so close to the Pakistani border that it was thought wise to build a safer capital further within the borders of India. At first Shimla, the old imperial summer capital, served as capital, but Chandigarh, a new planned city, was conceived and built to serve as the capital of the new Punjab.

In 1966, however, the Punjab was to undergo another split. This time it was divided into the predominantly Sikh and Punjabi-speaking state of Punjab and the state of Haryana. At the same time some of the northern parts of the Punjab were hived off to Himachal Pradesh. Chandigarh, on the

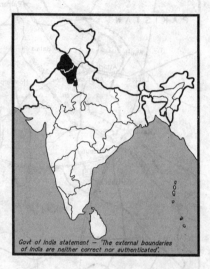

Govt of India statement — 'The external boundaries of India are neither correct nor authenticated'.

border of Punjab and Haryana, remained the capital of both states until 1986 when it was announced that it would be handed over to Punjab as an attempt to placate the Sikhs. However, with the continued violence in Punjab this didn't take place, although eventually it will. In the meantime, Chandigarh remains the capital of the two states, yet is administered as a Union Territory from Delhi.

At the time of partition the Punjab was devastated but the Sikhs' no-nonsense approach to life has won for it a position that statistics sum up admirably. The Punjab's per capita income is nearly double the all-India average (in second place is Haryana). Although Punjabis comprise less than 2½% of India's population, they provide 22% of India's wheat and 10% of its rice. The Punjab provides a third of all the milk produced in India.

Although the Punjab is predominantly an agricultural state, it also has a number of

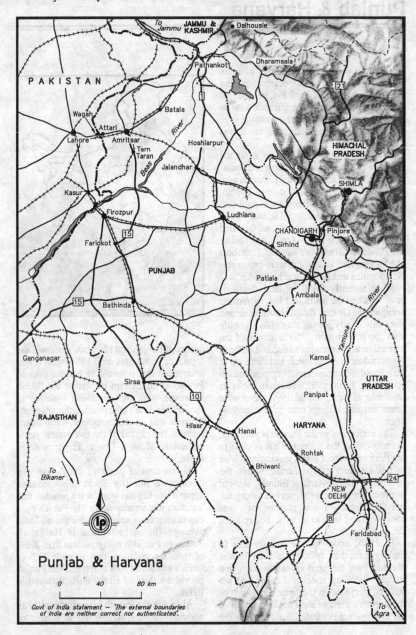

PAKISTAN

To Jammu
JAMMU &
KASHMIR
Dalhousie

Dharamsala

Pathankot

21

HIMACHAL
PRADESH

Wagah
Batala
Attari

River

Lahore   Amritsar
Tarn
Taran
Hoshiarpur

Beas
Jalandhar

SHIMLA

Kasur

Firozpur
15
Ludhiana
CHANDIGARH   Pinjore
Sirhind

Faridkot

PUNJAB
Patiala
Ambala

River

15   Bathinda

Ganganagar

Sirsa
Karnal

Yamuna

RAJASTHAN
10
Panipat
UTTAR
PRADESH

Hisar   Hansi   HARYANA

To
Bikaner
Rohtak

Bhiwani

24

NEW
DELHI

8

Faridabad

Punjab & Haryana

0   40   80 km

2

To
Agra

*Govt of India statement – 'The external boundaries
of India are neither correct nor authenticated'.*

thriving industries including Hero Bicycles at Ludhiana – India's (and the world's) biggest bicycle manufacturer. The Punjabis also have the highest consumption of alcohol in India – the iron bangle (kara), which all Sikh men must wear, is an ideal instrument for taking the caps off beer bottles!

From the traveller's point of view, neither Punjab nor Haryana has an enormous amount to offer and with the present uncertainty there are few visitors. The only major attraction is the Sikhs' Golden Temple in Amritsar. Apart from that, the two states are mainly places of transit for travellers on their way to the Himachal hill stations, Pakistan and Kashmir.

The Sikhs

The Sikhs are the reason for the Punjab's success story and they're amongst the most interesting people in India. See the Facts about the Country chapter for a description of their religion and customs.

Apart from anything else, the Sikhs are the most instantly recognisable people in India. The requirement that they do not cut their hair (kesha) ensures that all Sikh men are bearded and turbanned. For some reason they all seem to be big, bulky men too – you rarely see a weedy-looking Sikh. Sikh women also have a unique costume, the *salwar-kameez*: wide pyjama-style trousers fastened at the ankles, topped by a long shirt which almost reaches the knees. All Sikhs have adopted the Rajput surname Singh, meaning Lion.

Curiously, despite their undoubted success, the Sikhs have a reputation in India rather like that of the Irish in the West. The Indians have as many Sikh jokes as the West has Irish jokes. Not many translate very well but they basically follow the same line, which is strange since the stereotypical Sikh is quite unlike the stereotypical Irish person. The Irish-joke Irishman is supposed to be all thumbs; yet the Sikhs have a reputation for great dexterity and mechanical ability. Sikhs have always been at home with machines, and in India any activity with machines, from driving an auto-rickshaw to piloting a 747,

Punjabi Sikh

will employ a disproportionate number of Sikhs. Despite this, other Indians mock Sikhs as being blunt and straightforward to the point of stupidity!

Haryana

Population: 16.3 million
Area: 44,212 sq km
Capital: Chandigarh
People per sq km: 369
Main Language: Hindi
Literacy Rate: 55%

The state of Haryana has one of the most successful tourist departments in India, which is very interesting when you consider that the state has virtually no tourist attractions. What the clever Haryanans have done is take advantage of their geographical location. If you're going from Delhi to almost any major attraction in the north of India – Jaipur, Agra, Kashmir, Amritsar – you go through Haryana. So they've built a series of 'service centres' along the main roads – the sort of motel-restaurant-service station complexes that are quite common in the West, but are all too rare in India. They are all named after birds found in Haryana and are clean, well kept and, if you're after a place to stay, make travelling through Haryana a pleasure. Typically the complexes may have a camping site, camper huts (usually around Rs 100 to Rs 200) and rooms (usually in the Rs 150 to Rs 250 range if they have air-con, cheaper without). Some places also have dormitories. The main Haryana complexes with their distance from Delhi include the following:

Badkhal Lake (☎ 22-201, 32 km) – restaurants, swimming pool, boating, fishing, air-con rooms, camper huts

Barbet, Sohna (☎ 56, 56 km) – restaurant, cafe, sulphur springs, steam bath complex, swimming pool, air-con rooms, camper huts

Blue Jay, Samalkha (☎ 10, 60 km) – restaurant, rooms with and without air-con, camper huts

Bulbul, Jind (☎ 293, 127 km) – restaurant, camper huts

Dabchick, Hodal (☎ 91, 92 km) – elephant rides, boating, children's playgrounds, air-con rooms, camper huts with and without air-con

Flamingo, Hissar (☎ 2606, 160 km) – restaurant, air-con rooms, camper huts

Jangle Babbler, Dharuhera (☎ 25, Rewari, 70 km) – restaurant, cafe, camel riding, rooms with and without air-con

Kala Teetar, Abubshehr (325 km) – restaurant, boating, air-con rooms

Kingfisher, Ambala (☎ 58-352, 55 km from Chandigarh) – motel, restaurant, bar, health club, swimming pool

Koel, Kaithal, (☎ 2170) – Bidkiar Lake

Magpie, Faridabad (☎ 23-473, 30 km) – air-con rooms, restaurant

Mor Pankh (70 km) – restaurant, rooms without air-con

Myna, Rohtak (☎ 4594, 72 km) – restaurant, camper huts

Oasis, Karnal (☎ 4249, 124 km) – restaurant, cafe, kebab corner, boating, air-con rooms, camper huts

Parakeet, Pipli (☎ 250, 152 km) – restaurant, cafe, camping facilities, air-con rooms, camper huts

Rajhans, Surajkund (in the Union District of Delhi) (☎ 683-0766, 8 km) – swimming pool, boating, air-con rooms, camper huts, fishing

Rosy Pelican, Sultanpur (46 km) – restaurant, bird-watching facilities, camping site, air-con rooms, camper huts

Shama Restaurant (☎ 2683, 32 km) – restaurant, rooms without air-con

Skylark, Panipat (☎ 3579, 90 km) – restaurant, dormitory, air-con rooms

Tilyar, Rohtak (☎ 4606, 70 km) – restaurant, boating, rooms with and without air-con

Yadavindra Gardens Budgerigar, at the Moghul gardens in Pinjore (☎ Kalka 455, 281 km) – restaurant, open-air cafe, dosa shop, mini-zoo, children's games, air-con rooms, camper huts

Rajhans and *Badkhal Lake* are on the Delhi to Agra road. *Skylark, Parakeet* and *Kingfisher* are on the Delhi to Chandigarh road.

CHANDIGARH

Population: 574,000

Construction of Chandigarh from a plan by the French architect, Le Corbusier, began in the 1950s. Although to many Western visitors it appears to be a rather sterile and hopelessly sprawling city, Indians are very proud of it and Chandigarh's residents feel that it is a good place to live.

Chandigarh is a truly dreadful piece of town planning. It's a car city in a country where the general population don't own cars. It's as if Le Corbusier sat down and laid the city out having never visited India and without giving a second's thought to what India was like. The end result is a city where walking is a near impossibility, where cycle-rickshaws look lost and spend half their time taking shortcuts the wrong way around sweeping traffic circles, and where the huge expanses of road space in the shopping centre would be fine as car parks in the West but here are simply empty. Between the city's scattered buildings are long, ugly, barren stretches of wasteland. In Le Corbusier's home environment they might be parks or gardens, but in India empty ground is obviously doomed.

Orientation & Information

Chandigarh is on the edge of the Siwalik

Hills, the outermost edge of the Himalaya. It is divided into 47 numbered sectors, separated by broad avenues. The bus station and modern shopping centre are in Sector 17. In another brilliant bit of town planning, the railway station is eight km out of Chandigarh, so buses are much more convenient than trains.

The Secretariat and other important government buildings are in Sector 1, to the north. The museum is in Sector 10 and the Rose Garden in Sector 16, next to the bus station. The shopping centre has restaurants, ice-cream parlours, bookshops and a wide variety of other retail outlets.

The tourist office (☎ 22-548), upstairs in the bus station, is open from 9 am to 5 pm daily.

Chandigarh's telephone area code is 0172.

Government Buildings

The Secretariat and the Vidhan Sabha (Legislative Assembly) buildings are in Sector 1. Between 10 am and noon you can go to the top of the Secretariat, from where there is an excellent view over Chandigarh. The huge open hand here is a symbol of unity, and is supposed to be the centrepiece of the government sector.

Rock Garden

Close to the government buildings is a not-to-be-missed attraction, the bizarre Rock Garden – a sort of concrete maze with a lot of rocks and very little garden. This strange and whimsical fantasy has grown and grown over the years and is now very extensive. It's open from 9 am to 1 pm and 3 to 7 pm from 1 April to 30 September. The rest of the year it opens and closes an hour earlier in the afternoons.

Close by is the artificial Sukhna Lake, where you can rent rowboats or just stroll round its two-km perimeter.

Museum & Art Gallery

The art gallery in Sector 10 is open daily except Mondays and contains a modest collection of Indian stone sculptures dating back to the Gandhara period, together with some miniature paintings and modern art. The adjacent museum has fossils and implements of prehistoric humans found in India. Opening hours are 10 am to 5 pm Wednesday to Sunday.

Rose Garden

The rose garden in Sector 16 is claimed to be the biggest in Asia and contains more than a thousand varieties of roses.

Places to Stay – bottom end

Chandigarh is a disaster when it comes to budget accommodation. Cheapest is the *Panchayat Bhavan*, an institutional block with a sports club atmosphere – all smelly socks and towel flicking. Dorm beds cost Rs 8.50 or there are double rooms for Rs 60.

At the bus station there's an option which is even worse, the *Tourist Rest House* – a rather grandiose name for an upstairs room with four beds. Each bed costs Rs 12.50, but as this bus station is incredibly busy, you'd be lucky to get any sleep at all. The place is managed by the tourist office.

The *Chandigarh Yatri Niwas* is at the corner of Sectors 15 and 24 on the roundabout nearest the bus station. It's rather anonymously hidden behind a block of flats and is a Rs 10 rickshaw ride from the bus station. It's a bit hostel-like and the rooms only have common bathrooms, although there seems to be one bathroom for every two rooms. There's hot water and a cafeteria with hopelessly slow service. It's clean, and at Rs 100 for doubles, or Rs 150 with air-cooling, is the best value in town. It is, however, away from the main market and restaurants.

Opposite the bus station towards the Sector 21 roundabout is the *Hotel Jullundur* (☎ 28-458) with double rooms for Rs 140. This is about the best you'll do in a conventional hotel.

A number of the shops in the row directly opposite the bus station have signs offering rooms for rent. These are usually in another building away from the shopping centre, and can be a good fall back if you're stuck. One such place is the Royal Restaurant, which also has the *Peeush Motel* (☎ 20-683) in the

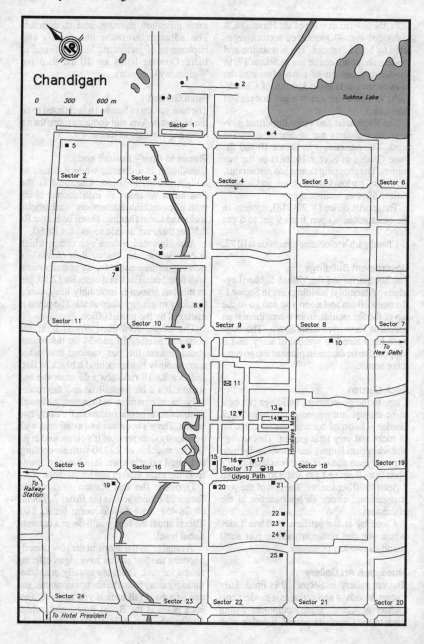

■ PLACES TO STAY		17 Kwality Restaurant
		23 Sai Sweets & Tasty Bite
5	Puffin Guest House	24 Golden Dragon Chinese Restaurant
6	Hotel Mount View	& Singh's Chicken
7	YMCA	
10	Panchayat Bhavan	OTHER
15	Hotel Siwalik View	
19	Chandigarh Yatri Niwas	1 Vidhan Sabha
20	Hotels Pankaj, Alankar & Amar	(Legislative Assembly)
21	Hotels Sunbeam & Jullundur	2 High Court
22	Piccadilly & Divyadeep Hotels	3 Secretariat
25	Aroma Hotel	4 Rock Garden
		8 Museum & Art Gallery
▼ PLACES TO EAT		9 Rose Garden
		11 GPO
12	Mehfil Restaurant	13 Indian Airlines
16	Indian Coffee House &	14 Air India
	Neelam Cinema	18 Bus Station & Tourist Office

street behind. Rooms here are small, and not wonderful value at Rs 140/160.

There are retiring rooms at the railway station, with beds at Rs 25, but it's a long way from anywhere.

Places to Stay – middle

Opposite the bus station on Udyog Path in Sector 22 there are three bottom to middle-range hotels side by side at the roundabout towards Sector 23. The *Hotel Pankaj* (☎ 41-906) is the pick of the bunch, with comfortable rooms at Rs 308/325. The *Alankar* (☎ 21-303) is cheaper at Rs 140/190 for singles/doubles, Rs 200 with air-cool and Rs 300 with air-con. The *Amar* (☎ 26-608) is cheaper still with rooms from Rs 120/150.

The *Hotel Divyadeep* (☎ 43-191) on Himalaya Marg has rooms at Rs 120/140, or Rs 170 for air-cooled doubles and Rs 240 with air-con. Just past the traffic lights, about 10 minutes walk from the bus station, is the long-running *Aroma Hotel* (☎ 23-359). Rooms with bath cost Rs 140/175, with air-con it's Rs 280/340, and it's clean and well kept. The *Puffin Guest House* (☎ 27-653) run by Haryana Tourism is in Sector 2 and has doubles with air-con for Rs 175/300.

Places to Stay – top end

There are a couple of options here. Opposite the bus station in Sector 22, by the Sector 21 roundabout, is the *Hotel Sunbeam* (☎ 46-840) with air-con rooms costing Rs 395/595.

There are several hotels along Himalaya Marg in Sector 22, including the *Hotel Piccadilly* (☎ 32-223) which charges Rs 350/450 for singles/doubles and is centrally located. The *Hotel President* (☎ 46-840) in Sector 26 is one of the best in Chandigarh and charges Rs 395/595 for singles/doubles.

The *Mount View* (☎ 67-141) in Sector 10 is Chandigarh's top hotel. It's less central than the other main hotels but has pleasant gardens and costs Rs 500/600 for singles/doubles.

The *Hotel Shivalik View* (☎ 67-131) is another modern upmarket place, and it's very centrally located in Sector 17. Rooms cost Rs 395/600.

Places to Eat

Chandigarh has plenty of places to eat. In the row of shops on Udyog Path opposite the bus station there are a number of cheap restaurants serving standard Indian food. These include the *Royal, Vince* and *Punjab* restaurants.

Around the corner on Himalaya Marg there's a few more choices. *Singh's Chicken* has a good range of chicken dishes, but their idea of half a chicken is a leg and a wing.

Close by is the *Golden Dragon* Chinese restaurant. It looks expensive but the prices are reasonable and the food is good. Also here is the *Tasty Bite*, a very ritzy take-away place with decent burgers and snacks. The *Bhoj Restaurant* at the Hotel Divyadeep serves slightly expensive vegetarian food in glossy surroundings. There are a few fast-food places in the Sector 17 shopping centre, including *Hot Millions* and two outlets of the *Indian Coffee House*. The bus station has a mediocre 24-hour restaurant.

Finally, still in the vast expanses of the Sector 17 shopping centre, there's a street with a cluster of top-end restaurants, including the *Mehfil Restaurant*. This tandoori specialist looks flashy – white tablecloths, soft music, etc – but it is not too extravagantly priced. The menu is the standard mix of Continental, Chinese and Indian dishes, and main courses are Rs 40 to Rs 60, desserts around Rs 15. Close by are the *Ghazal*, *Terminal One* and *Mughal Mahal* restaurants.

Things to Buy

Woollen sweaters and shawls from the Punjab are good buys, especially in the Government Emporium. The Sector 17 shopping centre is probably the most extensive in India.

Getting There & Away

Air The Indian Airlines office (☎ 40-539) is in the Sector 17 shopping centre. Vayudoot has no office in town so you'll have to make the trek out to the airport to make a booking.

There are Indian Airlines flights between Delhi and Chandigarh four times a week for US$32, and the flight continues to Jammu (US$50) and Srinagar (US$65). Twice a week there are flights to Leh for US$54.

Vayudoot has daily flights to Delhi (US$57) and Kulu (US$47). There are also Vayudoot flights from (but not to) Shimla (US$27) and Dharamsala (US$60).

Bus Chandigarh has a huge and noisy bus station – Indian chaos at its frenzied best. Buses depart regularly for the five-hour trip to Delhi. In fact there are nearly 200 every

day, at all hours of the day and night. Regular buses cost Rs 50, and there are also deluxe video buses (Rs 85) and even air-con deluxe video buses (Rs 145).

There are regular and deluxe buses to other places such as Shimla, Dharamsala, Manali and Jaipur. It takes about 10 hours to Manali by bus, only seven by taxi. Buses take five hours to Shimla (Rs 60 deluxe), eight hours to Kulu, six hours to Amritsar, 10 hours to Dharamsala and seven hours to Pathankot.

Train Buses are more convenient than trains to or from Chandigarh; if you prefer to travel by train, however, reservations can be made at the booking agency in Sector 22 (☎ 29-117) or at the office upstairs in the bus station. The latter is open daily from 7.30 am to 1.15 pm and 1.45 to 7.30 pm. Enquiries can be made by phoning 27-605.

It is 245 km from Delhi to Chandigarh and the daily superfast, air-con *Shatabdi Express* does the journey in just three hours. The fare is Rs 175 in a chair car, and Rs 350 in 1st class; this includes a meal.

Kalka is just 25 km up the line, and from there it takes nearly six hours to reach Shimla on the narrow-gauge mountain railway.

Getting Around

To/From the Airport The airport is 11 km from Sector 17 and it's Rs 80 by taxi or Rs 35 by auto-rickshaw. A better option is the minibus from the Indian Airlines office in Sector 17.

Local Transport Chandigarh is much too spread out to get around on foot, but a day is certainly sufficient to see all it has to offer. The extensive bus network is the cheapest way of getting around. Bus No 1 runs by the Aroma Hotel as far as the government buildings in Sector 1, and bus No 37 runs to the railway station from the bus station.

Cycle-rickshaws operate on the normal bargaining basis but Chandigarh is a bit big even for them. If you're planning a longer trip across the city consider taking an auto-rickshaw, of which there aren't so many.

There is a prepaid auto-rickshaw stand behind the bus station, but it's a joke. Despite the existence of a chart detailing all the set fares, no-one will accept any money in advance, nor will they adhere to the set fares.

Bicycle is the best form of transport, but they're hard to find; ask at your hotel. If you do want to try walking, start off at Sector 1 and stroll back through Sector 10 (museum and art gallery) and 16 (rose garden) to the bus station and shopping centre in Sector 17.

AROUND CHANDIGARH
Pinjore

The **Moghul gardens** at Pinjore were designed by Fidai Khan, Aurangzeb's foster brother, who also designed the Badshahi Mosque in Lahore, Pakistan. Situated 20 km from Chandigarh, near Kalka, the gardens include the Rajasthani-Moghul-style **Shish Mahal palace**. Below it is the Rang Mahal and the cubical Jal Mahal. There is an **otter house**, and other animals can be seen in the **mini-zoo** near the gardens. The fountains only operate on weekends.

Places to Stay The Haryana Tourism *Yadavindra Gardens Budgerigar Motel* (☎ Kalka 455) has air-con rooms from Rs 250.

Getting There & Away There are hourly buses from Chandigarh which stop at the Pinjore gardens gate.

CHANDIGARH TO DELHI

There are many places of interest along the 260-km route from Chandigarh to Delhi. The road, part of the Grand Trunk Road, is one of the busiest in India.

Karnal & Kurukshetra

Events in the *Mahabharata* are supposed to have occurred in Karnal, 118 km from Delhi, and also at the tank of Kurukshetra, a little further north. It was at Karnal that Nadir Shah, the Persian who took the Peacock Throne from Delhi, defeated the Moghul emperor, Mohammed Shah, in 1739.

The **Kurukshetra tank** has attracted as many as a million pilgrims during eclipses, as at these times the water in the tank is said to contain water from every other sacred tank in India. Thus its cleansing ability during the eclipse is unsurpassed. Kurukshetra also has an interesting small mosque, the **Lal Masjid**, and a finely designed **tomb**.

Gharaunda

The gateways of an old Moghul *serai* (rest house) stand to the west of this village, 102 km north of Delhi. Shah Jahan built *kos minars* (milestones) along the road from Delhi to Lahore and serais at longer intervals. Most of the kos minars still stand but there is little left of the various serais.

Panipat

Panipat, 92 km north of Delhi, is reputed to be one of the most fly-infested places in India – due, it is said, to a Muslim saint buried here. He is supposed to have totally rid Panipat of flies, but when the people complained that he had done too good a job he gave them all the flies back, multiplied by a thousand.

It is also the site of three great battles, although there is little reminder of these today. In 1526, Babur defeated Ibrahim Lodi, king of Delhi, at Panipat and thus founded the Moghul Empire in India. In 1556, Akbar defeated the Pathans at this same site. Finally in 1761, the Marathas, who had succeeded the Moghuls, were defeated here by the Afghan forces of Ahmad Shah Durani.

SULTANPUR

There are many birds, including flamingoes, at the bird sanctuary here. September to March is the best time to visit, and you can stay at the *Rosy Pelican* complex. To get there take a blue Haryana bus from Delhi to Gurgaon, and then take a Chandu bus (three or four times a day) to Sultanpur, 46 km from Delhi.

DELHI TO SIRSA

This route takes you north-west through Haryana towards the Punjab and Pakistan, south of the Delhi to Amritsar route. From

Delhi the railway line runs through **Rohtak**, 70 km north-west of Delhi, which was once a border town between the Sikhs' and Marathas' regions, and the subject of frequent clashes.

Hansi, north-west of Rohtak, was where Colonel Skinner (of the legendary regiment, Skinner's Horse) died. **Sirsa**, 90 km further north-west, is an ancient city but little remains apart from the city walls.

Punjab

Population: 20 million
Area: 50,362 sq km
Capital: Chandigarh
People per sq km: 401
Main Language: Punjabi
Literacy Rate: 57%

AMRITSAR
Population: 710,000

Until a second India-Pakistan border crossing is opened, travellers heading overland have to go through Amritsar, close to the only land crossing open to Pakistan.

Founded in 1577 by Ram Das, the fourth guru of the Sikhs, Amritsar is both the centre of the Sikh religion and the major city of Punjab state – where the majority of Sikhs live. Amritsar, or Pool of Nectar, is the name of the sacred pool by which the Sikhs' Golden Temple is built.

The original site for the city was granted by the Moghul emperor, Akbar, but in 1761 Ahmad Shah Durani sacked the town and destroyed the temple. It was rebuilt in 1764, and in 1802 was roofed over with copper-gilded plates by Ranjit Singh and became known as 'the Golden Temple'. During the turmoil of the partition of India in 1948, Amritsar was a flashpoint for the terrible events that shook the Punjab.

Whilst there is no end in sight of the political violence in the Punjab, things appear to be quieter in Amritsar than they have been in the recent past. The damage wrought on the Golden Temple by the tanks

of the Indian army has now been repaired. Fewer people were killed in terrorist attacks in 1992 than in the previous year and three of the leaders of the five Sikh separatist movements have now been rounded up.

The Sikhs are justifiably proud of their capital city and the Golden Temple, and travellers have commented on their friendliness and helpfulness.

Orientation & Information
The old city is south-east of the main railway station and is surrounded by a circular road which used to contain the massive city walls. There are 18 gates still in existence but only the north gate, facing the Ram Bagh gardens, is original. The Golden Temple and the narrow alleys of the bazaar area are in the old city.

The more modern part of Amritsar is north-east of the railway station, where you will also find the beautiful gardens known as Ram Bagh, The Mall and 'posh' Lawrence St. The bus station is two km east of the railway station on the road to Delhi.

The tourist office (☎ 51-558) is in the youth hostel, one km east of the bus station. It has very little information and is closed at weekends. (The youth hostel itself is closed. It's been taken over by the army and is fortified with piles of sandbags, a trench and gun turrets.)

Golden Temple
The holiest shrine of the Sikh religion, also known as the Hari Mandir, is in the centre of the old part of town. The temple itself is surrounded by the pool which gave the town its name, and is reached by a causeway. Open to all, it's a beautiful place, especially early in the morning. However, at the weekends it can get quite crowded.

During unrest in the Punjab during the early '80s the Golden Temple was occupied by Sikh extremists who were evicted by the Indian army in 1984 with much bloodshed. This action was a contributing factor to Indira Gandhi's subsequent assassination. The temple was again occupied by extremists in 1986.

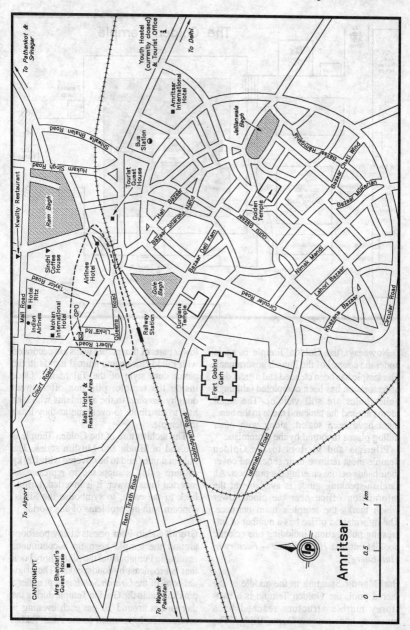

Amritsar

0   0.5   1 km

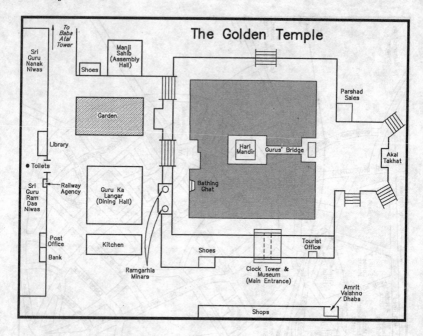

Nowadays the Golden Temple is again under the control of the Punjab government. The temple has been cleaned and a great deal of restoration has been completed (although bullet holes are still visible). The small rooms around the tank and those in the basement have been sealed, along with other hiding places favoured by the extremists.

Pilgrims and visitors to the Golden Temple must remove their shoes and cover their heads before entering the precincts. An English-speaking guide is available at the information office near the clock tower which marks the temple's main entrance. The information office has a number of interesting publications including one eclectic booklet entitled *Human Hair – Factory of Vital Energy*!

Hari Mandir Standing in the middle of the sacred pool, the Golden Temple is a two-storey marble structure reached by a causeway known as the Gurus' Bridge. The lower parts of the marble walls are decorated with inlaid flower and animal motifs in the pietra dura style of the Taj Mahal. Once inside the temple, pilgrims offer sweet doughy *parshad* to the attendants who take half to distribute to everyone as they leave the temple.

The architecture of the Golden Temple is a blend of Hindu and Muslim styles. The golden dome (said to be covered with 100 kg of pure gold) is supposed to represent an inverted lotus flower. It is inverted, turning back to the earth, to symbolise the Sikhs' concern with the problems of this world.

Granth Sahib Four priests at key positions around the temple keep up a continuous reading in Punjabi from the Sikhs' holy book that is broadcast by loudspeaker. The original copy of the *Granth Sahib* is kept under a pink shroud in the Golden Temple during the day and at around 10 pm each evening is ceremoniously returned to the Akal Takhat

(Parliament building). The morning processional ceremony takes place at 4 am in summer, 5 am in winter.

Sikh Museum The Central Sikh Museum is upstairs in the clock tower and comprises a gallery of paintings telling the story of the Sikhs and their martyrs.

Akal Takhat The Shiromani Gurdwara Parbandhak Committee, or Sikh Parliament, traditionally meets in this building, which is why it was almost completely destroyed by the Indian army in 1984. A new Akal Takhat is nearing completion.

Guru Ka Langar & Gurdwaras All Sikh temples have a community kitchen and in this one volunteers prepare free meals for thousands of people every day. The food is very basic – chapatis and lentils – but it's all prepared and dished out in a surprisingly orderly fashion. Nearby are the gurdwaras, offering free accommodation to all. Pilgrims are well provided for and there's a good library, a post office, bank and railway booking agent.

Other Buildings To the south of the temple enclosure is a garden in which stands the **Baba Atal Tower**. The tall **Ramgarhia Minars**, scarred by tank fire, stand outside the temple enclosure.

The Old City

A 15-minute walk from the Golden Temple through the narrow alleys of the old city brings you to the Hindu **Durgiana Temple**. This small temple, dedicated to the goddess Durga, dates back to the 16th century. A larger temple, built like the Golden Temple in the centre of a lake, is dedicated to the Hindu deities, Lakshmi and Narayan.

There are a number of mosques in the old city, including the mosque of **Mohammed Jan** with three white domes and slender minarets.

Jallianwala Bagh

This park is just five minutes walk from the Golden Temple and commemorates the 2000 Indians who were killed or wounded at this site, shot indiscriminately by the British in 1919. This was one of the major events in India's struggles for independence and was movingly re-created in the film *Gandhi*. Bullet marks and the well into which some people jumped to escape can still be seen. Officially, over 300 were killed.

Ram Bagh

This beautiful garden is in the new part of town and has a museum in the small palace built by the Sikh Maharaja Ranjit Singh. The museum contains weapons dating back to Moghul times and some portraits of the ruling houses of the Punjab. It's closed on Wednesdays.

Other Attractions

The **Fort Gobind Garh**, in the south-west of the city, has been taken over by the Indian army and is now off limits. It was built in 1805-09 by Ranjit Singh, who was also responsible for constructing the city walls.

Tarn Taran is an important Sikh tank about 25 km south of Amritsar. There's a temple, which predates Amritsar, and a tower on the east side of the tank, which was also constructed by Ranjit Singh. It's said that any leper who can swim across the tank will be miraculously cured.

Places to Stay – bottom end

Hospitality to pilgrims is part of the Sikh faith, and the most interesting place to stay in Amritsar is at the Golden Temple itself. The gurdwaras (*Sri Guru Ram Das Niwas* and *Sri Guru Nanak Niwas*) are staffed by volunteers. Accommodation is free but you must pay a deposit of Rs 50 (returnable on departure) and you can stay for up to three days. There are double rooms with bedding provided and the toilets and shower block are in the centre of the courtyard. There's no pressure from any of the staff but a donation is expected. In the Sri Guru Nanak Niwas there are also double rooms with attached bathrooms but these rooms are for rent. They're a bargain, though, at Rs 15.

The *Tourist Guest House*, east of the railway station, has singles/doubles from Rs 40/60 and is popular with travellers, but the food is expensive. At the front there are also a couple of air-con doubles for Rs 150. The manager is friendly and in his time has helped many travellers newly arrived from Pakistan to buy Enfields in Amritsar. Watch out for touts at the station who will direct you to the inferior *Hotel Tourist Bureau*. It's just outside the north entrance of the station and has rooms for Rs 75.

Station Links Rd, opposite the railway station, has several moderately priced hotels but they're nothing special. The *Hotel Chinar* has rooms from Rs 70/100 with attached bathroom, and the *Hotel Palace* has singles/doubles from Rs 55/75. At the northern end of this road is *Hotel Rosh* which is not bad with air-cooled doubles at Rs 125, air-con doubles at Rs 250. At the station, the *retiring rooms* are Rs 65 for doubles, Rs 125 with air-con.

Places to Stay – middle

The friendly *Grand Hotel* (☎ 62-977) on Queens Rd opposite the railway station has rooms at Rs 125/175, air-cooled rooms for Rs 150/200 or Rs 250/300 with air-con. Down an alley further east along Queens Rd, the *Hotel Shiraz Continental* (☎ 65-157) has air-cooled rooms for Rs 115/220 and air-con rooms for Rs 265/350, and the manager is very helpful. Next door, the *Hotel Veenus* is slightly cheaper.

On Mall Rd, in the new area of the city and about one km from the railway station, you'll find the pleasant *Hotel Blue Moon* (☎ 20-416) with double rooms at Rs 150/225, or Rs 295/350 with air-con.

The best place in this price range, *Mrs Bhandari's Guest House* (☎ 64-285), at 10 The Cantonment, is very good value for a group of people and a delightful place to stay. Rooms are Rs 350, Rs 450 with air-con, and some of these are four-bedded. The charming Mrs Bhandari controls operations from her spotless kitchen ('Commando Bridge'),

aided by her daughter, who's also a tour guide. Meals are available – breakfast is Rs 30, lunch and dinner Rs 75. The guest house is set in a large garden with a swimming pool (May to August) and resident cow. People on overland trips occasionally set up their tents here and camping charges are Rs 40 per person.

Places to Stay – top end

Punjab Tourism's centrally air-conditioned *Amritsar International Hotel* (☎ 31-991) is a modern building near the bus station. Rooms cost from Rs 250/300. The *Hotel Ritz* (☎ 26-606), at 45 The Mall, has singles/doubles for Rs 250/500 or Rs 390/600 with air-con. There's also a gym and swimming pool that nonresidents can use for a charge of Rs 40.

The top hotel here is the *Mohan International Hotel* (☎ 27-801) on Albert Rd with rooms from Rs 550/800 with bathtubs in the attached bathrooms. It has air-con, a swimming pool (Rs 40 for nonresidents) and a good restaurant.

Places to Eat

Free food is provided at the *Guru Ka Langar* at the Golden Temple, although you should make a donation when you eat here. Opposite the clock tower entrance to the temple are a number of cheap dhabas. *Amrit Vaishno Dhaba* (sign in Punjabi but it's at the end of the group, opposite the information office) does good chana bhatura for Rs 5.

There are a number of expensive restaurants in the new part of town, such as *Napoli, Kwality, Crystal* and *Sindhi Coffee House*. Main dishes in these places are around Rs 50 to Rs 60. Next door to the Kwality is *Salads Plus* and there's an ice-cream parlour nearby and the *Novelty* sweet shop.

Amritsar also has a number of cheaper and locally popular places such as *Kasar de Dhawa* near the Durgiana Temple and the telephone exchange in the old city. Parathas and other vegetarian dishes are the speciality here, and you can eat well for around Rs 25. *Kundan di Dhawa* near the railway station and *Mangal de Dhawa* are other popular cheapies, and *Sharma Vaishna Dhaba*, near the temple, also has good vegetarian food.

Things to Buy

Woollen blankets and sweaters are supposed to be cheaper in Amritsar than in other places in India, as they are locally manufactured. Katra Jaimal Singh, near the telephone exchange in the old city, is a good shopping area.

Getting There & Away

Air The Indian Airlines office (☎ 64-433) is in the centre of town at 48 The Mall. Amritsar is linked by a daily IA flight to Delhi (US$52). There's also a daily flight to Srinagar (US$45) and on Tuesday and Thursday it also stops in Jammu (US$27).

If things have settled down in Afghanistan and you can get a visa, there's the twice-weekly flight to Kabul (US$90) on Ariana Afghan Airlines (☎ 65-150).

Bus The bus journey to Delhi (Rs 76, 10 hours) is less comfortable than going by train. There are also early morning buses to Dehra Dun (Rs 75, 10 hours), Shimla (Rs 74, 10 hours), Kulu (Rs 80, 11 hours), Dalhousie and Dharamsala.

There are frequent buses to Pathankot (Rs 18, three hours), Chandigarh (Rs 38, six hours) and Jammu (Rs 32, five hours) for Srinagar. There are privately operated air-con buses to Jammu or Chandigarh (Rs 75) but these do not go from the bus station. Tickets must be bought in advance from the agents near the railway station.

Getting to Rajasthan from Amritsar can be a pain unless you go via Delhi. It's possible to get a direct bus as far as Ganganagar (just over the Rajasthan border); the journey takes around 10 hours.

Train There are direct rail links to Delhi (447 km, Rs 91/301 in 2nd/1st class) in eight to 10 hours. The *3008 Amritsar-Howrah Mail* links Amritsar with Lucknow (850 km, 17 hours), Varanasi (1251 km, 23 hours) and Calcutta (1829 km, 38 hours).

To/From Pakistan The rail crossing point is at Attari, 26 km from Amritsar, and the *4607 Indo-Pak Express* leaves Amritsar daily at 9.30 am, reaching Lahore in Pakistan at 1.35 pm. However, it can be delayed for hours at the border.

The road crossing at Wagah, 32 km from Amritsar, is less popular with travellers but can actually be quicker. The border is open from 9 am to 4 pm daily and there are frequent buses from Amritsar (Rs 5, one hour). Taxis cost Rs 100 to Rs 150. Punjab Tourism operates the *Neem Chameli Tourist Complex* at Wagah, with dorm beds and cheap double rooms.

See the introductory Getting There & Away chapter for further details.

Getting Around

The airport is 15 km from the city centre. An auto-rickshaw should cost around Rs 30, a taxi Rs 50 but drivers try for two or three times this amount.

Auto-rickshaws charge Rs 10 from the station to the Golden Temple. The same trip on a cycle-rickshaws will cost Rs 5 to Rs 7, or Rs 15 to Rs 20 per hour for sightseeing.

PATHANKOT

Population: 147,000

The town of Pathankot in the extreme north of the Punjab, 107 km from Amritsar, is important to travellers purely as a crossroad. It's the gateway to Jammu in the state of Jammu & Kashmir, which in turn is the starting point for the bus trip up to Srinagar.

Pathankot is also the bus centre for departures to the Himachal Pradesh hill stations, particularly Dalhousie and Dharamsala. Otherwise it's a dull little place, although there's the picturesque Shahpur Kandi Fort about 13 km north of the town on the River Ravi.

Places to Stay

The *Gulmohar Tourist Bungalow* (☎ 20-292) has a cheap dorm, and reasonably priced rooms. There are also cheap hotels like the *Green Hotel* and the *Imperial Hotel*, both close to railway and bus stations.

Getting There & Away

The dusty bus station and the railway station are only a hundred or so metres apart. Buses from Pathankot to Jammu take about three hours. The trip to Dalhousie takes about four hours, to Dharamsala five hours. You can also get taxis for these longer trips next to the bus station; to both Dalhousie or Dharamsala it's two hours and Rs 525, but if things are quiet you should be able to get this down to Rs 450 with bargaining.

PATIALA

Population: 269,000

Located a little south of the road and rail lines from Delhi to Amritsar, Patiala was once the capital of an independent Sikh state. There is a museum in the Motibagh Palace of the maharaja in the Baradari Gardens.

SIRHIND

Population: 31,000

This was once a very important town and the capital of the Pathan Sur dynasty. In 1555, Humayun defeated Sikander Shah here and a year later his son, Akbar, completed the destruction of the Sur dynasty at Panipat. From then until 1709 Sirhind was a rich Moghul city, but clashes between the declining Moghul and rising Sikh powers led to the city's sacking in 1709 and complete destruction in 1763.

The Pathan-style **Tomb of Mir Miran** and the later Moghul **Tomb of Pirbandi** Nakshwala, both ornamented with blue tiles, are worth seeing. The mansion or **haveli of Salabat Beg** is probably the largest private home remaining from the Moghul period. South-east of the city is an important Moghul **serai**.

LUDHIANA

Population: 1,012,000

An important textile centre, Ludhiana was the site of a great battle in the First Sikh War. Hero bicycles, the world's largest manufacturer, with a production of nearly three million bikes annually, are manufactured here.

There's little here to see; but if you're sick,

the Christian Medical Hospital (affiliated with the hospital of the same name in Vellore in Tamil Nadu) is a good place to head for.

Places to Stay

The PTDC *Amaltas Hotel* (☎ 51-500) has a cheap dormitory and reasonably priced rooms, some with air-con. The best hotel is the *Hotel City Heart*, a short walk from the railway station and just beyond the clock tower. Good rooms cost Rs 260/400, or Rs 360/600 with air-con. It also has an excellent restaurant and bar.

JALANDHAR

Population: 519,000

Only 80 km south-east of Amritsar, this was once the capital of an ancient Hindu kingdom. It survived a sacking by Mahmud of Ghazni nearly a thousand years ago and later became an important Moghul city. The town has a large **serai** built in 1857.

Places to Stay

Not far from the bus stand, the *Skylark Hotel* (☎ 76-981) has fine food and good rooms from Rs 165/225, or Rs 225/385 with air-con. Other places include the *Plaza Hotel* (☎ 75-886), with rooms from Rs 95/150, and the *Hotel Ramji Dass* (☎ 3252).

Getting There & Away

Trains take about six hours from Delhi to Jalandhar, and there's also a bus stand where frequent services run to other northern centres.

SOUTH-WEST PUNJAB

The railway line from Sirsa (Haryana) to Firozpur stops at **Bathinda**, which was an important town of the Pathan Sur dynasty.

Faridkot, 350 km north-west of Delhi and close to the Pakistan border, was once the capital of a Sikh state of the same name and has a 700-year-old fort.

Firozpur, almost on the border, is 382 km north-west of Delhi; prior to Partition, the railway line continued to Lahore, now in Pakistan.

Himachal Pradesh

Population: 5.1 million
Area: 55,673 sq km
Capital: Shimla
People per sq km: 92
Main Languages: Hindi, Pahari
Literacy Rate: 63%

The state of Himachal Pradesh came into being in its present form with the partition of the Punjab into Punjab and Haryana in 1966. Himachal Pradesh is essentially a mountain state – it takes in the transition zone from the plains to the high Himalaya, and in the trans-Himalayan region of Lahaul and Spiti actually crosses that mighty barrier to the Tibetan plateau. It's a delightful state for visitors, particularly during the hot season when people flock to its hill stations to escape the searing heat of the plains.

High points for the visitor include Shimla, the 'summer capital' of British India and still one of India's most important hill stations. The Kulu Valley is simply one of the most beautiful areas on earth – a lush, green valley with the sparkling Beas River running through it and the snow-capped Himalayan peaks forming the background. From Manali the trip along the spectacular mountain road to Leh is breathtaking, and it takes you across the highest mountain road pass in the world – only open for a few brief months each year. Then there's Dharamsala, home-in-exile for the Dalai Lama, and a host of other hill stations, lakes, walks and mountains.

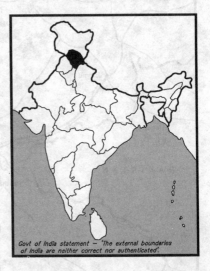

Govt of India statement – 'The external boundaries of India are neither correct nor authenticated'.

Trekking & Mountaineering

See Lonely Planet's *Trekking in the Indian Himalaya* for more information on trekking in this region. The Himachal Pradesh tourist office has a brochure on trekking which briefly details a number of treks in the state. They also have three excellent large-scale maps of Himachal Pradesh, which are invaluable for trekkers.

The trekking season in Himachal Pradesh runs from mid-May to mid-October. In Manali there is a Department of Mountaineering & Allied Sports which can advise you on trekking possibilities in the state and also on the numerous unscaled peaks. Dharamsala also has a Mountaineering Institute, and from here it's possible to take organised climbs. For more serious mountaineering, the Indian Mountaineering Foundation in Delhi is the place to go for information. Unlike in Nepal, no trekking permits are necessary in Himachal Pradesh and this helps to make trekking here relatively cheap.

Equipment and provisions will depend very much on where you trek. In the lower country in the Kulu or Kangra valleys, or around Shimla, there are many rest houses and villages. On the other hand, in Lahaul and Spiti the population is much less dense and conditions are more severe. You will need to be better equipped in terms of cold-weather gear, food and provisions. Some of the better known treks are detailed in the appropriate sections. There are many forest

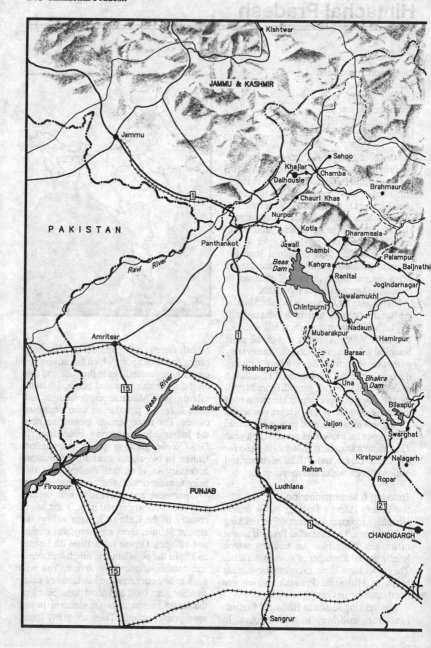

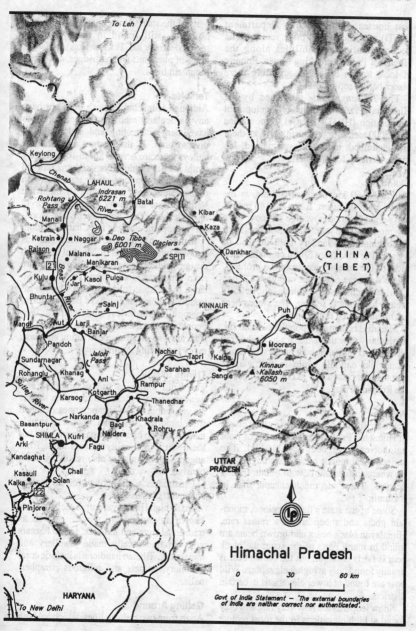

Himachal Pradesh

0   30   60 km

Govt of India Statement – 'The external boundaries of India are neither correct nor authenticated'.

rest houses, Public Works Department (PWD) rest houses and other semi-official accommodation possibilities along the Himachal Pradesh trekking routes. Enquire at local tourist offices about using these places before setting off.

The *Trekking Guide* published by the Himachal Pradesh Tourism Development Corporation (HPTDC) lists 136 mountains over 5000 metres high. The majority of them are unclimbed, most not even named. It's virgin territory for mountaineers.

Skiing

Narkanda, 60 km north of Shimla, is the state's main ski resort. It lies at 3143 metres and so gets a good coverage of snow for a few months of the year. The season runs from the beginning of January until the end of March. The road from Shimla remains open most of the time, so access isn't a problem. There's a range of slopes, one with a T-bar. Kufri is much closer to Shimla, and at 2501 metres has a short season. The slopes here are mainly suited to beginners.

Manali is becoming a popular place to ski, particularly now that Gulmarg in Kashmir is virtually off limits. Solang Nala is the area's winter ski capital, while in the warmer months it is possible to ski on the slopes of the Rohtang Pass.

Wildlife

There are fishing possibilities in many places in Himachal Pradesh and a number of trout hatcheries have been established. The various local tourist offices can advise you on where to fish and how to obtain fishing licences. These are much cheaper than in Kashmir.

Some of the state's deer, antelope, mountain goats and sheep are now rather rare. Himalayan black bears and brown bears are found in many parts of the state; the black bear is fairly common but the brown bear is usually found only at higher elevations. Wild boar are found at lower elevations in certain districts.

Snow leopards are now very rare and only found at high elevations in the most remote parts of the state. Panthers and leopards are, however, still found in many forested regions. Himachal Pradesh has numerous kinds of pheasants and partridges, and many mountain birds.

Temples

Although Himachal Pradesh does not have any particularly renowned temples, it does have many interesting and architecturally diverse ones. In the Kangra and Chamba valleys there are several 8th to 10th-century temples in the Indo-Aryan *sikhara* (curved spire) style. Pagoda-style temples with multi-tiered roofs are found in the Kulu Valley. There are many temples of purely local design, often with interesting wood-carvings, particularly in the Chamba region.

In the south of the state there are numerous temples with elements of Moghul and Sikh design, while in several locations there are cave temples. Finally, the Tibetans, who came to the state following the Chinese invasion of their country, have built colourful *gompas* (monasteries) and temples. The people of Lahaul and Spiti in the north of the state are also of Tibetan extraction and have many interesting gompas.

Things to Buy

The Kulu Valley is full of spinners and weavers, mostly men, and their fine shawls are very popular. The cheapest ones are made from imported Australian wool. The shawls made from the hair of the pashmina goat are the finest. Fine quality scarves made from angorra rabbit hair are also relatively inexpensive.

Chamba is well known for its leather chappals (sandals).

In the high Himalaya, soft, fleecy blankets known as *gudmas* are woven, as well as traditional rugs and numdas. In the bazaars you can find locally made jewellery and metalwork. Tibetan handicrafts include coral jewellery, carpets and religious paraphernalia.

Getting Around

Apart from two railway lines, which are both

narrow gauge and hence have more tourist appeal than practical travel significance, getting around Himachal Pradesh means taking a bus – unless you can afford a taxi. The two trains run from Kalka (just north of Chandigarh) to Shimla, and from Pathankot in Punjab along the Kangra Valley to Jogindarnagar.

Himachal Pradesh buses are generally the Indian norm – slow, crowded, uncomfortable and tiring. Things are made a little worse by the mountainous terrain. If you can manage to average 20 km/h on a bus trip, you're doing well. Taxis are readily available but rather expensive. One way you can make a saving is to find a taxi on a return trip – in that case you can often knock the price down a bit. Ask the people running your hotel; they're sometimes in the know as to who is going where and when.

The HPTDC has a number of deluxe tourist bus services. They often operate overnight but usually only in the high seasons or on demand. Typical fares are: Delhi to Manali (16 hours), Rs 250 or Rs 400 air-con; Shimla to Manali (11 hours), Rs 80 to Rs 160, according to the quality of the service.

SHIMLA
Population: 110,000
In the days before independence, Shimla was the most important British hill station, and in the hot season became the 'summer capital' of India. Shimla was first 'discovered' by the British in 1819, but it was not until 1822 that the first permanent house was erected and not until many years later that Shimla became the summer capital.

As the heat built up on the plains each year, first the women, then the men (or at least those who could escape) made their way to the cool mountain air of Shimla. The high-flown social life here in the summer was legendary – balls, bridge, parties, parades – and with many husbands being absent, romance, intrigue and gossip were always in the air.

Every summer huge baggage trains would cart all the necessary paraphernalia from Delhi so that the efficient running of the country could continue. At the end of the summer it would then get carted all the way back to Delhi, and a 'hang the expense' mentality prevailed.

At an altitude of 2130 metres, Shimla sprawls along a crescent-shaped ridge with its suburbs clinging to the slopes. Along the ridge runs The Mall – from which the British not only banned all vehicles but also, until WW I, all Indians. Today it's a busy scene each evening with throngs of holiday-makers. The Mall is lined with stately English-looking houses bearing strangely displaced English names. Shimla's English flavour is enforced by buildings like Christ Church which dates from 1857, Gorton Castle, and the former Viceroyal Lodge (Rashtrapati Niwas) on Observatory Hill which dates from 1888. Lajpat Rai Chowk is better known as Kipling's 'Scandal Corner'.

Following independence Shimla was initially the capital of the Punjab until the creation of Chandigarh. When the Punjab was broken into Punjab and Haryana, Shimla became the capital of Himachal Pradesh.

Orientation & Information
The ridge along which The Mall runs dips away westward. From it there are good views of the valleys and peaks on both sides. You'll find the tourist office (☎ 3311), the best restaurants and the main shopping centre along The Mall.

From the ridge the streets fall away steeply with the colourful local bazaars (Upper, Middle, Lower and a few in between) on the southern slopes. The streets are narrow, some of them with verandah-like 'sidewalks'. The bus station is in the middle of the crowded southern slope. In winter the southern slope is warmer than the northern side, where the ice-skating ground is located.

At the western end of The Mall as you enter the town, most buses stop at the Tourist Reception Centre, and here you'll be besieged by porters who will insist that you should get off the bus. Stay put, and the bus will continue on to the main bus stand.

For changing money the best bet is the Punjab National Bank on The Mall. ANZ

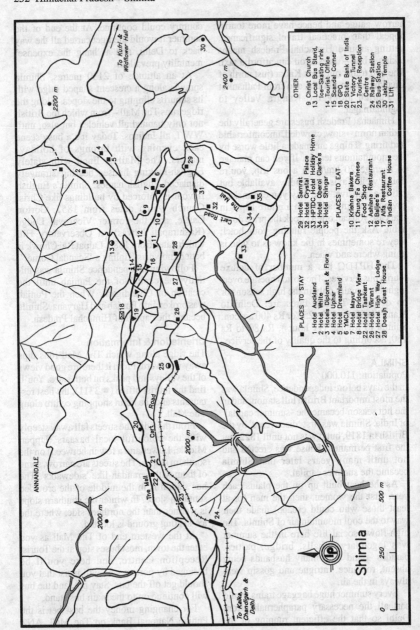

■ PLACES TO STAY
1 Hotel Auckland
2 Hotel White
3 Hotels Diplomat & Flora
4 Hotel Uphar
5 Hotel Dreamland
6 YMCA
7 Hotel Mayur
8 Hotel Bridge View
22 Hotel Tashkent
26 Hotel Vikrant
27 Hotel High Way Lodge
28 Hotel Doaajh Guest House

29 Hotel Samrat
32 Hotel Crystal Palace
33 HPTDC Hotel Holiday Home
34 Hotel Oberoi Clarkes
35 Hotel Shingar

▼ PLACES TO EAT
10 Krishna Bakers
11 Chung Fa Chinese Food Shop
12 Ashiana Restaurant
16 Baljee's Restaurant
17 Alfa Restaurant
19 Indian Coffee House

OTHER
9 Christ Church
13 Local Bus Stand,
15 Scandal Corner
14 Tourist Office
18 GPO
20 State Bank of India
21 Victory Tunnel
23 Tourist Reception Centre
24 Railway Station
25 Bus Station
30 Jakhu Temple
31 Lift

Shimla

To Kufri &
Wildflower Hall

2400 m

2200 m

The Mall

Cart Road

2000 m

The Mall

Cart Road

ANNANDALE

To Kalka,
Chandigarh &
Delhi

2000 m

500 m

250

0

Grindlays also changes money but often it doesn't receive the current rates until late in the day, and refuses to change until these rates are available. When I asked the clerk what happens if they don't receive the rate by closing time (2 pm), he replied: 'I am completely helpless, sir'.

Maria Brothers, 78 The Mall, has many interesting old maps and books.

The telephone area code for Shimla is 0177.

Rashtrapati Niwas

About one km west of the centre of Shimla, on Observatory Hill, this was formerly the Residence of the British Viceroy. Many decisions affecting the destiny of the subcontinent were made in this historic building. The huge, fortress-like building has six storeys and magnificent reception and dining halls. It now houses the Institute of Advanced Studies.

State Museum

An hour's pleasant walk down from the church on The Mall, this nice little museum has a modest collection of stone statues from different places in Himachal Pradesh. The Indian miniatures on exhibit include pictures from the Kangra school. The museum is open from 10 am to 5 pm; closed on Mondays.

Jakhu Temple

Dedicated to the monkey god, Hanuman, this temple is at an altitude of 2455 metres near the highest point of the Shimla ridge. It offers a fine view over the surrounding valleys, out to the snow-capped peaks, and over Shimla itself. The temple is a 45-minute walk from The Mall and, appropriately, there are many monkeys around the temple.

Walks

Apart from a promenade along The Mall and the walk to the Jakhu Temple, there are a great number of interesting walks around Shimla. The network of motorable roads offers access to other scenic spots.

Summer Hill There are pleasant, shady walks in this Shimla suburb on the Shimla to Kalka railway line. It's five km from Shimla at 1983 metres.

Chadwick Falls Reached via Summer Hill, the falls are 67 metres high and are at their best during the monsoon. They're seven km from Shimla at 1586 metres.

Prospect Hill It's a 15-minute climb from Boileauganj to this popular picnic spot with fine views over the surrounding country and a temple of Kamna Devia. It's five km from Shimla at 2145 metres.

Sankat Mochan Seven km from Shimla at 1875 metres, this spot, with its Hanuman Temple and fine view of Shimla, can be reached on foot or by car.

Tara Devi At 1851 metres and seven km from Shimla, you can reach this hilltop temple by rail and car. There's a *PWD Rest House* (☎ 3675) here, with double rooms for Rs 40.

Wildflower Hall On the road to Kufri, 13 km from Shimla and at 2593 metres, this was the former Residence of Indian Commander-in-Chief Lord Kitchener. The present huge mansion, surrounded by pine trees, is not the actual one built for Kitchener. From here you have a fine view back to Shimla and out to mountain peaks in the Pir Panjal and Badrinath ranges.

The run-down HPTDC *Wildflower Hall* (☎ Chharabra 8/212) has rooms from Rs 200/300 and cottages from Rs 400 to Rs 900.

Kufri This is the best known ski resort in Himachal Pradesh, 16 km from Shimla at 2501 metres. The skiing season is at its peak in January and February but the snow cover can sometimes be problematical. An annual winter sports festival is usually held the first week of February. If you'd like to try skiing in India, equipment can be rented very cheaply. The *Indira Rest House* is two km from Kufri, or there's the more upmarket *Kufri Holiday Resort*.

Mashobra Also accessible by car, this picnic spot has pleasant forest walks. It is 13 km from Shimla at 2149 metres.

Other Activities

In winter there's ice skating on the rink on the north side of the ridge, just down below ANZ Grindlays Bank.

On The Mall, in the area of the Indian Coffee House, there's at least two billiards halls where, for a few rupees, you can have a game on a full-sized table.

Organised Tours

The HPTDC conducts a number of tours to places around Shimla. Local tours, which operate more frequently in the summer season, cost Rs 50, last from 10 am to 5 pm, and are booked from the tourist office on The Mall.

Longer tours include the 64-km trip out to the skiing centre of Narkanda where there is a very fine panoramic view of the Himalaya.

Places to Stay

Accommodation in Shimla is expensive, especially during the summer season, which lasts from mid-April to mid-September. From June to September accommodation can be difficult to find at any price. Outside this season many places offer a discount – sometimes as much as 50% – so bargaining is definitely in order.

As The Mall offers the best views and is the city centre, it's the most popular address and the cost of hotels is highest here. Generally, the further you move from The Mall, the cheaper the prices. Most places do not have a rate for single occupancy.

Places to Stay – bottom end

The very clean and quiet *YMCA* (☎ 3341) is by far the best value. Rooms cost Rs 50/75 with common bath and cold water, Rs 60/80 with hot water, and there's one double with attached bath for Rs 110. There's also a Rs 20 temporary membership charge. Treks to

other places in Himachal Pradesh can be organised from here.

Filling but unexciting thali meals are available for Rs 18 for vegetarian dishes, and Rs 25 non-veg. The views from the terrace are terrific, and activities such as billiards and table tennis are offered. In summer this place is full virtually the whole time, so it's a good idea to phone ahead. The path up to the YMCA heads off between the Hotel Mayur and the Ritz Cinema. The touts at the bus and train stations will spin the usual stories about the YMCA being closed, full, far away, flooded, etc.

The *Hotel Tashkent*, just down the north side from The Mall and virtually above the Victory Tunnel, about a 10-minute walk from the centre, has rather primitive rooms with bath for Rs 60/80.

Closer to the centre is the *Hotel High Way Lodge* on Cart Rd, along from the bus station and a steep climb down from The Mall. It's very basic, noisy and about as cheap as you'll find. Rooms cost Rs 60 with common bath and lumpy beds, and bucket hot water costs Rs 4. On a small street off Cart Rd is the *Dosajh Guest House*. The rooms here are very cramped and gloomy, and cost Rs 85 with common bath.

Also on this side of the ridge, and an easy walk from the bus station, is the *Hotel Vikrant* (☎ 3602). It's a notch up the scale from the High Way Lodge, with good clean rooms for Rs 75/125 with common bath and Rs 175 with attached bath. In the season these prices jump to Rs 95/150 and Rs 225 respectively.

In between Cart Rd and The Mall, on Lower Bazaar is the *Malook Restaurant*. This place has a few rooms, but they're poor value and are best left till last. Doubles with attached bath and no window are Rs 125, while with a view it's Rs 165.

On the north side of the ridge there's a couple of places worth trying. The *Hotel Uphar* (☎ 6768), just past the Hotel Dreamland on the upper part of The Mall, is clean, friendly and fairly new. It's very good value, with rooms costing Rs 150 with bath and hot water, and Rs 200 with a view – a good deal in a town where good deals are like hens' teeth. The *Hotel Dreamland* (☎ 5057) is reasonable value, although it's not kept as clean as it might be, and the ground floor rooms are marred by ugly security mesh. The cost for basic double rooms is Rs 120 to Rs 160 with bath, and Rs 150 to Rs 180 with view.

On the next road down the slope is the *Hotel Flora* (☎ 78-027). It's an older place with an amazingly unimaginative design that does nothing to take advantage of the spectacular views. Rooms are Rs 100/200 with attached bath and hot water.

Places to Stay – middle

There are a number of good places in this range. One of the best is the *Hotel White* on the north side of the ridge. It's a very clean place run by an elderly, no-nonsense Sikh couple. Rooms vary from Rs 200/250 with no view, to Rs 300/350 with views and TV. All rooms have attached bath and hot water.

Just a few doors away is the *Hotel Diplomat* (☎ 72-001). In the high season the room rates range from Rs 200 to Rs 375, but in the off season there's a 50% discount. Also on this same street is the *Hotel Auckland* (☎ 72-621). It's a very pleasant place, and is about as far away from The Mall as it's convenient to be. Ordinary double rooms cost Rs 250, while deluxe rooms with a view cost Rs 300. The off-season discount is 20%.

On the south side of the ridge there's a whole group of places at the lower (eastern) end of The Mall, near the passenger lift. The *Hotel Bridge View* (☎ 78-537) looks attractive but the management is far from friendly and there's no off-season discount. The rooms range from Rs 175 to Rs 325.

The *Hotel Samrat* (☎ 78-572) has a range of rooms, many of them small and with no view. These are the cheapest at Rs 250, while bigger rooms with a view cost Rs 375. Discounts of 20% to 30% are offered in the off-season.

Close to the Samrat, on the lower level, is the *Hotel Crystal Palace* (☎ 5088). It's quite good value at Rs 200 for rooms at the back, and Rs 250 with a view.

Moving further along The Mall is the *Hotel Shingar* (☎ 2881), just past the Oberoi Clarke's. It's a very appealing place, although the views are certainly limited. Rooms cost Rs 340, more with colour TV. The off-season discount of 50% makes it good value at that time.

The HPTDC *Hotel Holiday Home* (☎ 72-375) is further along the lower road, about 10 minutes walk downhill from the centre. This place doesn't seem to suffer from the attitude of indifference by the staff which seems to affect so many state-run hotels. There's a bar and coffee shop, and the more expensive rooms have colour cable TV. The cost is Rs 300 for an ordinary double, up to Rs 625 for a deluxe room.

Places to Stay – top end

Without doubt the most pleasant top-end place is the *Woodville Palace Resort* (☎ 72-763), 1½ km past the Oberoi Clarke's. This ivy-covered building was constructed by Raja Rana Sir Bhagat Chandra, the ruler of Jubbal princely state in 1938, and is currently owned by his grandson. It's only a small place, but it has a very pleasant garden, and activities such as table tennis and billiards are available. The tariff ranges from Rs 800/900 up to Rs 2300/2400 for the suites, and a 20% discount applies out of season.

Back towards the centre of town is the Tudor-style *Oberoi Clarke's Hotel* (☎ 6091), one of Shimla's earliest hotels. The facilities are what you'd expect to get for US$60/80. The off-season price is the same, but it does include all meals.

Other top-end places include the *Asia the Dawn* (☎ 5858), and the *Himland Hotel (East)* (☎ 3595) on Circular Rd.

Places to Eat

Curiously Shimla is not as well endowed with restaurants as other hill stations – it's a long way behind Darjeeling for example. Overall the food is fairly mediocre; Shimla is not going to be anybody's culinary highlight. All the better known restaurants are along The Mall.

Baljee's is often crowded in the evening –

it has the standard Indian non-vegetarian menu, uninspiring decor and reasonable food. Upstairs there is an associated restaurant known as *Fascination*. Count on around Rs 60 for a meal.

A little further down The Mall, the *Alfa Restaurant* also has the standard non-veg menu. Just beyond the Alfa there is a branch of the *Indian Coffee House* with south Indian food and snacks at reasonable prices – a good place for an omelette, toast and coffee breakfast.

Along The Mall, the other way from Baljees, is the *Hotel Himani*, directly below the Ashiana Restaurant. The food is Indian, Western and Chinese, and although the service is lousy, the food is pretty good and the views are excellent.

The state tourism department has two restaurants at the main square on the ridge, close to the tourist office. The *Ashiana Restaurant* upstairs is much brighter than the gloomy *Goofa* down below. Prices are much the same in both restaurants. The ritzier Ashiana is supposed to be a cut above the cafe-like Goofa, although the latter does have good pizzas.

As you move down into the bazaar area the prices also start to descend. Right at the bottom end of the scale is a couple of basic, one-person Chinese eating places. The 'kitchens' are tiny, as are the restaurants themselves, but the food that comes out of them is excellent and cheap. The *Chung Fa Chinese Food Shop* is on Middle Bazaar, just down the steps, behind 62 The Mall. The other place is *Kwon Tung Aunty's Chinese Food Shop* at 44/31 Middle Bazaar. To find it take the steps down next to Baljee's on The Mall, and it's signposted along the first lane to the right.

Between these two Chinese places is the *Malook Restaurant*, run by a very friendly Sikh. It's a bit more expensive and offers Chinese and Tibetan dishes.

Along Lower Bazaar there are a number of standard Indian eating houses, including *Brothers*, *Shere-e-Punjab* (separate veg and non-veg restaurants) and *Metro*. None of them stand out.

Finally, there is a couple of bakeries, such as *Krishna Bakers*, along the eastern end of The Mall. You can get very good chicken or vegie burgers here for Rs 6, which they heat in a microwave oven – not a bad snack. These places also sell quite good cakes and pastries.

Things to Buy

There are quite a number of craft shops along the road near the Hotel Diplomat. Woodcarvings are the main item on sale, but you should be able to find just about anything.

Getting There & Away

Air The Vayudoot agent is the tourist office on The Mall. The agent for the new operator, Jagsan Airlines, is Span Tours N Travel (☎ 5279) at 4 The Mall.

Vayudoot has a daily flight to Delhi (US$95) via Chandigarh (US$27). Jagsan operates a flight three times weekly to Delhi for Rs 1040.

Bus All deluxe buses should be booked from the tourist office in The Mall. Semi-luxe buses are booked from the window outside the same building. It is open daily from 10 am to 1 pm and 2 to 4 pm.

A bus from Chandigarh is the easiest way to get to Shimla. The 117-km trip takes five hours and costs Rs 40 in an ordinary bus or Rs 60 in a deluxe bus. You can reach Chandigarh from Delhi by a variety of buses. The trip straight through from Delhi takes around 10 hours and costs Rs 145 in a deluxe bus.

There are buses north from Shimla to other hill stations in Himachal Pradesh such as Dharamsala or the Kulu Valley. From Shimla to Manali costs Rs 80 ordinary, Rs 105 semi-luxe and Rs 160 deluxe and takes 11 hours. To Dharamsala costs Rs 80 and takes 10 hours. To Mandi it's about six hours for Rs 65. Dehra Dun is a weary nine-hour trip for Rs 65.

Train There's a railway reservation office at 1 The Mall, just down the hill from the Indian Coffee House. It has quotas on all the trains

Top: Street scene, Old Delhi (RI)
Bottom: Street market, New Delhi (RI)

Top: On the Leh to Manali road near Darcha, Himachal Pradesh (BT)
Bottom: Lotus flower, Dal Lake, Srinagar, Jammu & Kashmir (GW)

from both Shimla and the broad-gauge line from Kalka.

The journey to Shimla by rail involves a change from broad gauge to narrow gauge at Kalka, a little north of Chandigarh. The narrow-gauge trip to Shimla takes nearly six hours. It is great fun as the little train winds its way around the mountains, although in summer it can get uncomfortably hot and crowded. If travelling from Shimla to Chandigarh, you can just catch the train for the three-hour journey to Solan, than take a bus to Chandigarh from there.

By train all the way from Delhi it's 364 km at a cost of Rs 79/263 in 2nd/1st class. The 6 pm departure from Shimla connects with the *Kalka-Howrah Mail*, which arrives in Delhi at 6.30 am. If you want to do the whole trip by train in daylight, the *Himalayan Queen* leaves New Delhi at 6 am, and with connections you arrive in Shimla at 4.50 pm. In the opposite direction the 10.55 am departure from Shimla also connects with the *Himalayan Queen*, which arrives back in New Delhi at 9.45 pm.

Taxi A taxi to Manali costs Rs 1900.

Getting Around

Local bus services operate from the Cart Rd bus stand on the north side of the ridge. It's just below the ice-skating rink, on the path which leads off The Mall from beside ANZ Grindlays Bank.

Half a km to the east of the main bus stand a two-part 'tourist lift' takes you up to The Mall for Rs 1. It saves a long and tedious climb and it's the only lift I've ever seen with a fire to keep the operator warm!

AROUND SHIMLA
Craignano

At 2279 metres and 16 km from Shimla, Craignano, with its hilltop *Municipal Rest House*, is only three km from Mashobra. Contact the Water Works Engineer in Shimla (☎ 2815) for bookings.

Chail

This was once the summer capital of the princely state of Patalia. Today the old palace is a luxurious hotel. Chail is 45 km from Shimla via Kufri, or you can reach it via Kandaghat on the Shimla to Kalka road or narrow-gauge rail line.

Chail, at an altitude of 2250 metres, is built on three hills, one of which is topped by the Chail Palace, and one by the ancient Sikh Temple. Chail also boasts a temple of quite another religion – cricket. Here you will find the highest cricket pitch in the world!

Places to Stay In the *Chail Palace Hotel* (☎ Chail 43) rooms are Rs 250 to Rs 600 but the Maharaja and Maharani suites are Rs 850 and Rs 1000. Chail also has a number of HPTDC cottages and log huts from Rs 200 to Rs 400, and the *Himneel Hotel* with rooms from Rs 50 to Rs 90. There are also a number of local hotels.

Getting There & Away There are direct buses to Chail from Kalka and Shimla.

Solan
Population: 22,000

This town is between Kalka and Shimla, on both the railway line and the road. It's named after the Soloni Devi Temple on the southern side of the town although it's more famous these days as the home of Golden Eagle beer; the Mohan Meakin brewery is about four km from town along the road to Shimla, and tours can be arranged on request.

Places to Stay & Eat The comfortable and quiet HPTDC *Tourist Bungalow* (☎ 2497) has rooms from Rs 97, or Rs 108 with a separate sitting room. It is on the edge of town on the way to Shimla, half a km from the bus station and 800 metres from the railway station.

There are also a couple of basic local hotels near the bus stand, but don't expect too much.

Kasauli

This pleasant little hill station at 1927 metres is only a short distance north of Kalka. It's an interesting 15-km trek from Kalka to

Kasauli, or you can get there from Dharampur, which is on the Kalka to Shimla railway line.

Only four km from Kasauli is Monkey Point, a picnic spot and lookout with a very fine view over the plains to the south and to the mountains in the north. Sabathu, 38 km from Kasauli, has a 19th-century Gurkha-built fortress.

Places to Stay & Eat There is a *PWD Rest House* with rooms for Rs 40, and a number of private guest houses such as the *Alasia, Morris* and *Kalyan*. The *Hotel Ros Common* (☎ 5) has rooms from Rs 175 to Rs 300. In Dharampur the simple *Mazdoor Dhaba* restaurant near the station has good (and cheap) vegetarian meals and a dormitory upstairs.

Kalka

The narrow-gauge railway line from Kalka to Shimla was built between 1903 and 1904. Although going by road is cheaper and quicker, the rail trip is more fun.

Pinjore (Haryana), which is 5 km south-west of Kalka near Chandigarh, has a Moghul summerhouse and garden, built by Fidai Khan, who also built the Badshahi Mosque in Lahore, Pakistan.

Naldera

At 2044 metres Naldera is 23 km from Shimla and has a golf course (supposedly the oldest in the country) and cafeteria. You can stay at the *Golf Club* for Rs 50 for a double room, or the *Hotel Golf Glade* (☎ 8/265) has double rooms for Rs 100 to Rs 125.

Chabba

This *Rest House*, 35 km from Shimla, is a pleasant five-km walk from Basantpur, on the road to Tattapani. For reservations see the Electricity Engineer in Shimla.

Tattapani

There's a direct bus to these popular sulphur hot springs, located at only 655 metres, and 51 km from Shimla. Doubles in the *Tourist Bungalow* are Rs 80 to Rs 120.

Fagu

Fagu, at 2510 metres, has very fine views. It's 22 km from Shimla, and receives a lot of snow in winter. This town also has a potato research centre (!). *Hotel Peach Blossom* (☎ 8/205) has double rooms for Rs 125 and Rs 150.

Narkanda

Population: 700

At 3143 metres, 64 km from Shimla, this is a popular spot for viewing the Himalaya, particularly from the 3300-metre Hattu peak. Narkanda has recently been developed as a skiing centre. The season lasts from late December to early March and you can take 10-day courses which include your room and board.

From Narkanda you can make trips to Baggi and Khadrala, which are on the Hindustan to Tibet road leading to the Tibetan border. Alternatively, you can visit the apple-growing area around Kotgarh or continue to the Kulu Valley via Luhri.

Places to Stay The HPTDC *Hotel Himview* (☎ 33) has doubles at Rs 150 to Rs 175, and dorm beds for Rs 20. Reservations are made through the tourist office in Shimla. There's also a *PWD Rest House*, with rooms for Rs 50 and Rs 95.

Baggi & Khadrala

Due east from Narkanda there are *Rest Houses* in both these places, and Khadrala also has a *Forest Rest House*. Baggi is 82 km from Shimla at 2648 metres, Khadrala is 11 km further on at 2987 metres.

Thanedhar

This is a centre for apple growing, 82 km from Shimla on the route past Narkanda. There is a *PWD Rest House* here.

Rohru

Situated 129 km from Shimla, this is the site for the Rohru Fair which takes place during two days each April. The temple of Devta Shikri is the centre for this colourful fair. The Pabar River, which runs through Rohru, is noted for its trout; there's a trout hatchery 13 km upstream at Chirgaon. Haktoti, a little before Rohru, has an interesting ancient Hindu temple dedicated to the goddess Durga. The temple contains a metre-high image of the eight-armed goddess, made of copper and bronze.

Places to Stay There's a *Rest House* in Rohru, a small *Forest Rest House* (booked in Rohru) at Chirgaon and *log cabins* at Seema, two km upstream towards Chirgaon. The log cabins cost Rs 15 per person and should be booked at the tourist office in Shimla.

SIRMUR DISTRICT

There are a number of other places of interest in the south of the state, where Himachal Pradesh borders Uttar Pradesh and Haryana. This district is known as Sirmur.

Paonta Sahib

Population: 13,000

Situated on the Yamuna River, on the border with Uttar Pradesh, Paonta Sahib is a transit point for travellers from the hill stations of northern Uttar Pradesh to Shimla and other hill stations in Himachal Pradesh.

Paonta Sahib is linked with Gobind Singh, the 10th of the Sikhs' gurus who lived here. At Bhangani, 23 km away, he achieved a great military victory when his forces defeated the combined might of 22 hill-country kingdoms. His weapons are displayed in the town and his gurdwara still overlooks the river.

Places to Stay There's the HPTDC *Hotel Yamuna* with doubles from Rs 100 to Rs 200. There are also local hotels.

Nahan

At 932 metres, Nahan is in the Siwalik Hills, where the climb to the Himalayan heights commences. There are a number of interesting walks around the town, including the trek to Choordhar (3647 metres) from where there are fine views of the plains to the south and the Sutlej River.

Saketi, 14 km south of Nahan, has a fossil park with life-sized fibreglass models of pre-historic animals whose fossilised skeletons were unearthed here.

Places to Stay There is a *PWD Rest House* with rooms for Rs 40, and a number of local hotels.

Renuka

North-west of Paonta Sahib, a major festival is held each November at this lake. There's a small zoo and a wildlife sanctuary with deer and many water birds.

Places to Stay The HPTDC has a *Tourist Inn* (☎ 41) at the lake with rooms for Rs 50, and the *Hotel Renuka* has rooms from Rs 90 to Rs 200.

THE SOUTH-WEST

Bhakra-Nangal

The giant Bhakra Dam, one of the largest in the world, provides irrigation water for a vast area of the Punjab and also produces hydro-electric power. The public relations office at the dam arranges permits to inspect this major project.

Bilaspur & Naina Devi

In Bilaspur, on the route from Chandigarh to Mandi, and on the shore of the Gobind Sagar (lake), are the interesting Vyas Gufa, Lakshmi Narayan and Radhashyam temples. There are fine views over the lake from Naina Devi.

MANDI

Population: 23,000

The town of Mandi, on the Beas River, is the gateway to the Kulu Valley. From here you climb up the narrow, spectacular gorge of the river and emerge from this grey and barren stretch into the green and inviting Kulu Valley. At an altitude of only 760 metres, temperatures are higher here and Mandi mainly serves as a travel crossroads as its name, which means 'market', might suggest.

Mandi is 202 km north of Chandigarh and 110 km south of Manali. Dharamsala is 150 km to the north-west on the road to Pathankot.

Sivarati Festival

This is one of the most interesting festivals in Himachal Pradesh. It lasts for a week and deities from all over Mandi district are brought here. Large numbers of people have *darshan* (viewing of a deity) at the Bhutnath Temple.

Places to Stay & Eat

Mandi has the HPTDC *Hotel Mandav*, on the ridge behind the bus stand, across the river from the main part of the town. Beds in the gloomy dorm are Rs 30, or there are doubles for Rs 125 to Rs 370. The service is lacking and the reception desk seems to be in constant darkness as someone is too lousy to turn the lights on. There is a footpath up to the hotel from the bus station, but this is the local shithouse and is putrid, even by Indian standards. The main driveway entrance is about 100 metres beyond the bus station.

On the other side of the river there are a number of cheap hotels, but most are filthy, and many are not licensed to take foreigners.

Up the scale is the *Hotel Ashoka Holiday Inn* (☎ 2800), a modern place with good rooms for Rs 200 with bath and hot water.

The rambling old *Raj Mahal* is a strange old place, but it has plenty of atmosphere if nothing else. Rooms start at Rs 75/95 with bath and cold water, Rs 125/175 with hot water. It has the only bar in town, and the restaurant serves amazingly good food – about the only place in town that does.

The *Cafe Shiraz* at Gandhi Chowk in the centre of town is run by the state tourist office and serves snacks.

Getting There & Away

There are three buses to Dharamsala daily (six hours, Rs 45), to Kulu (three hours) and Manali (five hours) they leave hourly, and there are also departures to Shimla and Pathankot.

REWALSAR LAKE

The Rewalsar Lake, a pilgrimage centre for Hindus, Buddhists and Sikhs, is high up in the hills 24 km south-east of Mandi. There is a mountain cave-refuge near here. The small lake is revered by Tibetan Buddhists and every year, shortly after the new year (sometime in March), many make a pilgrimage here, especially those from Dharamsala.

The festival, known as Tso-Pema, is particularly important in the Year of the Monkey, which falls every 12 years. At this time there are literally thousands of people here, and His Holiness the Dalai Lama gives puja in the monastery, and then does a circuit around the lake. It's a very colourful event, and was last held in 1992.

Places to Stay

The HPTDC *Tourist Inn* has dorm beds for Rs 20, doubles with common bath for Rs 120 and with attached bath for Rs 175 to Rs 300. There are also a number of local hotels, such as the *Lomush, Lake View* and *Shimla*.

Getting There & Away

There are regular buses from Mandi (Rs 7), and the trip takes one hour.

KANGRA VALLEY

The beautiful Kangra Valley starts near Mandi, runs north, then bends west and extends to Shahpur near Pathankot. To the north the valley is flanked by the Dhauladhar mountain range, to the side of which Dharamsala clings. There are a number of places of interest along the valley, including the popular hill station of Dharamsala.

The main Pathankot to Mandi road runs through the Kangra Valley and there is a narrow-gauge railway line from Pathankot as far as Jogindarnagar. The Kangra school of painting developed in this valley.

Baijnath

Only 16 km from Palampur, the small town of Baijnath is an important pilgrimage place due to its very old Siva temple. The temple is said to date from 804 AD. There is a *PWD Rest House* in Baijnath.

Palampur

A pleasant little town surrounded by tea plantations, Palampur is 35 km from Dharamsala and stands at 1260 metres. The main road runs right through Palampur and there are some pleasant walks around the town.

Places to Stay & Eat The HPTDC *Hotel T-Bud* is about a km from the bus station and has rooms for Rs 150 and Rs 200, and dorm beds for Rs 20. Meals are available.

The *Silver Oaks Motel*, 2½ km from the bus station, has great views. Double rooms cost Rs 150. For something cheaper, try the *Hotel Sawney*, near the bus station.

The HPTDC *Neugal Cafe* is 1½ km from the Hotel T-Bud.

Kangra

There is little to see in this ancient town, 18 km almost directly south of Dharamsala, but at one time it was a place of considerable importance. The famous temple of Bajreshwari Devi was of such legendary wealth that every invader worth their salt took time to sack it. Mahmud of Ghazni carted off a fabulous fortune in gold, silver and jewels in 1009. In 1360 it was plundered once again by Tughlaq but it was still able to recover and, in Jehangir's reign, was paved in plates of pure silver.

The disastrous earthquake which shook the valley in 1905 destroyed the temple, which has since been rebuilt. Kangra also has a ruined fort on a ridge overlooking the Baner and Manjhi rivers. It too was sacked by Mahmud, captured by Jehangir in 1620 and severely damaged in the 1905 quake.

Kangra has a *PWD Rest House*.

Jawalamukhi

In the Beas Valley, 34 km south of Kangra, the temple of Jawalamukhi is famous for its eternally burning flame. It's the most popular pilgrimage site in Himachal Pradesh.

Places to Stay The HPTDC *Hotel Jwalaji* (☎ 81) has rooms from Rs 125 to Rs 175, and

Rs 200 with air-con; and there's a Rs 20 dorm. There's also a *PWD Rest House*.

Nadaun, south of Jawalamukhi on the Beas River, has another *Rest House*.

Chintpurni

Chintpurni, near Bharwain, 80 km south of Dharamsala and across the Beas River, has an important temple.

Masrur

Three km from Haripur, and about 15 km south of Kangra, Masrur has 15 richly carved rock-cut temples in the Indo-Aryan style. They are partly ruined but still show their relationship to the better known and much larger temples at Ellora in Maharashtra.

Nurpur

Only 24 km from Pathankot on the Mandi to Pathankot road, this town was named by Jehangir, after his wife, Nurjahan. Nurpur fort is now in ruins but still has some finely carved reliefs. A ruined Krishna Temple, also finely carved, stands within the fort. Nurpur has a *PWD Rest House*.

TREKS FROM KANGRA VALLEY

From Baijnath you can make an interesting trek to Dharamsala, Chamba or Manali. The first day's trek to Bir Khas can be done by bus. At Bara Bhangal, reached on Day 6, you can choose to go east to Manali or west to Dharamsala or Chamba. Before setting out, obtain a good trekking map, such as the Survey of India's *Trekking Route Map of Himachal Pradesh*, sheet No 1 (scale 1:250,000).

Day 1	Baijnath to Bir Khas	1600 m	26 km
Day 2	Bir Khas to Rajgaunda	2500 m	13 km
Day 3	Rajgaunda to Palachak Deota	2750 m	8 km
Day 4	Palachak Deota to Panardu Got	3700 m	8 km
Day 5	Panardu Got to Thamsar Jot	4750 m	6 km
Day 6	Thamsar Jot to Bara Bhangal	2541 m	14 km

From here you can turn west and in four days reach Chanota which is on the Chamba to Dharamsala trek – see Treks from Chamba for details. The walks are:

Day 7	Bara Bhangal to Dhardi	21 km
Day 8	Dhardi to Naya Graun	24 km
Day 9	Naya Graun to Holi	16 km
Day 10	Holi to Chanota	13 km

Alternatively you can turn east, and a day's trek will bring you to the Manali Pass treks described in the Treks from Manali & Kulu Valley section. There are a number of possible routes down to Manali.

DHARAMSALA
Population: 17,000

The hill station of Dharamsala is actually split into two totally separate parts. Close to the snow line, the town is built along a spur of the Dhauladhar range and varies in height from 1250 metres at the Civil & Depot Bazaar up through Kotwali Bazaar and Forsyth Ganj to nearly 1800 metres at McLeod Ganj. There's quite a temperature variation between the top and bottom of the town.

As in other hill stations there is a wide variety of short and long walks, but Dharamsala has the additional attraction of its strong Tibetan influence. It was here that the Dalai Lama and his followers fled after the Chinese invasion of Tibet.

The Dalai Lama is the recipient of the 1989 Nobel Peace Prize, awarded to him not only for his spiritual activities but for 'his struggle for the liberation of Tibet'. It can also be seen as a reproach to the Chinese government in the wake of the Tiananmen Square massacre. Throughout his more than 30 years of exile, for religious as well as practical reasons, the Dalai Lama has worked for a peaceful settlement with China, which is in line with his pacifist approach to all personal and political conflicts in the world. Tibetans in exile view the award not only as well-deserved recognition for their leader but as acknowledgement of the long struggle for peaceful negotiation in the face

of extreme provocation. As the Dalai Lama said in his acceptance speech: 'I hope this prize will provide courage to the six million people of Tibet...(it) is a profound recognition of their faith and perseverance'.

For the serious student of Tibetan culture there's the monastery up at McLeod Ganj and the school of Tibetan studies and its library, one of the best in the world for studying Tibet and its culture, about midway between McLeod Ganj and the lower town.

For the not so serious, McLeod Ganj is a small freak centre with lots of Tibetan-run hotels and restaurants, all the menu favourites, low prices, crowds of Western travellers – almost another Kathmandu in fact. McLeod Ganj is full of colour and energy: those little Tibetan terriers (yappy but spry) scoot around everywhere; in the middle of the main street there's a small temple with a giant prayer wheel; and strings of multi-coloured Tibetan prayer flags wave in the breeze above many buildings.

Orientation & Information
Tourist Office The tourist office (☎ 363) is in the lower town close to the bus stand and the Dhauladhar Hotel. Although there is a timetable of buses on the wall and the tourist officer insists it is correct, double-check at the bus station.

Money For moneychanging there's branches of the State Bank in both McLeod Ganj and Dharamsala.

Telecommunications & Travel Agencies In the main street of McLeod Ganj are a couple of travel agents who can arrange all sorts of tickets. They also have facilities for long-distance/ISD phone calls.

Bookshops In one of the main streets of McLeod Ganj the Tibetan Charitable Trust has a small handicraft shop and bookshop. It's a good place for books about Tibetan Buddhism. The Tibetan Information Centre is on the same street and has some good photos of what the Chinese are up to in

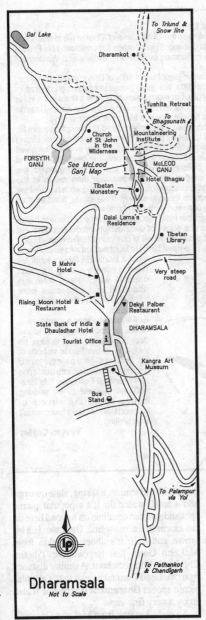

Dharamsala
Not to Scale

(Map labels:) Dal Lake; To Triund & Snow line; Dharamkot; Tushita Retreat; To Bhagsunath; Mountaineering Institute; Church of St John in the Wilderness; FORSYTH GANJ; See McLeod Ganj Map; McLEOD GANJ; Hotel Bhagsu; Tibetan Monastery; Dalai Lama's Residence; Tibetan Library; B Mehra Hotel; Very steep road; Rising Moon Hotel & Restaurant; Dekyi Palber Restaurant; State Bank of India & Dhauladhar Hotel; DHARAMSALA; Tourist Office; Kangra Art Museum; Bus Stand; To Palampur via Yol; To Pathankot & Chandigarh

Lhasa. For a bit of lighter reading material, try the Bookworm shop near the State Bank.

Medical Services The Tibetan Medical Centre, just across from the Koko Nor Hotel, will be of interest to followers of alternative medicine. There are also two other medical centres which get a considerable number of Indian and Western patients.

Church of St John
Of course Dharamsala was originally a British hill resort and one of the most poignant memorials of that era is the pretty Church of St John in the Wilderness. It is only a short distance below McLeod Ganj and has beautiful stained-glass windows. Here Lord Elgin, Viceroy of India, was buried in 1863.

Kangra Art Museum
This museum is in Dharamsala, down the road from the tourist office. It houses miniature paintings from the famous Kangra school of art, which flourished in the Kangra Valley in the 17th century. It's open Tuesday to Saturday from 10 am to 5 pm.

Meditation Courses
His Holiness the Dalai Lama gives teachings every year in March, and this is obviously a popular time to be in Dharamsala. As there are so many Westerners in town at this time, it's also a busy time for meditation courses.

At the library in McLeod Ganj they have courses for beginners, as well as Tibetan language courses. It costs Rs 50 per month and the teachers are all Tibetans.

The Tushita Retreat Centre has facilities for a retreat, and also has Buddhism courses. The monks here are either Tibetan or Western. Even if you don't stay at the Retreat Centre it is possible to attend some of the courses. Course fees are Rs 60 per day, plus Rs 60 for meals. Live-in accommodation is available for Rs 25 in a dorm, or Rs 45/70 with common bathroom and Rs 55/80 with attached bathroom.

An Audience with His Holiness the Dalai Lama

Travellers may request an audience with His Holiness the Dalai Lama of Tibet at his residence in Dharamsala. However, you need to do so at least one month in advance (by contacting his Private Office in McLeod Ganj) because he is so much in demand by Tibetans, Indians and Westerners alike.

Meeting this 14th incarnation of Chenresig, Tibetan Buddhism's deity of Universal Compassion, is no ordinary event. Not so much because of his title, nor even because of the high degree of reverence in which he is held by the Tibetan people; but more because of how it feels to be in his company. As an American friend put it: 'When you look at him, he is the size of a normal human being; but when you look away; you realise that his presence is filling the whole room'.

After waiting, strangely nervous, in the anteroom, we were ushered into his reception room for our audience with His Holiness, which seemed to speed by in a flash. However, several strong

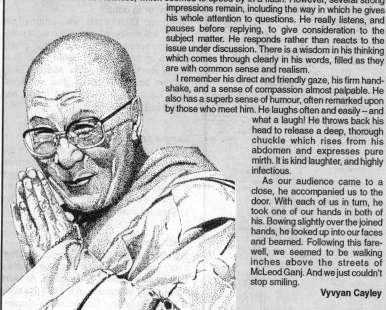

impressions remain, including the way in which he gives his whole attention to questions. He really listens, and pauses before replying, to give consideration to the subject matter. He responds rather than reacts to the issue under discussion. There is a wisdom in his thinking which comes through clearly in his words, filled as they are with common sense and realism.

I remember his direct and friendly gaze, his firm handshake, and a sense of compassion almost palpable. He also has a superb sense of humour, often remarked upon by those who meet him. He laughs often and easily – and what a laugh! He throws back his head to release a deep, thorough chuckle which rises from his abdomen and expresses pure mirth. It is kind laughter, and highly infectious.

As our audience came to a close, he accompanied us to the door. With each of us in turn, he took one of our hands in both of his. Bowing slightly over the joined hands, he looked up into our faces and beamed. Following this farewell, we seemed to be walking inches above the streets of McLeod Ganj. And we just couldn't stop smiling.

Vyvyan Cayley

There are also many courses offered by individual monks who live in monasteries.

Activities

There are many fine walks and even finer views around Dharamsala. The sheer rock wall of Dhauladhar rises behind McLeod Ganj. From the road up from the lower town it seems just an arm's length away.

From McLeod Ganj interesting walks include the two-km stroll to **Bhagsu** where there is an old temple, a spring, slate quarries and a small waterfall. It's a popular picnic spot and you can continue on beyond here on the ascent to the snow line. **Dal Lake** is a bit brown and dull; it's about three km from McLeod Ganj, just beyond the Tibetan Children's Village School. A similar distance from McLeod Ganj takes you to the popular picnic spot at **Dharamkot** where you'll also enjoy a very fine view.

An eight-km trek from McLeod Ganj will

bring you to **Triund** (2827 metres) at the foot of Dhauladhar. It's another five km to the snow line at **Ilaqa**. There is a *Forest Rest House* here for overnight accommodation.

The Mountaineering Institute, half a km north of McLeod Ganj, runs eight to 10-day high-altitude treks from April to December. A minimum of 10 people is required, and the cost is Rs 1200 to Rs 1480 per person all inclusive. Rock-climbing training is also available on application.

If you want to organise your own trek, guides and porters can be hired from the institute, as can tents and sleeping bags. Also for sale is a guide book (Rs 75) which gives details of treks in the area. It's called *Treks & Passes of Dhauladhar & Pir Panjal*, and is written by Shiv Ram Saini, the director of the institute.

Places to Stay

Dharamsala Dharamsala has two accommodation areas – the lower part of town and the upper part known as McLeod Ganj. The accommodation in the lower part is generally poor, and there's little reason to stay there.

Dharamsala's only attempt at a deluxe hotel is the HPTDC *Dhauladhar Hotel* (☎ 2107) with a dorm bed for Rs 24 or doubles from Rs 175 to Rs 250. There's a restaurant and a pleasant garden patio – ideal for sipping a sunset beer while you look out over the plains below.

There's the extremely laid-back and rather basic *Rising Moon Hotel & Restaurant* with dorm beds and rooms for around Rs 40, some with bathroom. Behind it is the *Tibet United Association Hotel* with rooms at similar prices. The *B Mehra Hotel* has basic rooms for Rs 50 with common bath or Rs 80 attached.

Finally there's the *Hotel Shimla* opposite the tourist office, which has good rooms with bath for Rs 95, and down the hill a bit further is the *Sun & Snow*.

McLeod Ganj Most Western visitors to Dharamsala stay not in the main part of town but 500 metres (and 10 km by road) higher up the hill at McLeod Ganj. Here the Tibetan

community who followed the Dalai Lama into exile have set up a whole series of hotels and restaurants. McLeod Ganj is very popular and many places are often full, especially during the time around Tibetan New Year (early March).

The Bhagsu road from the bus stop is a good bet. The long-running *Hotel Tibet* (☎ 2587) is simple and straightforward. Rooms cost Rs 76 with common bath, or Rs 92 with attached bath. There are also more expensive deluxe rooms for Rs 165 to Rs 275, and these all have hot water. Right opposite is the modern *Lhasa Guest House*, which has good rooms for around Rs 100.

Further along the Bhagsu road, the *Koko Nor Hotel* has rooms for Rs 40 to Rs 80. The *Green Hotel* is a popular cheapie and has doubles for Rs 40 with common bath, and Rs 60 with bath. On the road just above and north of the Bhagsu road there are a couple of good places. The *Kalsang Guest House* (☎ 2813) has singles/doubles for Rs 35/60 with common bath. Hot water costs Rs 5 by the bucket, or there are doubles with attached bath and hot water for Rs 146. It's a good place.

Just above this is the *Paljor Gakyil Guest House* (☎ 2571). This immaculate place is run by a very friendly Tibetan couple who have lived in Europe for some years and speak French, German and English. The rooms are good value at Rs 60/90 with bath and cold water, or Rs 200 with carpet, hot water and a wonderful view. They also have a few dorm beds for Rs 25.

On Jogibara Rd in the heart of town there's quite a few more places, including the *Shangrila Guest House* and the very basic *Hotel Snow Palace*. Further along, down a narrow lane off to the left, is the *Ashoka Guest House*. This is a popular budget place with rooms for Rs 50 with common bath.

Right next door to the Ashoka is the *Drepung Loseling Guest House*. This very new place is owned and run by the Drepung Monastery in Karnataka, and so the monks staffing it are not the most experienced when it comes to hotel services, but they are very friendly and eager to please. The rooms are

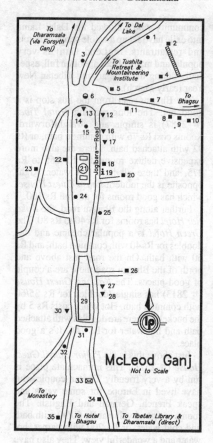

McLeod Ganj
Not to Scale

some of the best in Dharamsala, and cost Rs
165 for a double with attached bath and hot
water.

On Temple Rd the *Kailash Hotel* is an old
favourite, while the *Om Hotel* on the next
level down is so popular it often has a waiting
list during peak times, although it's hard to
see quite why. Rooms here cost Rs 50 with
common bath.

In the southern part of town, on a spur
which juts out towards the plains, is the new
Hotel Natraj (☎ 2076). It's perched right on
the edge of a long, steep drop and looks none
too stable. However, the views are unbeatable, the rooms are comfortably furnished
and range from Rs 275 to Rs 440. Right next
door is the similar *Hotel Him Queen*.

Right at the end of this ridge is the HPTDC
Hotel Bhagsu (☎ 3191), which charges Rs
200 for an ordinary double, or Rs 225 to Rs
350 for deluxe rooms.

Places to Eat

Just as accommodation is hard to find during Tibetan New Year, so is a restaurant that stays open. The options are very limited for a week or so in early March each year.

Dharamsala The *Rising Moon*, at the hotel of the same name, is a friendly place with a long menu, good food, good music and amazingly slow service. There are various other small restaurants around town, or you can try the restaurant in the *Dhauladhar Hotel*. As with accommodation, there's more choice of places to eat up at McLeod Ganj.

McLeod Ganj For those heartily sick of dhal and rice the restaurants here offer a wide range of Tibetan/Chinese dishes plus Western travellers' favourites such as banana pancakes. Overall, food in McLeod Ganj is a pleasant change from the Indian norm. The *Hotel Tibet* has an excellent and busy restaurant.

Right on the corner by the bus stop is the new *McLLo Restaurant*. This place is definitely a cut above the average Tibetan cheapie, and the atmosphere and the views are good. The limited menu features Western snacks and a few Indian dishes.

There are a number of places along Jogibara Rd from the bus stop. Right on the corner is the *Tashi Restaurant*, and a couple of doors down is the popular little *Malabar Restaurant*. A couple of doors further still is the *Cafe Shambhala* – all take a while to serve you, but the food is generally worth the wait.

Also in this area is the *Shangri La*, which apart from the usual Chinese and Tibetan dishes, has superb lemon curd cake and apple pie.

A bit further along Jogibara Rd there's another grouping of basic restaurants, including the *Gakyi, Snowlord, Tibet Memory* and *Aroma*.

Friend's Corner, on Temple Rd near the bus stop, is a good place for a drink.

Getting There & Away

The main bus station is in Dharamsala, about 300 metres below the tourist office. Take the new road next to Laj Printers, and then the flight of stairs to the left. All long distance buses leave from here; the buses from McLeod Ganj only ferry passengers to the Dharamsala bus station. The first bus down to Dharamsala from McLeod Ganj is at 4 am, so even if you have an early departure there's no need to stay the night down in Dharamsala, unless of course you absolutely must have that extra half-hour or so of sleep.

You can also make train reservations at the railway booking office in the bus stand, although they have a quota of only two reservations per day per train.

There are about four buses a day to Shimla and Delhi, and just one or two to other destinations. Approximate distances, times (in hours) and fares from Dharamsala are:

	Distance	Time (hrs)	Fare
Manali	253 km	12½	Rs 105
Kulu	214 km	10	Rs 90
Shimla	317 km	10	Rs 80
Chandigarh	248 km	9	Rs 47
Pathankot	90 km	3½	Rs 25
Delhi	526 km	13	Rs 91

Getting Around

It's about 10 km from the lower part to McLeod Ganj – a 45-minute ride for Rs 2. There are buses every hour, or plenty of Maruti van-taxis which do the trip for Rs 50. Walking down, take the steep short cut round to the left of the monastery and down to the cantonment via the library. It takes about 30 or 40 minutes to walk.

DALHOUSIE

Population: 9000

Sprawling over and around five hills at around 2000 metres, Dalhousie was, in the British era, a sort of 'second string' hill station – a place where those who could not aspire to Shimla went. The town was founded by Lord Dalhousie, and has some pleasant walks.

Orientation & Information

Dalhousie is very scattered; most of the

shops are clustered around Gandhi Chowk, while the 'town' – if Dalhousie can be called such a thing – is crowded down the hillside close to Subhash Chowk, a steep uphill climb from the bus stand. The houses almost stand on top of one another.

The tourist office (☎ 2136) is by the bus stand in a half-completed building. The State Bank of India here does not change money; the nearest places are either Pathankot or Dharamsala.

Things to See & Do

Today Dalhousie has a busy population of Tibetan refugees – if you take the footpath from Subhash Chowk to Gandhi (GPO) Chowk, you'll pass brightly painted **low-relief pictures** the Tibetans have carved into the rocks. There is a nice little Tibetan refugee handicrafts shop with carpets whose unusual designs feature rabbits and elephants; it's near Gandhi Chowk.

With its dense forest, old English houses and colourful Tibetans, Dalhousie can be a good place to spend some time, although very few travellers pass through here. About two km from Gandhi Chowk along Ajit Singh Rd, **Panch Pulla** (Five Bridges) could be quite a pleasant spot, but it's disfigured by the series of horrible concrete steps and seats built over the stream. Along the way there's a small, and easily missed, freshwater spring known as **Satdhana**.

Kalatope is 8½ km from the GPO and offers a fine view over the surrounding country. There's a *Forest Rest House* here. Lakhi Mandi, 15 km out and at around 3000 metres, has stupendous mountain views.

Places to Stay

Dalhousie has plenty of hotels, although a fair number of them have a run-down, left-by-the-Raj feel to them.

Prices fluctuate with the season; in the off season, hotels offer discounts of up to 30%.

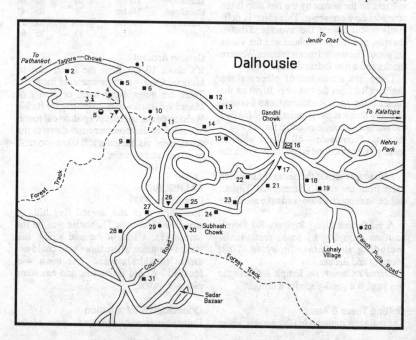

As is the case at most hill station hotels, single rooms are virtually nonexistent, and even a single tariff is hard to get.

Places to Stay – bottom end

The tourist bungalow, known as the *Hotel Geetanjali* (☎ 2155), is on the hill just above the bus stand and has doubles for Rs 150. The rooms are extraordinarily large and even contain separate living rooms. There's a 30% off-season discount, and an additional 20% single-occupancy rate.

The *Youth Hostel* near the bus stand has dorm beds for Rs 20, or Rs 10 if you are a member.

Places to Stay – middle

The *Hotel Shangrila* (☎ 2316) is an old house which has been converted. It is within walking distance of Gandhi Chowk and has very good views. Doubles cost between Rs 300 and Rs 475, all with TV and hot water.

The *Hotel Surya* (☎ 2158) in The Mall also has rooms from Rs 300. It's closed during the off season. Right next door is the family-run *Hotel Him Dhara* (☎ 286), which is good value at Rs 250/300 with bath and

hot water. The off-season rates of Rs 75/100 are a real bargain.

The *Grand View Hotel* (☎ 23) near the bus stand has good views of the surrounding area and charges Rs 300 for ordinary doubles, or Rs 350 for deluxe rooms. The views of the snow-capped Pir Panjal range are superb. An off-season discount of 30% applies.

The *Mount View Hotel* next door charges Rs 200/300, less 30% in the off season.

The *Hotel Shivali* is a modern place with good rooms at Rs 250/350 with bath and TV. Close by is the *Hotel Raviview* (☎ 390), which is similar.

Places to Stay – top end

The *Aroma-n-Claire Hotel* on Court Rd near The Mall has large rooms with a touch of the Raj for Rs 400, all with TV and fridge. In the off season it's Rs 200.

Places to Eat

During the off season it's hard to find a place to eat. The *Shere-e-Punjab Dhaba* at Subash Chowk and the *Punjab Restaurant* at Gandhi Chowk are about the only possibilities.

Seasonal restaurants include the *Kwality, Preet Palace* and *Milan Restaurant*.

	PLACES TO STAY		PLACES TO EAT
2	Youth Hostel	7	Lall's Restaurant
5	Mount View Hotel	17	Punjab Restaurant
6	Grand View Hotel	26	Restaurant Preet Palace
9	Hotel Kumar's	30	Shere-e-Punjab Dhaba
11	Hotel Geetanjali		
12	Hotel Surya		OTHER
13	Hotel Him Dhara		
14	Hotel Shangrila	1	English Cemetery
15	Mehar's Hotel	3	Tourist Office
18	Hotel Samrat	4	Dalhousie Club
19	Hotel Taj Palace	8	Bus Stand
21	Sunrise Cottage	10	Cinema
22	Hotel Highland	16	GPO & Kwality Restaurant
23	Green's Hotel	17	Tibetan Refugee Shop & Punjab
24	Hotel Crags		Restaurant
25	Hotel Super Star	20	Satdhana Spring
27	Hotel Shivali	29	Church
28	Hotel Himview		
31	Aroma-n-Claire		

Getting There & Away

Pathankot, 80 km away, is the usual departure point for buses to Dalhousie. The trip takes about four hours and costs Rs 25.

There are also direct buses to Amritsar, Jammu, Dharamsala (10 hours) and Shimla (15 hours!). For Shimla and Dharamsala it's far quicker to catch a bus back to Pathankot, and take another from there.

For Chamba there are four buses daily doing the two-hour trip.

Taxis between Dalhousie and Pathankot cost Rs 525 and take two hours.

KHAJIAR

This grassy 'marg' is 22 km from Dalhousie. Over a km long and nearly a km wide, it is ringed by pine trees with a lake in the middle. There's a golf course here and a golden-domed temple. The wood carvings in the temple are very impressive and date back to the 14th century.

Places to Stay

The tourist bungalow, *Hotel Deodar*, has dorm beds at Rs 20 and doubles at Rs 125 to Rs 175. Other alternatives are the *Youth Hostel* and the *PWD Rest House*.

Getting There & Away

You can walk there in a day from Dalhousie, or go by bus.

CHAMBA

Population: 17,000
Situated 56 km from Dalhousie, beyond Khajiar, Chamba is at 926 metres – quite a bit lower than Dalhousie, so it's warmer in the summer. Perched on a ledge high above the River Ravi, it has often been compared to a medieval Italian village and is famed for its temples, many of them within walking distance of the town centre.

For 1000 years prior to independence, Chamba was the headquarters of a district of the same name, which included Dalhousie, and was ruled by a single dynasty of maharajas. There are many reminders of this period, including the palace (now a hotel) and the museum.

The town is a centre for the Gaddis, traditional shepherds who move their flocks up to the high alpine pastures during the summer and descend to Kangra, Mandi and Bilaspur in the winter. The Gaddis live only on the high range which divides Chamba from Kangra.

Chamba has a grassy promenade known as the *chaugan* – it's only 75 metres wide and less than a km long. The village is a busy trading centre for villagers from the surrounding hills and each year it's the site for the Minjar festival in August, with a colourful procession and busy crowds of Gaddi, Churachi, Bhatti and Gujjar people. An image of Lord Raghuvira leads the procession and other gods and goddesses follow in palanquins.

Temples

The Chamundra Temple on top of a hill gives an excellent view of Chamba with its slate-roof houses (some of them up to 300 years old), the River Ravi and the surrounding countryside. It's a steep half-hour climb.

Next to the maharaja's palace is the temple complex of Lakshmi Narayan which contains six temples, three dedicated to Siva and three to Vishnu, the oldest dating back to the 10th century, the newest to 1828. The Hariraya Temple is also dedicated to Vishnu and is in the Sikhara style of architecture.

Bhuri Singh Museum

Chamba also has the Bhuri Singh Museum, which has an interesting collection relating to the art and culture of this region – particularly the miniature paintings of the Basohli and Kangra schools. It is open from 10 am to 5 pm daily except Sunday. The Rang Mahal in the upper part of town was badly damaged by fire, but some of its murals are now in the museum.

Places to Stay & Eat

The HPTDC has two tourist bungalows: the *Hotel Champak* with doubles from Rs 75 to Rs 100, dorm beds at Rs 20; and the *Hotel*

Iravati with rooms at Rs 150 and Rs 175 for doubles.

The *Hotel Akhand Chandi* (☎ 2371) on College Rd has air-con rooms at Rs 140/210. For something cheaper try the *Janta Hotel*.

Meals are available in the *Ravi View Cafe* and the *Hotel Iravati*. Despite its grotty appearance, the *Gupta Dhaba*, opposite RK Tailors near the GPO, has excellent food. At the *Khalsa Tea Stall* you can get butter toast with real Chamba butter.

Getting There & Away

Taxis and jeeps can be hired in Dalhousie but they're expensive at Rs 525 return. The local bus is Rs 15 and takes two hours, or you can walk there in two days, resting overnight in Khajiar. Buses from Pathankot take five hours and leave every two hours.

From Chamba trekkers can make an interesting, but hard-going, trek through Brahmaur and Triund to Dharamsala. Or via Tisa you can trek all the way into Lahaul or Kashmir.

TREKS FROM CHAMBA

There are a number of interesting treks from Chamba, both short out-and-back treks and longer treks to places like Dharamsala. The shorter ones include the eight-km walk to Sarol, 24 km to Bandal and the 40-km trek to Chhatrari. In Chhatrari, on the route to Brahmaur, the temple of Devi Adi Shakti is dedicated to the goddess of primeval energy.

On all treks you need to be self-sufficient, and it is a good idea to hire a guide/porter. Ample time should be allowed for acclimatisation, as some of the treks go as high as 5000 metres.

Brahmaur (Brahmpura)

Vehicles can cover the whole 65 km from Chamba to Brahmaur, although the last 16 km from Kharamukh require 4WD. Buses run up to Kharamukh.

Also known as Shivbhumi, this is the heart of the Gaddi's land. There are some very old temples grouped in a compound known as the *chaurasi* in Brahmaur, and accommodation is available in a *Forest Rest House*.

From Brahmaur it is about 80 km to Dharamsala and takes about six days to walk:

Day 1	Brahmaur to Chanota	22 km
Day 2	Chanota to Kuarsi	13 km
Day 3	Kuarsi to Chatta	13 km
Day 4	Chatta to Lakagot	10 km
Day 5	Lakagot to Triund	6 km
Day 6	Triund to Dharamsala	13 km

The Chatta to Lakagot sector crosses the 4300-metre Indrahas Pass with fine views over the Kangra Valley. For a more detailed description of this trek, see Lonely Planet's *Trekking in the Indian Himalaya* by Garry Weare.

From Brahmaur you can make the 35-km trek to Manimahesh Lake at 3950 metres. This important pilgrimage spot is at the base of the 5575-metre Manimahesh Kailash. Thousands flock here on the 15th day after Janmashtami (Krishna's birthday), which falls in August or September each year.

Pangi Valley

Kilar, 167 km north-east of Chamba, is in the deep and narrow gorge of the Chenab River. Here you are in the high Himalaya, in the scenic but lightly populated Pangi Valley, between the Pangi and Zanskar ranges. From Kilar you can trek north-west to Kishtwar in Jammu & Kashmir, or turn east about halfway to Kishtwar and cross the Umasi La pass into the Zanskar Valley, or trek southeast to Keylong and Manali.

Kulu Valley

The fertile Kulu Valley rises northward from Mandi at 760 metres to the Rohtang Pass at 3978 metres, the gateway to Lahaul and Spiti. In the south the valley is little more than a narrow, precipitous gorge, with the Beas River (pronounced 'bee-ahs') sometimes a sheer 300 metres below the narrow road.

Further up, the valley widens and its main part is 80 km long, though rarely more than a couple of km wide. Here there are stone-fruit and apple orchards, rice paddies and wheat fields along the valley floor and lower slopes, and deodar forests higher up the slopes, with snow-crowned rocky peaks towering behind. The main towns, Kulu and Manali, are in this fertile section of the valley.

The light-skinned people of the Kulu Valley are friendly, devout, hard working and relatively prosperous. The men wear the distinctive Kulu cap, a pillbox with a flap around the front in which they may stick flowers. The women wear lots of silver jewellery and long garments of homespun wool secured with great silver pins; they are rarely without a large conical basket on their backs, filled with fodder, firewood or even a goat kid.

The other people of the valley are the nomads (Gaddis) who take their flocks of black sheep and white goats up to the mountain pastures in the early summer and retreat before the winter snows. You don't really know what wool smells like until you've travelled in a bus overcrowded with rain-soaked villagers.

The valley also has many Tibetan refugees, some running restaurants and hotels in Manali, but many others in camps near the rivers, prayer flags fluttering. The Tibetans are great traders – you'll find them in all the bazaars – but many work in road gangs, whole families toiling together.

The Kulu Valley was always a popular place, but it managed to retain a very peaceful and unhurried atmosphere. With the troubles in Kashmir, however, the valley in general and Manali in particular, have largely replaced Kashmir as the place to go to see the snow. The result is that it is going ahead at an enormous rate – Manali now has over 150 hotels, compared with less than 50 just five years ago, and more are appearing each month. Unfortunately the expansion seems to be largely unplanned, and so the landscape is changing rapidly, often for the worse as more and more insensitively designed buildings get thrown up. One can only wonder just what will happen to all the hotels when and if the problems in Kashmir are resolved.

KULU
Population: 14,500

At an altitude of 1200 metres, Kulu is the district headquarters but it is not the main tourist centre; that honour goes to Manali. Nevertheless there are a number of interesting things to see around Kulu, and some fine walks.

The town, which sprawls on the western bank of the Beas, is dominated by the grassy maidans on the southern side of town. They're the site for Kulu's fairs and festivals, in particular the colourful Dussehra Festival, from which the Kulu Valley gained the name 'Valley of the Gods'.

Orientation & Information

The tourist office (☎ 2349) is by the maidan at the southern end of town. It's open daily from 9 am to 7 pm in summer, and from 10 am to 5 pm in winter.

The State Bank of India by the maidan is a shambles and it takes an eternity to change money.

There's a bus and taxi stand on the opposite side of the maidan, and all the HPTDC accommodation units and several of the hotels are around the maidan. The main bus stop is in the northern area of town.

Temples

Some of the main temples in and around Kulu are:

Raghunath Temple About a km from Dhalpur in Raghunathpura (or Sultanpur), the temple of the principal god is actually not very interesting. It is only open from 5 pm.

Jagannathi Devi Temple This temple is in the village of Bhekhli, three km from Kulu. It's a stiff climb, but from the temple there are fine views over the town. Take the path off the main road to Akhara bazaar after crossing the Sarawai bridge.

Vaishno Devi Temple This small cave has

an image of the goddess Vaishno and is four km along the Kulu to Manali road.

Bijli Mahadev Temple A jeep track links Kulu with Bijli Mahadev, eight km away. Across the river, high on a projecting bluff, the temple is surmounted by a 20-metre-high rod said to attract blessings in the form of lightning. At least once a year the image of Siva in the temple is supposed to be shattered by lightning, then miraculously repaired by the temple *pujari*.

Bajaura On the main road, 15 km south of Kulu, the famous temple of Basheshar Mahadev has fine stone carvings and sculptures. There are large image slabs facing north, west and south. There is a *PWD Rest House* in Bajaura.

Activities
The Shyamananda Meditation Centre holds meditation courses, although students must make their own accommodation arrangements.

Dussehra Festival
The Dussehra Festival, in October after the monsoons, is celebrated all over India but most particularly in Kulu. The festival starts on the 10th day of the rising moon, known as Vijay Dashmi, and continues for seven days. Dussehra celebrates Rama's victory over the demon king Ravana but in Kulu the festival does not include the burning of Ravana and his brothers, as it does in other places around India.

Kulu's festival is a great gathering of the gods from temples all around the valley. Approximately 200 gods are brought from their temples down to Kulu to pay homage to Raghunathji from the temple in Raghunathpura in Kulu. The festival cannot commence until the powerful goddess Hadimba, tutelary deity of the Kulu rajas, arrives from Manali. Like the other gods she is pulled in her own temple car, or *rath*, and Hadimba likes speed so she has to be pulled as fast as possible. She not only arrives before all the other gods but also leaves

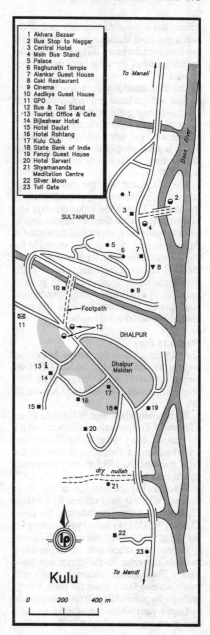

1 Akhara Bazaar
2 Bus Stop to Naggar
3 Central Hotel
4 Main Bus Stand
5 Palace
6 Raghunath Temple
7 Alankar Guest House
8 Gaki Restaurant
9 Cinema
10 Aadikya Guest House
11 GPO
12 Bus & Taxi Stand
13 Tourist Office & Cafe
14 Bijleshwar Hotel
15 Hotel Daulat
16 Hotel Rohtang
17 Kulu Club
18 State Bank of India
19 Fancy Guest House
20 Hotel Sarvari
21 Shyamananda
   Meditation Centre
22 Silver Moon
23 Toll Gate

To Manali

Beas River

SULTANPUR

Footpath

DHALPUR

Dhalpur
Maidan

dry nullah

To Mandi

Kulu

0   200   400 m

before them. Another curiosity is that the Jamlu god from Malana comes to the festival but does not take part – this god stays on the opposite side of the river from the Dhalpur maidan.

The Raghunathji rath is brought down, decked with garlands and surrounded by the other important gods. Priests and the descendants of Kulu's rajas circle the rath before it is pulled to the other side of the maidan. There is great competition to aid in pulling the car since this is a very auspicious thing to do.

The procession with the cars and bands takes place on the evening of the first day of the festival. During the following days and nights of the festival there are dances, music, a market and festivities far into the night. On the penultimate day the gods assemble for the 'Devta darbar' with Raghunathji, and on the final day the temple car is taken to the river bank where a small heap of grass is burnt to symbolise Ravana's destruction. Raghunathji is carried back to his main temple in a wooden palanquin.

Places to Stay

Only a little south of the maidan, but a short walk off the main road, is the HPTDC *Hotel Sarvari* (☎ 2471). It's a well-run place with doubles from Rs 200, and dorm beds at Rs 30.

Right behind the tourist office is the *Hotel Bijleshwar* The position is excellent and it's the best value in town at Rs 60/75 for rooms with bath and a fireplace. In summer the tariff goes up to Rs 150. Hot water is supplied by the bucket (Rs 4).

Also beside the maidan is the *Hotel Rohtang* which is good value at Rs 100/185. Up the road behind the Maidan, the *Hotel Daulat* (☎ 2358) has rooms with balcony for Rs 125 to Rs 150, half that in the off season.

Across the other side of the maidan, towards the river, is the cheap and basic *Fancy Guest House*, although there's certainly nothing fancy about the place, except perhaps the price of Rs 100 for a basic room.

On the path which connects the northern and southern parts of town is the *Aadikya*

Guest House, right by the footbridge. The roar of the river can be amazingly loud at times, so it's a bit like trying to sleep beside an aeroplane! At Rs 300 for rooms with TV, attached bath and hot water, it's definitely overpriced; the off-season rates of Rs 100/150 are far more realistic.

There are other rock-bottom places at the Manali end of town, by the main bus stand, such as the *Kulu Valley Lodge* or the *Central Hotel*, but this is a noisy area as the road is very narrow and traffic snarls are common. The *Alankar Guest House*, on the first floor above the little Telegraph Office, has a couple of nice clean rooms, and the little verandah overlooking the small maidan is a pleasant place to sit and watch the world go by.

Finally, the HPTDC *Silver Moon* is to the left of the road just as you enter town from the south. It has six double rooms at Rs 400. There is a 25% off-season discount.

Places to Eat

The *Hotel Sarvari* has the usual sort of dining hall. By the tourist office there's the HPTDC's *Monal Cafe* with good light meals and snacks, but sometimes painfully slow service. The *Marigold Restaurant* near the taxi stand is a popular place.

For ultra-basic Tibetan food, try the *Gaki Restaurant* near the main bus stand. It only has momos and thukpa, and no English is spoken, but it's very cheap.

Getting There & Away

Air The Vayudoot office is at the airport at Bhuntar, 10 km south of Kulu. Jagsan Airlines has its office (☎ 2286) in the Hotel Amit, also in Bhuntar.

Vayudoot has a daily Delhi/Chandigarh/Kulu and return flight. The fares from Kulu are US$47 to Chandigarh, and US$107 to Delhi. Jagsan Airlines has flights to Kulu from Delhi daily except Thursday; the fare is US$107. Their flight stops at Shimla on the way out but the return flight is direct to Delhi, unlike Vayudoot's. Another new airline, Trans-Bharat Aviation (☎ 2381), flies between Delhi, Chandigarh and Kulu on Monday, Thursday and Saturday. Prices are the same as Vayudoot's.

Bus & Taxi There are direct buses to Kulu from Dharamsala, Shimla (235 km), Chandigarh (270 km) or Delhi (512 km). The Kulu to Chandigarh buses do not go via Shimla. All these direct buses continue to Manali, 42 km further north.

A direct bus from Delhi takes 14 hours. Regular express buses cost Rs 150, but there are various classes right up to the HPTDC air-con superdeluxe bus which costs nearly Rs 350.

Buses run regularly along the main road from Kulu to Manali for Rs 12; the trip takes under two hours. There are fewer buses on the east side of the Beas River and the trip can take a long time, up to two hours from Manali to Naggar alone. Add another 1½ hours from Naggar to Kulu. The combined fare is not much different from the direct one.

Cars can get to Naggar by crossing the river at Patlikuhl near Katrain – the bridge is very narrow. Or you can get off the Kulu to Manali bus there and walk up. It's six km up to the castle by road but much less on foot, although the path is very steep.

Plenty of taxis make the trip up from the plains, but count on around Rs 1600 or more for Shimla or Chandigarh to Kulu or Manali. A taxi from Kulu to Manali costs Rs 300.

AROUND KULU

You can make some interesting excursions from Kulu to the adjoining valleys which run into the Kulu Valley. See also the Treks from Manali & Kulu Valley section later in this chapter.

Parvati Valley

The Parvati Valley runs off north-east from Bhuntar, which is south of Kulu. You can travel up the valley by bus. Manikaran is built near sulphur hot springs and it's interesting to watch the locals cook their food in the pools of hot water at the Sikh temple. There are also hot baths (separate baths for men and women) at the temple and, of course, free accommodation. Hot water is nice to have in Manikaran because the sides of the valley are very steep, and not much sun gets in. It's said that Siva sat and meditated for 2000 years at Kihr Ganga, a 30-km walk from Manikaran.

There are a lot of French and Italian freaks in the area. There's great trekking and wonderful scenery here.

Places to Stay The HPTDC *Hotel Parbati* (☎ 35) has 12 double rooms at Rs 150, and there's a 30% off-season discount.

Rooms in shops or houses are easily available if you ask around. The *Padha Family House*, near the bridge, is an excellent place where quite a few travellers stay. There are big, clean rooms with rope beds for Rs 40, and there's a private sulphur rock-bath indoors. You can get food and expensive, but beautiful, wild bee honey.

In the local chai shops try *kihr*, a delicious rice dessert made with milk, sugar, fresh coconut and sultanas.

Getting There & Away Buses from Kulu to Bhuntar take 1½ hours and cost about Rs 5. Bhuntar to Manikaran is another 1½ hours for about the same price.

Sainj Valley

The area from Aut to Sainj is not as beautiful as the other valleys but it has a charm of its own. It's also very rarely visited by travellers so the locals are friendly. There is no accommodation as such, but rooms are easily available if you ask around.

Getting There & Away A bus from Bhuntar to Aut takes an hour and costs Rs 5.

KULU TO MANALI

There are a number of interesting things to see along the 42-km road between Kulu and Manali. There are actually two Kulu-to-Manali roads; the direct road runs along the west bank of the Beas, while the much rougher and more winding east bank road is not so regularly used, but does take you via Naggar with its delightful Forest Rest House.

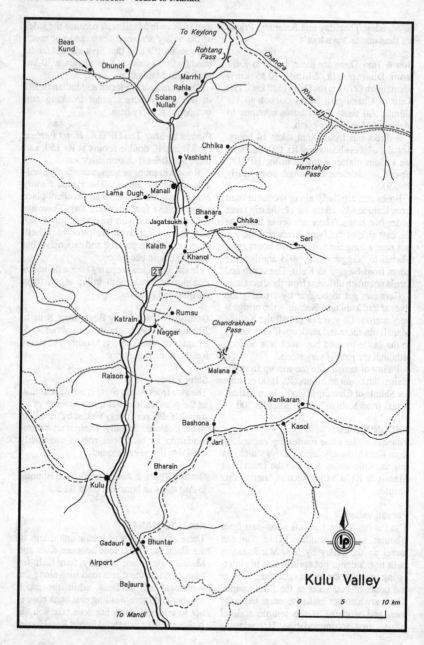

To Keylong

Beas Kund

Dhundi

Marrhi

Rohtang Pass

Rahla

Solang Nullah

Chandra River

Chhika

Vashisht

Hamtahjor Pass

Lama Dugh

Manali

Bhanara

Jagatsukh

Chhika

Kalath

Seri

Khanol

Rumsu

Katrain

Naggar

Chandrakhani Pass

Malana

Raison

Manikaran

Bashona

Kasol

Jari

Bharain

Kulu

Gadauri

Bhuntar

Airport

Bajaura

To Mandi

Kulu Valley

0   5   10 km

Raison

Only eight km from Kulu there's a camping place on the grassy meadow beside the river. It's a good base for treks in the vicinity. There are 14 *Tourist Huts* at the site with doubles at Rs 100, which can be booked through the Kulu tourist office.

Katrain

At about the midpoint on the Kulu to Manali road, this is the widest point in the Kulu Valley and is overlooked by the 3325-metre Baragarh peak. Two km up the road on the left side is a trout hatchery.

Places to Stay There's a small *Rest House* and a pleasant HPTDC tourist bungalow known as the *Hotel Apple Blossom* with doubles at Rs 150, cottages from Rs 250 and a five-bedded dorm for Rs 30 per bed. It's an interesting alternative to staying in Kulu or Manali. There's also the very expensive riverside *Span Resort* (☎ 40), which costs Rs 1400/1800 for singles/doubles with all meals.

Naggar

High above Katrain, on the east bank of the river, is Naggar with its *castle hotel*. Transport to the castle is a little problematical but the effort is worthwhile, for it is a stunning place to look around or stay at.

Naggar Castle At one time Naggar was the capital of the Kulu Valley and the castle was the raja's headquarters. Around 1660 Sultanpur, now known as Kulu, became the new capital. The quaint old fort is built around a courtyard with verandahs right round the outside and absolutely stupendous views over the valley. It feels an eon away from any of the hassles India can dish up! Inside the courtyard is a small temple containing a slab of stone with an intriguing legend about how it was carried there by wild bees.

Temples There are a number of interesting temples around the castle. The grey sandstone Siva Temple of Gauri Shankar is at the foot of the small bazaar below the castle and dates from the 11th or 12th century. Almost opposite the front of the castle is the curious little Chatar Bhuj Temple to Vishnu. Higher up the hill is the pagoda-like Tripura Sundri Devi Temple and higher still, on the ridge above Naggar, the Murlidhar Krishna Temple.

Roerich Gallery Also up the hill above the castle is the Roerich Gallery, a fine old house displaying the artwork of both Professor Nicholas Roerich, who died in 1947, and his son, Svetoslav Roerich, who died in Bangalore in 1993. Its location is delightful and the views over the valley are very fine.

Places to Stay The HPTDC *Castle Hotel* has just four double rooms with common bath for Rs 250 and two with bath at Rs 250, plus a larger family suite for Rs 350. There's also a five-bed dorm. This place is deservedly popular and often booked out; the Kulu tourist office can make reservations, but plan ahead. There's a *Forest Rest House* in Naggar.

The friendly *Poonam Mountain Lodge & Restaurant* (☎ Katrain 12), is opposite Naggar Castle near the post office. The owner is extremely helpful and can arrange trekking. The rooms are very large and spartan, and cost Rs 80. Meals and picnic lunches are available.

MANALI

Population: 2600

Manali, at the north end of the Kulu Valley, is the main resort in the valley. It's beautifully situated and there are many pleasant walks around the town, as well as a large number of hotels and restaurants. It's also very much a 'scene' – at the height of the tourist season it's packed out with Indian and Western tourists. Smaller villages around Manali have semipermanent 'hippie' populations. The nearby country and villages are truly beautiful and not to be missed.

The town itself is not particularly pretty; in fact, with the spate of hotel construction that's occurred in the last few years, it's now decidedly scrappy – it's the area around the town that is the attraction. Apple growing has traditionally been the mainstay of the local economy, although judging by the way many orchards have been turned into building sites, tourism must now be the area's number one money spinner.

Manali is also the starting point for a number of interesting treks, as well as for the two-day journey along the spectacular road to Leh in Ladakh.

It stays cold in Manali until surprisingly late in the season; there may still be snow on the ground in late March.

Orientation & Information

Manali has one main street where you'll find the bus stand and most of the restaurants. The tourist office (☎ 2325) is also on this main street, and the taxi stand is right outside. It's a very well-organised office and has a list of hotels and tariffs, and of taxi routes and fares.

Hotels are scattered all over town, some of them within easy walking distance of the bus stop, some of them, like the Tourist Bungalow (Hotel Manalsu), a good long stretch uphill.

If you want to organise a trek, there are any number of agencies in the main shopping area. Many of these operators have moved in from Kashmir as there is not much happening on the trekking scene there now.

Warning Manali is famous for its marijuana, which is not only esteemed by connoisseurs, but also grows wild all around. Don't be fooled by the fact that you see it growing everywhere; like anywhere else it's still illegal, police will still bust you and you can still end up in a situation which is better avoided. Take care.

Hadimba Temple

The temple of the goddess Hadimba, who plays such a major part in Kulu's annual festival, is a sombre wooden structure in a clearing in the dense forest about a km from the tourist office.

Hadimba is supposed to be the wife of Bhima in the epic *Mahabharata*. It's a pleasant stroll up to the temple, which was built

in 1553. Also known as the Dhungri Temple, it's the site of a major festival held in May. Non-Hindus are allowed to enter.

Old Manali Village

The current town of Manali is actually a new creation which has superseded the old village, a couple of km away. Follow the road across the cascading Manalsu stream, from where you can climb up to this interesting little village.

Tibetan Monastery

The colourful, pleasant new Tibetan Monastery has a carpet-making operation; you can buy carpets and other Tibetan handicrafts here.

Fishing

The tourist office will arrange a fishing licence if you want to try your luck with the Beas River trout – you'll need your own gear though.

Skiing

Skiing is also arranged by many of the agencies in town. The North Face Ski School, run by the national ski coach, has been recommended by a number of travellers. Two-day packages cost Rs 350 including ski hire and accommodation, and extra days are Rs 200.

Organised Tours

Guy Robins and Gerry Moffat, who operate Equator Expeditions, run excellent one to three-day rafting trips on the Beas River, and organise treks throughout the area, including Spiti. They can also arrange mountain biking tours and day trips, and kayaking tours for experts and beginners. They can be contacted through their agent, Iqbal Sharma, Himalayan Journeys (☎ 2365), PO Box 15, Manali, 175131. You can find them next to the State Bank of India.

In season there are daily bus tours to the Rohtang Pass (Rs 80) which last from 9 am to 4pm; they're basically for the locals who want to come and go and touch the snow. There are also tours to Manikaran (Sikh temple and hot springs) for Rs 100 and to Naggar Castle for Rs 50.

Places to Stay

Prices in Manali vary considerably according to the season. The high seasons are April to June and mid-September to early November, when the place is flooded with Indian tourists and prices go sky high. In July-August prices drop considerably and you can get a room priced at Rs 250 for around Rs 100. From December to February, when there are no tourists at all, the prices are even lower but some hotels close down completely. In winter expect to pay Rs 30 to Rs 40 for a bar heater. All hotels are required to display a tariff card at reception, so from this you can find out what is the maximum they should be charging.

As your bus pulls into the bus station chances are you'll be besieged by touts, all trying to entice you into their place, which is of course the 'best', 'quietest', 'closest' or whatever. The hotels in the heart of town have the least attractive location, although if you arrive late in the day they can be convenient for a night until you can hunt up something better. The most attractive area is the rise on the western side of the town. Here quite a few of the apple trees have survived, and so the atmosphere is much more rustic.

An alternative to staying in a hotel is to rent a house. As development spreads, the number of houses available drops, but it is still possible to find one for Rs 500 a month at the height of the season. For that price, however, conditions are likely to be a little primitive. There may be a stove but you'll need your own cooking utensils, and you may have a long walk to get water.

Places to Stay – bottom end

The cheapest places are across the bridge in old Manali. To the right across the bridge there's a small group of cheap places, although these are becoming increasingly cramped by more modern and expensive places. The *Rising Moon* and the *Riverside* guest houses both charge around Rs 80 a double.

Up to the left after you cross the bridge there's the *Hotel New Bridge View*, with rooms for Rs 50/75 with common bath. Bucket hot water costs Rs 3. A little further up are the *Beas View Paying Guest House* and the *Hotel Kirishan*. The *Veer Paying Guest House*, one of the best places in this area, charges around Rs 70 for a double. These guest houses are all small, intimate and family-run.

In the back streets in the main part of town, the *Sukhiran Guest House* is hardly the friendliest place in the world, but it is definitely one of the cheapest in town at Rs 15 for a dorm bed and Rs 125 for a double room.

Moving up to the area north-west of the centre, the *Hotel Kalpana* is one of the originals, and has large rooms in the old part of the house for Rs 150 with bath and hot water, or newer rooms for Rs 175. Another long-time stayer is the *Bombay Guest House*.

The HPTDC *Yatri Niwas*, above the tourist office, should be opening soon and promises dorm beds for around Rs 30 and some double rooms. Another possibility, although a pretty uninteresting one, is the HPTDC *Tourist Lodge* down by the edge of the river. Spartan four-bedded rooms here are Rs 120 or Rs 30 per bed. The HPTDC *Beas Hotel* is also by the riverside, and has double rooms from Rs 150 to Rs 275. There's also one single room at Rs 75.

Places to Stay – middle

The main concentration of places is in the streets between the main road and the rise. Here virtually every building is a hotel, so if you want to stay in this area it's just a matter of finding one to suit. They all have the tariff displayed, and charge around Rs 200 to Rs 300 in the season, dropping to Rs 50 to Rs 100 at other times. Places in this area include the *Rock Sea, Diamond, Skylark, Chelsea, Karma, Shiwalik, Raj Palace, Hill View, Mona Lisa* and *Park View*. There are many others.

The *Samiru Hotel* (☎ 2280), in the centre of town near the Mayur Restaurant, is a

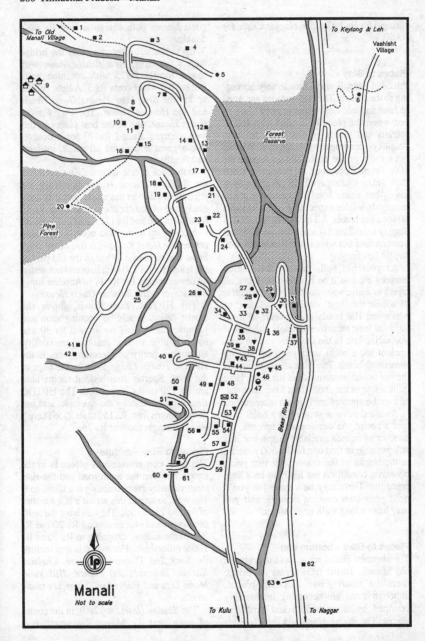

Manali

Not to scale

■ PLACES TO STAY

1 Beas View Paying Guest House
2 Hotel New Bridge View
3 Hotels Dreamland & Riverbank
4 Hema, Riverside, Him View & Rising Moon Guest Houses
7 Honeymoon Huts
9 Log Huts
10 Hotel Pankaj
11 Hotel Highlands
12 Pinewood Hotel
13 Negi's Mayflower Guest House
14 Sunshine Guest House
15 Hotels Kalpana & Rajhans
16 Hotels Chetna & Devi Dyar
17 John Banon's Hotel
18 Hotel Paradise
19 Hotel Rohtang Manalsu
21 Hotel Montesque
22 Hotel Tourist
23 Hotel Zarim & Bombay Guest House
24 Hotel Gilbert
25 Hotel Sunflower
26 Hotel Hilltop
31 Tourist Lodge
34 Hotel Gandhara
35 Hotel Solang
37 Beas Hotel
39 Samiru Hotel
40 Hotel Himgiri
41 Honeymoon Cottages
42 Grand View Hotel
44 Sukiran Guest House
48 Lhasa Hotel
49 Skylark Guest House

50 Ambika Guest House
51 Mt View Guest House
54 Hotel Ibex
55 Central View Guest House
56 Aroma Hotel
57 Samrat Hotel
58 Hotel Sunflower
59 Hotel Piccadily
61 Hotel Snow Drop
62 Ashok Travellers' Lodge

▼ PLACES TO EAT

8 Cafe Rohtang
29 Sa-Ba Restaurant
30 Chandratal Restaurant
33 Peter's
38 Adarsh Restaurant
43 Mayur Restaurant
45 Mona Lisa Restaurant
53 Ashiana Restaurant

OTHER

5 HPTDC Club House
6 Baths
20 Hadimba Temple
27 State Bank of India
28 Ambassador Travels
32 Taxis
36 Tourist Office
46 Temple
47 Bus Stop
52 Post Office
60 Tibetan Monastery
63 Mountaineering Institute

modern place with well-appointed rooms. These cost Rs 350 in the season, dropping to Rs 200 in the off season.

The HPTDC has a few places in this range. The *Honeymoon Cottages* and the *Honeymoon Huts*, both out of the centre, consist of huts with a couple of beds and attached baths for Rs 400. The *Hotel Rohtang Manalsu* is not a bad option and there are decent views across the valley. Double rooms cost Rs 200 to Rs 300 and there are some four-bedded rooms for Rs 250.

Once again, the best places are out of the centre of town. The *Hotel Tourist* (☎ 2297) is a quiet and pleasant place, just off the road to Old Manali. All rooms have a small balcony with a view, TV, attached bath and

hot water. At Rs 375 these are good value for expensive Manali, and the off-season rate of Rs 100 is a bargain.

Close to the Tourist is the *Hotel Zarim* (☎ 2225), which is a bit more upmarket. The rooms are modern and well appointed, and meals are available. The cost here is Rs 450 to Rs 800.

Further along this road is one of Manali's oldest places, the *John Banon's Hotel*. It's a very nice older-style building with good facilities, and it's good value at Rs 300. Surprisingly this place doesn't offer discounts.

The *Sunshine Guest House* is just a little further on, and it too is in an older building. The rooms are spacious, there's a lawn for relaxing on and the views aren't bad either. Cost for all this is Rs 250 to Rs 400 for a double with attached bath.

Higher up the hill is another Manali oldie, the *Hotel Highlands*. Rooms in this atmospheric place go for Rs 250 to Rs 350. The *Hotel Pankaj* (☎ 2444) next door has similar prices but lacks appeal.

Near the Highlands a footpath leads to the Hadimba Temple, and there are a few new places along here. The *Hotel Rajhans* (☎ 2208) has a good position and the view from the front rooms is excellent. For doubles with attached bath and hot water the rate is Rs 350, or Rs 200 in the off season. The bright and airy *Hotel Chetna* is yet another newie, and as it's the last along this track it has uninterrupted views of the pine forest, as well as over the town. The tariff is Rs 350 with TV, bath and hot water, but it's closed during the off season.

Across the river in Old Manali, the *Hotel Hema* is perhaps overpriced at Rs 250 with attached bath but hot water by the bucket. However, during the off season it's an incontestable bargain at Rs 50.

Places to Stay – top end

Manali also has its share of upmarket places. The *Hotel Piccadily* (☎ 2114) and the *Hotel Ibex* (☎ 2440) are both on the main street, just south of the shopping centre. The Piccadily charges Rs 850 for a double and the Ibex charges Rs 660.

Dominating the western ridge above the town is the *Hotel Shingar Regency*, while on the left bank of the Beas River, about 1½ km from town, is the expanded ITDC *Hotel Manali Ashok* (☎ 2331). Doubles here range from Rs 1000 to Rs 1600 and most are really suites, with a sitting room and fine views of the snow-capped peaks around Manali. There's a 50% off-season discount.

The HPTDC has self-contained *Log Huts*, up the road past the Cafe Rohtang; these cost Rs 1200 to Rs 1400.

Places to Eat

Manali is remarkably well endowed with places to eat. On the main street the *Mount View Restaurant* has good food and, in winter, it's pleasantly warm from the stove in the middle of the room. The food is mainly Chinese and Tibetan – the thalumein soup is excellent – and there's good music to eat by. Down a side street nearby is the *Mayur Restaurant* which is so popular with travellers that you may need to reserve a table in the evening.

Just off the main street the smaller *Mona Lisa* is another place with a pot-belly stove. Once again, the food and music are both good, and the fresh trout (Rs 30) is very popular. The *Chinese Room* near the post office serves good Chinese, Indian and Continental food.

The cavernous *Chandratal Restaurant* is run by the HPTDC with the standard Tourism Corporation menu. Thalis are Rs 20 vegetarian and Rs 25 non-veg. Up the hill overlooking the river, the HPTDC's *Cafe Rohtang* has fine views.

Tucked away near the State Bank of India, there's *Peter's*, an old Manali favourite. It's a bit passé these days but is still a popular (if slightly grubby) place, especially with those looking for goodies to take trekking – homemade jams, peanut butter, wholewheat bread and muesli are all tried and tested. A better place perhaps is the *Tibetan Coffee House* at the Beas River below Vashisht.

If you want to keep costs to a minimum there are a number of basic dhaba places on the main street opposite the tourist office. One which seems to have a bit more variety than the others is the *Kamal*.

Also near the tourist office is the *Sa-Ba Restaurant*. It serves south Indian snacks, and when the sun is shining it's pleasant to sit at the outdoor tables.

The *Ashiana* and the *Adarsh*, both on the main street, also serve decent food, but they're nothing outstanding.

Entertainment

If you're really stuck for something to do, a couple of places on the main street have nightly video shows, but the fare is usually the typical Indian 'masala movies'.

The HPTDC has the Club House on the

far side of the river. It's basically a sporting complex where you can hire equipment (where necessary) and play billiards (Rs 30 per hour), badminton (Rs 30 per hour), table tennis (Rs 20), board games and squash. There's also a bar and a restaurant – and a cover charge of Rs 5 just to step inside the place.

Getting There & Away

Bus The bus station is well organised and – surprise, surprise – the timetable is in English! Pity it's out of date. There are deluxe buses daily to Delhi and Shimla, and semideluxe buses to Shimla and Dharamsala. Demand for all these buses is heavy in summer, so make a reservation as far in advance as possible. Deluxe buses are booked, and leave from, the tourist office, while semideluxe are handled from the bus station itself. In the off season both the deluxe and semideluxe services are subject to demand, although there's a better chance of the semideluxe running.

Deluxe bus fares are Rs 275 (Rs 400 aircon) to Delhi (16 hours), and Rs 160 to Shimla. The semideluxe fares are Rs 105 to Shimla (10 hours) or Dharamsala (12½ hours).

Ordinary buses run to many destinations including Shimla (Rs 80), Dharamsala (Rs 80), Mandi (Rs 33), Chandigarh (Rs 86), Amritsar (Rs 132), Jammu (Rs 124) and Delhi (Rs 140).

There are many buses to Kulu (Rs 12), a few of which travel via the left bank of the Beas River. For Keylong there are buses hourly in summer. The trip take six hours and costs Rs 24.

To/From Leh For the two-day trip to Leh, there's a choice of buses. Most comfortable are the HPTDC's luxury coaches. Tickets must be bought in advance from the tourist office and cost Rs 500. At the bus station you can book HPSRTC's ordinary bus for Rs 320. If there's a J&KSRTC bus at the station you can buy a ticket from the driver for Rs 350. These last two buses are equally ram-shackle – take whichever one is leaving earlier or you'll have a very long second day.

Avoid the seats at the back of any of the buses as the road is very bumpy – so bumpy in fact that we all actually hit the roof at one point! When the road is open (July to mid-September) there's usually a bus every day with one of these companies. See the Leh section (Jammu & Kashmir chapter) for more information about this route.

Taxi The taxi stand is right outside the tourist office, and all drivers are members of the local union, which sets the taxi fares to all the main destinations. Typical fares are Rs 300 to Kulu, Rs 1900 to Shimla and Rs 9000 to Leh, but these are negotiable if you approach the driver direct.

AROUND MANALI
Vashisht

Vashisht is a picturesque little place, clinging to the steep hillside about three km out of Manali. On foot the distance is a bit shorter since you can follow paths up the hillside, whereas cars have to wind up the road.

On the way up to the village you'll come upon the HPTDC Vashisht Hot Bath Complex, where a natural sulphur spring is piped into a modern bathhouse. It's open from 7 am to 1 pm and 2 to 8 pm. The cost for a 20-minute soak is Rs 15 for the ordinary baths (you can fit two people in these) or Rs 30 for the larger baths. Twenty minutes isn't really long enough as this includes the time to fill the bath; however, if you've suffered a long, rough bus trip from Leh there's no better way to soak away the strain. The public hot baths are at the top of the road by the temple and there are separate tanks for men and women.

Places to Stay Vashisht is a centre for Manali's longer-term Western residents and there are a number of basic guest houses here, offering rooms from Rs 30 to Rs 60 with discounts for longer stays. One of the best is the *Dharma Guest House* with doubles for Rs 50 and triples for Rs 60. Follow the path up from the public hot baths to reach it. A new place is being built high above it with even better views. Down by the road the *Janata* and *Sanam* guest houses are cheaper and rooms are also available at *Dreamland Restaurant* and *Cafe Kanyakumari*.

The *Hotel Bhrigu* has doubles from Rs 275 (around Rs 100 off-season) with attached bathrooms and superb views. Right at the top of the price range is the *Ambassador Resort* with doubles from Rs 1200 to Rs 3500 and heli-skiing and white-water rafting on offer.

Places to Eat The *Freedom Cafe* is very laid back and has a good range of food. There are no set prices – just put what you think is about right in the box on the way out. The *Snack & Bite* is a similar place. On the village square there's the *Tibetan Cafe* with a good cake shop beside it. The *Cafe Kanyakumari* here is also popular and has a video parlour that often shows English-language movies.

Jagatsukh

About 12 km north of Naggar and six km south of Manali on the left-bank road, Jagatsukh was the capital of Kulu state until it was supplanted by Naggar. There are some very old temples in the village, particularly the sikhara-style Siva Temple. Shooru village nearby has the old and historically interesting Devi Sharvali Temple.

Kothi

Kothi is a pretty little village, 12 km from Manali on the Keylong road.

There are very fine views from Kothi, and the Beas River flows through a very deep and narrow gorge at this point. The trip to Rahla Falls, 16 km away, is another popular excursion.

Places to Stay The *Rest House* is a popular resting place for trekkers heading for the Rohtang Pass. It's surrounded by glaciers and mountains, two old tea stalls and nothing else. Doubles have bathroom, two big beds, carpets and a balcony. The food is good and it's quiet.

Other Places

Five km from Manali, **Arjun Gufa**, with a legendary cave, is near the village of Prini. A cold-water spring, named the **Nehru Kund** after former prime minister Nehru, is six km from Manali on the Keylong road.

The **Solang Valley** is north-west of Manali, before Kothi. The glacier nearest Manali is here, only 13 km from town. Take a bus to Palchan village, and then follow the jeep track. In Solang village there is the small *Friendship Hotel*, and from here you can organise downhill skiing for Rs 100 per day. Accommodation is Rs 50.

TREKS FROM MANALI & KULU VALLEY

There are many treks from Manali, both round trips and journeys further afield.

Malana Valley

It is less than 30 km from Katrain, on the Kulu to Manali road, across the Chandrakhani Pass to the interesting Malana Valley. The pass is at less than 3600 metres and is open from March to December. Malana can also be reached from the Parvati Valley – either from Manikaran over the 3150-metre Rashol Pass or from Jari. Jari is connected with the Kulu Valley by a jeep track and is only 12 km from Malana.

There are about 500 people in Malana and they speak a peculiar dialect with strong Tibetan elements. It's an isolated village with its own system of government. When visiting the village it is important not to touch *anything*, as local customs are very strict about this. Wait at the edge of the village for an invitation to enter.

The 6000-metre peak of Deo Tibba overlooks Malana and from the top of the Chandrakhani Pass you can see snow-capped peaks on the border of Spiti to the east. Starting from Naggar, it is possible to climb up to the pass summit and return to Naggar in the same day – but it is fairly hard going.

Local legends relate that when Jamlu, the main deity of Malana, first came there, he bore a casket containing all the other Kulu gods. At the top of the pass he opened the casket and the breeze carried the gods to their present homes, all over the valley.

At the time of the Dussehra Festival in Kulu, Jamlu plays a special part. He is a very powerful god with something of the demon in him. He does not have a temple image so, unlike the other Kulu gods, has no temple car to be carried in. Nor does he openly show his allegiance to Raghunathji, the paramount Kulu god, as do the other Kulu gods. At the time of the festival Jamlu goes down to Kulu but stays on the east side of the river, from where he watches the proceedings.

Every few years a major festival is held for Jamlu in the month of Bhadon. In the temple at Malana there is a silver elephant with a gold figure on its back which is said to have been a gift from Emperor Akbar.

It takes three days to trek from Naggar to Malana. You can either spend a day there, then return to Naggar or continue to Jari. A seven-day trek from Manali to Malana could be:

Day 1	Manali to Rumsu	2060 m	24 km
Day 2	Rumsu to Chandrakhani	3650 m	8 km
Day 3	Chandrakhani to Malana	2100 m	7 km
Day 4	Malana to Kasol	1580 m	8 km
Day 5	Kasol to Jari	1560 m	15 km
Day 6	Jari to Bhuntar	900 m	12 km
Day 7	Bhuntar to Manali by bus		

The trek can be extended by continuing from Jari along the east bank of the Beas via Bijli Mahadev, with its famous temple, and Naggar to Manali.

Deo Tibba Trek

This is an easy trek east of Manali to the base of 6000-metre Deo Tibba. The trek offers fine views and pleasant walking through forests and alpine meadows. From Manali you start via Jagatsukh to Khanol and Chhika (not the Chhika north-east of Manali on the way to the Hamta Pass). Seri is at the base of Deo Tibba and from here you can make an excursion to Lake Chandratal.

Day 1	Manali to Khanol	8 km
Day 2	Khanol to Chhika	6 km
Day 3	Chhika to Seri	5 km
Day 4	Seri to Bhanara	14 km
Day 5	Bhanara to Manali	7 km

Chandratal Trek

This circular trek from Manali over the Hamta, Chandratal and Baralacha La passes is one of the finest in Himachal Pradesh and takes 11 days to complete. From Manali you start at Jagatsukh, on the east bank road to Kulu. At the village of Prini you turn north-east and climb up to Chhika – a steep climb at first but later it becomes easier over grassy downs and pleasant meadows.

The next day involves a long and wearisome climb over the 4270-metre Hamta Pass, then a quick descent to Chhatru on the Chandra River. The pass is generally open from June to September, although it may be open longer. There are fine views of Deo Tibba (6001 metres) and Indrasan (6221 metres) from the pass. Two days' walk takes you through Chhota Dara to Batal, where the route branches off north-east to Spiti through the Kunzam Pass. There are magnificent views of the Bara Shigri glacier from here.

Succeeding days take you north over the Chandratal (Lake of the Moon) Pass, the Likhim Gongma (upper) and Likhim Yongma (lower), and the Topko Yongma before you reach the Keylong to Leh road at the Baralacha La pass. Three more days of walking bring you to Keylong, from where you can bus back to Manali. It may be possible to get a bus earlier and shorten the time to Keylong.

Day 1	Manali to Chhika	2960 m	21 km
Day 2	Chhika to Chhatru	3360 m	16 km
Day 3	Chhatru to		
	Chhota Dara	3740 m	16 km
Day 4	Chhota Dara to Batal	3960 m	16 km
Day 5	Batal to Chandratal	4270 m	18 km
Day 6	Chandratal to		
	Likhim Yongma	4320 m	12 km
Day 7	Likhim Yongma to		
	Topko Gongma	4640 m	11 km
Day 8	Topko Gongma to		
	Baralacha La	4885 m	10 km
Day 9	Baralacha La		
	to Patsio	3820 m	19 km
Day 10	Patsio to Jispa	3320 m	14 km
Day 11	Jispa to Keylong	3340 m	21 km

Parvati Valley

The Parvati Valley is accessible by bus from Kulu or Bhuntar. The last part of the Malana Valley trek descends the Parvati Valley to its junction with the Kulu Valley. An interesting alternative is to ascend the Parvati Valley to its upper reaches; it is much wilder and more rugged than the Kulu Valley. From Bhuntar, near the junction of the Beas and Parvati rivers, you can visit the Adibrahma Temple in Khokhan, about a km away, or the pagoda-shaped temple of Triyugi Narain in Diar village. The first day's walk takes you to Jari, on a hillside high above the Parvati River and near where the Malana River joins the Parvati.

It's a short trek to Kasol with its pleasantly sited *Tourist Hut* and *Forest Rest House*. There is good trout fishing here. Manikaran is a very short walk away and the river is wild at this point. Manikaran's famous hot spring, almost at boiling temperature, is near the river as you enter the village. There are several guest houses in Manikaran. Be sure not to miss the evening worship accompanied by harmonium, tablas and singing.

It's a long walk, rough and stony at first, to Pulga, where again there is a very pleasant *Forest Rest House*. The pretty little village is 300 metres above the river and is the usual end point of this trek, although hardy and well-equipped trekkers could continue further up the Parvati River and cross the Pin Parvati Pass into Spiti. Khirganga, just 10 km upstream from Pulga, has more hot springs. Or you could explore the Tos Nullah, which joins the Parvati River from the north-east, just upstream from Pulga.

Day 1	Bhuntar to Jari	15 km
Day 2	Jari to Kasol	8 km
Day 3	Kasol to Manikaran	3 km
Day 4	Manikaran to Pulga	16 km

Seraj Valley to Narkanda

The Seraj Valley branches off south-east from the southern end of the Kulu Valley and makes an interesting alternative route between the Kulu Valley and Shimla. Aut, on the main road which runs between Kulu and Manali, is the starting point; and Larji, at the junction of the Sainj and Tirthan rivers, is the first stop. There's a *PWD Rest House* here and good fishing is available during March, April and October – when the Sainj River runs clear.

In the lower reaches of the Tirthan Valley is Banjar, with an interesting group of temples. Continuing south you reach Shoja, where there is another *PWD Rest House* with a scenic setting. From here you can make excursions to the old ruined fort of Raghupur Gahr where there is a beautiful view; even Shimla can be seen on a clear day. Another interesting day trip from Shoja is to the beautiful flower-strewn meadow of Dughu Thatch.

From Shoja you cross the 3135-metre Jalori Pass. The view of the surrounding mountains from the pass crest is stunning. Khanag, at 2500 metres, is on the other side of the pass and has a *PWD Rest House*. Ani, again with a *PWD Rest House*, is the next stop, and from here you can either continue straight on to the main highway where buses run to Narkanda and Shimla, or turn east to Nirmand with its temple of Devi Ambika. There is a bus service between Ani and Luhri, on the north side of the Sutlej River.

Day 1	Aut to Larji	5 km
Day 2	Larji to Banjar	20 km
Day 3	Banjar to Shoja	13 km
Day 4	Shoja to Khanag	10 km
Day 5	Khanag to Ani	20 km
Day 6	Ani to Luhri	15 km

As an alternative to this route, you can branch off at Banjar and follow the Tirthan River to Rampur. The first day's walk takes you from Banjar to Goshaini, but you can get that far by bus. It's then a gentle climb to Bathad where there is a *PWD Rest House*, followed by a very hard climb to the Bashleo Pass at 3250 metres, 13 km on. A steep descent takes you to Sarahan, only three km further.

There is another beautifully situated *Rest House* here. From here it is an easy, pleasant walk to Arsu (which has another *PWD Rest House*) and then to Rampur on the main road.

Day 3	Banjar to Goshaini	13 km
Day 4	Goshaini to Bathad	16 km
Day 5	Bathad to Sarahan	16 km
Day 6	Sarahan to Arsu	13 km
Day 7	Arsu to Rampur	13 km

Solang Valley

There are a number of treks from Manali to the Solang Valley looping back to Manali, either from the north or the south. A seven-day trek takes you to Beas Kund, the source of the Beas River, and across the remains of dying glaciers. The first day takes you to Solang Nullah, where there is a mountain hut with rooms for 80 people. There are ski-runs here in the winter.

The second day's trek continues to Dhundi, on an alpine plateau, where you can see Deo Tibba and Indrasan, and admire the many alpine flowers. The third day takes you to Beas Kund and back to Dhundi, and the next day continues to Shagara Dugh, with a good chance of seeing red bears along the way. On the fifth day you reach Marrhi over a small 4000-metre pass with views to the Kulu Valley and Rohtang Pass. Finally, on Day 6 you continue down the Keylong-Manali road to Kothi, via the Rahla waterfall. On the last day you return to Manali.

Day 1	Manali to Solang Nullah	2480 m	11 km
Day 2	Solang Nullah to Dhundi	2840 m	8 km
Day 3	Dhundi to Beas Kund and return	3540 m	10 km
Day 4	Dhundi to		

	Shagara Dugh	3600 m	8 km
Day 5	Shagara Dugh to Marrhi	3380 m	10 km
Day 6	Marrhi to Kothi	2500 m	6 km
Day 7	Kothi to Manali		13 km

Manali Pass Treks

These two treks continue on from the Solang Valley trek but loop back to Manali from the south. They are both difficult treks involving long, hard ascents over rugged terrain. The first alternative continues from Beas Kund over the Tentu Pass (an arduous and tiring climb) to Phulangot through an uninhabited region. You then cross the Manali Pass to Rani Sui and go via Bhogi Thatch to Kalath, a little south of Manali on the Kulu to Manali road.

Day 3	Dhundi to Beas Kund	3540 m	6 km
Day 4	Beas Kund to Tentu Pass	4996 m	4 km
Day 5	Tentu Pass to camping ground	3856 m	10 km
Day 6	camping ground to Phulangot	4000 m	6 km
Day 7	Phulangot to Manali Pass	4988 m	6 km
Day 8	Manali Pass to Rani Sui	4200 m	8 km
Day 9	Rani Sui to Bhogi Thatch	2800 m	6 km
Day 10	Bhogi Thatch to Kalath	1800 m	12 km

The second alternative is to join the Manalsu Nullah from the Manali Pass and follow this

straight back to Manali – up to Day 8 this trek is the same as the first alternative.

An easy trek, which includes the last two days of the first alternative, involves going to Rani Sui via Lama Dugh. You leave Manali via the Hadimba Temple and climb through pleasant country to the camp site at Lama Dugh. On the second day you cross the Thanpri Tibba ridge to Rani Sui, and then Day 3 and Day 4 are as Day 9 and Day 10 of the first Manali Pass trek.

Day 1	Manali to		
	Lama Dugh	3380 m	6 km
Day 2	Lama Dugh to		
	Rani Sui	4200 m	5 km

Lahaul & Spiti

Fifty-one km north of Manali, the road to Leh crosses the Rohtang Pass and enters the Tibetan regions of Lahaul and Spiti, which are quite unlike the Kulu Valley. The Rohtang Pass has the same 'gateway' nature as the Zoji La between Kashmir and Ladakh. The region is bound by Ladakh to the north, Kulu to the south and Tibet to the east.

Although a lot of this territory is off limits to foreigners, things are slowly changing, and more and more of this fascinating region is becoming accessible. Permits are no longer necessary for the two-day bus ride between Manali and Leh. There are also numerous trekking possibilities, a popular one being the Keylong to Padum trek via the 5100-metre Zingo La. From Padum, in the heart of the isolated Zanskar region, there are buses to Kargil on the Leh to Srinagar road. A Restricted Area Permit is required and can be obtained from the Senior District Magistrate (SDM) in Keylong or from the Deputy Commissioner in Kulu or Shimla and also from the Ministry of Home Affairs in Delhi. Two photographs are required. Until recently only groups of four or more people were being given permits but it's likely that individuals will soon be granted permits too.

See the Lonely Planet guides *Kashmir, Ladakh & Zanskar* and *Trekking in the Indian Himalaya* for more information on treks in this region.

Climate
As in Ladakh, little rain gets over the high Himalayan barrier so Lahaul and Spiti are dry and, for the most part, barren. The air is sharp and clear and the warm summer days are followed by cold, crisp nights. Beware of the burning power of the sun in this region – you can get burnt very quickly even on cool days. The heavy winter snow from September to May closes the passes except for a few months of each year.

Culture
The people of Lahaul and Spiti follow a Tibetan form of Tantric Buddhism with a panoply of demons, saints and followers. The monasteries, known as gompas, are colourful places where the monks or lamas lead lives ordered by complicated regulations and rituals. There are many similarities between these people and the Ladakhis, further north. The people of Spiti are almost all Buddhists of Tibetan stock, but Lahaul is split roughly 50/50 between Buddhists and Hindus.

ROHTANG PASS
The 3978-metre Rohtang Pass is the only access into Lahaul and is open only from June to September each year, although trekkers can cross the pass a little before it opens for vehicles. During the short season it's open, there are regular buses from Manali to Keylong. The weather can change very quickly up here and before the road was built many travellers never made it over the pass. The name means Pile of Dead Bodies in Tibetan!

The tourist office operates a daily Rs 80 bus up to the pass, mainly for tourists to 'see the snow'. It's a very spectacular trip over the pass.

KEYLONG
Keylong is the main town in the Lahaul and

Top: Children from Manapiya village, Rajasthan (MH)
Bottom: Villagers at the base of Konke La, Ladakh, Jammu & Kashmir (RI)

Top: Himalaya on the Srinagar to Leh flight, Jammu & Kashmir (TW)
Left: Shy monks at Tikse Gompa, Ladakh, Jammu & Kashmir (TW)
Right: Tikse Gompa, Ladakh, Jammu & Kashmir (TW)

Spiti region; there are a number of interesting monasteries within easy reach of this oasis-like town. The old Kharding Monastery, formerly the capital of Lahaul, overlooks Keylong, only 3½ km away. Other monasteries include Shashur (three km), Tayal (six km) and Guru Ghantal (11 km).

Places to Stay & Eat
The HPTDC *Tourist Bungalow* has just three doubles at Rs 125, but during the summer season they set up tents which cost Rs 75. There is also a *PWD Rest House*. The *Lamayuru* serves up good food and music in a pleasant atmosphere, although the cheap rooms are dark and dirty.

The *A-Ha Tibetan Restaurant* is gloomy but has good cheap food.

Getting There & Away
Between Manali and Keylong there are buses hourly from 5 am in summer. The trip takes six hours and costs Rs 24. You can also pick up ordinary buses from here on Monday, Wednesday and Friday for the two-day trip to Leh (Rs 300) but at present the more comfortable HPTDC buses run only from Manali. As the route becomes more popular it's likely that more buses will be laid on and it may also be possible to get a seat in a jeep. See the Leh section (Jammu & Kashmir chapter) for more information about this route.

AROUND KEYLONG
A short distance before Keylong on the Manali to Keylong road, is **Gondhla** with its eight-storey castle of the Thakur of Gondhla and the historically significant gompa. You can trek back to Gondhla from Keylong, cutting across the loop the road makes. Between Gondhla and Keylong is **Tandi**, where the Chandrabagha or Chenab River meets the road.

Following the Chenab Valley to the north-west towards Kilar (see treks from Chamba) will bring you to **Triloknath** with its white-marble, six-armed image of Avalokitesvara. Close by is the village of **Udaipur**, with a finely carved wooden temple from the 10th

or 11th century which is dedicated to Mrikula Devi.

SPITI
The 4500-metre **Kunzam Pass** connects the Lahaul and Spiti valleys. Eventually a road will be completed from Kaza, the principal Spiti village, south-east through Samdoh to meet the Hindustan to Tibet road (see Kinnaur).

There are few settlements in this barren, high region. **Kaza** (or Kaja) is the main village. Slightly north-west of it is **Kibar** (or Kyipur), which at 4205 metres is reputed to be the highest village in the world. Tabo Kye and Dhankhar are two of the most important gompas.

Getting There & Away
Although the pass may be open by mid-May, a safer date is mid-June. The bus trip from Keylong takes eight hours.

KINNAUR
Most of this region, in the valley of the Sutlej River extending up towards the Tibetan border, is off limits unless you have a Restricted Area Permit (see Lahaul & Spiti above). The permit is also available from the SDM in Rampur and without it you can only go as far as the Wangtu Bridge just beyond Nachar.

Rampur
Rampur, 140 km from Shimla, beyond Narkanda, is the gateway to the region. It's the site for a major trade fair in the second week of November each year, and was once a major centre for trade between India and Tibet. There are direct buses from Shimla to Rampur, which has a *PWD Rest House*.

Sarahan
The last village in the district before entering Kinnaur, Sarahan is a beautiful little place with the interesting Bhimkali Temple which shows a curious blend of Buddhist and Hindu architecture.

Nachar

This picturesque village on the Hindustan to Tibet road is four km from the Wangtu Bridge, beyond which you need a permit to continue. Like Sarahan, Nachar is on the old road, which has been replaced by the new Hindustan to Tibet road nearby. There's a *Rest House* in the orchards.

Tapri & Choltu

Only 15 km further up the valley from Nachar, three roads meet at this scenic spot. One is the main road continuing up the valley to Kalpa. The second is the old road, also continuing to Kalpa via Rogi. The third is a small road which crosses the river and passes through Choltu and Kilba to the Sangla Valley. Choltu has a pleasant *Rest House*.

Sangla

The main village in the Sangla Valley is 18 km from Karcham, on the Hindustan to Tibet

road, and can be reached by jeep or on foot. It's a good base for trekking and there's a *Rest House*.

Kalpa

The main town in Kinnaur is close to the foot of 6050-metre-high Kinnaur Khailash. This is the legendary winter home of Lord Siva; during the winter the god is said to retire to his Himalayan home here and indulge his passion for hashish. In the month of Magha (January-February) the gods of Kinnaur supposedly meet here for an annual conference with Lord Siva.

Kalpa has a *Rest House* and from here you can continue on the northern side of the river to Puh and Namgia, close to the Tibetan border. Only 14 km from Kalpa, the tiny village of Pangli has a small *Rest House* and a fine view of Kinnaur Khailash. Rarang, eight km further on, is another centre for trade to Tibet.

Jammu & Kashmir

Population: 7.7 million
Area: 222,236 sq km
Capital: Srinagar
People per sq km: 35
Main Languages: Kashmiri, Dogri, Urdu,
                              Ladakhi
Literacy Rate: 26.2%

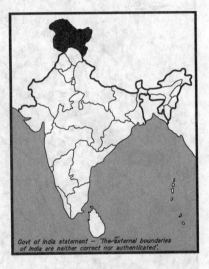

Govt of India statement — The external boundaries
of India are neither correct nor authenticated'.

The state of Jammu & Kashmir, J&K for short, is a region of widely varying people and geography. In the south, Jammu is a transition zone from the Indian plains to the Himalaya. Correctly the rest of the state is Kashmir but in practice this title is reserved for the beautiful Vale of Kashmir, a large Himalayan valley in the north of the state. Here the people are predominantly Muslim and in many ways look towards Pakistan and central Asia rather than towards India.

Finally, to the north-east is the remote Tibetan plateau region known as Ladakh, primarily Buddhist and Tibetan in its culture and a very clear contrast to the rest of Kashmir, indeed to the rest of India. Sandwiched between the Kashmir and Ladakh regions is a long narrow valley known as Zanskar. This valley is even more isolated than Ladakh although, with the improvement of the road into the valley, the number of visitors has soared in recent years and things are changing rapidly.

The recent escalation of political violence in the Kashmir Valley has discouraged most travellers from visiting what was once one of India's most popular tourist regions. A spell on a houseboat on Dal Lake has always been one of India's real treats and Kashmir also offers some delightful trekking opportunities and unsurpassed scenery. Before 1990 over 600,000 Indian tourists and 60,000 foreign visitors were visiting Srinagar each year but by 1992 this had dropped to a total of just 5000. The Kashmiris say that the Government of India is trying to dissuade tourists from visiting the area in order to starve the local tourist industry of earnings. The actions of a few militant Kashmiris in the past have not been helpful, though. In 1991 seven Israeli tourists, one of them a journalist, were kidnapped by the pro-Pakistan group, the Pasdaran-i-Inquilab-i-Islam. After a bizarre scenario in which the Israelis managed to get hold of some arms to stage a shoot-out, six escaped and the journalist was passed on to the JKLF (Jammu & Kashmir Liberation Front). He was finally released with the warning that any Israeli tourists venturing into Kashmir would be treated as spies in league with the Indian government.

J&K Tourism insists that whatever the future may bring for Kashmir, tourism will still be of vital importance to the local economy, so terrorist attacks and kidnappings will not be targeted on tourists. However, before visiting Srinagar and the Kashmir Valley check the current situation with your embassy and talk to recently returned travellers.

Ladakh, on the other hand, is far removed from the troubles and has greatly benefited from the slump in tourism to the west of the state. A regular bus service now runs between Leh and Manali in Himachal Pradesh, a spectacular two-day trip over the world's second highest motorable road. Ladakh offers a chance to study a region which, in today's world, is probably even more Tibetan than Tibet. It's one of the most otherworldly parts of India.

No special permits are required to visit Kashmir or Ladakh, but your movements are restricted in that you are not allowed to approach within a certain distance of the border. In Ladakh this means you are not allowed more than 1.6 km north of the Srinagar to Leh road without permission. In the Kashmir Valley all foreigners are required to register their arrival. In Srinagar this is done at the airport or can be handled by your houseboat owner if you come by bus.

Warning

Security in this region is very tight and all travellers in J&K are thoroughly searched at airports and stopped at roadblocks. In 1992 several foreigners were caught and prosecuted for 'drug trafficking' even though they were carrying only minute quantities of hashish. One German guy was caught at Leh airport with just a tola (11.6 grams) of hash hidden in his socks. He was refused bail and since the judge was away on holiday faced three weeks in jail before his case could be heard.

History

Jammu & Kashmir has always been a centre of conflict for independent India. When India and Pakistan became independent, there was much controversy over which country the region should go to. The population was predominantly Muslim but J&K was not a part of 'British India'. It was a 'princely state' and as such the ruler had to decide which way his state would move – to Muslim Pakistan or Hindu India. As *Freedom at Midnight*, by Larry Collins and Dominique Lapierre, relates the indecisive

maharaja only made his decision when a Pakistani-prompted invasion was already crossing his borders and the inevitable result was the first Indo-Pakistani conflict.

Since that first battle Kashmir has remained a flash point for relations between the two countries. Two-thirds of the region is now Indian and one-third is Pakistani; both countries claim all of it. Furthermore, Kashmir's role as a sensitive border zone applies not only to Pakistan. In 1962 the Chinese invaded Ladakh, prompting India to rapidly reassess its position in this remote and isolated region.

Since 1988 militant activities in Kashmir have increased substantially and it's estimated that as many as 10,000 Kashmiris have died in the fighting. The main combatants are: the Hizb-ul-Mujahedin, who are backed by Pakistan and want to be united with that country; the Jammu & Kashmir Liberation Front (JKLF), who want nothing less than complete independence; and the Indian army which has moved into the area in large numbers, supposedly to keep the peace. There are continuing reports of horrific atrocities committed by all three of these groups and in spite of talks between India and Pakistan it is unlikely that the situation will improve in the near future.

Lonely Planet Guides

If you'd like a lot more information about Kashmir and Ladakh, look for our guidebook *Kashmir, Ladakh & Zanskar* by Rolf & Margret Schettler or our trekking guide *Trekking in the Indian Himalaya* by Garry Weare.

Jammu Region

JAMMU

Population: 230,000

Jammu is the second-largest city in the state, but for most travellers it is just a transit point on the trip north to Kashmir. If you have time there are several interesting attractions in the town.

Jammu is still on the plains, so in summer

it is a sweltering, uncomfortable contrast to the cool heights of Kashmir.

In mid-1992 there were a number of confrontations between Kashmiri militants and the armed forces in the Jammu area. You should check the current situation before coming here or continuing to Kashmir.

Orientation

Jammu is actually two towns – the old town sits on a hilltop overlooking the river. Here you'll find most of the hotels, the Tourist Reception Centre and the tourist office, from where deluxe buses depart for Kashmir. Down beside the hill is the station for buses to other parts of north India and for the standard buses to Srinagar.

Several km away across the river is the new town of Jammu Tawi and the railway station where you'll find a second Tourist Reception Centre.

If you're en route to Srinagar and arrive in Jammu by train (as most people do), then you

have two choices: you can keep going straight through to Srinagar or stay overnight in Jammu.

If you choose the first option you have to take one of the buses which wait at the railway station for the arrival of the trains. If these buses don't leave Jammu early enough they stop for the night at Banihal, just below the Jarwarhal Tunnel, and continue on to Srinagar the following day. Following the political problems in Kashmir the tunnel is closed at night. Accommodation in Banihal is usually in the *Tourist Lodge* and is very basic.

The second choice is to stay overnight in Jammu and take a bus to Srinagar the first thing next day. These early buses complete the journey to Srinagar in one day.

If you decide to stay overnight then it's important first to find yourself a room and then book a ticket on the bus. Don't hang about as competition for both can be fierce during the tourist season.

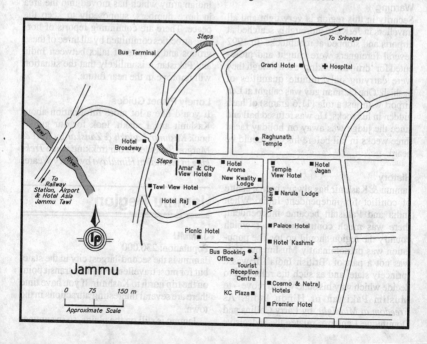

Information

The J&K tourist office (☎ 48-172) is at the Tourist Reception Centre on Vir Marg but they have very little information. However, the deputy director of tourism here, Mr SS Bhalla, is very knowledgeable about trekking routes in the Patnitop and Bhadarwah areas. Trekking gear can be hired from the Tourist Reception Centre at the station. Daily charges are Rs 20 to Rs 40 for a tent and Rs 8 to Rs 12 for a rucksack.

Raghunath & Rambireswar Temples

The Raghunath Temple is in the centre of the city, only a short stroll from the Tourist Reception Centre. This large temple complex was built in 1835 but is not especially interesting, although it makes a good sunset silhouette. The Rambireswar Temple, also centrally located, is dedicated to Lord Siva and dates from 1883.

Dogra Art Gallery

The Dogra Art Gallery, in the Gandhi Bhavan near the new Secretariat, has an important collection of miniature paintings including many from the locally renowned Basohli and Kangra schools. The gallery is open from 7.30 am to 1 pm in summer and from 11 am to 5 pm in winter but is closed on Mondays; admission is free.

Amar Mahal Palace

On the northern outskirts of town, just off the Srinagar road, is the Amar Mahal palace, a curious example of French architecture. The palace **museum** has a family portrait gallery and another important collection of paintings.

Places to Stay – bottom end

At the bottom end of the market, the popular *Tawi View Hotel* (☎ 47-301), Maheshi Gate, is the best of the bunch at Rs 50/60 for singles/doubles with bath. There's a restaurant here. Another simple place is the *Hotel Kashmir*, Vir Marg, with doubles at Rs 50/60, or Rs 60/80 with attached bath.

There are many other budget hotels but there's not much to choose between them;

it's usually a question of which ones have rooms available. Reasonable places include the *Hotel Aroma*, Gumat Bazaar, which charges Rs 50 for doubles with bath, and the similarly priced *Hotel Raj*. Doubles with attached bath go for Rs 80 at the *New Kwality Lodge* and the *Palace Hotel*, both on Vir Marg.

The railway station has *retiring rooms* at Rs 65 for doubles (Rs 125 with air-con) and dorm beds at Rs 12. Also at the station there's Jammu's second *Tourist Reception Centre* with four doubles at Rs 80. Above the bus station is the basic *Hotel JDA* with rooms from Rs 75/100 with attached bathroom. There's also a room where you can unroll your sleeping bag and spend the night for just Rs 5.

The *Hotel Cosmo* (☎ 47-561) is on Vir Marg. It's rather overpriced with singles from Rs 80 to Rs 150, doubles from Rs 150 to Rs 200 or Rs 400 with air-con. The *Hotel Jagan* (☎ 42-402), Raghunath Bazaar, is similarly priced but much better value.

Back on Vir Marg the *Natraj Hotel* has rooms with bath at Rs 80/100. Down the road from the Raghunath Temple are a number of other bottom and middle-range hotels.

Places to Stay – middle

The large *Tourist Reception Centre* (☎ 48-172) has doubles with attached bathrooms for Rs 125, or Rs 200 with air-cooling, Rs 250 with air-con but it can be difficult to get a room here. Nearby is the spotless *Narula Lodge* with just five rooms for Rs 125/200. Residents have their own bathrooms but these are not attached to the rooms.

Near the Hotel Raj and beside the Jewel Cinema, *Hotel Jewel's* (☎ 46-447) is a good clean place with air-cooled rooms for Rs 250/310 and air-con rooms for Rs 350/410. All rooms have attached bathroom and cable TV. There's a fast-food restaurant downstairs. On Vir Marg, the *Premier Hotel* (☎ 43-234) is not quite so good with ordinary rooms at Rs 215/275 or Rs 250/310 for air-cooled rooms, Rs 350/410 with air-con. Rooms have TV and there are two restaurants and a bar.

Other middle-bracket hotels include the *Broadway, Gagan, Amar* and *City View*, all in Gumat Bazaar.

Places to Stay – top end

The *Hotel Asia Jammu Tawi* (☎ 49-430) charges Rs 750/850 for its air-con rooms and is midway between the bus and railway stations. There's a bar (with champagne for Rs 500 a bottle), a good restaurant and a swimming pool. The *Hotel Jammu Ashok* (☎ 46-154) is on the northern outskirts of town, close to the Amar Mahal palace and is similarly priced.

A new luxury hotel, the *KC Plaza* on Vir Marg, should be open by now.

Places to Eat

Many of the hotels have their own restaurants. At the Tourist Reception Centre, there's a vegetarian restaurant and the plush air-con *Wazwan Restaurant* serving Kashmiri food. Rogan Josh costs Rs 36 and they have kahwa (Kashmiri tea) for Rs 6.

At the trendy *KC's Food Station*, at the KC Plaza, you can have a 'Huggy Buggy Paneer Burger' for Rs 14, reasonable pizzas from Rs 20 and hot dogs for Rs 17. There's an ice-cream parlour upstairs.

There are numerous cheap restaurants along Vir Marg and towards the bus station. At the railway *refreshment room* a vegetarian thali is Rs 10.

The air-con restaurant at the *Cosmo Hotel* is better than the hotel – good for a cold beer and a pleasant meal in cool surroundings. Main dishes are around Rs 40. A few doors down the *Premier* has Chinese and Kashmiri food and is similarly priced.

Getting There & Away

Air The offices of Indian Airlines (☎ 42-735) and Vayudoot (☎ 49-618) are at the Tourist Reception Centre.

Indian Airlines has daily flights to Delhi (US$74) and Srinagar (US$27) and two flights a week to Chandigarh (US$50), Leh (US$39) and Amritsar (US$27). Vayudoot flies to Delhi five times a week but charges a hefty US$134.

Bus Srinagar buses depart from various locations: superfast mini-coaches, A class and deluxe go from the Tourist Reception Centre; B class leave from the bus station; and private buses depart from various parts of the city. Buses also run from the railway station where they meet arriving trains – thus you can take the overnight *4645 Shalimar Express* from Delhi and catch a bus as soon as you arrive at around 7 am. Buses normally depart between 6 and 7 am in order to reach Srinagar by nightfall. It is vital to book your bus ticket as soon as you arrive.

Jammu to Srinagar bus fares are Rs 53 for B class, Rs 70 for A class, Rs 85 deluxe, Rs 100 video and Rs 160 for the mini-coaches. The journey takes 10 to 12 hours on most of the buses and under 10 hours on the mini-coaches.

Southbound, there are frequent buses from Jammu to Delhi (14 hours, Rs 120 to Rs 180), Amritsar (five hours, Rs 32), Pathankot (three hours) and other cities. Pathankot is the departure point for Dharamsala, Dalhousie and the other Himachal Pradesh hill stations.

Train The *4645 Shalimar Express* leaves Delhi at 4.10 pm and arrives in Jammu at 7 am. This is the only train that arrives early enough to link up with the early buses to Srinagar. The fare for the 585-km trip from Delhi is Rs 97 in 2nd class, Rs 368 in 1st.

There are also direct rail links with Madras, Bombay, Calcutta, Varanasi and Gorakhpur.

Taxi As a faster alternative to the buses, you could take a share taxi to Srinagar, from outside the railway station in Jammu. Seats cost Rs 300 and they depart as soon as they've collected five passengers.

Getting Around

To/From the Airport The airport is seven km out of town. Auto-rickshaws charge Rs 35 for the trip and a taxi costs around Rs 50.

Local Transport Jammu has metered taxis, auto-rickshaws, a minibus service and a tempo service between a number of points. A minibus from the railway station to the bus station costs Rs 1 (plus Rs 1 for a rucksack). This is much cheaper than taking an auto-rickshaw as the drivers refuse to use their meters and it's difficult to do the trip for less than Rs 25.

JAMMU TO SRINAGAR

Although most people simply head straight through from Jammu to Srinagar, there are a few places of interest between the two centres. Some can also be reached using Jammu as a base. Prior to the completion of the Jawarhar Tunnel into the Kashmir Valley, the trip from Jammu took two days with an overnight stop at Batote.

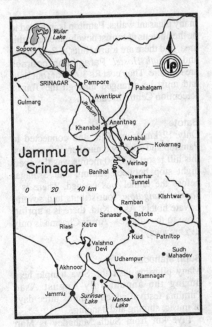

Akhnoor

The Chenab River meets the plains here, 32 km north-west of Jammu. This used to be the route to Srinagar in the Moghul era. Jehangir, who died en route to Kashmir, was temporarily buried at Chingas.

Basohli

Situated fairly close to Dalhousie, which is across the border in Himachal Pradesh, this is the birthplace of the Pahari miniature painting style.

Billawar, Sukrala, Babor & Permandal

All these places have ruined and uncompleted temples of some interest.

Surinsar & Mansar Lakes

East of Jammu, these lakes are picturesque and the scene for an annual **festival** at Mansar.

Vaishno Devi

This important cave temple is dedicated to the three mother goddesses of Hinduism. Thousands of pilgrims visit the cave each year after making a steep 12-km climb from the roadhead at Katra or taking a shorter and easier climb from a new road.

Riasi

Near this town, 20 km beyond Katra, is the ruined **fort** of General Zorawar Singh, renowned for his clashes with the Chinese over Ladakh. Nearby is a **gurdwara** with some interesting old frescoes and another important **cave temple**.

Ramnagar

The Palace of Colours has many beautiful Pahari-style wall paintings. Buses run here from Jammu or Udhampur. Krimchi, 10 km from Udhampur, has Hindu **temples** with fine carvings and sculptures.

Kud

This is a popular lunch stop at 1738 metres on the Jammu to Srinagar route. It's also popular in its own right as a hill resort and has a *Tourist Bungalow*. There's a well-known **mountain spring**, Swamai Ki Bauli, 1½ km from the road.

Patnitop

At 2024 metres this popular hill station has

many pleasant walks. Patnitop is intended to be the nucleus of tourist developments in this area, and there are tourist huts, a *Rest House* and a *Youth Hostel*. **Paragliding courses** are run here. They cost Rs 3000 for four days and must be arranged through the Tourist Reception Centre in Jammu.

Batote

Only 12 km from Kud, and connected to Patnitop and Kud by a number of footpaths, this hill resort at 1560 metres was the overnight stop between Jammu and Srinagar before the tunnel was opened. There is a *Tourist Bungalow*, tourist huts and several private hotels. As in Kud, there is a **spring** close to the village – Amrit Chasma is only 2½ km away.

Sudh Mahadev

Many pilgrims visit the Siva temple here during the annual July-August Asad Purnima festival which features three days of music, singing and dancing.

Five km from Sudh Mahadev is **Man Talai**, where some archaeological discoveries have been made. An eight-km walking or jeep track leads to Sudh Mahadev from Kud or Patnitop.

Sanasar

At 2079 metres, this beautiful valley is a centre for the Gujjar shepherds each summer. There is a *Tourist Bungalow*, tourist huts and several private hotels.

Bhadarwah

Every two years a procession of pilgrims walks from this beautiful high-altitude valley to the 4400-metre-high **Kaplash Lake**. A week later the three-day Mela Patt festival takes place in Bhadarwah. There is a *Rest House* in this scenic location.

Kishtwar

Well off the Jammu to Srinagar road there is a trekking route from Kishtwar to Srinagar. You can also trek from Kishtwar into Zanskar. There are many waterfalls around

Kishtwar, and 19 km from the town is the pilgrimage site of **Sarthal Devi**.

Jawarhar Tunnel

During the winter months Srinagar was often completely cut off from the rest of India before this tunnel was completed. The 2500-metre-long tunnel is 200 km from Jammu and 93 km from Srinagar and has two separate passages. It's extremely rough and damp inside.

From Banihal, 17 km before the tunnel, you are already entering the Kashmiri region and people speak Kashmiri as well as Dogri. As soon as you emerge from the tunnel you are in the green, lush Vale of Kashmir.

Kashmir Valley

This is one of the most beautiful regions of India but over the last few years it's been wracked by political violence. See the warnings at the beginning of this chapter before venturing up here.

The Moghul rulers of India were always happy to retreat from the heat of the plains to the cool green heights of Kashmir, and indeed Jehangir's last words, when he died en route to the 'happy valley', were a simple request for 'only Kashmir'. The Moghuls developed their formal garden-style art to its greatest heights in Kashmir, and some of their gardens are beautifully kept even to this day.

One of Kashmir's greatest attractions is undoubtedly the Dal Lake houseboats. During the Raj period Kashmir's ruler would not permit the British (who were as fond of Kashmir's cool climate as the Moghuls) to own land here. So they adopted the superbly British solution of building houseboats – each one a little bit of England, afloat on Dal Lake. A visit to Kashmir, it is often said, is not complete until you have stayed on a houseboat.

Of course Srinagar, Dal Lake and houseboats are not all there is to Kashmir. Around the edges of the valley are Kashmir's delightful hill stations. Places like Pahalgam and Gulmarg are pleasant in their own right and also good bases for trekking trips.

SRINAGAR
Population: 650,000

The capital of Kashmir stands on Dal Lake and the Jhelum River, and is the transport hub for the valley as well as the departure point for trips to Ladakh.

Srinagar is a crowded, colourful city with a distinctly Central Asian flavour. Indeed the people look different from those in the rest of India; and when you head south from Srinagar it is always referred to as 'returning to India'.

Srinagar now has the feel of an occupied city and there's a strictly enforced curfew after dark. There are roadblocks everywhere and soldiers in bunkers on all street corners. Most of the fighting takes place in the old city, usually during the night. This part of town looks like Beirut at the height of the troubles and should be avoided if you value your life. Information below on the sights within the old city is included in the hope that the situation may improve. At present, the safest areas are the lakes, and the houseboat owners are the best sources of information for which places in Srinagar to avoid. Be sure to take their advice.

Orientation

Srinagar is initially a little confusing because Dal Lake, so much a part of the city, is such a strange lake. It's actually three lakes, separated by dykes or 'floating gardens', and at times it's hard to tell where lake ends and land begins.

On the lake there are houseboats that are firmly attached to the bottom, and houses that look like they could float away. Most of the houseboats are at the southern end of the lake, although you will also find them on the Jhelum River and north on Nagin Lake. The Jhelum River makes a loop around the main part of town, and a canal connecting the river with Dal Lake converts that part of town into an island. Along the south of this 'island' is the Bund, a popular walk where you will find

the GPO and the handicrafts centre. The large Tourist Reception Centre is just north of the Bund.

There are many restaurants, shops, travel agents and hotels in the island part of town. The more modern part of Srinagar stretches away south of the Jhelum River while the older parts of town are north and north-west of here.

The Boulevard, running alongside Dal Lake, is an important address in Srinagar with the *shikara* ghats providing access to the houseboats, hotels, restaurants and shops along the way. Other main roads are Residency Rd, linking the Tourist Reception Centre with the downtown area, and Polo View Rd, lined with handicraft shops and travel agencies.

Information

Tourist Office The J&K Department of Tourism office (☎ 77-305) is at the Tourist Reception Centre, which is a large complex housing (among other things) the various tourist departments and Indian Airlines. It's also the departure and arrival point for Jammu and Leh buses. In 1992 it was partly occupied by the Indian army but the tourist counter, railway agency and bus booking offices were still operating.

Complaints J&K was the first Indian state to instigate legislation to protect tourists from being ripped off. According to the 1978 Act tourists may report any person found 'cheating, touting or obstructing in allowing free choice for shopping or stay or travel arrangements'. The offender is liable to be blacklisted, fined up to Rs 1000 or imprisoned for up to three months! It may be enough just to threaten someone with the Act. If this doesn't work go to the Deputy Director of Tourism in the Tourist Reception Centre.

Money The J&K Bank on The Boulevard is open later in the day than other banks, and is usually less crowded.

The American Express office is at Kai Travels, on The Boulevard by the driveway

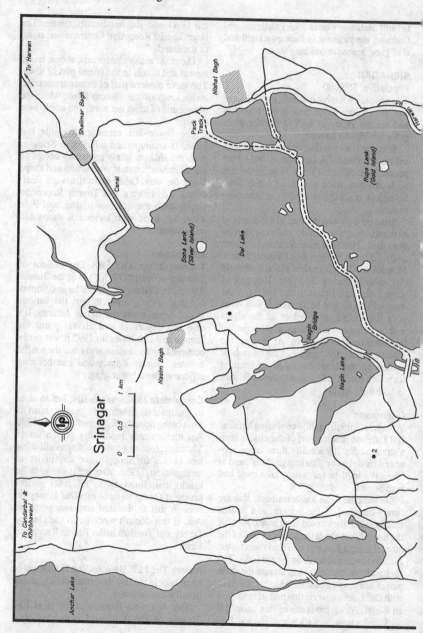

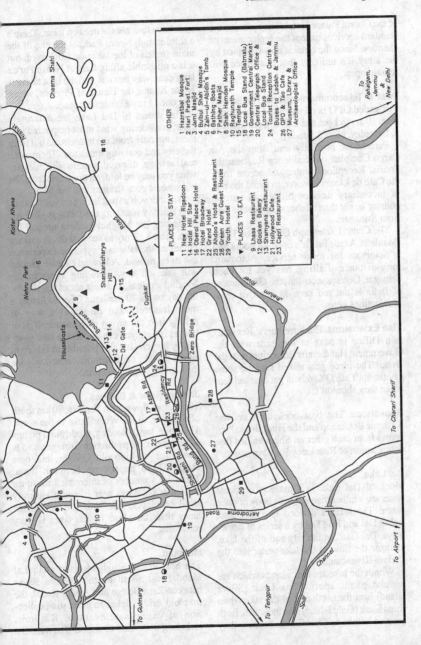

PLACES TO STAY

11 New Hotel Rigadoon
14 Hotel Hill Star
16 Oberol Palace Hotel
17 Hotel Broadway
22 Grand Hotel
25 Ahdoo's Hotel & Restaurant
28 Green Acre Guest House
29 Youth Hostel

PLACES TO EAT

9 Lhasa Restaurant
13 Glocken Bakery
15 Shamyana Restaurant
21 Hollywood Cafe
23 Capri Restaurant

OTHER

1 Hazratbal Mosque
2 Hari Parbat Fort
3 Jami Masjid
4 Bulbul Shah Mosque
5 Zain–ul–Abidin's Tomb
6 Bathing Boats
7 Pather Masjid
8 Shah Hamdan Mosque
10 Raghunath Temple
12 Temple
18 Local Bus Stand (Batmalu)
19 Government Central Market
20 Central Telegraph Office &
   Local Bus Stand
24 Tourist Reception Centre &
   Buses to Ladakh & Jammu
26 GPO & Tao Cafe
27 Museum, Library &
   Archaeological Office

of the Oberoi Palace Hotel. They provide the standard services except the replacement of cheques. Since the hotel is now occupied by the army it's unlikely that this office will remain open.

Post & Telecommunications The heavily barricaded GPO is on the Bund and is open from 10 am to 1 pm and 1.30 to 3 pm Monday to Saturday, closed Sunday.

Parcels are normally sent from the Air Cargo Complex on Residency Rd, near the Tourist Reception Centre and across from the Cafe de Linz. However, to avoid the risk of incendiary devices hidden in parcels nothing larger than a letter may now be sent from Srinagar.

The Central Telegraph Office is on Hotel (Maulana Azad) Rd. It's open 24 hours and is notorious for lousy service. Automatic long-distance dialling has yet to reach Srinagar. One suspects that the Government of India is not too keen to improve communications here.

Visa Extensions The Foreigners' Registration Office is next to the park with the Government Handicrafts Emporium near the Bund. The place gets mixed reports; some say the staff are OK, others get charged fees when they shouldn't.

Bookshops The best bookshops are the Kashmir Bookshop and the Hind Bookshop, across from each other on Sherwani Rd (the continuation of Residency Rd downtown).

Dal Lake

Much of Dal Lake is a maze of intricate waterways rather than a simple body of open water. The lake is divided into Gagribal, Lokut Dal and Bod Dal by a series of causeways. Dal Gate, at the city end of the lake, controls the flow of the lake water into the Jhelum River canal.

Within the lake are two islands which are popular picnic spots. Sona Lank (Silver Island) is at the north end of the lake while Rupa Lank (Gold Island) is to the south. Both are also known as Char Chinar because they

each have four *chinar* trees on them. There's a third island, Nehru Park, at the end of the main stretch of the lakeside Boulevard, but it is a miserable affair. East of Nehru Park a long causeway juts out into the lake towards Kotar Khana, the House of Pigeons, which was once a royal summer house.

The waters of Dal Lake are amazingly clear, considering what must be poured into them, not only from the houseboats but from the city and outlying areas too. There is no real sewage disposal system and, despite what you may be told, all the waste from the houseboats goes straight into the lake.

Whether you're just lazing on your houseboat balcony watching the shikaras glide by, or visiting the Moghul gardens around the lake, there's plenty to see and do. A shikara circuit of the lake is a sybaritic experience not to be missed. A leisurely cruise around will take all day, including visits to the Moghul gardens, and cost about Rs 100 for the day or Rs 20 per hour. There's hardly a more leisurely and pleasurable way of getting into the swing of Srinagar. If your budget is tight you can circuit the lake yourself by bicycle. It's also possible to ride right across the lake on the central causeway – see the Getting Around section.

Jhelum River & Bridges

The Jhelum flows from Verinag, 80 km south of Srinagar, to the Wular Lake to the north. This wide, swift-flowing, muddy and picturesque river sweeps through Srinagar, and is famed for its nine old bridges, but new bridges have popped up between them. There are a number of interesting mosques and other buildings near it, and a leisurely stroll or bicycle ride through the narrow lanes that run close to the river is very rewarding.

Museum

The Shri Pratap Singh Museum is in Lal Mandi, just south of the Jhelum River between Zero Bridge and Amira Kadal, the first 'old' bridge. It has an interesting collection of exhibits relevant to Kashmir, including illustrated tiles from Harwan. It's open every day from 10.30 am to 4 pm, closed all day Mondays and on Fridays between 1 and 2.30 pm; admission is free.

Shah Hamdan Mosque

Originally built in 1395, the all-wooden mosque was destroyed by fire in 1479 and 1731. The present mosque is shaped like a cube with a pyramidal roof rising to a spire. Non-Muslims are not allowed inside.

Pather Masjid

On the opposite bank of the Jhelum River is the unused and run-down Pather Masjid. This fine stone mosque was built by Nur Jahan in 1623.

Tomb of Zain-ul-Abidin

Back on the east bank between the Zaina Kadal and Ali Kadal bridges is the slightly decrepit tomb of King Zain-ul-Abidin, the highly regarded son of Sultan Sikander. Built on the foundations of an earlier temple, the tomb shows a clear Persian influence in its domed construction and glazed tiles.

Jami Masjid

This impressive wooden mosque is notable for the 300-plus pillars supporting the roof, each made of a single deodar tree trunk. The present mosque, with its green and peaceful inner courtyard, was rebuilt to the original design after a fire in 1674.

The mosque has had a chequered history: first built in 1385 by Sultan Sikander, it was enlarged by Zain-ul-Abidin in 1402 and then destroyed by fire in 1479. Rebuilt in 1503, it was destroyed by another fire during Jehangir's reign. Again it was rebuilt only to burn down once more before its most recent rebuilding.

Shankaracharya Hill

Rising up behind The Boulevard beside Dal Lake, this hill was once known as Takht-i-Sulaiman, the Throne of Solomon. A temple is said to have first been built here by Ashoka's son around 200 BC, but the present **Hindu temple** dates from Jehangir's time. It's a pleasant stroll to the top, from where you have a fine view over Dal Lake. The Srinagar TV tower is also here. There's also a road right to the top.

Moghul Gardens

Chasma Shahi (9 km from Srinagar) Smallest of the Moghul gardens at Srinagar, the Chasma Shahi are well up the hillside, above the Nehru Memorial Park. The gardens were laid out in 1632 but have been recently extended. These are the only gardens with an admission charge.

Pari Mahal (10 km) Just above the Chasma Shahi is this fine old Sufi college. The ruined, arched terraces have recently been turned into a very pleasant and well-kept garden with fine views over Dal Lake. From the Pari Mahal you can descend straight down the hill to the road that runs back to the Oberoi Palace Hotel.

Nishat Bagh (11 km) Sandwiched between the lake and the mountains, the Nishat gardens have a superb view across the lake to the Pir Panjal mountains. Designed in 1633 by Nur Jahan's brother Asaf Khan, these are the largest of the Moghul gardens and follow the traditional pattern of a central channel running down a series of terraces.

Shalimar Bagh (15 km) Set some distance back from the lake but reached by a small canal, the Shalimar gardens were built for Nur Jahan, 'light of the world', by her husband Jehangir in 1616. During the Moghul period the topmost of the four terraces was reserved for the emperor and the ladies of the court.

Since the curfew began the nightly Son et Lumière (Sound & Light show) that used to be put on in these beautiful gardens during the tourist season (May to September) has been suspended.

Nasim Bagh (8 km) Just beyond the Hazratbal Mosque, these gardens were built by Akbar in 1586 and are the oldest of Kashmir's Moghul gardens. Today, they are used by an engineering college and not maintained as gardens. Before the political troubles it was possible to camp in these gardens with prior permission from the Tourist Reception Centre.

Hazratbal Mosque

This shiny new mosque is on the north-west shore of Dal Lake. The mosque enshrines a hair of the prophet, but to nonbelievers it is most interesting for its stunningly beautiful setting on the shores of the lake with the snow-capped peaks as a backdrop.

Nagin Lake

The 'jewel in the ring' is held to be the most beautiful of the Dal lakes and is ringed by trees. There are a number of houseboats on this quieter, cleaner lake – ideal if you want to get away from it all.

Hari Parbat Fort

Clearly visible on top of the Sharika hill, to the west of Dal Lake, this fort was originally built between 1592 and 1598 during the rule of Akbar, but most of the present construction dates from the 18th century. Visits were only possible with written permission from the Archaeology Department but since the army has moved into the fort, this is unlikely to be granted. At the southern gate there is a shrine to the sixth Sikh Guru.

Pandrethan Temple

This small but beautifully proportioned Siva temple dates from 900 AD and is in the military cantonment area on the Jammu road out of Srinagar.

Organised Tours

Since travel around Kashmir is severely restricted all tours have been suspended. J&K Road Transport Corporation used to operate tours to Pahalgam, Daksum, Gulmarg, Aharbal, Verinag, Wular Lake, Yusmarg, Sonamarg and the Moghul gardens with departures from the Tourist Reception Centre. Private bus companies, particularly the KMDA (Kashmir Motor Drivers' Association), also had several tours.

No doubt these will be resumed when the political situation improves.

Places to Stay

The houseboats are the prime attraction of a stay in Srinagar and with so few tourists visiting Kashmir there are remarkable bargains to be found. There are also plenty of hotels but only a very few are open, many having been commandeered as barracks for the Indian army. The rest remain closed since their Kashmiri owners would rather they remained empty than occupied by the Indian 'invaders'.

The houseboats are grouped in three areas, Dal Lake, the more peaceful Nagin Lake and the banks of the Jhelum River (mainly cheaper houseboats).

Opposite the Tourist Reception Centre is the Houseboat Owners' Association hut which is where the tourist office will direct you for accommodation. However there is no reason why you shouldn't just go out to the lake and look around for yourself. Booking through the tourist centre only means you get less choice in the matter and pay a higher price. It's now very much a buyer's market and you can afford to be choosy and bargain hard.

Srinagar is, however, notorious for its houseboat touts. They'll grab you at the airport, hassle you as you walk through town, and even try to snare you in Jammu or Delhi! Don't consider any houseboat until you've actually been out and looked at it for yourself. It may sound terrific on paper but turn out to be a miserable dump overdue for downgrading to a lower category, or it might be a fine place in a terrible location. Despite this advice, it's amazing the number of letters we've had from people who committed themselves to a particular boat without seeing it and ended up regretting it.

Houseboats There is no greater escape from the noise and hassle of Srinagar, a typically noisy Asian city, than the superbly relaxing houseboats. As soon as you get out on the lake traffic, pollution and hassles fade away.

Basically most houseboats are the same. There's a small verandah at one end where you can sit and watch the world pass by, and behind this is a living room, usually furnished in British '30s style. Then there is a dining room and beyond that two or three bedrooms, each with a bathroom. Officially houseboats come in five categories, each with an officially approved price for singles/doubles, with and without meals. There are different charges for children or for renting an entire boat.

	Full Board	Lodging Only
Deluxe or 5-star	Rs 500/700	Rs 350/450
A class	Rs 275/400	Rs 190/275
B class	Rs 200/350	Rs 140/230
C class	Rs 150/275	Rs 100/200
D class*	Rs 100/150	Rs 75/100

* doonga boats

In practice these 'official prices' were always a bit meaningless and with most of the boats now standing empty you can negotiate substantial discounts. You should be able to get around 50% off the price of the cheaper boats and discounts of up to 75% on the more expensive ones. I even met one traveller who was paying just Rs 75 (with food) to stay on a deluxe houseboat!

There is a wide variance between boats – some are five-star and others FIVE-STAR! A good C-class boat can be better than a poor A-class boat. Also, most houseboats are managed in groups of three or more. You can be sure the food is not going to differ much from the best boat in the group to the worst.

To find a houseboat, go down to the shikara ghats along the lakeside and announce that you want one. Either there will be somebody there with a boat available or you can hire a kid with a shikara to paddle you around the boats to ask. Check if shikara trips to shore are included; they should be. Pin down as many details as possible. Check what breakfast is going to be, for example – exactly how many eggs? Check if they'll supply a bucket of hot water for washing each morning – Kashmir can be chilly. If you decide to miss a meal (eg lunch) each day,

then that can generally be negotiated into a lower price.

It's virtually impossible to recommend a particular boat; there are about 1000 of them, they all only have a few rooms and there are so many variable factors. A pleasant shikara man, who runs you back and forth between boat and shore, makes tea, supplies hot water and so on, can make a nondescript boat into a pleasant one. A pleasant boat can be ruined by a poor cook. Or simply having some pleasant fellow houseboaters to chat with in the evening can make all the difference. Even on the best boats the food can get rather monotonous but there are plenty of 'supermarket' boats cruising by if you need soft drinks, chocolate, toilet paper, hashish or any other of life's necessities.

A peaceful life out on the lake depends, to some extent, on avoiding the attentions of the vendors who continually paddle by. If you don't want to spend your whole time going through everything from woodcarvings to carpets and embroidery to papier mâché, it's necessary to be very firm and decisive with these people. You can always retreat from the houseboat verandah to the more secluded roof, but why should you have to? Equally important is the attitude of the houseboat owners who rake off a handy little commission from everything that gets sold on their houseboat. On some houseboats you may actually find that the service, food or general attitude take a disastrous dip if you don't spend, spend, spend. The only answer to this policy is to move to a better houseboat, where the owners have more respect for their guests' comfort.

Hotels In 1992 virtually all the hotels in Srinagar were closed. Exceptions were the *Grand Hotel* on Residency Rd, with doubles with attached bath from Rs 80, and *Ahdoo's Hotel* (☎ 72-593) which is almost opposite. Rooms here are Rs 300/400 with attached baths and TV and there's an excellent restaurant in the hotel. Information on other hotels is included below in case the political situation changes, allowing them to reopen.

Bottom-end hotels that were popular

before the political disturbances began were to be found in three main areas: amongst the houseboats around Dal Gate; along Buchwara Chowk, which runs parallel with The Boulevard; and in the Raj Bagh area across the Jhelum River.

The hotels on small Dal Lake islands were spartan and catered mainly to Indian tourists. The *Hotel Sundowna* and, next door, the *Hotel Savoy* were popular with budget travellers and reached by shikara from the first ghat by Dal Gate. The *New Hotel Rigadoon* was much cleaner and more pleasant and had a range of rooms including dorm beds. To find it cross over Dal Gate and it's on the right after the bridge. The *Hotel Hill Star* was recommended for its garden and friendly management. Nearby are the *Rubina Guest House, Hotel Sultan, Hotel Raj* and *Hotel Heeven*. Owned and operated by Bengalis, these were also above average by local standards. The *Tibetan Guest House*, east along Buchwara Rd, was another favourite.

Raj Bagh, a quiet residential area, is on the south bank of the Jhelum River, opposite the Bund. The *Bhat Guest House* was one of the cheapest places in Srinagar, and surprisingly clean and comfortable. There are several other places in this area. The *Tourist Reception Centre* had some rooms but they were often full and have now been taken over by the army. Across the river from the city centre on Wazir Bagh, the Srinagar *Youth Hostel* is rather out of the way but was very cheap.

One of the most popular mid-range places was the *Green Acre Guest House* (☎ 73-349), a large private house in Raj Bagh. It was a delightful haven from Srinagar's hustle and bustle with a nice garden, pleasant management, a wide choice of rooms and consistently good food. To find it, cross Zero Bridge, turn right, then left by the Snow Hut Cafe, and it's on the left at the foot of the slope.

Also in this price range was the *Pinegrove Hotel* (☎ 72-405), adjacent to the Lhasa Restaurant. On The Boulevard facing Dal Lake, the *Hotel Mazda* (☎ 72-842) was good value and the *Lake Isle Resort* (☎ 78-446) was

more expensive but beautifully located on an island in the middle of Dal Lake. There are several similarly priced hotels along The Boulevard, the best of which were probably the *Welcome* (☎ 74-104) and the *Asia Brown Palace*. The only hotel by Nagin Lake is the elegant *Hotel Dar-es-Salan* (☎ 77-803).

At the top end the *Oberoi Palace Hotel* (☎ 75-641) is the ex-palace of the Maharaja of Kashmir and was Srinagar's top establishment. Its comfortable amenities are now being enjoyed by the elite of the Indian army. The actual building is rather uninspiring, particularly if you've seen the sumptuous palace hotels of Rajasthan, but the gardens in front provide superb views over the lake. The *Hotel Broadway* (☎ 79-001) was a good modern alternative to the Oberoi Palace, and more conveniently located on Maulana Azad Rd across from the polo field.

Places to Eat

Probably because so many people eat on board their houseboats, Srinagar is not a very exciting place for eating out.

The *Tao Cafe* on Residency Rd, by the turnoff to the GPO, has a lovely garden which makes a nice place to chat or write postcards while you wait for your order. The food is mainly Chinese and generally good (the chicken in garlic sauce, for Rs 33, was excellent). It's a very popular place with travellers. The nearby *Cafe de Linz* is cheaper, with good mutton seekh kebabs for Rs 17 and good nan. As in all the restaurants, you can get excellent Kashmiri tea here.

On The Boulevard there's the new *Shamyana Restaurant* which does surprisingly good pizza from Rs 30 to Rs 38 and excellent garlic bread (Rs 13). The tiny *Alka Salka* on Residency Rd across from Polo View Rd serves very good Chinese and Indian food but it's quite expensive.

Ahdoo's, in the hotel of the same name on Residency Rd, has long been one of Srinagar's best places for Kashmiri food and Indian specialities. Main dishes are around Rs 30 to Rs 40 and there's a good bakery downstairs.

The *Mughal Darbar* is another of

Srinagar's better places for Kashmiri and Indian food. This is despite its often filthy appearance, its scruffy and inefficient waiters and the loud and overbearing locals. It's adjacent to the Suffering Moses store and across from the polo field on Residency Rd.

The *Lhasa Restaurant* serves good Chinese-Tibetan style food and is popular with travellers. It's near Dal Lake, just off The Boulevard. The Tourist Development Corporation runs the plush *Nun Kun* Chinese restaurant by Dal Lake. Main dishes are around Rs 35.

The bakeries near Dal Gate do a roaring trade with travellers. The *Glocken Bakery* is the most popular. It's run by a German-Kashmiri couple and has apple pie, delicious walnut honey cake, brown bread and chocolate cake. There are a few tables to sit at and they also serve hot and cold drinks. *Sultan Bakery* has excellent gingernut biscuits, apple pie and cheesecake. Stock up with goodies before heading to Leh.

Things to Buy

Kashmir is famous for its many handicrafts, and selling them is an activity pursued with amazing energy. You can visit workshops to see many of them being made. Popular buys include carpets, papier mâché articles, leather and furs, woodcarvings, shawls and embroidery, tailor-made clothing, pleasantly coarse-knitted sweaters and cardigans, expensive spice saffron and many other items.

There is a whole string of government handicraft emporiums scattered around Srinagar, but the main one is housed in the fine old British Residency building by the Bund. The flashiest shops are along The Boulevard by Dal Lake. The Bund also has some interesting shops, including Suffering Moses with high-quality goods. On Polo View Rd there's the elderly and engaging Cheerful Chippendale. Shikaras patrol Dal Lake like sharks, loaded down with goodies.

Kashmir is also famous for its high-quality honey, which goes very well with the Middle Eastern-style bread available in Leh. It's quite expensive and you should try before you buy since sugar is occasionally substituted. The best shop is the Oriental Apiary, midway between Dal Gate and Nagin Lake, where there's a wide range of honeys including lotus blossom, saffron and even marijuana flower honey!

Getting There & Away

Air The Indian Airlines office (☎ 77-370) is at the Tourist Reception Centre and is open from 10 am to 4 pm. There's an Air India office (☎ 77-141) in the Hotel Broadway Annexe on Maulana Azad Rd.

Indian Airlines has daily flights to Delhi (US$77), Amritsar (US$45) and Jammu (US$27). There are flights on Monday and Saturday to Chandigarh (US$65) and on Tuesday and Thursday to Leh (US$39).

Security at the airport is currently very tight so don't carry anything you shouldn't have on you (ie hash). You must arrive two hours before the flight and no hand luggage is allowed. Even cameras must be consigned to the hold.

Bus The routes between Jammu and Leh are reserved for the Jammu & Kashmir Road Transport Corporation buses which go from the Tourist Reception Centre. For Jammu, they leave at 7.30 am and cost Rs 160 for mini-coaches, Rs 100 for super deluxe and Rs 70 for A class. B class buses (Rs 53) go from the Lal Chowk bus stand.

For Leh, J&KRTC buses leave from the Tourist Reception Centre at 8 am. They cost Rs 165 for A class, Rs 250 for super deluxe. Buses to Kargil cost Rs 85 for A class, Rs 125 for super deluxe. Also from the Tourist Reception Centre there's a daily bus to Delhi for Rs 260. The journey is supposed to take 24 hours but can take up to 36 hours.

If the buses around the Kashmir Valley are running, they go from the Batmalu bus stand, which has two sections: buses to Pahalgam (Rs 13), Sonamarg (Rs 13) and the Mughal gardens depart from the Eastern bus stand; buses to Gulmarg (Rs 12), Tangmarg (Rs 7) and Wular Lake leave from the Western bus stand.

It's best to book a seat as soon as possible

for long-distance buses since they're often fully booked the day before.

Train There's no railway line to Srinagar, but train reservations can be made at the railway booking office at the Tourist Reception Centre for train departures from Jammu. However, their quota is just two 2nd-class berths per train to Delhi, Bombay, Madras, Calcutta and Gorakhpur.

Taxi For those with thick wallets, taxis are available for long-distance trips such as Jammu or Kargil (Rs 1500 for the whole vehicle or Rs 300 per seat) and Leh (Rs 4600 for the whole vehicle). You can also arrange day trips to Gulmarg (Rs 500) and Pahalgam (Rs 600).

Getting Around
To/From the Airport From Srinagar airport, which is about 13 km out of the city, the airport bus (Rs 12.50) runs only occasionally so you may have to take a taxi. The rate is posted outside the airport and is currently Rs 100 but the drivers will try for Rs 150. They will also attempt to steer you into the hands of the Houseboat Owners' Association. If that's not what you want insist they take you right to the lake.

Shikaras These are the graceful, long boats which crowd the Srinagar lakes. They're used for getting back and forth from the houseboats or for longer tours. Officially there is a standard fare for every trip around the lake and these are prominently posted at the main landings (ghats); in practice the fares can be quite variable. To be shuttled across to your houseboat should cost Rs 3 in a covered ('full spring seats') shikara, but the kids who are always out for a little money will happily paddle you across for Rs 1 in a basic, open shikara. If the curfew is still in operation no-one is allowed out after dark and near this time getting back to your houseboat at a reasonable price may require a little ingenuity!

Try paddling a shikara yourself sometime

– it's nowhere near as easy as it looks. You'll spend lots of time going round in circles.

Bus Take a No 12 bus to Nagin Lake or the Hazratbal Mosque.

Taxi & Auto-Rickshaw There are stands for these at the Tourist Reception Centre and other strategic locations in town. Srinagar's auto-rickshaw-wallahs are extremely reluctant to use their meters so you'll have to bargain hard. You should pay about Rs 5 from the Tourist Reception Centre to Dal Gate, Rs 10 from the bus stand at Batmalu to the Tourist Reception Centre. For longer trips the official fares are all posted by the stands.

Bicycle Cycling is an extremely pleasant way of getting around, especially as the valley is fairly flat. You can hire bikes for Rs 15 per day and there are several stores along The Boulevard close to Dal Gate. Following are some suggested trips but check with your houseboat owner that these areas are currently safe to visit.

Around Dal Lake – an all-day trip going by the Moghul gardens. It's particularly pleasant around the north of the lake where the villages are still relatively untouched.

Across the lake – you can ride across the lake on the causeway, a nice trip since there are no traffic problems and there is plenty of opportunity to observe lake life without being in a boat.

Nagin Lake – you can ride out to the Hazratbal Mosque via Nagin Lake and then make a complete loop around the lake on the way back. This trip can easily be combined with a trip along the Jhelum, taking in the various mosques close to the river. The streets here are very narrow so vehicles keep away and bike riding is pleasant.

AROUND SRINAGAR
There are a number of interesting places in the Kashmir Valley for day trips from Srinagar, and several popular hill stations which serve as good bases for short or long treks into the surrounding mountains. Pahalgam and Gulmarg are the two main Kashmiri hill resorts. However travel around the valley is currently restricted and you are

likely to be stopped and searched at the numerous roadblocks.

Harwan

At the northern end of Dal Lake, archaeologists have discovered unusual ornamented tiles near Harwan. The tiles are believed to have been from a 3rd-century Buddhist monastery which was built on the site, and examples of them can be seen in the Srinagar museum. The water supply for Srinagar is pumped from here and piped along the causeway across the lake.

Sangam

Sangam, 35 km north-east of Srinagar, is a centre for production of (would you believe) cricket bats. They're lined up by the road in their thousands.

Verinag

Verinag is in the extreme south of the Kashmir Valley. The spring here is said to be the actual source of the Jhelum River. Jehangir built an octagonal stone basin at the spring in 1612 and Shah Jahan laid out a garden around it in 1620.

SRINAGAR TO PAHALGAM

The route to Pahalgam passes through some interesting places including, if you take the bus tour to Pahalgam, enough Moghul gardens to leave you botanically saturated. Only 16 km south-east of Srinagar is Pampore, centre of Kashmir's saffron industry. Saffron is highly prized for its flavouring and colouring properties and is consequently rather expensive.

At Avantipur are two ruined Hindu temples, built between 855 and 883 AD. The Avantiswami Temple, the larger of the two, is dedicated to Vishnu and still has some fine relief sculptures and columns of an almost Grecian appearance. The smaller temple, dedicated to Siva, is about one km before the main temple and close to the main road.

At Anantnag the road forks, and the Pahalgam road turns north. Just beyond the Pahalgam turnoff is Achabal, a Moghul

garden laid out in 1620 by Shah Jahan's daughter, Jahanara. This carefully designed garden was said to be a favourite retreat of Nur Jahan. Kokarnag, further on, is certain to give you garden overload but is famous for its rose gardens. Back on the Pahalgam route Mattan has a fish-filled spring which is an important pilgrimage spot. Above Mattan on a plateau is the huge ruined temple of Martland.

PAHALGAM

Pahalgam is about 95 km from Srinagar, and at 2130 metres the night-time temperatures here are warmer than in Gulmarg, which is higher up.

The beautiful Lidder River flows right through the town, which is at the junction of the Sheshnag and Lidder rivers and is surrounded by soaring, fir-covered mountains with snow-capped peaks rising behind them.

There are many short walks from Pahalgam and it is an ideal base for longer treks to Kolahoi Glacier or Amarnath Cave – see Treks in Kashmir later in this chapter. Pahalgam is also famous for its many shepherds. They're a common sight, driving their flocks of sheep along the paths all around town.

In 1992, although trekkers were still visiting this region, most of the hotels and restaurants were closed. Bus services were suspended but it was possible to reach Pahalgam by taxi from Srinagar.

Information

The rather useless tourist office (☎ 24) is just around the corner from the bus stop. There is a bank and a post office open in the tourist season.

Fishing permits have to be obtained in Srinagar. Trekking supplies can be obtained here, although they are cheaper to buy in Srinagar.

Pahalgam Walks

Mamaleswara Only a km or so downstream and on the opposite bank of the Lidder, this small Siva temple with its square stone tank is thought to date back to the 12th century.

Baisaran There are excellent views over the town and the Lidder Valley from this meadow, five km from Pahalgam. A further 11 km takes you to the **Tulian Lake** at 3353 metres. It is covered with ice for much of the year.

Aru The pleasant little village of Aru makes a very interesting day walk, following the Lidder River for 11 km upstream. Unfortunately, the main track on the left bank also takes cars, although there is a less used (and more difficult) track on the right bank. This is actually the first stage of the Kolahoi Glacier trek.

Places to Stay

Before the political troubles began most travellers stayed in the lodges on the western bank. The hotels on the main street of Pahalgam catered mainly to Indian tourists. The basic *Aksa Lodge* (☎ 59) was the most popular cheapie. Hot water was always available and the food was good.

The other lodges were not as good. The best among them was probably the *Brown Palace*, although it is a long way from town. Another option was the *Windrush House*. To get there, continue past the path leading up to Aksa Lodge and go down to the right, on the riverbank. The government *Tourist Bungalow* and the adjacent *Tourist Huts* would also be worth checking out.

The *Hotel Kolahoi Kabin*, between the two rivers, was not bad but the other places, including the *White House* and *Bentes Lodge*, were a lot more decrepit.

Just outside Pahalgam on the Amarnath route the *Yog Niketan* ashram was an interesting place to stay. It offered yoga and meditation courses.

The *Pahalgam Hotel* (☎ 26) was the top hotel with all the facilities you'd expect in the Rs 600/800 price range, including heated swimming pool, sauna and massage. The *Woodstock Hotel* (☎ 27) next door was somewhat cheaper.

Places to Eat

People staying on the west bank area used to

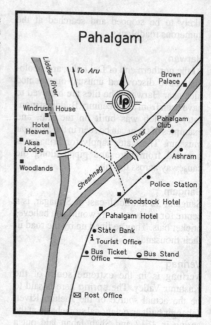

Pahalgam

eat in this area too. In the main street on the west bank, the *Lhasa Restaurant* was not as good as its namesake in Srinagar. The *Pahalgam Hotel* did expensive set meals.

Getting There & Away

When they're operating, local buses from Srinagar to Pahalgam cost Rs 13 and take 2½ to four hours. There were also more expensive tour buses operated by J&K Road Transport. Taxis cost about Rs 600 return.

Ponies can easily be hired in Pahalgam for trekking trips. The fixed costs to popular destinations are clearly posted, although they're basically bargaining guidelines.

GULMARG

The large meadow of Gulmarg is 52 km south-west of Srinagar at 2730 metres. The name means Meadow of Flowers and in spring it's just that. This is also an excellent trekking base. In winter it used to be India's premier skiing resort, until the activities of the militants frightened off the tourists. The skiing equipment available was fairly good and the costs very low. The area was also wonderful for ski-touring although very little cross-country equipment was available.

Gulmarg can get pretty cold at times, even compared to Pahalgam, so come prepared with plenty of warm clothes. In 1992, the hotels and ski-lifts here remained closed. The following information is included in the hope that the situation may improve.

Information
The tourist office, in the valley bottom about half a km beyond the golf course, is the green-blue building complex with three patches of new wooden roof.

Skiing
There is one chairlift, one T-bar, four pomas and a cable car to the top of Mt Apharwat. The slopes vary from beginner to intermediate and equipment could be hired cheaply. All lifts operated from 10 am to 5 pm, closing for one hour at lunch. Limited amounts of cross-country equipment were available from S D Singh, Hut 209A.

Gulmarg Walks
Outer Circular Walk A circular road, 11 km in length, runs right round Gulmarg through pleasant pine forests with excellent views over the Kashmir Valley. Nanga Parbat is visible to the north, and Haramukh and Sunset Peak are visible to the south-east.

Khilanmarg This smaller valley is about a six-km walk from the Gulmarg bus stop and car park. The meadow, carpeted with flowers in the spring, is the site for Gulmarg's winter ski runs and offers a fine view of the surrounding peaks and the Kashmir Valley. During the early spring, as the snow melts, it can be a very muddy hour's climb up the hill.

Alpather Beyond Khilanmarg, 13 km from Gulmarg at the foot of the 4511-metre Apharwat peak, this lake is frozen until mid-June, and even later in the year you can see lumps of ice floating in its cold waters. The walk from Gulmarg follows a well-graded pony track over the 3810-metre Apharwat Ridge, separating the lake from Khilanmarg, and proceeds up the valley to the lake at 3843 metres.

Ningle Nallah Flowing from the melting snow and ice on Apharwat Peak and Alpather Lake, this pretty mountain stream is 10 km from Gulmarg. The stream continues down into the valley below and joins the Jhelum River near Sopore. The walking path crosses the Ningle Nallah by a bridge and continues on to the **Lienmarg**, another grassy meadow and a good spot for camping.

Ferozpore Nallah Reached from the Tangmarg road, or from the outer circular walk, this mountain stream meets the Bahan River at a popular picnic spot known as **Waters Meet**. The stream is reputed to be particularly good for trout fishing; it's about five km from Gulmarg. You can continue on from here to **Tosamaidan**, a three-day, 50-km walk to one of Kashmir's most beautiful meadows.

Ziarat of Baba Reshi This Muslim shrine is on the slopes below Gulmarg and can be reached from either Gulmarg or Tangmarg. The *ziarat*, or tomb, is of a well-known Muslim saint who died here in 1480. Before renouncing worldly ways he was a courtier of the Kashmir king, Zain-ul-Abidin.

Places to Stay
Budget accommodation in Gulmarg was always in short supply, as was hot water. The *Tourists Hotel* (☎ 53), opposite the bus stand, is a remarkably baroque and weathered fantasy in wood, like something out of *Lord of the Rings* although rather grubby inside, albeit cheap. The similarly priced *City View* had a friendly manager, fine food and superb views. The nearby *Tourist Bungalow* was a little more expensive but was probably the most comfortable of the cheap places.

The pleasant *Green View* was a good mid-range hotel. The shabby *Kingsley Hotel* was overpriced.

The *Hotel Highlands Park* was Gulmarg's overrated topnotch hotel, in the Rs 750/900 price range. *Nedou's Hotel* and *Welcome Hotel* were better value.

Places to Eat

Limited and not very good summed up the situation. For cheap meals there were the south Indian cafes by the bus stand. Elsewhere, prices were considerably higher. *Ahdoo's* next to the bus stand was probably the best in Gulmarg.

Getting There & Away

There used to be a variety of buses running from Srinagar to Gulmarg, many of them on day tours. These tours enabled only a few hours at the hill resort, just long enough for one of the shorter day walks.

In 1992 it was only possible to get a bus from Srinagar as far as Tangmarg (Rs 7), seven km in distance and 500 metres in altitude below Gulmarg. The last stretch must be completed on foot or by pony. The winding road from Tangmarg to Gulmarg is 13 km in length, nearly twice as far as the more direct pony track.

SOUTH OF SRINAGAR

Interesting places in the south-west of the Kashmir Valley include **Yusmarg**, reputed to have the best spring flowers in Kashmir, and a good base for treks further afield. **Chari Sharif** is on the road to Yusmarg and has the shrine, or ziarat, of Kashmir's patron saint. **Aharbal** was a popular resting place for the Moghul emperors when they made the long trip north from Delhi.

SINDH VALLEY

This is a scenic area north of Srinagar through which the road to Ladakh passes. The Zoji La pass marks the boundary from the Sindh Valley into Ladakh. From Srinagar you pass the **Dachigam Wildlife Reserve**, once a royal game park; you need a signed

permit from the Srinagar tourist office to enter the reserve.

Anchar Lake, rarely visited, is close to Srinagar and has a wide variety of water birds. There is a Moghul garden built by Nur Jahan at **Manasbal Lake**. **Wular Lake** is possibly the largest freshwater lake in India, the Jhelum River flows into it.

Sonamarg, at 2740 metres, is the last major town before Ladakh and an excellent base for trekking. Its name means Meadow of Gold, which could derive from the spring flowers or from the strategic trading position it once enjoyed. There are *Tourist Huts*, a *Rest House* and some small hotels here.

The tiny village of **Baltal** is the last place in Kashmir, right at the foot of the Zoji La. When conditions are favourable you can walk to the **Amarnath Cave** from here. The Zoji La is the watershed between Kashmir and Ladakh – on one side you have the green, lush scenery of Kashmir while on the other side everything is barren and dry.

TREKS IN KASHMIR

There are various treks both within Kashmir and from Kashmir to Ladakh or Zanskar. Access to some of the treks described below is liable to be restricted by the activities of militants and the army. Check the current situation in Srinagar.

The short Pahalgam to Kolahoi Glacier trek is particularly popular and even in 1992 travellers were still doing this trek. The Pahalgam to Amarnath Cave trek is well known not only for the superb scenery, but for the great religious festival that takes place here.

Porters in Kashmir are used less frequently than they are in Nepal; ponies carry the gear. Although trekking companies are not as widespread as in Nepal they were starting to pop up. Summit Treks and Choomti Trekkers, both in Srinagar, have been recommended. Most houseboat owners can also help organise treks. Typical daily charges vary greatly, from as little as US$5 to as much as US$50, depending on the length of the trek, the number of people and your bargaining skills. Some travellers were

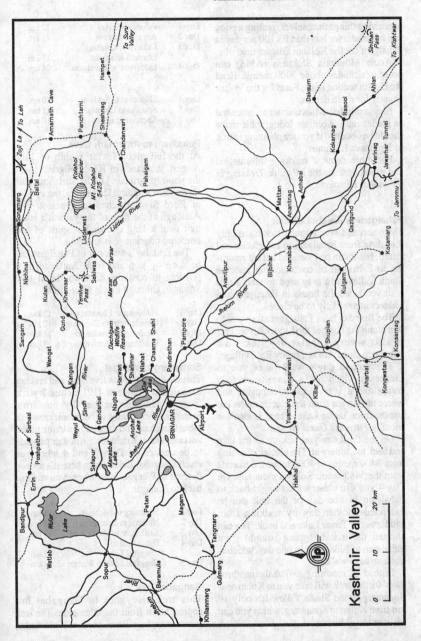

Kashmir Valley

organising things themselves, renting a pony and horseman for less than Rs 100 per day in Pahalgam for the Kolahoi Glacier trek.

Acute Mountain Sickness (AMS) can occur at altitudes above 3000 metres. Read the Health section in the Facts for the Visitor chapter for more details.

Maps included in this chapter are intended as guides only. Accurate topographic maps should be obtained if you are planning to trek in Jammu & Kashmir.

For more detailed trekking information and itineraries, see the LP guide *Trekking in the Indian Himalaya*.

Pahalgam to Kolahoi Glacier

This short and very popular trek takes only four days from Pahalgam to the glacier and return, but it can be extended before returning to Pahalgam or continued up into the Sindh Valley. You may need to take a tent with you since the hotels in Pahalgam and Lidderwat are likely to be closed.

The first day from Pahalgam takes you to Aru along the bank of the Lidder River. This is also a very popular day trek from Pahalgam since Aru is a pretty little village.

The second day's walk takes you to Lidderwat which has a *Government Rest House* and a very pleasant campsite, and where the stream from the glacier meets the stream from Tarsar Lake. There is also the friendly *Paradise Guest House*.

On the third day you trek up to the lake and back to Lidderwat. The glacier, climbing from 3400 metres to 4000 metres, descends from the 5485-metre Kolahoi mountain. On Day 4 you can either walk straight back to Pahalgam in one day or the trek can be extended another day by walking from Lidderwat to Tarsar Lake and back. You can shorten the trek by going straight from Pahalgam to Lidderwat in one day, which is quite an easy walk.

Instead of returning to Pahalgam, three days' further trek will take you to Kulan near Sonamarg in the Sindh Valley. It's only 16 km from Kulan to Sonamarg, which you can walk or travel by bus.

Day 1	Pahalgam to Aru	12 km
Day 2	Aru to Lidderwat	12 km
Day 3	Lidderwat/Kolahoi Glacier/Lidderwat	13 km
Day 4	Lidderwat to Pahalgam	24 km

or

Day 4	Lidderwat to Sekiwas	10 km
Day 5	Sekiwas to Khemsar	11 km
Day 6	Khemsar to Kulan	10 km

Pahalgam to Amarnath Cave

At the full moon in the month of July-August, thousands of Hindu pilgrims make the *yatra* (pilgrimage) to the Shri Amarnath Cave when a natural ice lingam, the symbol of Lord Siva, reaches its greatest size. Although at the time of the yatra it's less a trek than a long queue, the spirit of this immense pilgrimage is amazing.

The first day's walk out of Pahalgam can be done by jeep and from Amarnath it is possible to continue north to Baltal near Srinagar, although that is a hard trek.

Day 1	Pahalgam to Chandanwari	13 km
Day 2	Chandanwari to Sheshnag	12 km
Day 3	Sheshnag to Panchtarni	11 km
Day 4	Panchtarni to Amarnath	8 km

Sonamarg to Wangat

This 81-km trek takes five days and reaches a maximum altitude of 4191 metres. It starts from Sonamarg (reached by bus from Srinagar), then climbs to Nichinai, crosses a mountain chain and drops down to the pleasant campsite at Krishansar. Another pass has to be crossed on Days 3 and 4 when you reach Gangabal Lake. From here it's a steep descent to Wangat, from where you can bus back to Srinagar.

Day 1	Sonamarg to Nichinai	15 km
Day 2	Nichinai to Krishansar	13 km
Day 3	Krishansar to Dubta Pani	17 km
Day 4	Dubta Pani to Gangabal Lake	17 km
Day 5	Gangabal Lake to Wangat	19 km

Gangabal Trek

This trek also goes to Gangabal but approaches it from the other side. The trek commences from Errin, north of Wular Lake, and takes five days in all. On Day 4 you need ropes and ice-axes to cross the glacier between the Kundsar and Gangabal lakes. The final day's trek also ends at Wangat. At Narannag, just before Wangat, there is an interesting old temple.

Day 1	Errin/Chuntimula/	
	Poshpathri	11 km
Day 2	Poshpathri to Sarbaal	11 km
Day 3	Sarbaal to Kundsar Lake	9 km
Day 4	Kundsar Lake to	
	Gangabal Lake	11 km
Day 5	Gangabal Lake to Wangat	19 km

Konsarnag Trek

This short trek in the south of the Kashmir Valley ascends into the Pir Panjal mountains. The first day's trek is a short walk only taking about three hours. With an early start from Srinagar you can bus to Aharbal and complete the first walk in the same day. Konsarnag Lake is a beautiful deep-blue stretch of water at 3700 metres.

Day 1	Aharbal to Kongwatan	9 km
Day 2	Kongwatan to Mahinag	8 km
Day 3	Mahinag/Konsarnag/	
	Kongwatan	12 km
Day 4	Kongwatan to Aharbal	9 km

Daksum to Kishtwar

Starting from the south of the Kashmir Valley at Daksum, this trek is an interesting route to Jammu, although you can also trek from Kishtwar into the Zanskar Valley or to Himachal Pradesh. Daksum is 100 km from Srinagar and takes about three hours by road. The maximum altitude is reached on the first day's trek to the Sinthan Pass. On the last day it is only a short walk to Dadhpath from where buses depart at 10 am and 4 pm to Kishtwar.

Day 1	Daksum to Sinthan Pass	16 km
Day 2	Sinthan Pass to Chatru	8 km
Day 3	Chatru to Mughal Maidan	9 km
Day 4	Mughal Maidan to	
	Dadhpath	8 km

Pahalgam to Pannikar

This is a hard trek into the Suru Valley which leads to Zanskar. The first two days of the trek follow the Amarnath Cave route. The following days cross the Gulol Gali Pass, climb to the Lonvilad Gali, go over the Chalong Glacier and continue down to Pannikar. From Pannikar you can take the road north to Kargil or east into the Zanskar Valley.

Day 1 & 2	As Amarnath Cave trek	
Day 3	Sheshnag to Rangmarg	8 km
Day 4	Rangmarg to Hampet	6 km
Day 5 & 6	Hampet to Lonvilad Gali	22 km
Day 7	Lonvilad Gali to	
	Chalong Glacier	14 km
Day 8	Chalong Glacier to	
	Pannikar	15 km

Ladakh

'Little Tibet', 'the moonland' and 'the last Shangri-la' are names that have been applied to Ladakh, all with a bit of truth. Ladakh is a high-altitude plateau north of the Himalaya situated geographically in Tibet. It's a miniature version of Tibet, the people are Tibetan in their culture and religion, and there are many Tibetan refugees.

The Himalaya are a very effective barrier to rain – few clouds creep across their awesome height and as a result Ladakh is barren beyond belief. Only where rivers, running from faraway glaciers or melting snow, carry water to habitation do you find plant life – hence the moonland label, since Ladakh is as dry as the Sahara.

Finally, Ladakh could well be a last Shangri-la, although since the troubles in the Kashmir Valley began there has been quite an increase in the number of tourists visiting Ladakh. Only in the mid-70s was it opened to outside visitors. Its strategic isolation is matched by its physical isolation – only from June to September are the roads into Ladakh from Kashmir and Himachal Pradesh not covered by snow and only since 1979 have there been airline flights into Ladakh. That flight is one of the most spectacular in the world.

Ladakh is well worth the effort of getting there. It's an otherworldly place – strange gompas perched on soaring hilltops, ancient palaces clinging to sheer rock walls, and shattered-looking landscapes splashed with small but brilliant patches of green. But most of all there are the delightful Ladakhis, friendly as only Tibetan people can be and immensely colourful.

General Advice

A sleeping bag is very useful in Ladakh even if you're not trekking or camping. The nights can get very cold and visiting many of the gompas by public transport will require an overnight stop. Be prepared for dramatic temperature changes and for the extreme burning power of the sun in Ladakh's thin air (Leh is at 3505 metres). A cloud across the sun will change the air temperature from T-shirt to sweater level in seconds. Without a hat and/or sunscreen you'll have sunburn and a peeling nose in hours.

Acclimatise to Ladakh's altitude slowly – don't go scrambling up mountainsides as soon as you arrive. A spell in Kashmir is a good halfway acclimatisation, but people who fly straight from Delhi to Ladakh may feel very uncomfortable for a few days.

Outside Leh it is not easy to change money and in the tourist season there is often a severe shortage of small change. One very important word to learn for Ladakh is the all-purpose and frequently used greeting 'Jullay'. Finally, remember that this is a sensitive border region disputed by India, Pakistan and China. You are not allowed more than a 1.6 km north of the Srinagar to Leh road without permission.

Religion

At Kargil, on the Srinagar to Leh road, the Islamic influence dies out and you are in a Buddhist region. The people follow Tibetan Tantric Buddhism which has much emphasis on magic and demons. All around Ladakh are gompas, the Buddhist monasteries. They're fascinating to visit, although they have become very commercially minded since Ladakh's tourist boom commenced. There's

a good side to this though. Prior to tourism the gompas were gradually becoming more and more neglected. Today many of them are being refurbished and repaired with the profits from visiting Westerners. The monks are happy to have visitors wander around the gompas, sit in on the ceremonies, try the appalling (to the Western palate) taste of butter tea (bring your own cup) and take photographs.

SRINAGAR TO LEH

It's 434 km from Srinagar to Ladakh and the road is surfaced most of the way. It follows the Indus River for much of the distance. Buses run along this road daily during the summer season (see Getting There & Away for Leh) and take two days with an overnight stop at Kargil. With the military roadblocks and numerous passport checks these are currently two very long days. Sonamarg is the last major town in the Vale of Kashmir, shortly before you climb up over the Zoji La pass (3529 metres) and enter the Ladakh region.

There is accommodation of some form or other at Drass, Kargil, Mulbekh, Bodh Kharbu, Lamayuru, Khalsi, Nurla, Saspul and Nimmu.

Zoji La

This is one of the few unsurfaced stretches on the route. It's also the first pass to snow over in winter and the last to be cleared in summer. At 3529 metres it's not, however, the highest pass along the route. The other passes get less snow because they are across the Himalaya and in the mountain rain shadow.

The road up the pass is breathtaking, even more so than the road up the much higher Taglang La pass (5328 metres) on the Leh to Manali road. The road clings to the edge of sheer drops and there are times when you'll wonder if you were sane to make this trip!

Drass

This is the first village after the pass and the place from where road crews clear the road up to the pass for the start of the summer season. In winter, Drass is noted for its heavy snowfalls and extreme cold.

The buses stop here and tourists have to register their names and passport numbers.

Kargil

Once an important trading post, Kargil is now simply an overnight halt on the way to Leh or the point where you turn south for the Zanskar Valley. The people of Kargil are chiefly Muslim and noted for their extreme orthodoxy. Already you are in a region where irrigation is vitally important.

Places to Stay On the main street, the *Popular Chacha*, *De Lux*, *New Light*, *Puril*, *Punjab Janta* and *Argalia* provide rock-bottom accommodation at around Rs 40 a bed. The *Naktul View*, between the main street and the truck park, and the *Crown* on the other side of the truck park, are of a better standard. The *International* is overpriced at Rs 70 a double.

The *Marjina Tourist Home* has a range of rooms of varying degrees of cleanliness. They ask what they think you'll pay (as do most of the hotel owners here) but you should be able to get a clean double with attached bathroom for around Rs 100. The *Greenland Hotel* is similarly priced as is the *Tourist Bungalow*, which used to be the best deal in town.

Top-end accommodation includes the *Caravan Serai*, *Siachen*, *Broadway Suru View* and the *D'Zojila*.

Places to Eat The food is little better than the accommodation but with buses arriving late at night and leaving at crack of dawn, it's unlikely you'll get much of a chance to sample Kargil cuisine. The *Naktul* is easily the best in town and provides Chinese dishes. Otherwise the *Marjina Tourist Home* leads the pack, with the *Babu* and *New Light* taking the overflow and those fooled by the rash promises of French, Italian, German, Chinese and Tibetan cuisine.

Getting There & Away As well as the daily buses to Leh and Srinagar, there are daily services to Mulbekh, Drass and Pannikar, and twice-daily services to Sauku and Trespone.

The Zanskar bus service is a lot less reliable. Basically a bus leaves for Padum twice a week (Rs 65), although the frequency decreases at either end of the summer. Check with the Tourist Reception Centre, and consider hitching with a private truck (around Rs 100). Jeep hire to Padum will set you back about Rs 4500.

Shergol

Between Kargil and Shergol you cross the dividing line between the Muslim and Buddhist areas. The small village of Shergol has a tiny **gompa** perched halfway up the eastern slope of the mountain.

Mulbekh

There are two gompas on the hillside above the village of Mulbekh. As in other villages, it is wise to enquire if the gompa is open before making the ascent. If not, somebody from the village may have keys and will accompany you to the gompas.

Just beyond Mulbekh is a huge **Chamba statue**, an image of a future Buddha, cut into the rock face beside the road. It's one of the most interesting stops along the road to Leh. Those with time to spare can make a short trek from Mulbekh to the village of **Gel**.

Lamayuru

From Mulbekh the road crosses the 3718-metre Namika La, passes through the large military encampment of Bodh Kharbu and then crosses the 4094-metre Fatu La, the highest pass on the route.

Lamayuru is the first of the typical Ladakhi gompas perched on a hilltop with its village at the foot of the hill. In its heyday the **gompa** had five buildings and as many as 400 monks, but today there is only one building, tended by 20 or 30 monks.

Rizong

On beyond Khalsi, and a few km off the road, is the **nunnery of Julichen** and the **monastery** of Rizong. If you stay here overnight

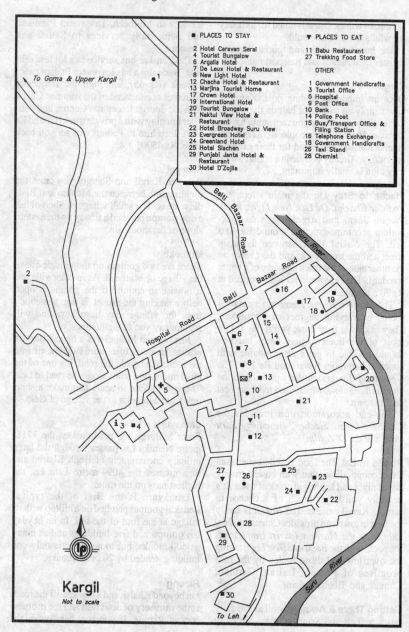

■ PLACES TO STAY

2 Hotel Caravan Seral
4 Tourist Bungalow
6 Argalia Hotel
7 De Leux Hotel & Restaurant
8 New Light Hotel
12 Chacha Hotel & Restaurant
13 Marjina Tourist Home
17 Crown Hotel
19 International Hotel
20 Tourist Bungalow
21 Naktul View Hotel & Restaurant
22 Hotel Broadway Suru View
23 Evergreen Hotel
24 Greenland Hotel
25 Hotel Siachen
29 Punjabi Janta Hotel & Restaurant
30 Hotel D'Zojila

▼ PLACES TO EAT

11 Babu Restaurant
27 Trekking Food Store

OTHER

1 Government Handicrafts
3 Tourist Office
5 Hospital
10 Post Office
14 Bank
14 Police Post
15 Bus/Transport Office & Filling Station
16 Telephone Exchange
18 Government Handicrafts
26 Taxi Stand
28 Chemist

To Gorna & Upper Kargil

Balti Bazaar Road

Balti Bazaar Road

Bazaar Road

Suru River

Balti

Hospital Road

Kargil

Not to scale

Suru River

To Leh

men must stay in the monastery, women in the nunnery.

Alchi

Near Saspul, this gompa is unusual in that it is built on lowland, not perched on a hilltop. It is noted for its massive **Buddha statues** and lavish woodcarvings and the only examples of Kashmiri-style wall paintings in the area. There are many *chortens* around the village.

There are two hotels here with basic rooms (Rs 80 to Rs 120 for doubles) and some dormitory accommodation. There's also a pleasant little hotel in Saspul; it makes a good base for visiting Rizong, Alchi and Lekir.

Lekir & Basgo

Shortly after Saspul a steep road turns off to the Lekir Gompa, which also has a monastery school. Closer to Leh there is a badly damaged **fort** at Basgo. The Basgo Gompa has interesting **Buddha figures**, although its wall paintings have suffered much water damage.

LEH

Population: 22,000

Centuries ago this was an important stop on the old caravan silk route from China. Today it's merely a military base and tourist centre, but wandering the winding back streets of the town is still fascinating. It's about 10 km north-east of the Indus River in a fertile side valley.

Orientation

Leh is small enough to make finding your way around very easy. There's one main street with the Leh Palace rising up at the end of it. The bus station and jeep halt is on the southern or airport side of town. The airport, with its steeply sloping runway, is several km out of town near the Spitok Gompa.

Information

The tourist office (☎ 497) is inconveniently located in the Tourist Reception Centre, on the road to the airport. It has very little information but is a good place to rent trekking gear. They have surprisingly high quality tents for Rs 20 per day (Rs 100 per week) as well as jackets (Rs 16 per day) and boots (Rs 20 per day). Trekking equipment can also be rented from the Nezer View Guest House for similar prices.

The Ladakh Ecological Development Group (LEDeG) has a solar demonstration house and a good library on Ladakh. Pick up a copy of their leaflet with important guidelines for tourists in Ladakh. Shorts and bare shoulders, as well as public displays of affection, are not the cultural norm here. It's a sad fact that in recent years visitors have been acting with decreasing sensitivity towards the local people.

Telegrams can be sent from the telegraph office for Rs 5 per word. International calls can be booked here for Rs 180 for three minutes. More convenient is the communications office, Gypsy's World (opposite the Hotel Yak Tail), where you can make international calls without waiting.

Artou Bookshop has the best selection of books on Ladakh and also sells novels and postcards.

If you're feeling the effects of the altitude (3505 metres) and your symptoms do not subside (or get worse) after 36 hours, phone 560 for medical help. The clinic is staffed 24 hours.

Leh Palace

Looking for all the world like a miniature version of the Potala in Lhasa, Tibet, the palace was built in the 16th century. It is now deserted and badly damaged, a legacy of Ladakh's wars with Kashmir in the last century.

The main reason for making the climb up to the palace is for the superb views from the roof. The Zanskar mountains, across the Indus River, look close enough to touch. The palace was recently sold to the Archaeological Survey of India by the Ladakhi royal family (who now reside at nearby Stok) and an ambitious renovation project is underway. Try to get a monk to unlock the preserved, but now unused, central prayer room; it's dusty and spooky, with huge masks looming out of the dark. There's a Rs 5 entry charge and you should watch out for the holes in the floor.

Leh & Tsemo Gompas

The Leh Gompa stands high above the palace and houses manuscripts and paintings. The Red (Tsemo) Gompa, built in 1430, contains a fine three-storey-high seated Buddha image. It's open from 7 to 9 am. The gompa above the Leh and Tsemo gompas is in a very ruined condition but the views down on Leh are superb.

Sankar Gompa

It's an easy stroll to the Sankar Gompa, a couple of km north of the town centre. This interesting little gompa is only open from 7 to 10 am and from 5 to 7 pm, and there's a Rs 10 entry fee. The gompa has electric lighting so an evening visit is worthwhile. Upstairs is an impressive representation of Avalokitesvara complete with 1000 arms and 1000 heads.

Centre for Ecological Development

Next door to the Tsemo-La Hotel is the HQ of the Ladakh Ecological Development Group (LEDeG), which initiates and promotes 'a development strategy for Ladakh that is carefully tailored to its environment, available resources and culture'. This includes solar energy, environmental and health education, strengthening the traditional system of organic farming and publishing books in the local language. Visitors are welcome to hear what LEDeG is all about, and to use the library and the restaurant.

At 3 pm on Monday, Wednesday and Friday the video *Ancient Futures – Learning from Ladakh* is shown. It's well worth seeing but the voice of Helena Norberg-Hodge, who started the Ladakh project and appears in the video, bears a chilling resemblance to that of a recent British prime minister!

Students' Educational & Cultural Movement of Ladakh (SECMOL)

This recently formed movement organises cultural shows to promote traditional art forms. You can meet Ladakhi students and help them practise their English at the meetings held here on Monday and Thursday at 4

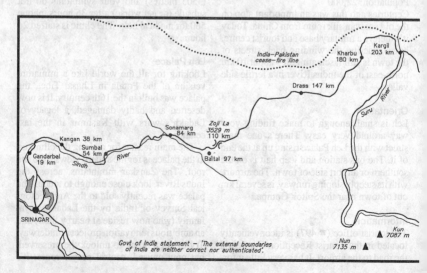

Govt of India statement – 'The external boundaries of India are neither correct nor authenticated'.

pm. SECMOL can also arrange for you to stay with a Ladakhi family.

Meditation

The Mahabodi Society (opposite Hotel Ri-Rab) has a daily group meditation session at 5 pm and sometimes runs meditation courses at Choglamsar.

Places to Stay

There's an amazing number of hotels and guest houses in Ladakh, many of which are only open during the tourist season. Prices are variable – soaring in the peak season, plummeting at other times. Prices quoted here are for the high season. The cheaper guest houses are usually rooms rented out in private homes. Many of the older places still have a traditional Ladakhi stove in the kitchen.

Places to Stay – bottom end

The long-established *Old Ladakh Guest House* has rooms with common bathroom for Rs 40/60 and doubles with attached bath from Rs 100. Other good places in this area with similarly priced rooms include the *Shalimar Guest House*, a clean friendly place

and the nearby *Tak Guest House* which is also popular. The larger *Palace View Kiddar* is much the same. More central and better is the friendly *Khan Manzil Guest House*.

Also away from the more touristy areas of Leh, the *Namgyal Hotel* is popular with budget travellers. Doubles are from Rs 45 or Rs 60 for the upstairs rooms, all with common bath. Beside the archery stadium, *Firdous Hotel* is a friendly little place with doubles for Rs 60 or Rs 100 with attached bath.

In the northern part of the town, the *Hotel Shangrila* is a very pleasant place run by a helpful family. Rooms are Rs 40/80, all with common bath but hot water is supplied free of charge. The *Antelope Guest House* is another clean and friendly place with great views up to Leh Palace. They have some small singles at Rs 50 and doubles for Rs 120 or Rs 180 with attached bathroom. The nearby *Hotel Himalaya* is rather run down, with doubles from Rs 100 or Rs 150 with bath.

The *Hotel Tse Mo View* (just north of the Hotel Himalaya) is in a very quiet location (follow the signs through the fields) with rooms with attached bath for Rs 80/120.

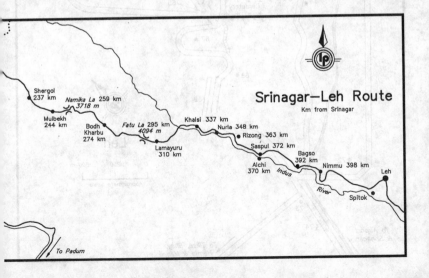

Srinagar–Leh Route
Km from Srinagar

Shergol 237 km
Namika La 259 km
3718 m
Mulbekh 244 km
Bodh Kharbu 274 km
Fatu La 295 km
4094 m
Khalsi 337 km
Lamayuru 310 km
Nurla 348 km
Rizong 363 km
Saspul 372 km
Alchi 370 km
Bagso 392 km
Nimmu 398 km
Leh
Indus River
Spitok

To Padum

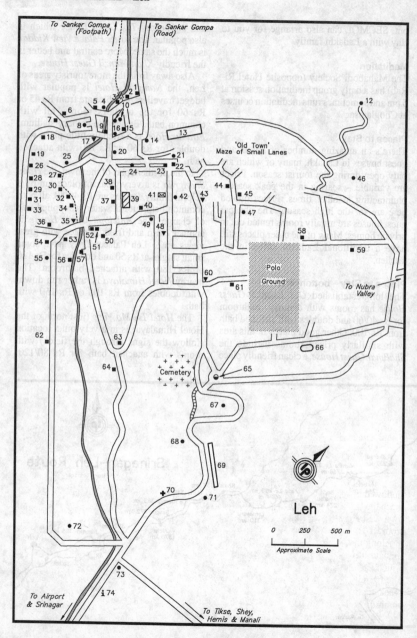

Leh

0   250   500 m

Approximate Scale

To Sankar Gompa
(Footpath)

To Sankar Gompa
(Road)

To Nubra
Valley

'Old Town'
Maze of Small Lanes

Polo
Ground

Cemetery

To Airport
& Srinagar

To Tikse, Shey,
Hemis & Manali

■ PLACES TO STAY

1 Antelope Guest House
2 Hotel Himalaya
3 Hotel Shangrila
5 Tsemo-La Hotel
6 Two Star Guest House
7 Rainbow Guest House
9 Hotel Khang-la-Chhen
15 Khan Manzil Guest House
18 Eagle Guest House
19 Tsavo Guest House
23 Hilltop Hotel & Restaurant
26 Hotel Omasila
27 Indus Guest House
28 Otsal Guest House
29 Asia Guest House
30 Ti-sei Guest House
31 Larchang Guest House
32 Dehlux Hotel
33 Hotel Ri-Rab
34 Bimla Guest House
36 Lung-Se-Jung Hotel
37 Hotel Galdan Continental
38 Hotel Lingzi
40 Hotel Ibex
44 Tak Guest House
45 Old Ladakh Guest House
50 Khangri Hotel & Restaurant
51 Dreamland Hotel & Restaurant
52 Hotel Yak Tail
53 Hotel Rockland
54 Hotels Lha-ri-Mo & K-Sar
56 Padma Guest House
57 Hotel Choskor
58 Palace View Hotel
59 Namgyal Hotel
61 Palace View Kiddar Hotel
62 Mandala Hotel
63 Dragon Hotel & Nezer
   View Guest House
64 Hotel Hills View

▼ PLACES TO EAT

17 Mentokling Restaurant
35 German Bakery Restaurant
43 Chang Pubs
48 La Montessori Restaurant
60 Burman Restaurant

OTHER

4 Ecological Development Centre
8 Circuit House
10 Police Station
12 Leh & Tsemo Gompas
13 Palace
14 Syed Ali Shah's Postcards
16 Moravian Church
20 Artou Bookshop
21 Mosque
22 Small Plaza
24 State Bank
25 SECMOL
39 Vegetable Market
41 Post Office
42 Telegraph Office
46 Buddha Picture
47 Delite Cinema (no sign)
49 Taxi Stand
55 Indian Airlines
65 Bus Station
66 National Archery Stadium
67 Large Chorten
68 Handicraft Training Centre
69 Mani Wall
70 Hospital
71 Radio Station
72 Mani Wall
73 Stone Signpost
74 Tourist Reception Centre

Follow the path towards Sankar Gompa to reach the spotless *Hotel Kailash*, surrounded by a walled garden and fields. Doubles are from Rs 100, all with common bathroom.

Along the path from the German Bakery Restaurant is a group of popular places which have lovely gardens and great views. The friendly *Bimla* is at the top of this price bracket, charging Rs 80/150 for rooms with common bath, Rs 150/200 with bath. The *Indus* has singles/doubles for Rs 60/100 or Rs 150 for a double with an attached bath-

room and solar-heated water. The *Dehlux* is similarly priced, as is the last in the row, the *Ti-sei* with a nice garden and a traditional Ladakhi kitchen.

Up past the Tsemo-La Hotel, the *Karzoo Guest House* has doubles from Rs 60. The nearby *Two Star Guest House* is another favourite, with doubles from Rs 70 and dorm beds for Rs 30. Further along this road is the *Mansoor Guest House* with a friendly family atmosphere and rooms from Rs 40. To the south of the road is the *Rainbow Guest*

House, good value at Rs 30/40 for rooms with common bath.

Changspa village is about 10 minutes walk from Leh and is a good place to escape the noise. The *Eagle Guest House* has double rooms for Rs 50/70. The *Tsavo* is very basic but is an authentic Ladakhi home and has doubles from Rs 40. The *Otsal, Asia* and *Larchang* have rooms for Rs 40/60 and the *Greenland Guest House* opposite is a little cheaper. The *Rinchens Guest House* further down this road has clean rooms for Rs 50 a double or Rs 150 with attached bath. A further 10 minutes walk away is the popular *Oriental Guest House* which has doubles from Rs 50 and is run by a very friendly family.

South of the centre of Leh are two recommended places. The *Padma Guest House* is very clean and has a pleasant garden. Rooms are Rs 50/75 for singles/doubles or Rs 120/200 with attached bath. They do a good Ladakhi dinner here for Rs 20. The *Nezer View Guest House* has rooms from Rs 40/60, Rs 120 with attached bath. The guy who runs it is very helpful and also rents out trekking equipment.

Places to Stay – middle

The *Yasmin Guest House* (opposite Hotel Rockland) has doubles for Rs 150, with hot water supplied in buckets. Their prices will probably have risen considerably following recent renovations. The *Hotel Choskor* has doubles with attached baths for Rs 150. The *Hotel Rockwood* charges Rs 250 for doubles with attached baths and *Hotel Bijoo* (near Hotel Choskor) has singles/doubles for Rs 255/355, all with baths.

The *Lung-Se-Jung*, down past the Dreamland Restaurant is popular, if only because of the reliable evening supply of hot water. Rooms cost Rs 150/250. The *Ibex* is similarly priced. Below the main town, the *Dragon Hotel* has nice surroundings and better rooms for the same price. Nearby is the *Hotel Hills View*, with rooms for Rs 70/100 with common bath or Rs 200 for a double with attached bath. The new *Hotel Horzay* is nearby with doubles for Rs 300.

The *Siachen Hotel* has rooms from Rs 200/300 with attached bathrooms but has nothing to recommend it other than being right beside the bus stand.

Places to Stay – top end

With singles/doubles at Rs 595/775 including meals, Leh's top-end places include the *Tsemo-La* (☎ 281), the central *Khangri* (☎ 251), the *Lha-ri-Mo* (☎ 301) and the *K-Sar* (☎ 548) next door, the *Mandala* further down the road, the *Hotel Galdan Continental* (☎ 373) in the town centre, and the *Shambala* out of town towards the edge of the valley.

The *Hotel Omasila* has an attractive garden and is in a peaceful location. Without meals, doubles are Rs 400.

Places to Eat

The centrally located *Dreamland Restaurant* has good food at reasonable prices. The Tibetan specialities and noodle dishes are a pleasant change from rice and more rice. They also make nice jasmine tea. This is a Leh favourite which has been able to outlast any of the competition. The basic *Tibetan Restaurant Devi* has managed to maintain its reputation for great, cheap, nourishing food. Vegetable thukpa costs Rs 10. It's just up the road from the vegetable market, or down the road from the State Bank of India.

La Montessori serves up big portions of very tasty Chinese, Tibetan and some Western favourites and is popular with local monks. The *Tibetan Friends Corner Restaurant*, near the taxi stand, is another established favourite. Although most of the dishes are Tibetan and very good, it has the reputation for producing the best French fries in Ladakh.

The open-air *Mentokling Restaurant* is a good place to go in the evening. They serve up interesting versions of hummus, falafel, cakes, pies and generally unusual dishes for this part of the world. There's a bar and good music. The newer *Mona Lisa* (near the Ecological Development Centre) is a similar place with tables in the garden and it gets quite lively in the evening. There's also a bar here and as well as the usual drinks it serves chang for a steep Rs 15 a shot. It's much cheaper in the unofficial (illegal) chang pubs behind the main street.

The *Ecological Development Centre* offers good coffee, herbal tea, walnut cookies and cakes. Service is rather slow but the boiled potatoes and fried spinach with garlic are very good. They do a special Ladakhi dinner (which must be ordered in advance) for Rs 70. It's all cooked by solar power and cake is only included in the menu if the sun's been shining all day.

The *German Bakery Restaurant* (near the Hotel Yak Tail) is a great place for a cup of coffee and a cream cheese and tomato sandwich. Other popular items on the menu include carrot juice, cinnamon rolls and pizza. They also have a shop near the vegetable market where you can buy excellent trekking bread (Rs 32) that keeps fresh for several days, and they will make up packed lunches (Rs 45 to Rs 60) for long bus trips. Lastly, there's good fresh bread in the early mornings from the bakery stalls in the street behind the mosque. This Middle Eastern-style bread is excellent with honey – bring some from Srinagar.

Entertainment

The Cultural & Traditional Society (CATS) puts on a cultural show each evening opposite the Hotel Yak Tail. Tickets are Rs 50. It's a bit touristy but the performers take it very seriously, sometimes rehearsing late into the night.

Things to Buy

After a number of greedy tourists spirited important antiquities out of Ladakh, the government sensibly clamped down on the sale of important older items. You must be able to prove that anything you buy is less than 100 years old. Baggage is checked on departure from Leh airport.

Things you might buy include *chang* and tea vessels, cups and butter churns, knitted carpets with Tibetan motifs, Tibetan jewellery or, for just a few rupees, a simple prayer flag. Prices in Ladakh are generally quite high – you might find exactly the same Tibetan-inspired item on sale at far lower prices in Kashmir, Dharamsala or Nepal.

Syed Ali Shah's postcard shop is well worth a visit. What the elderly proprietor sells is not actually postcards but a range of photographs he's taken himself over the years. They cost from Rs 10 to over Rs 100.

Getting There & Away

Air Indian Airlines has flights from Delhi (US$86), Srinagar (US$39), Jammu (US$39) and Chandigarh (US$54). The flight from Srinagar is very short (30 minutes) and extremely spectacular (you cross right over the Himalaya) but also very problematic.

Flights can only be made into Leh in the morning and only when weather conditions are good. If there's a possibility that conditions could deteriorate after arrival in Leh and the aircraft could not leave, the flight will be cancelled. The end result is a lot of cancellations, a lot of flights that actually leave Srinagar but are not able to land at Leh (since conditions can change very rapidly) and a lot of frustrated passengers.

At difficult times of the year, such as when the season is about to start but the roads are still closed, the flights can be heavily overbooked. The answer is to book well ahead but be prepared for disappointment. If you're unable to get on a flight from Srinagar ask your houseboat owner for help – every Kashmiri has 'connections'.

The Indian Airlines office (☎ 276) is near the Hotel Lha-ri-Mo, not far from the centre of town.

Bus There are two overland routes into Leh: the road from Srinagar and the recently opened road from Manali (Himachal Pradesh).

A complication when trying to leave Leh for Srinagar or Manali is that you may not be able to buy tickets on the local buses until the evening before departure, because buses may not turn up from either of these places. Thus you can't be certain you will be leaving until the last moment. These two routes are very heavily booked in both directions at the height of the season (August). You have to book days ahead.

To/From Srinagar The Srinagar-Leh road should be open from the beginning of June to October, but in practice the opening date can be variable – sometimes mid-May, sometimes mid-June. The trip takes two days, about 12 hours travel on each day. The overnight halt is made at Kargil. There is a variety of bus classes with fares from around Rs 120 to Rs 250. Jeeps, which take up to six passengers, will cost Rs 4600 but will permit additional stops and diversions along the interesting route.

Before the Srinagar-Leh road officially opens it's possible to cross the Zoji La on foot or by pony, although if there is still a lot of snow the Beacon Patrol will only let you through if you're properly equipped. The pass is cleared of snow before the road is repaired and ready for vehicles, and there is usually transport running along the roads on both sides of the pass before the through buses start to operate. Locals cross the pass regularly on foot in the pre-season so it is easy to tag along with a larger group or find a guide. But it can be hard work!

To/From Manali The new Manali-Leh road is open for a shorter period, usually from mid-July to mid-September, but again the opening and closing dates can be variable. At present the most comfortable bus is the one operated by Himachal Tourism from their office opposite the Dreamland Hotel. Since the road goes up to 5328 metres at its highest point most people suffer the effects of the altitude (headaches, nausea) unless they have spent some time acclimatising in Leh. If you plan to fly one way, then fly into Leh and take the bus out since the altitude gain on the bus journey will not be so great as doing the journey in the other direction.

Tickets to Manali on Himachal Tourism's bus cost Rs 500 and go on sale from 9 am on the day before the bus departs. No advance booking is possible and in the high season you may need to join the queue several hours

early. The bus leaves at 6 am and the journey takes two days with an overnight stop at Sarchu. Himachal Tourism has dormitory accommodation here in tents for the outrageously high price of Rs 75. The alternative to this bus is the less comfortable local buses which run from Leh bus station for Rs 350, departing at 4 am. An even cheaper option is to hitch a lift in a truck, which costs around Rs 100. At the other end of the scale, a jeep will set you back Rs 8625.

Getting Around
To/From the Airport The bus service from Leh to the airport costs Rs 5 but it doesn't run regularly; a jeep or taxi costs Rs 58.

Bus The enquiry office (☎ 285) is in the dirty stone building with green windows on the north side of the bus station.

There's a reasonably extensive network around Leh of both state road transport and private buses. The main services from Leh are:

To	Distance	Buses Daily	Fare
Choglamsar	8 km	4	Rs 1.75
Chushot	25 km	3	Rs 5.00
Hemis	45 km	1	Rs 12.00
Khalsi	98 km	2	Rs 25.00
Matho	27 km	2	Rs 5.00
Phyang	22 km	3	Rs 7.00
Sabu	9 km	3	Rs 2.00
Sakti	51 km	2	Rs 12.00
Saspul	62 km	2	Rs 14.00
Shey	16 km	5	Rs 3.50
Spitok	8 km	5	Rs 2.00
Stok	17 km	2	Rs 5.00
Tikse	20 km	3	Rs 6.00

There are buses to Alchi (Rs 19) on Wednesday and Sunday at 8.30 am. You can walk to Saspul (2 km from Alchi) to catch a bus back to Leh. There are also buses to further afield. The enquiry office at the bus station has the full details. Services are much less frequent in winter.

Jeep & Taxi Jeeps can also be hired and, although not cheap, for a group of people they can be a good alternative to the crowds and delays of the buses. The fares are set by the Taxi Drivers' Union for certain popular routes. A return trip to Spitok with an hour at the gompa costs Rs 150. A six-hour return trip from Leh covering Shey, Tikse and Hemis costs Rs 621, with an hour's wait at each monastery. Other set charges include Manali (Rs 8625), Srinagar (Rs 4600), Kargil (Rs 2070) and Leh airport (Rs 58). Per km, charges for taxis and jeeps are Rs 7 plus a waiting charge of Rs 20 per hour or Rs 200 per night. Check the current charges at the taxi union office at the taxi stand and try to negotiate a lower price directly with the drivers.

AROUND LEH
Rafting

Several agencies in Leh are now running white-water rafting trips on the Indus. Prices are around Rs 600 per person for a day trip. Himalayan Adventure Extraordinary (near Hotel Ibex) and Fargo Tours & Travels are two companies that have been recommended.

Spitok Gompa

On a hilltop above the Indus and beside the end of the airport runway, the Spitok Gompa is 10 km from Leh. The temple (Gonkhang) is about 1000 years old. There's an entry fee of Rs 13 and there are fine views over the Indus from the gompa. The walk out here from Leh is uninteresting as it's straight through the large army camp – 'rather like walking round Aldershot', remarked one reader!

Phyang

About 24 km from Leh, on the road back towards Srinagar, the gompa has 50 monks and the entry fee is Rs 10. There is an interesting little village below the gompa.

Beacon Highway & Nubra Valley

At present, you are not allowed to visit the Nubra Valley without special permission, but this whole area may soon be open to foreigners. Check the latest situation with the tourist office in Leh. Access to the Nubra Valley is

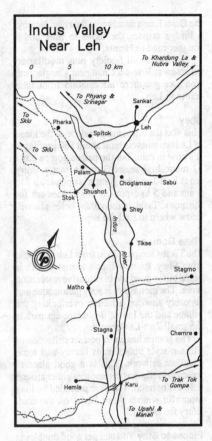

over the Khardung La (5606 metres) which makes this the highest motorable road in the world. It's only open in September and October – it takes the whole summer for the snow and ice to melt for that brief time.

Tibetan Refugee Camp

The refugee camp at Choglamsar has become an important centre for the study of Tibetan literature and history, and Buddhist philosophy. Don't indulge the kids who demand 'bonbons' – it turns them into beggars.

The impressive temporary residence of

the Dalai Lama stands near the river. Nearby, a bridge crosses the Indus to Stok and a rougher road to Hemis.

The Mahabodi Society runs **meditation courses** at Rde-wa Chan near Choglamsar. You can get more information from their centre in Leh.

Shey

This was the old summer palace of the kings of Ladakh and was built about 560 years ago. It's now in ruins but the palace gompa has a 12-metre-high seated **Buddha image**. Entry fee is Rs 10 and the gompa is open from 7 to 9 am and 5 to 6 pm. At other times ask for the monk, Tashi, in the village below; he will know where to find the key.

Tikse Gompa

The Tikse Gompa, 17 km from Leh, is visible from Shey. Its new-found tourist wealth is being put to good use in extensive restoration work. The monastery is very picturesque and superbly sited on a hilltop overlooking the village and the Indus. Beside the car park is the small **Zan-La Temple**.

The gompa has an important collection of Tibetan-style books in its library and some excellent artwork. This is a good place to watch the religious ceremonies either around 6.30 am or noon. They are preceded by long mournful sounds from horns on the roof. Entry fee is Rs 15.

Places to Stay You can get good doubles at the *Skalzang Chamba Hotel*. There are no dorm beds or singles here.

Karu

The road to Manali climbs out of the Indus Valley after this village. Twenty minutes beyond Karu there is a stop at the police checkpoint at Upshi. There are a number of tea shops here.

Hemis Gompa

Hemis Gompa, one of the largest and most important gompas in Ladakh, is 45 km from Leh on the western side of the Indus. It's easy to get there by car or jeep, but on public transport you will have to spend the night at the monastery as it is not easy to bus out there from Leh, walk the six km up from the river to the gompa, see it, walk back down and get back to Leh in one day.

The Hemis Gompa is famous for its **Hemis Festival**, which usually falls in the second half of June or in early July. This is one of the largest and most spectacular of the gompa festivals and at one time was virtually the only one which took place in the summer tourist season. The business-minded monks at some other gompas are now switching their festivals to more lucrative dates. The festival takes two days and features elaborate mask dances and crowds of eager spectators.

The gompa has an excellent library, well-preserved wall paintings and good Buddha figures. Entry fee is Rs 15.

If instead of turning right at Karu to climb up to Hemis you turn left, you reach the **Chemre Gompa**, five km off the road, and the **Trak Tok Gompa**, 10 km further on. Both lie in the restricted zone but tourists are allowed to visit them.

Guru Padmasambhava, Hemis Festival

Places to Stay At Hemis there's a *rest house/restaurant* with rather dirty dorm beds. You'll find cheaper and much cleaner rooms in local homes. The *Parachute Restaurant*, next to the bus stand, has good food.

Matho Gompa

The west-bank road on the Indus is not in as good condition as the more frequently used east-bank road, but you can return from Hemis on it and there are several interesting places to visit. Matho is in a side valley five km from Stagna, and in an important festival here the monks are possessed by spirits and go into a trance. **Stagna**, on the west-bank road, has a gompa too.

Stok Palace

Close to the Choglamsar bridge, a road turns off the west-bank road to the palace of Stok. The last king of Ladakh died in 1974 but his widow, the Rani of Stok, still lives in this 200-year-old palace. It is expected that her eldest son will become king when he reaches an auspicious age. You can only enter the museum here, which costs Rs 20 and is open from 7 am to 7 pm.

Pharka Gompa

This small cave gompa is almost directly opposite the Spitok Gompa on the Stok side of the Indus. You can reach it by crossing the Choglamsar bridge or the bridge near Spitok, but the last few km must be made on foot.

LEH TO MANALI

This road was opened to foreigners only in 1989 and has rapidly become a popular way into and out of Leh. It's the world's second-highest motorable road, reaching an elevation of 5328 metres at Taglang La. Buses run along this route during the summer season (see Getting There & Away for Leh and Manali). Since only about half of the total distance of 485 km between Leh and Manali is paved it can be a rough journey, especially if you're in the back of the bus.

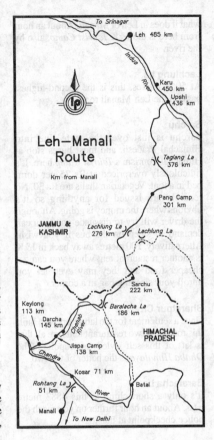

Leh–Manali Route

Km from Manali

- To Srinagar
- Leh 485 km
- Karu 450 km
- Upshi 436 km
- Taglang La 376 km
- Pang Camp 301 km
- Lachlung La 276 km
- Sarchu 222 km
- Baralacha La 186 km
- Darcha 145 km
- Jispa Camp 138 km
- Keylong 113 km
- Kosar 71 km
- Rohtang La 51 km
- Batal
- Manali
- To New Delhi

JAMMU & KASHMIR

HIMACHAL PRADESH

Indus River, Chenab River, Chandra River

Taglang La

A rough road leads to this pass, at 5328 metres, the highest on the road. There's a little **temple** here and you can get a free cup of tea at the government tea shop. The two other structures up here are clearly labelled: 'Gents Urinal' and 'Ladies Urinal'! There are superb views back down the valley.

Pang Camp

A number of restaurants in tents have been set up by the river and most buses stop here for lunch. A plate of rice, dhal and veg costs Rs 15. A bottle of mineral water costs twice what it does in Leh or Manali. About an hour from here is the J&K *Tourist Camp*, also by the river.

Lachlung La

At 5065 metres, this is the second-highest pass on the Leh-Manali road.

Sarchu

Sarchu is just over the state line into Himachal Pradesh, and most buses stop at Himachal Tourism's *Tourist Camp* here. It's ridiculously overpriced at Rs 75 per dorm bed in a tent. Vegetarian thalis are Rs 30. No receipts are issued for anything so it's obvious where the money is going. Although the driver will try to dissuade you, you can demand to sleep on the bus if you wish. Alternatively, 100 metres away back in J&K is another restaurant tent where you can get cheaper food and they may even let you unroll your sleeping bag in a corner.

Bharatpur City

Once a settlement for the labourers who built this road, just two restaurant tents are all that is left of this self-styled 'metropolis'. The *Dhaba Himalaya* is the better of the two.

Baralacha La

It's only a short climb to this 4883 metre pass. About an hour further on you reach the police checkpoint at Patsio.

Darcha

There are half a dozen small restaurants in this small community by the Chenab River. Shortly after Darcha you pass through Jispa, where there is a large army camp.

Keylong to Manali

Keylong is the first town of any size on the journey from Leh to Manali, and the administrative capital of Lahaul and Spiti in which several interesting treks can be made. See the Himachal Pradesh section for more details. After a lunch stop at **Kosar**, where there's an impressive waterfall, you cross the Rohtang La (3978 metres) and descend to Manali.

Zanskar

The long, narrow Zanskar Valley was opened even more recently than Ladakh. A jeep road has now reached all the way from Kargil to Padum, the capital, and although it is not open all the time, it has opened the area up to more outside influence.

For the moment at least, it remains an area for trekkers, and some of the treks are definitely hard going. You can make a number of interesting ones either down the valley or out of it to Ladakh, Kashmir or Himachal Pradesh.

PADUM

The 'capital' of Zanskar has a population of around 1000, of whom about 300 are Sunni Muslims. It's on the southern part of a wide fertile plain where two rivers join to form the Zanskar River.

There is a tourist bureau where you can arrange accommodation and the hire of horses. On arrival in Padum you must register with the Tourism Department.

Places to Stay

There's a limited choice of a few basic hotels, and rooms in private houses. The *Shapodok-la*, in the centre of town, has cheap dorm beds. The *Haftal View* and *Ibex* hotels have rooms from Rs 35 to Rs 60 but the similarly priced *Chora-la* is probably the best of the bunch. The *Tourist Bungalow* is more expensive but has doubles with attached bath.

AROUND PADUM
Zangla & Karsha Gompa

This is an interesting four-day trek around Padum. The first day takes you to **Thonde** on the riverbank with a monastery high above it. Since horses cannot cross the rope bridge from Padum, this is the first place on this side of the river where they can be hired for treks further afield to places like Lamayuru.

The second day takes you from Thonde to **Zangla**, where the king of Zanskar has his castle. On day three you backtrack towards Thonde, cross the river and continue to **Karsha**, the most important gompa in Zanskar. On the final day you can cross the river directly by ferry or continue down to the wooden Tungri Bridge and double back to Padum.

Tungri-Zongkhul Gompa Round Trip
This four-day trek around Padum takes you to the Sani and Zongkhul gompas by following the route up towards the Muni La, then cutting across to the base of the Umasi La.

TREKS IN LADAKH & ZANSKAR
Trekking in Ladakh and Zanskar can be hard going and you should be equipped for every eventuality. You can get basic supplies and rent gear in Srinagar and Leh but you won't find trekking gear like that available in Kathmandu, Nepal. There are a number of agencies in Leh that will organise things for you for between Rs 500 and Rs 1000 per day depending on the length of the trek and the number of people. Many travellers organise their treks independently, renting a horse and horseman at the start of the trek (eg at Stok or Spitok) for Rs 150 to Rs 250 per day. This is a good idea as the horseman can then also act as a guide.

Treks into Zanskar are principally down the valley from the north (from Kargil) or up the valley from the south (from Manali in Himachal Pradesh). Remember to take your garbage out with you; many areas are already becoming fouled with trekkers' rubbish.

Drass to Sanku
This is a short three-day trek into the Suru Valley joining the Kargil to Padum road at Sanku. It's simply an alternative route to the road down from Kargil.

Kargil to Padum
Although there is a road all the way to Padum, it is not always open all the way and is rough going at the best of times. The seven-day trek from Kargil on the Srinagar to Ladakh road can be shortened by four days if you can get a ride all the way from Kargil to the Pensi La. When all bridges are open the route is accessible from early June to late October.

The first day's travel is mainly on a surfaced road by bus to Sanku. Beyond Parkutse you pass close to Kun and Nun. The Rangdum Gompa is the first gompa reached in Zanskar; the road is still reasonably good to this point. Beyond the gompa you have to cross the 4401-metre Pensi La into Zanskar proper. On the last day's walk from Phe to Padum you cross the river and pass by the Sani Gompa, one of the most important in Zanskar.

Day 1	Kargil to Namsuru
Day 2	Namsuru/Pannikar/Parkutse
Day 3	Parkutse/Parkachik/Yuldo/ Rangdum Gompa
Day 4	Rangdum Gompa to Pensi La
Day 5	Pensi La to Abran
Day 6	Abran to Phe
Day 7	Phe to Padum

Manali to Padum
This 10-day trek used to be very hard going at its southern end. But with the opening of the motor road from Leh to Manali you can now go by bus to Baralacha La. Alternatively you can take a bus across the Rohtang Pass from Manali to Keylong and start the trek at Darcha. On the second day you cross the Baralacha La, a double pass where even the lower side is higher than Europe's highest mountain and twice the height of Australia's highest.

At the end of Day 6 you continue north to Padum or turn back south and cross the Shingo La back to Darcha in two days. You are not, however, allowed to take the alternative route if you're heading north. On Day 7 you can make a detour to the spectacular Phuctal Gompa. Continuing all the way north to Kargil on this route would take, with a few days for shorter treks around Padum, something like 20 days.

Day 1	Darcha to Mane Bar
Day 2	Mane Bar to Sarai Kilang
Day 3	Sarai Kilang to Debni
Day 4	Debni to Chumik Marpo
Day 5	Chumik Marpo to Shingsan
Day 6	Shingsan/Kargiakh/Purni
Day 7	Purni to Phuctal Gompa
Day 8	Phuctal Gompa to Katge Lato
Day 9	Katge Lato to Reru
Day 10	Reru to Padum

Padum to Lamayuru

There are a number of alternatives for this trek from Padum into Ladakh, intersecting the road at Lamayuru, about halfway from Kargil to Leh. The trek starts from Padum to Thonde, as on the short trek to the Zangla and Karsha gompas. On Day 3 the difficult ascent to the 4500-metre Shing La pass has to be made, but on Day 4 the Nerag La, at 4900 metres, is even more difficult and a local guide is a necessity. From Photosar, a small village, it is only two days walk to Lamayuru. There is an alternative route from Photosar that takes a day longer. The alternative route from Padum starts out on the opposite side of the Zanskar River and takes you to the Linghsot Gompa before joining up with the first route at Day 5.

Day 1	Padum to Thonde
Day 2	Thonde to Honia
Day 3	Honia/Shing La/Kharmapu
Day 4	Kharmapu to Nerag La
Day 5	Nerag La to Nerag
Day 6	Nerag/Yulching/Singi La/Photosar
Day 7	Photosar/Shirshi La/Hanupatta
Day 8	Hanupatta/Wanla/Shill/Prikiti La/Lamayuru

or

Day 1	Padum to Pishu
Day 2 - 4	Pishu to Linghsot Gompa
Day 3	Linghsot Gompa to Yulching

Padum to Kishtwar

This trek into the southern part of Kashmir is not especially difficult although it crosses the 5234-metre Umasi La, which can only be done in fine weather. You cannot use horses on this route but must take porters.

On the second day you reach the Zongkhul Gompa, which can also be visited on a short trek from Padum. Day 3 is a long climb and long descent over the snow-covered Umasi La. On Day 4 your Zanskari porters will not continue further and you must hire local porters or a pony.

The last few days are hard work with many ascents and descents but the road from Kishtwar, already extending to Galar, is gradually being lengthened.

Day 1	Padum to Ating
Day 2	Ating to Ratrat
Day 3	Ratrat/Umasi La/Bhuswas
Day 4	Bhuswas to Matsel
Day 5	Matsel to Atholi
Day 6	Atholi to Shasho
Day 7	Shasho/Galar/Kishtwar

Other Treks

Padum to Nimmu follows the Padum to Lamayuru route for most of its length, then turns off eastwards to join the Srinagar to Leh road at Nimmu.

Padum to Leh by the Markha Valley is a hard but rewarding trek which goes via Zangla before turning east over the Charcha La and the Ruberung La to the Markha Gompa, and eventually reaching Hemis near Leh. This trek can only be made in late August. Earlier than that the rivers which must be crossed are too high from melting snow and after that it's too cold.

You can trek from Padum to the Phuctal Gompa by an alternative route to that described in Manali to Padum, but the trail is poor and little used.

Uttar Pradesh

Population: 138.8 million
Area: 294,411 sq km
Capital: Lucknow
People per sq km: 471
Main Language: Hindi
Literacy Rate: 41.7%

In terms of population Uttar Pradesh is the largest state in India. In terms of variety and problems, it's also India larger than life. This is one of the great historical and religious centres of India. The Ganges River, which forms the backbone of Uttar Pradesh, is the holy river of Hinduism, and there are several important pilgrimage towns along it. The main ones are Rishikesh and Haridwar, where the river emerges from the Himalaya and starts across the plains, but there's also Varanasi, the most holy city of all. Buddhism also has its great shrine in the state, for it was at Sarnath, just outside Varanasi, that the Buddha first preached his message of the middle way.

Geographically and socially the state varies greatly. Most of it consists of the vast Ganges plain, an area of awesome flatness which often suffers dramatic floods during the monsoon. The people of this region, which is often referred to as the cow belt or the Hindi belt, are predominantly poorly educated farming peasants who scratch a bare existence from the overcrowded land. The north-west corner of the state is a part of the soaring Himalaya, with excellent treks, beautiful scenery and some of India's highest mountains. It's a state of strong contrasts.

In the last few years the state has also become the focus for the right-wing Hindu party, the BJP. The dispute at Ayodhya over the construction of a Hindu temple on the site of an ancient mosque, known as the Ranajanambhumi issue, brought the state to flash point on several occasions in 1992. It also led to riots and killings in other parts of India. The BJP is stirring the pot, and the issue remains unresolved thus far.

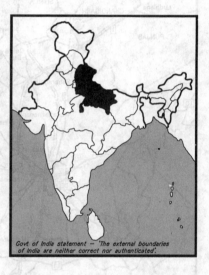

Govt of India statement — 'The external boundaries of India are neither correct nor authenticated'.

History

Over 2000 years ago the state was part of Ashoka's great Buddhist empire. More recently it was part of the Moghul Empire, and for some years Agra was its capital. Today, of course, Agra is famed for that most perfect of Moghul masterpieces, the Taj Mahal. More recently still, it was in Uttar Pradesh that the Mutiny broke out in 1857 (at Meerut) and some of its most dramatic (Lucknow) and unfortunate (Kanpur) events took place.

The state was first known as United Province when Agra was merged with Oudh after the British took over, but was renamed Uttar Pradesh (Northern State) after Independence.

Uttar Pradesh has produced seven of the nine Indian prime ministers since Independence in 1947 – Jawaharlal Nehru, Lal Bahadur Shastri, Indira Gandhi, Charan Singh, Rajiv Gandhi, VP Singh and Chandrasekhar.

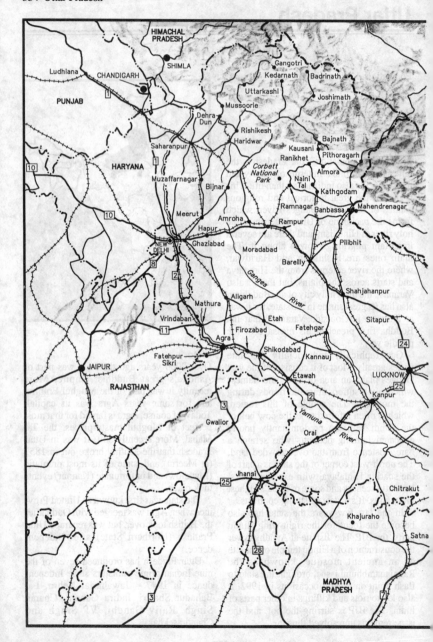

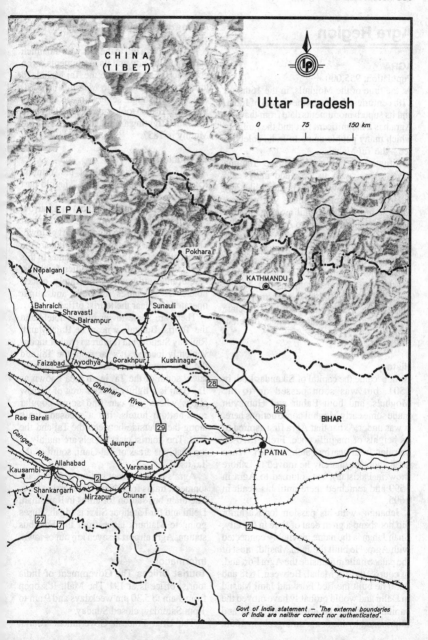

Uttar Pradesh

0   75   150 km

CHINA
(TIBET)

NEPAL

Pokhara

KATHMANDU

Nepalganj

Bahraich
Shravasti
Balrampur

Sunauli

Faizabad   Ayodhya   Gorakhpur   Kushinagar

Ghaghara River   28

                                            28

Rae Bareli

29   BIHAR

Jaunpur   PATNA

Ganges River

Kausambi   Allahabad

Shankargarh   Mirzapur   Chunar   Varanasi

2

27   7

2

Govt of India statement — 'The external boundaries
of India are neither correct nor authenticated'.

Agra Region

AGRA

Population: 955,000

At the time of the Moghuls, in the 16th and 17th centuries, Agra was the capital of India, and its superb monuments date from that era. Agra has a magnificent fort and the building which many people come to India solely to see – the Taj Mahal.

Situated on the banks of the Yamuna River, Agra, with its crowded alleys and predatory rickshaw riders, is much like any other north Indian city, once you're away from its imposing Moghul monuments. It's possible to take a day trip to Agra from Delhi (there's an excellent train service making this eminently practicable); however, Agra is worth more than a day's visit, particularly if you intend to visit, as you certainly should, the deserted city of Fatehpur Sikri. In any case, the Taj certainly deserves more than just a single visit if you want to appreciate how its appearance changes under different lights.

History

Agra became the capital of Sikandar Lodi in 1501, but was soon passed on to the Moghuls, and both Babur and Humayun made some early Moghul constructions here. It was under Akbar that Agra first aspired to its heights of magnificence. From 1570-85 he ruled from nearby Fatehpur Sikri. When he abandoned that city he moved to Lahore (now in Pakistan), but returned to Agra in 1599 and remained there until his death in 1605.

Jehangir, with his passion for Kashmir, did not spend a great deal of time in the city; Shah Jahan is the name inevitably connected with Agra. He built the Jami Masjid, most of the palace buildings inside the Agra Fort and, of course, the Taj Mahal. Between 1638 and 1650 he built the Red Fort and Jami Masjid in Delhi and would probably have moved the capital there had he not been deposed and imprisoned by his son, Aurangzeb, in 1658.

Aurangzeb transferred the capital to its current site.

In 1761, Agra fell to the Jats who did much damage to the city and its monuments, even going so far as to pillage the Taj Mahal. In turn, it was taken by the Marathas in 1770 and went through several more changes before the British took control in 1803. There was much fighting around the fort during the Mutiny in 1857.

Orientation

Agra is on the west bank of the Yamuna River, 204 km south of Delhi. The old part of the town, where you'll find the Kinari Bazaar (the main market place) in a narrow street, is north of the fort. The cantonment area to the south is the modern part of town, known as Sadar Bazaar. On The Mall are the tourist office, GPO and poste restante. In this area you will also find handicraft shops, restaurants and many moderately priced hotels. Deluxe buses for Delhi and Jaipur operate from near the tourist office.

There are some lower priced hotels and the Tourist Bungalow near the Raja Mandi Railway Station, but this area is rather inconveniently located. It's far from the Taj and the main hotel and restaurant area. Immediately south of the Taj in an area known as Taj Ganj is a tightly packed area of narrow alleys where you can find some popular rock-bottom hotels. It's a pleasant walk along the riverside between the Taj and the Fort. The 'tourist class' hotels are mainly in the spacious areas of Taj Ganj, south of the Taj itself.

Agra's main railway station is Agra Cantonment; trains from New Delhi arrive here. The main bus station for cities in Rajasthan, Delhi and for Fatehpur Sikri is Idgah. Buses going to Mathura leave from the Fort bus station. Agra airport is seven km out of town.

Information

Tourist Offices The Government of India tourist office is at 191 The Mall. It's open from 9 am to 5.30 pm weekdays and 9 am to 1 pm Saturday; closed Sunday.

The Uttar Pradesh Government Tourist

Office (☎ 75-034) is on Taj Rd, near the Clarks Shiraz Hotel. There's yet another tourist information counter at the railway station. This counter offers hotel information, but it seems to be caught up in the commission racket and so their recommendations may be biased.

Post & Telecommunications At the time of writing, Agra's phone system was being upgraded. The result is that the old five-digit numbers will probably be six-digit numbers by the time you're reading this. The telephone area code for Agra is 0562.

The post office is on The Mall, opposite the Government of India tourist office.

Bookshops The Modern Book Depot (☎ 36-3133), Sadar Bazaar, has a good selection of general books, including travel guides. Most of their stock is in English, and they also sell cards and stationery.

Commission, Touts & Rip-Offs Of all the cities in India, Agra is the city most seriously entangled in the nefarious activity of giving commission – it seems virtually everyone is into it. From the minute you step off the train or bus, there'll be a rickshaw driver wanting to take you to a hotel, handicraft shop or on a sightseeing tour. They can be tenacious and persistent, and some visitors find this mars their visit to Agra.

The next approach will probably be from a well-dressed young man, complete with cool sunglasses, on a moped, who insists he is a student (often from Punjab) and is interested in learning about your country as a place of study. Well, no genuine Indian student has the sort of funds necessary to be turned out in the manner that these blokes are, and so it can be assumed that they, too, are simply commission agents. An invitation to visit their home inevitably leads straight to a craft shop of some kind (usually belonging to an 'uncle' or 'brother'), where you will be pressured to buy at highly inflated prices. If when first approached you are cool and show a reluctance to talk, they'll try to hang the old guilt trip on you with comments such as: 'Don't you like to talk to Indians?'.

See the section on Things to Buy in the Facts for the Visitor chapter for more details.

Taj Mahal

If there's a building which represents a country – like the Eiffel Tower for France, the Sydney Opera House for Australia – then it has to be the Taj Mahal for India.

This most famous Moghul monument was constructed by Emperor Shah Jahan in memory of his wife Mumtaz Mahal, the 'lady of the Taj'. It has been described as the most extravagant monument ever built for love, for the emperor was heartbroken when Mumtaz, to whom he had been married for 17 years, died in 1629 in childbirth, after producing 14 children.

Construction of the Taj began in 1631 and was not completed until 1653. Workers were recruited not only from all over India but also from central Asia, and in total 20,000 people worked on the building. Experts were even brought from as far away as Europe – the Frenchman Austin of Bordeaux and the Italian Veroneo of Venice had a hand in its decoration. The main architect was Isa Khan, who came from Shiraz in Iran.

The most unusual (but almost certainly apochryphal) story about the Taj is that there might well have been two of them. Shah Jahan, it is said, intended to build a second Taj as his own tomb in black marble, a negative image of the white Taj of Mumtaz Mahal. Before he could embark on this second masterpiece he was deposed by his son, Aurangzeb. Shah Jahan spent the rest of his life imprisoned in the Agra Fort, looking out along the river to the final resting place of his wife.

The Taj is definitely worth more than a single visit as its character changes with the differing lights during the day. Dawn is a magical time, and it's virtually deserted. Fridays tend to be impossibly crowded and noisy – not very conducive to calm enjoyment of this most serene of buildings.

The main entrance to the Taj is a high red sandstone gate, set on the northern edge of

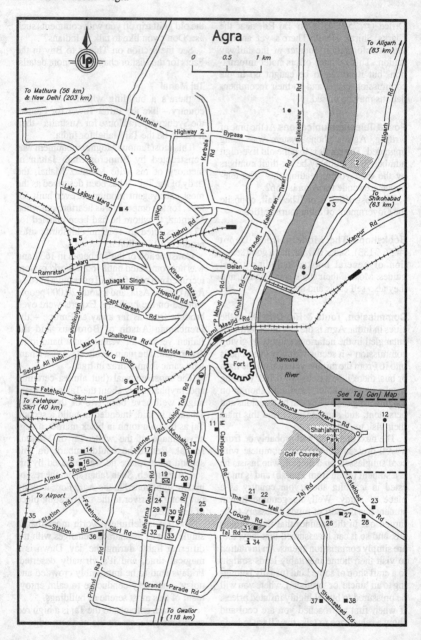

■ PLACES TO STAY		▼ PLACES TO EAT	
4	Youth Hostel	29	Zorba the Buddha Restaurant
5	Tourist Bungalow	30	Prakash Restaurant
10	Kapoor Tourist Rest House	33	Park Restaurant
11	Agra & Akbar Hotels		
13	Tourist Rest House		OTHER
14	Rose Hotel		
16	Seetal Lodge	1	Dayal Bagh Temple
17	Lauries Hotel	2	Ram Bagh
18	Major Bakshi's Tourist House	3	Chini Ka Rauza
20	Agra Ashok Hotel	6	Itimad-ud-daulah's Tomb
21	Hotel Akbar Inn	7	Agra Fort Railway Station
23	Mughal Sheraton Hotel	8	Agra Fort Bus Stand &
26	Mumtaz Hotel		Tourist Guest House
27	Shahanshah Inn	9	Central Methodist Church
28	Taj View Hotel &	12	Taj Mahal
	Mayur Tourist Complex	15	Idgah Bus Station
31	Clarks Shiraz Hotel &	19	GPO
	Indian Airlines Office	22	Archaeological Survey of India
32	Jaiwal Hotel, Kwality &	24	Government of India Tourist Office
	Gaylord Restaurants	25	Telegraph Office
36	Grand Hotel	34	UP Government Tourist Office
37	Highway Inn	35	Agra Cantonment Railway Station
38	Safari Hotel		

an ornamental courtyard, which is lined on the western side with tourist shops, while the eastern side has a police station and administrative offices. You can enter the courtyard from any of the three sides, but tickets (Rs 2; free on Friday) are sold at the eastern and western gates only, a bit of a nuisance if you're coming through the south gate from Taj Ganj. In the very early morning only the western ticket office is open. Opening hours are from 6 am to 7 pm.

The high red sandstone **entrance gateway** is inscribed with verses from the Koran in Arabic, but these days you only exit through here. The entrance is now through a small door to the right of the gate, where everyone has to undergo a security check. If you are carrying a video camera, photography is only allowed from inside the main gate; once you have shot from there (Rs 25) the camera must be deposited in one of the lockers at the desk inside the main gate.

Paths leading from the gate to the Taj are divided by a long **watercourse** in which the Taj is beautifully reflected – if the pool is filled with water! The ornamental gardens through which the paths lead are set out along the classical Moghul lines of a square quartered by watercourses. In spring the flower beds by the paths are a profusion of colour.

The Taj Mahal itself stands on a raised marble platform on the northern edge of the ornamental gardens. Tall, purely decorative white **minarets** grace each corner of the platform – as the Taj Mahal is not a mosque, nobody is called to prayer from them. Twin red sandstone buildings frame the building when viewed from the river; the building on the west side is a mosque, the identical one on the east is purely for symmetry. It cannot be used as a mosque as it faces the wrong direction.

The central Taj structure has four small domes surrounding the huge, bulbous, central dome. The **tombs of Mumtaz Mahal and Shah Jahan** are in a basement room. Above them in the main chamber are false tombs, a common practice in Indian mausoleums of this type. Light is admitted into the central chamber by finely cut marble screens. The echo in this high chamber, under the soaring marble dome, is superb and there is always somebody there to demonstrate it.

Although the Taj is amazingly graceful from almost any angle, it's the close-up detail which is really astounding. Semi-precious stones are inlaid into the marble in beautiful patterns and with superb craft in a process known as *pietra dura*. The precision and care which went into the Taj Mahal's design and construction is just as impressive whether you view it from across the river or from arm's length.

A final sad note about the Taj – scientists fear that after centuries of undiminished glory the modern world may finally be shortening its life. From the Red Fort, a distance of only two km, it is often almost impossible to see the Taj through the cloud of smoke, smog and haze which envelops it. There's a government-owned refinery less than 50 km upstream from the Taj, and this place dumps huge amounts of sulphur dioxide into the atmosphere – legally. To add to that, there are more than 150 registered iron-foundries in the vicinity. The UP government insists that all is fine, but the amount of suspended particles in the air is more than five times what the government itself says is the maximum the Taj can sustain without being damaged.

Environmentalists have finally managed to get a hearing in the supreme court, but unless the state government has the will to tackle the problem seriously, the Taj's future is less than assured. So far the government has only banned new industries within a 50-km radius of the Taj, although existing operations can remain. Not that people haven't damaged the Taj in the past – in 1764 silver doors fitted to the entrance gate were ripped off and carted away, and raiders have also made off with the gold sheets that once lined the subterranean vault.

Agra Fort

Construction of the massive Agra Fort was begun by Emperor Akbar in 1565, and additions were made up until the time of his grandson, Shah Jahan. While in Akbar's time the fort was principally a military structure, by Shah Jahan's time it had become partially a palace. A visit to the fort is an Agra 'must' since so many of the events which led to the construction of the Taj took place here.

There are many fascinating buildings inside the massive walls which stretch for 2½ km, surrounded by a moat over 10 metres wide. The fort is on the banks of the Yamuna River and only the Amar Singh Gate to the south is open. Inside, the fort is really a city within the city. It is open from sunrise to sunset and admission is Rs 2 except on Fridays when it is free. Some of the important buildings within the fort include:

Moti Masjid The Pearl Mosque was built by Shah Jahan between 1646 and 1653. This marble mosque is considered to be perfectly proportioned and a Persian inscription inside the building compares it to a perfect pearl. The mosque's courtyard is surrounded by arcaded cloisters and a marble tank stands in the centre.

Taj Patterns

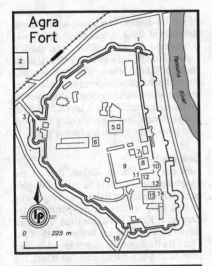

Agra Fort

1	Northern Tower
2	Jami Masjid
3	Delhi Gate
4	Elephant Gate
5	Moti Masjid
6	Ladies' Bazaar
7	Nagina Masjid
8	Diwan-i-Khas
9	Diwan-i-Am
10	Octagonal Tower
11	Mina Mosque
12	Grape Garden
13	Shish Mahal
14	Khas Mahal
15	Jehangir's Palace
16	Amar Singh's Gate

Diwan-i-Am The Hall of Public Audiences was also built by Shah Jahan and replaced an earlier wooden structure. Shah Jahan's predecessors had a hand in the hall's construction, but the throne room, with its typical inlaid marble work, indisputably bears Shah Jahan's influence. Here he sat to meet officials or listen to petitioners. Beside the Diwan-i-Am is the small **Nagina Masjid** or Gem Mosque and the Ladies' Bazaar where merchants came to display and sell goods to the ladies of the Moghul court.

Diwan-i-Khas The Hall of Private Audiences was also built by Shah Jahan in 1636-37. Here the emperor would meet important dignitaries or foreign ambassadors. The hall consists of two rooms connected by three arches. The famous Peacock Throne was kept here before being moved to Delhi by Aurangzeb. It was later carted off to Iran and its remains are now in Tehran.

Octagonal Tower The Musamman Burj, or Octagonal Tower, stands close to the Diwan-i-Khas and the small, private Mina Masjid. Also known as the Saman Burj, this tower was built by Shah Jahan for Mumtaz Mahal and is another of his finely designed buildings. It was here, with its views along the Yamuna to the Taj, that Shah Jahan died in 1666, after seven years' imprisonment. Unfortunately the tower has been much damaged over the years.

Jehangir's Palace Akbar is believed to have built this palace, the largest private residence in the fort, for his son. This was one of the first constructions demonstrating the fort's changing emphasis from military to luxurious living quarters. The palace is also interesting for its blend of Hindu and central Asian architectural styles – a contrast to the unique Moghul style which had developed by the time of Shah Jahan.

Other Buildings Shah Jahan's **Khas Mahal** is a beautiful white marble structure used as a private palace. The rooms underneath it were intended as a cool retreat from the summer heat. The **Shish Mahal** or Mirror Palace is reputed to have been the harem dressing room and its walls are inlaid with tiny mirrors. The **Anguri Bagh** or Grape Garden probably never had any grapevines but was simply a small, formal Moghul garden. It stood in front of the Khas Mahal. The **Delhi Gate** and **Hathi Pol**, or Elephant Gate, are now closed.

In front of the Jehangir Palace is the **Hauz-i-Jehangri**, a huge 'bath' carved out of a single block of stone – by whom and for what purpose is a subject of conjecture. The **Amar**

Singh Gate takes its name from a Maharaja of Jodhpur who was killed beside the gate, along with his followers, after a brawl in the Diwan-i-Am in 1644! Justice tended to be summary in those days; there is a shaft leading down to the river into which those who made themselves unpopular with the great Moghuls could be hurled without further ado.

Itimad-ud-daulah

There are several interesting sights on the opposite bank of the Yamuna and north of the fort. You cross the river on a narrow two-level bridge carrying pedestrians, bicycles, rickshaws and bullock carts. The first place of interest is the exquisite Itimad-ud-daulah – the tomb of Mirza Ghiyas Beg. This Persian gentleman was Jehangir's *wazir*, or Chief Minister, and his beautiful daughter later married the emperor. She then became known as Nur Jahan, the Light of the World, and her niece was Mumtaz Mahal, the lady of the Taj. The tomb was constructed by Nur Jahan between 1622 and 1628 and is very similar to the tomb she constructed for her husband, Jehangir, near Lahore in Pakistan.

The tomb is of particular interest since many of its design elements foreshadow the Taj, construction of which started only a few years later. The Itimad-ud-daulah was the first Moghul structure totally constructed of marble and the first to make extensive use of *pietra dura*, the inlay work of marble which is so characteristic of the Taj. The mausoleum is small and squat compared to the soaring Taj, but the smaller, more human scale somehow makes it attractive, and the beautifully patterned surface of the tomb is superb. Extremely fine marble lattice-work passages admit light to the interior. It's well worth a visit. The Itimad-ud-daulah is open from sunrise to sunset and admission is Rs 2; free on Fridays. The tomb is often referred to locally as the 'baby Taj', although the comparison is largely irrelevant and inappropriate.

Chini Ka Rauza

The China Tomb is one km north of the Itimad-ud-daulah. The squat, square tomb, surmounted by a single huge dome, was constructed by Afzal Khan, who died at Lahore in 1639. He was a high official in the court of Shah Jahan. The exterior was covered in brightly coloured enamelled tiles and the whole building clearly displayed its Persian influence. Today it is much decayed and neglected, and the remaining tile work only hints at the building's former glory.

Ram Bagh

Laid out in 1528 by Babur, first of the Moghul emperors, this is the earliest Moghul garden. It is said that Babur was temporarily buried here before being permanently interred at Kabul in Afghanistan. The Ram Bagh is two to three km further north of the Chini Ka Rauza on the riverside and is open from sunrise to sunset; admission is free. It's rather overgrown and neglected.

Jami Masjid

Across the railway tracks from the Delhi Gate of Agra Fort, the Jami Masjid was built by Shah Jahan in 1648. An inscription over the main gate indicates that it was built in the name of Jahanara, Shah Jahan's daughter, who was imprisoned with Shah Jahan by Aurangzeb. Large though it is, the mosque is not as impressive as Shah Jahan's Jami Masjid in Delhi.

Other Attractions

The **Kinari Bazaar**, or old market place, is a fascinating area to wander around. It's in the old part of Agra, near the fort, and the narrow alleys of the market start near the Jami Masjid. There are several market areas, or *mandis*, in Agra with names left over from the Moghul days, although they have no relation to what is sold there today. The **Loha Mandi** (Iron Market) and **Sabji Mandi** (Vegetable Market) are still used, but the **Nai Ki Mandi** (Barber's Market) is now famous for textiles.

In the **Malka Bazaar**, you'll see women beckoning to passing men from the upstairs balconies.

Swimming

A couple of the larger hotels allow non-residents to use their pools, for a fee of course. Cheapest is the Lauries Hotel, which charges Rs 50. A dip at the Sheraton will set you back Rs 120, at the Agra Ashok it's Rs 100, and at the Clarks Shiraz they'll welcome you for US$5.

Organised Tours

If you're just day-tripping from Delhi, tours commence from Agra railway station and tickets are sold on the *Taj Express* or *Shatabdi Express*. The tours start when the trains arrive (10 am for the *Taj Express*, 8.30 am for the *Shatabdi*). They last all day and include visits to the Taj, the Fort and Fatehpur Sikri. Tickets cost Rs 50.

In Agra itself, you can book for the tours (and get picked up) from the tourist office in The Mall. At the Cantonment Railway Station tickets are sold at the enquiry window near platform 1.

There are also tours just to Fatehpur Sikri. These start at 10.30 am and cost Rs 30.

Places to Stay – bottom end

The two main areas for cheap accommodation are the Taj Ganj tangle of narrow streets directly south of the Taj, and the Sadar area, close to the Cantonment Railway Station, the tourist office and the GPO, and only a short rickshaw ride from the Taj.

Taj Ganj Area Many of the hotels in this area boast of Taj views, but often it's just wishful thinking. The only one with a truly uninterrupted view from the rooftop is the *Shanti Lodge*. The five-star places would kill for the location of this friendly little place. It's not the cheapest in Taj Ganj, but is still good value at Rs 30/50 with common bath, Rs 40/60 with bath and Rs 80 with bath and hot water. Some rooms are definitely better than others, so try to look at more than one. On the ground floor there's a cheap restaurant, or you can take meals on the roof and feast your eyes on the Taj.

Another very good place is the modern and clean *Hotel Siddhartha* (☎ 36-0235), not far from the western gate. It's run by very friendly Sikhs, and has a pleasant garden courtyard. It's also very cheap at Rs 40/60 with bath and cold shower, Rs 60/80 for a bigger room, and Rs 100/150 with hot shower. There are limited views from the roof.

There are a couple of places worth considering by the eastern gate. The friendly *Hotel Pink* (☎ 36-0677) is indeed pink, but it's not too offensive. The somewhat gloomy rooms are ranged around a small courtyard, and cost Rs 40/70 with a bucket shower, and Rs 120 for a double with attached bath and hot water.

Also in this area is the small *Hotel Sheela*. It has just a few basic rooms set in a spacious garden. For these the charge is Rs 30/40 with common bath, or Rs 50/60 with bath attached. Hot water is available by the bucket. It's also possible to camp in the garden for Rs 20 per person. A good place.

A little further along the same road is the *Taj Khema Hotel* (☎ 36-0140) run by the UP state government. It's an unusual place with tents with attached bath for Rs 125/150, or there are a few rooms at the same price. As you can probably imagine, the tents get fiercely hot in summer, and inept service is the order of the day. There are, however, good views of the Taj, especially in the early mornings.

Along the lane which leads from the southern gate is the long-running *India Guest House*. This small, family-run place has just a few spartan rooms with charpoys for Rs 25/40 with common bath, or there's one room with a view on the roof for Rs 60, although this would be intolerably hot in summer.

The *Shahjahan Lodge* is run by a friendly Muslim man, and is in a good spot in the heart of Taj Ganj. Rooms cost Rs 30/40 with a bathroom shared with one other room, Rs 60 and Rs 75 for doubles with attached bath and hot water, and there's one large four-bed room, complete with attached bath (with tub) for Rs 150.

Just along the street is the *Gulshan Lodge*, which is a bit gloomy but for Rs 20/30 with

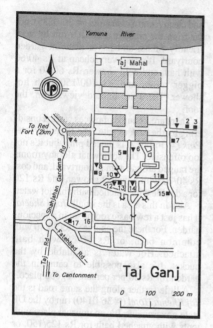

Legend:

1 Relax Restaurant
2 Hotel Sheela
3 Taj Khema Hotel
4 ITDC Taj View Restaurant
5 India Guest House
6 Sikander Restaurant
7 Hotel Pink
8 Nice Point Restaurant
9 Hotel Siddhartha
10 Joney's Place
11 Shanti Lodge
12 New Star & Taj View
    Restaurants, Shahjahan Lodge
13 Gulshan Lodge
14 Shankari Vegis Restaurant
15 Veshali Lodge
16 Jehangir Lodge
17 Taj View Lodge & Bicycle Hire

common bath it's as cheap as you'll find. There are also some doubles with bath attached for Rs 60.

Not far from the traffic roundabout is the *Taj View Lodge*. It has just four rooms for Rs 30/40 with common bath, but unfortunately these cop the noise from the street. Despite the name, the Taj is largely obscured from view. Further into Taj Ganj is the *Jehangir Lodge*. It's a bit rough around the edges but is otherwise OK, and the price is right – Rs 15 for a bed in a three-bed dorm, Rs 30/40 for a single/double, Rs 50 for a double with attached bath, and Rs 80 for a double with attached bath and hot water.

In the middle-range hotel area south of Taj Ganj, there's the popular *Safari Hotel* (☎ 36-0013) on Shamsabad Rd. It's run by the same people who own the Tourist Rest House in the Sadar area. It's new, clean and remarkably good value at Rs 75/100 with air-cool, hot water and a real bathtub. There are also rooms with three and four beds for Rs 150

and Rs 175 respectively. Meals are available, and the Taj is visible from the rooftop.

Also in this area is the *Paradise Guest House* on Fatehbad Rd. It hardly lives up to its name, but the owner doesn't seem to mind. The only advantage to this place is that it has a generator – Agra has chronic power problems, with blackouts virtually every night. Rooms cost Rs 80/100 with attached bath.

Sadar The very popular and long-running *Tourist Rest House* (☎ 36-3961) is on Kachahari Rd, not far from The Mall. This place is run by two helpful brothers who will even make train reservations for you. This pleasant though slightly dog-eared hotel has a variety of rooms with and without bath. Good-sized singles/doubles with bath and hot water are Rs 65/75, and this includes air-cooling in the hot months.

Rickshaws may be unwilling to take you there, and will instead take you to a couple of other places purporting to be the Tourist Rest House.

One such place is the *Kapoor Tourist Rest House*, right on a busy intersection on Fatehpur Sikri Rd. This place is a real dive and, no matter what they tell you, if the Central Methodist Church is across the road, you're at the Kapoor. Another pretender is the so-called *Tourist Rest House*. This one is easy to pick as it's right next to the Agra Fort bus station.

Down the scale a bit is the *Deepak Lodge* at 178 Ajmer Rd. The rooms are somewhat small and dark, and the 'attached bath' is virtually part of the room. All this is yours for Rs 40/60.

On Field Marshal Cariappa Rd, in a spacious residential area closer to the Taj and just a few minutes walk from the Red Fort, there's a couple of good places. The friendly *Agra Hotel* (☎ 36-3331) is a quiet place with a good range of rooms, some with the most amazing antediluvian plumbing. The cheapest rooms are Rs 75/100 with attached bath. Larger rooms are Rs 125/200, or with air-con it's Rs 225/300. Right next door is the *Hotel Akbar*, which is a little more basic, but is also cheaper at Rs 30/60 for small rooms, Rs 50/80 for bigger rooms with bath. Because this is an older place with high ceilings, it remains tolerably cool in summer.

Also in Sadar, in the heart of the main shopping and restaurant area, is the *Jaiwal Hotel* (☎ 36-3716), which is actually two hotels – the other is called *The Jaiwal Hotel*! It was originally owned by two brothers, but it seems they had a disagreement and so divided the hotel literally down the middle. The result is that you walk in and there are reception desks on either side of the partitioned lobby – it's a real circus! The one on the left is marginally the better of the two, and is clean and good value at Rs 125/150 with bath, TV and air-cooling.

At the top of this range is a place which has been popular for years – *Major Bakshi's Tourist Home* (☎ 67-2043). The rooms are comfortable and well furnished, and are quite good at Rs 100/200 with attached bath and hot water. With so much other cheap accommodation around, however, this place is generally fairly empty, and so lacks atmosphere.

Midway between Sadar and Taj Ganj is the *Hotel Akbar Inn* (☎ 36-3212), as distinct from the previously mentioned Hotel Akbar. It has a convenient location right on The Mall, although there's nowhere cheap to eat

in the immediate vicinity. The lawn and garden are added bonuses. The small rooms in the separate wing are cheap at Rs 25/30, while those in the main building are very good value at Rs 50/70 with attached bath, and Rs 80 for a double with air-cooling.

Elsewhere The *Youth Hostel* is in the north of the city on Mahatma Gandhi Rd. It's certainly cheap at Rs 10, but the location is such a detraction that you'd need a pretty good reason to stay here. Agra's *Tourist Bungalow* is also in this part of the city.

There's a couple of options if for some reason you want to be near the bus and railway stations. The *Seetal Lodge* is just a couple of minutes walk from the bus stand, but has little else going for it. Rooms cost Rs 50/100 with attached bath. A better bet is the *Rose Hotel* (☎ 67-049) at 21 Old Idgah Colony, just off Ajmer Rd. Double rooms (no singles) cost Rs 150 with attached bath, or Rs 250 with bath, TV and disagreeable wallpaper.

Places to Stay – middle

One of the nicest places in this range is the elderly *Lauries Hotel* (☎ 72-536) in the Sadar area. It has a relaxed garden area, a swimming pool (not always full) and is run by very pleasant people. The rooms are a tad shabby and cost Rs 250/325, although there's a 25% discount in the off season. Camping is possible at Rs 25 per person, including access to a hot shower.

The *Grand Hotel* (☎ 74-014) is another friendly place, this time near the railway station in the Cantonment area. Rooms cost Rs 280/330, or Rs 340/415 with air-con. Meals are available for Rs 35 for breakfast, or Rs 80 for lunch or dinner.

The *Bakshi's Guest House* (☎ 61-292) by the airport is at 5 Lakshman Nagar. The owner is the son of the late Major Bakshi whose guest house is in the Sadar area. Very pleasant rooms in this well-equipped and clean place are Rs 250/400. The food is good and they can also arrange to pick you up from the station or airport.

The main group of middle and top-end

places is in the area south of Taj Ganj, about
1½ km from the Taj itself. The *Mayur
Tourist Complex* (☎ 36-0302) is one of these
places, and has very pleasant cottages
arranged around a lawn, complete with a
kids' park with some positively deadly
looking play equipment. The cottages cost
Rs 250/325 with air-cool, Rs 310/400 with
air-con and Rs 385/525 for air-con deluxe
cottages. It's very well done, although the
service is erratic and the management gruff.

The centrally air-con *Hotel Shahanshah
Inn* (☎ 36-0110) is in this same area, and has
rooms for Rs 275/350, or Rs 375/450 with
carpet and TV. The *Mumtaz Hotel* is a
modern place which has good rooms at Rs
395/780.

Close by is the *Hotel Amar* (☎ 36-0695),
which has a popular swimming pool. Room
rates are Rs 360/450 with bath, or Rs
395/625 with air-con.

Places to Stay – top end

Agra's tourist-class hotels are generally in
the open area south of the Taj. The *Mughal
Sheraton Hotel* (☎ 36-1701) on Fatehbad Rd
has elegant, fort-like architecture and offers
everything from camel or elephant rides to
an in-house astrologer who, for a small fee
of course, will tell your fortune. There are
300 rooms with singles/doubles ranging
from US$125/135 to US$165/175. Suites are
available for US$400 to US$525.

The older *Clarks Shiraz Hotel* (☎ 36-
1421) is a long-standing Agra landmark. It
too is fully air-conditioned and has a swimming pool; the Indian Airlines office is here.
Singles/doubles cost US$65/70, and it is one
of the better expensive Agra hotels.

The ITDC *Agra Ashok Hotel* (☎ 36-1223)
in The Mall is one of the better managed in
the ITDC chain, although it has probably
been privatised by now, in which case the
service should be impeccable. Room rates
are Rs 1200/1350 for single/double rooms.

The *Taj View Hotel* (☎ 36-1171) is another
in the group south of Taj Ganj, and it has
standard rooms for US$90/100, or 'superior'
rooms for US$110.

Places to Eat

In the Taj Ganj area, the tiny *Joney's Place*
is one of the area's longest running places,
although it's nothing great. It is, however, a
good meeting place and the breakfast for Rs
10 is good value, as are the banana lassis.

Also in Taj Ganj is the popular little *Sikander Restaurant*. It has good food, reasonable
prices and a varied menu, although the servings are small. The *Shankari Vegis
Restaurant* has a less ambitious menu, and
the servings are a good size. I only hope
they've replaced the aging ghetto-blaster
which used to run about 1½ times normal
speed, making Jim Morrison sound like a 14
year old in tight pants (instead of a 24 year
old in tight pants!). The *New Star* and the *Taj
View* are other restaurants in this area. At the
Taj View the food is average and takes an
eternity to arrive.

The ITDC *Cafeteria & Restaurant* just
outside the west gate to the Taj has fine
Indian and Western food, although the
waiters are obviously used to high tipping,
and look thoroughly downcast if you are less
generous. The *Nice Point Restaurant* near
the west gate also has good travellers' food.
At the east gate the *Relax Restaurant* does
excellent real coffee and desserts.

The *Tourist Rest House* in the Sadar area
is a pleasant place to eat. The tables are
outside and at night the candles are a nice
touch.

The *Kwality Restaurant* on Taj Rd is air-
conditioned and excellent, certainly one of
the best in Agra. The *Hotel Gaylord* in the
same street also serves good food. The *Park
Restaurant* is an open-air place just along
from the Kwality, and it serves south Indian
and Chinese dishes.

Between Taj Rd and The Mall is the Oshi-
run *Zorba the Buddha* restaurant. The food
is good, the atmosphere pleasant and the
service excellent. In the same block of shops
is the *Savitri Restaurant*, which specialises
in barbecue kebabs and chicken tikka. In the
same street, but on the opposite side of the
road, is the *Chung Wah* Chinese restaurant.

The deluxe hotels have excellent food –
for a major splurge *Clarks Shiraz* is worth

considering; their lunchtime buffet is good value, as is the one at the *Mughal Sheraton*, although it is expensive at US$11.

Agra has a local speciality, the ultra-sweet candied melon called petha.

Things to Buy

Agra is well known for leather goods, jewellery and marble items inlaid like the *pietra dura* work on the Taj. The Sadar and Taj Ganj areas are the main tourist shopping centres, although the prices here are likely to be more expensive. Around Pratapur there are many jewellery shops, but precious stones are cheaper in Jaipur.

About one km along the road running from the east gate of the Taj is Shilpgram, a crafts village and open-air emporium. At festival times there are live performances by dancers and musicians; the rest of the time there are displays of crafts from all over the country. Prices are certainly on the high side, but the quality is good and the range hard to beat.

Getting There & Away

Air The Indian Airlines office (☎ 36-0153) is at the Clarks Shiraz Hotel. It is open daily from 10 am to 1.15 pm and from 2 to 5 pm.

Agra is on the popular daily tourist route Delhi/Agra/Khajuraho/Varanasi and return. It's only a 40-minute flight from Delhi to Agra. Fares from Agra are: Delhi US$23, Khajuraho US$39, and Varanasi US$57.

Bus Most buses leave from the Idgah bus station. Buses between Delhi and Agra operate about every hour and cost Rs 44; deluxe buses cost Rs 50, and super deluxe are Rs 55; the trip takes about five hours.

There are deluxe buses between Agra and Jaipur every half an hour for Rs 58.50. They leave from a small booth right outside the Seetal Lodge on Ajmer Rd, very close to the Idgah bus station.

There's an early morning bus to Khajuraho at 5 am. The fare is Rs 74 and the journey takes 10 to 12 hours. It's better to take the *Shatabdi Express* train to Jhansi

(two hours), from where it's only three hours by bus to Khajuraho.

Train The Cantonment railway booking office is not yet computerised, so reservations can take some time. Also the tourist-quota allotment here is not great, so getting a booking, especially to Varanasi, can be difficult. Try to plan as far in advance as possible.

Agra is on the main Delhi to Bombay broad-gauge railway line, so there are plenty of trains coming through. Agra is 200 km from Delhi and 1344 km from Bombay. The fastest train between Delhi and Agra is the daily air-con *Shatabdi Express*, which does the trip in a shade under two hours. It leaves Delhi at 6.15 am, returning from Agra at 8.15 pm, and so is ideal for day-tripping. The fare is Rs 200 in a chair car, or Rs 400 1st class, and this includes meals.

There is also the daily *Taj Express* to and from Delhi, but this is slower and gives you less time in Agra. Take great care at New Delhi station; pickpockets, muggers and others are very aware that this is a popular tourist route and they work overtime at parting unwary visitors from their goods.

To Bombay the journey takes 29 hours at a cost of Rs 172/682 in 2nd/1st class. There are also direct trains to Goa, Madras and Thiruvananthapuram (Trivandrum). If you're heading north towards the Himalaya there are trains through Agra which pass straight through Delhi, which means you don't have to stop and get more tickets.

Agra Fort Station is on the metre-gauge system, and this links Agra with Rajasthan. The daily *Agra-Jaipur Express* does the 208-km trip in five hours for Rs 47/161 in 2nd/1st class. The line also passes through Bharatpur. There are daily connections with Ajmer and Jodhpur.

Getting Around

To/From the Airport Agra's airport is seven km from the centre of town. The taxi fare is set at Rs 60, but an auto-rickshaw would take you for less.

Taxi There is a set taxi fare of Rs 50 from the Cantonment Railway Station to any hotel, but this is the top whack and you should certainly be able to get it for less.

Cycle-Rickshaw & Bicycle Agra is very spread out so walking is really not on – even if you could. It's virtually impossible to walk because Agra's hordes of cycle-rickshaw wallahs pursue would-be pedestrians with unbelievable energy and persuasive ability. Beware of rickshaw-wallahs who take you from A to B via a few marble shops, jewellery shops and so on – just great when you want to catch a train, and it can also work out very expensive!

A simple solution to Agra's transport problem is to hire a rickshaw for the day. You can easily negotiate a full-day rate (Rs 50 to Rs 60) for which your rickshaw-wallah will not only take you everywhere, but will wait outside while you sightsee or even have a meal. Agra is so touristy that many rickshaw-wallahs speak fine English and, like Western cabbies, are great sources of amusing information – like how much they can screw out of fat-cat tourists for a little pedal down to the Taj and back to the hotel's air-conditioning. Rs 5 to Rs 10 will take you from pretty well anywhere in Agra to anywhere else.

If, however, you really don't want to be pedalled around, Agra is sufficiently traffic-free to make pedalling yourself an easy proposition. There are plenty of bicycle hire places around. The cost is typically Rs 2 per hour and Rs 12 per day.

AROUND AGRA
Dayal Bagh Temple
In Dayal Bagh, 10 km north of Agra, the white marble *samadhi* (or temple) of the Radah Soami religion is currently under construction. It was started in 1904 and is not expected to be completed until sometime next century. You can see *pietra dura* inlaid marblework actually being worked on. Although the building is architecturally nothing remarkable (some would go so far as to call it gaudy, disproportioned and somewhat ugly), the level of artisanship has to be admired.

Dayal Bagh can be reached by bus or bicycle.

Akbar's Mausoleum
At Sikandra, 10 km north of Agra, the tomb

Full moon in Agra and what else could we do but make the recommended pilgrimage to the Taj. Finding transport was no problem with all the rickshaw-wallahs shouting 'Tajtajtaj' at every tourist on the street. Negotiating a price, we hopped in and set off. After a while we stopped and the driver shouted something to a passer-by. We turned round and disappeared down smaller and smaller side streets as we became more and more worried. Surely the driver couldn't not know the way to India's top tourist destination, so were we about to be mugged? A few minutes later the rickshaw came to a halt. The driver got out slowly and looked into the back. Clutching his hands to his head he said: 'I am sorry – I have lost Taj'!

We ended the journey on foot – about five minutes walk!

Chris Jenney (UK)

of Akbar lies in the centre of a large garden. Akbar started its construction himself but it was completed by his son, Jehangir, who significantly modified the original plans, which accounts for the somewhat cluttered architectural lines of the tomb.

The building has three-storey minarets at each corner and is built of red sandstone inlaid with white marble polygonal patterns.

Four red sandstone gates lead to the tomb complex: one is Muslim, one Hindu, one Christian, and one is Akbar's patent mixture. Like Humayun's Tomb in New Delhi, it is an interesting place to study the gradual evolution in design that culminated in the Taj Mahal. Akbar's mausoleum is open from sunrise to sunset and entry is Rs 2, except on Fridays when it is free.

Sikandra is named after Sultan Sikandar Lodi, the Delhi ruler who held power from 1488 to 1517, immediately preceding the rise of Moghul power on the subcontinent. The **Baradi Palace**, in the mausoleum gardens, was built by Sikandar Lodi. Across the road from the mausoleum is the **Delhi Gate**. Between Sikandra and Agra are several tombs and two kos minars, or milestones.

It's a fair way out to Sikandra; count on Rs 50 for the return trip in an auto-rickshaw.

FATEHPUR SIKRI
Population: 25,000

Between 1570 and 1586, during the reign of Emperor Akbar, the capital of the Moghul Empire was situated here, 40 km west of Agra. Then, as suddenly and dramatically as this new city had been built, it was abandoned. Today it's a perfectly preserved example of a Moghul city at the height of the empire's splendour – an attraction no visitor to Agra should miss.

Legend says that Akbar was without a male heir and made a pilgrimage to this spot to see the saint Shaikh Salim Chishti. The saint foretold the birth of Akbar's son, the future emperor, Jehangir, and in gratitude Akbar named his son Salim. Furthermore, Akbar transferred his capital to Sikri and built a new and splendid city. Later, however,

the city was abandoned mainly due, it is thought, to difficulties with the water supply.

Although a Muslim, Akbar was known to be very tolerant towards other religions, and he spent much time discussing and studying them in Fatehpur Sikri. He also developed a new religion called Deen Ilahi which attempted to synthesise elements from all the major religions. Akbar's famous courtiers, such as Bibal, Raja Todarmal and Abu Fazal, had their houses near his palace in the city.

Orientation & Information
The deserted city lies along the top of a ridge while the modern village, with its bus stand and railway station, is down the ridge's southern side. Fatehpur Sikri is open from sunrise to sunset and entry is Rs 1; free on Fridays. The Jami Masjid is outside the city enclosure.

As Fatehpur Sikri is one of the most perfectly preserved 'ghost towns' imaginable, you may well decide it is worthwhile spending a few rupees to hire a guide. When you arrive, look for the Shahi Darwaza, not Buland Darwaza. Shahi Darwaza is the official entrance to the fort where licensed guides are available. At the Buland Darwaza, the gateway to the mosque and shrine, unlicensed guides will try to lure you into hiring them. The mosque and shrine are not inside the city walls; you have to go there separately.

Jami Masjid (Dargah Mosque)
Fatehpur Sikri's mosque is said to be a copy of the mosque at Mecca, and is a beautiful building containing elements of Persian and Hindu design. The main entrance is through the 54-metre-high **Buland Darwaza**, the Gate of Victory, constructed to commemorate Akbar's victory in Gujarat.

The impressive gateway is reached by an equally impressive flight of steps. A Koranic inscription inside the archway includes the useful thought: 'The world is a bridge, pass over it but build no house upon it. He who hopes for an hour may hope for eternity'. Just outside the gateway is a deep well and, when there is a sufficient number of tourists assem-

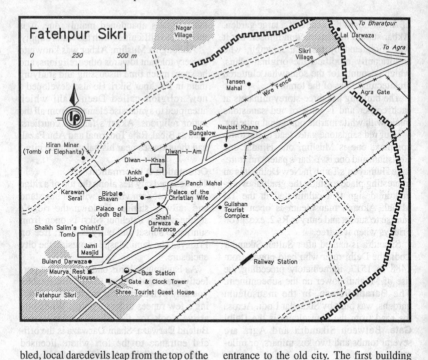

Fatehpur Sikri

bled, local daredevils leap from the top of the entrance into the water.

The eastern gate of the mosque is known as the **Shahi Darwaza** (King's Gate), and was the one formerly used by Akbar.

Inside the mosque is the dargah or **tomb of Shaikh Salim Chishti**. Just as Akbar came to the saint four centuries ago looking for a son, so do childless women visit his tomb today. The saint's grandson, Islam Khan, also has his tomb within the mosque. Abul Fazi and Faizi, adviser and poet to Akbar, had their homes just outside the mosque.

The superb perfect white marble tomb, built in 1570, is in the northern part of the courtyard, opposite the main gate. The carved marble lattice screens (*jalis*) are probably the finest examples of such work you'll see anywhere in the country.

Palace of Jodh Bai

North-east of the mosque is the main entrance to the old city. The first building inside the gate is the Palace of Jodh Bai, named after Jehangir's mother, who was the daughter of the Maharaja of Amber, and was also a Hindu.

Here again the architecture is a blend of styles with Hindu columns and Muslim cupolas. The **Hawa Mahal** (Palace of the Winds) is a projecting room with walls made entirely of stone latticework. The ladies of the court probably sat in here to keep a quiet eye on events below.

Birbal Bhavan

Built either by or for Raja Birbal, Akbar's favourite courtier, this small palace is extremely elegant in its design and execution. Victor Hugo, the 19th-century French author, commented that it was either a very small palace or a very large jewellery box. Birbal, who was a Hindu and noted for his wit and wisdom, unfortunately proved to be a hopeless soldier and lost his life, and most of his army, near Peshawar in 1586. Enormous stables adjoin the Jodh Bai Palace, with nearly 200 enclosures for horses and camels. Some stone rings for the halters are still in place.

Karawan Serai & Hiran Minar
The Karawan Serai or Caravanserai was a large courtyard surrounded by the hostels used by visiting merchants. The **Hiran Minar** (Deer Minaret), which is actually outside the fort grounds, is said to have been erected over the grave of Akbar's favourite elephant. Stone elephant tusks protrude from the 21-metre-high tower from which Akbar is said to have shot at deer and other game which were driven in front of him. The flat expanse of land stretching away from the tower was once a lake which even today occasionally floods.

Palace of the Christian Wife
Close to the Jodh Bai Palace, this house was used by Akbar's Goan Christian wife, Maryam, and at one time was gilded throughout – giving it the name the 'Golden House'.

Panch Mahal
This amusing little five-storey palace was probably once used by the ladies of the court and originally had stone screens on the sides. These have now been removed, making the open colonnades inside visible. Each of the five storeys is stepped back from the previous one until at the top there is only a tiny kiosk, its dome supported by four columns. The lower floor has 56 columns, no two of which are exactly alike.

Ankh Micholi
The name of this building translates as something like 'hide and seek', and the emperor is supposed to have amused himself by playing that game with ladies of the harem! It is more likely that the building was used for storing records, although it has some curious struts with stone monsters carved into them. By one corner is a small canopied

enclosure where Akbar's Hindu guru may have sat to instruct him.

Diwan-i-Khas
The exterior of the Hall of Private Audiences is plain, but its interior design is unique. A stone column in the centre of the building supports a flat-topped 'throne'. From the four corners of the room stone bridges lead across to this throne. Akbar spent much time here with scholars of many different religious persuasions, discussing and debating.

Diwan-i-Am
Just inside the gates at the north-east end of the deserted city is the Hall of Public Audiences. This consists of a large open courtyard surrounded by cloisters. Beside the Diwan-i-Am is the **Pachisi courtyard**, set out like a gigantic gameboard. It is said that Akbar played the game pachisi here, using slave girls as the pieces.

Other Monuments
Musicians would play from the **Naubat Khana**, at one time the main entrance to the city, as processions passed by beneath. The entrance road then ran between the mint and the treasury before reaching the Diwan-i-Am. The **Khwabgah**, in front of the Daftar Khana, or record office, was Akbar's own sleeping quarters. Beside the Khwabgah is the tiny but elaborately carved **Rumi Sultana** or Turkish Queen's House.

Near the Karawan Serai, badly defaced elephants still guard the **Hathi Pol**, or Elephant Gate. There is also a **Hakim**, or Doctor's House, and a fine **hammam**, or Turkish bath, beside it. Outside the **Dargah Mosque** are the remains of the small stonecutters' mosque. Shaikh Salim Chishti's cave was supposedly at this site and the mosque predates Akbar's imperial city.

Places to Stay & Eat
Although most people day trip from Agra, you can stay at the *Archaeological Survey Rest House* for only Rs 9. It's great value although the staff sometimes seem to regard guests as a nuisance. Bookings must be made

in advance at the Archaeological Survey of India, 22 The Mall, Agra.

There are a couple of cheap guest houses in the village area below the Buland Darwaza. The *Shree Tourist Guest House* is new and clean, although overpriced at Rs 60/100 with common bath, Rs 80/120 with attached bath. Better value is the *Maurya Rest House* just below the Buland Darwaza. The rooms are small, but cheap at Rs 30/40 with common bath.

At the top of the scale is the new UP state-run *Gulishan Tourist Complex* (☎ 251), about half a km back along the main road. The design is sympathetic to the local surroundings, and the facilities good, although I suspect it will go into the rapid decline so typical of many state-run hotels. The rooms are large and well appointed, and cost Rs 150/200, or Rs 275/325 with air-con. A dormitory is advertised at Rs 40 per bed, but it is definitely an afterthought, and they haven't even bothered to put any beds in it! The complex also houses a restaurant and a bar.

Getting There & Away

The tour buses only stop for an hour or so at Fatehpur Sikri. If you want to spend longer (which is recommended) it is worth taking a bus from Agra's Idgah bus station for about Rs 5; the trip takes a bit over an hour. Along the way you pass milestones, known as kos minars, about every three km. There's a train service but it's very slow. Along the road you'll often see dancing bears – the villagers dance their trained bears out into the road to block your way while they demand money!

You can spend a day in Fatehpur Sikri and continue on to Bharatpur in the evening. The bus station restaurant will let you lock up your bags in their garage, but firmly agree on the price beforehand or they may try to overcharge you.

MATHURA

Population: 233,000

This area, popularly known as Brij Bhoomi, is a major pilgrimage place for Hindus – there are literally thousands of temples here.

Krishna, the popular incarnation of Vishnu, is believed to have been born in Mathura and the area is closely linked with many episodes in his early life. Nearby is Vrindaban where Krishna 'sported' with his gopis (milkmaids) and where the Hare Krishnas have their headquarters.

The tourist office is at the old bus stand in Mathura and guided tours covering the main Krishna sites are sometimes available, departing at 6.30 am. Most temples are closed between about 11 am and 4 pm, siesta-time for the deities and their attendants.

History

Mathura (Muttra) is an ancient cultural and religious centre. The Buddhist monasteries here received considerable patronage from Ashoka, and Mathura was mentioned by Ptolemy and by the Chinese visitors Fa Hian (in India 401-410 AD) and Hiuen Tsang (634 AD). By then the population of the 20 monasteries had dropped from 3000 to 2000 as Buddhism began to give way to Hinduism here.

In 1017, Mahmud of Ghazni arrived on his rape, burn and pillage trip from Afghanistan, damaging the Hindu and remaining Buddhist shrines. Sikandar Lodi continued the destruction in 1500 and the fanatical Aurangzeb flattened the Kesava Deo Temple, which had been built on the site of one of the most important Buddhist monasteries, and built a mosque in its place.

Shri Krishna Janmbhoomi

Amongst the foundations of the Kesava Deo Temple is a small room made up to look like a prison cell. Here pilgrims file past the stone slab onto which Krishna is supposed to have been born, 3500 years ago. He was obliged to make his entry into the world in these undignified surroundings as his parents had been imprisoned by the tyrannical King Kansa. Aurangzeb's mosque rises above the site and there's a more recent Hindu temple beside it. There is, of course, an alternative birthplace 200 metres away and nearby is the **Potara-Kund**, where baby Krishna's

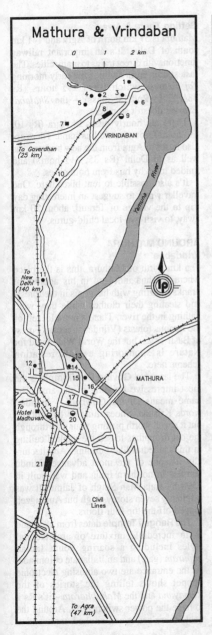

Mathura & Vrindaban

1 Nidhi Van Temple
2 Radha Ballabh Temple
3 Govind Dev Temple
4 Bankey Bihari Temple
5 Madan Mohan Temple
6 Rangaji Temple
7 ISKCON
8 Vrindaban Railway Station
9 Bus Stand
10 Pagal Baba Temple
11 Gita Mandir Temple
12 Shri Krishna Janmbhoomi & Mosque
13 Kans Qila
14 Jami Masjid
15 Vishram Ghat
16 Dwarkadheesh Temple
17 Archaeological Museum
18 Hotel Nepal
19 New Bus Stand
20 Old Bus Stand & Tourist Office
21 Mathura Junction Railway Station

nappies (diapers) are supposed to have been washed.

Along the Yamuna River

The 300-metre-wide Yamuna River, which flows through Mathura, is lined with ghats and full of large turtles. **Vishram Ghat** is the most important bathing ghat and is where Lord Krishna is said to have rested after killing King Kansa. Boats take pilgrims out for short river trips from here.

The **Sati Burj**, beside Vishram Ghat, is a four-storey tower built by the son of Behari Mal of Jaipur in 1570 to commemorate his mother's sati. Aurangzeb knocked down the upper storeys, but they have since been rebuilt.

The ruined **Kans Qila fort** on the riverbank was built by Raja Man Singh of Amber; Jai Singh of Jaipur built one of his observatories here, but it has since disappeared.

Set back from the river in the main part of the town are the **Jami Masjid**, which was built by Abo-in Nabir Khan in 1661, and the **Dwarkadheesh Temple**. Built in 1814 by Seth Gokuldass of Gwalior, this is Mathura's main temple and is dedicated (surprise, surprise) to Krishna.

Archaeological Museum

The Archaeological Museum is worth a visit for its large collection of examples of the Mathura school of ancient Indian sculpture. This includes the famous, 5th-century standing Buddha found here. There are many other sculptures, terracotta work, coins and bronze objects and there's a pleasant garden. It's open daily from 10.30 am to 4.30 pm (7.30 am to 12.30 pm from 16 April to 30 June). Admission is free.

Gita Mandir

This modern temple was funded by the Birla family (the wealthy industrialists). Pilgrims stop off on their way to Vrindaban to see the Gita Stambh, a pillar on which the whole of the *Bhagavad Gita* is carved. At the entrance vendors sell cassettes of devotional music – although much of it seems to be more for devotees of masala movies than for the religiously inclined.

Places to Stay & Eat

The most interesting cheap place is the *International Guest House* right beside Shri Krishna Janmbhoomi. It's excellent value with singles/doubles for as little as Rs 15/25 and there are doubles with attached bathrooms for Rs 50, or Rs 90 with air-coolers. There's a good vegetarian restaurant and a garden. For something more upmarket there's the *Hotel Brijraj* nearby with doubles for Rs 90 or Rs 175 with air-con. All rooms have hot water and TV, and there's also a restaurant.

Opposite the new bus stand is the *Hotel Nepal* with rooms from Rs 50/60 to Rs 85/125. The *Kwality Hotel*, near the old bus stand, is similarly priced. There's a *Tourist Bungalow* with doubles from Rs 75 but it's inconveniently located in Civil Lines.

The top hotel in the area is the *Hotel Madhuvan* (☎ 5058) with rooms for Rs 240/310 and Rs 310/460 with air-con. There's a swimming pool that nonresidents can use for Rs 40. Main dishes are Rs 40 to Rs 50 in the restaurant and service is slow.

Getting There & Away

Mathura is 57 km north of Agra and 141 km south of Delhi. It's an important railway junction with direct trains to many cities. The fastest train from Delhi is the early morning *Taj Express* which takes 2½ hours (Rs 33/122 in 2nd/1st class) – the *Shatabdi Express* doesn't stop here.

There are hourly buses to Agra (Rs 10, 1½ hours) from the old bus stand. There are also buses to Agra from the new bus stand as well as to Delhi (Rs 35, 3½ hours) and guided tours by bus from both cities.

It's also possible to rent bikes here. One traveller wrote to suggest an interesting day trip to the village of Terauli, about 20 km away, to visit two local child-gurus.

AROUND MATHURA
Vrindaban

Ten km north of Mathura, this is the place where Krishna indulged in his adolescent pranks – flirting with his gopis in the forests and stealing their clothes while they were bathing in the river. There's not a lot left of the famous forests (Vrindaban means Forest of Basil Trees) but the World Wide Fund for Nature is sponsoring a reafforestation scheme here.

The large red **Govind Dev Temple** is the most impressive building in the area. The name means Divine Cowherd – in other words Krishna. Shoes must be left outside but it's well worth picking your way through the bat droppings to see the vaulted ceiling in this cathedral-like building. Architecturally it's one of the most advanced Hindu temples in northern India and was built in 1590 by Raja Man Singh of Jaipur. It was originally seven storeys high but Aurangzeb lopped off the top four floors.

The **Rangaji Temple** dates from 1851 and is an incredible mixture of architectural styles including a soaring South Indian *gopuram* (gate) and an Italianate colonnade. At the entrance are two amusing electronic puppet shows telling the stories of the *Ramayana* and the *Mahabharata* – it's Rs 1 to have the power switched on. Around the back there's a weed-choked tank and a garden. Non-Hindus are not allowed in the middle enclosure of the temple, where there is a 15-metre gold-plated pillar.

There are 4000 other temples in Vrindaban including the popular **Bankey Bihari**, **Radha Ballabh** (built in 1626), **Madan Mohan**, the 10-storey **Pagal Baba**, and the **Nidhi Van** – where some of the monkeys are said to have learnt to steal cameras, only returning them in exchange for food!

The International Society of Krishna Consciousness (ISKCON) has its Indian base in Vrindaban. By the **Krishna Balaram Temple** here an impressive marble mausoleum is being built for their founder Swami Prabhupada, who died in 1977. Some of the most skilled masons in the country have been working on it since then and it's not due for completion until the mid 1990s. The Swami's rooms have been turned into a museum where you can see hallowed objects including the British Airways complimentary slippers from his UK trip and the last piece of soap he used. Every year several hundred Westerners attend courses and seminars here on everything from astrology to ayurvedic medicine. Phone (05664) 82-478 for details.

Places to Stay & Eat The *ISKCON Guest House* (☎ 82-478) has a range of good rooms where you may stay for a donation. The restaurant is the best place to eat in Vrindaban (pure veg, of course) and serves fruit juices, milk shakes and thalis.

Getting There & Away From Mathura there are tempos (Rs 3) from Shri Krishna Janmbhoomi and from the railway station. Tongas charge Rs 30. There are three steam trains a day on the metre-gauge run to Vrindaban (Rs 6 in 2nd).

Gokul & Mahaban

Sixteen km south-east of Mathura, this is where Krishna was secretly raised. Hordes of pilgrims flock here during his birthday

festival each July-August. There's a very basic *Tourist Bungalow*.

Mahaban, 18 km north of Mathura, is another place from the Krishna legend, where he also spent some of his youth.

Barsana & Goverdhan

Krishna's consort, Radha, was from Barsana, 50 km from Mathura. This is an interesting area to be during the festival of Holi when the women of Barsana attack the men of nearby Nandgaon with coloured water.

At Goverdhan, 26 km from Mathura, Krishna is said to have protected the inhabitants from Indra's wrath (rain) by holding the hilltops, neatly balanced on top of his finger, over the town for seven days.

Northern Uttar Pradesh

The northern part of Uttar Pradesh, an area of hills, mountains and lakes, is known as Uttarakhand, or Land of the North, and there's some local agitation to make it a separate state. The western half is known as the Garhwal region and the eastern part is the Kumaon.

There are several popular hill stations here, including Naini Tal and Mussoorie, and many trekking routes – most of them little known and even less used. In the summer pilgrims trek to the source of the holy Ganges near Gangotri, not far from the border with China. More accessible pilgrimage centres include Haridwar and Rishikesh, where the Ganges leaves the Himalaya and joins the plains for its long trip to the sea.

The region hit the world news in October 1991 when the Garhwal earthquake caused US$130 million of damage in the northern Uttarkashi district; 800 people died and 2000 were injured.

Recently a number of travellers have entered Nepal from the northern Uttar Pradesh region. See under Banbassa at the end of this section for more details.

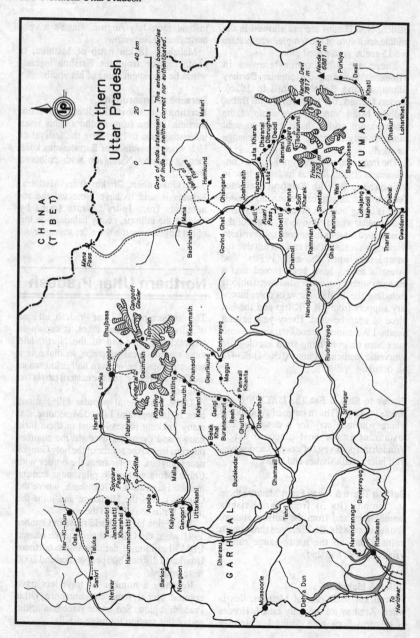

Northern
Uttar Pradesh

0   20   40 km

Govt of India statement — The external boundaries
of India are neither correct nor authenticated.

Toll Taxes

On some of the mountain roads in UP, bus passengers have to pay a Rs 2 toll, which is collected on the bus.

MEERUT

Population: 847,000

Only 70 km north-east of Delhi, this was the place where the 1857 Mutiny first broke out, when Meerut was the largest garrison in northern India. There's little to remember that event by today – just the cemetery near St John's Church, which also has the grave of General Ochterlony, whose monument dominates the Maidan in Calcutta. The Suraj Khund is the most interesting Hindu temple in Meerut and there's a Moghul mausoleum, the Shahpir, near the old Shahpir Gate.

Meerut is a green revolution boom town and the new-found wealth, indicated by the many well-stocked stores, has led to inter-communal tensions which sometimes result in violence.

At **Sardhana**, 18 km north of Meerut, is the palace of Begum Samru. She was converted to Roman Catholicism and built the basilica here in 1809, which has an altar of white Jaipur marble. The Begum's tomb can be found in the basilica.

There are several hotels in Meerut; the best is *Hotel Shaleen* and there's also the cheaper *Anand Hotel* – both in the Begum Bridge area.

SAHARANPUR

Population: 374,000

Situated 178 km north of Delhi, the large botanical gardens here, known as the Company Bagh, are over 175 years old.

DEHRA DUN

Population: 367,000

Also spelt Dehra Doon, this pleasant town is situated in an intermontane valley in the Siwaliks, the foothills of the Himalaya. The hill station Mussoorie can be seen, 34 km away, on the high mountain range above Dehra Dun.

Dehra Dun is at the centre of a forest area and the impressive Forest Research Institute

is here. Apart from this there's not much else of interest. The town is a major academic and research centre and the Indian Military Academy and the Survey of India (which sells very good maps of many Indian cities) are both based here. There are also several prestigious boarding schools including the Doon School, India's most exclusive private school, which numbers Rajiv Gandhi among its ex-pupils.

Orientation & Information

The UP tourist office (☎ 23-217) is in the Hotel Drona close to the bus stands and the railway station. The clock tower is the hub of the town and most of the budget hotels are near it or close to the railway station. The top-end hotels are all in the area known as Astley Hall, north of the clock tower. The main market is Paltan Bazaar and one of the main items sold here is basmati rice, for which the region is famous.

There's a subsidiary tourist office known as Garhwal Mandal Vikas Nigam or GMVN (☎ 26-817) which specifically covers the Garhwal region and pilgrimages (yatras) to the holy places north of here. Among the 10 packages organised by GMVN (mainly in the summer season) is a seven-day trip to Yamunotri and Gangotri for Rs 1600, which one traveller reported was 'an interesting experience'. Their brochure suggests that the trip is no picnic:

You have to reach the elevation of 10,000 and 11,000 feet hence you are required to take on warm pant, warm shirt, warm coat, sweater, maflor or monkey cap, warm shocks, shoes to walk comfortably need not to take beds and luggage, but if you like you can take general medicines with you, which will be helping to put off from the tireness, cold, vomiting & headack.

Forest Research Institute

Established by the British earlier this century the FRI is now reputedly one of the finest institutes of forest sciences in the world. It's set in large botanical gardens, with the Himalaya providing a spectacular backdrop.

In the six galleries of the extensive museum, exhibits are laid out in glass cases with Victorian attention to detail. They include examples of wood types, before and after models for social forestry programmes, a furniture gallery, stuffed examples of forest dwellers from bugs and pests to tigers, and a cross-section of a deodar which is over 700 years old.

The institute is open Monday to Friday from 10 am to 5pm and there's no admission charge. To get there take a six-seater from the clock tower to the institute gates.

Other Things to See

At the **Wadia Institute of Himalayan Geology** there's a museum containing rock samples, semiprecious stones and fossils. It's open Monday to Friday from 10 am to 5 pm.

The main temple is **Tapkeshwar Temple**, dedicated to Siva. It's beside a stream, which (when there's water in it) is directed to flow onto the lingam. A large fair is held here on Sivaratri Day (usually in March).

Other places to visit include the **Lakshman Sidh Temple**; **Sahastradhara** (14 km from Dehra Dun) with cold sulphur springs and a Tourist Rest House; the **Robbers Cave**, a popular picnic spot just beyond Anarwala village; and **Tapovan** where there is an ashram.

Places to Stay – bottom end

Most of the really cheap places in Dehra Dun aren't keen to let foreigners stay since they don't have the required 'C' form. You can stay at the *Victoria Hotel* which is excellent value at Rs 45/65 for singles/doubles with basic bathrooms attached. The *Oriental Hotel*, an old place in the bazaar, is not so good at Rs 55/90. North of the clock tower, the *Vikas Tourist Lodge* is a bit better with rooms at Rs 50/100. *The White House*, set in a garden, is a good place with pleasant rooms from Rs 80.

The *Hotel Meedo* ('Famous for Hospitality, Comfort and Glamour') has good rooms at the back for Rs 88/165 with attached baths and little balconies. These rooms are quieter than the more expensive front rooms above the rather sleazy bar. (Don't confuse this place with the top-end Hotel Meedo's

Grand.) Another reasonable place in the station area is *Hotel Prince* where rooms cost Rs 85/138 with attached baths. There are dorm beds for Rs 25 and doubles for Rs 80 at the railway *retiring rooms*.

The large *Hotel Drona* (☎ 24-371) is run by UP Tourism's local branch GMVN and has dorm beds with lockers for Rs 30, and rooms with attached bathrooms and hot water from Rs 120/160 to Rs 270/360 with air-con.

Places to Stay – middle

Middle-range places include the *Hotel Relax* (☎ 27-776) with good rooms from Rs 185/300, the similarly priced *Kwality Motel* (☎ 27-001) and the *Motel Himshri*. The *Hotel President* (☎ 27-386) has doubles for Rs 350.

Places to Stay – top end

In Astley Hall, along Rajpur Rd, there are several top-end hotels, all with air-con rooms from about Rs 395/550. They include the glitzy *Shahenshah* (☎ 28-508), the *Hotel Meedo's Grand* (☎ 27-171), the *Shipra* (☎ 24-611), *Inderlok* (☎ 28-113) and *Hotel Ajanta Continental* (☎ 29-595) which is the best of them and has a swimming pool. The *Hotel Madhuban* (☎ 24-094) is definitely overpriced at Rs 1260/1540, but is being renovated.

Places to Eat

In the station area the *Sammaan Veg Restaurant* (by the Oriental Hotel) is a good clean place with thalis from Rs 10. Two other popular thali restaurants are the *Vishal* and the *Kasturbi*. At all these places you can follow your thali with kheer (rice pudding) for Rs 4. Somewhat more expensive but definitely worth it is the *Kumar* – the best vegetarian restaurant in town. Their nan bread is excellent – thick and flecked with spinach. Main dishes are between Rs 16 and Rs 32 and in winter they have the sweet Gajar ka Halwa, made from carrot, spices and milk.

There are popular fast-food places like *Daddy's* (with pizzas from Rs 18) and a *Kwality* branch – often crowded with rich

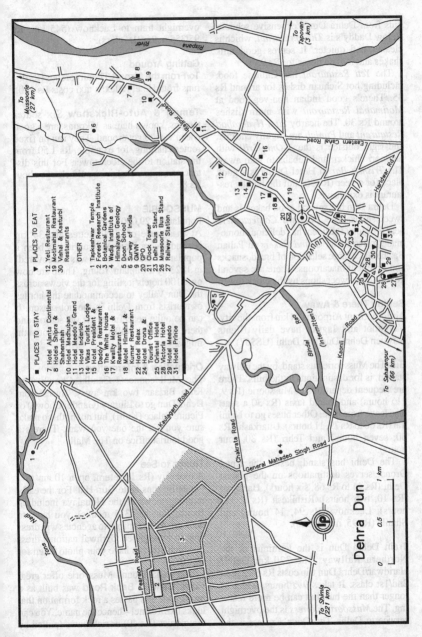

Dehra Dun

0   0.5   1 km

To Tapovan (3 km)

To Mussoorie (27 km)

To Saharanpur (66 km)

To Shimla (221 km)

Rispana River

Rajpur Road

Eastern Canal Road

Hardwar Rd

Bindal Rao (intermittent)

Kaoni Road

Chakrata Road

General Mahadeo Singh Road

Pearson Road

Kaulagarh Road

Tons

Nesi

PLACES TO STAY

7   Hotel Ajanta Continental
8   Hotels Shipra & Shahenshah
10   Hotel Madhuban
11   Hotel Meedo's Grand
13   Hotel Inderlok
14   Vikas Tourist Lodge
15   Hotel President & Daddy's Restaurant
16   The White House
17   Kwality Motel
18   Motel Himshri & Kumar Restaurant
22   Hotel Relax
24   Hotel Drona & Tourist Office
25   Oriental Hotel
28   Victoria Hotel
29   Hotel Meedo
31   Hotel Prince

PLACES TO EAT

12   Yeti Restaurant
19   Motimahal Restaurant
30   Vishal & Kasturbi Restaurants

OTHER

1   Tapkeshwar Temple
2   Forest Research Institute & Botanical Gardens
3   Wadia Institute of Himalayan Geology
4   Doon School
5   Survey of India
6   GMVN
20   GPO
21   Clock Tower
23   Delhi Bus Stand
26   Mussoorie Bus Stand
27   Railway Station

kids from Dehra Dun's expensive schools. Below Daddy's is *The Vegetarian*, which is cleaner and quieter. It serves good milk shakes and masala dosas for Rs 9.

The *Yeti Restaurant* has Chinese food, including hot Sichuan dishes for around Rs 35. There's good Indian non-veg food at *Motimahal Restaurant* with main dishes around Rs 30. The nearby *Sind-Hyderabad Restaurant* and *Punjab* are slightly cheaper, and right outside is the *A-One Grill* with tandoori chicken and kebabs to take away. The *Trishna Bar* in Hotel Drona is a good place for a beer (Rs 30) but the hotel's restaurant is expensive.

Dehra Dun has several good bakeries and sweet shops. The *Standard Confectioners* near the Hotel President has delicious homemade toffees. The *Grand Bakers* in Paltan Bazaar has a large selection of bread, snacks and excellent macaroons. There are several good Indian sweet shops by the clock tower.

Getting There & Away
Air Jolly Grant Airport is 24 km from the city. Vayudoot and Jagsan have daily flights between Dehra Dun and Delhi (US$67).

Bus The Mussoorie bus stand, by the railway station, is for destinations in the hills. There are frequent departures to Mussoorie (Rs 9, 1½ hours) and shared taxis (Rs 30 a seat) also leave from here. Other buses go to Naini Tal (Rs 66 to Rs 79, 11 hours), Uttarkashi (Rs 50, seven hours) and Tehri (Rs 30, four hours).

The Delhi bus stand, beside the Hotel Drona, serves destinations on the plains: Delhi (Rs 44 to Rs 68, six hours), Haridwar (Rs 10, two hours), Rishikesh (Rs 8, 1½ hours), Lucknow (Rs 94, 14 hours) and Shimla (Rs 95, nine hours).

Train Dehra Dun is the terminus of the Northern Railway. The 320-km Delhi/Haridwar/Dehra Dun trip costs Rs 64/228 in 2nd/1st class. It takes 9½ hours, which is longer than the bus, but can be more relaxing. The *Mussoorie Express* is the overnight service to Delhi. The *Doon Express* is the

overnight train to Lucknow (545 km, Rs 95/355 in 2nd/1st class).

Getting Around
To/From the Airport The airport bus (Rs 45) runs from Hotel Relax; a taxi costs Rs 180.

Tempo & Auto-Rickshaw Six-seater tempos, known here as Vikrams, are a good cheap way to get around. They run on fixed routes charging, for example, Rs 1.50 from the station to the clock tower. For this distance an auto-rickshaw would charge about Rs 8.

MUSSOORIE
Population: 29,000

At an altitude of 2000 metres and 34 km beyond Dehra Dun, Mussoorie has been a popular hill station since it was 'discovered' in 1823 by a Captain Young. There are now over 100 hotels jostling for the views across the Dun Valley to accommodate the hordes of tourists from Delhi in the hot season. It can be quite peaceful in the off season and there are good walks along the mountain ridges.

Orientation & Information
The Mall connects Gandhi Chowk with Kulri Bazaar, two km away. Buses from Dehra Dun go to Library (Gandhi Chowk) or Picture Palace (Kulri), but not both, so make sure you get the one you want. There's a good tourist office on The Mall.

Things to See
A ropeway (Rs 10 return, open 10 am to 7 pm daily) runs up to **Gun Hill**. For the early morning views of the Himalaya including Bandar Punch (6315 metres), you have to walk up. At the top, photo agencies will dress you up in sequined Garhwal national dress in which you can have your photo taken for Rs 10.

The walks around Mussoorie offer great views. **Camel's Back Road** was built as a promenade and passes a rock formation that looks like a camel – hence the name. You can rent ponies (Rs 40) or rickshaws (pulled by two rickshaw-wallahs and often pushed by a third) for Rs 70. Another good walk takes you down to Happy Valley and the **Tibetan Refugee Centre** where there's a temple and a small shop selling hand-knitted jumpers. An enjoyable longer walk takes you through Landour Bazaar to **Childers Lodge** (five km), the highest point in Mussoorie.

If you don't want to walk, you can rent fairly new 100cc motorcycles from Bertz (sounds like?!) for Rs 25 per hour or Rs 200 per day. They can also supply crash helmets and insurance.

GMVN (booth at Library bus stand) run tours to **Kempty Falls** (Rs 20) and **Dhanolti** (Rs 50) where there are good Himalayan views.

Other suggestions for passing the time here include a visit to the astrologer (Rs 50 per consultation), video games at the Tourist Complex, billiards at Hotel Clarks (Rs 30), joining the library (Rs 25) or roller skating (Rs 27) on the wooden floor of 'The Rink'.

Places to Stay – bottom end

With so many hotels competing for customers, prices vary enormously according to the season. Rates given here are for the off season (November to March) but you may be able to negotiate a further reduction. Most hotels have only double rooms with attached bathrooms and checkout time is usually 10 am. Prices rise by up to 300% in the summer. Porters from either bus stand to any hotel expect about Rs 8.

Kulri Bazaar With northern views, the *Hotel Broadway* was a small English guest house run by a Miss Lee until 1954. It's still a good clean place and the helpful manager has doubles for Rs 75 and a few singles for Rs 30. Basic doubles at the old *Regal Hotel* are Rs 50. The *Hotel Hill Queen*, under the ropeway, is good value with rooms from Rs 50 to Rs 150.

The *Hotel Nand Villa* is a large friendly place offering 'service with heart in it' and a range of rooms from Rs 75. With rooms from Rs 60, or Rs 80 with a sitting room, the *New Bharat Hotel*, below The Mall, is a creaky

old building run by an equally creaky old caretaker who's very helpful. He's a keen gardener and the place is filled with flourishing potted plants.

The small *Hotel Valley View* (☎ 2324) is an excellent place set in a small garden above The Mall, with clean rooms from Rs 100 and Rs 150, and a good restaurant. Le Suisse bakery, owned by the same family, supply the bread and pastries here. The *Hotel Mussoorie International* (☎ 2943) is another recommended place with similar prices.

If you fancy doing your own catering the *Hotel Walnut Grove* has suites with kitchens from Rs 120. Gas stoves cost Rs 30 per day to hire so this is probably only worth it if you get a group of people together. The nearby *Hotel Connaught Castle* is a similar place. Both also have rooms without kitchens.

Out of the tourist area past the clock tower in Landour Bazaar is the basic *Hotel Nishima* with doubles for Rs 55.

Library Area Right opposite the library, the *Hotel Imperial* is a rickety place with rooms from Rs 50. The nearby *Hotel Vishnu Palace* has some reasonable doubles from Rs 85 in the older building. The Sikh-run *Hotel India* is recommended, with great views to the north and good rooms from Rs 75. The similarly priced *Hotel Eagle* is nearby.

The *Tourist Complex* is a concrete monstrosity on The Mall run by UP Tourism's branch, GMVN. It has dorm beds for Rs 25 and doubles from Rs 126. The *Hotel Palki* next door has some good rooms for Rs 80.

The rooms at the small *Hotel Kanak* for Rs 100 are pleasant. High above The Mall is the *Hotel Prince*, a large old building with superb views from the terrace. Big tatty rooms are Rs 125.

The *Hotel Paramount* is a friendly place on The Mall with good doubles from Rs 125.

The well-kept *Hotel Vikram* has some nice doubles with balconies from Rs 150, and there's a great view over the Dun Valley from the double bed in room 25.

Places to Stay – middle & top end

In Kulri the more expensive places include

the large and characterless *Hotel Shipra*, right by the Picture Palace, with rooms for Rs 220; and the pleasant *Hotel Filigree* (☎ 2380) with northern views from the roof terrace and doubles for Rs 200.

On The Mall, rooms are Rs 200 at *Hakman's Grand Hotel*, a large run-down place full of Raj-reject furniture and with a cash register still calibrated in annas. Similarly priced places include the *Hotel Roselynn Estate* and *Hotel Classic Heights*.

For a special occasion you could try the *Honeymoon Inn* – Rs 300 for a double bed and giant-size bathtub (bring your own plug). However, the schizophrenic decor doesn't encourage romance. Much better is the *Hotel Shining Star* with big double beds, cable TV and a sauna for Rs 400.

The *Hotel Padmini Nivas* (☎ 2793) once belonged to the Maharaja of Rajpipla but this English-style villa is now a small hotel, one of the few here that combines character with

comfort. There are some rooms with sitting areas for Rs 250. Room 10, at Rs 350, has a great view over the Dun Valley, and is particularly recommended.

Opened in 1890, the *Savoy Hotel* (☎ 2010) is the largest place in Mussoorie. There's a huge ballroom (complete with band in the high season), tennis, squash courts and a beer garden. The touches of the Raj are very faded here including peeling gloss paint and moth-eaten deer heads. Rooms are rather overpriced at Rs 396/495.

Places to Eat

There's no shortage of places to eat. In Kulri, *Madras Cafe* has good South Indian food and the popular *The Green* nearby is the best vegetarian place in town. Main dishes are Rs 20 to Rs 28. The *President Restaurant* is a very good non-veg place with a nice sitting area outside. At the *Tavern*, main dishes are Rs 35 to Rs 50 and beer is Rs 35. There's a

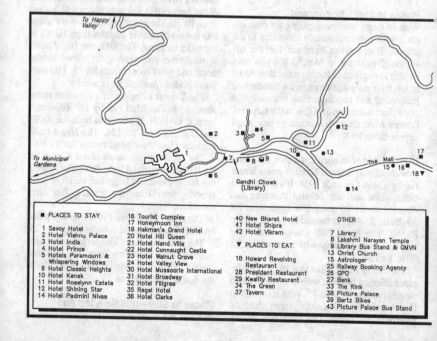

■ PLACES TO STAY		▼ PLACES TO EAT	OTHER
1 Savoy Hotel	16 Tourist Complex		7 Library
2 Hotel Vishnu Palace	17 Honeymoon Inn	18 Howard Revolving	8 Lakshmi Narayan Temple
3 Hotel India	19 Hakman's Grand Hotel	Restaurant	9 Library Bus Stand & GMVN
4 Hotel Prince	20 Hotel Hill Queen	28 President Restaurant	13 Christ Church
5 Hotels Paramount &	21 Hotel Nand Villa	29 Kwality Restaurant	15 Astrologer
Whispering Windows	22 Hotel Connaught Castle	34 The Green	25 Railway Booking Agency
6 Hotel Classic Heights	23 Hotel Walnut Grove	37 Tavern	26 GPO
10 Hotel Kanak	24 Hotel Valley View		27 Bank
11 Hotel Roselynn Estate	30 Hotel Mussoorie International		33 The Rink
12 Hotel Shining Star	31 Hotel Broadway		38 Picture Palace
14 Hotel Padmini Nivas	32 Hotel Filigree		39 Bertz Bikes
	35 Regal Hotel		43 Picture Palace Bus Stand
	36 Hotel Clarks		
	40 New Bharat Hotel		
	41 Hotel Shipra		
	42 Hotel Vikram		

Kwality branch with the usual menu and cable TV to watch as you eat.

Places for snacks include the sweet shop *Luxmi Misthan Bhandar* near the library, the ice-cream parlour at *Whispering Windows*, the *Le Suisse* bakery (near Kwality Restaurant) which has great bread and chocolate doughnuts for Rs 6, *Le Chef*, which is close to the bank, for fast food and takeaway pizzas from Rs 17, and *Chit Chat*, which is near Le Chef.

For a novel dining experience try the *Howard Revolving Restaurant* and admire the Dun Valley at one revolution every nine minutes. The food's not bad but is quite expensive.

Getting There & Away

There are hourly buses between the railhead at Dehra Dun and Mussoorie (Rs 9), and these go to either Library or Kulri Bazaar (Picture Palace). Shared taxis cost Rs 30 per

seat. For Delhi (Rs 80, eight hours) there's a bus at 8 am from Picture Palace bus stand and a deluxe night bus from Library. Overnight DTC buses leave from the Hotel Vishnu Palace (☎ 2932). Buses to Tehri (Rs 22, four hours) with connections to Uttarkashi and Gangotri, leave from Tehri bus stand – marvellous mountain scenery but a rough ride.

When travelling to Mussoorie from the west or north (ie Jammu), it is best to get off the express train at Saharanpur and catch a bus from there to Dehra Dun or Mussoorie. These buses run even in the middle of the night.

Taxis charge Rs 150 for Dehra Dun, Rs 350 for Rishikesh, Rs 450 for Haridwar and Rs 1200 for Delhi.

Rail tickets can be arranged through the Northern Railway booking agency (☎ 2846), which has quotas for trains from Dehra Dun to Delhi, Calcutta and Bombay.

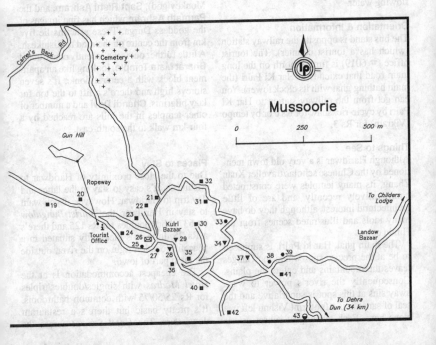

Mussoorie

0   250   500 m

HARIDWAR

Population: 189,000

Haridwar's propitious location at the point where the Ganges emerges from the high Himalaya to begin its slow progress across the plains makes it a particularly holy place. There are many ashrams here but you may find Rishikesh (24 km to the north) more pleasant, especially if you wish to study Hinduism. Haridwar means Gateway to the Gods, but despite its sanctity it's really just another noisy Indian city.

Every 12 years the Kumbh Mela attracts millions of pilgrims who bathe here. Kumbh Mela takes place every three years, consecutively at Allahabad, Nasik, Ujjain and then Haridwar. It is next due to take place in Haridwar in 1998. At the 1986 Kumbh Mela, despite extensive safety precautions, 50 people were killed in one stampede to the river (there are precise times for an especially holy dip), and dozens were drowned when they lost their footing in the swift-flowing water.

Orientation & Information

The bus stand is opposite the railway station (which has a tourist counter). The tourist office (☎ 6019) is further north on the long main road that extends to Har Ki Pairi (the main bathing ghat with its clock tower). You can get from the railway station to Har Ki Pairi by cycle-rickshaw for Rs 6 or by tempo (Vikram) for Rs 3.

Things to See

Although Haridwar is a very old town mentioned by the Chinese scholar/traveller Xuan Zhang, its many temples were constructed comparatively recently, and are of little architectural interest, although they do have many idols and illustrated scenes from the Hindu epics.

The main ghat, **Har ki Pairi**, is supposed to be at the precise spot where the Ganges leaves the mountains and enters the plains. Consequently the river's power to wash away sins at this spot is superlative and the seal of sanctity is a footprint Vishnu left in a stone here. Each evening at sunset priests perform the Ganga Aarti, or river worship, ceremony here. Non-Hindus can watch only from the bridge on the other side of the river.

It's worth taking the chairlift (Rs 8 return) to the **Mansa Devi Temple** on the hill above the city. The lift is not exactly state of the art, but it's well maintained. It's open from 8 am to noon and 2 to 5 pm. Vendors sell *prasad* of coconuts, marigolds and other offerings in colourful party-packs, to take up to the goddess. Mansa is one of the forms of Shakti Durga and, as the signs inform you, is not keen on photographers.

The **Daksha Mahadev Temple** is another important temple. Daksha, the father of Sati (Siva's first wife) performed a sacrifice here but neglected to invite Siva. Sati was so angry at this snub to her husband that she managed to spontaneously self-immolate!

Other temples and buildings of lesser interest include the **Bhimgoda Tank** (said to have been formed by a blow of Bhima's knee – Bhima is the brother of Hanuman, the Monkey god), **Sapt Rishi Ashram**, and the **Parmath Ashram** which has fine images of the goddess Durga. These ashrams lie five km from the centre on the road to Rishikesh. A little further out is the recently constructed **Bharat Mata Temple**, looking like an apartment block with a central dome. It's seven storeys high and there's a lift to the top for lazy pilgrims. **Chandi Devi** and a number of other temples in the hills are reached by a four-km walk to the south-east.

Places to Stay

Due to the close proximity of Haridwar to Rishikesh, it's easy to stay in the latter and day trip to Haridwar. However, if you want to stay in Haridwar, the *Tourist Bungalow* (☎ 6379) has doubles for Rs 125 and there's a Rs 25 dorm. It's pleasantly situated in a peaceful location right on the river, outside the main part of town.

The cheapest accommodation is at the *Hotel Madras* with singles/doubles/triples for Rs 25/50/75 with common bathrooms. It's pretty basic but there's a restaurant downstairs. The *Hotel Samrat* across the

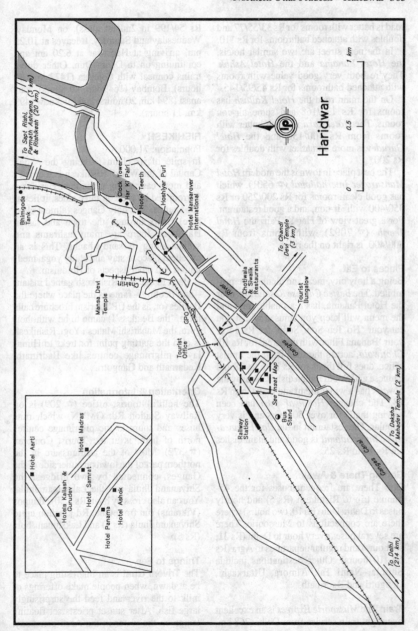

Haridwar

1 km
0.5
0

To Sapt Rishi,
Parmath Ashrams (3 km)
& Rishikesh (20 km)

Bhimgoda
Tank

Clock Tower
Har Ki Pairi
Hotel Teerth
Hoshyar Puri

Hotel Mansarover
International

Mansa Devi
Temple

Chartik

River

To Chandi
Devi Temple
(3 km)

Chattiwala
& Siwallik
Restaurants

GPO

Tourist
Bungalow

Tourist
Office

See Inset Map

Railway
Station

Bus Stand

Ganges

Ganga Canal

Upper Ganga Canal

To Daksha
Mahadev Temple (2 km)

To Delhi
(214 km)

Hotel Aarti
Hotels Kailash &
Gurudev
Hotel Samrat
Hotel Panama
Hotel Ashok
Hotel Madras

road is better with rooms for Rs 33/55/77 and doubles with attached bathrooms for Rs 110.

In the next street are two similar hotels, the *Hotel Panama* and the *Hotel Ashok*. They're both very good value with rooms with attached bathrooms for Rs 45/95/145.

On the main road the *Hotel Kailash* has rooms for Rs 133/168 and some air-con rooms. The *Hotel Aarti* is much better with rooms from Rs 100/150 and the *Hotel Gurudev* is more upmarket with doubles for Rs 200.

The best place in town is the modern *Hotel Mansarover International* (☎ 6501), which has good clean rooms for Rs 200/250 or Rs 350/400 with air-con, and a good restaurant. For a great view of Har Ki Pairi the *Hotel Teerth* (☎ 7092), with rooms from Rs 300/400, is right on the river.

Places to Eat

Being a holy city, meat and alcohol are prohibited. The *Bestec Chinese Restaurant*, near the Hotel Panama, has reasonable food and the menu will keep you amused whilst you eat your 'Ho Ten Sour Soup' for Rs 14 or your 'Banana Filter with custered' for Rs 10. *Chotiwala*, across the road from the tourist office, does full thalis for Rs 15 to Rs 28 and Chinese and South Indian dishes. Nearby the *Siwalik* has a wider menu and thalis from Rs 18. The cheaper *Hoshiyar Puri* has been serving thalis for over 50 years and is very popular. The restaurant in the *Hotel Mansarover International* is good and main dishes are Rs 16 to Rs 25.

Getting There & Away

Bus There are frequent buses for the 45-minute trip to Rishikesh (Rs 5) and hourly buses to Dehra Dun (Rs 10, two hours) where there are connections to Mussoorie. There are several buses every hour to Delhi (Rs 31, six hours) and regular departures to Agra (Rs 60, 10 hours). Other destinations include Shimla, Naini Tal, Almora, Uttarkashi, Gangotri and Badrinath.

Train The *Mussoorie Express* is an excellent overnight train service from Delhi (268 km,

Rs 54/199 in 2nd/1st class), on Monday, Wednesday and Saturday. It leaves at 10.25 pm, arriving at Haridwar at 6.20 am and continuing on to Dehra Dun. Other direct trains connect with Calcutta (1472 km, 35 hours), Bombay (1649 km, 40 hours), Varanasi (894 km, 20 hours) and Lucknow (493 km, 11 hours).

RISHIKESH

Population: 71,000

In spite of its claim to being the 'Yoga Capital of the World' Rishikesh is a quieter and more easy-going place than Haridwar. Surrounded by hills on three sides, it lies at 356 metres. The holy Ganges (almost clear here) flows through the town and, as in Haridwar, there are many ashrams and sadhus along its sandy banks. This is an excellent place to stay and study yoga, meditation and other aspects of Hinduism.

Back in the '60s Rishikesh gained instant – and fleeting – fame as the place where the Beatles (or, as the UP Tourism brochure calls them, 'the Beatless'!) came to be with their guru, the Maharishi Mahesh Yogi. Rishikesh is also the starting point for treks to Himalayan pilgrimage centres like Badrinath, Kedarnath and Gangotri.

Orientation & Information

The helpful tourist office (☎ 209) is on Railway Station Rd. GMVN, which runs buses and tours to the pilgrimage centres north of here, is at the Tourist Complex (☎ 372). Most of the ashrams are in the northern part of the town on either side of the Ganges, connected by two bridges: the Shivanand Jhula and the Lakshman Jhula. You can also cross by boat (Rs 1.50). Tempos (Vikrams) run from Ghat Rd junction up to Shivanand Jhula (Rs 2) and Lakshman Jhula (Rs 5).

Things to See

The **Triveni Ghat** is an interesting place to be at dawn, when people make offerings of milk to the river and feed the surprisingly large fish. After sunset priests set floating lamps on the water in the Aarti ceremony.

Nearby is the **Bharat Mandir**, the oldest temple here.

The suspension bridge, **Lakshman Jhula**, was built in 1929 to replace a rope bridge. This is where Rama's brother Lakshmana is said to have crossed the river on a jute rope and the old **Lakshman Temple** is on the west bank. Across the river are some turretted architectural oddities including the 13-storey **Kailashanand Mission Ashram** – there's a good view from the top. It's a pleasant two-km walk along this east bank to the Shivanand Jhula.

Pilgrims take Ganga water to offer at **Neel Khanth Mahadev**, a four-hour walk from Lakshman Jhula on the east bank. There are fine views on the way up to the temple at 1700 metres but take something to drink and start early as it can get very hot.

There are great views from **Kunjapuri**, in the hills north of Rishikesh. It's a three-km walk from Hindola Khal (45 minutes by bus from Rishikesh) which all buses to Tehri pass through.

A number of travel agents in the Ghat Rd area organise river rafting trips from Shivpuri, 15 km upstream.

Meditation

Studying Hinduism has, naturally, become somewhat commercialised at Rishikesh. However, once you've found a place to suit your needs, spending some time here can be a fulfilling experience. There are many ashrams to choose from. Most charge Rs 30 to Rs 60 per day for a basic room with food included. It's worth first talking to other travellers and going to a few lectures (free) at different ashrams to find a guru who gets through to you.

Many ashrams post up a 'code of conduct' advising you to bath daily, avoid unnecessary chatting, and abstain from eggs, meat, fish, liquor, onions, garlic, tobacco and pan. Notices also state that women are not allowed into temples or the courtyard when having *masik dharma* (menstruating).

Many travellers head for Ved Niketan where there are over 100 rooms arranged around a large courtyard. Rooms are Rs 25 or Rs 30 with attached bathroom. It's a very relaxed place and you don't have to attend the yoga class (6 am) or the evening lectures but you shouldn't treat the place like a hotel and should stay for at least a few days. Nearby is the Maharishi Mahesh Yogi's Transcendental Meditation Centre but it's not a place at which you can just turn up. Write in advance to Maharishi Mahesh Yogi Ashram, Rishikesh, 249201.

On the other side of the river is Shivanand Ashram (The Divine Life Society), founded by Swami Shivanand. You can stay for short-term study or for longer three-month courses, although to do this you need to write one month in advance. Or simply drop by for the daily lectures at 10 am and 5 pm. In the same area is Yog Niketan which has good double rooms for Rs 50. The yoga and meditation classes here have been recommended. Another popular place is the Yoga Study Centre at Koyalghati.

Places to Stay

If you're not staying in an ashram, there's a good range of other accommodation here.

GMVN's Tourist Bungalow, *Tourist Complex Rishilok* (☎ 373), is pleasantly situated close to the ashrams. It's a bit run down but has doubles from Rs 60 and rooms with attached bathrooms from Rs 93/124. There's a reasonably priced dining hall and a pleasant garden to relax in.

Across the river, near the Lakshman Jhula, there's the very basic *Bombay Kshettra* with rooms for Rs 30/50 with common bathrooms. The *Green Hotel* (☎ 1242) has excellent rooms for Rs 50/100 with attached bathrooms and some air-cooled doubles for Rs 250. There's a good restaurant where you can try their 'African Breakfast' with fruit for Rs 22.

By the main bus stand are the *Hotel Menka* and the *Hotel Gaurev*, both very similar with singles/doubles for Rs 50/80. A short distance behind them is a much better place, the *Hotel Ashoka*, with clean rooms for Rs 45 or Rs 55 with attached bathroom, and a helpful manager.

More upmarket places in the town centre

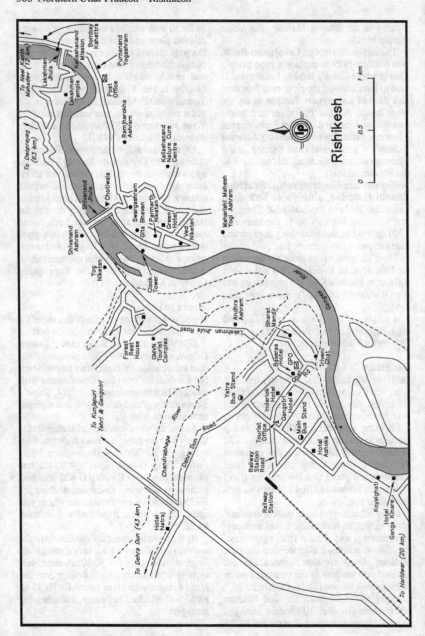

include the *Baseraa Hotel* (☎ 767), close to Triveni Ghat, with good rooms from Rs 110/150, and the similarly priced but rather glitzy *Gangotri Hotel*. Opposite is the *Inderlok Hotel* (☎ 555) whose resident yoga teacher gives free lessons on the lawn on the roof if you stay. Rooms range from Rs 150/200 to Rs 350/400 with air-con and bathtub.

The well-located *Hotel Ganga Kinare* (☎ 566) is right on the river and has a private ghat, but rooms are a bit overpriced at Rs 395/695. The *Hotel Natraj* has rooms at Rs 395/675 and a swimming pool that nonresidents can use for Rs 30.

Places to Eat

Meat and alcohol are prohibited in this holy town. The most famous restaurant is *Chotiwala* ('Two children or one adult can eat in a thali, Rs 15') just across the Shivanand Jhula. Next door is the equally good *Luxmi Hotel*. On the other side of the river near the boat landing the *Madras Restaurant* does great masala dosas.

The restaurant at the *Baseraa Hotel* is good, and the *Indrani Restaurant* at the Hotel Inderlok is probably the best place to eat in Rishikesh, although it is quite expensive. Dhal-of-the-Day is Rs 25 and cheese kebabs are Rs 20.

Getting There & Away

It's 18 km along the Dehra Dun road to Jolly Grant Airport and taxis charge Rs 150. There are daily flights to Delhi with Vayudoot or Jagsan (US$67).

A small branch railway line runs from Haridwar up to Rishikesh but the buses are more convenient. From the government bus stand there are four buses an hour to Haridwar (Rs 5, 45 minutes) from 4 am to 10 pm. There are shared taxis to Dehra Dun for Rs 20 and buses for Rs 8 (1½ hours) with connections to Mussoorie. There are hourly buses to Delhi (Rs 40, 6½ hours), an early morning bus to Ramnagar (for Corbett; Rs 40, six hours) and Naini Tal (Rs 59, 10 hours). Buses leave at 5.30 am and 10.30 pm

for Shimla (Rs 50, 11 hours) and early in the morning for Uttarkashi (Rs 45).

In the summer there are regular departures to Gangotri (Rs 70) and other pilgrimage centres from the Yatra bus stand.

CORBETT NATIONAL PARK

Established in 1936 as India's first national park, Corbett is famous for its wide variety of wildlife and its beautiful location. It covers 520 sq km on the banks of the Ramganga River in the foothills of the Himalaya. It may seem incongruous for a national park to be named after a famous British hunter – Jim Corbett is best known for his book *The Man-Eaters of Kumaon*, and was greatly revered by local people for shooting tigers that had developed a liking for human flesh. However, he was instrumental in setting up the reserve and eventually shot more wildlife with his camera than with his gun.

By 1973 the tiger population in the whole of India had fallen to around 1800 and it was from Corbett that Project Tiger was launched with the assistance of the World Wide Fund for Nature (WWF). There are now 18 reserves in this conservation scheme and the total tiger population has grown to about 4000, 92 of them in this park. It seems that the tiger has been saved from extinction but as the human population of the country snowballs, competition for land increases and attacks by tigers on people are no longer the stuff of memoirs. Also, Project Tiger is now beset by scandal – see Flora & Fauna in the Facts about the Country chapter.

Seeing a tiger here is dependent on chance, since baiting has been discontinued and there is no tiger tracking (unlike at Kanha in Madhya Pradesh). However, your best chance is if you come late in the season (April to mid-June) and stay for several days.

More commonly seen wildlife includes wild elephant, langur monkey (black face, long tail), rhesus macaque, peacock, and several types of deer including chital (spotted deer), sambar, hog deer and barking-deer. There are also crocodile, the odd-looking gavial or gharial (a thin-snouted, fish-eating crocodile often spotted from High Bank), monitor lizard, wild boar and jackal. Leopard (referred to as panther in India) are occasionally seen.

Corbett is also a birdwatcher's paradise, and since the creation of the Kalagarh Dam on the Ramganga River, large numbers of water-fowl have been attracted here.

Information

Dhikala is the main accommodation centre in the park, 51 km from Ramnagar (the nearest railhead). Outside Corbett there are some expensive resorts and a few hotels in Ramnagar. Apart from the daily bus service to Dhikala the only form of transport available there is elephants. Jeeps can usually only be rented at Ramnagar (Rs 6 per km).

Permits for an overnight stay in the park have to be obtained from the Reception Centre at Ramnagar (☎ 85-3189) where accommodation is booked. At the park gates you must pay an entry fee of Rs 35 (Rs 2 for students) for a stay of up to three days, then

Rs 12 per day. Corbett is open from mid-November to mid-June but you should avoid the crowded weekends. The gates are closed at sunset and no night driving is allowed.

At Dhikala there's a library and interesting wildlife films are shown (free) in the evenings. The elephant rides at sunrise and sunset are not to be missed and cost Rs 25 for about two hours. During the day you can sit in one of the observation posts to watch for animals.

There's a bank for foreign exchange in Ramnagar.

Places to Stay & Eat

Dhikala There's a wide range of accommodation here. There's a very basic dormitory (like three-tier sleepers on the trains!) for Rs 12 in the *Log Huts* but it's better to go for the triples (Rs 60) in the *Tourist Hutment*, or the four-bedded *Green Hut* (Rs 45). An extra charge of Rs 15 is made for mattresses and sheets in all these places. More comfortable

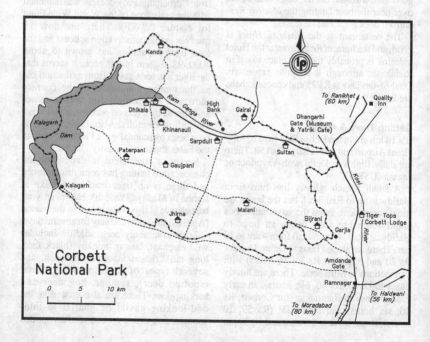

doubles at Rs 150 are in the cabins and *Forest Rest Houses*. There's only one restaurant but the food is good (main dishes Rs 20 to Rs 30).

With your own transport and food, you can also stay in forest rest houses at Sarapduli, Bijrani, Gairal, Kanda, Sultan and Khinanauli. Don't forget to get a 'clearance certificate' at Dhikala before you leave the park.

Ramnagar Note that if you use Ramnagar as a base you'll have to rent a jeep here and you won't be able to go out on elephant rides in the centre of the park, as day visits to Dhikala are not allowed.

There's a good *Tourist Bungalow* (☎ 85-3225), next to the Reception Centre. It has doubles for Rs 100 and dormitory beds for Rs 30. The *Hotel Govind* has a reasonable restaurant and grotty doubles for Rs 60. The *Hotel Everest* is much better – doubles with bathrooms for Rs 80.

There are some upmarket resorts, but they're outside the park. *Quality Inn Corbett Jungle Resort* (☎ Delhi 67-1327) has attractive cottages high above the river for Rs 925 and offers elephant rides and excursions into Corbett. *Tiger Tops Corbett Lodge* (☎ Delhi 77-1055) is a very luxurious place with prices to match – US$108 per person. It's designed and operated like their resort in Chitwan (Nepal) and there are elephant rides, jeep trips and a swimming pool.

Getting There & Away
Ramnagar is connected by train with Moradabad and by bus with Delhi (Rs 46, six hours), Lucknow, Naini Tal and Ranikhet. The bus station is near the Reception Centre and the hotels; the railway station is 1½ km south.

A bus runs from Ramnagar to Dhikala (Rs 13, two hours) at 3.30 pm, returning from Dhikala at 9 am next day. The airport at Pantnagar is 110 km away – too far to be of any use. There are also three-day package tours operated by UP Tourism (Rs 800) and others from Delhi.

KATHGODAM & HALDWANI
These two towns, six km apart, form an important travel junction for travellers to Naini Tal and most of the hill stations in the Kumaon region. Kathgodam is the railhead and there are evening trains to Lucknow, Agra and Jodhpur. There are retiring rooms, a good refreshment room and a tourist bureau. Bookings can be made in the out-agencies in many hill stations. There's supposed to be a connecting bus to Naini Tal but if the train is late you'll miss it. If you're coming up to this area it may be better to get off the train at Haldwani, where there's a big bus station.

NAINI TAL
Population: 31,000
At 1938 metres in the Kumaon Hills is the attractive hill station of Naini Tal, once the summer capital of Uttar Pradesh. The hotels and villas of this popular resort are set around the peaceful Naini lake or *tal*, hence the name.

Naini Tal is very much a green and pleasant land that immediately appealed to the homesick Brits, who were reminded of the Cumbrian Lake District. It was discovered by a Mr Barron and he had his yacht carried up here in 1840. The Naini Tal Boat Club, whose wooden clubhouse still graces the edge of the lake, became the fashionable focus of the community. Disaster struck on 16 September 1880 when a famous landslip occurred, burying 151 people in the Assembly Halls area and creating the recreation ground now known as the Flats.

This is certainly one of the most pleasant hill stations to visit and there are many interesting walks through the forests to points with superb views of the Himalaya.

The high season, when Naini Tal is packed and hotel prices double or triple, corresponds to school holidays. Avoid Christmas and the New Year, mid-April to mid-July and mid-September to early November.

Orientation & Information

The two bazaars, Tallital and Mallital, are at either end of the lake, connected by The Mall. A toll keeps most motorised traffic off this road and for some inexplicable reason the traffic laws of India are reversed here – on The Mall you drive on the right!

There's a UP Tourism office (☎ 2337) and a travel company (Parvat Tours) run by its local subsidiary, Kumaon Mandal Vikas Nigam (KMVN, ☎ 2543). The bus stand (☎ 2641) and railway booking agency (☎ 2518) are in Tallital.

Naini Lake

This attractive lake is said to be one of the emerald green eyes of Siva's wife, Sati. She had jumped into a sacrificial bonfire and as her mourning husband dragged her charred remains across the country, various appendages dropped off. India is now littered with places 'formed' by parts of her body. Her eye falling here makes this a holy spot and the popular **Naina Devi Temple** is by the northern end of the lake.

You can rent rowing boats and pedal-boats for Rs 20 to Rs 30 per hour from a number of places along The Mall. The Naini Tal Boat Club has a few yachts for Rs 40 per hour and you may be able to persuade them to waive the temporary membership fee (Rs 200) if you don't want to use the clubhouse facilities (bar, restaurant, ballroom and library). The club is less exclusive than it was. When Jim Corbett lived here he was refused membership because he'd been born in India, and hence was not a pukkah sahib.

St John's Church

Built in 1847, soon after the British arrived, this church contains a brass memorial to the victims of the famous landslip. The few bodies that could be uncovered from the rubble were buried in the graveyard here.

Ropeway to Snow View

A chairlift (ropeway) takes you up to this popular viewpoint at 2270 metres. The lift is open from 10 am to 4 pm and costs Rs 15. It's a pleasant walk down. The Rs 25 return ticket gives you only one hour at the top and a set time for your return. A sign says: 'Don't be panicy in case of power failure'!

At the top there are powerful binoculars (Rs 2) for a close-up view of Nanda Devi (7817 metres), which was, as the old brass plate here tells you, 'the highest mountain in the British Empire'. Nanda Devi was India's highest peak until Sikkim (and thus Kanchenjunga) was absorbed into the country. You can be dressed in Kumaon national costume and have your photo taken for Rs 15, with a spectacular Himalayan backdrop.

Walks

There are several other good walks in the area, with views of the snowcapped mountains to the north. China Peak, also known as Naini Peak is the highest point in the area (2610 metres) and can be reached either from Snow View or from Mallital (five km). Climb up in the early morning when the views are clearer.

A four-km walk to the west of the lake brings you to Dorothy's Seat (2292 metres) where a Mr Kellet built a seat in memory of his wife, killed in a plane crash. Laria Kanta is at 2480 metres on the opposite side of the lake and Deopatta (2435 metres) is west of Mallital.

Hanumangarh & Observatory

There are good views and spectacular sunsets over the plains from this Hanuman

Temple, three km south of Tallital. Just over one km further on is the State Observatory, which is sometimes open at weekends. Check with the tourist office.

Other Activities

If you don't feel like walking you can rent ponies (which are in surprisingly good condition) to climb to any of the viewpoints. Expect to pay around Rs 20 to Rs 30 per hour, or Rs 40 to Rs 50 for China Peak (3½ hours). You can play billiards for Rs 25 per hour at Naini Billiards or rent fishing gear at the lake at Bhim Tal, an overrated excursion spot 23 km from Naini Tal.

Organised Tours

KMVN's *Parvat Tours* (☎ 2656) operates tours to the nearby lakes (Sat Tal and Bhim Tal) and to places further north, like Kausani and Ranikhet. In the summer they offer a six-day pilgrimage to Badrinath and Kedarnath. Along The Mall there are lots of private travel agents (even one called Altruist Travels!) offering similar tours and selling bus tickets to Delhi. They have day trips to Corbett National Park for Rs 110. A taxi would charge Rs 900 for up to five people.

Places to Stay – bottom end

There are over 100 places to stay here. Off-season rates are given here but you may be able to get a further discount. It's worth paying a bit more for a room with a view over the lake and you often get a better deal for a more expensive room in a cheaper hotel, than for a cheap room in an upmarket place.

KMVN's *Tourist Reception Centre* in Tallital has only dormitory accommodation (Rs 20) in eight-bedded rooms, with lots of hot water. The other *Tourist Reception Centre* (doubles from Rs 100) is away from the lake on the road to Delhi – not a great location. The *Hotel Himalaya*, near the Tourist Reception Centre in Tallital, has some tiny singles for Rs 30 and some nice doubles (with attached bathrooms) facing the lake for Rs 70.

Behind the big Hotel Mansarover, the *Hotel Gauri Niwas* has some good value rooms with attached bathrooms for Rs 40. Nearby, the *Hotel Punjab* is not so good and the *Lake View* has rooms from Rs 75. On The Mall the *Hotel Merino* is an old place worth checking out, with doubles from Rs 80.

There are a couple of hotels in this area that have been popular with travellers for many years, but they are starting to move upmarket. The *Hotel Prashant* has rooms with attached bathrooms from Rs 100 to Rs 300 and good views from the balconies. The *Evelyn Hotel* has doubles from Rs 150 to Rs 300, a pleasant terrace overlooking the lake and a good restaurant. The *Hotel Regency* behind it is a little cheaper.

On The Mall there are doubles from Rs 150 at the large *Alka Hotel* and from Rs 125 at the *Hotel Sheela*. The *Hotel Krishna Mountain View* has some singles/doubles for Rs 75/95 and they do have views, but of hills rather than mountains.

There are some cheaper places further along The Mall. The *Standard Hotel* has some basic singles/doubles from Rs 50/90. The *Alps Hotel* is a creaky old place with vast rooms for Rs 45/50 – the front rooms have a balcony. Behind it is the *Hotel Madhuban* which has some doubles with attached bathrooms from Rs 60 and is very good value.

In Mallital the *Kohli Cottage* is an excellent, clean guest house, run by a friendly Sikh, with doubles for Rs 60 and rooms upstairs with great views. The three hotels nearby, the *Coronation Hotel*, *Lalit Guest House* and *Hotel Ajanta*, all have rooms for Rs 35/50. The Lalit Guest House is the best of them but they're all pretty basic.

The *Youth Hostel* has dorm beds for Rs 12 (members) or Rs 22 (nonmembers) and there are also two doubles. It's a well-run place in an excellent peaceful location, a 25-minute walk from Mallital Bazaar. The set meals for Rs 10 are great value and you can get information on the Pindari Glacier trek here.

On the way to the YH is the *Hotel Moon*, a friendly place with sunny doubles with attached bathrooms on the top floor for Rs 60, and a vegetarian restaurant. Nearby is the *Virdi Guest House*, which is run by a Sikh

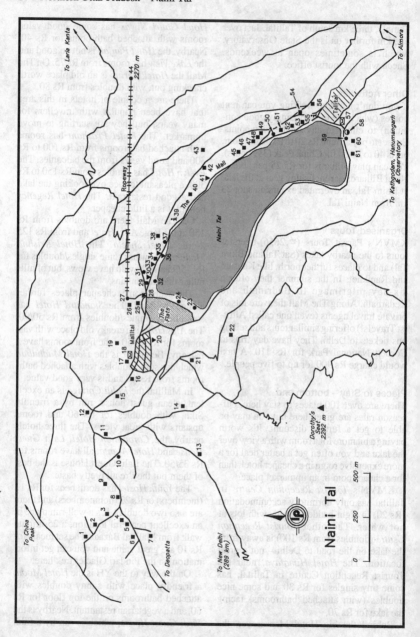

Naini Tal

To Larin Kanta

To Almora

To Kathgodam, Hanumangarh & Observatory

Ropeway

The Mall

The Mall

Naini Tal

The Flats

Mallital

Tallital

To China Peak

To Deopatta

To New Delhi
(289 km)

Dorothy's Seat
▲ 2292 m

▲ 2270 m

500 m

250

■	PLACES TO STAY	52	Hotel Elphinstone
		53	Hotel Mansarover
1	Shervani Hilltop Inn	54	Hotel Gauri Niwas
2	Arif Castles	56	Hotel Prashant
3	Hotel Armadale	60	Hotel Himalaya
4	Virdi Guest House	61	Tallital Tourist Reception Centre
5	Hotel Moon		
6	Vikram Vintage Inn	▼	PLACES TO EAT
7	Youth Hostel		
8	Hotel Earlscourt	20	Sher-E-Punjab (Mallital)
9	Swiss Hotel	28	Kumaon Restaurant
11	Manu Maharani Lake Resort	30	Flattis and Capri Restaurant
12	Hotel New Pavilion	33	Embassy Restaurant
13	Mallital Tourist Reception Centre	35	Nanak's Restaurant
14	Hotel Langdale Manor	36	Kwality Restaurant
15	Royal Hotel	41	Sher-E-Punjab (The Mall)
16	Lalit Guest House		
17	Kohli Cottage		OTHER
19	Hotel Belvedere		
21	Hotel Aroma	10	St John's Church
22	Vatika Naini Retreat	18	GPO
25	Alps Hotel	23	Naini Devi Temple
26	Hotel Madhuban	24	Assembly Rooms
29	Standard Hotel	27	Ropeway (Lower Station)
34	Hotel Channi Raja	31	Naini Tal Mountaineering Club
38	Grand Hotel	32	Naini Tal Boat Club
40	Hotel Natraj	37	Naini Billiards
42	Hotel Krishna Mountain View	39	UP Tourism
43	Hotel Silverton	44	Snow View (2270 m)
45	Hotel Sheela	50	Church
46	Alka Hotel	55	KMVN
47	Hotel India	57	Post Office
48	Evelyn Hotel	58	Bus Stand
49	Hotel Regency	59	Railway Booking Agency
51	Hotel Merino		

piano tuner. Rooms here with common bathroom are Rs 50.

Places to Stay – middle & top end

The *Grand Hotel* (☎ 2406) is one of the oldest places here with rooms from Rs 250/400. The better rooms are upstairs, with views over the lake. It's much better than the other similarly priced Raj leftover, the *Royal Hotel*, which is vast and dilapidated, with disinterested staff and peculiar sculptures in the garden.

Back on The Mall the *Hotel Channi Raja* (☎ 2624) is a flashy new place done up in Bombay glitz, with rooms from Rs 350. Set back above the lake, there are good views

from the *Hotel Silverton*, which is in the same price range.

Most of the other upmarket places are above Mallital and they operate a free Jeep service down to The Mall. The *Swiss Hotel* (☎ 3013) has large, high-ceilinged rooms for Rs 300/400 and discounts are sometimes available. Nearby is the *Hotel Earlscourt* (☎ 3381) which was once an English family house. The shelves are lined with the books they left behind – edifying publications like 'A Handbook for Girl Guides' and 'Hymns Ancient & Modern'. Rooms with bathrooms are Rs 300/650 and there's a pricey restaurant.

Further up is the resort hotel *Arif Castles*

(☎ 2801) with rooms for Rs 350/700, and above it the *Shervani Hilltop Inn* (☎ 3128) which has a pleasant garden and is good value at Rs 365 for a double.

The *Hotel Belvedere* (☎ 2082) is an old whitewashed maharaja's palace which is rather run down, with moth-eaten tiger-skins on the walls, but it has a certain character to it, and there are good views. The suites for Rs 600 are good, there are some cheaper rooms, and the manager is most helpful and friendly.

The *Vatika Naini Retreat* (☎ 2105) is in a secluded spot above Mallital. Only a few rooms have views of the lake but there's a nice garden and good restaurant. The *Vikram Vintage Inn* (☎ 2877) is a solid plush hotel with rooms for Rs 900, and at the top of the pile is the *Manu Maharani Lake Resort* (☎ 2531), with good lake views and all the mod cons. Doubles cost Rs 990.

Places to Eat

For a cheap snack, there's a stall outside the Standard Hotel serving great masala dosas for Rs 6. In Mallital bazaar there's the *Sher-E-Punjab* and the nearby *Sharma Vaishnek* with good vegetarian thalis.

Along The Mall there's quite a range of places to choose from. The *Kumaon* does veg and video games but the best vegetarian food is at the *Purohit Restaurant*, next to Embassy Restaurant. The *Capri Restaurant* is rather dark and main dishes are Rs 28 to Rs 40. *Flattis* is another popular place, and it's a bit cheaper. *Sakley's Restaurant* by the Alps Hotel has a bakery attached and some good pastries. At the other end of The Mall is another branch of *Sher-E-Punjab* and the *Merino Restaurant*, which has been recommended.

The best place for pizzas, hamburgers and ice cream is *Nanak's* but it's also expensive and trendy. Pizzas cost Rs 25 to Rs 40 and a masala dosa here will set you back Rs 12. Outside Nanak's, stalls sell candy-floss for Rs 3.

The *Kwality Restaurant* has a great location right on the water, and its Indian food is excellent. Main dishes are Rs 30 to Rs 40.

The *Embassy Restaurant* is more expensive but is supposedly the best place to eat in town.

Getting There & Away

The nearest airport is Pantnagar, 71 km away, with Vayudoot flights three times a week to Delhi (Rs 786). Book with KMVN which also runs the airport bus (Rs 55, 2½ hours).

Kathgodam (35 km south) is the nearest railway station, and the railway booking agency in Naini Tal has a quota for trains to Agra, Lucknow and Jodhpur. There are shared taxis to Kathgodam and Haldwani for Rs 25, and buses (Rs 9, 1½ hours) every 30 minutes. Morning and evening buses take nine hours to Delhi (Rs 50 to Rs 76) and private operators run video coaches and air-con buses (Rs 175).

Other bus destinations include Bhim Tal (Rs 6, one hour), Ramnagar (Rs 19, 3½ hours), Almora (Rs 19, three hours), Ranikhet (Rs 19, three hours), Kausani (Rs 29, five hours), Pithoragarh (Rs 39, nine hours), Bareilly (Rs 26, five hours), Haridwar (Rs 55, nine hours), Rishikesh (Rs 59, 10 hours) and Dehra Dun (Rs 65, 10½ hours). There's one early morning bus to Song (for the Pindari Glacier Trek).

Getting Around

KMVN operates an airport bus service (Rs 55, 2½ hours).

Getting up and down The Mall is no problem as there are speedy cycle-rickshaws charging a fixed Rs 2 between Tallital and Mallital. If you can't find an empty one you may need to join the queue at either end of The Mall for a few minutes.

RANIKHET

North of Naini Tal and at an altitude of 1829 metres, this peaceful hill station offers excellent views of the snow-capped Himalaya including Nanda Devi (7817 metres). It's an important army town and the HQ of the Kumaon Regiment. There are a couple of churches that have been converted into tweed and shawl mills with hand-operated looms.

There are several good walks – to **Jhula Devi Temple** (seven km) and the orchards at **Chaubatia** (three km further on), and for Rs 20 you can tee off on a golf course with a 300-km panoramic view of the Himalaya!

The tourist office is by the government bus stand.

Places to Stay & Eat

There are several hotels in the bazaar area between the bus stops. The *Hotel Raj Deep* is the best of the cheap places with doubles for Rs 40, or Rs 65 with bathroom, and a vegetarian restaurant. The *Alka Hotel* has good doubles from Rs 100 and a pleasant balcony with mountain views. Similarly priced places include the *Hotel Tribuwan* by the private bus stand and the *Moon Hotel* which has a good restaurant (main dishes Rs 25).

The three-star *Parwati Inn* by the government bus stand has rooms from Rs 275. The *Tourist Bungalow* with rooms at Rs 125 (with kitchens) and dorm beds at Rs 20 is five km from the bazaar.

Getting There & Away

As with the other hill stations in the Kumaon region, Kathgodam is the nearest railhead. There are buses to Kathgodam (Rs 24, four hours), Naini Tal (Rs 19, three hours), Almora (Rs 15, 2½ hours), Kausani (Rs 20, 3½ hours), Ramnagar (Rs 26, five hours), Delhi (Rs 72 to Rs 93, 12 hours) as well as to Lucknow, Haridwar and Badrinath. Buses depart from the government and the private bus stands, which are one km apart on the main road.

ALMORA

Population: 27,000

This picturesque hill station, at an altitude of 1650 metres, is one of the few not created by the British. Some 400 years ago it was the capital of the Chand rajas of Kumaon.

Almora is larger than Ranikhet and Kausani, there's an interesting bazaar, excellent views of the mountains and some great walks. The eight-km walk up to the **Kasar Devi Temple** is a good one – this is where Swami Vivekananda came to meditate. You can also visit the tweed mills above the Holiday Home, and the town **museum**. The clock tower was built in 1842 and carries the motto 'Work as if thou hadst to live for aye, Worship as if thou wert to die today'. There's a small Siva shrine in the room below it.

Places to Stay & Eat

There are several hotels in the bazaar including the very basic *Tourist Cottage* with rooms from Rs 40. The *Hotel Pawan*, further up the street, is much cleaner with singles/doubles from Rs 53/80 with attached bathrooms, and billiards upstairs. The top hotel is the large *Hotel Shikhar* with rooms from Rs 80 to Rs 400. The *Glory Restaurant* in this area is a good place to eat with masala dosa for Rs 7.50 and 'expresso' coffee.

Many people prefer the hotels outside the bazaar as they're rather more peaceful. The *Kailash Hotel* ('Junction of East and West Managed by House Wives') is an interesting place, opposite the GPO. Most travellers who stay here seem to enjoy the eccentricities of the hotel and its elderly proprietor, Mr Shah. Mrs Shah's cooking is very good and there are rooms from Rs 50 although, as the sign above the door says, 'The Kingdom of Heaven is not a Place but a State of Mind'. In the same area is the *Savoy Hotel* with rooms from Rs 50 to Rs 150.

At KMVN's Tourist Bungalow *Holiday Home* (☎ 2250) the doubles at Rs 50 are very good value. There's a Rs 20 dorm, and twin-bedded cottages with good views are available for Rs 125.

Getting There & Away

The nearest railhead is Kathgodam, where buses connect with arriving trains. From Almora there are buses to Naini Tal (Rs 19, three hours), Kausani (Rs 10, two hours), Ranikhet (Rs 15, 2½ hours), Pithoragarh (Rs 30, seven hours) and north to Song for the Pindari Glacier trek.

AROUND ALMORA
Katarmal & Jageshwar
There are a number of ancient temple sites in the area. At Katarmal (17 km from Almora) is the 800-year-old Sun Temple. A much larger group is 34 km away at Jageshwar in an attractive valley of deodars. They date back to the 7th century AD. There's a *Tourist Bungalow* (Rs 60 for doubles) and a small museum at Jageshwar.

PITHORAGARH
Population: 28,000
Situated at 1815 metres, Pithoragarh is the main town of a region that borders both Tibet and Nepal. It sits in a small valley that has been called 'Little Kashmir' and there are a number of picturesque walks in the area. You can climb up to Chandak (seven km) for a view of the Pithoragarh Valley.

There's a KMVN *Tourist Bungalow* here, with doubles from Rs 50 with attached bathroom, and several other hotels. There are buses to Almora, Naini Tal, Haldwani, Delhi and Tanakpur (the railhead, 158 km south).

KAUSANI
For an even closer view of the Himalaya, Kausani, 53 km north of Almora, is the place to head for. At 1890 metres, it's a small peaceful place that is perfect for quiet contemplation. Gandhi stayed at the Anashakati Ashram in 1929 and was inspired by the superb Himalayan panorama, and the Hindi poet laureate Sumitra Nandan Pant grew up here.

Among the numerous hikes in the area, the 14-km walk to the 12th-century temples at **Baijnath** is definitely worth it. Don't follow the road, as it's six km further, but ask for the path through the forest.

Places to Stay & Eat
The best places are over the ridge from the bus stop, a one to two-km walk. The cheapest is *Anashakati Ashram* (Gandhi Ashram) with rooms for Rs 25 and a good library that is open to all. The *Uttarakhand Hotel* is a friendly place with rooms from Rs 40. The KMVN *Tourist Bungalow* (☎ 26) has doubles from Rs 75 with good views, balconies and hot water, as well as some cottages for Rs 175 and dorm beds for Rs 20.

The top hotel is the *Hotel Krishna Mount View* (☎ 28), a well-appointed modern place run by a friendly manager. There is a range of rooms from Rs 130 to Rs 400 for doubles. It's near the Anashakati Ashram.

Getting There & Away
Kathgodam is the nearest railhead and there are buses from Kausani to Almora (Rs 10, two hours), Ranikhet (Rs 20, 3½ hours) and Naini Tal (Rs 29, five hours).

OTHER TOWNS
Bareilly
Population: 608,000
Former capital of the region known as Rohilkand, Bareilly came under British control when the Rohillas, an Afghan tribe, became too involved with the Marathas and the Nawab of Oudh.

Banbassa
To/From Nepal Banbassa is the closest Indian village to the Nepalese border post of Mahendrenagar. In 1992, a trickle of intrepid travellers entered Nepal at this point. There are daily buses from New Delhi to Banbassa, taking 11 hours and costing Rs 56. Banbassa is also connected by rail to Bareilly and by bus with Almora. From Banbassa, you can catch a rickshaw (20 minutes) to the border and across to Mahendrenagar.

There are direct night buses from Mahendrenagar to Kathmandu, but they take a gruelling 25 hours. The countryside is beautiful and fascinating, so it's much better to travel during the day and to break the journey at Nepalganj. In 1992 there was only one direct bus from Mahendrenagar to Nepalganj; it left at 4 am, and took around nine hours. Alternatively, buses run to Ataria (at the junction for Dhangadhi) and from there to Nepalganj. There are plenty of buses from Nepalganj to Kathmandu (day and night journeys; 16 hours) and to Pokhara (night, 15 hours).

Rampur

Population: 243,000

In this former Rohilla state capital, the State Library has an important collection of old manuscripts and miniatures, some of great importance, housed in a fine building in the old fort. There's a large Jami Masjid nearby and interesting bazaars around the walls of the palace.

TREKKING IN GARHWAL & KUMAON

The whole of this Himalayan region of northern Uttar Pradesh has traditionally been referred to as the Garhwal Himal by Western trekkers and expeditions. This is something of a misnomer since Garhwal is only the western part (Kumaon is the eastern part) of this region.

Although not many trekkers visit this region, there are a number of famous peaks, including Trisul (7120 metres) and Nanda Devi (7817 metres), India's second-highest mountain. There are also many important pilgrimage sites, such as Badrinath, Yamunotri, Kedarnath and Gangotri, near the source of the Ganges. The trekking routes pass through rich, green forests and cross beautiful meadows carpeted with flowers in summer. Glistening glaciers complement the soaring Himalayan peaks and there are many excellent state government tourist bungalows along the routes to simplify the question of shelter.

The best times to trek here are May-June and September-October. Some places, like the Valley of Flowers and the high-altitude *bugyals* (meadows), are at their best during the July-August rainy period. Although high-altitude trekking is difficult in the winter due to snow, the hill country itself is still very pleasant.

UP Tourism has two regional subsidiaries, Garhwal Mandal Vikas Nigam (GMVN) and Kumaon Mandal Vikas Nigam (KMVN) which are good sources of information. GMVN has offices in Dehra Dun, Mussoorie and Rishikesh; KMVN is based in Naini Tal. Both have smaller offices, usually in the numerous Tourist Bungalows they operate. Uttar Pradesh Mountaineering Division has branches in Rishikesh (at the Tourist Complex) and Naini Tal that can be helpful. You should also check the Lonely Planet guide *Trekking in the Indian Himalaya*.

Har-Ki-Dun Valley

This popular trek up the beautiful Har-Ki-Dun Valley can be undertaken from April to November. No high passes are crossed. Accommodation is available in PWD Rest Houses along the way and food can be bought in the villages. The roadhead, which used to be at Netwar, is now being pushed north and buses may soon be available to Sankri. Har-Ki-Dun is at 3566 metres.

Day 1	Mussoorie to Netwar	147 km*
Day 2	Netwar to Sankri	12 km
Day 3	Sankri to Taluka	12 km
Day 4	Taluka to Osla	12 km
Day 5	Osla to Har-Ki-Dun	14 km
Day 6 - 8	Return by same route	

* by bus

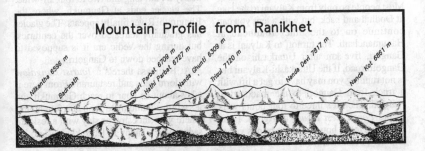

Mountain Profile from Ranikhet

Nilkantha 6596 m — Badrinath — Gauri Parbat 6709 m — Hathi Parbat 6727 m — Nanda Ghunti 6309 m — Trisul 7120 m — Nanda Devi 7817 m — Nanda Kot 6861 m

During July and August it would be possible to cross from Har-Ki-Dun Valley to Yamunotri via the Majhakanda Pass. The trail starts at Osla and since it's sometimes difficult to follow, it's advisable to hire a guide there. Osla to Yamunotri takes four to five days.

Yamunotri

Yamunotri is the source of the Yamuna River – it emerges from a frozen lake of ice and glaciers on the Kalinda Parvat at an altitude of 4421 metres. The temple of the goddess Yamunotri is on the left bank of the river and, just below it, there are several hot springs. Buses go as far as Hanumanchatti from Mussoorie or Rishikesh. From Hanumanchatti to Yamunotri takes five to six hours for there's a *Tourist Rest House* just past the halfway point, at Jankichatti. You can also stay at Yamunotri in the dharamsalas. Pilgrims cook their food in the boiling water of the hot springs.

Day 1	Mussoorie to	
	Hanumanchatti	81 km*
Day 2	Hanumanchatti to	
	Jankichatti	7 km
Day 3	Jankichatti/Yamunotri/	
	Jankichatti	14 km
Day 4	Jankichatti to	
	Hanumanchatti	7 km
Day 5	Hanumanchatti to	
	Mussoorie	81 km*

* by bus

Dodital

Most people go only from Kalyani to the lake at Dodital and back, but with a tent you can continue on to the other roadhead at Hanumanchatti. The turnoff to Kalyani is at Gangori, five km after Uttarkashi on the Gangotri road. If the Uttarkashi-Kalyani bus is not running you may have to get a lift with a truck from Gangori to the roadhead at Kalyani. Then it's three to four hours walk to the *Forest Rest House* at Agoda. From there five to six hours walking brings you to another *Forest Rest House* at Dodital. Set in

a forest of oak, pine, deodar and rhododendron, the lake is filled with trout. It's at 3307 metres and is fed by natural springs in its depths.

Day 1	Rishikesh to Uttarkashi	154 km*
Day 2	Uttarkashi/Gangori/	
	Kalyani/Agoda	17 km
Day 3	Agoda to Dodital	15 km
Day 4	Dodital to Agoda	15 km
Day 5	Agoda/Kalyani/Gangori/	
	Uttarkashi	17 km
Day 6	Uttarkashi to Rishikesh	154 km*

* by bus

To continue from Dodital to Hanumanchatti, ascend to the fields below Sonpara Pass (3953 metres), a good place to camp. Cross the pass next day and descend to the treeline for the second night. Then it's a steep descent to Hanumanchatti, where there are buses to Mussoorie and Rishikesh.

Gangotri & Gaumukh

The popular pilgrimage destination of Gangotri can be reached from Rishikesh by bus via Tehri and Uttarkashi, a 10 to 12-hour journey. There are also some buses from Mussoorie. The trek to the source of the holy Ganges starts from the tiny village of Gangotri which stands at 3140 metres. The temple of the goddess Ganga is on the right bank of the Bhagirathi River, which eventually becomes the holy Ganges. Gaumukh, the actual source of the river, is at the base of the Bhagirathi peaks.

At 4225 metres, the Gangotri Glacier is nearly 24 km long and two to four km wide. The glacier ends at Gaumukh, where the Bhagirathi River finally appears. The glacier has gradually retreated over the centuries, but during the Vedic era it is supposed to have reached down to Gangotri.

At Bhujbasa there's a *Tourist Bungalow* with dorm beds and restaurant. From here it takes about an hour to reach Gaumukh and it's worth continuing to Tapovan (four hours) where you can camp or stay with a resident sadhu who's happy to let trekkers share his cave – bring food from Gangotri.

Day 1	Gangotri to Bhujbasa	14 km
Day 2	Bhujbasa to Tapovan	10 km
Day 3	Tapovan to Bhujbasa	10 km
Day 4	Bhujbasa to Gangotri	14 km

From Gangotri it's also possible to trek up to Kedartal Lake. Although this takes only two days, some acclimatisation is necessary as the glacial lake is at 4500 metres.

Kedarnath

Like Badrinath, this is an important Hindu pilgrimage centre. The temple of Lord Kedar (Siva) is surrounded by snow-capped peaks, and said to date back to the 8th century.

To get to Kedarnath you can either make the short, direct trek from Sonprayag, 205 km north-east of Rishikesh, or you can follow the longer and more arduous yatra (pilgrimage) route from Gangotri. Along the way you pass through beautiful scenery and many colourful mountain villages. The trek starts from Malla, 20 km beyond Uttarkashi towards Gangotri.

Day 1	Malla to Belak Khal	15 km
Day 2	Belak Khal to Budakedar	14 km
Day 3	Budakedar to Ghuttu	16 km*
Day 4	Ghuttu to Panwali Khanta	12 km
Day 5	Panwali Khanta to Maggu	8 km
Day 6	Maggu to Sonprayag	9 km
Day 7	Sonprayag to Kedarnath	20 km**
Day 8	Kedarnath to Sonprayag	20 km**

* It's possible to set out from Tehri, getting a bus from there to Ghuttu (three hours), which will shorten the trek by three days.
** Taxis are available for the five km between Sonprayag and Gaurikund, on the route to Kedarnath.

Khatling Glacier

The Khatling Glacier is a lateral glacier from the centre of which the Bhilangana River emerges. The rich pasturelands here make ideal camping sites – the summer rains turn the flat land on the glacial moraines into excellent pastures. The glaciers are associated with the giant hanging glaciers of Ratangian, Jogin and Phating. Around Khatling Glacier are the snow-capped peaks of the Jogin ground (6466 metres), spectacular Sphetic Prishtwan (6905 metres), Kirti

Stambh (6402 metres) and Barte Kanta (6579 metres).

Ghuttu is three hours by bus from Tehri which is five hours from Rishikesh. There are hotels at Ghamsali and at Ghuttu, a *Forest Rest House* at Buranschauri (above Reeh) and at Gangi you can stay in the school shelter. Gangi is the last proper village before the glacier, and still very much cut off from the outside world. The people here are so isolated that they have been forced to frequently intermarry and as a result many are sterile.

Day 1	Rishikesh/Tehri/Ghamsali	99 km*
Day 2	Ghamsali/Ghuttu/Reeh	40 km**
Day 3	Reeh to Gangi	10 km
Day 4	Gangi to Khansoli	15 km
Day 5	Khansoli to Khatling	11 km
Day 6	Khatling to Naumuthi	14 km
Day 7	Naumuthi to Kalyani	12 km
Day 8	Kalyani to Reeh	15 km
Day 9	Reeh/Ghuttu/Ghamsali	40 km**
Day 10	Ghamsali/Tehri/Rishikesh	99 km*

* by bus
** 30 km by bus

The Khatling Glacier trek can also be made from the Kedarnath side. In that case the first three days of the trek are like Days 6, 5 and 4 of the Kedarnath Trek. On Day 3 you reach Ghuttu and then the route is the same as from the Gangotri side.

Nanda Devi Sanctuary

There are restrictions on entry to this national park so you should first check with KMVN to see if it is open.

Some of the most outstanding peaks in the central Himalaya are clustered between the glaciers of Gangotri and Milam. Nanda Devi with its camel-humped summit is the most important peak at 7817 metres. The Nanda Devi Sanctuary is surrounded by almost 70 white peaks which form a natural fortress, enclosing an area of 640 sq km. It's dotted with meadows and waterfalls and is the base camp for mountaineering assaults on Nanda Devi.

The seven-day trek from Lata, the roadhead 15 km from Joshimath, to

Tilchaunni is at times difficult and tedious but the scenic grandeur compensates for weary bodies and frayed nerves. The first six km, from Lata to Lata Kharak, is a tiring 1524-metre climb but there are glorious views from the broad grassy ridge of Lata Kharak. Another long uphill trek crosses the 4253-metre Dharansi Pass to Dharansi.

From Dharansi the trail winds across the Malatuni Pass (4238 metres), and then descends 750 metres to a stream. Cross the stream to the hospitable meadows of Dibrugheta, where a camp can be made by the river. From here to Deodi the track rises steeply at first, then makes a long traverse across several ridges. Cross a bridge over the Rishi Ganga to Deodi, then it's an eight-km trek through rhododendron forests to Ramani.

Nanda Devi comes ever closer as you approach Tilchaunni 'slate quarry'. It's a delightful birch clearing, the last on the Rishi gorge, but it means climbing *down* from the Bhujgara trail. Porters prefer to climb up to Patalkhan, a km above, where there is a cave and water. Many people prefer to camp at Dibrugheta.

There are three other routes in the sanctuary: Dunagiri and Changabang base (the ultimate mountain); Trisul base (with a new route into the inner south sanctuary discovered in 1979); and Nanda Devi north base (Rishi Tal above the Changabang Glacier).

Day 1	Joshimath to Lata	25 km*
	Lata to Lata Kharak	6 km
Day 2	Lata Kharak to Dharansi	10 km
Day 3	Dharansi to Deodi	13 km
Day 4	Deodi to Ramani	8 km
Day 5	Ramani to Bhujgara	6 km
Day 6	Bhujgara to Tilchaunni	8 km
Day 7	Tilchaunni to Nanda Devi base camp	5 km
Day 8	Nanda Devi base camp to Bhujgara	6 km
Day 9	Bhujgara to Ramani	6 km
Day 10	Ramani to Dibrugheta	17 km
Day 11	Dibrugheta to Dharansi	4 km
Day 12	Dharansi to Joshimath	31 km**

* by bus
** last 15 km by bus

Kuari Pass – The Curzon Trail

The route from Joshimath to the Kuari Pass is also known as the Curzon Trail – Lord Curzon was an enthusiastic Himalayan hiker. There are two routes: one goes through Auli and Gorson, Tali and Chitrakhanta and is more rewarding than the other route via Tapovan to Kuari Pass. From Auli the path trails its way through green forests, with the mountains always in view. The camping grounds are a delight – undulating slopes, carpeted in grass and set in beautiful natural surroundings. From Tali to Chitrakhanta there is only a narrow goat track which horses and mules cannot use.

At 4268 metres, Kuari, reached by a narrow pass, offers a superb panorama of the Himalaya to the north-east and the vast stretches of verdant valleys to the south-east. Nanda Devi, Dunagiri, Bethartoli, Hathi Parvat and Devastan are some of the peaks which can be seen. On a clear day it is possible to make out the Nanda Devi Sanctuary. Gailgarh, just five km from Kuari, is a little gem in wonderful surroundings. Six km south-east of Gailgarh is the snow-capped 5183-metre peak of Pangarchulia. It can be easily scaled with only normal trekking gear and, from its summit, Badrinath and other snow-covered peaks can be seen.

Delisera, six km east of Gailgarh, is a little hamlet at 3354 metres. In the local dialect *sera* means Rice Fields, and the terraced slopes around here date back countless years. In late June the entire land is a tapestry of flowers. Bore Kund, six km north-east of Gailgarh, is a lovely lake reputed to be very deep.

Day 1	Joshimath to Auli	15 km*
Day 2	Auli to Chitrakhanta	9 km
Day 3	Chitrakhanta to Kuari	8 km
Day 4	Kuari to Donabetti	7 km
Day 5	Donabetti to Panna	8 km
Day 6	Panna to Son Kharak	14 km
Day 7	Son Kharak to Rammani	6 km
Day 8	Rammani to Ghat	14 km
Day 9	Ghat to Nandprayag	29 km**

* until road is built, partly by taxi
** by taxi

Badrinath, Valley of Flowers & Hemkund

The beautiful Valley of Flowers National Park and the holy Hemkund Lake can be reached from Govind Ghat. In addition, you can visit the pilgrimage centre of Badrinath on the same trip. From Rishikesh it is 252 km (10 hours) by bus to Joshimath, where there's a *Tourist Bungalow* and hotels, and a further 44 km to Badrinath. You then have to backtrack 30 km to Govind Ghat for the start of the trek. From June to September the trail up to Hemkund Sahib is crowded with Sikh pilgrims.

Surrounded by snow-capped peaks, Badrinath, just a short distance from the Tibetan border, has been a Hindu pilgrimage centre since time immemorial. There are many temples, ashrams and dharamsalas here. The most important temple, on the left bank of the Alakananda, shows clear Buddhist influence in its architecture, indicating that in an earlier period this must also have been a Buddhist centre. The shrine is open between May and October and there is a *Tourist Bungalow* here.

The mountaineer Frank Smythe is believed to be the 'discoverer' of the Valley of Flowers. Between mid-June and mid-September the valley is an enchanting sight

with a dazzling variety of flowers fluttering in the gentle breeze. As a backdrop, snow-clad mountains stand in bold relief against the skyline. The valley is nearly 10 km long and two km wide, and is divided by the Pushpawati stream, into which several tiny streams and waterfalls merge. The huge Ghoradhungi mountain blocks one end of the valley. This national park has suffered intense tourist pressures and is periodically closed. No camping is allowed but if the park is open a day trip can be made from Ghangaria, where there is a *Tourist Rest House* and pilgrim accommodation.

From Ghangaria, you can follow the Laxma Ganga to the lake of Hemkund – quite a steep climb. In the Sikh holy book, the *Granth Sahib*, the Sikh Guru Gobind Singh recounts that in a previous life he had meditated on the shores of a lake surrounded by seven snow-capped mountains. Hemkund Sahib, Sikh pilgrims have decided, is that holy lake.

Day 1	Govind Ghat to Ghangaria	14 km
Day 2	Ghangaria/Hemkund & back	12 km
Day 3	Ghangaria/Valley of Flowers & back	11 km
Day 4	Ghangaria to Govind Ghat	14 km

Roopkund Lake

At an altitude of 4778 metres, below the 7120-metre-high Trisul massif, Roopkund Lake is sometimes referred to as the 'mystery lake' because of the skeletons of humans and horses found here. Every 12 years thousands of devout pilgrims make an arduous trek when following the Raj Jay Yatra from Nauti village, near Karnaprayag. The pilgrims are said to be led by a mysterious four-horned ram which takes them from there through Roopkund to the Shrine of Nanda Devi, where it disappears. A golden idol of the goddess Nanda Devi is carried by the pilgrims in a silver palanquin.

The small market town of Gwaldam is 78 km from Almora or 131 km from Naini Tal and there are bus connections. There's a *Tourist Rest House* at Gwaldam and it's an eight-km walk to Debal. Alternatively you

can catch a bus from Gwaldam to Debal via Tharali. The road continues through Debal to Mandoli (which you can reach by shared jeep) and is being pushed further north. There are *Forest Rest Houses* at Debal, Lohajang (just above Mandoli) and Wan. The route passes through delightful alpine pastureland and snow fields, with magnificent views of the Trisul and Nanda Ghunti peaks. On the way back you can either follow the route below to Nandprayag and Rishikesh or return to Naini Tal via Gwaldam.

Day 1	Naini Tal to Gwaldam	131 km*
Day 2	Gwaldam/Debal/Mandoli/	
	Lohajang	25 km**
Day 3	Lohajang to Wan	14 km
Day 4	Wan to Badni Bugyal	8 km
Day 5	Badni Bugyal to Baggubasa	8 km
Day 6	Baggubasa/Roopkund/	
	Baggubasa	8 km
Day 7	Baggubasa to Wan	16 km
Day 8	Wan to Kannual	9 km
Day 9	Kannual to Sheetal	9 km
Day 10	Sheetal to Ghat	14 km
	Ghat to Nandprayag	30 km***
Day 11	Nandprayag to Rishikesh	192 km*

* by bus
** 17 km by bus or jeep
*** by taxi

Pindari Glacier

The magnificent Pindari Glacier is the most easily accessible in the region, and is formed by snow from Nanda Kot and other lofty peaks. The glacier, three km long and nearly half a km wide, is at an altitude of 3353 metres. Close to it is an undulating meadow, and to the east a moraine projects into the glacier.

This popular trek offers views of the soaring peaks all the way and passes through pine forests, glades of ferns and wildflowers and tumbling waterfalls. From mid-May to mid-June there are many wildflowers, while from mid-September to mid-October the air is exceptionally clear and it has not yet got too cold.

From Naini Tal there's an early morning bus to Song, a km or so before Loharkhet. Alternatively you can stay in Bharari,

between Kapkot and Loharkhet, and catch a bus or jeep the next day for the hair-raising ride to Song. It's also possible to stay in the excellent *Tourist Bungalow* in Bageshwar and catch one of the several daily buses to Song.

The first couple of days from Song through Loharkhet and up to the Dhakuri Pass is a long, hard uphill slog. Nevertheless this is a fine walk with wonderful scenery. A km or two over the pass is the *Dhakuri Dak Bungalow*. There is an excellent view of the glacier from Purkiya, where some trekkers stop. On the return trek you can travel by road from Bajnath to Rishikesh or return via Almora to Naini Tal.

Dorm beds (Rs 20) are available at the *KMVN Tourist Bungalows* at Loharkhet, Dhakuri, Khati, Dwali and Purkiya and there are also *PWD Bungalows* at all these places as well as at Kapkot but they tend to fill up relatively early in the day. At Khati there is also the small *Himalayan Hotel* (with restaurant).

Day 1	Naini Tal/Song/Loharkhet	179 km*
Day 2	Loharkhet to Khati	18 km
Day 3	Khati to Purkiya	16 km
Day 4	Purkiya to Pindari	7 km
Day 5	Pindari to Khati	21 km
Day 6	Khati to Loharkhet	18 km
Day 7	Loharkhet/Bajnath/Almora	118 km*

* mostly by bus

SKIING IN UTTAR PRADESH
Auli

This skiing resort, reportedly the best equipped in the country, boasts 'over three km of satisfying run' and a portable skilift. A ski-descent of Trisul (7120 metres) would probably be more satisfying but it's already been done – by the Italians Alberto Re and Ezio Laboria in 1978.

Open from January to March, Auli is 15 km from Joshimath and until the road is built you have to walk the last eight km. GMVN operates the resort and has *Tourist Bungalows* at Joshimath and Auli. Skis and boots can be hired here and seven or 15-day ski courses are offered.

Central Uttar Pradesh

DELHI TO KANPUR
Aligarh
Population: 480,000

Formerly known as Koil, this was the site of an important fort as far back as 1194. During the upheavals following the death of Aurangzeb and the collapse of the Moghul Empire, the region was fought for by the Afghans, Jats, Marathas and Rohillas – first one coming out on top, then another. Renamed Aligarh (High Fort) in 1776, it fell to the British in 1803, despite French support for its ruler Scindia. The **fort** is three km north of the town, and in its present form dates from 1524.

Aligarh is best known today for the **Aligarh Muslim University** where the 'seeds of Pakistan were sown'. Muslim students come here not just from India but from all over the Islamic world.

Etawah
This town rose to some importance during the Moghul period, only to go through the usual series of rapid changes during the turmoil that followed the Moghuls. The **Jami Masjid** shows similarities to the mosques of Jaunpur, and there are **bathing ghats** on the riverbank, below the ruined fort.

Kannauj
Only a few dismal ruins indicate that this was once a mighty Hindu city, the capital of the region in the 7th century (AD). It quickly fell into disrepair after Mahmud of Ghazni's raids. This was where Humayun was defeated by Sher Shah in 1540, forcing him to temporarily flee India. There's not much to see now – just an archaeological museum, a mosque and the ruins of the fort.

KANPUR
Population: 2,110,000

Although Lucknow is the capital of Uttar Pradesh, Kanpur (79 km south west) is the largest city in the state. A major business and industrial centre on the Ganges, it attracts very few tourists.

During the 1857 Mutiny, some of the more tragic events took place here when the city was known as Cawnpore, the headquarters of a large Indian garrison. General Sir Hugh Wheeler defended a part of the Cantonment for most of the month of June but, with supplies virtually exhausted and having suffered considerable losses, he surrendered to Nana Sahib, only to be massacred with most of his party at Sati Chaura Ghat. Over 100 women and children were taken hostage and imprisoned in a small room. Just before relief arrived on 17th July, they were murdered and the dismembered bodies thrown down a well.

General Neill, their avenger, behaved just as sadistically as Nana Sahib. Some of the mutineers he captured were made to drink the English blood that still lay in a deep pool in the murder-chamber, before they were executed. Others suffered what must have been regarded as a far worse fate for a Hindu or Muslim – being force-fed beef or pork.

The site of General Wheeler's entrenchment, two km from the station, can be visited. Nearby is **All Souls' Memorial Church**, completed in 1875, which has some rather moving reminders of the tragic events of the Mutiny. There are also several temples, none of them very old, the most interesting being **JK Glass Temple**. This is actually made of white marble but has some unusual glass statues. Kanpur also has a large zoo.

The main shopping centre, **Navin Market**, is famous for its locally produced cotton goods. The main leather market is on Matson Rd and articles such as bags and shoes are very cheap.

Places to Stay & Eat
Kanpur has a large range of accommodation mainly centred along The Mall and around the railway station. The *Hotel Ganges*, with a good vegetarian restaurant, is a cheap place near the station.

The *Yatrik Hotel*, which has singles/

doubles for Rs 75/125 and air-con rooms for 185/225 is also near the station. On Civil Lines the small but popular *Attic* has similarly priced, air-con rooms.

Middle-range hotels include the *Geet Hotel* (☎ 21-1024) and the *Hotel Gaurav* (☎ 26-9599), both on The Mall, and the *Hotel Swagat* (☎ 24-1923) with air-con rooms for Rs 175/230 at 80 Feet Road. The *Grand Trunk Hotel* on Grand Trunk Road is more expensive.

The best hotel in town is the *Hotel Meghdoot* (☎ 21-1999) on The Mall with air-con singles/doubles for Rs 700/900 and three expensive restaurants, which local people rate as the best place for Mughlai cuisine.

Getting There & Away

There are daily flights (except Sunday) to Delhi operated by Vayudoot (US$120) via Lucknow (US$27).

Kanpur is on the main Delhi to Calcutta railway line and less than five hours from Delhi on the *Shatabdi* or *Rajdhani Express* (air-con chair car is the cheapest ticket on both these trains, at Rs 310). Other expresses take five to six hours from Delhi to Kanpur (435 km, Rs 81/301 in 2nd/1st class).

There are also direct rail links to Calcutta (18 to 25 hours, 1007 km), Bombay (24 hours, 1342 km), Agra (six hours, 254 km), Allahabad (2½ hours, 192 km) and Varanasi (six hours, 329 km). By train, Lucknow takes 1½ hours on the *Shatabdi* (Rs 105 in air-con chair-class, or just over two hours in an ordinary express (Rs 22 in 2nd class) and there's also a frequent bus service (Rs 15).

JHANSI

Situated at the neck of a 'peninsula' of Uttar Pradesh which is almost entirely surrounded by Madhya Pradesh, Jhansi is a major transport hub for the north of that state. As it is also the most popular transit point for Khajuraho, we have included Jhansi in the Madhya Pradesh chapter. For details, see the Northern Madhya Pradesh section of that chapter.

LUCKNOW

Population: 1,640,000

The capital of Uttar Pradesh, Lucknow rose to prominence as the capital city of the nawabs of Oudh (Avadh). These ultimately decadent Muslim rulers controlled a region of north-central India for about a century after the decline of the Moghul Empire, and most of the interesting monuments in Lucknow date from this period. The nawabs were:

Burhan-ul-mulk	1724-39
Safdar Jang	1739-53
Shuja-ud-Daula	1753-75
Asaf-ud-Daula	1775-97
Sa'adat Ali Khan	1798-1814
Ghazi-ud-din Haidar	1814-27
Nasir-ud-din Haidar	1827-37
Mohammad Ali Shah	1837-42
Amjad Ali Shah	1842-47
Wajid Ali Shah	1847-56

It was not until Asaf-ud-Daula that the capital of Oudh was moved to Lucknow from Faizabad. Safdar Jang lived in and ruled from Delhi and his tomb is a familiar landmark near Delhi's Safdarjang Airport. After Sa'adat Ali Khan the rest of the Oudh nawabs were uniformly hopeless at running affairs of state. Wajid Ali Shah was so extravagant and indolent that to this day his name is regarded by many in India as synonymous with lavishness. However the nawabs were great patrons of the arts, especially dance and music, and Lucknow's reputation as a city of culture and gracious living stems from this time.

In 1856 the British annexed Oudh, exiling the incompetent Wajid Ali Shah to a palace in Calcutta with an annual pension of £120,000. Satyajit Ray's 1977 film *The Chess Players* was based on these events. It was not a box-office success, suggesting as it did that Indians had themselves to blame for the British move. The annexation was one of the sparks that in 1857 lit the Indian Mutiny (or Uprising, as Indians understandably prefer to call it). Lucknow became the scene for some of the most dramatic events of the Mutiny, as the British residents held out in the Residency for 87 harrowing days, only to be besieged again for a further two months after being relieved.

The huge crumbling mausoleums of the nawabs and the pock-marked ruins of the Residency make Lucknow an interesting place to visit. However, it's not really on the tourist trail which makes a stay even more worthwhile. It's recently become popular with Western followers of the octogenarian guru, Poonjaji, who spends some of the year here. If you're interested, contact the Carlton Hotel to see if he's in town.

Orientation

Lucknow is rather spread out and there is quite a distance between the various places of interest. The historic monuments are mainly in the north-eastern part of the old city around the Chowk area. The main shopping area, with its narrow alleys, is Aminabad, while the modern area with wide avenues and large shops is the fashionable Hazratganj.

Information

Tourist information is available at the Hotel Gomti from UP Tours who run the half-day sightseeing tour (Rs 45, departing 8.30 am). The tourist office is hidden down an alley opposite the Hotel Kohinoor at 10/4 Station Rd (☎ 24-6205) and there's a branch in the main railway station building.

There's a British library (☎ 24-2144) in the Mayfair Building in Hazratganj. The Universal Bookseller at 82 Hazratganj is an excellent bookshop as is the British Bookshop opposite. Ram Advani's bookshop, next to the Mayfair Cinema on Hazratganj, is another good one.

The telephone area code for Lucknow is 0522.

Bara Imambara

The Bara or Great Imambara (an *imambara* is the tomb of a Shi'ite Muslim holy man) was built in 1784 by Asaf-ud-Daula as a famine-relief project. The central hall of the Imambara, 50 metres long and 15 metres high, is one of the largest vaulted galleries in

the world. An external stairway leads to an upper floor laid out as an amazing labyrinth known as the *bhulbhulaiya*, where a guide may be useful. From the top there's a fine view over the city and the Aurangzeb Mosque. Entry is Rs 6 and includes a visit to the ancient well *(baoli)* and to Rumi Darwaza.

There's a mosque with two tall minarets in the courtyard of the Imambara but non-Muslims are not allowed in. To the right of this, in a row of cloisters, is the baoli, the 'bottomless' well. The Imambara is open from 6 am to 5 pm.

Rumi (Roomi) Darwaza

Beside the Bara Imambara and also built by Asaf-ud-Daula, this huge and finely designed darwaza (gate) is a replica of one in Istanbul. 'Rumi' (relating to Rome) is the term Muslims applied to Istanbul when it was still Byzantium, the capital of the eastern Roman Empire.

Lakshman Tila

This high ground on the right bank of the River Gomti was the original site of the town which became known as Lucknau in the 15th century. Aurangzeb's Mosque now stands on this site.

Hussainabad Imambara

Also known as the Chhota, or Small Imambara, this was built by Muhammad Ali Shah in 1837 to serve as his own mausoleum. Thousands of labourers worked on the project to gain famine relief. The large courtyard encloses a raised rectangular tank with small imitations of the Taj Mahal on each side. One of them is the tomb of Muhammad Ali Shah's daughter, the other that of her husband. The main building of the Imambara is topped with numerous domes (the main one is golden) and minarets, while inside are the tombs of Ali Shah and his mother. The nawab's silver-covered throne and other paraphernalia of state are here.

The watchtower opposite the Imambara is known as Satkhanda, or the Seven-Storey Tower, but it actually has four storeys

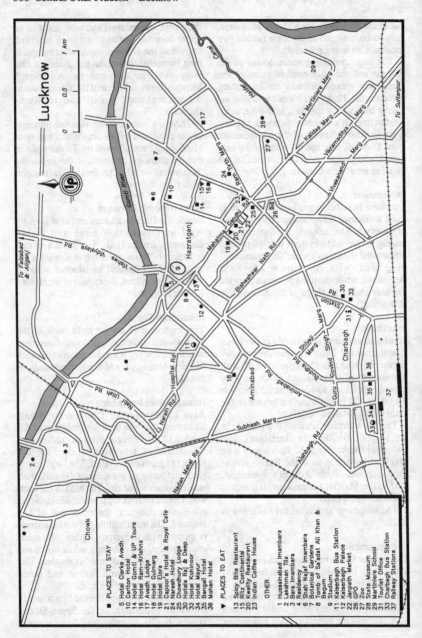

Lucknow

0   0.5   1 km

PLACES TO STAY

5 Hotel Clarks Avadh
10 Carlton Hotel
14 Hotel Gomti & UP Tours
16 Hotel Ram-Krishna
17 Avadh Lodge
18 Hotel Gulmarg
19 Hotel Elora
21 Capoor's Hotel & Royal Cafe
24 Naresh Hotel
30 Chowdhury Lodge
35 Hotels Raj & Deep
32 Hotel Kohinoor
34 Hotel Mayur
35 Bengali Hotel
36 Mohan Hotel

PLACES TO EAT

13 Spicy Bite Restaurant
15 Ritz Continental
20 Kwality Restaurant
23 Indian Coffee House

OTHER

1 Hussainabad Imambara
2 Lakshman Tila
3 Bara Imambara
4 Residency
6 Shah Najaf Imambara
7 Botanical Gardens
8 Tomb of Sa'adat Ali Khan &
   Begum
9 Stadium
11 Kaiserbagh Bus Station
12 Kaiserbagh Palace
22 Janpath Market
26 GPO
27 Zoo
28 State Museum
29 Martiniere School
31 Tourist Office
33 Charbagh Bus Station
37 Railway Stations

because construction was abandoned at that level when Ali Shah died in 1840. The Imambara is open from 6 am to 5 pm.

Clock Tower

Opposite the Hussainabad Imambara is the 67-metre-high clock tower (reputed to be the tallest in the country) and the Hussainabad Tank. The clock tower was built between 1880 and 1887.

Picture Gallery

Also facing the Hussainabad Tank is a *baradari* or summer house, built by Ali Shah. Now restored, it houses portraits of the various nawabs of Oudh. It's open from 10 am to 5 pm; admission is Rs 1.

Jami Masjid

West of the Hussainabad Imambara is the great Jami Masjid with its two minarets and three domes. Construction was started by Muhammad Ali Shah but completed after his death. This is one of the few mosques in India not open to non-Muslims.

Residency

Built in 1800 for the British Resident, this group of buildings became the stage for the most dramatic events of the 1857 Mutiny/Uprising – the Siege of Lucknow.

The British inhabitants of the city all took refuge with Sir Henry Lawrence in the Res-idency upon the outbreak of the Mutiny, expecting relief to arrive in a matter of days. In fact it was 87 days before a small force under Sir Henry Havelock broke through the besiegers to the remaining half-starved defenders. But once Havelock and his troops were within the Residency the siege immediately recommenced and continued from 25 September to 17 November, when final relief arrived with Sir Colin Campbell.

The Residency has been maintained exactly as it was at the time of the final relief, the shattered walls scarred by cannon shot. Even since Independence little has changed apart from the lowering of the Union Jack that flew night and day from one of the towers, and the unveiling of an Indian Martyrs' Memorial directly opposite the Residency.

There's a **model room** in the main Residency building which is worth visiting to get your bearings from the rather tatty model. Downstairs you can see the cellars where many of the women and children lived throughout the siege. The **cemetery** at the nearby ruined church has the graves of 2000 men, women and children, including that of Sir Henry Lawrence, 'who tried to do his duty' (according to the famous inscription on his weathered gravestone).

The whole place would make an excellent film set and indeed during the winter months there's supposed to be a Sound & Light show

---

1857 Mutiny

Numerous accounts of the 1857 Mutiny, the turning point in the history of British India, have been published. In *The Siege of Lucknow*, Julia Inglis (whose husband took command on the death of Sir Henry Lawrence) records the day-to-day activities of the imprisoned Europeans:

> July 1st – ...Poor Miss Palmer had her leg taken off by a round shot to-day, she, with some other ladies, having remained in the second storey of the Residency house, though warned it was not safe... July 4th – Poor Sir Henry (Lawrence) died to-day, after suffering fearful pain... July 8th – Mr Polehampton, one of our chaplains, was shot through the body to-day whilst shaving... October 1st – I was with Mrs Couper nearly all day, watching her baby dying...My baby was ill today. Sharp musketry firing at 10 am.

With stiff upper lip the Europeans watched the Residency population drop from almost 3000 to 980 during the siege. Many who did not die from bullet wounds succumbed to cholera, typhoid or smallpox. ■

here. There are no set opening hours for the Residency but the model room is open only from 9 am to 5.30 pm. Admission is Rs 1 to the Residency gardens, Rs 1 to the model room, except on Fridays when it's free.

Shah Najaf Imambara

Opposite the Carlton Hotel, this mausoleum takes its name from Najaf, the town 190 km south-west of Baghdad in Iraq where Hazrat Ali, the Shi'ite Muslim leader, is buried. The Imambara is the tomb of Ghazi-ud-din Haidar Khan, who died in 1827. His wives are also buried here. This was the scene of desperate fighting in November 1857 during the second relief of Lucknow.

The domed exterior is comparatively plain, but inside are chandeliers and it's said that at one time the dome was covered with gold. The building is used to store *tazia*, elaborate creations of wood, bamboo and silver paper which are carried through the streets at Muharram, the festival which commemorates the martyrdom of Mohammed's grandson, Iman Hussain. They are usually models of the Kerbala in Iraq. Many precious items from the mausoleum were looted following the Mutiny. The Imambara is open from 8 am to 5 pm.

Martiniere School

Outside the town is this strange school built by the Frenchman Major-General Claude Martin. Taken prisoner at Pondicherry in 1761, he joined the East India Company's army, then in 1776 entered service with the Nawab of Oudh, while at the same time maintaining his East India Company connections. He quickly made a substantial fortune from his dual occupations of soldier and businessman, and started to build a palatial home which he named Constantia.

Martin designed much of the building himself, and his architectural abilities were, to say the least, a little mixed – Gothic gargoyles were piled merrily atop Corinthian columns to produce a finished product which a British marquess sarcastically pronounced was inspired by a wedding cake. Martin died in 1800 before his stately home could be completed, but left the money and directions that it should become a school. He now keeps watch from his tomb in the basement.

'Kim', the boy hero of Kipling's story of the same name, went to school here, and there are similar establishments, also financed from Martin's fortune, in Calcutta and Lyon, France. The school can be visited but you should get permission from the Principal first. It's still run like a very British private school – the boys sing hymns in chapel every morning even though, a teacher reported with almost a tinge of regret, 'very few of them are Christians'.

Other Attractions

The **Kaiserbagh palace** was built for Nawab Wajid Ali Shah in 1850. Near the Hotel Clarks Avadh and the Kaiserbagh palace are the stone **tombs** of Sa'adat Ali and his wife. There is also a summer house in the well-kept garden. The **State Museum** (open 10.30 am to 4.30 pm, closed on Mondays) is in the Banarsi Bagh. The **zoo**, founded in 1921, is also here and has a large collection of snakes. It is open from 5 am to 7 pm.

Sikandarbagh, scene of pitched battles in November 1857, is now the home of the **National Botanical Research Institute**. The gardens are open from 6 am to 5 pm. General Havelock, who led the first relief of Lucknow, has his grave and memorial in the Alambagh, three km south of the railway station.

Nadan Mahal is the tomb of the first governor of Oudh appointed by Akbar, and it is one of the earliest buildings in Lucknow, dating from around 1600. Other buildings nearby include the small **Sola Khamba pavilion** and the **tomb of Ibrahim Chisti**.

Festivals

Local people say that these days it is only during the **Lucknow Festival** in February that something of the old cultured atmosphere of the city returns. There are processions, plays, *kathak* dancing, *ghazal* and sitar recitals as well as kite-flying and cock-fighting during the 10-day festival of nostalgia.

Lucknow is a good place to see the **Shi'ite Muharram** celebrations (dates vary from year to year; see under Holidays & Festivals in the Facts for the Visitor chapter) since it has been the principal Indian Shi'ite city since the nawabs arrived. The other major Muslim cities like Delhi and Agra are mainly Sunnite. The activity during Muharram, which centres on the Bara Imambara, can get very hectic as penitents scourge themselves with whips; keep a low profile.

Places to Stay – bottom end

Don't get caught out by the 24-hour check-out which most Lucknow hotels operate.

Best value in the railway station area has to be the *retiring rooms* at Rs 20 for a dorm bed or doubles from Rs 50 to 125 with air-con. There are numerous hotels in the vicinity but many are noisy and overpriced. The *Bengali Hotel*, has very basic singles/doubles without bath for Rs 50/60 or Rs 85/95 with bath.

There are clean dorm beds for Rs 35 in the expensive-looking *Mohan Hotel* and there's also an air-cooled dorm here (Rs 45 per bed). This hotel has a wide range of accommodation and prices. On the roof the singles/doubles at Rs 60/90 may not seem great value with no bathroom attached but they're clean and quiet, and are arranged around a courtyard. Opposite the station, the *Hotel Mayur* has overpriced rooms from Rs 90/110 to Rs 250/300 (with air-con).

Along the road between the station and Hazratganj there's the *Deep Hotel* with rooms from Rs 100/120 with attached bath to Rs 230/280 with air-con. Nearby, the *Hotel Raj* has a similar range of rooms that are a few rupees more.

Most travellers head for the Hazratganj area. *Chowdhury Lodge* down a little alley opposite the GPO is a popular place with singles from Rs 45 (Rs 70 with bath), doubles with bathroom from Rs 90. The rooms are OK and there's an annex nearby. Hot water is available in buckets for Rs 3 and air-coolers are Rs 40.

There are several places along Ram Tirth Marg, a lane which runs through a pleasant market area. The *Naresh Hotel* has a friendly manager and the rooms are good value at Rs 60/90 with attached bathroom. Also in Hazratganj, there's the *Hotel Ram-Krishna* with air-cooled rooms from Rs 115/155, and a good restaurant.

The *Avadh Lodge* (☎ 24-3821) at 1 Ram Mohan Rai Marg is a great old place with vast, tatty rooms and marble floors. Unfortunately the previous owner was a pretty good shot and large quantities of the local fauna, including the now rare gavial (fish-eating crocodile), decorate the walls. It's an interesting place to stay in a quiet area and rooms cost Rs 130/180 to Rs 240/320 (with air-con). Tempos run from the station to Sikhandarbagh which is a short walk away.

Centrally located on Hazratganj, *Capoor's* (☎ 24-3958) is a long-established hotel with good air-cooled rooms for Rs 150/250.

The *Hotel Gulmarg* (☎ 23-1227) has a range of rooms from Rs 90/160 to Rs 250/300 but it's in a rather inconvenient location. The *Hotel Elora* (☎ 23-1307) is right in the centre at 3 Lalbagh and has rooms from Rs 140/200 to Rs 300/350 (with air-con). The rooms are small and not great value but the restaurant is good.

Places to Stay – middle & top end

In the Hazratganj area near the Hotel Gomti is the *Carlton Hotel* (☎ 24-4021) which was once a palace and is still an impressive building with a musty air of decaying elegance. The large gardens around the hotel make this a wonderfully relaxing place to stay. Rooms cost from Rs 200/300 to Rs 370/650 (with air-con). It's popular with Westerners and often full.

UP Tourism's big *Hotel Gomti* (☎ 23-4708) is rather shabby and indifferently run. Rooms are Rs 200/250 to Rs 390/500 (with air-con). A bed in the dorm costs Rs 75 (!) but it is air-con.

The *Hotel Kohinoor* (☎ 23-5421) is a modern place one km from the railway station and charges Rs 400/600 for air-con singles/doubles.

The *Hotel Clarks Avadh* (☎ 40-130) may look like an apartment block but it's Lucknow's best hotel. It's the only real 'international' standard hotel in fact, but service and facilities don't match the prices and there's no pool. Singles/doubles start at Rs 1620/1740.

Places to Eat

The *refreshment room* in Lucknow Junction Station is good value and there are also numerous cheap places to eat in the alleys across the road.

In Hazratganj there's a great selection of places. The *Indian Coffee House* is where the local intelligentsia meet over a coffee and snack – the masala dosas are good. There are several Chinese restaurants in Hazratganj including the *Hong Kong Restaurant* where the food is not bad. Near the Hotel Ram-Krishna is the *Ritz Continental*, a trendy vegetarian restaurant serving pizza (Rs 20 to 30), masala dosas and sweets.

In the Mayfair Building there's a *Kwality Restaurant* with the usual menu. Around the corner in the Hotel Elora is *Seema Restaurant* which has been recommended by several travellers. The *Royal Cafe* is another good place.

Spicy Bite, in the Tulsi Theatre Building, is rated very highly by locals. It offers pizzas (Rs 25), burgers and Chinese food (main dishes Rs 50) and a wide range of ice creams. Downstairs you could treat yourself to a packet of excellent home-made biscuits (chocolate, cashew chocolate, even masala) from the *Baker's Hat*.

At the *Carlton Hotel* there's an all-you-can-eat buffet lunch and dinner for Rs 110 and occasionally there's an open-air barbecue. At Rs 65 the beer's no bargain.

For a special occasion the *Falaknuma*, in Hotel Clarks Avadh, would be the best place to try Lucknow cuisine. Main dishes are Rs 80 to 100, the food is good and there are great views across the city.

Entertainment

In winter there are often excellent classical music performances and dances at the Rabindralaya auditorium, in a garden down Vidhan Sabha Marg towards the new city from Charbagh Station. The Mayfair Cinema often shows English-language movies.

Things to Buy

The bazaars of Aminabad and Chowk are fascinating places to wander through, even if you're not buying. Down the narrow lanes of Aminabad you can buy *attar* – perfume made in the traditional way from essential oils which are mixed with flower fragrances. In Chowk, Nakkhas is the bird-sellers' district. Pigeon-keeping and cock-fighting have been popular since the time of the nawabs.

Several states have their government emporia in Hazratganj. The Gangotri government emporium is a good place for local handicrafts including the hand-woven embroidery known as *chikan* for which Lucknow is famous. It's made into saris for women and kurtas for men. Prices are lower in Aminabad, but you have to bargain.

Lucknow Cuisine

The refined palates of the nawabs have left Lucknow with a reputation for rich Mughlai cuisine. The city is famous for its wide range of kebabs and for dum pukht – the 'art' of steam pressure cooking, in which meat and vegetables are cooked in a sealed clay pot. Huge paper-thin chapatis (rumali roti) are served in many small Muslim restaurants in the old city. They arrive folded up and should be eaten with a goat or lamb curry like bhuna ghosht or roghan josh. Kulfi falooda, ice cream with cornflour noodles, is a popular dessert, and there are several places in Aminabad that serve it. The sweet orange-coloured rice dish known as *zarda* is also popular. In the hot months of May and June, Lucknow has some of the world's finest mangoes, particularly the wonderful *dashhari* variety grown in the village of Malihabad, west of the city. ■

Getting There & Away

Air The Indian Airlines office (☎ 24-0927) is at the Hotel Clarks Avadh and Vayudoot bookings can be made through Span Motels (☎ 23-214) on Vidhan Sabha Marg.

There are daily connections to Delhi (US$46) and three flights a week to Patna (US$49), Calcutta (US$92), Varanasi (US$29) and Bombay (US$152) on Indian Airlines. Vayudoot also operates flights to Kanpur (US$27) and Delhi (US$120).

Bus There are two bus stations: Charbagh near the railway station, and Kaiserbagh. You should check which bus station your bus leaves from as this is subject to change.

Currently from Charbagh there are several buses an hour to Kanpur (Rs 15, two hours), regular departures to Allahabad (Rs 34 to Rs 39, six hours), early morning buses to Varanasi (Rs 48, nine hours) and evening departures for Agra (Rs 62, 10 hours).

From Kaiserbagh there are buses for Delhi from 9 am to 10 pm (Rs 87, 12 hours); Gorakhpur (Rs 46, seven hours), Sunauli (Rs 62, 11 hours) and Faizabad (Rs 21, three hours) from 4 am to 10.30 pm; and an overnight bus to Naini Tal.

Train The two main stations are side by side in Charbagh: Lucknow and the mainly metre-gauge Lucknow Junction. Few trains stop at the third station, Lucknow City.

On the *Shatabdi Express*, Lucknow is only 6½ hours from Delhi (Rs 330 in air-con chair-class) and 1½ hours (Rs 105) from Kanpur. Other express trains take eight to nine hours to Delhi (507 km, Rs 92/337 in 2nd/1st class), five to six hours to Gorakhpur (276 km, Rs 57/210 in 2nd/1st class, with services on broad gauge and metre gauge), 27 hours to Bombay (1414 km), 23 hours to Calcutta (979 km), 22 hours to New Jalpaiguri (1121 km, for Darjeeling), 4½ hours to Allahabad (129 km) and three hours to Faizabad (106 km).

Varanasi is 4½ hours on the *Himgiri Express* (three times a week), five to six hours on other expresses (301 km, Rs 78/282 in 2nd/1st). There are overnight trains to Agra (486 km, Rs 87/327 in 2nd/1st class), Dehra Dun (545 km, stopping at Haridwar) and Kathgodam (399 km, for Naini Tal).

To/From Nepal From the border at Sunauli, where you enter Nepal, it's an 11-hour, Rs 62 bus ride to Lucknow.

Getting Around

To/From the Airport Amausi Airport is 15 km out of Lucknow and there's an airport bus (Rs 15) which leaves the Hotel Clarks Avadh to connect with flights. Telephone 24-4030 to check departure times.

Local Transport Tempos are more convenient than the buses and run along fixed routes connecting the railway station (Charbagh) with the GPO (Hazratganj), Sikandarbagh (for the Botanical Gardens), Kaiserbagh (for the other bus station) and Chowk (for the imambaras). Most journeys cost Rs 2 to Rs 3. Auto-rickshaws seem to be in short supply but there are plenty of cycle-rickshaws which charge local people around Rs 5 for the four km between the station and Hazratganj. A cycle-rickshaw for a day's sightseeing costs around Rs 50 and you can also tour the historic areas of Lucknow by tonga. UP Tours (Hotel Gomti) rents cars from Rs 200 for four hours within the city.

ALLAHABAD

Population: 858,000

The city of Allahabad is 135 km west of Varanasi at the confluence of two of India's most important rivers – the Ganges and the Yamuna (Jumna). This meeting point of the rivers, the *sangam*, is believed to have great soul-cleansing powers and is a major pilgrimage site. It is even more holy because the invisible Saraswati River is supposed to join the Ganges and the Yamuna at this point. Every 12 years the Kumbh Mela, the world's largest pilgrimage gathering, draws millions for a holy dip here.

Allahabad also has an historic fort built by Akbar which overlooks the confluence of the rivers and contains an Ashoka pillar. The Nehru family home, Anand Bhavan, is in

Allahabad and is worth a visit. Not many foreign visitors pause in this peaceful city, but it can be an interesting and worthwhile stop.

History

Built on a very ancient site, Allahabad was known in Aryan times as Prayag, and Brahma himself is said to have performed a sacrifice here. The Chinese pilgrim Hiuen Tsang described visiting the city in 634 AD, and it acquired its present name in 1584, under Akbar. Later Allahabad was taken by the Marathas, sacked by the Pathans and finally ceded to the British in 1801 by the Nawab of Oudh.

It was in Allahabad that the East India Company officially handed over control of India to the British government in 1858, following the Mutiny. The city was a centre of the Indian National Congress and at the conference here in 1920, Mahatma Gandhi proposed his programme of nonviolent aggression to achieve independence.

Orientation & Information

Allahabad is less congested and more modern than its sister city, touristy Varanasi. Civil Lines, with its modern shopping centre (and numerous bookshops), has broad tree-lined avenues and the main bus station. The older part of town is near the Yamuna River. The hub of the older part of the city is known as Chowk, and this is also the location of the main produce market, Loknath.

The tourist office (☎ 60-1873) is at the Tourist Bungalow on Mahatma Gandhi Rd.

Indian Airlines have an office here (☎ 60-2832) but are not currently operating flights from Allahabad.

Sangam

At this point the shallow, muddy Ganges (about two km wide here) meets the clearer, deeper, green Yamuna. During the month of Magha (mid-January to mid-February) hundreds of thousands of pilgrims come to bathe at this holy confluence for the festival known as the **Magh Mela**. Astrologers calculate the holiest time to enter the water and draw up a 'Holy Dip Schedule'. The most propitious time of all happens only every 12 years when the massive **Kumbh Mela** takes place. There's a half-Mela (Ardh Mela) every six years.

A huge temporary township springs up on the vacant land on the Allahabad side of the river and elaborate precautions have to be taken for the pilgrims' safety – in the early '50s, 350 people were killed in a stampede to the water.

Sunrise and sunset can be spectacular here. Boats out to the confluence are a bit of a tourist trap and what you pay very much depends on how many other people are around. Right by the fort you should be able to get a boat for about Rs 6; from Saraswati Ghat further up the Yamuna it should be around Rs 20.

Fort

Built by Akbar in 1583, the fort, which stands at the confluence on the Yamuna side, has massive walls and pillars and three magnificent gateways flanked by high towers. It

Kumbh Mela

Aeons ago the gods and demons, who were constantly at odds, fought a great battle for a *kumbh* or pitcher. Apparently whoever drunk the contents of this pitcher would be ensured immortality. They had combined forces to raise the pitcher from the bottom of the ocean, but once it was safely in their hands Vishnu grabbed it and ran. After a struggle lasting 12 days the gods eventually defeated the demons and drank the nectar – it's a favourite scene in illustrations of Hindu mythology. During the fight for the pitcher's possession four drops of nectar spilt on the earth, at Allahabad, Haridwar, Nasik and Ujjain. The mela is held every three years, rotating among the four cities. Thus each has its own mela every 12 years (for a god's day is a human's year).

Holiest of these four sacred sites is Allahabad where the Kumbh Mela returns in 2001. ■

is made from huge bricks and is at its most impressive when viewed from the river.

The fort is in the hands of the army so prior permission is required for a visit. Officially, passes can be obtained from the Defence Ministry Security Officer but the amount of patience required to get a permit is out of all proportion to the sights to be seen.

Apart from one Moghul building the only item of antiquity inside the walls is an **Ashoka pillar** dating from 232 BC, with an inscription eulogising the victories of Samudragupta, plus the usual edicts.

Patalpuri Temple & Undying Tree A small door in the east wall of the fort near the river leads to the one area in the fort you can go without permission – the underground Patalpuri Temple and the 'Undying Banyan Tree'. Also known as Akshai Veta, this tree is mentioned by Hiuen Tsang, who tells of pilgrims sacrificing their lives by leaping to their deaths from it in order to seek salvation. This would be difficult now as there's not much of it left.

Hanuman Temple This popular temple, open to non-Hindus, is unusual because of the reclining position of Hanuman, in contrast to the usual standing position. It is said that every year during the floods the Ganges rises high enough to touch the feet of the sleeping Hanuman before it starts receding.

Anand Bhavan

This shrine to the Nehru family must be the best kept museum in the country, which indicates the high regard in which this famous dynasty is held in India. The family home was donated to the Indian government by Indira Gandhi in 1970. The exhibits in the house show how this well-off family became involved in the struggle for Indian independence and later produced four generations of astute politicians – Motilal Nehru, Jawaharlal Nehru, Indira Gandhi and Rajiv Gandhi.

Visitors and pilgrims walk round the verandahs of the two-storey mansion looking through glass panels into the rooms.

You can see Nehru's dressing room, the room where Mahatma Gandhi used to stay during his visits and the room where Indira was born, as well as many personal items connected with the Nehru family. Opening hours are from 9.30 am to 5 pm; closed Mondays. There's a Rs 2 charge to go upstairs.

In the well-manicured gardens is a **planetarium**, built in 1979. Several shows take place here each day. Tickets are Rs 4 and the programme lasts about an hour.

Khusru Bagh

This peaceful garden, close to the railway station, contains the tomb of Prince Khusru, son of Jehangir, who was executed by his own father. Nearby is the unoccupied tomb intended for his sister and the tomb of his Rajput mother who was said to have poisoned herself in despair at Khusru's opposition to his father.

All Saints Cathedral

This cathedral was designed more than a century ago by Sir William Emerson, the architect of the Victoria Memorial in Calcutta. The polished brass memorial plaques make interesting reading and show that even for the sons and daughters of the Raj, life was not all chukkas of polo and pink gins. The inscriptions morbidly record the causes of death: 'died of blood poisoning', 'accidentally killed', 'died of cholera', 'died in a polo accident' and probably even more likely today: 'died in a motor accident on the road to Naini Tal'. There are some attractive stained-glass windows and services in English on Sundays.

Allahabad Museum

Set in a peaceful park, this large museum has galleries devoted to local archaeological finds (terracotta figures, stone sculptures and fossils), natural history and also exhibits donated by the Nehru family. Part of the museum is an art gallery with a fine collection of Rajasthani miniatures and paintings by the artist Professor Nicholas Roerich. The museum is open from 10.30 am to 4.30 pm and is closed Mondays. Admission is Rs 1.

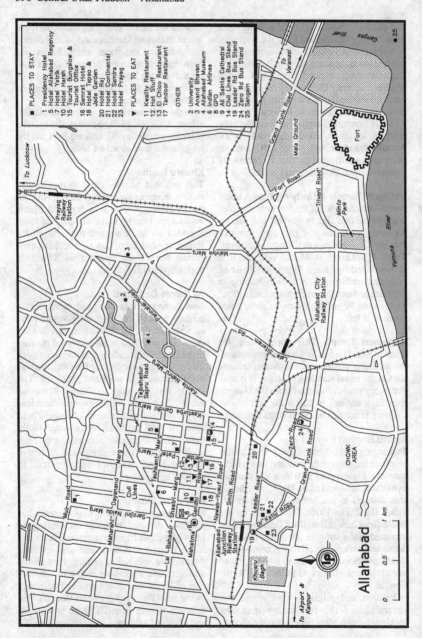

Allahabad

PLACES TO STAY	
1	Presidency Hotel
5	Hotel Allahabad Regency
7	Hotel Yatrik
10	Hotel Harsh
15	Tourist Bungalow & Tourist Office
16	Samrat Hotel
18	Hotel Tepso & Jade Garden
20	Hotel Raj
21	Hotel Continental
22	Hotel Samira
23	Hotel Prayag

PLACES TO EAT	
11	Kwality Restaurant
12	Hot Stuff
13	El Chico Restaurant
17	Tandoor Restaurant

OTHER	
2	University
3	Anand Bhavan
4	Allahabad Museum
6	Indian Airlines
8	GPO
9	All Saints Cathedral
14	Civil Lines Bus Stand
19	Leader Rd Bus Stand
24	Zero Rd Bus Stand
25	Sangam

Other Attractions

The Bharadwaja Ashram is mentioned in the *Ramayana* and the Allahabad University now occupies its site. The **Archaeological Museum** in the university has numerous artefacts from Kausambi. Opposite the university is the house where Rudyard Kipling lived, but it isn't open to the public.

In **Minto Park** a memorial marks the spot where Lord Canning read out the declaration by which Britain took over control of India from the East India Company in 1858. The **Nag Basuki Temple** is mentioned in the Puranas and is on the banks of the Ganges, north of the railway bridge.

Places to Stay – bottom end

There are hotels around the Leader Rd area and north of the railway line in Civil Lines, the more peaceful area to stay in.

Set back from the road the *Hotel Tepso* has rooms ranging from Rs 45 for singles without bath up to Rs 145/175 for deluxe singles/doubles with bath. It's near the market, GPO and railway station, and has a good restaurant in the small garden. Next door, the *Hotel Vishrant* has similar prices.

The UP *Tourist Bungalow* (☎ 60-1441) is at 35 Mahatma Gandhi Rd and is probably the best place for the money in Allahabad but it can be noisy if your room is overlooking the bus station. Rooms cost Rs 100/125 to Rs 275/300 (including air-con), and Rs 20 for dorm beds. It's a clean place set in a well-kept garden. A cycle-rickshaw from the City Railway Station costs about Rs 5.

Barnett's Hotel has been renamed *Hotel Harsh*. 'Stay once and become our permanent guest' is their proud claim, although poor Mr Barnett is probably turning in his grave at the dilapidated condition of his old hotel. Rooms in this wedding cake of a place certainly don't lack character and cost Rs 115/141 with bathrooms attached.

There are several cheap places south of Allahabad Junction Station. The *Hotel Prayag* is a modern block with a wide range of accommodation from singles (common bathroom) at Rs 40 to doubles with attached bath for Rs 80 to Rs 150. In the next street opposite the mosque is the *Hotel Continental*, with rooms from Rs 60/70 with attached bathrooms and some air-con rooms at Rs 170/210. Further down this street is the smaller *Hotel Samira* with rooms from Rs 50/75 with bath.

There are numerous other places to stay in this price bracket along Leader Rd. The *Hotel Raj* has rooms with bathrooms attached for Rs 65/90 or Rs 175 with air-cooling. The Ginza restaurant here is good.

At the City railway station there are a couple of *retiring rooms* for Rs 50. There are many more, including two dormitories, at the main station.

Places to Stay – middle & top end

Near the junction of Mahatma Gandhi Rd and Sardar Patel Marg, the *Samrat Hotel* (☎ 60-4888) has rooms from Rs 200/300, or Rs 300/400 with air-con.

Two-star is the best you can get in Allahabad and the *Presidency Hotel* (☎ 60-4097) is in a quiet residential area north of Civil Lines. Singles/doubles (all air-con) cost Rs 360/430 and the bathrooms have bathtubs. There's a pool, but as at the two hotels below, it's not used during the winter.

The *Hotel Allahabad Regency* (☎ 60-1519) is also two-star and charges Rs 350/450 for singles/doubles with air-con. There's a very pleasant garden and a pool. Nearby on Sardar Patel Marg, the *Hotel Yatrik* (☎ 60-1713) has had a face-lift and is obviously going for the stars as well. Rooms cost Rs 300/350 without air-con, Rs 360/550 with air-con. They boast of a 'Lush Green Lawn with Garden to Relax', and there's a pool.

Places to Eat

Most of the hotels have restaurants. At the *Tourist Bungalow* you can get a vegetarian thali for Rs 18 and there's the standard non-veg menu as well. The *Jade Garden* is the bamboo restaurant in the garden of the Hotel Tepso, and main dishes here cost Rs 30 to Rs 38. Just outside, on the pavement along

Mahatma Gandhi Rd, is a stand selling good masala dosas for Rs 6.

There are several snack bars. The bright young things in Allahabad hang out in *Hot Stuff*, an ice-cream parlour and fast-food place where pizzas are Rs 28. The *Kwality Restaurant* is also good for snacks. Burgers are Rs 14 and there's a great range of ice creams including the 'Killer Driller' for Rs 25. Sweet shops are popular here, and *Kamdhenu Sweets* (near the Hotel Tepso) is a clean place to try them.

The two best restaurants in the city are the *Tandoor*, with good service and excellent Indian food (main dishes Rs 30 to Rs 45, but no beer), and *El Chico* which is a little more expensive and does good Chinese. There's a pastry shop at El Chico.

There are also many restaurants in the crowded streets of the old town on the southern side of the railway tracks, plus many small dhaba places close to the station along Dr Katiu Rd. The *Ginza Restaurant*, next to the Hotel Raj, has a typical non-vegetarian menu and good food.

Getting There & Away

Allahabad is a good place from which to travel to Khajuraho. If you spend the night in Allahabad you can catch a morning train to Satna, from where buses go to Khajuraho (four hours). There are also buses to Satna from Allahabad but they take several hours longer than express trains.

Air Allahabad has been 'temporarily delinked' by Indian Airlines and Vayudoot.

Bus From Civil Lines bus stand, beside the Tourist Bungalow, there are regular buses to Varanasi (Rs 24, 3½ hours), Faizabad (Rs 35, 4½ hours), Gorakhpur (Rs 47, eight hours) via Jaunpur, and Sunauli (Rs 67, 12 hours) for Nepal. At 3 pm there's a deluxe bus to Lucknow (Rs 39, five hours) plus numerous others throughout the day. Buses to Jhansi and Satna go from the Leader Rd bus stand. There's a third bus stand at Zero Rd.

Train The main station is Allahabad Junction in the central part of the city. However, most trains to Varanasi leave from the Allahabad City Station at Ram Bagh, which is a metre-gauge line. The journey to Varanasi takes three to four hours (137 km, Rs 31/118 in 2nd/1st).

From the main station, direct expresses take 10 hours to Delhi (627 km, Rs 108/397 in 2nd/1st), 15 hours to Calcutta (814 km), 24 hours to Bombay (1373 km), 3½ hours to Lucknow (129 km) and four hours to Satna (180 km) for Khajuraho.

Getting Around

Use the back exit at Allahabad Junction Station for Civil Lines. There are plenty of cycle and auto-rickshaws. It's Rs 10 to Rs 12 for the six km to the Sangam in a cycle-rickshaw. Their seats are made to a uniform design without the Western bum in mind and must be the most uncomfortable in the country.

AROUND ALLAHABAD
Bhita

Excavations at this site, 18 km south of Allahabad, by the Yamuna River, have revealed the remains of an ancient fortified city. Layers of occupation dating from the Gupta period (320-455 AD) back to the Mauryan period (321-184 BC) and even earlier have been uncovered. There's a museum with stone and metal seals, coins and terracotta statues.

Garwha

The ruined temples in this walled enclosure are about 50 km from Allahabad. Garwha is eight km from Shankargarh and the last three km have to be completed on foot.

The major temple has 16 beautifully carved stone pillars, and inscriptions reveal that the temples date back to the Gupta period at the very least. Some of the better sculptures from Garwha are now shown in the State Museum in Lucknow.

Kausambi

This ancient Buddhist centre, once known as

Kosam, is 63 km from Allahabad. At one time it was the capital of King Udaya, a contemporary of the Buddha. There's a huge **fortress** near the village, and the broken remains of an **Ashoka pillar**, minus any pre-Gupta period inscriptions, can be seen inside the fort. Many of the archaeological finds here are on display in the museum at Allahabad University. A bus runs from Allahabad to Serai Akil which is 15 km from Kausambi.

Chitrakut

Rama is supposed to have spent some time in the hills here, making this a popular Hindu pilgrimage site. It's 132 km from Allahabad. **Bathing ghats** line the Mandakini River and there are over 30 temples in the town.

SHRAVASTI

The extensive ruins of this ancient city and Jetavana monastery are here, near the villages of Saheth-Maheth. It was at Shravasti that the Buddha performed the miracle of sitting on a 1000-petalled lotus and multiplying himself a million times, fire and water emanating from his body. Ashoka was among the early pilgrims and left a couple of pillars to commemorate his visit.

The site can be reached from Gonda on the Gorakhpur-Naugarh-Gonda loop line. The nearest station is Gainjahwa and the nearest large town is 20 km away at Balrampur.

FAIZABAD

Population: 177,000

Faizabad was once the capital of Oudh but rapidly declined after the death of Bahu Begum. Her mausoleum is said to be the finest of its type in Uttar Pradesh. Her husband, Nawab Shujaddaula, who preceded her as ruler, also has a fine mausoleum. There are three large mosques in the market (chowk) area and pleasant gardens in Guptar Park, where the temple from which Rama is supposed to have disappeared stands.

Places to Stay

Down a side street off the chowk area are three cheap places. The *Hotel Priya* (painted green, with its name in Hindi) has singles/doubles for Rs 35/44 with bath. The *Hotel Amber* run by a friendly Sikh is similarly priced and has a good restaurant. Opposite, the *Hotel Abha* has good air-cooled rooms with hot water and TV for Rs 80/100, and a dingy restaurant with poor service.

The more upmarket hotels are two km away, near the bus station. Rooms in the *Hotel Shan-e-Awadh* (☎ 3586) in Rikabganj range from Rs 80/100 to Rs 250/295 with air-con. The *Hotel Tirupati* next door has rooms from Rs 120/150 to Rs 250/295 and a good restaurant. Avoid the front rooms as both these places are right on the main Lucknow to Gorakhpur road.

Getting There & Away

Faizabad is three hours by train from either Varanasi or Lucknow. There are numerous buses for Allahabad (Rs 35, 4½ hours), Lucknow (Rs 21, three hours), Gorakhpur (Rs 24, three hours) and one direct early morning bus to Sunauli (for Nepal) for Rs 35. For Ayodhya there are many buses and tempos (Rs 2) from the main road near the chowk.

AYODHYA

Population: 41,000

Only six km from Faizabad, Ayodhya is a holy Hindu city and popular pilgrimage place. It's connected with many events in the *Ramayana* (including the birth of Rama), and has been very much in the news recently on account of the 'temple-mosque' dispute. The **Babri Masjid** was originally constructed on the site of Rama's birth by the Moghuls in the 15th century, but it eventually fell into disuse. Plans by the Hindus to build the Ram Mandir in its place have led to outbreaks of violence between Hindus and Muslims here and temples have been damaged in the riots. A fragile court order called for the maintenance of the status quo and armed guards attempted to keep the two communities from each others' throats.

In late 1992, however, gangs of Hindus moved in and destroyed the mosque, erecting a small Hindu shrine in its place. This caused rioting and many deaths in various places in India and unrest in neighbouring Muslim countries. The federal government has promised to rebuild the mosque and put a Hindu shrine alongside it. If demonstrations are taking place, it would be sensible to give them a wide berth.

The **Hanumangadhi** (dedicated to Hanuman) is the first major temple you come to. It was built within the thick white walls of the fortress and there are good views from the ramparts. There's also the **Kanak Mandir** (built by the Maharaja of Tikamgadh last century) and a ghat; the town is on the Gogra (Ghaghara) River. There are over 100 other temples (many open to non-Hindus) and the place sees few foreign visitors.

Places to Stay

Since Faizabad, with a larger range of accommodation, is so close it's easy to make a day trip from there. In Ayodhya, the Tourist Bungalow *Pathik Niwas Saket* (and tourist office) is next to the railway station. There's a pleasant dorm with beds (and lockers) for Rs 15 and singles/doubles from Rs 52/60 to Rs 214/237 for air-con. As this is a holy city, the restaurant serves only vegetarian food.

Getting There & Away

There are regular tempos and buses from Faizabad for Rs 2.

Varanasi Region

VARANASI

Population: 1,030,000

Varanasi, the 'eternal city', is one of the most important pilgrimage sites in India and also a major tourist attraction. Situated on the banks of the sacred Ganges, Varanasi has been a centre of learning and civilisation for over 2000 years. It was at Sarnath only 10 km away that the Buddha first preached his message of enlightenment, 25 centuries ago. Later the city became a great Hindu centre, but was looted a number of times by Muslim invaders from the 11th century on. These destructive visits climaxed with that of the Moghul emperor, Aurangzeb, who destroyed almost all of the temples and converted the most famous one into a mosque.

Varanasi has also been known as Kashi and Benares, but its present name is a restoration of an ancient name meaning the city between two rivers – the Varauana and Asi. For the pious Hindu the city has always had a special place. Besides being a pilgrimage centre, it is considered an auspicious place to die, ensuring an instant route to heaven. To this day Varanasi is a centre of learning, especially for Sanskrit scholars, and students flock here from all over India. Ironically it is in the centre of one of the most backward areas of India – a largely agrarian, rural and overpopulated area that has developed little since Independence.

On the other hand Varanasi has become a symbol of the Hindu renaissance and has a special role in the development of Hindi – the national language of India. The well-known novelist Prem Chand and the literary figure Bharatendu Harischand have played their parts in this development. Tulsi Das, the famous poet who wrote the Hindi version of the *Ramayana* known as the *Ram Charit Manas*, also lived in this city for many years.

Orientation

The old city of Varanasi is situated along the west bank of the Ganges and extends back from the riverbank ghats in a winding collection of narrow alleys. They're too narrow for anything but walking, and tall houses overhang the picturesque, though hardly clean, lanes. It's a fascinating area to wander around. The town extends from Raj Ghat, near the bridge, to Asi Ghat, near the university. Areas known as Chowk, Lahurabir and Godaulia (also spelt Godowlia and Gadaulia) are just outside the old city area along the river.

One of the best ways to get oriented in Varanasi is to remember the positions of the ghats, particularly important ones like Dasaswamedh Ghat. The big 'international hotels' and the national tourist office are in the Cantonment area north of the Varanasi Junction Railway Station. The TV tower is the most obvious landmark there. The broad, tree-lined avenues of the Cantonment are a great contrast to the crowds of people, bicycles and rickshaws in the old part of town.

Information

Tourist Office The most helpful place for information is the Government of India tourist office (☎ 43-744), at 15B The Mall in the Cantonment. The UP state tourist office is in the Tourist Bungalow and there's a useful kiosk in the railway station.

Money There are many places to change money including a bank in the international section at the airport. The State Bank of India has branches in all the larger Cantonment hotels.

Post & Telecommunications The Varanasi GPO is a good place to send parcels from, as there are tailors' stalls for wrapping and sealing right outside. You can send and receive faxes at the Central Telegraph Office in the Cantonment daily between 8 am and 8 pm. Varanasi's telephone area code is 0542.

Newspapers & Magazines The *Pioneer* is an informative local English-language newspaper. *Benares: City of Light* by Diana Eck (Princeton University Press) is a good guide to the city, with information on each ghat and temple and a good introduction to Hinduism.

Ghats

Varanasi's principal attraction is the long string of bathing ghats which line the west bank of the Ganges. Ghats are the steps which lead down to the river, and where, at the two 'burning ghats', bodies are cremated. The best time to visit the ghats is at dawn when pilgrims take their early morning dip – the city is coming alive, the light is magical and Varanasi is an exotic place.

There are over 100 ghats in all; Dasaswamedh Ghat is probably the most convenient starting point. A trip from there to Manikarnika Ghat makes an interesting short introduction to the river and will cost Rs 15 to Rs 20 an hour (with bargaining) if you hire

Bathing ghats

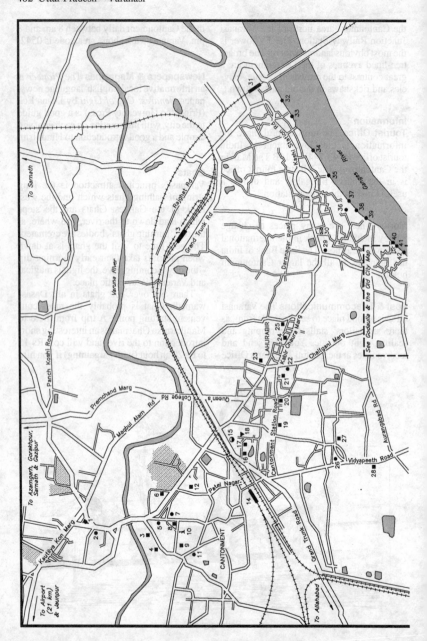

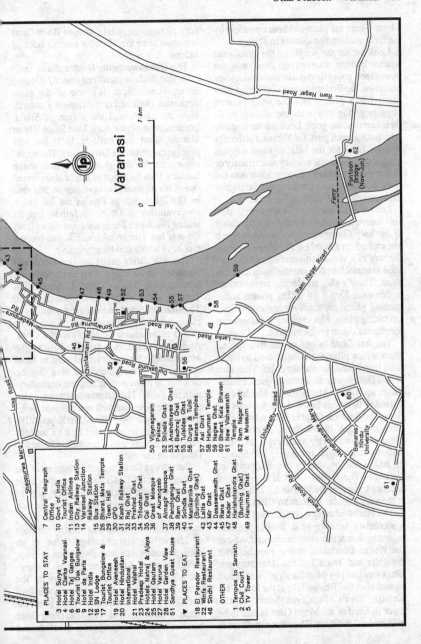

Varanasi

0   0.5   1 km

PLACES TO STAY

3 Hotel Surya
4 Hotel Clarks Varanasi
6 Hotel Taj Ganges
8 Tourist Dak Bungalow
9 Hotel de Paris
10 Hotel India
16 SN Lodge
17 Tourist Bungalow &
   Tourist Office
19 Hotel Avaneesh
20 Hotel Hindustan
   International
21 Hotel Valshal
23 Pradeep Hotel
24 Hotels Natraj & Ajaya
25 Hotel Gautam
27 Hotel Varuna
28 Hotel Garden View
51 Sandhya Guest House

PLACES TO EAT

18 El Parador Restaurant
22 Winfa Restaurant
46 Sindhi Restaurant

OTHER

1 Tempos to Sarnath
2 Civil Court
5 TV Tower
7 Central Telegraph
   Office
10 Govt of India
   Tourist Office
11 Indian Airlines
12 City Railway Station
14 Varanasi Junction
   Railway Station
15 Bus Station
26 Bharat Mata Temple
29 Town Hall
30 GPO
31 Kashi Railway Station
32 Raj Ghat
33 Prahlad Ghat
34 Trilochan Ghat
35 Ram Ghat
36 Great Mosque
   of Aurangzeb
37 Almagir Ghat
38 Panchganga Ghat
39 Ram Ghat
40 Scindia Ghat
41 Manikarnika Ghat
   (Burning Ghat)
42 Lalita Ghat
43 Mir Ghat
44 Dasaswamedh Ghat
45 Rana Ghat
47 Kedar Ghat
48 Harishchandra Ghat
   (Burning Ghat)
49 Hanuman Ghat
50 Vijaynagaram
   Palace
52 Shivala Ghat
53 Anandmayee Ghat
54 Bachraj Ghat
55 Tulsidas Ghat
56 Durga & Tulsi
   Rama Temples
57 Asi Ghat
58 Hanuman Temple
59 Nagwa Ghat
60 Bharat Kala Bhavan
61 New Vishwanath
   Temple
62 Ram Nagar Fort
   & Museum

a boat. There are plenty of boat operators by the river waiting for tourists to appear.

Look out for the people on the ghats – the women bathing discreetly in their saris, the young men going through contortionist yoga exercises, the Brahmin priests offering blessings (for a price) and the ever-present beggars giving others an opportunity to do their karma some good. Look for the lingams which mark each ghat, for Varanasi is the city of Siva. Look for the buildings and temples around the ghats, often tilting precariously or in some cases actually sliding down into the river. Each monsoon causes great damage to the riverbank buildings of Varanasi.

Look for the burning ghats where bodies are cremated after making their final journey to the holy Ganges swathed in white cloth and carried on a bamboo stretcher – or even the roof of a taxi. **Manikarnika** and the less used **Harishchandra** are the main burning ghats. There's also an electric crematorium at this ghat. Don't try taking photos at the burning ghats, especially when cremations are taking place. Just carrying a camera can sometimes cause problems here.

The **Asi Ghat** is one of the five special ghats which pilgrims are supposed to bathe from in order and on the same day. The order is Asi, Dasaswamedh, Barnasangam, Panchganga and finally Manikarnika. Much of the **Tulsidas Ghat** has fallen down towards the river. The **Bachraj Ghat** is Jain and there are three riverbank Jain temples. Many of the ghats are owned by maharajas or other princely rulers, such as the very fine Shivala or Kali Ghat owned by the Maharaja of Varanasi. The **Dandi Ghat** is the ghat of ascetics known as Dandi Panths, and nearby is the very popular **Hanuman Ghat**.

The **Harishchandra** or Smashan Ghat is a secondary burning ghat. Bodies are cremated by outcasts known as *chandal*. Above the **Kedar Ghat** is a shrine popular with Bengalis and south Indians. **Mansarowar Ghat** was built by Man Singh of Amber and named after the Tibetan lake at the foot of Mt Kailash, Siva's Himalayan home. **Someswar** or Lord of the Moon Ghat is said to be able to heal diseases. The **Munshi Ghat** is very picturesque, while **Ahalya Bai's Ghat** is named after the Maratha woman ruler of Indore.

The **Dasaswamedh Ghat's** name indicates that Brahma sacrificed *(medh)* 10 *(das)* horses *(aswa)* here. It's one of the most important ghats and is conveniently central. Note its statues and the shrine of Sitala, goddess of smallpox. Raja Man Singh's **Man Mandir Ghat** was built in 1600 but was poorly restored in the last century. The northern corner of the ghat has a fine stone balcony. Raja Jai Singh of Jaipur also erected one of his unusual observatories on this ghat in 1710. It is not as fine as the Jai Singh observatories in Delhi or Jaipur, but its setting is unique. There are good views from the top but you should watch out for the monkeys which can be aggressive.

The **Mir Ghat** leads to the **Nepalese Temple** with its erotic sculptures. Between here and the Jalsain Ghat is the Golden Temple, which stands back from the river. The **Jalsain Ghat**, where cremations take place, virtually adjoins one of the most sacred of the ghats, the **Manikarnika Ghat**. Above the steps is a tank known as the Manikarnika Well; Parvati is said to have dropped her earring here and Siva dug the tank out to recover it, filling the depression with his sweat! The **Charandpaduka**, a slab of stone between the well and the ghat, bears footprints made by Vishnu. Privileged VIPs are allowed to be cremated at the Charandpaduka. There is also a temple dedicated to Ganesh on the ghat.

Dattatreya Ghat bears the footprint of the Brahmin saint of that name in a small temple nearby. **Scindia Ghat** was originally built in 1830 but was so huge and magnificent that it collapsed into the river and had to be rebuilt. The **Ram Ghat** was built by the Raja of Jaipur. The **Panchganga Ghat**, as its name indicates, is where five rivers are supposed to meet. Above the ghat is Aurangzeb's smaller mosque, also known as the Alamgir Mosque, built over a Vishnu temple. The **Gai Ghat** has a figure of a cow made of stone upon it. The **Trilochan Ghat** has two turrets emerging from the river, and water between them is especially holy. **Raj Ghat** was the ferry pier until the road and rail bridge were completed here.

Golden Temple

Dedicated to Vishveswara (Vishwanath), Siva as Lord of the Universe, the Golden Temple is across the road from its original position. Aurangzeb destroyed the original temple and built a mosque over it – traces of the earlier 1600 temple can be seen behind his mosque.

The present temple was built in 1776 by Ahalya Bai of Indore, and the gold plating (three-quarters of a ton of it!) on the towers was provided by Maharaja Ranjit Singh of Lahore. Next to the temple is the Gyan Kupor well, the Well of Knowledge. Much esteemed by the faithful, this well is said to contain the Siva lingam removed from the original temple and hidden to protect it from Aurangzeb. Non-Hindus are not allowed into the temple but can view it from upstairs in a house across the street – soldiers sit downstairs.

Near the temple, which is interesting to visit in the evening, are narrow alleys filled with many shops.

Great Mosque of Aurangzeb

Constructed using columns from the Biseswar Temple razed by Aurangzeb, this great mosque has minarets towering 71 metres above the Ganges. Armed guards protect the mosque as the Indian government wants to ensure there are no problems between Hindus and Muslims.

Durga Temple

The Durga Temple is commonly known as the Monkey Temple due to the many monkeys that have made it their home. It was built in the 18th century by a Bengali maharani and is stained red with ochre. The small temple is built in north Indian Nagara style with a multitiered sikhara.

Durga is the 'terrible' form of Siva's consort Parvati, so at festivals there are often sacrifices of goats. Although this is one of the best known temples in Varanasi, it is, like

some other Hindu temples, closed to non-believers. However, you can look down inside the temple from a walkway at the top. Beware of the monkeys here who are daring and vicious – they'll snatch glasses off your face, and even scratch or bite if you get too close.

Next to the temple is a tank with stagnant water where, as usual, pilgrims bathe.

Tulsi Manas Temple

Next to the Durga Temple is this modern marble sikhara-style temple. Built in 1964, the walls of the temple are engraved with verses and scenes from the *Ram Charit Manas*, the Hindi version of the *Ramayana*. This tells of the history and deeds of Lord Rama, an incarnation of Vishnu. Its medieval author, Tulsi Das, lived here while writing it and died in 1623.

On the 2nd floor you can watch the production of moving and performing statues and scenes from Hindu mythology. If you are at all familiar with figures from the *Ramayana* or *Mahabharata*, you will find a visit here very enjoyable. Non-Hindus are allowed into this temple.

Benares Hindu University

A further 20-minute walk from the Durga Temple, or a Rs 3 rickshaw ride, is the Benares Hindu University (BHU), constructed at the beginning of the century. The large university covers an area of five sq km, and you can get there by bus from Godaulia or by a rickshaw for Rs 6.

The university was founded by Pandit Malaviya as a centre of education in Indian art, culture and music, and for the study of Sanskrit. The Bharat Kala Bhavan at the university has a fine collection of miniature paintings and also sculptures from the 1st to 15th centuries. In a room upstairs there are some old photographs and a map of Varanasi. It's open from 11 am to 4 pm (8 am to 12.30 pm in May and June) and is closed on Sundays.

New Vishwanath Temple

It's about a 30-minute walk from the gates of

the university to the new Vishwanath Temple which was planned by Pandit Malaviya and built by the wealthy Birla family of industrialists. A great nationalist, Pandit Malaviya wished to see Hinduism revived without its caste distinctions and prejudices – accordingly this temple, unlike so many in Varanasi, is open to all, irrespective of caste or religion. The interior has a Siva lingam and verses from Hindu scriptures inscribed on the walls. The temple is supposed to be a replica of the original Vishwanath Temple, destroyed by Aurangzeb.

Alamgir Mosque

Locally known as Beni Madhav Ka Darera, this was originally a Vishnu temple erected by the Maratha chieftain Beni Madhav Rao Scindia. Aurangzeb destroyed it and erected the mosque in its place, but it is a curious Hindu/Muslim mixture with the bottom part entirely Hindu.

Bharat Mata Temple

Dedicated to 'Mother India', this temple has a marble relief map of India instead of the usual images of gods and goddesses. It gives an excellent impression of the high isolation of the Tibetan plateau. The temple was opened by Mahatma Gandhi, and non-Hindus are allowed inside.

Ram Nagar Fort & Museum

On the other side of the river, this 17th-century fort is the home of the Maharaja of Benares. There are tours to the fort or you can catch a ferry across the river to get to it. The interesting museum contains old silver and brocade palanquins for the ladies of the court, elephant howdahs made of silver, old brocades, a replica of the royal bed and an armoury of swords and old guns. The fort is open from 9 am to noon and 2 to 5 pm; entry to the museum is Rs 1.50.

Activities

Swimming If you're staying in one of Varanasi's cheaper hotels and could do with a swim, the following hotels permit non-resident use of their pools: Hotel Hindustan International (Rs 50), Hotel Varanasi Ashok (Rs 60), Hotel Clarks Varanasi (Rs 75) and the Hotel Taj Ganges (Rs 78).

Yoga If you're interested in studying yoga, pay a visit to the Malaviya Bhavan at the university. They offer courses in yoga and also in Hindu philosophy.

There are also many private teachers and organisations offering courses. Some of these cost virtually nothing, and others are quite expensive. You could try the Yoga Clinic at D 16/19 Man Mandir (near Man Mandir Ghat) where Yogi Prakash Shankar Vyas runs a seven-day course in the principles of yoga.

Organised Tours & River Trips

Varanasi tours cost Rs 40 each for morning or afternoon tours. They start from the Tourist Bungalow or the major hotels in the Cantonment area in the morning and from the Government of India tourist office on The Mall in the afternoon. Telephone 43-744 for booking details.

The morning tour leaves at 6 am and takes you down the Ganges by the ghats, around the various temples and out to the university. The morning tour finishes at 12.15 pm and the afternoon tour commences at 2 pm and runs to 6 pm. The afternoon tour takes you out to Sarnath and to the Ram Nagar Fort – if there's time. In summer, all tours leave half an hour earlier.

The tours don't get unconditional recommendations and many people prefer to do things themselves. Organising a boat for sunrise over the ghats is easy and rickshaw-wallahs are keen to get a pre-dawn rendezvous arranged for the trip down to the river. Get them to take you to a large ghat such as Dasaswamedh, since there will be a number of boats to choose from. Travellers have reported being taken to smaller ghats where there was only one boat, placing them in a poor bargaining position. Aim to pay Rs 15 to Rs 20 per hour.

Places to Stay – bottom end & middle

There are three main accommodation areas

in Varanasi. The spacious Cantonment area is north of the railway tracks, and most of the hotels on the broad avenues in this peaceful area have pleasant gardens. The newer part of the city is south of the railway station and also near the bus station. However, the true atmosphere of this ancient holy city lies in the crowded, confused but colourful area by the river. These old city places are the cheapest you'll find, and staying close to the river has the advantage of being cooler during the hot season, and you can go down to the ghats at any time.

Wherever you stay in Varanasi, watch out for the rickshaw-wallahs who are heavily into hotel commissions. Suggest a hotel and if it doesn't give a commission you'll probably be told that it's 'closed', 'full up', or 'burnt down'. Hotels by the river may even be 'flooded'! For places in this Old City area it's better to ask the rickshaw-wallah for Dasaswamedh Ghat and walk to the hotel from there.

Railway & Bus Station Area There are several cheap places down the road opposite Varanasi Junction station. The *SN Lodge* is a friendly place with its own shrine and scenes from the *Ramayana* painted round the courtyard. It's pretty basic but there are singles/doubles for Rs 35/40 or Rs 40/50 with attached bathroom. Around the corner the *Hotel Glory* has rooms for Rs 50/90 with bathrooms. The *Hotel Amar* has rooms for Rs 45/70 or Rs 70/90 with attached bathrooms; the *Hotel Raj Kamal* and *Hotel Diwan* are slightly cheaper.

The *Tourist Bungalow* (☎ 43-413) is very popular since it's good value, has a pleasant garden and is within easy walking distance of the bus and railway stations. There are dorm beds for Rs 15, singles from Rs 45 to Rs 125, and doubles from Rs 100 to Rs 150. However the staff have a well-earned reputation for being less than helpful, as does the UP Tourist Office here. Just outside is the *Hotel Relax* (Rs 60/95 with attached bathroom) which, like the other hotels in the area, does good business when the Tourist Bungalow is full.

Beside El Parador Restaurant is the *Hotel Sandona*. It has singles/doubles/triples with attached bathrooms from Rs 45/85/105 but is being renovated so prices may go up.

There are a number of hotels right between the railway station and the bus station which could be noisy. The *Nar Indra* has rooms for Rs 70/90 or Rs 90/125 with bath and TV. On Vidyapeeth Rd, the *Hotel Malti* is more expensive with good rooms from Rs 150/200 to Rs 250/350 with air-con.

In the *retiring rooms* at Varanasi Junction station there are doubles for Rs 50 and Rs 75 (with air-con) or dorm beds for Rs 15.

Cantonment Area In this area, on the north side of Varanasi Junction station, hotels are mainly at the top of the price scale but there are a few cheaper places. The *Tourist Dak Bungalow* (☎ 42-182) on The Mall is very popular with overlanders and has a nice garden. There are camping facilities, dorm beds for Rs 20, singles/doubles from Rs 45/75 to Rs 70/200 and also some triples. There's a reasonable restaurant and they often have classical Indian dancing here in the evenings during the tourist season.

The *Hotel Surya* (☎ 43-014), just behind the Hotel Clarks Varanasi, is a recommended place with a garden that's great for relaxing in. It also has a good Chinese restaurant. All rooms have attached bathrooms. There are some doubles for Rs 80 and air-con rooms for Rs 125/150.

On Patel Nagar, the street that runs up from the station, there's another group of hotels. Cheapest here is the *Hotel Temples Town* (☎ 46-582) run by a friendly guy who has good rooms for Rs 90/130 with attached bathroom. The *Hotel Rudra* is similarly priced but rather run down.

Between them is the *Hotel India* (☎ 44-401) which has been recommended by several travellers. It's a more expensive place with rooms from Rs 175/250 or Rs 275 to Rs 350 with air-con; there's a restaurant and bar. Next door the smart new *Hotel Vaibhav* is providing formidable competition with similar facilities (but no bar yet) and slightly cheaper prices.

City Centre – Lahurabir Area Hotels in Lahurabir, between the station and Godaulia, are mainly in the middle-price bracket. An exception is the *Hotel Vaishal* which is a big place with singles/doubles/triples for 50/100/150 with bathrooms attached (bucket hot water). The *Hotel Natraj* has rooms for Rs 60/90/170 with bathrooms attached. Next door the *Hotel Ajaya* is slightly better and more expensive at Rs 80/100 with 24-hour checkout.

The two-star *Pradeep Hotel* (☎ 44-963) at Jagatganj near Lahurabir has rooms from Rs 140/175 to Rs 250/350 with air-con, and the Poonam Restaurant here is very good. Another good place is the *Hotel Gautam*, round the corner from the Hotel Natraj, with clean rooms from Rs 175/200 to Rs 250/300 with air-con. Back on Station Rd, the *Hotel Avaneesh* (☎ 53-465) is a new place with rooms from Rs 250/325 with air-con and in-house movies.

West of Lahurabir, halfway between Varanasi Junction Station and the ghats, in a quiet area is the *Hotel Varuna* (☎ 54-524). It's a friendly, recommended place where good singles/doubles/triples with attached bath are Rs 100/150/190. The *Hotel Garden View* is about one km away on the noisier Vidyapeeth Rd. The garden is tiny and the rooms not great value at Rs 50/80 without attached bathroom but they have some better doubles for Rs 130 to Rs 170.

East of Lahurabir near the GPO at Maidagin is the *Hotel Barahdari* (☎ 33-0346), well run by an aristocratic Jain family. It's right in the middle of the town and there are air-cooled rooms for Rs 165/190 or Rs 275/330 with air-con, a good vegetarian restaurant and a garden.

Godaulia The hotels around the Dasaswamedh Ghat Rd area tend to be a bit more spacious but rather less interesting than those right in the Old City. There are a few cheap places such as the *Hotel Binod*, the *Palace Hotel*, and the nearby *Hotel Samman* which is the best of these similarly priced hotels with rooms from Rs 60/100 with attached bath. *Banaras Lodge* and *Tripti Hotel* also

have cheaper rooms without bathrooms. The *Hotel Maharaja* near Dasaswamedh Rd is a similarly priced hotel that has been recommended.

The *Hotel Ganges* is a big place with a friendly manager and rooms from Rs 90/125 to Rs 200/250 with air-con and 'Video-Vision'. Opposite Aces Restaurant is the *Seema Hotel* (☎ 62-623), which has clean rooms for Rs 165/192 and hot water heaters in the attached bathrooms.

A number of places around here won't let you stay because they don't have 'C' forms for foreigner registration. *Dasaswamedh Lodge* is one place, the *Madras Hotel* another. Perhaps it's just as well since the sign for this last place advises you to 'Stay and Die in Varanasi'!

Old City & Ghats Area This is the place to look for rock-bottom hotels. The streets here are very narrow; you even have to abandon cycle-rickshaws and make your way down the convoluted alleys on foot.

There are a number of good lodges right on the river with superb views along the ghats. They all have roof terraces for relaxing on and in some you can watch the sunrise without even getting out of bed! A popular place is *Vishnu Rest House* with singles/doubles/triples with attached bathrooms for Rs 50/70/100 and vegetarian thalis for Rs 10. Nearby is *Kumiko House/Pension* with similar prices, run by a large and friendly Japanese woman with her large and friendly Indian husband. The Rs 15 dorm is often packed with Japanese travellers. Further south is the *Sun View Guest House* with basic rooms for Rs 30/60 and some doubles with bath for Rs 70. A yoga centre is run in the small garden here (Rs 30 a lesson).

In the north of this area, right above Scindia Ghat (beside Manikarnika Ghat), *Scindhia Guest House* (☎ 32-0319) is an excellent choice. It's small, clean and well run by a helpful manager. Singles/doubles are Rs 35/50, there are some doubles with attached baths for Rs 70 and dorm beds for Rs 20. The food here is a bit pricey but there are superb views along the river. Much further north is the cheaper *Tandon House Lodge* which is right on the river at Gai Ghat, but difficult to find.

Many travellers prefer the places down the alleys set back from the ghats. The *Yogi Lodge* (☎ 53-986) has long been a favourite with budget travellers and it's efficiently run by a friendly family. Dorm beds are Rs 20, and rooms are Rs 40/50 but they're quite small. There's a travellers' notice board, hot showers and a good restaurant. Its success has spawned the *Jogi Lodge* and the *New Yogi Lodge* which are inferior copies offering commissions to rickshaw-wallahs – be warned. Near the Yogi Lodge is *Golden Lodge* which is slightly cheaper and has a good roof terrace.

The *Sri Venkateshwar Lodge* (☎ 32-2357), beside the small blue temple, is a good place with singles/doubles/triples for Rs 35/60/75 and some rooms with attached bathrooms. The management is helpful and not overly keen on noxious substances. You must sign a form stating that you 'Solemnly Declare' that you will 'not Consume such type of Things' in case 'Unforeseen Things Happend'!

Trimurti Guest House (☎ 32-2616) is good value (although some of the rooms are a little cell-like) and has a popular restaurant. Rooms cost from Rs 30/45 upwards, some have attached baths and air-cooling, and there are great views from the roof over the Golden Temple. There are so many signs to the *Shanti Guest House* (near Manikarnika Ghat and Scindhia Guest House) that it's difficult to miss. It's a cheap place with dorm beds for Rs 15, rooms for Rs 30/40 and good views from the roof.

Further back from the river, *Om House Lodge*, in the Bansphatak area of the old city, is extremely cheap with dorm beds at Rs 10 to Rs 15 and rooms from Rs 25/30. It's popular with travellers and the owner gives yoga lessons. You have to wander down a maze of winding lanes to find it, but it's pleasantly quiet. The *Vaibav Lodge* is another very cheap and basic place. Even cheaper and more basic accommodation is available on the *houseboats* moored below

Kumiko Pension. For around Rs 10 a night you can't get closer to the river.

Away to the south of this area in a quiet location by the Shivala post office is the *Sandhya Guest House* (☎ 31-0644). It's run by a friendly, helpful manager and has a good restaurant on the roof with home-made soups and brown bread. There are dorm beds for Rs 12, rooms for Rs 40/60 or Rs 50/70 with attached bathrooms and it's only a few minutes from Shivala Ghat.

Places to Stay – top end

The *Hotel de Paris* (☎ 46-601) occupies a large rambling building of whitewashed arches in the Cantonment area. It's got a certain run-down style but probably doesn't deserve its three stars. Singles/doubles are Rs 395/575 with air-con, and there's a good restaurant.

The four-star *Hotel Hindustan International* (☎ 62-284) is a modern concrete block in the centre of the city with air-con rooms at Rs 700/850 and bathrooms with tubs. There's also a swimming pool. It's better value than the four-star *Hotel Varanasi Ashok* (☎ 46-020), next to Clarks in the Cantonment area, which has rooms for US$49/56. However the Ashok is in a quieter location with a better garden, and a pool.

The *Hotel Clarks Varanasi* (☎ 42-401) is the oldest hotel here, dating back to the British era but there's now a large modern extension. Air-conditioned singles/doubles cost US$65/70, and there's a swimming pool. It's considered the best place in town and is more popular than the equally upmarket *Hotel Taj Ganges*, which has air-con rooms from US$75/80 to US$185.

Places to Eat
Railway Station & Lahurabir Areas

Varanasi's railway station *restaurant* is the best value place in this area. Their breakfasts are particularly good as is their 'pot tea'. There's a restaurant at the *Tourist Bungalow* where the food is reasonable but overpriced. Just outside is the *Mandarin Chinese Restaurant*, which is cheaper although the food

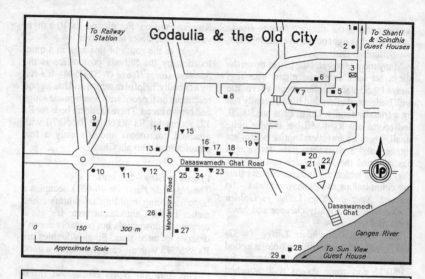

Godaulia & the Old City

■ PLACES TO STAY

1 Trimurti Guest House
5 Yogi Lodge
6 Golden Lodge
8 Om House Lodge
9 Hotel Binod
13 Palace Hotel
14 Seema Hotel
17 Tripti Hotel
18 Hotel Ganges
20 Sri Venkateshwar Lodge
21 Dasaswamedh Lodge
22 Vaibav Lodge
24 Banaras Lodge & Ayyars Cafe
25 Hotel Samman
27 Hotel Maharaja
28 Kumiko House/Pension
29 Vishnu Rest House

▼ PLACES TO EAT

4 Ganga Fuji Restaurant
7 Blue Moon Restaurant
11 Yelchico Restaurant
12 Jaljog
15 Aces New Deal Restaurant
16 Keshari Restaurant
19 Sunita Restaurant
23 Monga Restaurant

OTHER

2 Vishwanath (Golden) Temple
3 Vishwanath Post Office
10 St Thomas' Church
26 Universal Book Co

is only vaguely Chinese. Around the corner, the small *Most Welcome Restaurant* is OK.

The *Winfa Restaurant* in Lahurabir, behind the cinema, is the best Chinese restaurant here, with dishes at around Rs 30. In the Pradeep Hotel, the *Poonam Restaurant* does excellent Indian food. Main dishes are around Rs 40 and service is good. They even have the bizarre Mughlai dessert called

Shahi Tukra which will appeal to fans of bread-and-butter pudding – it's basically fried bread cooked in cream, with nuts and fruit.

However the best place to eat in this area, whether for a cappuccino or a splurge, is *El Parador*. It serves great soups and salads, fettucini, enchiladas, stews, crepes, chocolate cake and all the things you'd expect from a restaurant in Kathmandu rather than Varanasi – the owner is from Nepal. It's quite an expensive place with main dishes around Rs 50, but well worth it and very popular. They also do set brunches of waffles, pancakes, hash browns and cereal for Rs 30.

Cantonment Area The *Tourist Dak Bungalow* is noted for its Western breakfast, which includes porridge, eggs and toast for Rs 25. Good Chinese food is available at the Hotel Surya, with main dishes around Rs 28. If you want to dine in style in the Cantonment, there's the *Hotel Clarks* and the *Hotel Taj Ganges*.

Godaulia & the Old City Many of the lodges here offer room service, with vegetarian thalis ranging in price from Rs 10 to Rs 30. There are a number of places in Godaulia for breakfast and snacks including the *Aces New Deal Restaurant*, popular with travellers for many years though the food has received varied reports. It's now restyled itself as a vegetarian 'health food restaurant' and has a small courtyard.

For an Indian-style breakfast of puris and vegetables, known as kachauri, go to *Jaljog*, by the main square in Godaulia. The restaurant's name is in Hindi but as it was established nearly one hundred years ago everyone knows it. There are good samosas here too.

The best vegetarian restaurant in the area is *Keshari* down a small alley off Dasaswamedh Ghat Rd. The place is very clean and main dishes are around Rs 20. Another popular place is the basement restaurant *Yelchico*, which serves veg and non-veg food. It has the standard Indian/Chinese/Continental menu with main dishes at Rs 25 to Rs 30 and is one of the few restaurants around here where you can get a beer (Rs 40). *Monga* is a subterranean Chinese restaurant with similar prices, and *Ayyars Cafe* has good masala dosas and other light meals.

Blue Moon is a travellers' restaurant near Yogi Lodge with good lassi, but the prices aren't rock bottom (main dishes around Rs 25). *Ganga Fuji Restaurant* has a similar menu with similar prices. The restaurant in the *Trimurti Guest House* is another place popular with travellers. Near the Sri Venkateshwar Lodge is the *Sunita Cafe* which has good masala dosas for Rs 5.

In Bhelupura, near the Lalita Cinema, the *Sindhi Restaurant* does excellent vegetarian food. Rickshaw-wallahs all know the cinema but not the restaurant.

Varanasi is well known for its sweets, and *Madhur Jalpan Grih*, on the same side of the street as the cinema in Godaulia, is an excellent place to try them. The city is also known for its high quality pan. For greater highs the government *bhang* shop is on the way to the well-signposted Shanti Guest House.

Things to Buy

Varanasi is famous all over India for silk brocades and beautiful Benares saris. However, there are lots of rip-off merchants and commission people at work. Invitations to 'come to my home for tea' will inevitably mean to somebody's silk showroom, where you will be pressured into buying things. If you're 'only looking' they may even try to charge you for tea and electricity! Beware of anyone in your hotel (including the manager) who offers to take you to a cheap place. You'll be quoted at least 30% more for goods as commission has to be paid.

There's a market near the GPO called Golghar where the makers of silk brocades sell directly to the shops in the area. You can get cheaper silk brocade in this area than in the big stores, but you must be careful about the quality. Mixtures of silk and cotton can look very like pure silk to the untrained eye. The big shops selling silk brocades are all in the Chowk area of the old city. There's a fixed-price Cottage Industries Emporium in the Cantonment but since it's opposite the Hotel Taj Ganges the prices aren't fixed at the bottom end of the market.

The same care is necessary with sitars – yes, Ravi Shankar does live here (when he's not on tour in the West), but don't believe that every sitar maker is his personal friend! See the section under Music in the Facts about the Country chapter for details about purchasing musical instruments and tapes in Varanasi.

Getting There & Away

Air Varanasi is on several Indian Airlines routes including the popular daily tourist shuttle Delhi/Agra/Khajuraho/Varanasi and back. Delhi is US$74, Agra US$57 and Khajuraho US$39. Flights on this route are often delayed in winter by early morning fog in Delhi which throws out the schedules for the rest of the day. On Saturdays there's a direct flight to Delhi.

There are also three flights a week to Lucknow (US$29), Jaipur (US$97) and Bhubaneswar (US$69) plus a daily flight to Kathmandu (US$71).

The Indian Airlines office (☎ 43-746) is in the Cantonment near the Hotel de Paris.

Bus From the bus station opposite the main (Varanasi Junction) railway station there are frequent departures to Jaunpur (Rs 11, two hours), Allahabad (Rs 24, 3½ hours), Lucknow (Rs 48, nine hours), Faizabad (Rs 35, seven hours) and Gorakhpur (Rs 37, 6½ hours). There are morning and evening buses to Sunauli (Rs 56 to Rs 65, nine hours). No direct buses run to Khajuraho so take the train to Satna and a bus from there. The bus trip takes three to four hours.

Train There are three railway stations – Kashi, City and Varanasi Junction (also known as Varanasi Cantonment), which is the main station and has computerised booking. Railway reservations at the Varanasi Junction (Cantonment) station can be made by phoning 43-405.

There are not many trains running directly between here and Delhi or Calcutta but most Delhi to Calcutta trains do pass through Moghulserai, 12 km south of Varanasi. This is about 45 minutes by bus (Rs 2) or shared auto-rickshaw (Rs 8). The only reasonable accommodation in Moghulserai is the railway retiring rooms (Rs 60 for a good double) – the hotels opposite are fleapits.

From Varanasi Junction, expresses take 13 to 16 hours to Delhi (764 km, Rs 123/463 in 2nd/1st) and 13 hours to Calcutta (677 km, Rs 109/417 in 2nd/1st). The *Rajdhani Express* is the fastest train to Delhi or Calcutta but is not very convenient because it departs from Moghulserai in the middle of the night.

Other expresses take 28 hours to Bombay (1509 km, Rs 181/751 in 2nd/1st), 39 hours to Madras (2147 km, Rs 210/961 in 2nd/1st), three hours to Allahabad (137 km, Rs 31/120 in 2nd/1st), 4½ hours to Patna (228 km, Rs 49/175 in 2nd/1st), five hours to Lucknow (301 km, Rs 63/224 in 2nd/1st), two hours to Jaunpur (58 km, Rs 18/66 in 2nd/1st) and six hours to Gorakhpur (231 km, Rs 49/178 in 2nd/1st), but see the note below if you're going to Nepal.

For Khajuraho take the overnight 4248 *Varanasi-Bombay Express* to Satna (316 km, Rs 64/228 in 2nd/1st), and a bus from there to Khajuraho (three to four hours).

For the hill stations in UP, Himachal Pradesh or Kashmir, you can avoid going through Delhi. For Dehra Dun (Mussoorie) there's the daily *Doon Express* which stops in Haridwar.

To/From Nepal A bus may be better than the metre-gauge trains from here to the border. There are morning and evening government buses for Rs 56 to Sunauli (the border post) which go via Gorakhpur and take around nine hours.

Private companies operate buses to the Nepalese border and on to Kathmandu and Pokhara. They charge Rs 175 to Kathmandu or Pokhara which includes spartan accommodation at Sunauli. Alternatively, you can take one of their deluxe buses as far as the border for Rs 100 (or a much cheaper ordinary bus) and another bus from the border to Kathmandu or Pokhara for the Nepalese equivalent of Indian Rs 60. This gives you a choice of bus within Nepal and also of accommodation at Sunauli.

Getting Around

To/From the Airport Babatpur Airport is 22 km out of the city and a bus runs from the Indian Airlines office via the Cantonment hotels for Rs 20. Auto-rickshaws charge Rs 60 to Rs 80 and taxis around Rs 120.

Bus Godaulia is the midtown bus stop, just an easy walk from the ghats. Lanka is the bus stop closest to Benares Hindu University. Between the railway station and Godaulia a bus costs less than Rs 1, but unless you can get on at the starting point Varanasi buses tend to be very crowded.

Auto-Rickshaw & Tempo These operate on a shared basis with fixed prices (Rs 1 to Rs 3) along set routes. Once the driver realises you're not going to rent the whole rickshaw, these can be the best way to get around the city cheaply, although not with a lot of luggage as they're very cramped.

From the stand outside the north entrance of the station it's Rs 1 to the Cantonment TV tower or Rs 2 to the Civil Court (for auto-rickshaws to Sarnath). There's a stand outside the south entrance of the station for destinations including Lahurabir, the Civil Court and Godaulia (Rs 2).

Cycle-Rickshaw & Bicycle The main problem with cycle-rickshaws in Varanasi is the rickshaw-wallahs, who can be a major pain. A trip between the railway station and Godaulia, near Dasaswamedh Ghat, should be about Rs 6 but you'll probably have to pay twice that. The quoted 'two rupees any-where' fare only applies if you let them take you to one of their 'cheap' hotels where their commission is included in the room price.

There are several places to rent bicycles around Lanka; all-day rates are about Rs 10, although the Aces New Deal Restaurant in Godaulia has a few bikes for Rs 15 a day.

SARNATH
Only 10 km north-east of Varanasi, the most holy of Hindu cities, is Sarnath, one of the major Buddhist centres. Having achieved enlightenment at Bodhgaya, the Buddha came to Sarnath to preach his message of the middle way to final nirvana. Later, Ashoka,

the great Buddhist emperor, erected magnificent stupas and monasteries here.

Sarnath was at its peak when the indefatigable Chinese traveller Fa Xien visited the site early in the 5th century AD. In 640 AD when Xuan Zhang, another Chinese traveller, made his call Sarnath had 1500 priests, a stupa nearly 100 metres high, Ashoka's mighty stone pillar and many other wonders. The city was known as the Deer Park, after the Buddha's famous first sermon, The Sermon in the Deer Park.

Soon after, Buddhism went into decline and after the Muslim invaders destroyed and desecrated the city's buildings, Sarnath was little more than a shell. It was not until 1836 when British archaeologists started excavations that Sarnath regained some of its past glory.

It's an interesting place to spend an afternoon but is quite touristy and the UP government now has plans for a five-star hotel and convention centre. Although you can stay in some of the monasteries here, if you're interested in studying Buddhism you'd probably be better off going to Bodhgaya or Dharamsala.

Dhamekh Stupa
This 34-metre-high stupa dominates the site and is believed to mark the spot where the Buddha preached his famous sermon. In its present form it dates from around 500 AD but was probably rebuilt a number of times. The geometrical and floral patterns on the stupa are typical of the Gupta period, but excavations have revealed brickwork from the Mauryan period around 200 BC.

Originally there was a second stupa, Dharmarajika Stupa, but this was reduced to rubble by 19th-century treasure seekers.

Main Shrine & Ashoka Pillar
Ashoka is said to have meditated in the building known as the 'main shrine'. The foundations are all that can now be seen and to the north of it are the extensive ruins of the monasteries.

Standing in front of the main shrine are the remains of Ashoka's Pillar. At one time this stood over 20 metres high, but the capital is now in the Sarnath museum. An edict issued by Ashoka is engraved on the remaining portion of the column and below this are representations of a lion, elephant, horse and bull. The lion is supposed to represent bravery, the elephant symbolises the dream Buddha's mother had before his birth, and the horse recalls that Buddha left his home on horseback in search of enlightenment.

Archaeological Museum

The main attraction at this excellent Archaeological Museum is the superb capital from the Ashokan pillar. It has the Ashokan symbol of four back-to-back lions which has been adopted as the state symbol of modern India. Other finds from the site include many figures and sculptures from the various periods of Sarnath – Mauryan, Kushana, Gupta and later. Among them is the earliest Buddha image found at Sarnath, Buddha figures in various positions dating back to the 5th and 6th centuries, and many images of Hindu gods such as Saraswati, Ganesh and Vishnu from the 9th to 12th centuries. The museum is open from 10 am to 5 pm daily, but is closed on Fridays. Entry is Rs 0.50, and there is a booklet available for Rs 3 at the counter.

Mulgandha Kuti Vihar

This modern Mahabodhi Society temple has a series of frescoes by the Japanese artist Kosetsu Nosi in the interior. A bo tree growing here was transplanted in 1931 from the tree in Anuradhapura, Sri Lanka, which in turn is said to be an offspring of the original tree under which the Buddha attained enlightenment. There's a group of statues here showing the Buddha giving his first sermon to his five disciples.

Other Temples & Deer Park

You can visit the modern temples in the Thai, Chinese, Tibetan, Burmese and Japanese monasteries.

North of the Mulgandha Kuti Vihar is the deer park. This is now a mini-zoo with a few unhappy-looking deer foraging in the dust,

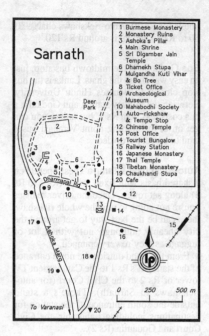

Sarnath

1 Burmese Monastery
2 Monastery Ruins
3 Ashoka's Pillar
4 Main Shrine
5 Sri Digamber Jain Temple
6 Dhamekh Stupa
7 Mulgandha Kuti Vihar & Bo Tree
8 Ticket Office
9 Archaeological Museum
10 Mahabodhi Society
11 Auto-rickshaw & Tempo Stop
12 Chinese Temple
13 Post Office
14 Tourist Bungalow
15 Railway Station
16 Japanese Monastery
17 Thai Temple
18 Tibetan Monastery
19 Chaukhandi Stupa
20 Cafe

and some large displays of Indian birds and waterfowl.

Places to Stay & Eat

The *Tourist Bungalow* (☎ 42-515) has singles/doubles from Rs 62/75 to Rs 132/155, all with bathrooms attached. There's also a very basic dorm at Rs 20 per bed. You can stay in some of the monasteries for a donation. The Burmese Vihara has 14 rooms, some with attached bathrooms, set around a peaceful courtyard.

The restaurant at the Tourist Bungalow does set lunches for Rs 30 (veg) and Rs 45 (non-veg). Cheaper snacks are available at the stalls on Dharmapal Rd and there's a cafe/ice-cream parlour 800 metres south of the Tourist Bungalow.

Getting There & Away

From Varanasi, an auto-rickshaw for the 20-minute journey costs Rs 25. For Rs 40 you could take the afternoon tour from Varanasi which returns via Ram Nagar Fort (though usually arriving there after it has closed). There's an infrequent bus service from Varanasi station to Sarnath for Rs 2 and a few trains stop here. It's easier to get a shared auto-rickshaw (Rs 5) from the stand by the Civil Court or from the stands in Lahurabir or Godaulia.

CHUNAR

If the narrow alleys of Varanasi are giving you a touch of claustrophobia, Chunar Fort overlooking the Ganges makes a good day trip. It's had a succession of owners representing most of India's rulers over the last 500 years. Sher Shah took it from Humayun in 1540, Akbar recaptured it for the Moghuls in 1575 and in the mid-18th century it passed to the nawabs of Oudh. They were shortly followed by the British, whose gravestones here make interesting reading. Chunar is 36 km from Varanasi and can be reached by bus.

JAUNPUR

Population: 136,000

This town sees very few travellers but is of great interest to architectural historians for its mosques, built in a unique style that is part Hindu and Jain, and part Islamic.

Founded by Feroz Shah Tughlaq in 1360 on an ancient site, Jaunpur became the capital of the independent Muslim Sharqui kingdom. The most impressive mosques were constructed between 1394 and 1478. They were built on the ruins of Hindu, Buddhist and Jain temples, shrines and monasteries and are notable for their odd mixture of architectural styles, their two-storey arcades and large gateways, and for their unusual minarets. Jaunpur was sacked by Sikandar Lodi, who left only the mosques undamaged, and the Moghuls took over in 1530.

Most of the mosques and the railway station are in the older part of the town north of the Gomti River. They are spread out over two or three sq km and although you can walk to them a cycle-rickshaw can be useful, and the wallahs can also act as guides.

The **Atala Masjid**, built in 1408 on the site

of a Hindu temple dedicated to Atala Devi, is one km from the station near the GPO. Continue 500 metres south of here and you come to **Jaunpur Fort** (built by Feroz Shah in 1360) and the stone **Akbari Bridge** constructed between 1564 and 1568. The largest of the mosques is the impressive **Jami Masjid** built between 1438 and 1478, one km north of the bridge. Other places to see include the Jhanjhri Masjid, the tombs of the Shaqui sultans, the Char Ungli Masjid and the Lal Darwaza Masjid.

Places to Stay & Eat

Jaunpur has a few very basic hotels and no fancy restaurants. Near the fort there's the *Hotel Gomti*, with doubles for Rs 60. Foreigners can also stay at the *Marwari Dharamsala* in the same area.

Getting There & Away

Varanasi is 58 km away, a journey of two hours by train (Rs 18) or bus (Rs 11).

Eastern Uttar Pradesh

GORAKHPUR

Population: 490,000

This is a city that most travellers (on their way to Kathmandu or Pokhara from Delhi or Varanasi) are happy to quickly pass through, spending a night here only if necessary. Apart from the Gorakhnath Temple which you pass on the road to Nepal, there's not a lot to see. And even if there were, the plagues of flies and mosquitoes early and late in the season would not encourage long stays.

Named after the sage, Yogi Gorakhnath, Gorakhpur is in the centre of a rich agricultural area which has nevertheless remained very undeveloped. The city is also a centre for the printing and publishing of Hindu religious literature, and the well-known Geeta Press is here.

Information

There are tourist offices at the railway station

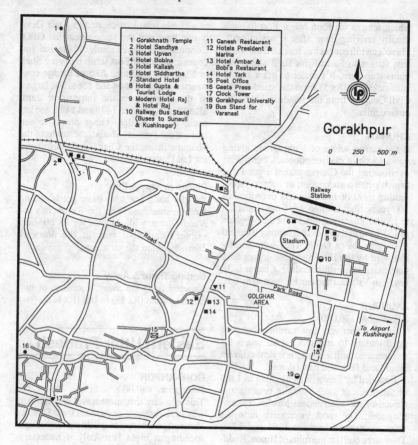

KEY

1 Gorakhnath Temple
2 Hotel Sandhya
3 Hotel Upvan
4 Hotel Bobina
5 Hotel Kallash
6 Hotel Siddhartha
7 Standard Hotel
8 Hotel Gupta &
   Tourist Lodge
9 Modern Hotel Raj
   & Hotel Raj
10 Railway Bus Stand
   (Buses to Sunauli
   & Kushinagar)
11 Ganesh Restaurant
12 Hotels President &
   Marina
13 Hotel Ambar &
   Bobi's Restaurant
14 Hotel Yark
15 Post Office
16 Geeta Press
17 Clock Tower
18 Gorakhpur University
19 Bus Stand for
   Varanasi

Gorakhpur

0   250   500 m

Cinema Road

Railway Station

Stadium

Park Road

GOLGHAR AREA

To Airport & Kushinagar

and in Park Rd (☎ 33-5450) on the way to the city centre. If you have just come from Nepal, Indrail Passes can be bought (with foreign currency) at the railway station.

Watch out for the ticket touts who home in like vultures as you get off the bus or train here. We've had numerous complaints about their through-tickets to Nepal by bus (which cost about 50% more than doing it yourself and are not always reliable) and about their hefty commissions on rail tickets. However they may be useful during the high season when things are booked up, and they're also able to change Nepalese rupees.

Places to Stay

If you're catching the 5 am bus to Sunauli (at the border) then the hotels opposite the railway station are the most convenient, but they're certainly nothing special. The *Modern Hotel Raj* has some unappealing singles for Rs 30 and single/doubles with attached bath for Rs 40/60. The *Hotel Gupta & Tourist Lodge* is no better, and has rooms with common bath for Rs 40/60 or Rs 50/80 with attached bath.

Much better is the *Standard Hotel*, with singles/doubles/triples with attached bathrooms for Rs 70/100/125 and they've got the

Left: Early morning at the ghats, Varanasi, Uttar Pradesh (HF)
Right: Flower sellers at the ghats, Varanasi, Uttar Pradesh (HF)
Bottom: Naini Tal, Uttar Pradesh (BT)

Left: The Mall, Mussoorie, Uttar Pradesh (BT)
Right: Mosque detail, Taj Mahal, Agra, Uttar Pradesh (RI)
Bottom: Cycle-rickshaw, Lucknow, Uttar Pradesh (BT)

mosquito problem under control with netting on the windows. Unfortunately this makes it rather hot from late March onwards. Air-cooled rooms are available in the *Hotel Raj* for Rs 150 a double.

The *Hotel Siddhartha* has some air-con rooms for Rs 200/225 as well as small rooms without air-con for Rs 75/110/145. At the railway station there are *retiring rooms* for Rs 50/80, air-con deluxe doubles for Rs 150 and dorm beds for Rs 20.

In the centre of the city there's the *Hotel Yark* with rooms from Rs 25/50 with common bath to air-con doubles for Rs 250. The similarly priced *Hotel Ambar* is close by. The *Hotel Marina* is a good place with rooms from Rs 60/95, air-cooled doubles for Rs 135 and air-con doubles with TV for Rs 225. It's directly behind the best place in town, the flashy *Hotel President* (☎ 33-7654). Ordinary rooms here are Rs 125/175, air-con Rs 200/300 with TV.

On the road to Nepal is the *Hotel Kailash* with singles from Rs 37 and doubles with bath from Rs 85.

Places to Eat

Around the railway station there are plenty of places to eat and the *refreshment room* in the station itself has good-value vegetarian meals.

In the city centre there's a much better range including the *Ganesh Restaurant* (good masala dosas) and *Bobi's*, which has a full menu (veg and non-veg) as well as an ice-cream parlour. Slightly more expensive but probably the best place to eat in Gorakhpur is the *Queen's Restaurant* in the Hotel President. It has good service, powerful air-conditioning and the added advantage of staying open until around midnight.

Getting There & Away

Air Gorakhpur has been 'temporarily de-linked' by Indian Airlines.

Bus There are regular departures for the border at Sunauli (Rs 17, three hours) between 5 am and 8 pm from the bus stand near the railway station. You'll need to take the 5 am bus from Gorakhpur to be sure of catching a day bus from the border to Kathmandu or Pokhara. There are also private buses from the road in front of the railway station.

Travel agents offer through-tickets to Kathmandu (Rs 125) or Pokhara (Rs 106) but doing it yourself is not only cheaper and more reliable, it also gives you a choice of bus at the border. Even with 'through' tickets you have to change buses at the border.

Buses to Varanasi (Rs 37 to Rs 45, 6½ hours) depart from the Katchari bus station which is a Rs 4 rickshaw ride from the city centre.

There are also regular buses to Lucknow (Rs 46) and Faizabad (Rs 24) as well as Kanpur and Patna. Buses to Kushinagar (Rs 10, 1½ hours) depart from the bus stand near the railway station.

Train Gorakhpur is the headquarters of the North Eastern Railway and is an important junction. There are evening departures for Delhi (783 km, 14½ hours, Rs 124/472 in 2nd/1st class) via Lucknow (276 km, 5½ hours, Rs 56/205 in 2nd/1st). There are early-morning departures for Bombay (1690 km, 35 hours, Rs 186/789 in 2nd/1st) and Varanasi (231 km, 5½ hours, Rs 49/178 in 2nd/1st). There are also metre-gauge trains to Nautanwa for Nepal, but the buses are more convenient as they take you right to the border.

KUSHINAGAR

It's here that the Buddha is reputed to have breathed his last words, 'Decay is inherent in all component things' and expired. Pilgrims now come in large numbers to see the remains of his brick cremation stupa, the large, reclining Buddha figure in the Mahaparinirvana Temple, the modern Indo/Japan/Sri Lanka Buddhist Centre and the monasteries.

Places to Stay

For a small donation it's possible to stay in some of the monasteries. *Pathik Nivas*, the UP State Tourist Bungalow, has singles/

doubles for Rs 125/150, air-con rooms and a restaurant. There's also the ITDC Ashok *Traveller's Lodge*.

Getting There & Away

Kushinagar is 55 km east of Gorakhpur and there are frequent bus services (Rs 10, 1½ hours).

SUNAULI

Right on the border with Nepal this sleepy village is just a bus stop, a couple of hotels, a few shops and the border post (open 24 hours).

The Nepalese border post is actually called Belhiya but everyone also refers to it as Sunauli. Nepalese visas are available here for US$20.

Places to Stay

The UP State *Hotel Niranjana* is a clean and friendly place 700 metres from the border. It's good value with dorm beds at Rs 15, singles/doubles (attached bath) for Rs 50/75 and some air-cooled rooms. By the border post is the dumpy *Sanju Lodge* (dorm beds Rs 15) and over on the Nepalese side there are several good cheap hotels.

Getting There & Away

From Sunauli there are direct buses to Vara-

nasi (Rs 56 to Rs 100, nine hours) in the early morning and early evening, and to Allahabad (Rs 67, 12 hours) and Lucknow (Rs 62, 11 hours). Buses to Gorakhpur (Rs 17, three hours) depart every half hour from 5 am to 7 pm. Be wary of touts offering combined bus/rail tickets since these are not 100% reliable. They're easy enough to arrange yourself at Gorakhpur railway station.

To/From Nepal There are numerous private buses from here to Kathmandu leaving hourly between 5 and 9 am (and sometimes additional buses at 10 and 11 am). The night buses leave between 3.30 and 8.30 pm but of course on these you miss the great views on the journey. Buses take 12 to 14 hours and cost Nepalese Rs (NRs) 97. The government 'Saja' buses are faster but leave from Bhairawa, four km from Sunauli, at 6.30 and 7.30 am, then at 6.30 and 7.30 pm. They're very popular and booking is essential (NRs 97 from the kiosk opposite the Hotel Yeti in Bhairawa).

From Sunauli there are also morning and evening buses to Pokhara, which take nine to 10 hours.

For Lumbini (the birthplace of the Buddha) there are numerous buses from Bhairawa for the 22-km journey.

Bihar

Population: 86 million
Area: 173,877 sq km
Capital: Patna
People per sq km: 497
Main Language: Hindi
Literacy Rate: 38%

Passing along the Ganges in the area that is now Bihar, the Buddha prophesied that a great city would arise here but added that it would be always in danger from 'feud and fire and flood'. Over 250 years later, in the 3rd century BC, the mighty Ashoka was ruling from Pataliputra, now Patna. It's difficult to imagine that this city, the capital of one of the most backward and depressed states in the country, was once the capital of the greatest empire in India.

The name 'Bihar' is derived from 'Vihara' meaning monastery. Bihar was a great religious centre for Jains, Hindus and, most importantly, Buddhists. It was at Bodhgaya that the Buddha sat under the bo tree and attained enlightenment, and a descendant of that original tree still flourishes there today. Nearby Nalanda was a world-famous Buddhist university in the 5th century AD, while Rajgir was associated with both the Buddha and the Jain apostle Mahavira.

Today the Buddha's predictions continue to come true. The rivers periodically flood causing disastrous problems for Bihar's dense population, which scratches a bare living from the soil. Per capita income is low yet the Chotanagpur plateau in the south produces 40% of India's mineral wealth. Bihar's literacy rate is one of the lowest in the country, and the state is considered to have the most widespread corruption. 'Feud and fire' take the form of outbreaks of inter-caste warfare and in 1992, 34 people were massacred in the village of Bara, near Gaya, by a rival caste.

Few travellers spend much time here, most just passing through Patna on their way to Calcutta or Kathmandu. However, Bodh-

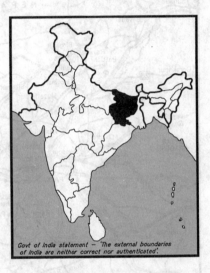

Govt of India statement – 'The external boundaries of India are neither correct nor authenticated'.

gaya is an excellent place to study Buddhism, and Rajgir, Nalanda and Sasaram are interesting places that are not on the tourist trail.

PATNA

Population: 1.1 million

Bihar's capital is a surprisingly pleasant city which sprawls along the southern bank of the Ganges. The river at this point is very wide; between Varanasi and Patna, it is joined by three major tributaries and triples in width. The Mahatma Gandhi Seti, one of the longest bridges in the world at 7½ km, crosses the Ganges here.

History

Ajatasatru shifted the capital of the Magadha Empire from Rajgir, early in the 5th century BC, fulfilling the Buddha's prophecy for a great city here. The remains of his ancient city of Pataliputra can still be seen at the site in Kumrahar, a southern district of Patna.

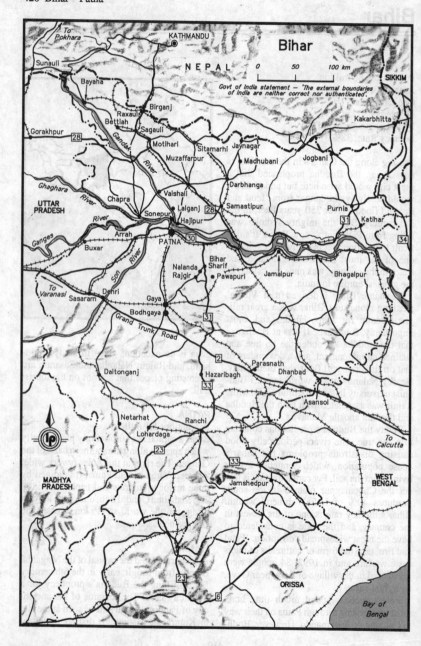

This was the capital of a huge empire spanning a large part of ancient India with Chandragupta Maurya and Ashoka among the emperors who ruled from here. For almost 1000 years Pataliputra was one of the most important cities on the subcontinent.

Renamed Azimabad, the city regained its political importance in the mid-16th century AD when Sher Shah, after defeating Humayun, made it his capital. It passed to the British in 1764 after the Battle of Buxar.

Orientation

The city stretches along the southern bank of the Ganges for about 15 km. The hotels, main railway station and airport are all in the western half of Patna, known as Bankipur, while the older and more traditional area is to the east, in Patna City. The 'hub' of the new Patna is at Gandhi Maidan. The main market area is Ashok Raj Path, which starts from Gandhi Maidan.

Two important roads near the railway station, Frazer and Exhibition Rds, have officially had their names changed to Muzharul Haque Path and Braj Kishore Path respectively but everyone still uses the old names. On the other hand, Gardiner Rd is now referred to as Beer Chand Patel Path.

Information

The state tourist office (☎ 25-295) is on Frazer Rd and there are counters at the railway station, the airport and at Hotel Pataliputra Ashok – but don't expect much from any of them. There's also a Government of India tourist office (☎ 26-721) at the Tourist Bungalow (Tourist Bhavan) on Beer Chand Patel Path.

There are a couple of reasonable bookshops along Frazer Rd and a British Library (☎ 24-198) on Bank Rd near the Bishuram Bhavan by Gandhi Maidan.

The telephone area code for Patna is 0612.

Golghar

Overlooking the maidan, this huge, beehive-shaped building was constructed in 1786 as a granary to store surpluses against possible famines. It was built by Captain John Garstin at the instigation of the British administrator, Warren Hastings, and although the Bihar government is making use of it now, it has hardly ever been filled. Standing about 25 metres high with steps winding around the outside to the top, the Golghar provides a fine view over the town and the Ganges.

Patna Museum

This excellent, albeit somewhat dog-eared, museum contains metal and stone sculptures dating back to the Maurya (3rd century BC) and Gupta (4th to 7th centuries AD) periods, terracotta figures and archaeological finds from sites in Bihar such as Nalanda. To the right as you walk in is the world's longest fossilised tree – 16 metres of it, 200 million years old. Stuffed wildlife includes the usual (tiger, deer, crocodile) and the unusual (a kid with three ears and eight legs). Upstairs are Chinese and Tibetan paintings and *thankas* (Tibetan cloth paintings). The museum is open from 10 am to 4.30 pm; closed on Mondays. Entry costs Rs 0.25.

Kumrahar Excavations

The remains of Pataliputra, the ancient capital of Ajatasatru (491-459 BC), Chandragupta (321-297 BC) and Ashoka (274-237 BC), have been uncovered in Kumrahar, south of Patna. The main points of interest are the assembly hall (a few large pillars are all that remain) dating back to the Mauryan period, and the foundations of the brick Buddhist monastery known as Anand Bihar. There's a small display of some of the clay figures and wooden beams discovered here.

The Kumrahar excavations are fairly esoteric, however, and are likely to attract only those with a keen interest in archaeology and India's ancient history. They are set in a pleasant park open daily (except Monday) from 9 am to 5 pm; entry costs Rs 0.50. Shared auto-rickshaws between Patna Junction railway station and Gulzarbagh pass right by here and cost Rs 2.

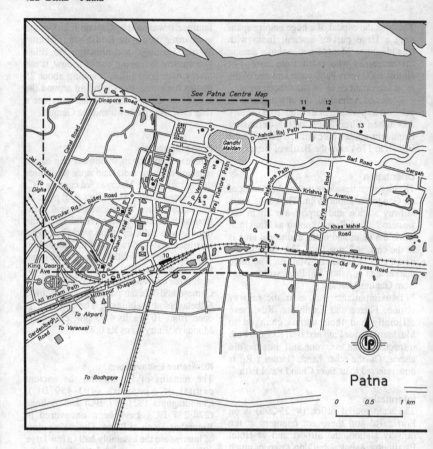

Patna

0   0.5   1 km

Har Mandir

At the eastern end of the city, in the Chowk area of old Patna, stands one of the holiest Sikh shrines. Built of white marble by Ranjit Singh, it marks the place where Gobind Singh, the 10th and last of the Sikh gurus, was born in 1660.

Not only must you go barefoot within the temple precincts, but your head must be covered. They lend cloths for this purpose at the entrance.

Qila House (Jalan Museum)

Built on the foundations of Sher Shah's fort,

Qila House contains an impressive private collection of antiques including a dinner-service that once belonged to George III, Marie Antoinette's Sèvres porcelain, Napoleon's four-poster bed, Chinese jade and Moghul silver filigree. Phone 42-354 for permission to visit.

Khuda Baksh Oriental Library

Founded in 1900, this library has a renowned collection of rare Arabic and Persian manuscripts, Moghul and Rajput paintings, and oddities like the Koran inscribed in a book only an inch wide. The library also contains

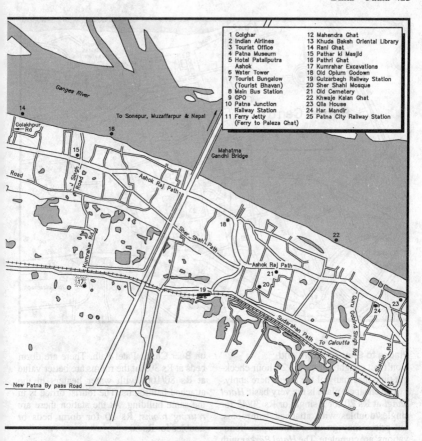

1 Golghar	12 Mahendra Ghat
2 Indian Airlines	13 Khuda Baksh Oriental Library
3 Tourist Office	14 Rani Ghat
4 Patna Museum	15 Pathar ki Masjid
5 Hotel Pataliputra Ashok	16 Pathri Ghat
6 Water Tower	17 Kumrahar Excavations
7 Tourist Bungalow (Tourist Bhavan)	18 Old Opium Godown
8 Main Bus Station	19 Gulzarbagh Railway Station
9 GPO	20 Sher Shahi Mosque
10 Patna Junction Railway Station	21 Old Cemetery
11 Ferry Jetty (Ferry to Paleza Ghat)	22 Khwaje Kalan Ghat
	23 Qila House
	24 Har Mandir
	25 Patna City Railway Station

the only books which survived the sacking of the Moorish University of Cordoba in Spain.

Other Attractions

Non-Hindus are welcome at the modern **Mahavir Mandir**, dedicated to the popular god, Hanuman. At night this place is lit up in garish pink and green neon – you can't possibly miss it as you leave the main railway station.

The heavy, domed **Sher Shahi**, built by the Afghan ruler Sher Shah in 1545, is the oldest mosque in Patna. Other mosques

include the squat **Pathar ki Masjid** and the riverbank **Madrassa**.

Gulzarbagh, to the east of the city, was the site of the East India Company's **opium warehouse**. The building is currently occupied by a Bihar state government printing works.

Organised Tours

The state tourist office operates a day trip which includes Patna, Rajgir, Nalanda and Pawapuri. It runs on Saturday and Sunday, and the cost is Rs 65. For departure times, contact the tourist office.

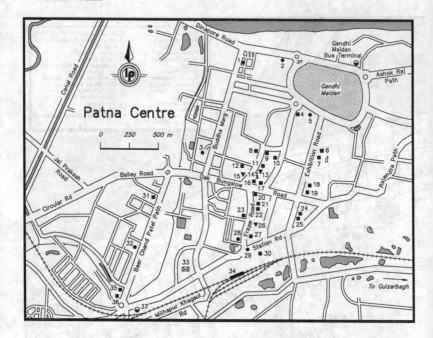

Patna Centre

Places to Stay – bottom end

Don't get caught out by the 24-hour checkout time that many of the hotels here apply.

The cheapest place is the very basic *Hotel Sangi* at Rs 20 for a single or Rs 30/45 for singles/doubles with attached bathrooms, but prices may go up a little when 'renovations' are complete. The *Hotel Parker* with rooms from Rs 40/50 is OK but rather dark. On the next block, the *Ruby Hotel* is spartan and charges Rs 40 for singles, Rs 50/70 for rooms with attached bathrooms.

The best of the cheap places is the *Hotel Shyama* where singles/doubles/triples with attached bathrooms cost Rs 40/60/85. On the way there you could check if the double room at the *AA of Eastern India* is available. It's clean and excellent value at Rs 50 with attached bathroom and TV and you don't have to be a member of the Automobile Association (AA).

The *Tourist Bungalow* (Kautilya Vihar Tourist Bhavan; ☎ 22-5411) is in 'R-block' on Beer Chand Patel Path. There are dorm beds at Rs 30 but the rooms are better value at Rs 80/100, with water heaters in the attached bathrooms. The tourist office is in the same building. At the station there are *retiring rooms*; Rs 20 for dorm beds or doubles for Rs 60.

Places to Stay – middle

The conveniently situated *Hotel Mayur* is good value with rooms for Rs 116/147 with water heaters in the attached bathrooms, and there's a restaurant. The *Hotel President* (☎ 22-0600) is down a side street off Frazer Rd and has rooms from Rs 135/150 or Rs 225/250 with air-con. Another good place is the small *Hotel Sheodar Sadan* with clean doubles from Rs 145 and air-con rooms for Rs 255.

Places to Stay – top end

The *Hotel Chanakya* (☎ 22-3141), near the Tourist Bungalow, is a newish place that has

PLACES TO STAY	
4	Maurya Patna Hotel
6	Hotel Shyama
7	Hotel Rajkumar
8	Hotel Parker
9	Hotel Sheodar Sadan
10	Ruby Hotel
11	Rajasthan Hotel
12	Hotel President
16	Hotel Rajdhani
17	AA of Eastern India
18	Republic Hotel
19	Rajdhani Guest House
20	Hotel Dai Ichi
21	Hotel Satkar International
22	Hotel Sangi
23	Hotel Samrat International
24	Hotel Vikram
25	Hotel Chaitanya
27	Hotel Mayur & Mamta Restaurant
30	Hotel Anand Lok
31	Hotel Pataliputra Ashok

35	Tourist Bungalow
36	Hotel Chanakya

▼ PLACES TO EAT	
13	Ashoka Restaurant
15	Jai Annapurna Restaurant
26	Mayfair Ice-cream Parlour

OTHER	
1	British Library
2	Golghar
3	Patna Museum
5	Indian Airlines
14	Tourist Office
28	Jail
29	Auto-rickshaw Stand (for Gulzarbagh)
32	Water Tower
33	GPO
34	Patna Junction Railway Station
37	Main Bus Station

already picked up three stars. Singles/doubles cost Rs 395/600.

Overlooking Gandhi Maidan, the *Welcomgroup Maurya Patna* (☎ 22-2060) is Patna's top hotel and has the usual mod cons, including a pool. Rooms cost from US$50/55. The *Hotel Pataliputra Ashok* (☎ 22-6270) is better value at Rs 650/800.

Places to Eat

Patna has plenty of places to eat, many of which are along Frazer Rd not far from the railway station. The *Mayfair Ice-cream Parlour* is a clean and popular place with good masala dosas (Rs 8.50) and other snacks, as well as 16-odd ice-cream flavours. The nearby *Mamta Restaurant* has main dishes for Rs 30 and beer is available for Rs 30. Further up Frazer Rd, the *Ashoka Restaurant* is rather dark but the non-vegetarian food is good.

Not far from the Ashoka, the *Rajasthan Hotel* has the best vegetarian restaurant in the city. It's not cheap but the food is excellent and they have a good range of ice-creams.

The *Jai Annapurna Restaurant* does good chicken kebabs and has a take-away service.

Getting There & Away

Air Indian Airlines (☎ 22-2554) has daily flights between Patna and Delhi (US$87), Calcutta (US$51) and Ranchi (US$32). A few flights a week connect Patna with Lucknow (US$47) and Bombay (US$157).

Bus The main bus station is at Harding Park, just west of Patna Junction railway station. It's a large place with departure gates spread out along the road. Buses for Siliguri (Rs 71 to Rs 105, 12 hours), Gaya (Rs 16, three hours), Ranchi (Rs 65, eight hours) and Sasaram (Rs 28, 4½ hours) go from Gate 7. Buses for Raxaul (Rs 38, five hours) on the Nepalese border go from Gate 6, via Muzaffarpur.

The Gandhi Maidan bus station is used by government buses to many places in Bihar. There are night buses to Ranchi and also a deluxe bus to Siliguri (Rs 105, departing at 7.30 pm).

Train Patna Junction is the main railway station. The fastest trains on the Calcutta-Delhi line take 15 hours to Delhi (992 km, Rs 143/534 in 2nd/1st) and nine hours to Calcutta (545 km, Rs 95/355 in 2nd/1st). The *Amritsar Mail* leaves early in the morning for Varanasi (228 km, five hours). There are direct trains to Ranchi (591 km, 10 hours), Bombay and a weekly service to Madras.

If you're heading to Darjeeling or the north-east region, the fast *North East Express* from Delhi leaves Patna at 9.20 pm, arriving in New Jalpaiguri at 9.35 am. It's 636 km and Rs 108/397 in 2nd/1st class. There's a daily direct train to Gaya (92 km, 3½ hours) but as it leaves in the evening and often gets delayed the bus is better.

To/From Nepal The flight from Patna to Kathmandu, which was quite popular with travellers, has been suspended indefinitely. If you're coming from Delhi or Varanasi, the Gorakhpur/Sunauli crossing point is much more pleasant than polluted Raxaul/Birganj.

There are no direct trains from Patna to the border town of Raxaul (you have to change at Muzaffarpur) so the buses are faster. From the main bus station, there are departures at 6.30 am, and 12.30, 2.20 and 10 pm, and other departures from the government bus stand. Buses take five hours and cost Rs 38.

It's also possible to buy through tickets to Kathmandu from a number of operators, including the Rajasthan Hotel. They offer a bus to Raxaul, a rickshaw for the border crossing and a voucher for a Nepalese bus on to Kathmandu for Rs 190 or Rs 280 with an overnight stay in a hotel at Raxaul. It's just as easy to do it yourself which not only gives you a choice of bus from the border, but is also cheaper.

Getting Around

To/From the Airport There's no bus service but the airport is so close you can get there by cycle-rickshaw for Rs 15. Taxis charge about Rs 60.

Auto-Rickshaw Shared auto-rickshaws shuttle back and forth between the main

Patna Junction Railway Station and Gulzarbagh for Rs 4 per person. The other main route is from the Patna Junction Railway Station to Gandhi Maidan Bus Station; it costs Rs 2.

PATNA TO NEPAL
Sonepur

A month-long cattle fair is held in October-November at Sonepur, 25 km north of Patna. It takes place around the full moon at Kartika Purnima, the most auspicious time to bathe at the confluence of the Ganges and the Gandak here. This is probably the largest animal fair in Asia and not only cattle but all types of animals are traded here. At the Haathi Bazaar, elephants change hands for anything from Rs 10,000 to Rs 100,000, depending on age and condition. If you'd like to purchase an alternative form of transport, Mark Shand's *Travels on my Elephant* is essential reading for the modern mahout.

Vaishali

As long ago as the 6th century BC, Vaishali was the capital of a republic. It's the birthplace of Mahavira, one of the Jain tirthankars and was where the Buddha preached his last sermon. There's very little to see – an **Ashoka pillar** (with its lion capital intact), a couple of dilapidated **stupas** (one contains an eighth of the Buddha's ashes) and a small **museum**. There are guided tours from Patna or buses from Lalganj and Muzaffarpur. There's a *Tourist Bungalow* at Vaishali.

Muzaffarpur
Population: 240,000

Apart from being a bus-changing point on the way to the Nepal border, Muzaffarpur is of limited interest. This is a poverty-stricken, agriculturally backward area. There are a number of places to stay, including the *Hotel Deepak* with reasonable food and very spartan rooms. The *Hotel Elite*, near the railway station on Saraiya Gunj, is more expensive.

Motihari & Raxaul
North of Muzaffarpur, the area becomes

even poorer. Motihari, where George Orwell was born, is a small provincial town which is also the district headquarters. Raxaul is right on the border and is virtually a twin town with Birganj, just across the border in Nepal. Both towns are crowded and dirty. Cycle-rickshaws take 30 minutes (Rs 15) to get from the border (open 4 am to 10 pm) to the bus station in Birganj. Nepalese visas are available at the border for US$20.

Places to Stay This is not a place to stick around. There are rooms at the *Hotel Kaveri* in Raxaul for Rs 30/40. The *Hotel Taj* is better but more expensive. Alternatively, you can cross the border and stay in equally unattractive Birganj.

Getting There & Away There are several buses a day from Raxaul to Patna (Rs 38, five hours) and more to Muzaffarpur. Beware of touts selling combined bus/train tickets as it's much more reliable to organise things yourself.

From Birganj there are morning and evening buses to Kathmandu taking around 12 hours (Nepalese Rs 110) or Pokhara (Nepalese Rs 100, 10 hours). To Kathmandu most buses take the much longer road via Narayanghat and Mugling, rather than the dramatically scenic Tribhuvan Highway via Naubise.

Warning Immigration procedures can be somewhat unorthodox at Birganj. Officials there have recently got into the habit of demanding the US$20 visa fee (if you don't already have a Nepalese visa) in US dollars cash *only*. They won't accept any other currency – Nepalese rupees and Indian rupees included.

As witnessed by our Nepal researcher, Richard Everist, two travellers got stuck entering Nepal from India as they only had a US$100 note. Even though the bank at the border was happy to change the $100 and give an exchange receipt so they could pay the visa fees in NRs, the immigration officials refused to accept NRs. They would only give change US dollars (thus necessitating a lengthy wait for other travellers to pass through with change) or give the US$60 change in NRs at a rate of their own choosing. So make sure you have some smaller denomination US dollars handy, or ensure you already have a visa before you cross the border – or choose another border crossing!

PATNA TO VARANASI
Sasaram

It's worth stopping off here between Varanasi and Gaya or Patna to see the impressive **mausoleum of Sher Shah** who died in 1545. Built of red sandstone in the middle of a large green pond, it's particularly striking in the warm light of sunset. The 46-metre dome has a 22-metre span, which is four metres wider than the Taj Mahal's dome.

Sasaram is on the Grand Trunk Road, the famous Indian highway that was built by Sher Shah in the mid-16th century. The narrow streets of this small town are interesting to wander round. There's also the **tomb of Hassan Khan** (Sher Shah's father) and several other Muslim monuments.

There are more Muslim tombs at Maner. At Dehri, 17 km from Sasaram, the railway and the Grand Trunk Road cross the River Son on a three-km bridge. The hill fort of Rohtas is 38 km from here.

Places to Stay & Eat The best place to stay is the friendly *Tourist Lodge* which is a 15-minute walk from the station. Turn left onto the Grand Trunk Rd outside the railway station and it's by the second petrol station. Doubles are Rs 50, or Rs 60 with attached bathrooms and Rs 75 with air-cooler. The *Ruchi Restaurant* is a good place to eat.

Getting There & Away There are frequent buses for Patna (Rs 28, 4½ hours). For Varanasi and Gaya it's better to take a train as buses start at Dehri, 17 km away, and few stop here.

PATNA TO GAYA
Nalanda

Founded in the 5th century BC, Nalanda was one of the world's great universities and an important Buddhist centre until it was sacked by the Afghans in the 12th century. When the Chinese scholar and traveller, Xuan Zhang, was here in the early 7th century AD, there were 10,000 monks and students in residence.

The brick-built remains are extensive and include the **Great Stupa**, with steps, terraces and a few intact votive stupas around it, and the monks' cells. There's an interesting **archaeological museum** (Rs 0.50; closed on Friday) housing the Nalanda University seal, sculptures and other remains found on the site. Pilgrims venerate the Buddha figures in spite of signs saying 'Do not offer anything to the objects in the museum'! Buy a guidebook at the booking office for Rs 3.

The newest building here is the **Hiuen Tsang Memorial Hall**, built as a Peace Pagoda by the Chinese. Xuan Zhang spent five years here as both student and teacher. There's also an international centre for the study of Buddhism, established in 1951. There are Burmese, Japanese and Jain dharamsalas at Nalanda as well as a PWD *Rest House*.

Getting There & Away Shared Trekkers (jeeps) cost Rs 2 from Rajgir to Nalanda village, and from there it's Rs 1 for the 10-minute ride on a shared tonga to the university site. Take another jeep (Rs 2) from Nalanda village to Bihar Sharif for buses to Patna (Rs 13, 2½ hours).

Rajgir

This was the capital of the Magadha Empire until Ajatasatru moved to Pataliputra (Patna) in the 5th century BC. Today, Rajgir is a thriving Indian holiday centre. In winter, visitors are drawn by the hot springs and the healthy climate of this hilly region, 19 km south of Nalanda.

Rajgir is an important Buddhist pilgrimage site since the Buddha spent 12 years here, and the first Buddhist council after the Buddha attained nirvana was held here. It's also an important place for Jains, as the Mahavir spent some time in Rajgir and the hills are topped with Digambara shrines. A

mention in the *Mahabharata* also ensures a good supply of Hindu pilgrims.

Most people rent a tonga for half a day to see the sites as they're spread out over several km. This costs about Rs 50; it's more for a cycle-rickshaw. Main sites include parts of the ruined city, caves and places associated with Ajatasatru and his father Bhimbisara whom he imprisoned and murdered. The pink building by the crowded hot springs is the **Lakshmi Narayan Temple**. There's also a Burmese temple, an interesting **Jain exhibition** (Rs 5), a modern Japanese temple and on the top of Ratnagiri Hill, three km south of the hot springs, the **Japanese Shanti Stupa**, reached by a chairlift (Rs 6, if it's running). If not it's only a 25-minute walk to the top where, as well as the stupa and the view, there's a fridge full of cold drinks.

The tourist office is near the bus stand. The *Archaeological Survey* guidebook to the sites which is available here is good value at Rs 3.

Places to Stay & Eat The *Hotel Siddharth* is a short walk from the bus stand. Set within a pleasant walled courtyard there are singles from Rs 50 or Rs 70/95 with attached bathrooms. Nearby is the *Hotel Ajatshatru Vihar* (Tourist Bungalow No 2) with only dorm beds (Rs 20). It's in a very peaceful location near the Burmese temple. You can also stay at the Burmese temple for a small donation and there's a good restaurant and coffee house in the grounds.

The *Hotel Gautam Vihar* (Tourist Bungalow No 1) is a good place with dorm beds for Rs 20, singles/doubles with water heaters in the attached bathrooms for Rs 80/100, and some air-con rooms.

There are lots of other cheap places catering to Calcuttan holiday-makers. The *Hotel Rajgir* has a pleasant garden and the rooms are good value at Rs 40/65 with attached bathrooms. *Triptee's Hotel* has some good rooms with balconies for Rs 100.

The top hotel here is the *Centaur Hokke* (☎ 245), an Indo-Japanese joint-venture, complete with tatami mats in the bedrooms

(US$61/92) and its own prayer hall. If you're getting bored with Indian cuisine try the Japanese dishes here (from Rs 50). Set meals with tempura cost Rs 140.

Getting There & Away Rajgir is on a branch line with daily trains to Patna but the buses are faster. There are also buses to Gaya (Rs 11, two hours) and Pawapuri. For Nalanda take a shared jeep for Rs 2.

Pawapuri

Mahavira, the final tirthankar and founder of Jainism, died and was cremated here in about 500 BC. It is said that the demand for his sacred ashes was so great that a large amount of soil was removed around the funeral pyre, creating the lotus-filled tank. A marble temple, the **Jalmandir**, was later built in the middle of the tank and is now a major pilgrimage spot for Jains. You can get here by bus from Rajgir or Bihar Sharif.

GAYA

Population: 294,000

Gaya is about 100 km south of Patna. Just as nearby Bodhgaya is a major centre for Buddhist pilgrims, Gaya is a centre for Hindu pilgrims. Vishnu is said to have given Gaya the power to absolve sinners. Pilgrims offer *pindas* (funeral cakes) at the ghats along the river here, and perform a lengthy circuit of the holy places around Gaya, to free their ancestors from bondage to the earth.

If you're on your way to Bodhgaya but only reach Gaya after dark, spend the night here as there have been a number of night-time muggings on the Gaya-Bodhgaya road. There are also reports of pilgrims being 'befriended' at the station, drugged with cups of tea and robbed.

Vishnupad Temple

In the crowded central part of the old town, this sikhara-style temple was constructed in 1787 by Queen Ahalya Bai of Indore on the banks of the River Falgu. Inside the temple the 40-cm-long 'footprint' of Vishnu is imprinted in solid rock and surrounded by a silver-plated basin.

During the monsoon, the river carries a great deal of water but it dries up completely in winter. You can see cremations taking place on the river banks. They seem to be relaxing the ban on non-Hindus entering the temple; it's worth trying to go in.

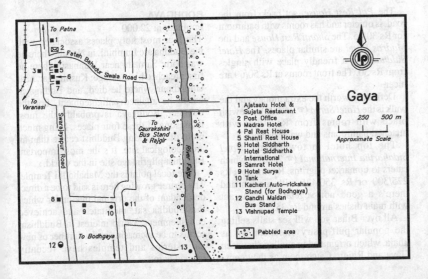

1 Ajatsatu Hotel &
   Sujata Restaurant
2 Post Office
3 Madras Hotel
4 Pal Rest House
5 Shanti Rest House
6 Hotel Siddharth
7 Hotel Siddhartha
   International
8 Samrat Hotel
9 Hotel Surya
10 Tank
11 Kacheri Auto-rickshaw
   Stand (for Bodhgaya)
12 Gandhi Maidan
   Bus Stand
13 Vishnupad Temple

Other Attractions

A flight of 1000 stone steps leads to the top of the **Brahmajuni Hill**, one km south-west of the Vishnupad Temple. There's a good view over the town from the top. Gaya has a small **archaeological museum** (closed on Mondays), near the tank.

A **temple of Surya**, the sun god, stands 20 km to the north at Deo. The **Barabar Caves**, dating back to 200 BC, are 36 km north of Gaya. These are the 'Marabar' caves of E M Forster's *A Passage to India*. Two of the caves contain inscriptions from Ashoka himself. To get there take the train to Bela, a tonga from there for 10 km and it's then a five-km walk to the two groups of caves.

Places to Stay & Eat

There are railway *retiring rooms* with a Rs 20 dorm and doubles at Rs 70 or Rs 125 with air-con. There are many other places to stay around the station, most of them spartan but OK for a short pause. The *Ajatsatu Hotel* is opposite the railway station and has reasonable singles/doubles with attached bathrooms for Rs 50/75. The hotel's *Sujata Restaurant* is quite good (main dishes cost Rs 25).

The *Pal Rest House*, set back from the road, is quieter and has rooms with bathroom for Rs 30/45. The *Shanti Rest House* and the *Madras Hotel* are similar places. The *Hotel Siddharth* is a friendly place with singles from Rs 30. The front rooms at Rs 50/60 are nicer.

Definitely worth the extra money and the walk is the *Hotel Surya* (☎ 24-004), a newish place with rooms from Rs 70/90 with attached bathrooms and water heaters.

The top hotel in town is the *Hotel Siddhartha International* (☎ 21-254) which caters to upmarket pilgrims. Rooms cost Rs 225/300 or Rs 350/425 with air-con and there's a good non-vegetarian restaurant with main dishes around Rs 35.

All over Bihar you will see stalls selling the popular puff-pastry sweet known as khaja, which originated in a village between Gaya and Rajgir. Catch them as they come

out of the oil – the flies are as partial to them as the Biharis are.

Getting There & Away

Buses to Patna (Rs 16, three hours) and Ranchi (Rs 36, seven hours) leave from the Gandhi Maidan bus stand. Buses to Rajgir (Rs 11, two hours) leave from the Gaurakshini bus stand which is across the river.

Gaya is on the main Delhi-Calcutta line and there are direct trains to Delhi, Calcutta, Varanasi, Puri and Patna.

The auto-rickshaws from the railway station cost Rs 40 for the 14-km trip to Bodhgaya but they'll try for twice as much. From the Kacheri auto-rickshaw stand, which is a 25-minute walk from the station, it's Rs 3 for a seat. Watch your head on the low roof in the back, though, or you'll attain a state of unconsciousness before you reach Bodhgaya!

Getting Around

It's Rs 5 by cycle-rickshaw to the Kacheri auto-rickshaw stand (for Bodhgaya) or to the Gaurakshini bus stand (for Rajgir) from the railway station.

BODHGAYA

Population: 22,000

The four most holy places associated with the Buddha are Lumbini, in Nepal, where he was born; Sarnath, near Varanasi, where he first preached his message; Kushinagar, near Gorakhpur, where he died; and Bodhgaya, where he attained enlightenment. For the traveller, Bodhgaya is probably the most interesting of these four places, being much more of a working Buddhist centre than an archaeological site. It's the most important Buddhist pilgrimage site in the world.

The focal point is the Mahabodhi Temple. The bo tree growing here is said to be a direct descendant of the original tree under which the Buddha sat, meditated and achieved enlightenment. World interest in Buddhism seems to be increasing and a number of new monasteries and temples have recently opened here.

Buddhists from all over the world flock to Bodhgaya, along with many Westerners who come here to learn about Buddhism and meditation. Bodhgaya is small and quiet and, if you are not planning a long study stay, a day is quite sufficient to see everything. The best time to visit Bodhgaya is when the Tibetan pilgrims come down from Dharamsala, during the winter. The Dalai Lama often spends December here. When the Tibetans leave in mid-February they seem to take some of the atmosphere of the place with them.

Mahabodhi Temple

A 50-metre high pyramidal spire tops the Mahabodhi Temple, inside which is a large gilded image of the Buddha. The temple is said to stand on the site of a temple erected by Ashoka in the 3rd century BC. Although the current temple was restored in the 11th century, and again in 1882, it is said to be basically the same as the one standing here in the 7th century. The stone railing around the temple, parts of which still stand, was originally thought to date from Ashoka's time but is now considered to be from the Sunga period around 184-172 BC. The carved and sculptured railing has been restored, although parts of it now stand in the museum in Calcutta and in the Victoria & Albert Museum in London. Stone stupas, erected by visiting pilgrims, dot the temple courtyard. Entry to the temple grounds costs Rs 0.50, and the temple is closed between noon and 2 pm.

Bodhi Tree

A sapling from the original bo tree under which the Buddha sat was carried to Sri Lanka by Sanghamitta (the Emperor Ashoka's daughter) when Ashoka took Buddhism to that island. That tree now flourishes at Anuradhapura in Sri Lanka and, in turn, a cutting from it was carried back to Bodhgaya when the original tree here died. A red sandstone slab under the tree is said to be the Vajrasan, or diamond throne, on which the Buddha sat.

Monasteries

Most countries with a large Buddhist population have a temple or monastery here, usually built in a representative architectural style. Thus the Thai temple looks very much like the colourful *wats* you see in Thailand. The Tibetan temple and monastery was built in 1934 and contains a large prayer wheel. The Tibetans have two other places here, the Sakya monastery and the Karma Temple.

The Burmese, who led the campaign to restore the Mahabodhi Temple in the 19th century, built their present monastery in 1936. The Japanese temple (Indosan Nipponji) has a very beautiful image of the Buddha brought from Japan and across the road is the Daijokyo Temple. There are also Chinese, Sri Lankan, Bhutanese and Vietnamese monasteries. The Tai Bodhi Kham monastery is being built by Buddhist tribes from Assam and Arunachal Pradesh. Laos is also working on a monastery. The newest is the Nepalese Tamang monastery, opened in 1992.

Other Attractions

The **archaeological museum** (open 10 am to 5 pm daily except Friday) has a small collection of Buddha figures and pillars found in the area. The Hindu Shankaracharya Math has a **temple**, and a sculpture gallery is due to open there. Across the river are the Dungeshwari and Suraya temples.

The 25-metre **Great Buddha Statue** in the Japanese Kamakura style was unveiled by the Dalai Lama in 1989. There's a plan to build a much bigger Maitreya Buddha statue in Bodhgaya as a symbol of world peace.

Meditation Courses

Courses and retreats take place in the winter, mainly from November to early February.

Some of the most accessible courses are run by the Root Institute for Wisdom Culture (☎ (06-3181) 714), set in a peaceful location on the edge of Bodhgaya. They run basic five-day meditation courses and hold retreats. Travellers who have spent some time here all seem impressed, not only with

Life of the Buddha

Legend tells that the birth of the prince of the Sakya clan who was to become the Buddha was attended by great portents and prophesies. He was named Siddhartha ('one whose aim is accomplished') because at his birth (in about 560 BC in Lumbini, now in Nepal) a soothsayer predicted that he would attain a position of immense power, either as a secular ruler or as a religious leader. Further predictions warned that if he ever laid eyes on the sufferings of the world he would have no choice but to follow the latter course and give up his family's kingdom.

His father, the king, anxious that this shouldn't happen, ensured that he was surrounded with youth, beauty and good health. He grew up happily, got married and had a son. As he grew older, however, the soothsayer's prediction came true. Outside the palace, amongst his father's subjects, he was confronted by the spectres of old age, sickness and death. Observing a wandering ascetic, and impressed by his tranquil countenance, he resolved to give up his privileged life in a search for absolute truth.

Subjecting himself to the most extreme deprivations, he spent nearly six years as an ascetic. He is said to have lived on just one grain of rice a day, fasting until he could feel his backbone when he clasped his stomach. He is also reputed to have spent long periods sitting on thorn bushes and sleeping amongst rotting corpses.

Barely alive and staggering along beside a river near Bodhgaya one day, he fainted and fell into the water. Coming to, he decided that such mortifications were counterproductive to his quest, and indulged in a restorative meal. After his meal he settled down beneath a bodhi tree to meditate.

While meditating, he came to the realisation that the human lot is one of an endless cycle of birth and death to which people are bound because of human desire. He realised that he had been unable to achieve enlightenment as an ascetic because he desired it and sought it so actively. Now that he had ceased to desire he became enlightened and could attain nirvana (escape from the cycle of birth and death into a state of perfect bliss).

the courses but by the way the Institute is working to put something back into the local community with health, agricultural and educational projects.

Courses are also run by the International Meditation Centre (☎ 734) near Magadh University (five km from Bodhgaya) and at their new centre (☎ 707) near the Mahabodhi Temple. In January there's a popular 10-day retreat run by Western Buddhists at the Thai monastery. Meditation courses are also offered at the Burmese and Tibetan monas-

teries. Some courses are advertised on the notice board in the Om Cafe.

If you're interested in working on social development projects in the area contact the Samanway Ashram.

Places to Stay – bottom end

The tourist bungalows (No 1 and No 2) are next door to each other and have been given more imaginative names: *Hotel Buddha Vihar* has only dormitory accommodation at Rs 20 a bed. *Hotel Siddharth Vihar*, next

The Buddha summarised his teachings into the Four Noble Truths:

1) Existence is comprised of conflict, dissatisfaction, sorrow and suffering;
2) This state is caused by selfish desire;
3) It is possible to escape from this and attain nirvana;
4) The key to achieving this is to follow the Eight-Fold Path, which consists of:

Right Understanding (uninhibited by superstition or delusion);
Right Thought (as befits human consciousness and intelligence);
Right Speech (honest and compassionate);
Right Action (peaceful and honest);
Right Mode of Living (without causing harm to other living creatures);
Right Endeavour (self-discipline and control);
Right Mindfulness (having an alert and contemplative mind);
Right Concentration (deep contemplation on the realities of life).

The Buddha first enunciated the Eight-Fold Path to five ascetics, former companions on his pilgrimage, at present-day Sarnath. This first sermon was known as the Dhammacakkappavatt-ana-sutta ('Setting in Motion the Wheel of Truth'). He maintained that it is inappropriate to follow two extremes, that is, self-indulgence and self-mortification. By avoiding these two extremes the Buddha had discovered the 'Middle Path'.

The Buddha died in Kushinagar (near Gorakhpur) in about 480 BC, reputedly after eating poisonous mushrooms.

The tenets encompassed in the Four Noble Truths and the Eight-Fold Path, transmitted orally by disciples of the Buddha after his death, form the basis of the philosophy of Buddhism today. ■

---

door, has singles/doubles with attached bathrooms for Rs 90/110, and air-con rooms for Rs 150/175.

The *Sri Lanka Guest House* run by the Mahabodhi Society charges Rs 100 for a double and is a popular and well-run place. On the road to Gaya, there are some basic little hotels like the *Amar* and the *Shashi*.

If you're planning a longer stay and/or don't mind roughing it a little, it's possible to stay at the monasteries. The Burmese monastery, which has a peaceful garden, is particularly popular with Westerners for its study courses. The rooms are extremely basic and you're expected to make a donation of Rs 5 to Rs 10 per night. Dignified conduct is expected but unfortunately some travellers have abused the monastery's hospitality by smoking or breaking the rules in other ways.

Western visitors have also made themselves unpopular at the Japanese monastery and they may not be keen to let you in. It's clean and comfortable but packed out with Japanese tour groups during the season.

Pilgrims can stay at most of the monasteries although some have better facilities than others. The Bhutanese monastery is a good place and rooms without bath cost between Rs 30 and Rs 50. The Tibetan monastery is somewhat more spartan and cheaper.

Other places to try include the Sakya Tibetan monastery, and the Thai and Nepalese monasteries.

Places to Stay – top end
The ITDC *Hotel Bodhgaya Ashok* (☎ 725) has been renovated and has singles/doubles at US$28/36 or US$38/46 with air-con. Prices and charges are reduced in the April to September off-season.

Places to Eat
The standard of food here is pretty low out of season and surprisingly high during the winter, when the pilgrims arrive. The

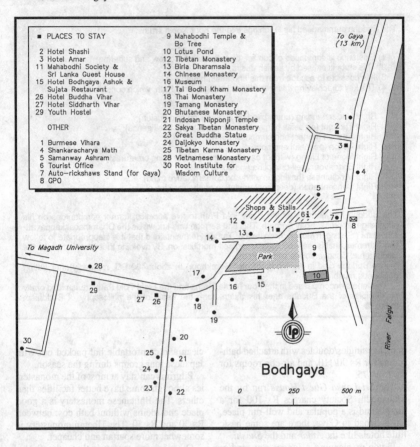

■ PLACES TO STAY

2 Hotel Shashi
3 Hotel Amar
11 Mahabodhi Society &
    Sri Lanka Guest House
15 Hotel Bodhgaya Ashok &
    Sujata Restaurant
26 Hotel Buddha Vihar
27 Hotel Siddharth Vihar
29 Youth Hostel

    OTHER

1 Burmese Vihara
4 Shankaracharya Math
5 Samanway Ashram
6 Tourist Office
7 Auto—rickshaws Stand (for Gaya)
8 GPO

9 Mahabodhi Temple &
   Bo Tree
10 Lotus Pond
12 Tibetan Monastery
13 Birla Dharamsala
14 Chinese Monastery
16 Museum
17 Tai Bodhi Kham Monastery
18 Thai Monastery
19 Tamang Monastery
20 Bhutanese Monastery
21 Indosan Nipponji Temple
22 Sakya Tibetan Monastery
23 Great Buddha Statue
24 Daijokyo Monastery
25 Tibetan Karma Monastery
28 Vietnamese Monastery
30 Root Institute for
    Wisdom Culture

To Gaya
(13 km)

To Magadh University

Shops & Stalls

Park

Bodhgaya

River Falgu

0   250   500 m

Mahabodi Canteen at the Sri Lanka Guest House is a reliable place serving quite reasonable Chinese food. The *Siva Hotel*, near the tourist office, does good pizzas, tomato soup and other Western food. *Roberto Italian Restaurant* is very popular since it's a clean place and Roberto grows everything himself for his salads. The restaurant outside the Burmese monastery is not bad.

There are also several restaurants run by Tibetans behind the Tibetan monastery. These restaurants operate in tents and only during the season. The two best places are the *Om Cafe* and *Loyak's*. Om Cafe does very

good Tibetan food and excellent brownies and chocolate-banana cake. Loyak's does good cheese and tomato sandwiches.

The *Sujata Restaurant* at the Hotel Bodhgaya Ashok is expensive and not very popular. Who wants to binge in a restaurant that faces a curio shop packed with skeletal fasting Buddha figures?

Getting There & Away

Bodhgaya is 13 km from Gaya and auto-rickshaws shuttle back and forth. They're phenomenally overloaded, carrying three passengers on each side on benches in the back, one squeezed between them at the front, and another standing up at the very back. Then the driver up front sits on a plank with two people see-sawing on each side of him. A total of 13 people (plus children, goods, etc) travel on a vehicle intended for three! The fare is Rs 3 or Rs 30 to rent the whole auto-rickshaw.

Buses depart less frequently. There's a daily bus to Patna and Rajgir, many more from Gaya. Don't travel on the Gaya-Bodhgaya road after dark.

SOUTHERN BIHAR

Ranchi

At 652 metres, Ranchi doesn't really deserve its title of hill station, especially since it's now lost most of its tree-cover. In British times it was Bihar's summer capital, with a reputation as a health resort. The Kanke hospital for the mentally handicapped is the best known in the country and was, until recently, a stop on the local tourist office's city tour.

One of the most interesting things to see here is the **Jagannath Temple**, a small version of the great Jagannath Temple at Puri, which celebrates its own, smaller festival of the cars. It's six km south-west of Ranchi and visitors are welcome.

There are a number of hills on the edges of Ranchi for sunset views over the rocky landscape. There's also a Tribal Research Institute with a **museum** here.

Places to Stay & Eat There are numerous hotels around the bus stand. The best small place is the friendly *Hotel Konark* with clean singles/doubles at Rs 60/85 with attached bathrooms and a good restaurant. Another good place is the *Hotel Paradise* at Rs 40/50.

The *Hotel Yuvraj*, 'a house of respectable living', is 15 minutes from the station with rooms from Rs 150/250. Nearby, the centrally air-conditioned *Hotel Yuvraj Palace* (☎ 30-0805) has rooms from Rs 500/650. This is Ranchi's best hotel.

Getting There & Away Ranchi has good air, bus and train connections. The railway station is 500 metres from the bus stand. There are buses to Gaya (Rs 36, seven hours), Hazaribagh (Rs 16, three hours) and Netarhat (Rs 20, four hours). A through bus to Puri takes 15 hours.

Hazaribagh

This pleasant leafy town lies 107 km north of Ranchi, at an altitude of 615 metres. About the only reason for coming here would be to visit **Hazaribagh National Park**, 19 km to the north. You can stay in the park at the *Tourist Lodge* or *Forest Rest House*. In Hazaribagh the *Hotel Upkar* (☎ 2246) is the best hotel and good value with singles/doubles for Rs 75/90.

The railway station, Hazaribagh Rd, is 67 km away. There are private minibuses for Gaya (Rs 20, four hours) from outside the bus station.

Parasnath

Just inside the Bihar state boundary from West Bengal, and only a little north of the Grand Trunk Road, Parasnath is the major Jain pilgrimage centre in the east of India. Like so many other pilgrimage centres, it's perched on top of a steep hill and is reached by a stiff climb on foot. Rich Calcuttan Jain pilgrims are carried up in palanquins by porters.

The 24 temples, representing the Jain tirthankars, stand at an altitude of 1366 metres. Parasnath, the 23rd tirthankar, achieved nirvana at this spot 100 years after his birth in Varanasi.

Calcutta

Population: 10.9 million
Main Language: Bengali

Densely populated and polluted, Calcutta is often an ugly and desperate place that to many people sums up the worst of India, yet it's also one of the country's more fascinating centres and has some scenes of rare beauty. Certainly the people are a friendly bunch and Bengali humour is renowned throughout India.

Don't let the squalor of first impressions put you off this city. There are a lot of jewels to be discovered and they're not far from the surface. However Calcutta is not a good introduction to India and is best visited after you've had a chance to get used to some of the country's extremes.

Calcutta isn't an ancient city like Delhi with its impressive relics of the past. In fact, it's largely a British creation which dates back only some 300 years and was the capital of British India until the beginning of this century.

In 1686, the British abandoned Hooghly, their trading post 38 km up the Hooghly River from present-day Calcutta, and moved downriver to three small villages – Sutanati, Govindpur and Kalikata. Calcutta takes its name from the last of those three tiny settlements. Job Charnock, an English merchant who later married a Brahmin's widow whom he dissuaded from becoming a sati, was the leader of the British merchants who made this move. At first the post was not a great success and was abandoned on a number of occasions, but in 1696 a fort was laid out near present-day BBD Bagh (Dalhousie Square) and in 1698, Aurangzeb's grandson gave the British official permission to occupy the villages.

Calcutta then grew steadily until 1756, when Siraj-ud-daula, the Nawab of Murshidabad, attacked the town. Most of the British inhabitants escaped, but those captured were packed into an underground cellar where,

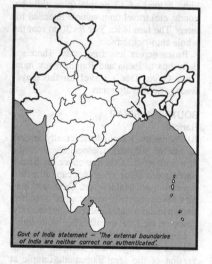

Govt of India statement – 'The external boundaries of India are neither correct nor authenticated'.

during the night, most of them suffocated in what became known as 'the black hole of Calcutta'.

Early in 1757, the British, under Clive of India, retook Calcutta and made peace with the nawab. Later the same year, however, Siraj-ud-daula sided with the French and was defeated at the Battle of Plassey, a turning point in British-Indian history. A much stronger fort was built in Calcutta and the town became the capital of British India.

Much of Calcutta's most enduring development took place between 1780 and 1820. Later in the 19th century, Bengal became an important centre in the struggle for Indian independence, and this was a major reason for the decision to transfer the capital to New Delhi in 1911. Loss of political power did not alter Calcutta's economic control, and the city continued to prosper until after WW II.

Partition affected Calcutta more than any other major Indian city. Bengal and the Punjab were the two areas of India with mixed Hindu and Muslim populations and the dividing line was drawn through them. The result in Bengal was that Calcutta, the jute-producing and export centre of India, became a city without a hinterland; while across the border in East Pakistan (Bangladesh today), the jute (a plant fibre used in making sacking and mats) was grown without anywhere to process or export it. Furthermore, West Bengal and Calcutta were disrupted by tens of thousands of refugees fleeing from East Bengal, although fortunately without the communal violence and bloodshed that Partition brought to the Punjab.

The massive influx of refugees, combined with India's own postwar population explosion, led to Calcutta becoming an international urban horror story. The mere name was enough to conjure up visions of squalor, starvation, disease and death. The work of Mother Teresa's Calcutta mission also focused worldwide attention on Calcutta's festering problems. In 1971, the India-Pakistan conflict and the creation of Bangladesh led to another flood of refugees, and Calcutta's already chaotic condition further deteriorated. The problem of having too many mouths to feed will undoubtedly get worse since the birth rate has been rising, not falling, over the last 10 years. Calcutta has the largest population, after Bombay, of any Indian city.

Economically it is still suffering further setbacks; the port has been silting up, making navigation from Calcutta down to the sea steadily more difficult and limiting the size of ships which can use the port. The Farakka Barrage (250 km north of Calcutta), designed to improve the river flow through the city, has been the subject of considerable dispute between India and Bangladesh because it will also affect the flow of the Ganges through Bangladesh.

Furthermore, Calcutta has been plagued by chronic labour unrest resulting in a decline of its productive capacity. Hindustan Motors is just one of the several major industries that have given up on the city and are in the process of transferring their operations to other states. The situation is summed up in the city's hopeless power-generation system. Electrical power in Calcutta has become so on-again off-again that virtually every hotel, restaurant, shop or small business has to have some sort of standby power generator or battery lighting system. The workers are blamed, the technicians are blamed, the power plants are blamed, the coal miners are blamed, even Indian railways are blamed for not delivering the coal on time, but it's widely pointed out that Bombay, for example, certainly doesn't suffer the frequency and extent of power cuts that are a way of life in Calcutta.

The Marxist government of West Bengal has come in for much criticism over the chaos currently existing in Calcutta but, as it is also pointed out, their apparent neglect and mismanagement of the city is combined with a considerable improvement in the rural environment. Threats of flood or famine in the countryside no longer send hordes of refugees streaming into the city as in the past.

Despite all these problems Calcutta is a city with a soul, and one which many residents are inordinately fond of. The Bengalis, so ready to raise arms against the British in the struggle for independence, are also the poets and artists of India. The contrast between the Bombay and Calcutta movie industries more or less sums it up. While Bombay, the Hollywood of India, churns out movies of amazing tinsel banality, the smaller number of movie makers in Calcutta make noncommercial gems that stand up to anything produced for sophisticated Western audiences.

The city's soul shows in other ways, too, and amongst the squalor and confusion Calcutta has places of sheer magic: flower sellers beside the misty, ethereal Hooghly River; the majestic sweep of the Maidan; the arrogant bulk of the Victoria Memorial; the superb collection of archaeological treasures exhibited in the Indian Museum. They're all part of this amazing city, as are massive Marxist and trade union rallies which can block traffic in the city centre for hours at a time. There's never a dull moment!

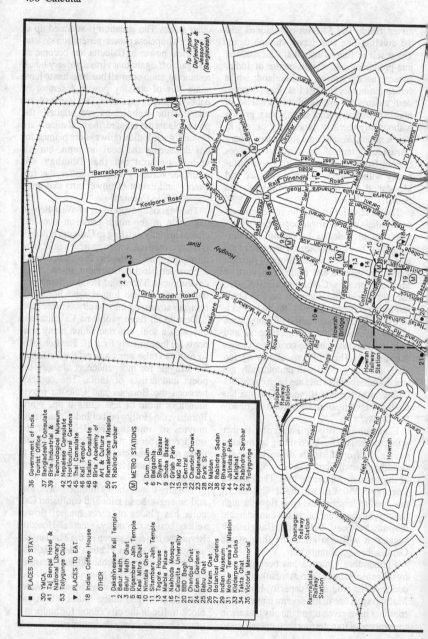

PLACES TO STAY

30 YMCA
41 Taj Bengal Hotel &
   National Library
53 Tollygunge Club

▼ PLACES TO EAT

18 Indian Coffee House

OTHER

1 Dakshineswar Kali Temple
2 Belur Math
3 Belur Math Ghat
5 Kasi Mitra Ghat
8 Digambara Jain Temple
7 Nimtala Ghat
11 Sitambara Jain Temple
13 Tagore House
14 Marble Palace
16 Nakhoda Mosque
17 Calcutta University
20 BBD Bagh
21 Chandpal Ghat
24 Eden Gardens
25 Babu Ghat
26 Outram Ghat
29 Botanical Gardens
31 Indian Museum
33 Mother Teresa's Mission
34 Takta Ghat
35 Victoria Memorial

36 Government of India
   Tourist Office
37 Bangladeshi Consulate
39 Birla Industrial &
   Technological Museum
42 Nepalese Consulate
43 Horticultural Gardens
45 Thai Consulate
46 Kali Temple
48 Italian Consulate
49 Birla Academy of
   Art & Culture
50 Ramakrishna Mission
51 Rabindra Sarobar

Ⓜ METRO STATIONS

4 Dum Dum
6 Belgachia
9 Shyam Bazaar
10 Shobh Bazaar
12 Girish Park
15 MG Rd
19 Central
22 Chandni Chowk
23 Esplanade
28 Park St
32 Maidan
38 Rabindra Sadan
40 Bhawanipore
44 Jatindas Park
47 Kalighat
52 Rabindra Sarobar
54 Tollygunge

Orientation

Calcutta sprawls north-south along the east bank of the Hooghly River, which divides it from Howrah on the west bank. If you arrive from anywhere west of Calcutta by rail, you'll come into the immense Howrah Station and have to cross the Howrah Bridge into Calcutta proper. Some of Calcutta's worst slums sprawl behind the station on the Howrah side.

For visitors, the more relevant parts of Calcutta are south of the bridge in the areas around BBD Bagh and Chowringhee. BBD Bagh, formerly Dalhousie Square, is the site of the GPO, the international telephone office, the West Bengal tourist office, and is close to the American Express office and various railway booking offices.

South of BBD Bagh is the open expanse of the Maidan along the river, and west from here is the area known as Chowringhee. Most of the cheap and middle-range hotels (and many of the upper-bracket ones) are concentrated in Chowringhee together with many of the airline offices, restaurants, travel agencies and the Indian Museum. At the southern end of Chowringhee you'll find the Government of India tourist office on Shakespeare Sarani, and, nearby, the Birla Planetarium and Victoria Memorial.

There are a number of landmarks in Calcutta and a couple of important streets to remember. The Ochterlony Monument at the northern end of the Maidan is one of the most visible landmarks – it's a tall column rising from the flat expanse of the Maidan. Sudder St runs off Chowringhee Rd and is the core of the Calcutta travellers' scene. Most of the popular cheap hotels are along Sudder·St so it is well known to any taxi or rickshaw-wallah, and the airport bus runs right by it. Furthermore, the Indian Museum is on the corner of Sudder St and Chowringhee Rd. Further south down Chowringhee Rd, which runs alongside the eastern edge of the Maidan, is Park St with a great number of more expensive restaurants and the Thai International Airlines office. The newest landmark is the recently completed cable bridge over the Hooghly, which is supposed to relieve the crush on the old Howrah Bridge.

Street Names As in many Indian cities, getting around Calcutta is slightly confused by the habit of renaming city streets, particularly those with Raj-era connotations. As usual this renaming has been done in a half-hearted fashion, and many street signs still display the old names, while some maps show old names and others show new ones; taxi-wallahs inevitably only know the old names. It's going to be a long time before Chowringhee Rd becomes Jawaharlal Nehru Rd!

Other renamed roads include:

Old Name	New Name
Ballygunge Store Rd	Gurusday Rd
Bowbazar St	Bepin Behary Ganguly
Buckland Rd	Bankim Ch Rd
Harrington St	Ho Chi Minh Sarani
Harrison Rd	Mahatma Gandhi Rd
Kyd St	Dr M Ishaque Rd
Lansdowne Rd	Sarat Bose Rd
Lower Chitpur Rd	Rabindra Sarani
Lower Circular Rd	Acharya Jagadish Chandra Bose Rd
Machuabazar St	Madan Mohan St & Keshab Sen St
Mirzapore St	Suryya Sen St
Theatre Rd	Shakespeare Sarani
Wellesley St	Rafi Ahmed Kidwai Rd
Wellington St	Nirmal Chunder St

There's a certain irony that the street the US Consulate is on was renamed Ho Chi Minh Sarani!

Information

Tourist Offices The Government of India tourist office (☎ 22-1402, 22-3521) is at 4 Shakespeare Sarani and is very helpful. They can give you computerised printouts of any destination in India. The West Bengal tourist office (☎ 28-8271) is at 3/2 BBD Bagh – the opposite side to the post office. Both the state and national tourist offices have counters at the airport and West Bengal has an office at Howrah Station.

Most other states have tourist offices here including the more obscure North-Eastern

Mother Teresa

Mother Teresa, the 'Saint of the Gutters', has come to epitomise selflessness in her dedication to the destitute, the suffering and the dying. Born Agnes Gonxha Bojaxhiu in Serbia in 1910 to Albanian parents, she joined the Irish Order of Loreto nuns in 1929 and was sent to Darjeeling as a teacher. Moving to a school in Calcutta in 1937 she was horrified at the numbers of poor people left to die on the streets of the city because there was nowhere else for them to go. She began to feel that behind the secure walls of the nunnery she was too far removed from the people she wanted to help.

The Missionaries of Charity was Mother Teresa's new order, formed in 1950. Amongst their vows is the promise 'to give wholehearted and free service to the poorest of the poor'. This vow was put into action with the setting up of several homes including Nirmal Hriday (the home for the dying), Shanti Nagar (for lepers) and Nirmala Shishu Bhavan (the children's home). There are now homes in many other places, staffed not only by nuns but also by volunteers or co-workers.

For all her saintliness, Mother Teresa is not without her critics. Germaine Greer, for example, has accused her of being a religious imperialist, although anyone who has spent some time with the nuns and seen them at work could hardly call them Bible-bashing evangelicals. Mother Teresa herself has said that hers is contemplative work. Her inspiration is spiritual and Christian but it is put into practice mainly by ministering to physical needs. In 1979 her work achieved world recognition when she was awarded the Nobel Peace Prize.

If you are considering undertaking voluntary work in India, see the relevant section in the Facts for the Visitor chapter. ■

Region states, Sikkim and the Andaman & Nicobar Islands, which are listed below:

Andaman & Nicobar Islands
   3A Auckland Place (☎ 22-2604)
Arunachal Pradesh
   4B Chowringhee Place (☎ 28-6500)
Assam
   8 Russell St (☎ 29-8331)
Manipur
   25 Asutosh Shastri Rd (☎ 35-6943)
Mizoram
   24 Old Ballygunge Rd (☎ 47-7034)
Nagaland
   13 Shakespeare Sarani (☎ 22-5269)
Sikkim
   5 Russell St (☎ 29-7516)
Tripura
   1 Pretoria St (☎ 22-3836)

To find out exactly what's happening on the cultural front, get hold of a free copy of the leaflet *Calcutta This Fortnight* from any tourist office.

Money American Express is at 21 Old Court House St (☎ 28-6281). On Chowringhee Rd there are branches of the State Bank of India and ANZ Grindlays (beside Maidan metro station). ANZ Grindlays has another branch on Shakespeare Sarani.

Post & Telecommunications The large Calcutta GPO is on BBD Bagh and has an efficient poste restante and a philatelic bureau for stamp collectors. The New Market post office is far more conveniently located if you're staying in the Sudder St area. The Park St post office is useful if you're staying in that area and more reliable for posting parcels than the GPO. There are people here who will handle the whole process for you (prices negotiable) and even the officials are friendly and helpful.

The Telephone Bhavan is also on BBD Bagh, while the Central Telegraph Office is at 8 Red Cross Place. There are lots of places to make international calls from, most with 'computerised' meters. There are several fax agencies, including one on Shakespeare Sarani.

International telephone calls are no problem but it takes several attempts to get through on a local call. When you eventually succeed, you invariably find that the number has been changed.

The telephone area code for Calcutta is 033.

Foreign Consulates Some of the useful addresses in Calcutta include:

Bangladesh
     9 Circus Ave (☎ 47-5208)
Bhutan
     48 Tivoli Court, Pramothesh Barua Sarani
     (☎ 41-301)
CIS (Russia)
     31 Shakespeare Sarani (☎ 47-4982)
Denmark
     18G Park St (☎ 24-9696)
France
     26 Park St (☎ 29-8314), inside the courtyard on
     the right-hand side of Alliance Française
Germany
     1 Hastings Park Rd (☎ 45-9141)
Italy
     3 Raja Santosh Rd (☎ 45-1411)
Japan
     12 Pretoria St (☎ 22-2241)
Nepal
     19 Sterndale Rd (☎ 45-2024)
Netherlands
     18A Brabourne Rd (☎ 26-2160)
Thailand
     18B Mandeville Gardens (☎ 74-0836)
UK
     1 Ho Chi Minh Sarani (☎ 47-5171)
USA
     5/1 Ho Chi Minh Sarani (☎ 22-3611, 47-2335)

The nearest Myanmar (Burmese) consulates
are in Dhaka, Kathmandu and Delhi. For
visas to Bangladesh, travellers have to go to
Delhi even though there's an embassy here.

Those requiring Thai visas also have a
problem as the Thai Consulate is hard to find.
It's probably best to take a taxi, though the
No 102 bus will get you close to it. It's near
South Point School (not South Point High
School) and closes at noon.

Visa Extensions & Permits The
Foreigners' Registration Office (☎ 47-3301)
is at 237 Acharya J C Bose Rd. Visa extensions and permits for the Andaman Islands
are issued here, although the latter are only
required if you are arriving by boat. If you
are flying to the Andamans, a permit can be
obtained on arrival in Port Blair. Tax clearance certificates are available from Room 11,
4th floor, Income Tax Building, Bentinck St.

Travel Agencies If you're looking for cheap
airline tickets, various places advertise their
services around Sudder St. Pan Asian Tours,

a tiny office on the 2nd floor at 20 Mirza
Ghalib St (Free School St), seem to know
what they're on about and have been recommended.

Books & Bookshops Geoffrey Moor-
house's classic 1971 study *Calcutta* is
available as a Penguin paperback. More
recently, VS Naipaul has some interesting
chapters on Calcutta in his *India – A Million
Mutinies Now*. Dominique Lapierre's *City of
Joy* has become *de rigeur* reading among
travellers to Calcutta and is available in
paperback at almost every bookshop (pirated
or otherwise). It's dangerous to criticise this
book given the guru-like status that many
readers accord him, but many parts of the
book seem a little fanciful though otherwise
interesting. What it certainly has done is to
put the Anand Nagar slums in Howrah onto
the tourist circuit, but we have a nagging
feeling that this is pure voyeurism. When the
book was filmed in 1991 a brand new slum
was specially built as the set.

The main bookshop area is along College
St, opposite the university. In the same building as the Indian Coffee House here, Rupa
has a good range including its own publications. Newman's, the publishers of the
railway timetable, run one of Calcutta's
oldest bookshops, in the same block as the
Great Eastern Hotel.

The Cambridge Book & Stationery
Company at 20D Park St is a good small
bookshop. Further down Park St towards
Chowringhee Rd, the Oxford Book Shop is
larger and also has some specialised stock.
The Bookmark, upstairs at 56D Mirza
Ghalib St, has a good general selection of
books. Classic Books, at 10 Middleton Row,
has a wide variety of both Indian and
Western books, and the owner, Bharat, is also
a mine of information. Booklands is a small
bookstall at the eastern end of Sudder St.

At the end of January a large book fair is
held on the Maidan.

Camera Repairs & Musical Instruments A
recommended place for camera repairs is
Camera Craft, Park Centre, 24 Park St, on

the 1st floor. Mr Choudhury here is a helpful, honest guy. Best place for strings, tunings, repairs and negotiable prices on musical instruments is Braganza & Co at 2A Marquis St. The character who runs it really knows his instruments. Another good place is J Reynold & Co, 15 Free School St, where there's a great selection of instruments.

Medical Services Two places which have been recommended are: Dr Paes at Vital Medical Services (☎ 22-4847), 6 Ho Chi Minh Sarani. A gamma globulin shot costs Rs 50 here, and hours are between 8 and 10 am. Dr Paes' residential telephone number is 47-2625. The Wockhardt Medical Centre (☎ 375-4096, 74-9165) has also been recommended. It is at 2/7 Lansdowne Rd, and hours are 10 am to noon. Alternatively, medical queries should be directed to any of the large hospitals.

Botanical Gardens

On the west bank of the Hooghly River, south of Howrah, are the extensive Botanical Gardens. They stretch for over a km along the riverfront and occupy 109 hectares. The gardens were originally founded in 1786 and initially administered by Colonel Kyd. It was from these gardens that the tea now grown in Assam and Darjeeling was first developed.

The gardens' prime attraction is the 200-year-old banyan tree, claimed to be the largest in the world. It covers an area of ground nearly 400 metres in circumference and continues to flourish despite having its central trunk removed in 1925, due to fungus damage. The cool and tropical tall-palm house in the centre of the gardens is also well worth a visit.

The gardens are at Sibpur over the Howrah Bridge and 19 km from Chowringhee on a No 55 or 56 bus. However it's much more pleasant to go by ferry and there are frequent departures from Chandpal and Babu Ghats (Rs 0.90). The gardens are open from sunrise to sunset, and although they tend to be very crowded on Sundays, on other days they are peaceful and make a pleasant escape from the hassles and crowds of Calcutta. Take something to drink as the cafes in the gardens are often closed during the week.

Calcutta children

Indian Museum

Conveniently situated on the corner of Sudder St and Chowringhee Rd, the Indian Museum was built in 1875. It's certainly the largest and probably the best museum in India, and one of the best in Asia. Unfortunately, it appears to have been starved of funds in recent years and many of the exhibits are literally falling apart. Some of the display cases are so dusty you can hardly see into them and Calcutta's power cuts don't help. Its widely varied collection includes oddities such as a whole roomful of meteorites. Other exhibits include the usual fossils, stuffed animals, skeletons and so on. There are a number of unique fossil skeletons of prehistoric animals, among them giant crocodiles and an amazingly big tortoise.

The art collection has many fine pieces from Orissan and other temples, and superb examples of Buddhist Gandharan art – an interesting meeting point between Greek artistry and Buddhist ideals centred around the North-West Frontier Province, now in Pakistan, that produced Buddha images and other sculptures of great beauty.

The museum is open from 10 am to 5 pm daily except Mondays. Between December and February it closes half an hour earlier. Entry fee is Rs 2 except on Fridays when it is free.

Rabindra Sarobar & Ramakrishna Mission

Rabindra Sarobar, in the south of the city, is a park and picnic spot with a central lake. Beside the park is the Ramakrishna Mission Institute of Culture, which has a library, reading rooms and lecture halls.

Maidan & Fort William

After the events of 1756, the British decided there would be no repetition of the attack on the city and set out to replace the original Fort William, in the Maidan, with a massive and impregnable new fort. First they cleared out the inhabitants of the village of Govindpur and in 1758 laid the foundations of a fort which, when completed in 1781, would cost them the awesome total, for those days,

of £2 million. Around the fort a huge expanse of jungle was cut down to give the cannons a clear line of fire but, as usually happens, the fort has never fired a shot in anger.

The fort is still in use today and visitors are only allowed inside with special permission (rarely granted). Even the trenches and deep fortifications surrounding the fort's massive walls now seem to be out of bounds. A traveller recently reported that, while walking innocently around the outside of the fort, he was arrested and interrogated for seven hours on suspicion of terrorism.

The area cleared around Fort William became the Maidan, the 'lungs' of modern Calcutta. This huge green expanse stretches three km north to south and is over a km wide. It is bound by Strand Rd along the river to the west and by Chowringhee Rd, lined with shops, offices, hotels and eating places, to the east. The stream known as Tolly's Nullah forms its southern boundary, and here you will find a racecourse and the Victoria Memorial. In the north-west corner of the Maidan is Eden Gardens, while Raj Bhavan overlooks it from the north.

Within the gardens are cricket and football fields, tennis courts, ponds, trees and Calcutta's latest attraction, the musical fountains. Cows graze, political discussions are held, people stroll across the grounds or come for early morning yoga sessions. And of course the place is used, like any area of open land in India, as a public toilet.

Ochterlony Monument Now officially renamed the Shahid (Martyr's) Minar, this 48-metre-high column towers over the northern end of the Maidan. It was erected in 1828 and named after Sir David Ochterlony, credited with winning the Nepal War (1814-16). The column is a curious combination of Turkish, Egyptian and Syrian architectural elements.

There's a fine view from the top of the column, but permission to ascend (not granted for the first and last week of each month) must be obtained from the Deputy Commissioner of Police, Police headquarters, Lal Bazaar St. It's only open

Monday to Friday and you should simply ask for a 'monument pass' at the Assistant Commissioner's office on the 2nd floor.

Eden Gardens In the north-west corner of the Maidan are the small and pleasantly laid-out Eden Gardens. A tiny Burmese pagoda was brought here from Prome, Myanmar (Burma) in 1856; it's set in a small lake and is extraordinarily picturesque. The gardens were named after the sister of Lord Auckland, the former governor general. The Calcutta Cricket Ground, where international test matches are held, is also within the gardens.

Near the gardens is a pleasant walk along the banks of the Hooghly River. Ferries run across the river from several ghats and there are plenty of boat operators around offering to take you out on the water for half an hour.

Victoria Memorial At the southern end of the Maidan stands the Victoria Memorial, the most solid reminder of British Calcutta – in fact probably the most solid reminder of the Raj to be found in India. The Victoria Memorial is a huge white-marble museum, a strange combination of classical European architecture with Moghul influences or, as some have put it, an unhappy British attempt to build a better Taj Mahal.

The idea behind the memorial was conceived by Lord Curzon, and the money for its construction was raised from 'voluntary contributions by the princes and peoples of India'. The Prince of Wales (later King George V) laid the foundation stone in 1906 and it was opened by another Prince of Wales (later the Duke of Windsor) in 1921.

Whether you're interested in the British Raj period or not, the memorial is an attraction not to be missed. It tells the story of the British Empire in India at its peak, just when it was about to begin its downhill slide. The imposing statue of Queen Victoria, at her bulky and least amused best, fronts the memorial and sets the mood for all the displays inside.

Inside you'll find portraits, statues and busts of almost all the main participants in British-Indian history. Scenes from military conflicts and events of the Mutiny are illustrated. There are some superb water-colours of Indian landscapes and buildings made by travelling Victorian artists. A Calcutta exhibit includes many early pictures of the city and a model of Fort William. Of course there are many fine Indian and Persian miniatures and rare manuscripts and books. Queen Victoria appears again inside, much younger and slimmer than her statue outside. There's also a piano she played as a young girl and other memorabilia. A huge painting depicts King Edward VII entering Jaipur in a regal procession in 1876. French guns captured at the Battle of Plassey are on exhibit along with the black stone throne of the nawab whom Clive defeated. To top it all off, there is a good view over the Maidan from the balcony above the entrance.

The booklet *A Brief Guide to the Victoria Memorial* is available in the building. The memorial is open from 10 am to 3.30 pm in winter, an hour later in summer. It is closed on Mondays, and entry costs Rs 2. The new Sound & Light show is worth going to; the English-language programme starts at 8.15 pm, daily except Mondays. Tickets are Rs 5 and Rs 10.

St Paul's Cathedral
Built between 1839 and 1847, St Paul's Cathedral is one of the most important churches in India. It stands just to the east of the Victoria Memorial at the southern end of the Maidan. The steeple fell during an earthquake in 1897 and, following further damage in a 1934 quake, was redesigned and rebuilt. Inside, the memorials are interesting and there's some impressive stained glass, including the great west window by Burne Jones. It's open to visitors from 9 am to noon, and from 3 to 6 pm. Sunday services are at 7.30 and 8.30 am, and 6 pm.

Birla Planetarium
This planetarium, near the Government of India tourist office, is one of the largest in the world. For Rs 8 you'll get a much better view of the stars in here than in the polluted atmos-

phere outside. There are shows in English
every day, but as times vary, check in
advance. Beware of pickpockets, especially
in the queue outside.

Nehru Children's Museum

This small museum, conveniently situated at
94/1 Chowringhee Rd, is worth visiting for
its models depicting the Hindu epics, the
Ramayana and the *Mahabharata*. It's open
from 1 to 7 pm daily except Monday; admission is Rs 2.

Kali Temple

Rebuilt in 1809 on the site of a much older
temple, Kalighat (as it is also known) is the
actual temple from which Kalikata
(anglicised to Calcutta) takes its name.
According to legend, when Siva's wife's
corpse was cut up, one of her fingers fell
here. Since then it has been an important
pilgrimage site.

Kali represents the destructive side of
Siva's consort and demands daily sacrifices.
In the mornings goats have their throats slit
here to satisfy the goddess' bloodlust.

The temple is about two km directly south
of St Paul's Cathedral and is easily accessible
by metro.

Zoo & Horticultural Gardens

South of the Maidan, Calcutta's 16-hectare
zoo was opened in 1875. Some of the
animals are displayed in near natural envir-
onments, others in the pitiful conditions
characteristic of Third World zoos. It's open
from sunrise to sunset; admission is Rs 1.50.

Just south of the zoo on Alipore Rd are the
pleasant and quiet horticultural gardens.
They're open from 6 to 10 am and 2 to 5 pm;
admission is Rs 1.

Howrah Bridge

Until 1943, the Hooghly River was crossed
by a pontoon bridge which had to be opened
to let river traffic through. There was considerable opposition to construction of a bridge
due to fears that it would affect the river
currents and cause silting problems. This
problem was eventually avoided by building

a bridge that crosses the river in a single
450-metre span with no pylons at all within
the river.

The cantilevered bridge is similar in size
to the Sydney Harbour Bridge but carries a
flow of traffic which Sydney could never
dream of – with a daily stream of 57,000
vehicles, and pedestrians too numerous to
count, it is the busiest bridge in the world.
It's intriguing to stand at one end of the
bridge at morning rush hour and watch the
procession of double-decker buses come
across. They heel over like yachts in a heavy
wind due to the weight of passengers
hanging onto the sides. In between are countless rickshaws, lumbering bullock carts,
hordes of bicycles and even the odd car. The
bridge is also known as Rabindra Setu and
during the morning and evening rush hours
it can take 45 minutes to get across. The
ferries running from below Howrah Station
are a more convenient way to cross the river
and give you a good view of the bridge.

The second bridge, two km downriver, has
been an on-off project for 22 years but was
finally completed in 1992. The problem now
is that the approach roads to it are too narrow
to handle the amount of traffic that uses the
bridge, and there are no funds left for further
development. A few days after opening, the
computers at the tollgate crashed, causing
several hours of chaos and banked-up traffic.

BBD Bagh (Dalhousie Square)

When Calcutta was the administrative centre
for British India, BBD Bagh was the centre
of power. On the north side of the square
stands the huge Writers' Building which
dates from 1880. In those days clerical
workers were known as 'writers' and the East
India Company's 'writers' have been
replaced by modern-day ones employed by
the West Bengal state government. That's
where all the quintuplicate forms, carbon
copies and red ink come from. Also on BBD
Bagh is a rather more useful place, the Calcutta GPO, and on the eastern side of the
square is the West Bengal tourist office.

Until it was abandoned in 1757, the original Fort William used to stand on the site of

the present-day post office. It stretched from there down to the river, which has also changed its course since that time. Brass markers by the post office indicate where the fort walls used to be. Calcutta's famous black hole actually stood at the north-east corner of the post office, but since Independence, all indications of its position have been removed. The black hole was actually a tiny guardroom in the fort and, according to the British version of the story, 146 people were forced into it on that fateful night when the city fell to Siraj-ud-daula. Next morning only 23 were still alive.

However, historians now suggest that the numbers of prisoners and fatalities were exaggerated in a propaganda exercise. There were probably about half as many people incarcerated and half as many deaths. However many or few there were, death by suffocation on a humid Calcutta night must have been a horrific way to go.

St John's Church

A little south of BBD Bagh is the Church of St John, which dates from 1787. The overgrown graveyard here has a number of interesting monuments, including the octagonal mausoleum of Job Charnock, founder of Calcutta, who died in 1692. Admiral Watson, who supported Clive in retaking Calcutta from Siraj-ud-daula, is also buried here. The obelisk commemorating the black hole was moved from near the GPO to a corner of this graveyard.

Other British Buildings

The Victoria Memorial is the most imposing reminder of the British presence in Calcutta, but the city's commercial wealth resulted in quite a few other interesting buildings. **Raj Bhavan**, the old British Government house, is now occupied by the governor of West Bengal and entry is restricted. The Marquis Wellesley built it between 1799 and 1805, modelling it on Lord Curzon's home, Kedleston Hall (Derbyshire, England), which was only completed a couple of years before. Raj Bhavan stands at the north end of the Maidan and contains many rare works

of art and other interesting items, including Tipu Sultan's throne. Next to Raj Bhavan is the Doric-style **Town Hall**, and next to that the **High Court**, which was copied from the Staadhaus at Ypres, Belgium, and completed in 1872. It has a tower 55 metres high.

Just south of the zoo in Alipur is the **National Library**, the biggest in India, which is housed in Belvedere House, the former residence of the Lieutenant-Governor of Bengal.

South Park St Cemetery has been restored and shows the high price paid by the early settlers from England. There are marvellous tombs and inscriptions at this peaceful site. The more famous occupants include Colonel Kyd, founder of the Botanical Gardens, and Rose Aylmer, remembered only because her unfortunate death was supposed to have been caused by her addiction to pineapples!

Other Museums

Calcutta has a number of other interesting museums apart from the magnificent Indian Museum and the Victoria Memorial. The **Asutosh Museum** at Calcutta University has a collection of art objects with emphasis on Bengali folk art. Admission is free and it is open from 10.30 am to 4.30 pm on weekdays, and 10.30 am to 3 pm on Saturdays.

At 19A Gurusday Rd is the **Birla Industrial & Technological Museum**, open from 10 am to 5 pm daily. Admission is Rs 1. Those philanthropic (and very wealthy) Birlas have also provided the **Birla Academy of Art & Culture** at 109 Southern Ave, open from 4.30 to 8 pm daily except Mondays; admission is Rs 1. It has a good collection of sculpture and modern art. They are also building a huge new Birla temple, just around the corner from the Industrial & Technological Museum.

The **Academy of Fine Arts**, on Cathedral Rd beside the cathedral in Chowringhee, has a permanent exhibition and runs an artists' studio. There are cultural shows in the evening. The Academy is open from 3 to 8 pm daily except Mondays. Entry is Rs 1.

On Muktaram Babu St, a narrow lane in

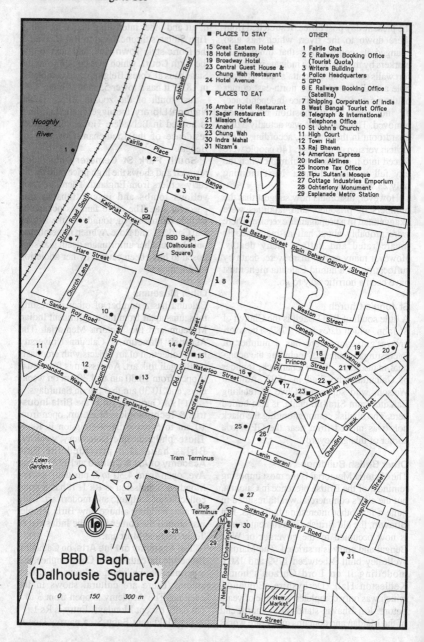

PLACES TO STAY
15 Great Eastern Hotel
18 Hotel Embassy
19 Broadway Hotel
23 Central Guest House &
   Chung Wah Restaurant
24 Hotel Avenue

PLACES TO EAT
16 Amber Hotel Restaurant
17 Sagar Restaurant
21 Mission Cafe
22 Anand
23 Chung Wah
30 Indra Mahal
31 Nizam's

OTHER
1 Fairlie Ghat
2 E Railways Booking Office
  (Tourist Quota)
3 Writers Building
4 Police Headquarters
5 GPO
6 E Railways Booking Office
  (Satellite)
7 Shipping Corporation of India
8 West Bengal Tourist Office
9 Telegraph & International
  Telephone Office
10 St John's Church
11 High Court
12 Town Hall
13 Raj Bhavan
14 American Express
20 Indian Airlines
25 Income Tax Office
26 Tipu Sultan's Mosque
27 Cottage Industries Emporium
28 Ochterlony Monument
29 Esplanade Metro Station

BBD Bagh
(Dalhousie Square)

0   150   300 m

Top: Bentinck street, Calcutta (RI)
Bottom: Sidewalk chess game, Calcutta (JH)

Top: Balloon seller, Babu Ghat, Calcutta (RI)
Bottom: Horse race crowd, Calcutta (RI)

north Calcutta, is the **Marble Palace**, an incongruous collection of statues and paintings, including works of Rubens and Sir Joshua Reynolds. It's open from 10 am to 4 pm except Mondays and Thursdays, and entry is free with a permit from the Government of India tourist office. Nearby is the rambling old **Tagore House**, a centre for Indian dance, drama, music and other arts. This is the birthplace of Rabindranath Tagore, India's greatest modern poet, and his final resting place. It's just off Rabindra Sarani and is open from 10 am to 5 pm daily, but closes at 2 pm on Saturday.

Sitambara Jain Temple
This temple, in the north-east of the city, was built in 1867 and dedicated to Sheetalnathji, the 10th of the 24 Jain tirthankars. The temple is an ornate mass of mirrors, coloured stones and glass mosaics. It overlooks a garden, and is open from 6 am to noon and 3 to 7 pm daily.

Nakhoda Mosque
North of BBD Bagh is Calcutta's principal Muslim place of worship. The huge Nakhoda Mosque is said to accommodate 10,000 people and was modelled on Akbar's tomb at Sikandra near Agra. The red sandstone mosque has two 46-metre-high minarets and a brightly painted onion-shaped dome. Outside the mosque you can buy attar, perfume made from essential oils and flower fragrances.

Belur Math
North of the city, on the west bank of the Hooghly River, is the headquarters of the Ramakrishna Mission, Belur Math. Ramakrishna, an Indian philosopher, preached the unity of all religions and, following his death in 1886, his follower Swami Vivekananda founded the Ramakrishna Mission in 1897. There are now branches all over India. Belur Math, the movement's international headquarters, was founded in 1899. It is supposed to represent a church, a mosque and a temple, depending on how you look at it. Belur Math is open from 6.30 to

11 am and from 3.30 to 7 pm daily, and admission is free.

Dakshineshwar Kali Temple
Across the river from Belur Math is this Kali temple where Ramakrishna was a priest, and where he reached his spiritual vision of the unity of all religions. The temple was built in 1847 and is surrounded by 12 other temples, dedicated to Siva.

Organised Tours
The Government of India tourist office (☎ 22-1402) at 4 Shakespeare Sarani has a full-day tour for Rs 50, departing daily (except Monday) from their office at 8 am. It covers Belur Math, Dakshineswar Temple, the Jain temple, the Victoria Memorial, the Indian Museum, the Academy of Fine Arts, Jawaharlal Sishu Bhavan and the zoo.

The West Bengal tourist office (☎ 28-8271) at 3/2 BBD Bagh has a similar tour for Rs 50 or Rs 40 if you just take the morning half (Belur Math, Dakshineswar and Jain temples, Victoria Memorial). It operates daily from 7.30 to 11.40 am and 12.40 to 5 pm but the museums are closed on Mondays. The morning tour is more popular since it covers the sights further out. Instead of taking the afternoon tour you could easily get around yourself and have more time for things like the Indian Museum. One of the problems with sightseeing in Calcutta is that an awful lot of time is spent just sitting in traffic jams.

Bus tours are also conducted for the various festivals and pujas around the state – consult *Calcutta This Fortnight* or a tourist office for details. West Bengal Tourism operates trips to the Sunderbans Wildlife Sanctuary twice a month. See the Sunderbans section in the West Bengal chapter for more information.

Places to Stay – bottom end
Calcutta suffers from a shortage of good cheap places to stay. Budget travellers' accommodation is centred on Sudder St, running off Chowringhee Rd beside the Indian Museum. Aim to arrive in Calcutta in

the morning or you may have great difficulty in finding a bed.

Chowringhee At 2 Sudder St the popular *Salvation Army Red Shield Guest House* (☎ 44-2895) has dorm beds at Rs 20 to Rs 30 and private rooms at Rs 50/60. The more expensive rooms have a bath. Although the water supply is decidedly erratic, the guest house is clean and well kept, and great value if you can get in. Much of the accommodation here is taken by volunteers working for Mother Teresa.

Further down Sudder St is the equally popular *Hotel Maria* (☎ 44-3311) with dorm beds for Rs 30 and Rs 40, some on the roof. They also have doubles for Rs 100 or Rs 150 with attached bathroom. They claim to have a strict no drugs, no alcohol policy.

Around the corner down Stuart Lane you'll find two of Calcutta's most popular budget establishments – the *Modern Lodge* (☎ 44-4960) at No 1, and the *Hotel Paragon* (☎ 44-2445) opposite at No 2. The Paragon has dorm beds at Rs 35 (downstairs) and Rs 40 (upstairs), tiny singles/doubles with common bath for Rs 70/90 and doubles with bath from Rs 140. There's a pleasant courtyard upstairs but the ground-floor rooms are rather gloomy. Baggage lockers and meals are available. The Modern Lodge is similar but a bit cheaper. Singles/doubles with common bath cost Rs 50/80 and doubles with bath are Rs 100 to Rs 150. There are also four-bed rooms and dorms, although these are currently being renovated. All the rooms have a fan, and the food is reasonable. The rooftop area is a popular meeting place in the evening, and tea and soft drinks are available.

The *Hotel Hilson* (☎ 44-5283) at 4 Sudder St has clean singles with common bath for Rs 70, doubles with bath from Rs 150 and some triples at Rs 200. The *Shilton Hotel* further down Sudder St has doubles with attached bathrooms for Rs 175.

There are several small places on Sudder St that are essentially private homes with a few rooms to let. The Sikh-run *Times Guest House* is a friendly place near the Blue Sky Cafe. It has an eight-bed dorm for Rs 40 per bed and three doubles with attached bathrooms for Rs 150. The *Tourist Inn* is fairly clean with rooms with common bath for Rs 50/100 and a four-bedded room with attached bath for Rs 200.

Opposite is the *Hotel Diplomat* with dark rooms from Rs 70/80. Next to it is the best of this bunch, the *Hotel Plaza* which has a few doubles for Rs 150. Currently this place also has good dorm beds for Rs 50 but these may be converted into doubles and triples. There's a nice verandah overlooking Sudder St. Down at the east end of Sudder St is the basic *Continental Guest House* with singles/doubles from Rs 50/80 and doubles from Rs 130 with bath.

Around the corner from Sudder St, at 20 Mirza Ghalib St (Free School St), is the popular *Centrepoint Guest House* (☎ 44-2867). This friendly place has a range of accommodation from Rs 125/150 for rooms with attached bath. There are also some air-con rooms for Rs 200/250 and there's a travel agent here. Down the alley between Centrepoint and Kathleen's, the *Calcutta Guest House* is similarly priced but not such good value.

Down Chowringhee Lane there's the *Hotel Palace* which has rooms for Rs 90/140 with attached bath, and the *Capital Guest House* which has similar rooms for Rs 100/160. Neither of them is anything special, nor is the *Timestar Hotel* on the next lane over, although it's a bit cheaper at Rs 75/120 for attached rooms. In the same area the *Woodland Guest House* (☎ 44-4729) has four doubles with attached bath at Rs 180.

Also south of Sudder St, there are two hotels right opposite each other along Dr M Ishaque Rd. The first is the *East End Hotel* (☎ 29-8921), an old, well-maintained place run by friendly people. It has singles/doubles with attached bath for Rs 120/200. The *Neelam Hotel* (☎ 29-9198) is better value with singles/doubles for Rs 75/150. Nearby is the *Classic Hotel* (☎ 29-7390), down an alley off Mirza Ghalib St, which has singles with common bath for Rs 90 and doubles with bath for Rs 170.

North of Sudder St, at 1 Chowringhee Rd, is the family-run *Chowringhee Hotel*, with singles/doubles from Rs 80/100 and an aircon room. It's conveniently close to the Esplanade metro station.

The Ys Calcutta has a collection of Ys but they're often full. The *YMCA* (☎ 44-3814) at 42 Surendra Nath Banerji Rd has doubles for Rs 50 and a dorm for Rs 20 plus Rs 15 for temporary membership. The *YMCA* (☎ 29-2192), at 25 Chowringhee Rd, is a big, gloomy building that's popular with Indian businessmen. There are some dorm beds for Rs 50, with breakfast. All other accommodation includes early-morning tea, breakfast and dinner; the rooms have attached baths. There are dorm beds for Rs 140 (in three, four and six-bedded rooms), singles/doubles for Rs 250/350 or Rs 450/600 with air-con. They've got some excellent full-size snooker and billiard tables in the lounge and, if you're discreet, it's possible to use them without being a resident.

The *YWCA* (☎ 29-0260), 1 Middleton Row, is for women only. It's a grand old place; airy, spotless and with a beautiful tennis court. Unfortunately, they won't take overnight guests – minimum stay is one week – but it's excellent value at Rs 850 per week including basic meals.

Other Places The *Youth Hostel* (☎ 67-2869) is at 10 Dr J B Ananda Dutta Lane in Howrah. It's small and a bit run down but OK; take a No 52 or 58 bus from Howrah Railway Station to Shamasri Cinema, or a No 63 bus to Khirertala. Dorm beds are Rs 15.

Howrah Railway Station has *retiring rooms* – four doubles with attached bathrooms for Rs 70. Next door is the recently opened *Railway Yatri Nivas* with dorm beds for Rs 50 and doubles with attached bathrooms for Rs 200, or Rs 300 with air-con. You can only stay here with a train ticket for 200 km or more, and then only for one night. There are also *retiring rooms* at Sealdah.

Finally, Calcutta airport has *rest rooms* if you're in transit, with dorm beds for Rs 40 and singles/doubles for Rs 125/190 or Rs 175/250 with air-con. Check at the reservations desk in the terminal.

Places to Stay – middle
BBD Bagh The *Central Guest House* (☎ 27-4876) is a recommended hotel that's good value with clean singles/doubles for Rs 150/200 or Rs 300 for air-con. All rooms have attached bathrooms. The hotel fronts onto Chittaranjan Ave but the entrance is round the back at 18 Prafulla Sarkar St.

In the same area is the *Hotel Avenue* (☎ 27-5546) but it's overpriced with dorm beds for Rs 70 and rooms from Rs 175/200. You could try the *Hotel City Heart* below which is better value but you may not get in as they have no 'C' forms for foreigner registration.

Nearby on Princep St is the old *Hotel Embassy* (☎ 27-9040) with singles/doubles for Rs 175/250 including attached bath. One block east is the *Broadway Hotel*, which has a range of rooms from Rs 100 for a single with common bathroom to singles/doubles/triples for Rs 130/160/250 with attached bath. It's popular and often full.

Chowringhee In the Sudder St area the *Gujral Lodge* (☎ 44-0620) is a small clean guest house with rooms at Rs 130/230 with attached bath and air-con doubles at Rs 350. On the floor above is the *Lindsay Guest House* (☎ 29-3202) with rooms at Rs 220/300 or Rs 360/460 with air-con. Their other place, the *Hotel Lindsay* (☎ 44-0817), at 8A Lindsay St, is better and worth the climb to the 6th floor. Rooms are Rs 220/300 for singles/doubles or Rs 300/400 with air-con.

At 12A Lindsay St is the amazingly plush *CKT Inn* (☎ 44-8246). It's a small friendly place with rooms for Rs 408/528 but this includes all taxes and service charge. The rooms are air-conditioned and have TVs and attached bathrooms.

The *Carlton Hotel* (☎ 23-3009), 2 Chowringhee Place, has been closed for renovations (which this fine old building desperately needed). It would be well worth

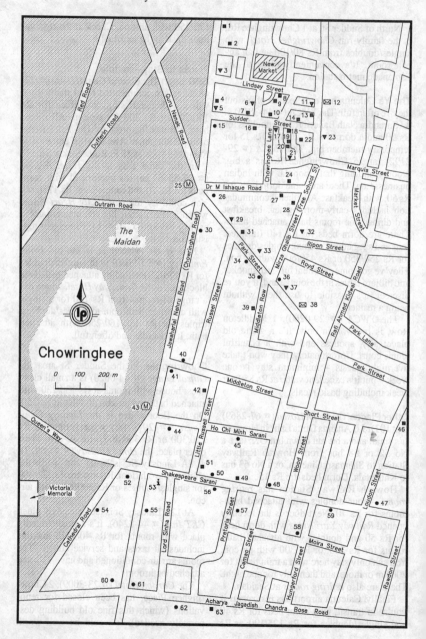

■	PLACES TO STAY
1	Oberoi Grand Hotel
2	Carlton Hotel
4	YMCA
7	Lytton Hotel
8	CKT Inn
9	Gujral Lodge & City Express Supermarket
10	Fairlawn Hotel
13	Centrepoint Guest House
14	Astoria Hotel.
16	Salvation Army Guest House
18	Hotel Maria
19	Hotel Paragon
20	Timestar Hotel
22	Modern Lodge
24	Neelam Hotel
27	East End Hotel
28	Classic Hotel
31	Park Hotel & Kwality Restaurant
39	YWCA
42	Old Kenilworth Hotel
46	Hotel Rutt Deen
49	Astor Hotel
51	New Kenilworth Hotel
63	Hotel Hindustan International

▼	PLACES TO EAT
3	Hindustan Restaurant
5	Zaranj Restaurant
6	Khalsa Restaurant
11	Kathleen's Restaurant & Bakery
17	Blue Sky Cafe
21	Abdul Khalique Hotel
23	Shamiana Bar & Restaurant
29	Gulnar Restaurant

32	Gupta Restaurant
33	Tandoor, Moulin Rouge & Blue Fox
37	Sky Room

	OTHER
12	New Market Post Office
15	Indian Museum
26	Bangladesh Biman Airlines
30	State Bank of India
34	Magnolia Bar & Singapore Airlines
35	Thai International & Flury's
36	French Consulate & Golden Dragon
38	Park St Post Office
39	YMCA
40	British Airways, RNAC & Air France
41	KLM & Cathay Pacific
44	British Consulate
45	US Consulate
47	CIS Consulate
48	ANZ Grindlays
50	British Council
52	Birla Planetarium
53	Government of India Tourist Office
54	St Paul's Cathedral
55	Air India
56	Fax Agency
57	Japanese Consulate
58	ISKCON
59	Vayudoot
60	Nehru Children's Museum
61	Aeroflot
62	Foreigners' Registration Office

Ⓜ	METRO STATIONS
25	Park St
43	Maidan

checking to see if it has reopened as it was once a very popular place to stay.

The *Astoria Hotel* (☎ 44-1359), 6/2 Sudder St, offers only air-con rooms which are rather overpriced. Rooms are variable and cost Rs 302/495 to Rs 440/550, including taxes. All the rooms have a bath, colour TV and telephone.

Places to Stay – top end

For an idea of how the other half lived and played in the days of the Raj, the *Tollygunge Club* (☎ 46-3141, fax (33) 74-1923), set in 44 hectares on the southern edge of Calcutta, is a wonderfully relaxing place to stay. It's

run by an Englishman, Bob Wright, along the exclusive lines set down almost 100 years ago. The elegant clubhouse was once the mansion at the centre of a large indigo plantation, now a championship golf course. Sitting by the swimming pool here, with a cold beer or an excellent club sandwich, it's hard to believe you're still in Calcutta.

Tolly (as it's affectionately called) is now the playground of the city's elite. As well as the two pools, there are seven tennis courts, two squash courts, a croquet lawn, billiards, badminton and table tennis, as well as a stable full of ponies. As a foreign visitor, so long as you telephone, fax, or write in advance (120 Deshapran Sasmal Rd, Calcutta 700033), you may stay here and are given temporary membership allowing you to use the facilities. Guests are expected to be reasonably tidy but jackets and ties are not necessary. The cheapest rooms are in 'Hastings' where doubles cost Rs 450, with air-con and attached baths. The cottages cost Rs 750/800 and have small sitting areas overlooking the golf course. Suites in Tolly Towers are Rs 1000. There are no additional taxes. It's a 10-minute walk from Tollygunge metro station.

There was a time when the only place to stay was the *Fairlawn Hotel* (☎ 44-4460), 13A Sudder St – a piece of Calcutta where the Raj simply never ended. Edmund Smith and his Armenian wife, Violet, the couple who still run the hotel more than 40 years after Independence, look like they've been time-warped from Brighton in the '50s. Their establishment is certainly atmospheric and packed with memorabilia but prices have risen while standards have not. Management and waiters can be curt to the point of rudeness and the English food is very variable.

However most of the rooms are comfortable, air-conditioned and have attached baths with constant hot water. They cost US$35/50/70 for singles/doubles/triples with all meals including afternoon tea on the lawn. It's been said that you don't really stay here so much as play your part in an on-going theatre performance. The current show seems to be *Fawlty Towers* and whether you find it funny or not depends on the part you're playing.

The *'Old' Kenilworth Hotel* (☎ 22-5325), 7 Little Russell St in Chowringhee, is another place brimming over with character. It's run by the very personable and loquacious Mrs Joyce Purdy who knows everything there is to know about Calcutta. It is not connected with the New Kenilworth Hotel, and is an old colonial-style house in its own grounds with the largest rooms in the city, all with south-facing balconies to catch the breezes. Mrs Purdy is keen on maintaining olde-worlde standards of comfort and

dignity and, on her own admission, has difficulty keeping staff because she's very strict about this. Some people enjoy the character of the place and its proprietor, others complain that it's overpriced. Singles/doubles are Rs 550/650 or Rs 700/800 with air-con. All the rooms have a bath, meals are available, drinking water is carefully boiled and filtered, and there's a refrigerator for guests' use.

The classic old *Great Eastern Hotel* (☎ 28-2311), 1-3 Old Court House St (south of BBD Bagh), is a rambling place that's distinctly tatty round the edges. This huge, Raj-style hotel with some 200 rooms is often full by late morning. There are singles/doubles from Rs 250/470 or Rs 860/960 with air-con. There are a number of restaurants and a coffee shop with the peculiar name, Dragon in Sherry's.

As far as modern places go, the centrally air-con *Lytton Hotel* (☎ 29-1875), 14 Sudder St, is a good choice. Singles/ doubles are Rs 600/750 with attached bathroom and TV. There's a laundry service, restaurant, bar, money exchange facilities and a small bookshop/newsagency. It's a popular place so get there early in the day if possible. The three-star *Hotel Rutt Deen* (☎ 47-3884), 21B Loudon St, is also good. It has singles/doubles from Rs 600/650 with air-con.

The *Astor Hotel* (☎ 22-9950), 15 Shakespeare Sarani, is in a good location and has singles/doubles from Rs 500/650 with air-con, TV and attached bath. The hotel has a very pleasant garden and there are daily barbecues.

The *New Kenilworth Hotel* (☎ 22-8394), 1-2 Little Russell St, has old and new wings. Air-con rooms are US$42/48, definitely overpriced for rooms in the old wing. All rooms have a fridge, TV and attached bath.

The *ITDC Airport Ashok* (☎ 56-9111), at the airport, is modern and convenient for passengers in transit. Singles/doubles with air-con cost Rs 1550/1700. It has all the facilities you would expect of a five-star hotel.

Going up in price, the *Park Hotel* (☎ 29-7336), at 17 Park St, is another modern hotel;

it costs Rs 1800/2000 for air-con singles/doubles, and there's a restaurant, bar and pool. Similar in price and standard is the 212-room *Hotel Hindustan International* (☎ 47-2394) at 235/1 Acharya J C Bose Rd.

Providing stiff competition for the Oberoi Grand, the new *Taj Bengal* (☎ 28-3939) is at the south end of the Maidan and has all the mod cons you'd expect, and an opulent atrium with a waterfall. Singles/doubles are US$160/175 right up to US$360. There are four restaurants, a nightclub, swimming pool and health club.

The *Oberoi Grand Hotel* (☎ 29-2323), 15 Chowringhee Rd, is pretty plain externally but very grand inside. Rooms range from US$160/175 to US$440 for the deluxe suite. There are four restaurants, and beneath the palm trees in the central courtyard there's a swimming pool. The Oberoi Grand has long been acknowledged as Calcutta's best hotel and the jewel in the Oberoi crown.

Places to Eat

Cheap Finding good food at reasonable prices is no problem in the Chowringhee/Sudder St area and everyone seems to have their own favourite place. *Blue Sky Cafe*, halfway down Sudder St, is always packed with travellers and does excellent breakfasts and snacks. They have good curd with fruit from Rs 7, milk shakes, fresh juice, great porridge and a range of burgers and snacks. It's a good place to start the day. At the *Delhi Durbar*, nearby on Chowringhee Lane, there are pizzas from Rs 12 to Rs 20 and boiled potatoes with cheese for Rs 12.

The other places less geared to the Western traveller are cheaper. Just south of Sudder St is the *Abdul Khalique Hotel* where you can get a delicious egg-roll (wrapped in newspaper) for Rs 3 and a cup of tea for Rs 1. The Sikh-run *Khalsa Restaurant*, across from the Salvation Army Guest House and down the street a few doors, has been popular with both locals and travellers for many years. The *Taj Continental*, opposite the entrance to Stuart Lane, is another good cheap place.

On nearby Mirza Ghalib St there are

several other places. The *Shamiana Bar & Restaurant* is clean and offers Indian and Chinese food; close by and similar is *Gypsy Fast Food*. Opposite the Shamiana Restaurant the *Moghul Durbar* gets mixed reports. The nearby *Cafe 48* has good veg thalis.

For good bread and take-away snacks there's the *Hare Krishna Bakery* on the corner of Middleton St and Russell St. Go early for the excellent brown bread. Nearer Sudder St is *Kathleen's Bakery* which has greater variety. This is where the Calcuttans who can afford to eat cake indulge themselves. A whole chocolate cake costs Rs 160 but there are also good cinnamon rolls for Rs 4. In the New Market on Lindsay St there are also good cake shops including *Nahoum*, a third-generation Jewish bakery in F row.

Also within reach of the Sudder St area is *Nizam's*, around the corner from the Minerva Cinema (see the BBD Bagh map). It's very popular among Calcuttans for mutton and chicken rolls, kebabs and Muslim food.

If you're staying near Chittaranjan Ave, the *Mission Cafe* is a good choice with masala dosa for Rs 9 and espresso coffee for Rs 4. In the same area is the *Chung Wah Chinese Restaurant*. It looks like something out of Shanghai in the 1930s and you sit in private wooden booths. Beer is Rs 30 and main dishes are around Rs 32. Nearby is the *Anand Restaurant*, probably the best vegetarian restaurant in the city. It's a smart place and main dishes are around Rs 20. There's a wide range of dosas and you can finish with an ice cream followed by coconut pan, wrapped in leaves specially brought in from Tamil Nadu.

Back in the Sudder St area, *Kathleen's Restaurant*, beside the bakery, is a good place for a full meal. They do good tandoori food, and most main courses are around Rs 30. A beer is Rs 32 here and there's a wide range of ice creams including a hot fudge sundae for Rs 22. Along the street opposite the Salvation Army Guest House, the *Oasis Restaurant* offers a similar menu. It's not bad and slightly cheaper than Kathleen's. South along Mirza Ghalib St is the *Gupta Restaurant*.

For reasonable Chinese food, try the *How Hua* on Mirza Ghalib St; they've even got northern Chinese dishes such as jiaozi, which is a bit like Tibetan momo. Other similar Chinese restaurants are the *Hong Kong Restaurant* and the *Golden Dragon Restaurant*, both on Mirza Ghalib St. The *Lung Fung Restaurant* at the junction of Stuart Lane and Marquis St is only mediocre. Calcuttans say the place to go for really good cheap Chinese food is the Tangra area, and they recommend the *Tangra Chinese Restaurant*. It's in the west of the city and you'll need a taxi to get there.

On Middleton Row, near the YWCA, *Peter Cat* has excellent kebabs. *Big Max*, on Park St, is the place to go for hamburgers and pizza.

A Calcutta institution is the *Indian Coffee House*, near Calcutta University, for years the meeting place of the city's intellectuals. Nowadays it's mostly younger undergraduates who congregate beneath the faded portrait of Rabindranath Tagore in this large cafe. Nevertheless it's a good place to meet people and is convenient for a coffee and snack if you've been looking round the many bookshops in this area.

The Bengali sweet tooth is legendary and *Indra Mahal* is a great place to try Bengali sweets. It's on Chowringhee Rd just up from the Grand Hotel; they also serve chat and other snacks. Bengali specialities are Moghul paratha and misthi dhoi (curd sweetened with jaggery), but curiously it's hard to find real Bengali food in Calcutta unless you dine at a Bengali's home. Just about the only restaurant specialising in this cuisine is *Suruchi*, on Elliot Rd, by the Mallik Bazaar bus stop.

More Expensive Right in the centre of town at 11 Waterloo St (the narrow street that runs by the Great Eastern Hotel) is the *Amber Hotel*. The food is excellent and the place is often voted by residents of Calcutta as the best place to eat in the city. Prices are very reasonable, with most dishes around Rs 35 and the tandoori items are very good. Beer is around Rs 30 and there's a range of ice

creams. Across the road is the *West End Takeaway* and nearby is the *Sagar*, both part of the same group.

Most of the other upmarket restaurants are on Park St though there are one or two cheap places amongst them. There are a whole stack of restaurants to choose from, some with very un-Calcutta names like *Blue Fox* and *Moulin Rouge*! Whichever you decide to eat at, remember that any restaurant or bar which has live music will attract a surcharge of between 30% and 100% depending on the establishment. Make sure you ask about this before sitting down to eat.

One of the cheapest of the restaurants on this street is the *Kwality* at 17 Park St, beside the Park Hotel. It has a small menu with main dishes around Rs 30 but is a good place to eat. Nearby is the similar *Tandoor* but the *Gulnar Restaurant* next to the Park Hotel is better. The food is excellent but quite expensive and you'll have to pay a surcharge if, as is usual, there's a band playing. It's very popular with relatively affluent local people. The restaurant is open from 5.30 to 11.30 pm and is licensed (last drinks 11 pm).

Another recommended place on Park St is the *Sky Room*, over the junction with Mirza Ghalib St, which offers good Indian and European food with fast service. *Flury's* is the place for tea and cakes, the *Magnolia Bar* is good for ice cream.

The *Astor Hotel*, on Shakespeare Sarani, has a very pleasant garden that's good for a relaxing drink (beers are Rs 35) or a barbecue (daily between 6 and 11 pm). On Saturday evenings there's live music here.

At the *Fairlawn Hotel* on Sudder St the food is English-style, and nonresidents can eat here for Rs 95. The set lunches and dinners can be fun and are certainly different, announced by a gong and served in impatient style by uniformed waiters. Check the day's menu before you decide to eat here as comments on the food vary enormously – from 'delicious roasts' to 'meat floating in gravy reminiscent of the transmission fluid from a '35 Bentley'! However the lawn in front of the hotel is an excellent place for afternoon tea or a beer (Rs 35) in the evening.

Also in Sudder St is the opulent *Zaranj Restaurant*, with a waterfall flowing through the middle of it. It's as expensive as its decor with most dishes around Rs 80, but is packed with rich Calcuttans who say it's worth it. If money is no object you could also try the restaurants at the Oberoi Grand and the Taj Bengal. The *Ming Court* at the Oberoi has excellent Chinese food but a three-course meal including beer and taxes will set you back Rs 450!

Entertainment

Calcutta is famous for its culture – film, poetry, music, art and dance all have their devotees here. Programmes are listed in the daily newspapers or in the leaflet *Calcutta This Fortnight*, available free from the tourist offices.

There are dances on at the Oberoi Grand Hotel on Chowringhee Rd every night at 6.30 pm. Even though there's no longer a charge, the audience is sometimes extremely small and it's worth going to.

A dance-drama performance, Bengali poetry reading or a similar event takes place on most nights at the Rabindra Sadan (☎ 47-9936) on Cathedral Rd. Foreign films and retrospectives are shown at the Nandan complex nearby.

Bars & Discos In the Sudder St area the Sun Set Bar at the Lytton Hotel is a good place for a drink. This bar is surprisingly popular with travellers, young expatriate workers and local young people involved on the fringes of the tourist trade. It's a friendly place and they have a good music system. Similar is the open-air bar in the forecourt of the Fairlawn Hotel where there's always an interesting crowd. There are plenty of other, much more basic, bars, some with bizarre names like Off cum On Rambo Bar! (Mirza Ghalib St).

Quite a few of the larger hotels have discos which go on until early morning. The best of them is probably the Pink Elephant at the Oberoi Grand Hotel but you have to be invited by a member or resident.

Thursday is a 'dry' day in Calcutta and the only places where you can get alcoholic drinks are in the four and five-star hotels, although some places seem to disregard this ruling. Several of the licensed restaurants are closed on Thursday.

Things to Buy

Calcutta has the usual government emporiums and quite a good Central Cottage Industries Emporium at 7 Chowringhee Rd. There are numerous interesting shops along Chowringhee Rd selling everything from carpets to handicrafts. The shops along the entrance arcade to the Oberoi Grand Hotel are particularly interesting. There's also an amazing variety of pavement vendors selling everything imaginable.

Amid this mêlée are many runners from other shops, particularly the New Market, looking for customers. Naturally, 'their' shop is only 'just round the corner', yet rarely is this true. If you follow them, it's going to take up quite a bit of your time and the prices of the goods which you're invited to examine will be relatively high. After all, it's a long way back and a lot of wasted time for them to find another punter.

New Market, formerly Hogg Market, is Calcutta's premier place for bargain shopping despite part of it being burnt out in late '85. Here you can find a little of almost everything, and it is always worth an hour or so wandering around. A particular bargain, if you're flying straight home from Calcutta, is caneware. This is ridiculously cheap compared to prices in the West and, of course, is very light if rather bulky. This market has also long been a good place to change money but with the liberalisation of the exchange-rate policy, things may change.

New Market is the place to sell things too. Whisky, cigarettes and watches are in demand but the prices offered for optical and electronic goods are nothing to write home about. Smuggled electronic goods are also bought and sold at the market in Kidderpore. There's another good street market (mainly clothes) along Lenin Sarani in the evenings.

Between Sudder St and New Market is an

expensive air-con market. In the basement is City Express Supermarket offering fully computerised checkout and at least one supermarket helper per customer, some even involved in product promotion!

Down Sudder St or in the lanes off there, those in search of highs derived from the plant kingdom are attended to by touts offering a range of services. Don't smoke openly; Uncle Sam doesn't like it and neither do the Indian authorities.

Getting There & Away

Air Most airline offices are around Chowringhee although Indian Airlines is on Chittaranjan Ave. A number of airlines, including Gulf Air, Kuwait Airways, Philippine Airlines and TWA, are handled by GSA Jet Air (☎ 47-7783), 230A Acharya JC Bose Rd.

Aeroflot
    58 Chowringhee Rd (☎ 22-1415)
Air France
    41 Chowringhee Rd (☎ 29-6161)
Air India
    50 Chowringhee Rd (☎ 22-2356)
Bangladesh Biman
    1 Park St (☎ 29-3709)
British Airways
    41 Chowringhee Rd (☎ 29-3430)
Cathay Pacific/KLM
    1 Middleton St (☎ 47-1221)
Indian Airlines
    39 Chittaranjan Ave (☎ 26-2548)
JAL
    35A Chowringhee Rd (☎ 24-8371)
Lufthansa
    30A/B Chowringhee Rd (☎ 24-8611)
Qantas
    (Hotel Hindustan International)
    235 Acharya JC Bose Rd (☎ 47-0718)
Royal Nepal Airlines (RNAC)
    41 Chowringhee Rd (☎ 29-8534)
SAS
    18G Park St (☎ 24-9696)
Singapore Airlines
    18D Park St (☎ 29-9297)
Swissair
    46C Chowringhee Rd (☎ 47-4643)
Thai International
    18G Park St (☎ 29-9846)
Vayudoot
    29B Shakespeare Sarani (☎ 47-7062)
    Dum Dum Airport (☎ 22-7062)

Calcutta is a good place for competitive air fares to other parts of Asia. You can expect to pick up tickets to Bangkok for around US$90 and to Kathmandu for around US$95 – payable in Indian rupees with bank certificates. Flights are usually with Air India, Indian Airlines, Thai International, Royal Nepal Airlines or Bangladesh Biman.

Indian Airlines prices are as follows: Agartala (US$34), Bagdogra (US$50), Bhubaneswar (US$41), Bombay (US$157), Delhi (US$132), Dibrugarh (US$74), Dimapur (US$69), Gawahati (US$46), Gorakhpur (US$70), Imphal (US$58), Jaipur (US$152), Lucknow (US$92), Madras (US$137), Patna (US$51), Port Blair (US$134) and Varanasi (US$69).

Calcutta's Indian Airlines office (☎ 26-2548) is fully computerised and it's a breeze buying tickets. It's open from 9 am to 9 pm seven days a week. There's a tourist counter which rarely has anyone waiting in front of it so it's very quick. Even refunds or a change of flight date are no hassle.

Vayudoot (☎ 47-7062) flies from Calcutta to Aizwal (Rs 1030), Cooch Behar (Rs 935), Jamshedpur (Rs 805), Kailashahr (Rs 805), and Shillong (Rs 855) but both prices and schedules for this airline are subject to change.

Bus Bus services from Calcutta are not as good an alternative as they are from a number of other Indian cities. It's generally better to travel from Calcutta by train, although there are several useful bus routes to other towns in West Bengal.

Buses generally depart from the bus stand area at the north end of the Maidan, near Chowringhee Rd, but there are a number of private companies which have their own stands.

The only buses which travellers use with any regularity are those from Calcutta to Siliguri and New Jalpaiguri (for Darjeeling). The 'Rocket Service' (!) costs Rs 115 and leaves Calcutta at 8 pm, arriving next morning. It's much rougher than going by train.

Train Calcutta has two major railway stations. Howrah, on the west bank of the Hooghly River, handles most trains into the city, but if you're going north to Darjeeling or the north-east region then the trains leave from Sealdah Station on the east side of the Hooghly. Beware of pickpockets and people of similar inclination at Howrah Railway Station.

The tourist railway booking office is on the 1st floor at 6 Fairlie Place near BBD Bagh. It's fully computerised and has a tourist quota but can be very crowded with foreigners. It's open Monday to Saturday from 9 am to 1 pm and 1.30 to 4 pm, and on Sunday between 9 am and 2 pm. They'll even handle bookings for trains that don't start or finish in Calcutta, but only if you have a rail-pass. If you don't, go to the other booking office nearby, at 14 Strand Rd, which has a satellite link. Here you can buy advance tickets on routes into and out of Delhi, Madras and Bombay (get a form and join the correct queue). Bookings can be made up to 60 days before departure for all trains apart from the *Shatabdi Express*, for which bookings are only open within 15 days of departure.

Both these places attract long queues and the staff at Fairlie Place office demand to see exchange certificates if you pay in rupees. There are other computerised booking offices which may be better for advance tickets out of Calcutta. The office at Tollygunge metro station is easy to get to and never seems to be very busy.

If you've just flown into Calcutta, it might be worth checking the rail reservation desk at the airport as they have an air-travellers' quota (!) for same-day or next-day travel on the main expresses.

Important trains departing from Howrah include the *Rajdhani Express*, which departs daily, except Wednesday and Saturday, at 4 pm taking 18 hours to New Delhi (1446 km, Rs 590 in air-con chair-car, Rs 1195 in air-con two-tier sleeper); and the *2381 AC Express*, which leaves on Tuesday, Wednesday, day and Saturday at 9.15 am, reaching Varanasi (678 km, Rs 109/417 in 2nd/1st) at

9 pm and New Delhi the following morning. The fastest service to Bombay (1968 km, 33 hours) is the daily *Gitanjali Express*.

The daily *Coromandal Express* leaves Howrah at 2.30 pm and at 9.38 pm reaches Bhubaneswar (437 km, Rs 81/301 in 2nd/1st) and Madras (1663 km, Rs 186/789 in 2nd/1st) at 5.35 pm the following day. During and soon after the monsoon season, the railway line can be cut off by the Godavari or Krishna rivers in north Andhra Pradesh. If this is the case the Calcutta to Madras service will make a loop inland and the trip takes a good deal longer.

For Darjeeling, trains go from Sealdah and Howrah to New Jalpaiguri or Siliguri, where you take a bus or the toy train (if running) up to the hill station. Trains go via Malda (344 km from Sealdah); the trip to New Jalpaiguri (566 km, Rs 97/388 in 2nd/1st) takes about 12 hours.

Boat See the Andaman & Nicobar Islands section for details on the shipping services from Calcutta.

Getting Around
To/From the Airport An airport bus costing Rs 17 runs past the Indian Airlines office and down Chowringhee Rd past Sudder St on its way in from the airport. On the way out to the airport it departs from the Indian Airlines office at 5.30, 7.15, 9.45 and 11.15 am, and 3.15 and 5.30 pm, and takes under an hour. There's also a public minibus (No S10) from BBD Bagh to the airport for Rs 3.50.

If you want to take a taxi from the airport, it's cheaper to go to the prepaid kiosk where you'll be assigned one. It costs Rs 65 to Sudder St or the Oberoi. In the opposite direction expect to pay at least an extra 25% or more. All the same, shared between four people, that's about as cheap as the airport bus.

Incidentally, Calcutta's airport takes its name, Dum Dum Airport, from the fact that this was the site of the Dum Dum Barracks, where the explosive dumdum bullet, banned after the Boer War, was once made.

Bus Calcutta's bus system is hopelessly crowded. It's an edifying sight to watch the double-decker buses come across Howrah Bridge during the rush hour. Fares are from Rs 0.70. Take a No 5 or 6 bus between Howrah Station and Sudder St; ask for the Indian Museum. There is a secondary private minibus service, which is rather faster and slightly more expensive, with fares a few paise more. You need to be a midget to ride in these buses though.

The second Howrah Bridge is now complete, and should reduce congestion on the original and make it easier to get across the river. Beware of pickpockets on any of Calcutta's public transport.

Tram Calcutta has a public tram service but the trams are like sardine tins. They may be pollution-free but since they're a major cause of the traffic jams, there's talk of abolishing them. Fares start at Rs 0.70 and they're least crowded on Sundays. Take a No 12A from Howrah to the Indian Museum.

Metro India's first underground railway system is being built at minimum cost and in maximum time almost totally by hand. The soggy soil makes digging holes by hand no fun at all, and after each monsoon it takes half the time to the next monsoon simply to drain out what has already been dug. Nevertheless, the northern and southern sectors are now open. It's the southern sector, from Esplanade to Tollygunge stations, that is of more use to visitors and there's a station near Sudder St. After using surface transport, you're in a different world down here. It's clean, efficient and almost a tourist attraction in itself. Movies are shown on platform TVs and the stations are air-conditioned and well decorated. (Rabindra Sadan has Tagore's poems on the walls.) Trains run from 8.15 am to 8.30 pm, Monday to Saturday and from 3 to 8.30 pm on Sunday. Tickets are from Rs 1.

Taxi Calcutta's taxi drivers are renowned not only for their passion for strikes, which in turn cause the buses to be even worse than usual, but also for their belligerent refusal to use the meter. Officially, the fare starts at Rs 5.50 and goes up by Rs 0.50 increments, but that's all in theory. In practice you have to agree on a price before setting off and that will always be more than it should cost. However, police stand guard over the taxi queue at Howrah Station and you can threaten to summon them if the driver doesn't turn on the meter here. It's about Rs 14 from Howrah to Sudder St.

Rickshaw Calcutta is the last bastion of the human-powered rickshaw, apart from at resorts like Mussoorie where they're just for the tourists. Calcutta's rickshaw-wallahs would not accept the new-fangled cycle-rickshaws when they were introduced elsewhere in India. After all, who could afford a bicycle? Most can't even afford their rickshaw and have to rent it from someone who takes the lion's share of the fares.

You may find it morally unacceptable to have a man pulling you around in a carriage – and these men are usually very thin, unhealthy and die early – but Calcutta's citizens are quite happy to use them. The only compensation is that they wouldn't have a job if people didn't use them and, as a tourist, you naturally pay more than local people. These sort of rickshaws only exist in central Calcutta, though. Across the river in Howrah or in other Calcutta suburbs, there are cycle-rickshaws.

Ferry The ferries can be a quicker and more pleasant way to get across the river than the congested Howrah Bridge. From Howrah to Chandpal Ghat or Fairlie Ghat there are several crossings an hour between 8.30 am and 8 pm for Rs 0.70. Ferries to the Botanical Gardens go from Chandpal Ghat or Babu Ghat and cost Rs 0.90.

Bicycle The Blue Sky restaurant on Sudder St rents bicycles but this is hardly prime bicycle country. As a taxi driver pointed out: 'We drive like Maradona playing football – we find a hole and move in!'.

West Bengal

Population: 68 million
Area: 87,853 sq km
Capital: Calcutta
Main Language: Bengali
People per sq km: 766
Literacy Rate: 58%

At the time of Partition, Bengal was split into East and West Bengal. East Bengal became the eastern wing of Pakistan and later, with the disintegration of that country, Bangladesh. West Bengal became a state of India with Calcutta as its capital. The state is long and narrow, running from the delta of the Ganges River system at the Bay of Bengal in the south to the heights of the Himalaya at Darjeeling in the north.

There is not a great deal of interest in the state apart from these two extremes – Calcutta, with its bewildering maelstrom of noise, culture, confusion and squalor at one end; and Darjeeling, serene and peaceful, at the other. This serenity was interrupted for a while in the 1980s when Gurkha agitators resorted to violence in their bid for a separate Gurkha state in the north. However, things have now calmed down and Darjeeling is a popular destination once more.

Outside these two centres the intrepid traveller will find a number of places to consider visiting, either south of Calcutta on the Bay of Bengal or north along the route to Darjeeling. Few foreign tourists visit the ruined mosques of Malda, the palaces of Murshidabad, the temples of Vishnupur or the Sunderbans Wildlife Sanctuary. If you do, the friendly Bengalis will make you feel all the more welcome for being an exception to the rule.

History

Referred to as Vanga in the *Mahabharata*, this area has a long history that dates back to before the Aryan invasions of India. It was part of the Mauryan Empire in the 3rd century before being overrun by the Guptas.

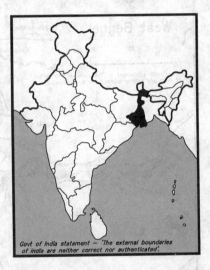

Govt of India statement – 'The external boundaries of India are neither correct nor authenticated'.

For three centuries from around 800 AD, the Pala dynasty controlled a large area based on Bengal and including parts of Orissa, Bihar and modern Bangladesh.

Bengal was brought under Muslim control by Qutb-ud-din, first of the Sultans of Delhi, at the end of the 12th century. Following the death of Aurangzeb in 1707, Bengal became an independent Muslim state.

Britain had established a trading post in Calcutta in 1698 which quickly prospered. Sensing rich pickings, Siraj-ud-daula, the Nawab of Bengal, came down from his capital at Murshidabad and easily took Calcutta in 1756. Clive defeated him the following year at the Battle of Plassey, helped by the treachery of Siraj-ud-daula's uncle, Mir Jafar, who commanded the greater part of the nawab's army. He was rewarded by succeeding his nephew as nawab but after the Battle of Buxar in 1764, the British took over full control of Bengal. For entertaining background reading on this

461

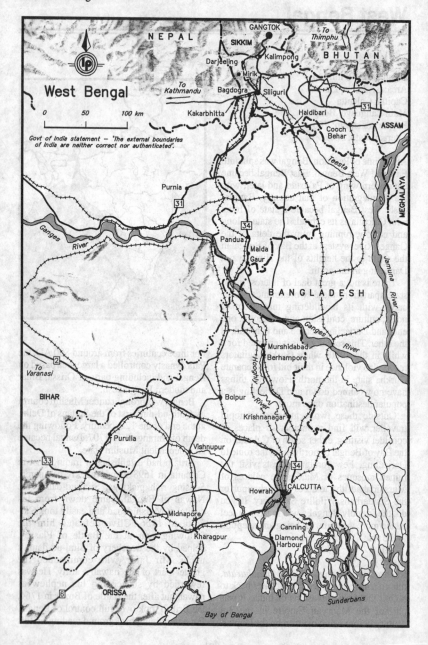

period as seen through the eyes of a modern-day traveller, Peter Holt's book, *In Clive's Footsteps*, is recommended. The author is five-times removed great grandson of Clive.

Permits

Permits are required for visits to Sikkim and the states of the north-eastern region – see the relevant chapters for information. All permit requirements for Darjeeling District including Darjeeling and Kalimpong have been lifted.

Permission is necessary if you wish to visit the Sunderbans. For Sajnekhali and the Project Tiger areas, it's available free of charge, while you wait (and wait) at the Forest Department (G Block, 6th floor) in the Writers' Building, Calcutta. You must bring your passport. For other areas in the Sunderbans go to the Divisional Forest Officer (☎ 45-1037), 24 Parganas, 35 Gopalnagar Rd, Calcutta.

SOUTH OF CALCUTTA
Down the Hooghly

The Hooghly River is a very difficult river to navigate due to the constantly shifting shoals and sandbanks. Hooghly River pilots have to continuously stay in touch with the river to keep track of the frequent changes in its course. When the Howrah Bridge was constructed it was feared that it would cause severe alterations to the river's flow patterns. The tide rises and falls 3½ metres at Calcutta and there is a bore, which reaches two metres in height, at the time of the rising tide. Because of these navigational difficulties and the silting up of the Hooghly, Calcutta is losing its importance as a port.

Falta, 43 km downriver, was the site of a Dutch factory. The British retreated here in 1756 when Calcutta was captured by Siraj-ud-daula. It was also from here that Clive recaptured Calcutta. Just below Falta the Damodar River joins the Hooghly. The Rupnarain River also joins the Hooghly nearby and a little up this river is **Tamluk**, an important Buddhist centre over 1000 years ago. The James & Mary Shoal, the most dangerous on the Hooghly, is just above the

point where the Rupnarain River enters. It takes its name from a ship which was wrecked here in 1694.

Diamond Harbour

A resort 51 km south of Calcutta by road, Diamond Harbour is at the point where the Hooghly turns south and flows into the open sea. It can be reached by bus or train from Calcutta. Launches run from here to Sagar Island.

Places to Stay Accommodation in the *Sagarika Tourist Lodge* can be booked through West Bengal Tourism in Calcutta.

Haldia

The new port of Haldia is 96 km south of Calcutta, on the west bank of the Hooghly. The port was constructed to try to regain the shipping lost from Calcutta's silting problems. There are regular buses between Calcutta and Haldia.

Sagar Island (Sagardwip)

At the mouth of the Hooghly, this island is considered the point where the Ganges joins the sea, and a great three-day bathing festival takes place here in mid-January. A lighthouse marks the south-west tip of the island but navigation is still difficult for a further 65 km south.

Digha

Close to the border with Orissa, 185 km south-east of Calcutta on the Bay of Bengal, Digha is another self-styled 'Brighton of the East'. The beach is seven km long and very wide but if a beach holiday is what you want, carry on south to Puri or Gopalpur-on-Sea.

There are daily buses between Calcutta and Digha (Rs 25, six hours) departing Calcutta at 6.15 am. The Chandaneshwar Siva Temple is just across the border in Orissa, eight km from Digha.

Places to Stay There's a *Tourist Lodge* with rooms and meals at reasonable prices. Digha has a wide range of other accommodation, including new and old *Tourist Cottages* and

শিব সদাগর

এপার গঙ্গা ওপার গঙ্গা মধ্যিখানে চর।
তারি মধ্যে বসে আছেন শিব সদাগর॥
শিব গেলেন শ্বশুরবাড়ি বসতে দিল পিঁড়ে;
জলপান করতে দিল শালিধানের চিঁড়ে।
শালিধানের চিঁড়ে নয় রে বিন্নিধানের খই—
মোটা মোটা সব রি কলা কাগমারি দই॥

Bengali children's poem

a *Youth Hostel* with dorm beds at Rs 20 (Rs 10 for members). The *Hotel Sea Hawk* has a range of rooms, with or without air-con.

Bakkhali

Also known as Fraserganj, this is another beach resort, 132 km from Calcutta, on the east side of the Hooghly. Accommodation here can again be reserved through West Bengal Tourism. From here you can get boats to the small island of Jambu Dwip to the south-west.

Sunderbans Wildlife Sanctuary

The innumerable mouths of the Ganges form the world's largest delta and part of this vast mangrove swamp is a 2585-sq-km wildlife reserve that extends into Bangladesh. It's designated a World Heritage Site and as part of Project Tiger has one of the largest tiger populations of any of the Indian parks. Tourist agencies capitalise on this fact but few visitors get even a glimpse of one of the 269 well-hidden tigers.

You wouldn't want to get too close to these animals. Partial to a little human flesh, they kill about 20 people each year, lying in wait beside the narrow channels that criss-cross the estuarine forest. Fishermen and honey-collectors have now taken to wearing masks, painted with human faces, on the back of their heads since a tiger is less likely to attack you if it thinks you're watching it.

An entry in the visitors' book at Sajnekhali seems to sum up the feelings of many visitors to the Sunderbans: 'Who came here but here is not see tiger, his visited is not success'. However, the area has other attractions and you may see some wildlife, mainly spotted deer, wild pig and monkeys. The journey here, by local boats and cycle-rickshaws through small traditional Bengali villages, can be fun. The whole area is wonderfully peaceful after frenetic Calcutta, and is teeming with birdlife.

There's a heron sanctuary (best between July and September) near Sajnekhali. At the Sajnekhali visitor centre there's a crocodile enclosure, shark pond, turtle hatchery and an interesting Mangrove Interpretation Centre. From here boats are available for excursions through the mangroves; it's Rs 300 for the whole day, Rs 200 for a four-hour trip plus Rs 57 for a guide and boat permits. There are watchtowers here and at several other points around the park. In the south of the Sunderbans are two other sanctuaries at Lothian and Halliday Islands, reached from Namkhana (three hours by bus from Calcutta).

Permission is required to visit the Sunderbans; see the permits section at the beginning of this chapter. Entry to the reserve costs Rs 6 for the first day, Rs 2 per day thereafter and cameras need a Rs 1 permit – all payable at Sajnekhali.

Places to Stay The *Sundar Chital Tourist Lodge* at Sajnekhali charges Rs 75 for a double with attached bathroom and there's a basic restaurant here. The signs say 'Movement prohibited after evening' and mean it. In 1991 a couple of tigers jumped over the fence and spent the night sniffing round the doors of the rooms where the tourists were sleeping!

Getting There & Away West Bengal Tourism organises a couple of boat tours each month including food and accommodation on board. A two-day trip with dormitory/cabin accommodation costs Rs 500/825 or Rs 1260/1640 for a three-day trip. Private operators have cheaper tours and day trips including lunch and a visit to Sajnekhali for Rs 125. They have offices opposite the railway station in Canning and if you just turned up early on a Sunday morning during the October and February season you could probably join a tour without booking.

Travelling independently is rather more complex. From Calcutta it's quickest to get a bus to Sonakhali/Basunti (Rs 12.50, three hours, from Babu Ghat) but alternatively you can take the train to Canning (Rs 7, 1¼ hours), then cross the river to Dok Kart opposite (Rs 0.30) by *bodbooti* (small overcrowded ferry) and go overland to Sonakhali by shared auto-rickshaw (Rs 5) or bus (Rs 1.30, 50 minutes). If you go via Canning you may be able to get a ride directly to Sajnekhali with one of the tour boats.

Continuing from Sonakhali/Basunti the next step is a boat to Gosava (Rs 2.50, 1¼ hours). From there get a cycle-rickshaw (no seats, just a wooden platform!) for the 40-

Around Calcutta

Govt of India statement – 'The external boundaries of India are neither correct nor authenticated'.

minute ride to Pakhirala (Rs 8) for a boat across the river to Sajnekhali. There's also a direct boat (Rs 2.50) leaving Gosava at 1 pm to reach Sajnekhali at 3.30 pm. In the morning it departs Sajnekhali at 8.30 am for Gosava.

A private boat to Sajnekhali costs Rs 400 from Canning or Rs 250 from Sonakhali/Basunti.

NORTH OF CALCUTTA
Serampore & Barrackpore
Twenty-five km from Calcutta on the Hooghly River, Serampore was a Danish

centre until their holdings in India were transferred to the East India Company in 1845. The old **Danish church** and **cemetery** still stand. The missionaries Ward, Marshman and Carey operated from here in the early 1800s.

Across the river is Barrackpore. A few dilapidated buildings are all that are left of the East India Company's cantonment here. There are also some gardens and a memorial to Gandhi by the river.

Mahesh, three km from Serampore, has a large and very old Jagannath Temple. In June-July of each year the Mahesh Yatra car festival takes place here. It is second in size only to the great car festival of Jagannath at Puri, Orissa.

Chandernagore

Also known as Chandarnagar, this was one of the French enclaves in India which were handed over at the same time as Pondicherry in 1951. Situated on the banks of the Hooghly, 39 km north of Calcutta, are several crumbling buildings dating from the French era. The first French settlers arrived here in 1673 and the place later became an important trading post, although it was taken by the British during conflicts with the French.

Hooghly & Satgaon

The historic town of Hooghly is 41 km north of Calcutta and very close to two other interesting sites – Chinsura and Bandel. Hooghly was an important trading port long before Calcutta rose to prominence. In 1537 the Portuguese set up a factory here; before that time Satgaon, 10 km further north, had been the main port of Bengal but was abandoned because of the river silting up. There are still a few traces of Satgaon's former grandeur, including a ruined **mosque**.

The Portuguese were kicked out of Hooghly in 1632 by Shah Jahan, after a lengthy siege, but were allowed to return a year later. The British East India Company also established a factory here in 1651. The **imambara**, built in 1836, with its gateway flanked by lofty minarets, is the main sight.

Across the road is an older imambara, dating from 1776-77.

Chinsura

Only a km or so south of Hooghly, Chinsura was exchanged by the Dutch for the British-held Indonesian island of Sumatra in 1825. The **Dutch church** is octagonal and dates from 1678. There is a fort and the Dutch **cemetery**, with many old tombs, a km to the west.

Bandel

A couple of km north of Hooghly, and 43 km from Calcutta, Bandel is the site of a Portuguese **church** and monastery which were built here in 1599. Destroyed by Shah Jahan in 1640, they were later rebuilt.

Getting There & Away Get off the train at Naihati and take the hourly shuttle service across the river.

Bansberia

A further four km north of Bandel, Bansberia has the **Vasudev Temple**, with interesting terracotta wall carvings, and the Hanseswari Temple.

Vishnupur

Also spelt Bishnupur, this interesting town of terracotta temples is a famous cultural centre. It flourished as the capital of the Malla kings from the 16th to the early 19th centuries. The Mallas were great patrons of the arts.

Since there is no stone in the area, the traditional building material for important buildings was brick. The facades of the dozen or so **temples** here are covered with ornate terracotta tiles depicting lively scenes from the Hindu epics. The main temples to see are the highly decorated Jor Bangla, the large Madan Mohan, the pyramidal Ras Mancha and the Shyam Rai, built in 1643.

Vishnupur is in Bankura district, famous for its pottery (particularly the stylised Bankura horse) and silk. In the markets here you can also find metalware, tussar silk and Baluchari saris, *ganjifa* (circular playing cards for a game long forgotten) and conch shell jewellery. In August the Jhapan Festival draws snake charmers to honour the goddess Manasa who is central to the cult of snake worship.

Places to Stay Accommodation is very limited. There's the good *Tourist Lodge* with dorm beds for Rs 20, and singles/doubles for Rs 75/100 with attached bathroom, or Rs 200 for an air-con double. It's about three km from the railway station. Cheaper hotels include the *Lali Hotel* and *Bharat Boarding*.

Getting There & Away There are buses from Calcutta (Rs 20, 4½ hours). The *Purulia Express*, from Howrah, is the fastest train, taking 3½ hours.

Jairambati & Kamarpukur

Ramakrishna was born in Kamarpukur, 143 km north-west of Calcutta, and there is a Ramakrishna Mission ashram here. Ramakrishna was a 19th-century Hindu saint who did much to rejuvenate Hinduism when it was going through a period of decline during the British rule. Jairambati, five km away, is another important point for Ramakrishna devotees.

Shantiniketan

The Visvabharati University is at Shantiniketan, three km from Bolpur. The brilliant and prolific poet, writer and nationalist Rabindranath Tagore (1861-1941) founded a school here in 1901. It later developed into a university with emphasis on humanity's relation with nature – many classes are conducted in the open air. Tagore went on to win the Nobel Prize in 1913 and is credited with introducing India's historical and cultural greatness to the modern world. In 1915, Tagore was awarded a knighthood by the British but he surrendered it in 1919 as a protest against the Amritsar massacre.

There are colleges of science, teacher training, Hindi, Sino-Indian studies, arts and crafts, and music and dance. It's difficult to get the real atmosphere of the place if you're not studying here but there are a number of things to visit. There's a **museum** and **art gallery** within the Uttarayan complex where Tagore lived. They are open from 10.30 am to 1 pm and 2 to 4.30 pm Thursday to Monday, mornings only on Tuesday. The university is open to visitors in the afternoons (mornings only on Tuesday and during vacations) but closed on Wednesday, the day the university was founded.

Four km away is **Sriniketan**, started as a project to revitalise traditional crafts such as *kantha* embroidery, weaving, batik and pottery.

Places to Stay The *International Guest House* has a large dorm with beds for Rs 4 and meals for Rs 10. *Shantiniketan Tourist Lodge* (☎ 699) is run by West Bengal Tourism and is a good place with singles/doubles for Rs 75/100 or Rs 225 for an air-con double. There are several other places including the new three-star *Mayurakhi Hotel* and university guest houses. At Bolpur railway station there are *retiring rooms*, with doubles for Rs 35 or Rs 70 with air-con.

Getting There & Away The *Shantiniketan Express* leaves Howrah daily at 9.55 am, reaching Bolpur at 12.30 pm. It departs from Bolpur at 1 pm for Howrah. Many other trains stop here.

Nabadwip

Also known as Nadia, the last Hindu king of Bengal, Lakshman Sen, moved his capital here from Gaur. It's an ancient centre of Sanskrit culture, 114 km north of Calcutta. There are many temples at this important pilgrimage centre.

Mayapur

Across the river from Nabadwip, this is a centre for the ISKCON (Hare Krishna) movement. There's a large new temple, gardens and accommodation available in the *ISKCON Guest House*. A bus tour is run from Calcutta on Sundays (daily during the winter). Details are available from ISKCON at 3C Albert Rd, Calcutta (☎ 47-6075).

Plassey

In 1757 Clive defeated Siraj-ud-daula and his French supporters here, a turning point in British influence in India. Plassey, or Palashi as it's now known, is 172 km north of Calcutta. There's nothing to see here apart from the 15-metre memorial a couple of km west of the village.

Berhampore

Eleven km south of Murshidabad is this large town, a notable centre for silk production. The Government Silk Research Centre is interesting to visit. In the old bazaar area of Khagra, in the northern part of Berhampore, the dilapidated mansions of European traders are quietly subsiding into the river.

Places to Stay & Eat The *Tourist Lodge* is good value and the best place to eat. Doubles are Rs 105 with attached bathroom, four-bedded rooms are Rs 131 and there are also air-con rooms for Rs 236. It's about 15 minutes from Berhampore Court Railway Station by cycle-rickshaw and close to the bus stand. At the railway *retiring rooms* there's a four-bedded dorm for Rs 11 a bed.

Getting There & Away On this branch line between Sealdah and Lalgola, there are several trains a day from Calcutta (186 km, four to six hours). There's a bus from Calcutta (Rs 26, five hours) leaving at 6.45 am and other buses to Malda (Rs 17.50, 3½ hours), Bolpur (Rs 15, four hours) and Siliguri (Rs 60, seven hours).

Across the river is Khagraghat Rd Station which is on the Howrah to Azimganj line.

Murshidabad

Population: 30,000

When Siraj-ud-daula was Nawab of Bengal, this was his capital, and it was here that he was assassinated after the defeat at Plassey. Murshidabad was also the major trading town between inland India and the port of Calcutta, 221 km south. Today it's a quiet town on the banks of the Bhagirathi River, a chance to see typical rural Bengali life.

Cycle-rickshaw-wallahs offer you guided tours of all the sites for Rs 30 to Rs 40 for a half-day. This is a good idea as everything's fairly spread out. The main attraction is the **Hazarduari**, the classical-style Palace of a Thousand Doors built for the nawabs in 1837. In the recently renovated throne room a vast chandelier, presented by Queen Victoria, is suspended above the nawab's silver throne. There are portraits of British dignitaries, an ivory sofa, ivory palanquins and silver sedan chairs. In the armoury downstairs is a cannon used at Plassey. It's open from 10 am to 4.30 pm daily except Friday; entry is Rs 0.50.

Across the grass from the palace is the rapidly deteriorating **Great Imambara**. Murshid Quli Khan, who moved the capital here in 1705, is buried beside the impressive ruins of the **Katra Mosque**. Siraj-ud-daula was assassinated at the **Nimak Haram Deohri** (Traitor's Gate). The Jain **Parswanath Temple** is at Kathgola and south of the railway station there's the **Moti Jhil**, or Pearl Lake, a fine place to view the sunset. It's worth taking a boat across the river to visit Siraj's **tomb** at Khusbagh, the Garden of Happiness. There are a number of other interesting buildings and ruins.

Places to Stay Accommodation here is very basic and rather overpriced, apart from the railway *retiring rooms* at Rs 18 for a double with attached bathroom. The *Hotel Anurag* overlooking the palace has grubby singles/doubles for Rs 40/60 but they may try for more. The *Hotel Historical* has a room for Rs 50 or you can sleep on the roof. The *Hotel Omrao* is the best (but nothing special) with singles for Rs 50 and doubles with attached bathroom for Rs 100. There's a reasonable restaurant here.

The *Tourist Lodge* in Berhampore is cleaner and much better value than most of these, but it's 11 km away by bus or train.

Getting There & Away Murshidabad is also on the Sealdah to Lalgola line and there are several trains daily from Calcutta (197 km, four to six hours). For long-distance buses you must go to Berhampore.

Malda & English Bazaar

On the route to Darjeeling, 349 km north of Calcutta, Malda is the base for visiting the ruins of the cities of Gaur and Pandua, although it's probably more famous now for its large Fajli mangoes. There's a small museum in Malda.

English Bazaar, also transliterated as Ingraj Bazar, is now a suburb of Malda. An English factory was established here in 1771. Old Malda is nearby, at the junction of the Kalindi and Mahananda rivers. It was once an important port for the former Muslim capital of Pandua.

Places to Stay Set around a garden of monster dahlias, the *Malda Tourist Lodge* is a reasonable place charging Rs 50 for an economy double room, Rs 75/100 for singles/doubles with attached bathroom, and Rs 225 for an air-con double. The tourist bureau is here and a rickshaw from the station costs Rs 3. Also OK and similarly priced are the *Hotel Samrat* opposite, and the *Hotel Natraj* on the road to the bus stand.

The top hotel is the *Hotel Purbanchal* with rooms from Rs 80/100 to Rs 250/325 with air-con but it's 20 minutes from the station by rickshaw. The railway *retiring rooms* are Rs 50 for a double or Rs 15 for a dorm-bed and there's a good refreshment room here.

Getting There & Away Situated on the main railway line, Malda is directly connected to Calcutta (344 km, seven hours) and New Jalpaiguri (233 km, five hours). There are buses to Siliguri (Rs 36, six hours) for Darjeeling, Berhampore (Rs 17.50, 3½ hours) for Murshidabad, and Calcutta (Rs 42, eight hours).

Gaur

Twelve km south of Malda and right on the border with Bangladesh, Gaur was first the capital of the Buddhist Palas, then the Hindu Senas and finally the Muslim nawabs. The ruins of the extensive fortifications and several large mosques are all that remain. (There are also some ruins on the other side of the ill-defined border.) Most impressive

are the **Bara Sona Mosque** and the nearby brick **Dakhil Darwajah** built in 1425. **Qadam Rasul Mosque** enshrines a footprint of the Mohammed but it looks as if he was wearing thongs when he made it! Fath Khan's tomb is nearby and a sign informs you that he 'vomited blood and died on this spot'. There are still some colourful enamelled tiles on the **Gumti Gate** and **Lattan Mosque** but few left on the **Firoz Minar**, although you can climb this tower for a good view.

Getting There & Away The monuments are very spread out and not all easy to find. Determined cycle-rickshaw-wallahs offer half-day trips from Malda for anything up to Rs 100. Taxis cost Rs 250 and also include Pandua.

Pandua

Gaur once alternated with Pandua as the seat of power. The main site is the vast **Adina Mosque**, built by Sikander Shah in the 14th century. Built over a Hindu temple, traces of which are still evident, it was one of the largest mosques in India but is now in ruins. Nearby is the **Eklakhi mausoleum**, so-called because it cost Rs 1 lakh to build. There are also several smaller mosques. The dusty deer park, 2½ km across the highway in the 'forest', is not worth going to.

Getting There & Away Pandua is on the main highway (NH34), 18 km north of Malda, and there are many buses that can drop you here. The main sites are at Adina, two km north of the village of Pandua, and right by the highway.

SILIGURI, NEW JALPAIGURI & BAGDOGRA

This crowded, sprawling, noisy place is the departure point for visits to Darjeeling, Kalimpong or Sikkim. Siliguri is a real boom town as the major trade centre for the north-east, Darjeeling, Sikkim and the east of Nepal, so it's packed with trucks and buses and is not a pleasant place to stay for a moment more than necessary. New

Jalpaiguri, the main railway junction, is eight km south of Siliguri though there's effectively no break in the urban sprawl between the two places.

Twelve km from Siliguri is Bagdogra, the airport serving this northern region.

Orientation & Information

Siliguri is very confusing at first, especially if you arrive at night. It's essentially just one north-south main road. New Jalpaiguri is the main railway junction, nothing more. The distance is about five km from there to Siliguri Town Station and another three or four km on to Siliguri Junction Station. You can catch the toy train (if it's running) to Darjeeling from any of these three stations. The new bus station is beside Siliguri Junction Railway Station.

There's a tourist information centre (☎ 21-632) in the centre of town and counters at the New Jalpaiguri and Siliguri Junction stations.

There's a useful railway booking office in the centre of town covering trains from all three stations here. Indian Airlines (☎ 26-689) have their office at Hotel Sinclairs.

Places to Stay

If you arrive in Siliguri too late to continue straight on to Darjeeling, there are over 40 hotels to choose from. There are good retiring rooms at New Jalpaiguri Station but they're often full.

Just past the Siliguri Town Station and to the left is the popular *Rajasthan Guest House* (☎ 21-815). It's a friendly place with dorm beds for Rs 30 and a range of singles/doubles from Rs 60/90 upwards and a triple for Rs 150 with bathroom. It's a fairly modern hotel and the vegetarian restaurant, though dark, is very good.

Continuing north along Hill Cart Rd, you come to two similar places, right beside each other and much in competition. The *Venus Hotel* has clean rooms from Rs 40/70 to Rs 90/140 and *Saluja Boarding* has rooms from Rs 60/125 with attached bathroom to Rs 250/300 with air-con. Both have restaurants.

North past the grubby *Airview Hotel* you

cross the bridge and come to a group of reasonable places. West Bengal Tourism's *Old Tourist Lodge* is a bit run down but the manager is friendly and it's fine for a night. There are dorm beds for Rs 30 and doubles with common bathroom for Rs 70 or Rs 100 with attached bathroom. The *Shere Punjab Hotel & Restaurant* is OK, with singles/doubles for Rs 50/90 with attached bathrooms. The *Hotel Kanchenjunga* nearby is slightly better and charges Rs 70/100.

Further along is the larger and newer *Mainak Tourist Lodge* (☎ 20-986), also run by West Bengal Tourism. Rooms are Rs 190/250 or Rs 350/450 with air-con and the hotel is set in a nice garden. Near it is the modern *Hotel Sharda* with singles/doubles for Rs 100/150 including attached bathrooms.

The best hotel here is the three-star *Hotel Sinclairs Siliguri* (☎ 22-674), but it's quite a distance from the railway station. Singles/doubles cost Rs 250/325, or Rs 395/700 with air-con, plus taxes. All rooms have attached bathrooms with hot water. The hotel has a good restaurant, bar, foreign exchange facilities and a swimming pool.

Places to Eat

There are several places to eat along Hill Cart Rd, including the *Amber Bar & Restaurant* and *Ranjit South Indian Restaurant*. For Punjabi food, there's the *Shere Punjab Hotel & Restaurant*. You can get a beer at all of these places as well. There's a good vegetarian restaurant at the *Rajasthan Guest House* and the food at *Hotel Sinclairs* is pricey but recommended.

Getting There & Away

Air Bagdogra airport is 12 km from Siliguri. There are daily flights to Calcutta (US$50), and flights daily, except on Monday and Saturday, to Delhi (US$128) and Gawahati (US$30). Flights to Dimapur (US$51) and Dibrugarh (US$61) go twice weekly.

Bus State Transport Corporation buses leave from the new Tenzing Norgay Central Bus Terminal, private buses from just outside.

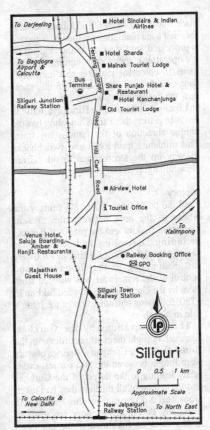

To Darjeeling

Hotel Sinclairs & Indian Airlines

To Bagdogra Airport & Calcutta

Hotel Sharda

Mainak Tourist Lodge

Bus Terminal

Shere Punjab Hotel & Restaurant

Hotel Kanchenjunga

Siliguri Junction Railway Station

Old Tourist Lodge

Tenzing Norgay Road

Hill Cart Road

Airview Hotel

Tourist Office

To Kalimpong

Venus Hotel, Saluja Boarding, Amber & Ranjit Restaurants

Railway Booking Office

GPO

Rajasthan Guest House

Siliguri Town Railway Station

Siliguri

0   0.5   1 km

Approximate Scale

To Calcutta & New Delhi

New Jalpaiguri Railway Station

To North East

toy train. From Siliguri there are several an hour from 6 am to 5 pm. There are also private Mazda buses for Rs 32 which are faster. Direct buses connect Siliguri with Kalimpong (Rs 18, three hours).

Sikkim Nationalised Transport (SNT) runs hourly buses to Gangtok (Rs 35, five hours) between 7 am and 4 pm from its office on Hill Cart Rd, opposite the main bus station.

The buses between Darjeeling and Kathmandu also run through Siliguri and regardless of which company you go with you'll have to change buses here. For further details see the Darjeeling section.

Train From Calcutta, trains go from Sealdah and Howrah to New Jalpaiguri or Siliguri, where you take a bus (or the toy train if it's running) up to the hill station. The *Darjeeling Mail* leaves Sealdah at 7 pm for the 12-hour trip to New Jalpaiguri (566 km, Rs 97/388 in 2nd/1st class).

The *NE Express* is the fastest train between New Jalpaiguri and New Delhi (1628 km, 33 hours). It also goes by Moghulserai (847 km, 19 hours) near Varanasi, and Patna (636 km, 16 hours). This train also links New Jalpaiguri with Gawahati (423 km, 8½ hours).

If the toy train from Siliguri/New Jalpaiguri to Darjeeling is running, it's possible to buy through tickets to Darjeeling all the way from your point of origin. For details on the toy train see the Darjeeling section.

Taxi Share taxis run between Siliguri and Darjeeling for Rs 75, leaving when there are five passengers.

Share taxis between Bagdogra and Darjeeling cost Rs 100 per person and leave when there are five people on board. They take 3½ hours. You can also get taxis from Bagdogra to Kalimpong and Gangtok. A taxi into Siliguri costs Rs 40.

Getting Around

A cycle-rickshaw from New Jalpaiguri Station to Siliguri Junction is about Rs 15.

There are day and overnight services between Siliguri and Calcutta (Rs 109 to Rs 127, 12 hours). Reservations can be made in Darjeeling.

Other destinations to the south include Malda (Rs 36, six hours), Berhampore (Rs 60, seven hours) and Patna (Rs 71 to Rs 105, 12 hours).

For Darjeeling there's a direct bus (Rs 55, 3½ hours) connecting with flights. Ask at the West Bengal tourist office at the airport as taxi drivers try to convince you this doesn't exist. Even the cheapest buses to Darjeeling (Rs 21, 3½ hours) are much faster than the

Buses run this route for Rs 2 and a taxi charges Rs 30.

MIRIK

Being promoted as a 'new' hill station, Mirik is about 50 km from both Siliguri and Darjeeling at an altitude of 1767 metres. The lake is the main attraction here and there's a 3½-km path around it. Mirik is surrounded by tea estates, orange orchards and cardamom plantations.

Accommodation is available at the *Tourist Lodge* with dorm beds for Rs 20 and doubles for Rs 250 in cottages. Cheaper places include *Chandrama Lodge* with doubles from Rs 65 and *Parijat Lodge* with doubles from Rs 120. Buses run to Darjeeling, Kurseong and Siliguri for Rs 14.

KURSEONG

Kurseong is the usual midtrip halting place between Siliguri on the plains and Darjeeling. If you want to overnight there's the *Tourist Lodge* (☎ 409) with doubles for Rs 200 or the much cheaper *Jeet Hotel*.

DARJEELING

Population: 73,000

Straddling a ridge at 2134 metres and surrounded by tea plantations on all sides, Darjeeling has been a very popular hill station since the British established it as an R&R centre for their troops in the mid-1800s. These days people come here to escape from the heat, humidity and hassle of the north Indian plain. You get an indication of how popular Darjeeling is from the 60 or so hotels recognised by the tourist office and the scores of others which don't come up to its requirements. Here you will find yourself surrounded by mountain people from all over the eastern Himalaya who have come to work, to trade or – in the case of the Tibetans – as refugees.

Outside of the monsoon season (June to September) the views over the mountains to the snowy peaks of Kanchenjunga and down to the swollen rivers in the valley bottoms are magnificent. Darjeeling is a fascinating place where you can see Buddhist monasteries, visit a tea plantation and see how the tea is processed, go for a ride on the chairlift (if it's operating), spend days hunting for bargains in colourful markets and handicraft shops, or go trekking to high-altitude spots near the border with Sikkim.

Like many places in the Himalaya, half the fun is in getting there and Darjeeling has the unique attraction of the famous toy train. This miniature train loops and switchbacks its way up the steep mountainsides from New Jalpaiguri to Darjeeling.

History

Until the beginning of the 18th century the whole of the area between the present borders of Sikkim and the plains of Bengal, including Darjeeling and Kalimpong, belonged to the rajas of Sikkim. In 1706 they lost Kalimpong to the Bhutanese, and control of the remainder was wrested from them by the Gurkhas who invaded Sikkim in 1780, following consolidation of the latter's rule in Nepal.

These annexations by the Gurkhas, however, brought them into conflict with the British East India Company. A series of wars were fought between the two parties, eventually leading to the defeat of the Gurkhas and the ceding of all the land they had taken from the Sikkimese to the East India Company. Part of this territory was restored to the rajas of Sikkim and the country's sovereignty guaranteed by the British in return for British control over any disputes which arose with neighbouring states.

One such dispute in 1828 led to the dispatch of two British officers to this area, and it was during their fact-finding tour that they spent some time at Darjeeling (then called Dorje Ling – Place of the Thunderbolt – after the lama who founded the monastery which once stood on Observatory Hill). The officers were quick to appreciate Darjeeling's value as a site for a sanatorium and hill station and as the key to a pass into Nepal and Tibet. The officers' observations were reported to the authorities in Calcutta and a pretext was eventually found to pressure the raja into granting the site to the British in return for an annual stipend of Rs 3000 (raised to Rs 6000 in 1846).

This transfer, however, rankled with the Tibetans who regarded Sikkim as a vassal state. Darjeeling's rapid development as a trading centre and tea-growing area in a key position along the trade route leading from Sikkim to the plains of India began to make a considerable impact on the fortunes of the lamas and leading merchants of Sikkim. Tensions arose and in 1849 two British travellers, Sir Joseph Hooker and Dr Campbell, who were visiting Sikkim with the permission of the raja and the British government, were arrested. Various demands were made as a condition of their release, but the Sikkimese eventually released both prisoners unconditionally about a month later.

In reprisal for the arrests, however, the British annexed the whole of the land between the present borders of Sikkim and the Bengal plains and withdrew the annual Rs 6000 stipend from the raja. The latter was restored to his son, raised to Rs 9000 in 1868 and raised again to Rs 12,000 in 1874.

These annexations brought about a significant change in Darjeeling's status. Previously it had been an enclave within Sikkimese territory and to reach it the British had to pass through a country ruled by an independent raja. After the takeover, Darjeeling became contiguous with British territory further south and Sikkim was cut off from access to the plains except through British territory. This was eventually to lead to the invasion of Sikkim by the Tibetans and the British military expedition to Lhasa.

When the British first arrived in Darjeeling it was almost completely forested and virtually uninhabited, though it had once been a sizeable village before the wars with Bhutan and Nepal. Development was rapid and by 1840 a road had been constructed, numerous houses and a sanatorium built and a hotel opened. By 1857 Darjeeling had a population of some 10,000.

Most of the increase in the population was accounted for by the recruitment of labourers from Nepal, who were brought in to work the tea plantations established in the early 1840s by the British, following the smuggling of tea seeds from China. Even today, the vast majority of people speak Nepali as a first language and the name Darjeeling continues to be synonymous with tea.

The immigration of Nepali-speaking peoples, mainly Gurkhas, into the mountainous areas of West Bengal, was eventually to lead to political problems in the mid-1980s. Resentment had been growing for a number of years among the Gurkhas over what they felt was discrimination against them by the government of West Bengal. Even their language was one of those not recognised by the Indian constitution and, that being so, government jobs were only open to those who could speak Bengali.

The tensions finally came to a head in widespread riots throughout the hill country which continued for some two years and in which hundreds of people lost their lives and thousands were made homeless. Tourism came to a grinding halt, the toy train was put out of action, and the Indian Army was sent in to maintain some semblance of order. The riots were orchestrated by the Gurkha National Liberation Front (GNLF), led by Subash Ghising, which demanded a separate state to be known as Gurkhaland. The Communist Party of India (Marxist) were also responsible for a good deal of the violence since they were afraid of losing the support which they had once enjoyed among the hill peoples.

A compromise was eventually hammered out in late 1988 whereby the Darjeeling Gorkha Hill Council was to be given a large measure of autonomy from the state government and fresh elections to the Council were to be held in December of that year. These resulted in the GNLF gaining 26 of the 28 seats in the Hill Council. Darjeeling remains part of West Bengal but with greater control over its own affairs as a Nepali-language administrative unit within it.

Outbreaks of violence between supporters of the GNLF and the Marxist CPI have all but died out. Even at the height of the troubles these were unlikely to affect travellers,

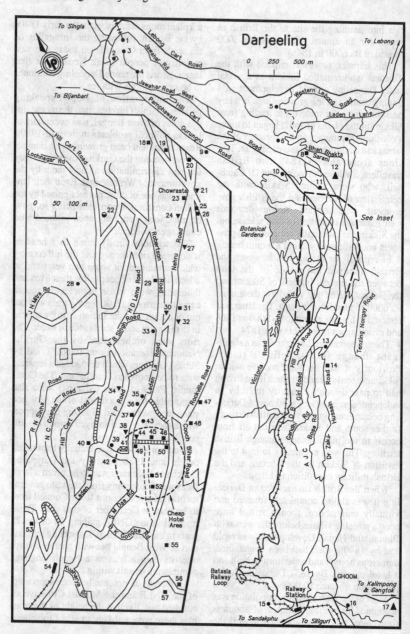

Darjeeling

To Singla
To Lebong

Lebong Cart Road
Jawahar Rd

0   250   500 m

To Bijanbari

Jawahar Road — West
Hill Cart
Pamphawati
Gurungni
Road

Western Lebong Road
Laden La Lane

Lochnagar Rd
Hill Cart Road

18
19
9
20
Chowrasta
23 21
25
24 26
27

Botanical
Gardens

5
6
7
Bhan Bhakta
8 Sarani
10
11
12

See Inset

22

28

0   50   100 m

Robertson Road
H D Lama Road
Nehru Road

29
30 31
33 32

Victoria Road
Sinha Road
Hill Cart Road
Tenzing Norgey Road

13
14

J N Mitra Rd
N B Singi Road
Laden La Road

34
35
36
37
38
40 39 41
42

I P Road
Rockville Road
Cooch Bihar Road

43
44 45 46
49 50
47
48
51
52

R N Sinha Road
N C Goenka Road
Hill Cart Road
Laden La Road
S M Das Rd
B K Gonopa Rd

Gandhi Rd
A J C Bose Rd
Dr Zakir Hussain Road

53
54
55
56
57

Cheap
Hotel
Area

Kutchery
GHOOM

Batasia Railway
Loop

Railway
Station

15
16
17

To Sandakphu
To Siliguri
To Kalimpong
& Gangtok

■ PLACES TO STAY

8	Tourist Lodge, Gymkhana Club & St Andrew's Church
14	Youth Hostel
18	New Elgin Hotel
19	Hotel Alice Villa
20	Windamere Hotel
23	Pineridge Hotel
25	Bellevue Hotel, Tourist Office & Indian Airlines
26	Main Bellevue Hotel
29	Central Hotel
31	Darjeeling Club
37	Shabnam Hotel & Grub Pub
40	Hotel Apsara
45	Hotel Prestige
46	Hotel Springburn
47	Hotels Valentino, Continental & Daffodil
48	Hotels Purnima & Broadway
49	Timber Lodge & Washington Restaurant
50	Hotel Tara
51	Hotel Pagoda
52	Shamrock Hotel
53	Hotels Kadambari & Nirvana
55	Everest Luxury Hotel
56	Hotel Sinclairs
57	Hotel Pradhan

▼ PLACES TO EAT

21	Star Dust Restaurant
24	Glenary's
27	Shangri La Restaurant
30	Kev's (Keventer's Snack Bar)
32	Dekevas Restaurant
34	New Dish Restaurant
38	Himalayan Restaurant
44	Tibetan Restaurants

OTHER

1	Ropeway Station
2	Snow Leopards
3	Himalayan Mountaineering Institute & Museums
4	Zoo
5	Tibetan Refugee Centre
6	Raj Bhavan
7	Bhutia Busty Monastery
9	Happy Valley Tea Estate
10	District Commissioner's Office
11	Natural History Museum
12	Observatory Hill
13	TV Tower
15	Ghoom Monastery
16	Monastery
17	Tiger Hill
22	Buses to Kalimpong & Siliguri
28	Market
33	Taxi Stand
35	ANZ Grindlays Bank
36	Foreigner's Registration Office
39	Buses to Gangtok (Sikkim Nationalised Transport)
41	GPO
42	Kathmandu Bus Agents
43	State Bank of India
54	Railway Station

although local tourists stayed away. It now looks as if the peace will hold and things have returned to normal in Darjeeling.

Climate

For mountain views, the best time to visit Darjeeling is from mid-September to mid-December, although it gets pretty cold by December. The season resumes around mid-March and continues to mid-June but as the haze builds up the views become less clear. During the monsoon months (June to September) clouds obscure the mountains and the rain is often so heavy that whole sections of the road from the plains are washed away,

though the town is rarely cut off for more than a few days at a time.

Average temperatures range from 8.5°C to 15°C in summer and from 1.5°C to 6°C in winter. It can get very cold indeed in winter, a real surprise if you've just come from Calcutta. If you go there during the monsoon an umbrella – available cheaply in the market – is essential.

People

Although the Buddhists, with their monasteries at Ghoom and Darjeeling, are perhaps the most conspicuous religious group, they constitute only a minority of the population – about 14%. The majority of the inhabitants

Darjeeling in the Monsoon

Those same clouds that obscure the distant crests and vales hover over the very ground one walks on. Making my way through this haze made me feel like an angel, or Enoch at the very least. No wonder the otherworldly is so inexorably intertwined with the real world in this part of the globe. But the best news for the budget traveller is that, because the monsoon season is low season, prices are automatically cut in half.

Sharon Packer, USA

are Hindus, reflecting their origins in the northern Indian states and Nepal. Christians and Muslims comprise little more than 3% each of the district's total population, though there are numerous churches scattered around Darjeeling dating mostly from the British period.

Orientation

Darjeeling sprawls over a west-facing ridge, spilling down the hillside in a complicated series of interconnecting roads and flights of steps. Hill Cart Rd has been renamed Tenzing Norgay Rd (even though there's already another road by the same name in Darjeeling) but the old name seems to stick. It's the main road through the lower part of the town, and the railway station and the bus and taxi stand are all on it. The most important route connecting this road with Chowrasta (the 'town square') at the top of the ridge is Laden La Rd and Nehru Rd. The Youth Hostel is further back up the ridge, virtually at the high point.

Along these two roads are a fair number of budget hotels and cheap restaurants, the GPO, the bus stations for Sikkim and Kathmandu, the Foreigners' Registration Office, the State Bank of India, curio shops and photographic supply shops. At the Chowrasta end of Nehru Rd and on Gandhi Rd above Laden La Rd are many of the mid-range hotels and restaurants. The bulk of the top-range hotels are clustered around Observatory Hill beyond Chowrasta. There are others along Dr Zakir Hussain Rd and A J C Bose Rd.

Information

Tourist Office The tourist office (☎ 2050) is below the Bellevue Hotel, Chowrasta. They

are helpful and have reasonably up-to-date pamphlets and a map of Darjeeling for Rs 5. They run a bus to Bagdogra airport for Rs 55, which leaves the Tourist Lodge at 8 am daily. Buy tickets in advance. The office is open from 10 am to 4.30 daily except Sunday.

Money The State Bank of India on Laden La Rd is the usual place to change money but there's also a branch of ANZ Grindlays very close by.

Post & Telecommunications The GPO is on Laden La Rd and the telegraph office is on Gandhi Rd.

Permits The Foreigners' Registration Office is on Laden La Rd. To get a 15-day permit for Sikkim you must first visit the Deputy Commissioner's Office, otherwise known as the 'DM' (District Magistrate). Then get an endorsement from the Foreigners' Registration Office and return to the DM to collect your permit. You should be able to get a permit in a few hours but one traveller reported having to wait five days.

Bookshops The Oxford Book & Stationery Company on Chowrasta is the best bookshop here.

Trekking Equipment Trekking gear can be hired from the Youth Hostel, but you must leave a deposit to cover the value of the articles you borrow (deposits returnable, less hire charges, on return of the equipment). Typical charges per day are: sleeping bag Rs 3, rucksack Rs 3, boots Rs 5, jacket Rs 3 and two-person tent Rs 20. The hostel keeps an interesting book in which trekkers write comments about the routes, and the very helpful Moni Rai Chhetri, who helps out here, has all the latest information.

Darjeeling Gorkha Hill Council Tourism also rents out gear for similar prices – contact the tourist office. There are a number of trekking agencies, including Trek Mate on Nehru Rd and U-Trek on N B Singh Rd, which have been recommended. Their gear is more expensive but some of it is good quality.

Tiger Hill

The highest spot in the area at 2590 metres, Tiger Hill is near Ghoom, about 11 km from Darjeeling. The hill is famous for its magnificent dawn views over Kanchenjunga and other eastern Himalayan peaks. On a clear day even Mt Everest is visible.

Every morning a large convoy of battered Land Rovers leaves Darjeeling at 4.30 am, which means that in the smaller lodges you get woken up at this time every day, whether you like it or not. A seat costs Rs 30 for the return trip. It can be very cold and very crowded at the top but coffee is available. There's a view tower and entry costs Rs 2 for the top or Rs 7 for the warmer VIP lounge. Halfway down the hill a temple priest causes a massive traffic jam by anointing the steering-wheel of each vehicle for the return trip!

The *Tourist Lodge* nearby closed during the disturbances but may be reopened soon – check with the tourist office. If it is, a pleasant excursion is to walk to the lodge from Darjeeling; it takes about two hours and there are several monasteries along the way. Next morning, after the sunrise view, you can walk to Ghoom station and catch the toy train back to Darjeeling. If you can't leave your gear elsewhere in Darjeeling the tourist office will look after it for you.

Senchal Lake

Close to Tiger Hill is Senchal Lake, which supplies Darjeeling with its domestic water. It's a particularly scenic area and popular as a picnic spot with Indian holiday-makers.

Kanchenjunga

At 8598 metres this is the world's third-highest mountain. From Darjeeling, the best uninterrupted views are to be had from Bhan Bhakta Sarani. From Chowrasta, take the road to the right-hand side of the Windamere Hotel and continue about 300 metres.

Ghoom Buddhist Monastery

This is probably the most famous monastery in Darjeeling and is about eight km from town, just below Hill Cart Rd and the railway station near Ghoom. It enshrines an image of the Maitreya Buddha (the coming Buddha). Foreigners are allowed to enter the shrine and take photographs. A small donation is customary and the monks are very friendly.

There is another monastery nearby in Ghoom itself and half an hour (by bus) further down the road to Siliguri is Sonada with a large and interesting monastery of the Kagyupa sect.

Aloobari Monastery

Nearer Darjeeling, on Tenzing Norgay Rd, this monastery welcomes visitors and the monks often sell Tibetan and Sikkimese handicrafts and religious objects (usually hand bells). If the monastery is closed ask at the cottage next door and they'll let you in.

Observatory Hill

Situated above the Windamere Hotel this viewpoint is sacred to both Hindus and Buddhists. There's a Kali shrine here and the multicoloured prayer flags double as trapezes for the monkeys. Watch out for them as they can be aggressive.

Bhutia Busty Monastery

Not far from Chowrasta is this colourful monastery, with Kanchenjunga providing a spectacular backdrop. Originally a branch of the Nygmapa sect's Phodang Monastery in Sikkim, it was transferred to Darjeeling in 1879. The shrine here originally stood on Observatory Hill. There's an old library of Buddhist texts upstairs.

Dhirdham Temple

The most conspicuous Hindu temple in Darjeeling, this is just below the railway station and is modelled on the famous Pashupatinath Temple in Kathmandu.

Natural History Museum

Established in 1903, a comprehensive but dusty collection of Himalayan and Bengali fauna is packed into this interesting museum. Amongst the 4300 specimens is the estuarine crocodile, the animal responsible for the greatest loss of human life in Asia. The museum is open daily from 10 am to 4 pm, but closes early on Wednesday at 1 pm. Entry is Rs 1.

Zoological Park

Conditions for some of the animals here are barely tolerable, made worse by the fact that they have no escape from the Indian male tourists who show off by teasing them mercilessly. The zoo houses India's only collection of Siberian tigers, and some rare species, such as the red panda. It's open daily from 8 am to 4 pm; entry is Rs 1.

Himalayan Mountaineering Institute & Museums

Entered through the zoo, on Jawahar Rd West about two km from the town, the HMI runs courses to train mountaineers. There are a couple of interesting museums here. The **Mountaineering Museum** contains a collection of historic mountaineering equipment, specimens of Himalayan flora and fauna (though not one of the Abominable Snowman!) and a relief model of the Himalaya. The **Everest Museum** next door traces the history of attempts on the great peak.

Sherpa Tenzing Norgay, who conquered Everest with Edmund Hillary in 1953, lived in Darjeeling and was the director of the Institute for many years. He died in 1986 and his statue now stands beside his cremation spot just above the Institute.

There are film shows at the Institute and for Rs 1 (minimum 10 people) you can view Kanchenjunga close up through a Zeiss telescope given to a Nepalese maharaja by Adolf Hitler.

The institute is open from 9 am to 1 pm and 2 to 4.30 pm and entry costs Rs 0.50. There's a reasonable vegetarian restaurant by Sherpa Tenzing's statue.

Snow Leopard Breeding Programme

In contrast to the animals in the rest of the zoo the snow leopards are kept in a large separate enclosure on the way to the ropeway. These rare animals are reputedly less keen to breed in captivity than the panda (whose disinterest in sex is legendary) but they've had some success here. Much credit must be given to the devoted attentions of Kiran Moktan who runs the programme and spends his days with the leopards. He welcomes interested visitors between 9 and 11 am, and from 2 to 4 pm, but you should not make too much noise. Ask to see his drawings as he's an accomplished artist.

Passenger Ropeway

At North Point, about three km from town, this was the first passenger ropeway to be constructed in India. It is five km long and connects Darjeeling with Singla Bazaar on the Little Ranjit River at the bottom of the valley. If the full route is open, this is a superb excursion, though not one for vertigo sufferers. However, the power problems in Darjeeling have meant that for some years only the first two km of the route has been operational. A return trip (including insurance and a very necessary standby generator!) is Rs 30. It's open from 8 am to 3.30 pm but closed on Sundays and holidays. You can phone to check it's running (☎ 2731).

Botanical Gardens

Below the bus and taxi stand near the market, these gardens contain a representative collection of Himalayan plants, flowers and orchids. The hothouses are well worth a visit. The gardens are open between 6 am and 5 pm; entrance is free.

Tibetan Refugee Self-Help Centre

A 20 to 30-minute walk from Chowrasta brings you down to this Tibetan centre. It was established in October 1959 to help rehabilitate Tibetan refugees who fled from Tibet with the Dalai Lama following the Chinese invasion. Religious importance is attached to this place, as the 13th Dalai Lama (the present is the 14th) stayed here during his visit to India in 1919-22. The centre produces superb carpets, woollens, woodcarvings and leatherwork, and has various Tibetan curios for sale (coins, banknotes, jewellery, etc).

You can wander at leisure through the workshops and watch the work in progress. The weaving and dyeing shops and the woodcarving shop are particularly interesting and the people who work there are very friendly. Their prices, however, are on a par with those in the curio shops of Chowrasta and Nehru Rd. It's an interesting place to visit even apart from the workshops, and the views are magnificent.

Tea Plantations

Tea is, of course, Darjeeling's most famous export. From its 78 gardens, employing over 40,000 people, it produces the bulk of West Bengal's crop, which is almost a quarter of India's total.

The most convenient garden to visit is the Happy Valley Tea Estate, only two km from the centre of town, where tea is still produced by the 'orthodox' method as opposed to the 'Curling, Tearing and Crushing' (CTC) method adopted on the plains. However, it's only worth going when plucking is in progress (April to November) because it's only then that the processing takes place. It's open daily from 8 am to noon and between 1 and 4.30 pm except on Mondays and Sunday afternoons.

If you're buying tea, Golden Flowery Orange Pekoe (unbroken leaves) is the top quality.

Gymkhana Club

Membership of the Darjeeling Gymkhana

Producing the World's Best Tea

Tea from some of the estates in the Darjeeling area is very high quality, attracting the highest prices at auction. Although the climatic conditions are just right for producing fine tea bushes, the final result is dependent on a complex drying process.

After picking, the fresh green leaves are placed 15 to 25 cm deep in a 'withering trough' where the moisture content is reduced from 70% to 80% down to 30% to 40% using high-velocity fans. When this is complete the withered leaves are rolled and pressed to break the cell walls and express their juices onto the surface of the leaves. Normally two rollings at different pressures are undertaken, and in between rolls the leaves are sifted to separate the coarse from the fine. Next the leaves, coated with their juices, are allowed to ferment on racks in a high-humidity room, a process which develops their characteristic aroma and flavour. This fermentation must be controlled carefully since either over or under-fermentation will ruin the tea.

The process is stopped by passing the fermenting leaves through a dry air chamber at 115°C to 120°C on a conveyer belt to further reduce the moisture content to around 2% to 3%. The last process is the sorting of the tea into grades. In their order of value they are: Golden Flowery Orange Pekoe (unbroken leaves), Golden Broken Orange Pekoe, Orange Fannings and Dust (the latter three consisting of broken leaves).

In the last few years modern agricultural practices have been brought to the tea estates to maintain and improve their viability. They were one of the first agricultural enterprises to use clonal plants in their replanting schemes, though very little of this has been done and most of the tea trees are at least 100 years old and nearing the end of their useful or even natural lives. The ageing plants and deteriorating soil causes grave concern since tea is not only a major export item but also provides much employment in the area.

Although the auction prices for the lower qualities of tea are often disappointing for producers, the top qualities continue to achieve record prices. At an auction in 1991, tea from the Castleton Estate in Darjeeling went to a Japanese bidder for Rs 6010 (US$275) per kg – a world record! ■

Club costs just Rs 15 per day but the activities here are not equestrian. The word gymkhana is actually derived from the Hindi *gendkhana* meaning ball-house. Ball games on offer here include tennis (mornings only, Rs 5 racquet hire), squash, badminton, table tennis, billiards and roller skating.

The club must have been magnificent when it was the playground of the Raj. Partly occupied by the army since the disturbances, it's an impressive place with large panelled rooms and a grand ballroom. Not much dusting's been done since the British left in 1948 and any old members would say the place has definitely gone to seed. In the billiard room extension, donated by the Maharaja of Cooch Behar in 1918, there's now a poster of Marilyn Monroe!

Other Activities

Beware of the pony-wallahs who congregate in Chowrasta. They'll come along with you as a guide and at the end you'll find you're paying for a second pony and for their guiding time! Usual charge is around Rs 20 an hour, but make sure of the price first.

The video craze has hit India everywhere, particularly in Darjeeling and some other hill stations. Lots of places have set themselves up as mini-cinemas; a blackboard outside indicates what's showing. Often it's Western films that would have had trouble getting by the censor in the old days.

In the autumn and spring you could go to the races. A lap round Lebong racecourse may only be 440 metres but it's the world's highest racecourse, at 1809 metres above sea level.

Three-month courses in Tibetan language are offered by the Manjushree Centre of Tibetan Culture at 8 Burdwan Rd.

Organised Tours

The tourist office offers a sunrise trip to Tiger Hill which leaves daily at 4.30 am. Tickets are Rs 40 and must be booked in advance. Most people go with the independent operators who charge a little less and some send a runner to your hotel to make sure you get up! Depending on demand, the tourist office also organises a local sightseeing tour (Rs 40), a trip to Mirik (Rs 75) and a two-day tour to Kalimpong and Gangtok (Rs 255).

There are numerous travel agents and tour operators. Jupiter Tours & Travels (☎ 2625), near the clock tower on Laden La Rd, seems to be reliable and also organises trips to Gangtok.

Places to Stay

There are a great number of places to stay in Darjeeling. Those that follow are only a limited selection. Prices vary widely with the season; as far as possible those listed are for the high season (15 March to 15 July and 15 September to 15 November). In the low season prices drop by 50% to 75% and discounts are open to negotiation.

The infrastructure suffered greatly during the disturbances and there are now not only frequent power cuts in Darjeeling but often severe water shortages as well. It's worth asking the other guests about the water situation before checking in at a hotel.

Places to Stay – bottom end

For cheap accommodation and the best views in Darjeeling many travellers head for the area around the Youth Hostel and TV tower. It's about 15 minutes from the railway station; you simply walk straight up the hill.

The *Youth Hostel* (☎ 2290), above Dr Zakir Hussain Rd right on the top of the ridge, used to be very popular with budget travellers. Unfortunately it's now pretty run down, having been starved of funds in recent years. However, the people who run it are very friendly and informative about trekking in this region and the views up here are great. With dorm beds at Rs 20 for nonmembers (Rs 10 for members) and a couple of doubles (Rs 40) it's still worth checking out as it may have been done up.

If you don't fancy the YH, right opposite is the excellent *Triveni Guest House*, well run by a friendly family. There are dorm beds for Rs 25 and doubles for Rs 60 with common bathroom. Below it is *Nabin Lodge* with doubles from Rs 60 and a tiny sign that's easy to miss. It's a bit spartan and can be cold as it's on the shadowed side of the ridge, but it's good value.

Back up on the road between the YH and the TV tower is the recommended *Aliment Restaurant & Hotel*, a great restaurant with a few clean doubles at Rs 60. The friendly manager just can't do enough for you. On the same road, but nearer the TV tower, there's *Lodge Cryptomeria*. It's another good small place, offering beds at Rs 25 each in spotless doubles and triples. Hot water is Rs 3 a bucket.

From the TV tower, the road over the ridge brings you to the popular *Hotel Tower View B&B*. Doubles with attached bathroom are Rs 80 including hot water in buckets, and there's a four-bedded room with a great view for Rs 220. The food here is good and the management very helpful. A little further down this road is the appropriately named *View Point Lodging*. Doubles and triples here are Rs 79/105.

Just beyond the post office there is a whole cluster of cheap hotels either on Laden La Rd or on the alleys and steps running off it. The *Shabnam Hotel* has some basic doubles for Rs 80. Take the stone steps uphill just beyond the post office and on the right is the *Timber Lodge*. It's decrepit and hardly a bargain at Rs 50 for a dorm bed! Much better value is the popular *Hotel Prestige* (☎ 2699) further up the steps. It offers clean, carpeted rooms with bathroom and geyser (hot water) for Rs 100/120 for singles/doubles. Kerosene heaters are available on request (for an extra charge), the staff are very friendly and there are good views.

At the top of the steps and left a few metres along Nehru Rd is the tatty *Hotel Spring-burn*, which is OK for a short stay. Nearby is the *Hotel Tara*, similarly tatty and more expensive but run by friendly Tibetans.

If you turn right after the Timber Lodge you reach the *Shamrock Hotel*, similar in price, quality and popularity to the Prestige. The upstairs rooms are more expensive (Rs 120 for a double) than the downstairs ones, but this Tibetan-run place is very friendly and well kept and there is a fire at night in winter. Hot water is heated in buckets by

immersion heater in your room. Travellers who have failed to turn off the mains before testing the water have had electric shocks! The smarter-looking *Hotel Pagoda* next door is not as good.

Going up in price a little, there's another collection of hotels above the taxi stand on Nehru Rd, including the *Hotel Crystal, Holiday Home, Kundus, Shree Anapurna*; and the *Capital*, which has doubles from Rs 125. There's not too much to choose between them and they're all similar in price but the views from the front rooms are definitely superior to those from the hotels further down the hill off Laden La Rd.

Further up the hill from this cluster on Rockville Rd is another group of Indian holiday hotels which includes the *Purnima, Broadway, La Bella, Ashoka, Rock Ville, Continental* and *Daffodil*. The Hotel Purnima, for example, charges Rs 180 to Rs 330 a double. The rooms have a bathroom and hot water and the hotel has its own restaurant. There are no singles. The flashy Rock Ville has some nice doubles from Rs 250 and is full of incomprehensible notices like '201 – I am the unseen guest of this hotel'!

Further away from this area along Nehru Rd are a number of other places. The *Everest Luxury Hotel* is anything but luxurious though it does have good views. Nearby, the fairly modern *Hotel Pradhan* is overpriced at Rs 250 for a double with bathroom.

Places to Stay – middle

An old favourite in this price bracket is the excellent *Bellevue Hotel* (☎ 2221) right on Chowrasta. It's very well kept and run by a friendly Tibetan family. There are no singles but a variety of doubles and triples are available at Rs 250 to Rs 450, all with bathroom and hot water. Room 49 has the best views and also has a separate sitting room. The hotel has its own cafe for snacks and breakfast, overlooking Chowrasta. New heaters have been installed in most rooms and the sitting room, a must in the cold season.

Independently run by a member of the same Tibetan family is the confusingly named *Main Bellevue Hotel*, just above the other Bellevue. It's quieter and in an old building with doubles with attached bathrooms for Rs 350.

Back down Nehru Rd there's a couple of restaurants which also have a few rooms. The *Shangri La* has three good doubles at Rs 450, with nice views and log fires in the bedrooms. Dekevas Restaurant runs the *Hotel Dekeling* (☎ 3459). It's another friendly Tibetan place, with eight rooms ranging from Rs 200 to Rs 500, most with views.

Opposite the Bellevue is the large *Pineridge Hotel* with doubles for Rs 310 and triples for Rs 395. All rooms have attached bathrooms.

Back on Laden La Rd is the overpriced *Hotel Apsara*, another typical Indian boarding house with doubles from Rs 350.

The *Hotel Alice Villa* offers singles/doubles for Rs 590/720 including breakfast and dinner. Outside the main season you can get a room without meals here for as little as Rs 120/150. A few of the rooms have fireplaces and there's a new extension.

West Bengal Tourism's *Tourist Lodge* is quite some way from the centre past Loreto College and next to the Gymkhana Club. Doubles with attached bathroom are Rs 300 to Rs 450 which includes breakfast and dinner. There are no reductions if you don't want to eat here. The rooms are OK and there are good views from the garden but it's nothing special. The Tourist Corporation also runs the *Tourist Lodge* at Tiger Hill near Ghoom. This has been closed for a while but may reopen. Advance booking was always essential.

Run by a Calcutta-based Chinese family, the *Hotel Valentino* (☎ 2228), on Rockville Rd, offers some of the best views in Darjeeling. Doubles here are Rs 600, including early-morning tea and breakfast. All rooms have a bathroom, hot water and optional heating. The hotel has its own bar and Chinese restaurant (one of the best in town).

Hotel Sinclairs (☎ 3431) at 18/1 Nehru Rd looks fairly run down outside and is nothing special inside. Singles/doubles cost Rs

395/625 or Rs 750/1175 including meals. All the rooms have bathroom, hot water and central heating. There's a restaurant and bar and the hotel has its own generator.

Along the road opposite the GPO is the flashy new *Hotel Chancellor*, a concrete block with singles/doubles for Rs 800/1000 with attached bathrooms. All meals are included and the staff is friendly.

Down the hill towards the market the *Central Hotel* (☎ 2033), Robertson Rd, has singles/doubles for Rs 750/1100 but this includes all meals. Without them a double is about Rs 600. Rooms have a bathroom and hot water and the doubles also have a sitting room with a fireplace. The hotel has its own bar and a restaurant with good Indian food.

Better value than the Central is the *New Elgin Hotel* (2182), off Robertson Rd, which is a delightful old place with resident labrador and pictures of the queen on the walls. The staff are friendly, singles/doubles cost Rs 750/1050 with food and doubles are Rs 660 without. The older rooms have fireplaces and fuel for them costs Rs 60. The other rooms have optional heating. It also has a popular bar, restaurant and garden/patio.

The *Darjeeling Club* above Nehru Rd was the Tea Planters' Club in the days of the Raj. You can get a suite here for Rs 500/600 or Rs 600/700 with a fire in the bedroom (buckets of coal are Rs 50). The upstairs suites are very pleasant but the cheaper rooms downstairs at Rs 400/500 are dark, overpriced and not recommended. There's a billiard room, a musty library, plenty of memorabilia and lots of nice sitting areas. The restaurant is only for residents.

Places to Stay – top end

There's no question about which is the best place to stay in Darjeeling – it's the *Windamere Hotel* (☎ 2841), on the slopes of Observatory Hill. This is one of the oldest established hotels here and a gem of a left-over from the Raj. It's set in beautifully maintained gardens and consists of a main block with detached cottages and dining room, and is for all lovers of nostalgia. The hotel, owned since the 1920s by Mrs Tenduf-

La, a Tibetan lady now in her mid-80s, describes its attitude to hotel management as defying 'fashion and the cramping dictates of an "amusement" industry which sees personalised service as an obsolete indulgence'.

The service is indeed excellent and the hotel is also characterised by its policy of deliberately side-stepping modern indulgences like TVs and central heating. There are, however, fires in almost every room and hot water bottles should you require them. There's a library and a bar, and a string quartet entertains you during dinner. Rooms cost US$50 a single, US$80 a double, and suites are US$90. The prices include all meals, which are excellent.

Places to Eat

If you're staying at the Youth Hostel and don't want to make the trek into town, the *Aliment Restaurant* (just down the road towards the TV tower) is very clean and has good food. Veg chow mein is Rs 12 and the excellent Tibetan bread is Rs 6. Opposite the *Ratna Restaurant* is not so good but is cheaper with veg momos at Rs 4 a plate.

There are numerous cheap restaurants along Laden La Rd all clustered together between the State Bank of India and the post office. Several of them are Tibetan-run while the remainder offer Indian cuisine of various sorts. It's probably unfair to make any particular recommendations since they're all pretty similar and everyone has their own favourite but some of them are definitely in need of a good scrub-down. Take your pick.

They include the *Grub Pub* at the Shabnam Hotel, *Cafe Himalaya* nearby for good Tibetan food, the *Golden Dragon, Vineet, Utsang, Potala, Lotus, Lhasa, Penang, Delhi, Soatlee, Washington* and *Beni's*. Opposite the Hotel Capital is the *Dafey Munal Restaurant* which offers 'chocolate pudding with fire'! .

Start the day with an excellent breakfast and great views on the terrace at *Kev's* (Keventer's Snack Bar). They've got ham, bacon, sausages, cheese, and other unusual delicacies from their own farm. Bacon or sausages and eggs cost Rs 25; service can be slow.

Across the road, on Nehru Rd overlooking the small square, is the *Dekevas Restaurant*. It's a neat, clean, shiny little place with good pizzas for up to Rs 22. They have other food in the same price bracket and also do breakfasts. Service isn't great here either but it's as popular with travellers as Kev's.

A short walk up the hill brings you to *Glenary's*, an excellent place with a definite ghost-of-the-Raj air to it. Tea time here is still an occasion that calls for freshly starched table linen. Prices are very reasonable and Darjeeling tea is Rs 5 per person. Everyone is given a large teapot – the amount of tea in it varies according to the order. You can also have full meals here (main dishes are Rs 25 to Rs 35) but the restaurant closes at 7 pm. It's licensed and beer is Rs 28, sweet red Golconda wine Rs 10 a glass. Downstairs is the bakery where, if you arrive early enough, you can get excellent brown bread. Their doughnuts (Rs 4) are legendary and they have a range of cakes (cherry, Madeira, Dundee) from Rs 27. You can also buy Kalimpong cheese here.

Nearby is the *Shangri La Restaurant* which offers Indian and Chinese food. Main dishes are between Rs 25 and Rs 40, and the restaurant has a log fire on winter evenings.

On Chowrasta itself the *Star Dust Restaurant* is an open-air restaurant offering south Indian vegetarian snacks. It's a good place to sit and watch the activity on the square and there are masala dosas for Rs 9 and espresso coffee for Rs 4. Also on Chowrasta is the *Golden Orchid* which does good egg rolls for Rs 5.

The best Chinese food is at the *New Embassy Chinese Restaurant* in the Hotel Valentino. Main dishes are Rs 30 to Rs 42, beer is Rs 30 and they don't let anyone in after 7 pm. Better value for an evening out is the *New Elgin Hotel* where set dinners are Rs 75. The food is good and the daily menu features such eclectic dishes as cream of cherry soup (delicious)!

For a real splurge you can't beat dinner at the *Windamere Hotel* but, if you are a nonresident, you must book in advance since they usually cater only for their guests. It's a set menu which costs US$9 and features four courses and coffee. A string quartet plays during dinner and afterwards you can retire to the library for a brandy (US$1.50) or a Johnny Walker Black Label (US$5) by the fire.

Things to Buy

Curio Shops The majority of these are on Chowrasta and along Nehru Rd. All things Himalayan are sold here – thankas, brass statues, religious objects, jewellery, wood-carvings, woven fabrics, carpets, etc – but if you're looking for bargains you have to shop judiciously and be prepared to spend plenty of time looking. Thankas in particular are nowhere near the quality of 10 years ago. They may look impressive at first sight, but on closer inspection you will find that little care has been taken over the finer detail. The brocade surroundings (said to originate from China) are often of much finer quality.

If you're looking for bronze statues, the real goodies are kept under the counter and cost in multiples of US$100! You have to indicate that you are not interested in the mass-produced stuff on display before they get the better ones out.

Woodcarvings tend to be excellent value for money. Most of the shops accept international credit cards. There is also a market off Hill Cart Rd next to the bus and taxi stands. Here you can find excellent and relatively cheap patterned woollen sweaters. If you need an umbrella these can be bought here cheaply. Made out of bamboo, they are collectors' items themselves!

For Tibetan carpets, the cheapest place in the area is at Hayden Hall, opposite the State Bank of India on Laden La Rd. It's a women's co-operative, excellent value and well worth checking out.

West Bengal's Manjusha Emporium, on Nehru Rd, is a fixed-price shop selling Himalayan handicrafts, silk and handloomed products. About two km from town on the way to Ghoom is the Ava Art Gallery, featur-

ing embroidered pictures done by the owner. Entry is Rs 0.25 and the pictures are for sale.

Getting There & Away

Air The nearest airport is 90 km away at Bagdogra down on the plains near Siliguri. See the Siliguri section for details.

Indian Airlines (☎ 2355) is in the Bellevue Hotel at Chowrasta and is open Monday to Saturday from 10 am to 1 pm and from 2 to 4 pm. On Sundays it is open from 10 am to 1 pm. The airport bus departs from the Tourist Lodge.

Bus Most of the buses from Darjeeling depart from the Bazaar bus stand (Hill Cart Rd). Most jeeps and taxis depart from the taxi stand, at Robertson Rd/Laden La Rd. There are many different companies operating buses, jeeps and taxis. Buses to Calcutta, Kathmandu and other points further afield generally go through Siliguri.

New Jalpaiguri/Siliguri There are numerous buses, jeeps and taxis in either direction daily between 6 am and 10 pm. The journey takes 3½ to 4½ hours by bus (sometimes less) and costs Rs 21 or Rs 32 for the express bus. A share taxi costs Rs 75 per person.

Bagdogra West Bengal Tourism buses connect with the arrival of flights from Calcutta and New Delhi. The fare is Rs 55 and the journey takes 3½ hours including a 15-minute stop at Kurseong for refreshments. In the opposite direction, they depart from the Tourist Lodge in Darjeeling at 8 am daily and also pick up from Alice Villa Hotel (below the Windamere) and the taxi stand. Buses from Darjeeling must be booked in advance at the tourist office.

Kalimpong Land Rovers, taxis and buses make this 2½-hour trip regularly. Land Rovers cost Rs 35 per person, taxis Rs 30 and are so much more convenient than the buses that they're worth the extra expense. Land Rovers and buses go from the Bazaar bus stand, taxis from the Robertson Rd/Laden La taxi stand.

Gangtok If you don't want to go by taxi or jeep, there is only one bus line to Gangtok. This is run by Sikkim Nationalised Transport (SNT), which has its Darjeeling office in the first building below the GPO on Laden La Rd. There is one minibus daily (Rs 50, seven hours) in either direction, and as there are few seats available, early booking is essential.

If you don't fancy the cramped conditions of the public bus then get a group together and hire a taxi. Your permit will be inspected before you cross the bridge at Rangpo, and at Rangpo itself you will have to visit the police station to fill in the visitors' book. On the way out your permit will be collected at Rangpo.

Kathmandu There are several companies which operate daily buses between Darjeeling and Kathmandu but the main ones are Assam Valley Tours & Travels, opposite the post office, and Mahendra Tours (☎ 3245) on Laden La Rd above the main block of budget restaurants. Neither of these companies runs direct buses and you have to change at Siliguri.

The usual arrangement is that the agents will sell you a ticket as far as Siliguri (Rs 21) but guarantee you a seat on the connecting bus with the same agency (for which you pay a further Rs 200 on average). You arrive at the border around 3 pm (Kakarbhitta is the name of the town on the Nepalese side), leave again around 4 pm and arrive in Kathmandu around 9 or 10 am the next day.

It's almost as easy to get from Darjeeling to Kathmandu on your own though it involves four changes – bus from Darjeeling to Siliguri (Rs 21), bus (Rs 5) or jeep (Rs 15) from Siliguri to Panitanki on the border, rickshaw across the border to Kakarbhitta (Rs 3), bus from Kakarbhitta to Kathmandu (Nepalese Rs 250). This is cheaper than the package deal, you get a choice of buses from the border, plus you have the option of travelling during the day and overnighting along the way. There are day buses from Kakarbhitta that go to a number of other towns on the Nepalese *terai* (plains) including Janakpur (NRs 90), and night buses direct to Pokhara (NRs 250).

A more comfortable alternative is to take the bus from the border as far as Biratnagar where there are several flights daily to Kathmandu (US$77).

There is no Nepalese consulate in Darjeeling; the nearest one is in Calcutta, but visas are available at the border for US$20 (which must be paid in cash), and these can be extended in Kathmandu.

Once in Nepal, buses travel west as far as Narayanghat on the Mahendra Highway, skirting the foothills and passing a number of interesting places and sights on the terai; from Narayanghat the road climbs through the Siwalik Hills to Mugling and the Trisuli River valley where you double back towards Kathmandu. If it isn't too hot, consider travelling by day, so you can see the sights and stop in Janakpur and/or the Royal Chitwan National Park.

Avalanches and floods can sometimes delay the bus. One traveller was held up for three days. The road is in very poor condition in the vicinity of the Kosi Barrage and there's another very bad section on the Prithvi Highway (the Pokhara to Kathmandu road) between Mugling and Kathmandu. Many travellers consider it one of the roughest bus journeys on the subcontinent!

Other Places Deluxe buses are also available to Calcutta, Patna, Gawahati, Shillong, Silchar and Agartala.

Train New Jalpaiguri/Siliguri is the railhead for all trains other than the narrow-gauge toy train. See the Siliguri section for rail details to or from Calcutta and other centres. If the toy train is operating, you can make reservations at the Darjeeling station for trains out of New Jalpaiguri.

Although a bus or taxi is the fastest means of getting from New Jalpaiguri or Siliguri to Darjeeling, the most interesting way of doing this last stage of the journey is to take the toy train – if it's working – though this will take at least twice as long – up to 10 hours.

Watch out for 'officials' on the Calcutta

train who sell you invalid tickets for the toy train and others who tell you it isn't running (on the rare occasions that it is) and get you to buy bus tickets.

Toy Train The journey to Darjeeling from New Jalpaiguri or Siliguri on the famous miniature railway is a superb experience which shouldn't be missed.

Unfortunately, in recent years it seems to have become more of a toy and less of a reliable form of transport. Services on the toy train line were discontinued in 1986 because of the political troubles which plagued the hill country area, and subsequent landslides appeared to have sealed its fate. Following the political accommodation between the GNLF and the West Bengal government, however, major repairs began on the line and it is now running between Darjeeling and Ghoom. The whole route to New Jalpaiguri should be operational in the near future; check before you go.

If the train is running there should be two or three departures daily (and sometimes more) in either direction though departure times from New Jalpaiguri don't necessarily follow the official timetable (though they may from Darjeeling). The journey takes 8½ to 10 hours and you stop en route long enough to grab something to eat. If you can't face the whole trip, you can simply make the short excursion between Ghoom and Darjeeling. If you walk up to Tiger Hill, near Ghoom, to watch the Himalayan dawn, you can ride the toy train back.

TREKKING IN THE DARJEELING REGION

The best months to trek in this region are April, May, October and November. There may be occasional showers during April and May but, in a way, this is the best time to go as many shrubs are in flower, particularly the rhododendrons. There may be occasional rains during the first half of October if the monsoon is prolonged. November is generally dry and visibility is excellent during the first half of December, though it's usually cold by then. After the middle of December there are occasional snowfalls.

In planning what clothes to take, bear in mind that you will be passing through valley bottoms as low as 300 metres and over mountain ridges as high as 4000 metres, so you'll need clothing for low, tropical climates and high mountain passes. No matter what time of year you go, it's a good idea to take a light raincoat which can be folded up and put inside your rucksack since the weather can be unpredictable, particularly at high altitudes. Another tip is to wear one thin pair of socks within a thicker pair and you'll get fewer blisters.

Darjeeling Toy Train

Until the late 1800s, all supplies for Darjeeling and all exports from the town had to be transported by bullock cart along the Siliguri road. This road, known as the Hill Cart Rd (although recently renamed to commemorate Tenzing Norgay), was so called because its gradient is such that only bullock carts could climb it. Naturally, this form of transportation was slow and expensive. Rice which sold in Siliguri for Rs 98 a ton fetched Rs 240 a ton by the time it reached Darjeeling.

The idea of a railway to Darjeeling was put forward by Franklin Prestage, an agent working for the Eastern Bengal Railway, in 1870. The scheme was accepted and construction begun in 1879. It was completed in 1881, and in 1885 a further km extension was added to take the line into the market area (now in disuse). Later on, in 1914, it was further extended south towards Kishanganj close to the Nepalese border to cope with the transport of jute and, in 1915, from Siliguri to 15 km beyond Sevok on the way to Kalimpong. The cost of the original section to Darjeeling was Rs 1,700,000 including rolling stock.

The whole line is an ingenious feat of engineering and includes four complete loops and five switchbacks, some of which were added after the initial construction had been completed to ease the line's gradient at certain points. One of the most important additions was the Batasia loop on the final descent into Darjeeling. Altogether, there are 132 unsupervised level crossings! ∎

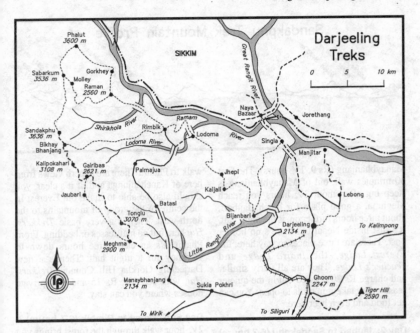

Acute Mountain Sickness (AMS) can occur at high altitudes. See the Health section in the Facts for the Visitor chapter for more details.

For the Sandakphu/Phalut trek below, you don't need to bring much with you since there's accommodation along the way. Most places have quilts but in the high season it might be worth bringing your own sleeping bag in case there's not enough bedding to go round.

Although you can get basic meals along the way everyone recommends bringing along some snacks like nuts, biscuits, raisins and chocolate. You need a water bottle – even a plastic mineral water bottle will do – as there are some stretches where there's no water or places to eat.

Guides and porters are not necessary but can be arranged through the Youth Hostel or the trekking agencies. A porter would cost about Rs 80, a guide Rs 150, per day. If you don't take a guide, you should ask directions

at every opportunity as the path is not always clear.

Sandakphu/Phalut Trek

This trek to the Himalayan viewpoint at Phalut (3600 metres) is the most popular trek in the area. It involves a short bus trip from Darjeeling to Manaybhanjang from where you walk steadily towards the mountains via Sandakphu. Here you can turn back or continue to Phalut and walk down to Rimbik for a bus to Darjeeling. The trek can be done in the opposite direction but you'll spend more time walking with your back to the mountains.

There's a rough jeep track from Manaybhanjang through Sandakphu but it's not used much; Rs 2500 will get you a return trip from Darjeeling to Sandakphu by Land Rover, if that's what you want.

Day 1: Darjeeling to Jaubari (8-9 hours)
From Darjeeling take the 7 am bus to

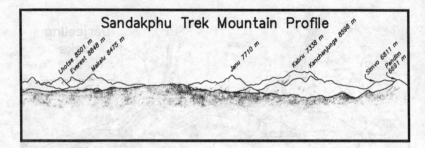

Sandakphu Trek Mountain Profile

Lhotse 8501 m Everest 8848 m Makalu 8475 m Janu 7710 m Kabru 7338 m Kanchenjunga 8598 m Simvo 6811 m Pandim 6691 m

Manaybhanjang (Rs 9, 1½ hours). The first 30 minutes walk out of Manaybhanjang is steep but after about 3½ hours you reach Meghma, a good place for lunch. Jaubari, about three hours further on, is the night halt. It's just inside Nepal but there's no border post. There are three places to stay here: the *Everest Lodge*, the *Indira Lodge* and *Teacher's Lodge*. They are all fairly similar and charge Rs 20 per bed but in the quieter season they take it in turns to open. You can get food and even beer here.

Day 2: Jaubari to Sandakphu (6-7 hours)
There are good views for most of the second day. Start with a half-hour descent to Gairibas then climb up to Kalipokhari, where there's a restaurant and a hotel. This is about 3½ hours from Jaubari. A further three hours takes you through Bikhay Bhanjang to Sandakphu; the last few km are steep. There are two *PWD bungalows* here with beds for Rs 10 and a new *Trekkers' Hut* also for Rs 10. Be careful with the drinking water here as the source is not very clean.

Day 3: Sandakphu to Molley (4½ - 5½ hours) Between Sandakphu and Sabarkum, a four to five-hour walk, there is nowhere to get food or water so you must bring both with you. For lodging, you have to go down to Molley, under half an hour's walk. The place to stay here is *Didi's* – it has good food and a warm fire.

Day 4: Molley to Gorkhey (5-6 hours) Go back up to Sabarkum and then it's a two-hour walk to Phalut. There are superb views from here of Kanchenjunga and, if it's clear, you should also be able to make out Everest in the centre of the group of mountains to the north-west. There's a very basic *Trekkers' Hut* here but no mattresses or bedding. From Phalut it's an easy three hours down to Gorkhey for a night halt. There's a new Darjeeling Gorkha Hill Council *Trekkers' Hut*, with beds for Rs 15 and also private houses where you can stay.

Day 5: Gorkhey to Rimbik (6-7 hours) A 2½-hour walk through the forest brings you to Raman where there's the friendly *Sherpa Hotel*, a nice place to stay. From here it's a level 3½-hour stroll through a number of small villages to Rimbik. There are only two hotels to choose from, and both are good. The *Shiva Pradhan Hotel*, with hot water and beer, operates a 'pay what you think it's all worth' system that seems to work. The *Sherpa Hotel* is also popular and has a 'great family atmosphere'.

Day 6: Rimbik to Darjeeling You can catch the early morning bus from here to Darjeeling (Rs 22, five hours). Alternatively you can walk on for 5½ hours to Bijanbari where buses also run to Darjeeling.

Shortcuts If you don't have time for a six-day trek, there are a number of shortcuts you can take. You can go just as far as Sandakphu where there are good views. Sandakphu is actually slightly higher than Phalut, although further back from the mountains. From here you can backtrack to Bikhay Bhanjang and cut straight across to Rimbik in five to six hours for a bus to Darjeeling. Bear in mind that there's no water or food on this stretch.

The other shortcut is between Molley and Raman, which takes around 3½ hours.

Note Before leaving Darjeeling you're advised to browse through the Darjeeling Youth Hostel's book in which trekkers write their comments about the routes.

KALIMPONG
Population: 41,000

Kalimpong is a bustling and rapidly expanding, though still relatively small, bazaar town set amongst the rolling foothills and deep valleys of the Himalaya at an altitude of 1250 metres. It was once part of the lands belonging to the rajas of Sikkim, until the beginning of the 18th century when it was taken from them by the Bhutanese. In the 19th century it passed into the hands of the British and thus became part of West Bengal. It became a centre for Scottish missionary activity in the late 19th century and Dr Graham's orphanage and school is still running today.

Kalimpong's attractions include three monasteries, a couple of solidly built churches, an excellent private library for study of Tibetan and Himalayan language and culture, a sericulture centre, orchid nurseries and the fine views over the surrounding countryside. The most interesting part of a trip to Kalimpong is the journey there from Darjeeling via the Teesta River Bridge. If you have no permit for Sikkim then the town is worth visiting just for the journey.

Orientation & Information
Though it's a much smaller town than Darjeeling, Kalimpong has a similar kind of layout, straddling a ridge and consisting of a series of interconnected streets and flights of steps.

Life centres around the sports ground and east through the market. The bus stand and Chowrasta is also a busy area, and it's here that most of the cheap cafes and hotels are situated.

Monasteries
The **Tharpa Choling Monastery** belongs to the Yellow Hat sect (Geluk-pa) of Tibetan Buddhism, founded in Tibet in the 14th century and to which the Dalai Lama belongs. Established in 1922, it's 40 minutes walk (uphill) from town; take the path to the right off K D Pradhan Rd, just before the Milk Collection and Extension Wing Building.

Lower down the hill, the **Thongsa Gompa** or Bhutanese Monastery is the oldest monastery in the area and was founded in 1692. The present building is a little more recent since the original was destroyed by the Gurkhas in their rampage across Sikkim before the arrival of the British.

Zong Dog Palri Fo-Brang Monastery was built in the mid-1970s at Durpin Dara Hill and was consecrated by the Dalai Lama. There are good mountain views from Durpin Dara Hill.

Flower Nurseries
Kalimpong is an important orchid-growing area and flowers are exported from here to many cities in northern India. The Sri Ganesh Moni Pradhan Nursery and the Sri L B Pradhan Nursery are among the most important in the area. The Standard and the Universal Nurseries also specialise in cacti. There's a flower festival in Kalimpong in October.

Sericulture Centre
The sericulture centre, where silkworms are bred and silk is produced, is on the road to Darjeeling and can be visited. Nearby is the Swiss Welfare Dairy, established by a Swiss missionary and the source of the delicious hard cheese you can buy here and in Darjeeling.

Arts & Crafts
Market days are Wednesday and Saturday and it's definitely worth strolling through on these days, especially if you want to meet and talk with local people, but it's otherwise overrated. It's certainly not a replica of

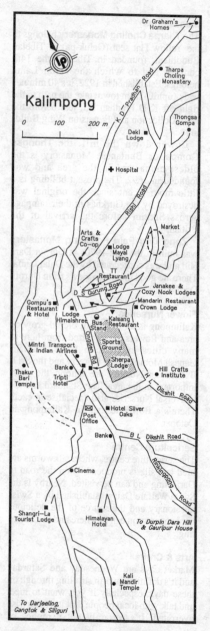

Kalimpong

0   100   200 m

Kathmandu and there's not much for sale here that you can't find in either Darjeeling or Gangtok. Antique (or imitation antique) Tibetan jewellery may be somewhat cheaper here, though.

Kalimpong tapestry bags and purses, copperware, scrolls and paintings from Dr Graham's Homes are sold at the Kalimpong Arts & Crafts Co-operative.

Rabindranath Tagore spent his summers here and started Chitrabhanu, a home for destitute women, at Gauripur House. Crafts produced here are also for sale.

Places to Stay – bottom end

There are a number of very basic places around the bus stand. *Lodge Himalshree* is a small family place on the third floor of a building on Ongden Rd. The owner is friendly and helpful and there are singles/doubles/triples for Rs 40/80/120, all with common bathroom. The *Punjab Lodge* cannot be described as spotless but has rooms with attached bathroom for Rs 60/90. *Lodge Cozy Nook* is a bit better and similarly priced.

Gompu's Restaurant & Hotel on Chowrasta is popular with travellers and is run by a friendly Tibetan family. There are good doubles for Rs 100, triples for Rs 150 and a four-bedded room for Rs 200, all with bathrooms attached. There's a good restaurant downstairs. The *Lodge Mayal Lyang* is a little cheaper but not quite so good. There are doubles for Rs 80 and hot water is supplied in buckets. *Sherpa Lodge* is nearer the bus stand and better value at Rs 50/100 for rooms with attached bathroom. It's run by very pleasant people.

The *Janakee Lodge* is a good place with a range of rooms from Rs 50/75 for doubles/triples with common bathroom or Rs 60/90 with bathroom. Hot water is supplied in buckets.

Away from this area on the road down to the Teesta Bridge is another very popular place – the *Shangri-La Tourist Lodge* (☎ 230). It's a clean, old wooden place with pleasant staff and it offers dorm beds for Rs 20 (seven in total) and double rooms with bathroom for Rs 100. Breakfast and dinner are available for Rs 40. The hotel isn't signposted so, if walking out of Kalimpong, watch for a cinema on the left-hand side and then take the small dirt path downhill on the right-hand side shortly afterwards.

The upmarket *Crown Lodge* (☎ 546) is a few metres down a side street off H L Dikshit Rd. It's quiet and clean with singles/doubles from Rs 140/165 with bathroom, water heater and TV. The staff are pleasant but the hotel has no restaurant.

Places to Stay – top end

If you have the money, there's no better place to stay in Kalimpong than the beautiful old stone-built *Himalayan Hotel* (☎ 248), on the right-hand side about 300 metres up the hill past the post office. It is the former home of a British trade agent with Tibet named David MacDonald who wrote *20 Years in Tibet* and *Land of the Lamas*. The hotel is surrounded by superb gardens looking across to the snow-covered peaks of Kanchenjunga. For many years it was run by Mrs Williams, David MacDonald's daughter. Dr R K Sprigg, a scholar of the Tibetan language from London University who spent much time here, added to the atmosphere of the place by serenading the guests with his bag-pipes at sunset.

The hotel is still in the MacDonald family, now run by Tim and Neelam MacDonald, and although the staff are the same, many of the valuable antiques which gave the place its character, including priceless thankas, were recently stolen. However it's still a great place to stay. The management is friendly and helpful, suggesting interesting walks in the neighbourhood and arranging picnics and birdwatching trips. Including all taxes, singles/doubles are US$20/25 with breakfast, US$30/45 with all meals. Tibetan food is available and is very good. Log fires in the rooms are extra.

By contrast, there is the *Hotel Silver Oaks* (☎ 260), Upper Cart Rd, about 50 metres uphill from the post office. It's not a patch on the Himalayan Hotel but, as modern hotels go, it is very pleasant if somewhat devoid of life and it does have good views. It's pretty expensive at Rs 950/1250 for singles/doubles including (good) meals.

Places to Eat

Kalsang Restaurant is an excellent Tibetan place where momos are Rs 1 each and you can try Mongolian alternatives, like shyaphaglevi for Rs 3, among many other dishes here. The people here are very friendly. *TT Restaurant* is a good Chinese/Tibetan place where you can have gyathuk, which is like thukpa (noodle soup), for Rs 12 or sweet and sour pork for Rs 20.

Gompu's Restaurant, Chowrasta, is a pleasant restaurant with friendly staff and is highly recommended by local people and travellers alike. They serve Tibetan, Indian and Chinese food and Western breakfasts. Roast chicken and chips is Rs 25, a plate of momos Rs 5. For Chinese food there's the *Mandarin Restaurant* opposite the bus stand. Another restaurant, similar in quality, is at *Lodge Mayal Lyang*.

The *Pure Veg Punjab Restaurant*, below Lodge Cozy Nook, is a good clean place. For a cheap simple meal, the *Usha Restaurant*, a tiny and very friendly chai shop between the Crown Lodge and the bus stand, is worth trying. For standard Indian food you could try one of the restaurants along the main street such as that at the *Tripti Hotel*.

If you give them a bit of notice you can eat at the *Himalayan Hotel*, where European, Indian and Tibetan food is available.

Getting There & Away

Darjeeling There are frequent jeeps (Rs 35 for a back seat, Rs 40 for the front) and a few taxis in either direction for the three-hour trip. The buses (Rs 25) are so much less frequent, slower and more uncomfortable that it's hardly worth the small cost saving. All the transport other than the taxis leaves from the Bazaar bus stand.

Siliguri Buses cost Rs 18 for this three-hour trip and there are also a few Land Rovers and taxis. The road to Siliguri follows the Teesta River after the bridge so it's much cheaper and quicker than going via Darjeeling. The views are magnificent.

Gangtok (Sikkim) Several bus companies operate this route from the bus stand – try Sikkim Nationalised Transport or Jayshree (sometimes spelt Joy Shree). They leave between 7 and 8 am for the four-hour trip, and the fare is Rs 21. They're fond of

dubbing the buses 'luxury', which is a joke and should be treated as such.

Bagdogra Mintri Transport operates one bus daily to Siliguri and the Bagdogra airport at 8 am from their office (which is also the Indian Airlines office; ☎ 241) on Main Rd. The trip takes about three hours and costs Rs 40. Mintri Transport can also book flights (including tickets on Royal Nepal Airlines).

Orissa

Population: 31.5 million
Area: 155,707 sq km
Capital: Bhubaneswar
People per sq km: 202
Main Language: Oriya
Literacy Rate: 48.7%

The tropical state of Orissa lies along the eastern seaboard of India, south of Bengal. Its main attractions are the temples of the capital Bhubaneswar, the long sandy beach at Puri and the great Sun Temple at Konark. These three sites make a convenient and compact triangle, and Bhubaneswar is on the main Calcutta to Madras railway route.

Orissa is predominantly rural, with fertile green coastal plains rising to the hills of the Eastern Ghats. The majority of the population live on or below the poverty line with annual per capita income one of the lowest in the country. Largely based on agriculture, Orissa's economy is often destabilised by natural disasters including flooding, drought, cyclone or tornado. However, flooding in the Mahanadi delta, which used to occur regularly, has been much reduced by the building of the Hirakud Dam. The state is mineral-rich and is a big exporter of iron ore, with a large factory at Rourkela.

Few visitors venture outside the Bhubaneswar/Puri/Konark triangle and although travel off the beaten track in Orissa is often rough, with few tourist facilities, it can be an interesting and rewarding experience. The Oriyas, 25% of whom are indigenous tribal peoples, are particularly friendly and hospitable.

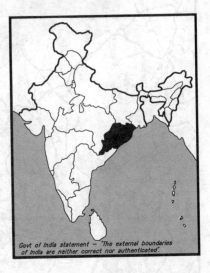

Govt of India statement – 'The external boundaries of India are neither correct nor authenticated'.

History

Orissa's hazy past focuses with the reign of Kalinga. In 260 BC he was defeated by Ashoka, the great Indian emperor, near modern Bhubaneswar. The bloody battle left Ashoka with such a bitter taste that he converted to Buddhism and spread that gentle religion far and wide. Buddhism soon declined in Orissa, however, and Jainism held sway until Buddhism reasserted itself in the 2nd century AD.

By the 7th century AD Hinduism had, in turn, supplanted Buddhism and Orissa's golden age began. Under the Kesari and Ganga kings the Orissan culture flourished and countless temples from that classical period still stand today. The Oriyas managed to defy the Muslim rulers in Delhi until the region finally fell to the Moghuls during the 16th century. Many of Bhubaneswar's temples were destroyed at that time.

Temple Architecture

Orissan temples – whether the mighty Lingaraj in Bhubaneswar, the Jagannath in Puri, the Sun Temple at Konark, or the many smaller temples – all follow a similar pattern. Basically there are two structures – the *jagamohan* or entrance porch, and the *deul* where the image of the temple deity is kept and above which the temple tower rises. The

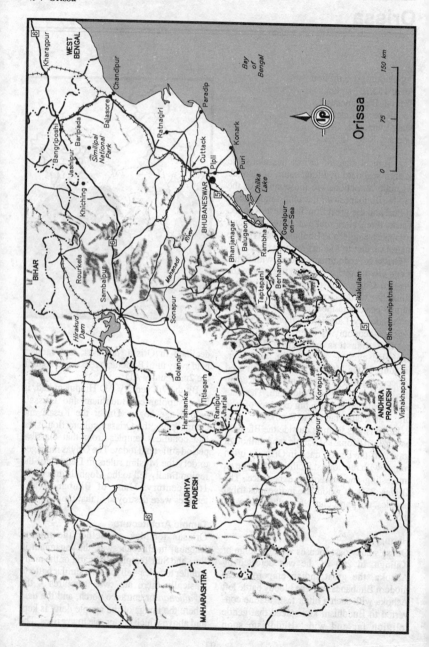

design is complicated in larger temples by the addition of other entrance halls in front of the jagamohan. These are the *bhoga-mandapa* or hall of offering and the *nata-mandir* or dancing hall.

The whole structure may be enclosed by an outer wall and within the enclosure there may be smaller, subsidiary temples and shrines. The most notable aspects of the temple design are the soaring tower and the intricate carvings that cover every surface. These may be figures of gods, men and women, plants and trees, flowers, animals and every other aspect of everyday life, but to many visitors it is the erotic carvings which create the greatest interest. They reach their artistic and explicit peak at Konark, where the close-up detail is every bit as interesting as the temple's sheer size.

Things to Buy

Orissa has a very wide and distinctive range of handicrafts. Best known is probably the appliqué work of Pipli. Brightly coloured patches of fabric, cut into animal and flower shapes, are sewn onto bed covers, cushions and beach umbrellas. The village of Raghurajpur is famous for its *patachitra*, paintings on specially prepared cloth.

Orissan Tribal People

Orissa has no less than 62 distinct tribal groups of aboriginal people who inhabited this region prior to the Aryan invasion of India. Officially known as 'tribals' they constitute more than a quarter of the state's population and live mainly in the hilly areas outside the small coastal plain. Many have adopted the ways of the invader and, as far as the foreign visitor is concerned, may not seem to look or dress very differently to the average Aryan Orissan – though an anthropologist or a caste-conscious Indian would hardly agree. Others, such as the Bonda, who wear very little, are rather more obviously different.

Kondhs The most numerous of the tribals are the 950,000 Kondhs. They still practise colourful ceremonies, although animal sacrifices have been substituted for the human ones which the British took so much trouble to stop – particularly around Russelkonda (Bhanjanagar).

Juang The Juang number only around 30,000 and live in thatched huts decorated with white wall paintings. Their small villages are mainly in the central districts of Dhenkanal and Keonjhar to the north.

Santal There are about 500,000 Santals, living in the northern Mayurbhanj and Balasore districts, particularly around Baripada and Khiching. Their marriage system is interesting in that it involves several different methods for a woman to get her man, including *nir balak bapla* or 'marriage by intrusion'. Unable to hook him by any other method, she can just move in and if he and his parents can't get her out after a week or so, he must marry her!

Saoras This tribe, numbering over 300,000, is divided into nine subdivisions. Now partially assimilated into the Indian community they are spread over a wide area in the central and southern districts. They speak an Austro-Asiatic language of the Munda family. The Lanjia Saoras of Ganjam and Koraput districts are still fairly traditional and are polygamous.

Bonda The Bonda, known as the 'naked people', are renowned for their wild ways and for the dormitories where young men and women are encouraged to meet for night-time fun and frolics. Only about 5000 remain, in the Bonda Hills of Koraput district. Women wear only a strip of cloth around their middle, long rows of beads and heavy metal neckbands.

Other major tribes are the Parajas, the colourful Godabas and the Koyas. Permission from the Orissa Home Ministry is needed to visit tribal villages, except for those along the main highways. ∎

Cuttack is known for its silver filigree jewellery.

Numerous types of Orissan handloomed fabrics are produced. Sambalpur is the centre of the area specialising in tie-dye and *ikat* fabrics. The complex ikat process involves tie-dying the thread before it is woven. This produces cloth with a slightly 'blurred' pattern which is particularly attractive. At Puri you can buy strange little carved wooden replicas of Lord Jagannath and his brother and sister. At Balasore, lacquered children's toys are manufactured.

BHUBANESWAR
Population: 411,000

Although it was only in 1950 that the state capital was moved from overcrowded Cuttack to Bhubaneswar, the town's history goes back over 2000 years, as excavations at Sisuphal Garh, the remains of a ruined city, have shown. Beside the site of the capital of ancient Kalinga, Bhubaneswar is known as Temple Town and Cathedral City on account of its many temples in the extravagant Orissan style. They date from the 8th to the 13th century AD and it is said that at one time the Bindu Sagar tank had over 7000 temples around it.

Today, the tour guides tell you that there are only 500 but even this seems like a bit of an exaggeration. Only about a dozen are of real interest, including the great Lingaraj Temple. It's one of the most important temples in India, but unfortunately is closed to non-Hindus.

During the last week of January the Tribal Festival is held here with dances, handicrafts and folk art on display.

Orientation & Information

A sprawling, rapidly expanding town, Bhubaneswar is divided by the railway line which runs roughly north-south through the middle of it. The new bus station is five km away on the western edge of town – further out from the centre than the airport. The temples are mainly in the south-east and the

closest hotel to them, the Panthanivas Tourist Bungalow, is within walking distance.

The tourist offices all seem very helpful. Orissa Tourism (☎ 50-099) is down the lane by the Tourist Bungalow and has branches at the airport and the railway station (open 24 hours). There's also an ITDC tourist office (☎ 54-203) not far from the Tourist Bungalow but it's closed on weekends.

The telephone area code for Bhubaneswar is 0674.

Lingaraj Temple

Surrounded by a high wall, the great temple of Bhubaneswar is off limits to all non-Hindus. Although the British Raj respected this ruling it did not deter them from building a viewing platform beside the northern wall. It was put up for the visit of Lord Curzon and is still used by tourists today. You'll be asked for a donation at the platform and shown a book to 'prove' that some people give over Rs 1000. How much you give is up to you but just a few rupees is more than enough. In fact you're now approached at many temples in Bhubaneswar with such persistence, you wonder whether these people really are the 'temple priests' they say they are.

The temple is dedicated to Tribhuvaneswar or Lord of the Three Worlds, also known as Bhubaneswar. In its present form it dates from 1090-1104, although parts of it are over 1400 years old. The granite block which represents Tribhuvaneswar is said to be bathed daily with water, milk and bhang. The temple compound is about 150 metres square and is dominated by the 40-metre-high temple tower.

The ornately carved tower is intricately sculptured. From the viewing platform you can easily see the lions crushing elephants, which are said to be a representation of the re-emergence of Hinduism over Buddhism. More than 50 smaller temples and shrines crowd the enclosure. In the north-east corner a smaller temple to Parvati is of particular interest.

There is also an annual chariot festival in the temple in April.

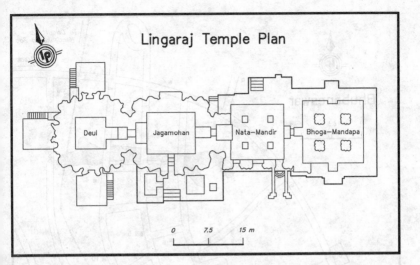

Lingaraj Temple Plan

Deul   Jagamohan   Nata–Mandir   Bhoga–Mandapa

0   7.5   15 m

Bindu Sagar Tank

The Ocean Drop tank just north of the great temple is said to contain water from every holy stream, pool and tank in India. Consequently, when it comes to washing away sin this is the tank that washes cleanest. There are a number of temples and shrines scattered around the tank, several with towers in imitation of the ones at the Lingaraj Temple. In the centre of the tank is a water pavilion where, once a year, the Lingaraj Temple's deity is brought to be ritually bathed.

Vaital Temple

Close to the Bindu Sagar Tank, this temple has a double-storey 'wagon roof', an influence from Buddhist cave architecture. It dates from the 8th century and was a centre of Tantric worship, the presiding deity being Chamunda (Kali). She can be seen in the dingy interior, although her necklace of skulls and the corpse she's sitting on are usually hidden beneath her temple robes.

Parsurameswar Temple

Close to the main Bhubaneswar to Puri road, on the same side as the Lingaraj Temple, the Grove of the Perfect Beings is a cluster of about 20 smaller temples, including some of the most important in Bhubaneswar. The best preserved of the early temples is the Parsurameswar, a Siva temple built about 650 AD. It has interesting and lively bas-reliefs of elephant and horse processions, lattice windows, Siva images and a temple 'priest' who won't leave you alone unless he considers your donation suitably generous.

Mukteswar, Siddheswar & Kedargauri

Not far from the Parsurameswar is the small 10th-century Mukteswar Temple, one of the most ornate temples in Bhubaneswar. The finely detailed carvings show a mixture of Buddhist, Jain and Hindu styles but unfortunately some of the figures have been defaced. The carvings of dwarves are particularly striking.

In front of the temple is a beautiful arched *torana* (architrave) showing clear Buddhist influence. The large green temple tank makes a perfect swimming pool for local children.

The later Siddheswar Temple is in the same compound. Although plainer than the Mukteswar, it has a fine standing Ganesh figure.

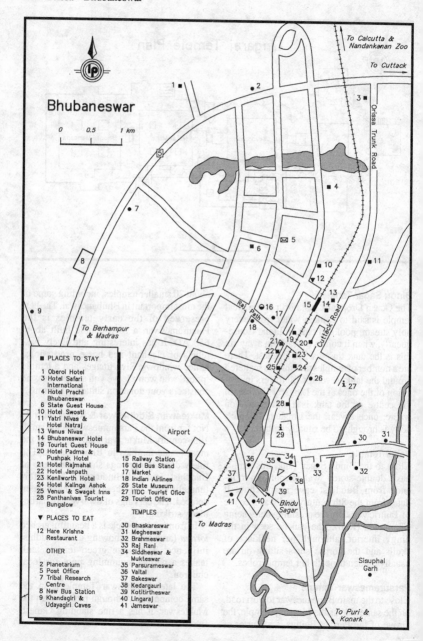

Bhubaneswar

0   0.5   1 km

To Calcutta &
Nandankanan Zoo

To Cuttack

Orissa Trunk Road

To Berhampur
& Madras

Raj Path

Cuttack Road

Airport

Bindu
Sagar

To Madras

Sisuphal
Garh

To Puri &
Konark

■ PLACES TO STAY

1   Oberoi Hotel
3   Hotel Safari
    International
4   Hotel Prachi
    Bhubaneswar
6   State Guest House
10 Hotel Swosti
11 Yatri Nivas &
    Hotel Natraj
13 Venus Nivas
14 Bhubaneswar Hotel
19 Tourist Guest House
20 Hotel Padma &
    Pushpak Hotel
21 Hotel Rajmahal
22 Hotel Janpath
23 Kenilworth Hotel
24 Hotel Kalinga Ashok
25 Venus & Swagat Inns
28 Panthanivas Tourist
    Bungalow

▼ PLACES TO EAT

12 Hare Krishna
    Restaurant

OTHER

2   Planetarium
5   Post Office
7   Tribal Research
    Centre
8   New Bus Station
9   Khandagiri &
    Udayagiri Caves

15 Railway Station
16 Old Bus Stand
17 Market
18 Indian Airlines
26 State Museum
27 ITDC Tourist Office
29 Tourist Office

TEMPLES

30 Bhaskareswar
31 Megheswar
32 Brahmeswar
33 Raj Rani
34 Siddheswar &
    Mukteswar
35 Parsurameswar
36 Vaital
37 Bakeswar
38 Kedargauri
39 Kotitirtheswar
40 Lingaraj
41 Jameswar

Also by the road, across the path from the Mukteswar, the Kedargauri is one of the older temples at Bhubaneswar, although it has been substantially rebuilt.

Outside the Mukteswar compound there are chai shops and curio-sellers.

Raj Rani

This interesting temple is surrounded by well-maintained gardens. It's one of the latest of the Bhubaneswar temples and is famous for its ornate deul, decorated with some of the most impressive Orissan temple sculptures. Around the compass points are statues of the eight *dikpalas* (temple guardians), who protect the temple, two for each side. Between them, nymphs, embracing couples, elephants and lions fill the niches and decorate the pillars. As it's no longer used for worship you are free to wander at will.

Brahmeswar

About a km east of the main road, the Brahmeswar Temple stands in a courtyard flanked by four smaller structures. It's notable for its very finely detailed sculptures with erotic and sometimes amusing elements – such as the young lady with the surprised look on her face, no doubt due to the location of her lover's hand! The temple dates from the 9th century.

Other Temples

There are two other temples near the Brahmeswar which are not of such great interest. The **Bhaskareswar** has an unusual stepped design in order to accommodate the unusually large three-metre lingam it once contained. About 300 metres east along the same road is the **Megheswar**, in a courtyard beside a tank.

North of the Bindu Sagar, the **Lakshamaneswar** is a very plain temple. Dating from the 7th century, it is one of the earliest specimens of Orissan architecture and acts as a gateway to the city.

State Museum

The museum is opposite the Hotel Kalinga

Ashok and has an interesting collection relating to Orissan history, culture and architecture and to the various Orissan tribes. The museum is open from 10 am to 5 pm daily, except Mondays. Entry is Rs 2.

Tribal Research Centre

Although this is primarily an anthropological research centre, visitors are welcome. There's an interesting outdoor display of reconstructed houses of Orissan tribal people, including the Santal, Juang, Gadaba, Saora and Kondh. Admission is free and it's open daily from 10 am to 5 pm, except on Sunday. Buses between the new bus station and the centre of town pass right by here.

Other Attractions

The partly excavated ruins at **Sisupal Garh** are thought to be the remains of an Ashokan city. In the north of the city, the **botanical gardens** and regional plant reserve have a large collection of plants including many cacti. A recent attraction is the city's **planetarium**, where there are shows at 3 and 4.30 pm daily except Mondays; tickets cost Rs 5.

Organised Tours

During the season, various tours operate from the Panthanivas Tourist Bungalow (☎ 54-515). If you really want to you can cover Orissa's main tourist sites (conveniently located in the Bhubaneswar/Puri/Konark triangle) in one long 12-hour tour for Rs 60. By taxi this tour would cost Rs 500. Travellers complain that the tours that include Nandankanan zoological park spend too long there and not long enough at the caves and temples.

Places to Stay – bottom end

Budget accommodation is available in Bhubaneswar municipality's *Yatri Nivas*. It's a friendly place, very much like a youth hostel, and has beds for Rs 15 in 18-bed dorms or Rs 20 in three or five-bed rooms. There's a cheap restaurant here. In the railway *retiring rooms* there are dorm beds for Rs 12 and doubles for Rs 50, or Rs 114 with air-con.

The *Hotel Janpath* is a recommended place that's good value, with singles from Rs 25 and single/double rooms with attached bathroom from Rs 40/50. It's clean and friendly. The *Hotel Gajapati* opposite the Kenilworth has basic rooms from Rs 35/50 with attached bathrooms, as well as more expensive rooms.

The *Venus Inn* has doubles for Rs 70 and a good South Indian restaurant downstairs. Nearby the *Swagat Inn* has rooms for Rs 70/90 and a fast-food restaurant. Both these places are fine but could be a bit noisy as they back onto the railway track.

On the eastern side of the railway station there's the *Bhubaneswar Hotel*, with a wide range of rooms from Rs 60/90/110 for singles/doubles/triples with attached bathrooms, or Rs 200/250 for air-con. It's OK and a popular place. There's also a restaurant here.

The *Hotel Padma* is a new hotel you can't miss at night, since it's covered with multicoloured illuminations. If they can maintain the standards of cleanliness then it's a recommended place with rooms for Rs 70/80 with attached bathroom and a good dorm for Rs 30 per bed.

Further north on Cuttack Rd is the *Venus Nivas*, quite a good place, with rooms with attached bathroom from Rs 60/70 and 24-hour checkout.

Places to Stay – middle

The *Panthanivas Tourist Bungalow* (☎ 54-515) is popular even though it's relatively poor value. On the plus side, it's conveniently located near the temples and has comfortable rooms. Doubles are Rs 165 or Rs 275 with air-con and all rooms have attached bathrooms and hot-water heaters. The 8 am checkout is a bit extreme.

The *Tourist Guest House* (☎ 40-0857) is a small place popular with foreigners. The owner claims that the Princess of Bhutan stayed here and that Prince Charles didn't (although the owner did give him a guided tour of Konark). It's clean and comfortable

with rooms for Rs 120/150 with attached bathrooms. Meals are available. The modern *Hotel Natraj* (☎ 54-842) has rooms from Rs 120/150 or Rs 250/300 with air-con, and 24-hour checkout.

Places to Stay – top end

Formerly the Hotel Konark, and with a good reproduction of a Konark chariot wheel outside it, the *Kenilworth Hotel* is recommended for its position and facilities. Air-con rooms are Rs 395/675. There's a swimming pool here that nonresidents can use for Rs 50 (closed between noon and 4 pm), a pastry shop, bookshop and resident masseur.

The air-conditioned *Hotel Prachi Bhubaneswar* (☎ 52-689) is also a good place with rooms at Rs 395/700. Facilities include the 'Wim Bul Don' (a tennis court!) and a pool that nonresidents can use for only Rs 25.

Not far from the Tourist Bungalow is the *Hotel Kalinga Ashok* (☎ 53-318), almost opposite the museum. This place is modern, air-conditioned, and has a good restaurant and bar. Singles/doubles cost US$20/37.

At the top of the pile is the impressive *Oberoi Hotel* (☎ 56-116), on the outskirts of town. Mimicking Orissan temple layout and design, it charges US$85/95 for rooms and has all mod cons including swimming pool, health club, floodlit tennis courts and jogging track.

Places to Eat

The *Modern South Indian Hotel*, behind the Hotel Rajmahal and under the Hotel Chand, is a good place for a cheap meal. They have vegetarian thalis for Rs 8 and a range of fruit juices. The best vegetarian eatery in Bhubaneswar is the *Hare Krishna Restaurant*, run by the organisation itself. It's a smart place with powerful air-con and excellent, though pricey, food.

The *Fahien Restaurant* at the Panthanivas Tourist Bungalow has quite good Chinese food with main dishes around Rs 28, but service is abysmally slow.

A recommended place for an evening out

is the *Kenilworth Hotel*. They have a barbecue on the roof terrace and the food is excellent. Food from their other restaurants can be served out here, too – the tandoori pomfret (Rs 65) is delicious and they also have lobster thermidor for Rs 110.

You can get a vegetarian thali for Rs 12 at the *Hotel Aahar*, near the Mukteswar Temple.

Things to Buy
Orissan handicrafts including appliqué work can be bought at the market off Raj Path in the Orissa State Handloom Co-operative or Utkalika.

Getting There & Away
Air Indian Airlines (☎ 40-0533) has daily flights between Bhubaneswar and Calcutta (US$41) and also Delhi (US$128). There are three flights a week to Madras (US$116), Raipur (US$52), Hyderabad (US$95), Nagpur (US$74) and Bombay (US$136). There are four direct flights a week to Bhubaneswar from Varanasi (US$69) but nothing direct from Bhubaneswar to Varanasi.

Bus The impressive new bus station (which looks more like an airport terminal) is on the main highway to Calcutta. Some buses still stop at the old bus stand which is much more conveniently located in the centre of town.

From the new bus station there are numerous departures to Calcutta (Rs 78, overnight), Cuttack (Rs 10, one hour) and Berhampur (Rs 27, five hours). Private video coaches are faster and run to most popular places including Berhampur (Rs 40, four hours), Baripada (Rs 50, seven hours) and Sambalpur.

The best way to get from Bhubaneswar to Puri is on the small Canter minibuses that leave from outside the old bus station. The trip takes a little over an hour and costs Rs 9.50. Numerous larger buses ply this route. They're a bit cheaper and much slower. It takes 1½ hours (Rs 8), to Konark. If it's not possible to get a direct bus to Konark, all Puri buses go through Pipli, where the Konark road branches off. It is then possible to catch another bus from there to Konark.

Train On the main Calcutta to Madras railway line, there are plenty of trains to Bhubaneswar as well as services terminating at Puri. The crack *Coromandal Express* departs Calcutta at 2.30 pm and arrives in Bhubaneswar just over seven hours later. Fares for the 437-km journey are Rs 81/301 in 2nd/1st.

There are also direct rail connections to Berhampur (166 km, 2½ hours), Madras (1226 km, 20 hours), Delhi (2077 km, 30 hours), Varanasi (998 km, 21 hours) and Agra (1874 km, 39 hours).

Getting Around
To/From the Airport The airport is very close to the town. There's no bus service and a taxi costs Rs 35 to the Tourist Bungalow or Rs 70 to the Oberoi. A cycle-rickshaw costs only Rs 10 but you may have to walk the last km between the entrance of the airport and the terminal.

Cycle-Rickshaw & Taxi Cycle-rickshaws offer 'five temple' tours for around Rs 20 covering the main temples; shorter journeys are less than Rs 5.

Taxis have set rates which are available from the tourist office. They charge Rs 150 for a one-way journey to Puri or Konark, Rs 100 for Dhauli, and Rs 100 for Nandankanan and the botanical gardens. Taxis outside the Tourist Bungalow may try to charge up to twice this much.

AROUND BHUBANESWAR
Udayagiri & Khandagiri Caves
A couple of km south of the new bus station in Bhubaneswar, these two hills facing each other across the road are riddled with caves, some of them ornately carved. Most are thought to have been chiselled out for Jain ascetics in the first century BC.

On the right of the road, **Udayagiri**, or Sunrise Hill, has the more interesting caves, which are scattered at various levels up the hill. All are numbered. At the base of the hill, round to the right, is the two-storey Rani ka Naur or Queen's Palace Cave (Cave 1). Both levels have eight entrances and the cave is extensively carved.

Return to the road via the Chota Hathi Gumpha (3), with its carvings of elephants coming out from behind a tree. The Jaya Vijaya Cave (5) is again double-storeyed and a bo tree is carved in the central compart-ment. Back at the entrance, ascend the hill to Cave 9, the Swargapuri, and 14, the Hathi Gumpha or Elephant Cave. The latter is plain but an inscription relates in 117 lines the exploits of its builder, King Kharaveli of Kalinga, who ruled from 168 to 153 BC.

Circle round the hill to the right, to the single-storey Ganesh Gumpha (10), which is almost directly above the Rani ka Naur. The carvings here tell the same tale as in the lower-level cave but are better drawn. Retrace your steps to Cave 14, then on to the Pavana Gumpha or Cave of Purification and the small Sarpa Gumpha or Serpent Cave, where the tiny door is surmounted by a three-headed cobra.

Only 15 or so metres from this is the Bagh Gumpha (12) or Tiger Cave, entered through the mouth of the beast. The hill is topped by the foundations of some long-gone building. The oldest of these various caves date back to the 2nd century BC. Some are of Jain origin.

Across the road, **Khandagiri Hill** is not so interesting, although there is a fine view back over Bhubaneswar from its summit. You can see the airport, the tower of the Lingaraj Temple rising behind it and, further away, the Dhauli Stupa. The steep path divides about a third of the way up the hill. The right path goes to the Ananta Cave (3) with carved figures of athletes, women, elephants and geese carrying flowers. The right path also leads to a series of Jain temples. At the top of the hill is an 18th-century Jain temple.

The caves are open from 8 am to 6 pm. There's a government restaurant here and lots of chai shops.

Getting There & Away Only a few buses go specifically to the caves, but there are plenty

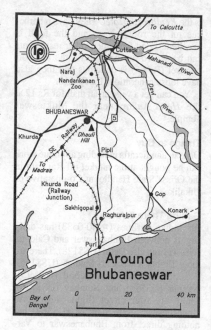

Around Bhubaneswar

which pass the nearby junction, the main Calcutta to Madras highway. It's about Rs 1 from town, or you can get there by rickshaw for about Rs 12.

Dhauli

Around 260 BC, King Ashoka had his famous edicts carved onto a large rock, halfway up the hill here at Dhauli, eight km south of Bhubaneswar, just off the Puri road. After murdering large numbers of his family to gain power, then hundreds of thousands on the battlefield as he enlarged his empire, Ashoka finally 'saw the light' after his bloody victory at nearby Kalinga, and con-verted to Buddhism.

Given his past record, Ashoka was wise to choose a pen name for these edicts, referring to himself as King Piyadasi (meaning He Who Looks on Everything with Kindness). In the edicts he tells his subjects 'Meritorious is abstention from killing living creatures, meritorious is abstention from reviling the unorthodox...'

At the top of the hill is a dazzling white Peace Pagoda built by the Japanese in the 1970s, with older Buddha figures set into the modern structure.

You can get to the place where you turn off the main road on any Puri or Konark bus for Rs 2, and from there it's a three-km walk to Dhauli.

Nandankanan Zoo

Famous for its white tigers (see the section on Bandhavgarh, Madhya Pradesh), this zoo is 25 km north of Bhubaneswar. There are also lion and tiger safaris in 'armoured buses', elephant rides and boating on the lake.

It's open daily from 8 am to 5 pm daily except Monday. The nearest railway station is Barang, a couple of km from the zoo.

PURI
Population: 125,000

The seaside resort of Puri, 60 km from Bhubaneswar, is one of the four *dhams* (holiest Hindu pilgrimage places in India). Religious life in the city revolves around the great Jagannath Temple and its famous Rath Yatra or Car Festival. It is thought that Puri was the hiding place for the Buddha tooth of Kandy before it was spirited away to Sri Lanka. There are similarities between the Rath Yatra and the annual Kandy procession.

Puri's other great attraction is its long sandy beach that draws large numbers of Western travellers and Indians, especially in the October to January high season. Parts of the beachfront are getting quite built up but it can still be a relaxing place to spend a few days. Many Indian companies and government departments have vacation homes here but the town is mostly visited by Bengali holiday-makers.

Orientation & Information

Grand Rd, a wide highway built to accommodate the hundreds of thousands of pilgrims who come to Puri for the Rath Yatra festival, runs from the Jagannath Temple to the Gundicha Mandir. The bus station is at the eastern end of this road. Most of the hotels are along the seafront but there are two distinct beach areas – Indians to the west, foreign travellers to the east.

The tourist office (☎ 3464) is on Station Rd and there's a counter (open 24 hours) at the railway station. Both are helpful.

Rath Yatra (Car Festival)

One of India's greatest annual events takes place in Puri each June or July when the fantastic festival of the cars sets forth from the Jagannath Temple. It commemorates the journey of Krishna from Gokul to Mathura. The images of Jagannath, his brother and his sister are brought out from the temple and dragged in huge 'cars', known as raths, down the wide Grand Rd to the Gundicha Mandir (Garden House), over a km away.

The main car of Jagannath stands 14 metres high, over 10 metres sq and rides on 16 wheels, each over two metres in diameter. It is from these colossal cars that our word 'juggernaut' is derived and, in centuries past, devotees were known to have thrown themselves beneath the wheels of the juggernaut in order to die in the god's sight. To haul the cars takes over 4000 professional car-pullers, all employees of the temple. Hundreds of thousands of pilgrims (and tourists) flock from all over India to witness this stupendous scene. The huge and unwieldy cars take an enormous effort to pull, are virtually impossible to turn and, once moving, are nearly unstoppable.

Once they reach the other end of the road the gods take a week-long summer break, then they are reloaded onto the cars and trucked back to the Jagannath Temple, in a virtual repeat of the previous week's procession. Following the festival the cars are broken up and used for firewood in the communal kitchens inside the temple, or for funeral-pyre fuel. New cars are constructed each year. At intervals of eight, 11 or 19 years (or combinations of those numbers depending on various astrological occurrences) the gods themselves are also disposed of and new images made. In the past 150 years there have been new images in 1863, 1893, 1931, 1950, 1969 and 1977. The old ones are buried at a site near the northern gate. ■

The State Bank of India offers the usual slow service for foreign exchange. It is also open on Sundays between 11.30 am and 1.30 pm.

Warning A number of swimmers have come to grief in Puri's treacherous surf – see the warning under Beach in this section.

Jagannath Temple

The temple of Jagannath, Lord of the Universe and an incarnation of Vishnu, is unfortunately closed to non-Hindus. As at the Lingaraj Temple in Bhubaneswar, non-believers have to be content with looking over the wall, this time from the roof of the library opposite, but you won't see much inside the temple. An additional platform on the roof was built for the viceroy's visit in 1939. The library is open from 9 am to noon and from 4 to 8 pm; a donation is required. Watch out for the monkeys. There's a good collection of ancient palm-leaf manuscripts in the library and another 'donation' is required if you wish to take a look.

The temple makes Puri one of the four dhams, cardinal centres of pilgrimage (the others being Dwarka in the west, Badrinath in the north and Rameswaram in the south). Its considerable popularity amongst Hindus is also partly due to the lack of caste distinctions – all are welcome before Lord Jagannath. Well, almost all – Indira Gandhi was barred from entering as she had married a non-Hindu.

The temple was built in its present form in 1198 and is protected by two surrounding walls. The outer enclosure is nearly square, measuring almost 200 metres on each side. The walls of the enclosure are six metres high. Inside, a second wall encloses the actual temple. The conical tower of the temple is 58 metres high and is topped by the flag and wheel of Vishnu, visible from far out to sea.

In front of the main entrance is a beautiful pillar, topped by an image of the Garuda, which originally stood in front of the temple at Konark. The main entrance is known as the Lion Gate due to the two stone lions guarding the entrance, and it is also the gate used in the chariot procession. The southern, eastern and northern gates are guarded by statues of men on horseback, tigers and elephants respectively.

In the central jagamohan, pilgrims can see the images of Lord Jagannath, his brother Balbhadra and sister Subhadra. Non-Hindus are not, of course, able to see them but the many shop stalls along the road outside the temple sell small wooden replicas. The curious images are carved from tree trunks, in a childlike caricature of a human face. The brothers have arms but the smaller Subhadra does not. All three are garlanded and dressed for ceremonies and the various seasons.

The temple employs 6000 men to perform the temple functions and the complicated rituals involved in caring for the gods. It has been estimated that in all, 20,000 people are dependent on Jagannath, and the god's immediate attendants are divided into 36 orders and 97 classes!

Gundicha Mandir

The Garden House, in which the images of the gods reside for seven days each year, is off limits to non-Hindus. The walls enclose a garden in which the temple is built. It's also known as the Aunt's House. Puri has a number of other temples, but most of these are off limits to non-Hindus.

Beach

Puri has a fine stretch of white sand from which Indian pilgrims bathe in their customary fully attired manner. Orissan fishers, wearing conical straw hats, guide bathers out through the surf. They're unlikely to be much help should trouble arise, as one traveller reported, witnessing a rescue attempt: 'To our amazement the lifeguards turned back having done only 10 yards and the swimmer (or non-swimmer) disappeared for good. Too late for anyone else to go by then. The victim was a young man of 19'. Another traveller reported two drownings in three days. The currents can be treacherous so don't go out of your depth unless you're a very strong swimmer.

Past the travellers' beach to the east is the local fishing village. Many of these fishing families come from Andhra Pradesh. It's worth getting up before sunrise to watch them head out to sea. For a little baksheesh they'll take you with them and one traveller said 'it was the highlight of my trip witnessing the dawn over the sea and fishing boats'. The crude construction of the boats is unusual – they're made of solid tree trunks and are enormously heavy. Buoyancy is achieved purely from the bulk of the wood. They're made in two or three pieces, split longitudinally and bound together. When not in use they're untied and the pieces laid out on the beach to dry.

For swimming, avoid the area opposite the Youth Hostel unless the sewage outlet here has been closed. As with all beaches this one doubles as a public lavatory, automatically flushed by the sea. Around the fishing village is the worst part and it really can stink here in the afternoon when the catch is being gutted on the beach. The cleanest area is just a 15-minute walk to the east, past the fishing village where the empty beach extends for miles.

Organised Tours

Tours operate out of Puri daily, except Monday, to Konark, Pipli, Dhauli, Bhubaneswar and the Udayagiri and Khandagiri caves. They depart at 6.30 am from the Panthabhavan, and return at 6.30 pm. The cost is Rs 60. On Monday, Wednesday and Friday there's a tour to Chilka Lake for Rs 75. There are a number of private operators running similarly priced tours. Tribe Tours (☎ 3781) can organise a car and interpreter for visits to tribal areas in the south of Orissa.

Places to Stay

Most of the budget hotels popular with travellers are at the east end of the beach towards the fishing village, along or off Chakra Tirtha Rd. In the centre are most of the middle-range and top-end hotels, while at the west end is a mixture of middle-range and budget hotels – the latter catering mainly to Indian pilgrims.

Prices below are for the high season (October to January) but you should be able to negotiate some healthy discounts outside this period, especially at the mid-price places. Because most people arrive in Puri on overnight trains, checkout times can be as early as 7 am in some hotels!

Places to Stay – bottom end

The big modern *Youth Hostel* has separate dormitory accommodation for men and women at Rs 20 per bed, Rs 10 if you're a YHA member. Some of the dorms have only two or three beds but others are larger. The restaurant is recommended for its excellent Orissan-style thalis (Rs 7.50).

In an old English villa, the *Bay View Hotel* is quiet and pleasant with rooms from Rs 35 to Rs 80 (most with attached bathrooms) and a nice verandah for sitting out on.

The *Hotel Dreamland* is a small, recommended place with singles/doubles for Rs 40/50 and a friendly manager. It's set back from the road in a secluded garden. Nearby there's the Japanese-run *Hotel Love & Life* with dorm beds for Rs 25 and rooms from Rs 60/70 with bath. The food is disappointingly mediocre.

The popular *Hotel Shankar International* (☎ 3637) is a good beachfront hotel with doubles from Rs 80 right up to Rs 350 for a triple with a sea-facing balcony. There's a walled garden and good food at the restaurant here.

By the Holiday Inn the *Hotel Tanuja* has doubles for Rs 60. Nearby, the *Hotel Sea 'n Sand* is a clean place with doubles with attached bathroom for Rs 70. The *Z Hotel* (that's Zed not Zee!) (☎ 2554) is an excellent place which is still very popular with travellers, which means it's often difficult to get a room. Formerly the palace of a very minor maharaja, it's an old, rambling building with large, airy rooms, many of them facing the sea. The management is friendly and easygoing, the hotel peaceful and the restaurant serves good seafood. There are some dorm beds for Rs 15, singles are Rs 40, doubles Rs

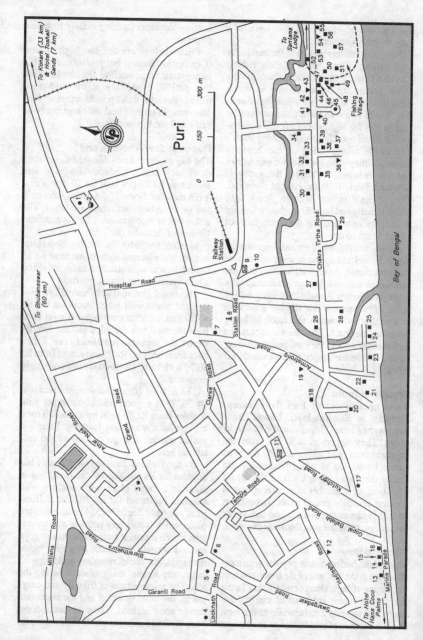

Puri

To Konark (33 km)
& Hotel Toshali
Sands (7 km)

To Bhubaneswar
(60 km)

Railway Station

Hospital Road

Station Road

Chakra Tirtha Road

Bay of Bengal

Mitiana Road

Grand Road

Clarke Road

Athar Nala Road

Armstrong Road

Bisarkhura Road

Gopal Ballabh Road

Temple Road

Kutchery Road

Garanti Road

Locknath Road

Swargadwar Road

Marine Parade

Hadesbi Road

To Hotel Hans Coco
Palms

Santana Lodge

Fishing
Village

300 m

150

0

To Hotel

100 to Rs 175 depending on whether they have shared or private bathroom. There's a nice roof terrace for sunbathing.

The basic *Travellers' Inn* is beside the Z, and has singles/doubles/triples from Rs 30/60/75 with common bathroom. There are several other similar places towards the beach here, including the *Hotel Derby, Nundy Cottage, Hotel Nilambu* and *Leo Castle*. The *Pink House* is a very mellow place right on the beach. Rooms are Rs 35/70 and there's a good restaurant.

Back across the road, the family-run *Hotel Sri Balaji* is a good choice, set in an enclosed garden. They charge Rs 40 to Rs 100 for a spotless double. In the fishing village, the *Durga Lodge* has six rooms for Rs 30/40 each, with mosquito net and common bath-

room. It's OK but the woman who runs it is a bit pushy.

Sagar Saikate looks like a small yellow castle and was a fortified English villa, right on the beach. It has a great roof area that is perfect for undisturbed sunbathing and big, high-ceiling rooms. Singles are Rs 25 and doubles with bathroom attached are Rs 60. There are smarter doubles for Rs 80 in the characterless modern annex, *Satya Lodge*, by the road.

Deep into the fishing village, set back from the sea, is the *Santana Lodge*. It's a recommended place run by a very friendly and helpful manager. Singles/doubles are Rs 25/50 with common bath, or Rs 60 per person including meals. They have some doubles with attached bathroom for Rs 55 and there's a nice roof terrace. It's a Rs 6 cycle-rickshaw ride from the station. The area is known as Pentakota; the rickshaw-wallah may not know the hotel.

At the other end of the beach, along Marine Parade, there are many other hotels patronised almost exclusively by Indian pilgrims. The *Sea View Hotel* is rather run down with doubles from Rs 80. The *Victoria Club* ('A Home Away From Home') is better and has doubles from Rs 100. The *Puri Hotel*, with doubles from Rs 180 upwards, claims to be Orissa's biggest and is very popular with middle-class Indians.

Places to Stay – middle & top end

The *Panthanivas Tourist Bungalow* (☎ 2562) is a good place where doubles with bathroom attached cost Rs 110 and there are air-con rooms for Rs 275. Some rooms in the new building have excellent views of the sea. It's well kept, well located and has a reasonable dining hall. In contrast, Orissa Tourism's other hotel, the *Panthabhavan*, on Marine Parade, is a gloomy converted palace with air-con doubles for Rs 275, ordinary doubles for Rs 165.

The friendly *Hotel Golden Palace* (☎ 3192) is in a good spot right on the beach, with doubles with balconies from Rs 160 to Rs 200. There's a beachside restaurant here.

There are several hotels along the beach from the Tourist Bungalow. The *Hotel Repose* charges Rs 220 for doubles. The *Hotel Vijoya International* (☎ 2702) is a modern block with single/double rooms at Rs 220/275 or Rs 390/450 with air-con. The smaller *Hotel Samudra* (☎ 2705) next door is the best of this group. It's right on the beach; most rooms have a balcony facing the sea and cost from Rs 125/165 to Rs 235/275.

Back on Chakra Tirtha Rd, the *Hotel Sealand* is a group of cottages with rooms for Rs 100/150 or Rs 150/200 with air-con. At the eastern end of this road is the new *Holiday Inn* (☎ 3782) which has good doubles with attached bathrooms from Rs 200.

Set back from the beach on the main road is the delightfully 'olde-worlde' *South-*

Eastern Railway Hotel (☎ 2063), also still referred to as 'the BNR' (Bengal Nagpur Railway, as it was once known). Ordinary singles/doubles, including all meals, cost Rs 330/575. These rooms have more character than the modern air-con rooms at Rs 450/650. The hotel has a pleasant lounge, bar, dining room and an immaculate stretch of lawn. Nonresidents can eat here with advance notice; lunch or dinner costs Rs 70 and the set meals are good.

You can't miss the ugly bulk of the *Hotel Holiday Resort* (☎ 2430) which has rooms with balconies overlooking the sea for Rs 320/450 and air-con cottages for Rs 600. If you stay here you'll feel more as if you are on the Spanish Costa Brava than in India. The *Hotel Nilachal Ashok* has not been open long but already has that run-down feel to it. It's set back from the beach and air-con rooms are Rs 395/695.

At the far western end of the beach is the excellent *Hans Coco Palms* (☎ 2638), with air-con rooms for Rs 395/795. This is a modern, well-run hotel in a private beach-front location. There's a good restaurant with main dishes from Rs 30 to Rs 40.

The *Hotel Toshali Sands* (☎ 2888) is a very secluded 'ethnic village resort', seven km from Puri on the road to Konark. Doubles in the cottages cost Rs 750. In the high season there's also accommodation in deluxe tents for a hefty Rs 300/395. It's a three-km walk through the Balukhand Forest and Turtle Reserve to the beach but the hotel does have a swimming pool which nonresidents can use for Rs 30. The food here is very good, although it's not cheap; main dishes are around Rs 50.

Places to Eat

You can get some excellent seafood here – good tuna steaks and occasionally even lobster. Some of the restaurants along the travellers' end of the beach manage passable cakes and pies – and do an interesting line in apple pies with a special extra ingredient!

The *Peace Restaurant* is an excellent place. It's clean, with efficient service and offers fish for Rs 5, prawns for Rs 14 and lobster (October to December) for Rs 45. *Sambhoo Restaurant* has long been a favourite with a similar menu and a variety of sweets. Two other places here are *Brady's* and *Harry's Place*. Across the road from the Z Hotel is the popular *Mickey Mouse Restaurant* but standards seem to be slipping here.

Raju's Restaurant is a cheap gathering place on the edge of the fishing village. Right on the beach is the *Pink House* with the usual travellers' fare including fish for Rs 5.

There are some good restaurants in the budget hotels. The best of them is at the *Z Hotel*, but with prices of most main dishes around Rs 25, a meal can be relatively pricey. The Hotel Shankar's *Om Restaurant* does quite good food.

There are a number of small cafes at the western end of the beach. In the old town there are countless vegetarian places like the *New Raj Restaurant* on Grand Rd, five minutes from the Jagannath Temple. Down the road beside the Puri Hotel there's a Chinese restaurant, the *Chung Wah* and another, the *Lee Garden* on Armstrong Rd.

For an evening out the set dinner at the *South East Railway Hotel* can be good, authentically Raj (often including puddings like trifle) and served in style by attentive uniformed waiters. It costs Rs 70 for four courses plus coffee and it's best to make a reservation. Alternatively the restaurants at the *Hans Coco Palms* and the *Toshali Sands* are both very good.

Things to Buy

Being a holy place, Puri is one of those delightfully eccentric Indian towns where the use of ganja is not only legal, the government very thoughtfully provides for smokers' requisites at special bhang shops. Ganga is available here at Rs 40 a tola but quality is reportedly not as good as in Kerala.

You'll come across quite a few craft and salespeople offering fabric, bead and bamboo work. Some of it is well worth a second look. Prices are negotiable, as always with this sort of thing. There are also plenty of people trying to sell snake and animal skins in such numbers that one dreads to think what is happening to the wildlife in the Orissan forests.

Getting There & Away

Bus Puri's new bus station is beside the Gundicha Mandir, though some of the private buses depart from around the nearby junction of Grand Rd and Hospital Rd. Take one of the new Canter minibuses for the trip to Bhubaneswar (Rs 9.50, one hour) as they're much quicker than the big buses.

Between 6 am and 4.30 pm there are frequent departures for Konark (Rs 5.50, one hour), early morning services for Berhampur (Rs 35, 5½ hours) and Taptapani (Rs 45, eight hours), a 6 am departure for Sambalpur (Rs 55, nine hours), and an overnight bus to Calcutta, but the trains are more comfortable for this route.

Train There are two overnight trains each way between Puri and Calcutta (500 km, Rs 87/327 in 2nd/1st) and a daily morning departure to Delhi (2140 km, 32 hours). There are several trains between Puri and Bhubaneswar (Rs 7, two hours) but the buses are quicker.

If you're travelling to or from Madras and stations in the south it's not necessary to go via Bhubaneswar. Khurda Road, 44 km from Puri is a convenient junction that all trains pass through.

The railway booking office is computerised. There's a second booking office with a 2nd-class quota on Grand Rd opposite the police station. It's advisable to book ahead in the pilgrim season when trains to Madras and Calcutta are often booked out five to 10 days ahead.

Getting Around

A cycle-rickshaw from the bus station to the hotels along the beach is around Rs 6. Buses shuttle between the Jagannath Temple and the bus station and between the railway station and the bus station for Rs 1.

The best way to get around is by bicycle and there are several places at the travellers' end of the beach where you can rent one for around Rs 10 per day. You can even try out an Enfield India from Tribe Tours for Rs 160 per day. They are also getting some cheaper mopeds and are planning self-drive car hire!

AROUND PURI

Raghurajpur

Famous for its patachitra painting, this artists' village, 10 km from Puri, makes an interesting excursion. The paintings are done on specially prepared cotton cloth which is coated with a mixture of gum and chalk and polished, before natural colours are applied.

The best way to get to the village is by taxi or bicycle as it's 1½ km off the main road. From Puri, take the Bhubaneswar road for nine km, almost to Chandapur. Turn right before the bridge, cross the railway line, then follow the right fork through the coconut plantation for a km until you come to Raghurajpur.

Pipli

Twenty-three km from Puri, at the junction where the Konark road branches from the Bhubaneswar to Puri road, this small village is notable for its appliqué craft. The colourful materials are used to make temple umbrellas and wall hangings.

KONARK

Population: 11,000

The great temple of Konark (also known as Konarak) is three km from the coast, 33 km from Puri and 64 km from Bhubaneswar. The site consists of little more than the temple and a handful of shops, stalls and places to stay. Although most people make a day trip to Konark from Puri or Bhubaneswar, it's a wonderfully peaceful place to spend a few days and the temple has even more atmosphere once the day-trippers have all gone home. However, there isn't a lot of accommodation here – yet. Several of the major hotel chains want to turn Konark into a new beach resort but planning permission for their hotels may be withheld on environmental grounds. Konark is now protected as a UNESCO World Heritage Site.

If you come to Konark for the day you can take an early morning bus from Puri and a late bus back (or on to Bhubaneswar) in the afternoon, which will give you plenty of time to have a look at the temple.

An open-air theatre has been built near the temple and the Konark Dance Festival is staged here in November. There's a smaller festival in February.

Sun Temple

Konark was constructed in the mid-13th century, but remarkably little is known about its early history. It's thought to have been built by the Orissan king, Narashimhadev I, to celebrate his military victory over the Muslims. It is believed to have fallen into disuse in the early 17th century after being desecrated by one of Jehangir's envoys. Until the early 1900s it was simply an interesting ruin of impressive size.

Then in 1904 debris and sand were cleared from around the temple base and the sheer magnitude of its architect's imagination was revealed. The entire temple was conceived as a chariot for the Sun God, Surya. Around the base of the temple are 24 gigantic carved-stone wheels. Seven mighty horses haul at the temple and the immense structure is covered with carvings, sculptures, figures and bas-reliefs. It is not known if the construction of the temple was ever completed. If the tower was completed it would have soared to 70 metres and archaeologists wonder if the sandy foundations could have supported such a structure. Part of the tower was still standing in 1837 but by 1869 had collapsed. Today the temple's interior has been filled in to support the ruins.

The main entrance, from the Tourist Bungalow side, is guarded by two stone lions crushing elephants. Steps rise to the main entrance, flanked by straining horses. The jagamohan still stands, but the deul behind it has collapsed. The three impressive chlorite images of Surya have been restored to their positions, aligned to catch the sun at dawn, noon and sunset. Between the main steps up to the jagamohan and the entrance enclosure is an intricately carved dancing hall. To the

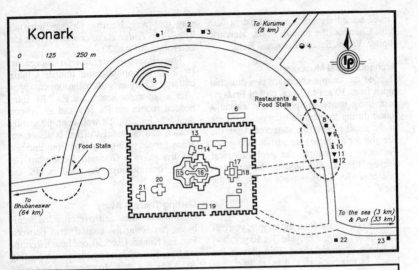

Konark

0   125   250 m

To Kuruma
(8 km)

Restaurants &
Food Stalls

Food Stalls

To
Bhubaneswar
(64 km)

To the sea (3 km)
& Puri (33 km)

1	Archaeological Museum	13	Elephants
2	Travellers' Lodge	14	Well
3	Yatri Nivas	15	Deul
4	Bus Stand	16	Jagamohan
5	Open-Air Theatre	17	Nritya Mandapa
6	Nine Planets' Shrine	18	Gajasimha
7	Bicycle Hire	19	Horses
8	Lodging Sunrise	20	Mayadevi Temple
9	Sun Temple Hotel	21	Brick Temple
10	Tourist Office	22	PWD Inspection Bungalow
11	Gitanjali Restaurant		(VIP's only)
12	Panthanivas Tourist Bungalow	23	Labanya Lodge

north is a group of elephants and to the south a group of horses rearing and trampling men.

At the western end of the temple, the rubble from the collapsed deul has been cleared allowing visitors to climb right down into the sanctuary. The image of the deity that was here is thought to have been moved to the Jagannath Temple in Puri in the 17th century.

Around the base of the temple and up the walls and roof is a continuous procession of carvings. Many are in the erotic style for which Konark, like Khajuraho, is famous. These erotic images of entwined couples, or solitary exhibitionists, can be minute images

on the spoke of a temple wheel or life-size figures higher up the walls.

Originally nearer the coast (the sea has receded), Konark was visible from far out at sea and was known as the Black Pagoda by sailors, in contrast to the whitewashed temples of Puri. It was said to contain a great mass of magnetic iron which would draw unwary ships to the shore.

Nine Planets' Shrine

The six-metre chlorite slab, once the architrave above the main entrance of the jagamohan, is now the centrepiece of a small shrine just outside the temple walls. The carved seated figures represent Surya (the sun), Chandra (the moon), Mars, Mercury, Jupiter, Venus, Saturn, Rahu and Ketu.

Archaeological Museum

Outside the temple enclosure is a museum (open from 10 am to 5 pm, closed Fridays) containing many sculptures and carvings found during the temple excavation. Some of the small pieces (the statue of Agni, the fire god for example) are particularly good. For more information, the Archaeological Survey of India's *Sun Temple – Konark* is on sale here (Rs 5.50) but not at the temple itself.

Konark Beach

The sea is three km from the temple; you can walk there or hire a bicycle (Rs 10 per day) or take a cycle-rickshaw. This part of the beach is much cleaner than at Puri, but beware of the strong current. It's also much quieter than Puri but if they're any children about you're likely to attract their attention, since not many foreigners swim here. With miles of open sand, you can of course always move along the beach a bit. A number of chai-shops sell drinks and snacks here.

Places to Stay & Eat

The cheapest accommodation is around the bus stand and is fairly basic. *Lodging Sunrise* has doubles for Rs 30 with common bathroom and the nearby *Banita Lodge* has rooms with attached bath. *Sun Temple Hotel* is only a restaurant but is a recommended place to eat. There are numerous chai-shops outside the temple entrance – the *Shanti Hotel* has cold beer for Rs 35. There are also a few chai-shops down by the beach.

In a quiet location, the *Labanya Lodge* is a good friendly place popular with travellers. Doubles are Rs 40, or Rs 60 with attached bathroom and there's a nice roof terrace for sunbathing. You can get meals here.

The newly opened *Yatri Nivas* is excellent value at Rs 60 for a double with attached bathroom, or Rs 90 for a four-bedded room. It's currently a good clean place but since it's government-run, there's no guarantee it'll stay that way. Nearby, Orissa Tourism's *Travellers' Lodge* is rather shabby with air-con rooms for Rs 220.

The *Panthanivas Tourist Bungalow* (☎ 223) is opposite the temple's main entrance. Doubles with bathroom equipped with a hot-water heater are Rs 110, four-bedded rooms are Rs 165 and an air-con double is Rs 220. It's well kept, pleasantly located and the tourist office is also here. Many people taking day trips from Puri use the Bungalow's *Gitanjali Restaurant* for meals, but although the food is OK the service can be slow.

Getting There & Away

Dilapidated buses and overcrowded mini-buses run along the coastal road between Puri and Konark (Rs 5.50, one hour). Returning from Konark is no problem – simply flag down any bus, minibus or jeep at any point along the road. Some people even cycle the 33 km from Puri and stay the night at Konark. Although it's a good flat road, make sure the bicycle you hire is in reasonable condition because there are few repair shops along the way.

There are buses fairly regularly to Bhubaneswar, including at least one express bus, usually at 10 am. The fare is Rs 8 and the trip takes around 1½ hours on the express tourist bus, longer on a stop/start local service.

CHILKA LAKE

South-west of Puri, Chilka Lake is dotted with islands and is noted for the many migratory birds which flock in winter (December to January) to the nesting sanctuary here. The shallow lake is about 70 km long and averages 15 km wide, and is supposedly one of the largest brackish-water lakes in the country. It's separated from the sea only by a narrow sand bar. The railway line and the main road run along the inland edge of the lake. It's a peaceful enough place but probably of greatest interest to ornithologists.

Places to Stay

Orissa Tourism is developing a resort on the

lake at Satapada, about 50 km from Puri, where a *Tourist Bungalow* is being built.

There are private hotels at Balugaon, which has a railway station and bus stand. Six km south at Barkul, Orissa Tourism has a *Tourist Bungalow* with doubles for Rs 165 or Rs 275 for air-con rooms. There are launches for hire here, from Rs 100 per hour for a seven-seater, and kayaks for Rs 25 per hour. The hotel is rather run down – even more so since being damaged by a bomb which some guests were apparently putting together in their bedroom when it accidentally went off!

The *Tourist Bungalow* (☎ 346) at Rambha, 130 km from Bhubaneswar, is far more pleasantly located and is a friendly place to stay. Doubles with attached bathrooms and balconies overlooking the lake are Rs 90 or Rs 220 with air-con. There's a good restaurant which sometimes serves crab and prawns from the lake. A launch is available for hire here or the fishers will take you out for Rs 25 per hour.

GOPALPUR-ON-SEA

The sea is clean and there's an excellent beach at this popular but decaying little seaside resort, 18 km south-east of Berhampur.

Places to Stay

Prices vary according to season and demand, and you should be able to get a 50% discount off the high-season (October to January) prices given below if they're aren't many people about.

By the lighthouse, the *Youth Hostel* is rather run down but has beds for Rs 10. Nearby is the friendly *Holiday Inn Lodge* with singles/doubles for Rs 70/100 with attached bathroom.

The *Hotel Kalinga* is a recommended place, right by the sea with good singles/doubles for Rs 100/150 or Rs 175 for a four-bedded room, all with attached bathrooms. It's well run and there's a restaurant here. The *Hotel Holiday Home* opposite is overpriced.

Two cheaper places are the *Hotel Rosalin*

and *Wroxham House*, which is an old bungalow at the far end of Beach Rd. The *Hotel Sea Breeze* has doubles for Rs 130 as well as some cheaper rooms, and it's beside the beach.

The *Motel Mermaid* on Beach Rd is flashy, clean and modern with rooms from Rs 250/350 but this includes all meals.

At the top end there is the 21-room *Oberoi Palm Beach Hotel* (☎ (06812) 8121) with rooms from Rs 1000/1300, also including all meals. It's a luxurious low-key retreat in a coconut grove right by the sea.

Getting There & Away

The only buses from Gopalpur are to Berhampur (Rs 2.50, 45 minutes) which is on the main Calcutta-Madras railway line. A cycle-rickshaw for the three km between the station and the Berhampur bus stand costs Rs 5. From the bus stand there are regular departures to Bhubaneswar (Rs 27, five hours), overnight buses to Jeypur in the south for Rs 65 and regular buses to Taptapani (Rs 6, two hours).

TAPTAPANI

Apart from the small hot springs in this peaceful place in the hills west of Gopalpur, there's not much else to see, and it's really not worth a day trip. However it would make a great winter splurge if you booked one of the two rooms at the *Panthanivas Tourist Bungalow* (☎ Podamari 431) which have hot spring water channelled directly to the vast tubs (accommodating several people) in their Roman-style bathrooms. Double rooms cost Rs 220 and there are also ordinary rooms for Rs 130, with ordinary bathrooms.

Near **Chandragiri**, 36 km away, there's a Tibetan refugee community and a temple. The Tibetans support themselves by weaving carpets, which you can buy here.

CUTTACK

Population: 439,000

Only 35 km north of Bhubaneswar, on the banks of the Mahanadi and Kathajuri Rivers, Cuttack was the capital of Orissa until 1950.

Today it's a chaotic and largely uninteresting place.

Only a gateway and the moat remain of the 14th-century Barabati Fort. The stone revetment on the Kathajuri River, which protects the city from seasonal floods, dates from the 11th century. The Kadam Rasul is a Muslim shrine which contains the Prophet's footprint and has become a place of pilgrimage for Hindus as well as Muslims.

Paradip, 90 km from Cuttack, is a major port and minor beach resort.

Places to Stay

The *Panthanivas Tourist Bungalow* (☎ 23-867) in Buxi Bazaar has doubles for Rs 130 or Rs 220 with air-con, and dorm beds for Rs 30. The *Hotel Neeladri* (☎ 23-831) has singles/doubles from Rs 80/120, and the *Hotel Ashoka* (☎ 25-708) offers rooms for Rs 200/250 or Rs 250/320 with air-con. The *Hotel Akbari Continental* has air-con rooms for Rs 325/390 and a restaurant. There are a number of other small hotels, but if you wish to visit Cuttack it is probably easier to take a day trip from Bhubaneswar.

LALITAGIRI, UDAYAGIRI & RATNAGIRI

Buddhist relics and ruins can be found at these three hilltop complexes, north-east of Cuttack and about 100 km from Bhubaneswar.

At Lalitagiri a gold casket was discovered, thought to contain relics of the Buddha, and excavations are continuing. In the village here artisans make replicas of stone sculptures. Eight km away is Udayagiri with another monastery complex and a brick stupa.

The Ratnagiri site, five km beyond Udayagiri, has the most interesting and extensive ruins and is well worth a visit. The two large monasteries here flourished from the 6th to the 12th centuries AD. There are beautifully carved doorways, a large stupa and enormous Buddha figures.

BALASORE & CHANDIPUR

Balasore is the first major town on the railway line from Calcutta in north Orissa. It was once an important trading centre with Dutch, Danish, English and French factories. In 1634 it was the first British East India Company factory in Bengal. Remina, eight km away, has the Gopinath Temple, an important pilgrimage centre.

Chandipur, 16 km away on the coast, is a beach resort where the beach extends five km at low tide and the sea can be very shallow. There are several buses a day from Balasore.

Places to Stay

The Municipal Tourist Bungalow in Balasore, known as *Deepak Lodging*, is pleasant and reasonably priced. Walk from the station to the main road, turn left and it's on the right-hand side, two blocks from the corner and across the street from the cinema. There are a few small hotels such as the *Hotel Sagarika* or the *Hotel Moonlight*.

In Chandipur there's a good *Panthanivas Tourist Bungalow* with dorm beds for Rs 30, doubles for Rs 150 or Rs 250 with air-con, and cheaper private accommodation.

SIMILIPAL NATIONAL PARK

In the north-east of the state, 250 km from Calcutta and 320 km from Bhubaneswar, this park covers 2750 sq km and is part of Project Tiger. There are leopard, tiger, elephant and several types of deer among the many species here. The scenery is beautiful and varied with hills, waterfalls and undisturbed forest in which the extensive wildlife manages to remain well hidden.

Tourist facilities are not well developed and you must bring all your food and arrange your own transport. The only entrance to the park that is currently open is on the western side at Jashipur. However, if you wish to stay in the park, your first stop has to be the Similipal park office at Baripada, to book your accommodation. Doubles at the six *Forest Rest Houses* dotted round the park range from Rs 40 to Rs 120. The one at Barheipani is recommended as it's near a 450-metre waterfall. More upmarket accommodation should by now be available at the *Similipal Resort* at Bangriposhi, between Baripada and Jashipur.

Jashipur is accessible by bus (or train and bus via Bangriposhi) from Baripada. Mr Roy charges Rs 50 for a double at his *Tourist Lodge* in Jashipur and you can arrange a jeep here (Rs 3.50 per km). You must get a permit from the Assistant Forest Conservator before entering the park.

OTHER ATTRACTIONS

In the north of Orissa, 50 km from Jashipur, **Khiching** was once an ancient capital and has a number of interesting temples, some in ruins, and a small museum. Further inland is the important industrial city of **Rourkela**, which has a major steel plant. A little north-west of Cuttack is the Siva temple of **Kapilas**. The crocodile sanctuary at **Bhitara-kanika** is on the coast north-east of Cuttack, but it's not easy to reach.

In the west on the border with Madhya Pradesh is the 24-km-long **Hirakud Dam**, built to control monsoon floods in the Mahanadi delta around Bhubaneswar. The large town of **Sambalpur**, 22 km south, is a textile centre but **Sonapur**, 80 km south, is more interesting. It's the heart of the ikat weaving district and there are Tantric temples here.

Bronze-casting is done in the **Bolangir** area. **Harishankar**, west of Bolangir, has a number of temples and a waterfall. The twin villages of **Ranipur-Jharial** are 30 km from Titlagarh and are noted for the extensive collection of temples on a rock outcrop. They include a circular 64-*yogini* temple, similar to the one at Khajuraho.

Gupteswar Cave is 85 km west of Koraput. This is in Orissa's large southern district which is inhabited by several tribal peoples including the Bonda.

Sikkim

Population: 421,000
Area: 7214 sq km
Capital: Gangtok
People per sq km: 57
Main Language: Nepali
Literacy Rate: 34%

Until 1975, Sikkim, or New House, was an independent kingdom, albeit under a treaty which allowed the Indian government to control Sikkim's foreign affairs and defence. However, following a period of political crises and riots in the capital, Gangtok, India annexed the country in 1975 and Sikkim became the 22nd Indian state. The move sparked widespread criticism, but tensions have now cooled. The central government has been spending relatively large sums of money to subsidise Sikkim's road building, electrification, water supply and agricultural and industrial development.

Much of this activity was no doubt motivated by India's fear of Chinese military designs on the Himalayan region. Even today, there's still a lot of military activity along the route from Darjeeling to Gangtok, though much of it has been connected over the last five years with the violence accompanying the Gurkha National Liberation Front's demand for their own separate state (Gurkhaland) in the Darjeeling and Kalimpong region.

For many years, Sikkim was regarded as one of the last Himalayan 'Shangri-las' because of its remoteness, spectacular mountain terrain, varied flora and fauna and ancient Buddhist monasteries. It was never easy to visit and, even now, you need a special permit to enter, though that's now easy to obtain (see the Permits section below). All the same, the eastern part of Sikkim along the Tibetan border remains out of bounds and trekking to the base of Kanchenjunga has to be organised through a recognised travel agent.

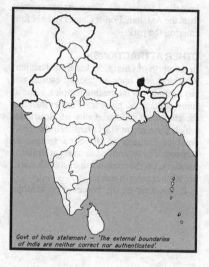

Govt of India statement — 'The external boundaries of India are neither correct nor authenticated'.

History

The country was originally home to the Lepchas, a tribal people thought to have migrated from the hills of Assam around the 13th century. The Lepchas were pacifist forest foragers and small-crop cultivators who worshipped nature spirits. They still constitute some 18% of the total population of Sikkim, though their ability to lead their traditional lifestyle has been severely limited by immigration from Tibet and, more recently, from Nepal.

The Tibetans started to emigrate into Sikkim during the 15th and 16th centuries to escape religious strife between various Lamaist sects. In Tibet itself, the Yellow Hat sect, or Geluk-pa (to which the Dalai Lama belongs), gradually gained the upper hand. In Sikkim, however, the Red Hat sect, or Nyingma-pa, remained in control and was the official state religion until the country became a part of India. In the face of the waves of Tibetan immigrants, the Lepchas

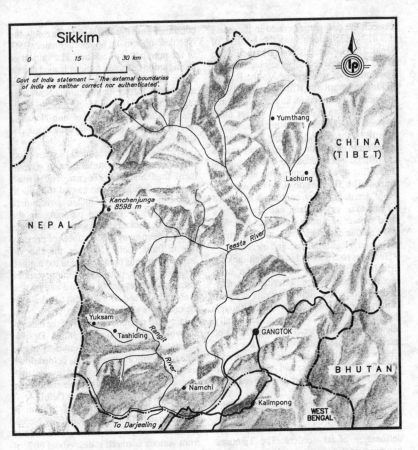

Sikkim

Govt of India statement — 'The external boundaries
of India are neither correct nor authenticated'.

NEPAL

Kanchenjunga
8598 m

CHINA
(TIBET)

Yumthang

Lachung

Teesta River

Yuksam

Tashiding

Rangit River

GANGTOK

BHUTAN

Namchi

Kalimpong

WEST
BENGAL

To Darjeeling

originally retreated to the more remote regions. A blood brotherhood was eventually forged between their leader, Thekong Tek, and the Bhutias leader, Khye-Bumsa, and spiritual and temporal authority was imposed on the anarchistic Lepchas.

In 1641, the Dalai Lama in Lhasa appointed Penchoo Namgyal as the first king of Sikkim. At that time, the country included the area encompassed by the present state as well as part of eastern Nepal, the Chumbi Valley (Tibet), Ha Valley (Bhutan) and the Terai foothills down to the plains of India, including Darjeeling and Kalimpong.

Between 1717 and 1734, during the reign of Sikkim's fourth king, a series of wars fought with the Bhutanese resulted in the loss of much territory in the southern foothills, including Kalimpong, then a very important bazaar town on the trade route between Tibet and India. More territory was lost after 1780 following the Gurkha invasion from Nepal, though the invaders were eventually checked by a Chinese army with Bhutanese and Lepcha assistance. Unable to advance into Tibet, the Gurkhas turned south where they came into conflict with the British East India Company. The wars between the two parties ended in the treaty of 1817 which delineated the borders of Nepal. The Gurkhas also ceded to the British all the Sikkimese territory they had taken; a substantial part was returned to the Raja of Sikkim in return for British control of all disputes between Sikkim and its neighbours. The country thus became a buffer state between Nepal, Tibet and Bhutan.

In 1835, the British, seeking a hill station as a rest and recreation centre for their troops and officials, persuaded the raja to cede the Darjeeling area in return for an annual stipend. The Tibetans objected to this transfer of territory. They continued to regard Sikkim as a vassal state, and Darjeeling's rapid growth as a trade centre had begun to make a considerable impact on the fortunes of Sikkim's leading lamas and merchants.

Tensions rose and, in 1849, a high-ranking British official and a botanist, who were exploring the Lachen region with the permission of both the Sikkimese raja and the British government, were arrested. Although the two prisoners were unconditionally released a month later following threats of intervention, the British annexed the entire area between the present Sikkimese border and the Indian plains and withdrew the Raja's stipend (the stipend was eventually restored to his son).

Further British interference in the affairs of this area led to the declaration of a protectorate over Sikkim in 1861 and the delineation of its borders. The Tibetans, however, continued to regard these actions as illegal and, in 1886, invaded Sikkim to reassert their authority. The attack was repulsed by the British, who sent a punitive military expedition to Lhasa in 1888 in retaliation. The powers of the Sikkimese raja were further reduced and high-handed treatment by British officials prompted him to flee to Lhasa in 1892, though he was eventually persuaded to return.

Keen to develop Sikkim, the British encouraged immigration from Nepal, as they had done in Darjeeling, and a considerable amount of land was brought under rice and cardamom cultivation. This influx of labour continued until the 1960s and, as a result, the Nepalese now make up approximately 75% of the population of Sikkim. The subject of immigration became a topic of heated debate in the late '60s and the raja was constrained to prohibit further immigration. New laws regarding the rights of citizenship were designed to placate those of non-Nepalese origin, but they served to inflame the opposition parties.

There was also a great deal of grass-roots support for a more popular form of government than Sikkim's *chogyal*. The British treaties with Sikkim had passed to India at independence and the Indian government had no wish to be seen propping up the regime of an autocratic raja while doing their best to sweep away the last traces of princely rule in India itself. However, the chogyal resisted demands for a change in the method of government until the demonstrations threatened to get out of control and he was eventually forced to ask India to take over the country's administration.

In a 1975 referendum, 97% of the electorate voted for union with India. Despite significant international resentment at the time, the political situation has cooled down and Sikkim is now governed by its own democratic congress with representatives in the central government in New Delhi.

The current population of Sikkim is approximately 18% Lepcha and 75% Nepalese; the other 7% are Bhutias and Indians from various northern states. About 60% of the population is Hindu and 28% Buddhist, although the two religions exist, as in many parts of Nepal, in a syncretic form. The ancient Buddhist monasteries, of which there are a great many, are one of the principal attractions of a visit to Sikkim.

Permits

With a view to promoting tourism in Sikkim, permit rules for foreigners have been considerably relaxed and permits can now be obtained either while you wait or within a few hours. You will need your passport and one photo. The permitted length of stay in Sikkim is usually 15 days though it could be only 10 days (extendible to 15 days in Gangtok without fuss). The places you are allowed to visit are Gangtok, Rumtek, Phodang, Pemayangtse, Tashiding, Naya Bazaar and the Yuksam-Dzongri trekking route. If your permit doesn't mention any of these places, you can get them added in Gangtok without fuss. There's no charge for permits.

Permits are best obtained in India itself from any of the following places:

Any Foreigners' Regional Registration Office (Delhi, Bombay, Calcutta, Madras)

Immigration at Delhi, Bombay, Calcutta or Madras airports

Resident Commissioner, Govt of Sikkim, 14 Panchseel Marg, Chanakyapuri, New Delhi (☎ 301-5346)

Sikkim Tourist Information Centre, SNT Bus Compound, Siliguri, West Bengal (☎ 24-602)

Assistant Resident Commissioner, Govt of Sikkim, 4C Poonam, 5 Russell St, Calcutta (☎ 29-7516)

Deputy Commissioner, Darjeeling, West Bengal

Deputy Secretary, Home Department, Govt of West Bengal, Calcutta

You can also have your Indian visa endorsed for Sikkim when you apply for it at an embassy or consulate. You should ask them to specify Gangtok, Rumtek, Phodang and Pemayangtse, which they are authorised to issue.

You are only allowed one 15-day permit for Sikkim per year. It's virtually impossible to get around this as your permit and passport are checked and stamped twice both on the way in and on the way out, so there's a record of your visit.

Trekking permits are obligatory for those wishing to trek in the Dzongri region. These are in addition to the normal permit and are issued at the Foreigners' Registration Office in Gangtok (above the tourist office). To get one, you must be part of a group of at least four people and have made a booking for a trek with a recognised travel agent. The government will arrange for a liaison officer/guide to accompany you. You can not simply go trekking on your own, or without a booking, or a trekking permit.

A trekking permit does not allow you to extend your stay in Sikkim beyond 15 days so it makes sense to have a trek organised before your arrival in Gangtok.

If you're on your way to Sikkim by train from Calcutta, you'll find a Foreigners' Registration Office on the platform at New Jalpaiguri Station, Siliguri (West Bengal). In theory, you're supposed to present your passport here but they don't stamp it so you can give it a miss. This office is a legacy of the days when a permit was required to visit Darjeeling/Kalimpong and should have been closed down a long time ago. Retrenchment of staff at redundant offices is obviously not a West Bengal government priority.

GANGTOK

Population: 25,000

Gangtok, the capital of Sikkim, occupies the west side of a long ridge flanking the Ranipool River. The scenery is spectacular and there are excellent views of the entire Kanchenjunga range from many points in the vicinity. Many people expect Sikkim to be a smaller version of Kathmandu overflowing with ancient temples, palaces, monasteries and narrow, colourful bazaars. It's not, but it is an interesting and pleasant place to stay and people here are exceptionally friendly. Gangtok only became the capital in the mid-1800s (previous capitals were at Yuksam and Rabdantse) and the town has undergone rapid modernisation in recent years.

Orientation

To the north is Raj Bhavan, the former British and later Indian Residency. Above this is the Tourist Lodge, Enchey Monastery and the telecommunications tower. The palace of the former chogyal and the impressive Royal Chapel (the Tsuk-La-Khang) are lower down along the ridge. Nearby is the huge Secretariat complex and, below it, the newly built Legislative Assembly, both executed in a style reminiscent of traditional architectural modes.

On a continuation of this ridge but much lower is the Institute of Tibetology, an orchid sanctuary and, not far beyond the institute, a large chorten (Tibetan stupa) and adjoining monastery.

All the main facilities – hotels, cafes, bazaars, bus stand, post office, tourist information centre and the Foreigners' Registration Office – are either on, or very near, the main Darjeeling/Rangpo road (Highway 31A).

Information

Tourist Office The tourist office is staffed by friendly and exceptionally helpful people and is open Monday to Saturday from 8 am to 4 pm; closed Sunday. The Foreigners' Registration Office is open Monday to Friday from 10 am to 1 pm; closed Sunday.

Money The State Bank of India, opposite the tourist office, is very helpful and efficient as is the State Bank of Sikkim, at the junction of the National Highway and Paljor Stadium Rd.

Post & Telecommunications The post office is open for mail Monday to Saturday and every day for long-distance/IDD telephone calls. International connections take seconds but domestic lines are subject to faults and long delays. New cables are being installed but the work is taking a long time. Gangtok's telephone area code is 0359.

Bookshops & Newspapers There are very few bookshops in Gangtok. The best is General Stores, M G Marg, diagonally opposite the tourist office. National daily newspapers are available here but are always a day old.

Tsuk-La-Khang

The Royal Chapel is the Buddhists' principal place of worship and assembly and the repository of a large collection of scriptures. It's a beautiful and impressive building, and its interior is covered with murals. Lavishly decorated altars hold images of the Buddha, bodhisattvas and Tantric deities and there are also a great many fine woodcarvings. A notice outside the entrance opposite the secretariat says, 'No sightseeing beyond this point'. However, if you approach the army officer inside the compound and courteously ask for permission to visit, it will be equally courteously granted, but you must remember that photography is forbidden.

The chapel is the site for such important festivals as the mid-September celebration which is dedicated to the god of Kanchenjunga, and the New Year celebration when the famous Black Hat dance portrays the triumph of good over evil.

Namgyal Institute of Tibetology

Established in 1958 and built in traditional style, this unique institute promotes research on the language and traditions of Tibet, as well as on Mahayana Buddhism. It has one of the world's largest collection of books and rare manuscripts on the subject of Mahayana Buddhism, many religious works of art and a collection of astonishingly beautiful and incredibly finely executed silk-embroidered thankas (cloth paintings). It also has a number of religious art and craft works, as well as books, for sale. The institute is open from 10 am to 4 pm, Monday to Saturday, and there is no entrance fee.

Chorten & Monastery

The gold apex of a huge white chorten, about 500 metres beyond the institute, is visible from many points in Gangtok and is surrounded by prayer flags attached to bamboo poles. Next to it is a monastery for young lamas with a shrine containing huge images of Guru Padmasambhava, the Indian teacher of Buddhism in Tibet, and his manifestation, Guru Snang-Sid Zilzon. As at other Buddhist monasteries, the chorten is surrounded by prayer wheels.

Orchid Sanctuary

Surrounding the institute and itself enclosed by a peaceful forest is the Orchid Sanctuary, where you can see many of the 454 species of orchid found in Sikkim. The best times to visit are April-May, July-August and October-November.

There is another, much larger, orchid sanctuary, off the main road to Rangpo alongside

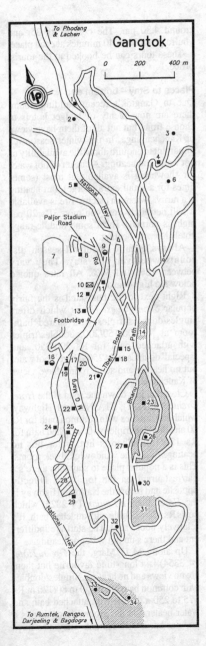

Gangtok

0   200   400 m

■ PLACES TO STAY

1   PWD Bungalow
4   Siniolchu Lodge
5   Hotel Himulchuli
8   Nor-Khill Hotel
11 Hotel Chumila
12 Hotel Tibet
13 Hotel Mayur
15 Modern Central Lodge
18 Hotel Lhakpa
19 Green Hotel
22 Hotel Tashi Delek
24 Hotel Shere-e-Punjab
25 Hotel Orchid
27 Tashi Lodge
29 Hotel Laden La

▼ PLACES TO EAT

20 House of Bamboo

OTHER

2   Cottage Industries Emporium
3   Telecommunications Tower
6   Enchey Monastery
7   Stadium
9   SNT Bus Station
10 GPO
14 Pavilion & Park
16 Private Bus Stand &
    Sunny Guest House
17 Tourist Office & Blue Sheep
    Restaurant
21 Indian Airlines
23 Palace
26 Tsuk-La-Khang (Royal Chapel)
28 Lall Market
30 Secretariat Complex
31 Deer Park
32 Legislative Assembly
33 Namgyal Institute of Tibetology &
    Orchid Sanctuary
34 Chorten & Monastery

To Phodang & Lachen

National Hwy

Paljor Stadium Road

Footbridge

M G Marg

Tibet Road

Bhanu Path

National Hwy

To Rumtek, Rangpo, Darjeeling & Bagdogra

the Teesta River, called the **Orchidarium**, which is accessible by public bus. It's also usually included on tours to the Rumtek Monastery.

Institute of Cottage Industries

High up on the main road above the town, the Cottage Industries Emporium specialises in producing handwoven carpets, blankets, shawls, Lepcha weaves, patterned decorative paper and 'Choktse' tables, exquisitely carved in relief. It's open from 9 am to 12.30 pm and 1 to 3.30 pm daily, except Sundays, and every second Saturday.

Deer Park

This popular viewpoint is on the edge of the ridge next to the Secretariat building. In it, as you might expect, are deer and a replica of the Buddha image at Sarnath in Uttar Pradesh, as well as a caged bear, which anyone with only a vague sympathy for the Animal Liberation movement would want to see released. The current obsession with human rights obviously does not extend to animal rights in this place.

Enchey Monastery

Above the Tourist Lodge, about three km from the centre of town, the 200-year-old Enchey Monastery is well worth a visit, particularly if you're in Gangtok when religious dances are performed in December. It's a relatively small place and doesn't compare with the other larger monasteries in Sikkim, but it does sit on a spectacular ridge overlooking Gangtok, and there are views across to Kanchenjunga.

Lall Market

If you've been to markets in Kathmandu or Darjeeling, this one may come as a disappointment due to its limited range of craft shops, but the vegetable market is certainly colourful and there's plenty of activity.

Organised Tours

The Department of Tourism offers tours of Gangtok, from Monday to Saturday at 10 am, returning at 12.30 pm, for Rs 25. The tour includes visits to Tashi Viewpoint, the Deer Park, Enchey Monastery, the Royal Chapel, the Secretariat, the Cottage Industries Emporium, the Institute of Tibetology and the nearby chorten and orchid sanctuary.

The other tour is to Rumtek Monastery and the Orchidarium. It operates from Monday to Saturday at 1.30 pm, returning around 4.30 pm. The cost is Rs 35, and you're given 30 to 40 minutes at each place.

These tours can be booked at the tourist office.

Places to Stay – bottom end

Due to Gangtok's recent building boom, there are now plenty of budget hotels to choose from, but not all of them have views of Kanchenjunga. In the winter season it's important to enquire about the availability of hot water and heating. A bucket of hot water for showering is available at most (sometimes for a small extra charge), but heating is a rarity. Where an electric fire is available it will definitely cost you more (Rs 20 per night is normal). Even some middle-range hotels have no heating.

Always enquire about off-season discounts wherever you stay. They vary between 15% and 30%. All rates quoted below are high-season rates.

Right next to the bus stand is the fairly popular *Sunny Guest House* which offers singles/doubles/triples with shared bathroom at Rs 100/150/200, doubles/triples with attached bath for Rs 200/250, and 'special' doubles at Rs 250. There's hot water but no heating and some rooms have views of Kanchenjunga.

Close by, just down the road is the *Hotel Orchid* (☎ 3151), 31A National Highway, which has doubles with common bath for Rs 80 and doubles/triples with attached bath for Rs 120/150. There's hot water but no heating. Avoid the windowless back rooms. This is a popular place to stay plus there's a bar/restaurant on the top floor. Directly opposite and below the National Highway is the *Hotel Shere-e-Punjab* (☎ 2823) which costs Rs 150 a double with attached bath. It's relatively poor value. The staff are indifferent and there's no hot water or heating.

Up along M G Marg, the *Green Hotel* (☎ 3354) is a long-time favourite but there are no views and no heating. Singles/doubles with common bath are Rs 70 to 80/120 or Rs 175 to 250 a double with attached bath and water heater. On the ground floor there's a popular bar and restaurant. They also have an annex elsewhere in town, the *New Green Hotel*, which does have views and costs Rs 120/175 for doubles/triples. Bucket hot water is available.

Further along M G Marg, the *Doma Hotel* has singles with common bath for Rs 50 and doubles with attached bath for Rs 100 but there's no hot water or heating. The hotel has a restaurant and bar. Others along this same road include the *Glacier Guest House* (Rs 150 a double); *Karma Hotel* (Rs 75 a double with attached bath; no views, no hot water or heating); *Sunshine Lodge, Crown Lodge* and *Hotel Hillview*. They're all similarly priced but most are featureless concrete boxes with no views and no hot water or heating.

Avoid the semi-derelict *Deepak Hotel* on this road.

Down in Lall Market, the *Hotel Laden La* is pleasant and would be a good place to stay but it's situated right next to the meat market and abattoir so the air doesn't smell too good.

Above M G Marg, along Tibet Road, are a number of new and almost new upper-range budget hotels. These are much better value in general and you can almost always get a room with a view of Kanchenjunga.

Excellent value and very popular is the *Modern Central Lodge*, run by a young Sikkimese man who is very friendly and helpful and will probably meet you as you get off the bus down at the bus stand. It's excellent value at Rs 120/140 for a triple/four-bed room with common bath or Rs 120/150 for doubles/triples with attached bath. Both bucket hot water and heating (Rs 20) are available. Cheap, tasty food is available in the restaurant/bar (which also has a good sound system) and there's even a snooker hall!

Almost next door is the *Hotel Lhakpa* (☎ 3002) which isn't as popular but is probably just as good. It has singles/triples and four-bed rooms with common bath for Rs 80/120/140 as well as doubles/triples with attached bath for Rs 120/150. There's bucket hot water but no heating, and the hotel has its own restaurant and bar.

Along Paljor Stadium Road below the GPO are another cluster of budget hotels.

Sikkimese Woman

They include the *Hotel Chumila* (☎ 3361), a small place with singles/doubles/triples and four-bed rooms with attached bath for Rs 80/125/180/250. Like the Modern Central Lodge, this is run by a very friendly and helpful young Sikkimese man, Kunzang Chewong Denzongpa, and his affable Keralan manager, Sebastian. The bar/restaurant here turns out excellent, cheap, tasty food.

Below the Chumila along the same road are other budget hotels – the *Hotel Orient, Hotel Sikkim* (very basic), *Hotel Lhakhar* and *Hotel Mount View*.

Further afield, the new *Hotel Himulchuli* (☎ 2714), National Highway, is an excellent little place with only five rooms but superb views, very friendly staff and both a rooftop and indoor restaurant. It's also where Yak & Yeti Travel have their trekking office. Singles/doubles/triples with attached bath, hot water, heating and TV cost Rs 150/275/375. There's even a telescope for viewing Kanchenjunga.

Very cheap but a long way out from the centre and a strenuous hike uphill is the

Siniolchu Lodge (☎ 2074), just below the entrance to Enchey Monastery. The lodge is run by Sikkim Tourism and has possibly the best views in town. Self-contained 'economy' singles/doubles are Rs 50/75, and Rs 80/120 for 'deluxe' rooms plus 10% tax. Only the 'deluxe' rooms have their own water heater. There's no heating. The easiest way to get there is by taxi.

Just below the Royal Palace is the *Tashi Lodge* (☎ 3014) on Bhanu Path. This also has excellent views but is a strenuous climb uphill if you're not taking a taxi.

Places to Stay – middle

The best hotel by far in this range is the *Hotel Tibet* (☎ 2523), Paljor Stadium Rd, next door to the GPO. Done out in traditional Tibetan style, it's very pleasant and comfortable and the staff will do almost anything for you. On the top floor is the residence of the Dalai Lama's Sikkim representative. Standard singles/doubles are Rs 305/395 and deluxe singles/doubles Rs 355/475 plus there are more expensive suites. All the rooms have hot water and TV, and heating is available. The views of Kanchenjunga from the back rooms are excellent. There's a bar and restaurant serving excellent Tibetan, Chinese, Indian and Continental dishes and credit cards are accepted. A discount of up to 30% applies in the off season.

Close to the above at the junction of National Highway and Paljor Stadium Rd is the *Hotel Mayur* (☎ 2825), another of the hotels run by Sikkim Tourism. This isn't such good value as, overall, it's more expensive though for no apparent reason and there's no heating available. Standard singles/doubles are Rs 200/250, deluxe singles/doubles Rs 325/400, and super deluxe singles/doubles Rs 400/475, excluding 10% service charges. All the rooms are self-contained with hot water. There's a bar and restaurant, and car-parking facilities are also available.

Places to Stay – top end

The best and most convenient hotel in this range is the *Hotel Tashi Delek* (☎ 2038), M

G Marg, which, like the Hotel Tibet, is done out in traditional decor. The staff are very friendly and eager to please and there are great views from the roof garden/restaurant (Sikkimese, Chinese, Continental and tandoori cuisine). There's also a bar. Singles/doubles are Rs 380/550 and there are double suites for Rs 750, with an additional 10% service charge. Full-board rates are Rs 750/1200 plus 10% service charge. Credit cards are accepted.

Further afield, the *Nor-Khill Hotel* (☎ 3187), just off the bottom of Paljor Stadium Rd and above the actual stadium, isn't such good value though it is spacious, and is cheaper in the off season. The trouble with this hotel is that they will only rent rooms without meals (European plan) in the off season. During the rest of the year, you must take a room with full board (American plan). Singles/doubles with full board are Rs 750/1050 and suites Rs 1150, all with an additional 10% service charge. There's a bar and restaurant (Indian, Chinese, tandoori and Continental cuisine).

Places to Eat

Most of the hotels in Gangtok have their own restaurants and some of them are very good. Those at the *Hotel Orchid, Green Hotel* and *Modern Central Lodge* are popular with budget travellers. All offer cheap, tasty and filling meals in a variety of cuisines – usually Tibetan, Chinese and Indian – plus most can usually rustle up what would pass for a Western-style breakfast (eggs, toast and the like).

Other than hotel restaurants, an excellent cheap place to eat which is popular with both local people and travellers is the *House of Bamboo*, M G Marg opposite the Green Hotel. The restaurant offers tasty Tibetan and Chinese dishes and is a cosy place to be on a cold day. As with most Sikkimese restaurants, there's an attached bar.

A new fast-food outlet has also opened diagonally opposite the Hotel Tibet. It's called *D'Zom's Pizza Point* but was closed when this edition was being researched.

For a splurge close by, there's the *Blue*

Sheep, also on M G Marg next to the tourist office. The speciality here is sizzlers but they also do Sikkimese and Chinese dishes. Further afield, try the *Snow Lion Restaurant* in the Hotel Tibet or the *Shaepi* in the Hotel Mayur.

Top of the line is a meal at the *Blue Poppy* in the Hotel Tashi Delek. Breakfast here costs Rs 45 and lunch or dinner is Rs 90.

Try thungba from a chang shop in the market – a large bamboo mug full of millet to which you add hot water to get fresh chang.

Entertainment
Gangtok is essentially early-to-bed territory, though there are cinemas. There are also numerous bars, most attached to restaurants but not all. Drinkers will find the price of beer and spirits in Sikkim refreshingly cheap after West Bengal.

Getting There & Away
Air Indian Airlines (☎ 3099) has an agency on Tibet Rd which is open Monday to Saturday from 10 am to 4.30 pm; closed Sunday. The nearest airport is at Bagdogra near Siliguri. The Indian Airlines' helicopter service between Bagdogra airport and Gangtok has been discontinued. There are no other air connections.

Public Bus Sikkim Nationalised Transport (SNT) is the main bus operator to Gangtok and their buses are not bad as long as you get one of the two-plus-two (2+2) seat buses. The three-plus-two (3+2) seat buses are a crush, and are very uncomfortable if you have normal to long legs. The advance booking office is open daily from 9.30 to 11 am and 1.30 to 2.30 pm. The early morning services are heavily subscribed so make sure you book in advance.

SNT operates the following interstate bus services:

To/From Siliguri There are 2+2 buses four times daily in either direction which take 4½ hours and cost Rs 65. There are also 3x2 buses six times daily in either direction

which take about the same amount of time but are somewhat cheaper. In Siliguri, these buses depart from and arrive at the SNT bus station which is different to but not far from the West Bengal state bus stand.

To/From Bagdogra There is one 2+2 bus daily in either direction which leaves Gangtok at 7 am, takes 4½ hours and costs Rs 65.

To/From Darjeeling There is one 2+2 bus daily in either direction which leaves at 7 am, takes seven hours and costs Rs 50.

To/From Kalimpong There is one 2+2 bus daily at 8.30 am and one 3+2 bus daily at 1.30 pm which take four hours and cost Rs 25.

Private Bus In addition to the SNT buses, there are private buses which run between Siliguri and Gangtok, and Darjeeling and Gangtok. However, although they're cheaper (Rs 30 and Rs 50), they're not much use if you're planning to leave Gangtok and get to New Jalpaiguri Station for the overnight *Darjeeling Mail* to Calcutta which leaves at 7 pm. Most leave Gangtok in the early afternoon and are scheduled to arrive in Siliguri between 6 and 6.30 pm which leaves you hardly enough time to get to New Jalpaiguri from Siliguri (about half an hour even in an auto-rickshaw). If there are any delays, you'll miss the train. In the opposite direction, of course, you don't face these problems.

The 3+2 Diamond Express bus which leaves Gangtok at 1.30 pm and arrives in Darjeeling at 6 pm at a cost of Rs 47 may, on the other hand, be of interest.

All the private buses depart from and arrive at the private bus stand adjacent to the Sunny Guest House in Gangtok. There's a booking office here and a timetable of the various bus trips, but the office rarely seems to be staffed in the mornings. In Siliguri, these buses leave from the West Bengal state bus stand. Private buses are a mixture of 2+2 and 3+2 buses.

The Hotel Tashi Delek in Gangtok also

operates a 3+2 bus from Gangtok to Darjeeling which leaves daily at 7.30 am and costs Rs 49 as well as a super deluxe bus to Calcutta daily at 2 pm which arrives at about 8 am and costs Rs 175. These buses also depart from the private bus stand but tickets should be bought from the hotel.

Local Buses There are plenty of domestic bus routes within Sikkim operated by SNT but, due to permit restrictions, only some of these are of interest to travellers.

To Phodang To get to this monastery (38 km from Gangtok) you need to take a bus going to Mangan or Singhik. They depart Gangtok daily at 8 am, 1.30 and 4 pm and take about two hours to Phodang and five hours to Mangan. In the opposite direction, the buses leave Mangan at 7 am and 1 pm which means they come through Phodang at approximately 10 am and 4 pm.

To Rumtek There is a daily bus from Gangtok at 4.30 pm which returns at 8 am the next day. The journey takes one hour and costs Rs 7. It obviously means you have to stay overnight in Rumtek.

To Jorethang This is the bus to take if you're heading for Darjeeling via Naya Bazaar. There are two daily buses from Gangtok at 8 am and 3 pm.

To Gezing This is the bus to take if you're heading for Pemayangtse, Dzongri or Tashiding in western Sikkim. There are daily buses from Gangtok at 7 am and 1 pm which take six hours and cost Rs 35. They return from Dzongri daily at 8 am and 1 pm. This service is heavily subscribed and advance booking is essential.

From Gezing (also spelt Gyalshing and Geyzing) there is a daily bus to Pelling (eight km) at 2.30 pm which costs Rs 3. This bus passes the turnoff to Pemayangtse Monastery (six km). Alternatively, you can walk from Gezing to Pemayangtse.

Your Sikkimese permit will be checked and your passport stamped at Legship, 16 km before Gezing.

Train The nearest railheads are at Siliguri/New Jalpaiguri and Darjeeling (though the toy train between Siliguri and Darjeeling has been suspended for a number of years; check the Darjeeling section in the West Bengal chapter for details).

There is a railway booking office in the SNT bus station which is open Monday to Saturday from 9.30 to 11 am and 1.30 to 2.30 pm. You can make reservations here for trains passing through or originating from Siliguri/New Jalpaiguri.

Taxi From the booking office at the private bus stand, you can also arrange private taxis to Siliguri, Darjeeling, Calcutta and Kathmandu. They're naturally much more expensive than the buses so you'd need enough people to fill one in order to keep costs reasonable.

Getting Around
Gangtok local taxis have fixed rates and carry a card showing these but there are no meters. All the taxis are new or near-new Maruti cars.

There are also quite a few private minivans which act as taxis and which park either below the Lall Market near the Hotel Orchid or along M G Marg. They're useful if you have a small group together and want to visit Rumtek or Phodang monasteries but wish to stay there longer than the 40 minutes which the tour buses allow. Average prices for the vehicle are Rs 138 one way or Rs 207 return plus Rs 28 per hour waiting time to Rumtek, and Rs 300 to Rs 350 (negotiable) return to Phodang.

AROUND GANGTOK
Rumtek Monastery
Rumtek, on the other side of the Ranipool Valley, is visible from Gangtok though it's 24 km away by road. The monastery is the seat of the Gyalwa Karmapa, the head of the Kagyu-pa sect of Tibetan Buddhism. The sect was founded in the 11th century by

Lama Marpa, the disciple of the Indian guru Naropa, and later split into several subsects, the most important of which are Druk-pa, Kagyu-pa and Karma-pa. The teachings of the sect are transmitted to the disciples orally.

The main monastery is a recent structure, built by the Gyalwa Karmapa in strict accordance with the traditional designs of his monastery in Tibet. Visitors are welcome and there's no objection to your sitting in on the prayer and chanting sessions. They'll even bring you a cup of salted butter tea when it's served to the monks. Mural work here is exquisite and a visit is a must if you're interested in the Tibetan style of religious painting.

If you follow the tarmac road for two or three km beyond Rumtek, through a gate off to the left you'll find another interesting, but smaller, monastery which was restored in 1983. Opposite is an old and run-down monastery with leather prayer wheels.

Places to Stay The *Kunga Delak Hotel & Restaurant* (no sign) is off the square in front of the monastery and has cheap rooms. It's dirty, with no water (although the rooms have bathrooms) and if you arrive late in the evening they may have no food for you. Better is the *Sangay Hotel*, 100 metres down the motor road from the monastery. It's basic but clean, and blankets and candles are provided (there's no electricity most of the time). It's run by friendly people and the price of a room is negotiable – reckon on Rs 30 per bed. Just below the hotel is a small chai shop where eggs and fresh bread are served in the morning, chow-chow in the evening.

The alternative to the hotels is to find a room with one of the villagers.

A new place to stay, the *Shambala Hotel*, is under construction not far from the main gate but will not be completed for some time. By the looks of what is being built, it will be a middle-range hotel.

Getting There & Away See the Gangtok section for details of local buses, tours and taxis to Rumtek.

Phodang & Labrang Monasteries

Phodang Monastery, some 38 km north of Gangtok along a winding and somewhat tortuous but largely tarmacked road, is much smaller and less ornate than Rumtek but it doesn't have the tourist hordes that Rumtek attracts. Here you can feel the timelessness of a part of Sikkim which tourists rarely visit. The monastery sits high up above the main road to Mangan and there are tremendous views down into the valley below.

Phodang is a fairly recent structure and there are far fewer monks here than at Rumtek, but they're very friendly and will take you around and explain the salient features of the monastery. The back room behind the altar has perhaps the most striking murals and was succinctly described by one of the authors' travelling companions as 'an acid-head's nightmare'! Executed largely in black, it depicts various demonic deities dismembering miscreants in the bowels of hell. Leave a donation.

Labrang Monastery is some two km further uphill from Phodang and is a much older structure. Unfortunately, if you're only visiting for the day and relying on public transport, you probably won't have time to walk up there and back in time to catch the last bus to Gangtok which comes through Phodang at around 4 pm. If you're intent on visiting Labrang, it's best to stay overnight.

Places to Stay & Eat Sikkim Tourism have a *Tourist Lodge* right next to Phodang Monastery with beds, sheets and blankets. The toilets and showers are spotless (cold water only) and food is available if requested in advance. It costs Rs 20 per person per night. It's best to book this place at the tourist office in Gangtok so that the caretaker can get things organised before you arrive.

Somewhat more comfortable is the *Yak & Yeti Hotel* about two km beyond the turnoff for the monastery. It costs Rs 110/130 for singles/doubles and those who have stayed there recommend it. There are no hotels as such in Phodang village.

Getting There & Away See the Gangtok

section for details of local buses and taxis to Phodang.

WESTERN SIKKIM

Until recently, this area of Sikkim was off limits to foreigners, but it has now been opened up and is attracting more and more visitors. Its main attractions, other than trekking up to Dzongri at the base of Kanchenjunga, are the two old monasteries of Pemayangtse and Tashiding.

Your Sikkim permit should allow you to visit Pemayangtse, Tashiding and to go from there to Jorethang on the Ranjit River (where you can cross over to West Bengal and go directly to Darjeeling). If it doesn't, get it altered to include these places in Gangtok – they'll do it on the spot. For Phodang and Pemayangtse, however, it is best to get your permit validated in a consulate overseas, as these places can be visited direct from Darjeeling.

In theory, these are the only places you're allowed to visit without a trekking permit but, in practice, there's a considerable amount of leeway. Many of the police checkpoints in this part of Sikkim are none too familiar with the permit system. There is also no longer a police checkpoint at Pelling. The next one is at Yuksam and the officer who staffs it is very friendly. He'll allow you to stay overnight there and may even allow you to do a half-day trek along the Dzongri trail *if you don't take your pack* but you will not be allowed to go further if that's clearly your intention (ie if you attempt to set off with a full pack).

Pemayangtse Monastery

Standing at a height of 2085 metres and surrounded on two sides by snow-capped mountains, Pemayangtse is one of the state's oldest and most important monasteries. It was originally founded in 1705 but was badly damaged in the earthquakes of 1913 and 1960. It has been reconstructed several times, and belongs to the Tantric Nyingmapa sect, which was established by the Indian teacher, Padmasambhava, in the 8th century. All the sect's monasteries are characterised by a prominent image of this teacher, together with two female consorts, and this monastery is the head of all others in Sikkim. The sect followers wear red caps.

The monastery is a three-storied structure filled with wall paintings and sculptures including a seven-tiered painted wooden model of paradise and hell complete with rainbows, angels and the whole panoply of Buddhas and bodhisattvas on the third floor. The model was built single-handedly by the late Dungzin Rinpoche in five years.

Pemayangtse is about six km uphill from Gezing or two km from Pelling. The SNT bus from Gezing to Pelling passes by the turnoff for Pemayangtse.

Places to Stay & Eat You have a choice of staying at Gezing, Pemayangtse or Pelling. Pelling is your best bet if you want something half decent but at budget rates. Pemayangtse is best if you want a degree of comfort in a middle-range hotel. Gezing would be the last choice.

Pelling Pelling is a pleasant town with good views and only two km from Pemayangtse. The *Hotel Kabur*, two km downhill away from Gezing, is a modern concrete building with good views from some of the rooms. A bed in a double room here with common bath costs Rs 25 per person, and a bucket of lukewarm water will be supplied on request. Sheets and pillows are provided and there is electricity and running water but you'll need a sleeping bag. There's a flat roof with deck chairs for sunny days. There's also a restaurant but the food is only mediocre.

One hundred metres further downhill is the *Hotel Garuda*, a classic travellers' hangout and the best one to use as a base for trekking up to Dzongri and for visiting Pemayangtse. The staff are very friendly and will store excess gear while you go trekking, and there's an excellent trekking map on the wall. The beds, which cost Rs 25 each, are not as good as those at the Kabur but the Garuda's Tibetan restaurant and bar is far better.

Further downhill from the Garuda, to the

right of the Magnolia Kindergarten, is a Tibetan family's house where you can buy woodcarvings and drink thugpa (chhang) all evening.

Pemayangtse At Pemayangtse there is a *Trekkers' Hut* but it's more or less derelict, there are no beds, and the toilets are gross, but this doesn't seem to prevent some people from staying here.

A few minutes walk downhill from the monastery is the *Hotel Mt Pandim* (☎ 73), run by Sikkim Tourism and known to the locals as the 'Tourist Lodge'. Standard rooms here without meals cost Rs 192/275 for singles/doubles or Rs 220/385 for deluxe rooms with a view of Kanchenjunga, all plus 10% service charge. They also offer full-board rates but this is expensive. The tourist office in Gangtok *may* make a reservation for you, but will usually tell you to go there and do it yourself.

Right next door to the Mt Pandim is a *PWD Rest House* which has huge rooms and great views but you won't be able to stay there, even if it's empty, unless you have made a booking in Gangtok.

Gezing Gezing is a bit of a dump, though there are at least four basic hotels, all pretty crummy and offering just bare-bones cubicles. Closest to the bus stand/market are the *Hotel Orchid, Hotel No Name, Hotel West End* and the *Hotel Mayalu*. They all charge Rs 15 per bed. The best place to eat is the Tibetan restaurant in the *Hotel No Name*. It has good food and a bar.

There's also a *PWD Rest House* but, again, you can't stay there unless you make a prior reservation in Gangtok.

Getting There & Away See the Gangtok section for details of SNT buses between Gangtok and Gezing but remember that it's worth making the effort to get the 7 am bus from Gangtok to Gezing because the views are great and you arrive in Gezing around 1 pm which gives you time to get to Pemayangtse or Pelling the same day by

foot, taxi or bus (SNT bus from Gezing to Pelling at 2.30 pm, Rs 3).

Gezing is something of a bus centre for West Sikkim. There are SNT buses daily to Siliguri (7 am), to Jorethang (8, 10 and 11 am and 4 pm, 1½ to two hours, Rs 13), to Yuksam (1 pm, three hours) and others to Darap and Dentam. There are also buses from Pelling to Jorethang (for Darjeeling) but make sure they are not doubling back to Pelling with a load of school children first!

If you want to get from Gezing to Darjeeling in one day, you must start early because jeep drivers will not leave from Jorethang for Darjeeling later than 1 pm – they say the Gurkhas will attack them and steal their vehicles if they attempt to drive after dark. The two-hour bus ride from Gezing to Jorethang/ Naya Bazaar goes via Legship and then along the Ranjit River. Permits are checked and passports stamped at Ramman beyond Jorethang just before you cross a suspension bridge into West Bengal. You may be searched for 'illicit' Sikkimese liquor entering West Bengal but most people are waved through.

From Jorethang to Darjeeling there are share taxis (up to 14 people crammed into a short wheelbase Mahindra jeep) at Rs 40 per head, or you can charter a whole jeep (six adults) for Rs 400. The journey takes about two hours (30 km) via Singla. There are no buses along this run.

Should you get stuck for the night in Jorethang, there are a number of basic hotels opposite the SNT bus stand.

Khechepari Lake

Pronounced 'catch a perry', and sometimes spelt Khecheopalri or Khechupherei, the standard hike from Pelling is to walk to the lake in one day by taking one of the several downhill trails to the Rimbi River, crossing either a bamboo or steel bridge, and then going uphill either by a steep trail or via the winding motor road. It takes between four and seven hours depending on the route you take and your fitness. Alternatively, you could hire a jeep and do it all by road, or take a Yuksam bus through Darap and Rimbi until you get to your choice of uphill routes to the lake. The road route is about 27 km from Pelling; the trail is somewhat shorter but is much steeper on foot.

The sacred lake lies in a depression surrounded by prayer flags and forested hills. It's not the most brilliant of tourist sights but it's rather a good excuse for a pleasant walk. The walk on the following day to Yuksam (about 11 km) takes four to five hours.

Just back from the lake, about five minutes' walk, is a good *Trekkers' Hut* with beds for Rs 20. It's run by a friendly caretaker and there are indoor toilets. At the lake are several basic chai shops serving noodles, eggs, dhal and hot raksi. There's also a fancy new *Government Rest House* but it may not be functioning.

Yuksam

Yuksam (also spelt Yoksum and Yuksom), 35 km by road from Pemayangtse, is the furthest north you can get by road. It's just a sleepy hamlet but is the trailhead for those intending to trek to Dzongri. It was also the place where the first monarch of Sikkim was crowned.

Places to Stay & Eat The popular *Trekkers' Hut* has beds, blankets and electricity but the caretaker tends to keep the inside toilets locked due to complications with the water system. There is, however, water outside and a row of toilets in a separate building. Beds cost Rs 25 per night and you can camp here on a large grassy area. Meals are not provided; you must bring your own or eat elsewhere.

Between the Trekkers' Hut and the police post is the *Dzongrila Hotel* with basic beds for Rs 25 as well as good food, beer and tongba (unfiltered chhang). It's run by a friendly, English-speaking family. Across the street is the large *Demazong Hotel* which was being expanded at the time this edition was being researched, and so was closed. It should be open again by the time you read this but it will be considerably more expensive than the other places.

The best place to stay is the beautiful

Forest Rest House No 1, up a hill just before you get to the police post, but you must make a booking for it in Gangtok at the Forest Department.

The *Arpan Restaurant*, downhill past the secondary school, is another possibility for food if you're staying at the Trekkers' Hut.

Getting There & Away See the section on Pemayangtse for details of buses between Gezing and Yuksam.

Tashiding Monastery

Founded around 1716, Tashiding Monastery is another of the more remote monasteries in western Sikkim and sees few foreign visitors. Coming from Yuksam, the trail to Tashiding goes via Norbugang chorten (one km), Dubdi Monastery (four km), Phamrung waterfalls (five km) and finally to Tashiding (19 km). It's a hard climb uphill to the monastery on top of the hill between the Ranjit and Ratong rivers from Tashiding village, but it's well worth it. Most people who do this trek stay and eat at the monastery – please leave a generous donation if you're offered hospitality. There's also a *Trekkers' Hut* available.

From Tashiding, there's a shortcut trail back to Pelling (about a day's walk) or it's about 16 km by road to Legship. There are no buses on the Yuksam-Tashiding-Legship circuit.

You may be told by the tourist office in Gangtok that Tashiding is off limits to foreigners but this is apparently not the case so long as you have Pemayangtse on your permit. Quite a few travellers have been there without any problems. There is a police check post in the village but no-one has been hassled – they just stamp your passport.

TREKKING IN SIKKIM

The only trekking route available in Sikkim at present is from Yuksam to Dzongri at the base of Kanchenjunga and on to Goechala. It's a beautiful trek but you can only do it with a trekking permit (which is required in addition to the normal Sikkim permit). For the regulations concerning the issue of these

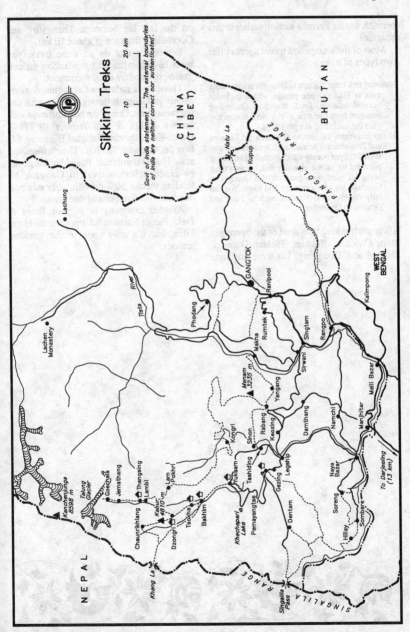

Sikkim Treks

Govt of India statement – 'The external boundaries of India are neither correct nor authenticated'.

0   10   20 km

CHINA (TIBET)

BHUTAN

PANGOLA RANGE

Natu La

Kupup

Lachung

GANGTOK

Ranipool

Tista River

Phodang

Makha

Rumtek

Singtam

Rangpo

Kalimpong

Lachen Monastery

WEST BENGAL

Melli Bazar

Sirwani

Menam 3235 ▲

Yangang

Mangola

Rabang

Keozing

Sinon

Kongri

Damthang

Namchi

Manjhitar

To Darjeeling (13 km)

Naya Bazar

Legship

Gezing

Soreng

Tashiding

Khechapari Lake

Pemayangtse

Dentam

Kanchenjunga 8598 m ▲

Talung Glacier

Goechala

Jemathang

Thangsing

Lamuni

Kabur 4810 m ▲

Pokhri

Lam

Tsokha

Bakhim

Dzongri

Chaunrikhang

Khang La

NEPAL

Singalila Pass

SINGALILA RANGE

Hillay

Sombare

permits, see the Permits section earlier in this chapter.

Most of the recognised travel agents offer two types of trek:

Nine-day trek from Yuksam to Dzongri: approximate cost is US$300 per person which includes accommodation, food, transport (including transport from Gangtok to Yuksam), porters and yaks but excluding sleeping bags.

12-day trek from Yuksam to Goechala via Dzongri and Zemathang (Chemathang): approximate cost is US$450 per person which includes everything provided for on the nine-day trek but you must bring all your own gear for the Dzongri to Goechala leg as it's over ice and snow. You can only do this trek during March to May and October to December.

There are trekking huts at all of the overnight stops (Yuksam, Bakhim, Tsokha, Dzongri, Bikbari and Thangsing) but there are none on the last leg between Thangsing and Goechala, a distance of about 10 km.

Remember that on all these treks, you must be accompanied by a liaison officer/guide provided by the government.

There are a number of recognised travel agents in Gangtok through which you can organise a trek. One of the best and most well known is *Yak & Yeti Travels* (☎ 2714), Harka-Kala Bhavan, National Highway, PO Box 56, Gangtok 737101. Their offices are at the Hotel Himulchuli. Postal bookings can be made before arrival in Gangtok by sending them a 50% deposit, your passport number, visa number and one photo.

Another company is *Bigfoot Tours & Treks*, Panjor Stadium Rd, opposite the Hotel Tibet, but it's only open in the trekking seasons.

North-Eastern Region

State	Capital	Area (sq km)	Population
Assam	Gawahati	78,000	22,000,000
Manipur	Imphal	22,300	1,800,000
Meghalaya	Shillong	22,400	1,800,000
Nagaland	Kohima	17,000	1,200,000
Tripura	Agartala	10,400	2,700,000
Arunachal Pradesh	Itanagar	84,000	858,000
Mizoram	Aizawi	21,000	686,000

Govt of India statement – 'The external boundaries of India are neither correct nor authenticated'.

The north-eastern region is the most varied and at the same time the least visited part of India. Before Independence the whole region was known as Assam Province, but it was finally split into five separate states and two Union Territories – Mizoram and Arunachal Pradesh.

In many ways the north-east is unlike the rest of India. It is the country's chief tribal area, with a great number of tribes speaking many different languages and dialects – in Arunachal Pradesh alone over 50 distinct languages are spoken! These tribal people have many similarities to the hill tribes who live across an arc which stretches from the eastern end of the Himalaya through Myanmar (Burma) and Thailand into Laos. Also, the north-east has a high percentage of Christians, particularly in the more isolated areas where the population is predominantly hill tribespeople.

For a number of reasons India has always been touchy about the north-east, and a visit to the region can involve a bureaucratic nightmare for foreigners. For a start the north-east is a sensitive border zone where India meets Bhutan, China, Myanmar and Bangladesh. Equally important, the region is remote – only the narrow Siliguri corridor connects it to the rest of India, and before Independence the usual route to Assam would have been through Bangladesh. Today, it involves making a long loop north and then east by metre-gauge rail. Roads have been improved dramatically but there

are still very few of them compared with the rest of India.

Until the early 1980s, permits for foreigners wishing to visit Assam and Meghalaya were relatively easy to procure, at least for specific tourist attractions, but the other states were, to all intents and purposes, off limits. Only with friends in high places and cast-iron references was it possible to get a permit for the more remote states and, even then, your movements would be carefully monitored.

By the mid-1980s, however, a dark cloud had descended over the north-east. A whole series of strikes and riots followed each other in quick succession which, in turn, led to widespread violence and terrorism. This put the whole area firmly off limits to outsiders. There were a number of reasons for this unrest, including a feeling of central government neglect (poor transport links and lack of infrastructure development were the main complaints). This feeling strengthened as oil

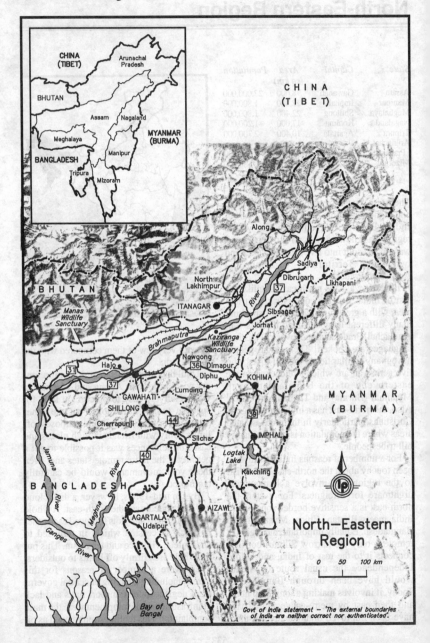

North-Eastern Region

0   50   100 km

Govt of India statement — 'The external boundaries
of India are neither correct nor authenticated'.

prices rose since Assam has a substantial part of India's small but important oil reserves. Very little of this oil wealth found its way back to improve Assam's industrial development, and the whole region remained overwhelmingly agricultural.

But economic neglect and exploitation was only a minor issue. The main issue was about the inflow of 'foreigners' into the region. Military repression and economic stagnation, combined with high birth rates in Bangladesh, pushed thousands of Bangladeshis over the lightly policed borders into the north-east region. The influx was so great that, in some cases, it threatened to outnumber the indigenous population, and demands for the Bangladeshis' repatriation became more and more strident. Such wholesale repatriation would have presented the central government with an extremely difficult problem since few of the 'foreigners' carried identification papers making it almost impossible to decide which of them had arrived recently and which had lived in the region for generations – legally or otherwise.

Lack of action in addressing the indigenous population's grievances, however, proved catastrophic. In 1983, wholesale massacres of 'foreigners' began to take place and photographs of their bodies floating down various tributaries of the Ganges and Brahmaputra rivers appeared in the world's press. The killings eventually subsided and events in the north-east were soon relegated to the back pages as a result of the greater unrest in the Punjab. Yet little had actually changed.

Then came the formation of the United Liberation Front of Assam (ULFA) pledged to the independence of Assam through armed struggle. Its military wing enjoyed a great deal of initial success and kept the Indian army on the run for many years, operating from bases deep in the jungle and from Bangladesh. Unwilling to countenance the loss of Assam, the Indian government was finally forced to mount a series of massive military operations to flush out the guerrillas, the latest, codenamed Operation Rhino, in 1991. With the movement almost crushed

and its leaders in hiding in Bangladesh, the state governor, Saikia, punted on a reconciliation by offering talks with the rebels on the basis of a cease-fire and the rebels laying down their arms.

The talks duly took place in Gawahati but it soon became apparent that not all of the ULFA's leaders were in favour of talks. Those who were in favour of continued armed struggle not only refused to attend but issued statements condemning those who agreed to the talks. It was also alleged that the cease-fire was conveniently used to give the recalcitrant rebels time to regroup and rearm. At the time of writing, little progress appears to have been made.

As if the trouble in Assam were not enough, the central government also had to contend with political and military agitation in Nagaland and Manipur at a time when they felt things in those states were under reasonable control. Nagaland has proved to be an intractable problem virtually since Independence, although it appeared that progress was being made in 1991 until the governor precipitously dissolved the state assembly and put the state back under President's rule. Manipur's complaints were more benign, amounting to not much more than a demand that Manipuri be added to the constitution as one of the official languages of India.

The states bordering Myanmar (Burma) were further hit with problems in 1991 following the Myanmar army's massive drive against the Muslim inhabitants in the country's north-west. As a result, tens of thousands of refugees fled over the border into Mizoram, Manipur and Nagaland. Feeding and sheltering these refugees has been a major burden on the Indian government and, although an agreement was signed between the Indian and Myanmar governments in early 1992 to allow the refugees to return, trust is an elusive commodity. Most of the refugees believe they will be shot if they return and few are keen to do so.

With all this violence and upheaval taking place in India's north-east states, it's not surprising that the central government is extremely reluctant to allow foreigners into this area of India. The fact is, we haven't heard of anyone being granted a permit for this area in years (except those with friends in high places or with relatives in the various states).

Permits
In theory, permits can be obtained for Assam and Meghalaya but, as far as Assam is concerned, you are restricted to the capital, Gawahati, and the game reserves at Manas and Kaziranga. In practice, you won't get one, or, if for some reason you do, it'll take months and a lot of hassle.

If your patience knows no bounds, they can be applied for at any overseas Indian consular office, or in India at the Foreigners' Registration Office, Hans Bhavan (near Tilak Bridge), Bahadur Shah, Zafar Marg, New Delhi 110002. You can also try at the Trade Adviser, Government of Assam, 8 Russell St, Calcutta 700071.

Permits for Assam allow for a maximum stay of 15 days, but *may* be extendible in Gawahati. If you fly to Gawahati and follow a specified route to Kaziranga and back, the regulations may be relaxed somewhat but these change constantly so you need to check this out.

Permits for Meghalaya can be applied for at the Meghalaya Information Centre in Calcutta which is next to the Assam office at 9 Russell St. They are usually for a seven-day visit though they *may* be extendible in Shillong, the capital.

Getting There & Away
Air Indian Airlines flies from Calcutta to Gawahati for US$46. Other regional flights from Calcutta include: Agartala (US$34), Dibrugarh (US$74), Dimapur (US$69), Imphal (US$58), Jorhat (US$69), Silchar (US$52) and Tezpur (US$57). Flights to Agartala are twice daily, to Gawahati at least twice daily, and to Silchar and Imphal once daily. Other flights are less frequent, usually once weekly.

Vayudoot flies from Calcutta to Agartala and Shillong (US$44) three times a week; to Aizawl four times a week, and to Gawahati

(US$46) three times a week, via Aizawl and Silchar (US$52).

Assam

The largest and most easily accessible of the north-east states, Assam grows 60% of India's tea and produces a large proportion of India's oil. The main visitor attractions are the Manas and Kaziranga wildlife reserves, home of India's rare one-horned rhinoceros.

GAWAHATI (Gauhati/Guwahati)
Population: 577,000
Capital of the state, Gawahati is on the banks of the Brahmaputra River. It has many ancient Hindu temples but its main importance is as a gateway to the north-east and the wildlife reserves.

Information
The state tourist office (☎ 27-102) is on Station Rd. There are also offices in Calcutta (☎ 39-8331), at 8 Russell St; and in Delhi (☎ 34-5897), at Kharak Sing Marg.

Temples
The **Umananda Temple** is a Siva temple on Peacock Island in the middle of the river. There's a pleasant ferry across the river. The **Navagrah Temple** is the Temple of the Nine Planets. In ancient times this was a centre for the study of astrology. It is on Chitrachal Hill, near the city.

Gawahati's best known temple is the **Kamakshya Temple** on Nilachal Hill, 10 km from the city. It attracts pilgrims from all over India, especially during the Ambuchi Festival in August. The temple is the centre for Shakti (energy) worship and Tantric Hinduism because when Siva sorrowfully carried away the corpse of his first wife, Sati, her *yoni* fell here. The temple was rebuilt in 1665 after being destroyed by Muslim invaders. In the centre of Gawahati the **Janardhan Temple** has an image of Buddha, indicating how Buddhism was assimilated back into Hinduism.

Other Attractions

The **Assam State Zoo** has tigers, lions, panthers and, of course, Assam's famous rhinos – plus the African two-horned variety for comparison. There is an **Assam State Museum** as well as the **Assam Government Cottage Industries Museum**.

Places to Stay

Cheaper hotels include the *Hotel Alka* (☎ 31-767) at Pt M S Rd in Fancy Bazaar, the *Hotel Ambassador* (☎ 25-587) and the *Happy Lodge* (☎ 23-409), both in Paltan Bazaar. Middle-range hotels include the *Nova Hotel* (☎ 23-258) in Fancy Bazaar and the *North-Eastern Hotel* (☎ 25-314) on G N Bordoloi Rd.

There's a government *Tourist Bungalow* (☎ 24-475) on Station Rd, and railway *retiring rooms* (☎ 26-688) with very cheap doubles, triples and dormitory accommodation.

At the top of the Gawahati price scale the *Belle Vue Hotel* (☎ 28-291/2) on Mahatma Gandhi Rd has rooms with and without aircon. However, it's quite a long way from the centre. The *Hotel Nandan* (☎ 31-281) on G S Rd is comparable at Rs 505 for an air-con double including tax, and is more conveniently located.

Getting There & Away

Air See Getting There & Away in the introductory section to this chapter for details about flights from Calcutta to Gawahati and other centres in the North-Eastern Region.

Train The most convenient points from which to get to Gawahati are Calcutta and New Jalpaiguri.

From Calcutta (Howrah) it's 993 km and about 24 hours to Gawahati on the *Kamrup Express* or 22 hours on the *Guwahati Express* at a cost of Rs 143/534 in 2nd/1st class. These trains pass through New Jalpaiguri station at 7.20 am and 2.45 am respectively. There is also the *North East Express* which comes from New Delhi and passes through New Jalpaiguri at 9.50 am.

The 424-km journey from here to Gawahati takes about eight hours and costs Rs 80/297 in 2nd/1st class.

If you're going further east than Gawahati, you must change here from broad gauge to metre gauge. There's a good network of metre-gauge lines to all the major centres of population in the north-east but as the area is essentially off limits to foreigners, there's little point in providing details. For further information, the best reference is *Newman's Indian Bradshaw* published monthly for Rs 30. It's available at most bookshops.

AROUND GAWAHATI
Hajo

Located on the north bank of the Brahmaputra, 24 km from Gawahati, Hajo is an important pilgrimage centre for Buddhists and Muslims. Some Buddhists believe that Buddha attained nirvana here, and they flock to the Hayagriba Madhab Temple. For Muslims the Pao Mecca Mosque is considered to have one-quarter *(pao)* the sanctity of the great mosque at Mecca.

Sualkashi

Also across the river from Gawahati, 20 km away, Sualkashi is a famous silk-weaving centre where the Endi, Muga and Pat silks of Assam are made in a small household weaving centre. There is a regular ferry across the river and a bus several times daily.

Other Attractions

The **Basistha Ashram** is 12 km south of Gawahati, and the *rishi* or sage, Basistha, once lived here. It's a popular picnic spot. The beautiful natural lagoon at **Chandubi** is 64 km from Gawahati.

Darranga, 80 km away on the Bhutan border, is a great winter trading area for the Bhutia mountain folk. **Barpeta**, with a monastery and the shrine of a Vaishnavaite reformer, is 145 km north-west of Gawahati.

NORTH-EAST ASSAM

A little beyond Kaziranga, **Jorhat** is the gateway to the north-east of Assam. **Sibsagar**, 55 km away, has the huge Jay

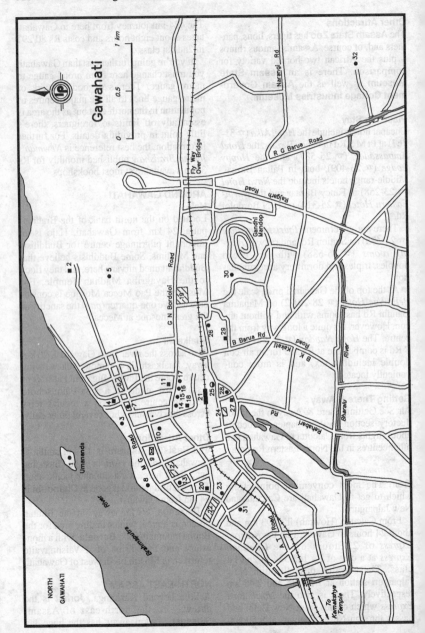

NORTH
GAWAHATI

Gawahati

0   0.5   1 km

Umananda

R G Barua Road

Narengi Rd

Fly Way
Over Bridge

Rajgarh Road

G N Bordoloi Road

Gandhi
Mandop

30

19

26   29   B Barua Rd

B K Kekati Road

River

Bharalu

Rehabari Rd

2

5

11

6
27
17
14 15 16
18

21

25 28

24

27

M G Road

4
7
3
10
9
22
8

13
20   23

1

22

31

A T Road

Brahmaputra River

Rehabari

To
Kamakshye
Temple

32

■ PLACES TO STAY

2	Belle Vue Hotel
4	Hotel Brahmaputra Ashok
11	North-Eastern Hotel
18	Tourist Bungalow
20	Nova Hotel
27	Hotel Nandan
29	Stadium Guest House

OTHER

1	Umananda Temple
3	D C Office
5	Nabagrah Temple
6	Uzan Bazar
7	High Court
8	Sukleswar Temple
9	General Post Office

10	Church
12	Panbazar
13	Police Station
14	District Library
15	Assam State Museum
16	Robindra Bhawan
17	Guwahati Emporium
19	Silphukhuri
21	Guwahati Railway Station
22	Fancy Bazaar
23	Sikh Temple
24	Paltan Bazar
25	ASTC Bus Station
26	Nehru Stadium
28	Indian Airlines Office
30	Hajimusafir Khana
31	Jain Mandir
32	Assam State Zoo

Sagar Tank and many temples in the environs; it was the old capital of the Ahom kingdom. There's a small *Tourist Bungalow* by the tank.

WILDLIFE PARKS

Assam is famous for its rare one-horned Great Indian Rhinoceros – when Marco Polo saw it he thought he had found the legendary unicorn! Kaziranga and Manas are the two well-known parks in Assam. There are smaller parks at Orang and Sonai.

Kaziranga

North-east of Gawahati, on the banks of the Brahmaputra River, is the Kaziranga Wildlife Reserve, famous as the last major home of *Rhinoceros unicornis*. The 430-sq-km park is thought to have a rhino population approaching 1000, although in 1904 they were on the verge of extinction. The park became a game sanctuary in 1926, and by 1966 the numbers had risen to about 400.

The park also has wild *gaur* (buffalo), deer, elephants, tigers, bears and many water bird species including pelicans, which breed here. One of the standard ways of observing the wildlife is from elephant-back, and the rhinos are said to have become accustomed to elephants carrying camera-toting tourists.

Information The park is at its best from February to May. There is a tourist information centre (☎ 23) at Kaziranga, but you're supposed to give 10 days notice for booking accommodation or transport. They have a minibus (Rs 0.30 per seat per km – minimum Rs 300 per trip) and a jeep (Rs 3.50 per km) and also organise those elephant rides (Rs 50 per person) into the long grass. The entry fees to the park are Rs 50 plus Rs 5 'viewing fee' and Rs 5 camera fee. Guides are free.

Avoid organised tours to Kaziranga from Gawahati since they're too short (two days) and you'll spend most of that time on the bus (some nine hours in all) and have only one game drive. You need at least three nights and four days in Kaziranga if you want to see anything.

Places to Stay There is a variety of accommodation around the park, including *Forest Inspection Bungalows* at Beguri (no bedding or mosquito nets), Arimarh (no electricity) and Kohora. Or there is a *Soil Conservation Inspection Bungalow*, a *PWD Inspection Bungalow* and two *Tourist Bungalows*. Bungalow No 1 (Bonani) has rooms for Rs 175/275 and Bungalow No 2 (Kunjaban) has rooms for Rs 120. Air-con at either costs an additional Rs 75.

At the top of the price scale there is the *Kaziranga Forest Lodge* (Aranya), which has rooms without air-con for Rs 250/325 or Rs 300/400 with air-con, including taxes. It's a good place to stay and is well run. The lodge provides a jeep and driver (Rs 65 for the first hour and Rs 40 for each subsequent hour) and the forest department provides a guide.

Getting There & Away Calcutta/Jorhat flights land 84 km from the park. Furketing is the most convenient railway station, 72 km away; from here buses and jeeps run to Kaziranga. Gawahati is 233 km away on Highway 37. There are state transport buses from Gawahati.

Manas

In the foothills of the Himalaya, north-west of Gawahati, Manas Wildlife Sanctuary is on the Bhutan border. Three rivers run through the sanctuary, which has abundant bird and animal life. The rare pygmy hog and the golden langur (monkey) are amongst the notable animals here, although you may also see rhinos.

Information Manas is best from January to March, although there is excellent fishing from November to December. Mothangiri is the main town in the park but the tourist information centre (☎ 49) is on Barpeta Rd. Entry and camera charges are the same as Kaziranga. Boats can be hired for excursions or fishing trips on the Manas River.

Places to Stay The *Manas Tourist Lodge* has a range of rooms which are all relatively cheap or you can camp if you have a tent. The *Forest Bungalow* doesn't have electricity but it is cheaper, and includes bedding and mosquito nets. There is a *Rest House* at the Barpeta Road Tourist Centre.

Getting There & Away Gawahati, 176 km away, has the nearest airport. Barpeta Road, 40 km from Mothangiri, is the nearest railway station. Transport from Barpeta Road to Mothangiri must be arranged in advance.

Meghalaya

Created in 1971, this state is the home for Khasia, Jantia and Garo tribespeople. The hill station of Shillong is the state capital while Cherrapunji, 58 km away, is said to be the wettest place on earth, with an average annual rainfall of 1150 cm, nearly 40 feet! In one year 26.46 metres of rain fell. It's no wonder Meghalaya means Abode of Clouds.

Other places of interest around the state include **Jakrem** with its hot springs, Kayllang Rock at **Mairang**, Mawjymbuin Cave at **Mawsynram** and **Umiam Lake**. Recently Mawsynram had an annual rainfall total that even surpassed the record at Cherrapunji.

SHILLONG
Population: 222,000

This pleasant hill station, standing at 1496 metres, is renowned for its climate and breathtaking views; it's even had the label 'Scotland of the East' applied to it! Around town you can pass the time observing the tiny red-light district behind the Delhi Hotel, as there's not a lot to do apart from pass through.

The people around Shillong, the Khasias, have a matrilineal social organisation, passing down property and wealth through the female rather than the male line.

Information
Police Bazaar has a Government of Meghalaya tourist office (☎ 6054) on Tirot Singh Syiem Rd and a Government of India tourist office (☎ 25-632) on G S Rd. The GPO is also on G S Rd.

Things to See

The **State Museum** covers the flora, fauna, culture and anthropology of the state. The town has a number of parks and gardens and a **Botanic Garden** and **Botanical Museum** beside the central Ward Lake. The **Crinoline Waterfalls** are near Lady Hydari Park, and there are various other waterfalls around Shillong. The town takes its name from the 1960-metre-high **Shillong Peak**, from which there are fine views. It's 10 km from the centre.

The Anglican graveyard and **All Saints' Cathedral** may be of interest to fans of the Raj; the gravestones have inscriptions such as 'killed in the great earthquake' or 'murdered by headhunters'.

Places to Stay & Eat

There's a good *Tourist Bungalow* near the polo grounds with rooms and dormitory accommodation. There are many other middle-priced hotels around, and cheap accommodation can be found in the Police Bazaar near the tourist office. There's good food at the *Lhasa Restaurant*, and there are several other restaurants around town.

Mr Bhuyan's *Snack Bar a la Carte* (☎ 24-909) also has good accommodation. Mr Bhuyan is very friendly and a good source of information.

The *Hotel Pinewood Ashok* (☎ 23-116, 23-765) is Shillong's premier hotel, though it's hardly up to the normal standard of the Ashok group of hotels.

Getting There & Away

A good road runs the 100 km from Gawahati in Assam to Shillong. Cherrapunji is 58 km south of Shillong, and there are daily buses; if it's not raining the views from here over Bangladesh are superb. Permission is required from the Commissioner of Police to visit the area.

Coming from Bangladesh, you cross the border (if it's open) at Dawki, from where it's a 1½-km walk to the town, and then a 3½-hour trip to Shillong.

Other States & Territories

All of these are essentially off limits to foreigners so the following information is for interest only.

Getting There & Away

The only railway to these states and territories terminates at Ledo, but the roads have been improved lately. Both Indian Airlines and Vayudoot operate a comprehensive service to the region from Calcutta.

ARUNACHAL PRADESH

The furthest north-east of the region, this Union Territory was known as the North-East Frontier Agency under the British. Arunachal Pradesh borders with Bhutan, China and Myanmar (Burma) and is a mountainous, remote and predominantly tribal area. The old 'Stillwell Road' used to run from Ledo in the south of Arunachal Pradesh to Myitkyinya in the north-east of Myanmar. Built in 1944 by General 'Vinegar Joe' Stillwell, it must rate as one of the most expensive roads in the world. The 430 km cost US$137 million way back then, and after opening for just a few months it has hardly been used since. All road routes into Myanmar are closed.

NAGALAND

South of Arunachal Pradesh and north of Manipur, the remote and hilly state of Nagaland is bordered by Myanmar. Kohima, the capital of Nagaland, was the furthest point Japanese troops advanced into India during WW II.

MANIPUR

South of Nagaland and north of Mizoram, Manipur also borders with Myanmar. The state is inhabited by over two dozen different tribes, many of them Christians. It is famous for its Manipuri dances and handloomed textiles.

Imphal (population 130,000), the capital,

is surrounded by wooded hills and lakes and has the golden Shri Govindaji Temple. During WW II a road was built from Imphal to Tamu on the Myanmar border but, as with the Stillwell Road further north, this route into Myanmar is also closed.

MIZORAM

This finger-like extension in the extreme south-east of the region pokes between Myanmar and Bangladesh. The name means Hill People's Land – from Mizo, Man of the Hill, and Ram, Land. It's a picturesque place where the population is both predominantly tribal and overwhelmingly Christian.

TRIPURA

The tiny state of Tripura is almost totally surrounded by Bangladesh. It's a lush, wooded region with many beautiful waterfalls. Agartala is the capital; near it is the lake palace of Nirmahal. Here, too, the population is largely tribal.

Rajasthan

Population: 48.9 million
Area: 342,239 sq km
Capital: Jaipur
People per sq km: 128
Main Languages: Rajasthani & Hindi
Literacy Rate: 38.8%

Rajasthan, the Land of the Kings, is India at its exotic and colourful best. It is the home of the Rajputs, a group of warrior clans who have controlled this part of India for 1000 years according to a code of chivalry and honour akin to that of the medieval European knights. While temporary alliances and marriages of convenience were the order of the day, pride and independence were always paramount. The Rajputs were therefore never able to present a united front against a common aggressor. Indeed, much of their energy was spent squabbling amongst themselves and the resultant weakness eventually led to their becoming vassal states of the Moghul Empire. Nevertheless, the Rajputs' bravery and sense of honour were unparalleled.

Rajput warriors would fight on against all odds and, when no hope was left, chivalry demanded that *jauhar* be declared. In this grim ritual, the women and children committed suicide by immolating themselves on a huge funeral pyre, while the men donned saffron robes and rode out to meet the enemy and certain death. In some of the larger battles, tens of thousands of Rajput warriors lost their lives in this way. Three times in Chittorgarh's long history, the women consigned themselves to the flames while the men rode out to their martyrdom. The same tragic fate befell many other fortresses around the state. It's hardly surprising that Akbar persuaded Rajputs to lead his army, nor that subsequent Moghul emperors had such difficulty controlling this part of their empire.

With the decline of the Moghul Empire, the Rajputs gradually clawed back their

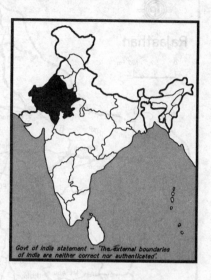

Govt of India statement — 'The external boundaries of India are neither correct nor authenticated'.

independence through a series of spectacular victories but, by then, a new force had appeared on the scene in the form of the British. As the Raj inexorably expanded, most Rajput states signed articles of alliance with the British which allowed them to continue as independent states, each with its own maharaja (or similarly titled leader), subject to certain political and economic constraints. The British, after all, were not there for humanitarian reasons, but to establish an empire and gain a controlling interest in the economy of the subcontinent in the same way as the Moghuls had done.

These alliances proved to be the beginning of the end for the Rajput rulers. Indulgence and extravagance soon replaced chivalry and honour so that, by the early 1900s, many of the maharajas spent most of their time travelling the world with a vast army of wives, concubines and retainers, playing polo, racing horses, gambling and occupying whole floors of the most expensive hotels in

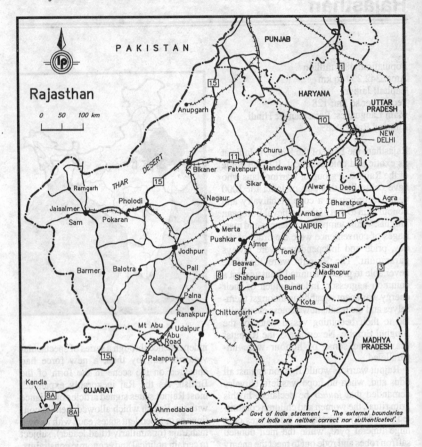

Govt of India statement – 'The external boundaries of India are neither correct nor authenticated'.

Europe and America. While it suited the British to indulge them in this respect, their profligate waste of the resources of Rajputana (the land of the Rajputs) was socially and educationally disastrous. When India gained its independence, Rajasthan had one of the subcontinent's lowest life expectancy and literacy rates.

At Independence, India's ruling Congress Party was forced to make a deal with the nominally independent Rajput states in order to secure their agreement to join the new India. The rulers were allowed to keep their titles, their property holdings were secured

and they were paid an annual stipend commensurate with their status. It couldn't last forever, given India's socialist persuasion, and the crunch came in the early 1970s when Indira Gandhi abolished both the titles and the stipends and severely sequestered their property rights.

While some of the rulers have survived this by turning their forts into museums and their palaces into luxury hotels, many have fallen by the wayside, unable to cope with the financial and managerial demands of the late 20th century.

Although the fortunes of its former rulers

may be in tatters, the culture of Rajasthan, with its battle-scarred forts, its palaces of amazing luxury and whimsical charm, its riotous colours and even its romantic sense of pride and honour, is still very much alive. It is certainly part of India, yet it's visibly unique. That visibility extends from the huge pastel-coloured turbans and soup-strainer moustaches sported by the men and the bright mirrored skirts and chunky silver jewellery of the women, to the manner in which these people deal with you. In some parts of India, you can never be sure that agreements will be kept. There are always exceptions, of course, but an agreement struck in Rajasthan is generally solid. Tourism has obviously made inroads here, but it will be a long time before it corrupts the traditional sense of honesty or destroys the cultural vitality of these people.

The land itself is somewhat dry and, in parts, inhospitable. Geographically, it's very varied. The state is diagonally divided into the hilly and rugged south-eastern region and the barren north-western Thar Desert, which extends across the border into Pakistan. Like all deserts, the Thar offers oases of magic and romance. There are plenty of historic cities, incredible fortresses awash with legends, and rare gems of impressionistic beauty, such as Udaipur, which combine water with earth and sky to create a pastiche of paradise. There are also a number of centres which attract travellers from far and wide, such as

peaceful Pushkar with its holy lake, and the exotic desert city of Jaisalmer which resembles a fantasy from *The Thousand & One Nights*.

No-one visits Rajasthan without taking home superb memories, an address book full of friends and, often, a bundle of embroidery and jewellery.

Festivals

Rajasthan has all the usual Hindu and Muslim festivals, some celebrated with special local fervour, as well as a number of festivals of its own. The spring festival of Gangaur (late March to early April) is particularly important, as is Teej (early to late August) which welcomes the monsoon. The state is at its most beautiful when the monsoon rains fill the many lakes and tanks.

Rajasthan also has many fairs, some traditional and others the creation of the Rajasthan Tourist Development Corporation (RJTC). Best known of the fairs is the immense and colourful Pushkar camel and cattle fair, held annually in early to mid-November. Similar, but less well known, are the Nagaur Festival (late January to early February; it's about halfway between Bikaner and Jodhpur), and the Kolayat Fair at Bikaner (mid to late November).

The Desert Festival at Jaisalmer (early to mid-February) is a modern creation designed to foster local folk arts and music and to promote tourism. It features camel races,

Festival Calendar

Festival	Location	1993	1994	1995
Nagaur Fair	Nagaur	30 Jan to 2 Feb	Feb 18-23	6-10 Feb
Baneshwar Fair	Dungarpur	3-6 Feb	22-26 Feb	11-15 Feb
Desert Festival	Jaisalmer	5-7 Feb	24-26 Feb	13-15 Feb
Elephant Festival	Jaipur	12-13 March	30-31 March	20-21 March
Gangaur Festival	Jaipur	26-27 March	14-15 April	3-4 April
Mewar Festival	Udaipur	26-27 March	14-15 Apr	3-4 Apr
Summer Festival	Mt Abu	1-3 June	1-3 June	1-3 June
Teej	Jaipur	22-23 July	10-11 Aug	30-31 July
Dussehra Mela	Kota	22-24 Oct	11-13 Oct	1-3 Oct
Marwar Festival	Jodhpur	29-30 Oct	18-19 Oct	7-8 Oct
Cattle Fair	Pushkar	26-29 Nov	15-18 Nov	4-7 Nov
Kolayat Festival	Bikaner	28-30 Nov	17-19 Nov	6-8 Nov
Chandrabhaga Fair	Jhalawar	28-30 Nov	17-19 Nov	6-8 Nov

Tribal People of Rajasthan

The main tribes of Rajasthan are the Bhils and the Minas, who were the original inhabitants of the area now called Rajasthan, but who were forced into the Aravalli ranges by the Aryan invasion. The warlike invaders fitted into the Kshatriya caste, which was later divided into 36 Rajput clans.

Smaller tribes include the Sahariyas, Damariyas, Garasias, and the Gaduliya Lohars. The tribal people of Rajasthan now constitute around 12% of the state's population.

Bhils The Bhils are an important tribal group and traditionally inhabited the south-eastern corner of the state – the area around Udaipur, Chittorgarh and Dungarpur – although the largest concentrations of them are found in neighbouring Madhya Pradesh.

Legend has it that the Bhils were fine archers, and Bhil bowmen are mentioned in both the *Mahabharata* and the *Ramayana*. They were highly regarded as warriors, and the Rajput rulers relied on them heavily to thwart the invading Marathas and Moghuls. The British even formed a Mewar Bhil Corps in the 1820s in recognition of their martial tradition.

Although originally food gatherers, the Bhils these days have taken up small-scale agriculture, or have abandoned the land altogether and taken up city residence and employment. The literacy rate of the Bhils, particularly the women, is amongst the lowest of any group in the country (7%) which has made them prime targets for exploitation and bonded labour.

The Baneshwar Festival is a Bhil festival held near Dungarpur in February each year, and large numbers of Bhils gather for four days of singing, dancing and worship. Holi is another important time for the Bhils.

Witchcraft, magic and superstition are deeply rooted aspects of Bhil culture.

Minas The Minas are the largest tribal group in the state, and are also the most widely spread, being found throughout Shekhavati and eastern Rajasthan. Originally they were a ruling tribe, but their downfall was a long drawn-out affair. It began with the Rajputs and was complete when the British government declared them a criminal tribe, mainly to stop them trying to regain their territory from the Rajputs. Their culture was totally destroyed and they have been given protection as a Scheduled Tribe.

tug-of-war teams, folk dancing and all the usual attractions, but is substantially over-rated.

The dates of the fairs and festivals are determined by the lunar calendar. See the table on the previous page.

Art & Architecture

Rajasthan has a school of miniature painting, the style deriving from the Moghul but with some clear differences – in particular, the palace and hunting scenes are complemented by religious themes, relating especially to the Krishna legends. This art carried through to the elegant palaces built by the Rajputs when they were freed from confrontation with the Moghuls. Many, such as Bundi, are liberally covered with colourful frescoes.

Most of Rajasthan's early architecture was damaged or destroyed by the first waves of Muslim invaders. Fragments remaining from that period include the Adhai-din-ka-jhonpra Mosque in Ajmer, which is basically a converted Hindu temple of great elegance, and the ruined temples at Osian, near Jodhpur. There are many buildings dating from the 10th to 15th centuries, including the superb Jain temples at Ranakpur, Mt Abu and Jaisalmer. Most of the great forts date, in their present form, from the Moghul period.

Accommodation

Palaces, Forts & Castles Rajasthan is famous for its delightful palace hotels. In these harder times, many of Rajasthan's maharajas have had to turn their palaces into hotels to make ends meet. The most famous are the super-luxurious Rambagh Palace in Jaipur, the Lake Palace Hotel and Shiv Niwas Palace in Udaipur, and the Umaid Bhawan Palace in Jodhpur. You don't have to spend a fortune to stay in a palace – there are plenty of smaller ones which are more moderately priced.

With the withdrawal of the Criminal Tribes Act, the Minas took to agriculture. As is the case with the Bhils, the literacy rate amongst the Minas is very low (8.3%).

The Minas are Siva worshippers, and one of their main deities is Sheetla Mata, the goddess of smallpox! Marriage is generally within the tribe. This is arranged by the parents and most marriages take place when the children are quite young.

Gaduliya Lohars The Gaduliya Lohars were originally a martial Rajput tribe, but these days are nomadic blacksmiths. Their traditional territory was Mawar (Udaipur) and they fought with the maharaja against the Moghuls. With typical Rajput chivalry, they made a vow to the maharana that they would only enter his fort at Chittorgarh after he had overcome the Moghuls. As he died without achieving this, the clan was forced to become nomadic. When Nehru was in power he led a group of Gaduliya Lohars into Chittorgarh fort, with the hope that they would then resettle in their former lands, but they preferred to remain nomadic.

Garasias The Garasias are a small Rajput tribe found in the Abu Road area of southern Rajasthan. It is thought that they intermingled with the Bhils to some extent, which is supported by the fact that bows and arrows are widely used.

The marriage ceremony is curious in that the couple elope, and a sum of money is paid to the father of the bride. If the marriage fails, the bride returns home, with a small sum of money to give to the father. Widows are not entitled to a share of their husband's property, and so generally remarry.

Sahariyas The Sahariyas are thought to be of Bhil origin, and inhabit the areas of Kota, Dungarpur and Sawai Madhopur in the south-east of the state. They are one of the least educated tribes in the country and, as unskilled labourers, have been cruelly exploited.

As all members of the clan are considered to be related, marriages are arranged outside the tribe. Their food and worship traditions are closely related to Hindu customs. ■

Tourist Bungalows On a more day-to-day level, the state Tourist Development Corporation operates a series of tourist bungalows in almost every large town. A few years ago they were very often the best value in town, but their prices are no longer the bargain they once were. In addition, the fabric and services (especially the bathroom facilities) have been allowed to deteriorate, with maintenance often nonexistent. However, they usually have a restaurant and bar and, for real shoestringers, frequently offer dormitory accommodation. The local tourist office is often found in the tourist bungalow.

Home Stays Staying with an Indian family can be a real education. It's a change from dealing strictly with tourist-oriented people, and the differences and curiosities of every-day Indian life can be very interesting.

Rajasthan has the only official home-stay programme, and it operates only in the cities of Jaipur, Jodhpur and Udaipur. The cost is anything from Rs 50 per day upwards, including meals, depending on the level of facilities offered. The tourist offices in the three cities have comprehensive lists of the families offering this service. It's known as the Paying Guest Scheme and is administered by the Rajasthan Tourist Development Corporation.

Getting Around

Bus Rajasthan has an extensive and reasonably good state bus system. On most sectors there is a choice of ordinary and express buses. You're advised to stick to expresses since the ordinary buses stop frequently, make a lot of detours off the main route and take a long time to get anywhere.

If you're taking a bus from a major bus stand, it's worth buying a ticket from the ticket office rather than on board the bus. It guarantees (or at least comes closer to guaranteeing) a seat, and you're also certain of getting on the right bus since the ticket clerk writes the bus registration number on your ticket. This can be an important consideration because timetables at bus stations are invariably in Hindi.

A number of private bus companies run luxury buses between the major population centres and many travellers prefer these to the state buses. Fares are higher than those on the state system but the buses are faster, more comfortable and don't take standing passengers. Their only drawback is that some are equipped with that curse known as the video cassette recorder. As elsewhere in India, this is always played at full volume and the film content is invariably macho trash. It's almost tolerable during the day but can be hell at night. Try to choose a bus without one of these infernal machines.

Train The RTDC 'Palace on Wheels' is a special tourist train service which operates weekly tours of Rajasthan, departing from Delhi every Wednesday from October to March. The itinerary takes in Jaipur, Chittorgarh, Udaipur, Jaisalmer, Jodhpur, Bharatpur and Agra. It's a hell of a lot of ground to cover in a week, but most of the travelling is done at night.

Originally this train used carriages which once belonged to various maharajas, but these became so ancient that newer carriages were refurbished to look like the originals. They were also fitted with air-conditioning. The result is a very luxurious mobile hotel, and it can be a memorable way to travel if you have limited time and limitless resources.

The cost includes tours, entry fees, accommodation on the train plus all meals. Depending on the berth, it ranges from US$150 per person per night for triple occupancy up to US$300 for single occupancy.

It's a very popular service and bookings must be made in advance at the RTDC Central Reservation Office in Delhi (☎ 332-1820).

Eastern Rajasthan

JAIPUR

Population: 1,500,000

The capital city of the state of Rajasthan is popularly known as the 'pink city' because of the pink paint applied to the buildings in its old walled city. (In Rajput culture, pink was traditionally a colour associated with hospitality.) In contrast to the cities on the Ganges plain, Jaipur has broad avenues and a remarkable harmony. The city sits on a dry lake bed in a wild and somewhat arid landscape, surrounded by barren hills surmounted by fortresses and crenellated walls. Jaipur long ago outstripped the confines of its city wall yet retains a less crowded and more relaxed atmosphere than its large size and population might suggest.

History

The city owes its name, its foundation and its careful planning to the great warrior-astronomer Maharaja Jai Singh II (1699-1744). His predecessors had enjoyed good relations with the Moghuls and Jai Singh was careful to cultivate this alliance.

In 1727, with Moghul power on the wane, Jai Singh decided the time was ripe to move down from his somewhat cramped hillside fortress at nearby Amber to a new site on the plains. He laid out the city, with its surrounding walls and six rectangular blocks, according to principles of town planning set down in the *Shilpa-Shastra*, an ancient Hindu treatise on architecture. In 1728, he built the remarkable observatory which is still one of Jaipur's main attractions.

Orientation

The walled 'pink city' is in the north-east of Jaipur, while the new parts have spread to the south and west. The city's main tourist attractions are in the old part of town. The principal shopping centre in the old city is Johari Bazaar, the jewellers' market. Unlike other shopping centres in narrow alleys in India and elsewhere in Asia, this one is broad and open. All seven gates into the old city remain but, unfortunately, much of the wall itself has been torn down for building material. There is now a preservation order on the remainder.

There are three main interconnecting roads in the new part of town – Mirza Ismail Rd (M I Rd), Station Rd and Sansar Chandra Marg. Along or just off these roads are most of the budget and mid-range hotels and restaurants, the railway station, the bus station, the GPO, many of the banks and the modern shopping centre.

Information

Tourist Offices The main tourist office (☎ 69-714) in Jaipur is on platform No 1 at the railway station. The people here are very helpful and offer a range of literature. It's open daily from 6 am to 8 pm. There's also a window at platform 2 at the bus station (☎ 73-261), but its hours seem to be infinitely flexible.

The Government of India tourist office is in the Khasa Kothi Hotel and, although it has the usual range of glossy leaflets, there's little other information, so it's of limited use. It's open from 9 am to 6 pm Monday to Friday, and 9 am to 1 pm Saturday.

Money The State Bank of India has a very quick and efficient foreign exchange counter on the 1st floor of its branch in M I Rd at the Sanganeri Gate. It's open six days a week.

Jaipur also has a number of bank branches which open later than the usual hours, such as the 'evening branch' of the State Bank of Bikaner & Jaipur opposite the GPO. It is open only from 2 to 6 pm and will change travellers' cheques.

Post & Telecommunications The GPO is pretty efficient. There's also a man who sets up shop in the entrance every day from 10 am to 4.30 pm and sews up parcels, sealing them with wax. He has supplies of cloth for this purpose and his prices are very reasonable.

The telephone area code for Jaipur is 0141.

Bookshops There's an excellent range of English-language hardbacks and paperbacks as well as magazines and guidebooks at Books Corner, next to Niro's Restaurant. The bookshop at the Rambagh Palace Hotel also has a good choice. A smaller but thoughtfully chosen selection can be found at the Arya Niwas Hotel.

Old City

The old city is partially encircled by a crenellated wall with seven gates – the major gates are Chandpol, Sanganeri and Ajmeri. Broad avenues, over 30 metres wide, divide the pink city into neat rectangles.

It's an extremely colourful city and, in the evening light, the pink and orange buildings have a magical glow which is complemented by the brightly clothed Rajasthanis. Cameldrawn carts are a characteristic of Jaipur's passing street scene, along with the ubiquitous Ambassador taxis and the more modern Maruti vans and cars, all jostling for space with the innumerable tempos, bicycles, autorickshaws and pedestrians.

The major landmark in this part of town is the Iswari Minar Swarga Sul, the Minaret Piercing Heaven, near the Tripolia Gate, which was built to overlook the city.

The main bazaars in the old city are Johari Bazaar (for jewellery and saris), Tripolia Bazaar (for brassware, carvings and lacquerware), Bapu Bazaar (for perfumes and textiles) and Chandpol Bazaar (for modern trinkets and bangles).

Hawa Mahal

Built in 1799, the Hawa Mahal, or Palace of the Winds, is one of Jaipur's major landmarks, although it is actually little more than a facade. This five-storey building, which looks out over the main street of the old city, is a stunning example of Rajput artistry with its pink, semioctagonal and delicately honeycombed sandstone windows. It was originally built to enable ladies of the royal household to watch the everyday life and processions of the city. You can climb to the top of the Hawa Mahal for an excellent view over the city. The palace was built by Maharaja Sawaj Pratap Singh and is part of the City Palace complex. There's a small archaeological museum on the same site.

Entrance to the Hawa Mahal is from the rear of the building. To get there, go back to the intersection on your left as you face the Hawa Mahal, turn right and then take the first right again through an archway. It's signposted. Hours are 9 am to 4.30 pm and there's a small entry fee.

City Palace

In the heart of the old city, the City Palace occupies a large area divided into a series of courtyards, gardens and buildings. The outer wall was built by Jai Singh but other additions are much more recent, some dating to the start of this century. Today, the palace is a blend of Rajasthani and Moghul architecture. The former maharaja still lives in part of the palace.

The seven-storey Chandra Mahal is the centre of the palace and commands fine views over the gardens and the city. The ground and 1st floor of the Chandra Mahal form the **Maharaja Sawai Man Singh II Museum**. The apartments are maintained in luxurious order and the museum has an extensive collection of art, carpets, enamelware and old weapons. The paintings include miniatures of the Rajasthani, Moghul and Persian schools. The armoury has a collection of guns and swords dating back to the 15th century, as well as many of the ingenious and tricky weapons for which the warrior Rajputs were famous. The textile section contains dresses and costumes of the former maharajas and maharanis of Jaipur.

Other points of interest in the palace include the **Diwan-i-Am**, or Hall of Public Audiences, with its intricate decorations and manuscripts in Persian and Sanskrit, and the **Diwan-i-Khas**, or Hall of Private Audiences, with a marble-paved gallery. There is also a clock tower and the newer Mubarak Mahal.

Outside the buildings, you can see a large silver vessel in which a former maharaja used to take drinking water with him to England. Being a devout Hindu, he could not drink the English water! The palace and museum are open daily, except on public holidays, between 9.30 am and 4.45 pm. Entry is Rs 10, plus Rs 5 if you wish to take photos.

Jantar Mantar

Adjacent to the entrance to the City Palace is the Jantar Mantar, or observatory, begun by Jai Singh in 1728. Jai Singh's passion for astronomy was even more notable than his prowess as a warrior and, before commencing construction, he sent scholars abroad to study foreign observatories. The Jaipur observatory is the largest and the best preserved of the five he built, and was restored in 1901. The others are in Delhi (the oldest, dating from 1724), Varanasi and Ujjain. The fifth, the Muttra observatory, has now disappeared.

At first glance, Jantar Mantar appears to be just a curious collection of sculptures but, in fact, each construction has a specific purpose, such as measuring the positions of stars, altitudes and azimuths, or calculating eclipses. The most striking instrument is the sundial with its 30-metre-high gnomon. The shadow this casts moves up to four metres an hour. Admission to the observatory is Rs 2; free on Mondays. Hours are 9 am to 4.30 pm.

Those interested in the theory behind the construction of these monumental instruments should buy a copy of *A Guide to the Jaipur Astronomical Observatory* by B L Dhama (Rs 15), which can be purchased on site.

Central Museum

The museum is housed in the architecturally impressive Albert Hall in the Ram Niwas Gardens, south of the old city. The upper floor contains portraits of the Jaipur maharajas and many other miniatures and artworks. The ground floor has a collection of costumes and woodwork from different parts of Rajasthan and a description of the people and life in the rural areas of the state. The collection, which started in 1833, is also notable for its brassware, jewellery and pottery. Entry to the museum is Rs 1, free on

Mondays. It is open every day except Friday from 10 am to 5 pm.

Other Attractions

The Ram Niwas Gardens also has a **zoo** with birds, animals and a crocodile breeding farm. Jaipur has a modern **art gallery** in the 'theatre' near the zoo. To visit it you need to make enquiries as it's normally locked.

Phone 62-227 to arrange a visit to the **Kripal Kumbh**, B-18/A Shiva Marg, where Jaipur's famous blue pottery is made.

The **Museum of Indology** is an amazing private collection of folk art objects and other bits and pieces of interest – there's everything from a map of India painted on a rice grain, to manuscripts (one written by Aurangzeb), jewellery, fossils, coins, old currency notes, clocks, watches and much more. It's worth a look, and is open daily from 10 am to 5 pm. Entry is Rs 10. The museum is in fact in a private house (although the living quarters seem to have been swallowed up by the ever-growing collection), and is signposted off Nehru Marg, south of the Central Museum.

Finally, if you go to only one Hindi movie while you're in India, see it at the **Raj Mandir**. This opulent, grandiose and extremely well-kept cinema is a Jaipur tourist attraction in its own right and is always full, despite its immense size. They don't build them like this in the West anymore.

Organised Tours

Jaipur City The RTDC offers half-day and full-day bus tours of Jaipur and Amber. They visit the Hawa Mahal, Amber Fort, Jantar Mantar, City Palace and Museum (except Friday) and include the inevitable stop at a craftshop. Here, the processes of production are explained and you'll be persuaded to buy something. The half-day tours are a little rushed but otherwise alright. If possible, take a full-day tour. Times are 8 am to 1 pm, 11.30 am to 4.30 pm and 1.30 to 6.30 pm. The full-day tours are from 9 am to 6 pm, including a lunch break at Nahagarh Fort. Half-day tours cost Rs 35, full-day tours Rs 60. They

all depart from the railway station, but you can arrange to be collected from any of the RTDC hotels.

Those who want to spend more time at places in the old town than tours allow should hire an auto-rickshaws, walk, or use a bicycle. Catch public buses to Amber.

Other Tours The RTDC operates a couple of other long-distance tours. On Saturdays and Sundays there are full-day tours to Nahargarh Fort for Rs 70; on Sundays only there's a day trip to Sariska (Rs 150).

Festivals

Jaipur's elephant festival is held in early to mid-March (depending on the lunar calendar) and is actually part of the Holi Festival. For the exact dates, ask at a tourist office.

Places to Stay

Getting to the hotel of your choice in Jaipur can be a problem. Auto-rickshaw drivers besiege every traveller who arrives by rail (less so if you come by bus). If you don't want to go to a hotel of their choice, they'll either refuse to take you at all or they'll demand at least double the normal fare. If you do go to the hotel of their choice, you'll pay through the nose for accommodation because the manager will be paying them a commission of at least 30% of what you are charged for a bed (and the charge won't go down for subsequent nights).

Many hotel owners cooperate with this 'mafia' but others refuse. It's very easy to find out which hotels don't cooperate – the auto-rickshaw drivers will either refuse to take you there or demand extortionate rates for transport. It's invariably cheaper and generally more satisfactory in the long run to pay double the normal fare to be taken to the hotel of your choice. If you want to stay at a mid-range hotel, you'll be charged double fare anyway because you can obviously afford it.

Places to Stay – bottom end

One of the most popular of Jaipur's budget hotels is the *Jaipur Inn* (☎ 66-057) in Bani

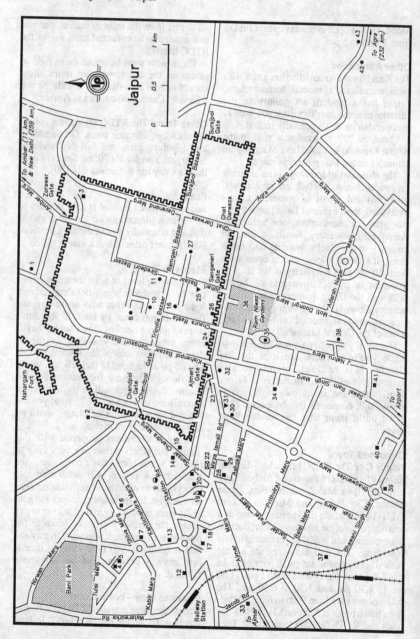

Jaipur

To Agra (232 km)

To Amber (11 km)
& New Delhi (259 km)

Zorawar Gate
Vinher Marg
Surajpol Gate
Surajpol Bazaar
Ghat Darwaza
Darwand Marg
Agra Marg
Govind Marg
Adarsh Nagar Marg
Ramganj Bazaar
Sireedeot Bazaar
Johari Bazaar
Sanganeri Gate
Ram Niwas Gardens
Moti Doongri Marg
Tripolia Bazaar
Chaura Rasta
Kishanpol Bazaar
Gangauri Bazaar
Ajmeri Gate
J Nehru Marg
Chandpol Gate
Chandpol Bazaar
Nahargarh Fort
Sawai Ram Singh Marg
Sansar Chandra Marg
Mirza Ismail Rd
Zaltak Marg
Bhagwandas Marg
Prithvi Marg
Station Rd
Kanti-chandra Marg
Shiva Marg
Palsi Marg
Tilak Marg
Sardar Marg
Bhawani Singh Marg
Bajai Marg
Nirwan Marg
Bani Park
Tulsi Marg
Kabir Marg
Waterworks Rd
Railway Station
To Ajmer
Jacob Rd
Prithviraj Marg
To Airport

Park, about a km west of Chandpol. It is clean, well run, helpful and friendly. It has a kitchen for guests to use or you can arrange to have meals prepared. Large dormitories cost Rs 30 per person and small single/double rooms are Rs 60/70, or there are some slightly larger rooms for Rs 80/90. You can even camp on the lawn if you have your own tent. It's also a good place to tune in to the travellers' grapevine.

Also very popular is the *Diggi Palace Hotel*, just off Sawai Ram Singh Marg, less than a km south of Ajmeri Gate. The building is the former palace of the thakur (similar to a lord or baron) of Diggi, and has a huge lawn area which gives the place a very spacious and peaceful ambience. The part which has been turned into a hotel is basically the old servant's quarters, but it's quite comfortable and the facilities are good. There's a range of rooms from Rs 60/80 with common bath up to Rs 175/250 with air-cool. Good meals are available.

Another option is the ever-expanding *Evergreen Guest House* (☎ 63-446), off M I Rd opposite the GPO. This large hotel, complete with restaurant, has buildings of various vintages arranged around a cramped garden courtyard. It has gone from being a small guest house to its present size in a few short years. Because of its size the personal touch has been lost, but it's still a good place to meet other travellers. There's a range of rooms and prices: from Rs 25 for dorm beds, to doubles (no singles) from Rs 60 with common bath, to Rs 140 with bath and hot water. It's bad news if you want a single room as there's no reduction on the double tariff. There are also more expensive air-cooled and air-con rooms.

The 60-bed *Youth Hostel* (☎ 67-576) is a long way from the centre of things and few people stay here. There are cheap dorm beds as well as single and double rooms.

The *retiring rooms* at the railway station might be a good option if you're just stopping overnight. Dorm beds are Rs 20, or for Rs 40/65 you can get a single/double room with attached bath, or there are air-con double rooms for Rs 155.

At the top of this range there are four excellent places, two in Bani Park and two near MI Rd. In Bani Park the *Marudhara Hotel*, D-250, behind the collectorate, has air-cooled double rooms for Rs 125 with attached bath. Just around the corner is the very pleasant *Madhuban* (☎ 79-033). This small, family-run place is well run and has a nice garden and lawn area. The air-cooled rooms all have attached bath and are good value at Rs 100/150, or Rs 200/250 for a very large room.

Closer to the centre is the *Arya Niwas Hotel* (☎ 73-456), just off Sansar Chandra Rd. It has spotlessly clean, pleasantly furnished and decorated rooms, ranging in price from Rs 110/140 up to Rs 200/240 for deluxe rooms. All rooms have baths and, in the winter months, hot water. The hotel restaurant serves tasty vegetarian food at very reasonable prices. Also available are money exchange facilities, a parking area, bicycle hire, a pleasant front lawn with tables and chairs and a small bookshop.

Equally good, and with a beautiful home atmosphere, is the smaller *Atithi Guest House* (☎ 78-679), 1 Park House Scheme, Motilal Atal Rd, between M I Rd and Station Rd. Run by the Shukla family, it's superbly maintained, squeaky clean, very friendly and it offers excellent meals. Like the Arya Niwas, it's excellent value at Rs 140/175, up to Rs 200/250 for deluxe rooms. All rooms have air-cooling, and attached bath with hot water. The family here are very keen to please and nothing is too much trouble.

Another possibility is the *Mumal Guest House* (☎ 60-053) on Ajmer Marg opposite the Jai Mahal Hotel. Rooms here cost Rs 150/200.

RTDC Places Of the four RTDC tourist bungalows in Jaipur, two are bottom-end places, although one of the others offers cheap dormitory accommodation.

The *Jaipur Tourist Hotel* (☎ 60-238) is housed in the rambling former Secretariat building on M I Rd. It's a bit shabby and in need of renovation, and so is not the best value. Dorm beds are Rs 30, single/double rooms with common bath are Rs 50/80, or 'deluxe' rooms with air-cooling are Rs 125/175.

The *Swagatam Tourist Bungalow* (☎ 67-560) near the railway station is a good choice if you have an early morning train to catch. Dorm beds are Rs 30, or there are single/double rooms from Rs 60/80 with attached bath, Rs 150/200 with air-cool and Rs 120/150 for 'super deluxe' air-cooled rooms. There's a restaurant with typically predictable and unexciting but good value food.

Although it's a mid-range place, the *Teej Tourist Bungalow* in Bani Park also has dorm beds for Rs 30. See the middle-range accommodation section below for full details.

Places to Stay – middle
Close to the Atithi Guest House on Motilal Atal Rd is the *Hotel Neelam* (☎ 72-215), which is pleasant but not used much by travellers. There are no singles but single occupancy rates are offered. Air-cooled doubles cost Rs 295 and air-con doubles are Rs 450.

On Sansar Chandra Rd is another good mid-range hotel, the *Hotel Mangal* (☎ 75-216). It has ordinary singles/doubles for Rs 120/150, air-cooled rooms for Rs 160/220 and air-con rooms for Rs 300/350. There's a popular bar here, as well as a good, pure vegetarian restaurant and even a herbal beauty parlour, health club and sauna. Checkout time is 24 hours after check-in.

Right in the heart of the old city is the *LMB Hotel* (☎ 56-5844) in Johari Bazaar. Although it's probably better known for its restaurant, the hotel does have good rooms, and the location is hard to beat. All rooms have air-con and attached bath, and cost Rs 390/575.

Along Banasthli Marg, which connects the bus station on Station Rd with Sansar Chandra Rd, are a number of modern mid-range hotels including the *Hotel Archana, Hotel Kumar, Hotel Shalimar, Hotel Gauray,*

Hotel Goyal, Hotel Kohinoor, Hotel Purohit and the *Hotel Sagar*. They all offer much the same facilities and are similarly priced – expect to pay upwards of Rs 200/250.

The *Hotel Bissau Palace* (☎ 74-191) is full of old-world charm and is surrounded by its own well-maintained gardens. The rooms, however, vary greatly; some are very pleasant while others are definitely not as good. Prices have risen dramatically in the last few years and it now costs Rs 330/660 for air-cooled single/double rooms. The hotel has a restaurant, swimming pool (not always filled), tennis court and library. The approach to this place is along one of the dirtiest streets in the city.

The *Hotel Khasa Kothi* (☎ 75-151) was a former minor palace and, before that, the state hotel. Although it's in need of major rejuvenation, the huge gardens and lawns are quiet and relaxing. Huge singles/doubles, all with air-cooling and attached bath, range from Rs 300/375 up to Rs 395/475. Facilities include swimming pool, money exchange, the Government of India tourist office, bar and restaurant.

In the south of the city is yet another former palace, the *Narain Niwas Palace Hotel* (☎ 56-3448). It's a quiet and pleasant place, surrounded by the obligatory large garden; air-cooled rooms cost Rs 330/500, while with air-con it's Rs 450/770. The rooms are huge and have somewhat ancient furniture, including four-poster beds in some of them. Meals are good value at Rs 30/70/80 for breakfast/lunch/dinner.

At the top of this range is the superb *Samode Haveli* (☎ 42-407), in the north-east corner of the old city. This 200-year-old building was once the town house of the rawal (like a nobleman) of Samode, who was also Prime Minister of Jaipur. It has a beautiful open terrace area, a stunning painted dining room, and a couple of amazing suites – one totally covered with original mirror-work, the other one painted. The charge is Rs 450/650 for ordinary rooms, or Rs 850 for the suites.

RTDC Places The RTDC *Teej Tourist Bungalow* (☎ 74-206) is at Bani Park Circle, within walking distance of both the bus and railway stations. Air-cooled rooms cost Rs 200/250, or there are rooms with air-con for Rs 300/350. All the rooms have bath and hot water, and there's a bar and restaurant.

The RTDC *Ganguar Tourist Bungalow* (☎ 60-231) is just off Sansar Chandra Rd. Although it is the most expensive of the tourist bungalows in Jaipur, it's still pretty good value and is better maintained than most others in Rajasthan. Deluxe singles/doubles cost Rs 150/200, air-cooled rooms are Rs 250/300 and air-con rooms are Rs 350/400, all with bath and hot water. There's a pleasant lawn, a restaurant, 24-hour coffee shop and bar.

Places to Stay – top end

If you have the money, the *Rambagh Palace* (☎ 52-1241) is the only place to stay in Jaipur. Formerly the palace of the Maharaja of Jaipur, this is one of India's most prestigious and romantic hotels, offering the elegance of cool white marble, endless terraces overlooking manicured lawns, fountains and browsing peacocks. By any standards, it's superb. If you can't afford to stay here, at least come for an evening drink at the terrace bar. The cheapest singles/doubles are US$125, but they are poor value compared with the cheapest suites. Known as the Garden suites, these are much more sumptuous and spacious, and cost US$250 – if you are going to splurge, take one of these. Prices go right up to US$500 for the Royal Suites.

A little more modest is the *Jai Mahal Hotel* (☎ 68-381) on the corner of Jacob Rd and Ajmer Marg, south of the railway station. This building also used to belong to the Maharaja of Jaipur, and has rooms ranging from US$105/115 all the way up to US$350 for luxury suites. There's a swimming pool, coffee lounge, bar and a restaurant serving Indian and Western food.

The small *Rajmahal Palace* (☎ 52-1757) on Sardar Patel Marg in the south of the city is yet another former important building, this time the former British Residency. It is by no means as luxurious as the previous two, but it still offers top of the range facilities, such as a swimming pool and a quality restaurant. It's a much more personal place as it has just 11 rooms and suites, and these cost US$38/75, or US$180 for the suites.

The *Hotel Clarks Amer* (☎ 82-2616), Jawaharlal Nehru Marg, is less expensive but a long way (about 10 km) from the centre of town. It is centrally air-conditioned, and has a pool, 24-hour coffee shop, beauty parlour, sauna and a restaurant.

The *Mansingh Hotel* (☎ 78-771), off Sansar Chandra Rd behind the Central Bank of India building, is a modern place close to the centre of town. This fairly new five-star hotel has fully air-conditioned singles/doubles for US$70, suites for US$85, and all the facilities you would expect of a five-star hotel, including a swimming pool.

The four-star ITDC *Hotel Jaipur Ashok* (☎ 75-121), Jai Singh Circle, Bani Park, is one of those hotels which was fine when it first opened but has been on the rapid decline ever since. However, it is one which the ITDC intends to privatise, and if this has happened, standards should have improved markedly. Current rates are Rs 1050/1200 for single/double rooms.

Places to Eat

In Johari Bazaar, near the centre of the old city, *LMB* (Laxmi Mishthan Bhandar) is well known for its excellent vegetarian food, with main courses ranging from Rs 15 to Rs 30. It also has amazingly pristine '50s 'hip' decor – definitely worth seeing. A dessert speciality is LMB kulfi, including dry fruits, saffron and cottage cheese, for Rs 18. A complete meal costs around Rs 80 per person. Out the front, a snack counter serves good snacks and excellent ice cream and offers a wide range of Indian sweets.

Niro's, on M I Rd, is rated one of Jaipur's best restaurants. It's certainly very popular with both locals and tourists and has a bright, busy atmosphere. The food, though good, is not outstanding but everyone seems to eat here at least once. They offer Indian, Chinese and Continental dishes. Next door to Niro's

are two good vegetarian restaurants, the *Surya Mahal Restaurant* and the *Natraj Vegetarian Restaurant*.

Further up M I Rd, opposite the GPO, is the *Handi Restaurant*, which has excellent barbecue chicken and kebabs in the evening, although it is open at lunchtimes as well. It's tucked away at the back of the Maya Mansions building. Another good choice on M I Rd is the *Minar Restaurant*, between the GPO and Niro's.

For really cheap food in the same area, you could try one of the cheap eating houses, known as bhojnalyas, on the other side of the road, just along from the post office. There are plenty of similar places right outside the railway station.

On Station Rd, not far from the bus station, is the very popular *Shree Shanker Bhojnalya*, where a good bottomless thali sets you back Rs 15.

If you are suffering withdrawal symptoms from lack of a decent cup of coffee, head for the *Indian Coffee House* on M I Rd. It's one of the chain found all over the country, and here too the waiters are all trussed up in cummerbunds and turbans. It's a good place for snacks, breakfast and, of course, coffee. It's tucked away off the street, in a narrow arcade next to Snowhite Drycleaners.

For the best lassi in town try the *Lassiwala* stall directly opposite Niro's on M I Rd. The lassis are cool and fresh, and served in clay pots which you smash in the gutter when empty. They come in three sizes – mini (Rs 4), small (Rs 8) and large (Rs 15) – and are excellent. Also in this area is a number of ice-cream parlours, all with a good range of flavours.

For Chinese food there's the *Golden Dragon Chinese Restaurant* down the side street next to Niro's. It's nothing flash but the prices are reasonable and the food tasty.

Things to Buy

Jaipur is well known for precious stones, which seem cheaper here than elsewhere in India, and is even better known for semi-precious stones. For precious stones, find a narrow alley called Haldion ka Rasta off

Johari Bazaar (near the Hawa Mahal). Semi-precious stones are sold in another alley, called the Gopalji ka Rasta, on the opposite side of the street. There are many shops here which offer bargain prices, but you do need to know your gems.

Shops around the City Palace and Hawa Mahal are likely to be more expensive, although they do have many interesting items including miniatures and clothes. Marble statues, jewellery and textile prints are other Jaipur specialities. The Rajasthali government emporium in M I Rd is reasonably priced; it has a branch in Amber as well as a workshop/sales outlet en route where RTDC tour buses stop. Jaipur's salespeople are hard working and very persuasive, so take care. Many unwary visitors get talked into buying things for resale at inflated prices.

Beware of these 'buy now to sell at a profit later' scams – see the the warning under Things to Buy in the Facts for the Visitor chapter for more details.

For fixed-price khadi (homespun cloth) and cotton, there are two good places to try. For khadi, the Khadi Gramodyog shops are the best bet. These government-run shops have a wide range and everything is handmade. There's one just inside Sanganeri Gate in Bapu Bazaar, and another at the Panchbatti intersection. For cotton there's the Rajasthan Handloom House on M I Rd, next to the Rajasthali Emporium.

Getting There & Away

Air The Indian Airlines office (☎ 70-624) in Jaipur is on Ajmer Rd. The Air India office (☎ 65-559) is in Rattan Mansion on M I Rd.

Indian Airlines flies Delhi/Jaipur (US$28) twice daily, and all flights continue on to Bombay, via any one or all of Jodhpur (US$34), Udaipur (US$35) and Aurangabad (US$79). There's also a daily direct flight to and from Bombay (US$98), and a three times weekly connection to Calcutta (US$152) via Varanasi (US$97).

East West Airlines has daily flights to Bombay (US$98).

Bus Buses to all Rajasthan's main population centres and to Delhi and Agra are operated by the Rajasthan State Transport Corporation from the bus station. Some services are deluxe (essentially nonstop). The deluxe buses all leave from platform 3, which is tucked away in the right-hand rear corner of the bus station yard. These buses should be booked in advance, and the booking office is also at platform 3.

State transport deluxe buses to Delhi take five hours. The 306-km trip costs Rs 98, and there are many departures daily. Deluxe state transport buses leave for Agra five times daily, taking 4½ hours at a cost of Rs 56. Deluxe buses run nine times a day to Ajmer and cost Rs 35 for the 2½-hour trip. Five deluxe buses per day take seven hours to reach Jodhpur and cost Rs 79. To Udaipur, there are four deluxe buses daily; they take about 10 hours and cost Rs 101. There are also one or two deluxe buses daily to Kota, and one daily to Jaisalmer (10 pm, 13 hours, Rs 110).

A number of private companies cover the same routes and also offer services to Ahmedabad, other cities in Gujarat and Bombay. These companies have their own depots, but the most useful collection is opposite the Hotel Neelam on Motilal Atal Rd, just off M I Rd. The buses are not as frequent as those operated by the state transport corporation and often travel at night. Avoid video buses unless you want a thumping headache the next morning.

Train The computerised railway reservation office is open from 8 am to 8 pm Monday to Saturday, and from 8 am to 2 pm Sunday.

The train services from Jaipur are generally slower than buses because it's a metre-gauge line. The *Pink City Express* leaves Old Delhi railway station at 6 am and reaches Jaipur at 11 am. The Jaipur to Delhi service leaves at 5 pm and arrives at 10.10 pm. The *Ahmedabad Mail* runs overnight, leaving Delhi at 10 pm and arriving in Jaipur at 4.30 am, while the *Chetak Express* leaves Delhi at 1 pm and arrives in Jaipur at 8.30 pm. These are the most convenient trains from Delhi, though there are others. All Jaipur trains leave from the Old Delhi station. Fares for the 308-km trip are Rs 63/224 in 2nd/1st class.

The daily superfast express between Jaipur and Agra (the *Jaipur-Agra Fort Express*) takes only five hours. It leaves Jaipur at 6.10 am and Agra at 5 pm, and reservations should be made one day in advance. Fares for the 208-km journey are Rs 47/161 in 2nd/1st class. There are plenty of express trains to Ajmer, Abu Road and Ahmedabad. The only services to Jodhpur leave Jaipur in the afternoon and arrive late in the evening, and it's the same story in the opposite direction. The 318-km trip takes eight hours and costs Rs 64/228 in 2nd/1st class.

To Udaipur, the most convenient train is the *Chetak Express*, leaving Jaipur at 9 pm and arriving in Udaipur at 9.15 am. The 431-km journey costs Rs 81/301 in 2nd/1st class.

There are also daily connections with Sawai Madhopur (3½ hours) and Bikaner (519 km, 10 hours).

Getting Around

To/From the Airport The airport is 15 km out of town. The airport bus costs Rs 20; a taxi costs about Rs 100.

Local Transport Jaipur has taxis (unmetered), auto-rickshaws and a city bus service, which also operates to Amber. A cycle-rickshaw from the station to the Jaipur Inn or Arya Niwas Hotel should cost about Rs 5, and from the station to Johari Bazaar, Rs 10, while an auto-rickshaw should cost Rs 10 and Rs 15 on these trips. However, if you're going to a hotel with your baggage and the hotel doesn't pay the driver's commission, you'll be extremely lucky to get a ride for these prices. In such cases, expect to pay two to three times the usual price. If they quote you the normal fare to a hotel whose rates you don't know, it probably means they're guaranteed an especially big commission at your expense.

Bicycles can be hired from several of the budget hotels, as well as from the Arya Niwas Hotel, at Rs 15 per day.

AROUND JAIPUR

There are several attractions around Jaipur, including some on the road between Jaipur and Amber. Jaipur tours usually stop at some of these sites on the way to or from Amber.

Amber

About 11 km out of Jaipur on the Delhi to Jaipur road, Amber was once the ancient capital of Jaipur state. Construction of the fortress-palace was begun in 1592 by Raja Man Singh, the Rajput commander of Akbar's army. It was later extended and completed by the Jai Singhs before the move to Jaipur on the plains below. The fort is a superb example of Rajput architecture, stunningly situated on a hillside and overlooking a lake which reflects its terraces and ramparts.

You can climb up to the fort from the road in 10 minutes. Riding up on elephant-back is popular, though expensive at Rs 65 per elephant one way (an elephant can carry up to four people). A quick ride around the palace courtyard costs about Rs 5. You can get cold drinks within the palace if the climb is a hot one.

An imposing stairway leads to the **Diwani-Am**, or Hall of Public Audiences, with a double row of columns and latticed galleries above. Steps to the right lead to the small **Kali Temple**. There is also the white marble **Sila Devi Temple**.

The maharaja's apartments are on the higher terrace – you enter through a gateway decorated with mosaics and sculptures. The **Jai Mandir**, or Hall of Victory, is noted for its inlaid panels and glittering mirror ceiling. Regrettably, much of this was allowed to deteriorate during the '70s and '80s but restoration work proceeds. Opposite the Jai Mandir is the **Sukh Niwas**, or Hall of Pleasure, with an ivory-inlaid sandalwood door, and a channel running right through the room which once carried cooling water. From the Jai Mandir you can enjoy the fine views from the palace ramparts over the lake below.

Amber palace is open from 9 am to 4.30 pm and entry costs Rs 10.

Getting There & Away

A bus to Amber from the Hawa Mahal in Jaipur costs about Rs 1.50. The trip takes half an hour and buses depart every few minutes. A taxi costs about Rs 80.

Gaitor

The **cenotaphs** of the royal family are at Gaitor, 6½ km from Jaipur on the road to Amber. The white marble cenotaph of Maharaja Jai Singh II is the most impressive and is decorated with carved peacocks. Next to it is the cenotaph of his son.

Opposite the cenotaphs is the **Jal Mahal water palace** in the middle of a lake and reached by a causeway. Or at least it was in the middle of a lake; the water is now all but squeezed out by the insidious weed, water hyacinth. There is another Royal Gaitor just outside the Jaipur city walls.

Tiger Fort

The Nahargarh Fort overlooks the city from a sheer ridge 6½ km away, and is floodlit at night. The road from Amber through the hills can be travelled by jeep or by rickshaw, but the peak is at the end of 1½ km of zigzag path. The views fully justify the effort and the entry fee. There's a small, almost deserted, restaurant on the top. The fort was built in 1734 and extended in 1868.

Jaigarh Fort

The imposing Jaigarh Fort, built in 1726 by Jai Singh, was only opened to the public in mid-1983. It's within walking distance of Amber and offers a great view over the plains from the Diwa Burj watchtower. The fort, with its water reservoirs, residential areas, puppet theatre and the cannon, Jaya Vana, is open from 9 am to 4.30 pm.

Samode

The small village of Samode is nestled amongst rugged hills, about 50 km north of Jaipur, via Chomu. The only reason to visit it is to see or, if you can afford it, to stay in,

the beautiful **Samode Palace** (although strictly speaking it's not actually a palace, as it wasn't owned by a ruler but by one of his noblemen). Like the Samode Haveli in Jaipur, this building was owned by the rawal of Samode. It's a beautiful building built on three levels, each with its own courtyard. The highlight of the building is the absolutely exquisite Diwan-i-Khas, which is covered with completely original painting and mirrorwork, and is probably the finest example of its kind in the country. Unfortunately the palace is open only to guests, and public transport (overloaded jeeps from Chomu) is infrequent and risky.

To stay in the palace (☎ 34) will cost you Rs 720/900, or there are suites for Rs 1200. Breakfast is available for Rs 70, while lunch and dinner are Rs 120.

Galta

The temple of the Sun God at Galta is 100 metres above the city to the east, a 2½-km climb from the Surya Gate. A deep temple-filled gorge stands behind the temple and there are fine views over the surrounding plain.

Sisodia Rani Palace & Gardens

Eight km from the city on the Agra road and surrounded by terraced gardens, this palace was built for Maharaja Jai Singh's second wife, the Sisodia princess. The outer walls are decorated with murals depicting hunting scenes and the Krishna legend.

Vidyadhar's Garden

Nestled in a narrow valley, this beautiful garden was built in honour of Jai Singh's chief architect and town planner, Vidyadhar.

Balaji

The Hindu exorcism temple of Balaji is about 1½ km off the Jaipur to Agra road, about 1½ hours by bus from Bharatpur. The exorcisms are sometimes very violent and those being exorcised don't hesitate to discuss their experiences. Two morning buses leave for Balaji from the bus station in Delhi.

Sanganer

The small town of Sanganer is 16 km south
of Jaipur and is entered through the ruins of
two *tripolias*, or triple gateways. In addition
to its ruined palace, Sanganer has a group of
Jain temples with fine carvings to which
entry is restricted. The town is noted for
handmade paper and block printing.

BHARATPUR

Population: 157,000

A must for those with an interest in ornithol-
ogy, Bharatpur is now best known for its
World Heritage-listed bird sanctuary, the
Keoladeo Ghana National Park. In the 17th
and 18th centuries, however, the town was a
Jat stronghold. Before the arrival of the
Rajputs, the Jats inhabited this area and were
able to retain a high degree of autonomy,
both because of their prowess in battle and
because of their chiefs' marriage alliances
with Rajput nobility. They successfully
opposed the Moghuls on more than one
occasion and their fort at Bharatpur, constructed in the 18th century, withstood an
attack by the British in 1805 and a long siege
in 1825. This siege eventually led to the
signing of the first treaty of friendship
between the Indian states of north-west India
and the East India Company.

The town itself, which was once surrounded by an 11-km-long wall (now
demolished), is of little interest. Bring insect
repellent with you as the shallow lakes of the
bird sanctuary are ideal breeding grounds for
mosquitoes.

Information

There's a tourist office (☎ 3700) at the Saras
Tourist Bungalow, but it's a joke. The guy
staffing it speaks minimal English and has
no clues about anything very relevant to the
park and Bharatpur in general.

Bird Sanctuary

No less than 328 kinds of birds have been
sighted at the Keoladeo sanctuary, 117 of
which migrate from as far away as Siberia
and China. The sanctuary was formerly a
vast semi-arid region, filling during the

monsoon season only to rapidly dry up afterwards. To prevent this, the Maharaja of
Bharatpur diverted water from a nearby irrigation canal and, within a few years, birds
began to settle in vast numbers. Naturally, his
primary concern was not the environment
but, rather, his desire to take guests on shooting sprees. A 'bag' of over 4000 birds per day
was not unusual. The carnage continued until
shooting was banned in 1964 and, today,
some 80 types of ducks are among the
species which nest in the sanctuary.

The food requirements of the bird population can be enormous and it's hard to believe
that these shallow lakes would be capable of
meeting it – yet they do. For example, as
many as 3000 painted storks nesting in a sq
km need about three tonnes of fish every day,
which amounts to over 90 tonnes of fish over
their 40-day nesting period – and that's just
one species. The best time to visit the sanctuary is from October to February when
many migratory birds can be seen, though
population densities differ from year to year.

Entry costs Rs 25, plus Rs 10 for a still
camera and Rs 1500 (!) for a video camera.
There's also an entry fee for cycles (Rs 3),
scooters (Rs 10) and cycle-rickshaws (Rs 5).

A guidebook including a map is available
at the ticket checkpoint. It contains a short
history of the park and an endless list of bird
species, but is otherwise of little help to
anyone without an understanding of orni-
thology.

Vehicles are prohibited in the park, so the

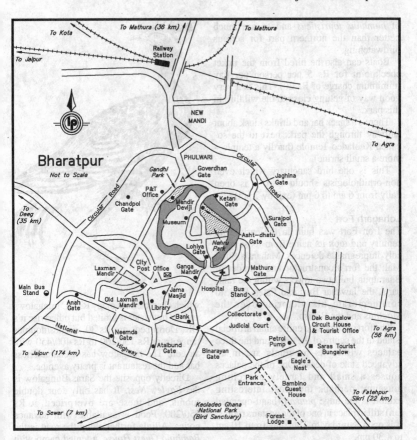

Bharatpur

Not to Scale

only way of getting around is by bicycle or cycle-rickshaw. Only those cycle-rickshaws authorised by the government (recognisable by the yellow plate bolted onto the front) are allowed inside the park – beware of anyone who tells you otherwise! Although you don't pay entry fees with these cycle-rickshaws, you'll be up for Rs 20 per hour if you take one and they'll expect a tip on top of that. Some of the drivers actually know a lot about the birds you'll see and can be very helpful, so a tip is a reasonable request.

The best way to see the park is to hire a bicycle. This allows you to easily avoid the

bottlenecks which occur at the nesting sites of the larger birds. It's just about the only way you'll be able to watch the numerous kingfishers at close quarters – noise or human activity frightens them away. You can also avoid clocking up a large bill with a rickshaw driver. Some of the hotels rent bicycles; otherwise, they can be hired from near the Saras Tourist Bungalow, but these are not cheap at Rs 30 per day. If you plan to visit the sanctuary at dawn (one of the best times to see the birds), you'll have to hire your bicycle the day before. The southern reaches of the park are virtually devoid of *humanus touristicus* and so are much better than the northern part for serious birdwatching.

Boats can also be hired from the ticket checkpoint for Rs 5 per person per day (minimum charge of Rs 20). This is a very good way of getting close to the wildlife in this park.

There's a snack bar and drinks kiosk about halfway through the park, next to the so-called Keoladeo Temple (hardly a temple – more a small shrine).

This is one bird sanctuary which even non-ornithologists should visit. It is open daily from 6 am to 6 pm (exit by 7 pm).

Lohagarh Fort

The Iron Fort was built in the early 18th century and took its name from its supposedly impregnable defences. Maharaja Suraj Mal, the fort's constructor and founder of Bharatpur, built two towers within the ramparts, the Jawahar Burj and Fateh Burj, to commemorate his victories over the Moghuls and the British.

The fort occupies the entire small artificial island in the centre of the town, and the three palaces within its precincts are in an advanced state of decay. One of the palaces houses a small and largely unexciting museum; perhaps the most interesting exhibit is the huge *punkah* (hand-operated fan) still in place in one of the upstairs rooms. It is open Saturday to Thursday from 10 am to 4.30 pm.

Places to Stay

If, like most people, you've come to Bharatpur to see the bird sanctuary, bear in mind the fact that the park entrance is about seven km from the railway station. If you stay near the station, transport is going to cost you quite a lot unless you hire a bicycle. Christmas and New Year are very busy times so, if possible, book accommodation in advance.

Most travellers stay at the *Saras Tourist Bungalow* (☎ 3700), about 500 metres from the park entrance, as it is about the best value place. It suffers from the lack of maintenance

which characterises many RTDC bungalows and the hot water is limited but otherwise it's OK. Dorm beds are Rs 30, singles/doubles range from Rs 150/200 to Rs 400/450 with air-con. The bungalow has a characterless bar and the restaurant is pretty average.

Directly opposite the Saras Bungalow is the *Eagle's Nest*. It has only four double rooms, and these are overpriced at Rs 150/200. Food is available with advance notice. A little further along the road is the *Bambino Guest House*, a tented camp with dorm beds for Rs 25 and large double tents for Rs 100. Although it's a nice concept, the hot weather in summer and the mosquitoes definitely do not help this place. There's also a few double rooms in the building for Rs 140 with bath, but these too are overpriced.

If you want to stay in the national park itself, the ITDC *Forest Lodge* (☎ 2722) is about one km beyond the entrance gate. It's a very pleasant place to stay but not cheap at US$41/49 from October to March. During the rest of the year it costs US$21/27, or US$28/36 with air-con. Meals are available and there's also a bar.

All the other hotels are much closer to the

railway station. They also seem to pay the rickshaw drivers commission, so you pay more. These hotels include the *Hotel Alora* (☎ 2616), Kumher Gate; the *Hotel Avadh* (☎ 2462), Kumher Gate; the *Hotel Tourist Complex*; the *Hotel Nannd* (☎ 3119); and the *Hotel Kohinoor* (☎ 3733).

The *Park Palace Hotel* (☎ 3222) near Kumher Gate is a good, clean and friendly place. Doubles with bath cost Rs 200, although the rickshaw-wallahs will try to tell you it's Rs 400. The *Shagun Tourist Home* inside Mathura Gate is run by a friendly guy who charges Rs 45 for double rooms.

Getting There & Away
Bus Bharatpur is on the Agra to Jaipur road, just two hours by bus from Agra or an hour from Fatehpur Sikri – buses cost about Rs 6. The Fatehpur Sikri buses pass the front door of the Tourist Bungalow and will stop there if you ask.

Buses from Jaipur take about 4½ hours and the fare is Rs 28. However, as the state transport corporation seems to select their most decrepit buses for this run, the train is preferable.

Train Bharatpur is on the New Delhi to Bombay broad-gauge line as well as the Delhi/Agra/Jaipur/Ahmedabad metre-gauge line, ensuring a good choice of trains. Be certain that the one you choose is going to stop at Bharatpur – not all trains do. The 188-km journey from Jaipur takes about three hours and costs Rs 42/151 in 2nd/1st class.

Getting Around
You can use tongas, auto-rickshaws and cycle-rickshaws to get around town, and the state tourist office has a minibus (see the tourist officer in the Tourist Bungalow). You can hire bicycles for Rs 30 a day.

DEEG
Population: 34,000
Very few travellers ever make it to Deeg, about 36 km north of Bharatpur. This is unfortunate because this small town with its massive fortifications, stunningly beautiful

palace and busy market is much more interesting than Bharatpur itself. It's an easy day trip from Bharatpur, Agra or Mathura.

History
Built by Suraj Mal in the mid-18th century, Deeg was formerly the second capital of Bharatpur state and the site of a famous battle in which the maharaja's forces successfully withstood a combined Moghul and Maratha army of some 80,000 men. Eight years later, the maharaja even had the temerity to attack the Red Fort in Delhi! The booty he carried off included an entire marble building which can still be seen.

Gopal Bhavan
Suraj Mal's palace, Gopal Bhavan, has to be one of India's most beautiful and delicately proportioned buildings. It's also in an excellent state of repair and, as it was used by the maharajas until the early 1970s, most of the rooms still contain their original furnishings.

Built in a combination of Rajput and Moghul architectural styles, the palace fronts onto a tank, the Gopal Sagar, and is flanked by two exquisite pavilions which were designed to resemble pleasure barges. The tank and palace are surrounded by well-maintained gardens which also contain the Keshav Bhavan, or Summer Pavilion, with its hundreds of fountains, many of which are still functional though only turned on for local festivals.

The palace is open daily from 8 am to noon and 1 to 7 pm; admission is free. Deeg's massive walls (up to 28 metres high) and 12 bastions, some with their cannons still in place, are also worth exploring.

Places to Stay
Deeg is essentially an agricultural town and few visitors ever come here with the intention of stopping overnight, so the choice of accommodation is very limited. The *Deeg Dak Bungalow* (☎ 18) is a possibility, with beds for less than Rs 20.

SARISKA TIGER RESERVE & NATIONAL PARK

Situated 107 km from Jaipur and 200 km from Delhi, the sanctuary is in a wooded valley surrounded by barren mountains. It covers 800 sq km (including a core area of 498 sq km) and has blue bulls, sambar, spotted deer, wild boar and, above all, tigers. Project Tiger has been in charge of the sanctuary since 1979.

As at Ranthambhor National Park, also in Rajasthan, this park contains ruined temples as well as a fort, pavilions and a palace (now a hotel) built by the maharajas of Alwar, the former owners of this area. The sanctuary can be visited year-round, except during July-August when the animals move to higher ground, but the best time is between November and June.

You'll see most wildlife in the evening, though tiger sightings are becoming more common during the day. The best way to see game is to book a 'hide' overlooking one of the waterholes. Take along food, drink and a sleeping bag (mattresses are provided).

Places to Stay

Most travellers stay at the RTDC *Tiger Den Tourist Bungalow* (☎ 42). It is very good, but somewhat expensive at Rs 150/200 for deluxe singles/doubles, Rs 250/300 air-cooled and Rs 400/450 with air-con, though they do have a Rs 30 dormitory. The bungalow has a bar and restaurant. There's also a very pleasant *Forest Rest House* where rooms cost Rs 200.

The two-star *Hotel Sariska Palace* (☎ 222), at the park entrance, is the former hunting lodge of the maharajas of Alwar. It offers air-cooled singles/doubles for Rs 500/600, and air-con doubles/suites for Rs 800/1000. All rooms have heating in winter and bath with constant hot water. There's a bar and restaurant so, even if you don't stay here, it warrants a visit.

Getting There & Away

Sariska is 35 km from Alwar, which is a convenient town from which to approach the sanctuary. There are direct buses to Alwar from Delhi (170 km) and Jaipur (146 km). Though some people attempt to visit Sariska on a day trip from Jaipur, this option is expensive and, largely, a waste of time.

ALWAR

Population: 211,000

Alwar was once an important Rajput state, which emerged in the 18th century under Pratap Singh by pushing back the rulers of Jaipur to the south and the Jats of Bharatpur to the east, and by successfully resisting the Marathas. It was one of the first Rajput states to ally itself with the fledgling British Empire, though British interference in Alwar's internal affairs meant that this partnership was not always amicable.

There is a tourist office (☎ 21-868) near the Purjan Vihar Garden.

Bala Quila Fort

This huge fort, with its five km of ramparts, stands 300 metres above the city. Predating the time of Pratap Singh, it's one of very few forts in Rajasthan which was constructed before the rise of the Moghuls. Unfortunately, because the fort now houses a radio transmitter station, it can only be visited with special permission.

Palace Complex

Below the fort sprawls the huge city palace complex, its massive gates and tank lined by a beautifully symmetrical chain of ghats and pavilions. Today, most of the complex is occupied by government offices, but there is a museum (closed on Fridays) housed in the former City Palace. Examples of miniature writing, miniature paintings of the Bundi school and ivory, sandalwood and jade *objets d'art*, as well as the usual armoury displays, are among the museum's unusual exhibits.

Places to Stay

If you're in the area, the RTDC *Lake Castle Tourist Bungalow* (☎ 22-991) at Siliserh is an ideal place to unwind, though it is some 20 km from Alwar. It is a former palace, built by Vinay Singh, Alwar's third ruler, and overlooks a lake. It's also relatively cheap at Rs 160/200 for deluxe singles/doubles, with more expensive air-cooled rooms for Rs 200/250 or with air-con for Rs 400/500, and there's a Rs 30 dormitory. It also has a bar and restaurant.

In Alwar itself there is a variety of cheaper hotels, including the *Alka Hotel* (☎ 2796) and the *Ashoka Hotel* (☎ 2027). The *Aravali Hotel* near the railway station is clean and costs Rs 120 for a double. The railway station also has *retiring rooms*.

SHEKHAWATI

The semidesert Shekhawati region lies in the triangular area between Delhi, Jaipur and Bikaner. Starting around the 14th century, a number of Muslim clans moved into the area and the towns which developed in the region became important trading posts on the caravan routes emanating from the ports of Gujarat.

The merchants prospered and in later years, encouraged by the British, established themselves as traders across the country. Some of India's richest industrialists of the 20th century, such as the Birlas, were originally Marwars (as the people from Shekhawati came to be known).

Although the towns have long since lost any importance they may once have had, what they have not lost is the amazing painted havelis (houses) built by the merchants for their families, who had stayed behind in their home towns. Most of the buildings date from the 18th century to early this century, and such is their splendour that the area has been dubbed by some as the 'open-air gallery of Rajasthan'. There is also the obligatory (for Rajasthan) forts, a couple of minor castles, distinctive wells, stepwells, chhatris, and a handful of mosques.

The major towns of interest in the region are Fatehpur, Mandawa, Ramgarh, Jhunjhunu and Sikar, although virtually every town has at least a few surviving havelis.

So far Shekhawati has been bypassed by the tourist boom, but with so much to see, and some interesting places to stay, it's an area well worth exploring for a few days. The best plan is to just wander at random through these small, dusty towns. There's no chance of getting lost, and there's surprises around every corner.

Havelis

With large amounts of money coming from trade, the merchants were keen to build mansions on a grand scale. The popular design was a building which from the outside was relatively unremarkable, the focus being the one or more internal courtyards. This served the purposes of security and privacy for the women, as well as offering some relief from the fierce heat which grips the area in summer. The plain exteriors also made the houses easily defendable.

The main entrance is usually a large wooden gate leading into a small courtyard, which in turn leads into another larger courtyard. The largest mansions had as many as four courtyards and were up to six storeys high.

Having built a house of grand proportions, the families then had them decorated with murals, and it is these murals which are the major attraction today. The major themes found are Hindu mythology, history (both old and contemporary), folk tales, eroticism (many now defaced or destroyed), and – one of the most interesting – foreigners and their modern inventions such as trains, planes, telephones, record players and bicycles. Animals and landscapes are also popular.

It is thought that the complex and sophisticated murals on the interiors of the buildings were executed by specialist painters from outside the area, while the more crude exterior ones were done by the local masons, after they had finished building the haveli. Originally the colours used in the murals were all ochre-based, but in the 1860s artificial pigments were introduced from Germany. The predominant colours are blue and maroon, but other colours such as yellow, green, and indigo are also featured.

Most of the havelis these days are not inhabited by the owners, who find that the small rural towns in outback Rajasthan have little appeal. Many are occupied just by a single chowkidah (caretaker), while others may be home to a local family. None are open as museums or for display, and consequently many are either totally or partially locked. While the locals seem fairly tolerant of strangers wandering into their front courtyard, be aware that these are private places, so tact and discretion should be used – don't just blunder in as though you own the place. Local custom dictates that shoes should be removed when entering the inner courtyard of the haveli.

One unfortunate aspect of the tourist trade

is also beginning to manifest itself here – that is the desire for antiques. A couple of towns have antique shops chock a block full of items ripped from the havelis – particularly doors and window frames, but anything that can be carted away is fair game.

Guidebooks

For a full rundown of the history, people, towns and buildings of the area, it's well worth investing in a copy of *The Guide to the Painted Towns of Shekhawati* (Ilay Cooper, Shri Om Printers, Jhunjhunu, Rs 35). It is widely available in Jaipur, but virtually

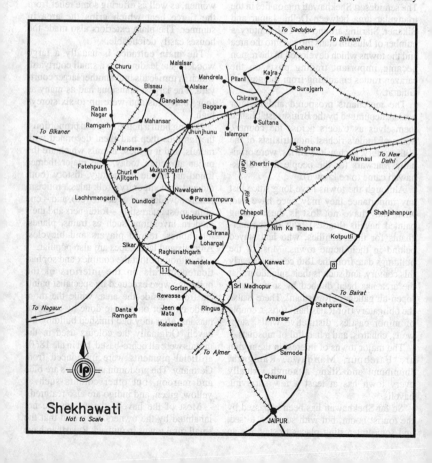

Shekhawati
Not to Scale

unobtainable in Shekhawati itself. It gives excellent details of the individual buildings of interest in each town, along with fine sketch maps of the larger towns in the area.

Getting There & Away

Access to the region is easiest from Jaipur or Bikaner. The towns of Sikar and Fatehpur are on the main Jaipur to Bikaner road and are served by many buses. Churu is on the main Delhi to Bikaner railway line, while Sikar, Nawalgarh and Jhunjhunu have daily rail links with Jaipur.

Getting Around

The Shekhawati region is crisscrossed by narrow bitumen roads, and all towns are well served by buses, either STC or private ones, although using these buses can be very time consuming. The local services to the smaller towns can get very crowded and riding 'upper class' (on the roof!) is quite acceptable – and usually necessary.

If you have a group of four or five people, it is worth hiring a taxi for the day to take you around the area. It's easy to arrange in the towns which have accommodation, although finding a driver who speaks English is more of a problem. The rate for a diesel Ambassador is Rs 2 per km, plus lunch for the driver.

Fatehpur

While not the most interesting town, Fatehpur is just off the main Bikaner to Jaipur road, and so is easily accessible. It also has a brand new RTDC Tourist Bungalow, and is fairly central, making it a good place to base yourself for further explorations.

The town was established in 1451 as a capital for Muslim nawabs, but it was taken by the Shekhawat Rajputs in the 18th century.

One of the main points of interest is the **Goenka Haveli**, which, although still lived in, is in a semi-derelict state. Built in 1860, it has just a single courtyard, and the main feature is the painted room upstairs, which features mirrorwork and some fine murals. A

tip is usually expected by the man living here, especially if you want to take pictures.

There's the remains of a huge **17th-century step-well** in the middle of town opposite the cinema. Unfortunately it is half full with rubbish, and at least one building has collapsed into it. Before long it will be beyond restoration.

Places to Stay The RTDC *Haveli Tourist Bungalow* (☎ 293) is on the southern edge of town, about one km from the bus stand. It is brand spanking new and so is currently a very pleasant and comfortable place to stay – if only it remains that way. Dorm beds are Rs 30, or there's large single/double rooms – where everything still works! – for Rs 100/150, or Rs 125/200 with air-cooling. Good meals are available and transport to other villages can be arranged.

Mandawa

The compact and busy little market town of Mandawa was settled in the 18th century, and was fortified by the dominant merchant families. Today it has some of the finest painted havelis in the region, and is a perfect place for wandering at random.

The **fort**, dating back to 1760, dominates the town and now houses a comfortable mid-range hotel. Of the havelis, the **Bansidhar Newatia Haveli** (c. 1910) has some curious paintings on its outer eastern wall – a boy using a telephone, and other 20th-century inventions such as an aeroplane and a car. The haveli is in the main street, almost opposite the lane which leads to the fort. The **Gulab Rai Ladia Haveli** (c. 1870) is one of the finest in the region, and has some superb murals. In the forecourt there's a very low-key souvenir stall, selling, among other things, the previously mentioned guidebook to the region. The haveli is a few minutes walk from the main street, south and east of the fort – just ask. Other buildings worth seeking out are the **Harlalka well**, in the western part of town, and the **Majisa ka Kuan well**, north of the central bazaar.

Places to Stay The *Mandawa Castle* (☎ 224) is wildly atmospheric. The rooms have been tastefully modernised, while the medieval feel of the place has remained undiminished. It's a wonderful place to stay if you can afford the price of Rs 600/650 for ordinary rooms, Rs 700/750 for larger deluxe rooms, or Rs 1000 to Rs 1500 for deluxe suites. Meals are available for Rs 75/110/125 for breakfast/lunch/dinner.

If the castle is out of reach, there's a few other alternatives, but two of them are inconveniently located well out of the town centre – the *Thar Hotel* and the *Desert Camp*, both on the road to Mukundgarh. The Desert Camp is actually part of the Mandawa Castle operation, and costs around Rs 200 per night.

The *Hotel Rath Mandawa* is on the northern edge of town and charges Rs 150/200.

Dundlod

Dundlod is a tiny town right in the heart of the Shekhawati region. Although it has little of interest, the **fort** here dates back to 1750, although much of it is more recent. It is owned by a direct descendent of the *rawal* who built the place. The Diwan-i-Khas audience hall is still in very good condition.

Places to Stay The fort, known as *Dera Dundlod Kila* (☎ 98), is a very low-key affair offering comfortable but far from palatial accommodation. The cost is Rs 400/500 for singles/doubles, and meals are available for Rs 50/80/100.

Nawalgarh

The main building in this town is also the fort, founded in 1837 but today largely disfigured by modern accretions. It houses government offices and a branch of the Bank of Baroda. One of the main havelis is the **Anand Lal Paddar Haveli**, built in the 1920s. Today it houses a school, but has many fine paintings; also worth a look is the **Kulwal Haveli**.

Places to Stay The *Hotel Natraj* is in the Sabzi Mandi, right outside the entrance to the fort. It is a very primitive Indian hotel, with just a couple of rooms for Rs 25/40 with common bath. It also has a restaurant serving extremely basic meals.

A much more pleasant alternative is the *Roop Niwas Palace* (☎ 2008), right on the eastern edge of town, about one km from the fort. It was formerly the country house of the Rawal of Nawalgarh, and has a pleasant garden setting. The quaintly furnished rooms cost Rs 390/500, and for meals you're looking at Rs 50 for breakfast, and Rs 100 for lunch or dinner.

Jhunjhunu

Jhunjhunu is one of the largest towns of Shekhawati and is the current district headquarters. It has some of the region's most beautiful buildings and should not be missed.

The town was founded by the Kaimkhani nawabs in the middle of the 15th century, and remained under their control until it was taken by the Rajput ruler Sardul Singh in 1730.

It was in Jhunjhunu that the British based their Shekhawati Brigade, a troop raised locally in the 1830s to try to halt the activities of the *dacoits* (bandits), who were largely local petty rulers who had decided it was easier to become wealthy by pinching other peoples' money than by earning their own.

Jhunjhunu has a few hotels, a bank and the only tourist office in the region – at the Shiv Shekhavati Hotel. It is also on the bus and railway routes, so it has good connections with other parts of the state.

The main item of interest here is the **Khetri Mahal**, a fine minor palace dating back to around 1760. It has very elegant lines and is architecturally the most sophisticated building in the region, although it's not in the greatest condition. The **Sri Bihariji Temple** is from a similar period and contains some fine murals, although these too have suffered over the years. The **Modi and Tibrewala havelis**, both in the main bazaar, are covered with murals, and the latter one is particularly interesting. The town also has a number of chhatris and wells.

Places to Stay Jhunjhunu has the widest range of accommodation of any of the Shekhawati towns. The bus stand is one km south of the centre, and close to it are a number of budget hotels, including the *Hotel Sangam* and the *Hotel Rukhali*. Both are OK at Rs 60/100, but they are on a noisy road and the distance from the centre is a hassle.

A better bet is the *Hotel Shiv Shekhavati* (☎ 2651) on the eastern edge of town, but still close to the centre. Rooms cost Rs 50/80 with common bath, Rs 150/200 with air-cooling and attached bath, and Rs 250/300 with air-con. Meals are available and there's also a bar.

Ramgarh

The town of Ramgarh was founded by the powerful Poddar merchant family in 1791, after they had left the village of Churu following a disagreement with the thakur. It had its heyday in the mid 19th-century and was one of the richest towns of the area. As a result, today it has probably the greatest concentration of painted havelis anywhere – it's a fascinating place to wander around.

The **Poddar Chhatris** near the bus stand, and the **Poddar havelis** near the Churu Gate (northern) are all fine examples. Down the side street next to the well near the northern gate is one of the antique shops which makes its living from pieces ripped out of the buildings in the area.

AJMER

Population: 402,000

South of Jaipur is Ajmer, a green oasis on the shore of the Ana Sagar, hemmed in by barren hills. Historically, Ajmer always had great strategic importance and was sacked by Mahmud of Ghazni on one of his periodic forays from Afghanistan. Later, it became a favourite residence of the great Moghuls. One of the first contacts between the Moghuls and the British occurred in Ajmer when Sir Thomas Roe met with Jehangir here in 1616.

The city was subsequently taken by the Scindias and, in 1818, it was handed over to the British, becoming one of the few places in Rajasthan controlled directly by the British rather than being part of a princely state. Ajmer is a major centre for Muslim pilgrims during the fast of Ramadan but, although it has some superb examples of early Muslim architecture, a fort overlooking the town and a lively bazaar, Ajmer is just a stepping stone to nearby Pushkar for most travellers.

Orientation & Information

The tourist office (☎ 21-626) is in the Khadim Tourist Bungalow and has a good range of literature. The tourist officer, Mr Hazarilal Sharma, is very keen to help – he's one of those rare tourist officers who takes an active interest in his job.

The bus stand is close to the Tourist Bungalow on the Jaipur side of town. The railway station and most of the hotels are on the other side of town.

Ana Sagar

This artificial lake was created in the 12th century by damming the River Luni. On its bank is a fine park, the **Dault Bagh**, containing a series of marble pavilions erected in 1637 by Shah Jahan. It's popular for an evening stroll.

The lake tends to dry up if the monsoon is poor, so the city's water supply is taken from **Foy Sagar**, five km further up the valley. There are good views from the hill beside the Dault Bagh.

Dargah

At the foot of a barren hill in the old part of town, this is one of India's most important places for Muslim pilgrims. The Dargah is the tomb of a Sufi saint, Khwaja Muin-ud-din Chishti, who came to Ajmer from Persia in 1192. Construction of the shrine was completed by Humayun and the gate was added by the Nizam of Hyderabad. Akbar used to make the pilgrimage to the Dargah from Agra once a year.

As you enter the courtyard, removing your shoes at the gateway, a mosque constructed by Akbar is on the right. The large iron cauldrons are for offerings which are cus-

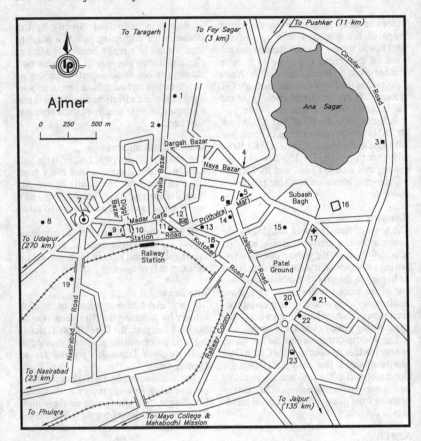

Ajmer

0   250   500 m

To Taragarh

To Foy Sagar
(3 km)

To Pushkar (11 km)

Circular Road

Ana Sagar

Dargah Bazar

Naya Bazar

Nalla Bazar

Diggi Bazar

Madar Gate

Station Road

Railway Station

To Udaipur
(270 km)

To Nasirabad
(23 km)

Nasirabad Road

To Phulera

To Mayo College &
Mahabodhi Mission

Kutchery Road

Jaipur Road

Railway Colony

Subash Bagh

Prithvira

Marj

Patel Ground

To Jaipur
(135 km)

1
2
3
4
5
6
7
8
9
10
11
12
13
14
15
16
17
18
19
20
21
22
23

tomarily shared by families involved in the shrine's upkeep. In an inner court, there is another mosque built by Shah Jahan. Constructed of white marble, it has 11 arches and a Persian inscription running the full length of the building.

The saint's tomb is in the centre of the second court. It has a marble dome and the actual tomb inside is surrounded by a silver platform. The horseshoes nailed to the shrine doors are offerings from successful horse dealers! The tomb attracts hundreds of thousands of pilgrims every year on the anniversary of the saint's death, in the seventh month of the lunar calendar. Beware of 'guides' hassling for donations around the Dargah using the standard fake donation books – all the donations registered in these books are over Rs 50!

Adhai-din-ka-jhonpra

Beyond the Dargah, on the very outskirts of town are the ruins of this mosque. According to legend, its construction, in 1153, took 2½ days, as its name indicates. It was built as a Jain college but in 1198 Muhammad Ghori took Ajmer and converted the building

1	Adhai-din-ka-jhonpra	12	GPO
2	Dargah Khwaja	13	Bank of Baroda &
3	Mansingh Hotel		Rajmahal Lodge
4	Agra Gate	14	Church
5	Nasiyan (Red) Temple	15	College
6	Bhola Hotel	16	Circuit House
7	Kaisar Ganj	17	JLN Hospital
8	Government College	18	Hotel Samrat
9	KEM Rest House & Honeydew Res-	19	Super Bazaar
	taurant	20	Collectorate
10	Hotels Ashoka, Surya, Chalsa & Sirtaj	21	Khadim Tourist Bungalow
	Tourist Hotel	22	State Bank of India
11	Pushkar Buses	23	Bus Station

into a mosque by adding a seven-arched wall in front of the pillared hall.

Although the mosque is now in need of repair, it is a particularly fine piece of architecture – the pillars are all different and the arched 'screen', with its damaged minarets, is noteworthy.

Three km and a steep 1½-hour climb beyond the mosque, the Taragarh, or Star Fort, commands an excellent view over the city. The fort was the site of much military activity during Moghul times and was later used as a sanatorium by the British.

Akbar's Palace

Back in the city, near the railway station, this imposing fort was built by Akbar in 1570 and today houses the Ajmer Museum, which is really not worth the bother. It is closed on Fridays and charges a small admission fee.

Nasiyan Temple

The Red Temple on Prithviraj Marg is a Jain temple built last century. Its double-storey hall contains a series of large, gilt wooden figures from Jain mythology which depict the Jain concept of the ancient world. It's certainly worth a visit. A sign in the temple warns that 'Smoking and chewing of beatles is prohibited'.

Places to Stay – bottom end

With some exceptions, most of Ajmer's budget hotels are typical Indian boarding houses with little to choose between them.

They offer basic essentials and are OK for a night, but those in Pushkar are far preferable. When exiting the railway station you'll be accosted by cycle and auto-rickshaw drivers all keen to take you 'anywhere' for Rs 2 or less – unfortunately 'anywhere' always means to a hotel where they get commission.

To the left as you exit the railway station is the huge *King Edward Memorial Rest House* (☎ 20-936), Station Rd, known locally as 'KEM'. Very few travellers seem to stay here and it's mainly used by Muslim pilgrims. Rooms range from Rs 30 for a '2nd class' single to Rs 50/100 for '1st class' single/doubles and Rs 80/120 for deluxe rooms. It's good value in what is quite an expensive town.

Better budget hotels can be found along Prithviraj Marg, between the GPO and the Red Temple. First down this road, opposite the GPO, the *Rajmahal Lodge* (☎ 21-347) is one of the most basic hotels in town with rooms for Rs 40/60. Further up, the *Anand Hotel* (☎ 23-099) has singles/doubles with bath and hot water for Rs 60/90, less with common bath.

Opposite the church at Agra Gate, the noisy *Bhola Hotel* (☎ 23-844) has singles/doubles for Rs 60/80 with bath and constant hot water. The vegetarian restaurant is excellent.

Most travellers stay at the RTDC *Khadim Tourist Bungalow* (☎ 20-490), only a few minutes walk from the bus station or about Rs 7 by auto-rickshaw from the railway

19th-century Rajasthani maharaja

station. There's a range of rooms available priced from Rs 100/125 to Rs 250/300 with air-con, as well as a Rs 30 dormitory. It's certainly a pleasant setting but hotel maintenance is virtually nonexistent.

On Kutchery Rd just a few minutes walk from the railway station is the *Hotel Samrat* (☎ 31-805). It's a friendly place, and although the rooms are on the small side, it's very convenient for early morning departures with the private bus companies, as they have their offices just across the road. The rooms cost Rs 100/150, or for a double with air-cooling Rs 250.

Places to Stay – top end

The only top-end hotel in Ajmer is the *Mansingh Hotel* (☎ 30-855), Circular Rd, overlooking Ana Sagar. While it looks OK, closer inspection reveals poor maintenance and lack of attention to detail. The position is ideal but it's poor value at Rs 395/780.

Places to Eat

Few restaurants in Ajmer stand out as worthy of special mention. One exception is the vegetarian restaurant at the *Bhola Hotel*. The food is very tasty, the restaurant is well maintained and few items cost more than Rs 15.

For a minor splurge, try the *Honeydew* restaurant near the KEM Rest House near the railway station. *Sweets in Paradise* on Kutchery Rd has an excellent range of Indian sweets.

Getting There & Away

Bus There are buses from Jaipur to Ajmer every 15 minutes, some nonstop. The trip costs Rs 33 and takes 2½ hours. From Delhi, 20 buses run daily in either direction at a cost of Rs 78.

State transport buses also go to Jodhpur (210 km, 4½ hours, Rs 41), Udaipur (303 km via Chittorgarh, Rs 58), Chittorgarh (190 km, Rs 34), Kota (200 km via Bundi, Rs 32 to Rs 40), Ranakpur (237 km, Rs 43), Bharatpur (305 km, Rs 62) and Bikaner (277 km, Rs 55). In addition, buses leave for Agra (385 km, Rs 73) each morning at 7.30, 8 and 10 am and for Jaisalmer (490 km, Rs 84) daily at 8 am. There are also regular buses to Kota and Bundi. As not all these buses are deluxe, limited stop or nonstop, you need to check beforehand.

Also available are private deluxe buses to Ahmedabad (Rs 120), Udaipur (Rs 60), Jodhpur (Rs 65), Jaipur (Rs 35) Mt Abu, Jaisalmer, Bikaner, Delhi (Rs 120) and Bombay. Most of the companies have offices on Kutchery Rd. If you book your ticket to one of these destinations through an agency in Pushkar, they will provide a free jeep transfer to Ajmer to commence your journey.

Train Ajmer is on the Delhi/Jaipur/ Marwar/ Ahmedabad line and most trains on this line stop at Ajmer. The 135-km journey from Jaipur costs Rs 31/118 in 2nd/1st class. The *Pink City Express* takes about the same time as the buses to cover the distance.

To Udaipur the fastest express takes 7½ hours at a cost of Rs 73/273 in 2nd/1st class.

Getting Around

Ajmer is a relatively small town and easy enough to get around on foot, but there are plenty of auto and cycle-rickshaws.

PUSHKAR

Population: 11,000

Like Goa or Dharamsala, the mellow, quiet and interesting little town of Pushkar is one of those travellers' centres where people go for a little respite from the hardships of life on the Indian road. It's only 11 km from Ajmer but separated from it by Nag Pahar, the Snake Mountain, and is situated right on the edge of the desert.

The town clings to the side of the small but beautiful Pushkar Lake with its many bathing ghats and temples. For Hindus, Pushkar is a very important pilgrimage centre. Unfortunately after a poor monsoon the lake doesn't get refilled and can be almost empty. This is a great pity, as it is a big factor in the town's appeal.

Pushkar is also world famous for the huge camel and cattle fair which takes place here each October or November. At this time, the town is thronged with tribal people from all over Rajasthan, pilgrims from all over India and film-makers and tourists from all over the world. If you're anywhere within striking distance at the time, it's an event not to be missed.

Being a holy place, alcohol and meat are banned.

Information

As yet there are no long-distance/ISD phones in Pushkar, but you can either go through the operator (often a lengthy process) or dial direct from phones in Ajmer.

Camel Fair

The exact date on which the Camel Fair is held depends on the lunar calendar but, in Hindu chronology, it falls on the full moon of Kartik Purnima. Each year, up to 200,000 people flock to Pushkar for the Camel Fair, bringing with them some 50,000 camels and cattle for several days of pilgrimage, horse dealing, camel racing and colourful festivities.

The Rajasthan tourist office has promoted the fair as an international attraction by adding Rajasthan dance programmes and other cultural events and by putting up a huge tent city for the Indian and foreign visitors. It's one of India's biggest and most colourful festivals. In 1993 it's on 26 to 29 November, in 1994 it's 15 to 18 November and in 1995 it's 4 to 7 November.

Temples

Pushkar boasts temples, though few are as ancient as you might expect at such an important pilgrimage site since many were destroyed by Aurangzeb and subsequently rebuilt. The most famous is what is said to be the only **temple** in India dedicated to Brahma. It's marked by a red spire, and over the entrance gateway is the *hans*, or goose symbol, of Brahma, who is said to have personally chosen Pushkar as its site. The **Rangji Temple** is also important.

The one-hour trek up to the **hilltop temple** overlooking the lake is best made early in the morning; the view is magnificent.

Ghats

Numerous ghats run down to the lake, and pilgrims are constantly bathing in the lake's holy waters. If you wish to join them, do it with respect – remove your shoes, don't smoke and don't take photographs. This is not Varanasi and the pilgrims here can be very touchy about insensitive intrusions by non-Hindus.

Places to Stay

Pushkar is such a small but popular town that it can be difficult to find accommodation, especially if you arrive late in the day. Most of the available hotels are very basic, and rooms have just a bed, common bathroom facilities and no hot water. Many have only charpoys (string beds) with no mattress or sheets. On the other hand, they're generally clean and freshly whitewashed. You should ask to see a few rooms before deciding as many have a cell-like atmosphere due to the small or nonexistent windows. Mosquitoes come with most rooms, so bring insect repellent.

One of the best places is the *Hotel White House* (☎ 147), run by a very friendly Brahmin family. There's rooms to suit most budgets, from doubles with common bath for Rs 50 up to large rooms with bath attached for Rs 125/150. It's a very peaceful and quiet place, there's an excellent view from the roof, and there's a large market-garden attached. The mango tea is also delicious.

Another very popular place is the *Pushkar Palace Hotel* (☎ 1), which has a lawn right at the lakeside. It's very clean, pleasant, freshly whitewashed and has a vegetarian restaurant. The hotel offers a variety of rooms, ranging from single/double rooms with common bath at Rs 60/80, right up to air-con suites for Rs 375/400. The cheaper rooms actually have a view of the lake.

Next to the Pushkar Palace Hotel, but approached from a different entrance, the RTDC *Sarovar Tourist Bungalow* (☎ 2040) is set in its own spacious grounds at the far end of the lake and has a vegetarian restaurant. It's much better value than the Tourist Bungalow in Ajmer, and has ordinary singles/doubles for Rs 50/70 with common bath, Rs 75/100 with attached bath, and air-cooled deluxe rooms for Rs 200/250. Part of this hotel was once a small palace belonging to the Maharaja of Jaipur.

The *Prince Hotel* is in a quiet location and has a small courtyard, complete with a couple of gum trees for homesick Aussies. The rooms are basic but pleasant, and cost Rs 40/50 with common bath. Close by is the *Hotel Pushkar-Lake*, which has just six small rooms around a tiny courtyard. It's pokey but pleasant and relaxed, and the rooms cost just Rs 25/50.

The popular *Everest Guest House* is also excellent value. It's a warren of a place, but it is mellow, quiet and very clean. There are also great views from the roof. Dorm beds are Rs 10, while small single/double rooms cost Rs 20/40 with common bath and Rs 50/60 with bath. Constant hot water is available and meals can be arranged.

A similar place is the *Payal Guest House*, right in the middle of the main bazaar. It's a very nice place with rooms from Rs 35/50 with common bath, and Rs 45/60 with attached bath.

At the western edge of the town is the *Krishna Palace Guest House*. It's typically basic but quite OK, and hot water is available for Rs 2 per bucket. Rooms are a bargain at Rs 20/30 with common bath. The *Hotel Brahma* is a similar place, right opposite the Marwar bus stand on the northern edge of town. The rooms are a good size, but the location is not great and the place cops the noise from the bus station.

Also good is the *Oasis Hotel* (☎ 100), near the Ajmer bus stand. It has an internal garden area, comfortable beds and good views from the roof. Singles/doubles with common bath cost Rs 30/45, Rs 75/80 with bath, and constant hot water is available. There's also one very large room with a balcony for Rs 200.

Another good choice on the outskirts of town is the *Peacock Hotel* (☎ 88). The rooms surround a large, shady courtyard, and the swimming pool is a big drawcard. Singles/doubles with bath cost Rs 50/80, Rs 30/50 with common bath. There are also larger air-cooled rooms at Rs 250/350. All the rooms have fans, hot water is available at a very reasonable price and meals can be arranged. Outsiders can use the pool for Rs 25. The travel agency here is not a good place to make travel arrangements though.

The *Hotel Navratan Palace* is a new and characterless place near the Brahma Temple. At Rs 100 for a single/double with bath it's overpriced considering what else is available in Pushkar.

Tourist Village During the Camel Fair, the RTDC sets up a tented 'Tourist Village' (☎ 2155) on the *mela* ground right next to the Camel Fair, with accommodation for up to 1600 people. It's a self-contained village with a dining hall, coffee shop, toilets, bathrooms (bucket hot water), foreign exchange facilities, post office, medical centre, safe

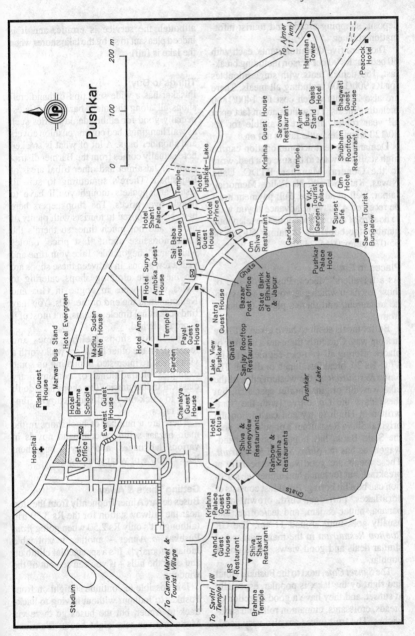

Pushkar

To Ajmer (11 km)

To Ajmer

Hamman Tower

Peacock Hotel

200 m

100

0

Krishna Guest House

Sarovar Restaurant

Ajmer Bus Stand

Oasis Hotel

Bhagwati Guest House

Temple

Shubham Rooftop Restaurant

Om Hotel

V.K. Tourist Palace

Garden Palace

Sunset Cafe

Sarovar Tourist Bungalow

Temple

Hotel Pushkar-Lake

Hotel Shanti Palace

Hotel Prince

Laxmi Guest House

Sai Baba Guest House

Om Shiva Restaurant

Garden

Hotel Surya

Ambika Guest House

Bazaar Ghats

State Bank of Bikaner & Jaipur

Pushkar Palace Hotel

Post Office

Natraj Guest House

Hotel Amar

Temple

Madhu Sudan White House

Payal Guest House

Garden

Pushkar Lake

Marwar Bus Stand

Rishi Guest House

Hotel Evergreen

Garden

Lake View Pushkar

Sanjay Rooftop Restaurant

Ghats

Hospital

Hotel Brahma

School

Everest Guest House

Post Office

Chanakya Guest House

Hotel Lotus

Shiva & Honeyview Restaurants

Rainbow & Krishna Restaurants

Ghats

Lake

Stadium

To Camel Market & Tourist Village

To Savitri Hill Temple

Krishna Palace Guest House

Anand Guest House

RS Restaurant

Shiva Shakti Restaurant

Brahma Temple

deposit, shopping arcade and tourist information counter.

There are five dormitory tents, each with 60 beds, at Rs 90 per person including breakfast, 150 deluxe tents with singles/doubles for Rs 900/1200 including all meals. There are also 20 huts which cost Rs 1400/1800 including meals. These huts are in fact open all year round, and are available for Rs 80/120 when the cattle fair is not on.

Demand for tent accommodation can be high so, if you want to be sure of a bed, write to the General Manager, RTDC, Usha Niwas, Kalyan Path, Nr Police Memorial, Jaipur, well in advance. Full payment must be received 45 days in advance if you want to be sure of accommodation. The telephone number for bookings is Jaipur 60-586 or 65-076 (telex 0365-2479).

Places to Eat

As a travellers' Mecca, Pushkar is one of those towns in which everyone has a favourite restaurant, and there's plenty to choose from.

Buffet meals seem to have taken off here in a big way. Currently there are a number of places offering all-you-can-eat meals for Rs 17 to Rs 20, breakfast, lunch or dinner. The *Shiva Restaurant* on the western edge of the lake was the original buffet specialist, but these days the *Om Shiva* (with the 'Om' written in Hindi to try and cash in on the original Shiva Restaurant's popularity), near the State Bank, has hopped on the bandwagon, as has the *Shiva Shakti Restaurant*. These meals are good value, especially at breakfast, but for lunch and dinner the selection can be a bit boring. Breakfast consists of cornflakes, porridge, curd, brown toast, banana, butter & jam, and tea/coffee, and usually goes until around 11 am. The *GR Rooftop Restaurant* in the main bazaar has similar deals and good views, but is not as popular.

The *Sunset Cafe*, next to the Pushkar Hotel and right by the lake, is popular, especially at sunset, and they have a good selection of breads, croissants, cinnamon rolls and sandwiches. The fruit juices are also very good, although the service is erratic, and it is indeed pleasant to sit by the lake shore (when the lake is full).

Things to Buy

Pushkar has a wide selection of handicraft shops all along the main bazaar and is especially good for embroidered fabrics such as wall hangings, bed covers, cushion covers and shoulder bags. A lot of what is stocked here actually comes from the Barmer district south of Jaisalmer and other tribal areas of Rajasthan. There's something to suit all tastes and pockets though you'll have to haggle over prices. The shopkeepers here have been exposed to tourists with plenty of money and not much time, so there's the usual nonsense about 'last price' quotes which aren't negotiable. Take your time and visit a few shops. In between these shops are the inevitable clothing shops catering to styles which were in vogue in Goa and Kathmandu at the end of the '60s. You may find occasional timeless items, but most of it is pretty clichéd.

The music shops (selling tapes and records), on the other hand, are well worth a visit if you're interested in picking up some examples of traditional or contemporary classical Indian music. The shops here don't seem to stock the usual banal current film-score rages.

There are a number of bookshops in the main bazaar selling secondhand novels in various languages, and they'll buy them back for 50% of what you pay.

Getting There & Away

Buses depart Ajmer frequently from the stop near the railway station for the Rs 3.50 trip (although it's only Rs 2.50 when going *from* Pushkar *to* Ajmer – another inexplicable Indian anomaly!). It's a spectacular climb up and over the hills – if you can see out of the window.

It is possible to continue straight on from Pushkar to Jodhpur without having to backtrack to Ajmer, but the buses go there via Merta and can take eight hours. It's much faster to go to Ajmer and take the 4½-hour express bus.

There are a couple of agents in Pushkar offering tickets for private buses to various destinations. These buses all leave from Ajmer, but the agents provide you with free jeep transport to Ajmer in time for the departures. See the Ajmer section for destinations.

RANTHAMBHOR NATIONAL PARK

Near the town of Sawai Madhopur, midway between Bharatpur and Kota, Ranthambhor National Park is one of the prime examples of Project Tiger's conservation efforts in Rajasthan. Sadly, it also demonstrates that program's overall failure; experts (see *BBC World* Jan/Feb '93) state that the tiger population may now be as low as 15. Officially, there are 40 tigers in the park and so you have a good chance of a sighting on your first safari. To be sure, plan on two or three safaris. Other game, especially the larger and smaller herbivores, are more numerous. Even if you don't see a tiger, it's worth the effort for the scenery alone: in India it's not often you get the chance to visit such a large area of virgin bush, and the contrast with the often denuded land elsewhere is stark.

The park itself covers some 400 sq km and its scenery is very beautiful. A system of lakes and rivers is hemmed in by steep high crags and, on top of one of these, is the extensive and well-preserved fortress of Ranthambore, built in the 10th century. The lower-lying ground alternates between open bushland and fairly dense forest and is peppered with ruined pavilions, *chhatris* (tombs) and 'hides' – the area was formerly a hunting preserve of the maharajas.

A good network of four gravel tracks crisscrosses the park and safaris are undertaken in open-sided jeeps driven by a ranger. If you've ever been on safari in Africa, you might think this is an unduly risky venture but the tigers appear unconcerned by jeep loads of garrulous tourists touting cameras only metres away from where they're lying. No-one has been mauled or eaten – yet!

The best time to visit the park is between October and April, and the park is actually closed during the monsoon from 1 June to 1 October. Early morning and late afternoon are the best times to view game.

Orientation & Information

There's a tourist office (☎ 2223) in the Project Tiger office in Sawai Madhopur. It is tucked away half a km south of the railway station. Just follow the tracks south from the station, through the overpass, and the office is on the left, just before the cinema, which is on the other side of the tracks.

There are four trails within the park, and on each safari six jeeps take each trail. While this may sound like a lot, they usually spread themselves out so it's not just a noisy convoy.

It's 10 km from Sawai Madhopur to the first park gate, where the jeeps queue and you pay the entry fees, and a further three km to the main gate and the Jogi Mahal. The accommodation is strung out all the way along the road from the town to the park. Advance booking is essential during the busy Christmas and New Year periods.

If you are taking photos, it's worthwhile bringing some 400 or 800 ASA film, as the undergrowth is dense and surprisingly dark.

There's a Rs 25 entry fee to the park, plus Rs 10 for a camera. You'll also have to pay the entry fee of Rs 75 per vehicle. The park entrance is about 10 km from the Sawai Madhopur railway station.

Places to Stay

There's some basic accommodation in the town itself, while the better places are along the park road. When stepping off the train you'll be besieged by touts and jeep drivers trying to drum up business. Don't be intimidated into taking a jeep to yourself (if you don't want one), or into staying somewhere you don't want to.

Right in town itself, about half a km from the railway station, is the *Hotel Swagat* (☎ 2601). It's pretty basic, but reasonable for what it offers, at Rs 40/60 or Rs 70 for a double with bath attached. The *Hotel Vishal*, in the same street, is similar.

Also in town, just by the railway flyover, is the more upmarket *Hotel Pink Palace*, where a double with bathroom attached and hot water is Rs 150.

Moving out of town along the road to the park, the first place is *The Cave* (one km from town), which is a tented camp of a dozen or so large tents, each fitted with a bathroom (!), supplied with bucket hot water. It's not cheap at Rs 100 per person; try bargaining.

Next up is the *Sawai Madhopur Lodge* (☎ 2541; 1½ km), formerly belonging to the Maharaja of Jaipur. It is suitably luxurious, and has a bar, restaurant and beautiful garden. The price for full-board accommodation is US$70/85, and jeeps are available for trips around the park.

A further 500 metres brings you to the small and very pleasant *Ankur Resort* (1½ km). This is a clean and modern place with good-sized rooms, all with bath attached. The price is Rs 150/200 for standard rooms, or Rs 200/300 with air-cool. There's an attached dining room, and good-value vegetarian meals are available for Rs 30. It's certainly one of the best places for the money. Very similar is the *Anurag Resort* (☎ 2451), a further 500 metres towards the park (2 km from town). Prices here are Rs 150/250, or Rs 200/300 with air-cooling.

The next place is the first of the RTDC places, the *Kamdhenu Tourist Bungalow* (☎ 2334; three km). It's a fairly modern and characterless building, offering unremarkable accommodation. The price is Rs 30 for dorm beds, Rs 200/250 for single/double rooms with bath attached, or Rs 250/300 with air-cool. Meals are available.

The other RTDC place is a total contrast. The *Castle Jhoomar Baori* (☎ 2495; five km, then two km off the road) is a former royal hunting lodge, and is stunningly sited on the hillside to the right of the road. The 11 rooms are comfortable, spacious and well furnished and have modern toilet and bathroom facilities with hot water. There's also a beautiful lounge as well as open rooftop areas. The ordinary air-cooled rooms cost Rs 300/350, but there's also a Panther Suite for Rs 400/450 and a Tiger Suite for Rs 500/600.

If you're most interested in wildlife and the sounds of the jungle then the best, though certainly not the cheapest, place to stay is the *Jogi Mahal*, three km inside the park from the main gate and overlooking one of the lotus-studded lakes. It's the only accommodation within the park itself. This former hunting lodge, which once belonged to the maharajas, is the one featured in all the glossy tourist brochures. It's a beautiful place to stay but, as they have only four rooms which are always in heavy demand, advance booking is essential. Rooms cost Rs 550 per person, including all meals. Meals are not available to nonresidents.

Getting There & Away

Sawai Madhopur is on the main Delhi to Bombay broad-gauge railway line and, as most trains stop here, there's a wide range to choose from. The 108-km trip to Kota takes two hours 10 minutes and costs Rs 27/104 in 2nd/1st class, while to Agra Fort it's 226 km, which takes eight hours and costs Rs 48/175.

Sawai Madhopur is also the junction of the metre-gauge spur to Jaipur and Bikaner. Three trains a day travel this line in either direction. But, the early morning departure from Sawai Madhopur can be packed solid, even in 1st class. The 130-km trip takes around three hours and costs Rs 31/111.

Getting Around

Jeeps can be hired from most of the lodges, and you'll be approached regularly by hopeful drivers. The fee for jeep hire is set at Rs 400 for a morning or afternoon safari, and this can be shared by up to six people, although four is preferable. This includes all km charges, so staying further from the park entrance isn't going to cost more.

Safari times are 6.30 to 10 am, and 2.30 to 5 pm (one hour later in summer). Only 24 jeeps are allowed in the park at any one time, and during the peak winter season it means getting a jeep and arriving at the park gate at least 30 minutes before it opens (6.30 am and 2.30 pm) to be sure of getting in. If you are alone and can't find others to share the cost of a jeep, it's possible to hire a bicycle and ride the 10 km to the gate. Here you can ask around, as many jeeps have only one or two passengers and often they don't mind taking an extra person, often for free.

The other alternative for a safari is the open-backed RTDC minibus, although this has the disadvantage of not venturing far into the park. However, it is cheaper at Rs 250 (minimum of five people) and will pick up from the Project Tiger Office, the Sawai Madhopur Lodge, the Ankur Resort, the RTDC places and at the park gate itself. For reservations phone 2223.

DHOLPUR

Although the town of Dholpur is in Rajasthan, this place can be more easily accessed from Madhya Pradesh. Hence, details are given in that chapter.

Southern Rajasthan

KOTA
Population: 536,000

Following the Rajput conquest of this area of Rajasthan in the 12th century, Bundi was chosen as the capital with Kota as the land grant of the ruler's eldest son. This situation continued until 1624 when Kota became a separate state, remaining so until it was integrated into Rajasthan following independence.

Building of the city began in 1264 following the defeat of the Bhil chieftains but Kota didn't reach its present size until well into the 17th century when Rao Madho Singh, a son of the ruler of Bundi, was made ruler of Kota by the Moghul emperor, Jehangir. Subsequent rulers have all added to the fortress and palaces which stand here today.

Today, Kota serves as an army headquarters. It's also Rajasthan's industrial centre (mainly chemicals), powered by the hydroelectric plants on the Chambal River – the only permanent river in the state – and the nearby atomic plant, which made headlines in 1992 when it was revealed that levels of radioactivity in the area were way above 'safe' levels. Very few tourists visit Kota, which is surprising because the fortress and

part of the palace complex are open to the public and the Rao Madho Singh Museum has to be one of the best in Rajasthan.

Orientation & Information
Kota is strung out along the east bank of the Chambal River. The railway station is well to the north, the Tourist Bungalow, a number of other hotels and the bus stand are in the middle, and Chambal Gardens, the fort and the Kota Barrage are to the south.

The tourist office (☎ 27-695) is at the Chambal Tourist Bungalow. The staff here are keen and a range of leaflets is available. It's open from 8 am to noon and 3 to 6 pm Monday to Saturday.

Changing money in Kota can be a problem. The only bank which will change travellers' cheques is the State Bank of Bikaner & Jaipur on Aerodrome Circuit, quite a way from the centre of things. The Hotel Brijraj Bhawan will change cheques for guests at the standard rate, but they don't issue an exchange certificate.

City Palace & Fort
Standing beside the Kota Barrage, overlooking the Chambal River, the City Palace and Fort is one of the largest such complexes in Rajasthan. Some of its buildings are now occupied by schools but most of the complex is open to the public. Entry is from the south side through the **Naya Darwaza**, or New Gate.

Just inside the New Gate is the small **Government Museum**. It has a collection of stone idols and other such fragments but is otherwise of only mild interest and desperately needs a major revamp. In theory, it's open between 10 am and 4.30 pm daily, except Friday, but the staff rarely arrive before 11 am.

The **Rao Madho Singh Museum**, in contrast, is superb. It's on the right-hand side of the complex's huge central courtyard and is entered through a gateway topped by rampant elephants like those at the Bundi Fort. Inside, you'll find displays of weapons, clothing and some of the best preserved murals in the state. Indeed, everything about this former palace is colourful. The museum is open daily, except Friday, from 11 am to 5 pm and there's a small entry fee.

After visiting the museum, it's worth wandering around the rest of the complex just to appreciate how magnificent this place must have been in its heyday. Unfortunately, a lot of it is falling into disrepair and the gardens are no more, but there are some excellent views over the old city, the river and the huge industrial complex with its enormous twin chimneys across the river.

Chambal Gardens

The gardens south of the fort at Amar Niwas are popular for picnics and feature a pond well stocked with crocodiles. In the past, these reptiles were common all along the river but, by the middle of this century, they had been virtually exterminated through overhunting. The pond is also home to some flamingoes, which appear remarkably unbothered by their reptilian companions.

Jagmandir

Between the City Palace and the Tourist Bungalow is the picturesque artificial tank of Kishore Sagar, constructed in 1346. Right in the middle of the tank, on a small island, is the enchanting little palace of Jagmandir. Built in 1740 by one of the maharanis of Kota, it's best seen early in the morning but is exquisite at any time of day. It doesn't appear to be open to the public, though you might be able to persuade one of the boat owners to take you around it.

Just below the tank, beside the Tourist Bungalow, is a curious collection of somewhat neglected but impressive royal tombs, or chhatris, in the Chhattar Bilas Gardens.

Places to Stay

Although there are a number of pretty good hotels close to the railway station, few people choose to stay such a long way from the centre of things. If you do want accommodation in this area, try either the *Hotel Shri Anand* or the *Gaytri Hotel* (☎ 23-230).

Most travellers to Kota head for the RTDC *Chambal Tourist Bungalow* (☎ 26-527). The staff are friendly and the hotel is surrounded by gardens, and although it's a bit rough around the edges these days, it probably offers the best value in Kota. The mosquitoes at this place are tenacious, but this is a problem common to all hotels here. Dorm beds are Rs 30, while single/double rooms with bath cost Rs 70/100, or Rs 150/200 with bath and air-cool, or Rs 250/300 with air-con.

The *Hotel Navrang* (☎ 23-294), close to the GPO on Station Rd, Civil Lines, is a very clean and pleasant place, but you have to pay for these privileges. Comfortable singles/doubles with bath and hot water cost Rs 132/275 with air-cool, or Rs 275/385 with air-con. For something cheaper, try the *Chaman Hotel* (☎ 23-377), closer to the bus station, also on Station Rd. It's grubby but undeniably cheap at Rs 30/45 with common bath and bucket showers.

By far the best hotel in Kota is the *Hotel Brijraj Bhawan* (☎ 23-071), once a palace of the maharaos of Kota and also the former British Residency. This superb place sits on an elevated site overlooking the Chambal River and is surrounded by beautifully maintained gardens, complete with peacocks. Everything has been left exactly as it was in those unhurried days before socialist India swept aside the princely states.

The lounge is awash with photographs of the former maharao and his son (now a general) shaking hands with everyone who was anyone during the '50s and '60s, from Indira Gandhi to J G Diefenbaker (Canadian Prime Minister) to Giscard d'Estaing (French President). There are more antelopes' and tigers' heads brooding over the diners in the period dining hall than there are live animals in Ranthambhor National Park. The rooms, better described as suites, are furnished with armchairs, a writing table and enormous beds, and have verandahs on which you could stage a June Ball.

Prices for all this are a bargain at Rs 440/790 including meals, or Rs 320/630 without. This place is understandably popular, and you should try to make reservations in advance.

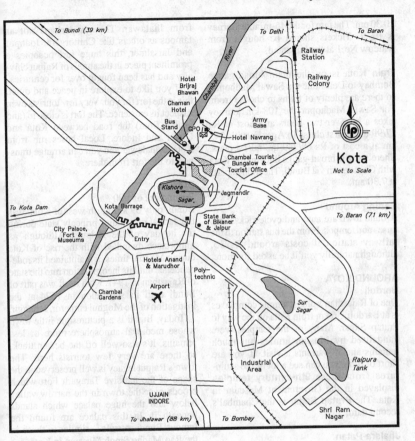

To Bundi (39 km)
To Delhi
To Baran

Chambal River

Railway Station

Railway Colony

Hotel Brijraj Bhawan

Chaman Hotel

Bus Stand

GPO

Army Base

Hotel Navrang

Chambal Tourist Bungalow & Tourist Office

Kota
Not to Scale

Kishore Sagar

Jagmandir

To Kota Dam

Kota Barrage

State Bank of Bikaner & Jaipur

To Baran (71 km)

City Palace, Fort & Museums

Entry

Hotels Anand & Marudhor

Poly-technic

Airport

Chambal Gardens

Sur Sagar

Industrial Area

Raipura Tank

UJJAIN INDORE

Shri Ram Nagar

To Jhalawar (88 km)
To Bombay

Places to Eat

Virtually all the cheap restaurants are up by the railway station; there are very few around the Tourist Bungalow or the bus station.

On the footpath outside the GPO many omelette stalls set up in the early evening, and this can be a cheap way to eat. The only other alternative in this area is the restaurant in the *Hotel Navrang*. It offers quite reasonable food, but check the prices carefully as it seems that some dishes are definitely overpriced – chicken biryani is Rs 60, yet vegetable biryani is only Rs 20.

If you're staying at the *Hotel Brijraj*

Bhawan, you'd be mad to eat anywhere else – it's certainly an experience. Unfortunately the dining room is not open to nonresidents.

Getting There & Away

Bus There are bus connections to Bundi, Ajmer, Chittorgarh (six hours), Jaipur, Udaipur and other centres in Rajasthan. If you're heading into Madhya Pradesh, several buses a day go to such places as Gwalior, Ujjain and Indore. None of the timetables at the bus stand are in English.

Buses leave for Bundi every hour, usually on the half-hour, from around 6.30 am to

10.30 pm. The fare for the 45-minute journey is Rs 7. Tickets should be bought from window No 1 at the bus stand.

Train Kota is on the main broad-gauge Bombay to Delhi line via Sawai Madhopur, so there are plenty of trains to choose from. For Sawai Madhopur the 108-km journey takes a bit over two hours at a cost of Rs 27/99 in 2nd/1st class. To Agra Fort it's 343 km at a cost of Rs 68/249 in 2nd/1st class. There's a new broad-gauge line linking Kota with Chittorgarh via Bundi. The train departs at 7.30 am.

Getting Around
Around town are auto and cycle-rickshaws, buses and tempos. From the bus station to the railway station it costs around Rs 15, although naturally you'll be asked for more.

AROUND KOTA
Bardoli
One of Rajasthan's oldest temple complexes is at Bardoli, 56 km from Kota on the way to Pratap Sagar. Many of the temples were vandalised by Muslim armies but much remains and it warrants a visit. If you are short of time, you can see a lot of the sculptures from these **9th-century temples** displayed in the Government Museum in Kota. The **Pratap Sagar** is the Chambal's second dam.

Jhalara-Patan
At Jhalara-Patan, some 80 km south of Kota on the Jhalawar road, are the ruins of a huge 10th-century Surya, or Sun God, **temple** containing magnificent sculptures as well as one of the best preserved idols of Surya in the whole of India.

Jhalawar, about seven km from the temple, is also worth a visit and has a good collection of sculptures from nearby temples displayed in the Government Museum in Kota.

Gagron Fortress
While you're in this area, you should also take a look at the Gagron Fortress, 10 km

from Jhalawar. Though perhaps not as famous as others like Chittorgarh, Jodhpur and Jaisalmer, this huge fort occupies a prominent place in the annals of Rajput chivalry and has been fought over for centuries.

If you like to explore in peace and quiet, this is the fort for you. Very few tourists even suspect its existence. The fort is close to (and visible from) the road between Kota and Ujjain and Indore. Local buses run from Kota to Jhalawar and you can arrange transport to the fort from there.

BUNDI
Population: 65,000
Bundi, only 39 km north-west of Kota, was the capital of a major princely state during the heyday of the Rajputs. Although its importance dwindled with the rise of Kota during Moghul times, it maintained its independence until its incorporation into the state of Rajasthan in 1947. Kota itself was part of Bundi until its separation in 1624 at the instigation of the Moghul emperor, Jehangir.

Today, Bundi is a picturesque little town whose medieval atmosphere more or less remains. It's also well off the beaten track, so there are very few tourists here. The town's Rajput legacy is well preserved in the shape of the massive Taragarh Fort which broods over the town in the narrow valley below and the huge palace which stands beneath it. In this palace are found the famous Bundi **murals** – similar to those in the Rao Madho Singh Museum in Kota.

There is some accommodation available, although many people visit Bundi on a day trip from Kota.

Orientation & Information
There's a small tourist office (☎ 2697) in the grounds of the Circuit House. The tourist officer is helpful, but as usual is limited by lack of printed information.

Taragarh Fort
The Star Fort was built in 1354. It is reached by a steep road leading up the hillside to its enormous gateway, topped by rampant elephants. Inside are huge reservoirs carved out

of solid rock and the Bhim Burj, the largest of the battlements, on which is mounted a famous cannon. Views over the town and surrounding countryside are excellent. It's just a pity that the national broadcaster, Doordarshan, decided to build a huge concrete transmission tower right next to the fort – it's a real eyesore.

Palace

The palace itself is reached from the north-western end of the bazaar, through a huge wooden gateway and up a steep cobbled ramp. Only two parts of the outer perimeter of the palace, known variously as the Chitra Mahal and Ummed Mahal, are open to the public. Some of the famous Bundi murals can be seen on the upper level. Photography is prohibited.

Unfortunately the rest of the palace, which houses the bulk of the absolutely superb Bundi murals, is closed to the public, mainly because of a dispute between the current maharaja and his sister. It seems that the maharaja sold all of the family properties (Taragarh Fort, this palace and the Phool Sagar Palace) to the Oberoi hotel chain, but his sister is now claiming her share of the proceeds. Until the dispute is settled (if it is in fact settled), it seems likely the palace will remain closed. What is more, maintenance seems to be nonexistent and the palace is already rapidly deteriorating, which is tragic.

Nawal Sagar

Also visible from the fort is the square artificial lake of Nawal Sagar. In the centre is a temple to Varuna, the Aryan god of water.

Baoris

Bundi has a couple of beautiful *baoris* (stepwells) right in the centre of town. The **Ranijiki Baori** is 46 metres deep and has some superb carving, and is one of the largest of its kind. It was built in 1699 by the Rani Nathavatji. The **Nagar Sagar Kund** is a pair of matching step-wells just outside the Chogan Gate to the old city, right in the centre of the town,

Other Attractions

Bundi's other attractions are all out of town and are difficult to reach without transport. The modern palace, known as the **Phool Sagar Palace**, has a beautiful artificial tank and gardens, and is several km out of town on the Ajmer road. It is closed to the public but you can gain glimpses from over the brick wall.

There's another palace, the smaller **Sukh Mahal**, closer to town on the edge of Jait Sagar. **Shikar Burj** is a small hunting lodge and picnic spot along the road which runs along the north side of the Jait Sagar.

Places to Stay

There is really only one place worth staying, and that is the *Haveli Braj Bhushanjee*, just below the palace. It's part of the Bundi Cafe Crafts shop, and is run by the very friendly and helpful Braj Bhushanjee family. The shop and rooms are housed in the family's 150-year-old haveli just below the palace, and the views from the rooftop terrace are excellent, especially at night when the palace is illuminated. The accommodation is good value at Rs 125/250 with breakfast, or there are a few dorm beds at Rs 50. Good vegetarian meals are available in the downstairs cafe. If you arrive after hours, when the shop is closed, just ring the doorbell.

In the noisy and bustling bazaar area there are two basic Indian hotels with rooms for Rs 40: the *Hotel Bundi Tourist Paradise* (wishful thinking!) near Azad Park, and the *Hotel Shivirani* near the Diamond Restaurant. Don't expect too much from these places.

The only other option is a government place, and so priority goes to travelling government officials. The *Circuit House* (☎ 2336), is in the south of town, and rooms here cost Rs 165/220. Meals are available for Rs 13 for breakfast, and Rs 18 for lunch or dinner. It's often full.

Places to Eat

The cafe in the *Bundi Cafe Crafts* shop below the palace has a good range, and the vegetarian set meals are good value. Other

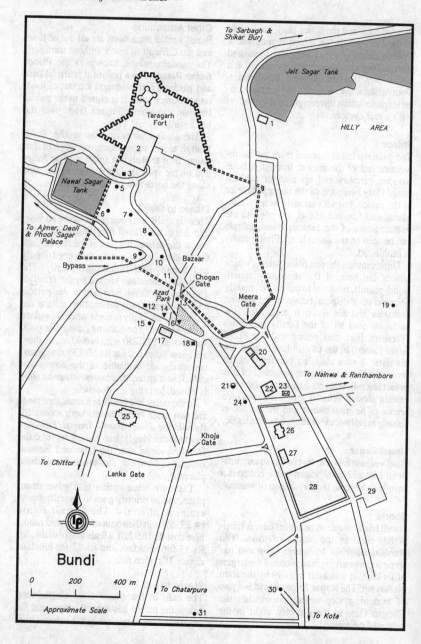

To Sarbagh &
Shikar Burj

Jait Sagar Tank

HILLY AREA

Taragarh
Fort

Nawal Sagar
Tank

To Ajmer, Deoli
& Phool Sagar
Palace

Bypass

Bazaar

Chogan
Gate

Azad
Park

Meera
Gate

To Nainwa & Ranthambore

To Chittor

Khoja
Gate

Lanka Gate

Bundi

0   200   400 m

Approximate Scale

To Chatarpura

To Kota

	PLACES TO STAY		7	Laxminath Temple
			8	Charbhuja Temple
3	Haveli Braj Bhushanjee &		9	Mordi Cenotaph
	Bundi Cafe Crafts		10	City Kotwali
12	Shivirami Hotel		11	Library
18	Hotel Bundi Tourist Paradise		13	Nagar Sagar Kund
27	Dak Bungalow		15	Bank of Baroda
			17	Ranijiki Baori
	PLACES TO EAT		19	Meera Sahib Masjid
			20	General Hospital
14	Diamond Restaurant		21	Bus Stand
16	K N Singh Restaurant		22	Ranjit Talkies
			23	GPO
	OTHER		24	Collectorate
			25	Kund Near Jail
1	Sukh Burj		26	Circuit House & Tourist Office
2	Palace		28	Police Parade Ground
4	Bhim Burj		29	Police Lines
5	Ayurvedic Hospital		30	84 Pillars Cenotaph
6	Motimahal		31	Railway Station

than that your choice is a couple of basic restaurants in the bazaar area.

Things to Buy

The Bundi Cafe Crafts shop has a good range of local souvenirs, including miniatures and jewellery. And just so you can see what you're missing, ask to see their photos of the Bundi murals which were taken inside the closed part of the palace – amazing!

Getting There & Away

It takes about five hours by bus from Ajmer to Bundi. From Kota, it's only 45 minutes to Bundi. Buses also go from Bundi to Chittorgarh, Sawai Madhopur and Udaipur.

Bundi also has broad-gauge rail links with Chittorgarh and Kota.

Getting Around

The bus station is at the Kota (east) end of town. It's relatively easy to find your way to the palace on foot through the bazaar – once you pass through the city gate, there are only two main roads through town and the palace is visible from many points. Auto-rickshaws are also available and can be hired for Rs 5 from outside the bus station.

CHITTORGARH

Population: 71,000

The hilltop fortress of Chittorgarh epitomises the whole romantic, doomed ideal of Rajput chivalry. Three times in its long history, Chittor was sacked by a stronger enemy and, on each occasion, the end came in textbook Rajput fashion as jauhar was declared in the face of impossible odds. The men donned the saffron robes of martyrdom and rode out from the fort to certain death, while the women and children immolated themselves on a huge funeral pyre. Honour was always more important than death.

Despite the fort's impressive location and colourful history, Chittor is well and truly off the main tourist circuit and sees surprisingly few visitors. It's well worth the detour.

History

Chittor's first defeat occurred in 1303 when Ala-ud-din Khilji, the Pathan King of Delhi, besieged the fort in order to capture the beautiful Padmini, wife of the Rana's uncle, Bhim Singh. When defeat was inevitable the Rajput noblewomen, including Padmini, committed sati and Bhim Singh led the orange-clad noblemen out to their deaths.

In 1535 it was Bahadur Shah, the Sultan

of Gujarat, who besieged the fort and, once again, the medieval dictates of chivalry determined the outcome. This time, the carnage was immense. It is said that 13,000 Rajput women and 32,000 Rajput warriors died following the declaration of jauhar.

The final sack of Chittor came just 33 years later, in 1568, when the Moghul emperor, Akbar, took the town. Once again, the fort was defended heroically but, once again, the odds were overwhelming and the women performed sati, the fort gates were flung open and 8000 orange-robed warriors rode out to their deaths. On this occasion, Maharana Udai Singh fled to Udaipur where he re-established his capital. In 1616, Jehangir returned Chittor to the Rajputs but there was no attempt at resettlement.

Orientation

The fort stands on a 280-hectare site on top of a 180-metre-high hill, which rises abruptly from the surrounding plain. Until 1568, the town of Chittor was also on the hilltop within the fort walls but today's modern town, known as Lower Town, sprawls to the west of the hill. A river separates it from the bus stand, railway line and rest of the town.

Information

The tourist office (☎ 3089) is in the Janta Avas Grah (the RTDC Tourist Bungalow), near the railway station. It's open from 10 am to 5 pm Monday to Saturday.

Fort

Bhim, one of the Pandava heroes of the *Mahabharata*, is credited with the fort's original construction. All of Chittor's attractions are within the fort. A zigzag ascent of over one km leads through seven gateways to the main gate on the western side, the Ram Pol.

On the climb, you pass two chhatris, memorials marking spots where Jaimal and Kalla, heroes of the 1568 siege, fell during the struggle against Akbar. Another chhatri, further up the hill, marks the spot where Patta fell. The main gate on the eastern side of the

fort is the Suraj Pol. Within the fort, a circular road runs around the ruins and there's a deer park at the southern end.

Today, the fort of Chittor is a virtually deserted ruin, but impressive reminders of its grandeur still stand and those with imagination should easily be able to tune in to the romantic heroism which lingers in the air of this incredible monument. The main sites can all be seen in half a day (assuming you're not walking) but, if you like the atmosphere of ancient sites, then it's worth spending longer as this is a very mellow place and there are no hassles whatsoever.

Rana Kumbha Palace Entering the fort and turning right, you come almost immediately to the ruins of this palace. It contains elephant and horse stables and a Siva temple. One of the jauhars is said to have taken place in a vaulted cellar. Across from the palace is the archaeological office and museum, and the treasury building or Nau Lakha Bhandar.

Fateh Prakash Palace Just beyond the Rana Kumbha Palace, this palace is much more modern (Maharana Fateh Singh died in 1930). It houses a small and poorly lit **museum,** and the rest of the building is closed. The museum is open daily from 10 am to 5 pm. Entry costs Rs 1.

Tower of Victory Continuing anticlockwise around the fort, you come to the Jaya Stambh, or Tower of Victory. Erected by Rana Kumbha to commemorate his victory over Mahmud Khilji of Malwa in 1440, the tower was constructed between 1458 and 1468. It rises 37 metres in nine storeys and you can climb the narrow stairs to the top. Watch your head on the lintels!

Hindu sculptures adorn the outside of the tower, but the dome was damaged by lightning and repaired during the last century. Close to the tower is the Mahasati, an area where the ranas were cremated during Chittorgarh's period as the Mewar capital. There are many sati stones here. The Sammidheshwar Temple stands in the same area.

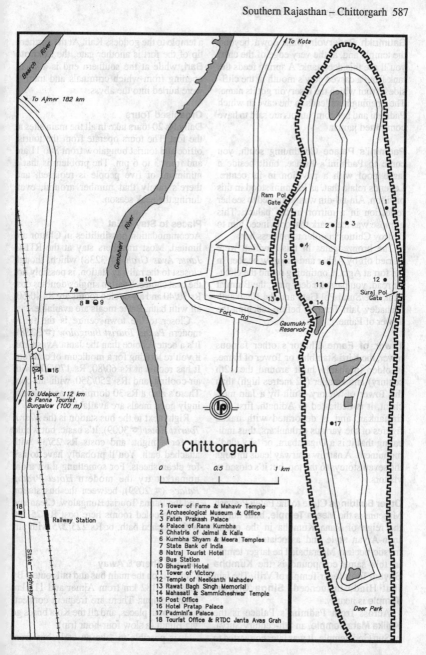

Chittorgarh

0   0.5   1 km

1 Tower of Fame & Mahavir Temple
2 Archaeological Museum & Office
3 Fateh Prakash Palace
4 Palace of Rana Kumbha
5 Chhatris of Jaimal & Kalla
6 Kumbha Shyam & Meera Temples
7 State Bank of India
8 Natraj Tourist Hotel
9 Bus Station
10 Bhagwati Hotel
11 Tower of Victory
12 Temple of Neelkanth Mahadev
13 Rawat Bagh Singh Memorial
14 Mahasati & Sammidheshwar Temple
15 Post Office
16 Hotel Pratap Palace
17 Padmini's Palace
18 Tourist Office & RTDC Janta Avas Grah

Gaumukh Reservoir Walk down beyond the temple and, at the very edge of the cliff, you'll see this deep tank. A spring feeds the tank from a carved cow's mouth in the cliffside – from which the reservoir got its name. The opening here leads to the cave in which Padmini and her compatriots are said to have committed jauhar.

Padmini's Palace Continuing south, you come to Padmini's Palace, built beside a large pool with a pavilion in its centre. Legends relate that, as Padmini stood in this pavilion, Ala-ud-din was permitted to see her reflection in a mirror in the palace. This glimpse was the spark that convinced him to destroy Chittor in order to possess her.

The bronze gates in this pavilion were carried off by Akbar and can now be seen in the fort at Agra. Continuing round the circular road, you pass the deer park, the Bhimlat Tank, the Suraj Pol Gate and the Neelkanth Mahadev Jain Temple, before reaching the Tower of Fame.

Tower of Fame Chittor's other famous tower, the Kirti Stambha, or Tower of Fame, is older (probably built around the 12th century) and smaller (22 metres high) than the Tower of Victory. Built by a Jain merchant, it is dedicated to Adinath, first Jain tirthankar, and is decorated with naked figures of the various tirthankars, thus indicating that it is a Digambara, or 'sky clad', monument. A narrow stairway leads through the seven storeys to the top, but it's closed to visitors.

Other Buildings Close to the Fateh Prakash Museum is the **Meera Temple**, built during the reign of Rana Kumbha in the ornate Indo-Aryan style and associated with the mystic-poetess Meerabai. The larger temple in this same compound is the **Kumbha Shyam Temple**, or Temple of Vriji. The Jain (but Hindu-influenced) **Singa Chowri Temple** is nearby.

Across from Padmini's Palace is the **Kalika Mata Temple**, an 8th-century Surya, or Sun God, temple. It was later converted to a temple to the goddess Kali. At the northern tip of the fort is another gate, the **Lokhota Bari**, while at the southern end is a small opening from which criminals and traitors were hurled into the abyss.

Organised Tours

Daily Rs 20 tours take in all the main sites at the fort. The tours operate from the tourist office and tourist bungalow from 8 to 11 am and from 3 to 6 pm. The problem is that a minimum of five people is required, and there's rarely that number around, even during the peak season.

Places to Stay & Eat

Accommodation possibilities in Chittor are limited. Most travellers stay at the RTDC *Janta Avas Grah* (☎ 3238) which, though closest to the railway station, is possibly not the best choice. Spartan singles/doubles cost Rs 30/40 and air-cooled rooms are Rs 40/60, all with bath. Basic meals are available.

Closer to the town centre is the fairly modern *Panna Tourist Bungalow* (☎ 3238). It's a better choice than the Janta Avas Grah if you're looking for a modicum of comfort. It has rooms at Rs 60/80, Rs 170/200 with air-cooling and Rs 250/350 with air-con. There's also a Rs 30 dormitory and surprisingly good meals are available.

Right next to the bus station is the *Natraj Tourist Hotel* (☎ 3009). It's basic, but would do for a night, and costs Rs 25/35 with attached bath. You'll probably have to ask for clean sheets. For something a bit more upmarket try the modern *Hotel Pratap Palace* (☎ 2099), between the bus station and the Panna Tourist Bungalow. Clean and airy air-cooled rooms here cost Rs 75/100 with attached bath, or Rs 225/275 with air-con.

Getting There & Away

Chittor is on the main bus and rail routes. By road, it's 182 km from Ajmer and 112 km from Udaipur. There are frequent connections to both places, and all the Kota buses go via Bundi (a slow four-hour trip).

It is possible to take an early bus from

Udaipur to Chittorgarh, spend about three hours visiting the fort (by auto-rickshaw or tonga), and then take a late afternoon bus to Ajmer, but this is definitely pushing it. Chittorgarh also has rail links with Ahmedabad, Udaipur, Ajmer, Jaipur and Delhi. The new broad-gauge line to Kota and Bundi would be convenient, except that the only passenger train on this route leaves Chittor at 3 pm, arriving in Kota four hours later. In the opposite direction, it leaves Kota at 7.30 am.

Getting Around

It's six km from the railway station to the fort, less from the bus station, and seven km around the fort itself, not including the long southern loop out to the deer park. Either way, if you're not taking a tour you'll need transport. Auto-rickshaws charge Rs 50 from either the bus or railway station, and this includes waiting time at the various sites. Bicycles can also be rented to visit the fort but, as Indian bicycles never have gears, you'll have to push the machine to the top. Still, they're great on the top and for the journey back down.

AROUND CHITTORGARH

Menal

On the Bundi to Chittorgarh road, 48 km from Bundi, Menal is a complex of Siva temples built during the Gupta period.

Bijolia

Bijolia, 16 km from Menal, was once a group of 100 temples. Today, only three are left standing, one of which has a huge figure of Ganesh.

Mandalgarh

A detour between Menal and Bijolia takes you to Mandalgarh. It is the third fort of Mewar built by Rana Kumbha – the others are the great fort of Chittorgarh and the fort at Kumbhalgarh.

Nagri

One of the oldest towns in Rajasthan, Nagri is 14 km north of Chittor. Hindu and Bud-

dhist remains from the Mauryan to the Gupta period have been found here.

Jagat

At this small town, 20 km south of the road between Udaipur and Chittorgarh, is a small 10th-century **Durga temple**. There are some fine carvings, including a couple of small erotic carvings, which has inspired some people to call the town the Khajuraho of Rajasthan, which is total nonsense.

UDAIPUR

Population: 308,000

Possibly no city in Rajasthan is quite as romantic as Udaipur, even though the state is replete with fantastic hilltop fortresses, exotic fairy-tale palaces and gripping legends of medieval chivalry and heroism. The French Impressionist painters, let alone the Brothers Grimm, would have loved this place and it's not without justification that Udaipur has been called the 'Venice of the East'. Jaisalmer is certainly the 'Beau Geste' of the desert and Udaipur is the 'Versailles'.

Founded in 1568 by Maharana Udai Singh following the final sacking of Chittorgarh by the Moghul emperor, Akbar, Udaipur rivals any of the world-famous creations of the Moghuls with its Rajput love of the whimsical and its superbly crafted elegance. The Lake Palace is certainly the best late example of this unique cultural explosion, but Udaipur is full of palaces, temples and havelis ranging from the modest to the extravagant. It's also proud of its heritage as a centre for the performing arts, painting and crafts. And, since water is relatively plentiful in this part of the state (in between the periodic droughts), there are plenty of parks and gardens, many of which line the lake shores.

Until recent times, the higher uninhabited parts of the city were covered in forests but, as elsewhere in India, most of these have inevitably been turned into firewood. There is, however, a movement afoot to reverse this process. The city was once surrounded by a wall and, although the gates and much of the wall over the higher crags remain, a great deal of it has disappeared. It's sad that this fate should have befallen such a historic place but the essence remains.

In common with all Indian cities, Udaipur's urban and industrial sprawl goes beyond the city's original boundaries and pollution of various kinds can be discouraging. This will be your first impression of Udaipur if you arrive at the railway or bus stations. Ignore it and head for the old city where a different world is waiting for you.

Orientation & Information

The old city, bounded by the remains of a city wall, is on the east side of Lake Pichola. The railway and bus stations are both just outside the city wall to the south-east.

The tourist office (☎ 29-535) and the Tourist Bungalow are also outside the city wall, to the north-east and only a km or so from the bus stand. Tourist office hours are 10 am to 1.30 pm and 2 to 5 pm Monday to Saturday. There are also tourist information counters at the railway station and airport.

The GPO is directly north of the old city, behind the movie theatre at Chetak Circle, but the poste restante is at the post office at the junction of Hospital Rd and the road north from Delhi Gate, close to the Tourist Bungalow. It's efficient and the staff are friendly and helpful.

Udaipur's telephone area code is 0294.

Lake Pichola

The beautiful Lake Pichola was enlarged by Maharana Udai Singh after he founded the city. He built a masonry dam, known as the Badi Pol, and the lake is now four km in length and three km wide. Nevertheless, it remains fairly shallow and can actually dry up in severe droughts. At these times, you can walk to the island palaces from the shore. Fortunately, this doesn't happen often. The City Palace extends a considerable distance along the east bank of the lake. South of the palace, a pleasant garden runs down to the lake. North of the palace, you can wander along the lake, where there are some interesting bathing and dhobi ghats.

Out in the lake are two islands – Jagniwas and Jagmandir. One-hour boat rides around the lake can be boarded at the City Palace jetty (known as Bansi Ghat) at any time during daylight hours. They cost Rs 30 per person.

A new Oberoi hotel is planned for the western shore of the lake, but it will be some time before it gets under way.

Jagniwas Island

Jagniwas, the Lake Palace island, is about 1½ hectares in size. The palace was built by Maharana Jagat Singh II in 1754 and covers the whole island. Today, it has been converted into a luxury hotel with courtyards, fountains, gardens and a swimming pool. It's a delightful place and, even if you can only dream of staying there, it's worth the trip out to have a look around.

Launches cross to the island from the City Palace jetty but casual visitors are discouraged. It used to be possible to visit the palace by splurging on the smorgasbord buffet lunch (Rs 250) or dinner (Rs 300) which was available to both guests and nonresidents. The cost included a free barge trip in either direction and a dance show (dinner only). It was also possible to visit for morning or afternoon tea, but this was expensive at Rs 150. However, the hotel is currently not open to nonresidents. This situation may change, so it may be worth checking out.

Jagmandir Island

The other island palace, Jagmandir, was commenced by Maharana Karan Singh, but takes its name from Maharana Jagat Singh (1628-52) who made a number of additions to it. It is said that the Moghul emperor, Shah Jahan, derived some of his ideas for the Taj Mahal from this palace after staying here in 1623-24 while leading a revolt against his father, Jehangir. The view across the lake from the southern end, with the city and its great palace rising up behind the island palaces, is a scene of rare beauty.

City Palace & Museums

The huge City Palace, towering over the lake, is the largest palace complex in Rajasthan. Actually a conglomeration of buildings added by various maharanas, the palace manages to retain a surprising uniformity of design. Building was started by Maharana Udai Singh, the city's founder. The palace is surmounted by balconies, towers and cupolas and there are fine views over the lake and the city from the upper terraces.

The palace is entered from the northern end through the Bari Pol of 1600 and the Tripolia Gate of 1725, with its eight carved marble arches. It was once a custom for maharanas to be weighed under the gate and their weight in gold or silver distributed to the populace.

The main part of the palace is now preserved as a museum with a large and varied, although somewhat run-down, collection. The museum includes the Mor Chowk with its beautiful mosaics of peacocks, the favourite Rajasthani bird. The Manak, or Ruby, Mahal has glass and porcelain figures while Krishna Vilas has a remarkable collection of miniatures. In the Bari Mahal, there is a fine central garden. More paintings can be seen in the Zanana Mahal. The Moti Mahal has beautiful mirrorwork and the Chini Mahal is covered in ornamental tiles.

Enter the City Palace Museum through the Ganesh Deori which leads to the Rai Angam, or Royal Courtyard. The museum is open from 9.30 am to 4.30 pm and entry is Rs 7, plus Rs 15 for a camera. There's also a government museum within the palace complex. Exhibits include a stuffed kangaroo and Siamese-twin deer.

The other part of the palace is up against the lake shore and, like the Lake Palace, it has been converted into a luxury hotel – two, in fact, known as the Shiv Vilas Palace and the Fateh Prakash Palace hotels.

Jagdish Temple
Only 150 metres north of the entrance to the City Palace, this fine Indo-Aryan temple was built by Maharana Jagat Singh in 1651 and enshrines a black stone image of Vishnu as Jagannath, Lord of the Universe. A brass image of the Garuda is in a shrine in front of the temple and the steps up to the temple are flanked by elephants.

Bagore ki Haveli
This 18th-century house is on the lake shore, below the Jagdish temple. It was built by a nobleman, and was once used as a royal guest house. It is one of the finest examples of its type, and now houses the Western Zone Cultural Centre. The labyrinthine haveli houses a **graphics studio**, **art gallery** (which occasionally has exhibitions by local artists), and some fine coloured glass and inlay work. It is open daily from 9.30 am to 6 pm, and entry is Rs 20.

Fateh Sagar
North of Lake Pichola, this lake is overlooked by a number of hills and parks. It was originally built in 1678 by Maharana Jai Singh but, after heavy rains destroyed the dam, it was reconstructed by Maharana Fateh Singh. A pleasant lakeside drive winds along the east bank of the lake. In the middle of the lake is Nehru Park, a popular garden island with a boat-shaped cafe. You can get there by boat from near the bottom of Moti Magri Hill for Rs 5 return. Pedal boats are also available for Rs 20 per hour.

Pratap Samak
Atop the Moti Magri, or Pearl Hill, overlooking Fateh Sagar, is a statue of the Rajput hero Maharana Pratap, who frequently defied the Moghuls. The path to the top traverses elegant gardens, including a Japanese rock garden. The park is open from 9 am to 6 pm and there's a small admission fee.

Bhartiya Lok Kala Museum
The interesting collection exhibited by this small museum and foundation for the preservation of folk arts includes dresses, dolls, masks, musical instruments, paintings and – the high point of the exhibits – puppets. The museum is open daily from 9 am to 6 pm and admission costs Rs 5. Regular puppet shows are held daily from 6 to 7 pm; entry is Rs 20. Call 24-296 for details.

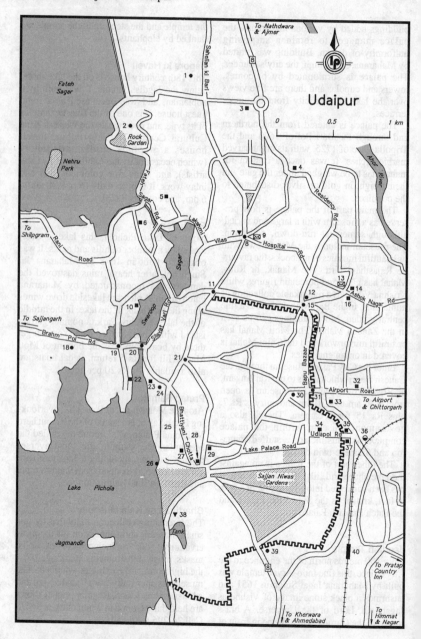

Udaipur

To Nathdwara
& Ajmer

0   0.5   1 km

Saheliyon ki Bari

The Saheliyon ki Bari, or Garden of the Maids of Honour, is in the north of the city. This small ornamental garden, with its fountains, kiosks, marble elephants and delightful lotus pool, is open from 9 am to 6 pm. Entry is Rs 2. It costs Rs 5 to have the fountains turned on and a camera fee of Rs 10 is charged.

Ahar Museum

East of Udaipur are the remains of an ancient city. Here, you'll find a small museum and the cenotaphs of the maharanas of Mewar.

Other Attractions

Patel or Sukhadia Circle is north of the city. The huge **fountain** in the centre is illuminated at night. **Sajjan Niwas Gardens** have pleasant lawns, a zoo and a children's train (if it's operating). Beside it is the Rose Garden, or **Gulab Bagh**. Don't confuse the **Nehru Park** opposite Bapu Bazaar with the island park of the same name in Fateh Sagar. The city park has some strange topiary work, a giant cement teapot and children's slides incorporating an elephant and a camel.

On the distant mountain range, the gleaming white edifice visible from the city is the former maharaja's **Monsoon Palace**. Now deserted, the views from the top are incomparable. The round trip takes about three hours.

Organised Tours

A five-hour tour starts at the Tourist Bungalow at 8 am each day. It costs Rs 25 and takes in all the main city sights. An afternoon tour (2 to 7 pm) goes out to Eklingi, Haldighati and Nathdwara and costs Rs 50.

Places to Stay

Home Stays Udaipur has what is called a 'paying guest scheme', where tourists can stay with an Indian family and get an insight into local life, something which it's impossible to do in a hotel environment. There are over 130 families in Udaipur participating in this scheme, which also operates in Jaipur and Jodhpur. Expect to pay Rs 50 to Rs 150, depending on what level of comfort and facilities you want. The tourist office has a list detailing all the places and the services offered.

Obviously the experience you have depends to a large degree on the host family, but travellers who have stayed in homes through this scheme generally speak very highly of it.

Places to Stay – bottom end

There are four main clusters of budget hotels in Udaipur, but those around the Jagdish Temple are definitely preferable to the others. Next best are those between the City Palace and the bus station, along Lake Palace Rd and Bhattiyani Chotta. The third cluster is along the main road between the bus station and the Delhi Gate. This is a very noisy and polluted road and you have to be desperate or totally lacking in imagination to stay here. The last cluster is around the Tourist Bungalow and, although it's better than staying on the main road, it's somewhat inconvenient.

Jagdish Temple Area You'll pay more for a hotel in this area, but there is no traffic noise, most places have fantastic views over the lake, and the central location is ideal. As it's the most popular area to stay in, you get a lot of the 'yes, have a look, change money sell something' from the touts and shop-owners, but this is not Agra.

One popular place is the *Badi Haveli* (☎ 23-500). This little labyrinth has narrow staircases, terraces, a leafy courtyard and two rooftops with superb views over the lake and old city. The eight rooms (one single and seven doubles) are all different and vary in price between Rs 60 and Rs 91 with fan and common bath.

Close by, well signposted towards the ghat, is the long-running *Lalghat Guest House* (☎ 25-301). This has been a very popular place for many years and has been recently renovated. It has a large courtyard with tables and chairs, rooftop areas with excellent views across the lake and a back terrace which overlooks the ghats. A variety of different rooms are available, ranging from dorm beds for Rs 40, small single/double rooms for Rs 60/80, larger rooms for Rs 100, or Rs 125 with a lake view and Rs 200 with view and bath. All the rooms have fans and mosquito nets. It's certainly not the cheapest, but it's still very popular.

Across the road from the Lalghat, the *Lake Ghat Guest House* is also popular. Again, there's a wide range of accommodation, although none of the rooms here have a view. Singles/doubles without bath cost Rs 50/80 and doubles with bath go for Rs 125 to Rs 150. While some of the cheaper rooms are very dark and cell-like, there's a good restaurant and terrace area and the management are friendly.

Just behind the Lake Ghat Guest House is the much smaller *Shri Karni Guest House*. It's very basic and has only five rooms (all doubles or triples) but, if the visitors' book is any indication, people who stay here really like it. It costs Rs 31/51 downstairs and Rs 61/71 upstairs, all with common bath and free hot water by the bucket.

Right next door to the Lal Ghat Guest House is the small and comfortable *Evergreen Guest House*. It has just seven rooms around a small courtyard, soft beds and a pleasant terrace area with limited views. The management are friendly and helpful, and hot water is available by the bucket at no extra charge. Rooms cost Rs 80 for a double with common bath, or Rs 125 with attached bath.

Also close to the Badi Haveli is the *Anjani Hotel* (☎ 25-420). It's a modern place, with a range of rooms, many with a lake view. They start at Rs 90 for a double with common bath.

The friendly *Jheel Guest House* (☎ 28-321) is right at the bottom of the hill, by the ghat. It is housed in an old haveli and has a good deal of character and charm – and amazingly steep stairs! Rooms cost Rs 50/90 with common bath, Rs 100 for a double with a view, and Rs 150 for a large double with bath attached. A good place.

Still in the same area, but towards the ghat from the City Palace entrance, is the modern

Shiva Guest House. This place has cramped and gloomy rooms, but it is still reasonable value at Rs 50/80 with common bath. The *Centre View Guest House* is also here, but it's cramped and there's not even the compensation of good views.

If you want to escape the bustle and the touts, try the *Lake Shore Hotel*, next to the Lake Pichola Hotel, across the Chand Pol bridge, about a 10-minute walk from the Jagdish Temple. This place has just a few rooms, and a fine terrace with views back across to Lal Ghat. It's fairly basic, but is definitely quiet and peaceful. Rooms start at Rs 30 for a small single up to Rs 80 to Rs 100 for doubles, most with a lake view.

A similar place, but even further away, is the funky *Hotel Natural* (☎ 28-451). This place has been described as the Yogi Lodge of Udaipur, although the comparison is largely irrelevant. It is basic and quiet, and there are good views along the arm of the lake to the Lake Palace. Rooms cost Rs 40/80 with common bath. The Natural Attic restaurant next door is about the only place to eat in this area.

Lake Palace Rd Area On Lake Palace Rd are two places right next to each other – the *Hotel Shambhu Vilas* (☎ 28-109) and the *Hotel Mahendra Prakash* (☎ 23-015). They're both modern buildings and similar in standard. Smaller rooms at either hotel cost Rs 80 and larger air-cooled rooms are Rs 150 to Rs 250. All rooms have bath and hot water and both hotels have garden areas.

Not far away is the *Ranjit Niwas Hotel* (☎ 25-774). It's a small place in quite a good location, and is friendly and well run. Dorm beds cost Rs 25, while single/double rooms with attached bath are Rs 50/90, and there's a discount if you stay for three days or more. There's a small garden courtyard, and meals are available.

Tourist Bungalow Area On the other side of the road from the Tourist Bungalow and back one block is a group of three hotels. The *Prince Hotel* (☎ 25-355) offers ordinary rooms for Rs 80 and deluxe doubles for Rs 120. All rooms have a bath and the deluxe rooms have constant hot water. Bucket hot water is available for the other rooms at Rs 2.

The *Alka Hotel* (☎ 25-130) is similar. It is a very large place with singles/doubles for Rs 45/80 and bigger rooms for Rs 90/130. The more expensive rooms are air-cooled and have constant hot water. Reasonably priced vegetarian meals are served. The nearby *Ashok Hotel* is very similar in price and standard.

Bus Terminal Area For those who don't mind the noise and pollution of the main road, there are a number of choices. Best of the group is probably the *Hotel Apsara* (☎ 23-400), a huge place where the rooms front onto an internal courtyard making them relatively quiet. There are dorm beds for Rs 30 and singles/doubles for Rs 60/80 to Rs 250. The more expensive rooms have constant hot water and air-con.

Closer to the bus station, next to Udai Pol, is the *Hotel Yatri* (☎ 27-251). It has little to recommend it, apart from the location. It offers singles/doubles with bath and constant hot water for Rs 75/85. Better, and only marginally more expensive, is the *Hotel Welcome* (☎ 25-375) on the other side of the gate. Rooms here cost Rs 75/95 with bath attached, or Rs 250 for an air-con double.

The *Hotel Shalimar Palace* (☎ 27-730) on Udaipol Rd is hardly palatial, but again is convenient for the bus station. As is the case with most of the hotels in this area, the front rooms can be horrendously noisy. The charge here is Rs 90/110 with air-cooling and Rs 300/350 with air-con.

The *Keerti Hotel* on Airport Rd is a squalid dump, but it is the place to come if you want to visit the Pratap Country Inn (see the following section).

Elsewhere The only other option in town is the *Mewar Inn* (☎ 27-093). Although it slags off at this book in its leaflet, it is a cheap and friendly place well away from the centre. The rickshaw drivers hate the place, and you'll have difficulty persuading one to take you there. Basic but clean rooms go for Rs 22/28, bigger rooms cost Rs 52 to Rs 78, there are dorm beds for Rs 10, and a discount is given to YHA members. It is on a busy road, and one visitor commented that there were great views of the accidents and many near-misses from the rooftop! The slightly inconvenient location is no great disadvantage as there are bicycles for hire.

There's also an interesting place at Titadha village, seven to eight km outside Udaipur – the *Pratap Country Inn*. It's operated by the same people who manage the Keerti, so go there first and they'll arrange transport to Titadha. City buses run there every hour for about Rs 1, or you can ride out on a bicycle. Accommodation in tents and rooms costs as little as Rs 30 or as much as Rs 400. There's a swimming pool, restaurant, a free two-hour horse ride daily (if you stay more than one night), beautiful surroundings and a very relaxed atmosphere, but it's straightforward and fairly primitive. If you come out here expecting any luxuries, you'll be disappointed. They also organise longer safaris – from Rs 600 to Rs 1800 per person per day, depending on the level of luxury you choose.

Places to Stay – middle

One of the best mid-range places is the *Rang Niwas Palace Hotel* (☎ 23-891), Lake Palace Rd. This interesting, pleasant and very relaxed hotel is surrounded by its own gardens and, as its name suggests, was formerly a small palace. Large rooms in the old building start at Rs 100/150 with common bath, and go up to Rs 300 and Rs 350 with attached bath. Very modern and comfortable rooms in the tasteful new building cost Rs 400 and Rs 450, and have air-con, balcony and attached bath with hot water. A restaurant in a separate building offers a limited range of Indian and Continental dishes, as well as standard breakfast fare. It's a very popular hotel and close to the centre of things. The owners also have a farm property 25 km from town, where you can stay for Rs 150 for a double.

An excellent place in this bracket is the very friendly and popular *Hotel Jagat Niwas*

(☎ 29-728), back in the Lal Ghat area. It is right on the lake shore, and has a very pleasant open-air restaurant area, complete with marble floor. There's a range of rooms, starting at Rs 100/200 with common bath and ranging up to Rs 400.

An excellent place, about midway along Bhattiyani Chotta down from the Jagdish Temple at No 103, is the *Hotel Raj Palace* (☎ 23-092), which from the terrace offers good views of the city side of the City Palace. This friendly place has a pleasant and spacious feel, aided immensely by the cool and shady garden. All the rooms are a good size, have attached bath and are either air-cooled or air-con. The charge is Rs 150 for a double, with suites up to Rs 450.

Another good place in the Lal Ghat area is the *Hotel Sai-Niwas* (☎ 24-909), just down the hill towards the ghat from the City Palace entrance. The rooms (all doubles) are all imaginatively decorated, and the more expensive ones have balconies with a lake view. The cost is Rs 200 to Rs 350, all with attached bath and hot water.

Like many of the RTDC tourist bungalows in the state, the *Kajri Tourist Bungalow* (☎ 29-509), at the traffic circle on Ashoka Rd, has seen better days. Still, it isn't too bad if you're prepared to take one of the higher-priced rooms. Deluxe singles/doubles are Rs 100/150, air-cooled rooms Rs 200/250 and air-con rooms Rs 300/400. Dorm beds cost Rs 30. There's a bar and restaurant and you can arrange boating and bus tours from here.

Between Lakes Pichola and Fateh Sagar are two other mid-range hotels. The *Hotel Hill Top* (☎ 28-708), 4 Ambavgarh, offers air-con rooms with bath and constant hot water for Rs 400. There's a bar and restaurant, and folk dances and puppet shows can be arranged on request. As the name suggests, the hotel overlooks Fateh Sagar.

Not far away along Rani Rd is the cheaper *Hotel Lakend* (☎ 23-841). Rooms are Rs 200/300, Rs 375/600 with air-con. There's a swimming pool, bar, restaurant and a garden running down to the Fateh Sagar lakeside.

Places to Stay – top end

Without a doubt, the best of the lower-priced top-range hotels is the *Lake Pichola Hotel* (☎ 29-387), Chand Pol, which looks out across to the ghats, the Jagdish Temple and the northern end of the City Palace. It's a modern building built in the traditional style, and is extremely well maintained and managed. All rooms have air-con, telephone, carpet and bath with constant hot water, and are very good value at Rs 395/600. There's a money exchange facility, bar and restaurant.

Between Pichola and Fateh Sagar lakes are two upper-notch hotels side by side. The ITDC-operated *Laxmi Vilas Palace Hotel* (☎ 24-411) is a four-star hotel where air-con rooms cost Rs 1000/1150. There's a swimming pool, bar and restaurant. Next door is the *Hotel Anand Bhawan* (☎ 23-256) which has air-con rooms with bath and constant hot water for Rs 450/600. The restaurant serves vegetarian and non-vegetarian food.

About three km out of town on the Ahmedabad road is the four-star *Shikarbadi Hotel* (☎ 83-200) where air-con singles/doubles cost Rs 395/695. It's a small but pleasant hotel set in beautiful grounds with swimming pool, lawns and a small lake. It has a deer park and a stud farm – horse and elephant rides are available. The food here is excellent and there's a choice of Continental, Indian and tandoori dishes.

At the very top end of the scale are two of India's most luxurious hotels, facing each other across Lake Pichola. The incomparable *Lake Palace Hotel* (☎ 23-241) is on the smaller of the lake's two islands. It's the very image of what a maharaja's palace should be like and most people with sufficient money to spend would not pass up an opportunity to stay here. It offers every conceivable comfort, including a mango tree-shaded swimming pool. The cheapest rooms are US$95/105, but with a lake view you'll pay US$145, while suites cost US$185 to US$450.

The equally luxurious *Shiv Niwas Palace Hotel* (☎ 28-239) forms part of the City Palace complex. It's a good deal cheaper at US$30 for standard air-con rooms, with suites ranging from US$125 to US$375. If you want accommodation in either of these 'palace' hotels, you have to plan ahead – there's heavy demand for rooms.

The small and intimate *Hotel Fateh Prakash Palace* (☎ 28-239) is also in part of the City Palace complex. It has just eight rooms, and most of them overlook the lake. If you can't get into the Lake Palace, this is a good alternative. Standard rooms cost Rs 1000, and the superb suites cost Rs 2250/3000. This hotel doesn't have its own dining room, so guests have to cross the courtyard and use the one in the Shiv Niwas.

Places to Eat

Udaipur is not overendowed with good places to eat. In the Lal Ghat area there are a couple of places popular with travellers. The *Gokul Restaurant* is just outside the City Palace entrance. The food is good, as is the music, although the service is a little slow. Further down the hill, almost opposite the Jagdish Temple, is the small *Mayur Cafe*, which has good south Indian food. Just behind the Lal Ghat Guest House is the very popular *Four Seasons Restaurant*. Apart from these places, some of the guest houses in this area, such as the Jagat Niwas, have good, cheap restaurants.

About a 15-minute walk from the Jagdish Temple is the *Natural Attic Restaurant*. It's next to the Hotel Natural, on the other side of the northern arm of Lake Pichola. The extensive menu features Mexican, Chinese, Western, Indian and Tibetan dishes, and there's a free puppet show each evening at 8 pm.

The *Kajri Tourist Bungalow* restaurant has the usual menu with variable results. Sometimes the food is surprisingly good, sometimes not, but you'd probably only eat here if you were staying in one of the rooms.

Just round the corner from the Rang Niwas Palace Hotel, facing the City Palace, the *Roof Garden Cafe* has the appearance of a Hanging Gardens of Babylon. The food here is slightly expensive but there's a good menu and live folk music several nights per week.

For a minor splurge, *Berry's Restaurant* on Chetak Circle is popular with middle-class Indians and Western tourists and, although relatively expensive, the food is good. A soup, main course and drink will cost you around Rs 70. Opposite is a branch of *Kwality* which offers the usual selection and is somewhat cheaper than Berry's. Another good place for a treat is *The Feast* at Saheliyon ki Bari.

South of the Sajjan Niwas Gardens, on the hill overlooking Lake Pichola, the *Cafe Hill Park* is worth a visit just for the views. They offer cheap south Indian dishes and snacks.

Just about everybody with a bit of spare cash who couldn't afford to stay at the *Lake Palace Hotel* (☎ 23-241) went there for a buffet dinner at least once while they were in Udaipur. At Rs 300 it was not that cheap, and many travellers felt that it wasn't worth it. Certainly the dining room is not all that flash and, while the food was certainly of a high quality, the range was not all that great. However, the live sitar music and the attentive service made it a very pleasant place to eat. After your meal you could take a drink in the bar, and watch the folk dancing which takes places each evening at 9 pm. A lunchtime buffet (12.30 to 2.30 pm) for Rs 250 was also an option, although there was no folk dancing.

Currently the palace is not open to non-residents, but this situation may change. It may be worth telephoning to check this out.

Entertainment

Rajasthani Folk Dances & Music From August to April there are daily performances at 7 pm at the Meera Kala Mandir (☎ 23-976), Sector 11, Hiran Magari, near the Pars Theatre. They cost Rs 20 per head and are well worth attending. You can expect to see not only a whole range of tribal dances, but also some more spectacular acts which involve balancing numerous pots on top of the head while dancing on broken glass or unsheathed sabres. An auto-rickshaw to the

auditorium from the City Palace area costs Rs 15 (shared by up to three people).

Things to Buy

Udaipur has countless small shops and many interesting local crafts, particularly miniature paintings in the Rajput-Moghul style. There's a good cluster of these shops on Lake Palace Rd, next to the Rang Niwas Palace Hotel, and others around the Jagdish Temple.

Getting There & Away

Air Indian Airlines has twice-daily flights to Delhi (US$58), via Jodhpur (US$28) and Jaipur (US$35), and also twice daily to Bombay (US$70), one direct and one via Aurangabad (US$63). The direct flight between Udaipur and Aurangabad can save a great deal of bus or train time. The Indian Airlines office (☎ 24-433) is at Delhi Gate.

Bus Frequent state transport buses run from Udaipur to other regional centres, as well as to Delhi and Ahmedabad. If you use these buses, make sure you take an express bus since the ordinary buses take forever, make innumerable detours to various towns off the main route and can be very uncomfortable. For long-distance travel, it's best to use private buses. The tourist office is the best source of bus schedules and prices. Trying to get these from the information counter at the frenetic bus stand is like pulling teeth.

Destinations served by express buses include Jaipur (nine hours, nine daily), Ajmer (eight hours, 11 daily), Kota/Bundi (six hours, six daily), Jodhpur (eight to 10 hours) via either Ranakpur (four hours, six daily) or Nathdwara (two daily) and Chittorgarh (three hours, five daily). Express and deluxe buses should be booked in advance.

There are quite a few private bus companies which operate to such places as Ahmedabad (Rs 60), Vadodara (Rs 90), Bombay (Rs 160), Delhi (Rs 130), Indore (Rs 100), Jaipur (Rs 60), Jodhpur (Rs 60), Kota (Rs 60) and Mt Abu (Rs 60). Most have their offices along the main road from the bus station to Delhi Gate (Khangipir Rd). Book at least one day in advance.

Train The best train between Delhi and Udaipur is the daily *Pink City/Garib Nawaz Express* which covers the 739 km in 15½ hours, and goes via Jaipur, Ajmer and Chittorgarh. Fares for the trip are Rs 118/446 in 2nd/1st class. This train operates during the day, and so reaches its destination in the late evening. If you'd rather do the journey overnight and arrive at a more civilised hour, the *Chetak Express* does the trip, but it takes 20 hours.

There is also a daily express in either direction between Udaipur and Ahmedabad on a metre-gauge line. The 297-km trip takes nine hours and costs Rs 57/218 in 2nd/1st class.

The daily (overnight) Udaipur-Jodhpur *Fast Passenger* does the 221-km trip to Jodhpur in 12 hours at a cost of Rs 48/175 in 2nd/1st class.

Getting Around
To/From the Airport The airport is 25 km from the city and, as there's no airport bus, the cheapest way to get into the city is to walk to the main road (about 500 metres) and take a regular bus from there. A taxi costs around Rs 100.

Local Transport Udaipur has a reasonably good city bus service. Auto-rickshaws and taxis are unmetered so you need to agree on a fare before setting off. The standard fare for tourists anywhere within the city appears to be Rs 10, and you'll be very lucky to get it for less since there are too many well-heeled tourists around who pay the first price asked.

The commission system is in place with a vengeance, and so rickshaw drivers will try to take you to a place of their choice rather than yours, especially if you want to go to the Lal Ghat area. If that's the case, just ask for the Jagdish Temple, as all the guest houses in that area are within easy walking distance of the temple.

Udaipur is small enough and vehicle

traffic slow enough to make getting around on a bicycle quite enjoyable. You can hire bicycles all over town for around Rs 2 an hour or Rs 10 per day. Two places are opposite the Anjani Hotel in the Lal Ghat area, and next to the Hotel Raj Palace on Bhattiyani Chotta.

AROUND UDAIPUR
Shilpgram
Shilpgram, a crafts village 3 km away west of Fateh Sagar, was inaugurated by Rajiv Gandhi in 1989. It's an interesting place with traditional houses from four states – Rajasthan, Gujarat, Goa and Maharashtra – and there are daily demonstrations by musicians, dancers, or artisans from the various states. Although it's much more animated during festival times (see the tourist office for details), there's always something happening.

The site covers 80 hectares but most buildings are in a fairly compact area. It's open daily from 2 to 8 pm, and is well worth an afternoon visit.

The open-air *Shilpi Restaurant* next to the site serves very good Indian and Chinese food, and snacks.

Getting There & Away There's no public transport to Shilpgram, so you'll have to rent a bicycle, or take an auto-rickshaw or taxi.

Eklingi
This interesting little village with a number of ancient **temples** is only 22 km and a short bus ride north of Udaipur. The Siva temple in the village itself was originally built in 734 AD, although its present form dates from the rule of Maharana Raimal between 1473 and 1509. The walled complex includes an elaborately pillared hall under a large pyramidal roof and features a four-faced Siva image of black marble. The temple is open at rather odd hours – 5 to 7 am, 10 am to 1 pm and 5 to 7 pm.

At **Nagada**, about a km off the road and a km before Eklingi, are three old temples. The Jain temple of Adbudji is essentially ruined, but its architecture is interesting and it's very old. The nearby Sas Bahu, or Mother and Daughter-in-Law, group has very fine and intricate architecture and carvings, including some erotic figures. You can reach these temples most conveniently by hiring a bicycle in Eklingi itself, though this isn't always easy.

Getting There & Away Buses run from Udaipur to Eklingi every hour from 5 am onwards. There's a small guest house in the village if you want to stay overnight.

Haldighati

This site, 40 km from Udaipur, is where Maharana Pratap valiantly defied the superior Moghul forces of Akbar in 1576. The site is a battlefield and the only thing to see is the chhatri to the warrior's horse, Chetak, a few km away.

Places to Stay The RTDC runs a *Rest House* here. It has just one room, which costs Rs 40/60, or there are dorm beds for Rs 30. Good meals are available on request.

Getting There & Away A state transport bus to Haldighati leaves Udaipur daily at 9 am and private buses depart at 11.45 am and 12.30 pm.

Nathdwara

The important 18th-century **Vishnu temple** of Sri Nathji stands here, 48 km from Udaipur. It's a popular pilgrimage site, but non-Hindus are not allowed inside. The black stone Vishnu image was brought here from Mathura in 1669 to protect it from Aurangzeb's destructive impulses. According to legend, when an attempt was later made to move the image, the getaway vehicle, a wagon, sank into the ground up to the axles, indicating that the image preferred to stay where it was!

Places to Stay The RTDC *Gokul Tourist Bungalow* (☎ 2685) offers air-cooled rooms for Rs 150, air-con rooms for Rs 150/200 and there's a dormitory with beds for Rs 30, as well as a bar and restaurant.

Getting There & Away There are state transport buses from Udaipur every hour from 5 am onwards.

Kankroli & Rajsamand Lake

At Kankroli, Dwarkadhish (an incarnation of Vishnu) has a **temple** similar to the temple at Nathdwara and, like that temple, is open at extremely erratic hours.

Nearby is a lake created by the dam constructed in 1660 by Maharana Raj Singh. There are many ornamental arches and chhatris along the huge bund.

Kumbhalgarh Fort

This is the most important fort in the Mewar region after Chittorgarh. It was built by Maharana Kumbha in the 15th century and, due to its inaccessibility on top of the Aravalli range at 1100 metres, it was taken only once in its history. Even then, it took the combined armies of the Moghul emperor, Akbar, and those of Amber and Marwar to breach its defences. It was here that the rulers of Mewar retreated in times of danger. The walls of the fortress stretch some 12 km and enclose many temples, palaces, gardens and water storage facilities. The fort was renovated in the last century.

There's also a game reserve here. The scarcity of waterholes between March and June makes this the best time to see animals. There is a lot of wildlife including antelope, panther and bear, and it's a good area for walking.

Places to Stay There's a *PWD Rest House*, or the small *Aodhi Hotel* (☎ Kelwara 22), where double rooms cost Rs 300.

Getting There & Away Kumbhalgarh Fort is 84 km from Udaipur. There are state transport buses from Udaipur to Kumbhalgarh at 7.30 and 11 am, and 3.30 and 5 pm. Private buses are also available. From where the bus drops you, you'll have to walk or hire a jeep, so it's a good idea to come here as part of a small group and share the cost.

Ranakpur

One of the biggest and most important Jain temples in India, the extremely beautiful Ranakpur complex lies in a remote and peaceful valley of the Aravalli range. The main temple in the complex is the **Chaumukha Temple**, or Four-Faced Temple, dedicated to Adinath. Built in 1439, this huge, beautifully crafted and well-kept marble temple has 29 halls supported by 1444 pillars, no two alike. Within the complex are two other Jain temples to Neminath and Parasnath and, a little distance away, a Sun Temple. One km from the main complex is the Amba Mata Temple.

The temple is open to non-Jains from noon to 5 pm. Shoes and all leather articles must be left at the entrance.

Places to Stay & Eat The RTDC *Shilpi Tourist Bungalow* has singles/doubles for Rs 80/100, air-cooled rooms for Rs 125/175, good dormitory beds for Rs 30 and a dining room.

For a donation, you can stay at the dharamsala within the temple complex. If you arrive at a meal time, you can get a good thali in the dining hall, just inside the main entrance to the complex on your left, again for a small donation. Staying overnight at Ranakpur breaks up the long trip between Udaipur and Jodhpur.

Getting There & Away Ranakpur is 39 km from Palna (or Falna) Junction on the Ajmer to Mt Abu rail and road routes. From Udaipur, there are five state transport express buses per day, and even these take up to five hours. Although it's just possible to travel through from Ranakpur to Jodhpur or Mt Abu on the same day, it's hardly worth it since you'll arrive well after dark. It's better to stay for the night and continue on next day. There's also a daily bus from Mt Abu which terminates at Sadri, only seven km from Ranakpur.

Ghanerao

The attractive town of Ghanerao can make a good base for explorations of the various

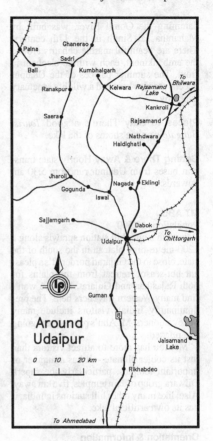

Around Udaipur

0   10   20 km

attractions around Udaipur. The Ghanerao Royal Castle's helpful owners can arrange a trek from Ghanerao to Kumbhalgarh with an overnight stay at their hunting lodge, Bagha ka Bagh, en route.

Places to Stay About a km out of town, the *Ghanerao Royal Castle* is a small castle/palace with six well-kept rooms for Rs 275/300.

Jaisamand Lake

Located 48 km south-west of Udaipur, this stunningly sited artificial lake, created by damming the Gomti River, was built by Maharana Jai Singh in the 17th century. There are beautiful marble chhatris around the embankment, each with an elephant in front. The summer palaces of the Udaipur queens are also here and a wildlife sanctuary is nearby.

Places to Stay There's a good *Tourist Bungalow* on the shores of the lake.

Getting There & Away Hourly state transport buses from Udaipur run from 5.30 am onwards.

MT ABU
Population: 15,500
Rajasthan's only hill station sprawls along a 1200-metre-high plateau in the south of the state, close to the Gujarati border. It's a pleasant hot-season retreat from the plains for both Rajasthan and Gujarat, but you won't find many Western travellers here. The predominantly Indian visitors include many honeymooners. Mt Abu's pace is easy-going and relaxed.

Mt Abu has more to attract visitors than just its cooler climate – it has a number of important temples, particularly the superb Dilwara group of Jain temples, five km away. Also, like many other hill stations in India, it has its own artificial lake.

Orientation & Information
Mt Abu is on a hilly plateau about 22 km long by six km wide, 27 km from the nearest railway station, Abu Road. The main part of the town extends along the road in from Abu Road, down to Nakki Lake. Coming in by bus, you first pass the Tourist Bungalow, up a hill to your right, then a string of hotels, before you arrive at the bus stand. The tourist office (☎ 3151) is opposite the bus stand and is open from 8 to 11 am and 4 to 8 pm.

Continuing through the town, you pass more hotels and restaurants, the small market to your right and, eventually, arrive at the lake. The GPO is on Raj Bhavan Rd, opposite the art gallery and museum. Several banks and a number of top-end hotels will change money.

Nakki Lake
Virtually in the centre of Mt Abu, the small lake takes its name from the legend that it was scooped out by a god, using only his nails, or *nakk*. It's a short and easy stroll around the lake – look for the strange rock formations. The best known, Toad Rock, looks just like a toad about to hop into the lake. Others, like Nun Rock, Nandi Rock or Camel Rock, require more imagination. The 14th-century Ragunath Temple stands beside the lake.

You can hire boats and row (or be rowed) out on the lake. Costs are around Rs 20 per half hour.

Viewpoints
Of the various viewpoints around town, **Sunset Point** is the most popular. Hordes stroll out here every evening to catch the setting sun, the food stalls and all the usual entertainments. Other popular points include **Honeymoon Point**, which also offers a view of the sunset, **The Crags** and **Robert's Spur**.

For a good view over the lake the best point is probably the terrace of the Maharaja of Jaipur's former **summer palace**. No-one seems to mind if you climb up here for the view and a photo.

Museum & Art Gallery
Maintenance of the small museum leaves a lot to be desired. Although it's not very interesting, the museum does have some items from archaeological excavations which date from the 8th to 12th centuries, as well as Jain bronzes, carvings, brasswork and local textiles. 'Art gallery' is hardly an accurate description of the collection of half a dozen pictures. The museum, on Raj Bhavan Rd, is open from 10 am to 4.30 pm daily, except Fridays, and admission is free. There is also a **Rajasthan Emporium** back towards the market.

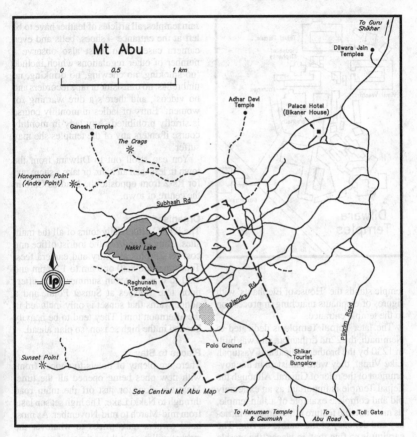

Mt Abu

0   0.5   1 km

To Guru
Shikhar

Dilwara Jain
Temples

Adhar Devi
Temple

Palace Hotel
(Bikaner House)

Ganesh Temple

The Crags

Honeymoon Point
(Andra Point)

Subhash Rd

Nakki Lake

Raghunath
Temple

Rajendra Rd

Pilgrim Road

Polo Ground

Shikar
Tourist
Bungalow

Sunset Point

See Central Mt Abu Map

To Hanuman Temple
& Gaumukh

To
Abu Road

To Toll Gate

Adhar Devi Temple

Three km out of the town, 200 steep steps
lead to this Durga temple built in a natural
cleft in the rock. You have to stoop to get
through the low entrance to the temple.
There are good views over Mt Abu from up
here.

Madhuban

This is the Brahma Kumaris World Spiritual
University, not far from the lake. Meditation
and Raja Yoga courses are held here regularly; they offer free introductory courses.
There's also a museum on the site.

Dilwara Temples

These Jain temples are Mt Abu's main attraction and amongst the finest examples of Jain
architecture in India. The complex includes
two temples in which the art of carving
marble reached unsurpassed heights.

The older of the temples is the **Vimal
Vasahi**, built in 1031 and dedicated to the
first tirthankar, Adinath. The central shrine
has an image of Adinath, while around the
courtyard are 52 identical cells, each with a
Buddha-like cross-legged image. Forty-
eight elegantly carved pillars form the
entrance to the courtyard. In front of the

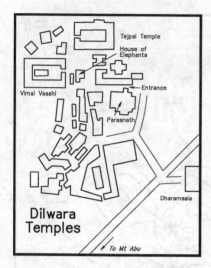

Tejpal Temple

House of
Elephants

Entrance

Vimal Vasahi

Parasnath

Dharamsala

**Dilwara
Temples**

To Mt Abu

temple stands the 'House of Elephants' with figures of elephants marching in procession to the temple entrance.

The later **Tejpal Temple** is dedicated to Neminath, the 22nd tirthankar, and was built in 1230 by the brothers Tejpal and Vastupal. Like Vimal, they were ministers in the government of the ruler of Gujarat. Although the Tejpal Temple is important as an extremely old and complete example of a Jain temple, its most notable feature is the fantastic intricacy and delicacy of the marble carving. The carving is so fine that, in places, the marble becomes almost transparent. In particular, the lotus flower which hangs from the centre of the dome is an incredible piece of work. It's difficult to believe that this huge lace-like filigree actually started as a solid block of marble. The temple employs several full-time stone carvers to maintain and restore the work. There are three other temples in the enclosure, but they all pale beside the Tejpal and Vimal Vasahi.

The complex is open from noon to 6 pm and there is a Rs 20 camera charge (or Rs 50 if you have a zoom or wide-angle lens, which to the ticket clerk seems to mean any camera that's not a pocket automatic). As at other Jain temples, all articles of leather have to be left at the entrance – shoes, belts and even camera cases. You must also observe a number of other regulations which include 'no smoking, no chewing, no drinking, no umbrellas, no transistor or tape recorders and no videos', and there's a dire warning for women: 'Entry of ladies in monthly course is strictly prohibited. Any lady in monthly course if enters any of the temples she may suffer'.

You can stroll out to Dilwara from the town in less than an hour, or take a share taxi for Rs 2 from opposite the Madras Cafe in the centre of town.

Organised Tours

The RTDC offers daily tours of all the main sites. They leave from the tourist office and cost Rs 25 plus all entry and camera fees. Tour times are 8.30 or 9 am to 1.30 pm and 1.30 to 6 pm (later in summer). The afternoon tour finishes at Sunset Point, and a notice warns that sunset is only included in the afternoon tour! They tend to be heavily booked in the high season, so plan ahead.

Places to Stay

There are plenty of hotels to choose from, with new ones being opened all the time. Most are along or just off the main road through to Nakki Lake. The high season lasts from mid-March to mid-November. As most hotel owners raise prices to whatever the market will bear at those times, it can be an expensive place to stay. The real peak time is 15 May to 15 June and a room of any kind for less than Rs 200 is very hard to find. During the five days of Diwali (November), rooms are virtually impossible to find without advance booking. A Rs 40 room in a dump will cost upwards of Rs 200, and anything mildly comfortable is simply outrageous. Avoid the place at this time.

In the low season (with the exception of Christmas and New Year), discounts of up to 50% are available and mid-range accommodation can be an absolute bargain. Most places are definitely open to a bit of bargaining, and the rates get cheaper the longer you stay. The hotels usually have a 9 am checkout time as most of the buses leave Mt Abu early in the morning.

At all times of year there are plenty of touts working the bus and taxi stations. In the off season you can safely ignore them and head for the place of your choice; at peak times they can save you a lot of legwork as they'll know exactly where the last available room is.

Places to Stay – bottom end

The popular *Hotel Lake View* (☎ 240) overlooks picturesque Nakki Lake but, although the views are certainly good, it's really only an average hotel. In winter, rooms on the front side are Rs 100 a double and, on the back side, Rs 60 (no window) to Rs 80. The minimum summer rate is Rs 200. All rooms have a bath, and hot water is available between 6 and 11 am.

Close by is the *Hotel Panghat* (☎ 286), which is cheap at Rs 25/30, or Rs 50 with a view. All rooms have common bath, and hot water is available from 7 to 9 am.

Also in this lakeside area is the *Hotel Nakki Vihar* (☎ 3481), which is not a bad place, despite the hideous paint job. Rooms here cost Rs 40/50 with attached bath, or Rs 60 for a double with a view. Hot water costs Rs 2 per bucket.

A bit higher up the hill is the *Shree Ganesh Hotel* (☎ 3591). The location is certainly quiet and the owner is friendly. The rooms are clean and well kept, although some lack windows, and there are good views from the rooftop terrace. As this place is a little further from the centre of things, the high-season rates tend to be little more sensible than elsewhere, and bargaining is definitely possible. Low-season rates are Rs 30/40.

If you take the right-hand fork going up the hill opposite the taxi stand and polo ground, you'll find several other budget hotels. The *Hotel Natraj* (☎ 3532) has reasonable rooms at Rs 60 at the back and Rs 120 at the front, all with balcony and hot water. The owner is a bit of a fast talker, but is friendly and helpful. Right across the road is the *Hotel Rajendra* (☎ 74), which is one of the cheapest places at Rs 25/40, although you get what you pay for – very little. Bucket hot water costs Rs 2.

Moving further away from the lake along the main road, there are a number of other possibilities. The *Hotel Rajdeep* is right opposite the bus station, and it has just a few basic rooms at Rs 50 with attached bath. The *Hotel Veena* is just a little further along, and good-sized rooms with balcony and attached bath go for Rs 80. There's not really a view of anything much from here, and while the main road is generally quiet by Indian standards, the noise can be annoying.

Set back from the road in this same area is the *Hotel Vrindivan* (☎ 47). It's quite a bit more upmarket, but it's a very pleasant place. Rooms cost Rs 120 with attached bath, and Rs 200 for larger rooms with TV.

Further still from the lake is the popular *Tourist Guest House* (☎ 3200), just off the main road below the Tourist Bungalow. It's a quiet and pleasant place with a small garden and the owner is very friendly. In winter it's the best value in Mt Abu, with rooms for Rs 60 and hot water in the early morning. Food is available in the rooms between 6.30 and 11 pm at reasonable prices. Close by is the *Hotel Vishram*, on the main road. It is somewhat more primitive but clean and reasonably good value at Rs 40 for a double with bath. There are no singles. Bucket hot water is available for Rs 2.

The 82-room RTDC *Shikar Tourist Bungalow* (☎ 3219), back from the main road and up a steepish path, is the biggest place in Mt Abu. Although fairly popular, it's certainly not the best value in town. Ordinary singles/doubles cost Rs 125/150, deluxe rooms are Rs 250/300, and cottages are Rs 400. These are the high-season prices, but there is a 30% discount in the off season. All rooms have bath and hot water some of the time. There's also a somewhat indifferent bar and a restaurant.

On the far side of the polo ground there's a string of hotels, which are definitely midrange in the season, but offer quite good rates in the off season. The *Hotel Mount View* (☎ 3320) is a nice older building and is very

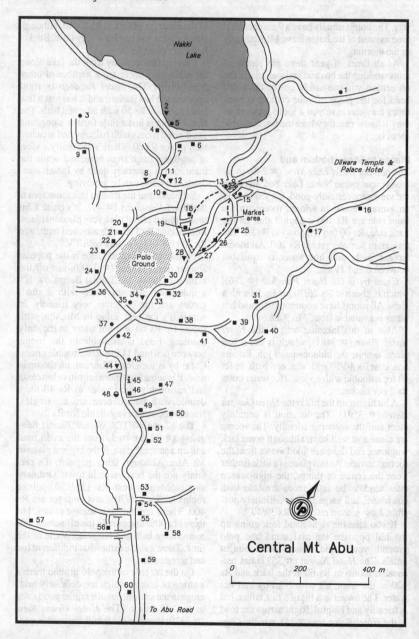

Nakki Lake

Dilwara Temple & Palace Hotel

Market area

Polo Ground

Central Mt Abu

0   200   400 m

To Abu Road

■ PLACES TO STAY

4	Hotel Nakki Vihar
6	Hotel Lake View
7	Hotel Panghat
9	Shree Ganesh Hotel
16	Mount Hotel
18	Hotel Ambika
19	Gujarat Hotel
20	Hotel Mount View
21	Asha Hotel
22	Hotel Surya Darshan
23	Hotel Saraswati
24	Hotel Abu International
25	Hotel Ashoka
26	Shere Punjab Hotel
29	Neelam Hotel
30	Hotel Maharaja International
31	Hotel Sudhir
32	Hotels Samrat & Navijan
36	Hotels Chanakya & Polo View
38	Hotels Natraj & Neelkanth
39	Laxman Guest House
40	Hotel Connaught House
41	Rajendra Hotel
46	Hotel Rajdeep
47	Hotel Vrinidavan
49	Hotel Veena
50	Hotel Hilltone
51	Hotel Madhuban
52	Hotel Sheratone
53	Tourist Guest House
55	Hotel Vishram
56	Hotel Hillock
57	Hotel Sunrise Palace

58	Shikar Tourist Bungalow
59	Hotel Maharani
60	Hotel Aravali

▼ PLACES TO EAT

2	Sarovar Restaurant
8	Bharti & Haveli Restaurants
11	Hencky Francky
12	MK Restaurant
28	Madras Cafe
34	Veena Restaurant
44	Kanak Dining Hall

OTHER

1	Universal Peace Hall
3	Maharaja of Jaipur's Old Summer Palace
5	Boats
10	Pony Hire
13	State Bank of India
14	GPO
15	Church
17	Telephone Exchange
27	Share Taxis to Dilwara
33	Bank of Baroda
35	Taxi Stand
37	State Emporium
42	Shanti Sadan
43	Police
45	Tourist Office
48	Bus Station
54	Railway Agency

good value at Rs 80 with attached bath, and hot water is available from 7 to 10 am. The rooms on the 1st floor have a terrace and good views. The *Hotel Surya Darshan* (☎ 3165) is a friendly place with rooms from Rs 50/60, and there's hot water in the morning.

Next door is the *Hotel Saraswati* (☎ 3237). The purple paint job is a bit radical, but the rooms are good value at Rs 40 for a double with bucket hot water, and Rs 60 to Rs 80 for doubles with bath and hot water.

Places to Stay – middle
The fairly new *Hotel Sheratone* (☎ 273),

alongside the main road, is a friendly place. The rooms are large and airy, and they have attached baths and channel music. Prices start at Rs 100/150 in the off season. Close by, a little further up the main road, is the *Hotel Madhuban*. Singles/doubles with bath cost Rs 150/250 and hot water is available from 7 to 10 am.

The *Hotel Samrat* and *Hotel Navijan* (☎ 73), on the main street, are basically the same hotel although they appear to be separate. It's a large place with off-season singles/doubles for Rs 120/150, all with bath and hot water. High season prices are double these rates. The hotel also has a restaurant. The *Hotel Maharaja International* (☎ 61), directly opposite, has doubles from Rs 80 to Rs 180, depending on the view and facilities offered.

At the bottom end of the polo ground is the *Hotel Abu International*. Doubles here cost Rs 350 in the high season, but are a bargain in the off season at Rs 75. The hotel restaurant offers Punjabi and Gujarati meals.

Those looking for the fading splendour of the Rajputs or the Raj should seriously consider staying at either the *Mount Hotel* (☎ 55) or the *Hotel Connaught House* (☎ 260). The Connaught is a little further up the road from the Natraj and Rajendra Hotels and belongs to the former Maharaja of Jodhpur.

This beautiful old place is set in extensive gardens and its somewhat gloomy and claustrophobic interior features numerous period photographs of members of the Indian aristocracy and polo-playing British officers. It offers off-peak doubles for Rs 350, all with bath and hot water. There's also a new wing of bright and airy rooms, and these are good value at Rs 250/350. In the season all rooms are Rs 500, and this is comparatively good value. Meals are available but should be ordered in advance.

The Mount Hotel once belonged to a British army officer and has changed little since those days, except for the installation of hot water in the bathrooms. Although the place is full of nostalgia and old-world charm and surrounded by well-maintained gardens, it is really quite spartan. There are only a few rooms, and these cost Rs 150 (negotiable) in the off season, and only Rs 300 in the high season. All meals are available with advance notice.

Places to Stay – top end

The delightful *Palace Hotel (Bikaner House)* (☎ 3121) is a worthwhile treat but is usually heavily booked in season and it can be hard to get in. The hotel was once the summer residence of the Maharaja of Bikaner and is now managed by the maharaja's very amiable and helpful son-in-law. There are 24 elegantly decorated rooms,

each with separate sleeping and living areas, and four magnificent suites.

The hotel is in a beautiful location near the Dilwara Temples and has well laid-out gardens, a private lake, two tennis courts and pony rides by arrangement. The cost is a very reasonable Rs 355/440 all year round, and meals are available at Rs 95 for vegetarian and Rs 120 for non-veg.

The very modern *Hotel Hilltone* (☎ 3112) is centrally located and is a good choice. It has a swimming pool, restaurant, bar, sauna and in-house videos. (They rarely show the puerile rubbish churned out for general consumption by the Bombay film industry.) Singles/doubles cost Rs 395/625, suites are Rs 700 and cottages Rs 790. There's no off-season discount.

On the opposite side of the road from the Tourist Bungalow and Tourist Guest House, the new *Hotel Hillock* (☎ 3467) is also excellent value. It's large, spotlessly clean and beautifully furnished and decorated. Its year-round tariff is Rs 650 to Rs 750 plus taxes.

On the hill above the Hotel Hillock is the very pleasant *Sunrise Palace Hotel* (☎ 3214). This place is yet another former summer residence of a Rajput maharaja (this time the Maharaja of Bharatpur) and is a very quiet and comfortable place with fabulous views. The rooms are well furnished and have attached bath, TV and phone, and range in price from Rs 500 to Rs 700. Capacious suites with views cost Rs 1000, and there is a 30% discount in the off season, making this one of the best value places in this range.

Places to Eat

Just uphill from the bus stand, the *Kanak Dining Hall* looks expensive but isn't. It's very clean and offers excellent south Indian vegetarian dishes ranging from Rs 6 to a maximum of Rs 12. The Rs 22 lunchtime thalis are very tasty, making this a popular place at that time.

Further uphill, next to the junction at the bottom end of the polo ground, you'll find a couple of restaurants on the main road. The *Veena Restaurant* has good Gujarati thalis with plenty of refills, and their 'super masala

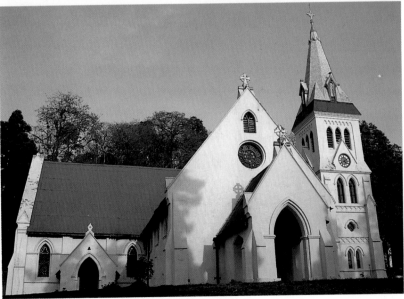

Top: Dakhil Darwaza, Gaur, West Bengal (BT)
Bottom: St Andrew's Church, Darjeeling, West Bengal (BT)

Top Left: Sun Temple, Konark, Orissa (BT)
Top Right: Dhauli Peace Pagoda, Orissa (BT)
Bottom Left: Beach at Gopalpur-on-Sea, Orissa (BT)
Bottom Right: Lingaraj Temple, Bhubaneswar, Orissa (BT)

dosas' are equally good. In the bazaar area, the *Shere Punjab Hotel* has excellent Punjabi food and is warmly recommended by local residents as well as travellers.

The *Madras Cafe* is in this same area, and while the food, such as vegie burgers, is quite good, the place suffers from inept management, and the lassis are terrible. The *Neelam Hotel* close by is one of the few places serving non-veg food, although it's nothing to get excited about.

There are several other good restaurants close to the crest of the hill leading down to the lake. The *MK Restaurant* has been popular for a number of years for its ice cream and thalis. Around the corner on the opposite side of the road, the equally popular *Bharti Restaurant* also serves Gujarati thalis. The amazingly named *Hencky Francky* is a fast-food place offering pizzas, burgers, dosas and idlis (rice dumplings). From here down to the lake are a number of small snack places. On the lake itself there's a large concrete 'boat' restaurant, the *Sarovar Cafe*, which is OK for a cup of tea or coffee but offers little else. It is closed in the off season.

For a splurge, go to a hotel restaurant. In the Samrat International Hotel, the *Taksha Shila* is recommended by local hotel owners and serves vegetarian Punjabi and Western food. The *Hotel Maharaja* restaurant features Gujarati, Punjabi and south Indian food. At the Hotel Hilltone, the *Woodlands Restaurant* is one of the chain with branches in Bombay, Bangalore, Delhi and Singapore. Despite that, it only has a limited menu of vegetarian snacks.

Things to Buy

The Rajasthan Emporium is on Raj Bhavan Rd and there are quite a few shops on the road down to the lakefront. Jewellery shops have a good selection. As in most of India, jewellery is usually sold by weight.

Getting There & Away

Bus From 6 am onwards, regular buses make the 27-km climb from Abu Road up to Mt Abu. The trip takes about an hour and costs Rs 8. A taxi, which you can share with up to

five people, costs Rs 120. As you enter Mt Abu, there's a tollgate where passengers are charged Rs 5. Some state transport buses go all the way to Mt Abu, while others terminate at Abu Road, so make sure you get the one you want.

The bus schedule from Mt Abu is extensive and, to many destinations, you will find a direct bus faster and more convenient than going down to Abu Road and waiting for a train. To Udaipur, STC buses take seven hours at a cost of Rs 40. To Ajmer (eight hours) and Jaipur (11 hours) there's one departure daily. For Ahmedabad there are many departures and the journey takes seven hours.

Private buses are more expensive but definitely preferable to state transport buses and there's plenty of choice. There are seemingly many companies with offices on the main street, but all but two are just ticketing agents; only Shobha and Maharaja are the actual bus operators. Buses to Udaipur take 4½ hours and cost Rs 70. Other destinations served include Ahmedabad, Ajmer and Jaipur.

Train Abu Road, the railhead for Mt Abu, is on the metre-gauge line between Delhi and Ahmedabad via Jaipur and Ajmer. In Mt Abu there's a railway agency at the HP service station near the Tourist Bungalow, and it has quotas on most of the express trains out of Abu Road. It is open daily from 9 am to 1 pm and 2 to 4 pm.

There's a variety of trains; the best is the daily superfast Delhi to Ahmedabad *Ashram Express*. Fares for the five-hour, 187-km journey from Ahmedabad are Rs 42/151 in 2nd/1st class. The 440-km journey from Jaipur takes eight hours and costs Rs 81/301 in 2nd/1st class.

Direct trains also run from Abu Road to Ajmer, Jodhpur and Agra. For Bhuj and the rest of the Kathiawar peninsula in Gujarat, change trains at Palanpur, 53 km south of Abu Road.

Getting Around

Buses from the bus stand go to the various

sites in Mt Abu, but it takes a little planning to get out and back without too much hanging around. Some buses go just to Dilwara, while others will take you out to Achalgarh, so you'll need to decide which place to visit first, depending on the schedule. For Dilwara it's easier to take a share taxi, and these leave when full from opposite the Madras Cafe in the centre of town; the fare is Rs 2.

There are plenty of taxis with posted fares to anywhere you care to mention.

AROUND MT ABU
Achalgarh

The Siva temple of **Achaleshwar Mahandeva**, 11 km away, has a number of interesting features, including a toe of Siva, a brass Nandi and, where the Siva lingam would normally be, a deep hole said to extend all the way to the underworld.

Outside, by the car park, is a tank beside which stand three stone buffaloes and the figure of a king shooting them with a bow and arrows. A legend states that the tank was once filled with ghee, but demons in the form of buffaloes came down and drank each night – until the king shot them. A path leads up the hillside to a group of colourful **Jain temples** with fine views out over the plains.

Guru Shikhar

At the end of the plateau, 15 km from Mt Abu, is Guru Shikhar, the highest point in Rajasthan at 1721 metres. A road goes almost all the way to the summit. At the top is the Atri Rishi Temple, complete with a priest and good views all around.

Below the temple is a cafe selling soft drinks and snacks.

Gaumukh Temple

Down on the Abu Road side of Mt Abu, a small stream flows from the mouth of a marble cow, giving the shrine its name. There is also a marble figure of the bull Nandi, Siva's vehicle. The tank here, Agni Kund, is said to be the site of the sacrificial fire, made by the sage Vasishta, from which four of the great Rajput clans were born. An image of Vasishta is flanked by figures of Rama and Krishna.

ABU ROAD

This station down on the plains is the rail junction for Mt Abu.

Places to Stay

In the main market area, the *Bhagwati Guest House* is only five minutes from the train and bus stations. It has cheap rooms and dorm beds. It's OK for one night and there are other simple places around. The station has railway *retiring rooms*.

Getting There & Away

Although there are state transport buses from Abu Road to other cities such as Jodhpur, Ajmer, Jaipur, Udaipur and Ahmedabad, there's little point in catching them here as they're all available from Mt Abu itself. Buses operated by private companies also run from Mt Abu.

The railway and bus stations are right next to each other on the edge of town.

Western Rajasthan

JODHPUR

Population: 648,000

Jodhpur stands at the edge of the Thar Desert and is the largest city in Rajasthan after Jaipur. The city is totally dominated by the massive fort, topping a sheer rocky hill which rises right in the middle of the town. Jodhpur was founded in 1459 by Rao Jodha, a chief of the Rajput clan known as the Rathores. His descendants ruled not only Jodhpur, but also other Rajput princely states. The Rathore kingdom was once known as Marwar, the Land of Death.

The old city of Jodhpur is surrounded by a 10-km-long wall, built about a century after the city was founded. From the fort, you can clearly see where the old city ends and the new begins. It's fascinating to wander around the jumble of winding streets in the old city. Eight gates lead out from the walled city. It's one of India's more interesting cities and, yes, it was from here that those baggy-tight horse-riding trousers, jodhpurs, took their name. Today, you're more likely to see them worn in Saurashtra in Gujarat than here.

Orientation

The tourist office, railway stations and bus stand are all outside the old city. High Court Rd runs from the Raika Bagh Railway Station, directly across from the bus stand, past the Umaid Gardens, the Tourist Bunga-low and tourist office, and round beside the city wall towards the main station and the GPO. Most trains from the east stop at the Raika Bagh Station before the main station – which is quite handy if you want to stay at the Ghoomar Tourist Bungalow.

Information

The tourist office (☎ 45-083) is at the Tourist Bungalow and is open Monday to Saturday from 8 am to noon and 3 to 6 pm.

Meherangarh Fort

Still run by the former Maharaja of Jodhpur, the Majestic Fort is just that. Sprawled across the 125-metre-high hill, this is the most impressive and formidable fort in fort-studded Rajasthan. A winding road leads up to the entrance from the city below. The first gate is still scarred by cannon ball hits, indi-cating that this was a fort which earned its keep. The gates include the Jayapol, built by Maharaja Man Singh in 1806 following his victory over the armies of Jaipur and Bikaner, and the Fatehpol, or Victory Gate, erected by Maharaja Ajit Singh to commem-orate his defeat of the Moghuls.

The final gate is the Lahapol, or Iron Gate, beside which there are 15 hand prints, the sati marks of Maharaja Man Singh's widows who threw themselves upon his funeral pyre in 1843. They still attract devotional atten-tion and are usually covered in red powder.

Inside the fort, there is a whole series of courtyards and palaces. The palace apart-ments have evocative names like the Moti Mahal, or Pearl Palace, the Sukh Mahal, or Pleasure Palace and the Phool Mahal, or Flower Palace. They house a fantastic collec-tion of the trappings of Indian royalty, including an amazing collection of elephant howdahs (used when the maharajas rode their elephants in glittering procession through their capitals), miniature paintings of a variety of schools, superb folk music instruments and the inevitable Rajput armoury, palanquins, furniture and cos-tumes. In one room, there's even an exhibit of rocking cradles. Finally, there's an enor-mous, luxurious and stunningly beautiful tent, originally made for the Moghul emper-ors but carried off as booty by the Rajputs following one of their many battles. The palace apartments are beautifully decorated and painted and have delicately carved lat-ticework windows of red sandstone. It's one of the best palace museums in Rajasthan.

At the southern end of the fort, old cannons look out from the ramparts over the sheer drop to the old town beneath. There's no guard rail and you can clearly hear voices and city sounds carried up by the air currents from the houses far below. The views from these ramparts are nothing less than magical. From here, you can also see the many houses painted blue to distinguish them as those of Brahmins. The Chamunda Temple, dedi-cated to Durga, stands at this end of the fort.

The fort is open from 9 am to 5 pm and admission is Rs 20, or just Rs 3 if you only want to visit the ramparts. There's an addi-tional charge of Rs 20 to use a camera. The fee includes a guided tour by liveried atten-dants, but they generally expect a small tip at the end. A group of musicians usually sit outside the cafe near the museum entrance and strike up a merry Rajasthani number to herald your arrival – it helps set the mood for a visit to this superb fort and they, too, appre-ciate a tip.

Jaswant Thanda

This white marble memorial to Maharaja Jaswant Singh II is a short distance from the fort, just off the fort road. The cenotaph, built in 1899, was followed by the royal cremato-

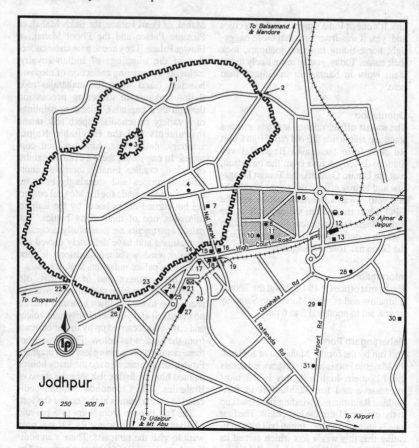

Jodhpur

0   250   500 m

To Balsamand & Mandore

To Chopasni

To Udaipur & Mt Abu

To Ajmer & Jaipur

To Airport

Nai Sarak

High Court Road

Gavghala Rd

Ratanada Rd

Airport Rd

---

rium and three later cenotaphs which stand nearby. Inside are portraits of the various Jodhpur rulers.

Clock Tower & Markets

The clock tower is a popular landmark in the old city. The colourful Sardar Market is close to the tower, and narrow alleys lead from here to bazaars selling textiles, silver and handicrafts.

Umaid Gardens & Museums

The Tourist Bungalow is on the edge of the Umaid Gardens on High Court Rd. The Government Museum, within the gardens, has a small and fairly uninteresting collection. There are lots of badly moth-eaten stuffed animals, including a number of almost featherless desert birds in two glass cases, each with a thorn bush. The military section includes cumbersome wooden biplane models and an extraordinary brass battleship. The museum is open daily, except Friday, from 10 am to 4.30 pm and admission is Rs 1. You can safely skip it.

The gardens also contain a zoo and a library.

■ PLACES TO STAY

7	Shree Laaxmi Hotel
11	Tourist Bureau & Ghoomar Tourist Bungalow
13	Hotel Akshey
15	Hotel Soner
16	Hotel Priya
18	Arun Hotel
19	Galaxy Hotel
25	Shanti Bhawan Lodge
29	Ajit Bhawan Hotel
30	Umaid Bhawan Palace Hotel

▼ PLACES TO EAT

17	Agra Sweet Home
24	Kalinga Restaurant

OTHER

1	Jaswant Thanda
2	Nagauri Gate
3	Fort Meherangarh & Museum
4	Sardar Market
5	State Bank of India
6	Bicycle Rental
8	Government Museum
9	Bus Stand
10	Zoo
12	Raika Bagh Railway Station
14	Sojati Gate
20	GPO
21	Railway Booking Office
22	Siwanchi Gate
23	Ranchodji Temple
26	Jalori Gate
27	Jodhpur Railway Station
28	Antique Shops
31	Indian Airlines

Umaid Bhawan Palace

Maharaja Umaid Singh, who died in 1947, initially lived in the Raika Bagh Palace but, in 1928, began building the Umaid Bhawan Palace on the outskirts of town. Constructed of marble and red sandstone, this immense palace is also known as the Chhittar Palace because of the local Chhittar sandstone used. It was designed by the president of the British Royal Institute of Architects and was not completed until 1943.

Probably the most surprising thing about this grandiose palace is that it was built so close to Independence. It seems to have escaped the attention of the maharaja and his British advisers that the upheavals of Independence were just around the corner, and that maharajas, princely states and the grand extravagances common to this class would soon be a thing of the past, or that works of a socially beneficial nature might have been more appropriate. Such considerations, however, seem rarely to have impinged on the consciences of rulers anywhere in the world. It has been suggested by some that the palace was built as some sort of royal job-creation programme!

Today, part of the palace has been turned into a hotel – and what a hotel! While it lacks the charm of Udaipur's palace hotels, it certainly makes up for it in spacious grandeur. Few who could afford it would miss the chance of staying here and the hotel corridors echo with languages from around the world. Unfortunately the palace is not open to nonresidents, unless you want to pay the visiting fee of Rs 120, although this is deductible from any food or drink you might purchase. A beer on the terrace overlooking the gardens is very pleasant, and the buffet meal in the grand dining room is well worth the Rs 320.

The maharaja still resides in another part of the palace, and yet another part has been turned into an excellent museum. On display here is an amazing array of items belonging to the maharaja – model aeroplanes, weapons, antique clocks and fob watches, priceless crockery, and hunting trophies – and there's even a private cinema! It's well worth a look, and is open daily from 10 am to 5 pm; entry is Rs 10 and tickets are sold in the gate house.

Organised Tours

The RTDC operates daily tours of Jodhpur from 9 am to 1 pm and 2 to 6 pm. These take in all the main sites including the Umaid Bhawan Palace, Meherangarh Fort, Jaswant Thanda, Mandore Gardens and the museum. The tours start from the Tourist Bungalow and cost Rs 30.

The Ajit Bhawan Hotel runs 'village

safaris', which are an ideal way to get out into the villages and see a bit of the local way of life – something that is not always easy to do in India. The cost is Rs 350 for a full day, including lunch, but as the trips don't run every day, ring in advance (☎ 20-409).

A private tour guide, the 60-year-old Mr N L Tak (☎ 30-637) has been recommended for day tours to local villages. It costs Rs 650 for up to five people and the trips last all day.

Places to Stay – bottom end

There's not a great deal of budget accommodation in Jodhpur and, unfortunately, the main budget hotel area around the railway station is extremely noisy, chock-a-block full of vehicles, dusty and polluted. Right opposite the railway station is the *Shanti Bhawan Lodge* (☎ 21-689). Singles/doubles with common bath cost Rs 35/65, rooms with attached bath and air-cooling are Rs 65/120. Next door, the *Charli Bikaner Lodge* (☎ 23-985) is similarly priced but scruffier.

There are better hotels near the Sojati Gate and the road which goes over the railway lines. Here, you'll find the *Hotel Soner* (☎ 25-732), which charges Rs 40/80 for rooms with common bath, and Rs 60/120 with attached bath. Hot water is available by bucket. The *Galaxy Hotel* (☎ 20-796) is by the railway bridge, and charges Rs 35/65 with common bath, Rs 50/80 with attached bath and Rs 105/200 with air-cooling. It's a popular place, although the front rooms can be noisy.

Along Nai Sarak towards the clock tower there's the *Shree Laaxmi Hotel* (☎ 22-047). This friendly little place has good clean rooms for Rs 60/100 with common bath, and Rs 120/150 with bath, and as a bonus, all rooms are air-cooled.

Most people stay at the *Ghoomar Tourist Bungalow* (☎ 44-010), High Court Rd. It has ordinary singles/doubles for Rs 120/150, air-cooled rooms for Rs 200/250 and air-con rooms for Rs 300/400. Dorm beds cost Rs 30. There's a bar and restaurant here, as well as the tourist office. It's a reasonably good place to stay and there's generally live folk music and dancing each evening between

6.30 and 7.30 pm, except Sundays, in the upstairs lounge (open to nonresidents). There's no charge for this, but the performers are paid so little that a tip is appreciated.

The *retiring rooms* at the railway station are good value at Rs 30 for a dormitory bed, and Rs 70 for a double, and all accommodation is air-cooled.

Places to Stay – middle

At the bottom end of this bracket is the modern and well-maintained *Hotel Akshey* (☎ 21-549), just behind Raika Bagh Palace Railway Station, and just five minutes walk from the bus station. All rooms are air-cooled, have attached bath and hot water, and checkout is based on the 24-hour system. The tariff is Rs 150/200 – a good place.

If you want to be close to the railway station a good choice is the *Adarsh Niwas Hotel*. The rooms have TV, phone and attached bath with hot water, and cost Rs 180/240 with air-cooling, and Rs 300/380 with air-con.

Moving up the scale there's the delightful *Ajit Bhawan Palace Hotel* (☎ 20-409) on Airport Rd, a very popular place to stay and great for a small splurge. The rooms actually consist of a series of 20 stone cottages arranged around a well-tended and very relaxing garden with fish-stocked pools. All the cottages are differently furnished in their own whimsical style but they're all equipped with very clean, modern bathrooms. It's a whole world away from the noise and pollution around the railway station. The cottages cost Rs 450/550, or there are suites for Rs 650/750. The Rs 65 buffet meals here are excellent. Rajasthani folk music and dancing is put on every evening between 6 and 8 pm and a skeleton band continues until late.

Places to Stay – top end

Jodhpur's finest hotel is the *Umaid Bhawan Palace* (☎ 22-316), the residence of the former Maharaja of Jodhpur. As the sales blurb says, 'To create luxury we did not change history'. They are not wrong! This has to be one of the world's most incredible hotels but, in comparison to what you would pay for something vaguely similar anywhere else in the world, it's an absolute bargain. It has everything from an indoor swimming pool to golf, badminton, tennis and croquet, a billiard room, endless manicured lawns, bars, a vast dining hall which would seat the entire United Nations Assembly, countless tigers' heads hanging from the walls and every conceivable service. Armies of cleaners keep every square inch squeaky clean and there are fine views across to the fort.

The rooms cost US$85/90, and suites range from US$200 to US$660 per night. If you can possibly afford it, opt for a suite, as the cheaper rooms are modern and while they are very comfortable and offer all the mod cons, they are hardly palatial.

The only other hotel in this category is the *Hotel Ratanada Polo Palace* (☎ 31-910), a new place on Residency Rd, some distance out towards the airport. Rooms cost Rs 1100/1200, and there's a 30% off-season discount.

Places to Eat

Surprisingly, one of the best places to eat is the veg/non-veg *refreshment room* on the 1st floor of the railway station. It's a cool and quiet haven, and the food is cheap and quite good. This place is thronged with travellers each evening, most of them catching the night train to Jaisalmer. It's open from 7 am to 10 pm.

The south Indian snacks cafe in *Shanti Bhawan Lodge* opposite the station is another place popular with travellers waiting for a train. Their vegie burgers are excellent, and the lassis enormous. The *Kalinga Restaurant* in the Adarsh Niwas Hotel next door has excellent non-vegetarian food, although it's not all that cheap at around Rs 30 to Rs 40 for vegetarian dishes and Rs 45 to Rs 60 for non-veg dishes.

Most people staying at the *Tourist Bungalow* eat in the restaurant there. The food is OK but nothing fantastic, the service is haphazard and arithmetic is not one of their strong points when it comes to preparing a bill.

While you're in Jodhpur, try makhania

lassi, a delicious saffron-flavoured variety of that most refreshing of drinks. The *Agra Sweet Home* opposite the Sojati Gate is so popular that in summer they claim to sell over 1500 glasses a day – at Rs 4.50 each. Other popular dessert specialties in Jodhpur include mawa ladoo and the baklava-like mawa kachori. Dhood fini is a cereal dish consisting of fine threads of wheat in a bowl with milk and sugar.

There are essentially only two places to go for a splurge and you should make sure that you go to one or the other whilst you're in Jodhpur, if only for the experience and the live music and dance which each present. The cheaper of the two is the *Ajit Bhawan Palace Hotel* where a fixed-price smorgasbord dinner in the main courtyard costs Rs 65, plus tax. The food is excellent and comes complete with a bonfire, as well as Rajasthani folk music and dances. Nonresidents should book in advance, though it's not always necessary.

More expensive of the two is the *Umaid Bhawan Palace*. A meal here is better described as a memorable banquet because it's served in what has to be the largest of the palace's halls and is accompanied by a live sitar, sarod and tabla recital. The food is superb and the range of dishes endless. At Rs 320 this buffet is quite good value – try to make it here at least once. Advance booking is not necessary as a rule, but it's a good idea to check beforehand in the high season. The Umaid Bhawan Palace also organises evening meals at the fort, with absolutely everything laid on – unforgettable and expensive (US$50!). These only take place when demand warrants it, so phone ahead (☎ 22-316).

Things to Buy

The usual Rajasthani handicrafts are available here, but Jodhpur specialises in antiques. The greatest concentration of antique shops is along the road connecting the Ajit Bhawan with the Umaid Bhawan and the well-known Abani Handicrafts is next to the Tourist Bungalow. However, the existence of these shops is well known to Western antique dealers who come here with suitcases full of money and wallets stuffed with plastic cards. As a result, you'll be hard pressed to find any bargains, though this is no reflection on the generally excellent quality of the goods available.

Certain restrictions apply to the exportation from India of items over 100 years old – see the section under Things to Buy in the Facts for the Visitor chapter for more details.

Getting There & Away

Air The Indian Airlines office (☎ 28-600) is south of the centre on Airport Rd, and is open daily from 10 am to 1.15 pm and 2 to 4.30 pm.

Indian Airlines flies twice daily to Delhi (US$56), Jaipur (US$34), Udaipur (US$28) and Bombay (US$87), and four times a week to Aurangabad (US$78).

Bus State transport buses (from the State Roadways bus stand at Raika Bagh) and private luxury buses connect Jodhpur with other cities and places of interest in Rajasthan.

The best bus to Jaisalmer is the daily super deluxe which departs from the Ghoomar Tourist Bungalow at 6 am and arrives in Jaisalmer five hours later. The fare is Rs 65. The cheaper buses from the State Roadways bus stand take up to 10 hours. The private buses to Jaisalmer only run during the off-season months.

Buses to Udaipur take eight to 10 hours and are much faster than the train. The fare is Rs 56 to Rs 63, depending on the bus. The six-hour trip across the desert to Bikaner costs Rs 51. Buses to Ajmer go hourly, take 4½ hours and cost Rs 50. The fastest state transport buses to Mt Abu leave from the bus stand at 6.30 am and 6 pm, take six hours and cost Rs 52. Private luxury buses are also available.

Train The railways booking office is on Station Rd, between the railway station and Sojati Gate. As only three windows deal with computerised reservations, it can take up to half an hour before you are served. Demand for tickets is heavy, so it pays to come here soon after you arrive, especially if you want to catch the night train to Jaisalmer on the same evening.

The office is open from 8 am to 1.45 pm and 2 to 8 pm Monday to Saturday, and to 1.45 pm on Sunday.

Tourist quota tickets are issued at the International Tourists Bureau at the railway station. This office (Room 5, 1st floor) was set up largely to provide help for foreign railway passengers. It makes an excellent base if you just want to visit Jodhpur for the day and catch the night train to Jaisalmer, as there are comfortable armchairs, and a shower and toilet. Unattended luggage must be deposited in the railway station cloak room, however.

Many people take the night train to Jaisalmer; so many, in fact, that it became a happy hunting ground for petty thieves and other characters of dubious ilk. In the high season, all foreigners are booked into the same carriages, and each carriage has a policeman stationed on it for the first part of the journey. There are both overnight and day trains to Jaisalmer, both taking around nine hours. The 295-km journey costs Rs 57/218 in 2nd/1st class.

There are superfast expresses between Delhi and Jodhpur (12 hours) and Ahmedabad and Jodhpur (nine hours). Fares for the 626-km trip from Delhi are Rs 108/397 in 2nd/1st class. There's also a daily train to Agra Fort, but it can get horrendously crowded. The 439-km trip takes an agonising 22 hours.

To Udaipur there's a nightly train which takes 10½ hours to cover the 113 km at a cost of Rs 27/104 in 2nd/1st class. For Barmer in the west of the state the daily train takes 5½ hours and costs Rs 31/118 in 2nd/1st class.

Not many people make the trip from Delhi straight through; most take the train from Jaipur, which takes eight hours to Jodhpur. The 318-km trip costs Rs 64/228 in 2nd/1st class.

Getting Around

To/From the Airport The airport is only five km from the centre. It costs about Rs 15 in an auto-rickshaw, but drivers often demand more. A taxi costs around Rs 40.

Bus There are regular city buses to places around Jodhpur like Mandore, Balsamand and Mahamandir.

Taxi & Auto-Rickshaw Jodhpur has unmetered taxis and allegedly metered auto-rickshaws as well as tongas. Auto-rickshaw drivers are rapacious, particularly if they pick you up from outside the Ajit Bhawan Palace Hotel or the Umaid Bhawan Palace. Quite rightly, they assume that if you can afford to stay or eat at either place, you're not short of money. You'd have difficulty getting through the narrow lanes of the old city in anything wider than an auto-rickshaw.

Bicycle Jodhpur is a good place to explore by bicycle. They can be rented from several places, including one right next to the Charli Bikaner Lodge opposite the main railway station. Expect to pay Rs 12 per day.

AROUND JODHPUR

Maha Mandir

The Great Temple is a small walled town north-east of the city. It is built around a 100-pillared Siva temple but is not of great interest.

Balsamand Lake & Palace

Originally constructed in 1159, this lake and garden are to the north of the city. A palace, built in 1936, stands by the lakeside. This is a popular excursion spot and the gardens are open from 8 am to 6 pm.

West of Jodhpur, the larger Pratap Sagar and Kailana Sagar (where there is also a garden) provide the city's water supply.

Mandore

Further north, Mandore was the capital of Marwar prior to the foundation of Jodhpur. Today, its extensive gardens with high rock terraces make it a popular local attraction. The gardens also contain the cenotaphs of Jodhpur rulers, including Maharaja Jaswant Singh and, largest and finest of all, the soaring temple-shaped memorial to Maharaja Ajit Singh.

The Hall of Heroes contains 15 figures carved out of a rock wall. The brightly painted figures represent Hindu deities or local heroes on horseback. The Shrine of 33 Crore (330 million) Gods is painted with figures of gods, spirits and divinities. Regular buses run to Mandore from Jodhpur.

Osian

The ancient Thar Desert town of Osian, 55 km from Jodhpur, was a great trading centre between the 8th and 12th centuries when it was dominated by the Jains. Today, it's a desert oasis with numerous peacocks. The wealth of Osian's medieval inhabitants allowed them to build lavish and beautifully sculpted temples, most of which have withstood the ravages of time. The largest of the 16 Jain and Brahmanical temples is dedicated to Mahavira, the last of the Jain tirthankars. The sculptural detail on the Osian temples rivals that of the Hoysala temples of Karnataka and the Sun Temple of Konark in Orissa; so, if you have the time, make the effort to visit this place.

The rickshaw-driver seemed to know very few English words but we managed to negotiate a price for the ride up to the fort (in Jodhpur). We set off and tried to make polite conversation with simple phrases. The driver didn't seem to be able to reply so we soon gave up. However, when we arrived, he turned to us and said, in perfect English: 'Excuse me, kind sirs. Pray tell me what country is being made anxious by your absence'. We were left speechless!

Chris Jenney (UK)

Getting There & Away About six buses a day make the two-hour trip from Jodhpur.

Nagaur

Nagaur has a historic fort and palace and also sports a smaller version of Pushkar's cattle and camel fair. The week-long fair takes place in late January or early February and attracts thousands of rural people from far and wide. As at Pushkar, the fair includes camel races and various cultural entertainment programmes. There is very little in the way of accommodation here, however.

Sardar Samand Lake

The route to this wildlife centre passes through a number of colourful villages. The maharaja's summer palace is here and accommodation can be arranged.

Dhawa, or Doli, is another wildlife sanctuary with many antelope, 45 km from Jodhpur on the road to Barmer.

JAISALMER

Population: 39,000

Nothing else in India is remotely similar to Jaisalmer. Jodhpur certainly has one of the country's most spectacular fortress-palace complexes and both Chittorgarh and Kumbhalgarh far surpass Jaisalmer in fame and sheer size. Yet this desert fortress is straight out of the *Tales of the Arabian Nights* and you could easily be forgiven for imagining that you'd somehow been transported back to medieval Afghanistan. This magic, incomparably romantic and totally unspoiled city has been dubbed the 'Golden City' because of the colour imparted to its stone ramparts by the setting sun. Jaisalmer is all of this and much more besides. No-one who makes the effort to get to this remote outpost leaves disappointed.

Centuries ago, Jaisalmer's strategic position on the camel train routes between India and central Asia brought it great wealth. The merchants and townspeople built magnificent houses and mansions, all exquisitely carved from wood and from golden-yellow sandstone. These havelis can be found elsewhere in Rajasthan but nowhere are they

quite as exotic as in Jaisalmer. Even the humblest shops and houses display something of the Rajput love of the decorative arts in its most whimsical form. It's likely to remain that way, too, for a long time to come since the city fathers are keen to ensure that all new buildings blend in with the old.

The rise of shipping trade and the port of Bombay saw the decline of Jaisalmer. At Independence, Partition and the cutting of the trade routes through to Pakistan seemingly sealed the town's fate, and water shortages could have pronounced the death sentence. However, the 1965 and 1971 Indo-Pakistan wars revealed Jaisalmer's strategic importance, and the Rajasthan Canal, to the north, is beginning to restore life to the desert. Paved roads and a railway link it to the rest of Rajasthan.

Today, tourism will soon rival military bases as the pillar of the city's economy. The military bases hardly impinge at all on the life of the old city and only the occasional sound of war planes landing or taking off in the distance ever disturbs the tranquillity of this desert gem.

It's not always been so peaceful, of course, since fortresses have rarely been constructed for aesthetic reasons and medieval desert chieftains were not known for their pacific temperaments. Chivalric rivalry and ferocity between the various Rajput clans were the order of the day and the Bhatti Rajputs of Jaisalmer were regarded as a formidable force throughout the region. While Jaisalmer largely escaped direct conquest by the Muslim rulers of Delhi, it did experience its share of sieges and sackings with the inevitable jauhar being declared in the face of inevitable defeat. There is perhaps no Rajasthani city in which you can more easily conjure up the spirit of those times.

Orientation & Information

Finding your way around Jaisalmer is not really necessary – it's a place to simply wander around and get lost. The streets within the old city walls are a tangled maze, but it's small enough not to matter. You simply head off in what seems like the right direction and you'll get somewhere eventually.

The old city was once completely surrounded by an extensive wall, much of which has sadly been torn down for building material in recent years. Much remains, however, including the city gates and, inside them, the massive fort which rises above the city and is the essence of Jaisalmer. The fort itself is a warren of narrow, paved streets complete with Jain temples and the old palace of the former ruler, still flying his standard.

The central market area is directly below the hill, while the banks, the new palace and several other shops and offices are near the Amar Sagar Gate to the west. Continue outside the walled city in this direction and you'll soon come to the Tourist Bungalow, which also houses the tourist office (☎ 2406). The tourist office is open Monday to Saturday from 8 am to noon and 3 to 6 pm.

The State Bank of India, not far from the Amar Sagar Gate, will not change travellers' cheques. This can be done at the Bank of Baroda, closer to the same gate.

The bus and railway stations are outside the walls to the south-east, while the taxi stand is at the roundabout not far from the Amar Sagar Gate.

The booklet *Jaisalmer – the Golden City* by N K Sharma (Rs 15) is worth buying if you want to read more about the city. It's available from bookshops in the old city and inside the fort.

The hospital here is a nightmare – it's dirty, overcrowded, there's often no running water and the staff are overworked – avoid it if at all possible.

Jaisalmer's telephone area code is 02992.

Havelis

The beautiful mansions built by the wealthy merchants of Jaisalmer are known as havelis, and several of these fine sandstone buildings are still in beautiful condition.

There are no entry fees to the havelis, but they are keen to get you to buy stone carvings and the like – there's some beautiful material to choose from. The havelis are open between 10.30 am and 5 pm.

Patwon ki Haveli This most elaborate and magnificent of all the Jaisalmer havelis stands in a narrow lane. One of its apartments is painted with beautiful murals. You can go inside the mansion and there is a fine view from the roof.

Salim Singh ki Haveli This haveli was built about 300 years ago and part of it is still occupied. Salim Singh was the prime minister when Jaisalmer was the capital of a princely state, and his mansion has a beautifully arched roof with superb carved brackets in the form of peacocks. The mansion is just below the hill and, it is said, once had two additional wooden storeys in an attempt to make it as high as the maharaja's palace. The maharaja had the upper storeys of the prime minister's haveli torn down!

Nathmal ki Haveli This late 19th-century haveli was also a prime minister's house. The left and right wings of the building were carved by brothers and are very similar, but not identical. Yellow sandstone elephants guard the building, and even the front door is a work of art.

Gadi Sagar Tank

This tank, south of the city walls, was once the water supply of the city and there are many small temples and shrines around it. A wide variety of water birds flock here in winter.

The beautiful gateway which arches across the road down to the tank is said to have been built by a famous prostitute. When she offered to pay to have this gateway constructed, the maharaja refused permission on the grounds that he would have to pass under it on going down to the tank, and he felt that this would be unseemly. While he was away, she built the gate anyway, adding a Krishna temple on top so the king could not tear it down.

Fort

Built in 1156 by Rawal Jaisal, the fort crowns the 80-metre-high Trikuta Hill. About a

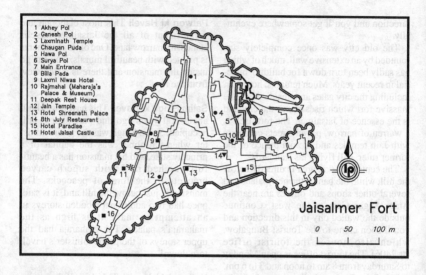

1 Akhey Pol
2 Ganesh Pol
3 Laxminath Temple
4 Chaugan Puda
5 Hawa Pol
6 Surya Pol
7 Main Entrance
8 Billa Pada
9 Laxmi Niwas Hotel
10 Rajmahal (Maharaja's Palace & Museum)
11 Deepak Rest House
12 Jain Temple
13 Hotel Shreenath Palace
14 8th July Restaurant
15 Hotel Paradise
16 Hotel Jalsal Castle

Jaisalmer Fort

0   50   100 m

quarter of the old city's population resides within the fort walls, which have 99 bastions around their circumference. It's fascinating to wander around this place. Nothing has changed here for centuries and if ever an effort were made to pack as many houses, temples and palaces into the smallest possible area, this would be the result. It's honeycombed with narrow, winding lanes, all of them paved in stone and with a remarkably efficient drainage system which keeps them free of excrement and effluent. It's also quiet – vehicles are not allowed up here and even building materials have to be carried up by camel cart. The fort walls provide superb views over the old city and surrounding desert. Strolling around the outer fort ramparts at sunset is a popular activity, but be warned that the entire outer rampart is used as a public toilet, so watch your step!

The fort is entered through a forbidding series of massive gates leading to a large courtyard. The former maharaja's seven-storey palace fronts onto this. The square was formerly used to review troops, hear petitions and present extravagant entertainment for important visitors. Part of the palace is open to the public, but there's little to see

inside; although one room has some beautiful murals. Opening hours are 8 am to 1 pm and 3 to 5 pm; entry is Rs 5.

Jain Temples Within the fort walls are a group of beautifully carved Jain temples built between the 12th and 15th centuries. They are dedicated to Rikhabdevji and Sambhavanthji.

The Gyan Bhandar, a library containing some extremely old manuscripts, is also in the temple complex. The temples are only open in the morning until 12 noon and the library only opens between 10 and 11 am. There are also Siva and Ganesh temples within the fort.

Organised Tours

Few travellers visit Jaisalmer without taking a camel safari into the desert. For details, see the comments under Places to Stay (below), and the info on Camel Safaris in the Around Jaisalmer section.

Festivals

The annual Desert Festival is supposed to have camel races and dances, folk music, desert ballads and puppeteers, but it seems to have quickly become a purely commercial tourist trap. The state Tourist Development Corporation sets up a special 'Tourist Village' at this time, similar to the one in Pushkar. The festival takes place between late January and mid-February, depending on the lunar calendar. Make enquiries at a tourist office for the exact dates.

Places to Stay

Jaisalmer is a very popular place, and many hotels, both cheap and not so cheap, have sprung up to meet the demand. More than anywhere else, the thing you'll notice on arrival, whether by bus or train, is the number of touts who swarm around, trying to grab the new arrivals. Unfortunately some of them are less than honest about the service they provide – don't believe *anyone* who offers to take you 'anywhere you like' for Rs 1, and take with a grain of salt claims that the hotel you want to stay in is 'full', 'closed', 'no good anymore' or has suffered some other inglorious fate. They'll only lead you to a succession of hotels, where of course they get commission if you stay. If, after being carted from one hotel to another, you still insist on staying where *you* want and not where *they* want, you'll be dropped unceremoniously outside the main fort gate, from where you'll have to walk to the hotel of your choice. If you have made no decision about where to stay and just want a lift into the centre, then these people may be of use, but just be prepared for the roundabout tour and pressure to stay in a particular place.

Many of the popular budget hotels send their own vehicles to meet the bus or train. They display their own sign and offer free transport; otherwise you can take an auto-rickshaw. The touting situation has reached such drastic proportions that the district magistrate has set up a Tourist Protection Squad. The aim of this squad is to keep the touts at a distance, so that travellers can at least gather their wits and baggage in peace before running the gauntlet. Their aims are very laudable – it's just a pity they are totally ineffective; the cynical might even say they work in collusion with the touts.

Unfortunately quite a few of the cheap places are really into the high-pressure selling of camel safaris. Some places can get quite ugly if you book a safari through someone else. Not only will they refuse to hold your baggage, but in many cases they'll actually evict you from the hotel!

Staying at one of the hotels within the fort itself is the most imaginative choice, but don't take this to imply that there aren't equally good hotels outside the fort walls. Jaisalmer is also one of those places where travellers fervently defend their choice of hotel over all others, so this selection will undoubtedly create controversy.

As is so often the case in Rajasthani towns, if there's a festival on, prices skyrocket and accommodation of any kind can be hard to get.

Places to Stay – bottom end

There's a good choice of budget hotels in the streets around the Amar Sagar Gate. The popular *Hotel Swastika* (☎ 2483), Chainpura St, is very well kept and has friendly staff and great views from the roof. Dorm beds are Rs 20, singles/doubles cost Rs 40/60 and rooms with bath are Rs 80 to Rs 100. Bucket hot water is available.

The *Hotel Renuka* (☎ 2757), a little further up the same street, is equally good and very pleasant. It's run by an exceptionally friendly family and, like the Swastika, has great rooftop views. It offers dorm beds at Rs 15, singles/doubles at Rs 30/40 with common bath, and doubles with bath for Rs 80.

Another reasonable alternative is the *Hotel Pleasure* (☎ 2323) on the next street over. It's very small and exceptionally clean, but the rooms are small and many have no windows. The charge is Rs 30/40, all with common bath. Also here is the *Hotel Pushkar Palace*, but at Rs 50 for small rooms with common bath, it's not great value.

Across the other side of the old town is another group of budget hotels, close to the entrance to the fort. By far the most popular is the *Fort View Hotel*, mainly because of the fine views from the roof and some rooms.

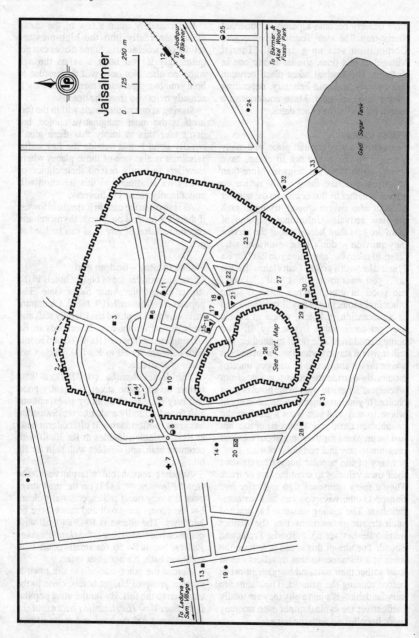

Jaisalmer

0   125   250 m

To Jodhpur & Bikaner

To Barmer & Akal Wood Fossil Park

Gadi Sagar Tank

See Fort Map

To Leduva & Sam Village

- **PLACES TO STAY**

3   Naryan Niwas Palace Hotel &
    Shri Naryan Vilas Hotel
4   Hotels Swastika, Renuka, Pleasure &
    Pushkar Palace
6   Hotel Rajdhani
10 Hotel Jaisal Palace
13 Tourist Bungalow &
    Tourist Office
15 Shree Giriraj Palace Hotel
17 Fort View & Flamingo Hotels
23 Hotel Pooja
27 Hotels Madhuvan & Anurag
28 Hotel Neeraj
29 Hotel Tourist
30 Hotel Rama

▼   **PLACES TO EAT**

9   Trio Restaurant, Skyroom Restaurant
    & Bank of Baroda
16 8th July Restaurant

21 Monica Restaurant
22 Seema & Moti Mahal Restaurants

OTHER

1   Chhatris & Sunset Point
2   City View & Sunset Point
5   Amar Sagar Gate
7   Hospital
8   Bus Stand
11 Patwon ki Haveli
12 Jaisalmer Railway Station
14 Police Station
18 Salim Singh ki Haveli &
    Natraj Restaurant
19 Museum
20 Post Office
24 Petrol Pump
25 Main Bus Station
26 Fort
31 Petrol Pump
32 Gadi Sagar Pol
33 Tilon Ki Pol

There are dorm beds for Rs 11, doubles with bath on the lower floors for Rs 44 to Rs 55 and doubles on the top floor for Rs 66 and Rs 88. Bucket hot water is available. There's also a couple of rooms with fort view and geyser, and these cost Rs 120 and Rs 150. This is one of the few budget hotels which actually has a restaurant – it has great views of the fort and overlooks the small square below. You can change money, make long-distance and ISD calls and arrange air, rail and bus tickets here. The *Hotel Flamingo* next door has just a few cheap rooms. It's very basic but popular.

Also in this area is the *Shree Giriraj Palace Hotel*. It's in an old haveli, so has heaps of character – and chronic plumbing problems. However, it's a friendly place and is clean enough. The rooms are odd shapes and sizes, and cost Rs 40 with common bath, and Rs 60 with attached bath. The *Hotel Sunil, Bhatia Rest House, Hotel Sri Lekha* and the *New Tourist Hotel* are nearby.

Further away from this area, to the south and south-east of the fort and quite a walk from the bazaar, you'll find several other places, some of which are popular. The *Hotel*

Madhuvan has rooms at Rs 50 with common bath and Rs 70 with attached bath. The *Hotel Anurag* (☎ 2596) next door is similar.

The *Hotel Pooja* (☎ 2608) is a small and friendly place, not far from Gadi Sagar Pol. It's in an old house, and rooms are Rs 35/60 with common bath, or there's just one double with bath for Rs 90.

The cheapest budget hotel within the fort itself is the *Deepak Rest House*. It's actually part of the fort wall and offers stunning views from its rooftops. The hotel is very quiet and well run. It has a total of 14 rooms, six with bath and eight with common bath. Room No 9 is the best one since it has its own balcony (the top of one of the bastions). Next best is room No 8. Both of these rooms cost Rs 80 a double. Other doubles are upwards of Rs 50. There are also singles for Rs 30 and Rs 40 and a dorm for Rs 15, or you can sleep on the roof for Rs 10. The cheaper rooms are somewhat cell-like and have no views. Hot water is available round the clock at no extra charge. To find this place, keep your eyes skinned for a tiny sign on the main alley and then go under an archway.

Of a similar standard, and equally hard to

find, is the *Hotel Laxmi Niwas*. If anything it's even smaller, and rooms cost Rs 50/80, or you can sleep on the roof for Rs 20. It's a great little place with plenty of atmosphere, and is often full.

Also in the fort, and of a much better standard, is the relatively new *Hotel Paradise* (☎ 2674). You'll see it on the far side of the main square from the palace as you come through the last gate into the fort. It's a kind of haveli, with 18 rooms arranged around a leafy courtyard and excellent views from the roof. It has just a couple of cheaper rooms (usually full) at Rs 60 with common bath; the rest cost from Rs 120 to Rs 300, depending on size and views.

At the top of this bracket is the modern *Hotel Rajdhani* (☎ 2746), not far from the Patwon ki Haveli. It's the cheapest place with a hot shower, and the rooms are clean and comfortable. Rooms with common bath cost Rs 60/80, doubles with bath and bucket hot water are Rs 100, or rooms with bath and hot water go for Rs 150/200. It's friendly, good value and the views from the roof are excellent.

Places to Stay – middle

The *Hotel Jaisal Castle* (☎ 2362) is a restored haveli in the south-west corner of the fort. It has superb views of Jaisalmer and would without doubt be the best place in town were it not for the attitude of the staff – indifference and outright surliness are the order of the day. If you can put up with this, it will cost you Rs 300/400 for a tastefully decorated single/double room with attached bath. It's not well signposted, but entry is through a large wooden doorway in front of a small courtyard at the far side of the fort.

A better bet in the fort is the *Hotel Shreenath Palace*, which is a haveli. In this one the family still lives on the ground floor, while upstairs there are four big guest rooms. Don't expect too many modern facilities here, as this place is totally authentic. Rooms cost Rs 200/250 with common bath and bucket shower, and breakfast is available.

Down in the Amar Sagar Gate area, the *Hotel Jaisal Palace* (☎ 2717) is not a bad

choice. There's a range of rooms, from Rs 100/150 with no window, to Rs 200/250 with a window. All rooms have attached bath and constant hot water. They also have a number of cheaper rooms in a separate building, but these are definitely not as good.

The RTDC *Moomal Tourist Bungalow* (☎ 2392) is reasonable value, although it's out of the walled city and is pretty deadly dull. Dorm beds cost Rs 30, while ordinary single/double rooms are Rs 150/200, air-cooled rooms are Rs 250/300 and rooms with air-con go for Rs 400/450. Off-season rates are offered between April and August. There's a reasonable restaurant, and a bar that gets quite lively at times.

The only other hotel in this category is the *Hotel Neeraj* (☎ 2442), which offers singles/doubles with bath and hot water for Rs 270/330. The hotel is often used by overland tour groups, but it's pretty characterless and poor value. It's also inconveniently located and is a long walk from anywhere else.

Places to Stay – top end

There are only two top-end hotels in Jaisalmer. The better of the two is the *Narayan Niwas Palace* (☎ 2408), on the hill at the back of the old town. Beautifully designed to simulate the atmosphere of a Rajput ruler's desert camp, it's festooned with local crafts and *objets d'art*. It's very pleasant and well run, and rooms cost Rs 650/900, or Rs 850/1100 with air-con. Meals are available and local musicians play in the courtyard while dinner is served.

Next door, the much smaller *Sri Narayan Vilas* (☎ 2283) has tried to capture the same atmosphere, with mixed success. It is, however, significantly cheaper at Rs 375/450, although the rooms vary widely – try to see at least a couple before deciding.

Places to Eat

Like all travellers' centres, Jaisalmer sports a clutch of budget restaurants/juice bars which seem to attract their own cliques of long-time stayers. All the usual travellers' favourites are offered – muesli, pancakes, spaghetti, juices and lassis – and most places do a pretty good job.

One of the most popular places is the restaurant on the top floor of the *Fort View Hotel*. The food is the same as you'll find anywhere, but the views across to the fort in the early morning are excellent. Although there is shade, it gets pretty hot up here in the afternoons.

Another good place is the *Monica Restaurant*, not far from the Fort View. It is an open-air place popular in the early mornings and evenings.

In a small lane behind the Fort View is the diminutive *Kanchan Shree Restaurant*, which is popular for its 18 varieties of lassi – the chocolate banana ones are positively addictive!

For a meal with a view of something different, try the *Natraj Restaurant*, just down the hill from the Monica. The open-air top floor has an excellent view of the upper part of the Salim Singh ki Haveli next door, and away to the south of town. The Natraj is a little more upmarket than the average places, but the food is good and the prices still reasonable.

Also a little more upmarket is the *8th July Restaurant*, which has two branches, one on the main street, and another on the square up in the fort. The latter is an excellent place to sit and watch the world go by – and the apple pie is worth it too!

Down near the Amar Sagar Gate there's a couple of very good restaurants. The *Trio* is one of Jaisalmer's longest running, and also one of the best. Although it's not all that cheap, the atmosphere is elegant, musicians play in the evenings, and they have their own generator for when the power fails – which is often in this desert town. Western dishes are in the Rs 30 to Rs 50 range, while Indian vegetarian dishes typically cost between Rs 15 and Rs 30.

Close by is the *Skyroom Restaurant*, on the top floor of an old haveli, above the State Bank of India. The menu features Indian, Continental and Chinese dishes, and main courses are in the Rs 20 to Rs 35 range. Live music is also a feature here.

Things to Buy

Jaisalmer is famous for embroidery, Rajasthani mirrorwork, rugs, blankets, old stonework and antiques. Tie-dye and other fabrics are made at the Kadi Bundar, north of the city.

Getting There & Away

Air There are no longer any flights into Jaisalmer, but this may change, so make enquiries locally.

Bus The main bus station is some distance from the centre of town, near the railway station. Fortunately, all buses start from the traffic roundabout just outside Amar Sagar Gate, and then call at the main station. Reservations are only needed on the night buses, and these should be made at the main bus station.

There are eight daily STC buses on the route to Jodhpur, the deluxe one leaving at 5 pm. For Bikaner there are departures at 6 (deluxe) and 11 am, and 8 and 9.30 pm. The trip takes eight hours and costs Rs 69.

Every day there are five state transport buses each way between Jaisalmer and Barmer. They take around four hours and cost Rs 30.

Private buses only run to Jaisalmer in the off season.

Train At the railway station there's an International Tourists Bureau, similar to the one at Jodhpur. It has comfortable armchairs, and a toilet and shower for use by rail patrons. The reservations office at the station is only open from 8 to 11 am, 2 to 4 pm and in the chaotic period just before departure.

There's a day and a night train in either direction between Jodhpur and Jaisalmer. The 295-km trip takes around nine hours; fares are Rs 57/218 in 2nd/1st class.

Getting Around

Unmetered taxis, auto-rickshaws and jeeps are available. From the railway station, expect to pay Rs 15 to the Tourist Bungalow and less to the old town.

Quite a few of the hotels provide their own

transport from the station which is free if you're going to stay there. Those hotels which own jeeps generally also hire them out for visits to the surrounding area. A visit to the sand dunes at Sam, for instance, is about Rs 80 per person.

The best way to get quickly around Jaisalmer itself is to hire a bicycle. There are a number of hire places, including one in Gandhi Chowk just inside Amar Sagar Gate, and another just outside the main gate of the fort.

AROUND JAISALMER

There are some fascinating places to see in the area around Jaisalmer, although it soon fades out into a barren sand-duned desert which stretches across the lonely border into Pakistan.

Camel Safaris

The most interesting means of exploring the desert around Jaisalmer is on a camel safari and virtually everyone who comes here goes on one of them. Indeed, you can hardly avoid doing so, especially if you stay at a budget hotel, since the managers will hassle you until you agree to book with them. Naturally, they all offer *the best* safari and spare no invective in pouring scorn on their rivals' safaris.

The truth is more mundane. None of the hotels have their own camels – these are all independently owned – so the hoteliers and the travel agents are just go-betweens, though the hotels often organise the food and drink supplies. In addition, there's a lot of cut-throat competition to offer the cheapest safaris and this has resulted in many complaints when promises have been made and not kept.

Everyone has a different tale to tell, so you need to consider a few things before jumping at what appears to be a bargain. Hotel owners typically pay the camel drivers Rs 60 per camel per day to hire them so, if you're offered a safari at Rs 100 per day, this leaves only a small margin for food and the agent's profit. It's obvious that you can't possibly expect three reasonable meals a day on these

margins, but this is frequently what is promised. As a result, a lot of travellers feel they've been ripped-off when the food doesn't eventuate. It's a moot point which of the parties ought to shoulder the responsibility for this – is it the agents who make impossible promises or the travellers who have unrealistic expectations?

The minimum price for a basic safari is Rs 150 per person per day. For this you can expect a breakfast of porridge, tea and toast, and lunch and dinner of rice, dhal and chapatis – pretty unexciting stuff. Blankets are also supplied. For Rs 250 you should also get fruit, mineral water and some relief from the rice-dhal-chapati tedium. Of course you can pay still more for greater levels of comfort – tents, stretcher beds, better food, beer, etc – and the sky is pretty much the limit.

However much you decide to spend, make sure you know exactly what is being provided and make sure it's there before you leave Jaisalmer. You should also make sure you know where they're going to take you. Attempting to get a refund on your return for services not provided is a waste of time. Try to talk to other travellers for feedback on who is currently offering good, reliable and honest service.

Most safaris last three to four days and, if you want to get to the most interesting places, this is a bare minimum. Bring something very comfortable to sit on – many travellers neglect to do this and come back with very sore legs and/or backsides! A wide-brimmed hat (or Rajput-style turban), sun cream and a personal water bottle are also essential. October to February is the best time for a safari.

The usual circuit takes in such places as Amar Sagar, Ludharva, Mool Sagar, Bada Bagh and Sam, as well as various abandoned villages along the way. Usually it's one person per camel, but check this when booking. The reins are fastened to the camel's nose peg, so the animals are easily steered. At resting points, the camels are completely unsaddled and hobbled. They limp away to browse on nearby shrubs while the cameleers brew sweet chai or prepare food. The whole crew rests in the shade of thorn trees by a tank or well.

It's a great way to see the desert, which is surprisingly well populated and sprinkled with ruins. You constantly come across tiny fields of millet, girls picking berries or boys herding flocks of sheep or goats. The latter are always fitted with tinkling neckbells and, in the desert silence, it's music to the ears. Camping out at night in the Sam sand dunes, huddling around a tiny fire beneath the stars and listening to the camel drivers' yarns can be quite romantic. The camel drivers will expect a tip or gift at the end of the trip. Don't neglect to do this.

If you don't have the time, money or inclination to do an extended safari, there are any number of shorter options available. One currently in favour is a 2½-day trip which involves transport out to Sam by jeep, the return journey being made by camel. The cost of a trip like this is around Rs 430 per person. For those with even less time, a one-day, half-jeep/half-camel safari costs around Rs 180 per person. On any of these trips which include jeep transport try to establish how many people will be in the group, and therefore how crowded the jeep will be. I've seen jeeps heading out of Jaisalmer loaded to the eyeballs with 10 travellers, a driver, a couple of camel drivers, *plus* bedding and provisions for all these people! Five travellers plus drivers and gear is a safer and more comfortable number.

Due to the troubles in Punjab and alleged arms smuggling across the border from Pakistan, most of Rajasthan west of National Highway No 15 is a Restricted Area. Special permission is required from the Collector's office in Jaisalmer if you want to go there, and this is only issued in exceptional circumstances. The only places exempted are Amar Sagar, Bada Bagh, Lodhruva, Kuldhara, Akal, Sam, Ramkunda, Khuri and Mool Sagar.

Bada Bagh & Cenotaphs

Only a km or so north of Jaisalmer, Bada Bagh is a fertile oasis with a huge old dam. Much of the city's fruit and vegetables are grown here and carried into the town each day by colourfully dressed women.

Above the gardens are royal cenotaphs with beautifully carved ceilings and equestrian statues of former rulers. In the early evening, this is a popular place to watch the setting sun turn Jaisalmer a beautiful golden brown.

Amar Sagar

North-west of Jaisalmer, this once pleasant formal garden has now fallen into ruins. The lake here dries up several months into the dry season.

A beautifully carved Jain temple is being painstakingly restored by craftspeople brought in from Agra. Commenced in the late '70s, this monumental task is expected to take many years.

Lodhruva

Further out beyond Amar Sagar, 15 km from Jaisalmer, are the deserted ruins of this town which was the ancient capital before the move to Jaisalmer. The **Jain temples**, rebuilt in the late '70s, are the only reminders of the city's former magnificence. The temples have ornate carved arches at the entrance and a **Kalputra**, the Divine-Tree, within. In the temple is a hole from which a snake is said to emerge every evening to drink an offering of milk. Only the 'lucky' can see it.

At the same time that they rebuilt the temples, Jain benefactors had the road out from Jaisalmer sealed, but it deteriorates into a desert track immediately beyond Lodhruva.

Mool Sagar

Nine km directly west of Jaisalmer, this is another pleasant, small garden and tank. Continuing in this direction you reach the Sam sand dunes, about 40 km from the town. This is the nearest real Sahara-like desert to Jaisalmer.

Khuri

Khuri is a village 40 km south-west of Jaisalmer, out in the desert, in the touchy area near the Pakistan border. It's a delightfully peaceful place with houses of mud and straw decorated like the patterns on Persian carpets.

As it's right on the 40-km limit from Jaisalmer, permits must be obtained from the Chief Magistrate's office, opposite the hospital, before setting out.

There are infrequent buses between Jaisalmer and Khuri, and the trip takes 2½ hours.

Places to Stay Mr Singh owns the only hotel in town, which is basic and costs Rs 110 per day, including all the food you like. You sleep on cane beds in mud huts. Camel treks can also be arranged for Rs 150 per day.

Other Places

Three km off the road to Barmer, at a point 14 km from Jaisalmer, the 180-million-year-old fossils of trees at the **Akal Wood Fossil Park** can be seen.

A desert national park has been established in the Thar Desert near Sam village, but a separate permit is required to enter it.

POKARAN

The junction where the Jaisalmer to Bikaner and Jaisalmer to Jodhpur roads split is the site of another magnificent Rajasthan fortress. The yellow sandstone fort rises from the yellow desert sands and shelters a tangle of narrow streets lined by balconied houses decorated with parrots, elephants and Rajasthan's inevitable peacocks. The usually quiet town springs to life during its annual cattle fair. It must also have sprung to life in May 1974 when a nuclear explosion took place nearby!

Places to Stay

The RTDC *Motel Midway* is a brand new place on the edge of town. It has just two rooms with attached bath for Rs 150/200, and meals are available.

BARMER

Barmer is a centre for woodcarving, carpets, embroidery, block printing and other handicrafts and its products are famous throughout

Rajasthan. Otherwise, this desert town, 153 km from Jaisalmer and 220 km from Jodhpur, isn't very exciting. There's no fortress here and the most interesting part is probably the journey to Barmer through small villages, their mud-walled houses decorated with the characteristic geometrical designs of each different village. Whilst walking around Barmer, I was stopped by an army captain driving a jeep. He asked me, 'Why have you come to Barmer? There's nothing here!' By the end of the day, I found myself in substantial agreement with him.

There's also hardly anywhere to stay here. The only obvious hotel I came across was the *Agra Rest House* on Station Rd, though there must be others.

Buses run between Barmer and Jaisalmer, and south to Palanpur in Gujarat. Barmer is also connected to Jodhpur by metre-gauge railway. Although the line continues on to the Pakistani border, there are no through trains to that country and, in any case, foreigners are not allowed to cross the border at this point.

BIKANER

Population: 415,000

This desert town in the north of the state was founded in 1488 by Rao Bikaji, a descendant of the founder of Jodhpur, Jodhaji. Like many others in Rajasthan, the old city is surrounded by a high crenellated wall and, like Jaisalmer, its smaller sister to the south, it was once an important staging post on the great caravan trade routes.

The city is chiefly interesting for its superb large fort, but it is also known for the fine camels bred here. There is a government camel breeding farm near the city. The Gang Canal, built between 1925 and 1927, irrigates a large area of previously arid land around Bikaner.

Orientation & Information

The old city is encircled by a seven-km-long city wall with five entrance gates, constructed in the 18th century. The fort and palace, built of the same reddish-pink sandstone as Jaipur's famous buildings, are outside the city walls.

The helpful tourist office (☎ 27-445) is in Junagarh Fort and is open from 10 am to 5 pm, closed on Sundays. The GPO is at the collectorate, while the city post office is inside Kote Gate.

Junagarh Fort

Constructed between 1588 and 1593 by Raja Rai Singh, a general in the army of the Moghul emperor, Akbar, the fort has a 986-metre-long wall with 37 bastions and two entrances. The Suraj Pol, or Sun Gate, is the main entrance to the fort. The palaces within the fort are at the southern side and make a picturesque ensemble of courtyards, balconies, kiosks, towers and windows. A major feature of this fort and its palaces is the superb quality of the stone carving – it rivals the best anywhere in the world.

Among the places of interest are the Chandra Mahal, or Moon Palace, with paintings, mirrors and carved marble panels. The Phool Mahal, or Flower Palace, is also decorated with glass and mirrors. The Karn Mahal was built to commemorate a notable victory over the Moghul Aurangzeb.

Other palaces include the Rang Mahal, Bijai Mahal and Anup Mahal. The contents include the usual Rajput weapon collection, not to mention the decaying pieces of a couple of old WW I biplanes. The Durga Niwas is a beautifully painted courtyard while the Ganga Niwas, another large courtyard, has a finely carved red sandstone front. Har Mandir is the royal temple, dedicated to Lord Siva.

The fort is open from 10 am to 4.30 pm and is closed on Fridays.

Lalgarh Palace

About three km north of the city centre, the Red Fort was built by Maharaja Ganga Singh (1881-1942) in memory of his father Maharaja Lal Singh. The Bikaner royal family still lives in part of the palace, which is made of red sandstone and has beautiful latticework. The rest of the palace has been turned into a luxury hotel, and a museum known as the Shri Sadul Museum. The museum, covering the entire 1st floor of the palace, houses an incredible array of photos, and an extraordinary collection of the former maharaja's personal possessions – golf clubs, camera, clothes, books, passport, glasses, earplugs and electric toothbrush! There's also the usual exhibition of Indian wildlife, shot and stuffed.

The museum is open from 10 am to 5 pm, closed Wednesdays; entry is Rs 5, and you'll need to take an auto-rickshaw from the centre of town (Rs 10 each way).

Places to Stay – bottom end

The pleasantly quiet *Dhola Maru Tourist Bungalow* (☎ 25-002) is on Pooran Singh Circle, about a km from the centre of the city. The deluxe singles/doubles for Rs 75/100, air-cooled rooms for Rs 100/150, air-con rooms for Rs 200/300 and dorm beds for Rs 30 are reasonably good value, but the fabric has been allowed to deteriorate and cleaning standards leave much to be desired. There's a bar and restaurant, but the food is very average and somewhat expensive.

There is a string of low-priced hotels near the station on Station Rd. This is an amazingly busy road so the noise level in any room fronting it can be diabolical – choose carefully. The *Hotel Shantiniwas* is down a large side street opposite the railway station. It's quite clean although not that friendly, and is often full later in the day. The rooms are OK at Rs 40/75. A little further along the same street is the small *Indra Lodge*. It's a friendly place, although the rooms are a bit gloomy and poorly lit. At Rs 35/60 for a room with attached bath it's not a bad place for a night's stopover.

In a small lane which runs off Station Rd from beside the Deluxe Hotel, the *Hotel Akashdeep* (☎ 6024) is a fairly typical grubby flophouse, but at least it's relatively quiet. There's dorm beds for Rs 20, or singles/doubles with attached bath for Rs 40/60.

The railway *retiring rooms* are surprisingly quiet for such a busy place, and cost Rs

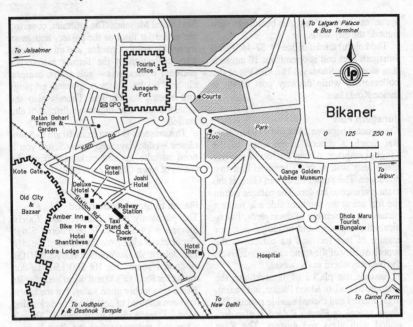

To Jaisalmer

Tourist Office

Junagarh Fort

GPO

Ratan Behari Temple & Garden

Kem Rd

Kote Gate

Old City & Bazaar

Green Hotel

Deluxe Hotel

Joshi Hotel

Station Rd

Amber Inn

Bike Hire

Railway Station

Taxi Stand & Clock Tower

Hotel Shantiniwas

Indra Lodge

To Jodhpur & Deshnok Temple

To New Delhi

Courts

Park

Zoo

To Lalgarh Palace & Bus Terminal

Bikaner

0   125   250 m

Ganga Golden Jubilee Museum

To Jaipur

Dhola Maru Tourist Bungalow

Hotel Thar

Hospital

To Camel Farm

---

25 for dorm beds, and Rs 30/60 for single/double rooms.

Places to Stay – middle

The *Joshi Hotel* (☎ 6162) is also on Station Rd near the railway station. It's a comfortable place offering air-cooled deluxe singles/doubles for Rs 130/160, and with air-con for Rs 225/300. All rooms have bath and hot water.

Another fairly new mid-range hotel is the *Hotel Thar* (☎ 7180), on the left-hand side of Hospital Rd on the way to the Tourist Bungalow. Rooms with bath and constant hot water cost Rs 200/300. There's a discount of 20% between April and August. The hotel has a restaurant, and Rajasthani music and folk dances are put on during the high season.

Places to Stay – top end

Bikaner's sole top-end hotel is the *Lalgarh Palace Hotel* (☎ 3263), which is part of the maharaja's modern palace of the same name. It offers ordinary rooms for Rs 500/700, air-cooled rooms with bath and constant hot water for Rs 760, and Rs 700/800 for a single/double with air-con. There's a restaurant and Rajasthani music and folk dances can be arranged if you're willing to pay for the troupe.

Places to Eat

Bikaner has very few outstanding places to eat. The *Chhotu Motu Joshi Restaurant* is just down from the Green Hotel towards the station and has good, cheap vegetarian food, icy-cold lassi and lots of Indian sweets. The *Green Hotel* and the *Deluxe Hotel* both have similar small, clean restaurants serving snacks and drinks.

Across the road from these hotels, you can get cheap vegetarian food at a number of open-air places like *Krishan*, *Laxmi* and *Ganesh*, but they're all pretty grubby. The more expensive *Amber Restaurant* is also here.

Getting There & Away

Bus The bus station is three km north of the city centre, right opposite the Lalgarh Palace. There is a sealed national highway to Jaipur (320 km) and to Jaisalmer (330 km).

There are two state transport buses daily between Jaisalmer and Bikaner. The journey takes nine hours and costs Rs 69. Private companies operate on this route in the off season.

To Jaipur there are at least six buses daily, including one deluxe bus at 9.30 pm. The journey takes seven hours at a cost of Rs 70. These buses go via the Shekhawati town of Fatehpur.

Other places served by bus from Bikaner include Agra, Delhi, Ajmer, and Udaipur.

Train Day and night trains take about 12 hours to make the 463-km trip from Delhi to Bikaner. Fares are Rs 85/314 in 2nd/1st class. There are also trains to Jodhpur and Jaipur.

Getting Around

Auto-rickshaws are unmetered. Bikaner also has tongas and there are bicycle-hire places along Station Rd, across from the railway station.

AROUND BIKANER

Bhand Sagar Temple

The 16th-century Jain temple to the 23rd tirthankar, Parasvanath, is the most important of the complex. Others include the **Chintamani Temple** of 1505 and the **Adinath Temple**. There is a fine view of the city wall and surrounding countryside from the park behind the temple.

Devi Kund

This is the site of the royal chhatris (cenotaphs) of many of the Bika dynasty rulers. The white marble chhatri of Maharaja Surat Singh is among the most imposing.

Camel Breeding Farm

This government-managed camel breeding station is probably unique in Asia. There are hundreds of camels here and it's a great sight at sunset as the camels come back from grazing. The British army had a camel corps drawn from Bikaner during WW I. Rides are available.

You'll have no difficulty finding transport to the camel farm – half the auto-rickshaw and taxi drivers in Bikaner appear to be on the lookout for tourists to take out there. The round-trip cost by taxi is around Rs 40, including a half-hour wait at the farm.

Gajner Wildlife Sanctuary

A number of animals can be seen in this reserve, 32 km from Bikaner on the Jaisalmer road. Imperial sand grouse migrate here in winter.

The old royal summer palace stands on the bank of the lake and is sometimes used as a hotel.

Karni Mata Temple

At Deshnok on the Jodhpur road, this temple is dedicated to the mystic Karni Mata. The huge silver gates to the temple and the marble carvings were donated by Maharaja Ganga Singh; a golden umbrella tops the temple.

The main interest here, however, is the rats. Like cows in the rest of India, the rats here are regarded as holy and are fed by the priests, who care for them in the belief that they will be reincarnated as mystics or holy men. Strolling around this temple with rats playing leapfrog over your bare feet can be a little unnerving. There's a Rs 5 camera fee at the temple.

Getting There & Away You can reach the temple on the hourly bus from Bikaner for about Rs 6, or hire a taxi or jeep from in front of the railway station for about Rs 120 for the round trip.

Gujarat

Population: 41 million
Area: 196,024 sq km
Capital: Gandhinagar
People per sq km: 210
Main Language: Gujarati
Literacy Rate: 60.9%

The west coast state of Gujarat is not one of India's busiest tourist destinations. Although it is quite easy to slot Gujarat in between Bombay and the cities of Rajasthan, few people pause to explore this interesting state. Yet Gujarat has a long and varied history and a great number of interesting places to visit. If you want to go right beyond history into the realms of legend, then the Temple of Somnath was actually there to witness the creation of the universe! Along the south coast are the sites where many of the great events in Lord Krishna's life took place.

On firmer historic footing, Lothal was the site of a Harappan or Indus Valley civilisation city over 4000 years ago. The main sites of this very ancient culture are now in Pakistan, but it is thought that Lothal may have survived the great cities of the Sind by as much as 500 years. Gujarat also featured in the exploits of the great Buddhist emperor, Ashoka, and one of his rock edicts can be seen near Junagadh.

Later, Gujarat suffered Muslim incursions from Mahmud of Ghazni and subsequent Moghul rulers, and was a battlefield between the Moghuls and the Marathas. It was also an early point of contact with the West and the first British commercial outpost was established at Surat. Daman and Diu survived as Portuguese enclaves within the borders of Gujarat until 1961. Gujarat also had close ties with the life of the father of modern India, Mahatma Gandhi. It was in Gujarat that the Mahatma was born and spent his early years, and it was to Ahmedabad, the main city of Gujarat, that he returned to wage his long struggle with the British for independence.

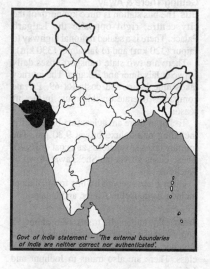

Govt of India statement — 'The external boundaries of India are neither correct nor authenticated'.

Gujarat has always been a centre for the Jains, and some of its most interesting sights are Jain temple centres like those at Palitana and Girnar Hill. The Jains are an influential and energetic group and, as a result, Gujarat is one of India's wealthier states with a number of important industries, particularly textiles and electronics, and has the dubious distinction of having the largest petrochemical complex in the country. Apart from its Jain temples, Gujarat's major attractions include the last Asian lions, in the Gir Forest, and the fascinating Indo-Saracenic architecture of Ahmedabad.

Geographically, Gujarat can be divided into three areas. The eastern (mainland) region includes the major cities of Ahmedabad, Surat and Vadodara (Baroda). The Gulf of Cambay divides the mainland strip from the flat, often barren, plain of the Kathiawar peninsula, also known as Saurashtra. This was never incorporated into British India, but survived in the form of more than 200

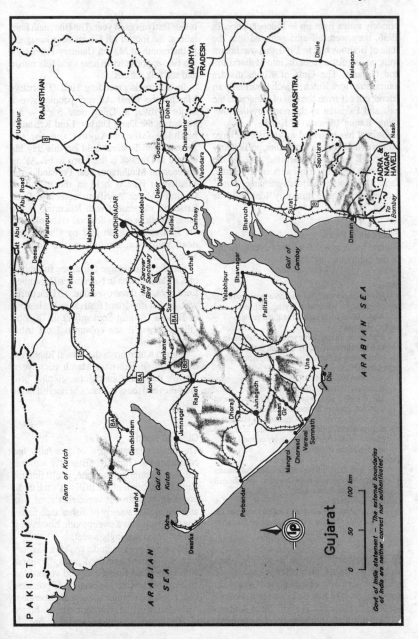

Gujarat

0   50   100 km

Govt of India statement – 'The external boundaries
of India are neither correct nor authenticated'.

princely states right up to Independence. In 1956, they were all amalgamated into the state of Bombay but, in 1960, this was in turn split, on linguistic grounds, into Maharashtra and Gujarat. The Gulf of Kutch divides Saurashtra from Kutch, which is virtually an island, cut off from the rest of Gujarat to the east and Pakistan to the north by the low-lying 'Ranns' (deserts) of Kutch.

Gujarat has provided a surprisingly large proportion of India's emigrants, particularly to the UK and USA. Around 40% of the Indians in the New York area are Gujaratis; there, the popular Gujarati surname 'Patel' has come to be commonly identified as Indian.

Festivals & Fairs

Gujarat has a busy calendar of events. Some of the main ones include:

January
> *Makar Sankranti* This end-of-winter festival is celebrated with kite-flying contests, and Ahmedabad hosts an international contest.

January-February
> *Muharram* Tazias, large replicas of the tombs of two Muslim martyrs, are paraded in the evening, particularly in Surat, Junagadh and Ahmedabad.

September-October
> *Navaratri* Nine nights of music and dancing celebrate this festival of the mother goddess, Amba. The Dandiya Ras, which Lord Krishna danced with his gopis (milkmaids), is featured. Other folk dances, such as the Gujarati Ras Garba, are also performed. Vadodara (Baroda) is a good place to be for Navaratri as many cultural events are organised at this time.

October
> *Dussehra* The 10th day of Navaratri culminates in the celebration of Rama's victory over the evil Ravana in the *Ramayana*.

October-November
> *Sharad Purnima* Song and dance celebrate the end of the monsoon on the night of the full moon in the month of Kartika.

Gujarat has many fairs in its temple towns and small villages. They offer a chance to see religious festivals and celebrations and, in the villages, also function as a shop window for local handicrafts. The village of Ambaji, 177 km north of Ahmedabad, celebrates four major festivals each year. The Bhavnath Fair, held at the foot of Mt Girnar near Junagadh in the month of Magha (January-February), is a fine opportunity to hear local folk music and see folk dances.

In the week preceding Holi (February-March), the tribal Adivasi people have a major festival at Dang near Surat – it's known as the Dang Durbar. Lord Krishna's birthday falls in August and for the Janmashtami Festival held on this day his temple at Dwarka is the place to be. Along the coast at Madhavpur near Porbandar, the Madhavrai Fair is held in the month of Chaitra (March-April) to celebrate Lord Krishna's elopement with Rukmini. In the same month, a major festival takes place at the foot of Pavagadh Hill by Champaner, near Vadodara, honouring the goddess Mahakali.

Somnath has a large fair at the full moon of Kartika Purnima in November-December. Lord Siva, the three-eyed one, or Trinetreshwar, has an important festival in his honour in Bhadra (August-September) in Tarnetar village – you'll see colourful local tribal costumes here.

Bhuj in Kutch hosts the annual Rann Festival held in February-March each year. There's craft demonstrations, cultural programmes and tours to places of interest in the region.

Gujarati Food

The strict vegetarianism of the Jains has contributed to Gujarat's distinctive regional cuisine. Throughout the state, you'll find the Gujarati variation of the thali – it's the traditional all-you-can-eat vegetarian meal with an even greater variety of dishes than usual. For those without a sweet tooth, however, it can be overpoweringly sweet.

Popular dishes include *kadhi*, a savoury curry of yoghurt and fried puffs, flavoured with spices and finely chopped vegetables. *Undhyoo* is a winter speciality of potatoes, sweet potatoes, broad beans and aubergines roasted in an earthenware pot which is buried upside down (undhyoo) under a fire. In

Surat, the local variation of this dish is more spicy and curry hot. *Sev ganthia*, a crunchy fried chickpea-flour snack, is available from *farsan* stalls.

In winter, try Surat's *paunk*, a curious combination of roasted cereals; or *jowar*, garlic chutney and sugar. Then there's *khaman dhokla*, a salty, steamed chickpea flour cake, and *doodhpak*, a thick, sweetened, milk-based dessert with nuts. *Srikhand* is a dessert made from yoghurt and spiced with saffron, cardamom, nuts and candied fruit. *Gharis* are rich sweets made of milk, clarified butter and dried fruits – another Surat specialty. In summer, *am rasis* is a popular mango drink.

The Gujaratis make superb ice cream, available throughout western India under the brand name of Vadelal. It comes in about 20 flavours, some of which are seasonal.

Things to Buy

With its busy modern textile works, it's not surprising that Gujarat offers a number of interesting buys in this line. Extremely fine, and often extremely expensive, Patola silk saris are still made by a handful of master craftspeople in Patan. From Surat comes the *zari*, or gold-thread embroidery work. Surat is also a centre for silk saris. Less opulent, but still beautiful, are the block prints of Ahmedabad. At Madhupura Rani-no-Hajiro on Mirzapur Rd, near the Ahmedabad GPO, you will also find cloth, hand painted in the traditional black, red, maroon and ochre.

Jamnagar is famous for its tie-dye work, which you'll see in Saurashtra as well as in the bazaar shops of Jamnagar. Brightly coloured peasant embroideries and beadwork are also found in Saurashtra, along with woollen shawls, blankets and rugs, while brass-covered wooden chests are manufactured in Bhavnagar and embroidered stuffed toys are made in Kutch. In Ahmedabad, antique shops sell wooden carvings, such as window frames, shutters and doorways from old houses, and most Gujarati handicrafts are on display at Gujari or Handloom House, both on Ashram Rd.

Eastern Gujarat

AHMEDABAD

Population: 3,300,000

Ahmedabad, Gujarat's principal city, is one of the major industrial cities in India. It has been called the 'Manchester of the East' due to its many textile industries. Ahmedabad is also very noisy and incredibly polluted; Tilak Rd (Relief Rd) gets the authors' votes as the most polluted, congested and thoroughly chaotic strip of barely controlled mayhem in the country. Only on Sunday mornings is there any respite.

Visitors in the hot season should bear in mind the derisive title given to Ahmedabad by the Moghul emperor, Jehangir: Gardabad, the City of Dust. Nevertheless, this comparatively little-visited city has a number of attractions for travellers. Gandhi's ashram at Sabarmati is open to tourists and features a small museum. In the city, there are some of the finest examples of Islamic architecture in India, as well as a number of other interesting buildings, both religious and secular. Ahmedabad is one of the best places to study the blend of Hindu and Islamic architectural styles known as the Indo-Saracenic.

The new capital of Gujarat, Gandhinagar, is 23 km from Ahmedabad.

History

Over the centuries, Ahmedabad has had a number of periods of grandeur, each followed by decline. It was originally founded in 1411 by Ahmed Shah and, in the 17th century, was thought to be one of the finest cities in India. In 1615, the noted English ambassador, Sir Thomas Roe, judged it to be 'a goodly city, as large as London' but, in the 18th century, it went through a period of decline. Its industrial strength once again raised the city up, and, from 1915, it became famous as the site of Gandhi's ashram and the place where he launched his famous march against the Salt Law.

In recent years, Ahmedabad has seen outbursts of communal violence, mainly between Muslims and Hindus. Some people fear that the city will eventually be divided into areas, strictly segregated on religious grounds but, at the moment, there is little evidence of this.

Orientation

The city lies on both sides of the Sabarmati River. On the eastern bank, two main roads run away from the river to the railway station, about three km away. They are Tilak Rd (Relief Rd) and Gandhi Rd. The airport is off to the north-east of the city, while the Gandhi Ashram is on the west bank of the Sabarmati River, to the north of the city. Virtually all the city walls are now demolished, but some of the gates remain.

Information

Tourist Office The state tourist office (☎ 44-9683) is just off Sri R C Rd, across the river from the town centre. Hours are 10.30 am to 1.30 pm and 2 to 5.30 pm; they're late starters, even by Indian standards. The office has excellent maps of Ahmedabad (Rs 4) and Gujarat state (Rs 1) and a free list of their own chain of hotels/resort centres with current prices. They can also arrange various tours of the state in their own buses, as well as car hire. Many rickshaw drivers don't understand where you want to go if you ask for the tourist office, but asking for HK House on Ashram Rd usually does the trick – the tourist office is in this building.

Visa Extensions The Foreigners' Registration Office (☎ 33-3999) is in the office of the Commissioner of Police in Shahibaug, north of the city centre on Balvantrai Mehta Rd.

Money The large State Bank of India branch at Lal Darwarja is a shambles, and the staff less than eager to help. Changing money takes around half an hour, and they don't give an encashment certificate unless prompted.

Post & Telecommunications The poste restante at the GPO routinely pigeonholes

letters according to the first name on the address, so you need to check all combinations.

The Central Telegraph Office is just south of Sidi Saiyad's Mosque. Ahmedabad's telephone area code is 0121.

Bookshops & Libraries There are a number of good bookshops at the Nehru Bridge end of Tilak Rd. International magazines can be bought from the Cama Hotel.

The British Library, in the British Council Building, opposite the Sidi Saiyad Mosque, has air-conditioning, a drinking fountain and spotless toilets.

Bhadra Fort & Teen Darwaja

The ancient citadel, the Bhadra, was built by Ahmed Shah in 1411 and later named after the goddess Bhadra, an incarnation of Kali. It now houses government offices and is of no particular interest. There is a post office in the former Palace of Azam Khan, within the citadel. In front of the citadel stands the triple gateway, or Teen Darwaja, from which sultans used to watch processions from the palace to the Jami Masjid.

Jami Masjid

The Jami Masjid is beside Gandhi Rd, a short distance from Teen Darwaja. This large mosque was built in 1424 by the city's founder, Ahmed Shah. Although 260 columns support the roof with its 15 cupolas, the two 'shaking' minarets lost half their height in the great earthquake of 1819, and another tremor in 1957 completed the demolition.

Much of this early Ahmedabad mosque was built using items salvaged from demolished Hindu and Jain temples. It is said that a large black slab by the main arch is actually the base of a Jain idol, buried upside down for the Muslim faithful to tread on.

Tombs of Ahmed Shah & his Queens

The Tomb of Ahmed Shah, with its perforated stone windows, stands just outside the east gate of the Jami Masjid. His son and grandson, who did not long survive him, also have their cenotaphs in this tomb. Women are not allowed into the central chamber. Across the street on a raised platform is the tomb of his queens – it's now really a market and in very poor shape compared to Ahmed Shah's tomb.

Sidi Saiyad's Mosque

This small mosque, which once formed part of the city wall, is close to the river end of Tilak Rd. It was constructed by Sidi Saiyad, a slave of Ahmed Shah, and is noted for its beautiful carved stone windows, formed by the intricate intertwining of the branches of a tree.

Ahmed Shah's Mosque

Dating from 1414, this was one of the earliest mosques in the city and was probably built on the site of a Hindu temple, using parts of that temple in its construction. It is in the south-west of the Bhadra. The front of the mosque is now a garden.

Rani Rupmati's Mosque

A little north of the centre, Rani Rupmati's Mosque was built between 1430 and 1440 and named after the sultan's Hindu wife. The minarets were partially brought down by the disastrous earthquake of 1819. Note particularly the way the dome is elevated to allow light in around its base. As with so many of Ahmedabad's early mosques, this one displays elements of both Hindu and Islamic design.

Rani Sipri's Mosque

This small mosque is also known as the Masjid-e-Nagira, or Jewel of a Mosque, because of its extremely graceful and well-executed design. Its slender delicate minarets again blend Hindu and Islamic styles. The mosque is said to have been built in 1514 by a wife of Sultan Mahmud Begara after he executed their son for some minor misdemeanour. It's to the south-east of the town centre.

Sidi Saiyad's Mosque

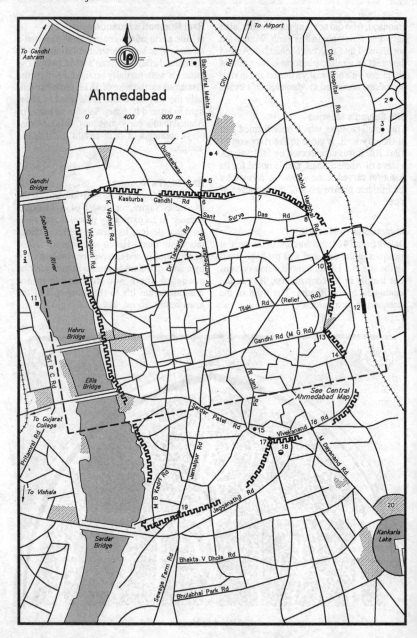

1	Commissioner of Police & Foreigners' Registration Office
2	Mata Bhavani's Well
3	Dadi Hari Wav (Step Well)
4	Hathee Singh Temple
5	Punjab Travels
6	Delhi Gate
7	Dariapur Gate
8	Prem Gate
9	Tourist Office
10	Kalupur Gate
11	Hotel Karnavati
12	Railway Station
13	Panchkuva Gate
14	Sarangpur Gate
15	Rani Sipri's Mosque
16	Raipur Gate
17	Astodia Gate
18	Long Distance Bus Station
19	Jamalpur Gate
20	Zoo

Sidi Bashir's Mosque & Shaking Minarets

Just south of the railway station, outside the Sarangpur Gate, the Sidi Bashir Mosque is famed for its shaking minarets, or Jhulta Minar. When one minaret is shaken, the other rocks in sympathy. This is said to be a protection against earthquake damage. It's a fairly fanciful proposition, and one which you'll be unable to test, unless of course you happen to be on the spot during an earthquake – or you know of some other way to make a solid stone tower vibrate.

Raj Babi Mosque

The Raj Babi Mosque, south-east of the railway station in the suburb of Gomtipur, also had shaking minarets, one of which was partially dismantled by an inquisitive Englishman in an unsuccessful attempt to find out how it worked. It's worth a visit but, once again, you're specifically prohibited from shaking the remaining minaret (even if that were possible). Expect to be hassled for a contribution when visiting this mosque.

A little to the north of the railway station, other minarets are all that remain of a mosque which was destroyed in a battle between the Moghuls and Marathas in 1753.

Hathee Singh Temple

Just outside the Delhi Gate, to the north of the old city, this Jain temple is built in typical style and, as with so many Jain temples, is made of white marble. Built in 1848, it is dedicated to Dharamanath, the 15th Jain tirthankar.

Dada Hari Wav (Step Well)

Step wells (wavs or baolis) are strange constructions, unique to northern India, and this is one of the best. The curious well, built in 1499, has a series of steps leading down to lower and lower platforms, eventually terminating in a small octagonal well. The depths of the well are cool, even on the hottest day, and it must once have been quite beautiful. Today, it is completely neglected and often bone dry, but it's a fascinatingly eerie place with galleries above the well and a small portico at ground level.

The best time to visit and/or photograph the well is between 10 and 11 am; at other times, the sun is in the wrong place and doesn't penetrate to the various levels. There's no entry or camera fee. Behind the well is the equally neglected Mosque and Rauza (Tomb) of Dada Hari. The mosque has a tree motif like the one on the windows of Sidi Saiyad's Mosque.

There is a second step well, that of **Mata Bhavani**, a couple of hundred metres north of Dada Hari's. Ask children to show you the way. Thought to be several hundred years older, it is much less ornate and is now used as a crude Hindu temple.

Kankaria Lake

South-east of the city, this artificial lake, complete with an island summer palace, was constructed in 1451 and has 34 sides, each 60 metres long. Once frequented by Emperor Jehangir and Empress Nur Jahan, it is now a local picnic spot. The huge **zoo** and children's park by the lake are outstanding and the Ghattamendal pavilion in the centre houses an **aquarium**.

Other Mosques & Temples

It's very easy to get bored with mosques in

Ahmedabad. If your enthusiasm for them is limited, don't go further than Sidi Saiyad's and the Jami Masjid. If you have real endurance, you could continue to **Dastur Khan's Mosque** near the Rani Sipri Mosque. Or try Haibat Khan's Mosque, Saiyad Alam's Mosque, Shuja'at Khan's Mosque, Shaikh Hasan Muhammed Chisti's Mosque and Muhafiz Khan's Mosque.

Then, for a complete change, you could plunge into the narrow streets of the old part of town and seek out the brightly painted **Swami Narayan Temple**. Enclosed in a large courtyard, it dates from 1850. To the south of this Hindu temple are the nine tombs known as the Nau Gaz Pir, or Nine Yard Saints.

Other Attractions

Ahmedabad can be an interesting place around which to wander. The bazaar streets are narrow, crowded and colourful, and lots of the houses have ornately carved wooden facades. In many streets, there are Jain bird-feeding places known as *parabdis*. Children catch and release pigeons for the fun of it. The older parts of the city are divided into totally separate areas known as *pols*. It's easy to get lost.

The **Victoria Gardens** beside M G Rd are pleasant and about the only place where you'll get some relief from the weekday noise and pollution.

The western side of Ahmedabad across the river is a late 20th-century creation full of modern buildings such as the Ahmedabad Mill Owner's Association Building and the museum, both designed by Le Corbusier, who also had a hand in the new capital of Gandhinagar.

Unlike so many other large cities, Ahmedabad has little evidence of the British period. The chief landmarks of the era are the tall smokestacks that ring this industrial city. On the sandy bed of the Sabarmati River, traditional block-printed fabrics are still stretched out to dry, despite the 70-plus large textile mills. The river dries to a mere trickle in the hot season.

Other places of interest in and around town include the ruined **Tomb of Darya Khan**, north-west of the Hathee Singh Temple. Built in 1453, the tomb has a particularly large dome. Nearby is the **Chhota Shahi Bagh**, across the railway line. Ladies of the harem used to live in the *chhota* (small) garden. In Saraspur, east of the railway line, the **Temple of Chintaman** is a Jain temple originally constructed in 1638 and converted into a mosque by Aurangzeb.

Museums

Ahmedabad has a number of museums. The **Calico Museum of Textiles** exhibits antique and modern textiles including rare tapestries, wall hangings and costumes. Also on display are old weaving machines. The museum is in Sarabhai House, a former haveli, in the Shahi Bagh gardens. It is open from 10 am to 12.30 pm and 2.30 to 5 pm, closed on Wednesdays, and admission is free. The interesting little museum shop sells cards, books and reproductions of some of the pieces.

The **N C Mehta Museum of Miniatures** at Sanskar Kendra, Paldi, has excellent examples of the various schools of Indian miniature painting. It is open from 9 to 11 am and 4 to 7 pm daily, except Mondays. The building was designed by Le Corbusier.

The **Shreyas Folk Museum** (closed Wednesdays) displays the folk arts and crafts of Gujarat. There's also the **National Institute of Design**, the **Tribal Research & Training Institute Museum** on Ashram Rd, and a **Philatelic Museum**.

The **Institute of Indology** on the university campus has an important collection of illustrated manuscripts and miniatures and one of the finest collections relating to Jainism in India. It is only open in the afternoons from around 3 pm.

Sabarmati Ashram

Six km from the centre of town, on the west bank of the Sabarmati River, this was Gandhi's headquarters during the long struggle for Indian independence. His ashram was founded in 1918 and still makes handicrafts, handmade paper and spinning wheels. Gandhi's spartan living quarters are pre-

Top: Camels in the Thar Desert, Jaisalmer, Rajasthan (RI)
Middle Left: Festive camel, Pushkar, Rajasthan (RI)
Middle Centre: Basket weaving, Jodhpur, Rajasthan (RI)
Middle Right: Jewellery, Pushkar, Rajasthan (RI)
Bottom: Pushkar Camel Fair, Rajasthan (RI)

Top: Udaipur at dusk, Rajasthan (GC)
Bottom: Temple carving, Rajasthan (GC)

served as a small museum and there is a pictorial record of the major events in his life. There's also a bookshop selling books by and about the Mahatma.

The ashram is open from 8.30 am to 6.30 pm (till 7 pm between April and September). Admission is free. At 8.30 pm on Sunday, Tuesday, Thursday and Friday evenings, there is a Sound & Light show in English for a small admission fee. Bus No 81, 82, 83 or 84 will take you there.

Organised Tours

The municipal corporation runs tours from the local bus station (Lal Darwaja) near Nehru Bridge, which depart daily at 8 am and 2 pm.

Places to Stay – bottom end

Most of the cheap hotels are scattered along or close to Tilak Rd and around the railway station, but there's nothing very special about most of them, and indeed most are eminently forgettable. The real cheapies are opposite the railway station, but most are assailed by Ahmedabad's horrendous noise and air pollution and are probably best avoided unless you have a very early morning departure. The area around Sidi Saiyad's Mosque at the western end of Tilak Rd is better, although it's still far from serene.

The friendly but very basic *A-One Guest House* (☎ 34-9823) is in an older building opposite the railway station. The outer rooms with windows here are OK, but the internal ones are gloomy. Rooms cost Rs 55/70 with common bathroom, or there are dorm beds for Rs 25.

Just off Tilak Rd is the *Hotel Naigra* (☎ 38-4977). The rooms are definitely on the small side, but are quite OK and not too noisy. The cost is Rs 55 for a single with common bathroom, Rs 66/116 for singles/doubles with bathroom, and Rs 210 for a double with air-con. Checkout time is 24 hours after arrival.

The *Hotel Ashiana* (☎ 35-1114) on the same street as the GPO is also worth checking out. It offers doubles with bathroom for

Rs 90, or Rs 80 with common bathroom, and is often full. Checkout time is 24 hours after arrival.

The *Hotel Esquire*, right opposite Sidi Saiyad's Mosque and back off the main street, is better than most. It's very clean and run by an oldish couple who care about standards. It costs Rs 72 per person for singles/doubles and is often full.

Down the lane opposite the Advance Cinema is the small and friendly *Hotel Relax* (☎ 35-4301). It's one of the best in this bracket, and is good value at Rs 85/100 for singles/doubles, Rs 160/200 with air-con. All rooms have bathroom and constant hot water.

An old favourite in the centre of the city, near Lal Darwaja and adjacent to Ahmed Shah's Mosque, the *Hotel Natraj* (☎ 35-0048) is a typical Indian boarding house and is quite adequate for most people's needs. The windows open on to a corridor so privacy is limited, but it is well maintained and good value at Rs 50/100 for singles/doubles with bathroom.

Just to the north of the Sidi Saiyad Mosque is another good cheapie, the *Hotel Bombay* (☎ 35-1746). This clean and friendly place is on the third floor of the KB Commercial Centre, and is not very obvious from street level. Rooms cost Rs 60/100 with common facilities, Rs 90/150 with attached bathroom, and Rs 162/210 with attached bathroom and toilet.

Finally, there are *retiring rooms* at the railway station, and these cost Rs 50 per person, Rs 100/150 with air-con and bathroom, or there are dorm beds for Rs 30.

Places to Stay – middle

Almost at the end of Tilak Rd, down a side alley opposite Electric House and round the corner from the Hotel Capri, is a group of good middle-range hotels. Quite a few travellers stay at the *Hotel Metropole* (☎ 35-4988). It's pretty good value at Rs 133/244 for singles/doubles, Rs 289/336 with air-con, all with TV, bathroom and hot water. The *Hotel Mehul* (☎ 35-2862) is a

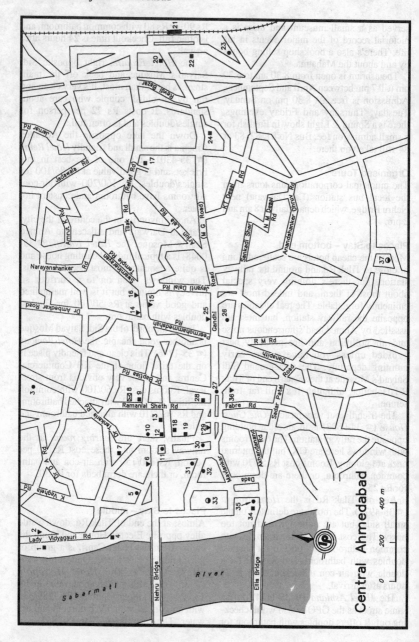

Central Ahmedabad

0   200   400 m

■ PLACES TO STAY

1	Cama Hotel
4	Ambassador Hotel
7	Hotel Bombay
9	Hotel Kingsway
12	Hotels Esquire, Good Night, Metropole & Mehul
13	Hotel Capri & Kwality Restaurant
17	Hotel Naigra
18	Balwas Hotel
19	Hotel Relax & Advance Restaurant
20	Hotel Shakunt
22	A-One Guest House
24	Hotel Payall
28	Hotel Ashiana
34	Hotel Natraj

▼ PLACES TO EAT

2	South Indian Restaurant
6	Roopalee Cream Station
14	Fruit Juice Stand
15	Havmor Restaurant & Ice-cream Bar

16	Chetna Restaurant
25	Sanman Restaurant
29	Paramount Restaurant
36	Neelam Restaurant

OTHER

3	Rani Rupmati's Mosque
5	Indian Airlines
8	GPO
10	British Council
11	Sidi Saiyad's Mosque
21	Ahmedabad Railway Station
23	Sidi Bashir's Mosque & Shaking Minarets
26	Jami Masjid
27	Teen Darwaja
30	Central Telegraph Office
31	Bhadra
32	State Bank of India
33	Lal Darwaja Local Bus Station
35	Ahmed Shah's Mosque
37	Central Bus Station

little more basic, but is still quite good at Rs 128/155.

In the same area is the new *Hotel Good Night* (☎ 35-1997). The pleasantly furnished rooms here are all marble-lined, have attached bathroom, TV and telephone. For all this you pay Rs 200/250, or Rs 275/325 with air-con, and the hotel has its own restaurant.

Similar to the Good Night in quality and price is the *Hotel Kingsway* (☎ 26-221), Ramanlal Sheth Rd, close to the junction with Tilak Rd. Singles/doubles cost Rs 250/325, or Rs 300/375 with air-con, and all rooms have bathroom, constant hot water and colour TV.

If you want to be near the railway station, the *Hotel Shakunt* (☎ 34-4615) is visible off to the right as you exit the station. The fact that the rooms don't have exterior windows is probably a blessing here as this cuts off the street noise to a large degree. The tariff is Rs 174/199, or Rs 335/385 with air-con, all with attached bathroom, hot water, TV and phone. The rooftop terrace gives good views of the chaos below.

The *Hotel Ambassador* (☎ 35-3244) is at the opposite end of Tilak Rd, close to the river. It's modern and very clean and all rooms have bathroom with constant hot water. In addition, the staff are pleasant and helpful. Rooms cost Rs 225/300, or Rs 300/375 with air-con.

If you don't mind staying some distance out of town, the modern, government-run *Ashram Guest House* (☎ 48-3742) is close to the river, right across the road from the Gandhi ashram. It has just nine rooms, each with bathroom and balcony, for Rs 133/210, or Rs 220/325 with air-con.

Places to Stay – top end
Close to the river end of Tilak Rd, the *Hotel Capri* (☎ 35-4643) is one of the cheapest of the top-end hotels, although it is perhaps overpriced. Rooms cost Rs 271/335, Rs 417/472 with air-con, all with bathrooms and constant hot water. Checkout time is noon.

The other main top-end hotel is alongside the river on Lady Vidyagauri Rd. The *Cama Hotel* (☎ 25-281) offers singles/doubles for

US$36/38, plus more expensive suites. It has all the facilities you would expect of a multi-star hotel including a swimming pool, liquor shop, currency exchange, bookshop and restaurants. Checkout time here is 9 am.

Across the river on Ashram Rd is the centrally air-conditioned *Hotel Karnavati* (☎ 40-2161) where singles/doubles cost Rs 700/850. On the same road, the four-star *Hotel Nataraj* (☎ 44-8747) has air-con rooms at Rs 395/650.

Places to Eat

Ahmedabad is a good place to sample a Gujarati thali; see the Gujarat food section earlier in this chapter. One of the best thali specialists in Ahmedabad is the *Chetna Restaurant* on Tilak Rd, where the all-you-can-eat thali costs Rs 15. It can be a little hard to locate since the sign is in Gujarati, but it almost adjoins the Krishna Cinema (although their sign is also in Gujarati) and is directly across the road from the Oriental Building. It's so popular that you may have to queue to get in, and a special waiter is provided to ply the waiting customers with water.

The *Advance Restaurant* opposite the cinema of the same name opens early and is a good place for breakfast and snacks. On Gandhi Rd opposite the Jami Masjid, the *Sanman Restaurant* has pretty reasonable south Indian dishes, and excellent lassis.

At the bottom end of the scale there's excellent Muslim (non-veg) street food available on Gandhi Rd between Teen Darwaja and the Jami Masjid. Each evening stalls are set up, and for around Rs 20 you can get a good feed. There's meat and fish dishes to choose from as well as vegetarian items. Another option for basic food, both veg and non-veg, is the *refreshment room* upstairs at the railway station. The food is nothing to get excited about, but it is cheap.

Near Teen Darwaja, the *Neelam Hotel* and the *Paramount* are good places for Western food, although a meal at the somewhat pretentious Neelam can set you back Rs 80. Likewise, at the *Kwality* on Tilak Rd near the Capri Hotel, a meal of ordinary fish & chips, alu gobi, nan, lemon soda and ice cream can cost Rs 80.

If you have this sort of money to spend on a meal, however, you might as well eat at the *Cama Hotel*. The restaurant here has surprisingly moderate prices, there's live music (Western cover bands) in the evenings and the steaks are just the thing for desperate carnivores.

On the other side of the river, the air-conditioned *Sankalp Restaurant*, off Ashram Rd near Dinesh Hall, is definitely worth at least one visit. This is an excellent south Indian vegetarian restaurant and the prices are very reasonable indeed. You won't find a crisper, fresher masala dosa anywhere and the restaurant boasts the longest dosas in India – four feet long! Get a group together and ask the extremely pleasant manager to cook you one of these culinary wonders (Rs 70). The Rs 20 south Indian thalis also make a very pleasant change from the sweet Gujarati cuisine. The restaurant is very close to the tourist office.

For ice-cream fans, there are any number of *Havmor* parlours – two along Tilak Rd alone – which also offer snacks and cold flavoured milk. There are a number of clean milk bars where you can get bottles of milk in curious flavours. On the corner of Tilak Rd and Dr Ambedkar Rd, across from the second Havmor, a large open-air fruit juice stand serves superb fruit juices. The *Roopalee Cream Station*, near Indian Airlines and the Roopalee Cinema, is good for drinks, ice cream and snacks. Very close to the Teen Darwaja Gate is the tiny *Gandhi Cold Drinks Bar* with more good ice cream and cold drinks.

For an interesting night out in Ahmedabad, try *Vishalla* (☎ 40-3357), a rural complex on the southern edge of town in Vasana which evokes the atmosphere of a Gujarat village. Here, you'll dine in Indian fashion, seated on the floor, while watching puppet shows and local dancing. It's peaceful, friendly and very well done, and the prices are very moderate. Lunch runs from 11 am to 1 pm, and dinner from 7 to 11 pm.

Things to Buy

On Ashram Rd, just before the tourist office, is the Gujarat state crafts emporium, called the Gujari. Handloom House is over the road.

Getting There & Away

Air Indian Airlines (☎ 35-3333) is on Tilak Rd, close to the Nehru Bridge, on the right-hand side coming from the railway station and near the Sidi Saiyad Mosque. Vayudoot is represented by Vyas Travels, Tilak Rd, not far from the railway station.

Air India (☎ 44-8853) is in Premchand House, near the High Court building on Ashram Rd, west of the river.

Ahmedabad has an international airport and there are direct flights with Air India to the UK and the USA.

Indian Airlines flies from Bombay to Ahmedabad at least once a day (US$47) and there are twice-daily direct flights to Delhi (US$79). Other destinations are Vadodara (daily, US$15), Indore (twice weekly, US$45), Goa (twice weekly, US$88), Bangalore (three times weekly, US$132) and Madras (three times weekly, US$143).

East West Airlines (☎ 25-285) flies daily in either direction between Ahmedabad and Bombay (US$47).

Bus Plenty of buses operate around Gujarat and to neighbouring states. The Gujarat State Transport Corporation buses are almost all standard-issue, battered meat wagons, but they're usually not too crowded and they run to schedule.

If you're travelling long-distance, private minibuses are a more expensive but much quicker alternative. There are a number of agencies running luxury buses to most of the main centres of population, and most hotels will book tickets for you. One such agency in Ahmedabad is Punjab Travels, with offices at Delhi Gate, Shahpur Rd (☎ 23-111), and Embassy Market (☎ 44-9777) off Ashram Rd. It operates luxury buses to many places within Gujarat, as well as to various cities in Rajasthan, Madhya Pradesh, Maharashtra and Bombay. To Bhavnagar, for instance, the fare is Rs 50 and the journey takes about six hours, leaving Ahmedabad at 5 pm and arriving in Bhavnagar at 11 pm. Another agency is Eagle Travels (☎ 77-477).

If you're heading north into Rajasthan, a direct bus to Mt Abu (Rs 70, seven hours) is probably faster than a train to Abu Road and a bus from there. A bus takes about six hours to Udaipur (Rs 70) and 11 hours to Bombay (Rs 150).

Train Ahmedabad is not on the main broad-gauge line between Delhi and Bombay, although there is a broad-gauge line running south to Bombay and a metre-gauge line running north to Delhi via the major towns of Rajasthan. There is a computerised booking office just outside the main station building, open Monday to Saturday from 8 am to 8 pm, and on Sunday from 8 am to 2 pm. Window No 2 handles the foreign tourist quota, and booking is a breeze.

The trip from Delhi to Ahmedabad is 934 km and takes 17 hours on the *Ashram Express*. Fares between Delhi and Ahmedabad are Rs 138/508 in 2nd/1st class.

There are plenty of daily trains between Ahmedabad and Bombay. The 492-km trip takes 10 to 15 hours, with the fastest mail trains making the journey in around nine hours. Fares are Rs 87/327 in 2nd/1st class. The Delhi trains on the northward metre-gauge line will get you to Abu Road in about five hours (186 km), to Ajmer in 12 hours (491 km) and to Jaipur in 15 hours (626 km).

If you're heading for Bhavnagar and Palitana, there's the overnight *Girnar Express*, which is a good alternative to the STC buses. For other places in Saurashtra, such as Rajkot and Jamnagar, there's the daily *Saurashtra Express*. For Bhuj and Kutch, the *Kutch Express*, departing at 2.05 am (!), takes you to Gandhidham in six hours, from where there are frequent connections for the two-hour journey to Bhuj.

Getting Around

To/From the Airport There's no bus to the airport. An auto-rickshaw will cost at least Rs 30.

Local Transport Ahmedabad has the usual local buses and taxis and hordes of completely reckless auto-rickshaw drivers. It is well on the way to displacing Lagos as the world's craziest city as far as traffic is concerned and the auto-rickshaw drivers are hellbent on making each journey a Rambo-like adventure. Venturing out in an auto-rickshaw is a nerve-shattering experience not to be undertaken lightly. Most drivers are willing to use the meter, but at the end of the journey will ask for something ridiculous. Demand to see the fare adjustment card, but be warned that this is entirely in Gujarati, so you'll need to learn the Gujarati numbers to make any sense of it. (This is worthwhile anyway, as all the numbers at the bus stations are also in Gujarati only.)

The local bus station is known as Lal Darwaja. The routes, destinations and fares are all posted in Gujarati.

AROUND AHMEDABAD
Sarkhej

The suburb of Sarkhej is only eight km from the centre of Ahmedabad. It is noted for its elegant group of buildings, including the **Mausoleum of Azam and Mu'assam**, built in 1457 by the brothers who were responsible for Sarkhej's architecture. The architecture here is interesting because the style is almost purely Hindu, with little of the Saracenic influence so evident in Ahmedabad.

As you enter Sarkhej, you pass the **Mausoleum of Mahmud Begara** and, beside the tank and connected to his tomb, that of his queen, Rajabai (1460). Also by the tank is the **Tomb of Ahmad Khattu Gaj Buksh**, a renowned Muslim saint and spiritual adviser to Ahmed Shah. The saint is said to have died in 1445 at the age of 111. Next to this is the fine mosque – 'the perfection of elegant simplicity'. Like the other buildings, it is notable for the complete absence of arches, a feature of Muslim architecture. The palace, with pavilions and a harem, is also around the tank.

The Dutch established a factory in Sarkhej in 1620 to process the indigo grown here.

Batwa

South-east of Ahmedabad, the suburb of Batwa has **tombs** of a noted Muslim saint (himself the son of another saint) and the saint's son. Batwa also has an important mosque.

Adalaj Vav

Nineteen km north of Ahmedabad, this is one of the finest of the Gujarati step wells, or baolis. It was built by Queen Rudabai in 1499 and provided a cool and secluded retreat during the hot summer months. Buses run here regularly.

Cambay

The old seaport of Ahmedabad is to the south-west, at the northern end of the Gulf of Cambay. At the height of Muslim power in Gujarat, the entire region was known as Cambay and, when the first ambassadors arrived from England in 1583, they bore letters from Queen Elizabeth addressed to Akbar, the 'King of Cambay'. Dutch and Portuguese factories were established in the port before the British arrived, but the rise of Surat eclipsed Cambay and, when its port silted up, the city's decline was inevitable.

Nal Sarovar Bird Sanctuary

Between November and February, this 116-sq-km lake is home to vast flocks of indigenous and migratory birds. Ducks, geese, pelicans and flamingoes are best seen early in the morning and in the evening.

Lothal

About 80 km south of Ahmedabad, towards Bhavnagar, this site is of great interest to archaeologists. The city which stood here 4500 years ago was clearly related to the Indus Valley cities of Moenjodaro and Harappa, both in Pakistan. It has the same neatly laid-out street pattern, the same carefully assembled brickwork and the same scientific drainage system.

The name Lothal actually means Mound of the Dead in Gujarati, as does Moenjodaro in Sindhi. At its peak, this was probably one of the most important ports on the subcontinent and trade may have been conducted with the civilisations of Mesopotamia, Egypt and Persia.

There is an **archaeological museum** at the site.

Places to Stay The Tourist Corporation of Gujarat runs the *Toran Holiday Home*, which has 10 dorm beds for Rs 15 each and two double rooms for Rs 50. Checkout time here is 9 am.

Getting There & Away Lothal is a day trip from Ahmedabad. You can reach it by rail, disembarking at Bhurkhi on the Ahmedabad to Bhavnagar railway line, from where you can take a bus. Alternatively, there are direct buses from Ahmedabad.

Modhera

The beautiful and partially ruined Sun Temple of Modhera was built by King Bhimdev I (1026-27) and bears some resemblance to the later, and far better known, Sun Temple of Konark in the state of Orissa, which it predates by some 200 years. Like that temple, it was designed so that the dawn sun shone on the image of Surya, the Sun God, at the time of the equinoxes. The main hall and shrine are reached through a pillared porch and the temple exterior is intricately and delicately carved. As with the Temple of Somnath, this fine temple was ruined by Mahmud of Ghazni. The temple is open from 8 am to 6 pm daily.

Places to Stay There is a *PWD Rest House* but foreigners find it difficult to get a bed here for the night.

Getting There & Away Modhera is 106 km north-west of Ahmedabad. There are direct buses to Modhera, or you can take the train to Mahesana and then catch a bus for the 40-km trip to Modhera.

Unjha & Sidhpur

A little north of Mahesana and a base for those visiting the Modhera Temple, the town of Unjha is interesting for the marriage customs of the Kadwakanbis who live in this region. Marriages occur only once every 11 years and, on that day, every unmarried girl over 40 days old must be wed. If no husband can be found, a proxy wedding takes place and the bride immediately becomes a 'widow'. She later remarries when a suitable husband shows up.

Further north again is Sidhpur where you'll find the very fragmented ruins of an ancient temple. This region was an important centre for growing opium poppies.

Patan

About 120 km north-west of Ahmedabad, this was an ancient Hindu capital before being sacked by Mahmud of Ghazni in 1024. Now a pale shadow of its former self, it still has over 100 **Jain temples** and is famous for the manufacture of beautifully designed Patola silk saris. There's also a renovated **step well** here.

Places to Stay The only hotel is the *Hotel Neerav*, about 500 metres from the bus station, next to Kohinoor Talkies. Double rooms cost Rs 80.

Getting There & Away Patan is 25 km north-west of the Mahesana Railway Station, which also serves as a departure point for Modhera.

Dasada

The small town of Dasada, north-west of Ahmedabad, is very close to the Little Rann of Kutch. Desert Coursers (☎ Ahmedabad 44-5068) is a safari company which organises tours and game drives on the Rann. They also provide tented accommodation and transport. The rate is Rs 950 per person per day, all inclusive.

GANDHINAGAR

Population: 121,000

Although Ahmedabad initially became the capital of Gujarat state when the old state of Bombay was split into Maharashtra and Gujarat in 1960, a new capital was planned 32 km north-east on the west bank of the

Sabarmati River. Named Gandhinagar after Mahatma Gandhi, who was born in Gujarat, it is India's second planned city after Chandigarh and, like that city, is laid out in numbered sectors, and is equally dull. Construction of the city commenced in 1965 and the secretariat was moved there in 1970.

Places to Stay
Gandhinagar has an excellent *Youth Hostel* in sector 16 and, in sector 11, there is the *Panthik Ashram* government rest house. You'll find other rest houses and guest houses at Pethapur and opposite Sachivalaya.

For more upmarket accommodation, the *Hotel Haveli* (☎ 23-905) in sector 11 charges Rs 295/350 for standard rooms, or Rs 395/550 with air-con.

Getting There & Away
Buses from Ahmedabad cost about Rs 2.

VADODARA (Baroda)
Population: 1,100,000
Baroda was the capital of the princely Gaekwad state prior to independence. Present-day Vadodara is a pleasant, medium-sized city with some interesting museums and art galleries and a fine park. The city's well-known Fine Arts College attracts students from around the country and abroad. It's a good place for a short pause.

Orientation & Information
The railway station, bus stand and a cluster of cheaper hotels are all on one side of the city. The tourist office is in a small, upstairs room across from the station to the left. Tilak Rd runs straight out from the station, across the river by the Sayaji Bagh and into the main part of town.

The State Bank of India, near the Kirti Mandir, is open from 11 am to 3 pm Monday to Friday, and 11 am to 1 pm Saturday.

Sayaji Bagh & Vadodara Museum
This extensive park, encircled by a mini-railway, is a popular spot for an evening stroll. Within the park is the Vadodara

Museum & Art Gallery, open from 9.30 am to 4.45 pm daily, except Saturday when it opens at 10 am. The museum has various exhibits, while the gallery has Moghul miniatures and a collection of European masters. Also within the park grounds is the relatively new **planetarium** where there is an English-language performance each evening, and there is also a small **zoo**.

Maharaja Fateh Singh Museum
A little south of the centre, this royal art collection includes European works by Raphael, Titian and Murillo and examples of Greco-Roman, Chinese and Japanese art, as well as Indian exhibits. The museum is in the palace grounds and is open from 9 am to noon and 3 to 6 pm between July and March, 4 to 7 pm from April to June. It is closed on Monday.

Other Attractions
The flamboyant **Laxmi Vilas Palace** has a large collection of armour and sculptures but is not normally open to the public. The **Naulakhi Well**, a fine baoli, is 50 metres north of the palace. These interesting multi-level wells are unique to western India. There are others in Ahmedabad as well as just outside the city.

The Railway Staff College now occupies the Pratap Vilas Palace; there are a number of other palaces in the city. The Gaekwad rulers' family vault, the **Kirti Mandir**, is decorated with murals created by Indian artist Nandial Bose. The town centre is built around a lake swarming with fish – vendors sell food to throw to them.

Organised Tours
Check with the tourist office about the daily tours of Vadodara.

Places to Stay – bottom end
There are a lot of cheaper hotels within walking distance of the railway station, although later in the day you may have little choice as places seem to fill up as the day wears on.

If you head straight out from the station

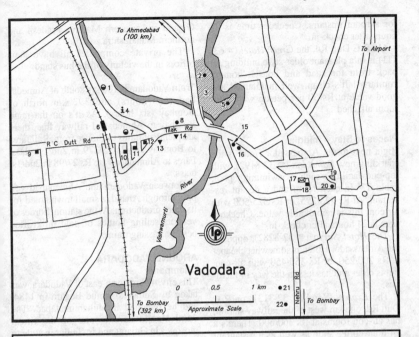

Vadodara

0   0.5   1 km
Approximate Scale

1 Long Distance Bus Stand	12 Jagdish Hindu Lodge
2 Museum & Art Gallery	13 Kwality
3 Sayaji Bagh	14 Havmor
4 Tourist Office	15 Kirti Mandir
5 Planetarium	16 State Bank of India
6 Railway Station	17 GPO
7 Local Bus Stand	18 Utsav Hotel
8 Fine Arts College	19 Jubilee Gardens
9 Green Hotel	20 Sursagar
10 Ambassador Hotel	21 Laxmi Vilas Palace & Naulakhi Well
11 Apsara Hotel	22 Maharaja Fateh Singh Museum

and take the third road on the right, you'll find the *Jagdish Hindu Lodge*, with gloomy and basic but reasonably clean rooms ranged around a courtyard. It's the best of the cheapies and also one of the cheapest, at Rs 50 for a double with bathroom attached. In the same street, and a notch up the scale, is the *Hotel Vikram* (☎ 32-7737), which charges Rs 80/125 for singles/doubles with bathroom attached, or Rs 140/180 with air-con.

In the next street back towards the station is the pleasant and well-kept *Apsara Hotel* (☎ 32-8251), with comfortable rooms at Rs 90/130 with bathroom. Across the road and a little further down is the big *Ambassador Hotel* (☎ 32-7653), with large, quiet rooms from Rs 105/166, or Rs 162/287 with air-con. They have a couple of gloomy, cupboard-sized cells on the ground floor which they may try to fob off on you, so ask for a room upstairs. Checkout time is 24 hours after check-in.

On R C Dutt Rd, the *Green Hotel* (☎ 63-111) is in a pleasant older-style building set back from the road and boasts 'homely comforts'! It's clean, well maintained and good value at Rs 50 per person with bathroom attached.

Places to Stay – middle

Right next to the Ambassador Hotel is the sparkling new *Rama Inn* (☎ 32-8192), with top-end facilities such as swimming pool, cable TV in each room and a decent restaurant. At Rs 225/375, or Rs 325/500 with air-con, this is remarkable value. Checkout time is 24 hours after check-in.

The *Hotel Surya* (☎ 32-8282), opposite the Ambassador Hotel, is somewhat cheaper at Rs 200/250, or Rs 350/450 with air-con, but is older and has less in the way of facilities.

The *Express Hotel* (☎ 32-3131) on R C Dutt Rd, one km west of the railway station, has air-con rooms at Rs 360/600. There's a 24-hour coffee shop as well as a restaurant which offers a variety of cuisines.

Places to Eat

Along the main road from the station towards the gardens and the river, there's a reasonable *Kwality* and a *Havmor*. Expect to pay at least Rs 40 for a meal at either place. The railway station also has a good restaurant.

For Chinese food try the *Chung Fa* on R C Dutt Rd.

Getting There & Away

Air The Indian Airlines office (☎ 67-677) is on University Rd, Fateh Ganj. There are Indian Airlines flights from Vadodara to Bombay (US$39), Delhi (US$88) and Ahmedabad (US$15).

Bus The long-distance bus stand is half a km north of the railway station, and there are STC buses to many destinations in both Gujarat and western Madhya Pradesh and northern Maharashtra.

The private companies all have their offices in the vicinity of the bus stand.

Train Vadodara is 100 km south of Ahmedabad (two hours) and 392 km north of Bombay (six hours). As it's on the main Bombay to Ahmedabad railway line, there are plenty of trains to choose from. Rail fares to Bombay are Rs 73/279 in 2nd/1st class. Fares to Ahmedabad are Rs 27/98 in 2nd/1st class.

Between Vadodara and Ahmedabad you pass through Anand, a small town noted for its dairy production. At the station, hordes of vendors selling bottles of cold milk often besiege passing trains.

AROUND VADODARA

Champaner

This city, 47 km north-east of Vadodara, was taken by Sultan Mahmud Begara in 1484, and he renamed it Muhammadabad. The **Jami Masjid** here is one of the finest mosques in Gujarat and is similar in style to the Jami Masjid of Ahmedabad.

The **Hill of Pavagadh**, with its ruined fort, rises beside Champaner in three stages. In 1553, the Moghuls, led by Humayun himself, scaled the fort walls using iron spikes driven into the rocks, and captured both the fort and its city. Parts of the massive fort walls still stand. According to Hindu legend, the hill is actually a chunk of the Himalayan mountainside which the monkey god Hanuman carted off to Lanka in an episode of the *Ramayana*, hence the name Pavagadh, which means Quarter of a Hill. Two important festivals are held here each year.

Places to Stay The state tourist organisation runs the *Hotel Champaner* (☎ 41). It has 15 dorm beds for Rs 10 per person and 32 double rooms for Rs 125. Checkout time is 11 am.

Dabhoi Fort

The 13th-century fort of Dabhoi is 29 km

south-east of Vadodara. A fine example of Hindu military architecture, it is notable for the design of its four gateways – particularly the Hira, or Diamond Gate.

Dakor

Equidistant from Vadodara and Ahmedabad, the Temple of Ranchodrai in Dakor is sacred to Lord Krishna and is a major centre for the **Sharad Purnima** festival in October or November.

BHARUCH (Broach)

Population: 138,000

This very old town was mentioned in historical records nearly 2000 years ago. In the 17th century, English and Dutch factories were established here. The **fort** overlooks the wide Narmada River from a hilltop and, located at its base, is the **Jami Masjid**, constructed from a Jain temple. On the riverbank, outside the city to the east, is the **Temple of Bhrigu Rishi**, from which the city took its name, Bhrigukachba, later shortened to Bharuch.

The Narmada River has featured in the news both locally and internationally recently as a large dam, the Sardar Sarovar, is being constructed upstream of Bharuch near the village of Manibeli. This is part of a hugely extravagant US$6 *billion* project in the Narmada Valley to provide massive amounts of irrigation water and electricity. The Sardar Sarovar dam is only a part of the entire project, which, if ever completed, will include 30 mega-dams, 135 medium dams and 3000 small dams.

The aim is laudable, but it's hard to see how the immediate disruption it causes will be effectively managed – the conservation lobby estimate that more than 100,000 people will need to be relocated as a result of the dam, a further 200,000 will be affected by associated canal and dam works, and the homes of at least one million people will be submerged. Typically, the reports prepared by the government and the World Bank, which is chipping in with US$450 million, do not fully examine the ramifications of the project.

The town of Suklatirth near Bharuch has a State Tourism Corporation of Gujarat *Toran Holiday Home* (☎ 38) with double rooms for Rs 30. The nearby island of Kabirwad, in the river, features a gigantic banyan tree which covers a hectare.

SURAT

Population: 1,500,000

Surat stands on the banks of the River Tapti and was once one of western India's major ports and trading towns. Two hundred years ago, it had a bigger population than it does today and was far more important than Bombay. Parsis first settled in Surat in the 12th century; they had earlier been centred 100 km south in Sanjan, where they had fled from Persia five centuries before. In 1573, the city fell to Akbar after a prolonged siege. It then became an important Moghul trading port and also the point of departure for Mecca-bound Muslim pilgrims.

Surat soon became a wealthy city and, in 1612, the British established a trading factory there, followed by the Dutch in 1616 and the French in 1664. Portuguese power on the west coast had been severely curtailed by a crushing naval defeat at the hands of the British. In 1664, Moghul power and prestige suffered a severe blow when the Maratha leader, Shivaji, sacked the town. In a classic display of the British stiff upper lip, Sir George Oxenden sent a message to Shivaji from the strongly defended English factory, saying that he should 'save the labour of his servants running to and fro on messages and come himself with all his army'. Perhaps Shivaji took the implied threat seriously, because the English factory was not attacked.

Although the English factory later transferred its 'presidency' to Bombay, Surat continued to prosper. A dock was built in 1720, followed by two British shipyards. By 1759, when the British took virtually full control over the city's ruler, Moghul power was long past its prime and, by 1800, the city was in British hands. Surat is no longer of any importance as a port, but it is a major industrial centre, especially for the manufacture of textiles and chemicals.

Despite its industrial importance, the city is of little interest to travellers, except those with a fascination for urban decay, noise and pollution. If Ahmedabad is bad in this respect, Surat is horrific. It might just be tolerable if the city had even one redeeming feature, but it doesn't.

Orientation

An eight-km-long wall once bordered Surat on one side, while the Tapti River borders the other. The walls were made of mud but, after the city was sacked by Shivaji, they were reconstructed in brick. The railway station, with many cheaper hotels in its immediate vicinity, is connected to the old fort beside the river by one of Surat's few wide roads.

Castle

Built in 1546, the castle is on the riverbank, beside the Tapti Bridge. Since most of it has been given over to offices it is no longer of great interest, but there is a good view over the city and river from its bastions. To get there, ask for the Tapti Bridge.

Factories

Without a guide, you would have difficulty finding the remains of the factories and, in any case, there is little to indicate their former importance. They are near the IP Mission High School. The English factory is about midway between the castle and the Kataragama Gate, out of the old city. Not too far away, standing close to the river, are the remains of the Portuguese Factory, French Lodge and Persian Factory. From the riverbank, you can see the Tapti Bridge to your left and across the river to your right is the mosque-studded suburb of Rander. There's a small temple by the river which is dedicated to Hanuman.

Cemeteries

The now very run-down, overgrown and neglected **English cemetery** is just beyond the Kataragama Gate, to the right of the main road. Many of the tombstones mark the graves of children under five years of age. As you enter the cemetery, the huge mausoleum to the right is that of Sir George Oxenden, who died in 1669. The structure is actually a tomb within a tomb, since his brother was buried here 10 years earlier and a larger mausoleum was constructed over that tomb. Another large tomb next to it is said to be that of Gerald Aungier, the next president of the English factory. Like any scrap of waste ground in India, the English cemetery has become a public toilet and the imposing mausoleums are in a sorry state.

Backtrack towards the city and, about 500 metres after the Kataragama Gate and some 100 metres off the road to the left (to the right if you are coming from the centre), you'll find the **Dutch cemetery**. The massive mausoleum of Baron Adriaan van Reede, who died in 1691, was once decorated with frescoes and woodcarvings. Note the inscription on the wall; 'Souratta' rates capital letters while lesser 'bombai' is in lower case. Adjoining the Dutch cemetery is the **Armenian cemetery**.

Other Attractions

Surat has a number of mosques and Jain, Hindu and Parsi temples. Cotton, silk and the manufacture of bangles are important industries here. Nearby **Rander**, five km across the Hope Bridge, was built on the site of a very ancient Hindu city which had been taken by the Muslims in 1225. **Swally** (Suvali) was the old port for Surat, 19 km to the west. It was off Swally, in 1615, that Portuguese colonial aspirations in India were ended by the British navy.

Places to Stay – bottom end

There are lots of hotels near the railway station but none stand out. They're all within walking distance. In the rock-bottom bracket, the *Rupali Hotel* has dorm beds for Rs 25, doubles with bathroom for Rs 85 and singles with common bathroom for Rs 40. Facilities are basic. On the left, down the road facing the station, the *Janta Hotel* has doubles with bathroom for Rs 55 and singles/doubles with common bathroom for

Rs 30/45. You'll get a good idea of the hotel's standards as you climb the greasy, filthy stairs to the 2nd-floor reception area. The staff are not particularly helpful.

On the same street, the *Simla Guest House* is better value but otherwise unremarkable. It has doubles with bathroom for Rs 130 and singles/doubles with common bathroom for Rs 44/80. Another cheapie close to the station is the large *Central Hotel*, where ordinary singles/doubles cost Rs 80/130 and deluxe singles/doubles are Rs 90/175.

Good value at the top end of this category is the *Sarvajanik Hotel*, close to the railway station. It's pleasant, though the staff are indifferent, and offers singles for Rs 90 to Rs 105 and doubles for Rs 140, all with bathroom and hot water. In the same block as the Rupali, the *Hotel Amar*, a new building with very friendly staff, is also good. Singles/doubles cost Rs 85/140 and deluxe air-con doubles are also available. All rooms have bathroom and hot water.

Places to Stay – middle

The *Hotel Yuvrav* (☎ 53-621), near the railway station, is a good middle-range air-con place with two vegetarian restaurants. Rooms cost Rs 250/330.

On the Ring Rd, about two km from the railway station, is the *Tex Palazzo Hotel* (☎ 62-3018), with singles/doubles for Rs 225/350, more with air-con. It has all the usual services and a restaurant.

Places to Stay – top end

Surat's best hotel is the *Hotel Rama Regency* (☎ 66-6565) near Bharti Park in Athwa Lines, five km from the central city area. Air-con rooms with plenty of buttons and switches cost Rs 800/900, and there are more expensive suites available. The hotel has a number of facilities, including a swimming pool, health club and two restaurants.

Places to Eat

The *Tex Palazzo Hotel* boasts India's first revolving restaurant and, as with so many revolving restaurants around the world, the food takes a distant second place to the view.

At least it's not outrageously expensive, but the splendours of Surat unfold below you through windows nearly as dirty as those on the average Indian bus! Back at ground level, the same hotel serves a good Gujarati thali.

Close to the railway station and next to the Central Hotel, the *Gaurav Restaurant* offers excellent and very cheap south Indian dishes. It's clean, popular and highly recommended. For a more substantial meal, try the *Hotel Ashoka* (actually a restaurant, not a hotel), next to the Simla Guest House. It's run by Sikhs and the food is good without being really special.

Getting There & Away

Surat is on the main Bombay to Ahmedabad railway line so there are many trains to both places.

AROUND SURAT

There are a number of beaches near Surat. Only 16 km away, **Dumas** is a popular health resort. **Hajira** is 28 km from the city and **Ubhrat** is 42 km out, while **Tithal** is 108 km away and only five km from Valsad on the Bombay to Vadodara rail line.

Twenty-nine km south of Surat, **Navsari** has been a headquarters for the Parsi community since the earliest days of their settlement in India. **Udvada**, only 10 km north of Vapi, the station for Daman, has the oldest Parsi sacred fire in India. It is said that the fire was brought from Persia to Diu, on the opposite coast of the Gulf of Cambay, in 700 AD. **Sanjan**, in the extreme south of the state, is the small port where they first landed. A pillar marks the spot.

Places to Stay

State-run *Holiday Homes* abound in this area. Hajira has one, with cottages for Rs 175 and double rooms for Rs 125, as does Ubhrat, where accommodation ranges from double rooms for Rs 40 up to four-bed bungalows for Rs 200.

There's another one at Tithal (☎ Valsad 2206), and here bungalows cost Rs 250, while double rooms are Rs 100 and Rs 150.

DAMAN

Right in the south of Gujarat, the 56-sq-km enclave of Daman was, along with Diu, taken from the Portuguese at the same time as Goa. For a time, Daman and Diu were governed from Goa but both now constitute the Union Territory of Daman & Diu, which is governed from New Delhi.

Daman's main role now seems to be as a place to buy alcohol, since the surrounding state of Gujarat is completely 'dry'. The streets of Daman are lined with bars selling beer, 'Finest Scotch Whisky – Made in India' and various other spirits such as feni (distilled from fermented cashew nuts or coconuts).

The Portuguese seized Daman in 1531 and were officially ceded the region by Bahadur Shah, the last major Gujarati sultan, in 1559. There is still a lingering Portuguese flavour to the town, with its fine old forts and a number of churches, but it is definitely not a smaller version of Goa. The town is divided by the Damao Ganga River. The northern section is known as Nani Daman, or Little Daman, and contains the hotels, restaurants, bars and so on. In the southern part, known as Moti Daman, or 'big' Daman, government buildings and churches are enclosed within an imposing wall.

Like Goa, Daman is beside the sea but its beaches bear no relation to the glowing, golden stretches of sand further south. Daman's beaches are grey, drab, dirty and dismal and function as local latrines.

Information

The main post office is south of the river in Moti Daman, but there's a more convenient subbranch near the Sun n Sea Hotel in Nani Daman.

Churches

The **Se Cathedral** in the Moti Daman fort dates from the 17th century and is totally Iberian. It's less impressive than the **Church of Our Lady of the Rosary**, where ancient Portuguese tombstones are set into the cool, damp floor. The altar is a masterpiece of intricately carved, gold-painted wood. Light filters through the dusty windows, illuminating wooden panels painted with scenes of Christ and the apostles.

Other Attractions

You can walk around the ramparts of the **Nani Daman fort** (Fort of St Jerome). They're a good place from which to watch the fish market and the activity on the small fishing fleet which anchors alongside, but there's otherwise nothing much of interest.

Near the river on the Nani Daman side is an interesting **Jain temple**. If you enquire in the temple office, a white-robed caretaker will show you around. The walls inside are completely covered with glassed-over 18th-century murals depicting the life of Mahavira, who lived around 500 BC.

It's also quite pleasant to wander round the wide streets of the old **Fort of Moti Daman**. The place has a very sleepy atmosphere, and the views across the river to Nani Daman from the ramparts near the lighthouse are not bad.

Places to Stay

Most of the hotels are on Seaface Rd. The cheaper places are pretty basic and uninspiring. Perhaps the best of them is the *Hotel Sovereign* (☎ 2823), where doubles on the ground floor cost Rs 60, while single/double rooms on the first floor are Rs 75/90. The *Hotel Brighton* across the road is even more spartan and is slightly cheaper, but seems to be permanently full.

Just off Seaface Rd, the *Hotel Marina* is one of the few surviving Portuguese-style houses. The reception area indicates that it must once have been a very fine house but, although it still has a lot of character, it's unfortunately been allowed to decay and can only be described as very basic. The rooms are large and airy but the bed sheets are far from clean and are full of holes. Doubles with bathroom cost Rs 60. The staff are friendly and there's a bar and restaurant downstairs.

For something a bit better try the *Hotel*

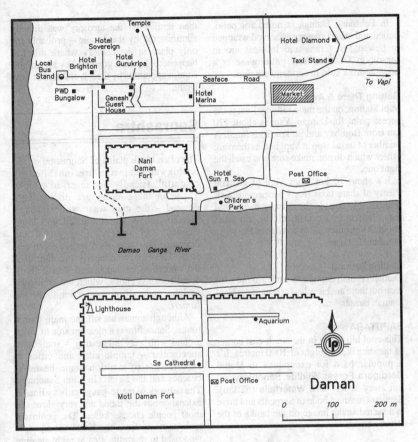

Daman

0   100   200 m

Diamond near the taxi stand. This friendly place has good-sized rooms with bathroom and hot water for Rs 80/110, and there are more expensive air-con rooms and an air-con bar and restaurant.

Better still is the *Hotel Gurukripa* (☎ 2846) on Seaface Rd, with rooms for Rs 100/125, or Rs 250/300 with air-con.

Daman's newest hotel is the *Hotel Sun n Sea* (☎ 2506), near the river. It's somewhat disorganised and chaotic – Basil Fawlty would feel right at home here. Rooms with balcony overlooking the river cost Rs 150/165, or with air-con it's Rs 250/300.

Places to Eat

The restaurant at the *Hotel Gurukripa* is air-con and the food is very good, with most dishes around Rs 30. The beer is cold and the service attentive. It's undoubtedly the best place to eat in town.

There are a number of places which claim to be a 'bar & restaurant', but this is just a function of the liquor laws – places selling liquor must provide food. Consequently most of these places are bars first and the food is something of an afterthought. A Kingfisher at any of them will set you back a mere Rs 15.

In February, Daman is noted for papri, boiled and salted sweetpeas served wrapped in newspaper. Crabs and lobsters are in season in October. *Tari* palm wine is a popular drink sold in earthenware pots.

Getting There & Away

Vapi Station, on the main railway line, is the access point for Daman. Vapi is about 170 km from Bombay and 90 km from Surat. A number of trains stop at Vapi but, as there are others which do not, make sure you catch the right one.

It's about 10 km from Vapi to Daman. Plenty of share taxis (Rs 5 per person) wait immediately outside the railway station and leave frequently for Daman. The trip takes about 20 minutes. Also available are some ramshackle buses.

Getting Around

Daman is small enough to walk around with ease but there are bicycles for rent in the Nani Daman bazaar.

SAPUTARA

This cool hill resort in the south-east corner of the state is at a height of 1000 metres. It's a popular base for excursions to **Mahal Bardipara Forest Wildlife Sanctuary**, 60 km away or the **Gira Waterfalls** (52 km). Saputara means Abode of Serpents and there is a sacred snake image on the banks of the River Sarpagana.

Places to Stay

The State Tourism Corporation of Gujarat runs the *Toran Hill Resort* (☎ 26) at Saputara. The resort offers dorm beds for Rs 20 to Rs 25 per person and a range of double rooms for Rs 150 to Rs 550.

DADRA & NAGAR HAVELI

This small Union Territory, covering less than 500 sq km, is in the extreme south-west corner of the state, on the Maharashtra border. It was administered by the Portuguese from 1779, when the Marathas assigned it to them for a fee of Rs 12,000, right up until it was 'liberated' in 1954. From then until 1961 the territory was directly administered by the people – probably the only place in the country where this had happened. It is now governed by an Administrator appointed by the government in New Delhi.

Saurashtra

The often bleak plains of Saurashtra on the Kathiawar peninsula are inhabited by colourful, friendly but reserved people. Those in the country are distinctively dressed – the men wear white turbans, pleated jackets (short-waisted and long-sleeved) and jodhpurs (baggy seat and drainpipe legs) and often sport golden ear-studs. The women are nearly as colourful as the women of Rajasthan and wear embroidered backless cholis, which are known by various names but most commonly the *kanjeri*.

Although somewhat off the main tourist routes, Saurashtra is a pleasant area to travel around with very interesting – sometimes spectacular – temple sites and cities to explore, not to mention some beautiful beaches and the Sasan Gir Lion Sanctuary. The network of metre-gauge railway lines is extensive but the trains are very slow and most people choose buses. The peninsula took its name from the Kathi tribespeople who used to roam the area at night stealing whatever was not locked into the many village forts, or *kots*. Around Kathiawar, you may notice long lines of memorial stones known as *palias* – men are usually depicted riding on large horses while women ride on wheels, showing that they were in carriages.

BHAVNAGAR

Population: 403,000

Founded as a port in 1723, Bhavnagar is still an important trading post for the cotton goods manufactured in Gujarat. The Bhavnagar lock gate keeps ships afloat in the city's port at low tide. On the surface, Bhavnagar isn't the most interesting place to

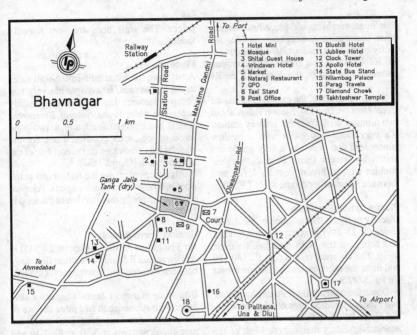

Bhavnagar

0   0.5   1 km

Railway Station

Station Road

Mahatma Gandhi Road

To Port

Diwanpara Rd

Ganga Jalia Tank (dry)

To Ahmedabad

To Palitana, Una & Diu

To Airport

1 Hotel Mini
2 Mosque
3 Shital Guest House
4 Vrindavan Hotel
5 Market
6 Nataraj Restaurant
7 GPO
8 Taxi Stand
9 Post Office
10 Bluehill Hotel
11 Jubilee Hotel
12 Clock Tower
13 Apollo Hotel
14 State Bus Stand
15 Nilambag Palace
16 Parag Travels
17 Diamond Chowk
18 Takhteshwar Temple

visit and few travellers get here. It does, however, have a beautiful old bazaar area with overhanging wooden balconies, thousands of little shops, lots of local colour and not a tourist in sight.

Orientation & Information

Bhavnagar is a sprawling city with distinctly separate old and new sections. The bus station is in the new part of town and the railway station is at the far end of the old town around 2½ km away. To complicate matters, private bus companies usually have their own depots which are sometimes a long way from the bus station.

There are no cheap hotels around the bus station so, if you're on a budget, take an auto-rickshaw into the old town. Even there, the choice is very limited.

Bazaar

The bazaar is well worth a day's exploration if you enjoy taking in the sights, sounds and smells of an extremely busy and colourful old town untouched by tourism.

Takhteshwar Temple

This temple sits on the highest hillock in Bhavnagar. The views over the city and out into the Gulf of Cambay are excellent but the temple itself is of minor interest.

Places to Stay – bottom end

The only cheap hotels in Bhavnagar are in the old bazaar area and there's very little choice. Perhaps the best value is offered by the *Shital Guest House* (☎ 28-360), Amba Chowk, Mali Tekra, right in the middle of the bazaar area. It's clean and the manager speaks English. Singles/doubles with bathroom cost Rs 35/50, Rs 30/40 with common bathroom. Dorm beds are also available for Rs 15 per person.

Not far from the Shital is the *Vrindavan Hotel* (☎ 27-391). It's well signposted but the entrance can still be quite difficult to find.

This huge, rambling old place has a somewhat Dickensian atmosphere. Inside, it's pretty basic. Singles/doubles with bathroom are Rs 45/80, double rooms with common bathroom cost Rs 60, and dorm beds are Rs 25.

Going up in price, the extremely pleasant *Hotel Mini* (☎ 26-813), Station Rd, is about two minutes walk from the railway station. It's very clean and quiet with a mellow atmosphere and is run by a very gentle old man who speaks fluent English. Singles/doubles with bathroom cost Rs 45/75, and there are some larger rooms at Rs 75/100.

Places to Stay – middle

Directly opposite the bus station, the *Apollo Hotel* (☎ 25-249) is somewhat overpriced, and being on the main road can be quite noisy. The cheapest rooms cost Rs 140/180 and there are more expensive air-con rooms for Rs 200/250.

Down the road a little from the Apollo are two modern middle-range hotels. The *Bluehill Hotel* (☎ 26-951) is extremely pleasant and immaculately maintained. Most of the rooms have a balcony and all have wall-to-wall carpeting, colour TV and bathroom with constant hot water. Singles/doubles cost Rs 175/250, Rs 225/350 with air-con, and there's a vegetarian restaurant. The *Jubilee Hotel* (☎ 20-045) next door offers similar facilities but is slightly more expensive at Rs 200/250 for singles/doubles and Rs 225/325 for air-con rooms. The hotel has a very good vegetarian restaurant.

If you can possibly afford it, the most interesting place to stay is the *Nilambag Palace* (☎ 21-337), west of the bus station on the Ahmedabad road. As its name suggests, the Nilambag is a former maharaja's palace, and is packed with memorabilia from a bygone age and surrounded by well-tended gardens, complete with strutting peacocks. Rooms are surprisingly cheap with singles/doubles at just Rs 162/267, and more expensive rooms at Rs 277/382 with air-con. Even the cheapest rooms are very capacious, with bathrooms the size of your average hotel room. Meals are available at very reasonable prices. The staff here are very friendly indeed.

Places to Eat

Apart from the usual hole-in-the-wall cafes in the bazaar area, Bhavnagar has very few cheap restaurants. Just about the only readily accessible place is the *Nataraj Restaurant* which has average food and a two-page menu of ice-cream goodies! Look for the Vadelal Ice Cream sign on the east side of the now-dry tank (Ganga Jalia).

Also convenient are the restaurants at the *Apollo, Bluehill* and *Jubilee* hotels. Prices at all three are pretty reasonable and the food is good.

Getting There & Away

Air The Indian Airlines office (☎ 24-745) is on Diwanpara Rd. Indian Airlines flies daily between Bombay and Bhavnagar for US$35.

Bus State transport buses connect Bhavnagar with Ahmedabad and other centres in the region. For Una (and Diu) there are morning departures at 5.30, 6.30, 7.45 and 8.30 am, and also departures later in the day. The journey takes 4½ hours and costs Rs 30. To Palitana there are frequent departures throughout the day for the 1½-hour journey (Rs 7.50). The timetable at the state bus stand in Bhavnagar is entirely in Gujarati.

The main private bus company is Punjab Travels (☎ 26-333), Parag Travel Agency, Waghawadi Rd, near the Takhteshwar Temple. It operates buses to Ahmedabad at 6.30 am daily. These cost Rs 50 and take about six hours.

Train Bhavnagar is 268 km by rail from Ahmedabad. The trip takes about seven hours and costs Rs 54/199 in 2nd/1st class. To Palitana there are a couple of steam trains daily and these cover the 47 km in a dazzling two hours.

AROUND BHAVNAGAR
Valabhipur

North of Palitana, this ancient city was once the capital of this part of India. Extensive ruins have been located and archaeological finds are exhibited in a museum, but there's little to see apart from scattered stones.

PALITANA
Population: 42,000

Situated 51 km south-west of Bhavnagar, the town of Palitana is little more than a gateway to **Shatrunjaya**, the Place of Victory. The 600-metre ascent from the town to the hilltop is a walk of some two km. Over a period of 900 years, 863 temples have been built here. The hilltop is dedicated entirely to the gods; at dusk, even the priests depart from the temples, leaving them deserted.

Almost all the temples are Jain and this hill, one of Jainism's holiest pilgrimage places, is another illustration of their belief that merit is derived from constructing temples. The hilltops are bounded by sturdy walls and the temples are grouped into nine enclosures or *tunks* – each with a central major temple and many minor ones clustered around. Some of the earliest temples here were built in the 11th century but, in the 14th and 15th centuries, the Muslims destroyed them, so the current temples date from the 16th century onwards.

The hilltop affords a very fine view in all directions; on a clear day you can see the Gulf of Cambay beyond Bhavnagar. The most notable of the temples is dedicated to **Shri Adishwara**, the first Jain tirthankar. Note the frieze of dragons around this temple. Adjacent is the Muslim shrine of **Angar Pir**. Women who want to have children make offerings of miniature cradles at this shrine.

Built in 1618 by a wealthy Jain merchant, the **Chaumukh**, or Four-Faced shrine, has images of Adinath facing out in the four cardinal directions. Other important temples are those to Kumar Pal, Sampriti Raj and Vimal Shah. There are so many marble temples on the hill summit that, from a distance, it looks like a giant, glistening, white wedding cake.

The temples are open from 7 am to 7 pm. You'll need a photography permit to take a camera up the hill – enquire at your hotel.

You will be asked for the permit at the main entrance. (There are two entrances – the main one is reached by taking the left-hand fork as you near the top and the other by the right-hand fork.)

A horse cart to the base of the hill costs Rs 3 per person or Rs 8 if you're alone, although you'll have to bargain for this rate. The walk is time consuming but not strenuous. You can be carried up the hill in a *dooli* swing chair for Rs 50, as do quite a few affluent and obese pilgrims.

Places to Stay
Palitana has scores of dharamsalas (pilgrims' rest houses) but, unless you're a Jain, you're unlikely to be allowed to stay at any of them. The *Hotel Sumeru* (☎ 227) on Station Rd is a Gujarat Tourism enterprise which offers excellent accommodation at reasonable prices. Double rooms with bathroom and balcony are Rs 150 a double, Rs 250 with air-con, and there are a total of 32 dorm beds at Rs 20 per person. Meals are available at the hotel.

The *Hotel Shravak* (☎ 2428), opposite the bus station, has single/double rooms at Rs 50/100 and more expensive rooms with air-con. Beds in the rather crowded dormitories cost Rs 20, but there are no lockers so the Sumeru's dorms are better.

Places to Eat
The *Hotel Sumeru* has a reasonable restaurant with Gujarati thalis as well as Punjabi food. Down the alley towards the cinema, beside the Shravak, a wildly busy 24-hour snack place offers puris, sabzi, curd, roasted peppers and ganthia – varieties of fried dough.

Getting There & Away
Bus If you're coming from the north, plenty of state transport buses make the 1½ trip from Bhavnagar. The fare is Rs 7. Express buses to and from Ahmedabad take 4½ hours, an hour less than the ordinary ones, and the fare is Rs 50.

There are a few direct buses daily to Una (for Diu), or you can take local buses in stages to Talaja (1½ hours), then to Mahuva (one hour) and another bus on to Una (two hours), but these tend to be crowded and it can be difficult to get a seat.

Train Express trains make the trip from Ahmedabad in nine to 11 hours with a change at Sihor shortly before Palitana. Local trains between Bhavnagar and Palitana take about 1½ hours.

DIU

Population: 21,000

One of India's undiscovered gems, this was the first landing point for the Parsis when they fled from Persia, although they stayed only three years. Like Daman and Goa, Diu was a Portuguese colony until taken over by India in 1961. Along with Daman, it is still governed from New Delhi as a Union Territory rather than as part of Gujarat. The former colony includes the island of Diu itself, about 11 km long by three km wide, separated from the coast by a narrow channel. There are also two tiny mainland enclaves. One of these, on which the village of Ghoghla stands, is the entry point to Diu if you arrive through the town of Una.

Diu's crowning glory is the huge fort, a sight which justifies the long trip here. The northern side of the island, facing Gujarat, is tidal marsh and saltpans while the southern coast alternates between limestone cliffs, rocky coves and sandy beaches, the best of which are at Nagoa. The somewhat windswept and arid island is riddled with quarries from which the Portuguese removed vast quantities of limestone to construct their huge fort, city walls, monuments and buildings.

The rocky or sandy interior reaches a maximum height of just 29 metres, so agriculture is limited although there are extensive stands of coconut and other palms. Branching palms *(Hyphaene* species) are very much a feature of the island and were originally introduced from Africa by the Portuguese.

The Indian government appears to have an official policy of playing down the Portu-

guese era. Seven Rajput soldiers (six of them Singhs) and a few civilians were killed in Operation Vijay, which ended Portuguese rule. After the Indian Air Force unnecessarily bombed the airstrip and terminal, near Nagoa, it remained derelict until the late 1980s. The old church in Diu Fort was also bombed and is now a roofless ruin. It's said that the Portuguese blew up Government House to stop it falling into 'enemy' hands.

History

These days, it's hard to understand why the Portuguese should have been interested in capturing and fortifying such an apparently unimportant and isolated outpost but, in the 14th to 16th centuries, Diu was an important trading post and naval base from which the Ottoman Turks controlled the shipping routes in the northern part of the Arabian Sea.

After an unsuccessful attempt to capture the island in 1531, during which Bahadur Shah, the Sultan of Gujarat, was assisted by the Turkish navy, the Portuguese finally secured control in 1535 by taking advantage of a quarrel between the sultan and the Moghul emperor, Humayun. Humayun had defeated Bahadur Shah the previous year and had forced him into exile in Malwa, but while he was distracted by clashes with the Afghan Sher Khan, Bahadur was able to return.

With pressure still being exerted by both the Portuguese and the Moghuls, Bahadur concluded a peace treaty with the Portuguese, effectively giving them control over the port at Diu. The treaty was soon cast to the wind and, although both Bahadur Shah and his successor, Sultan Mahmad III, attempted to contest the issue, the peace treaty which was eventually signed in 1539 ceded the island of Diu and the mainland enclave of Ghoghla to the Portuguese. Soon after the signing of this treaty, the Portuguese began constructing their fortress.

Information

The tourist office is in the new Tourist Complex at Ghoghla, but apart from a hope-

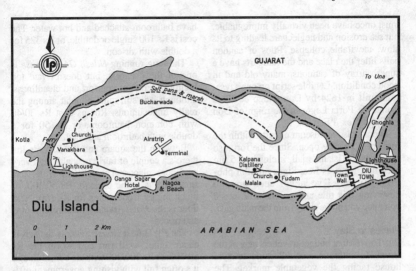

Diu Island

lessly verbose glossy brochure, they have little to offer.

The State Bank of Saurashtra is the most efficient place to change travellers' cheques. The main post office opens remarkably early for India and there's another post office at Ghoghla.

All the buses operate from the main 'town square' on the northern shore. The post office and banks (three of them) are nearby, along with Goa Travels, customs, and a few bars and restaurants.

Diu Town

The island's main industry would have to be fishing, followed by booze and salt. A distillery at Malala produces rum from sugar cane grown on the mainland. The town boasts quite a few bars where visitors from the 'dry' mainland can enjoy a beer (or stronger IMFL – 'Indian Made Foreign Liquor').

The town is sandwiched between the massive fort to the east and a huge city wall to the west. The main **gateway** in the wall has some nice carvings of lions, angels and a priest, while just inside the gate is a miniature chapel with an icon, dating to 1702. Diu Town has two churches, **St Paul's** and **St**

Francis of Assisi, and a third which has been converted into a hospital. It's said that there are now only 15 Christian families left on the whole island.

Unlike Daman, the buildings in Diu show a significant Portuguese influence. The town is a maze of narrow, winding streets and, although many of the wooden balconies have been allowed to decay, you could easily imagine yourself to be in one of the former Portuguese Moroccan enclaves such as Essaouira or El Jadida. Many of the houses are well ornamented and brightly painted. Further away from this tightly packed residential quarter, the streets turn into meandering and often leafy lanes reminiscent of rural Iberia.

At the back of the town square, there's also a tiny but interesting bazaar where most of life's necessities can be found. In a small park on the esplanade, between the square and the police station, the **Marwar Memorial**, topped by a griffin, commemorates the liberation of the island from the Portuguese. It also sports a tiny crocodile 'farm'.

Fort Constructed in 1547, the massive Portuguese fort with its double moat (one tidal) must once have been virtually impregnable, but sea erosion and neglect are leading to its slow, inevitable collapse. Piles of cannon balls litter the place and the ramparts have a superb array of cannons, many old and in good condition. Legible script on one says it was built in 1624 by Don Diego de Silva Conde de Porta Legre in the reign of Don Philippe, Rex d'Espana.

There's also a museum of sorts within the fort but it's rarely open. Since the fort also serves as the island's jail, it closes at 5 pm each day. Entry is free. Signs prohibit photography but I've never seen anyone observing this rule and no-one will hassle you once you move away from the main gate.

Places to Stay

Diu Town Most budget travellers stay at the *Hotel Mozambique*, an old Portuguese-style house facing the vegetable market. The potential of this place is enormous but, alas, unrealised and likely to remain so without more imagination on the part of the management. Doubles are overpriced at Rs 60 and there are views from the upstairs balcony. All rooms have common facilities but there's no hot water. There is, however, a bar and a basic restaurant on the ground floor.

Higher in price is the *Baron's Inn* which is also known as the *The Fun Club* – a most inappropriate name which gives a totally false impression of the place. On the Old Fort Rd, halfway between the ferry quay and the PWD Rest House, this fine old Portuguese villa is right by the sea, overlooking the channel between Diu Town and Ghoghla. Spacious rooms with fan and bathroom (cold water only) cost Rs 75/95 and excellent meals are available on request. Unfortunately this place is often full.

Another good place is the modern *Hotel Prince* (☎ 2265), not far from the fish market. Rooms here are good value at Rs 50 for a double at the back of the building, and Rs 75 with an ocean view, all with attached bathroom and hot water.

The *Hotel Samrat* (☎ 2354), a couple of blocks back from the main square, is new and clean although not overly friendly. All rooms

have bathroom attached and hot water. The cost is Rs 100 single or double, or Rs 325 for a double with air-con.

The long-running *Nilesh Guest House* is one of the cheapest, but doesn't rate too highly in terms of comfort and cleanliness, although it is still quite popular among the really impecunious. Rooms cost Rs 30/40 with common bathroom, or Rs 50 for a double with bathroom attached.

Between the square and the Baron's Inn there's a couple of fairly new although very mediocre places. The *Alishan Hotel* has small rooms at the back for Rs 50/100, or much bigger front rooms for Rs 150. Next door is the *Hotel Apana* with similar rooms and prices.

The *PWD Rest House* towards the fort is clean, quiet, well run and worth the Rs 50/100, or Rs 200/300 with air-con, although it's often full with visiting government officials. Meals are available on request and there are fine views from the 1st-floor rooms.

The *Hotel Ashiyana* (☎ 2260) is a new place not far from the main square. Although it has a bit of a men's club atmosphere, it is sparkling clean (at least so far) and good value at Rs 50 per person with bathroom attached.

Nagoa Beach The *Ganga Sagar Hotel* is the only hotel at Nagoa beach. It's very clean and run by a no-nonsense woman who decides which room you will get and how much you will pay (up to a point). It can seem a little like Fort Knox but it means no hassles for the guests (most of whom are Westerners) and security for your gear. The upstairs rooms have the best views over the beach. Singles/doubles cost Rs 50/100, and checkout time is a very uncivilised 8 am. None of the rooms have baths and there is no hot water, but the common facilities are adequate.

It's also possible to rent palm-roofed cottages in the village for around Rs 100 per week but all you get is a roof. You'll have to buy beds and cooking facilities for yourself so this is only a viable option if you plan to stay for a while.

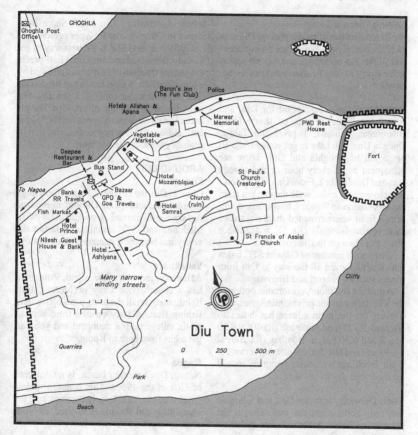

Diu Town

Ghoghla Post Office

GHOGHLA

Baron's Inn (The Fun Club)
Police
Hotels Alishan & Apana
Marwar Memorial
PWD Rest House
Vegetable Market
Fort
Deepee Restaurant & Bar
Bus Stand
Hotel Mozambique
St Paul's Church (restored)
To Nagoa
Bank & RR Travels
Bazaar
GPO & Goa Travels
Hotel Samrat
Church (ruin)
Fish Market
Hotel Prince
Nilesh Guest House & Bank
Hotel Ashiyana
St Francis of Assisi Church
Many narrow winding streets
Cliffs
Quarries
0   250   500 m
Park
Beach

Places to Eat

Although there are plenty of bars in Diu Town, there are very few restaurants. The bars may offer rice and dhal, or something similar, but that's about the limit. One of the few exceptions is the *Deepee Restaurant & Bar* on the main square. It has a limited menu of Indian dishes, but the food is quite good and the bar is separate from the restaurant.

The other restaurants are attached to the hotels. The *Alishan Hotel* has a reasonable restaurant serving pretty unexciting food, or there are a couple of very basic eateries

around the market square. Diu is certainly not going to be a gastronomic highlight.

Beer and drinks are exceedingly cheap (Rs 15 for a Kingfisher) but it's hardly a raging town – by 9 pm all the bars have closed up for the night. At Nagoa beach, in addition to the Ganga Sagar there is the *Mombasa Bar & Restaurant*, next door to the hotel. Though widely advertised all over Diu island, it's just a tiny place which is mainly a bar, but they'll cook food for you if they have it or if you order in advance. Don't expect anything elaborate as cooking facilities are relatively crude, but the staff are very friendly.

Getting There & Away

Air Rehabilitation of the airport on Diu was recently completed, but as yet no commercial flights are operating, and no-one seems to have any idea as to who will start flying, or when.

Bus Una is the access point for Diu, and there are direct buses to there from Bhavnagar, Palitana, Veraval and Talaja. Once in Una, you have to get yourself the 10 or so km to Ghoghla and Diu. There are infrequent buses every hour or so between Una and Diu for Rs 2. From Una, if you don't want to wait for a bus, walk the one km from the bus station to Tower Chowk (ask directions), from where crowded share rickshaws take you to Ghoghla (Rs 5), and another share rickshaw on to Diu costs Rs 2.

There are a number of Gujarat STC buses which actually run all the way to Diu from places such as Veraval and Bhavnagar.

A quicker and more comfortable option to the STC buses are the private minibuses. Goa Travels on the main square has buses to Veraval (Rs 25) and Junagadh (Rs 40) at 6.30 am, 2 and 6.30 pm; to Bombay (Rs 200) at 10.30 am; and RR Travels plies to Veraval at 6 am. Bookings with either company should be made one day in advance.

Train Delwada, between Una and Ghoghla and only about eight km from Diu, is the nearest railhead. A shared auto-rickshaw from there to Ghoghla costs about Rs 2. Trains run from Delwada to Veraval (96 km, 4½ hours), Sasan Gir and Junagadh (164 km, seven hours). Although extremely slow, the metre-gauge steam trains are great if you're not in a hurry, and you certainly get a much more relaxed and interesting ride than on the often crowded STC buses.

Getting Around

There are plenty of auto-rickshaws on the island, and they have a chart listing the fares set by the government. Officially it's Rs 25 from Diu to Nagoa, or Rs 40 return, although if things are slow you should be able to bargain this down. Rs 5 gets you anywhere within the town of Diu itself. Share rickshaws to Ghoghla cost Rs 2 per person.

Cycling around Diu is the best way to get to know this island and most travellers prefer the greater freedom of movement allowed by a bicycle. There's a cycle store in the bazaar that rents them out for Rs 12 per day. For more mobility with less effort, Goa Travels in the bazaar rents out mopeds for Rs 50 plus fuel, although this is negotiable, and they'll probably initially ask for more.

AROUND DIU

Fudam

Close to Diu, the village of Fudam has a huge abandoned church, Our Lady of Remedies. A large old carved wooden altar with Madonna and child remains inside but the vestry has become a manger, full of straw!

Vanakbara

At the extreme west of the island, Vanakbara has a church (Our Lady of Mercy), fort, lighthouse, small bazaar, post office and fishing fleet. A ferry crosses from here to Kotla village on the mainland and you can get a bus from here to Kodinar.

Nagoa

Nagoa, Diu's premier beach, is reminiscent of Goa in the 1960s. This beautiful palm-fringed beach is still largely deserted, safe for swimming and the place to shed all your worldly cares.

Ghoghla

In the village of Ghoghla on the mainland part of Diu is the new *Tourist Complex*. This building also houses the tourist office and is the first building in Diu after you come through the barrier which marks the border with Gujarat. The complex is a masterpiece of poor planning and thoughtless construction – two-storey blocks of 'cottages' which could have been orientated to face the sea, but instead give guests a view of nothing more exotic than the backside of the Samudra Beach Resort next door (and actually across the border in Gujarat). There are dorm beds for Rs 50, rooms in the 'cottages' cost Rs 150 for a double, or Rs 150/300 with air-con, and there's a small restaurant.

Samudra Beach

Just over the state border beyond Ghoghla stands one of Gujarat State Tourism's prestige developments, the *Samudra Beach Resort* (☎ Una 116). Crores of rupees have been spent on this ambitious but quite sensitively designed answer to the lures of Diu. It could be a beautiful place to stay and there's no criticising the ethnic furnishings, the decor or the maintenance.

Unfortunately, however, it's an organisational disaster, staffed by people who simply don't seem to care. And, despite the fact that the Diu border is within spitting distance, you cannot even have a beer with your meal, let alone anything stronger. This is puritanism with a vengeance. Meals are available for guests, but don't expect anything out of the ordinary. If you still feel you want to stay here, it will cost you Rs 400 for an air-con cottage, or Rs 575 for a four-bed air-con beach cottage.

VERAVAL

On the south coast of Saurashtra is Veraval, which was the major seaport for Mecca pilgrims before the rise of Surat. It still has some importance as one of India's major fishing ports (over 1000 boats are based here), and as the base for a visit to Somnath Temple, five km south of the town.

As you might imagine, the place stinks of fish depending on the prevailing wind. Wooden dhows of all sizes, from fishing dinghies right up to ocean-going vessels, are still being built totally by hand – you won't hear the buzz of a power saw or drill here. The largest dhows still make the journey from here to Dubai and other Middle Eastern destinations, and you may well see some of them tied up loading or discharging cargo. They are not allowed to take passengers, but you might just get lucky.

It's well worth a wander around the **port**, although photography is supposedly prohibited. If you're on a bicycle heading for Somnath, you can take a shortcut right through the port area. Apart from the port, there's not a lot to see in Veraval, despite its size. Pigs abound in the streets. Between Veraval and Somnath, a large ship lies (spectacularly) wrecked on the shore.

Places to Stay

Accommodation in Veraval can be hard to find; places are often full and prices get jacked up. There's the *Toran Tourist Bungalow* (☎ 20-488), College Rd, but it's an unattractive place to stay and the location is inconvenient. Double rooms cost Rs 120, and meals must be ordered in advance.

By far the best proposition is the well-maintained *Satkar Hotel* (☎ 20-120) near the bus stand. It has all sorts of rooms, from dorm beds at Rs 30 or regular rooms from Rs 50/75 to rooms with air-con for Rs 200/250. There are railway *retiring rooms* at the station, and the *Chandrani Guest House* is nearby, although it's very basic and no English is spoken.

Places to Eat

Veraval has few eating places. The *Satkar Hotel*, near the bus stand, does good Gujarati thalis with plenty of refills for Rs 25. The *New Apsara*, not far from the station, serves vegetarian thalis and dosas downstairs and non-vegetarian food (including local fish) upstairs, but it's fairly basic.

Getting There & Away

Air Keshod, the nearest airport, is serviced by Vayudoot but there's no Vayudoot office in Veraval. Somnath Travels (☎ 162) in Satta Bazaar will obtain tickets for a fee.

Bus Daily buses run from the bus station to Diu via Kodinar, Porbandar, Junagadh, Rajkot and Bhavnagar. For Sasan Gir there are departures at 8.30 and 10.30 am, and 3.45 and 4.30 pm for the 1½-hour journey. Mayur Travels opposite the bus station is the agent for the private bus companies. There are daily departures for Porbandar, Diu, Rajkot and Junagadh.

Train It's 431 km from Ahmedabad to

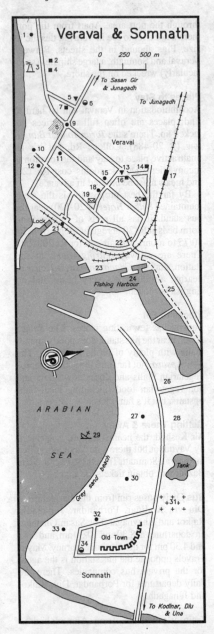

Veraval & Somnath

0   250   500 m

To Sasan Gir & Junagadh

To Junagadh

Veraval

Lock

Fishing Harbour

ARABIAN

SEA

Grey sand beach

Tank

Old Town

Somnath

To Kodinar, Diu & Una

■ PLACES TO STAY

2 Toran Tourist Bungalow
4 Circuit House
7 Satkar Hotel
14 Chandrani Guest House
16 Sri Niwas Guest House
20 Hotel Supreme

▼ PLACES TO EAT

5 Chetna Restaurant & Mayur Travels
13 New Apsara

OTHER

1 Temple
3 Lighthouse
6 Bus Stand
8 Municipal Gardens
9 Clock Tower
10 Temple
11 Bank
12 Fruit & Vegetable Market
15 Bank
17 Railway Station
18 Bank
19 GPO
21 Bank
22 Junagadh Gate
23 Sheds
24 Dhow Wharf
25 Dhow Building
26 Boatyard
27 Temple
28 Cold Stores
29 Shipwreck
30 Mosque
31 Cemetery
32 Museum
33 Temple of Somnath
34 Bus Stand

Veraval. Fares for the 12½-hour trip are Rs 81/301 in 2nd/1st class. There are slow steam passenger trains for Sasan Gir at 8.30 am and 1 pm, and one daily passenger service to Delwada (for Diu) at 3.15 pm, although it arrives at 8 pm.

To Rajkot there are daily trains at 6.35 (seven hours) and 11.15 am (5½ hours).

Getting Around

Bicycles can be hired opposite the railway

station for Rs 2 per hour, and these are the best way to see the port and Somnath.

An auto-rickshaw to Somnath, five km away, costs about Rs 15. There are local buses to Somnath for Rs 2.

AROUND VERAVAL
Chorwad

The summer palace of the Junagadh nawabs, situated at the popular beach resort of Chorwad, 70 km from Junagadh and 20 km from Veraval, was converted by the Gujarat State Tourism Department into the beautiful *Palace Beach Resort* (☎ 96). The hotel is surrounded by well-tended gardens and overlooks the sea. It has a total of 30 rooms in the main palace building, and 16 detached cottages. Doubles in the cottages cost Rs 125, in the palace they're Rs 175, while air-con rooms in the former palace itself cost Rs 250. All meals have to be ordered in advance.

SOMNATH
Temple of Somnath

This temple, at Somnath Patan near Veraval and about 80 km from Junagadh, has an extremely chequered past. Its earliest history fades into legend – it is said to have been originally built out of gold by Somraj, the Moon God, only to be rebuilt by Rawana in silver, then by Krishna in wood and Bhimdev in stone. A description of the temple by Al Biruni, an Arab traveller, was so glowing that it prompted a visit in 1024 by a most unwelcome tourist – Mahmud of Ghazni. At that time, the temple was so wealthy that it had 300 musicians, 500 dancing girls and even 300 barbers just to shave the heads of visiting pilgrims.

Mahmud of Ghazni, whose raids on the riches of India were to gain him quite a reputation, descended on Somnath from his Afghan kingdom and, after a two-day battle, took the town and the temple. Having looted its fabulous wealth, he destroyed it for good measure. So began a pattern of Muslim destruction and Hindu rebuilding which continued for centuries. The temple was again razed in 1297, 1394 and finally in 1706 by

Aurangzeb, that notorious Moghul fundamentalist.

After the 1706 demolition, the temple was not rebuilt until 1950. Outside, opposite the entrance, is a large statue of S V Patel (1875-1950), who was responsible for the reconstruction. Inside the temple there are fine views from the 2nd floor, as well as a photo collection (with English commentary) on the archaeological excavation of the seven temples and restoration work.

The current temple was built to traditional patterns on the original site by the sea. It is one of the 12 sacred Siva shrines known as jyoti lingas but, despite its long history and its holiness, it's not really very interesting. Hardly anything of the original temple remains and the new one is an unimaginative monstrosity far removed from what one imagines the original temple to have looked like. You can get lunch in the simple dining hall in the temple compound, north of the main gate. The grey sand beach right outside the temple is OK for a swim, although there's no shade.

Museum

Down the lane from the temple is a museum, open from 9 am to noon and 3 to 6 pm, closed Wednesdays and holidays. Admission is Rs 0.20, plus Rs 0.20 for each photograph you take. They're not very serious about keeping count. Remains of the old temple can be seen here as a jumble of old carved stones littering a courtyard. There are pottery shards, a seashell collection and a (strange) glass case of water bottles containing samples from the Danube, Nile, St Lawrence, Tigris, River Plate and even the Australian Murray, as well as seawater from Hobart and New Zealand.

Other Sites

The town of Somnath Patan is entered from Veraval by the **Junagadh Gate**. This very ancient triple gate was the one which Mahmud finally broke through to take the town. Close to the second gate is an old **mosque** dating from Mahmud's time. The **Jami Masjid**, reached through the town's picturesque **bazaar**, was constructed using parts of a Hindu temple and has interesting bo tree carvings at all four corners. It is now a museum with a collection from many of these temples.

About a km before the Junagadh Gate, coming from Veraval, the finely carved Mai Puri was once a **Temple of the Sun**. This Hindu temple was converted into a mosque during Mahmud's time and is surrounded by thousands of tombs and palias. Two old tombs are close by and, on the shore, the **Bhidiyo Pagoda** probably dates from the 14th century.

To the east of the town is the **Bhalka Tirth** where Lord Krishna was mistaken for a deer and wounded by an arrow while sleeping in a deerskin. The legendary spot is at the confluence of three rivers. You get to it through the small sangam (confluence gate), which is simply known as the Nana, or Small Gate. North of this sacred spot is the **Suraj Mandir**, or Temple of the Sun, which Mahmud also had a go at knocking down. This very old temple, with a frieze of lions with elephant trunks around its walls, probably dates from the same time as the original Somnath Temple. Back inside the small gate is a temple which Ahalya Bai of Indore built as a replacement for the Somnath Temple.

Places to Stay

About halfway between the bus stand and the temple and some 100 metres north of the road, the *Sri Somnath Temple Trust* has a vast guest house. The 200 double rooms are a bit dingy but they're not that old and, at Rs 25, they're good value. The signs for the guest house are in Hindi and Gujarati only, but you can ask for directions.

SASAN GIR LION SANCTUARY

The last home of the Asiatic lion *(Panthera leo lersica)* is 54 km from Junagadh via Visavadar. The sanctuary, which covers 1400 sq km, was set up to protect the lion and its habitat, and in this respect has been a success: in 1980 they numbered less than 200; at the time of writing there were 284 lions in the park. While the lions have been

the winners, the local herders (the *maldharis)* have lost valuable grazing land for their cattle. Although the lions seem remarkably tame, in recent years they have reportedly been wandering further afield, well outside the limits of the sanctuary, in search of easy game – namely calves – which in earlier times were found within the park itself.

The best time to visit the sanctuary is from December to April, and it is closed completely from mid-May to mid-October.

Apart from the lions there are also bears, hyenas, foxes and a number of species of deer and antelope. The deer include the largest Indian antelope (the nilgai), the graceful chinkara gazelle, the chousingha and the barking deer. You may also see parrots, peacocks and monkeys.

The lions themselves are elusive but you'd be unlucky not to see at least one on a safari, although it would be safer to allow for a couple of trips if you're determined to see one. Morning safaris are generally a better bet than those in the afternoons. Unfortunately the local guides are poorly trained and some are entirely lacking in enthusiasm, which can certainly reduce your chances of spotting a lion. Whatever else you do, take a jeep and not a minibus. While the latter stick to the main tracks, the jeeps can take the small trails where you're much more likely to come across lions.

Before you can go on safari, you must get a permit. These are issued on the spot at the Sinh Sadan Forest Lodge office and cost Rs 15 per person (valid for three days) plus Rs 7.50 for a camera. Jeeps cost Rs 6 per km and can take up to six people. There are three tracks in the park, so you will cover 25 to 35 km, depending on the track your jeep is assigned to. The guide's fee is set at Rs 7.50 (total, not per person), but expect to get hassled for a tip – if your guide's been keen and searched hard then a tip is certainly justified, otherwise it's up to you. Jeeps are available from the lodge office every day between 7 and 10 am and 4 and 6.30 pm. If possible, book in advance, though they're rarely full.

Places to Stay & Eat

There are two places to stay at Sasan Gir village. About a 10-minute walk from the railway station is the *Sinh Sadan Forest Lodge* (☎ 40). It is a very pleasant place to stay, with rooms set around a quiet green garden, which is complete with illuminated fountain at night! They also show a very aged and faded film about the park every evening at 7 pm.

Good singles/doubles with mosquito nets and baths cost Rs 80, and there are some air-con rooms for Rs 350, and deluxe rooms for Rs 450. It's popular because of the price, so try to make advance reservations, but even if you just turn up on the doorstep the chances of getting a room are good. Although you'll probably be told it's full, hang around and see what happens, as rooms often miraculously become available. Similarly, once you have a room you may well be told that it's only free for one night, but again, this seems to be remarkably flexible. There's a restaurant here which serves thalis but you need to order in advance – breakfast is Rs 20, and a thali lunch or dinner is Rs 20.

The State Tourism Corporation of Gujarat's *Lion Safari Lodge* (☎ 21) is down by the river, about 200 metres from the Sinh Sadan, surrounded by well-maintained gardens. It is not such a great place and suffers from poor service, although it is far better here than in some of the other state-run places. It has 20 dorm beds (four beds per dorm) for Rs 30, singles/doubles for Rs 162/212 and rooms with air-con for Rs 335/382. The restaurant on the ground floor serves good thalis and other dishes and, despite the notice at the dining-hall entrance, you don't have to order meals in advance.

You can also get snacks at the shacks opposite the Sinh Sadan Lodge, but the food is very basic.

Getting There & Away

State transport buses make the two-hour trip between Junagadh and Veraval via Sasan Gir four times a day. They leave Junagadh at 8.45 and 10 am and 12.30 and 1.30 pm and cost Rs 7. For buses from Sasan Gir to Veraval or Junagadh, ask the manager of the Sinh Sadan as he is the most reliable source.

Slow steam trains run to Veraval (two hours, Rs 7) twice daily, and to Delwada (for Diu) and Junagadh once a day.

JUNAGADH

Population: 167,000

Few travellers make the trip out to Junagadh, but it's an interesting town situated right at the base of the temple-studded Girnar Hill. Junagadh is also the departure point for visits to the Gir Forest.

The city takes its name from the fort which enclosed the old city. Dating from 250 BC, the Ashokan edicts near the town testify to the great antiquity of this site. At the time of Partition, the Nawab of Junagadh opted to take his tiny state into Pakistan. However, the inhabitants were predominantly Hindu and the nawab soon found himself in exile, perhaps explaining the sorry state of his former palace and fort.

This city is full of some very exotic old buildings, most in a state of disrepair. It is a fascinating place to explore, but very few tourists come to this very friendly and unspoilt town.

Information

Visiting the tourist office in the Hotel Girnar is a waste of time. The best source of current information is the Relief Hotel, the city's unofficial information centre and the only one worth checking out.

The State Bank of India near the Durbar Hall doesn't accept Amex travellers' cheques. To change these you must go to the Bank of India in the same area.

Just inside the entrance to the fort you'll see a man selling literature. It's worth paying Rs 3 for the booklet *Girnar Guide* by Mohanlal Desai. It supposedly describes the holy mountain of the same name but is somewhere between a barrel of laughs and a barrel of bullshit. If any publication deserves a Nobel Prize for pure, unadulterated nonsense (let alone typos), this is it. It's money well spent!

Uparkot

This very old fort, from which the city derives its name (*jirna* means old), stands on the eastern side of Junagadh and has been rebuilt and extended many times over the centuries. In places, the walls are 20 metres high and an ornate triple gateway forms the entrance to the fort. It's said that the fort was once besieged, unsuccessfully, for a full 12 years. In all, it was besieged 16 times. It is also said that the fort was abandoned from the 7th to 10th centuries and, when rediscovered, it was completely overgrown by jungle. The plateau-like area formed by the top of the old fort is covered in lantana scrub. Paths lead from one point of interest to the next and entry to the fort is free.

The **Jami Masjid**, the mosque inside the fort, was built from a demolished Hindu temple. Other points of interest include the **Tomb of Nuri Shah** and two fine baolis (step wells) known as the **Adi Chadi** and the **Naughan**. The Adi Chadi is named after two of the slave girls who fetched water from it. The Naughan is reached by a magnificent circular staircase.

Cut into the hillside close to the mosque are some ancient **Buddhist caves** which are thought to be at least 1500 years old. The double-storey cave has six pillars with very fine carvings. There are other caves in Junagadh, including some thought to date back to the time of Ashoka. The soft rock on which Junagadh is built encouraged the construction of caves and wells.

The colossal five-metre-long cannon, called **Nilam**, is another point of interest. Cast in Egypt in 1531, it was left behind by a Turkish admiral who was assisting the Sultan of Gujarat in his 1531 struggle with the Portuguese at Diu.

Mahabat Maqbara

This incredible mausoleum of one of the nawabs of Junagadh with its silver doors, intricate architecture, minarets and spiralling stairways predates Disneyland or *Lord of the Rings* by generations. A visit is a must, but it badly needs maintenance work. The mausoleum is generally locked but you may be able to obtain the keys from the adjacent mosque.

Durbar Hall & Museum

Another of Junagadh's half-derelict monuments, this must have been a very fine building in its heyday. The museum has the usual display of weapons and armour from the days of the nawabs, together with their collections of silver chains and chandeliers, settees and thrones, howdahs and palanquins, and a few cushions and gowns. There's a portrait gallery of the nawabs and local petty princes, including photos of the last nawab with his various beloved dogs.

It's open from 9 am to 12.15 pm and 3 to 6 pm daily, closed on Wednesday, the 2nd and 4th Saturday of every month and all public holidays.

Ashokan Edicts

On the way to the Girnar Hill temples, you pass a huge boulder on which Emperor Ashoka inscribed 14 edicts in around 250 BC. His inscription is in the Pali script. Later Sanskrit inscriptions were added around 150 AD by Rudradama and in about 450 AD by Skandagupta, the last emperor of the Mauryas. The 14 edicts are moral lectures, while the other inscriptions refer mainly to recurring floods destroying the embankments of nearby Sudershan Lake, which no longer exists. The boulder is actually housed in a small roadside building, on the right if you're heading towards Girnar.

Girnar Hill

The 600-metre climb up 10,000 stone steps to the 1118-metre-high summit of Girnar is best made early in the morning, preferably at dawn. The steps are well built and maintained and were constructed between 1889 and 1908 from the proceeds of a lottery. The start of the climb is in a scrubby teak forest, a km or two beyond the Damodar Kund, and the road actually takes you to around step No 3000 – which leaves you with only 7000 to the top!

There are frequent refreshment stalls on the two-hour ascent. These stalls also sell chalk, so you can graffiti your name onto the rocks beside the path. Walking sticks are also available for hire for Rs 1 plus Rs 2 deposit, or if you really can't face the walk, doolies (rope chairs) carried by porters can be hired; for these you pay by weight so, before setting off, you have to suffer the indignity of being weighed on a huge beam scale, just like a sack of grain. You'll see monkeys by the path and eagles soaring overhead. From the summit, the views are superb.

Like Palitana, the temple-topped hill is of great significance to the Jains. The sacred tank of **Damodar Kund** marks the start of the climb to the temples. The path ascends through a wood to the marble temples near the summit. Five of them are Jain temples, including the largest and oldest – the 12th-century **Temple of Neminath**, the 22nd Jain tirthankar. There is a large black image of Neminath in the central shrine and many smaller images around the temple.

The nearby triple **Temple of Mallinath**, the 9th tirthankar, was erected in 1177 by two brothers. During festivals, this temple is a favourite gathering place for sadhus and a great fair is held here during the **Kartika Purnima** festival in November or December. On top of the peak is the **Temple of Amba Mata**, where newlyweds are supposed to worship at the shrine of the goddess in order to ensure a happy marriage.

A local No 3 or 4 bus from the stand opposite the GPO will take you to Girnar Taleti at the base of the hill. Buses run about once an hour, cost Rs 0.50 and go by the Ashoka edicts. An auto-rickshaw from town costs Rs 10.

Other Attractions

If you are unable to visit the Gir Forest, Junagadh's **zoo** at Sakar Bagh, 3½ km from the centre of town on the Rajkot road, has Gir lions. The zoo was set up by the nawab in 1863 specifically to save the lion from extinction. It's surprisingly good with well-kept lions, tigers and leopards being the main attractions.

The town also has a fine local **museum** with paintings, manuscripts, archaeological finds and various other exhibits including a natural history section. The museum is open daily, except on Wednesday and the 2nd and 4th Saturday of each month. Take a No 1, 2 or 6 bus, or walk there by the old Majevadi Gate on your right.

The **Ayurvedic College** at Sadarbag on the western edge of town is housed in one of the ex-nawab's palaces, and has a small museum devoted to ayurvedic medicine. The staff are knowledgeable and it's a good place to obtain information on this ancient form of traditional medicine.

Other old buildings include the gate opposite the railway station on Dhal Rd, the clock tower near the GPO and the building opposite the Durbar Hall.

Places to Stay

Junagadh has neat, clean railway *retiring rooms* for Rs 25/40 and dorm beds for Rs 15. Just outside the railway station are two very basic hotels, the *Gita Lodge* and the *Sharada Lodge*, but you'd have to be penniless to consider staying there.

The hotels around Kalwa Chowk, one of the two main squares in Junagadh, are better, but are an inconvenient distance from the centre of town. In this area, you'll find the *Lake Guest House* and the *Capital Guest House*, which offer similar standards of accommodation. Singles/doubles cost Rs 25/40, all with common bathroom, and bucket hot water is available for Rs 2. As you might expect at that price, they're very basic. A good place in this area is the new *Hotel National* (☎ 20-736). Rooms in this friendly place are Rs 150/250, and meals are available for Rs 30 to Rs 65.

By far the best hotel, however, is the *Relief Hotel* (☎ 20-280), Chittakhana Chowk, within easy walking distance of both the bus stand and the railway station. The switched-on manager, Alex, is very keen to make sure you're comfortable and have everything you need. He is also full of accurate information about the area. None of the other hotels are a patch on this place. The Relief is immaculately clean and well maintained and the cheap restaurant on the ground floor here is

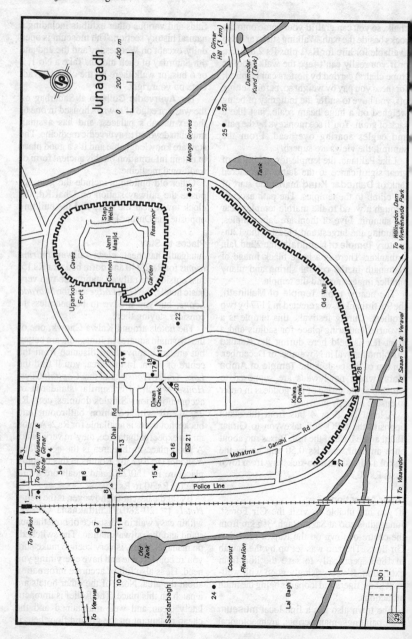

Junagadh

0   200   400 m

To Girnar Hill (3 km)

Damodar Kund (Tank)

Tank

Mango Groves

To Willingdon Dam & Vivekananda Park

To Sasan Gir & Veraval

Step Wells

Jami Masjid

Reservoir

Uparkot Caves Fort

Cannon

Garden

Old Wall

Dhal Rd

Diwan Chowk

Kalwa Chowk

To Visavadar

Mahatma Gandhi Rd

Police Line

Zoo, Museum & Hotel Girnar

To Rajkot

To Veraval

Old Tank

Coconut Plantation

Sardarbagh

Lal Bagh

To Veraval

excellent. It's not the cheapest hotel in town but is definitely worth the extra. It offers a variety of rooms ranging in price from Rs 40/60 for a single/double with common bathroom to Rs 80/100 with bathroom attached. All the bathrooms have hot water and the most expensive double (Rs 250) also has air-con. Bicycles and a motorcycle are available for hire, or a car can be arranged for longer trips.

Halfway between the Relief and the bus station is the *Hotel Vaibhav* (☎ 21-070) which costs Rs 40 for a dorm bed, Rs 60/80

for a room with attached bathroom, and Rs 155/160 with bathroom and air-con. The hotel also has an air-conditioned restaurant.

On the same road but across the railway line is the fairly new *Hotel Anand* (☎ 27-227). It's already showing signs of decay, and is not great at Rs 100 for a double with bathroom, and Rs 360 with air-con, TV and phone. There are no single rooms and the front rooms are noisy.

Junagadh's top-end hotel is the state-operated *Hotel Girnar* (☎ 21-201), Majwadi Darwaja, but it too is nothing special. It has dorm beds for Rs 20 to Rs 25, doubles for Rs 150 and air-con doubles for Rs 200. Check-out time is 9 am and the hotel is inconveniently located north of the town centre.

Places to Eat

Cheap all-you-can-eat thalis can be found at the *Sharada Lodge* opposite the railway station. Only slightly more expensive is the food at the *Relief Hotel*, which is probably where you'll eat if you're staying there.

For something of an eye-opener, try the restaurant at the *Hotel Vaibhav*. It has an amazingly flashy air-conditioned mirrored dining hall where you can get the 'ultimate' all-you-can-eat thali for Rs 20.

Junagadh is famous for its fruit, especially kesar mangoes and chiku (sapodilla) which are popular in milk shakes in November-December.

Getting There & Away

Air Keshod, 40 km from Junagadh, is the nearest airport. Vayudoot has daily flights to and from Bombay for US$120.

Bus The timetable at the state bus stand is entirely in Gujarati. Buses leave for Rajkot every hour (the 8.30 am bus is nonstop), Sasan Gir at 8.45 and 10 am, 12.30 and 1.30 pm, Una (for Diu) at 5, 6 and 7 am, Bhuj at 5.45 am and 7.30 pm, Palitana at 5.30 am, Veraval every hour and Ahmedabad daily at 9.45 pm.

Raviraj Travels at the Hotel Vaibhav has deluxe minibuses to Rajkot, Ahmedabad, Bombay, Porbandar and Jamnagar.

Train The *Somnath Mail* and *Girnar Express* run between Ahmedabad and Veraval via Junagadh. (The *Somnath Mail* is a multi-part train, so make sure you get into the right part.) The *Veraval-Rajkot Mail* runs between Rajkot and Veraval via Junagadh. The 380-km trip from Ahmedabad to Junagadh takes about 11 hours and costs Rs 72/265 in 2nd/1st class. A daily passenger train to Sasan Gir and on to Delwada, near Diu, leaves Junagadh daily at 6.10 am. As the steam train takes 2½ hours to do the 73-km trip to Sasan Gir, it's much quicker, although less interesting, to take a bus.

Taxi Share taxis between Junagadh and Rajkot leave when full from next to the bus station in Junagadh. The fare is Rs 30 per seat and the journey takes around one hour.

Getting Around

For Girnar Hill there are buses from outside the GPO at 5, 6 and 7 am.

You can rent bicycles for Rs 8 per day from either the Relief Hotel or the small yellow shack near the railway station. Junagadh's taxis seem to be mostly 1940s vintage Ford Plymouths, and there's dozens of them; probably the greatest concentration of working examples anywhere in the world – it would certainly bring a smile to old Henry Ford's face!

PORBANDAR

Population: 160,000

On the south-east coast, about midway between Veraval and Dwarka, modern-day Porbandar is chiefly noted as the birthplace of Mahatma Gandhi. In ancient times, the city was called Sudamapuri after Sudama, a compatriot of Krishna, and there was once a flourishing trade from here to Africa and the Persian Gulf. The Africa connection is apparent in the number of Indianised Blacks, called Siddis, who form a virtually separate caste of Dalits.

Porbandar has several large cement and chemical factories and a textile mill. A massive breakwater was recently constructed to shelter a deep-water wharf and

fishing harbour. Dhows are still being built here and fish-drying is an important activity, lending a certain aroma to the town!

Swimming near the Tourist Bungalow is not recommended. The beach, called Chowpatty, is used as a local toilet and there is a factory drain outlet by the Hazur Palace. Swimming is said to be OK a few km down the coast towards Veraval.

Kirti Mandir

The Kirti Mandir, Gandhi's birthplace, houses one of India's many collections of Gandhian memorabilia. A swastika on the floor in a small room marks the actual spot! There is also an exhibit of photographs, some with English captions, and a small bookshop.

Nehru Planetarium

Across the muddy creek, which is spanned by the Jynbeeli (once Jubilee) Bridge, are the Nehru Planetarium and the Bharat Mandir. Flocks of flamingoes are an unexpected sight along the creek. Men and women enter the planetarium from the verandah by separate doors whose panels celebrate Indian non-alignment, showing Shastri with Kosygin on one side and Nehru with JFK on the other! The planetarium has afternoon sessions in Gujarati. The projection equipment is a little antiquated and stars chase one another across the domed roof to the sound of whirring machinery.

Bharat Mandir

The large Bharat Mandir hall is in a charming irrigated garden opposite the planetarium. On the floor inside is a huge relief map of India and the building's pillars are brilliantly painted with bas-reliefs of over 100 religious figures and legendary persons from Hindu epics. The verandah's six distorting mirrors are popular with children.

Hazur Palace

This massive, forlorn-looking building near the shore has been deserted by the present maharana.

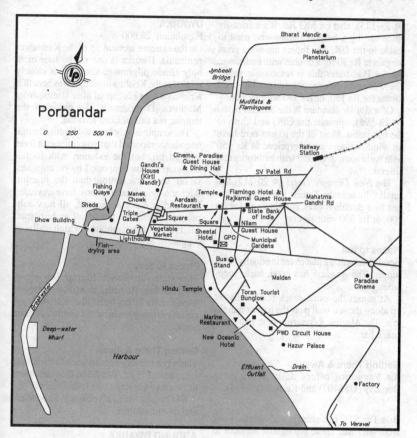

Porbandar

0   250   500 m

Places to Stay

Good cheap accommodation is hard to find
in this town. The state tourist organisation's
Toran Tourist Bungalow (☎ 22-745) on
Chowpatty is large and spacious. From its
very quiet location near the shore it has fine
views of sea, harbour and sunset, and inland
to the Barda Hills. Dorm beds cost Rs 20,
doubles are Rs 150 and doubles with air-con
cost Rs 250.

In the centre the best place for cheap
rooms is S T Rd, a small road which runs
from the bus station to Mahatma Gandhi Rd.
The *Nilam Guest House* (☎ 20-503) is a

mildly grubby place with rooms at Rs 30/40
with bathroom attached. Close by is the
Darami Guest House (☎ 21-239) and, while
it is hardly spotless, it is reasonably quiet,
although most rooms only have internal
windows. A double with bathroom costs Rs
50.

Cheaper still is the *Rajkamal Guest House*
(☎ 20-374) on Mahatma Gandhi Rd. It is
outrageously cheap at Rs 14/28 for single/
double rooms, or dorm beds for Rs 7. With
prices like these it's very popular with local
travelling salesmen, and is invariably full.

Up the scale a bit is the *Flamingo Hotel*

(☎ 23-123), also on MG Rd. It's a friendly place run by a helpful Indian who used to reside in the UK. The rooms are not a great bargain at Rs 70 for a double with bathroom, but for Porbandar this is reasonable value. There are also more expensive marble-lined rooms for Rs 150, or Rs 390 with air-con.

Of a similar standard is the *Sheetal Hotel* (☎ 23-596), opposite the GPO and close to the bus stand. Most of the rooms here have no windows, and are overpriced at Rs 150 with bathroom, or Rs 350 with bathroom and air-con.

The *New Oceanic Hotel* (☎ 20-717) is a small villa near the Tourist Bungalow. It has just four double rooms, and these go for Rs 200, or Rs 300 with air-con.

Places to Eat
Good cheap eating places are in equally short supply. The *Aardash* has good, basic vegetarian food.

At sunset the usual snack-food stalls set up along the sea wall near the tourist bungalow. The *Marine Restaurant* here is a basic snack bar.

Getting There & Away
Air Vayudoot offers daily services to Bombay (US$107) and Keshod (US$34).

Bus The STC bus stand is a 15-minute walk from MG Rd. There are regular services to Dwarka, Jamnagar, Veraval and Rajkot.

The private bus companies have their offices on MG Rd, in the vicinity of the Flamingo Hotel. They only have signs in Gujarati so you'll need to enlist some local help to find the one you want. The main companies are Jay, Eagle and Raviraj, and there are departures for Jamnagar, Veraval, Rajkot and Ahmedabad.

Train Porbandar is the terminus of a rail line; the main service is the *Saurashtra Express* to and from Bombay via Rajkot (4½ hours) and Ahmedabad (10 hours). Fares from Ahmedabad are Rs 85/314 in 2nd/1st class.

DWARKA
Population: 28,000
On the extreme western tip of the Kathiawar peninsula, Dwarka is one of the four most holy Hindu pilgrimage sites and is closely related to the Krishna legend. It was here that Krishna set up his capital after fleeing from Mathura. Dwarkanath, the name of the temple, is a title of Lord Krishna.

The temple is only open to Hindus (though one visitor reported that you can sign a form and go in), but the exterior, with its tall five-storey spire supported by 60 columns, is far more interesting than the interior. Archaeological excavations have revealed five earlier cities at the site, all now submerged. Dwarka is the site of an important festival at Janmashtami which falls in August or September.

Places to Stay
The state-run *Toran Tourist Dormitory* (☎ 313) has 70 beds, in six to eight-bed rooms, at Rs 20 per bed. Otherwise there are railway *retiring rooms* and a number of basic hotels.

Getting There & Away
There is a railway line between Dwarka and Jamnagar, 145 km away, and there are trains to Bombay via Rajkot and Ahmedabad.

STC buses run to all points in Saurashtra, and to Ahmedabad.

AROUND DWARKA
Island of Bet
A little north of Dwarka, a ferry crosses from Okha to the Island of Bet, where Vishnu is said to have slain a demon. There are modern Krishna temples on the island and other important religious sites around Dwarka.

JAMNAGAR
Population: 365,000
Prior to independence, the princely state of Jamnagar was ruled by the Jadeja Rajputs. The city was built around the small Ranmal Lake, in the centre of which is a small palace, reached by a causeway.

This bustling city has a long history of

pearl fishing and a local variety of tie-dyeing, but today is more well known for having the only Ayurvedic University in India and a temple listed in the *Guinness Book of Records*!

The old part of town has a number of interesting and impressive old buildings, such as the Mandvi Tower, and is very colourful and vibrant. The centre of the old town is known as Darbar Gadh, a semicircular gathering place where the former Maharaja of Nawanagar used to hold public audiences. As very few tourists make the effort to get to Jamnagar, you'll probably have the place to yourself.

Orientation

The state bus stand (known locally as 'ST') and the new railway station are several km apart and both are a long way from the centre of the city, so you'll need to take an auto-rickshaw.

Lakhota Palace

This diminutive palace once belonged to the Maharaja of Nawanagar. Today it houses a small museum with displays from archaeological sites in the area. The **museum** is reached by a short causeway from the northern side of the tank, and is open from 10.30 am to 1 pm and 3 to 5.30 pm daily except Wednesday.

Bala Hanuman Temple

The Bala Hanuman Temple is on the south-eastern side of Lakhota Tank, and here, 24 hours a day since 1 August 1964, there's been continuous chanting of the invocation 'Shri Ram, Jai Ram, Jai Jai Ram'. Early evening is a particularly good time to visit the temple as it's fairly animated then; at other times there's just a handful of people around. In fact this whole area on the south-eastern edge of the tank becomes very lively around sunset when people come to promenade, and the usual chai and kulfi stalls set up and ply their trade.

Places to Stay

At the bottom end of the market, Jamnagar offers some of the worst hotels in the whole of India and you'd be well advised to give these disgusting dosshouses a miss. They're mostly clustered around the old railway station and include the *Everest Lodge, Jai Hind Lodge, Palace Guest House, Dreamland Guest House* and the *Grand Hotel*, as well as the *Evergreen Lodge* further out. The Everest charges Rs 35 for a double with bathroom attached, but don't expect too much.

A good place for those on a budget is the centrally located *Hotel Ashiana* (☎ 77-421), New Super Market, a vast, rambling place on the top floor of the supermarket complex. The huge sign above the supermarket is easily seen from the road below. There's a range of singles/doubles here for Rs 60/85 with bathroom, Rs 170/200 with air-con.

On the floor below the Ashiana is the *Jyoti Guest House* (☎ 71-155), which has good sized rooms and is cheaper at Rs 40/60 for single/double rooms.

On the 2nd floor of the building across the road is the cheap and friendly *Shital Guest House* (☎ 74-288), where a typically shabby but habitable double room costs Rs 45.

The modern and clean *Hotel Punit* (☎ 70-559) is a notch up the scale, although the rooms facing the road can be hellishly noisy. Singles/doubles at this place go for Rs 120/160, or with air-con it's Rs 250 for a double.

If you want to be near the bus stand, the *Hotel Kama* (☎ 77-778) is right opposite, on the 4th floor of a modern high-rise building. There's a good range of rooms, from Rs 75/125 for singles/doubles with bathroom, up to huge deluxe air-con suites for Rs 350/400. The hotel serves food, and the view from the 8th-floor terrace is excellent.

Jamnagar's best hotel is the modern *Hotel President* (☎ 70-516), Teen Batti Chowk, right in the centre of town. Singles/doubles cost Rs 197/267, Rs 312/382 with air-con, all with bathroom and constant hot water. The hotel has a restaurant (the 7 Seas), currency exchange facilities and also accepts credit cards.

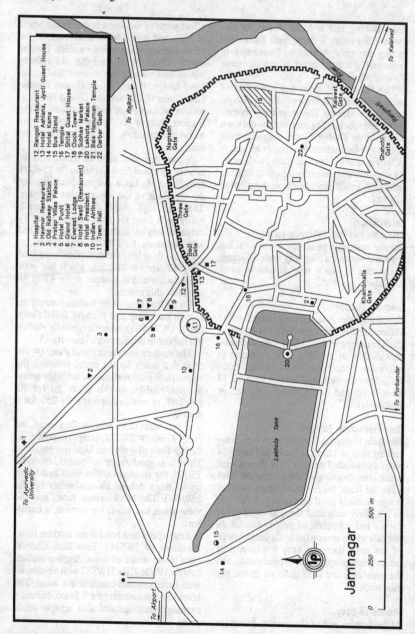

Jamnagar

1 Hospital
2 Havmor Restaurant
3 Old Railway Station
4 Pratap Villas Palace
5 Hotel Punit
6 Grand Hotel
7 Everest Lodge
8 Hotel Swati (Restaurant)
9 Hotel President
10 Indian Airlines
11 Town Hall
12 Rangoli Restaurant
13 Hotel Ashiana, Jyoti Guest House
14 Hotel Kama
15 Bus Stand
16 Temple
17 Shital Guest House
18 Clock Tower
19 Subhas Market
20 Lakhota Palace
21 Bala Hanuman Temple
22 Darbar Gadh

To Kalavad

To Rajkot

Nagnath Gate

Three Gate

Bedi Gate

Kalawat Gate

Ghachi Gate

Khambhalia Gate

To Porbandar

Lakhota Tank

To Ayurvedic University

To Airport

0   250   500 m

Places to Eat

For snack food in the evening try the various stalls that set up near the Bala Hanuman Temple.

In the centre of town, in the Teen Batti Chowk area, there are plenty of basic eating places. The *Ram, Kalpana* and *Laxmi Vilas* restaurants all serve cheap, honest and thoroughly unexciting meals. Also in this area is the *Hotel Swati*, a vegetarian place with an extensive range of south Indian, Jain and Punjabi dishes. Prices are surprisingly moderate (most dishes are in the Rs 15 to Rs 20 range), although servings are perhaps a little small. The restaurant has air-con, and is on the first floor of a line of shops, near the Grand Hotel.

Out along the road towards the Ayurvedic University is the *Havmor Restaurant*, one of the chain of restaurants found dotted throughout Gujarat and other states. For a splurge, the *7 Seas Restaurant* at the Hotel President offers reasonable food and is far from being expensive.

Around Mandvi Tower in the heart of the old town there's an extraordinary array of 'sweetmeat' shops selling a wide variety of sweet and sticky creations.

Getting There & Away

Air The efficient Indian Airlines office (78-569) on Bhid Bhanjan Rd is open from 10 am to 4.30 pm (closed for lunch from 1 to 1.45 pm).

Indian Airlines has flights five times weekly from Bombay (but not *to* Bombay) for US$52, and these continue on to Bhuj (US$15).

Bus There are STC buses to Rajkot every 30 minutes or less, and other departures to Dwarka, Porbandar, Bhuj, Junagadh and Ahmedabad.

Somnath Travels, in the lower level of the building opposite the bus station, is the agent for private bus companies, and these have services to Rajkot, Dwarka, Porbandar and Ahmedabad.

Train There are direct trains from Bombay and Ahmedabad via Rajkot. The fare for the 328-km trip from Ahmedabad is Rs 64/235 in 2nd/1st class.

To Dwarka the 138-km journey takes three hours by express train, or a tedious 5½ hours on the daily 'fast passenger' service. It costs Rs 31/120 in 2nd/1st class.

Getting Around

To/From the Airport There is no minibus service to the airport, which is a long way out. Auto-rickshaw drivers demand Rs 20 – it's a rip-off but they refuse to use the meters.

RAJKOT

Population: 651,000

This pleasant town was once the capital of the princely state of Saurashtra and is also a former British government headquarters. Mahatma Gandhi spent the early years of his life here while his father was the chief minister, or Diwan, to the Raja of Saurashtra. The Gandhi family home, the Kaba Gandhi no Delo, now houses a permanent exhibition of Gandhi items.

The Rajkumar College dates back to the second half of last century and is regarded as one of the best private schools in the country. It was originally one of five schools set up by the British for the education of the sons of the princely state rulers ('rajkumar' means son of a prince).

Information

Rajkot has a tourist office (☎ 31-616), but they obviously don't want anyone to know – it's hidden away behind the old State Bank of Saurashtra building on Jawahar Rd, almost opposite the Galaxy Hotel.

Watson Museum

The Watson Museum & Library in the Jubilee Gardens commemorates Colonel John Watson, Political Agent from 1886-89. The entrance is flanked by two imperial lions and among the exhibits are copies of artefacts from Moenjodaro, 13th-century carvings, silverware, natural history exhibits

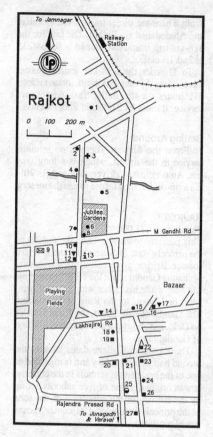

Rajkot

0   100   200 m

To Jamnagar

Railway
Station

Jubilee
Gardens

M Gandhi Rd

Bazaar

Playing
Fields

Lakhajiraj Rd

Rajendra Prasad Rd

To Junagadh
& Veraval

■ PLACES TO STAY

12 Galaxy Hotel
16 Himalaya Guest House
19 Ashok Hotel
20 Ashok Guest House
22 Jyoti Guest House
23 Jayshree Guest House
26 Jeel Hotel
27 Hotel Samrat

▼ PLACES TO EAT

11 Havmor Restaurant
14 Taj Ice Creams
17 Rainbow Restaurant

OTHER

1 Stadium
2 Ambedkar Square
3 Women's Hospital
4 Bank
5 Fruit Market
6 Watson Museum & Library
7 Telegraph Office
8 Gandhi School & Statue
9 GPO
10 Bank
13 Tourist Office
15 Library
18 Indian Airlines
21 Municipal Offices
24 Private Bus Companies
25 Bus Station

and textiles as well as dioramas of local tribal costumes and housing styles.

Perhaps the most startling piece is a huge marble statue of Queen Victoria seated on a throne and decidedly not amused – hardly surprising, given that she has to endure the indignity of a brass crown and thumblessly hold an orb and sceptre. This section also has two plaster Venuses and many splendid portraits of colonial bigwigs.

Places to Stay – bottom end

On Lakhajiraj Rd, the road leading into the heart of the bazaar area, are a number of hotels. The *Himalaya Guest House* is a huge place where singles/doubles with bathroom are Rs 40/80. It's basic, but clean and quite adequate, and bucket hot water is available at no extra charge. The entrance to this place is right inside the shopping complex over which it stands.

There are a couple of other cheapies at the back of the bus station: the *Jyoti Guest House* (no English spoken) and the *Jayshree Guest House* which offers singles/doubles with bathroom for Rs 40/70.

Very close to the bus station on the main road are the *Ashok Hotel* (☎ 32-047) and the *Ashok Guest House* (☎ 27-144). Both are basic, noisy boarding houses with rooms from Rs 35/60 with bathroom attached.

Places to Stay – middle

By far the best middle to top-end hotel in Rajkot is the *Galaxy Hotel* (☎ 31-781) on Jawahar Rd. It has a good atmosphere, the staff are pleasant and helpful and the beautiful spacious rooms are kept spotlessly clean. The front rooms overlook the maidan. Rooms cost Rs 170/280 for singles/doubles, Rs 310/500 with air-con. All rooms have TV, phone and bathroom with constant hot water. Most international credit cards are accepted and travellers' cheques can be cashed, but there's no restaurant.

The *Hotel Samrat* (☎ 22-269) is a comfortable place on the road behind the bus station. It's good value at Rs 162/267 for singles/doubles with TV and attached bathroom, and Rs 277/440 with air-con.

Another mid-range hotel is the *Hotel Jayson* (☎ 26-404) on S V P Rd (Canal Rd), where the rooms cost Rs 125/175, and Rs 200/280 with air-con.

Places to Eat

For cheap vegetarian food and thalis, try the popular *Vaibhav Restaurant* attached to the Ashok Hotel.

There's good, cheap south Indian food at the *Rainbow Restaurant* near the Himalaya Guest House. There's an air-con section upstairs.

The better class *Havmor*, near the Galaxy Hotel, serves Indian, Chinese and Western food.

Getting There & Away

Air The Indian Airlines office (☎ 27-916) is on Station Rd. Indian Airlines has daily direct flights between Rajkot and Bombay (US$46). A minibus between the Indian Airlines office in town and the airport connects with the flights.

Bus STC buses connect Rajkot with Jamnagar, Junagadh, Porbandar, Veraval and Ahmedabad. The trip from Rajkot to Veraval via Junagadh takes about five hours and costs Rs 20. Rajkot to Jamnagar is a two-hour journey and costs Rs 18.

There are also a number of private buses which operate to such places as Ahmedabad, Bhuj, Bhavnagar, Una (for Diu), Mt Abu, Udaipur, and Bombay. The offices of these companies are on the road behind the bus station. Make reservations one day in advance.

Train A number of broad-gauge express trains connect Rajkot with Ahmedabad, 246 km away. Fares are Rs 49/187 in 2nd/1st class. There are other fast trains to and from Jamnagar (broad gauge), Porbandar and Veraval (metre gauge).

Taxi Share taxis from Junagadh to Rajkot leave when full from next to the bus station. Cost is Rs 30.

AROUND RAJKOT
Wankaner

Like so many Indian palaces, the palace at Wankaner (☎ (02828) 324), about 50 km from Rajkot, has been put to good use as a place to stay. The difference between this place and the palace hotels of Rajasthan is that here guests are accommodated by the royal family, and the place is more a private guest house than a hotel. It was built in 1907 and is an amazing Greco-Roman Gothic Indo Scottish baronial extravagance trapped in a 60-year-old time warp.

As the royal family still live in the palace, guests are accommodated a couple of km away in a building known as the *Oasis House*, a wonderful Art Deco building built in the 1930s, complete with indoor swimming pool. While hardly palatial, the rooms are very comfortable and spacious, and meals are taken at the palace with the family. Rooms cost Rs 800 per person, including meals, so it's definitely not a cheap place to stay.

Right next to the palace is the *Royal Guest House*, a building originally built by the British in 1882 to house the resident they installed, who administered the state for 17 years until the then maharaja came of age (he was only three when his father died). Accommodation in this guest house is Rs 1000 per person, including all meals.

Getting There & Away There are regular buses to Rajkot every half hour, and Wankaner Junction is on the main railway line to Ahmedabad.

Surendranagar (Wadhwan)

This town on the route from Ahmedabad to Rajkot features the very old **Temple of Ranik Devi**, who became involved in a dispute between local rulers Sidh Raja (who planned to marry her) and Rao Khengar (who carried her off and did marry her). When Sidh Raja defeated Rao Khengar, she chose sati over dishonour and Sidh Raja built the temple as her memorial.

Tarnetar

Every year in the month of Bhadra (around September), the Trineteshwar Temple at Tarnetar, 65 km north-east of Rajkot, hosts the three-day **Tarnetar Fair**. There's much singing and dancing, although the fair is most well known for the different chhatris (umbrellas) made specifically for the occasion.

According to legend, Arjuna once danced at this site, and the River Ganges flows into the tank here once a year.

Kutch (Kachchh)

The westernmost part of Gujarat is virtually an island; indeed, during the monsoon period from May onwards, it really is an island. The Gulf of Kutch divides Kutch from the Kathiawar peninsula while, to the north, Kutch is separated from the Sind region of Pakistan by the Great Rann of Kutch.

The salt in the soil makes this low-lying marsh area almost completely barren. Only on scattered 'islands' which rise above the salt level is there vegetation. During the dry season, the Rann is a vast expanse of hard, dried mud. Then, with the start of the monsoon in May, it is flooded first by sea water, then by the fresh water from rivers as they fill. Kutch is also separated from the rest

of Gujarat to the east by the Little Rann of Kutch.

During the winter, the Gulf of Kutch is a breeding ground for flamingoes and pelicans. The Indian wild ass lives in the Little Rann of Kutch and part of the area has been declared a sanctuary for this rare animal. Because of their isolation, the people of Kutch have preserved their local customs and traditions to a much greater degree than elsewhere in the state and you're in for a very colourful experience. Very few tourists ever visit this part of India.

BHUJ

Population: 110,000

Bhuj, the major town of Kutch, is an old walled city – in the past the city gates were locked each night from dusk to dawn. It's one of those places which leaps right out of the pages of Rudyard Kipling. Bhuj is the Jaisalmer of Gujarat except that, in this case, the walls not only enclose the palace but almost the entire bazaar area and a lake too! The bazaar is lively and extremely colourful.

You can lose yourself for hours in the maze-like streets and alleyways of this town. There are walls within walls, crenellated gateways, old palaces with intricately carved wooden pavilions, Hindu temples decorated with the gaudy, gay abandon of which only tribal people seem capable, equally colourful tribespeople, and camels pulling huge cartfuls of produce into the various markets. All this exists right next to one of the largest Indian Air Force bases in the country, with aircraft taking off, on average, every 20 minutes. In short, there's never a dull moment.

Bhuj resembles much of India before the tourist invasion. People remain largely unaffected by what goes on outside the area, so you're much more likely to come across that disarming hospitality which was once the hallmark of rural India. Where else would someone offer you a lift on their bicycle?

Information

The Tourist Office (☎ 20-004) is housed in the Aina Mahal, and is staffed by the very helpful Mr P J Sethi, who is a mine of information on anything to do with Bhuj and Kutch.

The State Bank of India on Station Rd, near the Indian Airlines office, changes money with amazing speed.

Aina Mahal (Old Palace)

Rao Pragmalji's old palace, built in traditional Kutchi style, is in a small fortified courtyard in the old part of the city. It's a beautifully presented museum and is the highlight of Bhuj. The entrance to the palace houses the tourist office, and this is also the site of the **Maharao Sinh Madansinhji Museum**, which has a varied collection of paintings, photos and embroideries. There's also a collection of old princely-state coins, minted from the 17th century right up until 1948.

The real attraction here, though, are the rooms known as the Fuvara Mahal and Hira Mahal. The **Fuvara Mahal** is a room devoted entirely to decadence and leisure. Most of the floor area is an ornamental pool, lined with tiles which were manufactured by the maharao himself. (He had spent time travelling in Europe, and in Italy acquired the skills needed to make high quality glazed tiles.) In the centre of the pool is a small platform where the maharao used to sit and be entertained by local musicians and dancing girls. Fountains and sprays used to keep the air at a comfortable temperature, and the whole system of pool and fountain was filled by a complicated system of siphons and pumps (the room is on the 1st floor).

The **Hira Mahal** has some superb embroidery pieces and still contains the Maharao Shri Lakhpatji's bed and sword, and it remains largely untouched from when he died in the 18th century. The beautiful inlaid wood and ivory door of the palace was coveted for some time by the British Museum. The correspondence relating to the British attempt to 'borrow' this priceless object many years ago is solemnly set out next to the door.

On the 2nd floor you'll find all the marriage paraphernalia from the maharao's wedding in 1884.

This palace is well worth half a day, and is open from 9 am to noon and 3 to 6 pm; closed on Saturdays. Entry is Rs 2.

Prag Mahal (New Palace)

Across the courtyard from the Aina Mahal is the new palace, an ornate Italianate marble and sandstone building which was constructed in the latter part of the 19th century. Parts of it are now used for government offices but the vast and amazingly kitsch **Darbar Hall** and the **clock tower** are open to the public. High up on the walls of this unfurnished hall are portraits of past maharaos, while down below is the usual mausoleum of big game driven to the verge of extinction by egotism and pompous stupidity – all mounted but lying on the floor gazing blankly at the ceiling. The clock tower adjacent to the Darbar Hall is well worth climbing for the superb views over the town and surrounding countryside. Much of the rest of this fairly modern palace is empty, locked up and rapidly deteriorating.

Entry to the palace costs Rs 2; remove your shoes at the door. If you want to take photographs the fee is Rs 15, and there's a guard posted at the top of the clock tower to make sure you have a ticket.

Kutch Museum

The Kutch Museum was originally known as the Fergusson Museum after its founder, Sir James Fergusson, a governor of Bombay under the British Raj. Built in 1877, it's the oldest museum in Gujarat and has an excellent collection. The well-maintained and labelled (in English and Gujarati) exhibits include a picture gallery, an anthropological section, archaeological finds, textiles, weapons, musical instruments, a shipping section and, of course, stuffed animals. The museum is open every day, except Wednesdays and the 2nd and 4th Saturday of each month, from 9 to 11.30 am and 3 to 5.30 pm.

Sarad Bagh Palace

The last maharao died in the UK in 1991 and

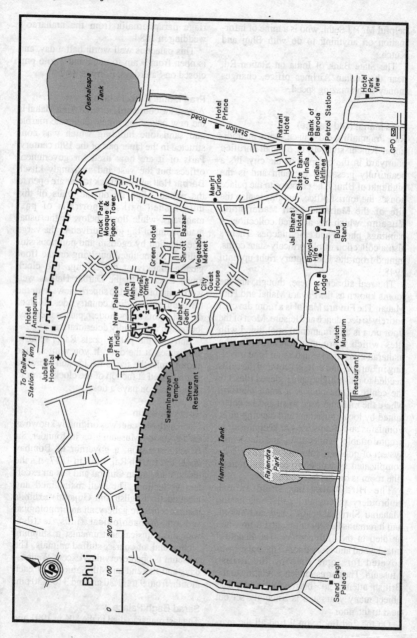

Bhuj

0   100   200 m

Deshalsapa Tank

Station Road

Hotel Prince

Ratrani Hotel

Bank of Baroda

Petrol Station

State Bank of India

Indian Airlines

GPO

Hotel Park View

Manjri Curios

Truck Park Mosque & Pigeon Tower

Jai Bharat Hotel

Bus Stand

Green Hotel

Shrott Bazaar

Vegetable Market

Bicycle Hire

VPR Lodge

Hotel Annapurna

Tourist Office

Aina Mahal

City Guest House

Darbar Gadh

To Railway Station (1 km)

Bank of India

New Palace

Jubilee Hospital

Kutch Museum

Restaurant

Swaminarayan Temple

Shree Restaurant

Hamirsar Tank

Rajendra Park

Sarad Bagh Palace

his palace to the east of the lake has been turned into a small museum. Set in spacious and beautifully tended gardens, the palace itself, built in 1867, is of very modest proportions, with just a drawing room downstairs and bedroom upstairs (closed). The dining room is in a separate building and on display here are a number of the maharao's personal possessions, including his video player. Also on display is his coffin, in which his body was brought back from the UK for cremation!

The palace is open from 9 am to noon and 3 to 6 pm daily except Friday.

Other Attractions

A huge old wall stretches around the hills overlooking the city – the view is best from near the railway station. Unfortunately, you cannot explore as this is all a restricted military area.

The very colourful and richly decorated **Swaminarayan Temple** is near the bazaar. Descriptions and photographs of this temple have featured in many travel magazines around the world. Non-Hindus are allowed inside but, if you want to take photographs, it's probably best to enlist (for a small fee) one of the people who hang around outside the temple offering their services as guides.

Places to Stay – bottom end

Most travellers stay at the *City Guest House*, right in the heart of the bazaar and quite close to the vegetable market and the palace. It's the only hotel right in the middle of the walled city. The rooms are pleasant and clean, and there's a courtyard area and a flat rooftop with good views over the bazaar. It's also good value at Rs 10 for a dorm bed (four beds per dorm) and Rs 30/50 for single/double rooms. Bathrooms are shared between three to four rooms, but they're adequate and kept very clean, and bucket hot water is available. It can be difficult to find this place so take an auto-rickshaw, or ask directions from Darbar Gadh.

Outside the bazaar, just off Station Rd, is the *Ratrani Hotel* (☎ 22-388) where you can also find cheap rooms. Singles/doubles with

bathroom cost Rs 40/60 and hot water is available on request for no extra charge. The restaurant serves Gujarati thalis and Punjabi food.

The *Hotel Park View* (☎ 23-598) on Hospital Rd charges Rs 30/45 for rooms with bathroom, and Rs 150/190 with air-con. It's one of those 'deteriorating rapidly' hotels in which India seems to specialise. Only a single sheet and one blanket is provided per bed, hot water is frequently not connected to the showers, the pretentious fittings have seen better days, the windows are all fitted with opaque glass and there's certainly no 'view' of any 'park' whatsoever. If you have a guest call to see you, they'll be charged up to Rs 60 per visit!

Places to Stay – middle

In terms of price, the *Hotel Prince* (☎ 20-370), Station Rd, is an excellent choice. The rooms are pleasant, clean and well kept, and cost Rs 150/200, or Rs 300/360 with air-con. All have TV and bathroom with constant hot water. The hotel restaurant has very good vegetarian and non-vegetarian food, and there's a special breakfast menu. Checkout time is based on the 24-hour system.

Equally good, and a good deal cheaper, is the *Hotel Anam* (☎ 21-390), also on Station Rd. It has a range of rooms, all with bathroom and constant hot water, with singles/doubles for Rs 90/180, or Rs 220/300 with air-con, and the hotel has its own vegetarian restaurant.

Places to Eat

You can get an excellent cheap breakfast (omelette and toast plus tea or coffee) from the *Omlet Center*, in the line of shops outside the bus station.

Perhaps the best vegetarian thalis in town can be found at the air-conditioned restaurant on the ground floor of the *Hotel Anam*. The restaurant is open for lunch from 10.30 am to 3 pm and for dinner from 7 to 10 pm, except on Sundays when it opens only for lunch. For a splurge, have a meal at the *Hotel Prince*. It has both veg and non-veg dishes but doesn't serve thalis. Another good thali specialist is the restaurant in the *VPR Lodge*, visible to the west of the bus station. Service here is erratic but the thali at Rs 22 is very good.

The nearest restaurant to the City Guest House is the *Green Hotel*, down a small alley opposite the vegetable market. It offers cheap vegetarian meals and snacks.

For a taste of Kutch food, try the restaurant at the *Hotel Annapurna*, outside the northern gate of the old town.

If you're wandering around the bazaar or visiting the palace, the *Shree Restaurant*, opposite the top end of the Swaminarayan Temple, is a good place to have a cold drink or a snack and watch the world go by. The staff are very friendly.

Things to Buy

If you are genuinely interested in the embroidery from the various Kutch villages, get in touch with Mr A A Wazir. Over the past 17 years or so he has been combing Kutch collecting embroidery and now has a priceless collection of over 1500 pieces, many of them very old. Some pieces are for sale (with prices starting at around Rs 200 for something very small) but most are for display and exhibition only. If you really want to buy a piece of genuine Gujarati embroidery, and not just something mass produced for the tourist trade, Mr Wazir is the person to contact. He can be reached through the tourist office, or you can call him on 24-187.

Getting There & Away

Air The Indian Airlines office (☎ 20-033) is open daily from 11 am to 1 pm and 1.45 to 6 pm. They have a minibus (Rs 5) which connects with all incoming and outgoing flights.

Indian Airlines flies Bombay-Jamnagar-Bhuj-Bombay five times a week. To Bombay it's US$62, while from Jamnagar to Bhuj costs US$15. Flights to or from Bhuj are often delayed because of military activity at the airport, so it's a good idea to call at the Indian Airlines office early to check if the flight is leaving according to schedule.

Bus Buses run to other centres in Gujarat

including Ahmedabad, Rajkot and Kandala Port. The private bus companies have their offices in the bus station area, and have services to Rajkot (daily except Sunday). STC buses to Rajkot take 5½ hours and cost Rs 30.

For Jaisalmer in Rajasthan there are no direct services, so you need to go first to Palanpur (by bus or overnight train), and take a bus from there to Barmer, and yet another on to Jaisalmer. If you take the overnight train to Palanpur, the entire trip can be done in 24 hours.

Train New Bhuj Railway Station is one km north of town along a very rough little back road from the north gate of the old town. An auto-rickshaw costs Rs 5. The reservation office at the station has a good quota of tickets on many broad and medium-gauge trains.

There are daily connections with Ahmedabad via Palanpur, and there are through carriages direct to Jodhpur and Delhi. As the direct train to Ahmedabad goes the long route via Palanpur (491 km, 16 hours), it's much quicker to take a local train or bus to Gandhidham (57 km), and then catch the nightly *Gandhidham-Kutch Express* which does the 300-km journey to Ahmedabad in six hours and costs Rs 57/218 in 2nd/1st class.

Getting Around

To/From the Airport You're advised to take the minibus which runs from the Indian Airlines office to the airport to connect with flights – the taxi and auto-rickshaw drivers are rapacious. They'll demand Rs 30 but accept Rs 20 after much haggling. Even so, it's a rip-off since the airport is only four km out of town (though they'll tell you it's more).

Local Transport When you're not just wandering around the bazaars there are plenty of auto-rickshaws, or there are places renting bicycles along the road outside the bus stand.

AROUND BHUJ

The city is connected by road with the old port of Mandvi to the south-west and by road and rail to the new port of Kandala. It is intended that Kandala should substitute Karachi as a port for this area. There is a boat service from Kandala to Navlakhi, which is on the Kathiawar peninsula and connected to Morvi and Wankaner by rail.

Gandhidham

Population: 104,000

The new town of Gandhidham, near Kandala, was established to take refugees from the Sind following Partition. The town has nothing of interest, but if you are stuck here for a night, there's the *Hotel Natraj* opposite the bus station, and the *Hotel Gokul* about 300 metres away.

Kutch Villages

The villages of the Kutch region each specialise in a different form of handicraft, be it embroidery, tie-dye, block printing or weaving. It's a fascinating area to explore, and it would be easy to spend a week visiting some of these villages, using Bhuj as a base.

Some of the more important villages, and the craft they specialise in, are: Bhujjodi, wool and cotton weaving; Padhar and Dhaneti, Ahir embroidery; Dhamanka, block printing; Lilpur, tie-dye; Anjar, nut-cutters, block printing and tie-dye. Anjar also has an old Deputy Collector's bungalow, which used to be inhabited by a Captain McMurdo, who was the first European to live in the area. The interior walls of the bungalow are decorated with interesting Kamagar paintings.

Dholavira is a small village on a small 'island' north-east of Bhuj. Here archaeologists have unearthed a city belonging to the Harappan (Indus Valley) civilisation, and excavation is still in progress. As this area is getting uncomfortably close to the Pakistan border (as far as the Indian authorities are concerned), you need a permit to visit Dholavira, and in fact any of the villages on the 'peninsula' north of Bhuj. These permits are available from the Collector's Office in Bhuj.

An interesting two-day trip would involve catching a bus from Bhuj to Lilpur, with an overnight stop in the Gandhi Ashram there (see the following section), then catch a bus the next morning to Dholavira, from where there is a direct bus back to Bhuj at 3 pm.

For more information on the area, contact Mr Pethi, the supervisor of the Bhuj tourist office.

Places to Stay Accommodation in the villages is predictably limited. Lilpur has a *Gandhi Ashram*, where you can stay for around Rs 50 per night including meals. Anjar village also has a couple of basic guest houses.

Mandvi

Mandvi is being promoted as a beach resort. It's on the coast, 60 km south-west of Bhuj, and there are regular bus connections between the two places. It was once a walled port town famous for shipbuilding.

Places to Stay The *Government Guest House* is two km out of town and costs Rs 100 for a double. More basic accommodation is available at either the *Vinayak Guest House* (Rs 15), or the *Shital Guest House* (Rs 30).

Madhya Pradesh

Population: 66 million
Area: 443,446 sq km
Capital: Bhopal
People per sq km: 149
Main Language: Hindi
Literacy Rate: 43%

Madhya Pradesh is India's largest state and the geographical heartland of the country. Most of the state is a high plateau and in summer it can be very dry and hot. Virtually all phases of Indian history have left their mark on Madhya Pradesh, historically known as Malwa. There are still many pre-Aryan Gond and Bhil tribal people in the state, but Madhya Pradesh is overwhelmingly Indo-Aryan with the majority of the people speaking Hindi and following Hinduism.

Some of Madhya Pradesh's attractions are remote and isolated: Khajuraho, in the north of the state, is a long way from anywhere and most easily visited when travelling between Agra and Varanasi; Jabalpur, with its marble rocks, is in the centre of the state; Kanha National Park, famous for its tigers, is 170 km south-east of Jabalpur.

Most of the state's other attractions are on or near the main Delhi to Bombay rail line. From Agra, just outside the state to the north, you can head south through Gwalior (with its magnificent fort), Sanchi, Bhopal, Ujjain, Indore and Mandu. From there you can head west to Gujarat or south to the Ajanta and Ellora caves in Maharashtra.

History

The history of Madhya Pradesh goes back to the time of Ashoka, the great Buddhist emperor whose Mauryan Empire was powerful in Malwa. At Sanchi you can see the Buddhist centre founded by Ashoka, the most important reminder of him in India today. The Mauryans were followed by the

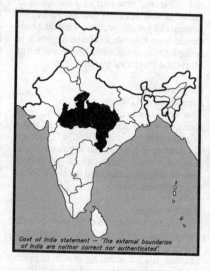

Govt of India statement — 'The external boundaries of India are neither correct nor authenticated'.

Sungas and then by the Guptas, before the Huns swept across the state. Around 1000 years ago the Parmaras ruled in south-west Madhya Pradesh – they're chiefly remembered for Raja Bhoj, who gave his name to the city of Bhopal and also ruled over Indore and Mandu.

From 950-1050 AD the Chandellas constructed the fantastic series of temples at Khajuraho in the north of the state. Today Khajuraho is one of India's main attractions, drawing visitors from both India and overseas.

Between the 12th and 16th centuries, the region saw continuing struggles between Hindu and Muslim rulers or invaders. The fortified city of Mandu in the south-west was frequently the scene for these battles, but finally the Moghuls overcame Hindu resistance and controlled the region. The Moghuls, however, met their fate at the hands of the Marathas who, in turn, fell to the British.

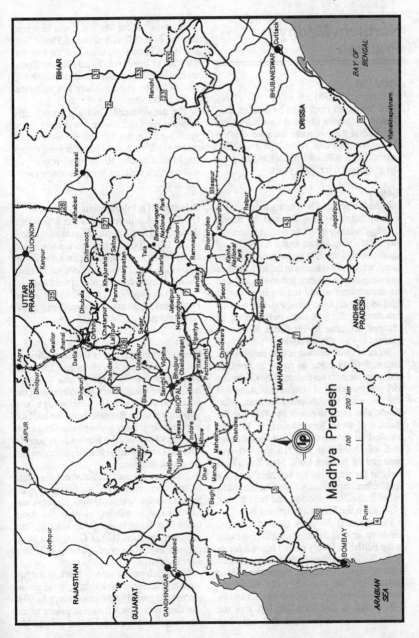

Madhya Pradesh

Northern Madhya Pradesh

GWALIOR

Population: 720,000

Just a few hours from Agra by train or road, Gwalior is famous for its old and very large fort. Within the fort walls are several interesting temples and ruined palaces. The dramatic and colourful history of the great fort goes back over 1000 years.

History

Gwalior's legendary beginning stems from a meeting between Suraj Sen and the hermit Gwalipa, who lived on the hilltop where the fort stands. The hermit cured Suraj Sen of leprosy with a drink of water from the Suraj Kund, which still remains in the fort. He then he gave him a new name, Suhan Pal, and said his descendants would remain in power so long as they kept the name Pal. His next 83 descendants did just that, but number 84 changed his name to Tej Karan and – you guessed it – goodbye kingdom.

What is more certain is that in 1398 the Tomar dynasty came to power in Gwalior and, over the next several centuries, Gwalior fort was the scene of continual intrigue and clashes with neighbouring powers. Man Singh, who came to power in 1486, was the greatest of these Tomar rulers. In 1505 he repelled an assault on the fort by Sikandar Lodi of Delhi, but in 1516 the fort was besieged by Ibrahim Lodi. Man Singh died early in the siege, but his son held out for a year before capitulating. Later the Moghùls, under Babur, took the fort and held it until 1754 when the Marathas captured it.

For the next 50 years the fort changed hands on several occasions, including twice to the British. It finally passed into the hands of the Scindias, although the British retained control behind the scenes. At the time of the Indian Mutiny in 1857, the maharaja remained loyal to the British but his troops didn't, and in mid-1858 the fort was the scene for some of the final, and most dramatic, events of the Mutiny. It was near here that the British finally defeated Tantia Topi and it was in the final assault on the fort that the Rani of Jhansi was killed. See the Jhansi section in this chapter for more details on this heroine of the mutiny. There is a memorial to her in Gwalior.

The area around Gwalior, particularly between Agra and Gwalior, was until recent years well known for the dacoits (armed robbers) who terrorised travellers and villagers. In the Chambal River valley region you still see men walking along the roads carrying rifles.

Orientation & Information

Gwalior is dominated by its fort which tops the long hill to the north of Lashkar, the new town. The old town clings to the north-east of the fort. The main market area, the Jayaji Chowk, is Lashkar's hub. Gwalior is a big place and everything is very spread out.

The tourist office (☎ 21-568) is in the Hotel Tansen, about one km south-east of the railway station.

Fort

Rising 100 metres above the town, the fort hill is about three km in length. Its width varies from nearly a km to less than 200 metres. The walls, which encircle almost the entire hilltop, are 10 metres high and imposingly solid. Beneath them, the hill face is a sheer drop away to the plains. On a clear day the view from the fort walls is superb: over old Gwalior at the north-eastern end and far across the plains.

You can approach the fort from the south or the north-east. The north-eastern path starts from the Archaeological Museum and follows a wide, winding slope to the doors of the Man Singh Palace (Man Mandir). The southern entrance (Urbai Gate) is a long, gradual ascent by road, passing cliff-face Jain sculptures.

The climb can be sweaty work in the hot season. A taxi or auto-rickshaw up the southern road is probably the easiest way in. You can then walk down from the palace to the museum when you've looked around the fort. If you're walking both ways then it's better to go the other way: in at the north-east and out at the south. No refreshments are available in the fort, so come prepared in summer.

Check at the gates to see if the Sound & Light show is operating, as it's worth going to. Indian megastar Amitabh Bachchan is the narrator.

There are several things to see in and around the fort, although most of the enclosed area is simply open space and fields. There's an admission charge here of Rs 0.20.

Southern Entrance The long ascent on the southern side climbs up through a ravine to the fort gate. Along the rock faces flanking this road are many **Jain sculptures**, some impressively big. Originally cut into the cliff faces in the mid-1400s, they were defaced by the forces of Babur in 1527 but were later repaired.

The images are in five main groups and are numbered. In the Arwahi group, image 20 is a 17-metre-high standing sculpture of Adinath, while image 22 is a 10-metre-high seated figure of Nemnath, the 22nd Jain tirthankar. The south-eastern group is the most important and covers nearly a km of the cliff face with more than 20 images.

Teli Ka Mandir Beyond the Suraj Kund tank, this temple probably dates from the 9th century and has a peculiar plan and design. The roof is Dravidian while the decorations (the whole temple is covered with sculptures) are Indo-Aryan. A Garuda tops the 10-metre-high doorway. This is the highest structure in the fort.

Between the Teli Ka Mandir and the Sasbahu temples is a modern Sikh gurdwara.

Sasbahu Temples The 'mother-in-law' and 'daughter-in-law' temples stand close to the eastern wall about midway along that side of the fort. The two temples are similar in style, and date from the 9th to 11th centuries. The larger temple has an ornately carved base and

figures of Vishnu over the entrances, and four huge pillars carry the heavy roof.

Man Singh Palace The palace, a delightfully whimsical building, is also known as the Chit Mandir or Painted Palace because of the tiled and painted decorations of ducks, elephants and peacocks. Painted blue, with hints of green and gold, it still looks very good today.

The palace was built by Man Singh between 1486 and 1516, and was repaired in 1881. It has four storeys, two of them underground and all of them now deserted. The subterranean ones are cool, even in the summer heat, and were used as prison cells during the Moghul period. The Emperor Aurangzeb had his brother Murad imprisoned and executed here. The east face of the palace, with its six towers topped by domed cupolas, stands over the fort entrance path.

Other Palaces There are other palaces clustered within the fort walls at the northern end. None is as interesting or as well preserved as the Man Singh Palace. The **Karan Palace**, or Kirti Mandir, is a long, narrow two-storey palace on the western side of the fort. At the northern end are the **Jehangir** and **Shah Jahan palaces** with a very large and deep tank, the **Jauhar Kund**. It was here that the Rajput women of the harem committed mass sati after the raja was defeated in battle in 1232.

North-East Entrance There is a whole series of gates as you descend the worn steps of the path to the archaeological museum. The sixth gate, the **Hawa Gate**, originally stood within the palace but has been removed. The fifth gate, the **Hathiya Paur**, or Elephant Gate, forms the entrance to the palace.

Descending, you pass a Vishnu shrine dating from 876 AD known as **Chatarbhujmandir**, Shrine of the Four-Armed. A tomb nearby is that of a nobleman killed in an assault on this gate in 1518. From here a series of steps lead to some rock-cut Jain and

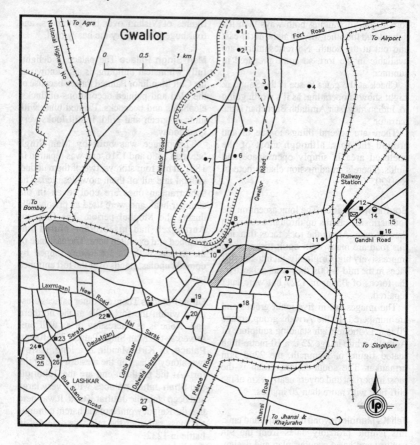

Gwalior

Hindu **sculptures** at the north-east of the fort. They are not as impressive as the sculptures on the southern side.

The interesting fourth gate was built in the 1400s and named after the elephant-headed god, Ganesh. There is a small pigeon house or **Kabutar Khana** here, as well as a small four-pillared **Hindu temple** to the hermit Gwalipa, after whom the fort and town were named.

The third gate dates from the same period as the Gujri Mahal and is known as the **Badalgarh**, after Badal Singh, Man Singh's uncle, or as the Hindola Gate after a swing,

or *hindol*, which used to stand here. The second gate, the Bansur, or Archer's Gate, has disappeared. The first gate is the **Alamgiri Gate**, dating from 1660. It was named after Aurangzeb, who took the title of Governor of Alamgiri in this region

Archaeological Museum The museum is within the Gujri Mahal palace. Built in the 15th century by Man Singh for his favourite queen, Mrignayani, the palace is now rather deteriorated. There's a large collection of Hindu and Jain sculptures and copies of the Bagh Caves' frescoes. It's open from 10 am to 5 pm daily except Mondays; admission is Rs 2 plus Rs 2 for a camera.

Jai Vilas Palace & Museum

Located in the new town, which actually dates from 1809, this was the palace of the Scindia family. Although the current maharaja still lives in the palace, a large part of it is now a museum. It's full of the bizarre items Hollywood maharajas are supposed to collect, such as Belgian cut-glass furniture (including a rocking chair), and what looks like half the tiger population of India, all shot, stuffed and moth-eaten. Modes of transport range from a Rolls Royce on rails to a German bubble-car. Then there's a little

room full of erotica, including a life-sized marble statue of Leda having her way with a swan. But the *pièce de résistance* is a model railway that carried brandy and cigars around the dining table after dinner.

If you go there by auto-rickshaw, get dropped off at the museum, not at the palace entrance as the two are far apart. The museum is open daily, except Mondays, from 10 am to 5 pm; guided tours are Rs 20 and photography is prohibited.

Old Town

The old town of Gwalior lies to the north and north-east of the fort hill. The 1661 **Jami Masjid** is a fine old building, constructed of sandstone quarried from the fort hill. On the eastern side of town is the fine **Tomb of Mohammed Gaus**, a Muslim saint who played a key role in Babur's acquisition of the fort. It has hexagonal towers at its four corners, and a dome which was once covered with glazed blue tiles. It's a very good example of early Moghul architecture.

Close to the large tomb is the smaller **Tomb of Tansen**, a singer much admired by Akbar. Chewing the leaves of the tamarind tree near his grave is supposed to do wonders for your voice, although some years ago some enthusiasts got somewhat carried away and ate the whole tree – roots and all! It is a place of pilgrimage for musicians during December-January. To find it, follow the Fort Rd from the north-eastern gate for about 15 minutes and turn right onto a small road.

Places to Stay – bottom end

The cheapest good places are near Bada, several km from the station. The friendly *Hotel Swagat* (☎ 22-520), in Lashkar, has singles from Rs 40 and doubles with bathroom from Rs 80. The *Hotel Bhagwati* on Nai Sarak is excellent value with rooms with attached bathroom for Rs 35/50 and good views of the fort from the terrace. Next door the *Ranjeet Hotel* has rooms with common bathroom for Rs 35/60. The *Hemsom Hotel* is a bit of a dive with singles from Rs 50 or rooms with attached bathrooms for 70/80/100. Beer is Rs 25 in the bar here.

The *Regal Hotel* also has great fort views from its roof terrace. There's a range of rooms from Rs 50/75 with common bathroom to doubles with bathroom for Rs 100 and some air-con rooms. The restaurant is reasonable and you can get a beer here. It's still a popular place with travellers in spite of complaints about a concealed peephole in a bathroom. Nearby is the *President Hotel* with rooms for Rs 125/150.

The best of the places near the station is the *Hotel India* with singles/doubles from Rs 75/110. It's run by the Indian Coffee Workers' Co-operative whose coffee houses you see in many Indian towns. There's one here too, staffed as usual by waiters in starched fan-shaped headgear.

In Topi Bazaar, near the GPO, is *Hotel Vivek*, a large place with rooms from Rs 95/125 and a dark restaurant.

Places to Stay – middle & top end

Beside the Indian Airlines office, the *Hotel Meghdoot* (☎ 27-374) is a clean place with air-cooled rooms from Rs 150/200 and some air-con rooms.

MP Tourism's *Hotel Tansen* (☎ 21-568) is pleasantly situated about one km from the station. It was recently upgraded but is now rather overpriced. Air-cooled singles/doubles are Rs 190/210 or Rs 335/350 with air-con.

The flashy *Hotel Gwalior Regency* has rooms for Rs 360/460. Nonresidents can use the health club and jacuzzi for Rs 100 and the swimming pool for Rs 25.

Gwalior's top hotel is the one-star *Welcomgroup Usha Kiran Palace* (☎ 32-2049). Set in a garden behind the Jai Vilas Palace, it was (as the name suggests) once a palace. The cheapest double rooms (US$55) are the nicest; the others are overpriced.

Places to Eat

The *Indian Coffee House* at the Hotel India is a good cheap place with masala dosas for Rs 5 and other vegetarian snacks.

There's a *Kwality Restaurant* with the usual menu and the nearby *Amber Restaurant* is another popular place with main dishes for around Rs 30 to Rs 40.

Near the Usha Kiran Palace is the *Volga Restaurant*. There's nothing Russian about it, but very good Indian food is served. Main dishes are around Rs 25. The restaurant at the *Usha Kiran Palace* is expensive (main dishes are Rs 55 to Rs 75) but the Indian dishes here are good.

Getting There & Away

Air Indian Airlines (☎ 24-433) has a daily flight from Delhi (US$33) through Gwalior to Bhopal (US$39), Indore (US$55) and Bombay (US$103) and vice versa.

Bus From the government bus stand there are regular services to Agra (Rs 25, three hours), Jhansi (Rs 23, three hours), Shivpuri (Rs 23, three hours) and Ujjain, Indore, Bhopal and Jabalpur. There's one bus in the morning to Khajuraho (Rs 51, nine hours). There are also departures from the private bus stand in Lashkar.

Train Gwalior is on the main Delhi to Bombay rail line with connections to most places. The superfast *Shatabdi Express* links Gwalior with Delhi (3¼ hours, Rs 255), Agra (1¼ hours, Rs 115), Jhansi (one hour, Rs 110) and Bhopal (4½ hours, Rs 275). If you've got the money but not the time you could use this reliable service for a day trip to Gwalior from Agra.

On other express trains it's five hours to Delhi (317 km, Rs 64/228 in 2nd/1st), two hours to Agra (118 km, Rs 31/111), 12 hours to Indore (652 km, Rs 108/408) and 24 hours to Bombay (1225 km, Rs 164/642 in 2nd/1st class).

Getting Around

To/From the Airport There's an airport bus (Rs 20) from the Indian Airlines office. Taxis charge at least Rs 100.

Auto-Rickshaw & Tempo Auto-rickshaw drivers will not use their meters, so arrange the fare before you depart. The tempos are good and run fixed routes around the city; the fare is Rs 2 from the railway station to Bada, the main square in Lashkar.

AROUND GWALIOR
Shivpuri

The old summer capital of the Scindias was at Shivpuri, 114 km south-west of Gwalior and 94 km west of Jhansi. Set in formal gardens, the **chhatris** are the main attraction here. With Moghul pavilions and sikhara spires these beautiful memorials to the Scindia rulers are inlaid in pietra dura style, like the Taj Mahal. The chhatri of Madho Rao Scindia faces his mother's chhatri across the tank.

Nearby is **Madhav National Park**, essentially a deer park. On the edge of the park is the Sakhya Sagar lake. Swimming from the old boat club pier here might not be wise as there are crocodiles in the lake.

The road from Gwalior passes through **Narwar**, with its large old fort.

Places to Stay The *Chinkara Motel* (☎ 2297) in Shivpuri has singles/doubles at Rs 120/140. On the main road right in the middle of town, the *Harish Lodge* has cheaper rooms and a restaurant. The *Tourist Village* (☎ 2600) is near Bhadaiya Kund and has comfortable rooms in attractive cottages for Rs 175/195 or Rs 325/350 with air-con.

Towards Agra

Between Gwalior and Agra, actually in a part of Rajasthan that separates Madhya Pradesh and Uttar Pradesh, is **Dholpur**. It was near here that Aurangzeb's sons fought a pitched battle to determine who would succeed him as emperor of the rapidly declining Moghul Empire. The Shergarh fort in Dholpur is very old and is now in ruins.

Near Bari is the **Khanpur Mahal**, a pavilioned palace built for Shah Jahan but never occupied.

Towards Jhansi

To the east of the railway line, 61 km south of Gwalior towards Jhansi, a large group of

white **Jain temples** is visible scattered along a hill. They're one of those strange, dreamlike apparitions that so often seem simply to materialise in India. Sonagir is the nearest railway station.

Only 26 km north of Jhansi is **Datia**, with the deserted seven-storey palace of Raj Bir Singh Deo. It's an impressive building, and some of the rooms still contain murals. It's worth the short bus trip from Jhansi. The town is surrounded by a stone wall and the palace is to the west.

CHANDERI

At the time of Mandu's greatest power, Chanderi was an important place, as indicated by the many ruined palaces, serais, mosques and tombs – all in a Pathan style similar to Mandu. The **Koshak Mahal** is a ruined Muslim palace which is still being maintained.

Today the town is chiefly known for its gold brocades and saris. Chanderi is 33 km west of Lalitpur, which is 90 km south of Jhansi on the main railway line. Accommodation in the town includes a *Circuit House* and the *Rest House* near the bus stand.

JHANSI
Population: 369,000

Jhansi, situated 101 km south of Gwalior, is actually just across the border in Uttar Pradesh, but for convenience we've included it here. Although Jhansi has played a colourful role in Indian history, most visitors to the town today go there simply because it's a convenient transit point for Khajuraho. This is the closest the Delhi to Bombay rail line runs to Khajuraho, and there are good connections with Delhi and Agra; it's 5½ hours by bus from Jhansi to Khajuraho.

In the 18th century, Jhansi became an important centre, eclipsing Orchha 18 km to the south, but in 1803 the British East India Company got a foot in the door and gradually assumed control over the state. The last of a string of none-too-competent rajas died without a son in 1853 and the British, who had recently passed a neat little law allowing

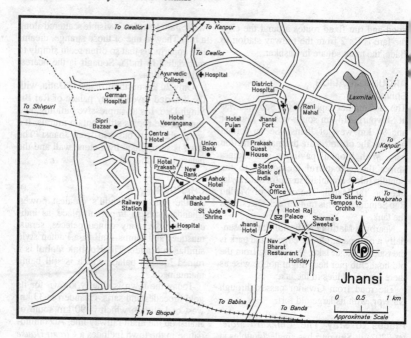

them to take over any princely state under their patronage when the ruler died without a male heir, pensioned the rani off and took full control.

The Rani of Jhansi, who wanted to rule in her own right, was unhappy about this enforced retirement, so when the Indian Mutiny burst into flame four years later, she was in the forefront of the rebellion at Jhansi. The British contingent in Jhansi were all massacred, but the following year the rebel forces were still quarrelling amongst themselves and the British retook Jhansi. The rani fled to Gwalior and, in a valiant last stand, she rode out against the British, disguised as a man, and was killed. She has since become a heroine of the Indian independence movement, a sort of central Indian Joan of Arc.

Orientation & Information

The old city is behind the fort, which is two km from the railway station. The town is quite spread out so you'll need to use autorickshaws to get around.

The Uttar Pradesh and Madhya Pradesh state governments have tourist booths at the railway station, although neither of them is particularly good.

Jhansi Fort & Rani Mahal Museum

Once used by the Indian Army, the fort can now be visited. It was built in 1613 by Maharaja Bir Singh Deo of Orchha. The British ceded the fort to the Maharaja of Scindia in 1858, but later exchanged it for Gwalior in 1866. There's nothing much to see, apart from the excellent views from the ramparts. Watch out for the band of aggressive monkeys by the temples here. It's open from 6 am to 5 pm daily, and entry is Rs 0.25.

Close to the fort, the Rani Mahal was the palace of the Rani of Jhansi. It's now a museum with a large collection of poorly displayed sculpture from the 9th to 12th century. It's open from 8 am to 5 pm; entry is free.

Places to Stay & Eat

There are dorm beds for Rs 20 in the railway *retiring rooms* and doubles here for Rs 80 or Rs 160 with air-con. The refreshment room is excellent value.

UP Tourism's *Hotel Veerangana* (☎ 1276) also has dorm beds (for Rs 20) and singles/ doubles from Rs 75/100 up to Rs 175/225 with air-con. It's a large place, but a bit run down although it has a good restaurant. It's a Rs 5 auto-rickshaw ride, or 15-minute walk, from the railway station.

The *Central Hotel* has a range of basic singles/doubles/triples from Rs 44/77/99 without bathrooms to Rs 110 for a double with attached bathroom. The rooms on the terrace upstairs are nicer than the dark cells downstairs. The *Hotel Shipra* nearby, furnished with Raj jumble including metal bedsteads and wooden hat stands, is cheaper but far from spotless.

The *Hotel Prakash* is much better with air-cooled rooms from Rs 60/110 with attached bathrooms and 24-hour checkout. It also has some air-con rooms for Rs 200/250 and is about a 10-minute walk along Station Rd.

The *Prakash Guest House* (☎ 1833) is a recommended place with good doubles from Rs 120 to Rs 250 with air-con. All rooms have attached bathrooms with hot-water heaters. It's clean, light and friendly.

The *Jhansi Hotel* (☎ 1360) is the best in town. It was a hotel in British times and faded touches of the Raj are still evident. The heads of animals shot in the area line the verandah walls and in the hot season the old method of cooling is still used here: *tatties* (large grass mats) are hung over the front of the hotel, kept damp to lower the air temperature as the water evaporates in the sun. Rooms are Rs 190/290 and some air-con rooms are also available at Rs 325/400. There's a good restaurant and bar.

Nearby is the modern *Hotel Raj Palace* (☎ 44-2554) with air-cooled rooms from Rs 140/170, more for air-con. The hotel features

'24 hours lightening service and Posh Location'. It's a good clean place, though it lacks the atmosphere of the Jhansi Hotel.

Most of the hotels have restaurants. Near the Jhansi Hotel the *Nav Bharat Restaurant* and the *Holiday* both serve good food.

Getting There & Away

Bus Buses to Khajuraho (Rs 35, 5½ hours) leave from the railway station at 6, 7 and 11 am (Shatabdi Link). There are sometimes later buses from the bus stand at 11.45 am and 1 pm. Also from the bus stand there are buses to many other places including Gwalior (Rs 23, three hours), Shivpuri (Rs 22, three hours) and Datia (Rs 7, one hour). For Orchha, the tempos from here are better. They cost only Rs 4 for the 40-minute journey and leave when full.

Train Jhansi is on the main Delhi/Agra/ Bhopal/Bombay railway line with good rail connections. Cheapest tickets on the crack *Shatabdi Express* cost Rs 300 for Delhi, Rs 165 for Agra, Rs 110 for Gwalior and Rs 240 for Bhopal. It departs at 10.47 am for Bhopal and 5.58 pm for Delhi.

Other expresses connect Jhansi with Delhi (414 km, Rs 80/289 in 2nd/1st), Agra (215 km, three hours), Gwalior (97 km, 1½ hours), Bhopal (291 km, four hours), Indore (555 km, 10 hours) and Bombay (1158 km, 21 hours). There are also direct trains from Jhansi to Bangalore, Lucknow, Madras, Pune and Varanasi.

Getting Around

The forecourt outside the railway station is filled with predatory auto-rickshaw drivers. They charge around Rs 10 for the trip to the bus station; there are also tempos for Rs 2.

ORCHHA

Once the capital city of the Bundellas, Orchha is now just a village, set amongst a complex of well-preserved palaces and temples. It's definitely worth a visit. Tour groups do it in a couple of hours but it's a wonderfully relaxing place to stay, and you can even get a room in part of the palace here.

Orchha was founded in 1531 and remained the capital of a powerful Rajput kingdom until 1783 when nearby Tikamgadh became the new capital. Bir Singh Deo ruled from Orchha between 1605 and 1627 and built the Jhansi Fort. A favourite of the Moghul Prince Salim, he feuded with Akbar and in 1602 narrowly escaped the emperor's displeasure; his kingdom was all but ruined by Akbar's forces. Then in 1605 Prince Salim became Emperor Jehangir, and for the next 22 years Bir Singh was a powerful figure. In 1627, Shah Jahan became emperor and Bir Singh once again found himself out of favour; his attempt at revolt was put down by 13-year-old Aurangzeb.

Orchha's golden age was during the first half of the 17th century. When Jehangir visited the city in 1606, a special palace, the Jehangir Mahal, was built for him. Later, both Shah Jahan and Aurangzeb raided the city.

If you're wondering what all the numbers and arrows painted on the palace floors are, they're for the Walkman tour! Go-ahead MP Tourism has 14 Walkmans that can be rented for Rs 25 (with Rs 500 deposit) from the Hotel Sheesh Mahal. In spite of the breathless enthusiasm of the narrator the recording really brings the empty palaces to life.

Palaces

The **Jehangir Mahal Palace** is of impressive size and there are good views of the countryside from the upper levels. The **Raj Mahal Palace** nearby has superb murals but you may need to find the attendant to unlock some of the rooms. Below the Jehangir Mahal is the smaller **Raj Praveen Mahal**, a palace built near a garden that is now being restored. The hammam (baths) and camel stables are nearby.

Dinman Hardaul's Palace is also interesting, as is his story. The son of Bir Singh Deo, he committed suicide to 'prove his innocence' over an affair with his brother's wife, and has achieved the status of a local god through his martyrdom.

The walled **Phool Bagh** gardens, a cool summer retreat, are also worth visiting. Other places to see include the dilapidated **Sundar Mahal** and the **chhatris** (memorials) to Orchha's rulers, down by the Betwa River.

Temples

Orchha's impressive temples date back to the 17th century. They're still in use today and are visited regularly by thousands of devotees. In the centre of the modern village is the **Ram Raja Temple** with its soaring spires. Originally a palace, it was turned into a temple when an image of Rama, temporarily installed, proved impossible to move. It now seems to have somehow made it's way into the nearby **Chaturbhuj Temple** where it is hidden behind silver doors. The **Lakshmi Narayan Temple** is worth the walk for its well-preserved murals.

Places to Stay & Eat

The *Hotel Mansarover*, run by SADA (Special Area Development Authority), has clean rooms for Rs 50/75 with common bathroom (with a big marble tub but only cold water). SADA also runs the roof-top *Betwa Tarang* restaurant nearby and the *Hotel Palki Mahal*, near the Phool Bagh gardens. The Hotel Palki has two triples at Rs 90 and dorm beds for Rs 25. A *Yatri Nivas* is under construction, not far from the Ram Raja Temple, which will have dorm beds for about Rs 20.

The most romantic place to stay in Madhya Pradesh must be the *Hotel Sheesh Mahal* (☎ 24), in a wing of the Jehangir Mahal Palace. Run by MP Tourism, there's one single for Rs 100, six singles/doubles for Rs 160/175 and an air-con suite for Rs 395/495. The best rooms are No 1 (the air-con suite) and No 2 below it. Both have great views, even from the toilet! There's a good restaurant here and it's a friendly place.

Getting There & Away

There are regular buses and tempos (Rs 4) from the Jhansi bus stand for the 18-km journey.

KHAJURAHO

Population: 6500

The temples of Khajuraho are one of India's major attractions – close behind the Taj and up there with Varanasi, Jaipur and Delhi. Once a great Chandella capital, Khajuraho is now just a quiet village of just over 6000 people. In spite of all the tourist attention it's still a very mellow place to spend a few days.

The temples are superb examples of Indo-Aryan architecture, but it's the decorations with which they are so liberally embellished that has made Khajuraho so famous. Around the temples are bands of exceedingly fine and artistic stonework. The sculptors have shown many aspects of Indian life 1000 years ago – gods and goddesses, warriors and musicians, real and mythological animals.

But two elements appear over and over again and in greater detail than anything else – women and sex. Stone figures of *apsaras* or 'celestial maidens' appear on every temple. They pout and pose for all the world like pin-up models posing for the camera. In between are the *mithuna*, erotic figures, running through a whole Kama Sutra of positions and possibilities. Some obviously require amazing athletic contortions, some just look like good fun!

These temples were built during the Chandella period, a dynasty which survived for five centuries before falling to the onslaught of Islam. Khajuraho's temples almost all date from one century-long burst of creative genius from 950-1050 AD. Almost as intriguing as the sheer beauty and size of the temples is the question of why and how they were built here. Khajuraho is a long way from anywhere and was probably just as far off the beaten track 1000 years ago as it is today. There is nothing of great interest or beauty to recommend it as a building site, there is no great population centre here and during the hot season Khajuraho is very hot, dry, dusty and uncomfortable.

Having chosen such a strange site, how did the Chandellas manage to recruit the labour to turn their awesome dreams into stone? To build so many temples of such monumental size in just 100 years must have required a huge amount of human labour. Whatever their reasons, we can be thankful they built Khajuraho where they did, because its very remoteness helped preserve it from the desecration Muslim invaders were only too ready to inflict on 'idolatrous' temples elsewhere in India.

Large numbers of visitors come to Khajuraho in March for the dance festival. This lasts 10 days and draws some of the best classical dancers in the country who perform by the western enclosure, with the floodlit temples providing a spectacular backdrop.

Orientation & Information

The modern village of Khajuraho is a cluster of hotels, restaurants, shops and stalls, near the western group of temples. The Government of India tourist office (☎ 2047) is here. There are also offices at the airport and the bus stand which can be helpful with booking accommodation in the height of the season. MP Tourism hides at the Tourist Bungalow and will sell you a T-shirt for Rs 120 or a poster for Rs 10 but don't expect anything else from them. The largest and most important temples are in the attractively landscaped western enclosure in this area.

A km or so east of the bus stand is the old village of Khajuraho. Around it are the temples of the eastern group and to the south are two further groups of temples.

During the tourist season, dance displays are staged at the modern purpose-built Chandella Cultural Centre. Foreigners have to pay a rip-off US$5 for tickets. The tourist office is said to be reviewing its discriminatory pricing policy.

As well as the usual opening hours, the State Bank of India is also open for foreign currency transactions between 4 and 5 pm Monday to Friday and 2.30 to 3.30 pm on Saturday. The chhatri behind the bank is a memorial to Maharaja Pratap Singh Ju Deo.

Temple Terminology

The Khajuraho temples follow a fairly consistent design pattern unique to Khajuraho. Understanding the architectural conventions

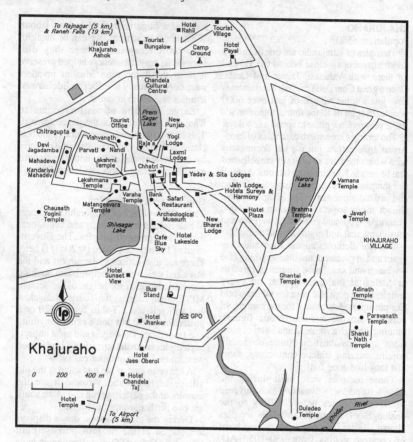

To Rajnagar (5 km)
& Raneh Falls (19 km)

Hotel Rahil
Tourist Village
Hotel Khajuraho Ashok
Tourist Bungalow
Camp Ground
Hotel Payal
Chandela Cultural Centre
Prem Sagar Lake
New Punjab
Tourist Office
Chitragupta
Vishwanath
Devi Jagadamba
Parvati ● Nandi
Mahadeva
Lakshmi Temple
Raja's ● Yogi Lodge
Laxmi Lodge
Chhatri
Kandariya Mahadev
Lakshmana Temple
Yadav & Sita Lodges
Jain Lodge, Hotels Sureya & Harmony
Chausath Yogini Temple
Varaha Temple
Matangesvara Temple
Bank
Safari Restaurant
Archeological Museum
New Bharat Lodge
Hotel Plaza
Narora Lake
Vamana Temple
Javari Temple
Brahma Temple
KHAJURAHO VILLAGE
Shivsagar Lake
Cafe Blue Sky
Hotel Lakeside
Hotel Sunset View
Ghantai Temple
Bus Stand
GPO
Hotel Jhankar
Adinath Temple
Parsvanath Temple
Shanti Nath Temple

Khajuraho

0   200   400 m

Hotel Jass Oberoi
Hotel Chandela Taj
Hotel Temple
To Airport (5 km)
Duladeo Temple
Khodar River

and some of the terms will help you enjoy the temples more. Basically all the temples follow a five-part or three-part layout.

You enter the temples through an entrance porch, known as the *ardhamandapa*. Behind this is the hall or *mandapa*. This leads into the main hall, or *mahamandapa*, supported with pillars and with a corridor around it. A vestibule or *antarala* then leads into the *garbhagriha*, the inner sanctum, where the image of the god to which the temple is dedicated is displayed. An enclosed corridor, the *pradakshina*, runs around this sanctum. The simpler three-part temples don't have a mandapa or pradakshina, but otherwise follow the same plan as the five-part temples.

Externally the temples consist of successive waves of higher and higher towers culminating in the soaring sikhara (spire), which tops the sanctum. While the lower towers, over the mandapa or mahamandapa, may be pyramid-shaped, the sikhara is taller and curvilinear. The ornate, even baroque, design of all these vertical elements is balanced by an equally ornate horizontal element from the bands of sculptures that run around the temples. Although the sculptures are superbly developed in their own right, they are also a carefully integrated part of the overall design – not some tacked-on afterthought.

The interiors of the temples are as ornate as the exteriors. The whole temple sits upon a high terrace, known as the *adisthana*. Unlike temples in most other parts of India, these had no enclosing wall but often had four smaller shrines at the corners of the terrace; many of them have now disappeared. The finely carved entrance gate to the temple is a torana, and the lesser towers around the main sikhara are known as *urusringas*.

The temples are almost all aligned east to west, with the entrance facing east. Some of the earliest temples were made of granite, or granite and sandstone, but all the ones from the classic period of Khajuraho's history are made completely of sandstone. At that time there was no mortar, so the blocks were fitted together. The sculptures and statues play such an important part in the total design that many have their own terminology:

apsara – heavenly nymph, beautiful dancing woman.
mithuna – Khajuraho's most famous image, the sensuously carved, erotic figures which have been shocking people from Victorian archaeologists to bus-loads of blue-rinse tourists.
nayika – it's really impossible to tell a nayika from a surasundari, since the only difference is that the surasundari is supposed to be a heavenly creature while a nayika is human.
salabhanjika – female figure with tree, which together act as supporting brackets in the inner chambers of the temple. Apsaras also perform this bracket function.
sardula – a mythical beast, part lion, part some other animal or even human. Sardulas usually carry armed men on their backs, and can be seen on many of the temples. They all look like lions but the faces are often different. They may be demons or *asuras*.
surasundari – when a surasundari is dancing she is an apsara. Otherwise she attends the gods and goddesses by carrying flowers, water, ornaments, mirrors or other offerings. She also engages in everyday activities like washing her hair, applying make-up, taking a thorn out of her foot, fondling herself, playing with pets and babies, writing letters, playing musical instruments or posing seductively.

Western Group

The main temples are in the western group, conveniently close to the tourist part of Khajuraho. Most are contained within a fenced enclosure which is very well maintained as a park. The enclosure is open from sunrise to sunset and entry is Rs 0.50. This includes entry to the archaeological museum across the road, so don't lose your ticket. Admission is free on Fridays. Just inside the enclosure you can buy an excellent Archaeological Survey of India guidebook to Khajuraho for Rs 5.

The temples are described here in a clockwise direction.

Lakshmi & Varaha Facing the large Lakshmana Temple are these two small shrines. The Varaha Temple, dedicated to Vishnu's boar incarnation or Varaha avatar, actually faces the Matangesvara Temple. Inside this small, open shrine is a huge, solid and intricately carved figure of the boar incarnation, dating from around 900 AD.

Lakshmana The large Lakshmana Temple is dedicated to Vishnu, although in design it is similar to the Kandariya Mahadev and Vishvanath temples. It is one of the earliest of the western enclosure temples, dating from around 930-950 AD, and is also one of the best preserved, with a full five-part floor plan and four subsidiary shrines. Around the temple are two bands of sculpture instead of the usual three; the lower one has fine figures of apsaras and some erotic scenes. Inside are excellent examples of apsaras acting as supporting brackets.

On the subsidiary shrine at the south-west corner you can make out an architect working with his students – it is thought this may be the temple's designer including himself in the grand plan. Around the base of the temple is a continuous frieze with scenes of battles, hunting and processions. The first metre or two of the frieze consists of a highly energetic orgy, including one gentleman proving that a horse can be a person's best friend, while a stunned group of women look aside in shock.

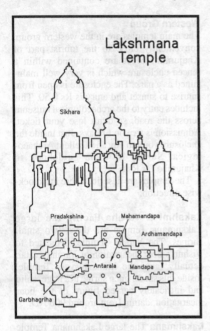

The temple platform gives you a good view of the Matangesvara Temple (see below). It's outside the western enclosure and the only temple in this area that is still in use today.

Kandariya Mahadev The first of the temples on the common platform at the back of the western enclosure is the one temple to see in Khajuraho above all others. The Kandariya Mahadev is not only the largest of the temples, it is also artistically and architecturally the most perfect. Built between 1025 and 1050, it represents Chandella art at its finest. Although the four subsidiary shrines which once stood around the main temple have long disappeared, the central shrine is in superb condition and shows the typical five-part design of Khajuraho temples.

The main spire is 31 metres high, and the temple is lavishly carved. The English archaeologist Cunningham counted 226 statues inside the temple and a further 646 outside – 872 in total with most of them nearly a metre in height. The statues are carved around the temple in three bands and include gods, goddesses, beautiful women, musicians and, of course, some of the famed erotic groups. The mithuna on the Kandariya Mahadev include some of the most energetic eroticism to be seen at Khajuraho.

Mahadeva This small and mainly ruined temple stands on the same base as the Kandariya Mahadev and the Devi Jagadamba. Although small and insignificant compared to its mighty neighbours, it houses one of Khajuraho's best sculptures – a fine sardula figure (man or woman, observers have been unable to decide), caressing a lion.

Devi Jagadamba The third temple on the common platform is slightly older than the Kandariya Mahadev and of a simpler, three-part design. It was probably originally dedicated to Vishnu, but later changed to Parvati and then Kali. Some students believe it may still be a Parvati temple and that the Kali image (or Jagadamba) is actually an image of Parvati, painted black. The sculptures around the temple are again in three bands. Many of the two lower band images are of Vishnu with sardulas in the inner recesses. But on the third and uppermost band the mithuna again come out to play, and some feel that this is Khajuraho's most erotic temple.

Chitragupta The fourth temple at the back of the western enclosure does not share the common platform with the other three. Similar in design to the Devi Jagadamba, this temple is probably slightly newer and is unique at Khajuraho in being dedicated to Surya, the Sun God.

Attempts have obviously been made at restoration, but it is not in as good condition as other temples. Nevertheless it has some very fine sculptures that include processions, dancing girls, elephant fights and hunting scenes. In the inner sanctum, Surya can be seen driving his chariot and seven horses, while on the central niche in the south facade you can see an 11-headed statue of Vishnu. The central head is that of Vishnu himself; the 10 others are of his incarnations.

Parvati Continuing around the enclosure, you come to the Parvati Temple on your right. The name is probably incorrect since this small and not so interesting temple was originally dedicated to Vishnu and now has an image of Ganga riding on the back of a crocodile.

Vishvanath Temple & Nandi Believed to have been built in 1002, this temple has the complete five-part design of the larger Kandariya Mahadev Temple, but two of its four subsidiary shrines still stand. That it is a Siva shrine is made very clear by the large image of his vehicle, the bull Nandi, which faces the temple from the other end of the

common platform. Steps lead up to this high terrace, flanked by lions on the northern side and elephants on the southern side.

The sculptures around the temple include the usual Khajuraho scenes, but the sculptures of women are particularly notable here. They write letters, fondle a baby, play music and, perhaps more so than at any other temple, languish in provocative poses.

Matangesvara Temple Standing next to the Lakshmana Temple, this temple is not within the fenced enclosure because it is still in everyday use, unlike all the other old Khajuraho temples. It may be the plainest temple here (suggesting that it was one of the first built) but inside it sports a polished linga, 2½ metres high.

Early in the morning, flower-sellers do a brisk trade in garlands for the statue of Ganesh outside. People drape them round the elephant-headed statue, say a prayer and as they walk away the flower-sellers whip them off to resell!

Khajuraho's Erotica

The most frequently asked question by visitors to Khajuraho is why all the sex? One theory has it that the erotic posturing was a kind of *Kama Sutra* in stone, a how-to-do-it manual for adolescent Brahmin boys growing up segregated from the world in special temple schools. Another claims that the figures were thought to prevent the temples being struck by lightning, by appeasing the rain god Indra. This old lecher is supposedly a keen voyeur who wouldn't want the source of his pleasure damaged.

Rather more convincing is the explanation that these are Tantric images. According to this cult, gratification of the baser instincts is one way to blot out the evils of the world and achieve final deliverance. *Bhoga* (physical enjoyment) and *yoga* (spiritual exercise) are seen as equally valid in this quest for nirvana.

Probably the most accurate theory is that the Khajuraho sculptors were simply representing life as it was viewed by their society, unhampered by Old Testament morality. In spite of the fact that modern visitors are drawn as much for reasons of prurience as for cultural appreciation, this is not pornography. Although there are certainly large numbers of erotic images here, many other day-to-day scenes are also shown. The carvings should be seen as a joyous celebration of all aspects of life. ∎

Chausath Yogini Standing beyond the tank, some distance from the other western group temples, this ruined temple is probably the oldest at Khajuraho, dating from 900 AD or earlier. It is also the only temple constructed entirely of granite and the only one not aligned east to west. Chausath means 64 – the temple once had 64 cells for figures of the 64 yoginis who attended the goddess Kali. A 65th cell sheltered Kali herself.

A further half km west is the **Lalguan Mahadev Temple**, a small, ruined shrine dedicated to Siva and constructed of granite and sandstone.

Archaeological Museum

Close to the western enclosure, this museum has a fine collection of statues and sculptures rescued from around Khajuraho. It's small and worth a visit but the attendants tend to hassle you for baksheesh. There's a wonderful dancing Ganesh figure in the entrance gallery. Admission is included in the western enclosure entrance fee and the museum is open from 10 am to 5 pm but is closed on Friday.

Opposite the museum, in the Archaeological Survey of India's compound beside the Matangesvara Temple, there are many more rescued sculptures – but this area is off limits.

Eastern Group

The eastern group of temples can be subdivided into two groups. The first is made up of interesting Jain temples in the walled enclosure. The other four temples are scattered through the small village of Khajuraho.

Jain Museum Outside the Jain enclosure is this recently constructed circular gallery, filled with statues of the 24 tirthankars. It's open every day from 7 am to 6 pm and entry is Rs 1.

Parsvanath The largest of the Jain temples in the walled enclosure is also one of the finest at Khajuraho. Although it does not approach the western enclosure temples in size, and does not attempt to compete in the sexual activity stakes, it is notable for the exceptional skill and precision of its construction, and for the beauty of its sculptures. Some of the best known figures at Khajuraho can be seen here, including the classic figure of a woman removing a thorn from her foot and another of a woman applying eye make-up. Although it was originally dedicated to Adinath, an image of Parsvanath was substituted about a century ago and the temple takes its name from this newer image.

Adinath Adjacent to the Parsvanath Temple, the smaller Adinath has been partially restored over the centuries. It has fine carvings on its three bands of sculptures and, like the Parsvanath, is very similar to the Hindu temples of Khajuraho. Only the striking black image in the inner sanctum indicates that it is Jain rather than Hindu.

Shanti Nath This temple is a relatively modern one built about a century ago, but it contains many components from older temples around Khajuraho. The 4½-metre-high statue of Adinath is said to have been sculpted in 1028. A triple padlocked metal chest beside it is labelled 'secret donation box'. Groups of Digambara Jain pilgrims occasionally stay at the dharamsala here, their nakedness causing raised eyebrows amongst package tourists.

Ghantai Walking from the eastern Jain temple group towards Khajuraho village, you come to this small, ruined Jain temple. Only its pillared shell remains, but it is interesting for the delicate columns with their bell and chain decoration and for the figure of a Jain goddess astride a Garuda which marks the entrance.

Javari Walk through the village, a typical small Indian settlement, to this temple. Dating from around 1075-1100 AD, it is dedicated to Vishnu and is a particularly fine example of Khajuraho architecture on a small scale. The exterior has more of Khajuraho's delightful women.

Vamana About 200 metres north of the

Javari Temple, this temple is dedicated to Vamana, the dwarf incarnation of Vishnu. Slightly older than the Javari Temple, the Vamana Temple stands out in a field all by itself. It's notable for the relatively simple design of its sikhara. The bands of sculpture around the temples are, as usual, very fine with numerous 'celestial maidens' adopting interesting poses.

Brahma & Hanuman Turning back (west) towards the modern village, you pass this granite and sandstone temple, one of the oldest at Khajuraho. It was actually dedicated to Vishnu and the definition of it as a Brahma temple is incorrect.

Taking the road directly from the modern village to the Jain enclosure, you pass a Hanuman Temple containing a large image of the monkey god. This 2½-metre statue has on it the oldest inscription here, dating it to 922 AD.

Southern Group

There are only two temples in the southern group, one of which is several km south of the river.

Duladeo A dirt track runs to this isolated temple, about a km south of the Jain enclosure. This is the latest temple at Khajuraho, and experts say that at this time the skill of Khajuraho's temple builders had passed its peak and the sculptures are more 'wooden' and 'stereotyped' than on earlier temples. Nevertheless, it's a fine and graceful temple with figures of women in a variety of pin-up poses and a number of mithuna couples.

Chaturbhuja South of the river, about three km from the village and a healthy hike down a dirt road, this ruined temple has a fine three-metre-high image of Vishnu.

Organised Tours

There are currently no guided tours operated by the tourist office, although they are planning to reintroduce them. Licensed private guides are available for hire, charging

around Rs 80 for a half-day. If you want a taxi this would be a further Rs 150.

Places to Stay – bottom end

MP Tourism has quite a few hotels here and they're good value at the height of the season but overpriced at other times when private hotels reduce their prices. If there aren't many people here it's worth trying to get a reduction.

The cheapest places are in the centre of the new village, close to the western group of temples. The *Gupta, Apsara* and *Laxmi* are side-by-side and are very similar, very basic and not too clean. Singles/doubles are around Rs 40/50 with attached bathrooms. Nearby are two more cheap lodges, in the same price range, the *Yadav* and the *Sita Lodge*. The Yadav Lodge is the best of this group.

The *Yogi Lodge* (☎ 2158) is very good value with singles/doubles with attached bathrooms from around Rs 50/60. It's run by a yoga teacher and lessons are sometimes available here. He's reputed to be a specialist in Tantric yoga. In a very quiet location on the way to the Jain temples, the *Hotel Plaza* is newly built with doubles with attached bathrooms from Rs 50.

An old favourite with travellers is the *Jain Lodge* (☎ 2052), which has a range of rooms from Rs 50/60 upwards, including air-cooled and air-con rooms. There's a good vegetarian restaurant here. Next door the *Hotel Sureya* (☎ 2145) is a clean place with a small garden and good rooms with attached bathrooms for Rs 80/100. Right beside this, the *Hotel Harmony* (☎ 2135) also claims to be 'the only hotel with a garden in the city'. Rooms are Rs 130/150 and there's a vegetarian restaurant. The small walled garden is immaculate. These three hotels are very much in competition with each other and they're all worth checking out.

To the north of the modern village of Khajuraho are a number of hotels run by MP Tourism. The *Tourist Village* (☎ 2128) is in a very peaceful location and the manager is friendly and helpful. It's an interesting collection of ethnic cottages (watch your head on the low doorways), decorated with local carpets and furnishings. Singles/doubles cost Rs 95/125 with attached bathrooms and there's an open-air restaurant. The *Hotel Rahil* (☎ 2062) is a large concrete block nearby with an institutional feel to it. The dorms are small and clean with beds for Rs 30 and there are rooms with attached bathrooms and hot water for Rs 126/146.

The *Hotel Sunset View* (☎ 2077) has a wide range of accommodation including dorm beds at Rs 15 and rooms from Rs 60 to Rs 150 for a double with bathroom. Clean and modern with a nice garden, it's a reasonable place to stay as long as the building work has finished. Be careful buying jewellery from its craft shop, though. It's on the main road from the airport, just before the town.

The *Hotel Lakeside* (☎ 2120) has very clean rooms set around a courtyard, right in the middle of the new village. There are dorm beds for Rs 25 and singles/doubles range from Rs 100/150 to Rs 250/300 with attached bathrooms.

Places to Stay – middle

MP Tourism's old *Tourist Bungalow* (☎ 2064) is a popular, conveniently located place. Spacious singles/doubles/triples cost Rs 150/175/205 with attached bathrooms and there's a restaurant here.

Also run by the state tourism organisation, the *Hotel Payal* (☎ 2076) is a modern place with a garden and spacious singles/doubles for Rs 170/195 or Rs 320/350 with air-con. It's clean, well kept and there's an information booth. Good food is available in the restaurant although the service is very slow.

MP Tourism's flagship here is the glitzy *Hotel Jhankar* (☎ 2063). Rooms are well decorated and cost Rs 170/195 or Rs 320/350 for air-con, all with attached bathrooms and hot-water heaters. The restaurant is not that great and there's no beer.

Places to Stay – top end

The *Hotel Khajuraho Ashok* (☎ 2024), a short walk north of the modern village, continues to get the thumbs down from visitors.

At US$36/44 for singles/doubles it cannot be called good value. Service is slow in the overpriced restaurant, and beer is hardly a snip at Rs 75 a bottle. You can, however, use the swimming pool for Rs 36 as a non-resident.

The *Hotel Chandela Taj* (☎ 2054), south of the modern village, is the best hotel in Khajuraho. Air-conditioned rooms cost US$70/80, with comfortable beds, and bathtubs in the attached bathrooms. Diversions for when guests are 'templed out' include tennis, yoga, archery, croquet and badminton. Nonresidents can use the swimming pool for Rs 120 or have a massage at the health club, also for Rs 120. There's a good bookshop and two excellent restaurants.

Almost as good is the *Hotel Jass Oberoi* (☎ 2085) nearby. These two hotels are in close competition with each other with identical prices and similar facilities. The pool at the Jass Oberoi is not open to nonresidents.

Places to Eat

The *Safari Restaurant* is currently the most popular travellers' place to eat. Prices aren't rock-bottom but it's good value as portions are generous. A big salad is Rs 8. Excellent grilled chicken & chips costs Rs 35 and there are lots of cheaper dishes. There's a shady patio, fairly quick service and Bob Marley goes nonstop on the tape deck.

For a cheaper meal the *Lovely Restaurant*, opposite the museum, does an excellent vegetarian thali for Rs 10 to Rs 15. It's much better value than the *Madras Coffee House* which is nearby. Their South Indian thali is Rs 36 and a pancake with 'hunney' will set you back Rs 25.

Raja's Cafe has been here for years and so has the Swiss woman who runs it. The large shady tree in the restaurant's courtyard is a popular gathering spot and there are good views over the temples from the terrace above. The quality of food here is variable and it's more expensive than the Safari. Much of it is rather bland although this seems to be what people like about it. Swiss rostis at Rs 15 are of course a speciality, pancake chicken béchamel is Rs 50 and chicken tempura Rs 35. They also do packed lunches, run trips to Panna National Park and have a limited book exchange.

The *New Punjab Restaurant* is cheaper and also has a nice terrace with umbrellas and views of the temples. The *Maharaja Terrace Restaurant* and the *Cafe Blue Sky* are similar places with reasonable food. Both have terraces and are obviously trying to compete with the Safari and Raja's. The *New Bharat Lodge* has two restaurants, one in the hotel and the other near the tourist office. Main dishes here are around Rs 35. Nearby is a liquor shop where Kingfisher beer costs Rs 35.

The *Hotel Chandela Taj* is the best place to eat although it's very expensive. Main dishes are Rs 75 to Rs 90 and a gin and tonic over Rs 100. Service is attentive and the food is excellent.

Getting There & Away

Getting to Khajuraho can be a major pain. It's really on the way from nowhere to nowhere, and is not near any railway station. Although many travellers slot it in between Varanasi and Agra, it involves a lot of travelling to cover not particularly great distances. If you can afford to fly, then do; although flights can be subject to delays.

Air Indian Airlines (☎ 2035) is in the Hotel Temple building. They have a daily Delhi-Agra-Khajuraho-Varanasi flight that returns by the same route to Delhi. It's probably the most popular tourist flight in India and can often be booked solid for days by tour groups. In winter early morning mist in Delhi can delay departures, which has a domino effect on the rest of the day's timetable.

If you've got one of those middle-of-the-night international flights out of Delhi don't rely on flying in from Khajuraho the day before. Problems with flights from here may lessen when the new runway beacons are installed and when Indian Airlines finally gets a computer link.

Prices from Khajuraho are: Agra US$39, Delhi US$53 and Varanasi US$39. Links with Bombay are planned.

Bus & Train From the west there are bus services from Agra (Rs 74, 12 hours), Gwalior (Rs 51, nine hours) and Jhansi (Rs 35, 5½ hours). Jhansi is the nearest approach to Khajuraho on the main Delhi to Bombay rail line, and there are half a dozen buses a day on this popular route. The Shatabdi Link leaves Khajuraho at 11.30 am and goes right through to Jhansi railway station, arriving at 4 pm in time to catch the *Shatabdi Express* to Gwalior, Agra and Delhi. MP Tourism are planning a luxury air-con bus, similar to their Bhopal-Indore service, for the Khajuraho to Jhansi route.

There is no direct route to Varanasi from Khajuraho. Satna (Rs 23, four hours from Khajuraho) is the nearest railhead for travellers from Varanasi and the east. It's on the Bombay to Allahabad line. To get from Varanasi to Khajuraho in the same day you'd have to catch the *Bombay Mail* from Mughal Sarai (near Varanasi), leaving at 7.58 am, reaching Satna at 2.10 pm. Go straight to the bus stand in Satna as there may not be another bus for Khajuraho after 3.30 pm.

Another alternative from Khajuraho to Varanasi is to take the bus to Mahoba (Rs 13, 2½ hours via Londi at 10.30 am and 2.30 pm) and a train from there, but it's a rather slow passenger train. There are also buses to Harpalpur, which is 99 km from Khajuraho (closer than Satna).

Overnight buses for masochists connect Khajuraho with Bhopal (Rs 83, 12 hours) and Indore (Rs 119, 16 hours). There's an early morning bus to Jabalpur (Rs 58, 11 hours) but it would be more comfortable to take a train from Satna.

Getting Around

To/From the Airport There's no airport bus; taxis charge Rs 50 for this short journey. If there aren't too many tourists about, you should be able to get a cycle-rickshaw to the airport for Rs 25.

Local Transport The best way to get around Khajuraho is by bicycle, since it's all flat and pleasantly traffic-free. Bicycles cost Rs 10 per day from several places in the new village. Cycle-rickshaws are a rip-off. This is hardly surprising with rich tourists willing to pay Rs 30 for the trip from the Hotel Chandela Taj to the western temples!

It's a long walk to the eastern group of temples. If you're planning to take a cycle-rickshaw it's best to arrange a number of stops, including the southern temples and waiting time.

AROUND KHAJURAHO
Dhubela
In the old fort in this town, 64 km from Khajuraho along the road to Jhansi, there's a small **museum**. Exhibits include Shakti cult sculptures, weapons, clothes and other personal belongings of the Bundella kings.

Panna National Park
The road to Satna passes through this recently created park, lying along the River Ken, 32 km from Khajuraho. It contains large areas of unspoilt forest and a variety of wildlife. There are tiger here but you'd be very lucky to see one. The numerous waterfalls in this area are popular picnic spots. Day trips often also take in a visit to the **diamond mines** at Majhgawan, the **Rajgarh Palace** and the **temples** of Panna town, 48 km from Khajuraho.

Ajaigarh & Kalinjar Forts
At Ajaigarh, 80 km from Khajuraho, is the large isolated hilltop fort, designed to protect the local population during attacks and sieges. It was built by the Chandellas when their influence in the area was on the decline. Kalinjar Fort, 25 km north (just inside Uttar Pradesh) is much older, built during the Gupta period and mentioned by Ptolemy in the 2nd century AD.

Chitrakoot
It was here that Brahma, Vishnu and Siva are believed to have been 'born' and taken on their incarnations, which makes this town a popular Hindu pilgrimage place. It's on the banks of the Mandakini River by the border with Uttar Pradesh, and is 195 km from Khajuraho and 132 km from Allahabad. Both MP Tourism and UP Tourism have *Tourist Bungalows* here.

SATNA
Population: 160,000
You may find it convenient or necessary to stay overnight here on your way to or from Khajuraho. The tourist office is at the railway station.

Places to Stay & Eat
The *Hotel India* is a good place near the bus stand. Singles/doubles are Rs 50/75 with attached bathroom and downstairs there's an excellent, cheap vegetarian restaurant. It's part of the Indian Coffee House chain. Nearby the *Hotel Star* has rooms for Rs 30/55 and the *Hotel Glory* has singles for Rs 25 but they're both very basic.

The *Hotel Park* is in a slightly quieter location, with clean singles/doubles for Rs 50/75, air-cooled doubles for Rs 140, and air-con rooms. It's 1½ km from the railway station and there's a vegetarian restaurant here.

MP Tourism's *Hotel Barhut* (☎ 2041) is the revamped Tourist Bungalow. It's a good clean place with singles/doubles at Rs 150/175 or Rs 245/275 with air-con. There's a restaurant and the bathroom here gives you the choice of urinal, Indian squat lavatory or Western throne – all in the one room!

Getting There & Away
There are buses to Khajuraho (Rs 23, four hours) at 6 and 10 am, and 2.30 and 3.30 pm and a morning bus to Tala (Rs 23, four hours) for Bandhavgarh National Park.

The railway station and the bus stand are about two km apart and cycle-rickshaws charge Rs 2, although you'll probably have to pay double that. There are direct trains from Satna to Varanasi (316 km, Rs 64/228 in 2nd/1st class) taking eight hours and other direct expresses connect with Allahabad (180 km, four hours), Calcutta, Bombay and Madras.

Central Madhya Pradesh

SANCHI

Beside the main railway line, 46 km north of Bhopal, a hill rises from the plain. It's topped by some of the oldest and most interesting Buddhist structures in India. Although this site had no direct connection with the life of Buddha, it was the great Emperor Ashoka who built the first stupas here in the 3rd century BC, and a great number of stupas and other religious structures were added over the succeeding centuries.

As Buddhism was gradually absorbed back into Hinduism in its land of origin, the site decayed and was eventually completely forgotten. In 1818 a British officer rediscovered the site, but in the following years amateur archaeologists and greedy treasure hunters did immense damage to Sanchi before a proper restoration was first commenced in 1881. Finally, between 1912 and 1919, the structures were carefully repaired and restored to their present condition by Sir John Marshall.

Despite the damage which was wrought after its rediscovery, Sanchi is a very special place and is not to be missed if you're anywhere within striking distance. The sculptures here are full of vitality and a freshness of perception only possible at the beginning of a cultural era. The site itself is one of the most mellow in India and Sanchi is a good base for a number of interesting cycle excursions.

Orientation & Information

Sanchi is little more than a small village at the foot of the hill. The site is open daily from dawn to dusk and tickets are available from the kiosk outside the museum. Entry costs Rs 0.50 which covers both the site and the museum. It's worth buying a copy of the guidebook *Sanchi* (Rs 4), published by the Archaeological Survey of India. There's also a museum guidebook (Rs 3) on sale here.

At the crossroads the Mrignayanee Emporium sells local handicrafts including batik bedcovers for Rs 90 and bell-metal figures. It's sometimes possible to visit the silkworm farm (Sericulture Centre). Ask at the MP Travellers' Lodge next door. If you are not well there's a very helpful doctor at the clinic near the Tourist Cafeteria.

The quickest way up to the site is via the stone track off to the right of the tarmac road. There's a bookshop and drink stall by the modern *vihara* on Sanchi hill.

Archaeological Museum

This museum has a small collection of sculpture from the site. The most interesting pieces are the lion capital from the Ashoka pillar, a yakshi (maiden) hanging from a mango tree and a beautiful Buddha figure in red sandstone. Note that, as museum rules state, 'no cooking or picnicing', is allowed nor may you 'sleep, run, sing or commit nuisance' here! It's open 10 am to 5 pm daily except on Fridays.

Great Stupa

Stupa 1, as it is listed on the site, is the main structure on the hill. Originally constructed by Ashoka in the 3rd century BC, it was later enlarged and the original brick stupa enclosed within a stone one. In its present form it stands 16 metres high and 37 metres in diameter. A railing encircles the stupa and there are four entrances through magnificently carved gateways or toranas. These toranas are the finest works of art at Sanchi and amongst the finest examples of Buddhist art in India.

Toranas The four gateways were erected around 35 BC and had all fallen down at the time of the stupa's restoration. The scenes carved onto the pillars and their triple architraves are mainly tales from the *jatakas*, the episodes of the Buddha's various lives. At this stage in Buddhist art the Buddha was never represented directly – his presence was always alluded to through symbols. The lotus stands for his birth, the bo tree represents his enlightenment, the wheel his teachings and the footprint and throne symbolise his presence. Even a stupa itself is a symbol of the Buddha.

Go round the stupa clockwise, as one should around all Buddhist monuments.

Northern Gateway The northern gateway, topped by a broken wheel of law, is the best preserved of the gateways. It shows many scenes from the Buddha's life, both in his last incarnation and in earlier lives. Scenes include a monkey offering a bowl of honey to the Buddha, whose presence is indicated by a bo tree. In another panel he ascends a road into the air (again represented by a bo tree) in the 'miracle of Sravasti'. This is just one of several miraculous feats he performs on the northern gateway – all of which leave his spectators stunned. Elephants, facing in four directions, support the architraves above the columns, while horses with riders and more elephants fill the gaps between the architraves.

Eastern Gateway One pillar on this gateway includes scenes of the Buddha's entry to nirvana. Across the front of the middle architrave is the 'great departure', where the Buddha (symbolised by a riderless horse) renounces the sensual life and sets out to find enlightenment. Maya's dream of an elephant standing on the moon, which she had when she conceived the Buddha, is also shown on one of the columns. The figure of a yakshi maiden, hanging out from one of the architraves, is one of the best known images of Sanchi.

Southern Gateway The oldest of the gateways, this includes scenes of the Buddha's birth and also events from Ashoka's life as a Buddhist. As on the western gateway, the tale of the Chhaddanta Jataka features on this gateway.

Western Gateway The western gateway, with the architraves supported by dwarves, has some of the most interesting scenes at the site. The rear face of one of the pillars shows the Buddha undergoing the temptation of Mara, while demons flee and angels cheer

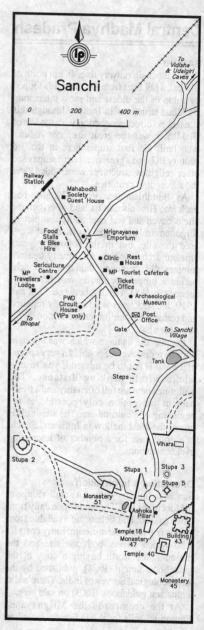

Sanchi

0   200   400 m

To Vidisha & Udalgiri Caves

Railway Station

Mahabodhi Society Guest House

Mrignayanee Emporium

Food Stalls & Bike Hire

Clinic   Rest House

Sericulture Centre

MP Tourist Cafeteria

MP Travellers' Lodge

Ticket Office

PWD Circuit House (VIPs only)

Archaeological Museum

To Bhopal

Post Office

Gate

To Sanchi Village

Tank

Steps

Vihara

Stupa 2

Stupa 1   Stupa 3
Stupa 5

Monastery 51

Ashoka Pillar

Temple 18
Monastery 47

Building 43

Temple 40

Monastery 45

his resistance. Mara also tempts on the back of the lowest architrave. The top front architrave shows the Buddha in seven incarnations, but since he could not, at the time, be represented directly, he appears three times as a stupa and four times as a tree. His six incarnations prior to the seventh, Gautama Buddha, are known as the Manushi Buddhas.

The colourful events of the Chhaddanta Jataka are related on the front face of the bottom architrave. In this tale the Buddha, in a lower incarnation, took the form of a six-tusked elephant, but one of his two wives became jealous; she managed to reincarnate as a queen and then arranged to have the six-tusked elephant hunted and killed. The sight of his tusks, sawn off by the hunter, was sufficient for the queen to die of remorse! Pot-bellied dwarves support the architraves on this gateway.

Pillars Scattered around the site are pillars or the remains of pillars. The most important is pillar 10, which was erected by Ashoka and stands close to the southern entrance to the great stupa. Only the base of this beautifully proportioned and executed shaft now stands, but the fine capital can be seen in the museum. The three back-to-back lions, which once topped the column, are an excellent example of the Greco-Buddhist art of that era at its finest. They now form the state emblem of India and can be seen on every bank note.

Pillars 25 and 35, both dating from the 5th century AD, are not as fine as the earlier Ashoka pillar. Pillar 35, also broken, stands close to the northern gateway of the great stupa; again, the capital figure is in the museum.

Other Stupas
There are many other stupas on the hill, some of them tiny votive ones less than a metre high. They date from the 3rd century AD. Eight were built by Ashoka but only three remain, including the great stupa. **Stupa 2**, one of the most interesting of the lesser stupas, is halfway down the hill to the west.

If you come up from the town by the main route you can walk back down via stupa 2. There are no gateways to this stupa, but the 'medallions' which decorate the surrounding wall are of great interest. Their design is almost childlike, but full of energy and imagination. Flowers, animals and people – some mythological – are found all around the stupa.

Stupa 3 stands north-east of the main stupa and is similar in design, though smaller in size, to the great stupa. It has only one gateway and is thought to have been constructed soon after the completion of the great stupa. Stupa 3 once contained relics of two important disciples of the Buddha. They were removed and taken to London in 1853 but returned to Sanchi in 1953. Stupa 2, down the hill, also contained relics of important Buddhist teachers, but it is thought this lower spot was chosen for their enshrinement because the top of the hill was reserved for shrines to the Buddha and his direct disciples.

Now almost totally destroyed, **stupa 4** stands right behind stupa 3. Between stupa 1 (the great stupa) and stupa 3 is **stupa 5**, which is unusual in that it once had an image of the Buddha, now displayed in the museum.

Temples
Immediately south of stupa 1 is **temple 18**, a *chaitya* hall which in style is remarkably similar to classical Greek-columned buildings. It dates from around the 7th century AD but traces of earlier wooden buildings have been discovered beneath it. Beside this temple is the small **temple 17**, also Greek-like in style. The large **temple 40**, slightly south-east of these two temples, in part dates back to the Ashokan period.

Temple 6 stands between 40 and 18. It is known as the Gupta Temple and dates back to the 4th century AD. The flat-roofed structure is made of stone slabs, and also shows a Greek influence, probably stemming from the work of Bactrian artisans. This temple is interesting in that it displays the Indian temple style with a porch leading to the central shrine, which was later developed in classical Hindu temples at Khajuraho and Orissa.

Monasteries

The earliest monasteries on the site were made of wood and have long since disappeared. The usual plan is of a central courtyard surrounded by monastic cells. **Monasteries 45 and 47** stand on the higher, eastern edge of the hilltop. They date from the later period of building at Sanchi, a time of transition from Buddhism to Hinduism, and show strong Hindu elements in their design. There is a good view of the village of Sanchi below and Vidisha in the distance from this side of the hill.

Monastery 51 is partway down the hill on the western side toward stupa 2. Close to it is the **'great bowl'** in which food and offerings were placed for distribution to the monks. It was carved out of a huge boulder.

The modern **vihara** (monastery) on the hill was constructed to house the returned relics from stupa 3. The design is a poor shadow of the former artistry of Sanchi. The *Sanchi* guidebook describes all these buildings, and many others, in much greater detail.

Places to Stay

It's possible to take in all that Sanchi has to offer in just two or three hours – less if you're pushed for time – so few people stay overnight. However this is such a peaceful place that it's really worth spending the night here.

Best value for money in Sanchi is probably (and surprisingly) the railway *retiring rooms*. There are just two of them but they're spacious and very clean. Charges are Rs 20 per bed for the first 24 hours, Rs 30 thereafter.

The *Sri Lanka Mahabodhi Society Guest House* is rather more spartan and has dorm beds and even some rooms with attached bathrooms. Donations of around Rs 25 per person should be made if you stay here. In theory you should make reservations in advance, but in practice you can just drop in.

Ask around for the caretaker if it looks closed. There's quite a good library here.

The creaky Gothic-looking *Rest House* is another cheap place. The rooms are very variable here and cost around Rs 40 a double but the water supply is rather erratic. If there's no-one around, ask at the house across the courtyard.

In front of the Rest House is MP Tourism's *Tourist Cafeteria* (☎ 243) which offers very clean rooms for Rs 130/150. As the name suggests, meals are available here and the restaurant is also open to nonresidents.

On the main road to Bhopal about 250 metres from the crossroads is MP Tourism's other place, the *Travellers' Lodge* (☎ 223). It's in a very peaceful location and has a range of rooms, all with attached bathrooms and water-heaters, from Rs 150/175 to Rs 300/350 for air-con. There's a restaurant and even conference facilities, should you need them.

Places to Eat

The best food is from the spotlessly clean *Tourist Cafeteria* and the dishes are also good value at Rs 15 to Rs 20. Selling drinks to the day-trippers is obviously the money-spinner, as these are quite expensive. However, pot tea does come complete with a tea-strainer.

The food in the *Travellers' Lodge* is also good but slightly more expensive. Apart from these two places there's the cluster of food stalls at the crossroads. The stalls don't look too sanitary but they're no worse than any others in India and there's plenty of choice.

Getting There & Away

Bus Local buses connect Bhopal with Sanchi (and other towns and villages in the area) about every hour from dawn to dusk, but there are two possible routes. The longer route goes via Raisen (an interesting town with an extensive hilltop fortress), takes three hours for the 68-km trip and costs Rs 12. The shorter route follows the railway line to Delhi, takes 1¾ hours and costs Rs 9.

Train Sanchi is on the main Delhi to Bombay railway line only 46 km north of Bhopal. A useful train from Bhopal is the *Bina Passenger* leaving at 8.50 am. It takes just over an hour and costs Rs 7. Though most express trains don't stop at Sanchi, 1st-class passengers who have travelled a minimum distance can request that the train be halted for them. Obviously it is necessary to arrange this in advance. The *Shatabdi Express* will not stop here for anybody.

Getting Around

In Sanchi itself everything's within easy walking distance. For excursions to places nearby like Vidisha (10 km) and the Udaigiri caves (14 km) you can rent bikes in Sanchi for Rs 1.50 per hour.

AROUND SANCHI

In the immediate vicinity of Sanchi there are more Buddhist sites, although none are of the scale or as well preserved as Sanchi's sites. Most are within cycling distance. **Sonari**, 10 km south-west of Sanchi, has eight stupas, two of them important. At **Satdhara**, west of Sanchi on the bank of the Beas River, there are two stupas, one 30 metres in diameter. Another eight km south-east is **Andher**, where there are three small but well-preserved stupas. These stupas were all discovered in 1851, after the discovery of Sanchi.

The main places of interest around Sanchi are listed below.

Vidisha

Vidisha was important in Ashoka's time and it was from here that his wife came. Then it was known as Besnagar and was the largest town in the area. The ruins of the 2nd-century BC Brahmanical shrine here show traces of lime mortar – the earliest use of cement in India. Finds from the site are displayed in the museum near the railway station.

From the 6th century AD the city was deserted for three centuries. It was renamed Bhilsa by the Muslims who built the now ruined Bija Mandal, a mosque constructed

from the remains of Hindu temples. You can reach Vidisha by bike (see Udaigiri below for directions), train or bus (Rs 3, every half-hour) from Sanchi.

Heliodorus Pillar

Between Vidisha and the Udaigiri caves, one km north of the Udaigiri turnoff, is this inscribed pillar, known locally as the Khamb Baba pillar. It was erected in about 140 BC by Heliodorus, a Greek ambassador to the city from Taxila (now in Pakistan). The pillar celebrates his conversion to Hinduism. It's dedicated to Vishnu and worshipped by local fishers.

Udaigiri Caves

Cut into the sandstone hill, five km from Vidisha, are about 20 Gupta cave shrines dating from 320-606 AD; two are Jain, the other 18 Hindu. In cave 5 there is a superb image of Vishnu in his boar incarnation. Cave 7 was cut out for King Chandragupta II's personal use. Cave 20 is particularly interesting with detailed Jain carvings. On the top of the hill are the ruins of a 6th-century Gupta temple.

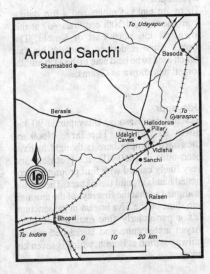

Around Sanchi

Getting There & Away From Bhopal take a Sanchi bus or train to Vidisha, and from there take a tonga to the caves (Rs 20 including waiting time).

To reach the caves by bike from Sanchi, cycle towards Vidisha until you cross the river (six km). One km further on turn left (or carry straight on if you want to visit Vidisha first). After three km you'll reach a junction in the colourful bazaar – turn left again. One km further is another left turn. Take this road for the caves (3½ km) or continue for one km for the Heliodorus Pillar.

Raisen

On the road to Bhopal, 23 km south of Sanchi, the huge and colourful hilltop fort of Raisen has temples, cannons, three palaces, 40 wells and a large tank. This Malwa fort was built around 1200 AD and although initially the centre of an independent kingdom, it later came under Mandu control. There are also ancient paintings in the caves in this area.

Gyaraspur

There are tanks, temples and a fort dating from the 9th and 10th centuries AD at this town, 51 km north-east of Sanchi. The town's name is derived from the big fair which used to be held here in the 11th month, sometimes known as Gyaras.

Udayapur

Reached via Basoda, Udayapur is 90 km north of Sanchi. The large **Neelkantheswara Temple** here is thought to have been built in 1059 AD. It's profusely and very finely carved with four prominent decorated bands around the sikhara. The temple is aligned so that the first rays of the morning sun shine on the Siva lingam in the sanctum. It's a particularly fine example of Indo-Aryan architecture and is reached via the railway station at Bareth, which is seven km away.

BHOPAL

Population: 1,064,000

The capital of Madhya Pradesh, Bhopal was built on the site of the 11th-century city of Bhojapal. It was founded by the legendary Raja Bhoj who is credited with having constructed the lakes around which the city is built. The present city was laid out by the Afghan chief Dost Mohammed Khan who was in charge of Bhopal during Aurangzeb's reign, but took advantage of the confusion following Aurangzeb's death in 1707 to carve out his own small kingdom.

Today, Bhopal presents a multifaceted profile. There's the old city with its crowded marketplaces, huge old mosques, and the palaces of the former begums who ruled over the city from 1819 to 1926. To the north sprawl the huge industrial suburbs and the slums which these developments inevitably attract in India. The new city with its broad avenues, sleek high-rise offices and leafy residential areas lies to the west. In the centre of Bhopal are two lakes which, while providing recreational facilities, are also the source of its plagues of mosquitoes.

The city, of course, is famous as the site of the world's worst industrial disaster. On the night of 2 December 1984, a tank at the Union Carbide plant containing methyl isocyanate (a base for the manufacture of pesticides) ruptured and released a deadly cloud of highly poisonous gas. By the time it had dispersed, over 2000 people had died and tens of thousands had their health destroyed for the rest of their lives. The Indian government demanded US$6 billion in compensation but was persuaded to accept US$470 million or have the case drawn out for at least a decade. All criminal charges were dropped and the money paid to the government. However, it was not until seven years after the accident and after another 2000 people had died that a little of this money began to reach the victims.

Outside the now closed factory, which lies just north of Hamidia Rd, is a memorial statue to the dead, and the death toll continues to rise. Researchers have now discovered that the repercussions may be enormous with birth defects and cancer eventually affecting as many as 300,000 people. Union Carbide is a profitable business once more and has just launched a new brand of battery on the Indian market. Read the small print when buying batteries in India.

Orientation

Both the railway station and bus station are within easy walking distance of the main hotel area along Hamidia Rd. When arriving by train, you need to leave the station by platform No 4 or 5 exit to reach Hamidia Rd.

The new part of the city is a long way from either of the transport terminals so you'll have to take an auto-rickshaw or taxi. Auto-rickshaw drivers almost always use their meters except at night when you'll have to negotiate the fare.

Information

There is a tourist information office at the railway station. The staff are helpful but have no street maps of Bhopal. The headquarters of MP Tourism (☎ 55-4340) is in the Gangotri Complex, 4th floor, T T Nagar, in the new town.

To cash travellers' cheques you must go to T T Nagar. Try the State Bank of India or the State Bank of Indore, below the Hotel Panchanan.

The telephone area code for Bhopal is 0755.

Taj-ul-Masjid

Commenced by Shah Jahan Begum, but never really completed, the Taj-ul-Masjid is one of the largest (if not the largest) mosques in India. It's a huge pink mosque with two massive white-domed minarets and three white domes over the main building.

Other Mosques

The **Jama Masjid**, built in 1837 by Qudsia Begum, is surrounded by the bazaar and has very squat minarets. The **Moti Masjid** was built by Qudsia Begum's daughter, Sikander Jahan Begum, in 1860. Similar in style to the Jama Masjid in Delhi, it is a smaller mosque

with two dark-red minarets crowned by golden spikes.

Lakes

The larger Upper Lake covers six sq km and a bridge separates it from the Lower Lake. You can rent boats to get out on the lakes, which are very picturesque when they reflect the lights of the surrounding city at night.

Lakshmi Narayan Temple & Birla Museum

There are good views over the lakes to the old town from the Lakshmi Narayan Temple, also known as the Birla Mandir. Beside it on Arera Hill is an excellent museum that is well worth visiting. It contains a small but very selective collection of local sculptures dating mainly from the Paramana period. The exhibits are all beautifully displayed and labelled in both Hindi and English. The stone sculptures are mainly of Vishnu, Siva and their respective consorts and incarnations. There's also a small selection of terracotta exhibits from Kausambi and a reconstruction of the Zoo Rock Shelter from Bhimbetka. Entry is Rs 1.

Bharat Bhavan

This complex for the verbal, visual and performing arts was designed by the well-known architect Charles Correa and opened in 1982. It's now regarded as one of the most important centres in the country for the preservation of traditional folk art. As well as the workshops and theatres here, there's the **Roopankar**, the impressive art gallery that 'shows you what is sadly missing from the folk art churned out for tourists', as one reader put it. The Bharat Bhavan is in the Shamla Hills and is open from 2 pm to 8 pm, daily except Monday; admission is Rs 0.50.

Tribal Habitat Museum

Tribal buildings from all over India are being reconstructed in what promises to be an interesting open-air exhibition. The display is at Rashtriya Manav Sangrahalaya in the Shamla Hills, on a 40-hectare site overlooking the Upper Lake. There are craft and

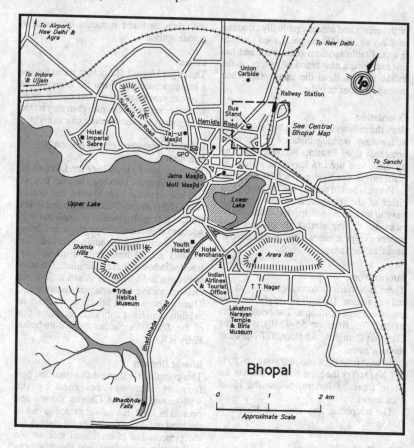

Bhopal

0   1   2 km

Approximate Scale

pottery demonstrations, and film shows on Saturdays at 4 pm.

Places to Stay – bottom end

There's not a great choice of decent cheapies in Bhopal although most are OK for a night. Some will turn you away as they have no 'C' forms for foreigner registration. Such places include the *Rainbow*, *International*, *Shalimar* and *Crown*.

In the railway *retiring rooms* there are dorm beds for Rs 15 and doubles for Rs 70. The cheapest rooms in the Hamidia Rd area are in the *Grand*, *Capital* or *Reem* close to

the flyover, but this is a noisy junction and the hotels are often filled with long-term lodgers. The Hotel Reem is the best of these, set back from the road, with singles/doubles with attached bathrooms from 45/60. The *Hotel Gulshan* is better with singles with common bathroom for Rs 40 and doubles with private bathroom for Rs 80. The *Hotel Maghdoot* and *Hotel Samrat* are similarly priced.

The *Hotel Rama International* is a recommended place, slightly quieter as it's set back from Hamidia Rd. Rooms are from Rs 60/90 to Rs 110/135 with air-con. The *Hotel Bharti* is also good, and is cheaper. Rooms without bathrooms are Rs 40/60/90. The *Hotel Manjeet* has rooms from Rs 65/90 and is quite clean and very popular.

The *Hotel Deep* has clean rooms with attached bathrooms from Rs 80/100. There are TVs showing soft porn movies in each room. The *Hotel Ranjit* (☎ 75-211) is very popular and good value with singles/doubles for Rs 70/90 and 'delux' rooms for Rs 90/100, all with air-cooling, bathroom, hot water, TV and telephone. Locals rate the restaurant here as one of the best in town.

Places to Stay – middle

There's a good choice of middle-range hotels available. Most have a very wide range of rooms from basic doubles to air-cooled and air-con rooms.

The *Hotel Jyoti* (☎ 76-838) is very clean, well maintained and costs Rs 120/160 for singles/doubles with TV and attached bathroom. One of the features they advertise is

the 'non alcoholic atmosphere' – the hotel is managed by Gujaratis so all the food is pure vegetarian and there's no bar. It's a recommended place.

The *Hotel Rajdoot* has a large number of rooms from Rs 85/135 to Rs 225/325 with air-con and a grubby bar. The *Hotel Srimaya* is a much better choice with air-cooled singles/doubles for Rs 110/160 and air-con rooms for Rs 200/225, all with bathrooms and hot water. There's no restaurant and checkout time is 24 hours after arrival.

The *Hotel Ramsons International* (☎ 75-298) has rooms for Rs 140/195 or Rs 230/290 with air-con, all with bathroom and hot water, colour TV, English and Hindi videos and a verandah. Checkout is noon, and there's an air-con bar and restaurant. Round the corner from Ramsons is the *Hotel Taj* (☎ 73-161) where the cheaper rooms are much better value than the rooms at Ramsons. Singles/doubles cost Rs 130/185 with bathrooms. However the air-con rooms

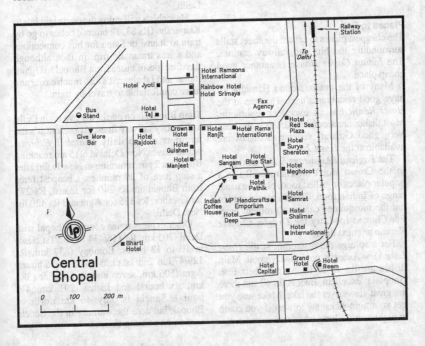

Central Bhopal

0   100   200 m

here at Rs 265/365 are definitely overpriced. The restaurant is very good, though.

MP Tourism's accommodation is in T T Nagar, the new town. There are rooms for Rs 195/215 or Rs 335/350 at the *Hotel Palash* (☎ 55-3006). There's a branch of the tourist office here.

Places to Stay – top end

The two best hotels are the *Hotel Lake View Ashok* (☎ 55-3399) and the *Jehan Numa Palace Hotel* (☎ 54-0100). The Lake View Ashok is a distinctive modern hotel in the Shamla Hills with good views over the lake, as the name suggests. Comfortable singles/doubles are US$31/41 and there is an excellent restaurant here. The Jehan Numa Palace is also in the Shamla Hills and was formerly a palace, built in the late 19th century. Rooms are Rs 395/595 and there's a restaurant and bar. The *Hotel Imperial Sabre* (☎ 54-0702) is similarly priced.

Places to Eat

The cheapest places to eat are the street stalls surrounding the bus and railway stations. The *Indian Coffee House* is another good cheap place.

Many of the hotels around Hamidia Rd have good restaurants/bars. The one at the *Hotel Ranjit* has an excellent reputation. Most dishes are around Rs 25, as is the beer. Very good Gujarati vegetarian dishes are available at the *Hotel Jyoti*.

The *Bagicha Restaurant & Bar* next door to the Crown Hotel on Hamidia Rd is a popular place for grilled food, plus the usual range of Indian food. There's also a garden but the mosquitoes can be a problem here. For Chinese food, try the *Dragon Chinese Restaurant* next door.

For a splurge the restaurant at the *Hotel Lake View Ashok* is particularly good. Main dishes are Rs 45 to Rs 55 and their Fish Bhopali is excellent. Beer is Rs 40 and there are great views over the lake. Make sure you get your auto-rickshaw to wait if you come at night as it's a long way from anywhere.

Getting There & Away

Air The Continental agent, Lucky Travel Agency (☎ 55-4121), is on the ground floor and Indian Airlines (☎ 55-0480) is in the building next door. Air India (☎ 55-1055) is also in T T Nagar.

Indian Airlines has daily connections between Bhopal and Bombay (US$70), Indore (US$21), Gwalior (US$39) and Delhi (US$62). The private airline, Continental, has taken over Vayudoot's routes and has flights on Tuesday, Thursday and Saturday between Bhopal and Bombay (Rs 1348), Indore (Rs 497), Jabalpur (Rs 875) and Raipur (Rs 1275).

Bus There are numerous daily buses to Sanchi (Rs 9, 1¾ hours). MP Tourism operates an impressive air-con bus to Indore (Rs 150, four hours) leaving at 8.45 am from the bus station. A second bus leaves at 2.30 pm from the railway station having collected passengers off the *Shatabdi Express* from Delhi.

Masochists will enjoy the overnight bus to Khajuraho (Rs 83, 12 hours); better to go by train to Jhansi or Satna for bus connections and a less traumatic trip. In fact, although there are lots of buses from Bhopal to Ujjain, Indore and Jabalpur, it's also much easier and more comfortable to travel by train.

Train Bhopal is on one of the two main Delhi to Bombay railway lines. At present it's the terminus of the daily *Shatabdi Express*, which leaves New Delhi at 6.15 am reaching Bhopal at 2 pm, returning to New Delhi after a stop here of 20 minutes. Cheapest fares from Bhopal are Rs 240 for Jhansi, Rs 275 for Gwalior, Rs 325 for Agra and Rs 420 for New Delhi.

Other express trains connect Bhopal with Delhi (705 km, Rs 116/434 in 2nd/1st class) in 10 to 12 hours, Bombay (837 km, Rs 129/473 in 2nd/1st class) in 12 to 15 hours, Agra (506 km, seven hours), Gwalior (388 km, six hours) and Jhansi (291 km, 4½ hours). Sanchi is only 46 km north of Bhopal, but note the warning in the Sanchi section on nonstop trains.

Getting Around

To/From the Airport Indian Airlines operates a bus (Rs 15) to the airport, leaving their office at 7 am.

AROUND BHOPAL

Bhojpur

The legendary Raja Bhoj (1010-53) not only built the lakes at Bhopal but also built another one, estimated at 400 sq km, in Bhojpur, 28 km south-east of the state capital. History records that the lake was held back by massive earthen dams faced on both sides with huge blocks of sandstone set without mortar. Unfortunately, the lake no longer exists having been destroyed by Hoshang Shah, the ruler of Mandu, in a fit of destructive passion in the early 15th century. It's said that the lake took three years to empty and that the climate of the area was radically affected by the loss of this enormous body of water.

What does survive here is the huge, but uncompleted, **Bhojeshwar Temple** which originally overlooked the lake. Dedicated to Siva, it has some very unusual design features and sports a lingam 2.3 metres high by 5.3 metres in circumference. The earthen rampart used to raise stones for the construction of the dome still remains. Nearby is another incomplete monolithic temple, this time a **Jain shrine** containing a colossal statue of Mahavira over six metres in height. Though a long way from rivalling the 17-metre-high statue of Gomateshvara at Sravanabelagola in Karnataka, this has to be one of the largest Jain statues in India.

Bhimbetka

Like the Aboriginal rock paintings in the outback of Australia, the cave paintings of the Bushmen in the Kalahari Desert in Africa or the Palaeolithic Lascaux caves of France, the Bhimbetka caves are a must. Amongst forests of teak and sal in the craggy cliffs of an almost African setting 45 km south of Bhopal, some 1000 rock shelters have been discovered. Almost half contain ancient paintings depicting the life and times of the different people who lived here.

Because of the natural red and white pigments which the painters used, the colours have been remarkably well preserved and it's obvious in certain caves that the same surface has been used by different people at different times. There's everything from figures of wild buffalo (gaur), rhinoceros, bears and tigers to hunting scenes, initiation ceremonies, childbirth, communal dancing and drinking scenes, religious rites and burials.

The extent and archaeological importance of the site was only recently realised and dating is still not complete. The oldest paintings are believed to be up to 12,000 years old whereas some of the crude, geometric figures probably date from as recently as the medieval period.

The caves are not difficult to find; a path connects the 15 that the local guide will show you. The 'Zoo Rock Shelter' is one of the first you come to, famous for its variety of animal paintings. There's nothing here other than the caves so bring something to drink.

Getting There & Away From Bhopal, 45 km away, take a Hoshangabad bus, although you may need to change at Obaidullaganj, 50 minutes south of Bhopal. Get off the Hoshangabad bus 6½ km after Obaidullaganj by the sign pointing right with '3.2' and some Hindi on it. Follow this sign, crossing the railway track for the 3.2-km walk to the hills in front of you. To get back you can flag down a truck on the main road. A taxi for the trip from Bhopal would cost about Rs 350.

Other Places

Of the less important sites, **Neori**, only six km from Bhopal, has an 11th-century Siva temple and is a popular picnic spot. **Islampur**, 11 km from Bhopal on the Berasia Rd, was built by Dost Mohammed Khan and has a hilltop palace and garden. At **Ashapuri**, six km north of Bhopal, there are ruined temples and Jain palaces with statues scattered on the ground. **Chiklod**, 45 km out, has a palace in a peaceful sylvan setting.

PACHMARHI

Madhya Pradesh's peaceful hill station stands at an altitude of 1067 metres. It was 'discovered' by a Captain Forsyth who realised the potential of the saucer-shaped valley as a health resort in 1857, when he first saw it from the viewpoint that now bears his name.

Things to See & Do

Although it's nothing like a Himalayan hill station, Pachmarhi is a very attractive place rarely visited by foreign tourists. The area draws quite a few artists; Ravi Shankar has a music school and the arts and crafts mela (fair) that has been held here a number of times may become an annual October event. Gurus occasionally hold retreats up here and up to 100,000 sadhus and tribals attend the **Sivaratri** celebrations (February-March) at Mahadeo Temple.

There are fine views out over the surrounding red sandstone hills, pools and waterfalls to bathe in, ancient **cave paintings** and some interesting walks through the sal forests. A recommended long day walk is to the hilltop **shrine of Chauragarh**, four km from Mahadeo. You can see the cave paintings at Marodeo on the way. There's a golf course, a couple of churches and if you don't feel like walking, bicycles can be rented from the shop near the New Hotel or in the bazaar.

Places to Stay & Eat

Almost all the accommodation in Pachmarhi is run by MP Tourism. The *New Hotel*, however, is a large, recommended place operated by the PWD. It's clean and good value with doubles from Rs 50 to Rs 125 and some cottages. There's a reasonable restaurant with main dishes around Rs 25.

If you want something cheaper try the *Youth Centre* which has a large open hall with 50 beds at Rs 20 each. The other cheap place is the friendly *Holiday Homes* although it's not in such a good location as the New Hotel. Doubles are Rs 75 with a small courtyard and attached bathrooms. Hot water comes in buckets.

The *Neelamber Cottages* are an excellent choice. They're right beside the TV relay centre on the top of a hill so the views are great. Doubles with attached bathroom with water heater are Rs 125. The *Panchvati Huts & Cottages* below the hill are not such good value with singles/doubles from Rs 145/165 to Rs 195 but the good *China Bowl* restaurant is here. *SADA Nandan Van* cottages are better value at Rs 125 a double.

The top hotel is the *Satpura Retreat* (☎ 2097), a former English bungalow with a large verandah around it, comfortable rooms and vast bathrooms. It's in a very quiet location along the Mahadeo Rd. Rooms are from Rs 275/295 or Rs 395/495 with air-con. *Amaltas* (☎ 2098) was also a Raj bungalow and has rooms for Rs 175/220 with attached bathrooms but no air-con.

Getting There and Away

From the bus stand near the bazaar in Pachmarhi there's one early morning bus to Bhopal and departures every couple of hours to Pipariya (Rs 12, 1½ hours). Jeeps also ply this route for Rs 20 per head or Rs 175 for the whole jeep. Signs by the winding road warn drivers that 'Overtakers provide job for undertakers'!

Sadhu

PIPARIYA

Pipariya is the nearest road/rail junction to Pachmarhi, 47 km away. It's on the railway line that runs from Bombay to Jabalpur. Opposite the railway station, there's an excellent little MP Tourism *Tourist Motel* with doubles at Rs 75 and a restaurant.

Western Madhya Pradesh

UJJAIN

Population: 367,000

Only 80 km from Indore, ancient Ujjain is one of India's holiest cities for Hindus. It gets its sanctity from a mythological tale about the churning of the oceans by the gods and demons in search of the nectar of immortality. When the coveted vessel of nectar was finally found there followed a mad scramble across the skies with the demons pursuing the gods in an attempt to take the nectar from them. Four drops were spilt and they fell at Haridwar, Nasik, Ujjain and Prayag (Allahabad). As a result, Ujjain is one of the sites of the Kumbh Mela which takes place here every 12 years. The 1992 Kumbh Mela drew millions (literally!) to bathe here in the River Shipra.

Ujjain ranks equal as a great religious centre with such places as Varanasi, Gaya and Kanchipuram, despite its relative obscurity today. Non-Hindus may very well find it a relatively boring city. There's not much of interest going on here most of the year and by no stretch of the imagination is this Varanasi.

History

On an ancient trade route, Ujjain has a distinguished history whose origins are lost in the mists of time. It was an important city under Ashoka's father, when it was known as Avantika. Later it was so attractive to Chandragupta II (380-414 AD) that he ruled from here rather than from his actual capital, Pataliputra. It was at his court that Kalidasa,

one of Hinduism's most revered poets, wrote the *Meghdoot*, with its famous lyrical description of the city and its people.

With the passing of the Guptas and the rise of the Paramaras, Ujjain became the centre of much turmoil in the struggle for control of the Malwa region. The last of the Paramaras, Siladitya, was captured by the Muslim sultans of Mandu, and Ujjain thus passed into the hands of Moghul vassals.

Muslim rule was sometimes violent, sometimes benign. An invasion by Altumish in 1234 resulted in the wholesale desecration of many temples but that was halted during the reign of Baz Bahadur of Mandu. Bahadur himself was eventually overthrown by the Moghul emperor, Akbar. Later on, under Aurangzeb, grants were provided to fund temple reconstruction.

Following the demise of the Moghuls, Maharaja Jai Singh (of Jaipur fame) became the governor of Malwa and during his rule the observatory and several new temples were constructed at Ujjain. With his passing, Ujjain experienced another period of turmoil at the hands of the Marathas until it was finally taken by the Scindias in 1750. When the Scindia capital was moved to Gwalior in 1810, Ujjain's commercial importance declined rapidly.

Orientation & Information

The railway line divides the city: the old section, including the bazaar and most of the temples and ghats, are to the north-west of the city, and the new section is on the south-east side. The majority of hotels are in front of the railway station. Tourist information is available at the station and the Shipra Hotel.

Temples

Mahakaleshwar Temple The most important temple in Ujjain, the Mahakaleshwar Temple is dedicated to Siva. The temple enshrines one of India's 12 *jyoti linga* – lingas believed to derive currents of power (*shakti*) from within themselves as opposed to lingas ritually invested with *mantra-shakti* by the priests.

The myth of the jyoti linga (the linga of

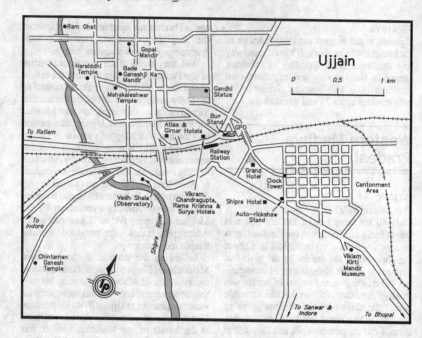

light) stems from a long dispute for primacy between Brahma and Vishnu. During this dispute, according to legend, the earth split apart to reveal an incandescent column of light. To find the source of this column, Vishnu became a boar and burrowed underground while Brahma took to the skies in the form of an eagle. After 1000 years of fruitless searching, Siva emerged from the linga of light and both Brahma and Vishnu acknowledged that it was he who was the greatest of the gods.

The temple was destroyed by Altamish of Delhi in 1235 but restored by the Scindias in the 19th century.

Bade Ganeshji Ka Mandir Above the tank near the Mahakaleshwar Temple, the large ornate statue of Ganesh here makes this temple a popular pilgrimage spot.

Harsiddhi Temple Built during the Maratha period, this temple enshrines a famous image of the goddess Annapurna. The two large pillars adorned with lamps were a special feature of Maratha art and are spectacular when lit at Navratri (Dussehra) in September-October.

Gopal Mandir The marble-spired Gopal Mandir was constructed by the queen of Maharaja Daulat Rao Scindia in the 19th century and is an excellent example of Maratha architecture.

The silver-plated doors of the sanctum have quite a history. They were originally taken from the temple at Somnath to Ghazni in Afghanistan and then to Lahore by Mahmud Shah Abdati. From there they were rescued by Mahadji Scindia and shortly afterwards installed in the temple. This is a very large temple but is easy to miss as it's so buried in the bazaar.

Chintaman Ganesh Temple On the opposite bank of the River Shipra, this temple is believed to be of considerable antiquity. The artistically carved pillars of the assembly hall date back to the Paramara period.

Ghats

Since most of the temples are of relatively recent construction you may find more of interest on the ghats. The largest of these is Ram Ghat fairly close to the Harsiddhi Temple. The others are some considerable distance north of the centre.

Vedh Shala (Observatory)

Since the fourth century BC, Ujjain has been India's Greenwich, with the first meridian of longitude passing through it, as far as Indian geographers were concerned. With modern calculations, the Tropic of Cancer is now actually just to the north. Maharaja Jai Singh built one of his quirky observatories here. This one is smaller than those in Jaipur or New Delhi but it's still in use and quite interesting. Astrologers can purchase the complete year's astronomical ephemeris in both English and Hindi at the observatory for Rs 13.

Kaliadeh Palace

On an island in the Shipra River, eight km north of town is the water palace of the Mandu sultans, constructed in 1458. River water is diverted over stone screens in the palace, and the bridge to the island uses carvings from the sun temple which once stood here. The central dome of the palace is a good example of Persian architecture.

With the downfall of Mandu, the palace gradually fell into ruin but was restored, along with the nearby sun temple, by Madhav Rao Scindia in 1920.

Places to Stay

There's quite a range of accommodation right opposite the railway station. Even the cheapest rooms seem to have attached bathrooms. At the bottom of the pile is the *Vikram Hotel* with singles/doubles from Rs 45/50. It's had a lick of paint but get them to change the sheets before you stay here. Next door

the *Surya Hotel* is much more impressive with rooms from Rs 60/75 to Rs 150/200.

The *Hotel Rama Krishna* and the *Hotel Chandragupta* are nearby, both quite good and in close competition with each other. Both have vegetarian restaurants and rooms from Rs 50/75 to Rs 100/125. Just outside the station, MP Tourism's new *Yatri Niwas* should now be open and worth checking out. Budget rooms and dorm-beds are planned.

Just over the railway bridge is the *Grand Hotel*. It's impressive from the outside with a cannon mounted in its ornamental gardens but there's nothing grand about the interior. The singles for Rs 40 are more like interrogation cells. Doubles range from Rs 84 to Rs 126; the front rooms are OK. All rooms have bathrooms.

The top hotel is MP Tourism's *Shipra Hotel* (☎ 28-262), down a quiet road in a very pleasant setting. All rooms have attached bathrooms with water heaters and range from Rs 165/195 with air-cooler to Rs 325/350 with air-con. There's an excellent restaurant.

Places to Eat

There are a number of places to eat opposite the station. The *Chanakya Restaurant* serves good vegetarian food and beer for Rs 30. The *Sudama Restaurant* next door has similar prices but flashier decor. The *Ankur Restaurant* in the Hotel Atlas is quite popular, with main dishes around Rs 25.

The best place to eat is the *Nauratna Restaurant* in the Shipra Hotel. Main dishes are around Rs 22 but they do an excellent veg pulao for Rs 12 and service is very attentive.

Getting There & Away

Bus There are frequent daily buses to Indore (Rs 11 to Rs 13, 1½ hours) which are generally faster than the train. Other buses go to Bhopal (Rs 37, five hours) and there are two buses a day to Mandu. A few buses connect Ujjain with Kota in Rajasthan.

Train The overnight *Malwa Express* is the fastest link with Delhi. It takes 15½ hours to New Delhi (885 km, Rs 133/492 in 2nd/1st), via Bhopal (184 km, 3½ hours), Jhansi (475 km) and Agra (690 km). It leaves Delhi at 7.15 pm, stops in Ujjain at 10.35 am and reaches Indore at 12.35 pm.

Another daily express connects Ujjain with Indore, Bhopal, Jabalpur and Bilaspur. To Bombay requires a change of train at Nagda.

Getting Around

Many of Ujjain's sights are a long way from the centre of town so you'll probably find yourself using quite a few auto-rickshaws. The drivers here are rapacious so make sure you fix the price before setting off.

INDORE

Population: 1,100,000

Indore is not of great interest, but it makes a good departure point for visiting Mandu. The affluence of this place is obvious when you first arrive. No cycle-rickshaws can be seen; auto-rickshaws are the most basic form of transport and they must be the best maintained in the country. Indore is a major textile-producing centre and at Pithampur, 35 km away, Hindustan Motors, Kinetic Honda, Bajaj Tempo and Eischer all have factories. Indians call Pithampur the Detroit of India, and Indore is its gateway.

The Khan and Sarasvati rivers run through Indore. Although it is on an ancient pilgrimage route to Ujjain, nothing much happened here until the 18th century. From 1733, it was ruled by the Holkar dynasty who were firm supporters of the British, even during the Mutiny.

Orientation & Information

The older part of town is on the western side of the railway line, the newer part on the east. If arriving by train, leave the station by platform No 1 for the east side of town and by platform No 4 for the west side.

The railway station and main bus station (Sarwate) are close together but are separated by a complicated flyover system. Not surprisingly a number of holes have appeared in the fence between the two and people just march straight through.

The tourist office (☎ 38-888) is by the Tourist Bungalow at the back of the R N Tagore Natya Griha Hall, R N Tagore Rd. They have a fair selection of leaflets and good maps of Madhya Pradesh and Indore for sale. This is the best place to make enquiries about tours to Mandu.

Travellers' cheques can be changed at the State Bank of India (Main Branch) near the GPO. Rupayana, by the Central Hotel, is a reasonably good bookshop.

Rajwada

In the old part of town, the multistorey gateway of the Rajwada or Old Palace looks out onto the palm-lined main square in the crowded streets of the Kajuri Bazaar. A mixture of French, Moghul and Maratha styles, the palace has been up in flames three times in its 200-year history. After the serious 1984 conflagration it's now not much more than a facade.

Kanch Mandir

On Jawahar Rd, not far from the Rajwada, is the Kanch Mandir or Seth Hukanchand Temple. This Jain temple is very plain externally, but inside is completely mirrored with pictures of sinners being tortured in the afterlife.

Museum

The museum, near the GPO, has one of the best collections of medieval and premedieval Hindu sculpture in Madhya Pradesh. Most are from Hinglajgarh in the Mandasaur district of western Madhya Pradesh and range from early Gupta to Paramana times.

Some pieces are stunning in their delicacy but one wonders why they were brought here. Many appear to have been carelessly hacked away from whatever they used to be attached to and a lot of damage has been done in the process. Not only that, but the pieces are poorly displayed, and much of the collection appears to have been dumped at random pending cataloguing, except that this latter task has never been done. It's a great pity to see such treasures treated so apathetically.

The museum is open from 10 am to 5 pm daily except Monday; admission is free.

Lal Bagh Palace

In the south-west, surrounded by gardens, lies the grand Lal Bagh Palace, built between 1886 and 1921. It has all the usual over-the-top touches like entrance gates that are replicas of those at Buckingham Palace, a wooden ballroom floor mounted on springs, marble columns, chandeliers, stained-glass windows and stuffed tigers. It's open from 10 am to 6 pm daily, except Mondays.

Other Attractions

The **chhatris**, or memorial tombs, of the region's former rulers are now neglected and forgotten. They stand in the Chhatri Bagh on the banks of the River Khan. The cenotaph of Malhar Rao Holkar I, founder of the Holkar dynasty, is the most impressive.

At the western end of MG Rd, the **Bada Ganapati Temple** contains an eight-metre-high day-glo orange statue of Ganesh – reputed to be the world's largest.

The **Kajuri Bazaar** streets are a good place to take a stroll. They're always very busy and there are many examples of old houses with picturesque overhanging verandahs. Unfortunately, these are disappearing fast as concrete rapidly replaces wood.

Places to Stay – bottom end

The railway station and the Sarwate bus station are only a few minutes walk apart, and it's in this area that you'll find the budget hotels. The area is lively, dirty, polluted and noisy. You may be approached by commission touts with a pocketful of hotel cards. Avoid them unless everywhere seems to be full. The mid-price hotels are much better value than the budget places.

Apart from the Rs 10 dorm beds in the rat-infested railway *retiring rooms*, the cheapest place is the *Janta Hotel* (sign in Hindi) next door to the Hotel Ashoka. Singles/doubles cost Rs 30/45 or Rs 45/60 with bathrooms and it's grubby but OK. There's a very popular cheap restaurant downstairs. The *Standard Lodge* nearby (sign in Hindi) has rooms from Rs 45/55 and also has a restaurant.

The *Hotel Shalimar* has rooms from Rs 40/65 with attached bathrooms, making it excellent value. One of the idiosyncrasies of this and a number of Indore hotels is that you reach your bathroom through the bedroom cupboard!

The *Hotel Sagar International* is quite a good place, with a range of rooms from Rs 85/110 to Rs 200/250. Walk under the flyover to reach the new *Hotel Payal*, which has very smart rooms from Rs 90/125 or Rs 130/180 with air-con.

The *YWCA* opposite the GPO takes only women but may be worth checking out.

Places to Stay – middle

The *Tourist Bungalow* (☎ 38-888), on R N Tagore Rd, is at the back of the Tagore Natya Griha Hall. It's recently been done up and singles/doubles are Rs 150/160, or Rs 260/290 with air-con.

The popular *Central Hotel* (☎ 38-521) is attractively old-fashioned with large, well-kept rooms. Singles/doubles (with TV and Gideons Bible) are Rs 120/160 or Rs 200/250 with air-con. Checkout time is noon, and the staff are pleasant. You'll be told by the auto-rickshaw drivers that this place is 'full', because they don't get any commission.

The *Samrat Hotel* (☎ 37-256) is a large modern place with comfortable rooms with TV from Rs 100/150, or Rs 175/200 with air-con. There's a restaurant and bar. Also good value is the *Siddhartha Hotel*, with singles/doubles from Rs 125/150 up to Rs 195/265 with air-con.

There are a number of upmarket hotels with air-cooled rooms from about Rs 150/200 and air-con from Rs 200/250. The *Surya Hotel* (☎ 38-465) is a recommended place in a quiet location. The doormat in the lift reminds busy executives which day of the week it is! Also good is the *Shreemaya Hotel* (☎ 43-1942) 'where the personal touch prevails'. It's a few rupees cheaper but easy to miss as the sign is in Hindi. Checkout time

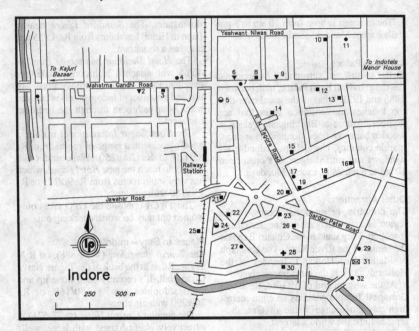

Indore

0   250   500 m

is 9 am, travellers' cheques can be cashed here and there's a good restaurant.

The *Hotel President* (☎ 34-913) is fully air-conditioned with rooms from Rs 225/325 and boasts a health club and sauna for residents. The top hotel is the *Indotels Manor House* (☎ 32-121), a four-star place with all the usual mod cons. Rooms cost from Rs 400/500 to Rs 1500 (for the Maharaja suite), and there's a good restaurant.

Places to Eat
There are several good places offering standard Indian fare close to the bus stand. The restaurant at the *Janta Hotel* is also good value. Near the Central Hotel is a branch of the *Indian Coffee House*. For lunch try the Rajasthani thali (Rs 25) beside the fountains and waterfalls of the *Status Restaurant*.

The *Volga Restaurant* has an extensive vegetarian menu with main dishes around Rs 20 and a set lunch/dinner for Rs 45. Locals

vote the *Apsara* the best vegetarian restaurant in Indore. It's in the Tagore Natya Griha Hall, in front of the Tourist Bungalow.

Most of the hotels have restaurants and bars. The *Shreemaya* is a recommended restaurant with main dishes around Rs 22. The restaurant at the *Surya Hotel* is a great place for a splurge. Main dishes are around Rs 50 and beer costs Rs 25. In the Surya Bar you can enjoy 'silent lights, sound of sips, soft & sweet heart music' and 'testy meals'.

Indore is famous for its variety of namkin snacks – 'Prakash' brand is the best. If you're here during one of the festivals watch out for the bhang gota – samosas with added spice!

Getting There & Away
Air Indore Aerodrome is 10 km from the city. Indian Airlines (☎ 21-211) has daily flights to Bombay (US$53) and Delhi (US$78), via Bhopal (US$21) and Gwalior (US$55).

There are also twice-weekly flights to Ahmedabad (US$45).

The small private airline Continental flies to Bhopal (Rs 497), Jabalpur (Rs 1075), Raipur (Rs 1475) and Bombay (Rs 1026).

Bus There are frequent departures from Sarwate bus station to Ujjain (Rs 13, 1½ hours). For Mandu, there are only a few direct buses (Rs 20, 4½ to 5½ hours) but if you can't get the deluxe bus it's actually quicker to go to Dhar and change there.

Getting to the Ajanta and Ellora caves and Aurangabad in Maharashtra can be tedious and complicated. From Sarwate bus station there's a direct bus to Ajanta (Rs 70) at 5 am and an evening bus that also goes to Ellora. Otherwise you may have to make a series of changes at Khandwa, Burhanpur, Bhusawal or Jalgaon and the trip may take up to 14 exhausting hours. The train journey is not much better since even this involves changes. One of the direct overnight video coaches is probably the best option after a direct day bus although the road is awful and sleep impossible.

The most impressive bus in the state, and possibly in the country, is the air-conditioned service between Bhopal and Indore. It's run by go-ahead MP Tourism from their tourist office and costs a hefty Rs 150! Departures are at 8 am and 3.15 pm. Alternatively there are frequent departure from Sarwate to Bhopal (Rs 36, five hours).

From Gangwal bus stand there are many buses for Dhar and a few departures to Udaipur (12 hours).

There are several private bus companies. Vijayant Travels (☎ 39-771) is a large one operating deluxe overnight buses to Bombay (Rs 150), Pune (Rs 150), Nagpur (Rs 140), Gwalior (Rs 100) and Aurangabad (Rs 110).

Train Indore is connected to the main broad-gauge lines between Delhi and Bombay by tracks from Nagda via Ujjain in the west and Bhopal in the east. The daily *Malwa Express* leaves Indore at 3.05 pm for New Delhi (969 km, Rs 143/526 in 2nd/1st), via Ujjain (80 km, 1½ hours), Bhopal (264 km, five hours), Jhansi (555 km, 10 hours), Gwalior (652 km, 12½ hours) and Agra (770 km, 14 hours).

The other broad-gauge line runs from Indore to Bilaspur via Ujjain, Bhopal and Jabalpur. The overnight *Narmada Express* reaches Jabalpur (600 km, Rs 97/373 in 2nd/1st) at dawn.

There is also a metre-gauge line through Indore. Services on this line run from Ajmer and Chittorgarh, north of Indore in Rajasthan, south-east to Khandwa, Nizamabad and Secunderabad.

Getting Around

To/From the Airport There's no airport bus; auto-rickshaws charge Rs 50 and taxis at least Rs 75.

Local Transport There are plenty of taxis, auto-rickshaws and tempos in Indore. The auto-rickshaws are cheap (most journeys are around Rs 5) and drivers automatically use their meters – if not, walk away and find another. The only trouble is that few auto-rickshaw-wallahs speak English, so they don't understand much more than hotel names, 'bus station' and 'railway station'. If you don't want to be taken on a very frustrating wild goose chase (at your expense), make sure they understand where you want to go before you set off.

AROUND INDORE

Omkareshwar

This island at the confluence of the Narmada and Kaveri rivers has drawn Hindu pilgrims for centuries on account of its jyoti linga, one of the 12 throughout India, at the Siva **Temple of Shri Omkar Mandhata**. (For an explanation of the myth of the jyoti linga refer to the section on Ujjain.)

The temple is constructed from local soft stone which has enabled its artisans to achieve a rare degree of detailed work, particularly in the friezes on the upper parts of the structure.

There are other temples on this island including the **Siddhnath**, a good example of early medieval Brahminic architecture, and a cluster of other Hindu and Jain temples. Though damaged by Muslim invaders in the time of Mahmud of Ghazni (11th century), these temples and those on the nearby riverbanks remain essentially intact. The island temples present a very picturesque sight and are well worth visiting.

Places to Stay There are many dharamsalas offering basic accommodation at Omkareshwar, and also the *Holkar Guest House* at Omkareshwar Mandir, but they're mainly for Hindu pilgrims.

Getting There & Away Omkareshwar Road, on the Ratlam-Indore-Khandwa line, is the nearest railway station. Omkareshwar itself is 12 km from here by road.

There are regular local buses to Omkareshwar from Indore (77 km), Ujjain and Khandwa.

Maheshwar

Maheshwar was once an important cultural and political centre at the dawn of Hindu civilisation and was mentioned in the *Ramayana* and *Mahabharata* under its former name of Mahishmati. It languished in obscurity for many centuries after that until revived by the Holkar queen, Rani Ahilyabai of Indore, in the late 18th century. It's from these times that most of the temples and the fort complex of this riverside town date.

The principal sights are the **fort** which is now a museum displaying heirlooms and relics of the Holkar dynasty (open to the public), the three **ghats** lining the banks of the Narmada River, and the many-tiered **temples** distinguished by their overhanging balconies and intricately worked doorways.

Maheshwar saris are famous throughout the country for their unique weave and beautifully complex patterns.

Places to Stay There is a *Government Rest House*, the *Ahilya Trust Guest House* and a number of basic dharamsalas.

Getting There & Away Maheshwar is best reached by road as the nearest railhead is 39 km away. Local buses run here on a regular basis from Barwaha and Dhar both of which, in turn, can be reached by local bus from Indore.

Maheshwar is often included on bus tours from Indore to Mandu.

Dhar

Founded by Raja Bhoj, the legendary founder of Bhopal and Mandu, this was the capital of Malwa until Mandu rose to power. There are good views from the ramparts of Dhar's well-preserved **fort**. Dhar also has the large stone **Bhojashala Mosque** with ancient Sanskrit inscriptions, and the adjoining **tomb** of the Muslim saint Kamal Maula.

Dhar is best visited en route to or from Mandu, 33 km away.

MANDU

The extensive and now mainly deserted hilltop fort of Mandu is one of the most interesting sights in central India. It's on an isolated outcrop separated from the tableland to the north by a deep and wide valley, over which a natural causeway runs to the main city gate. To the south of Mandu the land drops steeply away to the plain far below and the view is superb. Deep ravines cut into the sides of the 20-sq-km plateau occupied by the fort.

Although it's possible to make a day trip from Indore, it's really worth spending the night here, although accommodation is limited. If you're visiting at the height of the season it might be a good idea to phone and book a room in advance. In the winter, Mandu is quite popular with foreign visitors (mainly French and Italian tour groups) but the local tourist season is during the monsoon, when the place turns green and the buildings are mirrored in the lakes.

Entry to Mandu costs Rs 1 per person and Rs 4 for a car. There are soft drink and fruit stalls at most of the major sites.

History

Mandu, known as the 'city of joy', has had a chequered and varied history. Founded as a fortress and retreat in the 10th century by Raja Bhoj (see Bhopal), it was conquered by the Muslim rulers of Delhi in 1304. When the Moghuls invaded and took Delhi in 1401, the Afghan Dilawar Khan, Governor of Malwa, set up his own little kingdom and Mandu embarked on its golden age. Even after it was added to the Moghul Empire by Akbar, it retained a considerable degree of independence, until the declining Moghuls lost control of it to the Marathas. The capital of Malwa was then shifted back to Dhar, and Mandu became a ghost town. For a ghost town, however, it's remarkably grandiose

and impressive, and worth a day's inspection at the very least. Mandu has one of the best collections of Afghan architecture to be seen in India.

Although Dilawar Khan first established Mandu as an independent kingdom, it was his son, Hoshang Shah, who shifted the capital from Dhar to Mandu and raised it to its greatest splendour.

Hoshang's son ruled for only a year before being poisoned by Mahmud Shah, who became king himself and ruled for 33 years. During his reign Mandu was in frequent and often bitter dispute with neighbouring powers.

In 1469, Mahmud Shah's son, Ghiyas-ud-din, ascended the throne and spent the next 31 years devoting himself to women and song, before being poisoned at the age of 80 by – his son, Nasir-ud-din. The son lived only another 10 years before dying, some say of guilt. In turn his son, Mahmud, had an unhappy reign during which his underlings, like Gada Shah and Darya Khan, often had more influence than he did. Finally, in 1526, Bahadur Shah of Gujarat conquered Mandu.

In 1534 Humayun, the Moghul, defeated Bahadur Shah, but as soon as Humayun turned his back an officer of the former dynasty took over. Several more changes of fortune eventually led to Baz Bahadur taking power in 1554. In 1561 he fled from Mandu rather than face Akbar's advancing troops, and Mandu's period of independence ended. Although the Moghuls maintained the fort for a time and even added some new minor buildings, its period of grandeur was over.

Orientation & Information

The buildings of Mandu can be divided into three groups. When you enter through the north gate of the fort, a road branching off to the west leads to the group of buildings known as the Royal Enclave. If you continue straight on from the entrance you'll pass the Travellers' Lodge and come to the small village which is the only inhabited part of Mandu today. The buildings here are known as the village group. Continuing on, you'll

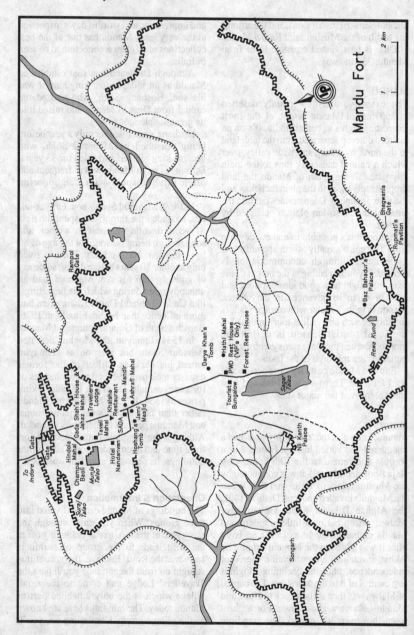

Mandu Fort

0   1   2 km

eventually reach the Rewa Kund group at the extreme south of the fort.

You can get a copy of the Archaeological Survey of India's excellent guidebook *Mandu* for Rs 4.25 from the Taveli Mahal in the Royal Enclave. There are many other buildings in Mandu apart from those we've described here.

The nearest bank for cashing travellers' cheques is in Indore.

Royal Enclave Buildings

Jahaz Mahal The Ship Palace is probably the most famous building in Mandu. It really is shiplike, being far longer (110 metres) than it is wide (15 metres), and the illusion is completed by the two lakes that flank it to the east and west.

It was built by Ghiyas-ud-din, son of Mahmud Shah for his harem, reputed to number more than 10,000 maidens specially selected for their beauty. The Jahaz Mahal with its lookouts, arches, cool rooms and beautiful pool was their magnificent playground, but the only sighs you'll hear today are those of the wind whistling through the empty ruins.

Just south of the Jahaz Mahal is the Taveli Mahal, now the Archaeological Survey of India's Rest House.

Hindola Mahal Just north of Ghiyas' stately pleasure dome, this churchlike hall is known as the Swing Palace because the inward slope of the walls is supposed to create the impression that the walls are swaying. The wide, sloping ramp at the northern end of the building is said to have been built to enable the ruler to be conveyed upstairs by elephant.

Champa Baoli To the west of the first two Royal Enclave structures is this interesting building on the north shore of the lake. Its subterranean levels featured cool wells and bathrooms and it was obviously a popular hot-weather retreat.

Other Enclave Buildings Several other buildings in the enclave include the 'house and shop' of Gada Shah and the 1405

Mosque of Dilawar Khan, one of the earliest Muslim buildings in Mandu.

Village Group Buildings

Jami Masjid This huge mosque built in 1454 dominates the village of Mandu. It is claimed to be the finest and largest example of Afghan architecture in India. Construction was commenced by Hoshang Shah, who patterned it on the great Omayyed Mosque in Damascus, Syria. The mosque features an 80-metre-square courtyard. It's open from 8.30 am to 5 pm daily.

Hoshang's Tomb Immediately behind the mosque is the imposing marble tomb of Hoshang, who died in 1435. Reputed to be India's oldest marble building, the tomb is entered through a domed porch. The interior is lit by stone jali screens – typical of the Hindu influence on the tomb's fine design. It has a double arch and a squat, central dome surrounded by four smaller domes. It is said that Shah Jahan sent his architects to Mandu to study this tomb before they embarked upon the design of the Taj Mahal.

To one side of the tomb enclosure is a long, low colonnade with its width divided into three by rows of pillars. Behind is a long, narrow hall with a typically Muslim barrel-vaulted ceiling. This was intended as a shelter for pilgrims visiting Hoshang's tomb.

Ashrafi Mahal The ruin of this building stands directly across the road from the Jami Masjid. Originally built as a *madrassa* (religious college), it was later extended by its builder, Mahmud Shah, to become his tomb. The design was simply too ambitious for its builders' abilities and it later collapsed. The seven-storey circular tower of victory, which Mahmud Shah erected, has also fallen. A great stairway still leads up to the entrance to the empty shell of the building.

Rewa Kund Buildings

Palace of Baz Bahadur About three km south of the village group, past the large Sagar Talao tank, is the Rewa Kund group. Baz Bahadur was the last independent ruler of Mandu. His palace, constructed around 1509, is beside the Rewa Kund and there was a water lift at the northern end of the tank to supply water to the palace. The palace is a curious mix of Rajasthani and Moghul styles, and was actually built well before Baz Bahadur came to power.

Rupmati's Pavilion At the very edge of the fort, perched on the hillside overlooking the plains below, is the pavilion of Rupmati. The Malwa legends relate that she was a beautiful Hindu singer, and that Baz Bahadur persuaded her to leave her home on the plains by building her this pavilion. From its terrace and domed pavilions Rupmati could gaze down on the Narmada River, winding across the plains far below.

It's a romantic building, the perfect setting for a fairytale romance – but one with an unhappy ending. Akbar, it is said, was prompted to conquer Mandu partly due to Rupmati's beauty. And when Akbar marched on the fort Baz Bahadur fled, leaving Rupmati to poison herself.

For the maximum effect come here in the late afternoon to watch the sunset, or at night when the moon is full. Bring a bottle or a loved one – preferably both.

Darya Khan's Tomb & Hathi Mahal To the east of the road, between the Rewa Kund and the village, are these two buildings. The Hathi Mahal or Elephant Palace is so named because the pillars supporting the dome are of massive proportions – like elephant legs. Nearby is the tomb of Darya Khan, which was once decorated with intricate patterns of mosaic tiles.

Nil Kanth Palace This palace, at the end of one of the ravines which cuts into the fort, is actually below the level of the hilltop and is reached by a flight of steps down the hillside. At one time it was a Siva shrine, as the name – God with the Blue Throat – suggests. Under the Moghuls it became a pleasant water palace with a cascade running down the middle. Though once one of Emperor Jehangir's favourite retreats, it has once

again become a Siva temple and a playground for monkeys.

At the top of the steps, villagers sell the seeds of the baobab tree. Although it is common in Africa, Mandu is one of the few places in India where the baobab is found. It's not difficult to miss – it's the tubby grey tree that looks as if it's been planted upside down with its roots in the air.

Organised Tours
From Indore, several private bus companies offer guided tours to Mandu, usually only at the weekends. If this is what you're looking for, one company to try is Vijayant Travels (☎ Indore 39-771). They have a full-day Sunday tour for Rs 60.

Places to Stay & Eat
The Special Area Development Authority (SADA) has some basic but adequate rooms with bathrooms (water in buckets) right opposite the Jami Masjid. The rooms cost only Rs 30 a double but they insist you deposit Rs 50 in case of 'dammige', as their notice points out. Don't fight this one – the chowkidah (nightwatchman) is only doing his duty and you'll get your change next day. The *Hotel Nandanvan* is the other cheap place but is not nearly such good value. It has bathroomless doubles for Rs 60, though this could be bargained down.

The most romantic place to stay is actually in one of the old buildings in the Royal Enclave. The *Archaeological Survey Rest House* (☎ 3225) is in the Taveli Mahal and there are two doubles here (Rs 100) with bathrooms attached, complete with bathtub and hot-water heater. There's also a dining hall with an interesting relief map of the fort. However they're often booked up.

The *PWD Rest House* is reserved for visiting VIPs. You can only stay in the *Forest Rest House* if you reserve at the Forest Department in Dhar.

The other accommodation below is run by MP Tourism and should be booked at the tourist office in Indore if you want to be sure of a bed.

The *Travellers' Lodge* (☎ 3221) has eight

double rooms at Rs 180/210 with bathroom and hot water and you can get meals here. Despite the fact that there are only eight rooms, the lodge can accommodate up to 24 people with extra beds at Rs 30 each. The manager is friendly and the lodge is well organised plus there are good views over the ghats.

The *Tourist Bungalow/Cottages* (☎ 3235) is a series of cottages in a very pleasant location overlooking the lake. Rooms with bathrooms attached cost Rs 180/210. Deluxe rooms are Rs 200/240 and there are also some air-con rooms for Rs 350. It's a nice place and has an outdoor restaurant but you can tell from the service that this is a state-run hotel.

Most of the lodges have restaurants. In addition there's the *Relax Point Restaurant* opposite the Jami Masjid which is a good cheap place. The *Khalsha Restaurant* has excellent vegetarian food.

Getting There & Away

There are numerous buses from Mandu to Dhar (Rs 7, 1½ hours) from 5.30 am to 6 pm and lots of buses from there on to Indore. There are two direct buses to Indore (Rs 20, 4½ to 5½ hours) at 7 am and 5 pm but they can take longer than if you change at Dhar. At 5.30 am there's a bus to Bhopal (Rs 60, eight to 10 hours). There are also buses to Mhow and Ujjain. The buses stop near the Jami Masjid.

The alternative to the erratic tours is to get a group together and hire a car. Taxis charge Rs 600 for the return journey from Indore plus Rs 200 for an overnight stay. They can be found outside the railway station or round the tourist office. MP Tourism has some cars but even their cheapest Ambassador costs more than a taxi.

Getting Around

You can hire bikes from the shop near the Jami Masjid for Rs 15 a day or Rs 1.50 an hour. This is really the best way to get around as the sights are quite far apart. On the other hand, this is a fine area for walking and it's pleasantly unpopulated.

There are only three auto-rickshaws here and they hang around the bus stand. They charge Rs 60 for a five-hour tour of the Mandu sights.

BAGH CAVES

The Bagh Caves are seven km from the village of Bagh and three km off the main road. Bagh is about 50 km west of Mandu, on the road between Indore and Vadodara in Gujarat. The Buddhist caves date from 400-700 AD and all are in very bad shape. Cave-ins, smoke and water damage have reduced them to such poor condition that restoration work is barely worthwhile. Compared to the caves of Ajanta or Ellora, the Bagh Caves are hardly worth the considerable effort of getting to them. There's a *PWD Dak Bungalow* here.

RATLAM & MANDSAUR

The railway line passes through Ratlam, capital of a former princely state whose ruler died in one of those tragically heroic Rajput battles against the might of the Moghuls.

At Mandsaur, north of Ratlam, a number of interesting archaeological finds were made in a field three km from the town. Some others are displayed in the museum at Indore. Two 14-metre-high sandstone **pillars** are on the site, and an inscription commemorates the victory of a Malwa king over the Huns in 528 AD. In the **fort** are some fine pieces from the Gupta period.

Eastern Madhya Pradesh

JABALPUR

Population: 887,000

Almost due south of Khajuraho and east of Bhopal, the large city of Jabalpur is principally famous today for the gorge on the Narmada River known as the Marble Rocks. It's also the departure point for a visit to the national parks of Kanha (175 km away) and Bandhavgarh (197 km).

The original settlement in this area was ancient Tripuri and the rulers of this city, the Hayahaya, are mentioned in the *Mahabharata*. It passed successively into Mauryan and then Gupta control until, in 875 AD, it was taken by the Kalchuri rulers. In the 13th century it was overrun by the Gonds and by the early 16th century it had become the powerful state of Gondwana.

Though besieged by Moghul armies from time to time, Gondwana survived until 1789 when it was conquered by the Marathas. Their rule was unpopular, due largely to the increased activities of the Thuggees who were ritual murderers and bandits. The Maratha were defeated in 1817 and the Thuggees subdued by the British who developed the town in the mid-19th century.

Today Jabalpur is a major administrative and educational centre and the army headquarters for the states of Orissa and Madhya Pradesh. It also has an unusual number of Christian schools, colleges and churches scattered throughout the cantonment area and, judging from the names on the houses, a large community of Goans.

Information

The tourist office (☎ 32-2111) is at platform No 1 at the railway station, and is open daily from 10 am to 5 pm, except Sundays and the second and third Saturdays of the month. They have the usual range of leaflets and can book MP Tourism accommodation for you at Kanha National Park a minimum of four days in advance, but they require a 50% deposit.

Money can be changed at the main branch of the State Bank of India and at Jackson's Hotel, where there's also a post office.

Bazaar

The old bazaar area of Jabalpur is huge and full of typically Indian smells, sights, sounds and goods for sale. Put aside a whole morning or afternoon to stroll through it. You'll be lucky to see another tourist though you may well meet quite a few students from Kenya and Somalia.

The **Rani Durgavati Museum**, south of the bazaar, is also worth a visit. It's open from 10 am to 5 pm daily except Mondays.

Madan Mahal

This Gond fortress, built in 1116 AD, is on the route to the Marble Rocks, perched on top of a huge boulder. The Gonds, who worshipped snakes, lived in this region even before the Aryans arrived, and maintained their independence right up until Moghul times.

Places to Stay – bottom end

The cheap places to stay are almost all down by the bus stand, about three km from the railway station. Most are very cheap and very basic but for Rs 20/30 you can get a single/double at the *New Central Lodge*, or for a few rupees more at the *Meenakshi Lodge* next door.

The *Hotel Mayur* is a recommended cheap place that's excellent value. Rooms with a bathroom are Rs 35/55. They have some deluxe doubles for Rs 57. Nearer the bus station, the *Hotel Park* is also recommended, but is more expensive at Rs 50/70 for clean rooms with attached bathrooms and TV.

North of the bus station is another group of similarly priced hotels. The *Hotel Sharda* is a reasonably clean place with rooms from Rs 30/50 or Rs 40/70 with attached bathroom. The *Hotel Anand* advertises itself as a 'House of Comforts'. It's a good choice and the staff are friendly. Rooms cost Rs 45/65 for singles/doubles with bathroom and hot water supplied on request, more for rooms with TV.

The modern (but run-down) *Hotel Rahul* is OK with rooms at Rs 70/95 with bathroom and hot water. The hotel also has some air-con rooms and a restaurant. Further south is the *Hotel Samrat*, Russel Crossing, with singles/doubles at Rs 60/80 to Rs 200/240 for an air-con room. All rooms have attached bathroom and TV.

Jackson's Hotel (☎ 32-2320) in Civil Lines must have been the best hotel in town

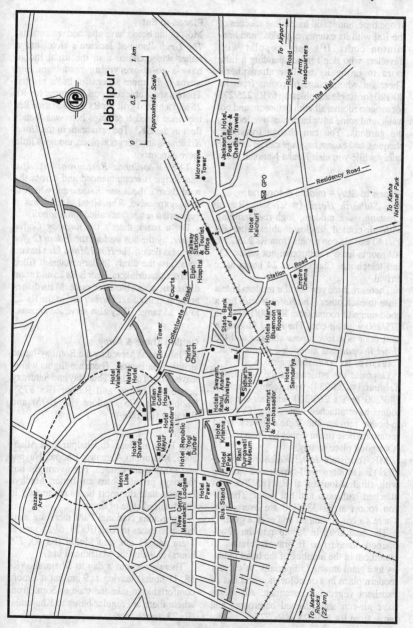

Jabalpur

To Airport

Ridge Road

The Mall

Army Headquarters

Jackson's Hotel, Post Office & Chadha Travels

Microwave Tower

GPO

Residency Road

To Kanha National Park

Hotel Kalchuri

Railway Station & Tourist Office

Station Road

Empire Cinema

Elgin Hospital

Courts

Road

State Bank of India

Hotels Maruti, Bluemoon & Roopali

Hotel Samdariya

Collectorate

Christ Church

Hotels Swayam, Rahul's and Shivalaya

Sidharth Hotel

Clock Tower

Hotel Vaishnalee

Natraj Hotel

Indian Coffee Houses

Hotel Mayur

Hotel Standard

Hotel Republic & Yogi Durbar

Hotels Semrat & Ambassador

Hotel Krishna

Hotel Sharda

Hotel Park

Rani Durgavati Museum

Mona Lisa

Bazzar Area

New Central & Meenakshi Lodges

Hotel Pawar

Bus Stand

To Marble Rocks (22 km)

Approximate Scale

0   0.5   1 km

at one time, and it still has fading touches of the Raj with its extensive gardens and badminton court. It's very popular with travellers who don't mind spending a little extra to enjoy its mellow atmosphere. There's a whole range of rooms from Rs 80/120 for singles/doubles up to Rs 225/275 for air-con rooms, all with bathroom and hot water, and some have balconies overlooking the gardens. You can change travellers' cheques, and excess baggage can be left here safely while you visit Kanha National Park.

Places to Stay – middle & top end

The *Sidharth Hotel* (☎ 27-580), Russel Crossing, is a modern, high-rise building with air-cooled singles/doubles from Rs 95/140 and air-con rooms from Rs 225/250. All rooms have a bathroom, hot water, TV and telephone. Checkout is 24 hours after arrival.

There are three very similar modern hotels close to each other. The *Hotel Maruti* has a good range of rooms from Rs 100/120 to Rs 175/250 with air-con. The *Hotel Bluemoon* next door is a few rupees cheaper and the *Hotel Roopali* has air-cooled rooms for Rs 150/170 or Rs 200/250 for air-con.

Opposite the museum is the new *Hotel Krishna* (☎ 28-984) with rooms from Rs 140/200 or Rs 260/320 with air-con. All rooms have attached bathrooms, TVs with in-house movies and there's a very good restaurant here (main dishes Rs 26 to Rs 36). It's a good place to stay.

MP Tourism's *Hotel Kalchuri* (☎ 321-4991) is a modern, well-maintained building with singles/doubles at Rs 185/205 with attached bathroom and hot water. The air-con rooms at Rs 335/350 are overpriced. There's a bar, restaurant and even a gym.

The best hotel in Jabalpur is the newly opened *Samdariya*. It bravely claims to 'stand out in the humbug of the hotel industry as a giant among Lilliputians'. It's a very modern place in a quiet location and has an excellent vegetarian restaurant. All rooms have air-con and attached bathrooms and range from Rs 225/325 to Rs 775.

Places to Eat

Most of the hotels have attached restaurants. *The Grub Room* at Jackson's Hotel has a rather wider choice than the usual Indian have-a-go-at-everything restaurant and seems to be more successful in its results. There's roast chicken, pork supreme for Rs 25 and a mixed grill for Rs 30. One traveller reckoned the fish & chips here was 'better than in the UK'. The restaurant in the *Hotel Krishna* is another good place, though a little more expensive.

The *Woodlands Restaurant* at the Samdariya is recommended and across the road there's the *Autar Restaurant* which is quite expensive. The Hotel Anand has a vegetarian restaurant called the *Roopali*.

For a snack there's the *Rajbhog Coffee House*, by the bus station; the *Indian Coffee House* is better. The *Hotel Mona Lisa* has no beds, just the dimly lit bar/restaurant filled with serious drinkers. Beer is Rs 25 and main dishes are about the same price. Main dishes at the popular *Yogi Durbar* are in the Rs 25 to Rs 35 range. They also serve ice creams.

Getting There & Away

Air Jabalpur is served by the Bombay-based airline, Continental. There are flights which leave every Tuesday, Thursday and Saturday between Jabalpur and Raipur (Rs 875), Bhopal (Rs 875), Indore (Rs 1075) and Bombay (Rs 1800).

Bus There are buses to Jabalpur from Allahabad, Khajuraho, Varanasi, Bhopal, Nagpur and other main centres. For overnight bus journeys private buses are better. Madhya Pradesh state transport buses are mostly in an advanced state of decay.

For Kanha National Park there are state transport buses to Kisli (Rs 31, 6½ hours) at 7 am and 11 am, and Mukki (Rs 40, 7½ hours) at 9 am (the Malakhand bus).

There's one bus a day to Khajuraho (Rs 58, 11 hours) leaving at 9 am but it's more comfortable to take the train to Satna from where there are regular buses to Khajuraho (Rs 23, four hours).

Train There are direct connections between Jabalpur and Satna (189 km, Rs 42/151 in 2nd/1st) in three hours, Varanasi (505 km, Rs 92/337 in 2nd/1st) in 13 hours and Bhopal (336 km, Rs 65/241 in 2nd/1st) in 7½ hours.

If heading for the Ajanta and Ellora caves, catch a train on the Bombay line to Bhusaval (all the trains stop here) and take another train to Jalgaon. There are buses to the caves from there.

Getting Around

To/From the Airport There's an airport minibus service from the office at the Sidharth Hotel which connects with all flights.

Local Transport Be careful with Jabalpur auto-rickshaw driver; they can be rapacious, so always agree on a fare first. You probably don't need one if you arrive by train and are staying at Jackson's or the Kalchuri. If arriving by bus, most of the budget and mid-range hotels are within 10 minutes walk of the city bus stand.

Cycle-rickshaw-wallahs are almost as bad but one of the cheapest is the elderly gent with bad teeth and a cackle who hangs around Jackson's Hotel. If you want to rent a bicycle there are several places where you can do this between Jackson's and the Hotel Kalchuri as well as across the other side of the railway tracks.

AROUND JABALPUR
Marble Rocks

Known locally as Bhedaghat, this gorge on the Narmada River is 22 km from Jabalpur. The gleaming white and pink cliffs rise sheer from the clear water and are a very impressive sight, especially by moonlight. However it's been heavily promoted by MP Tourism and views on this tourist spot vary from 'truly spectacular' to 'a total bust'. It really all depends on when you come. Steer clear of the place at weekends and on the night of the full moon as it's packed with local tourists.

The best way to see the km-long gorge is by shared rowboat – Rs 5 per person or Rs 75 for the whole boat. These go all day every day from the jetty at the bottom of the gorge where the sign advertises 'Boating without any thinking. Information regarding Marbal rockinboating. Monkey jomp, elephant leg, rockhorselegspot.'! The boaties give you a running commentary (in Hindi) and point out all these peculiar formations which they've named so imaginatively.

The cliffs at the foot of the gorge are floodlit at night. At the head of the gorge is the Dhuandhar or Smoke Cascade. All around the falls are hundreds of stalls selling marble carvings, much of it fairly clichéd but you can find some nice pieces if you shop around and bargain hard. Above the lower end of the gorge, a flight of over 100 stone steps leads to the Chausath Yogini or Madanpur Temple. The circular temple has damaged images of the 64 yoginis, or attendants of the goddess Kali.

Places to Stay & Eat Marble Rocks is a very mellow place to stay and the best accommodation is at MP Tourism's *Motel Marble Rocks* (☎ 424), which overlooks the foot of the gorge and has an excellent restaurant. The motel has only four rooms, for Rs 160/190 a single/double with bathroom, so it's best to book in advance. There are plenty of cheap cafes in the village and at the falls but there is nowhere to stay at the falls themselves.

Getting There & Away Tempos run to the Marble Rocks from the city bus stand in Jabalpur for Rs 6; buses from here are even cheaper. A taxi hired from Jabalpur costs about Rs 200 return including waiting time; auto-rickshaws charge Rs 130.

An alternative way to get there is to hire a bicycle for the 22-km trip. The road is mostly flat with plenty of stalls to stop along the way. Follow the road for Nagpur out of Jabalpur, then take the right fork below the Jain temples high on the hill. After about 15 km turn left at the crossroads following the 'Bhedaghat 5 km' sign.

Narsinghpur

It was from here in the early 19th century that Colonel Sleeman waged his war against a bizarre Hindu cult that, over the centuries, probably claimed as many as a million lives. It was largely due to his efforts that Thuggee (from which the word 'thug' is derived) was wiped out. For years its followers had roamed the main highways of India engaging in ritual murders, strangling their victims with a yellow silk scarf in order to please the bloodthirsty goddess Kali.

There's a fascinating account of Slee-man's detective work in Sir Francis Tuker's *The Yellow Scarf*, and the novel *The Deceivers* by John Masters was based on Sleeman and the Thugs.

Narsinghpur (84 km west of Jabalpur) is now just a sleepy provincial town but worth visiting if you're interested in following the Sleeman trail. You can visit Narsingh Mandir, an old temple with a honeycomb of underground tunnels beneath it. The caretaker will take you down to show the room where Sleeman cornered some of the Thuggee leaders.

Places to Stay Accommodation is available at the *Gunawat Inn*, which has doubles at Rs 75 and is near the station. Or else try *Nira Farm Guest House*. Here, Mrs Nagu has just one basic double at Rs 60 and this must be arranged in advance. You can write to Mrs Prem Nagu at Nira Farm, Narsinghpur, Madhya Pradesh, or phone Narsinghpur 238. She's an excellent cook and her husband, a retired colonel, is particularly knowledgeable about Sleeman as well as about places in the nearby Satpura Hills.

KANHA NATIONAL PARK

Kanha, 175 km south-east of Jabalpur, is one of India's largest national parks covering 1945 sq km including a core zone of 940 sq km. The setting for Kipling's *Jungle Book*, it's a beautiful area of forest and lightly wooded grassland with many rivers and streams, and it supports an excellent variety of wildlife. It is also part of Project Tiger, one of India's most important conservation efforts. A scandal within this project, though, mean tiger numbers may be decreasing.

Wildlife was first given limited protection here as early as 1933 but it wasn't until 1955 that the area was declared a national park. Additions to the park were made in 1962 and 1970. Kanha is a good example of what can be achieved under a determined policy of wildlife management: between 1973 and 1988 the tiger population increased from 43 to over 100, leopards from 30 to 62, chital from 9000 to over 17,000, sambar from 1058 to 1853 and barasinga from 118 to 547. In spite of a serious outbreak of rinderpest in 1976, the numbers of gaur rose from 559 to 671.

The park is very well organised and a popular place to visit. You're almost guaranteed one or even more sightings of tiger, gaur and many herbivores on every outing, especially if you go on elephant-back. Indeed, the tigers in this park appear to be so accustomed to bunches of camera-toting visitors on elephant-back that the mahout will take the elephant right up to a tiger. It can be quite disconcerting to be staring into the eyes of a wild tiger which is literally only a few feet away but, so far, no-one has come off the worse for wear. It's certainly a very exciting experience.

Excursions into the park are made in the early morning and evening; no night driving is allowed. Between 1 July and 31 October, Kanha is completely closed owing to the monsoons. Although the wildlife can be seen throughout the season, sightings increase as the weather gets hotter in March and April and the animals move out of the tree cover in search of water. The hottest months are May and June when the temperature can reach 42°C in the afternoons. December and January are the coldest months and, although it's warm enough to do without a sweater during the day, as soon as the sun sets the temperature quickly plunges to zero and below. Excursions into the park can be very cold so bring plenty of warm clothes.

There are no facilities for changing travellers' cheques here. The nearest places to do this are at Mandla and Jabalpur. There's

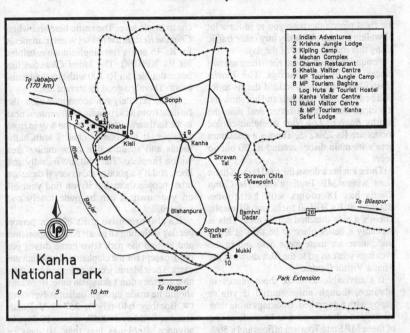

1 Indian Adventures
2 Krishna Jungle Lodge
3 Kipling Camp
4 Machan Complex
5 Chaman Restaurant
6 Khatia Visitor Centre
7 MP Tourism Jungle Camp
8 MP Tourism Baghira
  Log Huts & Tourist Hostel
9 Kanha Visitor Centre
10 Mukki Visitor Centre
  & MP Tourism Kanha
  Safari Lodge

Kanha National Park

0   5   10 km

a telephone and small shop at Kisli but no petrol – the pump here has been dry for years. Make sure you bring enough film. It needs to be fast film (400 ASA or higher) because of the low light of the early morning and evening excursions.

The local market at **Sarekha** on Fridays is worth going to, drawing the colourful Baiga tribal people.

Entry to the park costs Rs 10 per person per day and Rs 10 for a vehicle. A compulsory guide is Rs 4 and video cameras require a Rs 50 permit. Still-cameras are free.

Visitor Centres

In a joint project with the US National Park Service and the Indian Centre for Environment Education, three Visitor Centres have been set up. The interpretative displays in these centres at Khatia and Mukki gates and at Kanha itself are of a very high standard and well worth looking round. The Kanha display is the most impressive with five gal-

leries and a research hall. As well as displays of the animals and the environment, there's a novel Sound & Light show 'Encounters in the Dark'. Select the English or Hindi soundtrack and spend an enjoyable 20 minutes in a small dark room with five other people, 'there is no danger, all exhibits are artificial'!

A number of publications are on sale including informative brochures, posters and postcards, and a small guide to the roadside markers installed as part of the project. There's also a recently published full-colour handbook to the park for Rs 120. The Visitor Centres are open from 7 to 10.30 am and from 4 to 6 pm daily, and there are free film shows each evening at the Khatia Visitor Centre.

Places to Stay & Eat

Accommodation is strung out over a distance of about 6½ km along the road from Jabalpur so it's important that you get off the bus at the right place otherwise you're in for a lot of walking – there's hardly any other traffic along this road for most of the day.

Around the main gate at Kisli there are two places run by MP Tourism. The *Tourist Hostel* has three eight-bedded dorms at Rs 80 a bed including all meals and hot showers. It's clean and a much better deal than the nearby *Baghira Log Huts* where air-cooled rooms are Rs 250/275. There's a restaurant here with main dishes around Rs 20 but no beer.

Three km back down the road is the Khatia Gate where MP Tourism's *Jungle Camp Khatia* has 18 rooms with bathrooms attached at Rs 80/160 including all meals. There's a nice thatched sitting area. This is probably a better place to be than at Kisli, since there are more jeeps here and in the evenings you can go to the film shows at the Khatia Visitor Centre.

It's advisable to book these places in advance, though not essential if you're happy with a dorm bed. Bookings more than 10 days in advance have to be made at one of these MP State Tourism offices and a 50% deposit is required:

Bhopal
    4th Floor, Gangotri, T T Nagar (☎ 55-4340)
Bombay
    74 World Trade Centre, Cuffe Parade, Colaba (☎ 21-4860)
Calcutta
    Room 7, 6th Floor, Chitrakoot Bldg, 230A, A J C Bose Rd (☎ 47-8543)
New Delhi
    2nd Floor, Kanishka Shopping Plaza, 19 Ashok Rd (☎ 332-1187).

Bookings between four and 10 days in advance have to be made through the tourist office (☎ 32-2111) at the railway station in Jabalpur. If you can't book more than four days in advance then this same tourist office can tell you what accommodation will be available.

There are a few small private lodges at Katia. The *Machan Complex* is a basic place charging Rs 25 for a dorm bed or Rs 80 for a double with attached bathroom. There are

cheap meals here. The rustic blue and white *Chaman Restaurant* has set vegetarian meals for Rs 15 and a few singles/doubles/triples for Rs 30/60/90. The *Motel Chandan* has better doubles for Rs 100 with attached bathroom. There's a good restaurant here.

Of the privately run accommodation, the furthest from Kisli is *Indian Adventures*, next to the ford across the river on the way in from Jabalpur. It has double chalets with bathrooms and an attractive open dining area with a fireplace. The staff are friendly and keen, and it's a good place to stay if there are other people there, but if you find yourself on your own, it can be quite lonely and isolated.

It's also expensive at Rs 825 per person per day including all meals and transport into and around the park (two game drives per day), except for the elephant rides which are extra. Their Maruti jeep is quiet and comfortable and they don't skimp on time. Bookings should be made through Indian Adventures (☎ Bombay 640-6399), 257 S V Road, Bandra, Bombay 400050, at least 10 days in advance. Bookings less than 10 days in advance can be made through Chadha Travels (☎ Jabalpur 32-2178), Jackson's Hotel, Civil Lines, Jabalpur.

Nearby, a new camp, the *Krishna Jungle Lodge*, is under construction. It's likely to be very similar in price to Indian Adventures. Contact the Hotel Krishna in Jabalpur (☎ 28-984) for details.

Kipling Camp is the best place to stay at Kanha. Staffed by enthusiastic Brits and operated on the lines of an English house party it's run by Bob Wright, who can be contacted through the Tollygunge Club (☎ Calcutta 46-3141, fax 74-1923) 120 D P Sasmal Rd, Calcutta 700 033. It's not cheap at Rs 1400 per day, but prices include all meals, excursions into the park in open Land Rovers, guides, etc.

It's also the home of Tara, the central character in Mark Shand's book *Travels on My Elephant*. She takes guests for rides in the surrounding forest and you can even join her for her daily bathroom in the river. Kipling Camp is open from 1 November to early May and does not take people who just roll up, so bookings must be made in advance. Arrangements can be made to meet you in Jabalpur (3½ hours by car), Bilaspur (6½ hours) or Nagpur (6½ hours). If you come via Nagpur you could break your journey at Kawardha Palace (see Kawardha below).

Finally, there's MP Tourism's *Kanha Safari Lodge* at Mukki on the other side of the park from Kisli, where there's also a Visitor Centre. Singles/doubles cost Rs 225/250 or Rs 260/290 with air-con and there's a bar and restaurant. It's in a pleasant location and is hardly ever full so is a good place to try if you can't get accommodation at Kisli. However, Mukki isn't easy to get to without your own transport. Bookings can be made in the same way as for the MP Tourism accommodation at Kisli.

Getting There & Away

There are direct state transport buses from the city bus station in Jabalpur to Kisli Gate twice daily at 7 am (six hours) and 11 am (seven hours) which cost Rs 31. Tickets go on sale about 15 minutes before departure. In the opposite direction, the buses depart from Kisli at around 8 am and noon but the early bus can be late starting in winter. These are ramshackle old buses and crowded as far as Mandla though there are generally spare seats after that. Don't bring too much baggage as there's hardly anywhere to put it. On the Kisli to Jabalpur run you may have to change buses at Mandla.

The nearest railway station to Kisli is 1½ hours by bus at Chiraidongri. It's reached on a slow journey by narrow gauge trains that will appeal to rail enthusiasts, via Nainpur from either Jabalpur or Gondia (between Nagpur and Raipur).

Getting Around

Jeep Jeeps are for hire at both Khatia and Kisli Gates and cost Rs 6.50 per km shared by up to six people, plus Rs 4 per hour for a compulsory guide. Park entry fees are extra. Park gates are open from sunrise to noon and 3 pm to sunset from 1 November to 15

February; sunrise to noon and 4 pm to sunset from 16 February to 30 April, and sunrise to 11 am and 5 pm to sunset from 1 May to 30 June. An average distance covered on a morning excursion would be 60 km; less in the afternoon. At the height of the season there may not be enough jeeps to go round so book as soon as you arrive. As in other Indian national parks, drivers tend to drive too fast and not wait around long enough for game to appear. If you think they're being impatient, tell them to slow down. And stay in the jeep if it breaks down...

One evening we were travelling around the park in our rather old jeep when it decided to break down on us. After much fiddling around with the engine our driver decided that the only thing for us to do was to walk back to Kisli, a mere 15 km! So we gingerly jumped out of the back of the jeep and started to walk. Fifteen minutes earlier we had been searching for tigers. Now we hoped they weren't searching for us.

Relief was on everyone's face when another jeep picked us up after three km or so. Of course our jeep turned up again next morning at 6.30 am, the starter motor 'fixed'. However, yesterday's guide refused to go out with us again!

Linda & Paul Careling, Australia

Elephant The elephants are used only for the so-called 'Tiger Show' in the mornings between 8 and 11 am. What happens here is that certain tigers seem to favour certain spots in the park and the trackers go out on elephant early in the morning to find them. They report back to the Visitor Centre at Kanha on the hour and when a tiger is located you can collect a token for the 'show' from here or from Kisli gate. Your jeep then takes you to the spot where the tigers are and there you transfer to an elephant for the final 100 metres or so.

The 'show' costs Rs 5 per person plus Rs 10 per elephant shared between up to four people. If you're at the Kanha Visitor Centre find out how long you'll have to wait as it can be up to a couple of hours in the height of the season. You can either do some more game-viewing in your jeep or look round the Visitor Centre while you wait.

BANDHAVGARH NATIONAL PARK

This national park is 197 km north-east of Jabalpur in the Vindhyan mountain range. It's not part of Project Tiger but tiger are occasionally seen here, more frequently late in the season. There are 25 tiger in the core area of 105 sq km but a buffer zone of 343 sq km has recently been added, along with another 25 tiger.

Bandhavgarh's setting is impressive. It's named after the ancient fort built on the top of cliffs 800 metres high. There's a temple at the fort which can be visited by jeep and below it are numerous rock-cut cave shrines.

The core area of the park is fairly small with a fragile ecology but it supports such animals as nilgai, wild boar, jackal, gaur, sambar and porcupine as well as many species of birds. The ramparts of the fort provide a home for vulture, blue rock thrush and crag martin.

Like Kanha, the park is closed for the middle part of the day. Entry is Rs 10 per vehicle plus Rs 15 for the compulsory guide. Jeeps can be hired for Rs 6.50 per km. Elephants are only used for the 'Tiger Show' (see Kanha section) which takes place in the morning if a tiger is located.

Places to Stay & Eat

There's a small range of accommodation just outside the park gate in the village of Tala, where there are also several cheap places to eat.

Cheapest accommodation is at the ornate-looking *Tiger Lodge*, at Rs 50 a double with fan. The *Hotel Baghela* looks better and is worth checking out, if it's open. The *Nature*

Resort might be fun – it advertises 'lunch-time games for everyone' and charges Rs 50 for a bed in a tent and has some rooms at Rs 225 for a double.

MP Tourism's *White Tiger Forest Lodge* (☎ 308) is a good place, overlooking the river where the elephants bathe. Singles/doubles cost Rs 250/275 or Rs 350/395 with air-con, all with bathrooms attached. The food is good and the waiters and manager all very friendly. Advance booking is advisable. Phone the lodge directly less than five days in advance or see MP Tourism contact addresses in the Kanha section. They have new jeeps for hire at Rs 6.50 per km.

You can also stay in the former palace of the Maharaja of Rewa here, the *Bandhavgarh Jungle Camp*. It's an expensive place at Rs 900 but this includes all food and visits to the park. The address for bookings is 1/1 Rani Jhansi Rd, New Delhi 110 055 (☎ Delhi 52-3057).

Getting There & Away

Umaria, on the Katni to Bilaspur rail line, is the nearest railhead, 32 km away. Local buses are available from there to Tala (Rs 7, one hour). From Satna there's a morning bus to Tala which takes around four hours via Amarpatam.

MANDLA & RAMNAGAR

Mandla is about 100 km south-east of Jabalpur on the road to Kanha. Here there is a **fort** on a loop of the Narmada River built so that the river protects it on three sides while a ditch protects it on the fourth. Built in the late 1600s, the fort is now subsiding

---

White Tigers

The famous white tiger of Rewa was discovered as a cub near Bandhavgarh in 1951. He was named Mohun and as his mother had been shot he was reared by hand. Mated with one of his daughters in 1958, a litter of white cubs was produced and Mohun's numerous descendants can now be seen in several zoos around the world. The interesting thing about these white tigers is that although they have a white coat, they are not albinos. Their eyes are blue, rather than pink and with their dark stripes they are the result of a recessive gene. Inbreeding has led to their decline and the world population of white tigers has dropped from over 100 to about 20. The original white tiger can still be seen today – Mohun's stuffed body is in the Maharaja of Rewa's palace, now a hotel in Tala. ■

into the jungle although some of the towers still stand.

About 15 km away is Ramnagar with its ruined three-storey **palace** overlooking the Narmada. This palace, and the fort at Mandla, were both built by Gond kings, retreating south before the advance of Moghul power. Also near Mandla is a stretch of the Narmada where many temples dot the riverbank.

BHORAMDEO & KAWARDHA

At Bhoramdeo, 125 km east of Kisli (Kanha) is a small but interesting 11th-century **Siva temple** built in the style of the temples of Khajuraho. Carvings cover virtually every external surface with deities indulging in the usual range of activities including the familiar sexual acrobatics. Unlike most of the Khajuraho temples, this one's still very much in use today. A cobra lives in the temple and is fed by the priests. A few km away there are two other temples, the **Mandwa Mahal** and

the **Madanmanjari Mahal** which date from the same time.

Twenty km south of Bhoramdeo, well off the tourist trail, the Maharaja of Kawardha has recently opened part of his palace to guests. The *Palace Kawardha* is a delightfully peaceful place and you're made to feel very welcome here. As far as palaces go it's neither enormous nor particularly old (it was built in 1939) but it does have the touches you'd expect in a maharaja's palace – Italian marble floors, stuffed tigers and ancient English bathroom fittings.

If you can afford to stay here it's an experience not to be missed. It costs Rs 1300 per person, which includes all meals (taken with the charming ex-maharaja and his family) and outings in the jeep – to the temples or into the hills. Open from 1 October to 30 April, reservations must be made in advance. Write to Margaret Watts-Carter, Palace Kawardha, Kawardha, District Rajnandgaon, Madhya Pradesh 491995.

Bombay

Population: 12.6 million
Main Languages: Hindi & Marathi

Bombay is the capital of Maharashtra and the economic powerhouse of India. It's the fastest moving, most affluent and most industrialised city in India. It also has India's busiest international airport and the country's busiest port, handling nearly 50% of the country's total foreign trade. It's the stronghold of free enterprise in India and a major manufacturing centre for everything from cars and bicycles to pharmaceuticals and petrochemicals. It's the centre for India's important textile industry as well as the financial centre and an important base for overseas companies. Nariman Point, with India's tallest buildings, is rapidly becoming a mini-Manhattan. Yet once upon a time Bombay was nothing more than a group of low-lying, swampy and malarial mud flats passed on to the British by its Portuguese occupiers as a wedding dowry!

When the Portuguese arrived on the scene Bombay consisted of seven islands occupied by fisherfolk known as Kolis. In 1534 the seven islands, from Colava in the south to Mahim in the north, were ceded to Portugal by the Sultan of Gujarat in the Treaty of Bassein. The Portuguese did little with them and the major island of the group, Mumbadevi, was part of the wedding dowry when Catherine of Braganza married England's Charles II in 1661. In 1665 the British government took possession of all seven islands and in 1668 leased them to the East India Company for an annual UK£10 in gold.

Soon after the British takeover, Bombay started to develop as an important trading port. One of the first signs of this was the arrival of the Parsis, who settled in Bombay in 1670 and built their first Tower of Silence in 1675. In 1687 the presidency of the East India Company was transferred from Surat to Bombay and by 1708 it had become the

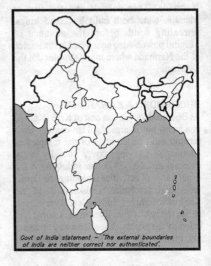

Govt of India statement — 'The external boundaries of India are neither correct nor authenticated'.

trading headquarters for the whole west coast of India.

Although Bombay grew steadily for the next century, it was around the middle of the 1800s that its most dynamic development took place. The first railway was laid out of Bombay in 1854, and one of the effects of the Mutiny of 1857 was to further improve the city's image as a 'safe' place, far from the insurrections of the north. Then the American Civil War provided Bombay's young cotton and textile industries with an enormous boost as supplies of cotton from the USA dried up. A major land-reclamation project in 1862 joined the original seven islands into a single land mass and a year later the governor, Sir Bartle Frere, dismantled the old fort walls, sparking a major building boom.

During this century Bombay has further extended its position as the major commercial, industrial, financial, trading and film centre of India. Its role as an economic magnet – the Indian city with streets paved with gold – has also contributed to enormous slum problems and overcrowding. The problem is exacerbated by the fact that there is no room for further expansion – except on the mainland where a 'new' city is in the making. Meanwhile, those who cannot afford the commuter fares from the mainland into the city continue to flock to and eke out a living on the peninsula itself in some of the worst slums in Asia.

In many ways it's no worse than New York, Mexico City, Manila or Bangkok, except that the poverty is more extreme. The (Indian) Mafia rules here and you do what you're told. Politics is dictated on communal lines and if you get out of line – you're dead. The Shiv Sena, a hardline Hindu political party, made that quite clear several years ago, though their influence is declining.

Despite this, Bombay is an active, alive city, full of interest in its own right and, for many people, the gateway to India. It has its Beverly Hills, its Bronx, its super-rich and abject poor, its Victorian monuments and Buddhist relics, mega-congestion, gleaming high-rises and cardboard shanty towns, pollution you've never seen the like of and opulence fit for a Moghul emperor. It's India in an oyster.

Orientation

Bombay is an island connected by bridges to the mainland. Low, swampy areas indicate where it was once divided into several islands. The principal part of the city is concentrated at the southern end of the island; the northern end is comparatively lightly populated. Sahar International Airport is in the suburb of Santa Cruz, 26 km north of the city centre.

There are three main railway stations in the city centre. Churchgate and Victoria Terminus are central, but Bombay Central is some distance out.

Orientation in Bombay is relatively simple. The southern promontory is Colaba Causeway and the northern end of this peninsula is known as Colaba. Most of the cheap hotels and restaurants, together with a

number of Bombay's topnotch establishments, are here. Bombay's two main landmarks, the Gateway of India and the Taj Mahal Hotel, are also at Colaba.

Directly north of Colaba is the area known as Bombay Fort, since the old fort was once here. Most of the impressive buildings from Bombay's golden period during the last 40 years of the last century are here, together with the GPO, offices, banks, tourist office and two of the main railway stations.

To the west of the fort is Back Bay, the city's beach, around which sweeps Marine Drive. The southern end of this drive is marked by Nariman Point. This is the modern business centre of Bombay with its international-class hotels, skyscrapers, airline offices (including Indian Airlines and Air India), consulates and banks. The other end of the drive is Malabar Hill, a classy residential area.

Information

Tourist Offices The Government of India tourist office (☎ 29-1585) is at 123 Maharishi Karve Rd, Churchgate, directly across from Churchgate Station. It's open from 8.30 am to 6 pm Monday to Friday, and 8.30 am to 1.30 pm every second Saturday and public holidays; it's closed on Sundays. This main office has a comprehensive leaflet and brochure collection and is one of the most helpful and efficient offices in the country. They also have a counter at the international (Sahar) airport (☎ 632-5331, ext 253) and in the domestic terminal (☎ 614-9200, ext 278) and these are supposedly open around the clock.

There is a Maharashtra Tourism Development Corporation office (☎ 202-6713) at CDO Hutments, Madame Cama Rd. It offers city and suburban tours of Bombay and operates long-distance buses to Mahabaleshwar, Aurangabad and Panaji. It also has a list of the hotels (including prices) which it operates around the state as well as the buses which it runs. Bookings can be made here.

Money The American Express office (☎ 204-8278) is in the Oriental Building,

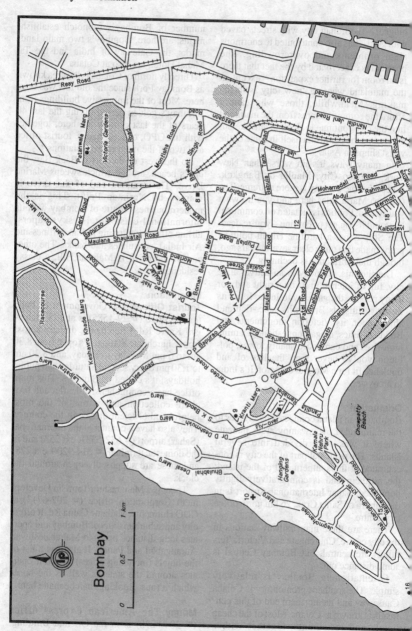

Bombay

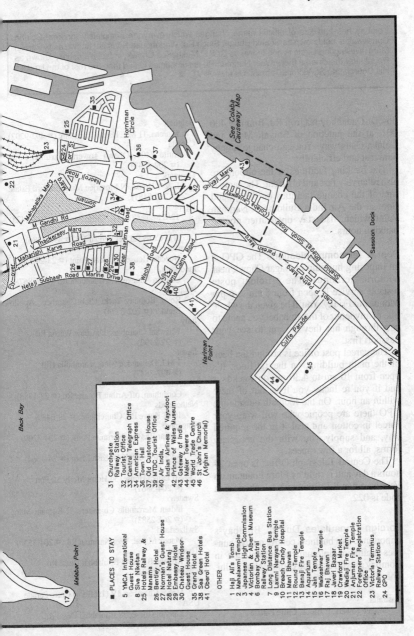

Malabar Point

Back Bay

● 17

Horniman Circle

See Colaba Causeway Map

Nariman Point

Cuffe Parade

Sassoon Dock

Netaji Subhash Road (Marine Drive)

Maharishi Karve Road

M Gandhi Rd

Mahapalika Marg

V Thackersey Marg

Naoroji Road

Soman

Veer Nariman Road

Wacha Road

Madame Cama Road

Colaba Causeway

Shivaji Marg

N Parekh Marg

Bhai Singh Road

Shahid Marg

Capt P P ... Marg

■ PLACES TO STAY

5   YMCA International
    Guest House
8   Siva Niketan
25 Hotels Railway &
    Manama
26 Bentley Hotel
27 Norman's Guest House
28 Hotel Natraj
29 Embassy Hotel
30 Chateau Windsor
    Guest House
35 Grand Hotel
38 Sea Green Hotels
41 Oberoi Hotel

31 Churchgate
    Railway Station
32 Tourist Office
33 Central Telegraph Office
34 American Express
36 Town Hall
37 Old Customs House
39 MTDC Tourist Office
40 Air India
    Indian Airlines & Vayudoot
42 Prince of Wales Museum
43 Gateway of India
44 Maker Towers
45 World Trade Centre
46 St John's Church
    (Afghan Memorial)

OTHER

1   Haji Ali's Tomb
2   Mahalaxmi Temple
3   Japanese High Commission
4   Victorian & Albert Museum
6   Bombay Central
    Railway Station
7   Long Distance Bus Station
9   Laxmi Narayan Temple
10 Breach Candy Hospital
11 Mani Bhavan
12 Round Temple
13 Banaji Fire Temple
15 Jain Temple
16 Walkeshwar Temple
17 Raj Bhavan
18 Javeri Bazaar
19 Crawford Market
20 Wadiaji Fire Temple
21 Anjuman Fire Temple
22 Foreigners Registration
    Office
23 Victoria Terminus
    Railway Station
24 GPO

Bombay has had lots of official name changes which everyone completely ignores. Colaba Causeway is not known as Shahid Bhagat Singh Rd, Wodehouse Rd is not known as N Parekh Marg. Wellingdon Circle is not known as Dr S P Mukherjee Chowk; in fact it's usually known as Regal after the cinema there. Veer Nariman Rd is sometimes called that; the rest of the time it's still Churchgate St. Victoria Terminus is always VT. ■

364 Dr Dadabhoy Naoroji Rd, Bombay 400 001, at the junction of Shivaji Marg and Colaba Causeway. You can change money here fast and efficiently.

The banking facilities at the airport are also relatively fast and efficient. The same is true of the change facilities on the ground floor at the Air India Building at Nariman Point which also stay open after normal banking hours.

Post & Telecommunications The GPO is an imposing building in Nagar Chowk near Victoria Terminus. The efficient poste restante service is open from 8 am to 6 pm Monday to Friday. You'll be given the whole pile of any letter of the alphabet you name to sort through but they'll want to see your passport first.

The parcel post office is around the back of the main building, on the 1st floor. It's open from 10 am to 4.30 pm on weekdays and if you're lucky you'll be out of there within an hour. On the footpath outside the GPO there are people who will wrap your parcel in cotton and seal it in the required way, and supply you with the necessary forms, all for a few rupees.

The Central Telegraph Office is open 24 hours a day and is right by Flora Fountain on Veer Nariman Rd. Bombay's telephone area code is 022.

Foreign Consulates Due to Bombay's importance as a business centre, many countries maintain diplomatic representation in Bombay as well as in the capital, New Delhi. They include:

Australia
    Maker Towers, E Block, Cuffe Parade
    (☎ 218-1071)

Belgium
    Morena, 11 M L Dahanukar Marg (☎ 492-9202)
Canada
    Suite 2401, Oberoi Towers, Nariman Point
    (☎ 202-4343)
Denmark
    L & T House, N Morarjee Marg, Ballard Estate
    (☎ 261-8181)
Egypt
    12/B Maker Towers, Cuffe Parade (☎ 218-2425)
France
    N G Cross Rd, off Peddar Rd (☎ 492-3386)
Germany
    Hoechst House, Nariman Point (☎ 23-2422)
Indonesia
    Lincoln Annexe, 17 Altamount Rd (☎ 36-8678)
Ireland
    Royal Bombay Yacht Club Chambers, Apollo
    Bunder (☎ 202-3774)
Italy
    Waswani Chambers, Dinshaw Wacha Rd
    (☎ 22-2192)
Japan
    1 M L Dahanukar Marg, Cumbulla Hill
    (☎ 492-3847)
Mauritius
    Corinthian, off Arthur Bunder Rd (☎ 23-1788)
Netherlands
    16 M Karve Rd, Churchgate (☎ 29-6480)
Singapore
    Sakhar Bhavan, Nariman Point (☎ 204-3209)
Spain
    Ador House, 6 K Dubash Marg (☎ 24-4664)
Sri Lanka
    Sri Lanka House, 34 Homi Mody St, Fort
    (☎ 204-5861)
Sweden
    Indian Mercantile Chambers, R Kamani Marg
    (☎ 261-2583)
Switzerland
    Manek Mahal, Veer Nariman Rd (☎ 204-3550)
Thailand
    Krishna Bagh, 43 Bhulabhai Desai Rd
    (☎ 822-6404)
UK
    Maker Chambers IV (1st floor) Cuffe Parade
USA
    Lincoln House, 78 Bhulabhai Desai Rd
    (☎ 363-3611, 822-3611)

Cultural Centres The British Council Library (☎ 22-3560) is at Mittal Tower A Wing, Nariman Point. Although it is ostensibly for members only, it is possible to get in to read the British newspapers.

The Alliance Française (☎ 29-1867) is at Sophy Hall, New Marine Lines.

Travel Agencies Travel Corner Ltd, Marine Drive, near the Ambassador Hotel, is a reliable agency for discounted tickets. Transway International (☎ 26-9941) at Pantaky House, 3rd floor, 8 Maruti Cross Lane, Fort, has also been recommended as quick, efficient and reasonably priced. Space Travels (☎ 286-4458) gives good service and is at Nanabhoy Mansion, Sir P M Rd.

Curiously enough, despite the great number of airlines flying through Bombay it is not as good a centre for cheap tickets as New Delhi.

If you need passport photos there's an automatic machine (typically, it provides a job for an attendant) at Central Station. According to one traveller, it's a real experience: 'You get a brief training course and your photos held in front of a fan by the attendant as part of the service'.

Bookshops & Publications The Nalanda Bookshop in the Taj Hotel is excellent. Other good bookshops are: Strand, just off Sir P M Rd (parallel to Churchgate behind Horniman Circle and Flora Fountain), and Bookpoint, in the Ballard Estate.

There are also a large number of street bookstalls under the arcades along Dr Dadabhoy Naoroji Rd and along the southern section of Mahatma Gandhi Rd.

City of Gold, the Biography of Bombay is a good book to read about the city. *The Bombay Guide* is a glossy, 80-page booklet with a chatty introduction to the city followed by a long list of airlines, hotels, restaurants and shops and several poor maps. At Rs 23 it's worth buying if you have a lot of official business to do; otherwise it's of limited use.

Gateway of India
In the days when most visitors came to India by ship and when Bombay was India's principal port, this was indeed the 'gateway' to India. Today it's merely Bombay's principal landmark. The gateway was conceived following the visit of King George V in 1911 and officially opened in 1924. Architecturally it is a conventional Arch of Triumph, with elements in its design derived from the Muslim styles of 16th-century Gujarat. It is built of yellow basalt and stands on the Apollo Bunder, a popular Bombay meeting place in the evenings.

The Taj Mahal Intercontinental Hotel overlooks the Apollo Bunder and launches run from here across to Elephanta Island. Close to the gateway are statues of Swami Vivekananda and of the Maratha leader, Shivaji, astride his horse.

Colaba Causeway
The streets behind the Taj Mahal Hotel are the travellers' centre of Bombay. Here you will find most of the cheap hotels and restaurants. Colaba Causeway, now renamed Shahid Bhagat Singh Rd, extends to the end of the Colaba promontory, the southern end of Bombay Island. Sassoon Dock is always interesting to visit around dawn, when the fishing boats come in and unload their catch in a colourful scene of intense activity. There's an old lighthouse at the end of the promontory, although the actual lighthouse used today is further south on a rocky island.

St John's Church
This church, also known as the Afghan Church, was built in 1847 and is dedicated to the soldiers who fell in the Sind campaign of 1838 and the First Afghan War of 1843.

Prince of Wales Museum
Beside the Wellingdon Circle, close to the Colaba hotel enclave, the Prince of Wales Museum was built to commemorate King George V's first visit to India in 1905 while he was still Prince of Wales. The first part of this interesting museum was opened in 1923. It was designed in the Indo-Saracenic style

and has sections for art and paintings, archaeology and natural history. Among the more interesting items is a very fine collection of miniature paintings, images and bas-reliefs from the Elephanta Caves, and Buddha images. Put aside at least half a day to explore this fascinating place.

The museum (☎ 24-4484) is open from 10 or 10.30 am to 6 or 6.30 pm, depending on the time of year. It is closed on Mondays and entry is Rs 2 (children Rs 1), except on Tuesdays when it is free.

Jehangir Art Gallery
Within the compound of the museum stands Bombay's principal art gallery. There are often special exhibitions of modern Indian art here. The gallery also has public phones, public toilets and a good snack bar. It opens at 10.30 am.

University & High Court
Along K B Patel Marg, overlooking Cross Maidan, there are several imposing public buildings erected during Bombay's period of great growth under the British. The university is in 14th to 15th-century Gothic style and is dominated by the 80-metre Rajabai Tower. This impressive clock tower rises above the university library.

Statues of Justice and Mercy top the huge High Court building beyond the university. It was built in Early English style and completed in 1878.

Flora Fountain
This is the business centre of Bombay, around which many of the major banks and business offices are centred. Now officially renamed Hutatma Chowk, it was erected in 1869 in honour of Sir Bartle Frere, who was governor of Bombay from 1862 to 1867, during which time Bombay experienced its most dramatic growth due to the worldwide cotton shortage caused by the American Civil War.

Close to the fountain is the Cathedral of St Thomas, begun by Gerald Aungier in 1672 but not formally opened until 1718. There are several interesting memorials inside the cathedral, which has had a series of additions and alterations over the years.

Horniman Circle
Several interesting old Bombay buildings stand close to Horniman Circle. If you're walking from the GPO back to Colaba some time, it's worth pausing to have a glance at some of these buildings. The old **Mint** was completed in 1829 and has an Ionic facade. It was built on land reclaimed in 1823 and adjoins the Town Hall. Behind the Town Hall stand the remains of the old **Bombay Castle**.

Opened in 1833, the **Town Hall** still houses the library of the Royal Asiatic Society. Ascend the imposing steps at the front of the Town Hall and have a short wander inside. You'll see statues of a number of the government officials and wealthy benefactors of Bombay's golden period, including Sir Bartle Frere and Sir Jamsetjee Jeejeebhoy. Continuing on, you pass the old **Customs House** built in 1720. The old Bombay dockyards are behind this building.

Marine Drive
Now officially renamed Netaji Subhash Rd, Marine Drive is built on land reclaimed in 1920. It runs along the shoreline of Back Bay, starting at Nariman Point and sweeping around by Chowpatty Beach and up to Malabar Hill. The road is backed with high residential buildings and is one of Bombay's most popular promenades.

Taraporewala Aquarium
Constructed in 1951, the aquarium on Marine Drive has both freshwater and salt-water fish. It's open Tuesday to Saturday from 11 am to 8 pm, Sunday from 10 am to 8 pm, and admission is Rs 1. It is closed on Mondays.

Also along Marine Drive, before the aquarium, is a series of cricket pitches where in summer there always seems to be games underway.

Chowpatty Beach
Bombay's famous beach attracts few bathers and even fewer sunbathers – neither activity

has much of a following in India, and in any case the water is none too healthy. Chowpatty has plenty of other activities though. It's one of those typical Indian slices of life where anything and everything can happen, and does. Sand-castle sculptors make elaborate figures in the sand, contortionists go through equally elaborate contortions and family groups stroll around. In between there are kiosks selling Bombay's popular snack, bhelpuri, and kulfi ice cream. Donkeys and ponies are available for children's rides.

Chowpatty Beach is also the scene for the annual Ganesh Chaturthi Festival, during which large images of the elephant-headed god are immersed in the sea.

Mani Bhavan
At 19 Laburnum Rd, near August Kranti Maidan, is the building where Mahatma Gandhi stayed during his visits to Bombay between 1917 and 1934. Today it has a pictorial exhibit of incidents in Gandhi's life and contains a library of books by or about the Mahatma. It is open from 9.30 am to 6 pm; entry is Rs 2.

Malabar Hill
At the end of Back Bay, Marine Drive climbs up to Malabar Hill. This is an expensive residential area, for not only is it a little cooler than the sea-level parts of the city, but there are fine views over Back Bay and Chowpatty Beach and right across to the central business district. At the end of the promontory is Raj Bhavan, the old British government headquarters and now the governor's residence.

Close by is the temple of Walkeshwar, the Sand Lord, an important Hindu pilgrimage site. According to the *Ramayana*, Rama rested here on his way from Ayodhya to Lanka to rescue Sita. He constructed a lingam of sand at the site. The original temple was built about 1000 years ago but was reconstructed in 1715.

Jain Temple
This marble temple was built in 1904 and is dedicated to the first Jain tirthankar, Adinath.

It's typical of modern Jain temples in its gaudy, mirrored style. The walls are decorated with pictures of incidents in the lives of the tirthankars.

Hanging Gardens
On top of Malabar Hill, these gardens were laid out in 1881 and are correctly known as the Pherozeshah Mehta Gardens. They take their name from the fact that they are built on top of a series of reservoirs that supply water to Bombay. The formally laid out gardens have a notable collection of hedges shaped like animals and there are good views over the city.

Kamala Nehru Park
Directly across the road from the Hanging Gardens, this park offers more superb views over Bombay. It was laid out in 1952 and was named after Nehru's wife. An unusual feature is a large nursery-rhyme 'old woman's shoe' which children love to play in.

Towers of Silence
Beside the Hanging Gardens, but carefully shielded from viewers, are the Parsi Towers of Silence. The Parsis hold fire, earth and water as sacred and thus will not cremate or bury their dead. Instead the bodies are laid out within the towers to be picked clean by vultures (if there are any vultures in Bombay; maybe it's crows).

Elaborate precautions are taken to keep ghoulish sightseers from observing the towers, despite which a *Time-Life* book on Bombay provided a bird's-eye view of one of the them. Parsi power in Bombay is sufficiently strong that the book was black-ink censored. Tour guides, always fond of a tall story for tourists, like to tell you that the reason the Hanging Garden reservoirs were covered over was that the vultures had an unpleasant habit of dropping the odd bit in the water supply.

Mahalaxmi Temple
Descending from Malabar Hill and continuing around the coastline, you come to the

Mahalaxmi Temple, the oldest in Bombay and, appropriately for this city of business and money, dedicated to the goddess of wealth. The images of the goddess and her two sisters were said to have been found in the sea.

Near here is the Mahalaxmi Racecourse, said to be the finest in India, where horse races are held each Sunday from December to May. The road along the seashore by the racecourse was once known as the Hornby Vellard, and was constructed in the 18th century to reclaim the swampland on which the course is now constructed.

Haji Ali's Tomb

This tomb and mosque are devoted to a Muslim saint who drowned here. The buildings are reached by a long causeway which can only be crossed at low tide. Here a scene of typical Indian ingenuity and resourcefulness takes place. Hundreds of beggars line the length of the causeway waiting for the regular stream of pilgrims. At the start of the causeway is a small group of moneychangers who, for a few paise commission, will change a Rs 1 or Rs 2 coin into lots of smaller denominations. Thus a pilgrim can do his/her soul the maximum amount of good for the minimum expenditure.

No doubt at the ebb tide the mendicants can change their low-value paise coins into something a little more manageable, thus giving the moneychangers their small change for the next low tide and no doubt providing them with another commission rake-off.

Victoria Gardens

These gardens, which contain Bombay's **zoo** and the **Victoria & Albert Museum**, have been renamed the Veermata Jijabai Bhonsle Udyan. The museum has some interesting exhibits relating to old Bombay. Just outside the museum building is the large stone elephant removed from Elephanta Island in 1864, and after which the island was named.

The museum (☎ 872-7131) is open from 10.30 am to 5 pm, the zoo from sunrise to sunset. Both are closed on Wednesday and charge Rs 0.50 admission.

Juhu

Close to Bombay's airports, Juhu is 18 km north of the city centre. It's the nearest beach to the city and has quite a collection of upper-notch hotels, but it's no place for a pleasant swim as the water is filthy.

On weekdays it is fairly quiet, but on weekends and in the late afternoons there are donkeys, camels, dancing monkeys, acrobats and every other type of Indian beach entertainment including thieves and hustlers. From Santa Cruz Station you can get there on a No 231 bus.

Other Attractions

The **Nehru Planetarium** (☎ 492- 0510) is on Dr Annie Besant Rd at Worli near the Haji Ali Tomb. There are shows in English at 3 and 6 pm daily except on Mondays when it is closed. Admission is Rs 6.

Falkland St is the centre for Bombay's notorious red-light district known as The Cages. The ladies stand behind metal-barred doors, hence the name. A No 130 bus from the museum passes through this fascinating area.

Organised Tours

Daily tours of Bombay are operated by the Maharashtra Tourist Development Council (MTDC) though, as elsewhere, they're a breathless rush-around. Morning tours generally last from 9 am to 1 pm and the afternoon tours from 2 to 6 pm. The fare is Rs 50.

The MTDC also has a suburban tour which operates from 9.15 am to 6.15 pm and costs Rs 85. This goes to the Kanheri Caves, Juhu Beach and other fascinating places such as the airport.

Of more interest to travellers are the launch tours to Elephanta Island. These four-hour tours depart daily (except during the monsoon) every hour from 9 am to 2.15 pm from the Gateway of India, Apollo Bunder. You have the choice of a luxury launch at Rs 40 (with guide) or an ordinary launch at Rs

25 (without guide). If you want to enquire about availability of seats, ring 202-6364 or 202-3585.

The MTDC also offers tours further afield to such places as Mahabaleshwar (suspended during the monsoon) and Aurangabad/Ajanta/Ellora, but it's better to go there independently even if you use one of their 'luxury' buses to get there in the first place (MTDC's buses are far from luxurious – better than a state bus but definitely not 'luxury').

Places to Stay

Bombay is India's most expensive city for accommodation, so if your funds are limited you should plan on spending as little time as possible here. Not only that, but it's a magnet for Middle East and Gulf Arabs who come here for holidays, shopping expeditions and business. They invariably bring with them their entire entourage. Not all of these visitors are super-rich oil sheikhs who can afford to stay in the Taj Mahal Intercontinental, so the pressure for accommodation – even at the bottom end of the market – is intense.

There is no guarantee that you will be able to find a room in your preferred price range, at least for the first night and especially if you arrive late in the day. You may have to settle for something considerably more expensive in the first instance until you've had time to walk around unencumbered with baggage. The standard of accommodation, too, at the bottom end of the market, is often poor in comparison with elsewhere in India.

It's a distinct advantage to be part of a small group (impromptu or otherwise), since if the first place you try is full, then one or two of you can look after the baggage while the rest fan out in search of somewhere else. If you should be unlucky enough not to find anything in the price range that you can afford on the first day, try making a booking for the following day.

Taxi drivers are fond of telling new arrivals that the hotel of their choice is 'full' and suggesting somewhere else. This will inevitably be an expensive hotel (they often have a sticker for the hotel they suggest on their dashboard). It's likely they pick up a commission for introducing a guest but this isn't always the case. What definitely is the case is that they haven't a clue whether a hotel is full or not. No taxi driver in Bombay routinely checks hotels for occupancy levels nor do they have intercoms. If you want to go to a specific hotel, insist on going there first.

And don't bother with the tourist information services, either in the city or at the airport, unless you intend staying at an expensive hotel (ie three to five-star). They know as much as the taxi drivers.

Places to Stay – bottom end

Colaba The majority of the budget hotels are in the Colaba area directly behind that useful landmark, the Taj Mahal Intercontinental.

The cheapest place is the *Salvation Army Red Shield Hostel* (☎ 24-1824), at 30 Mereweather Rd. It's a very popular place, with dorm beds including breakfast for Rs 55 or full board for Rs 85. There are also doubles at Rs 250 and family rooms at Rs 100 (per person) with full board but you must share the communal bathrooms. Safe-deposit lockers can be hired for a returnable deposit of Rs 50 plus Rs 3 per day. Checkout time is 9 am and there's a maximum limit of one week's stay.

Close by is the old *Carlton Hotel* (☎ 202-0642) at 12 Mereweather Rd. It's decidedly semi-derelict and only for those inured to rock-bottom Indian conditions plus there are only common showers and toilets. Prices, including taxes, are Rs 120 for a single and Rs 165 and Rs 190 a double (depending on the size of the room and whether you want a window).

Much better in terms of maintenance and the fabric of the building is *Hotel Prosser's* (☎ 24-1715), on the corner of Henry Rd and P J Ramchandani Marg, which has small hardboard partitioned singles/doubles with shared bath for Rs 180/250 including tax. Checkout time is noon.

Away from this immediate area, but within easy walking distance, is the very popular 3rd-floor *Hotel Lawrence* (☎ 24-3618), Rope Walk Lane, off K Dubash Marg

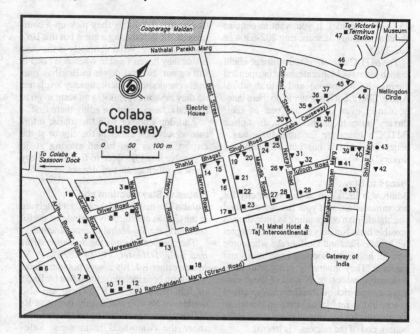

Colaba Causeway

To Victoria Terminus Station
Museum
Cooperage Maidan
Nathalal Parekh Marg
To Colaba & Sassoon Dock
0   50   100 m
Electric House
Wellingdon Circle
Best Street
Convent Street
Colaba Causeway
Shahid Bhagat Singh Road
Mandlik Road
Barrow Road
Henry Road
Walton Road
Garden Road
Oliver Road
Arthur Bunder Road
Mereweather Road
Navraji Road
Tulloch Road
Mahakav Bhushan Marg
Shivaji Marg
PJ Ramchandani Marg (Strand Road)
Taj Mahal Hotel & Taj Intercontinental
Gateway of India

at the back of the Prince of Wales Museum. It's often full since it only has nine rooms, but it's excellent value at Rs 70/120 for singles/doubles with common bath including taxes. Some of the rooms have balconies.

Back in Colaba, there's the friendly *Bentley's Hotel* (☎ 24-1733), 17 Oliver Rd, which offers singles/doubles for Rs 172/350 to Rs 196/400 for bed and breakfast including tax. The higher priced rooms have attached bath and the double rooms have colour TV. Also good is the small (but unsignposted) *Hotel Volga II* (☎ 287-3436), Navraji Rd, above street level and next door to the Leopold Restaurant. The manager is friendly and doubles/triples without bath are Rs 250/350 plus tax. There are three clean shared bathrooms.

Cheaper but basic is the *Apollo Guest House* (☎ 204-5540), 1st floor, Mathuradas Estate Building, Colaba Causeway, which has singles/doubles with shared bathroom for Rs 160/180 including tax. Don't confuse

this place with the hotel of the same name on Garden Rd. Also on Colaba Causeway near the Leopold Restaurant, the *Hotel Crystal* (☎ 202-0673) has reasonable rooms with windows but these are a mixed blessing as the street noise can be horrendous at times. It's somewhat more expensive than the Apollo.

There's a whole collection of small hotels on various floors along the noisy and somewhat sleazy Arthur Bunder Rd. The *Seashore Hotel* and the *Hotel Mukund* (☎ 287-3240) at Kamal Mansion are both fairly clean, friendly and have decent-sized rooms, although you'll be lucky to get a window. Prices depend on the size of the room and whether you get a window.

Others along Arthur Bunder Rd include the *Janata Guest House, Imperial Guest House, India Guest House, Gateway Guest House, Gulf Hotel* and *Hotel Al-Hijaz.* Many of these places look like they ought to be cheap, but don't let appearances fool you

■ PLACES TO STAY

1 Ascot Hotel
2 Apollo Guest House
3 Hotel Cowies
4 Godwin Hotel
5 Garden Hotel
6 Fariyas Hotel
7 Hotel Mukund
8 Bentley's Hotel
9 Hotel Kishan
10 Shelley's Hotel
11 Strand Hotel
12 Sea Palace Hotel
13 Whalley's Guest House
17 Salvation Army Red Shield Hostel
18 Hotel Prosser's
21 Hotel Moti International
22 Regent Hotel
23 Hotel Diplomat
24 Apollo Guest House
25 Hotel Volga II &
   Leopold Restaurant
28 Carlton Hotel
34 Hotel Crystal
39 Suba Guest House
41 Hotel Apollo
47 YWCA International Centre

▼ PLACES TO EAT

14 Kamat Hotel Restaurant
15 Ananda Punjabi
16 Dipti's Pure Drinks
19 Apsara Restaurant
20 Food Inn
26 Laxmi Vilas
30 Olympic Coffee House
31 Apollo Restaurant
32 Gohul Bar & Restaurant
36 Canteena
37 Hotel Majestic Restaurant
38 Cafe Mondegar
40 Naval & Military Restaurant
42 Mandarin & Hong Kong Restaurants
45 Sahakari Bhandar Canteen
46 Woodside Pizza

OTHER

27 Crown & Anchor Bar
29 Alps
33 Royal Bombay Yacht Club
35 Delhi Durbar
43 Central Cottage
   Industries Emporium
44 American Express

and remember that prices and standards vary enormously.

If you're really stuck there are a couple of ultra-basic places on Colaba Causeway which may have room. Most of these places have no signs but there are always touts hanging around who will willingly lead the way. In Bombay terms they're cheap, airless and grubby, and you wouldn't want to leave anything in your room while you're out.

Elsewhere There are several cheapies on P D'Mello Rd just to the east of the GPO/Victoria Terminus but they are certainly nothing special. The *Railway Hotel* (☎ 26-6705), 249 P D'Mello Rd, is probably one of the best as it's been renovated, but it costs Rs 220/305 including tax for rooms without air-con. Similar is the *Rupam Hotel* (☎ 26-6225), 239 P D'Mello Rd, which offers both air-con and non-air-con rooms. The management are friendly and it's clean despite being somewhat run down. Nearby is the *Hotel Manora* (☎ 26-7450) at No 243.

Cheaper is the *City Lodge* (☎ 26-5515) directly across from VT station and the GPO and above a tailor shop. The management are friendly and the rooms are extremely shabby but it would do at a pinch. None of the rooms have their own bath.

Between here and Colaba at Ballard Pier, the very pleasant and quiet *Fernandez Guest House* (☎ 26-0554) in the Balmer Lawrie Building, 5 J N Heredia Marg, is very similar in quality and price to the Lawrence Hotel but it's not easy to find and, like the Lawrence, is invariably full – there are just seven rooms.

There are only two cheap places to stay on Marine Drive. The first is *Bentley Hotel* (☎ 29-1244) on the corner of Marine Drive and D Rd, which offers bed and breakfast for Rs 160/185 in rooms with common bath. Some of the rooms are very small. The hotel is on the 3rd floor. Right opposite is *Norman's Guest House* (☎ 29-4234), on the corner of Marine Drive and D Rd, which has clean and simple rooms with attached bath for Rs 218/300 including tax.

The Ys Like other Indian cities, Bombay has its share of YMCAs and YWCAs. Although very good value for money, they're invariably full. The most popular is the *YWCA International Centre* (☎ 202-0445), in Colaba at 18 Madame Cama Rd. It takes both women and men and offers B&B for Rs 202/387 including tax plus Rs 10 membership charges (valid for one month). The rooms have attached bathrooms. It's sometimes booked out up to three months in advance.

The *YMCA International Guest House* (☎ 89-1191) is at 18 YMCA Rd near Central railway station. This is rather a long way from downtown Bombay and the popular Colaba area. The rooms are pleasant and well kept and charges are much the same as for the YWCA.

Other Accommodation For men only there is excellent dormitory accommodation for Rs 15 or rooms for three people at Rs 20 per person at *Siva Niketan* (☎ 37-2395) on J Jijibhoy Rd. This is in the northern part of the city, near Byculla Railway Station on the suburban line from VT.

There are no purpose-built youth hostels as such in Bombay, but during university/college vacations you may be able to find cheap accommodation at *Bhavan's College* (☎ 57-2192), Versova Rd, Bhavan's Camp, Andheri; *University Hostel* (☎ 47-2425), L A Kidwai Rd; or *Podar College of Commerce Hostel* (☎ 47-2414), 193 Sion Koliwada Estate.

There are *retiring rooms* at the domestic airport if you're departing in less than 24 hours, which are cheaper than checking into a hotel. Ask at the airport manager's office.

Finally, both Bombay Central and Victoria Terminus have *retiring rooms*. At Central they cost Rs 65 for a double, or Rs 130 with air-con.

Places to Stay – middle

Many of the middle-bracket hotels are in the Colaba area though there is another group clustered along Marine Drive (Netaji Subhash Rd) between Madame Cama Rd and Veer Nariman Rd, and along Veer Nariman Rd itself. The ones in the Colaba area tend to be less expensive than those along Marine Drive.

Colaba *Whalley's Guest House* (☎ 22-1802), 41 Mereweather Rd, is one of the cheapest in this range but it's nothing special and some of the rooms have no windows. Rooms without air-con cost Rs 200/250 or Rs 250/450 with air-con including tax. Only some of the cheaper rooms have attached bath.

At the south-western end of P J Ramchandani Marg are three hotels in a row. First is *Shelleys Hotel* (☎ 24-0229) at No 30, which has a range of doubles (no singles) at Rs 400, Rs 480 and Rs 560 including tax. They all have attached bath, air-con and the most expensive rooms also have a colour TV. The hotel has its own restaurant. Next door is the ageing *Strand Hotel* (☎ 24-1624) which offers rooms without air-con and shared bath for Rs 305/360 and rooms with attached bath, air-con, fridge and TV for Rs 360/440 including tax. Next door again at No 26 is the *Sea Palace Hotel* (☎ 24-1828) whose business card claims 'All rooms are exotically designed'! They might not be wrong but not in the expected sense. Singles are Rs 300, or it's Rs 345/675 for singles/doubles with air-con, plus there are suites for Rs 690. The hotel has its own restaurant and roof garden.

Back towards Colaba Causeway, the *Hotel Kishan*, Walton Rd, has air-con rooms with attached bath for Rs 260/360. It's popular with Japanese travellers. Similar in price is the *Hotel Moti International* (☎ 202-5714), 10 Best St, which has doubles (no singles) with attached bath and air-con for Rs 385. Few travellers stay here as it's used mainly by Indian family groups. Slightly more expensive is *Hotel Cowie's* (☎ 24-0232), 15 Walton Rd, which offers large air-con rooms with attached bath and colour TV for Rs 350 a single and Rs 400 and Rs 500 a double.

Up in price again, there are three popular hotels on Garden Rd which are rarely full despite what taxi drivers will tell you. The *Ascot Hotel* (☎ 24-0020), 38 Garden Rd, has air-con singles/doubles with bath, TV and fridge for Rs 390/680 including breakfast. A few doors down, the *Godwin Hotel* (☎ 287-2050), 41 Garden Rd, offers accommodation of a similar standard for Rs 400/710, also including breakfast. The hotel has its own bar and rooftop garden restaurant. The *Garden Hotel* (☎ 24-1476) at 42 Garden Rd has air-con doubles (no singles) with TV and fridge for Rs 400, Rs 480 and Rs 560 including tax. There are also more expensive suites. The hotel has its own bar and restaurant.

The brand new *Regent Hotel* (☎ 287-1854), 8 Best Rd, has been beautifully designed and built to high standards and offers air-con singles/doubles/triples with TV and fridge for Rs 605/825/880 including taxes. The staff are friendly and eager to please. Round the corner from here at the back of the Taj is the *Hotel Diplomat* (☎ 202-1661) at 24-26 Mereweather Rd. It's a small hotel and popular with business people so it's often full. Air-con rooms with TV and fridge go for Rs 437/633. There are also deluxe doubles for Rs 805. The hotel has its own bar and restaurant.

Further over behind the Regency Cinema is the *Regency Inn* (☎ 202-0292), 18 Lansdowne House, Mahakavi Bhushan Marg, which, from the appearance of the foyer, looks like it might be cheap. Yet it's surprisingly expensive for an old hotel at Rs 320 for a 'budget' room, Rs 425 for a 'standard' room and Rs 500 for a 'superior' room. There are also suites for Rs 600. All the rooms have air-con and a TV.

Round the corner is the *Hotel Apollo* (☎ 202-0223), 22 Lansdowne House, Mahakavi Bhushan Marg, which was recently renovated. The tariff is in the Rs 400/680 range, and all rooms are air-con.

VT Station Area At 221-225 P D'Mello Rd near Victoria Terminus the *Hotel Manama* (☎ 26-3860) is a reasonable choice but has only double rooms and is often full. Also on P D'Mello Rd, the *Embassy Hotel* (☎ 86-6255) is opposite the Dockyard Rd suburban

railway station and offers rooms of a similar standard. Both these hotels have air-con.

At the top end of this category in this area is the elegant *Grand Hotel* (☎ 26-8211), 17 Sprott Rd, Ballard Estate, which has been completely refurbished and is very popular with business people, yet few travellers seem to stay here. It's a large place with friendly staff and is rarely full. Air-con rooms with marbled bathrooms, traditionally designed furniture, TV and small balcony cost Rs 650/845 including tax. There's a restaurant, coffee shop and bar.

Marine Drive Moving to the Marine Drive (Netaji Subhash Rd) area, the two cheapest places to stay are the *Sea Green Hotel* (☎ 22-2294), 145 Marine Drive and the *Sea Green South Hotel* (☎ 22-1613), 145-A Marine Drive. They both charge Rs 250/340 without air-con and Rs 330/420 with air-con. They also have suites for Rs 350 (single) and Rs 450 (double). All the rooms have attached bath with hot water but there's no TV (except in the communal lounge area). Checkout time for advance reservations is 8 am (unusual in Bombay).

Nearby at 141 Marine Drive on the corner of Veer Nariman Rd is the old *Hotel Delamar* (☎ 204-2848) which offers singles with shared bath and without air-con for Rs 350, doubles with shared bath and air-con for Rs 680, and singles/doubles with attached bath and air-con for Rs 390/700. There's 24-hour hot water and all the rooms have a colour TV.

Close by is the popular *Chateau Windsor Guest House* (☎ 204-3376), 86 Veer Nariman Rd, which has a wide selection of rooms with and without air-con and bath, and varying widely in size. Some of the windowless little boxes are poor value so don't take a room until you've seen it. Singles go for Rs 225, Rs 275 and Rs 345 (attached bath). Doubles are Rs 350 (shared bath), Rs 520 and Rs 595. There are also triples and rooms with four beds ranging from Rs 595 to Rs 745, all with attached bath. All the higher priced rooms have air-con and most rooms have a colour TV but, if not, you can rent one for Rs 30 per day.

Airport Close to the domestic terminal and at the cheaper end of the scale is the *Hotel Aircraft International* (☎ 612-3667) at 179 Dayaldas Rd, Vile Parle, which has ordinary rooms at Rs 325, deluxe rooms at Rs 350 and super-deluxe rooms at Rs 425. The comfortable and well-kept *Hotel Jal* (☎ 612-3820) on Nehru Rd costs Rs 375/425 and has a vegetarian restaurant and bar. Also on Nehru Rd, the *Hotel Transit* (☎ 612-9325) has rooms of a similar quality at Rs 360/585 and suites for Rs 725. The hotel has its own restaurant. Another in this range is the *Hotel Avion* (☎ 611-3220), Nehru Rd, which has rooms for Rs 395/585 and suites for Rs 795.

Juhu The *Kings Hotel* (☎ 614-9775), 5 Juhu Tara Rd, provides air-con rooms for Rs 413/495 including tax. The *Sea Side Hotel* (☎ 620-0293), 39/2 Juhu Rd, offers air-con rooms with attached bath for Rs 345/450.

Other places to try at the cheaper end of the market are the *Sea View Hotel* and the *Purnima Guest House*.

Places to Stay – top end

Hotels in this category, like many of those in the mid-range, invariably have both state and central government taxes imposed on room tariffs, though in this range they can amount to as much as 30% if you pay in rupees. You can lop 20% off this if you pay in foreign currency or by credit card. In addition, there are usually service charges of at least 10% which you can do nothing about.

Colaba One of the cheapest (but only just) in this range is the *Fariyas Hotel* (☎ 204-2911), off Arthur Bunder Rd, Colaba (it's actually two streets west of Arthur Bunder Rd). The rooms are very pleasant, it's fully air-conditioned and the staff are friendly. Singles/doubles are Rs 990/1190 plus there are more expensive suites ranging from Rs 1700 to Rs 2100. There's a swimming pool, a bar and a good restaurant.

At the other end of Colaba is the *Taj Mahal Hotel & Taj Mahal Intercontinental* (☎ 202-3366), Apollo Bunder, reputedly the best hotel in India, though that's a moot point

these days. Certainly the affluence ostentatiously paraded in the Taj is amazing and it definitely has an air of Beverly Hills glamour about it. BMWs and Mercedes Benz vie for space in front of the main entrance while Gulf Arab sheikhs in gleaming white, flowing gowns glide across the immense, deliciously cool, marble-floored foyer. If you don't look mega-rich here, you don't exist though that doesn't prevent you from entering. The Taj, after all, does have one of the best bookshops in Bombay and most travellers are avid readers, so don a clean T-shirt and join the fashion parade. It also has the best public toilets in Bombay (though you're expected to tip the man who keeps them clean).

All of the 650 rooms are luxuriously appointed and range from US$155/170 for a standard room in the Intercontinental section to US$185/200 in the old wing. Also in the old wing are various theme suites ranging from 'Executive' at US$310 to US$450, to the 'Presidential' suites at US$650. Taxes (30%) and service charges are extra. The hotel has every conceivable facility you could imagine including four restaurants, three bars, coffee shop, disco (residents only) and swimming pool.

Nariman Point & Marine Drive Other top-end hotels are scattered around Nariman Point and Marine Drive. The *Ritz Hotel* (☎ 22-0141), 5 J Tata Rd, Churchgate, is one of the older establishments with the usual range of facilities but no swimming pool. It has rooms for Rs 1050/1200 and suites for Rs 2000 to Rs 2200, and is centrally air-conditioned.

More modern is the *Ambassador Hotel* (☎ 204-0004), Veer Nariman Rd, Churchgate, where the cheapest singles/doubles are Rs 1195/1395. More expensive singles/doubles are Rs 1495/1795 plus there are a range of suites from Rs 1795 to Rs 3995. Tax (30%) is extra. There's a bar and revolving rooftop restaurant but no swimming pool.

In the same price bracket is the recently opened but somewhat featureless (from the outside) *Hotel Nataraj* (☎ 204-4161), 135

Marine Drive, which has ordinary rooms for Rs 1200/1500 and deluxe doubles at Rs 1680 plus suites for Rs 2840. The hotel has a limited range of facilities and is used mainly for conferences and banquets.

Competing with the Taj for pride of place as Bombay's most luxurious and opulent hotel is the huge and thoroughly modern *Oberoi/Oberoi Towers* (☎ 202-4343), Nariman Point. The enormous atrium here, around which there's a shopping complex on two floors, is beautifully designed and well worth seeing even if you're not staying at the hotel. It's also deliciously cool! Rooms cost US$190/200 to US$200/215 plus there are a range of suites from US$375 to the Kohinoor suite at US$1150. There's a plethora of facilities including a swimming pool, three restaurants and a bar with superb views over the bay and dancing every evening from 6.30 pm onwards.

Somewhat further afield in the diplomatic/business enclave of Cuffe Parade is the *Hotel President* (☎ 215-0808), 90 Cuffe Parade, which has standard rooms at US$125/140 and superior rooms at US$140/155. There are also suites for US$210. The hotel has a range of facilities including a swimming pool and four banqueting halls. It's used mainly by business people and expatriates on long-term contracts.

Airport There are a number of hotels out by the airport. Unless you have some compelling reason to be near the airport, there's little incentive to stay there.

Right outside the domestic terminal (Santa Cruz) is the five-star *Centaur Hotel* (☎ 612-6660), a large circular hotel with all the usual amenities including a swimming pool, three restaurants and bar and rooms for US$77/87, plus suites at US$152 to US$278.

There are several other hotels very close by, either beside the Centaur or just across the road. They're all air-con and offer good but expensive facilities. The *Hotel Airport Plaza* (☎ 612-3390) is at 70-C Nehru Rd, Vile Parle (pronounced 'Veelay Parlay') and has rooms for Rs 600/900. It also has a swimming pool. The *Hotel Airport Inter-national* (☎ 612-2883), 5/6 Nehru Rd, Vile Parle, behind the Centaur Hotel, has rooms at Rs 395/600. The *Hotel Airport Palace* is even cheaper than this.

By the international terminal, the five-star *Leela Kempinski* (☎ 636-3636) has rooms for US$150 (single or double) and suites for US$215 to US$900. It has all the amenities you'd expect including a swimming pool, four restaurants, two bars and range of other sports facilities.

Juhu There are a lot of hotels along Juhu Beach. But it's hard to think of a good reason to stay there. Don't even consider swimming at Juhu – one look at the untreated sewage which slithers sluggishly out to sea from the vast slum encampments from Dadar to Juhu will convince you. The beach is also a favourite patch for thieves.

The four-star *Hotel Sands* (☎ 620-4512), 39/2 Juhu Beach, has rooms for Rs 625/725 and suites for Rs 1200. It has a restaurant and bar but no swimming pool.

Close by is the *Hotel Horizon* (☎ 614-8100), 37 Juhu Beach, with rooms for Rs 750 to Rs 1250 (single or double) and suites for Rs 1500 to Rs 2250. It has a swimming pool, restaurants, bar and discotheque. Next door is the five-star *Sun-n-Sand Hotel* (☎ 620-1811), 39 Juhu Beach, which has singles/doubles at Rs 1000/1200 and suites for Rs 1200 to Rs 2400. There's a swimming pool, health club, restaurant and bar. Similar is the *Hotel Sea Princess* (☎ 612-2661), Juhu Beach, another five-star hotel, with rooms at Rs 1100/1250 plus suites from Rs 2800. Like the others it has a swimming pool, restaurant and bar.

Up in price again, the *Ramada Inn Palm Grove* (☎ 611-2323), Juhu Beach, has rooms for Rs 1250/1500 plus suites for Rs 2000 and Rs 3500 plus tax. It offers all the facilities associated with Ramada Inns. More expensive still is the *Holiday Inn* (☎ 620-4444), Balraj Sahani Marg, Juhu Beach, which has rooms for US$96 (single or double) and suites for US$170 to US$335 plus tax. This has even more facilities than the Ramada including two swimming pools, garden barbecue, restaurants, pub and shopping arcade.

Top of the line is the five-star deluxe *Centaur Hotel Juhu Beach* (☎ 611-3090), Juhu Tara Rd, an enormous place offering a standard of luxury and exclusiveness rivalling that of the best hotels in the centre of Bombay. It has rooms for US$87/97 and suites for US$152 to US$278 and a full range of every conceivable amenity. There's also an Air India and Indian Airlines reservation office here.

Most of the top-end hotels at Juhu Beach have free courtesy buses to and from both the domestic and international airports so there's no need to take a taxi.

Places to Eat

The accommodation shortage certainly doesn't spill over into restaurants. Bombay probably has the best selection of restaurants of any major Indian city. As in other cities, a meal in a better class restaurant can be one of India's bargains. A foray into the more expensive places is a worthwhile investment, even for backpackers.

Cheap There are plenty of places to eat around Colaba. *Dipti's Pure Drinks*, Best St, is popular for its wonderful fruit juices, fruit salads and lassis. The relatively high prices don't put people off this tiny establishment.

On Navroji Furounji Rd, *Laxmi Vilas* has excellent vegetarian thalis and lassis. On Wodehouse Rd (alias the extension of Colaba Causeway alias Shahid Bhagat Singh Rd) the *Ananda Punjabi* is more expensive but tasty, say Rs 40 for two. A couple of doors down, the *Kamat Hotel* has excellent vegetarian food and it's air-conditioned upstairs.

The *Apsara Restaurant* is a popular place with good Indian and Chinese food at about Rs 40 for two. Nearby, the *Food Inn* is also popular and very clean and shiny-looking although their tea is, as one traveller put it 'in the face of some stiff competition, the worst in Bombay'.

The *Leopold Bar & Restaurant* is one of Bombay's legends and a very popular place, not only for breakfast, lunch or dinner, but for hanging around over a cold beer (they have draught and bottled) and watching the streetlife through the open doors. You'll meet travellers here you saw elsewhere in India – often months ago. It's even popular with expats working in Bombay and you may even see Gulf Arabs having a surreptitious beer! The Leopold has a very pleasant atmosphere, a good juice bar and an extensive veg/non-veg menu. The service is friendly and the kitchen hygienic but you must remember that, because of its popularity, prices are consistently higher than other nearby restaurants.

The *Cafe Mondegar*, a pleasant coffee bar in the next block towards Wellingdon Circle, is very similar. Across the road, the *Hotel Majestic* is a big vegetarian plate-meal specialist; it's Rs 10 for a standard thali, Rs 15 with pulao and sweets. Directly across from the Leopold, the *Olympic Coffee House* is a traditional old coffee bar with wonderful decor.

Right by Wellingdon Circle, the *Sahakari Bhandar Canteen* is tacked on to an old building but the food is good and very cheap. Also good and cheap in the Colaba area is the *Gohul Bar & Restaurant* on Tulloch Rd. It has much the same menu as the Leopold but is decidedly cheaper.

The *Maharajah Cafe*, four doors down from the British Bank of the Middle East at Elphinstone Circle, behind Flora Fountain, is a fairly new establishment which has a good reputation among travellers. The chicken korma here is particularly good plus there's a visitors' book with all manner of comments in it as well as a collection of books and magazines which you can read or swap.

The *Cafe Samovar* in the Jehangir Art Gallery is a good place for a cold drink or a quick snack. At the top of Garden Rd, next to the garage, the *Edward VIII Restaurant* is a well-kept little place with good fruit juices.

Colaba is renowned for fine prawns and seafood. You can get fish & chips in quite a few places, including right beside the Marine Drive aquarium!

Bhelpuri is a Bombay speciality – a tasty

snack of crisp noodles, spiced vegetables and other mysterious ingredients for Rs 2 or less. It's available from stalls all over town, but particularly on Chowpatty Beach. There are several restaurants along the beach road.

There's a couple of places to go if you want a meal, a snack or just a drink while you read the mail you've just picked up from the GPO. *Kohinoor* is virtually opposite the GPO. At 204 D Naoroji Rd, back towards Colaba from the GPO and Victoria Terminus, the small *Suvidha* restaurant in the National Insurance Building has excellent vegetarian food although it's crowded at lunchtime.

Bombay also has its own string of fast-food places called *Open House*. The closest one to the centre is on Veer Nariman Rd near the footbridge. They have good burgers for Rs 10 to Rs 15, and pizza for Rs 15 to Rs 20.

More Expensive The Taj Mahal Hotel has a whole range of restaurants, bars and snack bars. The *Apollo Bar/Rooftop Rendezvous* on the rooftop of the Intercontinental section caters for Western tastes and has fine views but beers are mega-expensive. If that's what you primarily want, take one in the much

cheaper *Harbour Bar*. For coffee and snacks, the *Shamiana* is the place to head for. The *Tanjore* is probably the best place for a splash-out meal – it has traditional Indian food accompanied by sitar music, and classical Indian dancing in the evenings. It also offers thalis. The lunchtime buffet at the rooftop restaurant costs Rs 190 but the choice is limited, the food leaves much to be desired and the waiters can be downright offhand. Formal dress is required in all the Taj's restaurants in the evening but smart casual wear is acceptable at lunchtimes.

A much better place for a lunchtime splurge is the Polynesian restaurant at the *Oberoi Towers Hotel* which costs Rs 200 for a splendid array of Indian, Oriental and Continental dishes. The waiters can be no less offhand than at the Taj but the food here is excellent.

Another similar place to splurge is in the revolving rooftop restaurant at the *Ambassador Hotel*.

Along K Dubash Marg, just across from the Jehangir Art Gallery and at the back of the Prince of Wales Museum, the newly renovated *Copper Chimney* offers North Indian and Mughlai dishes and is a good place to eat. It's a minor splurge.

Daba Lunches

Mr Bombay Business-Wallah sets off from home, boards his train or bus and heads into the city every morning – just like his office-worker counterpart in the West. Just like many of his overseas office-wallah brothers and sisters, he'd like to take his lunch with him and eat in the office. But an Indian lunch isn't as simple as a couple of sandwiches and an apple. A cut lunch could never satisfy an Indian – there has to be curry and rice and parathas and spices and a lot of things that take a lot of time to prepare and would hardly slip into a brown paper bag in the briefcase.

Naturally there's a supremely complex, yet smoothly working, Indian solution to this problem – it's called the *daba* lunch system. After he's left for work, his wife – or the cook or bearer – sets to and fixes his lunch. When it's prepared it's packed into a metal container about 15 cm in diameter and 30 cm high. On the lid there's a mysterious colour-coded notation. The container is then carried down to a street corner pick-up point where it meets up with lots of other lunch containers and heads towards their city office destination. From the pick-up point they're conveyed to the nearest train station where they're transported to the appropriate city station.

In the city they're broken down to their separate destinations, and between 11 and 12 in the morning thousands upon thousands of individually coded lunches pour out of Victoria Terminus, Churchgate, Bombay Central and other stations. On the heads of porters, carried in carts, slung from long poles, tied on bicycle handlebars, those lunch containers then scatter out across the city. Most of the daba-wallahs involved in this long chain of events are illiterate, but by some miracle of Indian efficiency, when Mr Business-Wallah opens his office door at lunchtime there will be his lunch by the door. Every day, without fail, they never lose a lunch. ■

Movies

Quickly, what are the biggest film-producing city and country in the world? Hollywood and the USA? Wrong twice – Bombay and India! The Indians turn out 500 to 600 full-length feature films a year and, of these, nearly half are made in Bombay. Calcutta makes some arty, intellectual films; Madras some family comedies or musicals; but for extravaganzas, action dramas, the 'starcast' A features, it's Bombay all the way.

A visit to a film studio is a real education, as we found when we turned up at Famous Film Studios. For a start the film production company and the studios are totally separate. Bombay has about 12 studios and far more film-makers. When they want to make a film they simply hire the studio by the day. Nor are Indian films made one at a time as in the West. A big star could be involved in a number of films simultaneously – shooting a day on one, a week on another, a morning on a third. This involves phenomenal scheduling problems and also means that Indian films generally take a long time to make.

A glance at Indian film posters or film magazines gives you the impression that Indian movie actors are a band of escapees from weight-watchers. Well, there's no glamour in being thin in India. Every beggar in the street is skinny; it's the well-padded look which appeals. It's amusing to see how this works on Western films shown in India – familiar European and American film stars become remarkably rotund when they're repainted for the Indian posters. Our image of these chubby, smug actors was quickly shattered when we were asked into the dressing room to meet the star of the film we went to see. He was friendly, very open about the problems involved in making films in India – and not a kg overweight!

Life for a lot of Indians is not all that much fun and illiteracy is still widespread. Bombay film-makers are not trying to produce something for a sophisticated and intellectual audience. It's pure, straightforward, down-to-earth entertainment: escapism and nothing more.

Bombay films always have a bit of everything – drama, action, suspense, music, dancing, romance – all mixed together into one extravagant blend. They've even got a name for them –

In Colaba the *Delhi Darbar* doesn't serve alcohol but it does have an extensive menu. This is a good place to try the Parsi dish dhaansak. They have very good milk shakes and ice cream (try the pista kulfi).

Bombay has a particularly good selection of Chinese restaurants. Some say the *Nanking*, on Shivaji Marg in Colaba, has the best Chinese food in India. Directly across the road, the *Mandarin* is marginally more expensive. The adjacent *Hong Kong* does excellent Szechuan food – 'the best Chinese food we've ever found anywhere', reported a Canadian traveller. The *Kabab Corner* in the Hotel Nataraj on Marine Drive has excellent food and a sitar player in the evenings.

At Nariman Point, past the Air India Building, is the *Rangoli Restaurant* in the performing arts complex. The excellent buffet lunch is fantastic value at Rs 80. Near Churchgate Station, the *Samrat* vegetarian restaurant has been recommended for its good food. Here you can try the local apéritif known as jal jeera – 'very popular but it

smells like rotten eggs and is very salty' according to one unimpressed drinker.

Entertainment

For a day of relaxation in pleasant surroundings and away from the hassle of the streets, try the Breach Candy Club, Wanden Rd (Bhulabhai Desai Marg), on the shoreline out near the racecourse. This exclusive swimming and volleyball club charges Rs 60 per day for nonmembers or Rs 75 on Saturday and Rs 150 on Sunday. There are two swimming pools, a bar and snack bar, all set in tropical gardens. It's quite popular with expatriates.

If you get jaded of sitting over cold Kingfisher beers at the Leopold Bar & Restaurant, give the back room of the Gohul Bar & Restaurant a go. It's just round the corner on Tulloch Rd and the beers are cheaper than at Leopold. Also, they have an excellent collection of tapes.

Far more down to earth but with an almost exclusively Indian clientele is the upstairs 'masala movies', since masala is the all-purpose word for spices, something you add to make it tasty.

Within their commercial constraints Indian movie-makers often do a surprisingly good job, particularly the camera operators and technicians, who manage to produce reasonable standard films from hopelessly outdated equipment. Apart from the restrictions on importing new equipment, a large slice of the proceeds goes to the Indian government. Film admission prices may be only Rs 3, 4 or 5, but the government gulps down about 75% of that figure. To make an Indian movie and earn money out of it, you really have to know what you're about.

Tony Wheeler

On the other hand, to Westerners with long exposure to quality American, European and Australian films (and even to certain grades of kung-fu movies), India's 'masala movies' are unadulterated rubbish. Many sophisticated Indians agree as the reviews in various magazines indicate.

Fight scenes, in particular, are unbelievably unconvincing – two men will beat the living daylights out of each other for up to five minutes at a time yet without sustaining a single cut or bruise or shedding a drop of blood. Even a knockout is rare. Romance scenes are sickly sweet and unashamedly male chauvinist. Everyone lives happily ever after and, naturally, no-one ever has sex. Perish the thought!

The songs written for the movies are pure bubble-gum and rely heavily on electronic effects. The leading lady (or her ghost singer) is *always* a soprano permanently hovering around top C and the leading man *always* a tenor with tight pants. It's guaranteed to make you reach for the earplugs.

Fortunately, India does have some good directors who make films with an international appeal so it's worth looking out for them.

Geoff Crowther

section of the Crown & Anchor Bar on the corner of Mandik Rd and Mereweather Rd. This is Colaba's answer to Bangkok's Patpong Rd girlie bars though, naturally, here it's pure silk saris instead of mini-bikinis. It's a pick-up joint but there's no pressure and decorum is the name of the game. You'll probably be the only non-Indian there unless you go along with a friend. Normal prices prevail and it's usually packed out every night.

Things to Buy

Bombay has a number of intriguing markets and some feel it's much better, for shopping than Delhi. Chor Bazaar is Bombay's 'thieves' market'. It's off Grant Rd (Maulana Shaukatali Rd) and here you'll find a phenomenal collection of 'antiques', jewellery, wooden items, leather and general bric-a-brac. Mutton St has a particularly interesting collection of shops for miscellaneous 'junk'. Shops are generally open from 10 am but are closed on Fridays. The shopkeepers here really know the value of their stuff but it's still possible to pick up some interesting items.

Crawford Market, officially renamed Mahatma Phule Market, is the centre for flowers, fruit, vegetables, meat and fish in Bombay. This is the place to look for Bombay's two famous fish – the pomfret and the 'Bombay duck'. The market building was constructed in 1867 and is one of the most colourful and photogenic places in Bombay. Nearby is Javeri Bazaar, the jewellery centre off Mumbadevi Rd. There is some fantastic stuff here, especially silver belts and old statues and charms. Nearby is the brass bazaar on Kalbadevi Rd.

There are all sorts of places selling handicrafts, artefacts, antiques and art around the Colaba area. Shops in the Taj Hotel specialise in high quality – and high prices. Check the Jehangir Gallery by the Prince of Wales Museum too. The street stalls along S B Singh Rd in Colaba are good places to buy things, especially 'export reject' clothes which are incredibly cheap – good men's shirts are Rs 25. Also good is the Khadi Village Industries Emporium (☎ 204-3288) at 286 D Naoroji Rd, and the Central Cottage Industries Emporium (☎ 202-2491) at Apollo Bunder.

One of the best places in Bombay to buy silver and gold (or at least have a look at what you can't afford) is at Gupta Prakash Emporium, next to the American Express Bank (not the Travel Service) at Flora Fountain. Another (particularly for Moghul jewellery) is Suite A43 at the President Hotel. Don't let the manager's gruff mien put you off!

For handcrafted shoes, you can't beat Wing Son Chinese Shoemaker next to the Regent Cinema behind the Taj Intercontinental. He's not cheap but he's famous and no other shoes will ever fit so well.

Those searching for a good selection of Indian music tapes should try the Asiatics Department Store facing Churchgate Station.

Mereweather Rd at the back of the Taj Hotel is the centre for Kashmiri carpets and there's a superb choice but, as you might imagine from the location, prices are high. Make sure you check out the Jammu & Kashmir Government Emporium first before buying from any of these shops.

If Bombay is your last (or only) stop, you can also pick up souvenirs from all over the country from the various state government emporiums. In the World Trade Centre near Cuffe Parade are the Madhya Pradesh, Himachal Pradesh, Maharashtra and Jammu & Kashmir emporiums. The Uttar Pradesh and Bihar emporiums are on Sir P M Rd.

If you need to ship things out of India, the best people to see are Perfect Cargo Movers (☎ 22-3131), 56 Abdullabmia Currimjee Building, 4th floor, Jamabhoomi Marg, Fort. They're extremely reliable people and many travellers have recommended them.

Getting There & Away

Air Most airline offices are in the Nariman Point area between Maharshi Karve Marg and Marine Drive. Air India and Indian Airlines are both in the tall Air India Building at the junction of Madame Cama Rd and Marine Drive. The airport buses also depart from here.

If you're staying in the Colaba area of Bombay and want to make reservations with Indian Airlines, you don't have to go all the way to Nariman Point as there's an Indian Airlines desk in the Taj Mahal Hotel.

Some of the airlines with offices in Bombay include:

Aeroflot
    241/242 Nirmal, Nariman Point (☎ 22-1743)
Air France
    Maker Chambers VI, Nariman Point
    (☎ 202-4818)
Air India
    Air India Building, Nariman Point (☎ 202-4142)
Air Lanka
    Mittal Towers, Nariman Point (☎ 22-3299)
Air Mauritius
    Air India Building, Nariman Point (☎ 202-8474)
Alitalia
    Dalamal House, 206 Nariman Point (☎ 22-2163)
Bangladesh Biman
    199 J Tata Rd (☎ 22-3342)
British Airways
    202 B Veer Nariman Rd (☎ 22-0888)
Cathay Pacific Airways
    Taj Mahal Hotel, Apollo Bunder (☎ 202-9561)
Czechoslovak Airlines
    308/309 Raheja Chambers, 213 Nariman Point
    (☎ 22-0736)
East West Airlines
    'Sophia', 18 New Kantwadi Rd, off Perry Cross
    Rd, Bandra (☎ 643-6678)
Egypt Air
    Oriental House, 7 J Tata Rd (☎ 22-1415)
Ethiopian Airways
    Taj Mahal Hotel, Apollo Bunder (☎ 202-8787)
Gulf Air
    Maker Chamber V, Nariman Point (☎ 202-4065)
Indian Airlines
    Air India Building, Nariman Point (☎ 202-3031,
    287-6161)
Iraqi Airways
    Mayfair Building, 79 Veer Nariman Rd
    (☎ 22-1399)
Japan Air Lines
    3 Raheja Centre, Nariman Point (☎ 23-3136)
Kenya Airways
    199 J Tata Rd (☎ 22-0064)
KLM
    Khaitan Bhavan, 198 J Tata Rd (☎ 22-1372)
Kuwait Airlines
    86 Veer Nariman Rd (☎ 204-5351)

LOT (Polish Airways)
    Maker Arcade, Cuffe Parade (☎ 21-1440)
Lufthansa
    Express Towers, Nariman Point (☎ 202-3430)
Pakistan International Airlines
    Oberoi Towers, Nariman Point (☎ 202-1480)
Qantas
    Oberoi Towers, Nariman Point (☎ 202-9288)
Sabena
    Nirmal, Nariman Point (☎ 202-3240)
SAS
    World Trade Centre, Cuffe Parade (☎ 21-4180)
Singapore Airlines
    Air India Building, Nariman Point (☎ 202-3855)
Swissair
    Maker Chambers VI, 220 Nariman Point
    (☎ 287-0122)
Thai International
    World Trade Centre, Cuffe Parade (☎ 218-4180)
Vayudoot
    Airport (☎ 614-6583)
Zambia Airways
    Stadium House, Veer Nariman Rd (☎ 24-1251)

There is an extensive network of flights operating to and from Bombay's Sahar and Santa Cruz airports. The domestic terminal (Santa Cruz) is some distance away from the international terminal and there are two parts to it – the old terminal and the new one – about five minutes walk from each other. Bombay is the main international gateway to India, with far more flights than Delhi, Calcutta or Madras. It also has the busiest network of domestic flights.

On the major trunk routes, Indian Airlines has direct flights six times daily in either direction between Bombay and Delhi (two hours, US$115); two daily to Calcutta (2¼ hours, US$157); at least two daily to Madras (1¾ hours, US$110); at least three daily to Hyderabad (about 1½ hours, US$74), and three times daily to Bangalore (1½ hours, US$88).

On other routes, there are flights at least twice daily to Ahmedabad (one hour, US$47 – one of these continues on to Indore); once daily to Aurangabad (45 minutes, US$34 – these flights continue on to Udaipur, Jodhpur, Jaipur and Delhi); once daily to Bhavnagar (50 minutes, US$35); three times a week to Bhubaneswar (three hours via Raipur, US$136 – these flights continue on

to Calcutta); once daily to Coimbatore (1¾ hours, US$94); twice daily to Goa (one hour, US$46); once daily to Indore (one hour, US$53 – this flight continues on to Bhopal (2¼ hours, US$70), Gwalior (3½ hours, US$103) and Delhi; once daily direct to Jaipur (1½ hours, US$98); five times weekly to Jamnagar (one hour, US$52); twice daily to Kochi (Cochin) (1¾ hours, US$109); at least once daily to Kozhikode (Calicut) (1½ hours, US$98); twice daily to Mangalore (1¼ hours, US$75); once daily to Nagpur (1¼ hours, US$73); twice a week to Patna (three hours via Ranchi, US$157); once daily to Rajkot (one hour, US$46); once daily to Thiruvananthapuram (Trivandrum, two hours, US$124); once daily to Udaipur (1¼ hours, US$70; this flight continues on to Jodhpur 2¼ hours, US$87, Jaipur and Delhi); once daily to Vadodara (one hour, US$39); and three times a week to Varanasi (two hours, US$148; these flights continue on to Lucknow 3¾ hours, US$152).

Vayudoot schedules tend to change at short notice so you need to check before making plans. It usually has two flights daily in either direction between Bombay and Pune (40 minutes, US$54); daily between Bombay, Kolharpur (1¼ hours, US$95) and Belgaum (two hours, US$114); daily between Bombay, Porbander (1½ hours, US$107) and Keshod (2¼ hours, US$120), and six times weekly between Bombay, Kandla (1¾ hours, US$147) and Rajkot (2¾ hours, US$107).

Continental Aviation (☎ Bombay 287-2012) flies twice daily in either direction between Bombay and Pune (30 minutes, Rs 620); three times weekly to Delhi (two hours, Rs 2200), Vadodara (1¼ hours, Rs 840), Goa (1¾ hours, Rs 1000), Indore (1¾ hours, Rs 1026), Bhopal (2¾ hours, Rs 1348), Jabalpur (four hours, Rs 1800) and Raipur (5½ hours, Rs 1800).

East West Airlines has flights once daily in either direction between Bombay and Ahmedabad (US$47), Bangalore (US$88), Coimbatore (US$94), Delhi (US$115), Goa (US$46), Hyderabad (US$74), Jaipur (US$98), Kochi (Cochin) (US$109),

Kozhikode (Calicut) (US$98), Madras (US$110), Mangalore (US$75) and Thiruvananthapuram (Trivandrum) (US$124).

Bus Long-distance buses depart from the State Transport Terminal opposite Bombay Central railway station. It's fairly chaotic and there are almost no signs or information available in English.

The state bus companies of Maharashtra, Gujarat, Karnataka and Madhya Pradesh all have offices here and bookings can be made (☎ 37-4272) between 8 am and 11 pm. There is computerised advance booking available for journeys by deluxe buses.

The MTDC operates daily deluxe buses to Mahabaleshwar (seven hours, Rs 130) except during the monsoon, and to Aurangabad (11 hours, Rs 145) as well as other places. These are better than a lot of other deluxe buses as they are not the dreaded video coaches and the drivers don't seem to have the suicide wish that is common among Indian bus drivers. Bookings should be made in advance at the CDO Hutments, Madame Cama Rd.

Train Two railway systems operate out of Bombay. Central Railways handles services to the east and south, plus a few trains to the north. The booking office (☎ 204-3535) at Victoria Terminus (VT) is fully computerised, air-conditioned and there are over 70 ticket windows. You can queue up at any one of them after you fill in a form (available downstairs) but it can still take you over half an hour to get to the front of the queue. Windows 1 and 2 are specifically for dealing with foreigners and this is where you buy Indrail Passes. Despite all this, however, if you want to get a tourist-quota ticket, it still has to be arranged through the Foreign Tourist Guide in the kiosk on the main railway station concourse. The booking office is open daily from 9 am to 1 pm and 1.30 to 5 pm.

The other system operating out of Bombay is Western Railways, which has services to the north from Churchgate and Central stations. Bookings in 1st class can be made at the Western Railways booking office (☎ 29-1952) next to the Government of India tourist office opposite Churchgate, between 8 am and 8 pm Monday to Saturday, and 9 am to 4 pm Sunday. Tourist-quota tickets are issued from here, but only between 9.30 am and 3 pm and they must be paid for in foreign currency. The exchange rate is the same as the bank so you don't lose out. Refunds and change are given only in rupees. With the exception of the tourist quota, 2nd class has to be booked from Bombay Central (☎ 37-5986) between 9 am and 4 pm.

There are a number of Central Railways trains that do not depart from either Central or Churchgate but from Dadar Station, further north of Central. These trains can still be booked at Central Station and include the *Dadar to Madras Express*, the fastest train to Madras.

From Bombay it is 1588 km and 17 hours to Delhi, and the fare is Rs 181/751 in 2nd/1st. The *Rajdhani Express* is the fastest train; it's a special one-class train which costs Rs 580 in the air-con chair car, Rs 1170 in the air-con 1st-class sleeper. Fares include tea, dinner, coffee and breakfast on board.

Bombay to Calcutta is a lengthy 1968-km trip taking 32 hours and costing Rs 201/881 in 2nd/1st. Bombay to Madras is 1279 km and takes from 27 hours at a cost of Rs 164/642 in 2nd/1st.

There are no direct trains between Bombay and Goa (Vasco da Gama/Margao) and you must change at Miraj. The best two routes are:

1. The *Mahalaxmi Express*, which leaves Dadar Station daily at 8.45 pm and arrives at Miraj at 6.10 am. At Miraj you change to the *Mandovi Express* which leaves at 7 am daily and arrives at Vasco da Gama at 5.15 pm.
2. The *Konya Express*, which leaves Bombay VT daily at 8.45 am and arrives at Miraj at 7.45 pm. At Miraj you change to the *Gomantak Express* which leaves daily at 8.45 pm and arrives at Vasco da Gama at 9 am.

Boat The Bombay to Panaji (Goa) ferry has been suspended for years and although there's talk of starting up the service again (in the form of a hovercraft), nothing has happened. Check with the tourist office in Bombay about resumption of service.

Whilst there are no scheduled ferry services, Odyssey Tours (☎ 627-1690/1) at 1307 Everest Apartments, JP Rd, Versova, Anheri (W) 400061 operates tours along the coast between Bombay and Goa. More details can be found under Coastal Boat Tours in the Goa chapter.

Shipping Companies The addresses of some shipping companies in Bombay are:

Moghul Lines
    GN Vaidya Marg (☎ 286-1835)
Shipping Corporation of India
    Shipping House, Madame Cama Rd
    (☎ 202-6666)

Getting Around

To/From the Airport The airport bus service operates between the Air India Building at Nariman Point and Santa Cruz (domestic) and Sahar (international) airports. The journey from Nariman Point to Santa Cruz takes about one hour and costs Rs 29. To Sahar it takes about 1½ hours and costs Rs 35. From Nariman Point, departures are at 4, 5 and 8 am then hourly until 4 pm then at 6, 7 and 9 pm then hourly until 1 am. In peak hour the trip through Bombay's horribly congested streets can take well over two hours so don't cut things too fine.

Tickets for the buses are bought either on the buses themselves, at the Air India Building or at the terminals. Buses between the domestic and international terminals depart every hour and are free if you can show a ticket for a connecting flight, otherwise they cost Rs 10.

For those die-hards determined to get there on the cheap regardless of inconvenience, it is possible to get from Sahar Airport to central Bombay for less than Rs 15. First, take the airport bus from the international to the domestic terminal, then an ordinary bus to Vile Parle (No 321), followed by a suburban train to Churchgate. If you're

carrying more than a toothbrush, avoid doing anything as defiant as this in rush hours.

A taxi to the domestic airport on the meter costs about Rs 120 from Colaba, Rs 50 from Juhu but they generally ask for more (Rs 140 and Rs 60 respectively). It's a bit further to the international airport. During rush hours you won't find anyone who's prepared to use the meter, so expect to pay more, but don't agree to pay the Rs 200 often asked.

From the airport there is a police-operated taxi booth where you pay a set fare and are then assigned to a taxi. You give the driver your slip and there's no further fuss. You do, however, pay a bit more than the meter fare (plus adjustment card).

Bus Bombay has one of the best public transport systems of any major Indian city. There are lots of well-kept double-decker buses with fares beginning from Rs 0.50. They tend to be crowded, especially during rush hours, and Bombay's pickpockets are notoriously adept. Take care.

The buses are operated by BEST (Bombay Electric Supply & Transport) and have separate route maps for their extensive city and suburban services. From the Victoria Terminus Railway Station take a No 1, 6 Ltd, 7 Ltd, 103 or 124 to Electric House, a useful landmark in Colaba. From Bombay Central take a No 43, 70 or a 124. Ltd means 'limited stops'.

Train Bombay has an extensive system of electric trains, and it's virtually the only place in India where it's worth taking trains for intracity travel. But *avoid* rush hours when they are so crowded that you have to make your way towards the door at least three stops before you want to get out to have any chance of getting off, *and* you need to know which side the platform will be on – forget it. First class is also packed solid even though it is comparatively expensive.

The main suburban route of interest to travellers is Churchgate to Bombay Central and Dadar, with many other stops in between. There's a train every two to five minutes in either direction between 4.30 am and 10.30 pm. The fare between Churchgate and Central is Rs 1.80 in 2nd class and Rs 21 in 1st. A taxi over the same distance would cost you about Rs 25 on the meter. If you arrive at Bombay Central on the main railway system, your ticket covers you for the journey from there to the more convenient Churchgate Station.

Taxi Bombay has a large fleet of metered taxis but you'll often have to try a few before you find one willing to go where you want, especially during peak periods. As usual, the meters are out of date so you pay according to a fare conversion card which all drivers carry, regardless of how reluctant they are to pull them out when they'd prefer to tell you the first figure that comes into their head.

Drivers will probably reset the meters from dawn until late evening, but between midnight and dawn they're reluctant to take you anywhere on the meter so you'll have to negotiate a price.

AROUND BOMBAY
Elephanta Island

The island of Elephanta is about 10 km north-east of Apollo Bunder and is Bombay's major tourist attraction due to its four rock-cut temples. They are thought to have been cut out between 450 and 750 AD, and at that time the island was known as Gharapuri, the Fortress City. When the Portuguese arrived they renamed it Elephanta after the large stone elephant near the landing place. This figure collapsed in 1814 and the remaining pieces were removed to the Victoria Gardens in Bombay in 1864 and reassembled in 1912.

Unfortunately the Portuguese took their traditional disdain for other religions to its usual lengths at Elephanta, and did considerable damage to the sculptures. Although some people feel that Elephanta is not as impressive as the rock-cut temples of Ellora, the size, beauty and power of the sculptures are without equal.

The caves are reached by a stairway up the hillside from the ferry landing. Palanquins

are available for anybody in need of being carried up. There is one main cave with a number of large sculpted panels, all relating to Siva, and a separate lingam shrine.

The most interesting of the panels includes one of Trimurti, or the three-headed Siva, where he also takes the role of Brahma, the creator, and Vishnu, the preserver. In other panels Siva appears as Ardhanari, where he unites both sexes in one body – one side of the sculpture is male, one side female.

There are figures of Siva and his wife Parvati and of their marriage. In another panel Siva dances the Tandava, the dance that shakes the world. Parvati and their son, Ganesh, look on a little astonished. One of the best panels is that of Ravana shaking Kailasa. The demon king of Lanka decided to carry Siva and his companions off by the simple expedient of removing their Himalayan home, the mountain Kailasa. Parvati became panic-stricken at his energetic attempts to jerk the mountain free, but Siva calmly pushed the mountain back down with one toe, trapping Ravana beneath it for 10,000 years.

Getting There & Away Launches leave regularly from Apollo Bunder by the Gateway of India. The economy boats cost Rs 25 return (children Rs 15) and the deluxe launches including a guide are Rs 40 (children Rs 25). A good guide (and there are some excellent ones) can considerably increase your enjoyment and understanding – even, as one tubby little gentleman with glasses does, show you how Siva danced the Tandava.

Both types of launch leave every hour from 9 am to 2.15 pm and return after four hours. During the monsoon, the economy boats are suspended. Elephanta gets very crowded on weekends.

Aarey Milk Colony

Fresh milk is produced at this model milk-production centre. It's notable also for its hilltop viewpoint with a fine view over the island. There's an entry fee and not much to see.

Left: Rupmati's Pavilion, Mandu, Madhya Pradesh (BT)
Right: Creating dust in the early morning, Mandu, Madhya Pradesh (BT)
Bottom: Pot-bellied dwarves on architraves, Sanchi, Madhya Pradesh (BT)

Top Left: Gateway of India, Bombay (TW)
Top Right: Tea vendors, Bombay (GE)
Bottom Left: Stone carving on the Aina Mahal (Old Palace), Bhuj, Gujarat (HF)
Bottom Right: Gandhi statue, meeting point for local cows, Porbandar, Gujarat (HF)

Krishnagiri Upavan National Park

Reached via Borivli Station, the national park contains the Kanheri Caves and lakes Vihar, Tulsi and Powari, which act as reservoirs for much of Bombay's water supply.

At the entrance to the park there's a huge outdoor movie lot, including a fort frontage partly constructed from old oil drums. Also near the park entrance is, believe it or not, a Lion Safari Park. It's open from 9 am to 5 pm daily except Mondays (Tuesdays if Monday is a public holiday) and trips are made through the park in a 'safari vehicle'.

Kanheri Caves

Within the national park, about 42 km from Bombay, 109 caves line the side of a rocky ravine. The caves are Buddhist and date from around the 2nd to 9th century AD. Although there are so many of them, most are little more than holes in the rock and only a handful are of real interest. The most important is cave 3, the Great Chaitya Cave, which has a long colonnade of pillars around the *dagoba* at the back of the cave. Further up the ravine are some good views out to the sea.

Kanheri can be visited on the regular MTDC suburban tours, or you can take a train to Borivli Station and then a taxi for the 10 km or so to the caves. On Sundays and holidays there is a bus service from the station to the caves.

Beaches

Bombay's best known beach, Juhu, is too close to the city and not sanitary enough for a pleasant swim, but there are more remote beaches on the island. Manori beach is about 40 km out of the city. You can get to it via the station at Malad, 32 km out. There's an interesting fishing village and an old Portuguese church nearby.

A nice place to stay near the village of Manori is the *Manoribel Hotel* (☎ 24-1707) or there's the friendly *Hotel Dominica*. To get there, take the suburban electric train to Malad, then a bus (No 272) to Marve ferry, cross on the ferry and walk to the Manoribel. The walk to the beach is a little over a km from where the ferry stops at Manori.

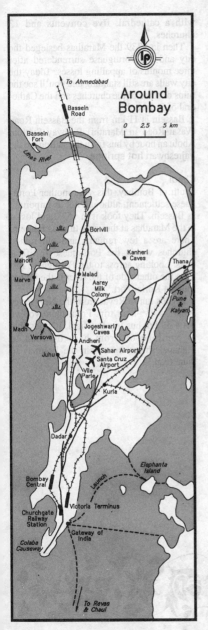

Around Bombay

To Ahmedabad

Bassein Road

Bassein Fort

Ulhas River

0   2.5   5 km

Borivli

Manori

Kanheri Caves

Malad

Thana

Marve

Aarey Milk Colony

To Pune & Kalyan

Madh

Jogeshwari Caves

Versova

Andheri

Sahar Airport

Juhu

Santa Cruz Airport

Vile Parle

Kurla

Dadar

Elephanta Island

Bombay Central

Launch

Churchgate Railway Station

Victoria Terminus

Colaba Causeway

Gateway of India

To Revas & Chaul

Other beaches around Bombay include Madh, 45 km out and reached via Malad. Versova is 29 km from the city, reached via Andheri Station, but it is very dirty. Getting to Uran involves a 74-km trip, the last 10 km by sea. Launches leave from the New Ferry Wharf.

Montpezir & Jogeshvari Caves

There are a few Hindu caves, one of which was converted into a Portuguese church, at Montpezir near Borivli. The Jogeshvari Caves are near Andheri Station.

Bassein

Just across the river which separates the mainland from Bombay island is Bassein, which was a Portuguese fortified city from 1534 to 1739. The Portuguese took Bassein at the same time as Daman, further north in Gujarat. They built a fort containing a city of such pomp and splendour that it came to be known as the Court of the North. Only the Hidalgos or aristocracy were permitted to live within the fort walls, and by the end of the 17th century there were 300 Portuguese and 400 Indian-Christian families here,

with a cathedral, five convents and 13 churches.

Then in 1739 the Marathas besieged the city and the Portuguese surrendered after three months of appalling losses. Today the city walls are still standing and you'll see the ruins of some of the churches and the Cathedral of St Joseph.

Bassein is 11 km from the Bassein Road (Vasai Road in Marathi) Railway Station. About an hour by bus from the station are the Vajreshwari **hot springs**.

Chaul

South of Bombay, this was another Portuguese settlement, although not as important as Bassein. They took it in 1522 and lost it to the Marathas at the same time as Bassein. There are a few remains and old ruined churches within the Portuguese fortifications. Looking across to the Portuguese fort from the other side of the river is the hilltop Muslim Korlai Fort.

Ferries run to Revas from the New Ferry Wharf, a 1½-hour trip. From there you've got a 30-km bus trip to Chaul. It's possible to continue on from here by road to Mahabaleshwar, or to join the Bombay to Pune road.

Maharashtra

Population: 79 million
Area: 307,690 sq km
Capital: Bombay
People per sq km: 256
Main Language: Marathi
Literacy Rate: 63%

The state of Maharashtra is one of the largest in India, both in terms of population and in area. Its booming capital, Bombay, makes it not only one of the most important states economically, but also a major gateway for overseas visitors. From Bombay you can head off into India in a number of directions, but most travellers will either be going south to Goa through Pune (Poona), with its famous ashram, or north-east to the amazing cave temples of Ajanta and Ellora. Most of the state stands on the high Deccan plateau. Historically this was the main centre for the Maratha Empire, which defied the Moghuls for so long, and which, under the fearless rule of Shivaji, carved out a large part of central India as its domain.

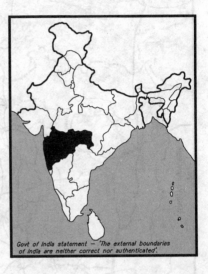

Govt of India statement — 'The external boundaries of India are neither correct nor authenticated'.

Cave Architecture

The rock-cut caves in Maharashtra have several distinct design elements. The Buddhist caves, which are generally the older ones, are either chaityas (temples) or viharas (monasteries). Chaityas are usually deep and narrow with a stupa at the end of the cave. There may be a row of columns down both sides of the cave and around the stupa.

The viharas are usually not as deep and narrow as the chaitya caves. They were normally intended as living and sleeping quarters for the monks and often have rows of cells along both sides. In the back there is a small shrine room, usually containing an image of the Buddha. At Ajanta, the cliff face into which the caves are cut is very steep and there is often a small verandah or entrance porch in front of the main cave. At Ellora the rock face is more sloping and the verandah

or porch element generally becomes a separate courtyard.

The cave temples reach their peak of complexity and design in the Hindu caves at Ellora, and particularly in the magnificent Kailasa Temple. Here they can hardly be called caves, for the whole enclosure is open to the sky. In design they are much like other temples of that era – except that instead of being built up from the bottom they were cut down from the top. They are an imitation of the conventional architecture of that period.

Though the caves are notable for their sculptures and paintings, the famous Ajanta 'frescoes' are not, technically speaking, frescoes at all. A fresco is a painting done on a wet surface which absorbs the colour. The Ajanta paintings are, more correctly, tempera, since they were painted on a dry surface. The rough-hewn rock walls were coated with a cm-thick layer of clay and cow dung mixed with rice husks. A final coat of lime was then applied to produce the finished

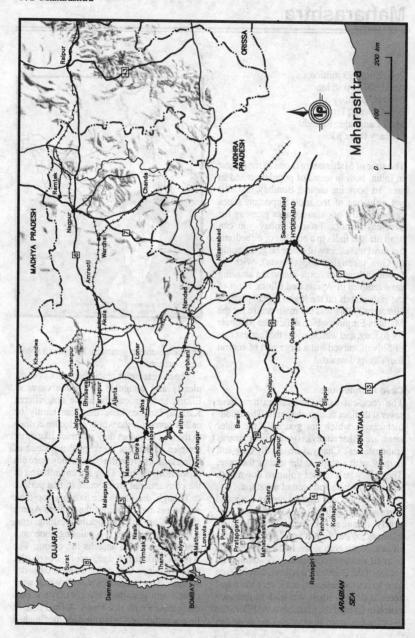

surface on which the artist painted. This surface was then polished to produce a high gloss.

Bombay Area

MATHERAN

Population: 4700

Matheran, the nearest hill station to Bombay, is 171 km from the city via Neral on the Bombay to Pune railway line. The name means Jungle Topped or Wooded Head, which is just what it is – an undulating hilltop cloaked in shady trees. It's the abundance of shade as much as the 700 to 800-metre altitude which makes Matheran a slightly cooler place than Bombay. Matheran became a popular hill station during the days of the Raj; Hugh Malet is credited with its 'discovery' in 1850.

Matheran sprawls north-south along the hilltop. Many km of walking tracks lead to the viewpoints that ring the station; at many of them the ground drops sheer to the plains far, far below. On a clear day the view can be fantastic and it's possible to see, and even hear, Bombay from Porcupine or Louisa Point. Even in the hazy air of the pre-monsoon dry season, the eerie views of surrounding hills are very fine.

Porcupine Point is a good place for catching the sunset, but Panorama Point, at the extreme north, is said to have the finest views. The western side, from Porcupine to Louisa Point, is known as Cathedral Rocks, and Neral can be seen far below, straddling the central railway line. At the south, near One Tree Hill, a trail down to the valley below is known as Shivaji's Ladder, so called because the Maratha leader is said to have used it.

These days Matheran has become the hangout of trendy young day-trippers from Bombay who come equipped complete with ghetto blasters and whisky. The result is that the quiet and peaceful atmosphere is well and truly disturbed. On weekdays there are far fewer than on weekends. During the Diwali

Festival in November it is impossible to find a place to stay unless you have made a reservation well in advance. It's a good time to avoid Matheran anyway as the overcrowding is severe.

During the monsoon season Matheran virtually closes up. Very few of the hotels and restaurants remain open, and the walking trails become very muddy (none of the roads are surfaced). The only advantage of visiting during the monsoon is that there are very few people around, and the hotels that do remain open reduce their tariffs significantly.

Getting to Matheran is half the fun; from Neral you take a tiny narrow-gauge toy train up the 26-km route to the hill station. It's a two-hour ascent as the train twists, turns and winds its way up the steep slopes. Food and drink vendors cling to the outside and at one point you pass through 'one kiss tunnel'. Alternatively, you can take a taxi or minibus from Neral which is much quicker (half an hour) but then you'll be faced with a 40-minute walk into Matheran or will have to hire a horse or cycle-rickshaw as motor vehicles are prohibited in Matheran itself. Only the toy train goes right into the centre of town.

Information

The tourist office is a kiosk diagonally opposite the railway station on M G Marg. It hands out maps of Matheran but not much else. It's open every day of the week.

There is a branch of the State Bank of India on M G Marg.

Entry to Matheran costs Rs 7 (Rs 2 for children). Coming by train, you pay this leaving the station. By road, you pay at the taxi stand.

Places to Stay

As Matheran is very spread out, much of the accommodation (and some of the best of it) is out of the actual town centre, and so is inconvenient if you are carrying a backpack. It may also mean that you are more or less compelled to eat at your hotel in the evening as none of the paths are lit at night. Many hotels, in any case, offer only full-board rates.

As with most hill stations, it's important to know the checkout time since this is often as early as 7 am.

Places to Stay – bottom end

Budget accommodation is limited. Most of it is along M G Marg and the road above it running parallel. The staff at quite a few places don't speak a word of English.

One of the cheapest places is *Khan's Cosmopolitan Hotel* (☎ 240) on M G Marg, which is a rather primitive rambling place, but is well run and has a range of rooms. Singles/doubles with common bath are Rs 60/120. English is spoken and there's a restaurant.

Better is the friendly, Christian-run *Hope Hall Hotel* (☎ 253), M G Marg, which is basic and offers lodging only at Rs 110 a double (no singles). Another is the *Hotel Prasanna* opposite the station on M G Marg. It offers full board at Rs 170 per person (vegetarian food) or Rs 210 per person (nonveg food).

Also relatively cheap but very inconvenient for the centre of town is the Maharashtra Tourism Development Corporation (MTDC) *Tourist Camp* (☎ 277), next to the taxi park, which has dorm beds for Rs 30 as well as double rooms for Rs 100 and Rs 120 plus tax. There are also cottages which sleep four and five people.

Places to Stay – middle

Right opposite the railway station is the *Hotel Rangoli* which is basic and nothing special. It charges Rs 350/400 for singles/doubles with full board.

Up on the road running parallel to M G Marg is the *Hotel Meghdoot* (☎ 266) which offers full board for Rs 212/243/318 for singles/doubles/triples. No English is spoken. The *Sayeban Lodge*, opposite the back of Khan's, has doubles at Rs 250 and four-bed rooms at Rs 600 with full board. It's clean and tidy and all the rooms have attached bath and fan but no English is spoken.

Better is the *Gujarat Bhavan Hotel* (☎ 278), a 'resort' hotel, which offers regular rooms at Rs 200 per person, deluxe rooms at Rs 250 per person and cottages at Rs 350 per person, all with full board. The hotel is strictly vegetarian and there's no bar.

Close by is the *Royal Hotel Matheran* (☎ 357), a two-star 'resort' hotel and a good choice. In the high season ordinary rooms with full board cost Rs 250 per person and air-con rooms with TV and full board are Rs 400 per person. In the low season it costs Rs 150 per person Monday to Thursday and Rs 180 per person Friday to Sunday. There's a bar, children's park and a variety of indoor and outdoor games. It's popular with Indian families.

Further afield are two friendly Goan-run lodges which have a more homely atmosphere. The first is the *Silvan Lodge* (☎ 1) which offers full board at Rs 300 a single and Rs 250 per person in a double room. Close by is the *West End Hotel* (☎ 259) which offers the same rates. There's a tennis court at the West End.

Places to Stay – top end

Up above the railway station is the *Rugby Hotel* (☎ 291), Vithalrao Kotwal Marg, an older type of place with a certain charm but somewhat run down, though the prices don't reflect this. The cheapest rooms, with full board and including all taxes, are Rs 961 a double plus there are more expensive rooms at Rs 1047 a double. Air-con rooms with full board are Rs 1160 a double, and there are more expensive suites at Rs 1221 a double.

Cheaper is the *Regal Hotel* (☎ 43) along with its quieter annex across the road which offers full board in the regular rooms at Rs 540 a double, Rs 665 in the deluxe rooms, Rs 840 in the superdeluxe rooms, and Rs 910 in the 'Regal' room. There are also more expensive suites and air-con rooms. It's a big place with Western disco music blaring out all day and is popular with Indian families.

Further up the same road is the *Brightlands Resort* (☎ 244), another lively place with a swimming pool and disco nights. Full board here for rooms without air-con is Rs

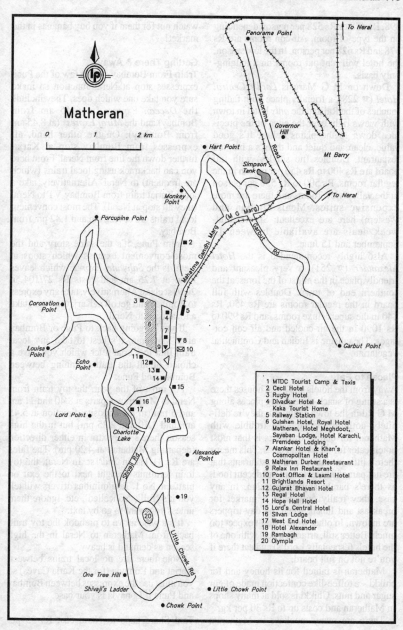

Matheran

0   1   2 km

To Neral

Panorama Point

Governor Hill

Panorama Road

Mt Barry

Hart Point

Simpson Tank

To Neral

Monkey Point

Garbut Rd

Mahatma Gandhi Marg (M G Marg)

Porcupine Point

Coronation Point

Louisa Point

Echo Point

Garbut Point

Lord Point

Charlotte Lake

Alexander Point

Shivaji Rd

Little Chowk Rd

One Tree Hill

Shivaji's Ladder

Little Chowk Point

Chowk Point

1 MTDC Tourist Camp & Taxis
2 Cecil Hotel
3 Rugby Hotel
4 Divadkar Hotel &
   Kaka Tourist Home
5 Railway Station
6 Gulshan Hotel, Royal Hotel
   Matheran, Hotel Meghdoot,
   Sayeban Lodge, Hotel Karachi,
   Premdeep Lodging
7 Alankar Hotel & Khan's
   Cosmopolitan Hotel
8 Matheran Durbar Restaurant
9 Relax Inn Restaurant
10 Post Office & Laxmi Hotel
11 Brightlands Resort
12 Gujarat Bhavan Hotel
13 Regal Hotel
14 Hope Hall Hotel
15 Lord's Central Hotel
16 Silvan Lodge
17 West End Hotel
18 Hotel Alexander
19 Rambagh
20 Olympia

398, Rs 478 or Rs 528 per person depending on the type of room. Air-con rooms are Rs 578 and Rs 628 per person. In the low season, the hotel will rent out rooms on a lodging-only basis.

Down on M G Marg is *Lord's Central Hotel* (☎ 228), a friendly place with fading touches of the Raj and the *only* hotel in town with views right over the edge of the precipice down to the plains below. It's good value, clean and quiet and there's a bar and restaurant. Doubles (no singles) with full board are Rs 400 to Rs 450 per person in the regular rooms, Rs 500 to Rs 550 per person in the valley view rooms and there are more expensive suites. Meals (Indian and Western) here are excellent. Special mid-week deals are available between 15 September and 15 June.

Also highly recommended is the *Hotel Alexander* (☎ 251), a very pleasant and friendly place in the midst of the forest at the southern end of town. Doubles with full board in the regular rooms are Rs 450, Rs 840 in the superdeluxe rooms, and Rs 990 to Rs 1090 in the air-cooled and air-con cottages. The cuisine is Indian and Continental vegetarian.

Places to Eat

Away from the hotels and guest houses there is a string of snack-style eating places along M G Rd in the town centre but they're definitely nothing special. The trouble with Matheran for budget travellers is that most hotels cater for their own guests. This means there's little incentive for the restaurants that are not part of a hotel to turn out decent food, as there's barely any competition. In any case, they really only have a market for breakfast and lunch, when the day-trippers are in town. In other words, don't expect too much. Better still, arrange a deal with one of the hotels (especially Lord's) and eat there if you're not on full board.

Matheran is famed for its honey and for chikki – a toffee-like confection made of gur sugar and nuts. Chikki is sold at many shops in Matheran and costs up to Rs 30 per kg.

There are many monkeys in Matheran; watch out for them if you buy bananas in the market!

Getting There & Away

Train From Bombay, only a few of the Pune expresses stop at Neral Junction so make sure you take one which does. They include the *Deccan Express* (at 6.45 am from Bombay) and the *Miraj Express* (at 8.45 am from Bombay). On the other hand, all expresses from Bombay stop at Karjat further down the line from Neral. From here you can backtrack using local trains (which are frequent) to Neral. Alternatively, take a local Karjat train from Bombay VT to Neral (they all stop at Neral). The most convenient local trains are at 7.22 am and 1.42 pm from Bombay.

From Pune, it's the same story and the most convenient express which stops at Neral is the *Sahyadri Express* which leaves Pune at 7.25 am and costs Rs 27/104 in 2nd/1st class. Alternatively, take any express to Bombay and get off at Karjat and then take a local train to Neral.

If you're going back to Pune or Bombay after Matheran, it's best to take any local train first to Karjat after which you have a choice of all the trains running between Bombay and Pune.

For most of the year, the toy train from Neral to Matheran departs at 8.40 and 11 am and 5 pm (in the opposite direction at 5.45 am, and 1.10 and 2.35 pm) but in the high season there's one extra in either direction (departing Matheran at 4.20 pm). The fares are Rs 31/111 in 2nd/1st. In Neral, the toy train terminus is right next to the exit on platform No 1. Taxi/minibus drivers will tell you it's 'full', 'cancelled', etc. Ignore them unless you want to go by taxi.

It's a wise move to prebook the toy train back from Matheran to Neral in the high season as demand is heavy.

Note there are no local trains between Karjat and Lonavla (for the Karla Caves) so you must use the expresses between Bombay and Pune if Lonavla is your base.

Taxi Share taxis to Neral cost Rs 35 per

person and they leave when full – usually four passengers. If you don't want to wait then you have the option of paying the full Rs 140 and they'll go immediately. There are plenty in either direction daily and the trip takes half an hour.

Getting Around
In Matheran itself the only transport is by horse or cycle-rickshaw – one man pulls, two push (or hold it back on the descents). If your gear is too heavy to carry very far, and you're staying a long way from the station, you may want to use one to get your bags to the hotel. Ponies can also be hired for riding on the many trails that wind around Matheran.

Taxis and minibuses stop 2½ km or 45 minutes walk from the centre. From here, you can either walk (quickest along the railway line), hire a horse (Rs 40) or a cycle-rickshaw (Rs 50) into the centre. It's quicker to walk *into* the centre than it is to hire a cycle-rickshaw but this isn't necessarily true in the opposite direction.

The railway station is right in the centre of town.

KARLA & BHAJA CAVES
Situated 126 km south-east of Bombay on the main rail line to Pune, Lonavla (sometimes spelt Lonavala) is the place from which to visit the Karla and Bhaja caves. There is nothing of interest in the town itself unless you're a Bombay yuppie with a country cottage or a real estate developer looking for a contract to build one. In that respect, the town has changed dramatically over the last few years from a sleepy little backwater into a major development area with new hotels, restaurants and exclusive country cottages going up all the time. The influx of money has also attracted a lot of beggars.

It is possible to visit the caves in a day trip from either Bombay or Pune if you don't mind rushing and hiring an auto-rickshaw from Lonavla for the day.

The Karla Cave is about 11 km from Lonavla, about 1½ km off the main road. The Bhaja Caves are about three km off the other side of the main road across the railway

tracks. If you plan on walking to the latter, take a local train from Lonavla to Malavli first.

Information
The 'Tourist Information' place on the main road opposite the Hotel Gurukripa is nothing of the sort – it's just an agency for two or three of the hotels in Lonavla and it doesn't have any other information.

Karla Cave
It's a steep 500-metre km climb up the hillside to Karla Cave. The cave temple is Hinayana Buddhist and was completed around 80 BC. One of the best preserved of its type in India, it dates from the time when this style of temple was at its height in terms of design purity.

A beautifully carved 'sun window' filters the light in towards the small stupa at the inner end of the deep, narrow cave. Unfortunately an ugly little modern temple has been erected just outside the cave entrance. Inside, the pillars are topped by two kneeling elephants and two seated figures. Generally the figures are male and female, but sometimes they are two women. The roof of the cave is ribbed with teak beams said to be original; there may once have been such beams at Ajanta and Ellora, but they are now gone. On the sides of the vestibule are carved elephant heads which once had real ivory tusks.

Other carvings can also be seen along the sides. A pillar topped by four back-to-back lions, an image usually associated with Ashoka, stands outside the cave. It may be older than the cave itself.

There are some small monastery, or vihara, caves at Karla, further round the hillside. Some of these have been converted into Hindu shrines.

If possible, avoid going to the Karla Cave at weekends or on public holidays, when it is invaded by the transistor radio and picnic mobs from Bombay and Pune. The noise and mess which they create isn't going to do anything for your appreciation of this beautiful site. Bhaja is too far from the main road for this to happen on the same scale, but it does get its fair share too.

Bhaja Caves

It's a fairly rough route from the main road to the 18 Bhaja Caves. They're in a lusher, greener setting than the Karla Cave's dry hillside, and are thought to date from around 200 BC. Cave 12, a chaitya cave similar in style to the Karla Cave, is the most important. About 50 metres past this is a strange group of 14 stupas, five inside and nine outside the cave. The last cave on the south side has some fine sculptures.

A few minutes walk past the last cave is a beautiful waterfall which, during the monsoon and shortly afterwards, has enough water for a good swim. From the waterfall you can see the old forts on the hilltops.

Other Caves & Forts

Further along the line, six km south-east of Kamshet station, are the **Bedsa Caves**. They are thought to be more recent than the better executed Karla Cave. At one time the roof of the main cave was probably painted.

There are a number of old forts in the

vicinity, including the hilltop **Lohagen Fort**, six km from Malavli, which was taken twice by Shivaji. Above the Bhaja Caves is **Visapur Fort**.

Khandala, before Lonavla, is picturesquely situated overlooking a ravine. In the wet season there is a fine waterfall near the head of the ravine.

Places to Stay

Lonavla Probably the best of the cheapies and certainly very friendly is the *Hotel Swiss Cottage* (☎ 2561) which is clean and tidy and has dorm beds for Rs 50, singles/doubles for Rs 125/225 and suites (four beds) for Rs 550. There's a 30% discount on these rates Monday to Thursday or if you are staying a minimum of one week. They also offer full board 'packages' at Rs 99 per person (dorm bed) and Rs 184 per person (in a double room) including tax and service charges. A 'Swiss cottage' it certainly isn't (it's a concrete block) but it is in a quiet and shady location. Recommended.

Cheaper is the *Janata Hotel*, another concrete block, which is simple and clean and costs Rs 50 per person in rooms with attached bath.

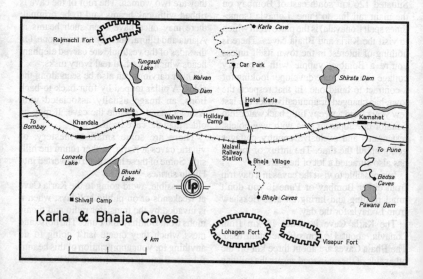

Karla & Bhaja Caves

0   2   4 km

Not far from here is the *Matruchhaya Lodge* (☎ 2875), an old-style house in quiet surroundings which is often full. It costs Rs 100/120 with attached bath.

Above the main road in the centre of town is the delightfully ramshackle *Pitale Lodging & Boarding* (☎ 359) with its wide verandahs and olde-worlde atmosphere, bar, garden restaurant, shady trees and friendly staff. It wouldn't suit everyone but it's cheap at Rs 100 a double with common bath.

Diagonally opposite here is the *Highway Lodge* which has a friendly owner who appreciates a joke. It's often full, and is somewhat overpriced at Rs 150 a double.

Avoid the *Hotel Gurukripa* next to the bus station (noisy and only vaguely habitable) and the *Hotel Mahalaxmi* (filthy).

Going up in price, you can't beat the *Hotel Chandralok* (☎ 2294), an excellent place with keen, friendly staff and very tasty, reasonably priced all-you-can-eat vegetarian Gujarati thalis for Rs 25 (Rs 30 to Rs 35 for 'special' thalis). They have dorm beds for Rs 50 per person plus single/double/triple rooms for Rs 140/180/270 including tax. All the rooms have attached bath with hot water 24 hours a day. Checkout time is 10 am.

On the same road is the older *Adarsh Hotel* (☎ 2353) which backs onto the bus station so avoid the rooms on that side. There are no singles; 'economy' doubles are Rs 110, 'luxury' doubles Rs 175 to Rs 300 and triples are Rs 250. There are also air-con suites for Rs 475.

Further afield is the *Hotel Nicky Resort* (☎ 2529) opposite the Janata Hotel. It's decidedly overpriced at Rs 300 a double (no singles). Facilities are minimal though the rooms do have attached bath. Next door is the *N T Shahani Health Home*, a brand new place with 62 rooms with attached bath 'run on a non-commercial basis' as the blurb has it. It's very popular with Indian couples and worth checking out.

Going into the top bracket, the brand new and very well appointed *Hotel Dhiraj* (☎ 3200) on the main road has doubles without air-con for Rs 390 or Rs 550 with air-con plus there are deluxe doubles for Rs 750. There's a swimming pool, car park, bar and restaurant. Pity about the location!

Tucked away down a quiet leafy lane but without a swimming pool is the *Hotel Star Regency* (☎ 3331), Justice Telang Rd, which has double rooms (no singles) for Rs 450 and Rs 550 as well as deluxe rooms for Rs 650.

Across the other side of the railway lines from the main town is the *Ryewood Retreat* (☎ Bombay 811-5315) which consists of a series of very spacious and comfortable cottages with all amenities. It costs Rs 515/750 for singles/doubles.

Top of the line is the *Fariyas Holiday Resort* (☎ 2701), 8 Frichley Hill, on the outskirts of town. It's a five-star hotel with all the facilities you'd expect including an indoor swimming pool. Full board costs Rs 750 a double plus there are suites (four beds) for Rs 1500.

Karla If you prefer to stay close to Karla Cave, there's the MTDC's *Holiday Camp* (☎ 30) just off the Bombay to Pune road near the caves. It has double rooms at Rs 125 and Rs 150 plus there are suites and cottages (all of which sleep four people) for Rs 250 to Rs 400. The more expensive of the latter are air-con. The Camp has its own bar and restaurant. From July to September there's a discount of 10% on weekends and 25% on weekdays.

The *Hotel Karla* is in a good location, at the Karla Caves junction, but the rooms are filthy and it's not in any way a pleasant place to stay.

Places to Eat
Lonavla Most of the best places to eat are the restaurants at the hotels mentioned above. Otherwise, try the *Lonavla Restaurant* on the main road which offers Sindhi-Punjabi veg and non-veg food as well as tandoori dishes. Close by is the *Mehfil Bar & Restaurant*, attached to the side of the Hotel Gurukripa, which is slightly more expensive.

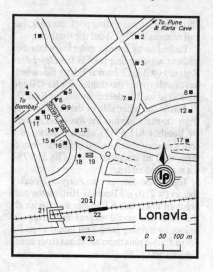

1 Ashok Hotel
2 Shamiana Lodge
3 Matruchhaya Lodge
4 Pitale Lodging & Boarding
5 Hotel Annapurna
6 Lonavla Restaurant & Mehfil Bar & Restaurant
7 Hotel Star Regency
8 Janata Hotel
9 Bus Stand
10 Hotel Dhiraj
11 Highway Lodge
12 Hotel Nicky Resort
13 Adarsh Hotel
14 Sagar Snacks
15 Hotel Chandralok
16 Hotel Mahalaxmi
17 Hotel Swiss Cottage
18 Bank of Baroda
19 Post Office
20 Tourist Office
21 Footbridge
22 Railway Station
23 Central Restaurant

Getting There & Away

Lonavla is on the main Bombay to Pune road and railway line so there are plenty of trains and buses from both cities.

Bus The timetable at Lonavla bus station is entirely in Marathi except for the buses to Dadar (a suburb of Bombay). Most of the buses are pretty rough and ready and you'd be better off using the trains.

Train Unlike getting to Neral (for Matheran), all express trains between Bombay and Pune stop at Lonavla. There's also a frequent local shuttle train between Pune and Lonavla. The 128-km trip to Bombay takes about three hours and costs Rs 31/111 in 2nd/1st. The 64-km trip to Pune takes about 1½ hours by express train and about two hours on the shuttle train and costs Rs 20/69 in 2nd/1st class.

Getting Around

In theory there are local buses about a dozen times a day between Lonavla and Karla and

to the Rajmachi Fort. Unfortunately the timetable seems to be imaginary; the buses arrive full and leave even fuller, everybody fights like crazy to get on and you never know which buses are going where because there are no signs.

You can save a lot of time and frustration by hiring an auto-rickshaw but this works out quite expensive, especially if you are alone. The prices are fairly standard: Lonavla to Karla Rs 50, Rs 80 for the return trip including waiting time, and Rs 150 for Lonavla-Karla-Bhaja-Lonavla including waiting time at both sites. Even if you do hire an auto, there is still quite a walk to both sites from the car parks. In the monsoon the road to Bhaja is closed to vehicles at the Malavli railway crossing.

If you don't mind doing some walking, you can keep costs down to less than Rs 5 and still get around comfortably in a day. Catch the 9 am bus from Lonavla to Karla Cave, then walk to Bhaja Cave (five km, 1½ hours), walk back to Malavli railway station (three km, one hour) and catch a local train back to Lonavla.

Southern Maharashtra

PUNE (Poona)

Population: 2,485,000

Shivaji, the great Maratha leader, was raised in Pune, which was granted to his grandfather in 1599. Later it became the capital of the Peshwas, but in 1817 went to the British, under whom it became the capital of the region during the monsoon. It has a rather more pleasant climate at that time than muggy Bombay.

With the express commuter train, the *Deccan Queen*, connecting Pune to Bombay in just over three hours, many people who can't afford the sky-high prices of accommodation in Bombay actually commute daily between the two cities. As a result some of the big-city influence has rubbed off on Pune, so fashion shops and fast-food outlets are springing up all the time.

Although Pune has a number of points of interest and can be conveniently visited if you're heading from Bombay to Aurangabad (for Ajanta and Ellora) or to Goa, its major attraction for Western visitors is the Shree Rajneesh (Osho) Ashram. Most Indians will assume that you're in Pune for just that and the ashram is so well known that it was formerly even included on the city bus tour, where, in a superb reversal of roles, Indians flocked to view Westerners.

Orientation

The city is at the confluence of the Mutha and Mula rivers. The main concentration of hotels and restaurants is around the railway station.

The main bus station, which is called Swargate, is in the south of town by the Nehru Stadium.

The main street of the city is Mahatma Gandhi Rd (M G Rd), which is lined with trendy fashion shops, electronic goods suppliers, banks, hotels and restaurants. Just to the east of it, though, the streets have the atmosphere of the traditional bazaar-town as you walk south.

Information

There's a tourist information counter at the railway station but it basically only sells tickets for the MTDC city bus tours and to Mahabaleshwar. It has no map of the city. The tours also leave from outside the station. The regional tourist office is in the government offices, known as Central Buildings, but is not of great use.

The best place to change money by far is Thomas Cook, Thakkar House, off East St (between East St and M G Rd). It's open during normal business hours and on Saturday morning until 12.30 pm. They change cheques in less than five minutes with no fuss and provide a certificate. Normal banks can be strange about changing cheques and often direct you elsewhere.

The best bookshop in Pune is Manney's Book Seller, Clover Centre, 7 Moledina Rd (near the junction with M G Rd).

Pune's telephone area code is 0212.

Rajneesh (Osho) Ashram

After a 4½-year sojourn in the USA at the agricultural commune and ashram of Rajneeshpuram in Oregon, Bhagwan Rajneesh was deported to India in November 1985 after having been found guilty of immigration fraud charges and fined US$400,000. Unfortunately, the Indian government was no more sympathetic to the Bhagwan than the Americans and, shortly after his return, refused visa extensions for Rajneesh's new American secretary, his British doctor and a number of other close followers.

For the next six months, the hierarchy set out on a world odyssey in an attempt to find a country which would allow them to settle and set up a new community. It was a futile effort and they were deported from or denied entry to a total of 21 countries!

Following this, Rajneesh returned to Bombay and, after a six month stay there, finally took up residence again at the Pune ashram in January 1987. Despite the interregnum, the ashram in Koragaon Park once again flourished and thousands of foreigners flocked to attend his nightly discourses and

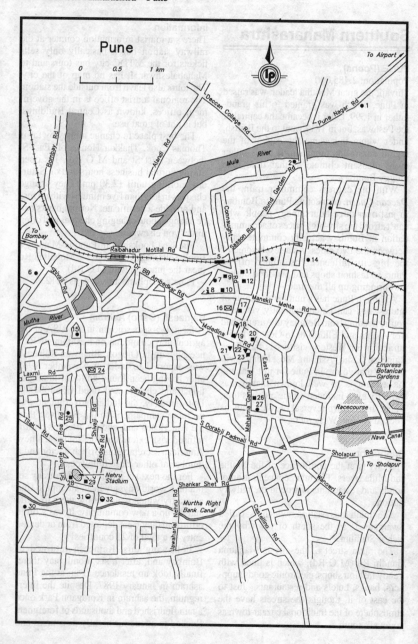

Pune

0   0.5   1 km

meditation courses. Most were from Germany, Italy and Japan. However, from early 1989 until his death in January 1990, Rajneesh (or Osho as he preferred to be called) once again reverted to silence as he had done so once previously whilst in America.

Before his death, the orange clothes and the *mala* (the string of beads and photograph of the Bhagwan worn around the neck), which used to be the distinctive mark of Bhagwan followers, had been discarded. This was done so that his followers could, according to the ashram press office, 'avoid harassment and molestation by the authorities'.

Rajneesh was one of the most popular of India's 'export gurus' and, without doubt, the most controversial. He followed no particular religion, tradition or philosophy and his often acerbic criticism and dismissal of various religious and political leaders made him many enemies the world over. What particularly outraged his Indian critics was his advocacy of sex as a path to enlightenment, an approach which earned him the epithet 'Sex Guru' from the Indian press.

Nevertheless, it was a curious blend of Californian pop-psychology and Indian mysticism which he used to motivate his followers. His last technique, tagged 'The Mystic Rose', involved following a regime of laughing for three hours a day for seven days, crying for three hours a day for seven days, followed by becoming a 'watcher on the hill' (whatever that might be) for three hours a day for seven days. The Bhagwan felt that it was 'the most important breakthrough in meditation since Buddha's vipassana, created 25 centuries ago'. Indeed, he began to lean heavily in favour of Zen Buddhism in the years before his death and, at one point, even declared himself to be the Buddha.

Since his death, the ashram at Pune has continued to prosper and still attracts thousands of devotees, but there has been a movement away from it in favour of a new living guru, Poonjaji, an octogenarian godman who has his ashram in Lucknow and is himself a devotee of Ramana Maharishi.

If your main reason for coming to India is to visit the Rajneesh Ashram, don't put that on your visa application as you may be knocked back. For people wishing to stay, ashram authorities demand that you provide an AIDS/HIV-negative certificate.

Raja Kelkar Museum

This interesting museum is one of Pune's real delights. The exhibits are the personal collection of Shri Dinkar Kelkar, a smiling old man in a white dhoti whom visitors will often see wandering around the building. The museum has recently expanded into the building next door so many of the pieces which used to be in storage are now on display.

Amongst the items you might see are Peshwa and other miniatures, a coat of armour made of fish scales, a bizarre collection of musical instruments, carved doors and windows, hookah pipes, strange locks, oil lamps and a superb collection of betel-nut cutters. The museum is housed in a quaint purple, red and green Rajasthani-style building and is open from 8.30 am to 12.30 pm and 3 to 6 pm daily; entry is Rs 2. It is also on the itinerary of the city tour but they rush you round in such a hurry that you'll see almost nothing. It's best to go on your own and spend several hours there.

Shanwarwada Palace

In a section of the town where narrow and winding streets form a maze stands the imposing, fortress-like Shanwarwada Palace. Built in 1736, the massive walls enclosed the palace of the Peshwa rulers – until it was burnt down in 1828. Today there is a pleasant two-hectare garden inside and little signs proclaiming which rooms used to stand where. The palace is entered through sturdy doors studded with spikes in order to dissuade enemy elephants from leaning too heavily against the entrance! In a nearby street the Peshwa rulers used to execute offenders by having elephants trample them to death.

Tribal Museum

Just south of the railway line and east of the railway station is this excellent museum. It is open daily from 10 am to 5 pm. City bus tours do not call here.

Temples & Gardens

The **Empress Botanical Gardens** have fine tropical trees and a small zoo nearby. The moated **Saras Buag Ganesh Temple** is in **Peshwa Park**. The **Bund Gardens**, on the banks of the river, are a popular place for an evening stroll. The bridge here crosses the river to Yeravda and the Gandhi National Memorial (formerly the Aga Khan's Palace). The **Parvati Temple** is on the outskirts of the town on a hilltop. There's a good view from the top, where the last Peshwa ruler is said to have stood and watched whilst his troops suffered defeat at the hands of the British at Kirkee.

The rock-cut **Panchaleshwar Temple**, a small 8th-century temple similar in style to the much grander rock temples of Ellora, is fairly central. The story goes that it was excavated in one night. There's a fine equestrian statue of Shivaji close by.

The 150-metre-long **Wellesley Bridge** crosses the Mutha River to Sangam, the promontory of land where the Mutha and Mula join. It dates from 1875.

Gandhi National Memorial

Across the river in Yeravda is this fine memorial set in 6½ hectares of gardens. In

Kasturba & Mahandas Gandhi

the past it was the Aga Khan's palace but he donated it to India in 1969.

At one time Mahatma Gandhi and other leaders of the movement for Indian independence were interned here, and today it is maintained as another memorial to Gandhi. Kasturba Gandhi, the Mahatma's wife, died here while interned and her memorial tomb stands in the palace grounds.

Some of the scenes from the movie *Gandhi* were shot in this building. It is open from 9 am to 4.45 pm daily; entry is Rs 2. The easiest way to see it is on the city tour which stops here for half an hour or so (too short if you want to read the blurb which accompanies the photographs).

Organised Tours

There are daily bus tours of Pune from 8 am to noon and 2 to 6 pm from the railway station which cost Rs 40 and cover all the main sights, but it's a breathless rush and you never get enough time at each site. Book at the MTDC kiosk in the station's main hall.

The MTDC also offers day trips to Mahabaleshwar which start at 7.30 am and return at 10 pm. The cost is Rs 150. Naturally, you spend most of the day on the bus.

Places to Stay – bottom end

Most of the cheapies close to the railway station are fleapits but there are some which are not – most are in the area known as Wilson Gardens, directly opposite the station and behind the National Hotel.

Here you'll find the *Hotel Jinna Mansion* (☎ 66-7158), Wilson Gardens, a big old house run by a very friendly woman which is popular with travellers. The paint is peeling but it's clean and there are good bathrooms. Singles cost Rs 110 and Rs 120 and doubles Rs 140, Rs 150 and Rs 160, all with attached bath. There's hot water from 7 to 9.30 am. Close by and also in Wilson Gardens are the *Hotel Alankar* with singles/ doubles/triples at Rs 78/100/130 with attached bath and including tax, and the *Hotel Milan* which has singles for Rs 60 with common bath or Rs 100 with attached bath,

and doubles for Rs 70 to Rs 80 with common bath or Rs 140 to Rs 160 with attached bath.

The *National Hotel* (☎ 68-054), 14 Sassoon Rd, opposite the railway station, is a beautiful, old mansion with verandahs and high ceilings. It's a very popular place to stay, friendly, and the best choice in this range. In addition to the rooms in the main house, there are a row of cottages at the back which are simple but very clean and peaceful. A single with common bath costs Rs 80 and a single/double with attached bath Rs 150/180. Breakfast is available if ordered in advance.

Further afield on Connaught Rd (left coming out of the station and then first main road right) is the *Ritz Hotel* (☎ 62-995), an old-fashioned wooden house with a friendly, mellow atmosphere and very close to the GPO. Quite a few travellers stay here. The rooms are large and clean though a little tatty and cost Rs 65/120. There's hot water in the mornings only.

Down on M G Rd to the north of Moledina Rd is the *Grand Hotel*, another old-style place in its own grounds and run by a friendly woman. Singles with common bath cost Rs 50 and doubles with attached bath Rs 100. The hotel has its own bar and restaurant.

If you want to be near Swargate bus station for an early morning departure, the *Hotel Avanti* (☎ 44-5975) is excellent value with clean, airy rooms and hot water, but is otherwise very inconvenient for the centre.

There are good *retiring rooms* at the railway station with rooms from Rs 25.

Places to Stay – middle

At the bottom of this category is the *Hotel Gulmohr* (☎ 66-1773), 15 A/1 Connaught Rd, within easy walking distance of the railway station. It has rooms without air-con from Rs 140/210 and doubles with air-con for Rs 345. There's hot water 24 hours day plus a bar and restaurant.

Not far from here is the huge *Hotel Woodland* (☎ 66-1111), off Sadhu Vaswani Circle, which has a range of rooms from Rs 200/250 (regular) to Rs 300/325 (regular air-con) and Rs 325/375 (deluxe air-con) as well as suites.

The rooms are good and well maintained but there's no bar or restaurant (though there is room service for both food and drinks – very strange!).

Closer to the station is the new *Hotel Ashirwad* (☎ 66-6142), 16 Connaught Rd, which offers spacious rooms with balcony for Rs 250/300 to Rs 275/340 without air-con and Rs 375/500 with air-con. There's a restaurant with good vegetarian food but no bar. Better and with a much greater range of facilities including a bar, restaurants (veg and non-veg), coffee shop (good for breakfast) and a shopping arcade is the *Hotel Amir* (☎ 66-1840) at 15 Connaught Rd. It has 'budget' rooms for Rs 250/300, 'First Class' rooms for Rs 350/450, and 'deluxe' rooms for Rs 360/550. The staff are friendly and helpful.

There are many others in this range but you'll undoubtedly find a room at the above, though if you want to be in the thick of things on M G Rd, try the *Marina Hotel* (☎ 66-9141) at No 77.

Places to Stay – top end

About one km from the railway station is the *Hotel Sagar Plaza* (☎ 66-1880), 1 Bund Garden Rd, off Moledina Rd, which is a new place and deliciously cool in the summer months. Air-con rooms cost Rs 620/750 plus there are deluxe doubles for Rs 795. Facilities include a bar, coffee shop, speciality restaurant, small swimming pool and bookshop.

Top of the line is the huge *Hotel Aurora Towers* (☎ 64-1818), 9 Moledina Rd at the junction of M G Rd (entrance on M G Rd). This centrally air-conditioned hotel has standard rooms at Rs 395/650 and deluxe doubles at Rs 750. There are also more expensive suites. Facilities include a shopping arcade, parking, swimming pool, bar and two speciality restaurants (Indian, Continental and Chinese).

Places to Eat

On Station Rd, near the corner of Connaught Rd, both the *Hotel Neelam* and the *Hotel Preetam* offer clean, reasonably priced veg and non-veg Indian and part-Western dishes and are open all day. The Preetam also serves cold beers. Further along in the large Hotel Metro building is the *Hotel Madhura* which serves excellent thalis.

The best place to go in the evening for a cheap meal and to mix with the bright young things of Pune is the street opposite the GPO. It's really popular, and has a whole string of cheap restaurants offering an amazing variety of food and cold drinks. There are tables and chairs strewn along the wide sidewalk. It's a great place to meet people but only operates in the evenings.

For something of a splurge, there are two excellent places opposite each other on Moledina Rd close to the junction with M G Rd. On the north side is the part open-air and part enclosed *Kabir's* at No 6 which offers Indian, Mughlai and tandoori dishes. The food is tasty and reasonably priced and it's a popular place to eat.

Right opposite and very popular with both Westerners and Indians is *The Place: Touché the Sizzler*, a two-tier indoor restaurant which specialises in sizzlers but also offers Indian, tandoori and Continental dishes. The food is excellent and the service fast though it's somewhat more expensive than Kabir's. Both restaurants have cold beers.

Also on Moledina Rd is the *Coffee House*, a trendy hangout and definitely the place to be seen. Nearby is *Venky's*, a fast-food outlet which has good burgers and milk shakes.

Getting There & Away

Air The Indian Airlines office (☎ 66-4189) is next to the Hotel Amir on Connaught Rd. Air India (☎ 66-8932) is on Moledina Rd.

Indian Airlines flies Delhi to Pune and vice versa daily (US$130). It also flies Madras/Bangalore/Pune and vice versa three days a week (US$102 to Madras and US$84 to Bangalore).

Vayudoot (☎ 54-785 city, 66-7538 airport) flies Pune to Bombay twice daily for US$54. Continental (☎ 66-1602) also flies Bombay to Pune twice daily in either direction. The fare is Rs 620.

Bus Pune has three bus stations: the Railway bus stand for points south, including Goa, Belgaum, Kolhapur, Mahabaleshwar and Panchgani; the Shivaji Nagar bus stand for points north and north-east – Ahmednagar, Aurangabad, Belgaum, Lonavla and Nasik; and the Swargate bus stand for Sinhagad.

The timetable at the Swargate state bus stand is entirely in Marathi with not a word of English anywhere.

There are daily regular and air-con buses between Bombay and Pune. The MTDC operates deluxe buses to Mahabaleshwar (Rs 150). Reservations can be made at the tourist information counter at the railway station.

To Aurangabad for the Ajanta and Ellora caves there are regular buses from the Shivaji Nagar bus stand. Pune to Aurangabad takes about six hours.

The state buses tend to be pretty rough and ready and most travellers prefer to use the railway system. If you don't want to do this, then there are plenty of private deluxe buses to most nearby centres of population but beware of going through agents (especially those advertising their services around the railway station) as you'll end up paying up to 50% commission and find yourself dumped on a regular state bus. This is a common scam. Don't get caught out, and avoid Satish Travels. Always go direct to the bus operators.

Try Bright Star Tours & Travels (☎ 66-9647), 13 Connaught Rd, which has luxury buses daily to Ahmedabad, Aurangabad, Bangalore, Goa, Hubli/Belgaum, Hyderabad, Mangalore, Nagpur and Sholapur; or Sohrab Tours & Travels (☎ 66-7392), 13 Moledina Rd, which has daily buses to Mapusa (Goa) at 6.30 pm which arrive at 6 am and cost Rs 130.

Train Pune is one of the Deccan's most important railway stations and all express and mail trains stop here. The computerised booking hall is to the left of the station as you face the entrance.

The fastest train to Bombay is the *Deccan Queen* which leaves Pune daily at 7.15 am and arrives at Bombay VT at 10.40 am. In the opposite direction it departs Bombay VT at 5.10 pm and arrives in Pune at 8.35 pm. The 192-km journey costs Rs 42/152 in 2nd/1st. This is a commuter train and heavily subscribed so you need to book well in advance, although the ticket superintendent on the platform at Pune can usually allocate you a seat at the last minute. The other expresses and mail trains to Bombay take four to five hours.

Going south-east, the best trains to take are the *Sahyadri Express* (10.42 pm) and the *Udyan Express* (12.10 pm). The 1029-km journey to Bangalore takes about 31 hours and costs Rs 150/572 in 2nd/1st. The *Sahyadri Express* continues on to Madras Central, a total of 1387 km and 40 hours for which the fare is Rs 172/682 in 2nd/1st. If you're heading for Matheran, the only express train which stops at Neral is the *Sahyadri Express*. See the Matheran section for further details.

Taxi Long-distance share taxis also connect Pune and Bombay. They leave from the taxi stand in front of the railway station.

Getting Around

Bus The local buses are relatively un-crowded. The main bus which you are likely to use is the No 4, which runs from the Railway bus stand to Swargate via the Shivaji Nagar bus station. The Marathi number '4' looks like an '8' with a gap at the top.

Auto-Rickshaw On average, half the auto drivers in Pune will use the meters; the other half will refuse and quote a price which they think you will pay (usually double the meter price). If you're strapped for cash, find one which will use the meter – or walk.

Bicycle This is a good place to get around by bicycle (except at rush hours when it's conceivably dangerous). They're available for rent in many places such as near the entrance to the National Hotel.

AROUND PUNE

Sinhagad

Sinhagad, the Lion Fort, is 25 km south-west of Pune and was the scene of another of Shivaji's daring exploits. It makes an excellent day trip from Pune, which will give you a good chance to get some fresh air into your lungs and clear your head.

The fortress stands near the telecommunications mast at 1270 metres, on top of a steep hill. Although the fort itself is largely ruined, there are a number of old bungalows up here, including one where Gandhi met with Tilak in 1915. Obviously the fort itself dates back much further. In 1670 Shivaji's general, Tanaji Malusre, led a force of men who scaled the steep hillside in the dark and defeated the unprepared forces of Bijapur.

Legends about this dramatic attack relate that the Maratha forces used trained lizards to carry ropes up the hillside! There are monuments at the spot where Tanaji died, and also at the place where he lost his left hand before his death.

The climb up from the end of the road takes a sweaty 1½ to two hours but the views from the top are superb. Although there is a tea stall, and cool drinks are available at the top, it's a good idea to bring some water and food with you from Pune. There are also lassi-wallahs at various intervals on the trail up but give them a miss unless you feel the need for some exotic germs in your stomach.

Getting There & Away The Pune city bus No 50 takes you to Sinhagad village at the end of the road. The buses run frequently from 5.25 am to 8 pm from the stop opposite the Nehru Stadium and the trip takes about 45 minutes.

MAHABALESHWAR

Population: 10,500

This popular hill station was the summer capital of the Bombay presidency during the days of the Raj. At an altitude of 1372 metres, Mahabaleshwar has pleasant walks and good lookouts (the sea is visible on a clear day), and the area has interesting historical con-

nections with Shivaji. The station was founded in 1828 by Sir John Malcolm.

As with most hill stations, Mahabaleshwar closes up tight for the monsoon season. During the period from mid-June to mid-September the local buildings are clad with *kulum* grass to stop them being damaged by the torrential rain. In this three-month period Mahabaleshwar receives an unbelievable six *metres* (around 235 inches) of rain!

Elphinstone Point, Babington Point, Bombay Point, Kate's Point and a number of other lookouts around the wooded plateau offer fine views over the plains below. Arthur's Seat, 12 km from Mahabaleshwar, looks out over a sheer drop of 600 metres to the coastal strip between the ghats and the sea, known as the Konkan. There are pleasant waterfalls such as Chinaman's Waterfall (2½ km), Dhobi Waterfall (three km) and Lingmala Waterfalls (six km).

Most of the walking trails are well signposted, although the moss growing over the signs can make them difficult to read these days. The riding paths have quaint old names such as Lamington Ride, Malcolm Path, Lady Wilingdon Gallop and Duchess Ride.

Venna Lake, within Mahabaleshwar, has boating and fishing facilities. In the village of Old Mahabaleshwar there are three old temples, although they are badly ruined. The Krishnabai or Panchganga (Five Streams) Temple is said to contain five streams, including the Krishna River.

Places to Stay

There are plenty of hotels at Mahabaleshwar but most are closed during the monsoon. The cheaper lodges are all in the town centre in the bazaar area, but even these are not cheap by local standards. If you arrive by bus there are plenty of touts at the station who will find you a room.

The *Hotel Saraswati* on Mari Peth has doubles with hot water for Rs 250 in season. The off-season price of Rs 60/80 for singles/doubles is good value. The *Poonam Hotel* (☎ 291) is very central but charges Rs 220 for a double. Other cheaper lodges near the centre include the *Vyankatesh* (☎ 397), *Samartha* (☎ 416), and the *Ajantha* (☎ 272), all on Mosque St.

The *Ripon Hotel* (☎ 257) is a 20-minute walk from the bus stand. It is run by a very friendly elderly gentleman and there are fine views over the lake. Rooms cost Rs 100 per person including breakfast (closed during the monsoon).

There is a MTDC *Holiday Camp* (☎ 318) about two km from the centre, which has a whole variety of accommodation available ranging from Rs 10 per person on the floor (without a bed) to Rs 30 per person for a dorm bed followed by doubles for Rs 100, Rs 125 and Rs 150, to cottages and suites which sleep three to four people for Rs 200 to Rs 400. Reservations can be made through the MTDC (☎ 202-4482) at Express Towers, Nariman Point, Bombay.

More expensive hotels include the *Dreamland Hotel* (☎ 228), *Regal Hotel* (☎ 317), *Dina Hotel* (☎ 246) and *Fredrick Hotel* (☎ 240). These places generally quote all-inclusive prices in the Rs 250 to Rs 350 per person range.

Places to Eat

The *Shere-e-Punjab* is right in the bazaar and does good non-veg food. During the monsoon this is about the only place open. At the far end of the same road, *Imperial Stores* does take-away toasted sandwiches, burgers and other small snacks.

Getting There & Away

Pune is the normal departure point for Mahabaleshwar although Satara Road is the closest convenient railway station. Mahabaleshwar is 120 km from Pune via Panchgani.

There are daily buses to Kolhapur (seven hours, Rs 30), Satara (one hour, Rs 10), Pune (three hours, Rs 20) and Panchgani (Rs 4). There is also an MTDC luxury bus daily in either direction (except during the monsoon) between Bombay and Mahabaleshwar (at 7 am from Bombay and 3 pm from Mahabaleshwar) which takes seven hours and costs Rs 130.

Getting Around

Mahabaleshwar has a wonderful collection of old Dodge limousines as its taxis. It's possible to hire one to take you around the main viewpoints for Rs 200. To Panchgani it costs Rs 80 to hire the whole vehicle.

AROUND MAHABALESHWAR
Panchgani

Panchgani (Five Hills) is just 19 km from Mahabaleshwar and, at 1334 metres, just 38 metres lower. It's also a popular hill station but is overshadowed by better known Mahabaleshwar. On the way up to Panchgani from Pune you pass through Wai, a site featured in the *Mahabharata*.

Places to Stay & Eat As in Mahabaleshwar, there are various hotels. The most expensive is the *Aman Hotel* (☎ 211). Cheaper places include the *Prospect Hotel* (☎ 263), *Hotel Western* (☎ 288) and the *Malas Guest House* (☎ 321).

The *Hotel Five Hills* is run by the MTDC and has rooms for Rs 125/175. The attached *Silver Oaks Restaurant* is reasonably priced and has excellent food.

Pratapgarh Fort

Built in 1656, this fort is about 24 km from Mahabaleshwar. It's connected with one of the more notable feats in Shivaji's dramatic life. (See the box called Pratapgarh Protagonists for more details.) There is another Shivaji fort at Raigarh, 80 km from Mahabaleshwar.

SATARA
Population: 95,000

On the main road from Pune to Belgaum and Goa, but 15 km off the railway line from Satara Road, this town houses a number of relics of the Maratha leader Shivaji. A building near the new palace contains his sword, the coat he wore when he met Afzal Khan and the *waghnakh* with which he killed him. The **Shivaji Maharaj Museum** is opposite the bus station.

The fort of **Wasota** stands in the south of the town – it has had a colourful and bloody

Pratapgarh Protagonists

Outnumbered by the forces of Bijapur, Shivaji arranged to meet with the opposing General Afzal Khan. Neither was supposed to carry any weapon or wear armour; but neither, it turned out, could be trusted.

When they met, Afzal Khan pulled out a dagger and stabbed Shivaji, but the Maratha leader had worn a shirt of mail under his white robe and concealed in his left hand was a *waghnakh*, a deadly set of 'tiger's claws'. This nasty weapon consisted of a series of rings to which long, sharpened metal claws were attached. Shivaji drove these claws into Khan and disembowelled him. Today a tomb marks where their encounter took place, and a tower was erected over the Khan's head. There is a statue of Shivaji in the ruined Pratapgarh fort. ■

history, including being captured from the Marathas in 1699 by the forces of Aurangzeb, only to be recaptured in 1705 by means of a Brahmin who befriended the fort's defenders, then let in a band of Marathas.

KOLHAPUR

Population: 417,000

This was once the capital of an important Maratha state. One of Kolhapur's maharajas died in Florence, Italy, and was cremated on the banks of the Arno where his chhatri (cenotaph) now stands. The last maharaja, Major General His Highness Shahaji Chhatrapati II, died in 1983.

There's little of interest in the town itself, although the palace is worth a visit if you're passing through.

Maharaja's Palace

The old maharaja's palace has been turned into the Shahaji Chhatrapati Museum and it contains a weird and wonderful array of the maharaja's old possessions including his clothes, old hunt photos and the memorial silver spade used by the maharaja to 'turn the first sod of the Kolhapur State Railway' in 1888. There's even his Prince Shiraji Pig-Sticking Trophy. The gun and sword collection is comprehensive, and the ashtrays and coffee tables made from tigers' and elephants' feet, not to mention the lamp stands from ostrich legs, are unbelievably gross.

Only a few rooms are open to the public and there are officious men employed to make sure you don't wander off. The palace is a few km to the north of town. Rent a

bicycle, or take an auto-rickshaw (Rs 5), but make sure you ask for the 'new palace' or you'll end up at the Shalini Palace Ashok Hotel by the lake.

Places to Stay

The main hotel and restaurant area is around the square opposite the bus station, five minutes walk from the centre of town and the railway station. The cheapest place is the *Hotel Anand Malhar* (☎ 25-091) which charges Rs 50 for a single without bath, Rs 80 for a double with bath. There's also a good restaurant. The *Hotel Sahyadri* (☎ 24-581) is of a similar standard but gets a bit noisy.

The *Hotel Maharaja* (☎ 29-025) is a bit better at Rs 70/100, while the *Hotel Girish* has good clean rooms for Rs 95/125. All the rooms in this friendly place have TV, phone and piped music (mercifully there's a switch to kill it).

At the top of the scale, the *Shalini Palace Ashok* (☎ 20-401) is in a grand old palace by the lake, five km from the bus or railway station. Simple rooms cost Rs 250/325, or with air-con Rs 375/480.

There are *retiring rooms* at the railway station, and these cost Rs 25/35.

Places to Eat

The restaurants are also concentrated around the square. The *Subraya Restaurant* has north Indian veg and non-veg dishes, and good thalis.

In the evening dozens of snack stalls are set up in the street to the right of the bus station (as you leave it). They whip up great omelettes and other goodies – it's a very economical and interesting place to eat.

Getting There & Away

Bus The bus station is not too chaotic but, as usual, there is nothing written in English. For buses originating in Kolhapur it is possible to book 24 hours in advance between 8 am and noon and 2 and 4.30 pm.

There are daily departures for Satara, Bijapur, Mahabaleshwar, Pune, Ratnagiri and Belgaum.

Train The railway station is close to the centre of town. The broad-gauge line connects Kolhapur with Miraj, from where there are daily trains to Pune, Bombay, Madras and Vasco da Gama (Goa).

The daily *Koyna Express* goes all the way to Bombay, taking 13 hours.

OTHER PLACES IN THE SOUTH
Ratnagiri

Ratnagiri, on the coast 135 km west of Kolhapur, was the place where Thibaw, the last Burmese king, was interned by the British from 1886 until his death in 1916.

Panhala & Pawangarh

These are interesting hill stations. At Panhala there is a fort with a long and convoluted history; it was originally the stronghold of Raja Bhoj II in 1192. The Pawala Caves are nearby, plus a couple of Buddhist cave temples.

Sholapur (Solarpur)

This rapidly developing and busy town north of Bijapur (in neighbouring Karnataka) is a major railway junction, and is on the broad-gauge system. You'll pass through here heading north or south to/from Bijapur or Badami and, depending on the state of the booking on the broad-gauge system, may have to stay the night. There's nothing much for the tourist here but it's worth checking out the superbly decorated municipal offices.

Places to Stay & Eat The *Hotel Rajdhani* near the railway station is a reasonable place to stay. Otherwise, for comfort, stay at the three-star *Hotel Pratham* (☎ 29-581), 560/61 South Sadar Bazar. It's excellent value at Rs 195 a double without air-con and Rs 275 with air-con. There are also more expensive deluxe rooms and suites. The hotel has its own vegetarian and non-veg restaurants (very tasty food) and a bar.

Northern Maharashtra

AHMEDNAGAR
Population: 222,000

On the road between Pune (82 km away) and Aurangabad, Ahmednagar has had a colourful history. It was here that Emperor Aurangzeb died in 1707, aged 97. The town's imposing fort was erected in 1550, and at one time Nehru was imprisoned here by the British.

Places to Stay

There are various hotels, including the *Ashoka Tourist Hotel* (☎ 3607) and the *Hotel Sablok*. The Ashoka is at King's Gate, about a km from the centre, and has rooms with and without air-con.

NASIK
Population: 722,000

This interesting town with its picturesque bathing ghats makes a good stopover on the way from Bombay to Aurangabad. The town itself is actually about eight km north-west of the station, which is 187 km from Bombay.

Temples & Caves

Nasik stands on the Godavari River, one of the holiest rivers of the Deccan. Like Ujjain, in neighbouring Madhya Pradesh, this is one of the sites for the triennial Kumbh Mela which takes place here every 12 years. The riverbanks are lined with steps above which stand temples and shrines. Although there are no particularly notable temples in Nasik, the **Sundar Narayan Temple**, to the west of the city, is worth seeing.

Other points of interest in Nasik include the **Sita Gupta Cave** from which, according to the *Ramayana*, Sita, the deity of agriculture and wife of Rama, was supposed to have been carried off to the island of Lanka by the evil king Ravana. Near the cave, in its grove of large banyan trees, is the fine house of the Panchavati family. Also nearby is the Temple of **Kala Rama**, or Black Rama, in a 96-arched enclosure. The **Kapaleswar Temple** upstream is said to be the oldest in the town.

Kumbh Mela

The Kumbh Mela alternates between Allahabad, Nasik, Ujjain and Haridwar every three years. Kumbh means Pot, and in Hindu mythology, four drops of the nectar of immortality fell to earth, one in each of these places. For more details about this extraordinary pilgrimage, see the section under Allahabad in the Uttar Pradesh chapter.

Places to Stay

A good place here is the *Hotel Siddhart* (☎ 73-288) on the Nasik to Pune road near the airport. Somewhat more expensive are the *Hotel Samrat* (☎ 77-211), near the central bus station on the old Agra Rd, and the *Green View Hotel* (☎ 72-231), 1363, M I Trimbak Rd, about two km from the centre of town.

More expensive is the two-star *Hotel Panchavati* (☎ 75-771), 430 Vakilwadi, which offers rooms without air-con for Rs 210/290 or Rs 320/390 with air-con. The hotel has its own restaurant. Similar is the two-star *Wasan's Hotel* (☎ 77-881), Old Agra Rd, which has a range of air-con and non-air-con rooms. Wasan's also has its own restaurant.

AROUND NASIK
Pandu Lena

About eight km south of Nasik, close to the Bombay road, are these 21 Hinayana Buddhist caves. They date from around the 1st century BC to the 2nd AD. The most interesting caves are Nos 3, 10 and 18. Cave 3 is

a large vihara (monastery) with some interesting sculptures. Cave 10 is also a vihara and almost identical in design to cave 3, although it is much older and finer in its detail. It is thought to be nearly as old as the Karla Cave. Cave 18 is a chaitya (temple) cave thought to date from the same time as the Karla Cave. It too is well sculpted and its elaborate facade is particularly noteworthy. Cave 20 is another large vihara. The other caves are not of great interest.

Trimbak

This is the source of the Godavari River, 33 km from Nasik. From this source high on a steep hill, the river dribbles into a bathing tank whose waters are reputed to wash away sins. From this tiny start the Godavari eventually flows down to the Bay of Bengal, clear across India.

AURANGABAD
Population: 592,000

It's easy to think of Aurangabad simply as a place to stay when visiting the cave temples of Ajanta and Ellora. In fact Aurangabad has a number of attractions and could easily stand on its own were it not so overshadowed by the famous caves. The city is named after Aurangzeb, but earlier in its history it was known as Khadke.

Orientation & Information

The railway station, tourist office and a variety of cheaper hotels and restaurants are clustered in the south of the town. There's a fairly open gap from here to the more crowded and older part of the town to the north, where you'll also find the bus station. In comparison to other Deccan towns, Aurangabad is remarkably uncrowded and quiet except for the occasional political rally.

The more expensive hotels are between the old town and the railway station or on the road out to the airport. There is a not particularly useful state tourist office (☎ 24-713) in the MTDC Holiday Resort, Station Rd (East), while on Station Rd (West) is a more useful Government of India tourist office (☎ 24-817). Even so, it's the usual 'sit around, do nothing and rely on what out-of-date publications they have'. The latter is open 8.30 am to 6 pm on weekdays, 8.30 am to 12.30 pm on Saturdays.

Bibi-ka-Maqbara

This poor-man's Taj was built in 1679 by Aurangzeb's son for Rabia-ud-Darani, Aurangzeb's wife. It's a poor imitation of the Taj in both design and execution – somehow it simply looks awkward and uncomfortable compared to the sophisticated balance of the Taj; and where the Taj has gleaming marble, this tomb has flaking paint, though restoration is being undertaken. Nevertheless it's an interesting building and the only example of Moghul architecture on the Deccan plateau.

It stands to the north of the city, and on the main gate an inscription reveals that it cost precisely Rs 665,283 and 7 annas to build. Admission is Rs 0.50.

Panchakki

This water mill takes its name from the mill which once ground grain for pilgrims. In 1624 a Sufi saint and spiritual guide to Aurangzeb was buried here, and the pleasant garden with its series of fish-filled tanks serves as his memorial. It's a cool, relaxing and serene place when not overflowing with tourists from MTDC bus tours, although the stream sometimes runs dry prior to the monsoons. Admission is Rs 0.75.

Aurangabad Caves

Although they're easily forgotten, standing as they do in the shadow of the Ajanta and Ellora caves, there is a group of caves in Aurangabad. They're a couple of km north of the Bibi-ka-Maqbara and were built around the 6th or 7th century AD. The 10 caves are all Buddhist; five are in the western group and five about a km away in the eastern group. Other caves further east are little more than natural ones.

Western Group – Caves 1 to 5 Except for

cave 4, with a ridged roof like the Karla Cave, all the caves are viharas rather than chaityas. Cave 4 is also fronted by a stupa,

now partially collapsed. Cave 3 is square and is supported by 12 highly ornate columns. It has an interesting series of sculptures depicting scenes from one of the jatakas.

Eastern Group – Caves 6 to 10 Cave 6 is fairly intact and the sculptures of women are notable for their exotic hairdos and ornamentation. There is a large Buddha figure here and Ganesh also makes an appearance. Cave 7 is the most interesting of the Aurangabad caves, particularly (as in the other caves) for the figures and sculptures – the figures of women, scantily clad but ornately bejewelled, are very well done.

To the left of Cave 7 a huge figure of a Bodhisattva prays for deliverance from eight fears which are illustrated as fire, the sword of the enemy, chains, shipwreck, lions, snakes, mad elephants and a demon (representing death).

You can walk up to the caves from the Bibi-ka-Maqbara or take an auto-rickshaw up to the eastern group. From this group you can walk back down the road to the western group and then cut straight back across country to the Bibi-ka-Maqbara. If you take an auto-rickshaw agree on a price first and make sure it includes waiting time.

Organised Tours

There are various tours from Aurangabad to the Ajanta and Ellora caves, Daulatabad Fort and the sights of Aurangabad. The MTDC operates a daily tour to the Ajanta Caves for Rs 100 which begins at 8 am and finishes at 5.30 pm, and to the Ellora Caves for Rs 65 which starts at 9.30 am and finishes at 5.30 pm. The tour buses start from the MTDC Holiday Resort but also pick up from the major hotels.

The Ellora tours include Daulatabad and the attractions in Aurangabad itself (but not the Aurangabad Caves), so they save a lot of travelling and waiting time compared to doing it yourself. On the other hand, these organised tours suffer from the usual attempt to pack in too many places (some of which aren't worth seeing) thus leaving you with not enough time at the Daulatabad Fort and

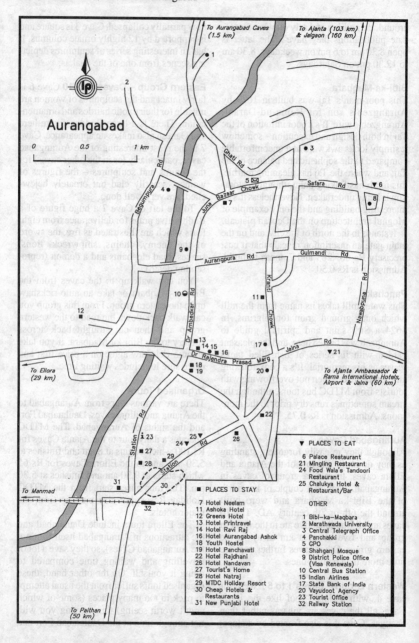

Aurangabad

To Aurangabad Caves (1.5 km)

To Ajanta (103 km) & Jalgaon (160 km)

0   0.5   1 km

To Ellora (29 km)

To Manmad

To Paithan (50 km)

To Ajanta Ambassador & Rama International Hotels, Airport & Jalna (60 km)

▼ PLACES TO EAT
6 Palace Restaurant
21 Mingling Restaurant
24 Food Wala's Tandoori Restaurant
25 Chalukya Hotel & Restaurant/Bar

■ PLACES TO STAY
7 Hotel Neelam
11 Ashoka Hotel
12 Greens Hotel
13 Hotel Printravel
14 Hotel Ravi Raj
16 Hotel Aurangabad Ashok
18 Youth Hostel
19 Hotel Panchavati
22 Hotel Rajdhani
26 Hotel Nandavan
27 Tourist's Home
28 Hotel Natraj
29 MTDC Holiday Resort
30 Cheap Hotels & Restaurants
31 New Punjabi Hotel

OTHER
1 Bibi-ka-Maqbara
2 Marathwada University
3 Central Telegraph Office
4 Panchakki
5 GPO
8 Shahganj Mosque
9 District Police Office (Visa Renewals)
10 Central Bus Station
15 Indian Airlines
17 State Bank of India
20 Vayudoot Agency
23 Tourist Office
32 Railway Station

Ellora. Likewise, because the Ajanta Caves are quite a long way from Aurangabad, these tours don't really give you enough time to fully explore them, so many travellers prefer to take local transport and stay overnight.

The state transport buses also run daily tours to the same places but only in season. They start from the railway station and are cheaper than the MTDC tours.

Places to Stay – bottom end

Most of Aurangabad's cheaper hotels are close to the railway station and there are infinite variations on the Punjab, Punjabi, New Punjabi and Shere-Punjab name theme.

The notable exception outside this area is the excellent *Youth Hostel* midway between the railway station and the main part of town. There are 40 dorm beds at Rs 10 each (Rs 6 for YHA members) and the place is spotlessly clean. It has hot and cold water, and breakfast and evening meals are available. There's also one family room for three people. Check-in times are 7 to 11 am and 4 to 8 pm; checkout time is 9 am. The people who run this place are very friendly but it's sometimes closed when there are water shortages.

A hundred metres or so from the station is the MTDC *Holiday Resort* (☎ 24-259), where you'll also find the state government tourist office. Doubles with bathroom cost Rs 150 and Rs 175 without air-con and Rs 250 with air-con. Mosquito nets are provided. The Holiday Resort staff are a long way short of helpful – checkout time is 8 am and they positively will not look after baggage for you, even if you are going on one of their tours.

Between the Holiday Resort and the station there is a string of very cheap and basic places such as the *Ashoka Lodging, Ambika Lodge, New Punjabi Hotel* and the *Ashoka Tourist Hotel*. They're all of a similar standard and there's not much to choose between them. Expect to pay around Rs 60 a double.

Better value are the two hotels on the west arm of Station Rd. The first is the *Hotel Natraj* which is a typical Indian boarding

house with singles/doubles at Rs 60/80 with bathroom. The hotel has a vegetarian restaurant. The other is the *Tourist's Home* which is basic but very clean and pleasant. Singles/doubles with common bath cost Rs 60 and doubles with bath cost Rs 80. Bucket hot water is available for Rs 2.

Over towards the old part of town, between the bus station and post office, is the *Hotel Neelam* (☎ 4561) which is a newer looking building with rooms at Rs 70 to Rs 80 with bath.

At the top of this range is the *Hotel Printravel* (☎ 4707) which has singles/doubles for Rs 80/120, all with attached bath and hot water. Checkout time is noon. Similar is the *Hotel Panchavati*, next to the Youth Hostel, which has singles/doubles at Rs 80/100 with attached bath, and hot water in the mornings. It's basic but the building is relatively new and the staff are friendly. Checkout time is 24 hours, and the hotel has a restaurant and bar.

Places to Stay – middle

The *Hotel Ravi Raj* (☎ 27-501), Dr Rajendra Prasad Marg close to the junction with Station Rd, is a convenient place to stay, but it's definitely seen better days. Singles/doubles without air-con cost Rs 270/300, and with air-con they're Rs 330/370. There are also more expensive suites at Rs 475/575 with/without air-con. All the rooms have bathrooms. The hotel has two restaurants, one indoor and the other outdoor, and there's a bar. Checkout time is noon.

Better value though less convenient is the *Hotel Rajdhani* (☎ 27-562), on Station Rd, which is a new building and very clean. Rooms are similar in price to those at the Ravi Raj. All rooms have a bath and hot water.

Similar but older is the *Hotel Nandavan* (☎ 3311), also on Station Rd, about one km from the railway station. Rooms are somewhat cheaper than the above but they all have a bath with hot water. The hotel has a restaurant and bar, travellers' cheques can be cashed and there's a same-day laundry service. Checkout time is noon.

At the top end of this range is the *Hotel Amarpreet* (☎ 23-422), Nehru Marg, but we suggest you avoid it as we've had a lot of complaints about it recently – overcharging (up to double the official rates), poor maintenance, and unfriendly, uncooperative staff. Rooms without air-con cost Rs 300/350 or Rs 360/470 with air-con.

Places to Stay – top end
Cheapest in this range is the two-star *Hotel Aurangabad Ashok* (☎ 24-520), Dr Rajendra Prasad Marg, which is air-conditioned and has rooms for Rs 395/695. It's good value with all the usual amenities including a swimming pool, restaurant (Indian and Continental), bar and currency exchange.

At the top of this category are two five-star hotels, the *Ajanta Ambassador Hotel* (☎ 82-211), Chikal Thana, and the *Welcomgroup Rama International* (☎ 82-241), R-3 Chikal Thana. Both of them have all the amenities you'd expect of a five-star hotel including swimming pool, bar, restaurants, shopping arcades and credit card facilities. The Ajanta Ambassador is the cheaper of the two at Rs 825/990 with more expensive suites priced between Rs 1095 and Rs 3025 plus tax. The Rama costs from Rs 1000/1200 to Rs 1600/1800, with more expensive suites at Rs 2000 to Rs 4000. Both hotels are centrally air-conditioned.

Places to Eat
There's a string of rock-bottom restaurants along Station Rd (East) near the railway station and this is where most budget travellers come to eat. None of these places stand out as deserving particular mention but the food is usually good and cheap. The *Prem Popular Punjab* must set a record for the number of switches on the panel above the cashier.

More expensive but excellent vegetarian food can be found at *Food Wala's Bhoj Restaurant* in front of the Hotel Printravel at the junction of Dr Rajendra Prasad Rd and Station Rd. This is a very popular place to eat and the food is very tasty. You can eat as

much as you like if you order a thali. They also have south Indian specialities including masala dosa – excellent! This restaurant has a branch on Station Rd (East) beyond the MTDC Holiday Resort called *Food Wala's Tandoori Restaurant & Bar* which offers what its name implies. Meals here are definitely more expensive, as you might expect, but it's good for a splurge.

Another very good place to splurge at is the *Chalukya Hotel & Restaurant/Bar*, which is a little further up the road from the tandoori restaurant.

Some travellers have recommended the *Mingling Restaurant* opposite the Hotel Amarpreet as having good, reasonably priced Chinese food, though it's quite a way from the centre of town. Others have recommended the *Palace Restaurant* in the centre of the old town at Shahganj opposite the Shahganj Mosque. It's a typical Muslim restaurant with so-so biryanis and other dishes.

For a major splurge, go for lunch or dinner to one of the three top-end hotels. The *Ajanta Ambassador* is particularly recommended but it is expensive.

Getting There & Away
The cave groups at Ajanta and Ellora are off the railway lines and are usually approached from either Aurangabad (Ellora 30 km, Ajanta 106 km) or from Jalgaon (Ajanta 59 km). Jalgaon is on the main broad-gauge line from Bombay to Allahabad, but Aurangabad is off the main line and getting there requires a change to metre-gauge line at Manmad. On the other hand Aurangabad is the access point from Pune (by road) or Hyderabad (by rail). Aurangabad also has an airport which is served by Indian Airlines.

Air The Indian Airlines office is on Dr Rajendra Prasad Marg next to the Aurangabad Ashok.

Indian Airlines flies from Bombay to Aurangabad daily, and these flights continue on to Udaipur, Jodhpur, Jaipur and Delhi. It's a popular tourist route and the flights can be booked up several days in advance. Fares

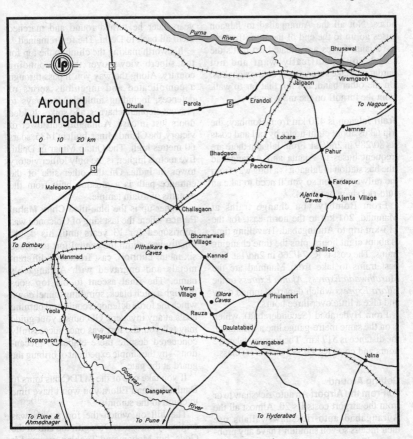

Around Aurangabad

0   10   20 km

from Aurangabad are US$34 to Bombay, US$63 to Udaipur, US$78 to Jodhpur, US$79 to Jaipur, and US$99 to Delhi.

Bus There are bus connections between Aurangabad and Pune, Nasik, Indore and Bombay. Several luxury buses are available to Bombay. TPH Tours & Travels at the Hotel Rajdhani, Station Rd, go daily to Bombay at 9 pm. The journey takes 10 hours and costs Rs 120. Likewise, MTDC offers daily luxury buses to Bombay which cost Rs 145. Other luxury buses can be booked at Food Wala's Bhoj Restaurant.

To Ellora & Ajanta Caves Aurangabad is a good base for visiting either the Ellora or Ajanta caves. Unless you're planning on doing a day tour from Aurangabad to Ajanta, you'll probably find it more convenient to actually stay at Ajanta. Bus fares from Aurangabad are Rs 7 to Ellora (every half-hour), Rs 18 to Ajanta (about every hour, takes three hours), and Rs 24 to Jalgaon (hourly, 4½ hours). From Ajanta to Jalgaon costs Rs 9 (takes 1½ hours).

Most of the Ajanta accommodation is actually at Fardapur, about five km from the caves – Rs 1 by the reasonably frequent buses. Not all the Aurangabad to Jalgaon buses go up to the end of the turnoff where the Ajanta Caves are situated, so if it's the caves you specifically want and not Fardapur, make sure you get on the right bus. On the other hand, it's not that far to walk from the turnoff on the main road.

Train Jalgaon is 420 km from Bombay; the trip takes about eight hours by rail and costs Rs 80/289 in 2nd/1st. From Jalgaon there are frequent buses to Ajanta and Aurangabad (the bus station in Jalgaon is a long way from the railway station so you'll need to take an auto-rickshaw or tonga).

From Bombay you change trains at Manmad, 261 km to the north-east, for the 113-km trip to Aurangabad. Travelling time is about eight hours, plus the time changing trains. The cost is Rs 74/266 in 2nd/1st. The best trains to take from Manmad are the *Marathwada Express*, *Ajanta Express* or the *Ellora Express* which depart Manmad daily and take a little over three hours.

From Hyderabad (Secunderabad), which is on the same metre-gauge line as Manmad, the distance is 517 km. The journey takes 12 hours and costs Rs 92/337 in 2nd/1st class.

Getting Around

To/From the Airport An auto-rickshaw to or from the airport costs Rs 20. Almost all the Aurangabad auto-rickshaw-wallahs use their meters so you shouldn't have any problems with overpricing.

DAULATABAD

Between Aurangabad and the Ellora Caves is the magnificent hilltop fortress of Daulatabad. The **fort** is surrounded by five km of sturdy walls, while the central bastion tops a 200-metre-high hill. In the 14th century the somewhat unbalanced Mohammed Tughlaq, Sultan of Delhi, conceived the crazy plan of not only building himself a new capital here, but marching the entire population of Delhi 1100 km south to populate it. His unhappy subjects proceeded to drop dead like flies on this forced march, and 17

years later he turned round and marched them all back to Delhi. The fort remained.

It's worth making the climb to the top for the superb views over the surrounding country. Along the way you'll pass through a complicated and ingenious series of defences, including multiple doorways to prevent elephant charges, and spike-studded doors just in case. A magnificent tower of victory, the Chand Minar, built in 1435, soars 60 metres high. The Qutab Minar in Delhi, five metres higher, is the only loftier victory tower in India. On the other side of the entrance path is a mosque built from the remains of a Jain temple.

Higher up is the blue-tiled **Chini Mahal Palace** where the last king of Golconda was imprisoned for 13 years until his death. Finally you climb the central fort to a huge six-metre **cannon**, cast from five different metals and engraved with Aurangzeb's name. The final ascent to the top goes through a pitch black, spiralling tunnel down which the fort's defenders could hurl burning coals at any invaders. Of course, your guide may tell you, the fort was once successfully conquered despite these elaborate precautions – by the simple expedient of bribing the guard at the gate.

If you take one of the MTDC bus tours to Daulatabad and Ellora you won't have time to climb to the summit.

The hill on which the fort stands was originally known as Devagiri, the Hill of the Gods, but Mohammed Tughlaq renamed it Daulatabad, the City of Fortune.

RAUZA

Also known as Khuldabad, the Heavenly Abode, this walled town is only three km from Ellora. It is the Karbala or holy shrine of Deccan Muslims. A number of historical figures are buried here, including Aurangzeb, the last great Moghul emperor. Aurangzeb built the crenellated wall around the town, which was once an important centre, although today it is little more than a sleepy village.

The emperor's final resting place is a simple affair of bare earth in a courtyard of the Alamgir Dargah at the centre of the town. Aurangzeb's pious austerity extended even to his own tomb, for he stipulated that his mausoleum should be paid for with money he earned himself by copying out the Koran. Within the building there is also supposed to be a robe worn by the Prophet Mohammed; it is only shown to the faithful once each year. Another shrine across the road from the Alamgir Dargah is said to contain hairs of the Prophet's beard and lumps of silver from a tree of solid silver, which miraculously grew at this site after a saint's death.

ELLORA CAVES

The caves of Ellora are about 30 km from Aurangabad. Whereas the Ajanta Caves are noted for their paintings, here it's the sculpture that is remarkable. Chronologically the Ellora Caves start where the Ajanta Caves finish – it's thought that the builders of Ajanta moved to Ellora when they suddenly ceased construction at their earlier site. The Ellora Caves are not all Buddhist like those of Ajanta; the earliest are, but during this time Buddhism was declining in India and a later series of Hindu and Jain cave temples were added.

In all there are 34 caves at Ellora: 12 Buddhist, 17 Hindu and five Jain. Although the temples are numbered consecutively, from 1 at the southern end to 34 at the northern end, and although the various religious groups do not overlap, the caves are not arranged chronologically. It is thought that construction of the Hindu caves commenced before the Buddhist caves were completed, for example. Roughly, the Buddhist caves are thought to date from around 600 to 800 AD, the Hindu caves to around 900 AD. The Jain caves were not commenced until about 800 AD and were completed by 1000 AD.

The caves are cut into a hillside running north-south. Because the hill slopes down rather than drops steeply, as at Ajanta, many of them have elaborate entrance halls to the main shrines. From south to north, the caves cover about two km.

Buddhist Caves

Apart from cave 10, all the Buddhist caves are viharas (monasteries) rather than chaityas (temples). They are not as architecturally ambitious as the Hindu caves, although 11 and 12 show signs of attempting to compete with the complex Hindu designs. The Buddhist caves chart the period of Buddhism's division and decline in India.

Caves 1 to 4 These are all vihara caves. Cave 2, with its ornate pillars and figures of the Buddha, is quite interesting. Caves 3 and 4 are earlier, simpler and less well preserved.

Cave 5 This is the biggest vihara cave. The rows of stone benches indicate that it may have been an assembly or dining hall.

Caves 6 to 8 In cave 6 there is a large seated Buddha in the shrine room, but this ornate vihara also has a standing figure thought to be either the Hindu goddess of learning, Saraswati, or her Buddhist equivalent, Mahamayuri. Caves 7 and 8 are not quite so interesting.

Cave 10 The Viswakarma or Carpenter's Cave is the only chaitya cave in the Buddhist group. It takes its name from the ribs carved into the roof, in imitation of wooden beams. The temple is entered by steps to a courtyard, followed by further steps to the main temple. A finely carved horseshoe window lets light in and a huge seated-Buddha figure fronts the nine-metre-high stupa.

Cave 11 The Do Thal (Two-Storey) Cave is also entered by a courtyard. Curiously, it actually has three storeys but the third was not discovered until 1876. Construction of the middle floor was never completed.

Cave 12 The Teen Thal (Three-Storey) Cave also has three storeys and is entered through a courtyard. It contains a very large seated Buddha and a number of other figures. The walls are carved with relief pictures, as in the Hindu caves.

Hindu Caves

The Hindu caves are the most dramatic and impressive of the Ellora cave temples. In size, design and energy they are in a totally different league from the Buddhist or Jain caves. If calm contemplation describes the Buddhist caves, then dynamic energy is the description for the Hindu caves. The sheer size of the Kailasa Temple (cave 16) is overwhelming. It covers twice the area of the Parthenon in Athens and is 1½ times as high. Remember that this whole gigantic structure was cut out of solid rock. It has been estimated that carving out the Kailasa entailed removing 200,000 tonnes of rock! It is, without doubt, one of the wonders of the world.

All these temples were cut from the top down, so that it was never necessary to use any scaffolding – their builders started with the roof and moved down to the floor. It's worth contemplating the skill and planning that must have gone into such a process – there was no way of adding a panel or a pillar if things didn't work out as expected.

Cave 14 The first Hindu cave, cave 13, is not impressive, but cave 14, the Rava Kakhai, sets the scene for the others. Like them it is dedicated to Siva, who appears in many of the carvings. You can see Siva dancing the *tandava*, a victory dance over the demon Mahisa, or playing chess with his wife Parvati, or defeating the buffalo demon. Parvati also appears in the form of Durga. Vishnu makes several appearances too, including one as Varaha, his boar incarnation. The seven 'mother goddesses' can also be seen, and Ravana makes yet another attempt to shake Kailasa.

Cave 15 The Das Avatara Cave is one of the finest at Ellora. The two-storey temple is reached by a long flight of steps. Inside there is a modern image of Siva's vehicle, the bull Nandi. Many of the familiar scenes involving Siva can be found again here, but you can also see Vishnu resting on a five-hooded serpent or rescuing an elephant from a crocodile. Vishnu also appears as the man-lion,

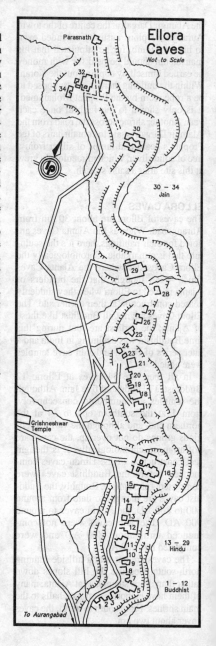

Top: Bhaja Caves, Maharashtra (HF)
Left: Bibi-ka-Maqbara, Aurangabad, Maharashtra (TW)
Right: Maharashtran tribal women at Ellora Caves (GC)

Top Left: Woman selling fruit, Benaulim beach, Goa (MH)
Top Right: Anjuna flea market, Goa (TW)
Bottom: Sravanabelagola, Karnataka (HF)

Narasimha, while Siva emerges from his symbolic lingam and in another panel he marries Parvati.

Cave 16 The mighty Kailasa Temple is the central attraction at Ellora. Here Indian rock-cut temple architecture reaches its peak. Kailasa is, of course, Siva's Himalayan home, and the Kailasa Temple is a representation of that mountain. The temple consists of a huge courtyard, 81 metres long by 47 metres wide and 33 metres high at the back. In the centre, the main temple rises up and is connected to the outer enclosure by a bridge. Around the enclosure are galleries, while towards the front are two large stone elephants with two massive stone 'flagstaffs' flanking the Nandi pavilion, which faces the main shrine.

As in the previous two caves, there is a variety of dramatic and finely carved panels, the most impressive being the image of Ravana shaking Kailasa. In the *Ramayana* the demon king Ravana flaunted his strength by lifting up Siva's mountain home. Unimpressed, Lord Siva simply put his foot down on the top and pressed the mountain and the upstart Ravana back into place. Vishnu also appears along one gallery as Narsimha once again; in this legend he defeats a demon, who could not be killed by man or beast, by the simple expedient of becoming a man-lion, neither man nor beast.

Other Caves The other Hindu caves pall beside the majesty of the Kailasa, but several of them are worth at least some study. Cave 21, known as the Ramesvara, has a number of interesting interpretations of scenes also depicted in the earlier temples. Siva once again marries Parvati and plays dice with her, and the goddesses Ganga and Yamuna once again appear. The figure of Ganga, standing on her crocodile or *makara*, is particularly notable.

The very large cave 29, the Dumar Lena, is similar in design to the Elephanta Cave at Bombay. It is thought to be a transitional model between the simpler hollowed-out caves and the fully developed temples exemplified by the Kailasa.

Jain Caves

The Jain caves mark the final phase of Ellora. They do not have the drama and high-voltage energy of the best Hindu temples nor are they as ambitious in size, but they balance this with their exceptionally detailed work. There are only five Jain temples, several hundred metres north of the last Hindu temple.

Cave 30 The Chota Kailasa or Little Kailasa is a poor imitation of the great Kailasa Temple and was never completed. It stands by itself some distance from the other Jain temples, which are all clustered closely together.

Cave 32 The Indra Sabha (Assembly Hall of Indra) is the finest of the Jain temples. The ground-floor plan is similar to that of the Kailasa, but the upstairs area, reached by a stairway, is as ornate and richly decorated as downstairs is plain. There are images of the Jain tirthankars Parasnath and Gomatesvara, the latter surrounded by vegetation and wild-life. Inside the shrine is a seated figure of Mahavira, the 24th and last tirthankar, and founder of the Jain religion. Traces of paintings can still be seen on the roof of the temple.

Other Caves Cave 31 is really an extension of 32. Cave 33, the Jagannath Sabha, is similar in plan to 32 and has some particularly well-preserved sculptures. The final temple, the small cave 34, also has interesting sculptures. On the hilltop over the Jain temples a five-metre-high image of Parasnath looks down on Ellora. An enclosure was built around it a couple of hundred years ago.

Grishneshwar

Close to the Ellora Caves in the village of Verul, this 18th-century Siva temple has one of the 12 jyoti lingas (important shrines to Siva) in India, so it's an important place of pilgrimage for Hindus.

Places to Stay

Although most people stay in Aurangabad, there is the *Hotel Kailasa* very close to the caves which offers rooms with attached bath at a reasonable price. The restaurant at the hotel is cheaper than the other government restaurant here, which is intended for tour groups.

AJANTA CAVES

The caves of Ajanta predate those of Ellora, so if you want to see the caves in chronological order you should visit these first. Although the Ellora Caves are easily visited using Aurangabad as a base, it's much easier to stay near the Ajanta Caves rather than make a day trip to them. Unlike the Ellora Caves, which are Buddhist, Hindu and Jain, the Ajanta Caves are all Buddhist; and whereas at Ellora the caves are masterpieces of sculpture, at Ajanta it's the magnificent paintings for which the caves are famous.

After their abandonment with the move to Ellora and the decline of Buddhism, the Ajanta Caves were gradually forgotten and their rediscovery was dramatic. In 1819 a British hunting party stumbled upon them, and their remote beauty was soon unveiled. Their isolation had contributed to the fine state of preservation in which some of the paintings remain to this day. The caves are cut into the steep face of a deep rock gorge. There are 29 caves in a curve of the gorge, and there is a good viewpoint across the ravine. They date from around 200 BC to 650 AD and do not follow the chronological order that the Ellora Caves generally do; the oldest are mainly in the middle and the newer ones are close to each end.

The cave paintings initially suffered some deterioration after their rediscovery, and some heavy-handed restoration also caused damage. Between 1920 and 1922 two Italian art experts conducted a meticulous restoration process and the paintings have been carefully preserved since that time. Many of the caves are dark, and without a light the paintings are hard to see – it's worth paying for a lighting ticket which will ensure that the cave guards turn the lights on for you. Or you could try tagging along with a tour party, although normally the doors are shut after each party enters a cave.

Five of the caves are chaityas or temples while the other 24 are viharas or monasteries. Caves 8, 9, 10, 12 and 13 are the older Hinayana caves, while the others are Mahayana. In the simpler, more austere Hinayana school the Buddha was never represented directly – his presence was always alluded to by a symbol such as the footprint or wheel of law. The Ajanta paintings are not, strictly speaking, frescoes but tempera paintings – a difference purely of technique. Although the Ajanta paintings are particularly notable, there are also many interesting sculptures here.

The caves are open daily from 9 am to 5.30 pm. Entry costs Rs 0.50 plus Rs 5 for a lighting fee (this is optional but more or less essential).

Avoid, if at all possible, coming here at weekends or on public holidays. On those days, Ajanta seems to attract half the population of India and it's bedlam. The Calcutta rush hour has nothing on this place at those times – hardly the contemplative atmosphere which its monks and builders had in mind!

Cave 1

This vihara cave is one of the most recent and also most fully developed of the Ajanta Caves. A verandah at the front leads to a large square hall which has elaborate carvings and paintings, as well as a huge Buddha statue. Cave 1 is notable for both its sculpture and its paintings.

Amongst the interesting sculptures is one of four deer sharing a common head. There are many paintings of women, some remarkably similar to the paintings at Sigiriya in Sri Lanka. Notable paintings include those of the 'black princess' and the 'dying princess'. Other paintings include scenes from the jatakas (events from the Buddha's previous lives), and portraits of the Bodhisattvas (near-Buddhas) Padmapani (holding a lotus flower) and Vajrapani.

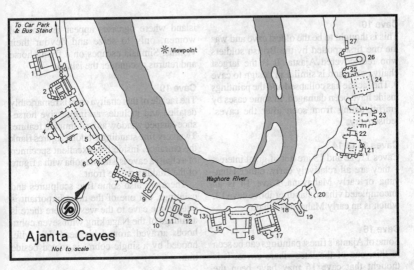

Ajanta Caves
Not to scale

Cave 2

Also a more recent vihara cave, this one has important paintings too, although unfortunately some are damaged. As well as murals, there are paintings on the ceiling. The scenes include a number of jatakas and events connected with the Buddha's birth, including his mother's dream of the six-tusked elephant which heralded the Buddha's conception.

Cave 4

This is the largest vihara cave at Ajanta and is supported by 28 pillars. Although it was never completed, the cave has some fine sculptures, including scenes of people fleeing from the 'eight great dangers' to the protection of the Buddha's disciple Avalokitesvara. One of the great dangers is an angry-looking elephant in pursuit of a man and woman. Caves 3, 5 and 8 were never completed.

Cave 6

This is the only two-storey cave at Ajanta, but parts of the lower storey have collapsed. Inside is a seated figure of the Buddha with an intricately carved door to the shrine.

Upstairs the hall is surrounded by cells with fine paintings on the doorways.

Caves 7 & 8

Cave 7 is of unusual design in that the verandah does not lead into a hall with cells down the sides and a shrine room at the rear. Here there are porches before the verandah, which leads directly to the four cells and the elaborately sculpted shrine. Cave 8 is used solely for the generating equipment which lights the caves.

Cave 9

This is a chaitya cave and one of the earliest at Ajanta. Although it dates from the Hinayana period, two Buddha figures flanking the entrance door were probably later Mahayana additions. Similarly, the paintings inside, which are not in excellent condition, show signs of having been refurbished at some time in the past. Columns run down both sides of the cave and around the three-metre-high dagoba at the far end. At the front there is a horseshoe-shaped window above the entrance, and the vaulted roof has traces of wooden ribs.

Cave 10

This is thought to be the oldest cave and was the one first spotted by the British soldiers who rediscovered Ajanta. It is the largest chaitya cave and is similar in design to cave 9. The facade has collapsed and the paintings inside have been damaged, in some cases by graffiti dating from soon after the caves' rediscovery.

Caves 11 to 14

Caves 11, 12 and 13 are not of great interest – they are all relatively early, either Hinayana or early Mahayana. Cave 14 is an uncompleted vihara, standing above cave 13, which is an early Mahayana vihara.

Cave 16

Some of Ajanta's finest paintings can be seen in this, one of the later vihara caves. It is thought that cave 16 may have been the original entrance to the entire complex, and there is a very fine view of the river from the front of the cave. Best known of the paintings here is the 'dying princess'. Sundari, wife of the Buddha's half-brother Nanda, is said to have expired at the hard news that her husband was renouncing the material life (and her) in order to become a monk. This is one of the finest paintings at Ajanta. Nanda features in several other paintings, including one of his conversion by the Buddha.

Cave 17

This is the cave with the finest paintings at Ajanta. Not only are they in the best condition, they are also the most numerous and varied. They include beautiful women flying overhead on the roof while carved dwarves support the pillars. A popular scene shows a woman, surrounded by attendants, applying make-up. In one there is a royal procession, while in another a couple engage in a little private lovemaking. In yet another panel the Buddha returns from his enlightenment to his own home to beg from his wife and astonished son.

A detailed panel tells the story of Prince Simhala's expedition to Sri Lanka. With his 500 companions he is shipwrecked on an island where ogresses appear as beautiful women, only to seize and devour their victims. Simhala escapes on a flying horse and returns to conquer the island.

Cave 19

The facade of this chaitya cave is remarkably detailed and includes an impressive horseshoe-shaped window as its dominant feature. Two very fine standing Buddha figures flank the entrance. Inside this excellent specimen of a chaitya cave is a tall dagoba with a figure of the Buddha on the front.

There are also some fine sculptures and paintings, but one of the most important is outside the cave to the west, where there is an image of the Naga king with seven cobra hoods arrayed around his head. His wife, hooded by a single cobra, is seated beside him.

Caves 20 to 25

These caves are either incomplete or not of great interest, although cave 24 would have been the largest vihara at Ajanta, if finished. You can see how the caves were constructed from this example – long galleries were cut into the rock, and then the rock between them was broken through.

Cave 26

The fourth chaitya cave's facade has fallen and almost every trace of its paintings has disappeared. Nevertheless there are some very fine sculptures remaining. On the left wall is a huge figure of the 'reclining Buddha', lying back as he prepares to enter nirvana. Other scenes include a lengthy depiction of the Buddha's temptation by Mara. In one scene Mara attacks the Buddha with demons, and then his beautiful daughters tempt him with more sensual delights. However, the Buddha's resistance is too strong, and the final scene shows a glum and dejected-looking Mara having failed to deflect the Buddha from the straight and narrow.

Caves 27 to 29

Cave 27 is virtually a vihara connected to the

cave 26 chaitya. There's a great pond in a box canyon 200 metres upstream from the cave. Caves 28 and 29 are higher up the cliff face and relatively hard to get to.

Places to Stay & Eat

There is an MTDC *Travellers' Lodge* (☎ 26) right by the entrance to the caves but it's in an appalling state of repair. Rooms cost Rs 75/100 with common bath. If the common bath is anything like the one attached to the restaurant then you're in for a shock. Check-out time is 8 am. The restaurant itself, however, is half-decent and the food reasonably good. Prices are moderate.

Most people stay at Fardapur, five km from the caves, where there is the excellent MTDC *Holiday Resort* (☎ 30) run by the state government. Rooms along the pleasant verandah cost Rs 100 for a single or double with bath (cold water only). Each room has two beds, clean sheets, mosquito nets and a fan. You have to pay in advance and there's a Rs 50 returnable deposit. You can also sleep on the floor here (no beds) for Rs 5. The hotel is run by a no-nonsense manager, so gear left in the rooms is secure.

The only other place in Fardapur is the *Pavan Tourist House* – at least, there's a sign to that effect nailed onto a tree outside the Holiday Resort, but I never found the place.

There are a number of shacks along the main road where you can buy cheap tea and snacks but nothing that you could vaguely call a meal. The only restaurant is the *Vihara Restaurant* attached to the Holiday Resort. It only functions in the evening, only offers thalis and the food is very average. If possible, order in advance or they may not buy sufficient food to cater for you.

Getting There & Away

It's Rs 18 from Aurangabad to Ajanta by local bus and it takes about three hours. From Jalgaon it's Rs 8 to Fardapur by local bus and this trip takes about 1½ hours. The caves are a couple of km off the main road from Aurangabad to Jalgaon, and Fardapur is a little further down the main road towards Jalgaon. There are regular buses between Fardapur and the Ajanta Caves which cost Rs 1 but not all buses travelling along the main road call at the caves. Make sure you get on the right one otherwise you'll have to walk the last two km.

There's a 'cloakroom' at the Ajanta Caves where you can leave gear, so it is possible to arrive on a morning bus from Jalgaon, look around the caves, and continue to Aurangabad in the evening, or vice versa.

JALGAON

The railway and bus stations in Jalgaon are a long way from each other and you'll need to take a tonga or auto-rickshaw between the two.

Places to Stay

For those en route to the caves, the *Morako* and the friendly *Tourist Hotel* are lower middle-range places. The *Tourist Hotel*, one km from the railway station, has rooms at around Rs 100 and a popular non-vegetarian restaurant. The *PWD Rest House*, just behind the Tourist Hotel, has also been recommended and is much better. The railway *retiring rooms* at Jalgaon are good value.

LONAR METEORITE CRATER

At the small village of Lonar, three hours by bus north-east of Jalna or 4½ hours south-east of Ajanta, is this huge and impressive meteorite crater. It's about two km in diameter and several hundred metres deep, with a shallow lake at the bottom. A plaque on the rim near the town states that this is 'the only natural hypervelocity impact crater in basaltic rock in the world'.

There are several **Hindu temples** on the crater floor, and langur monkeys inhabit the bushes by the lake. The crater is only about five minutes walk from the bus station – ask for Lonar Tank.

It's possible to visit Lonar in a day en route between Fardapur and Aurangabad, but this would be rushing things.

Places to Stay

There is a basic hotel by the bus station in

Lonar, and others in Buldhana, three hours to the north.

Getting There & Away

From Lonar there are buses to Buldhana from where it's easy to catch a bus for the bumpy 1½-hour journey to Fardapur. Heading south from Lonar there are direct buses to Jalna, from where there are trains and buses to Aurangabad, a total of about five hours.

NAGPUR

Population: 1,661,000

Situated on the River Nag, from which the town takes its name, Nagpur is the orange-growing capital of central India. It was once the capital of the central province, but was later incorporated into Maharashtra. Long ago it was a centre for the aboriginal Gond tribes who remained in power until the early 18th century. Many Gonds still live in this region. Later it went through a series of changes before eventually falling to the British.

Places to Stay

Among the centrally located cheaper places is the *Hotel Shyam* (☎ 52-4073) on Pandit Malaviya Rd, with rooms at Rs 95/125. The hotel has a good rooftop restaurant with a multi-cuisine menu and a bar. Similar is the *Hotel Jagsons* (☎ 48-611), 30 Back Central Ave, which has rooms for Rs 90/140 or Rs 175/250 with air-con. There's a restaurant and bar and all the rooms have a TV. Cheaper, as far as rooms without air-con are concerned, is the *Hotel Blue Diamond* (☎ 47-461) at 113 Dosar Square Central Ave which has rooms for Rs 35/55 to Rs 65/100 or Rs 150/200 with air-con. There's a restaurant and bar.

More expensive is the two-star *Rawell Continental* (☎ 52-3845), 7 Dhantoli, Wardha Rd, which is centrally air-con and has rooms for Rs 330/500 and suites for Rs 360 to Rs 700. Also in this category is the *Hotel Centre Point* (☎ 52-3093), 24 Central Bazar Rd, Ramdaspeth, which is about four km from the railway station. It has air-con rooms at Rs 360 for singles, Rs 550 to Rs 650 for

doubles, and Rs 720 for suites. There's a swimming pool, restaurant and bar.

OTHER PLACES IN THE NORTH

Ramtek

About 40 km north-east of Nagpur, Ramtek has a number of picturesque 600-year-old **temples** surmounting the Hill of Rama. In summer this is one of the hottest places in India. The old British cantonment of Kemtee is nearby, and a **memorial** to the Sanskrit dramatist Kalidasa is just along the road from the Tourist Bungalow, which has a spectacular view of the town.

Wardha & Sevagram

About 80 km south-west of Nagpur, near Wardha station, is Sevagram, the Village of Service, where Gandhi established his ashram in 1933. For the 15 years from then until India achieved independence, this was in some ways the alternative capital of India.

The Centre of Science for Villages (Magan Sangrahalaya) is a **museum** intended to explain and develop Gandhi's ideals of village-level economics. The huts of his ashram are still preserved in Sevagram and there is a photo exhibit of events in the Mahatma's life at Mahadev Bhawan, beside the Sevagram hospital.

Only three km from Sevagram is the **ashram of Vinoba Bhave**, Gandhi's follower who walked throughout India persuading rich landlords to hand over tracts of land for redistribution to the landless and poor.

Amraoti & Akola

These two towns are between Jalgaon and Nagpur. Amraoti has the biggest **cotton market** in India and is the site of the old Amba **temple** near the walled city. The town has a famous sports college which has old-fashioned wrestling pits.

Places to Stay You can try the *Maharaja Guest House* at Amraoti or the *Hotel Dreamland* at Akola – the latter is another of those places on the downhill path to Indian hotel oblivion.

Goa

Population: 1.2 million
Area: 3659 sq km
Capital: Panaji
People per sq km: 316
Main Languages: Konkani & Marathi;
   English is widely spoken and many of the
   older generation also speak Portuguese.
Literacy Rate: 77%

The former Portuguese enclave of Goa, one of India's gems, has enjoyed a prominent place in the travellers' lexicon for many years. The main reason for this is its magnificent palm-fringed beaches and 'travellers' scene'. Yet it offers much more than just the hedonism of sun, sand and sea. Goa has a character quite distinct from the rest of India. Despite more than three decades of 'liberation' from Portuguese colonial rule, Roman Catholicism remains the predominant religion, skirts far outnumber saris, and the people display an easy-going tropical indulgence, humour and civility which you'll find hard to beat, even in Kerala.

Gleaming whitewashed churches with Portuguese-style facades pepper the hillsides, rice paddies and dense coconut palm groves, while crumbling forts guard rocky capes and estuary entrances. Markets are lively colourful affairs, and siesta is widely observed during the hot afternoon hours. Carnival explodes onto the streets for four riotous days and nights prior to Lent. Not only that, but there seems to be a total lack of the excessive shyness which Hindu women display towards men, and there are very good reasons for that. One of them relates to the Goan laws of property which ensure that a married woman is entitled to 50% of the couple's estate – a far cry from what applies in the rest of India.

With a bit of luck you'll come across that peculiar colonial anachronism, the *escrivão*, an older Hindu civil servant wearing a three-piece suit with tie, socks and shoes, a solar hat and a dhoti!

Govt of India statement – 'The external boundaries of India are neither correct nor authenticated'.

Until recently, Goa was part of the Union Territory of Goa, Daman & Diu, but in 1987 it became the 25th state of the Indian Union. Daman & Diu remain a Union Territory, although the governor of Goa is also designated as the lieutenant governor of Daman & Diu. Those places are both dealt with in the Gujarat chapter of this book.

If you're interested in a sympathetic yet satirical cartoon essay on Goa from a Goan point of view, then get hold of the booklet *Goa with Love* by Mario Miranda (Goa Tours, Goa, 1982) – it's superb!

History

Goa's history stretches back to the 3rd century BC when it formed part of the Mauryan Empire. It was later ruled by the Satavahanas of Kolhapur at the beginning of the Christian era and eventually passed to the Chalukyans of Badami, who controlled it from 580 to 750 AD. Over the next few centuries it was ruled successively by the

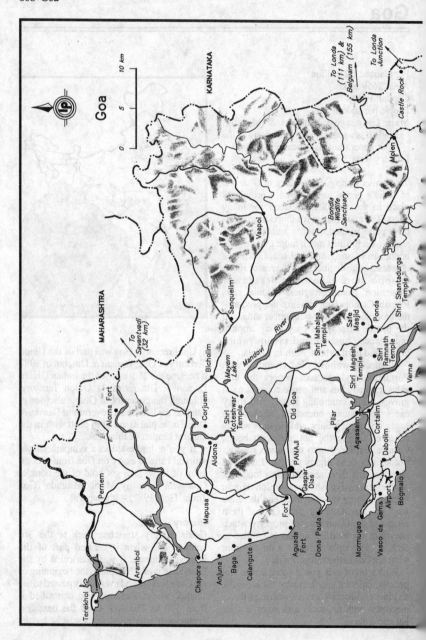

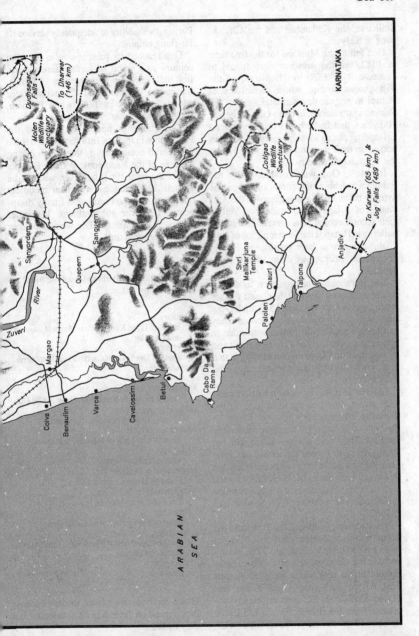

KARNATAKA

Dudhsagar
Falls

To Dharwar
(146 km)

Molem
Wildlife
Sanctuary

Cotigao
Wildlife
Sanctuary

Sanvordem

River

Sanguem

Quepern

Shri
Mallikarjuna
Temple

Chauri

To Karwar (65 km) &
Jog Falls (489 km)

Zuvari

Anjadiv

Margao

Palolen

Talpona

Betul

Colva

Benaulim

Varca

Cavelossim

Cabo Da
Rama

ARABIAN
SEA

Shilharas, the Kadambas and the Chaluk-yans of Kalyani.

Goa fell to the Muslims for the first time in 1312, but the invaders were forced to evacuate it in 1370 by Harihara I of the Vijayanagar Empire, whose capital was at Hampi in present-day Karnataka state. The Vijayanagar rulers held on to Goa for nearly 100 years, and its harbours became import-ant landing places for ships carrying Arabian horses on their way to Hampi to strengthen the Vijayanagar cavalry.

In 1469, Goa was conquered by the Bahmani Sultans of Gulbarga, and when this dynasty broke up, the area passed to the Adil Shahis of Bijapur, who made Goa Velhaa their second capital. The present Secretariat building in Panaji is the former palace of Adil Shah, and it was later taken over by the Portuguese viceroys as their official Resi-dence.

The Portuguese, having been unable to secure a base on the Malabar coast further south, arrived in Goa in 1510 under the command of Alfonso de Albuquerque. They had been unsuccessful further south due to opposition from the Zamorin of Calicut and stiff competition from the Turks who, at that time, controlled the trade routes across the Indian Ocean.

Blessed as it was by natural harbours and wide rivers, Goa was the ideal base for the seafaring Portuguese, who were intent on their quest for control of the spice route from the East. They were also possessed with the strong desire to further the spread of Chris-tianity. For a while their control was limited to a small area around Old Goa, but by the middle of the 16th century it had expanded to include the provinces of Bardez and Salcete.

The eventual ousting of the Turks and the fortunes to be made from control of the spice trade led to Goa's 'golden age'. The colony became the viceregal seat of the Portuguese Empire of the east which included various East Africa port cities, East Timor and Macau. Decline set in, however, due to com-petition from the British, French and Dutch in the 17th century, combined with Portugal's inability to adequately service its far-flung empire.

Goa reached its present size in the 18th century as a result of further annexations, first in 1763 when the provinces of Ponda, Sanguem, Quepem and Canacona were added, and later in 1788 when Pednem, Bicholim and Satari were added.

The Marathas nearly vanquished the Portuguese in the late 18th century and there was a brief occupation by the British during the time of the Napoleonic Wars in Europe. It was not until 1961, however, when India ejected the Portuguese in a near bloodless operation, that the Portuguese finally disap-peared from the subcontinent. The other enclaves of Daman and Diu were also taken over at the same time.

Festivals

The Christian festivals in Goa take place on the following dates:

6 January
    Feast of Three Kings at Reis Magos, Cansaulim and Chandor
2 February
    Feast of Our Lady of Candelaria at Pomburpa
February/March
    Carnival
Monday after 5th Sunday in Lent
    Procession of the Franciscan Order at Old Goa
1st Sunday after Easter
    Feast of Jesus of Nazareth at Siridao
16 days after Easter
    Feast of Our Lady of Miracles at Mapusa
24 August
    Festival of Novidades
1st fortnight of October
    Fama de Menino Jesus at Colva
3rd Wednesday of November
    Feast of Our Lady of the Rosary
3 December
    Feast of St Francis Xavier at Old Goa
8 December
    Feast of Our Lady of Immaculate Conception at Panaji and Margao
25 December
    Christmas

Hindu festivals are harder to date because they depend on the Indian lunar calendar, but they include:

January

Festival of Shantadurga Prasann at the small village of Fatorpa, south of Margao in Quepem province. There is a night-time procession of chariots bearing the goddess, and as many as 100,000 people flock to the festival.

The Shri Bodgeshwar *zatra*, or temple festival, takes place just south of Mapusa.

February

The three day zatra of Shri Mangesh takes place in the lavish temple of that name in the Ponda district.

In the old Fontainhas district of Panaji the Maruti zatra draws huge and colourful crowds. Maruti is another name for Hanuman.

March

In Goa the festival of Holi is called Shigmo. There's a parade in Panaji and numerous temple festivals around Goa.

In the Procession of Umbrellas at Cuncolim, south of Margao, a solid silver image of Shantadurga is carried in procession over the hills to the original temple site, which was wrecked by the Portuguese in 1580. The route taken is the same one by which the image was spirited away to safety outside the Portuguese borders. It's a colourful and dramatic event.

Nudism & Local Sensibilities

Goa is a part of the Indian subcontinent overlaid with much Hindu culture. You should never make the mistake of thinking that because Goa is so welcoming, friendly and liberal, that you're at liberty to exploit it or flagrantly disregard local sensibilities.

Too many people did that in the late '60s and '70s by nude (or seminude) bathing, and Goa became famous for it. Of course, there are still places where you can lie around in your birthday suit and plenty of people do, but don't do it where families bathe. Probably no-one v.ill bother you (that's Goa), but remember that it's merely tolerated.

This guidebook has come in for varying degrees of criticism for suggesting that nudism, whether partial or complete, was acceptable on Goan beaches. One newspaper article bitterly attacked the 'disgusting unabashedness' with which we suggested that, if you were tired of wearing clothes, to take them off since everyone else did. It went on to condemn the 'pernicious attempt to cash in on nudism by making it one of the artificially created resources for tourism promotion'.

The truth of the matter is that signs have been erected prohibiting nudism as a result of pressure by several citizens' action groups. In practice, however, this has had minimal effect away from the main tourist areas. And, while we accept the criticism, the fact is that nudism remains a common feature of the beaches north of Vagator, but no longer at Calangute or Baga, where G-strings are *de rigeur*. Signboards are one thing. The will to enforce what they prohibit is quite another. Just don't overdo it!

Ganja

The dreaded weed is readily available in Goa (it's usually from Kerala). Travellers who've come from Kashmir or the Kulu Valley may offer you resin but the quality varies. It is, of course, illegal.

Crackdowns by the local police are frequent and the consequences of being caught can be drastic. Be discreet, and read the warning in the Facts for the Visitor chapter.

Accommodation

Accommodation prices in Goa are based on high, middle and low seasons. This generally won't affect you if you stay in budget accommodation but certainly will if you stay in middle or top-range hotels. The high season covers the period from 15 December to 31 January, the middle (shoulder) period from 1 February to 30 June, and the low season from 1 July to 30 September. Prices quoted in this chapter are the high-season rates. If you're in Goa during the rest of the year then count on about 15% discount in the middle season and up to 50% in the low season.

The other thing to bear in mind are checkout times, which vary considerably and have no relation to the type of hotel you are staying in. They can be as early as 9 am; others set it at 10 am, others at noon and still others work on a 24-hour basis. Watch this carefully otherwise you could end up paying an extra 50% of the daily rate for overstaying a few hours. You'll come across this elsewhere in India but in Goa disorder seems to rule.

Goan Food & Drink

Although food in Goa is much like food anywhere else in India, there are several local specialities, including the popular pork vindaloo. Other pork specialities include the Goan sausage, or *chourisso*, and the pig's liver dish known as *sarpotel*. *Xacutí* is a chicken or meat dish. Seafood of all types is, of course, plentiful and fresh. *Bangra* is Goan mackerel, prepared in a variety of delicious ways. *Sanna* are rice 'cupcakes' soaked in palm toddy before cooking. There are a variety of special Christmas sweets called *dodol, bebinca* and so on. *Moira kela* are cooking plantains (banana-like fruit) from Moira village in Bardez. They were probably introduced from Africa and can be found in the vegetable market in Panaji close to Indian Airlines.

There are the usual travellers' menu items at the beach restaurants. Bread is usually excellent, as are the muesli, pancakes, porridge and other dishes which make such a welcome change from Indian food.

Although the ready availability (and low price) of commercially produced alcoholic beverages contrasts markedly with most other parts of India, the Goans also brew their own local varieties. Most common of these is feni, a spirit made from coconut or cashews. A bottle bought from a liquor shop costs only slightly more than a bottle of beer bought at a restaurant.

Reasonably palatable wines are also being turned out. The dry white is not bad; the red is essentially port. As you might expect, the quality depends on the price you pay.

Getting There & Away

Air & Bus See the Getting There & Away section of Panaji for details of long-distance air and bus travel.

Train At present Goa has only metre-gauge connections with Karnataka, and so for long-haul journeys (especially from Bombay) buses are generally faster. However, a new broad-gauge line running south along the coast from Bombay is currently under construction and once completed should speed the journey between the two places considerably.

The railhead in Goa is at Vasco da Gama (it actually continues on to Mormugao but very few of the main trains start from there). See the Getting Around section for details of getting to Vasco from Panaji. The other main station in Goa is at Margao. Seats and sleepers on the trains can be booked at Vasco da Gama, Margao or the South Central Out-Agency booking office at counter No 5 in the Panaji bus station, *except* for Indrail Pass holders who must book at Vasco da Gama and nowhere else (there's a special tourist quota allocated to them at this station). The Out-Agency booking office is open from 10 am to 1 pm and 2 to 4.30 pm daily except Sundays.

Trains to Bangalore take about 20 hours. Fares for the 689-km trip are Rs 110/421 in 2nd/1st class. There are also some through carriages which get unhooked at Arsikere and continue on to Mysore.

The 769-km trip to Bombay takes 24 hours and involves a change of train at Miraj. The fare is Rs 123/463 in 2nd/1st class. Getting to New Delhi from Goa also involves a change from metre to broad gauge at Miraj. Total journey time is about 44 hours and the fare for the 2400-km trip is Rs 221/1029.

If you are heading for inland Karnataka – Hampi, Bijapur or Badami – there are two through carriages on the No 7805 *Miraj Passenger* (departing Vasco da Gama at 9.15 pm), which get detached at Londa and hook up with the No 7838 *Miraj Link Express* to Hubli, arriving there at 6.15 am. Hubli is a major railway junction from where there are express trains to Bombay and Bangalore, and passenger steam trains to Hospet (for the Vijayanagar ruins at Hampi), Badami and Bijapur.

Coastal Boat Tours Since the unfortunate demise of the Bombay-Goa ferry service, there has been no way to take this interesting trip up the coast. However, it is now possible to go up the coast on a tour organised by Odyssey Tours. They have several programmes, some of which include a four-day cruise in a large yacht (maximum 20 passengers) along the coast between Bombay and Goa.

Odyssey Tours have offices in Bombay (☎ 627-1690/1) at 1307 Everest Apartments, JP Rd, Versova, Andheri (W) 400 061; and in New Delhi (☎ 344-225), Connaught Palace Hotel, 2nd Floor, 37 Shaheed Bhagat Singh Marg 110 001. For their foreign addresses, see Tours in the Getting There & Away chapter.

Getting Around

Bus The state-run Kadamba Bus Company is the main operator, although there are many private companies in operation too. They're cheap and they run to just about everywhere. Services are frequent and destinations at the bus stations are in English so there are no worries about finding the bus you want. Pay your fare on the bus.

The only trouble is that the conductors have the same mentality as sardine-can manufacturers so, if you want a seat, get on at a bus station otherwise you'll have to join the crush. The good news, on the other hand, is that Goans have a very mellow attitude to being packed into a tin can. There's no crazy panic and no-one will try to claw you out of the way in their manic attempt to board a bus. Seated passengers may even offer to take your bags if you're standing. The buses are, however, fairly slow since they make many stops.

Motorcycle Taxis Goa is the one place in India where motorcycles are a licensed form of taxi. If you don't mind travelling this way, they are much cheaper than other transport if you are travelling alone, and backpacks are no problem. Licensed motorcycles have a yellow front mudguard and are found in large numbers throughout the state.

Motorcycle Hire Hiring a motorcycle in Goa is easy, and many long-term travellers do just

that. The machines available are old Enfields (which often need loving care on the spark plugs), Rajdoots (of Indian manufacture which one of the authors of this book asserts, from experience, are the worst in the world) and more modern Yamahas and Hondas. Obviously what you pay for – with certain exceptions – is what you get, but Rs 800 per week would be about right for an Enfield. On a daily basis you're looking at around Rs 200 per day for a fairly new Yamaha. You'll need your passport and a sizeable deposit before they'll let you go.

While it might be more expensive than the buses – and with all due respect to the conservationist lobby – the freedom it gives you cannot be measured. If you don't agree then rent a bicycle – but getting down to Palolen or up to Terekhol is something else on a bicycle!

If you are in the market for a new or used motorcycle, try Auto Guides on Dr Dada Vaidya Rd, near the Hotel Samrat in Panaji.

If you hire a motorcycle, be warned that there are occasional licence checks on foreigners, particularly in Anjuna on market day (Wednesday). Make sure that you have the necessary paperwork for both yourself (licence) and the bike (registration and insurance).

Bicycle There are plenty of places to hire bicycles in all the major towns and beaches in Goa. Standard charges are Rs 2 per hour or Rs 15 to Rs 20 for a full day (8 am to 6 pm) plus Rs 5 if you keep it overnight. Occasionally you'll be asked for more. If you object, go to a different place.

Boat One of the joys of travelling around Goa are the ferries across the many rivers in this small state. Almost without exception they are combined passenger/car ferries. The main ferries are:

Panaji to Betim – These are the ferries that connect with buses, motorbikes and taxis going north of Panaji. There are nonstop passenger/car ferries around the clock across the Mandovi River. These ferries are free for passengers and bicycles but you have to pay a small charge for motorbikes and cars (buy the ticket for this before boarding the ferry). For Aguada, Calangute and Baga the ferry landing is opposite the Mandovi Hotel.

Dona Paula to Mormugao – This ferry runs between September and May only. There are regular crossings but they are infrequent and, at certain times of the day, you could find yourself waiting about two hours. The crossing takes 30 to 45 minutes and costs Rs 2. Buses wait on either side for the arrival of boats. This is a passenger ferry only, but it's the best way of getting from Panaji to Vasco da Gama.

Old Goa to Piedade – Ferries go every 30 minutes.

Other Ferries – These include: Aldona to Corjuem; Colvale to Macasana; Pomburpa to Chorao; Ribander to Chorao and Siolim to Chopdem. There are also launches from the central jetty in Panaji to Aldona (once daily), Britona (twice daily), Naroa (twice daily) and Verem.

PANAJI (Panjim)

Population: 85,000

Panaji is one of India's smallest and most pleasant state capitals. Built on the south bank of the wide Mandovi River, it officially became the capital of Goa in 1843, though the Portuguese viceroys shifted their Residence from the outskirts of Old Goa to the former palace of Adil Shah at Panaji as early as 1759.

The old town has preserved its Portuguese heritage remarkably well; there are narrow winding streets, old houses with overhanging balconies and red-tiled roofs, whitewashed churches and numerous small bars and cafes. Portuguese signs are still visible over many shops, cafes and administrative buildings. People are friendly and the atmosphere is easy-going. The main attraction is Old Goa, nine km east of Panaji, the former capital founded by Alfonso de Albuquerque in 1510, but Panaji is well worth a visit for its own sake.

Panaji's 'sights' are few, but among those worth visiting are the old **Church of the Immaculate Conception** (on the hillside at one end of the Municipal Gardens) and the **Mahalaxmi Temple**. If you're staying in Panaji rather than on the beaches of Goa then the nearest beach is at Miramar, three km along the road to Dona Paula.

Information

Tourist Offices The tourist office (☎ 45-715) is in the government-run Tourist Home between the bus stand and Ourem River (it's signposted). The staff here are very keen and their information is reliable. Excellent maps of Goa and Panaji are available for Rs 6.50.

The local government also operates a tourist counter at the airport, and it is open for incoming flights. There's another tourist counter at the interstate bus stand, and this is open from 9.30 am to 1 pm and from 2 to 5 pm daily.

To complete the picture there's also a Government of India tourist office (☎ 43-412) in the Communidade Building, Church Square.

Post & Telecommunications The poste restante at the GPO is efficient. They give you the whole pile to sort through yourself and will willingly check other pigeon holes if expected letters are not arriving. It's open from 9.30 am to 1 pm and 2 to 5.30 pm Monday to Saturday.

International telephone calls are handled at the Central Telegraph Office, Dr Atmaram Borkar Rd, which is open 24 hours, but it is quicker, easier and cheaper to use one of the many private long-distance/ISD booths around town. There's a 24-hour booth almost opposite the telegraph office, and you can bargain for a discount if your call is likely to be more than 10 minutes or so.

Visa Extensions Visa extensions are not granted as a matter of course in Panaji. The more respectable and upmarket you look, the more your application is likely to be viewed favourably. If you're unsuccessful here, Bombay and Bangalore are the nearest places. The Foreigners' Registration Office is in the centre of Panaji and is open from 9.30 am to 1 pm Monday to Friday.

Tax Clearance If you've stayed in India so long that you need a tax clearance certificate before you depart, then the Taxation Department is in the Shanta Building at the end of Emidio Gracia Rd.

Travel Agencies Georgeson & Georgeson (☎ 2150) opposite the GPO (1st floor) is a travel agent which seems to be reasonably reliable and efficient. MGM Travel is similar and has branch offices at Calangute and Anjuna. If you have to reconfirm international flights, check if Air India will do it first. Some travel agents charge heavily for this service.

Books & Newspapers The hotels Mandovi and Fidalgo both have good bookshops. *Inside Goa* by Manohar Mulgaokar with illustrations by Mario Miranda is excellent, though somewhat expensive. The *Herald Tribune, Time, Newsweek* and other international magazines are also available.

Three local English language newspapers are published in Panaji. The 'establishment' paper is the *Navhind Times* and the 'independent' papers are the *Herald* and the *Gomantok Times*.

Organised Tours

Tours of Goa are offered both by the tourist office (book there or at the Panaji interstate bus station (☎ 6515), and by private agencies. The tours aren't very good because they pack too much into a short day so you end up seeing very little. The beach tours are only for voyeurs hoping to catch a glimpse of nude or seminude Western bodies.

The North Goa tour visits Panaji, Datta Mandir, Mayem Lake, Mapusa, Vagator, Anjuna, Calangute and Fort Aguada. The South Goa tours take in Miramar, Dona Paula, Pilar Seminary, Marmugao, Vasco da Gama, Colva, Margao, Shantadurga Temple, Mangesh Temple and Old Goa. The tours cost Rs 45 and depart daily at 9 and 9.30 am respectively, both returning to Panaji at 6 pm. The beach tour is Rs 30, lasts from 3 to 7 pm and covers Calangute, Anjuna and Vagator. The Bondla Wildlife Sanctuary tour costs Rs 45 and departs daily at 9.30 am, returning at 5 pm.

There are also daily river cruises along the Mandovi River at 6 (Sunset Cruise) and 7.15 pm (Sundown Cruise) which last an hour and cost Rs 50. They're good value and include a cultural programme of Goan folk songs and dances. Drinks and snacks are available. On full-moon nights there are two-hour cruises from 8.30 pm for Rs 80, and dinner is available. Make sure you get the government-operated boat, the *Santa Monica*, which leaves from the former Bombay steamer jetty by the customs office. The other boats, in front of the Tourist Hostel, are privately owned and departures are more random.

Places to Stay

Whenever there is a religious festival in Goa – especially the festival of St Francis Xavier (several days on either side of 3 December) – it can be difficult to find accommodation in Panaji, especially at the small, inexpensive lodges. There is no accommodation at Old Goa.

In the high season many hotels have only a double tariff – bad news if you're travelling alone. At all times of year there's a 5% government tax on rooms over Rs 100, and it's 10% on rooms over Rs 500. Prices quoted in the following section do not include this tax.

Places to Stay – bottom end

Popular at the lower end of the scale is the *Republica Hotel* (☎ 44-630), José Falcão Rd, at the back of the Secretariat block. It's an old place with fine views over the Mandovi River, although it's decidedly shabby. Singles/doubles without bathroom cost Rs 30/60 and doubles with bathroom Rs 80 to Rs 100, depending on the size of the room and the view. The showers and toilets are kept passably clean and the staff are friendly. If possible, try to get one of the rooms overlooking the river – the others are a bit dingy. The *Palace Hotel* next door is for emergencies only. Rooms cost Rs 20/40, or Rs 60 with bathroom attached, but the atmosphere is gloomy and the management indifferent.

Just up the road from the Republica and at the back of the Tourist Hostel is the very popular *Mandovi Pearl Guest House* (☎ 46-852), but as it has only four rooms, it's often full. All rooms have common facilities and

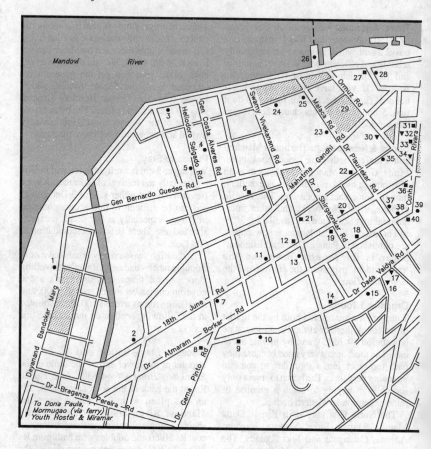

range from Rs 110 for a single to Rs 150 for a triple. Prices are less in the low season.

In the old part of town, in the narrow streets running parallel to the Ourem River, there are several good, cheap places to stay. The friendly *Hotel Venite*, 31 January Rd, has only four basic but clean rooms, but these are overpriced at Rs 75, or Rs 90 with a balcony. Close by are the *Udipi Boarding & Lodging* and the *Elite Boarding & Lodging*. These are much better value, with rooms for Rs 60 a double with common bathroom and Rs 75 a double with private bathroom.

Up on the hillside overlooking the Elite is the *Casa Pinho*, a large old house with basic and dingy but relatively clean rooms for Rs 50/75 with bathroom.

Travellers looking for dormitory accommodation have a couple of options. The *Tourist Home* (☎ 45-715), in a complex which includes the tourist office, is by the riverside between the bus station and town centre. It's quite popular with Westerners and Indians alike, and costs Rs 35 per bed per night in the high season, Rs 20 in the low season. There is a restaurant and bar.

The *Youth Hostel* (☎ 45-433) is out at Miramar Beach in a shady she-oak garden

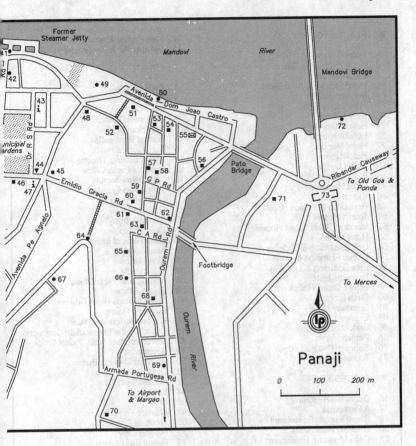

Panaji

0   100   200 m

right next to the beach. The drawbacks are the institutional air and the long distance from the centre of Panaji. Dorm beds cost Rs 10 (Rs 20 for nonmembers) and there's a solitary double room with bathroom for Rs 66. Officially the hostel is closed between 1 and 4 pm, but they're not strict about it.

Also at Miramar beach, the *Hotel Solmar* (☎ 4555), Avenida Gaspar Dias, and the *Belo Horizonte*, on the main road, have reasonably priced rooms.

Back in town but going up in price, there is the multistorey *Tourist Hostel* (☎ 47-103) fronting onto the Mandovi River. This place

is a bargain at Rs 135/150 for a single/double with bathroom and hot water, and off-season prices are Rs 90/100. Its only drawback is that it can be booked out for weeks in advance. Front rooms overlook the river but tend to be noisy, so try for a back room. There's a terrace restaurant, bar, bookshop and handicraft shop on the ground floor.

In the streets parallel to the Ourem River, in the old part of town, are a number of other places. Prominent among them is the family-run *Park Lane Lodge* at Rs 90/95 for a single/double. It's an older style building and has a pleasant lazy atmosphere.

■ PLACES TO STAY

6	Hotel Delmon
8	Hotel Palácio de Goa
9	Hotel Samrat
12	Hotel Fidalgo & Air India
14	Mayfair Hotel
18	Hotel Nova Goa
19	Keni's Hotel
21	Hotel Summit
22	Hotel Neptune
27	Hotel Mandovi
31	Hotel Aroma
33	Safari Lodge
36	Pure Gujarat Hotel
40	Hotel Rajdhani
46	Kamat Hotel
48	Republica & Palace Hotels
51	Tourist Hostel
52	Mandovi Pearl Guest House
53	Hotel Venite
54	Udipi Boarding & Lodging
56	Hotels Flamingo & Sona
57	Elite Boarding & Lodging
58	Baretons Hotel
59	Orav's Guest House
60	Casa Pinho
61	Embassy Hotel
63	Everest Lodge
65	Park Lane Lodge
68	Panjim Inn
70	Sangam Deluxe Lodge
71	Tourist Home

▼ PLACES TO EAT

16	Goenchin Restaurant
17	A Pastelaria
20	Shere Punjab Restaurant
30	Godinho Restaurant
32	Casa Moderna Restaurant
34	New Punjab Restaurant
44	George Bar & Restaurant

OTHER

1	Children's Park
2	Museum
3	Indian Airlines
4	El Dorado Theatre
5	Municipal Market
7	Budget Rent-a-Car
10	Auto Guides
11	Ashok Samrat Theatre
13	National Parks Office
15	Mahalaxmi Temple
23	Police Headquarters (visa extensions)
24	Collectorate
25	Central Library
26	Ferry Ramp
28	State Bank of India
29	Azad Maidan
35	Cine National
37	Municipality
38	Central Telegraph Office
39	Phone Office
41	Santa Monica River Cruises
42	Customs House
43	Karnataka Tourist Office
45	Church of the Immaculate Conception
47	Government of India Tourist Office
49	Secretariat
50	Ferry for Mapusa Buses
55	GPO
62	Income Tax Office
64	School
66	Church
67	Alliance Française
69	Archives Office
72	Fishing Jetty
73	Panaji Bus Station

Also good in this upper budget bracket is *Orav's Guest House*, 31 January Rd, which is a relatively new place and very clean. It costs Rs 150 a double with bathroom. There are no single rooms.

In the new part of town is the *Hotel Neptune* (☎ 47-727), Malaca Rd, which offers rooms for Rs 90/130 a single/double and Rs 200/250 with air-con. All the rooms have bathrooms and hot water, and there's a 'posh restaurant with bar attached'. It's often full.

Places to Stay – middle

One of the best places to stay at the lower end of this bracket is the *Panjim Inn* – a beautiful old mansion with a large 1st-floor verandah and leafy garden. It's a popular place and the staff are friendly. Rooms cost Rs 165/195 a single/double with bathroom; try to see a couple of rooms as some are definitely better than others. There's a TV lounge, and good meals are available for guests. Checkout time is 9 am.

Equally popular, and fronting onto the

Municipal Gardens, is the modern *Hotel Aroma* (☎ 3519), Cunha Rivara Rd, which has rooms for Rs 154/195 a single/double with bathroom. There are clean sheets, fans and a laundry service but hot water is often a figment of the imagination. The tandoori restaurant on the 1st floor is one of the best in Panaji.

Of a similar standard but less attractive is the *Hotel Sona* (☎ 44-426), on noisy Ourem Rd, which costs Rs 175 a double (no singles). All rooms have a bathroom with hot water in the mornings only.

The very pleasant *Mayfair Hotel* (☎ 46-174), Dr Dada Vaidya Rd, is good value at Rs 120/165 for a single/double, or Rs 165/210 with air-con. All rooms have their own bathroom with hot and cold water plus there's a bar and restaurant with Goan, Continental, vegetarian and non-vegetarian cuisine. Similar is the *Hotel Summit* (☎ 46-734), Menezes Braganza Rd, but it's more expensive at Rs 200 for a double with bathroom, and Rs 300 for an air-con double. All rooms have their own bathroom with hot and cold water 24 hours a day.

Other hotels in this bracket include the *Hotel Samrat* (☎ 44-546), Dr Dada Vaidya Rd, and *Keni's Hotel* (☎ 44-581), 18th June Rd. The Samrat charges Rs 145/250 for singles/doubles. All rooms have a bathroom with hot water plus there's a restaurant, bar and rooftop garden. They can also change travellers' cheques and accept most credit cards. Keni's Hotel is also popular with travellers in need of a touch of luxury. They offer singles/doubles for Rs 180/250 and air-con doubles for Rs 350 with bathroom, hot water and colour TV. The hotel includes a bar, restaurant and shopping arcade. Keni's Hotel is actually classified as a three-star hotel so don't be too surprised if you're quoted high prices when the rooms without air-con are full.

The *Hotel Palácio de Goa* (☎ 4289), Dr Gama Pinto Rd, is a sensitively designed five-storey hotel with each room having a Portuguese-style balcony overlooking the street. Rooms cost just Rs 225 for a double and Rs 295 for an air-con double – an incontestable bargain at today's prices. The only trouble with the Palácio is that it caters mainly for Gujarati families so it has pure vegetarian food and no alcohol. But so what? Goa is replete with seafood restaurants and bars.

Another good one in this bracket is the *Hotel Rajdhani* (☎ 45-362), Dr Atmaram Borkar Rd, which charges Rs 165/185 for singles/doubles, and air-con rooms are also available. Checkout time is 10 am.

The *Hotel Delmon* (☎ 45-616) is another relatively new place in the centre of Panaji. Rooms here are good value at Rs 200/250.

Places to Stay – top end

The *Hotel Fidalgo* (☎ 46-291), 18th June Rd, is one of Panaji's oldest top of the range hotels, but it is centrally located and has a good range of facilities. Rooms cost Rs 395/650, plus tax.

Another older place is the *Hotel Mandovi* (☎ 46-270), Dayamond Bandokar Marg. Rooms overlooking the river are the most expensive at Rs 700 for a double, while those at the rear are much cheaper at Rs 330/360.

One of the better newer places is the *Hotel Nova Goa* (☎ 6231), Dr Atmaram Borkar Rd, with rooms for Rs 360/480 a single/double. There are more expensive suites and a shaded swimming pool.

Places to Stay – Around Panaji

Most of the hotels outside Panaji – south of Calangute and north of Colva but excluding Vasco da Gama and Mormugao – are beach resorts that cater largely to affluent tourists and those seeking water sports. One of them was chosen during Indira Gandhi's time as the venue for a Commonwealth Heads of Government conference.

Seventeen km west of Panaji, on the opposite side of the Mandovi River, is the *Fort Aguada Beach Resort* (☎ 7501), Sinquerim. It has 120 rooms and costs Rs 2250 for singles or doubles in the high season, but discounts apply during the low season. It's a very pleasant, upmarket resort.

Seven km south of Panaji and facing Mormugao Bay is the *Cidade de Goa* (☎ 43-

301), Vainguinim Beach, Dona Paula, which has 101 rooms and costs US$90/95 for foreigners, and is very popular with tour groups. There are discounts during the low season.

At Dona Paula on the tip of the peninsula, the *Dona Paula Beach Resort* (☎ 47-955) is a small place with good views and beach access. Rooms cost Rs 250/300, and there's a restaurant on the premises.

Even further south, on the far side of the Mormugao peninsula but only three km from the airport, is the *Oberoi Bogmalo Beach* (☎ 2191) which has 119 rooms. They cost Rs 1700 a single or double in the high season and there are discounts for the low season. All these five-star hotels offer the usual luxuries plus a whole range of water and land-based sports facilities.

A little upriver from the Cidade de Goa but still facing Mormugao Bay is the fairly new *Green Valley Beach Resort* (☎ 6499), Bambolim Village, eight km south-east of Panaji. It offers air-con doubles at Rs 650, water sports and an open-air thatched restaurant surrounding an enormous banyan tree. The resort is owned by two Goan brothers, Vero and Savio Nunes, and with prices like these the place is deservedly popular.

Places to Eat

Panaji is full of restaurants, many of them attached to hotels, which cater for every taste and every pocket. One of the best is at the *Hotel Venite*, 31 January Rd. This beautiful old place on the 1st floor has polished wooden floors, flower-decked balconies overlooking the street and bags of atmosphere. This restaurant attracts a colourful crowd of local people and travellers every day of the week. The Goan and seafood cuisine is very good, the servings are generous and all the food is fresh. Meals generally take a while to arrive, but the tape selection is good so waiting is no real chore. Prices are surprisingly moderate – generally Rs 20 to Rs 30 per plate. It's also a great spot for a cold beer or two during siesta. The Venite is open for breakfast, lunch and dinner daily except Sunday.

Other restaurants have tried to copy the style of the Venite but without success. One of them is the *Udipi Boarding & Lodging*, one street east of the Venite. The Udipi also has a 1st-floor restaurant with balcony overlooking the street. Although cheap, it isn't anywhere near as popular, but is worth checking out. Another is the *Godinho* around the back of the Hotel Aroma. Its good range of Goan, seafood and Indian non-vegetarian dishes is about as close as you can get to anything with a Portuguese flavour in Panaji. The restaurant is partitioned into areas with and without air-con, and it's a popular place to eat, but servings are small. Lunchtime is probably the best time for a meal as most of the evening clientele come here to talk over bottles of beer rather than to eat.

The *New Punjab Restaurant* in the Municipal Gardens offers excellent Punjabi food and is a cheap and popular place to eat, though tandoori specialities are more expensive. It's closed on Saturdays. Diagonally opposite is the good vegetarian *Kamat Hotel*, while off the gardens at the opposite end is the *Jesmal Cafe* which has excellent milk shakes (particularly mango).

Upstairs at the Tourist Hostel is the *Chit Chat Restaurant* with its pleasant open-air verandah overlooking the Mandovi River. It's a good place for breakfast, the food is reasonable and it's used by many travellers, but the lunch and dinner servings (especially of seafood) are minuscule so it's not particularly good value. The breakfast menu is extensive and good value, and is served from 7 to 11 am and 3 to 7 pm!

Another good restaurant is the *Shere Punjab Restaurant* on 18th June Rd. This is a popular place serving excellent north Indian food, with most dishes in the Rs 15 to Rs 30 range. Also popular are the *Shalimar* and *Taj Mahal* restaurants next to each other on Mahatma Gandhi Rd. The former is non-vegetarian and the latter vegetarian.

Going up in price, the best place for a Chinese meal is the *Goenchin*, just off Dr Dada Vaidya Rd. The food here is excellent but it's definitely a splurge. It's open from 12.30 to 3 pm and 7.30 to 11 pm daily. Another excellent place to splurge is the

Chilliya Restaurant next to the Hotel Summit on Menezes Braganza Rd. This restaurant specialises in Mughlai vegetarian and non-vegetarian dishes and is open for lunch and dinner. The rooftop restaurant at the *Mandovi Hotel* is also worth trying both for the food and the views, but it's expensive. For much less expensive food and similar views, try the restaurant on the banks of the Mandovi River right opposite the Mandovi Hotel adjacent to the ferry landing.

For fruit juices, probably the best place in town is the *Juicy Corner* right opposite the Secretariat (Adil Shah's old palace) in the centre of town. It's a very popular place especially with travellers. Cake freaks should head for *A Pastelaria* next to the Goenchin Chinese restaurant. There's another cake shop of the same name which is part of the Mandovi Hotel complex.

Getting There & Away

Air Indian Airlines (☎ 4067) is at Dempo Building, D Bandodkar Marg, on the riverfront, and is open from 10 am to 1 pm and 2 to 4.30 pm. It's a busy place so try to get there 15 minutes before the doors open. Air India is at the Fidalgo Hotel on 18th June Rd. Business hours are 9.30 am to 1 pm and 2 to 5 pm Monday to Friday.

The Vayudoot agent is Alcon Travels (☎ 45-197) in the Hotel Delmon building.

Indian Airlines have two to three flights a day between Bombay and Goa (US$52). There are also daily flights to and from Delhi (US$150) and Cochin (US$68), and twice-weekly flights to Bangalore (US$52), Madras (US$79) and Ahmedabad (US$88).

East West Airlines (☎ 46291) flies daily in either direction between Bombay (US$46) and Thiruvananthapuram (Trivandrum) (US$84).

Bus Many private companies offer luxury/ deluxe, super deluxe and super deluxe video buses to Bombay, Bangalore, Pune and Mangalore from Panaji and Margao daily. The buses generally depart at night but if you have any designs on sleeping then avoid the video buses. Most of the companies have offices in Panaji, Mapusa and Margao, but they're scattered around the respective towns.

The state-operated Kadamba buses are pretty good, and the booking office at the bus station is open daily from 8 to 11 am and 2 to 5 pm.

The trip to Bombay is supposed to take 14 hours but can take up to 18. The cheapest fare is Rs 120, with others ranging from Rs 150 to Rs 215 depending on the type of bus.

Buses go to Londa (where you can get a direct railway carriage to Mysore every day), Hubli (a railway junction on the main Bombay to Bangalore line, where you can also get trains to Gadag for both Bijapur and Badami, and Hospet and Hampi) and Belgaum. A bus to Hubli takes seven hours and costs Rs 31.50. From Hubli to Hospet is another 4½ hours.

There are daily buses to Mysore which take 16 hours. Mangalore is an 11-hour trip for Rs 99 in a Kadamba luxury bus. Other buses include those to Pune and Bangalore (Rs 141).

To Karwar, the first major town across the southern border with Karnataka, there are five Kadamba buses daily.

Getting Around

To/From the Airport Kadamba operates buses from the Indian Airlines office in Panaji to Dabolim Airport near Vasco da Gama in time for flights. They generally leave two hours before flights depart but the posted timetable is a mass of alterations so turn up early. The fare is Rs 20.

A taxi costs about Rs 200 and takes about 40 minutes. You can share this with up to five people.

The cheapest way from the airport into Panaji or Vasco is to take a motorcycle taxi from the airport to the main road (Rs 5) and then take a local bus for Panaji (Rs 4) or Vasco.

Bus The bridge across the Mandovi River from Panaji to Betim collapsed in 1986 with the loss of several lives. The tragedy aside, the main joke going around Goa at the time was that it stood for only half as long as it took to construct. Construction of a new bridge was undertaken but it too met with disaster when one of the concrete spans collapsed into the river before the bridge was even completed! Construction continued, and the bridge was finally completed and opened to traffic in mid-August 1992.

Some of the more popular routes from Panaji include:

Vasco da Gama & Mormugao – There are two ways of getting there. You can either go via the ferry from Dona Paula to Mormugao, or road via Agassaim and Cortalim. Unless you know there will be a ferry waiting for you on arrival at Dona Paula, the route via Agassaim and Cortalim is the quicker of the two. Either way it costs about Rs 5 and takes about one hour.

Margao – You can get to Margao either via Agassaim and Cortalim or via Ponda. The former is the more direct route and takes about 1½ hours at a cost of Rs 5. Via Ponda it takes about an hour longer and costs Rs 6.

Old Goa – Take one of the frequent buses going straight to Old Goa or any bus going to Ponda. The journey costs Rs 1.50 and takes 20 to 30 minutes.

Calangute – There are frequent services throughout the day and evening. The journey takes about 35 to 45 minutes and costs Rs 2.

Mapusa – Buses cost Rs 2 and take about 25 minutes. There are also three buses daily direct to Chapora Village via Mapusa. Mapusa is pronounced 'Mapsa', and this is what the conductors shout.

Taxis & Auto-Rickshaws Taxis and auto-rickshaws are metered but getting the drivers to use them is extremely difficult, so you'll have to negotiate the fare with them before heading off.

Typical fares from Panaji include: Calangute, Rs 50; Colva, Rs 150; and Dabolim Airport, Rs 200 (negotiable) plus Rs 3 for the Zuari River bridge toll.

Other Transport See the Getting Around section at the start of this chapter for information on bike and motorcycle hire, and travel by boat within Goa.

OLD GOA
History

Even before the arrival of the Portuguese, Old Goa was a thriving and prosperous city and the second capital of the Adil Shahi dynasty of Bijapur. At that time it was a fortress surrounded by walls, towers and a moat, and contained many temples and mosques as well as the large palace of Adil Shah. Today none of these structures remain except for a fragment of the gateway to the palace. What is there dates from the Portuguese period.

Under the Portuguese the city grew rapidly in size and splendour, eventually coming to rival Lisbon itself, despite an epidemic in 1543 which wiped out a large percentage of the population. Many huge churches, monasteries and convents were erected by the various religious orders which came to Goa under royal mandates. The Franciscans were the first to arrive.

Old Goa's splendour was short-lived, however, because by the end of the 16th century Portuguese supremacy on the seas had been replaced by that of the British, Dutch and French. The city's decline was accelerated by the activities of the Inquisition and a devastating epidemic which struck the population in 1635. Indeed, if it had not been for the treaty between the British and the Portuguese, it is probable that Goa would either have passed to the Dutch or been absorbed into British India.

The city muddled on into the early 19th century as the administrative capital of Portugal's eastern empire, which consisted of Goa, Daman & Diu in India, a string of port cities along the East African coast, East Timor and Macau.

Today it's a small village surrounded by huge churches and convents built during its heyday. Some of them remain in active use while others have become museums maintained by the Archaeological Survey of India – a maintenance very necessary because if the lime plaster which protects the laterite structure was not renewed frequently, the monsoons would soon reduce the buildings to ruin.

Information

The Archaeological Survey of India publishes *Old Goa* by S Rajagopalan (New Delhi 1975), an excellent booklet about the monuments. It's available from the Archaeological Museum in Old Goa.

Se Cathedral

The largest of the churches in Old Goa, Se Cathedral was begun in 1562 during the reign of King Dom Sebastião (1557-78) and substantially completed by 1619, though the altars were not finished until 1652. The cathedral was built for the Dominicans and paid for by the Royal Treasury out of the proceeds of the sale of Crown property.

Architecturally, the building is Portuguese-Gothic in style with a Tuscan exterior and Corinthian interior. There were originally two towers, one on either side of the facade, but one collapsed in 1776. The remaining tower houses a famous bell, one of the largest in Goa, often called the 'Golden Bell' because of its rich sound. The main altar is dedicated to St Catherine of Alexandria, and old paintings on either side of it depict scenes from her life and martyrdom.

Convent & Church of St Francis of Assisi

This is one of the most interesting buildings in Old Goa. It contains gilded and carved woodwork, old murals depicting scenes from the life of St Francis, and a floor substantially made of carved gravestones – complete with family coats of arms dating back to the early 1500s. The church was built by eight Franciscan friars who arrived here in 1517 and constructed a small chapel consisting of three altars and a choir. This was later pulled down and the present building was constructed on the same spot in 1661.

The convent at the back of this church is now the **Archaeological Museum**. It houses many portraits of the Portuguese viceroys, most of them inexpertly touched

---

The Incorrupt Body of St Francis Xavier

Goa's patron saint, Francis Xavier, had spent 10 years as a tireless missionary in South-East Asia when he died on 2 December 1552, but it was through his death that his greatest power in the region was released.

He died on the island of Sancian, off the coast of China. His servant is said to have emptied four sacks of quicklime into his coffin to consume his flesh in case the order came to return the remains to Goa. Two months later the body was transferred to Malacca, where it was observed to be still in perfect condition – refusing to rot despite the quicklime. The following year it was returned to Goa where the people were declaring the preservation a miracle.

The Church was slower to acknowledge it, requiring a medical examination to establish that the body had not been embalmed. This was performed, in 1556, by the viceroy's physician who declared that all internal organs were still intact and that no preservative agents had been used. He noticed a small wound in the chest and asked two of the Jesuits with him to put their fingers into it. He noted, 'When they withdrew them they were covered with blood which I smelt and found to be absolutely untainted'.

In comparison to 16th and 17th-century Church bureaucracy, modern Indian bureaucracy seems positively streamlined, for it was not until 1622 that canonisation took place. The holy relic hunters were already at work on the 'incorrupt body' and in 1614 the right arm had been removed and divided between Jesuits in Japan and Rome. By 1636 parts of one shoulder blade and all the internal organs had been scattered through South-East Asia. By the end of the century the miracle appeared to be over: the body was in an advanced state of desiccation. The Jesuits decided to enclose it in a glass coffin out of view and it was not until the mid-19th century that the current cycle of 10-yearly expositions began.

The next exposition is scheduled to begin on 23 November 1993 and will continue until January 1994, but there are rumours that the Pope has forbidden the display of the body. Even if you can't file past the ghoulish remains of the Saint, the festival is still worth attending, drawing tens of thousands of Christians from all over India, with a fun fair and side shows, as well as high mass on a grand scale. ■

up; fragments of sculpture from Hindu temple sites in Goa, which show Chalukyan and Hoysala influences; stone Vetal images from the animist cult which flourished in this part of India centuries ago; and a model of a Portuguese caravel minus the rigging (surely someone could get it together to do the rigging!).

Professed House & Basilica of Bom Jesus

The Basilica of Bom Jesus is famous throughout the Roman Catholic world. It contains the tomb and mortal remains of St Francis Xavier who, in 1541, was given the task of spreading Christianity among the subjects of the Portuguese colonies in the east. A former pupil of St Ignatius Loyola, the founder of the Jesuit Order, St Francis Xavier made missionary voyages in the east that became legendary and, considering the state of communications at the time, were nothing short of miraculous.

See the aside on St Francis Xavier for details on the remarkable manner in which he attained his saintly status.

Apart from the richly gilded altars, the interior of the church is remarkable for its simplicity, and this is the only church which is not plastered on the outside (although it was originally). Construction began in 1594 and the church was completed in 1605. The centre of interest inside the church is, of course, the Tomb of St Francis, the construction of which was underwritten by the Duke of Tuscany and executed by the Florentine sculptor Giovanni Batista Foggini. It took 10 years to build and was completed in 1698. The remains of the body are housed in a silver casket which at one time was covered in jewels. On the walls surrounding it are murals depicting scenes from the saint's journeys, including one of his death on Sancian Island.

The Professed House, next door to the basilica, is a two-storey laterite building covered with lime plaster which was completed in 1585 despite much opposition to the Jesuits. Part of the building burned down in 1633 and was partially rebuilt in 1783.

There's a modern **art gallery** attached to the basilica.

Church of St Cajetan

Modelled on the original design of St Peter's in Rome, this church was built by Italian friars of the Order of Theatines, who were sent by Pope Urban III to preach Christianity in the kingdom of Golconda (near Hyderabad). The friars were not permitted to work in Golconda and so settled down at Goa in 1640. The construction of the church began in 1655. Historically, it's of much less interest than the other churches.

Church of St Augustine Ruins

All that is left of this church is the enormous 46-metre-high tower which served as a belfry and formed part of the facade of the church. What little is left of the other parts of the church is choked with creepers and weeds, and access is difficult. The church was constructed in 1602 by Augustinian friars who arrived at Goa in 1587.

It was abandoned in 1835 due to the repressive policies of the Portuguese government, which resulted in the eviction of many religious orders from Goa. The church fell into neglect and the vault collapsed in 1842. Many years later, in 1931, the facade and half the tower fell down, followed by more parts in 1938.

Church & Convent of St Monica

This huge, three-storey laterite building was commenced in 1606 and completed in 1627, only to burn down nine years later. Reconstruction started the following year, and it's from this time that the buildings date. Once known as the Royal Monastery due to the royal patronage which it enjoyed, the building is now used by the Mater Dei Institute as a nunnery which was inaugurated in 1964. Visitors are allowed inside if they are reasonably dressed. There are fading murals on the western inside walls.

Other Buildings

Other monuments of minor interest in Old Goa are the Viceroy's Arch, Gate of Adil

Shah's Palace, Royal Chapel of St Anthony, Church of St John of God, Chapel of St Catherine, the ruins of the Church of the Carmelites, and the Church of Our Lady of the Mount.

Getting There & Away

If you're a lover of old buildings and exotic ruins you'll need the best part of a day to wander around Old Goa. Otherwise, a morning or an afternoon would be sufficient.

There are frequent buses to Old Goa from the bus stand at Panaji; you can also use all buses from Panaji to Ponda as they also pass through Old Goa. The trip takes 20 to 30 minutes and costs Rs 1.50. Whenever there is a festival at Old Goa (such as the Festival of St Francis Xavier on 3 December) boats ply between Panaji and Old Goa. This 45-minute trip is a very pleasant way of getting there.

MARGAO (Madgaon)

Population: 72,000

The capital of Salcete province, Margao is the main population centre of southern Goa and a pleasant provincial town which still displays many reminders of its Portuguese past. In itself it's not of great interest to travellers, though the old Margao church is worth a visit and the covered market is the best of its kind in the whole of Goa. Its importance, however, is as a service and transport centre for people staying at Colva beach. If you're planning on staying at Colva you must first head for Margao, which is connected to the rest of Goa and to the neighbouring states by bus, train and taxi.

The covered market is a fascinating place to wander through, even if you don't want to buy anything. If you'll be staying at Colva for some time and renting a house, the other, smaller market behind the Secretariat building is excellent for pots, pans and other kitchen equipment.

If you're coming to Margao from outside Goa, the last bus to Colva Beach leaves at 8 pm. After that you will either have to hire a motorcycle or taxi to get to Colva or stay overnight in Margao.

Orientation & Information

The tourist office is in the Tourist Hostel in the centre of town. The staff are friendly and helpful, though, as elsewhere in India, they're limited in what they can offer due to lack of funds.

The main bus station (Kadamba Bus Station) is about 1½ km from the centre of town on the road to Panaji. Auto-rickshaws, motorcycles and taxis are available for transfer between the two.

The main taxi stand is behind the Secretariat building.

The State Bank of India is right opposite the Municipal Gardens. Unless you have a Visa card, this is the closest place to the beaches for changing money, although Visa travellers' cheques are not accepted.

Menezes, behind the Secretariat, is an Indian Airlines agent. The poste restante is not in the GPO on the north side of the Municipal Gardens, but in a separate office about 300 metres away.

Places to Stay – bottom end

Most of the cheapies are strung out along Station Rd between the central Municipal Gardens and the railway station. The friendly *Rukrish Hotel* (☎ 21-709), opposite the Bank of India, is probably the best of the bunch. Here you can get a good, clean single with a small balcony overlooking the street for Rs 60, or doubles with bathroom for Rs 95.

Other hotels of similar standard along Station Rd include the *Milan Kamat Hotel* (☎ 22-715), which charges Rs 30/40 (Rs 5 extra with bathroom) and is good for afternoon train departures as the checkout time is 5 pm, and the *Sanrit Hotel* (☎ 21-226) which is a shade more expensive at Rs 50 for a double with common bathroom, Rs 60 with attached bathroom.

Near the market in the middle of town the government-run *Tourist Hostel* (☎ 21-966) has singles/doubles for Rs 90/110 (or Rs 70/85 in the low season). It's of a similar standard to the Tourist Hostel in Panaji. Another place worth checking out is the *Twiga Lodge* (☎ 20-049), 413 Abade Faria

■ PLACES TO STAY

3	Hotel Metropole
7	Mabai Hotel
10	Woodlands Hotel
14	Tourist Hotel & Tourist Office
16	Rukrish Hotel
20	Milan Kamat Hotel
21	Vishranti Lodge
22	Sangram Boarding
23	Sanrit Hotel

▼ PLACES TO EAT

8	Marliz
12	Kamat Hotel
18	Bombay Cafe
19	Paradise Bar & Restaurant

OTHER

1	Kadamba Bus Station
2	Margao Church
4	GPO
5	Poste Restante
6	Buses to Colva
9	State Bank of India
11	Bank of Baroda
13	Secretariat
15	Menezes Air Travel Agent
17	Market
24	Railway Station

Rd, which has singles/doubles for under Rs 100. It's off the main road so there's no traffic noise.

At the top of this bracket, the *Mabai Hotel* (☎ 21-653), conveniently located on the north side of the Municipal Gardens, has singles/doubles for Rs 55/90, Rs 90/135 with air-con. The rooms are large, airy and pleasantly decorated. This place is very good value, although the front rooms tend to be noisy. There's also a restaurant, bar and roof garden.

A very pleasant place in this bracket is the quiet *Woodlands Hotel* (☎ 21-121), Miguel Loyola Furtado Rd, which has friendly staff and its own bar and restaurant. Singles/doubles are Rs 70/90 with bathroom, and air-con rooms are Rs 230/250.

Places to Stay – middle

The *Hotel Metropole* (☎ 21-566), Avenida Concessão, a short walk from the centre of town, offers doubles for Rs 250. There are two restaurants, a roof garden, bar, disco and bookshop. This place is a bit of a shambles, however, with the lobby looking more like a storeroom, and the reception desk is in a cupboard on the first floor.

Places to Eat

The *Kamat Hotel* opposite the Municipal Gardens is one of the chain found throughout south India. It offers cheap, no frills 'meals' for Rs 15 and other south Indian snack food. The *Bombay Cafe* is another popular 'meals' place.

Directly opposite the tourist office, the charming *Longuinhos* does ultra-hot curries and good sweets and cakes.

For snacks and breakfasts, the *Marliz* on the north side of the Municipal Gardens is an extremely popular cafe and has been so for many years. It's always crowded – and for very good reasons, as its snacks are excellent. They include sandwiches, vegetarian and non-vegetarian pasties, cakes and coffee.

Getting There & Away

Bus Margao has good connections with beaches and other towns in Goa.

Colva Beach – Buses run to Colva via Benaulim approximately every hour. The first bus from Margao leaves at about 7.30 am and the last at 8 pm. The fare is Rs 2 and the journey takes 20 to 25 minutes.

Panaji – Buses depart approximately every half-hour from dawn to 8 pm, take about 1½ hours and cost Rs 5. It's a picturesque journey, if you get a seat, as there are many old, whitewashed churches and monasteries to be seen en route. The alternative route taken by some buses is via Ponda, and this takes at least an hour longer (Rs 6).

Other Buses – You can find buses to most towns in Goa from the Kadamba bus stand in Margao. Timetables are approximate (the buses leave when full) but they're fairly frequent to the major centres of population in central and southern Goa. To the smaller towns, such as Betul south of Colva, they're much less frequent so it's best to make enquiries at the bus station in advance. Get there early if you want a seat.

Train Trains are dealt with in the Panaji section but bookings for all classes can be made at Margao station *except* for Indrail Pass holders who must go to Vasco da Gama to make bookings.

Taxi To get to Colva you can take a motor-cycle for Rs 12 (no objection to rucksacks) or a taxi. The fares of the latter are government regulated so it should cost Rs 35 during the day, but more at night because they're entitled to charge 50% of the cost of the return journey. You can share this with up to five people.

AROUND MARGAO
Rachol Seminary & Church

There are some interesting places around Margao. About three km from the small village of Raia, which is on the road from Margao to the Borim bridge, is the Rachol Seminary and Church. The old church dates from the early 1600s and the seminary has interesting architecture, a decaying library and paintings of Christian characters done in Indian styles. This is not a tourist site so you should ask before wandering around.

Christ Ashram

To the east of the Margao to Cortalim road near the village of Nuvem is the Christ Ashram exorcism centre. It has been condemned by Catholic authorities as the trappings are Catholic but the ambience definitely Hindu.

VASCO DA GAMA

Close to Mormugao Harbour and Dabolim Airport, Vasco da Gama is the terminus of the railway line to Goa – apart from a few local trains which continue to the harbour. If you arrive in Goa by train you can get off at Margao, near Colva Beach, but if you fly in it is possible to arrive in Goa too late to get much further than Vasco da Gama unless you're prepared to take a taxi. There are several hotels in this unexciting town.

Places to Stay

A good place is the *Hotel Annapurna*

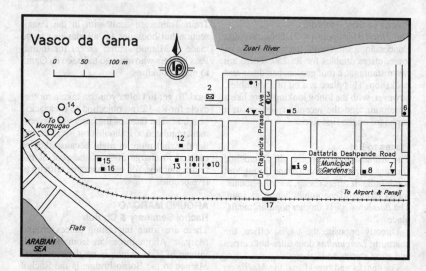

Vasco da Gama

Zuari River

0   50   100 m

Dr Rajendra Prasad Ave

Dattatria Deshpande Road

To
Mormugao

Municipal
Gardens

To Airport & Panaji

Flats

ARABIAN
SEA

1	Vegetable Market	10	Fish Market
2	Post Office	11	Vegetable Market
3	Bus Station	12	Hotel Annapurna
4	Little Chef Restaurant	13	Hotel Westend
5	Hotel Gladstone	14	Oil Refinery
6	State Bank of India	15	Hotel Rukmini
7	Nanking Chinese Restaurant	16	Tel-Jose-Mar Tourist
8	Hotel La Paz Gardens		Rest House
9	Tourist Hostel & Tourist Office	17	Railway Station

(☎ 3645), Dattatria Deshpande Rd, which offers singles/doubles for Rs 90/110. Good vegetarian food is served in the restaurant. Just opposite is the *Hotel Westend* (☎ 2288) with double rooms at Rs 110.

Another good choice is the relatively new and centrally located *Tourist Hostel* (☎ 3119), which, like others of its kind, is run by the Goa Tourist Development Corporation. Singles/doubles cost Rs 90/110 in the high season, Rs 70/85 in the low season. There are also rooms with four beds for Rs 140 (Rs 100 low season).

The small *Tel-Jose-Mar Tourist Rest House* is a friendly little place at the western edge of the centre, but still just a couple of minutes walk from the railway station. Dorm beds cost Rs 35, or there are basic double rooms for Rs 80, or Rs 100 with bathroom attached.

Also at the western edge of the centre is the *Hotel Rukmini* (☎ 2350), a fairly modern place which charges Rs 120/150 with bathroom, and Rs 200/240 with air-con.

The *Hotel Gladstone* (☎ 3966) is worth considering if you don't want to be more than a couple of minutes stagger from the bus or train station. Singles/doubles are good value at Rs 95/160, or Rs 160/220 with air-con.

For something a bit more upmarket try the *Hotel La Paz Gardens* (☎ 3302), where air-con rooms go for Rs 275/450.

Places to Eat

The *Nanking Chinese Restaurant*, three blocks east of the railway station, is a friendly place with good food. In the same area is the *Sweet N Sour* Chinese restaurant in the Hotel La Paz Gardens.

The 'meals' restaurant in the *Hotel Annapurna* is a good cheap option, or as a fall back there's the typically uninspired and uninspiring service and menu at the restaurant in the *Tourist Hostel*.

MAPUSA

Population: 31,500

Mapusa (pronounced locally as 'Mapsa') is the main centre of population in the northern provinces of Goa and the main town for supplies if you're staying either at Anjuna or Chapora. If you're staying at Calangute or Baga, you have a choice of Panaji or Mapusa as a service centre.

In itself, there's nothing to see in Mapusa, though the Friday market is worth a visit. You may, however, need to stay here overnight if you're catching a bus to Bombay the following day – there's no need to go to Panaji for long-distance buses unless you particularly want to. India Tours and Laxmi Motor Services, next to the Imperial Hotel, both have services to Bombay.

Places to Stay

There's no need to actually stay in Mapusa – accommodation at the nearby beaches of Anjuna, Vagator and Chapora is far preferable. If you have to stay here, the *Hotel Bardez* (☎ 42-607) is a good choice. It has rooms for Rs 95/125 with bathroom.

Also reasonable value is the *Tourist Hostel* (☎ 42-794), on the roundabout at the entrance to Mapusa, which has singles/doubles for Rs 90/110 and rooms with four beds for Rs 140 in the high season. In the low season the tariff is Rs 70/85 and Rs 100 respectively.

The *Satyahara Hotel* (☎ 42-849), near the Maruti Temple, is also good, with rooms for Rs 60/95, or Rs 225 for a double with air-con.

Places to Eat

The *Tourist Hostel* has a large dining hall. The *Imperial Bar & Restaurant* serves good non-vegetarian food and cold beers. It's clean, easy-going and popular with local people.

Getting There & Away

As at Panaji, schedules are only approximate (buses leave when full), but bus services are frequent. Buses to Anjuna and Chapora can be very crowded – mostly with Westerners staying on the beaches. Mapusa to Panaji takes about 25 minutes and costs Rs 1.50. There are also buses to Calangute and to other population centres in northern Goa.

Instead of buses you can take either a taxi or a motorcycle. A motorbike to Anjuna or Calangute costs Rs 20 and takes about 15 minutes. Taxi fares are government controlled so you should be paying Rs 30 (shared by up to five people).

Mapusa

Beaches

Goa is justifiably famous for its beaches, and Westerners have been flocking to them since the early '60s. They used to suffer from bad press in both the Western and Indian media, because of the real or imagined nefarious activities of a small minority of visitors. Since the mid-1980s, however, the situation has changed considerably. While the beaches are still awash with budget travellers of all ages and various degrees of affluence (or penury, depending on yo'r point of view), there's also a large contingent of Western package-tour visitors who arrive by direct charter flight and stay in the beach resort complexes which have sprung up in the main centres. Even the Indians from outside Goa have begun to come here in ever increasing numbers, though you won't find them swimming or sunbathing!

The only problem is deciding which beach to head for. Much depends on how long you intend to stay. Renting a room at a hotel is an expensive way of staying long-term and most budget travellers prefer to either rent a simple room at one of the beach cafes or to rent a private house on a monthly basis (shared, if desired, with a group of friends). Such rooms and houses can be found at all the main centres but there's heavy demand for the latter in the winter (high) season, so it might take you several days to track one down. In the meantime, stay at a cafe or hotel and do a lot of asking around.

Colva & Benaulim, Calangute & Baga, Vagator & Chapora and Anjuna are the main beaches where travellers congregate. Instant accommodation is easiest at Colva & Benaulim and Calangute & Baga. At the others you may have to do quite a bit of legwork before you find somewhere to stay as there are no real hotels as such (if you disregard the relatively expensive Vagator Beach Resort).

All these beaches are well touristed, so if what you have in mind is that near-deserted beach, then you'll have to look further afield.

Arambol (or Harmal as it's spelt on some maps), near the northern tip of Goa, is one such place. Betul, south of Colva, and Palolen, even further south, are two others. The 'real' freaks have gone even further south over the border into Karnataka, though a few still hang on at Arambol.

The Aguada, Bogmalo, Varca and Cavelossim beaches are essentially for affluent tourists staying at the beach resorts there.

Warning
When using the beaches, it pays to be a little security conscious. Things do get stolen, so don't leave valuables unattended. Better still, don't bring them to the beach at all unless you and a friend take turns looking after them.

COLVA & BENAULIM
Colva stretches sun-drenched, palm-fringed and virtually deserted for km after km. Twenty years ago precious little disturbed its soft white sands and warm crystal-clear turquoise waters, except the local fishers who pulled their catch in by hand each morning, and a few of the more intrepid hippies who had forsaken the obligatory drugs, sex and rock & roll of Calangute for the soothing tranquillity of this corner of paradise. Since there were only two cottages for rent and one restaurant (Vincy's), most people stayed either on the beach itself or in palm-leaf shelters, which they took over from departing travellers or constructed themselves.

Those days are gone forever. Even in days of yore the property speculators and developers had begun to sniff around in search of a fast rupee. Today, you can see the results of their efforts – air-conditioned resort complexes, close-packed ranks of tourist cottages, discos, trinket stalls and cold-drink stalls. You'll be lucky if you see an angler around the main area and, anyway, most have acquired motorised trawlers which stand anchored in a line offshore. Likewise, you won't come across anyone sleeping out on the beach these days or throwing up a palm-leaf shelter. The changing times and the determination of the average male Indian day-tripper to catch a glimpse of a scantily clad Western female body put paid to all that.

It's only fair to point out that this development is concentrated in a relatively small area at the end of the road from Margao, and that it's simplicity itself to get away from it. Walk two km either side of there, and you'll get close to what it used to be like before the cement mixers began chugging away. It could be said we have only ourselves to blame for making the beach so popular in the first place, but Colva still has a long way to go before it gets as developed as Calangute, or a lot of other beaches I could think of around the world. It's still the best of the Goan beaches, and if you like a really quiet life you can always head further south to Benaulim.

Information

The nearest post office is in Colva village. Letters can be sent poste restante there rather than to Margao if you like. There is no bank in Colva, but the Silver Sands Hotel may be prepared to change travellers' cheques. The nearest banks are in Benaulim village, where the Bank of Baroda handles Visa card cash advances only, and Margao.

Places to Stay

The best deal – if you're going to stay here for a while – is to rent a house with a number of other people. If you're not already part of a large enough group, ask around in the cafes at Colva and Benaulim, or take a walk along the road which runs parallel to the beach from Colva village in both directions, and ask every time you see a likely looking place. It shouldn't take more than a few days. Obviously you get what you pay for, but around Rs 800 per month would be reasonable. Between November and March competition is stiff, so get there before then if possible. There are very few places to rent on a long-term basis on the beach itself; most houses are a good 15 to 20 minutes walk from the beach.

The price of hotel accommodation varies according to the season. The peak season stretches from 16 November to 15 February, the shoulder from 16 February to 15 June and 16 September to 15 November, and the low season from 16 June to 15 September. Unless otherwise stated, peak season rates are quoted in what follows. In the shoulder period you can expect up to 20% less; in the low season it is 50% to 60% less.

Colva For short-term accommodation there is a wide choice. At the cheaper end of the market are various places strung out along the roads behind the beach, north of the main area.

The *Fishermen's* is one of the closest places to the beach, and there's just a few rooms at Rs 75/90 for a single/double with bathroom. It's quiet and friendly and just a short stagger to the beach. Across the road is *Rodrickson Cottages*, which are slightly more expensive. In this same area is the *Lucky Star Restaurant*, which has a few rooms and used to be popular, although these days it's relatively poor value.

On the next road back from the beach there's a couple of good places which offer the cheapest accommodation in Colva. The long-running *Tourist Nest* has rooms for Rs 60, or Rs 70 with attached bathroom. Just around the corner is the friendly *La Village*, a family-run place with just four rooms at Rs 40 for a double with common bathroom. The *Garden Cottages* close by are similar.

There's another couple of places right in the thick of things on the main street. The *Vailankanni Cottages* are very popular with travellers, mainly because of the friendly atmosphere generated by the family which runs the place. Rooms here cost Rs 90 for a double with attached bathroom, and there are good meals and snacks available.

A little closer to the beach, on the opposite side of the road and hidden behind the souvenir stalls which clutter the whole area, is the *Blue Diamond Cottages*. This is an older style place which offers rooms for Rs 100 with attached bathroom.

The only other really cheap option is *Jymi's Cottages*, very close to the beach just south of the main drag. The rooms are pretty basic and cost Rs 85, but the location is excellent.

More expensive but excellent value for money is the government-owned *Tourist Complex* (or Tourist Cottages) (☎ 22-287) which consists of a double-storeyed terrace of rooms facing the sea (each with its own balcony), a separate block of cottages, a restaurant, bar, reception area and garden. The rooms cost Rs 150/165 a double complete with clean sheets, fan and bathroom, or Rs 270 with air-con. There's also a dormitory for Rs 35 per bed. In the low season, prices drop to Rs 80/100 a double and Rs 20 for a dormitory bed. The place is very well maintained and the staff are friendly.

Similar, but without the favourable aspect, is the *Sukhsagar Hotel* (☎ 20-224) which offers doubles for Rs 180 and Rs 280 with air-con. All rooms have bathrooms with hot and cold running water. The hotel has a bar but no restaurant.

The *Hotel La Ben* is a fairly characterless new building on the main road. The rooms are comfortable but otherwise unremarkable, and are pretty good value at Rs 200 for a double with bathroom.

The *Skylark Cottages* cost Rs 210 for a double with bathroom, or Rs 400 with air-con. It's a fairly new place and the rooms are very clean. In the low season prices drop by around 30%.

The *Vincy Hotel* (☎ 22-276), once the only bar/restaurant in the area, has been through many changes as Colva changed from an obscure fishing village to a major resort area. The original Indo-Portuguese structure has sadly long since disappeared and Vincy's has joined the 20th century with a vengeance. It now offers plain double rooms with bathroom and hot and cold running water for Rs 180. There's a vast restaurant on the ground floor, and although it has no atmosphere, the food is good.

The *Colmar Hotel* (☎ 21-253) is pretty good value and has double rooms with bathroom for Rs 150 and chalets for Rs 350. The hotel has its own restaurant and bar, and

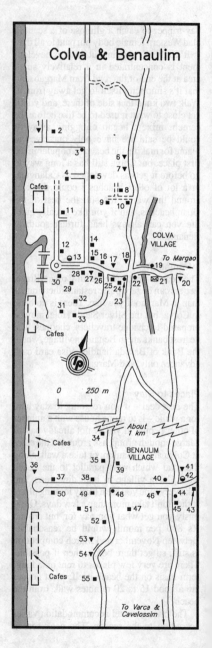

■	PLACES TO STAY		51	Rosario's Inn
			52	Savio Rest House
2	Longuinhos Beach Resort		55	Palm Grove Cottages
4	Fishermen's Cottages			
5	Rodrickson Cottages		▼	PLACES TO EAT
8	Tourist Nest			
9	Garden Cottages		1	Lucky Star Restaurant
10	La Village		6	Andorinho Restaurant
11	Colmar Hotel		7	Umita Corner Restaurant
12	Tourist Complex		17	Johnny Cool Restaurant
14	Skylark Cottages		18	Man Mar Inn
15	Colva Beach Resort		20	Paloma Restaurant
16	Blue Diamond Cottages		27	Lactancia Restaurant
24	Vailankanni Cottages		36	Pedro's Bar & Johney's
25	Williams Resort		41	Fridola's Restaurant
26	Hotel La Ben		46	Cacy-Rose Restaurant
28	Silver Sands Hotel		53	Bar Dominic
29	Mar E Sol Hotel		54	Malibu Bar & Restaurant
30	Vincy Hotel			
31	Penthouse Beach Resort			OTHER
32	Jymi's Cottages			
33	Sukhsagar Hotel		3	Mac-Cou Corner
34	D'Souza Guest House		13	Bus Stop
35	Pinto Tourist Cottage		19	Church
37	L'Amour Beach Resort		21	Post Office
38	Green Garden Tourist Cottages		22	General Store
39	Kencro Tourist Cottages		23	Worldlinkers Payphone
43	Brito's Tourist Home		40	Bank of Baroda
45	Caravan Tourist Home		42	Bus Stop
47	Peacock Guest House		44	Church
49	Liteo Cottages		48	Bike & Motorcycle Hire
50	O Palmar Beach Cottages			

money exchange facilities, and is used by overland tour groups.

Further away from the beach is the *Colva Beach Resort* (☎ 21-975) with doubles for Rs 250 and air-con doubles for Rs 450, both with bathroom and hot water. There's no restaurant at this hotel. Also in this category is *William's Resort* (☎ 21-077) which costs Rs 300 for a double, Rs 350 with air-con.

At the top of the scale is the *Silver Sands Hotel* (☎ 21-645) and the *Penthouse Beach Resort* (☎ 21-030). Rooms in the high season at the Silver Sands cost Rs 450/495 a single/double, or Rs 495/550 with air-con. There's a swimming pool, health club, water sports and indoor games facilities, an excellent bar and restaurant (live bands play in the high season), travel counter and money exchange facilities. It's good value for money, the staff are very friendly and the hotel operates an

airport shuttle bus. The Penthouse Beach Resort consists of five units plus facilities built in the Portuguese style of architecture and set amongst green lawns. It offers singles/doubles for Rs 350, and Rs 450 for a double with air-con. There are indoor games, currency exchange facilities, and live bands in the high season.

Benaulim If you hanker after the more tranquil parts of this coastline then Benaulim beach, less than two km south of Colva, is the place to head for. If you are planning to stay for a while, it's best to ask around for a house to rent or a room in a private house. They can be as little as Rs 30 per night. In the meantime, there's plenty of choice of immediate accommodation.

Right on the beach, *L'Amour Beach Resort* has good rooms from Rs 175 a double with bathroom and fan. Most of the rooms are cottages which are aligned so that they catch the sea breezes. Furthermore the staff are very friendly and helpful, and the restaurant is excellent. It's often full in the high season.

Opposite it are the *O Palmar Beach Cottages* which cost Rs 147 with fan and bathroom. Neither of these places have much in the way of shade and are fairly exposed, but you can't get much closer to the beach.

Most of the other places are scattered around the village of Benaulim about one km back from the beach, and accommodation here is much cheaper than that available at the beach itself. *Rosario's Inn* is a very pleasant little place, with a separate row of rooms with a verandah, each for Rs 70 with attached bathroom, or others in the larger main building for Rs 40 with common bathroom. It's a good, friendly place.

A short distance north along one of the roads to Colva is the *D'Souza Guest House*. This is another excellent little guest house, in an older style Goan bungalow with an extensive garden. Rooms at this friendly family-run place cost Rs 80. Also on this same road is the *Furitado Guest House* and the *Pinto Tourist Cottage*.

Along the same road, but south of the beach road, there's the *Palm Grove Cottages*. These are a bit more upmarket, with a couple of small doubles for Rs 75, or Rs 125 with bathroom, and larger rooms for Rs 140 with bathroom. Comfortable rooms in the new building cost Rs 225 with bathroom and hot water, or Rs 325 with air-con. It's a very friendly place with a shady garden, and meals are available.

Benaulim village is at the second crossroads back from the beach and, off to the right, you'll find the *Caravan Tourist Home*. This place has a beautifully furnished lounge room, although the rooms themselves are far more basic. Still, it's a pleasant place to stay, and is good value at Rs 40 to Rs 60 for double rooms. Right next door is the *Priti Kunj Tourist Home*.

Brito's Tourist Home is a modern building on the Margao road, near the main intersection in Benaulim. It's a fairly featureless place but is friendly and good value at Rs 80. Many people stay here for months and come back year after year. Attached to the building is a small general store, which is where you will find the owner, Edmund.

Varca & Cavelossim The 10-km strip of pristine beach south of Benaulim has become Goa's resort beach. It sports at least half a dozen resorts of varying degrees of luxury. As far as resorts go, some of them are quite good, and they are certainly isolated from anything which might disturb the peace. Access to the resorts is along the main road south from Benaulim, or you can hire a bicycle and cycle along the beach, at low tide at least.

Varca is five km south of Benaulim and the first resort you come to is the new *Resorte de Goa* (☎ 25-065). It's a reasonably small place with rooms and villas set around a swimming pool. Once the shade trees get established this should be a very pleasant place. Air-con rooms cost Rs 750, or villas with two double rooms are Rs 1500. Off-season rates are 50% less.

Half a km further on is the *Remada Renaissance Resort* (☎ 23-611). This is the most luxurious of all the places along here, and is a true five-star resort. All rooms have a balcony facing the sea, there's a pool, beachside bar, and even a six-hole golf course. As you'd expect, there's a couple of restaurants to choose from, and watersports are also available. Rooms here cost US$97/105 in the season, but are a bargain in the monsoon at US$37/45.

Cavelossim is another seven km south, and the first place here is the *Dona Sylvia* (☎ 6321). It's very clean and new, and is a popular place with package groups from sun-starved Europe. Again, when the shade trees get going this place will be much improved; at the moment it's a little bleak. Still, the facilities are excellent and it's probably the best value of all the places. In the high season rooms cost Rs 700, or Rs 795 with air-con; this drops to Rs 350 and Rs 535 respectively in the off season.

The *Old Anchor Resort* is next door to the Dona Sylvia. It's an older place which lacks a beach frontage, and is overpriced at Rs 1500 for a double, with meals available for Rs 90/130/155 for breakfast/lunch/dinner.

The *Averina Beach Resort* (☎ 20-643) has rooms ranged around a pool, just back from the beach. They cost Rs 1600 for a double, dropping to Rs 800/900 for a single/double in the off season.

Right at the end of the road, near the mouth of the small estuary, is the *Leela Beach Resort*. This is another upmarket place and is imaginatively designed with rooms ranged around a series of somewhat muddy lagoons. The main building is very airy and catches the sea breezes. There's a couple of open-air restaurants, and at least one swimming pool. Villas go for US$135, dropping down to US$70 in the monsoon.

Bogmalo North of Colva and close to the airport is Bogmalo where the *Oberoi Bogmalo Beach* (☎ 2191) has 118 rooms with singles/doubles for US$115 at the height of the season, dropping to US$50/55 during the monsoon. There's a swimming pool, water sports and all the other five-star facilities.

Places to Eat

If you're at the beach you naturally want to eat outside, and there's plenty of alfresco restaurants. It doesn't matter how good the food is if it's spoilt by having to eat it inside glass and concrete and away from the sights and sounds that attracted you to Goa in the first place.

Colva The most popular places to eat (and drink) around Colva itself are the string of open-air wooden restaurants which line the beach on either side of where the road ends. They're all individually owned and, because of the competition, the standard of food is pretty high. Seafood is, of course, *de rigeur* and the restaurants are well tuned in to what travellers like for breakfast. Virtually all of them have a sound system but the variety and quality of the tapes which they play varies

enormously. Cold beer and spirits are available at all of them.

It would be unfair to single out individual restaurants for special mention since every traveller has their favourite place and this often depends on the particular crowd which congregates there. This naturally changes constantly.

Apart from the beach huts, there are plenty of established restaurants to choose from. One of the cheapest is the *Lucky Star Restaurant*. It's been a popular place for years, although these days it seems to be living on its reputation.

Further back from the beach along the back road are a number of popular places. They include the *Man Mar Inn*, *Umita Corner Restaurant & Bar* and the *Andorinho Restaurant*. The improbably named *Johnny Cool* is also worth a try. The sort of night you have at any one of them depends largely on the crowd which turns up but the food is generally good.

The *Vincy Hotel* was Colva's original restaurant, but although it now occupies about three times its former space and still attracts a fair share of customers, it sports the atmosphere of a fast-food outlet. Prices, however, are still reasonable and, despite the lack of atmosphere, the food is very good and the portions generous. Going up somewhat in price, the *Dolphin* at the Hotel Colmar is good but the restaurant is enclosed so there are no sea breezes to enliven the cuisine. The same is true of the restaurant at the *Tourist Complex* though they do have a good variety of Indian curries, as opposed to seafood, on the menu.

For a splurge, there's a few choices – *Longuinhos Beach Resort*, *Silver Sands Hotel* and *Penthouse Beach Resort*. The cuisine and service at these places is what you would expect from multistar hotels and they all offer Goan, Indian and Continental dishes as well as seafood. Both the Silver Sands and the Penthouse have live bands during the high season and dinner is often an 'all you can eat' smorgasbord for a set price. They're all good value and not beyond a budget traveller's pocket but, if *alfresco* is your preference, then head for the Penthouse. The other restaurants are enclosed.

Benaulim Down at Benaulim, the *L'Amour Beach Resort* restaurant offers a wide variety of seafood plus chips. The food is good and the prices reasonable, although the service isn't what it might be. *Pedro's Bar & Restaurant* on the beach at Benaulim is a mellow place and has been popular for years, although it's somewhat *passé* these days. The only problem about this place is finding someone to order from, and the service tends to be erratic.

Very similar are the beach huts below Pedro's which include the popular *Johnney's*, and the *Red Lobster*. There are plenty of other cafes along this stretch of beach, including *Seaview, Meridien, Dominick, Argentina* and *Patrose*.

There are a number of places back from the beach at Benaulim village. One of the most popular is the *Cacy-Rose Bar & Restaurant*, very close to the crossroads opposite Maria Hall. It's also a good place to ask around for accommodation in the village.

If you're staying at Palm Grove Cottages then the *Malibu Bar & Restaurant* is convenient for a meal or snack.

Getting There & Away

Buses run from Colva to Margao about every hour and take 25 minutes. The fare is Rs 1.50. The first bus from Colva departs around 7.30 am and the last one back leaves about 8 pm. Buses from Margao to Benaulim are also frequent, and some of them continue south to Varca and Cavelossim.

A taxi from Colva to Margao costs Rs 30 shared between up to five or six people (or more if the driver is willing). Colva to Dabolim Airport costs Rs 180 and to Panaji costs Rs 200. All fares are negotiable. If you like the wind through your hair, the easiest way to get between Margao and Colva is to take a motorcycle. The standard fare is Rs 18. Backpacks are no problem.

Getting Around

There are plenty of places that rent bicycles in both Colva and Benaulim. The usual charge is Rs 2 an hour or Rs 15 for a full day plus a further Rs 2 if you keep it overnight. Some places charge more, so you'll have to negotiate. At low tide you can ride down the beach 12 km to the picturesque fishing port of Cavelossim at the southern end. It's possible to get a boat across the estuary to Betul and then cycle back via Margao.

For the weekly flea market at Anjuna beach, you will see large signs advertising buses in many of the beach restaurants and at some of the hotels in Colva and Benaulim. If you're not planning on staying at any of the northern beaches then it's worth making the day trip – but it will take you the best part of a day. The cost is minimal. Doing this trip by public buses involves umpteen changes and a lot of messing about. It's also possible to hire one of the wooden ex-fishing boats to take you there, but for this you're going to have to get a group together as they're relatively expensive.

CALANGUTE & BAGA

Seemingly not all that long ago, Calangute was the beach all self-respecting hippies headed for, especially around Christmas when all psychedelic hell broke loose and the beach was littered with more budding rock stars than most people have hot dinners. If you enjoyed taking part in those mass pujas with their endless half-baked discussions about 'when the revolution comes' and 'the vibes, man', then this was just the ticket. You could frolic around with not a stitch on, be ever so cool and liberated, and completely disregard the feelings of the local inhabitants. You could get totally out of your head every minute of the night and day on every conceivable variety of ganja from Timor to Tenochtitlan, exhibit the most bizarre behaviour, babble an endless stream of drivel and bore everybody shitless. Naturally, John Lennon or The Who were always about to turn up and give a free concert. Ah, Woodstock! Where did you go!

Calangute's heyday as the Mecca of all expatriate hippies has passed and the place has settled down to the more bourgeois pursuits of selling handicrafts, jewellery and woven fabrics to the tourists. It no longer provides the Indian press with a permanent shock-horror story about the decadent, drug-crazed (not to mention naked) fiends who were supposed to be rotting the moral fibre of Indian youth.

Calangute isn't one of the best Goan beaches – there are hardly any swaying palms to grace the shoreline, much of the sand is contaminated with red soil and the beach drops pretty rapidly into the sea – but there's plenty going on and people who find Colva too quiet may find Calangute just the place.

Only two km north of Calangute is Baga, where the beach is much better and where there's a good choice of restaurants and accommodation. Indeed, Baga has become more popular with travellers than Calangute and it's easy to see why. There's nowhere near the same degree of commercialisation as there is at Calangute, the atmosphere is much mellower and the landscape more interesting. Development is definitely creeping closer and closer but there's still a sort of *cordon sanitaire* between the two.

Orientation & Information

Where the road forks to Baga and Calangute beach there's an excellent second-hand bookshop offering books in most languages you could care to name. You can buy, sell or exchange here. Halfway between these places and Calangute market, and next to the Hotel Orfil, is a branch of the State Bank of India where you can change travellers' cheques and cash.

Close to the bookshop is MGM Travels, which offers discount tickets to other parts of the world at rates similar to those you can get in Bombay.

Places to Stay

Just like Colva beach, the price you pay for accommodation here depends on the season. The high season stretches from 15 December to 31 January, the shoulder from 1 February to 30 June and 1 October to 14 December, and the low season is from 1 July to 30

September. Finding budget accommodation – or even higher priced accommodation – in the high season is not always easy so you may initially have to stay in whatever is available and put a lot of effort into asking around. Baga is the place to head for if you don't want to pay through the nose for the first few days.

In recent years there's been a tremendous spate of building activity around Calangute and the place is now awash with hotels, most of them in the mid to upper-range bracket.

Calangute Despite the building boom it's still possible to find privately owned rooms or part houses here for as little as Rs 40 per night – but there aren't many of them. Don't expect anything other than a bed without linen, a couple of chairs and access to a well for this price.

There's a fair choice of budget accommodation south of the road which leads to the beach. The *Souza Lobo Restaurant* (☎ 79) has quite a few attractively constructed bamboo matting doubles for Rs 75 with common bathroom. They're clean and a table fan is provided but, unfortunately, the rooms don't have windows and the verandah is taken up by the restaurant.

Better perhaps is the *Angela P Fernandes Guest House* which is a large place offering doubles for Rs 75 with common bathroom and Rs 120 with private bathroom. It's good value, a popular place to stay and the staff are very friendly. All the rooms have fans.

Similar in price and standard is the *Calangute Guest Paradise* and the *Alfa Guest House* close to the end of this road.

Off to the left down a side track is the very pleasant *Coco Banana* where the rooms surround a quiet courtyard. Rooms in this mid-range place are very clean, the beds comfortable, fans are provided and the staff are friendly and helpful. Similar is the *Hotel A'Canôa* (☎ 2282) which has doubles for Rs 150 with bathroom.

Other places in the budget hotel bracket in this area include the *7 Eleven Guest House*, and the *Trinidade Guest House*, but there are others. The nearby *Calangute Beach Resort* is a modern place and looks more expensive than it is. The rooms are spacious and clean, the beds have mosquito nets, the management is very friendly and the hotel has its own restaurant.

Back in the centre of the village, dominating the beach, is the rather ugly government-owned *Tourist Resort* (☎ 2224), though the cottages constructed as an extension are much more attractively designed. Between 4 October and 15 June, rooms cost up to Rs 150 a single, Rs 165 a double and Rs 250 a triple, all with bathroom and fan. Between 15 June and 3 October they cost up to Rs 80, Rs 100 and Rs 160 respectively. There's also a dormitory for Rs 35 (Rs 20 low season). A restaurant forms part of the complex. Close by is *Meena's Lodge* which is also cheap but tends to be noisy.

Not very far from the bus stand is the attractively designed *Varma's Beach Resort* (☎ 2277) which is excellent value if you can afford the extra money. It's spotlessly clean, friendly, has its own bar and restaurant for the use of guests only and the rooms surround a leafy courtyard. Doubles cost Rs 350 to Rs 450 for rooms with bathroom, air-con and your own small verandah with table and chairs. The hotel is closed from June to September. Of a similar standard, and virtually right on the beach, is the *Concha Hotel* (☎ 2256).

Calangute to Baga There are a string of hotels and guest houses all the way along the road from Calangute to Baga as well as along the side roads which branch off for the beach. It would be pointless to mention them all as there are so many of them and it's fairly obvious which are the cheapies and which are not.

Johny's Hotel is a modern brick building just a short way from the Calangute bus stand. Rooms here go for Rs 100, and meals are available. Close by is the amazingly ugly and dilapidated *Hotel Chalston*, which is a monument to insensitive design and thoughtless planning. It's also far from cheap, despite its condition. Just north of the Chalston is the tiny *Ema Guest House*, a

quiet place set amongst the dunes. It's just a small family-run place with a few rooms for Rs 60 and a small restaurant.

Back on the main road heading north are a number of smaller places such as *Oseas Tourist Home*, *Rodrigues Cottages*, *Alben Joh Guest House*, the *Stay Longer Guest House* and the *Saahil Hotel*. All of these places are budget priced and of a pretty good standard.

The friendly *Hotel Shelsta* (☎ 42269) with its shady garden is very good value. Single/double rooms cost Rs 100/150, although they prefer stays of at least three days here. The only drawback is that the road can get noisy at times, at least by local standards.

The *Vinar Holiday Home* is a pleasant old building which hasn't altered much over the years. There are only six rooms but it's clean and costs Rs 100 a double with common bathroom and Rs 140 a double with private bathroom.

Between the Vinar and the beach are a number of new mid-range places. The somewhat cramped *Captain Lobo's Beach Hideaway* is the best value, with comfortable two-room units with small kitchen and fridge a bargain at Rs 460. There's a pool and restaurant, and the beach is just a short walk away. In the same compound is the *Colonia Santa Maria* (☎ 2571), which offers slightly more luxurious accommodation, but is perhaps overpriced at Rs 600 for a double.

Also in this region is the very comfortable *Vila Goesa Beach Resort* (☎ 6182), which is very close to the beach. It consists of a small modern building set in a lush garden. At Rs 400 (Rs 495 with air-con), it represents good value for money. In the off season prices drop to Rs 300 and Rs 400 respectively.

Back on the main road, the *Ronil Beach Resort* (☎ 2268) is popular with package groups. Rooms cost Rs 395/495, or Rs 700 for an air-con double. Right across the road is the well-known *Villa Bonfim*. This has been a very popular place for years and offers large, airy rooms with fans for Rs 350. It's run by a friendly family and most of the rooms have a bathroom except for the two enormous front rooms which would be spoiled by such additions. Despite the relatively high price, it's often full.

Continuing on down the road from the Villa Bonfim are the *Ancora Beach Resort Cottages* (☎ 2296) which are very pleasant and good value at Rs 160 a double. There's an attached restaurant and bar. Almost next door is the *Julma Resort* which offers a similar standard of accommodation but which is definitely overpriced at Rs 160 a double with bathroom.

Away across the sand dunes to the left of the Julma and closer to the sea are the *Sea View Cottages*. As far as sea views and breezes go, you probably won't find better, and each room has a shower, fan and verandah. Prices depend on your powers of persuasion but expect to pay up to Rs 250 a double. Another place along the road is the *Miranda Beach Resort*, which is good value at Rs 125.

One of the best places in this bracket, however, is the *Estrela do Mar* (☎ 2214). All the rooms are different and have their own character. Flowering vines cover the walls and the surrounding gardens are lush and colourful. The open-air bar and restaurant is an ideal place to relax and enjoy excellent food and the beach is only a short trip over the sand dunes. Doubles cost Rs 460 in the high season, and discounts are available in the low season. Advance booking is recommended in the high season.

Baga On the way into Baga, right next to the Casa Portuguesa Bar & Restaurant, you'll come across the *Villa Fatima Beach Resort* set back from the road amid the coconut palm groves. It's a somewhat grandiose name for what is essentially a three-storey building attached to a private house, but it's a very popular place to stay, especially long-term. The family who run it are really pleasant. Double rooms cost Rs 175 at the back, or Rs 250 facing the beach. It's often full in the high season.

Further in towards Baga is the *Cavala Motel* (☎ 2290) which offers doubles with their own verandah and bathroom for Rs 200

to Rs 300. There's also quite a decent restaurant at this hotel.

In Baga itself, you come across a cluster of bar & restaurants alongside the main road – Jack's, Britto's and St Anthony's, with the Two Sisters' Bar & Restaurant a little further off to the right. These are the places to ask around for a room or for a house to rent, and it shouldn't take long to turn up something. There are also a number of houses and cottages for rent across the river but they're often occupied for weeks and months at a time by long-term visitors, so you'll have to play it by ear.

You cross over to the northern side of the river by a most extraordinary bridge which has to be seen to be believed. Somebody was evidently given an unlimited amount of concrete and told to construct the ugliest and most extravagant bridge they could imagine. The result was a covered footbridge that could support an army of tanks and survive a direct nuclear hit.

As for hotel accommodation, there's little choice. The cheapest is the *Hotel Riverside* at Rs 230 a double with bathroom and fan. The rooms are very pleasant and clean, and the staff are friendly, plus the hotel has its own bar and restaurant.

More expensive is the two-star *Hotel Baia do Sol* (☎ 5207), a modern hotel set in an attractive flower garden. Singles/doubles here cost from Rs 250/300, or Rs 50 more with air-con. The hotel has its own restaurant and bar.

Across the river, *Nani's & Rani's* restaurant has a few basic but pleasant rooms to let, but it's a popular place and getting a room can be difficult at times.

Places to Eat

There are any number of small restaurants all the way from Calangute village to the beach, especially around the bus stand, and a whole collection of them on the beach at Baga. As at Colva, seafood features prominently on the menus of most restaurants though some do also offer meat dishes. Genuine vegetarian food is often hard to find – what you usually get if you order it is a double helping

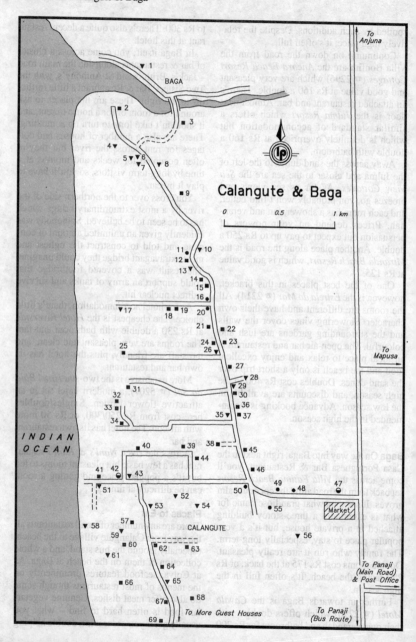

▪ PLACES TO STAY		▼ PLACES TO EAT	
2	Hotel Baia do Sol	1	Nani's & Rani's Bar & Restaurant
3	Hotel Riverside	4	Cafes
9	Cavala Motel	5	St Anthony's Bar & Restaurant
12	Villa Fatima Beach Resort	6	Britto's Bar & Restaurant
14	Sea Wolves Hotel	7	Jack's Bar & Restaurant
15	Miranda Beach Resort	8	Sea Breeze &
18	Ancora Beach Resort Cottages		Tropicana Restaurants
19	Julma Resort	10	Electric Cats Bar & Restaurant
21	Villa Bonfim	13	Casa Portuguesa Bar & Restaurant
22	Ronil Beach Resort	17	Tito's
23	Hotel Bonanza	26	Boutique Tatophanie Cafe
24	Hotel Linda Goa	28	Casa Nelar
25	Captain Lobo's Beach Hideaway	29	The Milky Way
	& Colonia Santa Maria	35	Blue Star Bar & Restaurant &
27	Vinar Holiday Home		Calangute Mahal
30	Hotel Shelsta	43	Alex Cold Drink House
31	Estrela do Mar & Bella Vista	51	Dinky Bar & Restaurant
32	Ema Guest House	52	Tibetan Kitchen
33	Hotel Chalston	53	Meena Lobo's Restaurant
34	Johny's Hotel	54	Sundowner Restaurant
36	Saahil Hotel	56	Jaqueline's Bar & Restaurant
37	Stay Longer Guest House	58	Souza Lobo Restaurant
38	Oseas Tourist Home	59	Epicure Bar & Restaurant
39	Varma's Beach Resort	61	Summervine Bar & Restaurant
40	Meena's Lodge	65	Pete's Bar & Restaurant
41	Tourist Resort		
44	Tourist Dormitory		OTHER
45	Alben Joh Guest House		
46	Rodrigues Cottages	11	Church
57	Hotel A'Canôa	16	Shobha Cold Drinks Stall
60	Concha Hotel	20	Bharat Bar
62	Calangute Guest Paradise	42	Bus Stand
63	Coco Banana	47	Bus Stop
64	Angela P Fernandes Guest House	48	Bank
66	Calangute Beach Resort	49	Space Travels
67	Alfa Guest House	50	Book Exchange
68	7 Eleven Guest House	55	MGM Travel Agent
69	Trinidade Guest House		

of whatever vegetables would be served with fish or meat. Indian curries are also hard to find, the *Tourist Resort* being one of the few places where they're available.

Right on the beach at Calangute, one of the best places to eat is the *Souza Lobo Restaurant* which has an excellent setting and is a perfect place to watch the sunset or relax in the early afternoon (though it closes between 3 and 6 pm for the benefit of the guests). The food is very good and cheap and it's a popular place to eat. Another popular place to eat or sit around with a few cold

beers is *Pete's Bar & Restaurant* near Angela P Fernandes Guest House.

For Chinese food, Meena's Lodge near the bus stand has the *China Town Restaurant*, or there's decent Tibetan food available from the *Tibetan Kitchen*, signposted one block off the main road.

Along the road to Baga there's the popular *Boutique-Tatophanie Cafe*, a very slick, German-run place with not only designer clothes but also a relaxing little cafe serving treats such as apple pie, chocolate cake and filter coffee.

Vila Goesa Beach Resort has an open-air restaurant and a pub, with live bands twice a week in the high season.

One of the most popular restaurants in this area, however, is *Tito's*, almost at the end of the road which branches off at the Villa Bonfim and heads towards the beach. This place has been a travellers' haunt for years on account of its excellent food and pleasant setting overlooking the sea. Prices are as much as double what you'd pay in the restaurants in Calangute and Baga but the ambience is agreeable, especially at night. Fish, chips and salad is Rs 50.

Further up along the main road to Baga is the *Casa Portuguesa Bar & Restaurant*. This is a good place for a minor splurge with its old-world charm and pleasant setting among the coconut palms, though not everyone rates the cuisine too highly.

At Baga itself, take your pick of the open-air restaurants – *Jack's Bar & Restaurant*, *Britto's Bar & Restaurant*, *St Anthony's Bar & Restaurant* or the *Two Sisters' Bar & Restaurant*. They're all popular and offer the same sort of fare at a similar price – Western breakfast staples, seafood, fruit juices, beer and other drinks.

For a very mellow afternoon or night out, try *Nani's & Rani's Bar & Restaurant* on the other side of the river from the Hotel Baia do Sol (cross the river via the bridge next to the Hotel Riverside). The food is good and the atmosphere relaxed.

The food at the *Hotel Baia do Sol* is fairly indifferent but there's live bands and dancing on weekends during the season. The restaurant at the *Hotel Riverside* is another pleasant spot and is worth the short walk from Baga.

Things to Buy

There are numerous stalls all the way from the crossroads to the beach selling genuine and reproduction Tibetan and Rajasthani crafts. Most of them are well made and some of them stunningly beautiful, but they aren't cheap. Interesting jewellery, bangles and other ethnic trinkets (usually Tibetan, Kashmiri and Indian tribal in origin) are available.

Getting There & Away

There are frequent buses to Panaji (north side of the river) and Mapusa from Calangute throughout the day. The fare is Rs 1.50 from Calangute to Panaji and the trip takes 35 to 45 minutes.

Taxis are also available and worth the extra cost if you have a small group and want to save time. Panaji to Calangute or Baga costs Rs 50 for the car and takes about 15 minutes. A motorcycle taxi costs Rs 20.

Getting Around

Most of the buses between Panaji and Calangute terminate at Calangute; very few continue on to Baga. Bicycles can be hired at many places in Calangute and Baga at the usual rates – Rs 2 per hour or Rs 15 for a full day plus Rs 2 for the night, though many places ask for Rs 20 per day. Get there early in the morning if you want the best bicycles – maintenance is only undertaken under duress.

Motorbikes – old Enfields and Rajdoots – are also available for hire at the usual rates (see under Panaji). Hiring by the week or the month is much more economical than by the day. You need basic maintenance skills to keep these machines running – spark plugs oil-up constantly. The Boutique-Tatophanie Cafe between Calangute and Baga has a whole fleet of new Enfields for rent at Rs 200 per day.

AGUADA

South of Calangute, near the mouth of the Mandovi River, Aguada is Goa's jet-set beach. Its main attraction is the 16th-century Portuguese Aguada Fort in which the main hotel is built.

Places to Stay

There are several hotels here, all very much at the top end. The five-star *Fort Aguada Beach Resort* (☎ 87-501) is built within the ramparts of the old fort and has standard air-con rooms for US$90/100, and deluxe rooms for US$110/130. The resort has a swimming pool, tennis courts, shops, boats and canoes to rent, and bicycles. They also have a number of villas known as the *Aguada Hermitage* costing Rs 1750/3250 for singles/doubles.

ANJUNA

This is the beach that everyone went to when Calangute had been filmed, recorded, reported and talked about into the sand. There's a weird and wonderful collection of overlanders, monks, defiant ex-hippies, gentle lunatics, artists, artisans, seers, searchers and peripatetic expatriates who normally wouldn't be seen out of the organic confines of their health-food emporia in San Francisco or London.

There's no point in trying to define what Anjuna is or what it's like – it's many different things to many different people. The only way to find out is to stay here for a while and make some friends. Full moon is a particularly good time to be here. Unlike Calangute, the place has retained its charm and there's no hotel development going on. Nude bathing, on the other hand, is very much on the decline as are the once freely available drugs. Local outrage and official concern about the excesses of a certain minority has led to periodic clampdowns and an exodus to more remote beaches like Arambol to the north and Gokarn over the border in Karnataka to the south.

Information

There is a post office to which you can have mail sent, and there's a branch of the Bank of Baroda not far away. Be warned that this bank will change travellers' cheques, but won't touch foreign cash. Halfway between Nelson's Restaurant and the beach is a branch of MGM Travels where you can make bookings and get flights confirmed.

Flea Market

The Wednesday flea market at Anjuna is a major attraction for people from all the Goan beaches. It's a wonderful blend of Tibetan and Kashmiri traders, colourful Gujarati tribal women, blissed-out '60s-style hippies plus just about anybody else you might meet in India. Whatever you need, from a used

paperback to read to a new *tanga* (G-string monokini) for the beach, you'll find it here. There's lots of good food, both Indian and Western – many long-term Western visitors seem to get out their favourite recipes from back home and cook up a batch of something to sell at the flea market. It's quite a scene.

Traditional-style fishing boats are available for transport to the market from Baga beach – you'll see notices advertising this in the restaurants.

Places to Stay

It isn't easy to find a place to stay between November and March. Most of the available houses are rented on a long-term basis, often six months to a year, by people who come back again and again. There are only two or three hotels, which are near the junction where the road from Chapora meets the road to the beach, but they're more or less permanently full. If you want to stay here you may initially have to make do with a very primitive shack or even sleep outside a restaurant, leaving your gear with the owner until you've made some friends or had a good scout around for a house. Quite a few places have 'Rooms to Let' signs displayed, so these are the ones to head for initially.

Anjuna is not a beach to head for if you're expecting immediate comforts in the shape of a hotel. This beach is definitely for people with plenty of initiative. If you're only planning on staying a few days then it's not really worth coming here except for the market.

Places to Eat

There are any number of restaurants and cafes strung out along the road to the beach and all along the beachfront. Which one you choose as your favourite will depend largely on what sort of person you are and who you meet. The *Rose Garden Restaurant* has excellent seafood and cold beer and is one of the more popular places. Other places include *Searock, Amigo, White Negro, Fernandes* and *Guru Bar*. *Xaviers* has excellent food and good service.

La Frenyas, however, has unbelievably poor service – it takes up to two hours

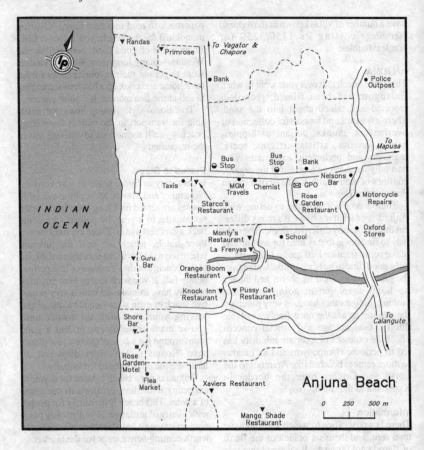

Anjuna Beach

0   250   500 m

between ordering and actually having a meal put in front of you. The *Shore Bar* is the current 'in' place to sit and watch the sunset. This is usually followed by a visit to *Primrose* for strawberries and ice cream, and to find out where the next party is, although the motorcycle taxi-wallahs are also a good sources for this.

Back from the beach there's a number of places south of the post office worth trying, and these include the *Knock Inn*, *Orange Boom* and *Pussy Cat*.

For a cultural night out, try the *Haystack Restaurant*, not far from Anjuna. On Friday

nights there's a Goan buffet, and the price of Rs 150 includes live music and performances by local dancers.

Getting There & Away

There are buses every hour or so to Anjuna and Chapora from Mapusa. They can be very crowded at certain times of the day. It's usually a lot easier and certainly quicker to take a motorcycle (Rs 20, about 15 minutes) or to get a group together and hire a taxi (Rs 50).

Licence and insurance checks on foreigners who have rented motorcycles are becoming more common, particularly on market day. See the warning under the Getting Around section at the beginning of this chapter for more details.

CHAPORA & VAGATOR

This is one of the most beautiful, interesting and unspoilt areas of Goa and a good deal more attractive than Anjuna for either a short or a long stay. Much of the inhabited area nestles under a canopy of dense coconut palms and the village is dominated by a rocky hill on top of which sits an old Portuguese fort. The fort is fairly well preserved and worth a visit, and the views from its ramparts are excellent. Secluded sandy coves are found all the way around the northern side of this rocky outcrop, though the main beaches face west towards the Indian Ocean, and this part is known as Vagator.

Many Westerners stay here on a long-term basis but it's not a tourist ghetto. The local people remain friendly and since the houses available for rent are widely scattered and there are many beaches and coves to choose from, only rarely will you see large groups of travellers together in one place.

Quite a lot of traditional boat building goes on along the shores of the Chapora River.

Places to Stay

There are few places where you can find cheap instant accommodation in Chapora. This is one of the things which makes it such a pleasant place to stay, particularly as most people who do come here stay for a long time. Initially, you'll have to take whatever is available and ask around, or stay at Mapusa, Calangute or Baga and 'commute' until you've found something.

It helps if you get here before the real height of the season – try September and October when there are only a few people about. On the other hand, it isn't particularly difficult to find somewhere to live – just make it your top priority and keep asking around in the stores and cafes. As at Anjuna, you'll see a number of places with 'Rooms to Let' signs out.

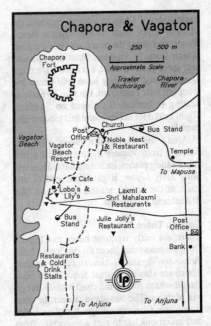

Wherever you decide to live, make sure you have a torch (flashlight) handy. There are no street lights, and finding your way along the paths through coconut palms late at night when there's no full moon is a devil of a job! Houses for rent cost between Rs 150 to Rs 400 a month depending on their size and location.

At the top end of the market is the *Vagator Beach Resort* (☎ Siolim 41), on the beach of the same name. The resort, in palm-shaded grounds, comprises a main block containing the restaurant, bar and reception area, and two types of cottages. It's a friendly place and, as beach resorts go in Goa, deserves top billing. The cottages cost Rs 550/590, falling to Rs 200/290 during the monsoon.

Slightly cheaper is the *Abu John Bungalows*, which are new and good value at Rs 250 for a double with bathroom.

Places to Eat

There are numerous restaurants along the

main street of Chapora village, opposite the church, at the back of the Vagator Beach Resort and along the beach south of the road which leads to Vagator. Most are pleasant and serve good seafood, but *Lobo's* is exceptionally good and they have cold beers. It's a superb little restaurant, but turn up early as seating is limited. It's closed on Sundays. Right next door is *Lily's*, and this place is also popular.

Along the road which heads inland to Mapusa from Vagator there are quite a few more eating places, including the *C Shell* and *Jolly Jolly Lester*. Right at the end of this road, at the beach, are the *Laxmi* and *Shri Mahalaxmi* restaurants.

Getting There & Away

There are fairly frequent buses to Chapora from Mapusa throughout the day for Rs 1.50. A bus to Vagator is almost as convenient. There are also occasional direct buses from Panaji which follow the coast and do not go via Mapusa. The bus stand is near the road junction in Chapora village. It's often easier and much quicker to rent a motorbike from Mapusa or to get a group together and hire a taxi.

ARAMBOL (Harmal)

Some years ago, when the screws were tightened at Anjuna in an attempt to control what local people regarded as the more outrageous activities (nudism and drug use) of a certain section of the travelling community, the diehards cast around for a more 'sympathetic' beach. Arambol, north of Chapora, was one of those which they chose.

Initially, only those willing to put up with very primitive conditions and a total lack of facilities came here. That has changed due to the laws of supply and demand, even if some of those who come here look askance at the developments. Nevertheless, development has so far been minimal, although there is talk of a Japanese-funded resort being built here, which would obviously dramatically change the pristine nature of the place – see it while you can.

Buses from Mapusa take you as far as Arambol where there is a chai shop and a few other tiny shops. From here a road branches off to the village by the sea where kids will offer you a room for around Rs 25 a day. All you get is bare walls and no beds. You can rent mattresses, cookers and all the rest from the shops at the village – obviously one comes here for at least a week. In the village there are 10 or so chai shops that serve 'Westernised-Indian' food.

The seashore is beautiful and the village quiet and friendly with just a few hundred locals, mostly fishers, and a couple of hundred Western residents in the November to February high season.

Getting There & Away

There are occasional buses from Mapusa to Arambol which take three hours. Alternatively, get a group together and hire a taxi but remember that if you do this you'll have to pay the fare both ways since the driver is unlikely to be able to pick up passengers for the return journey. Another way to get there is to take the ferry across the river from Siolim, north-east of Chapora, to Chopdem and hitch from there.

OTHER BEACHES

If you'd like to get right out of the way of all the tourist development in Goa then it's worth considering a trip to either Terekhol in the extreme north-west corner of Goa or Palolen way down south near Chauri.

At Terekhol there's a large old Portuguese fort which has been converted into a government-owned hotel, the *Terekhol Fort Tourist Rest House* (☎ Redi 48), which offers a range of accommodation. Doubles (there are no singles) cost Rs 150 (Rs 100 low season), while suites go for Rs 220 (Rs 160).

There are very occasional buses between Mapusa or Pernem to Querim on the opposite (south) side of the river from Terekhol. Between Querim and Terekhol there is a flat-bottomed ferry.

At Palolen there's only basic accommodation available as yet. To get there, take a bus from Margao to Chauri.

Other Attractions in Goa

BONDLA WILDLIFE SANCTUARY

Up in the lush foothills of the Western Ghats, Bondla is a good place to see sambar and wild boar, among other things. It's the smallest of the Goan wildlife sanctuaries (eight sq km) but the easiest one to gain access to at present. It's 52 km from Panaji and 38 km from Margao.

There is a botanical garden, fenced deer park and a zoo, which is better than most with spacious enclosures. It was originally started to house orphaned animals, but these days there are now breeding colonies of the larger species of deer.

Places to Stay & Eat

Bookings for accommodation should be made in advance at the office of the Department of Forestry, directly opposite the Air India office and beside the Hotel Fidalgo in Panaji. The accommodation is often booked out, and so it may be easier to get a room on Thursdays, when the park is closed. This may not sound like such a smart idea, but it's still a very pleasant place to stay and you're right there for when the gates open at 9 am on Friday.

The excellent chalets cost Rs 15 per night, or there are dorm beds for Rs 3. Drinks are always readily available in the large refectory, and a few hours notice will get you a very respectable fish curry thali for around Rs 18.

Getting There & Away

Take a bus to Ponda, and from here a taxi to the park costs Rs 110. Alternatively, you can take the Molen bus as far as Tiskar, from where a motorcycle taxi to the park will cost Rs 35.

Getting Around

There is a minibus around the park, but it is easier (and quieter) to walk. The minibus is essentially for the deer park, which opens for an hour or so at 4 pm.

MOLEN & COTIGAO WILDLIFE SANCTUARIES

Both these wildlife sanctuaries are larger than the Bondla sanctuary but neither is easy to get to and you would need your own transport.

Places to Stay & Eat

Cheap accommodation is available at Molen in the *Tourist Complex* (☎ 38), and meals are available for those who book in advance.

There's no accommodation available at the Cotigao sanctuary.

TEMPLES

When the Portuguese arrived in Goa they destroyed every Hindu temple and Muslim mosque they could lay their hands on, so temples in Goa are generally back from the coast and comparatively new, although some date back about 400 years. The temples have been rebuilt from the original temples destroyed by the Portuguese, and their lamp towers are a distinctive Goan feature. Despite their earnest attempts to spread Roman Catholicism, only 38% of Goans today are Christian.

Five of the most important Hindu temples are close to Ponda on the inland route between Panaji and Margao. The Siva temple of **Shri Mangesh** is at Priol-Ponda Taluka, about 22 km from Panaji. This tiny 18th-century temple with its white tower, a local landmark, is on top of a small hill. Less than two km further down the road is **Shri Mahalsa**, a Vishnu temple.

About five km from Ponda are **Shri Ramnath** and **Shri Nagesh**, and nearby is the **Shri Shantadurga Temple**. Dedicated to Shantadurga, the goddess of peace, the latter temple sports a very unusual, almost pagoda-like structure with a roof made out of long slabs of stone. Further south are the temples of **Shri Chandreshwar**, west of Quepem; the **Shantadurga**, east of Betul; and the **Shri Mallikarjuna**, east of Chauri.

MOSQUES

The only mosque remaining in Goa is the **Safa Shahouri Masjid** at Ponda, built by Ali

Adilshah in 1560. When first built it matched in size and quality the mosques at Bijapur, but was allowed to decay during the Portuguese period. Little remained of its former grandeur by the time the Portuguese left but the Archaeological Survey of India has now undertaken its restoration using local artisans. If what has already been completed is anything to go by, it will look superb when finished.

FORTS

There are quite a few old Portuguese forts dotted around Goa, mostly on the coast, and most are in a reasonable state of preservation. They're certainly worth visiting if you have the time. The one at **Chapora** is particularly recommended. Two of them – **Aguada** and **Terekhol** – have been converted into hotels.

Karnataka

Population: 44 million
Area: 191,773 sq km
Capital: Bangalore
People per sq km: 234
Main Language: Kannada
Literacy Rate: 56%

The state of Karnataka, formerly known as Mysore, is one of the more easy-going Indian states. It's a state of strong contrasts, with the modern, industrialised city of Bangalore at one extreme and expanses of rural farming areas at the other. Karnataka also has some of the most interesting historic architecture in India, and a varied and tumultuous history.

History

It was to Sravanabelagola, Karnataka, in the 3rd century BC that Chandragupta Maurya, India's first great emperor, retreated after he had renounced worldly ways and embraced Jainism. Later, the mighty 17-metre-high statue of Gomateshvara, which celebrated its 1000th anniversary in 1981, was erected at Sravanabelagola. Fifteen hundred years ago at Badami, in the north of the state, the Chalukyans built some of the earliest Hindu temples in India. All later south Indian temple architecture stems from the Chalukyan designs at Badami, the Pallavas at Kanchipuram and Mahabalipuram in Tamil Nadu.

Other important Indian dynasties, such as the Cholas and the Gangas, have also played their part in Karnataka's history, but it was the Hoysalas, who ruled between the 11th and 14th centuries, who left the most vivid evidence of their presence. The beautiful Hoysala temples at Somnathpur, Belur and Halebid are gems of Indian architecture with intricate and detailed sculptures rivalling anything to be found at Khajuraho (Madhya Pradesh) or Konark (Orissa).

In 1327, Hindu Halebid fell to the Muslim army of Mohammed bin Tughlaq but his triumph was brief and in 1346 it was annexed

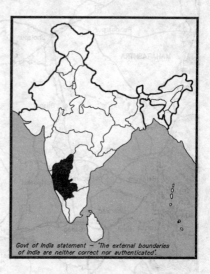

Govt of India statement – 'The external boundaries of India are neither correct nor authenticated'.

by the Hindu kingdom of Vijayanagar, founded in 1336 with its capital at Hampi. Hampi is one of the most beautiful, extensive and fascinating of India's ruined kingdoms, yet has been little visited by foreigners until recent years. Vijayanagar reached its peak in the early 1550s, but in 1565 it fell to the Deccan sultans and Bijapur became the most important city of the region. Today, Bijapur is just a small city surrounded by an imposing wall and packed with a fascinating collection of mosques and other reminders of its glorious past.

Following the demise of Vijayanagar, the Wodeyars of Mysore gradually grew in importance and, over a short period of time, established their own rule over a large part of southern India which included all of old Mysore state and parts of Tamil Nadu. Their capital was at Srirangapatnam. Their power remained more or less unchallenged until 1761 when Hyder Ali (one of their generals) rose to great strength and deposed them.

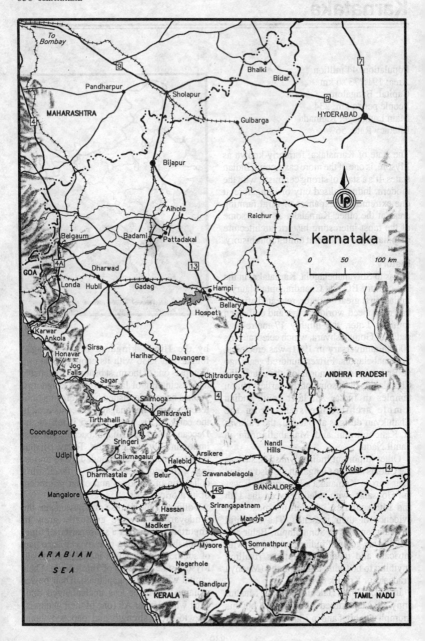

To Bombay

MAHARASHTRA

Bhalki
Bidar

Pandharpur
Sholapur

HYDERABAD

Gulbarga

Bijapur

Aihole

Raichur

Belgaum
Badami
Pattadakal

Karnataka

0   50   100 km

GOA
Dharwad

Londa   Hubli   Gadag   Hampi

Karwar
Ankola

Bellary

Hospet

Honavar

Jog
Falls

Sirsa

Harihar   Davangere

ANDHRA PRADESH

Sagar

Chitradurga

Coondapoor

Shimoga
Bhadravati

Tirthahalli

Udipi

Sringeri

Nandi
Hills

Chikmagalui

Halebid

Arsikere

Kolar

Dharmastala

Belur

Sravanabelagola

BANGALORE

Mangalore

Hassan   Srirangapatnam

Madikeri

Mandya

Nagarhole

Mysore   Somnathpur

ARABIAN
SEA

Bandipur

KERALA

TAMIL NADU

These were the years of bitter rivalry between the British and French for control of the Carnatic, and Hyder Ali, followed by his son, Tipu Sultan, were assisted by the French in consolidating their hold over the area in return for assistance in fighting the British.

In 1799, however, the British finally defeated Tipu Sultan (who himself was killed in the battle), annexed a part of his kingdom, and placed the Hindu Wodeyars back on the throne of Mysore.

The Wodeyars continued to rule Mysore state until Independence when they were pensioned off, yet they were enlightened and progressive rulers and so popular with their subjects that the maharaja became the first governor of the post-Independence state. The maharaja remains very popular in Mysore city itself but, since Indira Gandhi rescinded the pensions of all India's princes in the 1970s, the Wodeyars fell on hard times. Perhaps it was too many years of easy living and lack of business sense.

While they did convert many of their palaces and hunting lodges into hotels in the 1970s, the capital for maintenance, as well as managerial acumen, were obviously lacking. Since then, most have been franchised out to international hotel chains and relaunched as superdeluxe hotels. Meanwhile the erstwhile maharaja continues to live in the vast palace complex in Mysore, itself open to the public.

Under Nehru's premiership, vast irrigation schemes and dams to supply them were initiated in Karnataka state and most have now been completed, but since the dams tap two of the major rivers which flow through into Tamil Nadu (in particular, the Cauvery), the state governments of Karnataka and Tamil Nadu are currently in bitter dispute over water rights. A compromise is proving hard to find. Perhaps more serious, though, is the deforestation over major areas of central and northern Karnataka. You can travel for hours by train in this area yet rarely see a single tree. As a result, soil erosion is a major problem and should the monsoons ever fail, it would be a disaster for the people in the rural villages.

Southern Karnataka

BANGALORE

Population: 4.1 million

Though a modern, bustling city and an important industrial centre, Bangalore remains one of India's most pleasant cities. The central area is studded with beautifully laid out parks and gardens, wide tree-lined avenues, imposing buildings and lively bazaars. Situated 1000 metres above sea level and with a very pleasant climate, it's a city where people from all over India and abroad have come to look for work, business opportunities and higher education. In fact Bangalore has become India's yuppie heaven and is one of the country's fastest growing cities.

The pace of life, like the intellectual and political climate, is brisk, and hardly a day goes by without some new controversy boiling over across the front pages of its daily newspapers or onto the streets. It is also one of India's most progressive and liberal cities as far as social attitudes go. Bangalore's important industries include machine tools, aircraft, electronics and computers.

Bangalore is an excellent place to visit if you're looking for 'action'. It's a cosmopolitan melting pot and the young people here are some of the most Westernised in India. You may well be pleasantly surprised at their enthusiasm and the way they flout normal Hindu caste and social mores. The Tibetans who have settled here display an even greater divergence from the norm. There's also a wide range of hotels, restaurants, films and other cultural activities, excellent bookshops and craft shops. Make sure you have a reasonable set of clean clothes: you'll look very much out of place otherwise. This is a very fashion conscious city.

History

Now the capital of Karnataka state, Bangalore was founded by Kempegowda in the early 16th century and became an important fortress city under Hyder Ali and Tipu Sultan

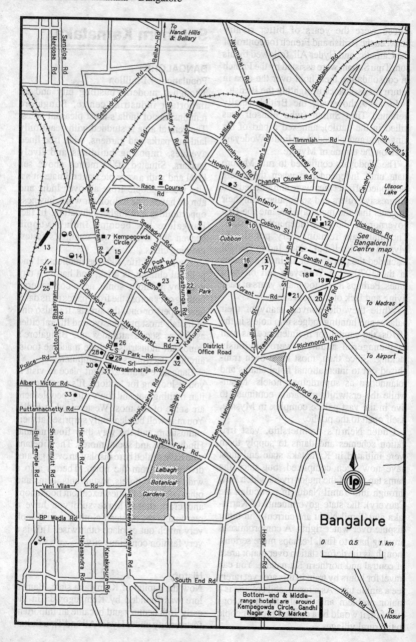

To Nandi Hills & Bellary

Race Course Rd

Kempegowda Circle

Cubbon Park

Lalbagh Botanical Gardens

Bangalore

0.5   1 km

To Madras

To Airport

To Hosur

Bottom–end & Middle–range hotels are around Kempegowda Circle, Gandhi Nagar & City Market

■ PLACES TO STAY

2	West End Hotel
4	Hotel Tourist
7	Sri Ramakrishna & Royal Lodges
11	New Central Lodge
12	YWCA Guest House
15	Gupta Lodge
18	Hotel Gautam
19	Nilgiris Nest Hotel
20	Hotel Imperial & Shansug Hotel
22	YMCA
24	Sri Ganesha Lodge
25	Sudha Lodge
31	Rainbow Hotel

OTHER

1	Cantonment Railway Station
3	Commissioner of Police
5	Racecourse
6	City Bus Station
8	Vidhana Soudha
9	GPO
10	Central Telegraph Office
13	City Railway Station
14	Central Bus Station
16	Government Museum & Technological Museum
17	KSTDC Head Office
21	Air France
23	Indian Airlines
26	Chandra Vihar
27	Badami House
28	City Market
29	City Market Bus Station
30	Fort
32	Air India
33	Tipu Sultan's Palace
34	Bull Temple

two centuries later, though there are few remains from this period except for the Lalbagh Botanical Gardens.

Orientation

Arrivals and departures in Bangalore revolve around Kempegowda Circle and in the narrow, busy streets of Gandhi Nagar and Chickpet adjacent to the bus and railway stations. This is where you will find one of the main shopping areas, many of the cinemas and the cheaper hotels. It's a very busy area at lunchtime and in the evening,

when workers spill out of their offices and into the numerous coffee bars, bars and restaurants and form long queues outside the cinemas.

On the other hand, the main centre of activity, particularly for the more affluent and the student population, is the area bounded by Mahatma Gandhi Rd (M G Rd), Brigade Rd and Regency Rd east of Cubbon Park and about four km from the railway station. It's here you'll find the more expensive hotels and restaurants, bars, discos, night clubs, the GPO, travel agents, airline offices, tourist information centres, bookshops and craft shops.

Most government offices and museums are either in or around Cubbon Park, while Bangalore's few remaining historical relics are all south of the City Market – some of them a considerable way to the south.

The old part of the city lies south of the railway station along Cottonpet Bhashyam Rd and around the City Market on Sri Narasimharaja Rd. Here there are narrow, winding streets, an endless variety of small cottage industries and manufacturing concerns, old temples, bullock carts and tea shops.

If you are in Bangalore for less than 24 hours, it's probably more convenient to stay close to the station. Otherwise it's well worth spending a little more and staying in the M G Rd area of the city.

Information

Tourist Offices The Government of India tourist office (☎ 57-9517) is in the KFC Building at 48 Church St in the M G Rd area. They have friendly staff and a lot of material to give away. It is open from 10 am to 6 pm Monday to Friday, 9 am to 1 pm Saturdays.

Karnataka State Tourism Development Corporation (KSTDC) has its head office (☎ 21-2901) at 10/4 Kasturba Rd, Queen's Circle. There are counters at 1 Badami House (☎ 21-5869), Narasimharaja Square, the City Railway Station (☎ 70-068, open 6 am to 9 pm), the airport (☎ 57-1467, open 7 am to 8.30 pm), and at the Hotel Mayura

Kempegowda (☎ 71-759), Dhanavanthri Rd.

Money Thomas Cook (☎ 57-1066) is at 55 M G Rd, and this is an excellent place to change money. They take virtually all travellers' cheques and you'll be out of the place in under five minutes.

Post & Telecommunications The GPO is on Cubbon St, opposite Cubbon Park. The efficient poste restante service is open from 10 am to 7 pm Monday to Saturday, and 10.30 am to 1.30 pm on Sunday.

The Central Telegraph Office is right next door to the post office and is open 24 hours a day. Bangalore's telephone area code is 0812.

Visa Extensions Bangalore is a good place to get a visa extension as these are issued without fuss in 24 hours, and sometimes even the same day or same morning. The office of the Commissioner of Police is on Infantry Rd, 10 minutes walk from the GPO.

Bookshops There are various bookshops on Brigade Rd, Residency Rd, Church St, Avenue Rd (west of Cubbon Park) and on M G Rd, but the best is Premier Bookshop, 46/1 Church St, round the corner from Berrys Hotel. There's no place quite like this – books on every conceivable subject are piled from floor to ceiling. It looks totally chaotic but the owner knows where everything is and, if it's in print, he's got it. Gangaram's Book Bureau on M G Rd is also very good, and almost next door is a branch of Higginbothams at 68 M G Rd.

The Bangalore Tract & Book Society on the corner of St Mark's Rd and M G Rd is also pretty good and is an agent of Oxford University Press.

The British Library on St Mark's Rd has lots of current British newspapers and magazines, and they don't seem to mind if you rest awhile and catch up on the news. It's open from 10.30 am to 6.30 pm Tuesday to Saturday.

Vidhana Soudha

This is one of Bangalore's, and indeed one of India's, most spectacular buildings. Built of granite in the neo-Dravidian style of architecture and located at the north-west end of Cubbon Park, it houses both the Secretariat and the State Legislature. The cabinet room is famous for its massive door made of pure sandalwood, and the building is floodlit on Sunday evenings and on public holidays.

If you want to pay a visit it is open from 3 to 5.30 pm on weekdays. The entrance is on the ground floor behind the grand steps. You are allowed only into the entrance lobby where you can admire the impressive dome and the gaudy colour scheme.

Cubbon Park & Museums

One of the main 'lungs' of the city, this beautiful shady park, full of flowering trees, covers an area of 120 hectares and was laid out in 1864. In it are the red Gothic buildings which house the Public Library, the High Court, the Government Museum and the Technological & Industrial Museum. Also in the gardens is a huge **children's park** where, in a reversal of the usual roles, adults are not allowed in unless accompanied by children.

The **Government Museum**, one of the oldest in India, was established in 1886 and houses collections on geology, art, numismatics and relics from Mohenjodaro (one of the cradles of Indian civilisation, dating back 5000 years). There are also some good pieces from Halebid and Vijayanagar. Admission costs Rs 0.50 and the museum is open daily, except Wednesdays and public holidays, from 9 am to 5 pm.

The **Technological & Industrial Museum**, also on Kasturba Rd and adjacent to the Government Museum, is open daily, except Mondays and public holidays, between 10 am and 5 pm; admission costs Rs 1. Its theme is the application of science and technology to industry and human welfare. It is full of happy children pressing the buttons of exhibits that reflect India's technological progress. However, it's nothing special and you could skip it if you are short of time.

Lalbagh Botanical Gardens

This is a beautiful and popular park in the southern suburbs of Bangalore. It covers an area of 96 hectares and was laid out in the 18th century by Hyder Ali and his son Tipu Sultan. It contains many centuries-old trees (most of them labelled), lakes, lotus ponds, flower beds, a deer park and one of the largest collections of rare tropical and sub-tropical plants in India. Refreshments are available at several places within the park.

The gardens are open daily from 8 am to 8 pm.

Fort

Located close to the City Market, this was originally a mud-brick structure built in 1537 by Kempegowda. It was later rebuilt in stone in the 18th century by Hyder Ali and Tipu Sultan, but much of it was destroyed during the wars with the British. It is supposed to be open daily from 8 am to 6 pm, but this isn't always the case.

Tipu Sultan's Palace

This palace was begun by Tipu Sultan's father, Hyder Ali, and completed by Tipu in 1791. It resembles the Daria Daulat Bagh at Srirangapatnam near Mysore, but has been sadly neglected and is falling into disrepair. You may find the temple next to it of far greater interest. The palace is open daily from 8 am to 6 pm; admission is free.

Bull Temple

Situated on Bugle Hill at the end of Bull Temple Rd, this is one of Bangalore's oldest temples. Built by Kempegowda in the Dravidian style, it contains a huge monolith of Nandi similar to the one on Chamundi Hill, Mysore. Non-Hindus are allowed to enter and the priests are friendly. You will be offered jasmine flowers and are expected to leave a small donation.

Other Attractions

The remains of the four **watchtowers** built by Kempegowda are worth a visit if you're in the vicinity of the Bull Temple. They are about 400 metres to the west of the temple.

Ulsoor Lake, to the north-east of Cubbon Park, has boating facilities and a swimming pool which is far from clean. The **Karnataka Folk Art Museum** at Kumara Park West has displays of folk art, costumes, toys and an extensive recorded music collection.

Organised Tours

The Karnataka State Tourism Development Corporation (KSTDC) offers the following tours, all starting at Badami House:

Bangalore City The tours operate twice daily from 7.30 am to 1.30 pm and 2 to 7.30 pm. The places visited are Tipu's Palace, Bull Temple, Lalbagh Botanical Gardens, Ulsoor Lake, Government Soap Factory, Vidhana Soudha, Government Museum, Technological & Industrial Museum and Art Gallery. The tours cost Rs 40 and about half of the time is spent at government-owned emporiums that sell silks and handicrafts.

Srirangapatnam, Mysore & Brindavan Gardens Daily tours begin at 7.15 am and return at 11 pm. The tour includes visits to Ranganathaswamy Temple, the Fort, Gumbaz and Daria Daulat Bagh at Srirangapatnam, St Philomena's Cathedral, Chamundi Hill, the Palace, Art Gallery, zoo and Cauvery Arts & Crafts Emporium at Mysore. The tour costs Rs 120 including all entrance fees. Mysore is such a pleasant city that it is better to visit it on your own unless your time is very limited.

Belur, Halebid & Sravanabelagola Daily tours begin at 7.15 am and return at 10 pm. The fare is Rs 150. This is a good tour to take if you don't want to go to the trouble of visiting these places independently using local transport.

Hampi & Tungabhadra Dam This is a weekend tour which departs on Fridays at 9 pm and returns to Bangalore at 10 pm on Sunday. It includes visits to Mantralaya (the village associated with the Hindu saint, Raghavendra Swami), Tungabhadra Dam and Hampi. Overnight accommodation is at the *Hotel Mayura Vijayanagar* at Tungabhadra Dam. The cost of the tour is Rs 320, including accommodation.

Nandi Hills Tours to Nandi Hills, a hill station north of Bangalore, operate daily in season (April and May) and on Saturday, Sunday and public holidays the rest of the year. They depart at 8.30 am and return by 6 pm. The fare is Rs 55 including a vegetarian lunch.

There are many other tours to places further afield (such as Tirupathi, Ooty, Jog Falls) which last from two to five days, but they're of little interest to most travellers. All the above tours can be booked at any of the KSTDC tourist offices.

Places to Stay – bottom end

Bus Station Area There are a couple of cheap and extremely noisy hotels along Cottonpet Bhashyam Rd, south of the bus station. An old favourite is the *Sudha Lodge* (☎ 60-542) at No 6, although these days it's definitely on the skids. Close by, and equally basic, is the *Sri Ganesha Lodge* (☎ 60-9144).

On the east side of the bus station are a dozen or more hotels and lodges to suit most budgets. One of the best is the *Royal Lodge* (☎ 28-951) on Subedar Chatram Rd. It has clean and fairly spacious double rooms for Rs 50, Rs 60 with bathroom, and there is hot water in the mornings. Just along from the Royal Lodge is the huge *Sri Ramakrishna Lodge* (☎ 73-041) which is also good value. Also in this area is the KSTDC *Hotel Mayura Kempegowda* (☎ 71-759), Dhanavanthri Rd, which has rooms with attached bathroom for Rs 100/120.

A little further afield is the *Hotel Tourist* (☎ 72-381), Race Course Rd, which is good value at Rs 40/60 with attached bathroom, and hot water in the mornings.

Up the scale a bit, the relatively new *Hotel Adora* (☎ 76-225) at 47 Subedar Chatram Rd has good rooms for Rs 60/95, and there's hot water in the morning. The *Samadhya Lodge*

(☎ 74-064) at 70 Subedar Chatram Rd has similar prices.

At the top end of this range is the new *Janardhana Hotel* (☎ 26-4444), Kumara Krupa Rd, High Grounds, opposite the Bangalore International, which has spacious rooms with balconies and attached bathrooms with hot water round the clock at Rs 90/130 and deluxe doubles at Rs 180.

There are also *retiring rooms* at City railway station though they are often full by the afternoon. Dorm beds cost Rs 25 and doubles Rs 75.

M G Rd Area Budget accommodation is limited in this area but there are a few good places. The *New Central Lodge* (☎ 58-6859), 56 Infantry Rd, is a clean and popular place. Rooms with attached bathrooms with hot water cost Rs 45/90 (ordinary), Rs 100/130 (standard) and Rs 110/140 (deluxe). Also good value is the *Sunflower Lodge*, 129 Brigade Rd, which has doubles with attached bathroom for Rs 95.

Also in this area is the *Hotel Vellara* (☎ 56-5684), 283 Brigade Rd, which has ordinary rooms with attached bathroom for Rs 120/160 and deluxe doubles for Rs 220. Similar is the *Hotel Imperial* (☎ 57-7421), 95 Residency Rd, which has clean, airy rooms with attached bathroom for Rs 63/115.

At the top end of this category is the *Brindavan Hotel* (☎ 57-371), 108 M G Rd, which has ordinary singles/doubles at Rs 130/165, deluxe doubles at Rs 220, and air-con singles/doubles at Rs 160/375. The hotel is set back from the road so it doesn't suffer too much from the traffic noise. Similar is the *Hotel Gautam* (☎ 56-0001), 17 Mission Rd, which has non-air-con singles/doubles with attached bathroom for Rs 120/150.

It might also be worth trying the *YMCA* (☎ 21-1848), Nirupathunga Rd, on the western edge of Cubbon Park, which has singles/doubles at Rs 60/80, but it only takes men. Women have the option of the *YWCA Guest House* (☎ 57-0997), 86 Infantry Rd, which has doubles at Rs 60, or the *YWCA Annexe* (☎ 23-8574), 32 Mission Rd, which

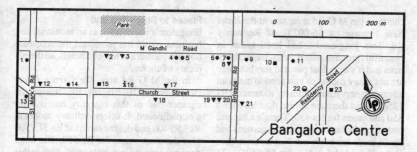

PLACES TO STAY

10 Brindavan Hotel
15 Berrys Hotel & Premier Bookshop
23 Hotel New Victoria

▼ **PLACES TO EAT**

2 Chit Chat Restaurant
3 Lakeview Milk Bar
8 Rice Bowl Restaurant
17 Oasis Bar & Restaurant
18 Blue Heaven Chinese Restaurant
19 Mac Fast Food
20 The Pub
21 Waikikee Restaurant

OTHER

1 Bangalore Tract & Book Society
4 Higginbothams Book Store
5 Gangaram's Book Bureau
6 Thomas Cook
7 The Cottage Arts
9 Cauvery Arts & Crafts Emporium
11 Karnataka Govt Sari Emporium
12 KC Das
13 British Library
14 Ginza
16 Govt of India Tourist Office
22 Bus from Station

offers B&B at Rs 200 a double. Both the YMCA and YWCA accommodation is heavily subscribed so it's best to make advance reservations if possible. There's also a temporary membership fee of Rs 10 payable at any of them.

City Market Area This is the place to stay if you want to be really in the thick of things. It's the area of Bangalore with the noise, bustle and local atmosphere. To get there on foot from either the railway or bus stations, go south down Cottonpet Bhashyam Rd as far as the Kangeri Police Station (on the right-hand side), and then turn left. This is Police Rd, though there are no signs to tell you this. Continue down Police Rd for several hundred metres and you will find yourself outside City Market. It is 25 minutes walk from the railway station.

The *Rainbow Hotel* (☎ 60-2235) is on Sri Narasimharaja Rd right opposite the City Market bus stand. It's very good value at Rs 40/60, and their air-con rooms at Rs 100 a double are some of the cheapest you'll find in Bangalore.

Close by on Avenue Rd, the *Delhi Bhavan Lodge* (☎ 75-045) is cheap and gloomy at Rs 35/55, while the *Chandra Vihar* (☎ 22-4146) opposite is marginally better.

Places to Stay – middle
Most of the hotels in this price range are in the more expensive M G Rd area but there are a few in the City railway station/State bus stand area.

Nearest to the City railway station area is the new *Hotel Raceview* (☎ 26-6147), 25 Race Course Rd, which has doubles without air-con for Rs 200 or Rs 325 with air-con. There are no singles.

For a touch of class and olde-worlde

charm in the M G Rd area, stay at the *Hotel New Victoria* (☎ 56-0025), 47 Residency Rd. This long-established hotel is set in beautiful grounds filled with huge shady trees and it's a popular place to stay but there are not many rooms so you need to make an advance reservation. Ordinary rooms cost Rs 125/250 and there are deluxe doubles for Rs 350 and suites for Rs 450. There's a bar and restaurant (eat indoors or in the garden) and credit cards are accepted. Not far from here is the *Hotel Nilgiris Nest* (☎ 58-8401), 171 Brigade Rd, which has spacious rooms without air-con for Rs 190/260 or Rs 250/320 with air-con.

Further to the west is the popular but relatively poorly maintained *Berrys Hotel* (☎ 58-7211), 48/1 Church St, just at the back of M G Rd. It's a large place so is rarely full and has ordinary rooms for Rs 140/170, deluxe rooms for Rs 200/250, and air-con rooms for 250/300 plus tax. There's a restaurant and the room staff are friendly but reception can be testy.

More expensive is the *Hotel Rama* (☎ 21-3381), Lavelle Rd, which offers very comfortable rooms without air-con for Rs 340/395 or Rs 395/450 with air-con. Breakfast is included in the price. The hotel has its own bar and restaurant (Indian, Chinese and Continental).

Similar in price but over in the Race Course Rd area are two hotels to choose from. The *Hotel Bangalore International* (☎ 26-8011), 2A/2B Crescent Rd, High Grounds, has ordinary rooms without air-con for Rs 210/280 or Rs 300/400. Ordinary/deluxe air-con rooms go for Rs 260/360 and Rs 350/450 respectively. All the rooms have a colour TV plus there's a range of facilities including a bar and restaurant with a live band every evening.

Not far from the Bangalore International is the relatively new *Hotel Abhishek* (☎ 26-2713), 19/2 Kumara Krupa Rd, High Grounds. This three-star hotel offers rooms without air-con for Rs 360/450 or Rs 450/540 with air-con. All the rooms have a colour TV and there are two vegetarian restaurants but no bar.

Places to Stay – top end

Bangalore's importance as an industrial and business centre has prompted the construction of a plethora of top-end hotels, so there's plenty of choice.

In the M G Rd area, the *Curzon Court* (☎ 58-2997), 10 Brigade Rd, lies at the cheaper end of this category but is fully air-conditioned. It offers ordinary rooms at Rs 350/400 and deluxe rooms at Rs 375/500 plus there are suites for Rs 550. The hotel does not have its own restaurant. Also in this category is the *Cauvery Continental* (☎ 26-6966), 11-37 Cunningham Rd, which has rooms for Rs 250/320 or Rs 320/400 with air-con.

More expensive but in the same area is the four-star *Gateway Hotel* (☎ 58-4545), 66 Residency Rd, which has standard rooms at Rs 825/950 and deluxe rooms for Rs 900/1025. Facilities include a coffee shop, restaurant, swimming pool and gymnasium.

Over in the Race Course Rd area, there is the three-star *West End Hotel* (☎ 26-9281), Race Course Rd, which has a pleasant garden and swimming pool. Air-con rooms are Rs 1400/1600.

At the top end of this category are five five-star hotels. The *Ashok Radisson Hotel* (☎ 26-9462), Kumara Krupa Rd, High Grounds, has rooms from Rs 1000/1150 plus more expensive suites. The *Taj Residency* (☎ 58-4444), 41/3 M G Rd, costs Rs 1100/1250.

The *Holiday Inn* (☎ 26-9451), 28 Sankey Rd, is similar to its clones elsewhere around the world and has rooms from Rs 1275/1575. Almost next door is the *Welcomgroup Windsor Manor* (☎ 26-9898), 25 Sankey Rd, with a range of rooms from Rs 1425 to Rs 2000 for singles and Rs 1625 to Rs 2200 for doubles. Similar is the *Oberoi Bangalore* on M G Rd. All these hotels have the usual full range of facilities including swimming pools, bars and restaurants.

Places to Eat

Bangalore has some excellent places to eat, with a whole range of different cuisines available. Most of the better restaurants are in the M G Rd area. The very popular and reasonably priced *Rice Bowl*, Brigade Rd, has excellent Chinese, Tibetan and Continental food and is run by friendly Tibetans. The wonton soups are superb value. You can also have a cold beer here, there's a good sound system (Western music) and the service is quick. Another good place for Chinese food is the *Blue Heaven* in Church St, although it's more expensive than the Rice Bowl.

Also on Church St, *Mac Fast Food* imitates, as you might expect, a Western food chain of a similar name. It's very popular with young, middle-class Indians and some of the food is good (eg the pizzas) but other dishes are not so good. There's an extensive menu and it's good for a snack but not really a meal, and it's not cheap.

Round the corner on M G Rd, the *Indian Coffee House* is considerably cheaper and you can get a good, simple Indian vegetarian meal here any time. As with the other cafes in this chain, the waiters are all done up in shabby white suits replete with cummerbunds and hats. Much more upmarket, but popular, is *Chit Chat*, also on M G Rd, which offers tasty food as well as good lassis and ice cream. In the same area, the *Lakeview Milk Bar* has excellent shakes and sundaes.

For an Indian meal in the M G Rd area, the *Shanbag Cafe* (not to be confused with the New Shanbag a couple of doors along) on Residency Rd does an excellent thali in its air-con dining hall. The meal starts with a sweet, followed by a soup, then you move on to puris, three vegetable curries, sambar, pepper water, papadam, chutney, pickles and curd, followed by a sizeable vegetable biryani and finally a fruit salad.

The *Waikikee Restaurant* on Brigade Rd does good north Indian non-veg dishes. The steaks and pizzas at *Casa Piccolo*, 131 Residency Rd, have received good raves from a number of travellers plus they do wicked ice cream. It has a good atmosphere, the staff are friendly and prices sensible.

For a modest splurge in splendid, shady surroundings, go for a meal (lunch or dinner) at the *Hotel New Victoria*, Residency Rd.

The food is good (Indian and Continental) and prices are reasonable plus they have cold beers. It's a great place to wind down.

For a somewhat expensive but sumptuous lunchtime splurge, try the buffet at the *Memories of China* restaurant in the Taj Residency Hotel. You can gorge yourself here on a whole string of Chinese specialities and follow it up with superb desserts and coffee: all-you-can-eat for Rs 90 in a setting of pure luxury.

K C Das, on the corner of Church St and St Mark's Rd, is a well-known snack-and-sweet shop whose headquarters are in Calcutta. Try their famous rasgullas. On Brigade Rd, opposite the Kwality Restaurant, is the *Nilgiris* supermarket where you can get such goodies as whole-wheat bread, cheese and Danish pastries as well as delicious samosas.

The many restaurants in the bus station area offer mainly Indian food. The *Kamat Hotel* on Subedar Chatram Rd has good vegetarian meals and snacks, while next door the *Sagar Hotel* has cheap vegetarian and non-veg meals. Most of these restaurants (eating rooms is perhaps a more accurate description) are typical cheap veg and non-veg Indian eateries, although the standards of hygiene in some leave much to be desired.

Entertainment

Hardly a week goes by in the M G Rd area without some new (and often very flash) bar opening its doors. All of these places imitate, to a greater or lesser degree, their counterparts in Western countries. They're very popular with well-heeled young people, office workers and businesspeople so you need a reasonable set of clean clothes in order not to feel out of place. They're also very well lit in the main – unlike the 'black holes' so familiar in Tamil Nadu where you feel like a social reprobate for drinking beer! Most of them have draught beer (the cheapest drink on order) and the price of this varies only slightly from one bar to the next but be careful when ordering anything other than beer – a fruit juice, for instance, can cost double the price of a glass of beer!

One refreshing aspect of these bars, other than the beverages which they sell, is that they are far from all-male. Bangalorians are a liberal bunch so women travellers need have no reservations about going into them. One of the best – and the most informal of the lot – is '19 Church St', next door to Berrys Hotel. It attracts a good crowd of Indian students, young Tibetans, artists, misfits and travellers and plays *loud* rock & roll plus there's a giant TV screen with MTV/Star TV. It's open daily, all day until around 11.30 pm. A glass of draught beer costs Rs 12.

Just round the corner from here, and also next door to Berrys Hotel, is the Night Watchman. It's pretty formal, there's (softer) Western music but little action, though it's fine if you're a couple. Less formal is The Pub, also on Church St, next door to Mac Fast Food. This is an older place and was designed to resemble an English pub.

Still on Church St is the Oasis Bar & Restaurant which is a good place to wind down and have an audible conversation when your ears have had enough of the loud music at No 19.

Another informal place is the Restaurant Charisma on Brigade Rd next to the Sunflower Lodge. It's a nightclub with live bands. Entry costs Rs 20.

For a splurge, try the very plush Time Again cocktail lounge and disco in the 5th Avenue Building, 183 Brigade Rd.

Things to Buy

Like its sister establishment at Mysore, the Cauvery Arts & Crafts Emporium (☎ 57-1418) at 23 M G Rd stocks a huge range of superb handcrafted tables, carvings (many of them in sandalwood), jewellery, ceramics, carpets and incense *(agarbathis)*. If anything, there is a better selection here than in the store in Mysore. Few things are cheap, but this emporium stocks some of the best craftwork in India, and they're good at packing and posting.

Another excellent place to look for hand-crafted items is The Cottage Arts (☎ 72-227), 52 M G Rd, close to the junction with Brigade Rd.

For silk saris the Government Emporium, next to the Symphony Theatre on M G Rd, sells good quality material.

Getting There & Away

Air Indian Airlines (☎ 21-1211) is in the Housing Board Buildings, Kempegowda Rd, and Air India (☎ 22-4143) is in the Unity Buildings, Jayachamaraja Rd. The Vayudoot agent is Paramount Travels, Embassy Centre, Race Course Rd. For East West flights telephone 58-6642.

Indian Airlines has flights three times daily connecting Bangalore with Bombay (US$88); at least once daily with Delhi (US$182); once daily with Hyderabad (US$56); twice daily with Madras (US$33), and daily to Calcutta (US$159).

There are also frequent connections to Ahmedabad (US$132), Goa (US$52), Madurai (US$39), Mangalore (US$35), Pune (US$84), Coimbatore (US$28), Tiruchirappalli (US$39), and Thiruvananthapuram (Trivandrum; US$62).

Vayudoot has flights from Bangalore to Puttarpathi (US$40) and Madras (US$80). East West Airlines has one flight daily to Bombay (US$88).

Bus Bangalore's huge and well-organised Central bus station is directly in front of the City Railway Station. All the regular buses within the state are operated by the Karnataka State Road Transport Corporation (KSRTC) (☎ 73-377). Interstate buses are operated by KSRTC as well as the state road transport corporations of Andhra Pradesh (☎ 28-915), Kerala (☎ 22-0286), Maharashtra (☎ 60-4806) and Tamil Nadu (Thiruvalluvar) (☎ 76-974). The interstate bus corporations have their offices at Stand 13 in the Central bus station. Computerised advance booking is available for all KSRTC superdeluxe and express buses as well as for the bus companies of neighbouring states.

It's advisable to book in advance for long-distance journeys.

There are so many departures from Bangalore to other major centres of population that anything other than a selection is pointless. KSRTC, for instance, has departures to Bombay (four times daily, 24 hours), Coimbatore (once daily), Kannur (Cannanore, five times daily), Kozhikode (Calicut, twice daily), Ernakulam (three times daily), Jog Falls (once daily), Kodaikanal (once daily, 12 hours), Madurai (twice daily), Madras (seven times daily, nine hours), Ooty (six times daily), Pondicherry (once daily), Panjim (once daily) and Tirupathi (nine times daily). To Mysore there are buses every 15 minutes from 5.45 am until 9.30 pm (3½ hours).

Thiruvalluvar also has frequent daily buses to Madras, Madurai and Coimbatore, and APSRTC have several daily buses to Hyderabad.

In addition to the various state buses, numerous private companies offer buses between Bangalore and the other major cities in central and southern India. You'll find them all over the bus station area. Their prices are higher than the state service but their buses are better and there's more leg room – important on long journeys. The thing you need to watch out for is the dreaded video coach. Find a non-video bus if you want to retain your sanity, let alone your hearing or any chance of a nap.

Train Train reservations in Bangalore are computerised but there are no tourist quotas on any trains and bookings are heavy on most routes. On the other hand, it's usually possible for travellers to get into the emergency quota. The booking and enquiry offices (☎ 74-172 for 1st class, 29-511 for 2nd) are adjacent to Bangalore City Station and are open from 7 am to 1 pm and 1.30 to 7 pm Monday to Saturday, but only in the morning on Sunday. You can leave luggage at the railway station.

Bangalore is connected by direct daily express trains with all the main cities in southern and central India. But, as elsewhere in India where there is more than one express per day, you should be careful to choose the right train if speed is your priority, as journey times vary considerably from one express to the next.

The daily *Karnataka Express* to New Delhi departs from Bangalore at 6.40 pm and arrives in New Delhi 42 hours later. Fares for the 2444-km journey are Rs 225/1065 in 2nd/1st class.

Various expresses operate between Bangalore and Bombay but most require a change of train at Miraj. The only direct service is the *Udyan Express* which leaves Bangalore daily at 8.30 pm and arrives at Bombay (VT) 11¾ hours later. The 1211-km trip costs Rs 164/649 in 2nd/1st class.

There are three daily express trains between Bangalore and Madras; the *Madras Express* at 7.25 am (seven hours), the *Brindavan Express* at 2.15 pm (6¼ hours) and the *Madras Mail* at 10 pm (7 hours). The 356-km journey costs Rs 70/253 in 2nd/1st class.

Various trains operate between Bangalore and Hyderabad/Secunderabad but the best to take is the daily *Hyderabad Express* which leaves at 5.15 pm. The 790-km trip takes about 17 hours and costs Rs 124/472 in 2nd/1st class.

The only direct express between Bangalore and Thiruvananthapuram (Trivandrum) is the *Rajkot-Trivandrum Express* which departs Bangalore at 5.20 pm on Sunday. The 855-km trip takes about 24 hours and costs Rs 139/473 in 2nd/1st class.

The only direct express between Bangalore and Goa is the *Vasco Mail* which departs Bangalore daily at 5.10 pm and arrives about 20 hours later. This particular express is on the metre-gauge system.

Those who want to go direct from Bangalore to Hampi (Vijayanagar) should take the convenient overnight *Hampi Express* to Hospet which leaves Bangalore daily at 9.40 pm and arrives next morning at 7.45 am. The 491-km journey costs Rs 87/327 in 2nd/1st class.

There are five daily express trains to Mysore, and these take between 2¾ and three hours. The fares for the 139-km journey are Rs 31/120 in 2nd/1st class.

Getting Around

To/From the Airport The airport is 13 km from the city centre (railway station) but less from the M G Rd area. Since it's outside the city limits, you'll have to haggle over a price for a taxi or auto-rickshaw as they'll refuse to use the meter.

Bus Bangalore has a comprehensive local bus network. The main bus station, near the railway station, is also the centre for local buses.

To get from the railway station to the M G Rd area, catch a No 131, 315 or 333 to the fire station on Residency Rd. For Kadugodi (Sai Baba Ashram), take a No 331 bus.

Auto-Rickshaw Any Bangalore resident will be proud to tell you that auto-rickshaw drivers are required by law to use the meters (which are properly calibrated, incidentally) and customers will *insist* on them being used. Do likewise! But don't be surprised if they refuse – after all, you're not a local. If that happens, find another. Flagfall is Rs 4 and less than Rs 1 for each extra km.

AROUND BANGALORE
Nandi Hills

This hill station, 68 km north of Bangalore, was a popular summer retreat even in Tipu Sultan's days. Tipu's Drop, a 600-metre-high cliff face, provides a good view over the surrounding country. There are two ancient temples here.

Places to Stay The cheapest places to stay are the *cottages* run by the Department of Horticulture. You can make a reservation either in Nandi Hills itself (☎ 21) or in Bangalore (☎ 60-2231).

The KSTDC operates the *Hotel Mayura Pine Top* (☎ 8624) in Nandi Hills. Rooms cost Rs 85/100 and it's best to make reservations in advance in Bangalore through one of their offices.

Getting There & Away Unless you want to stay overnight, Nandi Hills is best visited on one of KSTDC's one-day tours. For details,

see under Organised Tours (Bangalore). Alternatively, there are KSRTC buses from the central bus station in Bangalore daily at 8.30, 9.15 and 9.30 am.

MYSORE
Population: 652,000

Sandalwood City! Everywhere you go in this beautiful city you'll find yourself surrounded by the lingering aromas of sandalwood, jasmine, rose, musk, frangipani and many others. Whenever you smell them again, you'll be reminded of this place. It's one of the major centres of incense manufacture in India, and scores of small, family-owned agarbathi (incense) factories are scattered all over town, their products exported all over the world.

Every one of the incense sticks is handmade, usually by women and children, and a good worker can turn out at least 10,000 a day! They are made with thin slivers of bamboo, dyed red or green at one end, onto which is rolled a sandalwood putty base. The sticks are then dipped into small piles of powdered perfume and laid out to harden in the shade. You can see them being made if you enquire at any of the small firms you come across.

Mysore is also a crafts centre, and there are numerous shops selling a large range of sandalwood, rosewood and teak carvings, and furniture. Probably the most stunning display can be seen at the Cauvery Arts & Crafts Emporium in the centre of town. Their rosewood tables and elephants, intricately inlaid with ivory and other woods, are perhaps the best you will see anywhere.

There are plenty of other reasons why you would not want to miss Mysore. Until Independence the city was the seat of the maharajas of Mysore, a princely state covering about a third of present-day Karnataka, and their walled Indo-Saracenic palace in the centre of the city is a major attraction drawing visitors from all over the world. Just south of the city is Chamundi Hill, which is topped by an important Siva temple.

Outside the city to the north lie the extensive ruins of the former capital of Mysore, the fortress city of Srirangapatnam, built by Hyder Ali and Tipu Sultan on an island in the middle of the Cauvery River. Tipu Sultan fought the last of his battles with the British here in the closing years of the 18th century. Probably the biggest attraction outside the city is the beautiful temple of Somnathpur. Indian tourists prefer the Brindavan Gardens below the Krishnaraja Sagar (Dam).

Mysore, at an altitude of 770 metres, is a travellers' Mecca and it's easy to see why. Apart from offering many attractions, it's a friendly, easy-going city with plenty of shady trees, well-maintained public buildings, clean streets and a good climate, yet it's small enough not to overwhelm. The contrasts with the state capital, Bangalore, couldn't be greater. Mysore has chosen to retain and promote its heritage while Bangalore is hell-bent on confronting the 21st century with gusto and determination.

Orientation

The railway and bus stations (two km apart) are both conveniently close to the city centre and only 10 minutes walk from all the main hotels and restaurants. The main shopping street is Sayaji Rao Rd, which runs from New Statue Square on the north side of the maharaja's Palace, across Irwin Rd to the north of the city.

Chamundi Hill, one of the city's main features, is to the south.

The budget hotels are mostly along or off Dhanvantri Rd and around Gandhi Square, whereas the mid-range and top-end hotels are more scattered, though most are along Jhansi Lakshmi Bai Rd and the road which runs past the Central bus stand.

Information

Tourist Office The tourist office (☎ 23-652) is in the Old Exhibition Building, on Irwin Rd. There is a limited amount of literature available but the staff are friendly and helpful and know the best ways of getting to such places as Jog Falls, Hampi, etc, by bus and train. The office is open daily from 10 am to 5.30 pm.

Post & Telecommunications The GPO is on the corner of Irwin Rd and Ashoka Rd, and the poste restante mail is delivered through the window on the right. Make sure you check under all the initials of your name as letters are often filed incorrectly.

The Central Telegraph Office is on the main road around the eastern side of the palace, and is open 24 hours a day. There are also quite a few private long-distance/ISD outlets, though not as many as in other large cities.

Bookshops Two very good bookshops in Mysore are the Geetha Book House, New Statue Square (at the bottom of Sayaji Rao Rd), and the Ashok Book Centre, Dhanvantri Rd (near the junction with Sayaji Rao Rd). Both have plenty of English-language paperbacks and Penguin books.

Wildlife Sanctuaries If you're planning a visit to the wildlife sanctuaries of Bandipur (80 km south of Mysore) or Nagarhole (93 km south-west of Mysore), it's advisable to book accommodation and transport in advance with the Forest Officer, Woodyard, Ashokpuram (near the Siddhartha High School in a southern suburb of the city). Take a rickshaw or a No 61 city bus there.

Maharaja's Palace

The beautiful profile of this walled Indo-Saracenic palace, the seat of the maharajas of Mysore, graces the city's skyline. It was built in 1907 at a cost of Rs 4.2 million to replace the former palace which burned down.

Inside it's a kaleidoscope of stained glass, mirrors, gilt and gaudy colours. Some of it is undoubtedly over the top but there are also beautiful carved wooden doors and mosaic floors, as well as a whole series of mediocre, though historically interesting, paintings depicting life in Mysore during the Edwardian Raj. Note the beautifully carved mahogany ceilings, solid silver doors, white marble floors and superb columned Durbar Hall. The palace even has its own Hindu temple inside the walls, complete with

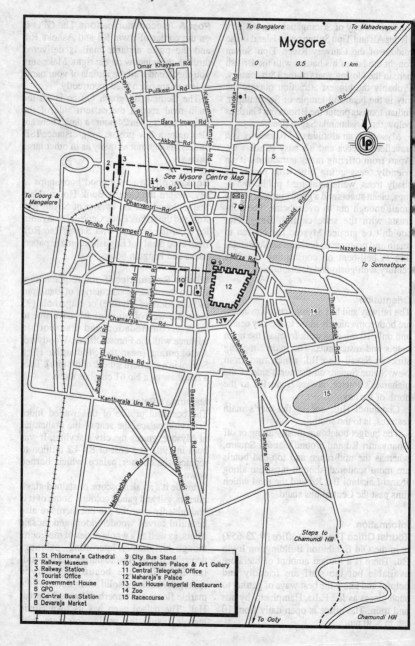

Mysore

0.5   1 km

To Bangalore
To Mahadevapur
Omar Khayyam Rd
Pulikesi   Rd
Sayyaji Rao Rd
Ashoka Rd
Kalamma Rd
Ashoka Rd
Bara Imam Rd
Bara Imam Rd
Akbar Rd
Temple Rd
See Mysore Centre Map
Irwin Rd
Dhanvantri Rd
Theobald Rd
To Coorg &
Mangalore
Vinoba (Sivarampet) Rd
Nazabad Rd
To Somnathpur
Mirza Rd
Chamudeshwari Rd
Sheshadri Rd
Chamaraja   Rd
Jhansi Lakshmi Bai Rd
Vanivilasa Rd
Kantharaja Urs Rd
Basaveshwara Rd
Harishchandra Rd
Thandi Sadak Rd
Chamudeshwari Rd
Madhachacharya Rd
Sankara Rd
Steps to
Chamundi Hill
To Ooty
Chamundi Hill

1 St Philomena's Cathedral
2 Railway Museum
3 Railway Station
4 Tourist Office
5 Government House
6 GPO
7 Central Bus Station
8 Devaraja Market
9 City Bus Stand
10 Jaganmohan Palace & Art Gallery
11 Central Telegraph Office
12 Maharaja's Palace
13 Gun House Imperial Restaurant
14 Zoo
15 Racecourse

gopuram (gateway tower). There's a good museum adjacent to it but it's often closed even during posted opening hours.

The former maharaja is still in residence at the back of the palace.

A good deal of the palace is open to the public but, depending on how many tourist coaches there are outside in the parking lot, the palace can sometimes rival the departure lounge of a major international airport. Check this out before you go in! Entry is from the south gate only and the palace is open daily from 10.30 am to 5.30 pm. Tickets cost Rs 2 and you must leave your shoes and camera at the deposit (there's a small charge for this).

On Sunday nights the palace is spectacularly illuminated between 7 and 8 pm.

Chamundi Hill

You can spend a very pleasant half-day walking up (or, more sensibly, down) the 1000-odd steps to the top of this hill, where the temple to Sri Chamundeswari stands 1062 metres above sea level. There's some shade on the way and the views over the city and surrounding countryside are superb.

Three-quarters of the way up the hill you will come across the famous Nandi (Siva's bull) carved out of solid rock which, at five metres high, is one of the largest in India. It's always garlanded in flowers and constantly visited by bevies of pilgrims offering prasad to the priest in attendance there.

The temple is a huge structure with a seven-storey, 40-metre-high gopuram which is visible from far away. The goddess Chamundi was the family deity of the maharaja, and the statue at the top of the temple is that of the demon Mahishasura who was one of Chamundi's victims. Visiting hours for the temple (non-Hindus are allowed inside) are from 8 am to noon and 5 to 8 pm. The priests will quite enthusiastically show you around.

There are buses approximately every half-hour from the City bus station in Mysore to the terminus on Chamundi Hill which is about 300 metres from the temple. Demand for buses can be very heavy on Sundays (I've seen 500 people waiting for a bus!). It's quite

a good walk down and this bypasses the problem of ridiculously overcrowded buses. Buses up the hill are not so crowded. Refreshments, snacks and south Indian vegetarian meals are available at cafes around the temple.

Though local guidebooks and tourist literature will tell you that the summit is 13 km from the city, this refers to the winding and switchbacked road only. Going via the steps it's only about four km.

Devaraja Fruit & Vegetable Market

This market stretches along Sayaji Rao Rd from Dhanvantri Rd to New Statue Square and is one of the most colourful in India. It provides excellent subject material for photographers.

Jaganmohan Palace

Another place worth a visit is the Jaya-chamarajendra Art Gallery in Jaganmohan Palace. Not only does it display paintings, particularly by Ravi Varma, but it has handicrafts, historical objects of interest and rare musical instruments. The palace itself was built in 1861 and served as a royal auditorium. Visiting hours are from 8 am to 5 pm daily and entry is Rs 2. Photography is prohibited.

St Philomena's Cathedral

This cathedral is interesting if you want to see what the Christians got up to in Mysore earlier this century. It's one of the largest churches in India and is built in neo-Gothic style.

Railway Museum

Across the line from the railway station is a small but interesting railway museum with a maharani's saloon carriage, complete with royal toilet, dating from around 1888. It's open from 10 am to 1 pm and 3 to 5 pm daily except Monday; entry is Rs 0.50.

Organised Tours

Mysore is one of southern India's major tourist destinations and both the KSTDC and private companies offer a variety of tours in comfortable buses. Prices vary only slightly but private companies will only commence a tour if there's sufficient demand.

The Mysore city tours include visits to Jaganmohan Palace (Art Gallery), the maharaja's palace, St Philomena's Cathedral, the zoo, Chamundi Hill, Somnathpur temple, Srirangapatnam and the Brindavan Gardens. The tours start daily at 7.30 am, end at 8.30 pm and cost Rs 70 with KSTDC. This isn't a bad tour though some of the sights are definitely rushed (particularly Srirangapatnam).

Another popular tour is that to Belur, Halebid and Sravanabelagola. KSTDC does this every Tuesday, Wednesday, Friday and Sunday (daily in the high season) starting at 7.30 am and ending at 9 pm. The cost is Rs 125. This is an excellent tour if your time is short or you don't want to go to the trouble of independently making your own way to these places. The time you get at each place is probably sufficient for most people.

There's another tour to Ooty with KSTDC which leaves every Monday, Thursday and Saturday (daily in the high season) at 7 am and returns at 9 pm. The cost is Rs 125. If you want to sit on a bus all day and see precious little of Ooty then it's ideal. Otherwise, forget it.

KSTDC tours can be booked through the main tourist office, the railway station tourist office branch (☎ 30-719), or at the Hotel Mayura Hoysala (☎ 25-349), 2 Jhansi Lakshmi Bhai Rd. Private companies include Modern Travels (☎ 25-242), Asha Suman Complex, Irwin Rd (near the Central bus stand), and Seagull Travels (☎ 31-467), Hotel Metropole.

Festivals

If you have the opportunity, don't miss coming to Mysore during the 10-day Dussehra Festival in the first and second weeks of October each year. At this time, the palace is illuminated every night and on the last day the maharaja leads one of India's most colourful processions.

Richly caparisoned elephants, liveried retainers, cavalry, and the gaudy and flower-bedecked images of deities make their way through the streets to the sound of jazz and brass bands, and through the inevitable clouds of incense. This festival is one of India's spectaculars.

Places to Stay

During the 10-day Dussehra Festival in the first and second weeks of October each year, accommodation becomes difficult to find, especially in the middle-range places. The real cheapies aren't as badly affected.

Places to Stay – bottom end

Mysore has plenty of budget hotels. The main areas are Gandhi Square, Dhanvantri Rd and Vinoba Rd and the streets between these two.

Starting from the railway station end of Dhanvantri Rd, but in no order of preference, one of the cheapest is the friendly *New Gayathri Bhavan* (☎ 21-224), a large place offering singles/doubles with common bathroom for Rs 30/53, singles with attached bathroom for Rs 42 and a range of other doubles with attached bathroom for Rs 63, 75, 84 and Rs 95 according to size. There are also triples for Rs 125 and Rs 140.

Round the corner is the *Hotel Sangeeth* (☎ 24-693), 1966 Narayana Shastry Rd, a fairly new place, very clean and with enthusiastic staff. Rooms with attached bathroom here are Rs 60/90 and there's hot water 24 hours a day. Similar in standard is the *Agrawal Lodge* (☎ 22-730) just off Dhanvantri Rd and down a side street. It has singles/doubles with attached bathroom for Rs 45/70, triples for Rs 85 and four-bed rooms for Rs 95.

Down the next side street is the *Hotel Aashriya* (☎ 27-088) which is good value and has rooms with attached bathroom for Rs 50/125 plus tax. It is possible to make long-distance/ISD calls from reception. Further down this street is the large *Hotel Chalukya* (☎ 27-374) which has singles for Rs 50, ordinary/deluxe doubles for Rs 75/95 as well as triples and four-bed rooms for Rs 137/176. All the rooms have attached bathroom.

Back on Dhanvantri Rd, the *Hotel Indra Bhavan* (☎ 23-933) is an older place and similar to the Gayathri Bhavan. It has ordinary singles/doubles at Rs 50/70, larger doubles for Rs 80 and Rs 90 and triple rooms for Rs 70, 90 and Rs 120. All the rooms have attached bathroom.

The *Hotel Anugraha* (☎ 20-768) right in the centre of town at the junction of Sayyaji Rao Rd and Sardar Patel Rd is excellent value. It looks like a middle-range hotel but is surprisingly cheap at Rs 50/80. They also have double rooms with TV for Rs 100 and triples for Rs 160. All the rooms have attached bathroom.

In the Gandhi Square area are three older-type places with very reasonable room rates. They are the *Hotel Madhu Nivas, Hotel Srikanth* (☎ 26-111) and the *Hotel Mona* which all have rooms with attached bathroom for Rs 30/75. The Srikanth has hot water in the mornings. Also in this area is the popular *Hotel Durbar* (☎ 20-029) which charges Rs 25/40 for rooms with bathroom, Rs 35/70 with private bathroom. The rooftop restaurant here is also good. Close by and better value is the *Hotel Maurya* (☎ 26-677) which has ordinary singles/doubles at Rs 45/80, deluxe doubles for Rs 140 and triples for Rs 120. All the rooms have attached bathrooms and there's hot water from 5 to 8 am. The hotel has its own restaurant and a long-distance/ISD facility.

Up in price, but still in the Gandhi Square area, the *Hotel Dasaprakash* (☎ 24-444) is one of a chain of hotels throughout south India. It's a huge place and has a variety of somewhat shabby rooms ranging from Rs 70/135 up to Rs 110/175 for 'deluxe' rooms, although the only difference between the rooms seems to be that you get a few more switches to play with. All rooms have hot water in the morning and you get a newspaper under your door.

Off Gandhi Square towards the bus station, the modern and spotlessly clean *Hotel Mannars* (☎ 35-060) is an excellent choice. The staff are very friendly and rooms with attached bathrooms cost Rs 75/95. They also have triples for Rs 150.

At the top end of this category is the clean and pleasant *Hotel Park Lane* (☎ 30-400), 2720 Curzon Park Rd, which has rooms with attached bathrooms for Rs 50/80 on the ground floor and Rs 70/99 on the upper floor. They also have triples at Rs 125. There's a popular bar and restaurant on the ground floor.

Up above the bus station is the modern, semi-high rise *Sri Nandini Hotel* (☎ 26-699), which has singles/doubles with attached bathrooms at Rs 70/100 including tax. The hotel is pleasant enough and there's a spit-and-sawdust bar on the ground floor but the area itself isn't particularly attractive. Right next to the bus station is the cheap *Woodside Lodge* but you can forget about it as the noise from the bus station is horrendous.

Lastly, right in the centre of town, is the older *Hotel Calinga* (☎ 31-310), 23 K R Circle, opposite the City bus stand. The staff are friendly and it's reasonably priced at Rs 60/99 for the ordinary rooms and Rs 80/120 for the deluxe rooms with colour TV. All the rooms have attached bathroom with hot water 24 hours a day. The hotel has its own bar and restaurant.

At the railway station there are good *retiring rooms* including dormitory beds. There's also a *Youth Hostel* (☎ 36-753) five km from the centre of town to the north-west. It's the usual price but its location makes it very inconvenient – surely you come to Mysore to soak up the atmosphere, sights and smells of the city rather than keep it at arm's length? If you're keen, take a bus No 27, 41, 51, 53 or 63 from the City bus station.

Places to Stay – middle

For a touch of class and friendly olde-worlde charm, you can't beat the *Ritz Hotel* (☎ 22-668) which has very spacious doubles (no singles) for Rs 95 and four-bed rooms for Rs 180. The rooms are on the upper floor and there's a lounge for residents' use. As they only have four rooms you need to get here early. Downstairs is a pleasant and equally spacious bar and restaurant. There's a sign up in the bar saying: 'There's no place like

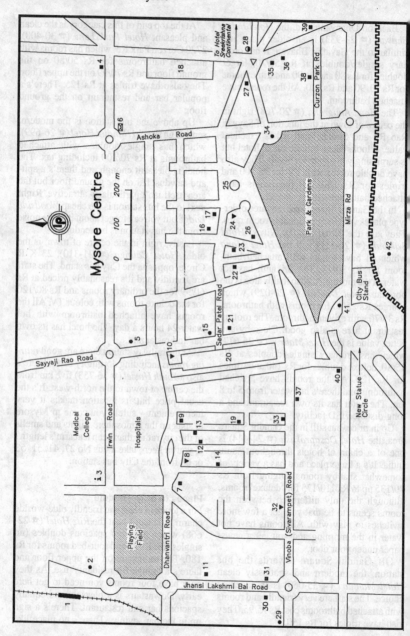

Mysore Centre

To Hotel
Sreekrishna
Continental

Ashoka Road

Park & Gardens

Mirza Rd

Curzon Park Rd

City Bus Stand

New Statue Circle

Sayyaji Rao Road

Sadar Patel Road

Irwin Road

Medical College

Hospitals

Dhanvantri Road

Playing Field

Vinoba (Sivarampet) Road

Jhansi Lakshmi Bai Road

0   100   200 m

■ PLACES TO STAY	
4	Sri Nandini Hotel
9	Hotel Indra Bhavan
11	Hotel Mayura Hoysala & Indian Airlines
12	Agrawal Lodge
13	Hotel Aashriya
14	Hotel Sangeeth
16	Hotel Dasaprakash
17	Hotel Durbar
19	Hotel Chalukya
21	Hotel Anugraha
22	Hotel Maurya
23	Hotel Mona
26	Hotel Srikanth
27	Hotel Mannars
30	Hotel Metropole
31	Kings Kourt Hotel
33	Lakshmi Lodge
35	Ritz Hotel
36	Mysore Hotel Complex
37	Sri Ram Lodge
38	Hotel Park Lane
39	Hotel Roopa
40	Hotel Calinga

▼ PLACES TO EAT	
8	Kwality Restaurant
10	Punjabi Restaurant & Bookshop
24	Shilpashri Restaurant & Bar
32	Shanghai Chinese Restaurant

OTHER	
1	Railway Station
2	Commercial Superintendent's Office (Tourist Quota)
3	Tourist Office
5	Cauvery Arts & Crafts Emporium
6	GPO
7	New Gayathri Bhavan
15	State Bank of Mysore
18	Central Bus Station
20	Devaraja Market
25	Gandhi Square
28	Bus to Somnathpur
29	South Star Mysore
34	Clock Tower
41	Geetha Book House
42	Maharaja's Palace

home – after the bar closes', which is 11 pm. It's very convenient for the bus station.

Equally good value but on the opposite side of the city centre is the KSTDC's *Hotel Mayura Hoysala* (☎ 25-349), 2 Jhansi Lakshmi Bai Rd, which offers spacious, pleasantly decorated singles/doubles with bathroom for Rs 90/110 and suites for Rs 145. The hotel has its own quiet gardens as well as a bar and restaurant. Indian Airlines has its offices here and the bus tours operated by KSTDC start from this hotel. It's the most convenient hotel for the railway station.

Close by but considerably more expensive is the *Kings Kourt Hotel* (☎ 25-250) at the junction of Jhansi Lakshmi Bhai Rd and Vinoba Rd. Despite being a large place, it's often full because it's used by business-people and the like for conventions. Rooms cost Rs 225/350, or from Rs 295/450 with air-con, plus there are more expensive deluxe rooms and suites. There's a whole range of facilities including a bar and restaurant and credit cards are accepted.

Right across the other side of town near the bus station, the cheapest middle-range hotel is the *Mysore Hotel Complex* (☎ 26-217). Non-air-con rooms with attached bathrooms with constant hot water in this huge, though somewhat characterless, place are Rs 125 (ordinary), Rs 175 (deluxe), and Rs 200 (deluxe with TV). They also have air-con deluxe rooms with TV for Rs 250. There are no singles and there's no deduction for single occupancy.

Close by on the opposite side of the road is the new *Hotel Roopa* (☎ 33-770) which has standard rooms for Rs 100 and a range of deluxe rooms at Rs 165, Rs 190 and Rs 210. It's reasonable value but the staff are unfriendly and indifferent.

Much better value, brand new and with friendly staff is the *Hotel Sreekrishna Continental* (☎ 37-042), Sri Madhvesha Complex, 73 Nazarbad Main Rd, which is excellent value at Rs 175 a double, or Rs 250 with air-con. There are no singles.

Places to Stay – top end
Superb value in this range and oozing with

character and olde-worlde charm is the *Hotel Metropole* (☎ 20-681), 5 Jhansi Lakshmi Bai Rd at the junction with Vinoba Rd. Set in its own well-kept grounds filled with flamboyant trees and frangipani bushes, it was once the maharaja's guest house. Some of the rooms here are enormous and the shady verandahs would have to be the widest of any hotel in India. Rooms cost Rs 250/325, or Rs 325/450 with air-con, plus there are air-con suites for Rs 500 and Rs 600. The staff are friendly and helpful and room service is prompt. There's also a pleasant bar and a very elegant restaurant serving very tasty Indian, Chinese and Continental food, as well as an evening barbecue on the lawns. Other facilities include a laundry service, currency exchange and travel counter. Credit cards are accepted. If you can afford it, there's no better hotel in Mysore

If you can't handle Edwardian elegance or prefer plush modernity, then just round the corner is the new *Southern Star Mysore* (☎ 27-217), 13-14 Vinoba Rd, which has superb rooms with all the facilities you would expect at Rs 699/949 as well as more expensive deluxe doubles and suites for Rs 1095, Rs 1295 and Rs 1795. The staff are friendly and facilities include a swimming pool, health club, two bars (one beside the pool), multi-cuisine restaurant, nightclub, bookshop and travel service. Credit cards are accepted.

Top of the line is the *Ashok Radisson Lalitha Palace Hotel* (☎ 27-650) on the eastern outskirts of town. This huge, gleaming white structure was formerly one of the maharaja's palaces and is the place to stay if you have money to burn. The cheapest singles/doubles are Rs 1300/1450 (US$67/74) plus there are deluxe doubles and suites for Rs 1650/2400 (US$85/123) as well as two superb 'theme' suites – the Dupleix Suite (Rs 5500/US$282) and the Viceroy Suite (Rs 9000/US$462). The hotel is centrally air-conditioned and most rooms have private terraces.

Facilities include a swimming pool, tennis and croquet courts, a huge bar with the best billiard table in India, a multi-cuisine restaurant with live traditional Indian instrumental music, and a shopping arcade. Even if you can't afford to stay here it's worth dropping in for a cold beer just to savour the luxury, but bring plenty of money with you – a beer costs Rs 93 including taxes!

Places to Eat

There are many reasonably good 'meals' restaurants in Mysore where you can get standard south Indian vegetarian food for Rs 8 to Rs 10. The majority are along Dhanvantri Rd and Sayyaji Rao Rd. The *Hotel Dasaprakash* also has a good vegetarian restaurant with 'Mysore meals' for Rs 12 and 'Bombay meals' for Rs 15. They also have an excellent ice-cream parlour.

The *Hotel Durbar* by Gandhi Square does good meals for Rs 10, and also has a popular rooftop restaurant open in the evenings. This is one of the few places where you can find an omelette in the morning.

The *Hotel Indra Bhavan* on Dhanvantri Rd has a good 'meals' hall, and their air-con restaurant, the *Samrat*, does excellent north Indian dishes. Close by is the *Kalpaka*, which has good ice cream and shakes, although a sign here asks you to 'please refrain from sitting idle'. Would dancing a jig do?

If you're looking for something more interesting than a 'meals' cafe, go to the *Shilpashri Restaurant & Bar*, Gandhi Square, in the evening. It's on the 1st floor above a liquor store and includes an open-air rooftop section. It's very popular with travellers and for good reason as the food, both vegetarian and non-vegetarian, is excellent and prices are very reasonable. They also have some of the coldest beers in Mysore.

For Chinese food the *Shanghai Restaurant* on Vinoba Rd does excellent wonton soups and ginger chicken, although the noodle dishes are definitely bland.

The *Hotel Park Lane* on Curzon Park Rd has a pleasant outdoor restaurant with unusual cubicles, although you can also eat inside. 'Sizzler' dishes are a speciality here. The *Punjabi Restaurant* on Dhanvantri Rd, near the junction with Sayyaji Rao Rd, is another good place for north Indian food.

The *Kwality Restaurant* on Dhanvantri Rd serves both vegetarian and non-vegetarian food as well as Chinese and tandoori specialities. You can eat here for around Rs 40 and they also serve spirits and beers.

For a splurge, go for a meal (lunch or dinner) at the *Hotel Metropole* where the food is excellent, the setting elegant, the service efficient, and where you have the choice of dining inside or out on the lawn (there's also a barbecue on the lawn in the evenings).

For a mega-splurge, the *Ashok Radisson Lalitha Palace Hotel* has an excellent evening buffet and the decor is impressive; 'like eating inside a giant Wedgewood pot' was how one overawed diner described it. It's very similar to the evening buffets at the Umaid Bhawan Palace in Jodhpur (Rajasthan). Get spruced up before you go otherwise you'll feel decidedly out of place.

Entertainment

Bangalore's explosion of classy pubs selling draught beer has finally reached Mysore. The *Royal Legacy* (otherwise known as 'Beer Junction') opened recently in the Sri Madhvesha Complex, No 73/3, 11, 12, 13, on Nazarbad Main Rd, not far from the state bus stand. Air-conditioned with a repro Victorian interior, it's open daily from 11 am to 11 pm and offers mugs of beer for Rs 12 (double mugs for Rs 23) as well as snacks.

The swimming pool at the Lalitha Palace Hotel is open to nonresidents but costs Rs 65 per day.

Things to Buy

Mysore is famous for carved sandalwood and ivory articles, inlay works, silk saris and incense. The best place to see the whole range is at the Cauvery Arts & Crafts Emporium on Sayyaji Rao Rd. It's open daily, except Thursdays, from 10 am to 2 pm and 3.30 to 7.30 pm (Sundays from 10 am to 2 pm). They accept credit cards, foreign currency or travellers' cheques and will arrange packing (they do a very good job) and export.

There are always a number of street hawkers outside the Cauvery Emporium. They sometimes have interesting and cheap bangles, rings and old coins. Few of the larger things are cheap by Indian standards (the smallest of the inlaid tables costs about US$100), but the place is worth a visit even if you're not going to buy anything.

There are many other craft shops along Dhanvantri Rd with similar prices. Some of them specialise in ivory chess sets, but a 10-cm set can cost you up to US$1500, and anyway, the ivory looks much better left on the elephant. The best bargains are the carved sandalwood images of Indian deities. They retain their scent for years and come in a huge array of sizes and configurations.

Getting There & Away

Air Indian Airlines (☎ 21-486) is in the Hotel Mayura Hoysala on Jhansi Lakshmi Bai Rd. It's open from 10 am to 5.15 pm daily except Sunday, but is closed for lunch from 1.30 to 2.15 pm.

There are no flights to Mysore at present though Vayudoot may resume the service depending on demand.

Bus The Central bus station is not far from the centre of Mysore, just north of the Ritz Hotel, and it handles all the KSRTC long-distance buses. There's a timetable in English and you can make reservations three days in advance. The City bus stand, near the Palace by New Statue Circle, is for city and Srirangapatnam buses. Other short-distance buses leave from opposite the Ritz Hotel (eg to Somnathpur).

From the Central bus stand there are nonstop buses to Bangalore every 15 minutes from 5.45 am to 9.30 pm as well as superdeluxe buses every hour from 6.30 am to 7 pm.

Buses to Arsikere depart 12 times daily. You can use Arsikere as a base from which to visit Belur, Halebid and Sravanabelagola, though Hassan is the more usual base. There are 12 buses daily from Mysore to Hassan and the journey takes 2½ hours. There's also the option of buses direct to Sravanabelagola at 6.30 and 8.15 am, 12.30 and 4 pm.

There are two buses daily to Hospet (for Hampi/Vijayanagar) at 6 and 11.45 am. These are the best ones to take if you're heading there direct rather than taking a bus first to Bellary and then changing .

To Mangalore there are 10 buses daily between 5.15 am and 10.40 pm; it's about six hours.

To Ooty there are buses 11 times daily between 1.45 am and 7 pm; they take about five hours. These buses pass through Bandipur National Park and you can use them to get there, but there are also three buses just to the park daily at 12.15, 2.30 and 5.15 pm.

To Ernakulam there are three buses daily at 5.30 and 8 am and 8.30 pm; it's about 13 hours. There are also five daily buses to Kozhikode (Calicut) and six buses daily to Kannur (Cannanore).

There are a few direct buses daily to Somnathpur from the corner diagonally opposite the Ritz Hotel. It's more likely that you'll have to catch a bus to T Narisipur first (from the same place), then change to another bus for Somnathpur. These buses leave often and the total journey time is around 1½ hours. You can also get to Somnathpur by taking a bus from Mysore to Bannur and then another one from there. There are also buses direct from Bannur to Srirangapatnam.

There are plenty of buses from the City bus stand to Srirangapatnam. The No 125 goes only as far as Srirangapatnam; others pass through on their way to somewhere else. There's no problem getting back to Mysore along the same route. It's also possible to catch a bus from Srirangapatnam on to Somnathpur.

In addition to the KSRTC buses, there are a number of private bus companies which run to such places as Bangalore, Bombay, Goa, Hyderabad, Madras, Mangalore, Ooty and Pune. Their offices are clustered on the street opposite the Hotel Mannars. Take your pick. Fares on these buses are more than those on the KSRTC buses but they are definitely more comfortable.

Train The booking office at Mysore station is very good and rarely has more than two or three people waiting. If you're trying to book sleeper tickets on trains from Mysore and you're told that the quota is full for the day you're hoping to leave, buy a ticket anyway and go to the Commercial Superintendent's Office; it's just near the railway station entrance. Find the office marked, 'Concession Orders Issued Here' (it's on your right as you enter) and ask for the Tourist Quota. Have your ticket handy – you can't do this without a ticket for the journey – fill in a form, wait for five minutes, and you'll get that sleeper. The quota here has precedence over the official waiting list compiled at the station ticket office.

Since Mysore is on the metre-gauge system and not on any of the major trunk routes, getting to any of India's other major cities, except Bangalore, involves a change of trains at some point. This is usually at Arsikere, Miraj or Hubli where you can pick up the broad-gauge trunk routes. Depending on how long you have to wait for a connection, this can soak up a considerable amount of time. In many cases, it's quicker to go first to Bangalore and take a direct long-distance train from there.

The most convenient way of getting to Bombay is to take any train as far as Hassan or Arsikere in time to pick up the daily *Mahalaxmi Express* which comes through those places from Mangalore at 5.10 and 7 am respectively and arrives in Miraj at 9.50 pm. It them continues on to terminate at Dadar Station in Bombay. The trip takes about 40 hours. If you prefer to be on a train which arrives at Bombay VT station, you'll have to change again at Miraj.

There are three passenger trains daily between Mysore, Hassan and Arsikere at 7.35 am, and 2.15 and 6.05 pm; they take 4½ hours to Hassan and six hours to Arsikere. The fare is Rs 40 in 2nd class (no 1st class). Hassan is the nearest place to the Hoysala temple towns of Belur and Halebid.

One of the daily passenger trains to Arsikere connects with the daily *Vasco Mail* train from Bangalore and goes right through to Vasco da Gama (Goa). You don't have to change trains on this service as one of the carriages from Mysore is tacked onto the *Vasco Mail* at Arsikere but you do need a reservation in that specific carriage to avoid a change. On the other hand, this journey is painfully slow as it runs as a passenger train as far as Arsikere and takes a full 50 hours from Mysore. The 700-km journey costs Rs 110/421 in 2nd/1st.

An alternative route to Goa is to take a train from Mysore to Talguppa (a few km from Jog Falls) via Arsikere and Birur and then a bus from there to Goa.

There are five daily express trains to Bangalore which take between 2¾ and three hours; the fares for the 139-km journey are Rs 31/120 in 2nd/1st class.

As an alternative to the bus to Srirangapatnam, it's also possible to get there by taking a Bangalore train from Mysore station.

Getting Around

Bus Bus No 150 goes to Brindavan Gardens. For Chamundi Hill, take No 101 from the City bus stand. They run approximately every 40 minutes and cost Rs 3.

Taxi & Auto-Rickshaw There are plenty of auto-rickshaws and drivers are usually willing to use the meters unless you get on outside a mid or top-range hotel, in which case you'll have to negotiate a fixed price. Flagfall is Rs 4 for the first km plus less than Rs 1 for each subsequent km.

Taxis are considerably more expensive and they don't have meters so it's best to negotiate an hourly or daily rate. Daily rates will be subject to a minimum of 14 hours or 150 km which makes the minimum charge Rs 675 including the driver's wages. A taxi to Bangalore, for instance, would cost about Rs 950 one way or return (no discount for one way).

AROUND MYSORE
Srirangapatnam

Sixteen km from Mysore on the Bangalore road stand the ruins of Hyder Ali and Tipu Sultan's capital from which they ruled much of southern India during the 18th century. In 1799, the British, allied with disgruntled local leaders and with the help of a traitor, finally defeated them. Tipu's defeat marked the real beginning of British territorial expansion in southern India.

There isn't much left of Srirangapatnam as the British did a good job of demolishing the place, but the extensive **ramparts** and battlements and some of the gates still stand. The dungeon where Tipu held a number of British officers has also been preserved. Inside the fortress walls there's also a mosque and the **Sri Ranganathaswamy Temple**, a popular place of pilgrimage for Hindus. Non-Hindus can go all the way inside except to the inner sanctum, where there is a black stone image of sleeping Vishnu. The population of the town inside the fort is about 20,000.

Across the other side of the main road from Srirangapatnam stands the **Daria Daulat Bagh** (Tipu's summer palace) and the **Gumbaz** (Tipu's mausoleum). These are perhaps the most interesting parts of a visit to Srirangapatnam. The Daria Daulat Bagh was later used as a residence by Colonel Arthur Wellesley. It is set in well-maintained ornamental gardens and is now a museum which houses some of Tipu's belongings as well as many ink drawings of him and his family.

It also has 'artists' impressions' of the last battle, drawn by employees of the British East India Company. All around the internal walls of the ground floor are paintings depicting Tipu's campaigns, with the help of French mercenary assistance, against the British. The Daria Daulat Bagh is open daily until 5 pm.

Places to Stay Srirangapatnam can comfortably be visited in a day trip from Mysore, but it is also possible to stay here. The KSTDC operates the beautifully located

Hotel Mayura River View (☎ 2114), a few km from the bus stand and railway station. Cottages cost Rs 150 for a double (no singles) and there is a restaurant.

Just up the main road from the bus stand in Srirangapatnam are a couple of basic lodges which would do for an overnight stay.

Getting There & Away There are scores of buses every day to and from the Central bus station in Mysore, and the fare is Rs 3. It's also possible to take any of the Mysore to Bangalore trains.

Getting Around Walking around the sights is not really an option as the points of interest are well spread out. The best plan is to hire a bicycle in Srirangapatnam. There are a couple of hire shops in the main street, about 500 metres from the bus stand or railway station. All the roads are well signposted so it's not difficult to find your way around.

There are also tongas and auto-rickshaws for hire.

Ranganathittoo Bird Sanctuary

The sanctuary is on one of three islands in the Cauvery River, three km from Srirangapatnam. If you're interested in birds this is a good place to visit at any time of year, though it's best between May and November. Access is by a motorable road, open all year. Boats are available for use on the river but there is no accommodation.

Somnathpur

The Sri Channakeshara, built around 1260 AD during the heyday of the Hoysala kings, is at Somnathpur, 45 km east of Mysore. It's an extremely beautiful and interesting building, although not as large as the other Hoysala temples at Belur and Halebid north-west of Mysore. Unlike these other two, however, it is complete.

The walls of the star-shaped temple are literally covered with superb sculptures in stone depicting various scenes from the *Ramayana, Mahabharata, Bhagavad Gita* and the life and times of the Hoysala kings. No two friezes are alike.

The Sri Channakeshara Temple is open daily from 9 am to 5 pm.

Information A useful booklet, *The Hoysalas* by P K Mishra, can be purchased at the temple for Rs 6.

Places to Stay Just outside the temple compound is the KSTDC *Hotel Mayura Keshav* (☎ Bannur 85) which has pleasantly decorated rooms with attached bathroom and carpeted floors for Rs 25/45 and they're rarely full. The restaurant serves decent food.

Getting There & Away See the Mysore section for details on how to get to Somnathpur by public transport.

Bandipur Wildlife Sanctuary

Eighty km south of Mysore on the Mysore to Ughagamandalam (Ootacamund) road, this wildlife sanctuary covers 874 sq km and is part of a larger national park which also includes the neighbouring wildlife sanctuaries of Mudumalai in Tamil Nadu and Wynad in Kerala. In the days of the Mysore maharajas this was their game reserve.

The sanctuary is one of the 15 selected across the country for Project Tiger, a scheme launched in 1973 by the World Wild Fund for Nature to save the tiger and its habitat. The sanctuary is noted for its herds of bison, spotted deer, elephant, sambar and leopard. There are supposed to be two dozen tigers but they are rarely seen.

Motorised transport and accommodation in the sanctuary must be booked in advance if you want to be sure of them.

Food and accommodation at the park are very good. The best time to go is May and June, and again from September to November, although one traveller wrote of seeing elephant, bison, jungle fowl, peacocks, monkeys, mongoose, sambar and deer in February! If there is a drought, the park may not be worth visiting, as the animals migrate to the adjoining park at Mudumalai in Tamil Nadu for water. Entry is only possible from 6 to 9 am and 4.30 to 6.30 pm. For reservations contact any of the following:

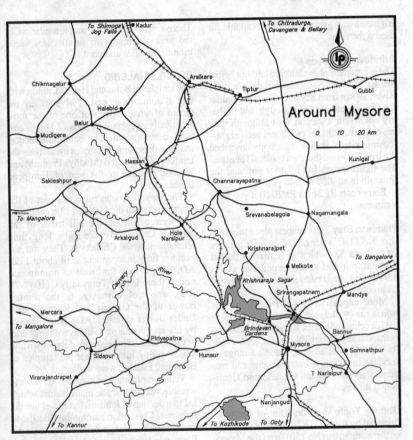

Around Mysore

To Shimoga/Jog Falls • Kadur

To Chitradurga, Davangere & Bellary

Chikmagalur

Arsikere

Tiptur

Gubbi

Halebid

Belur

Mudigere

Hassan

Kunigal

Sakleshpur

Channarayapatna

To Mangalore

Nagamangala

Sravanabelagola

Arkalgud

Hole Narsipur

Krishnarajpet

Cauvery River

Melkote

To Bangalore

Krishnaraja Sagar

Srirangapatnam

Mercara

Mandya

To Mangalore

Pirlyapatna

Brindavan Gardens

Mysore

Bannur

Somnathpur

Sidapur

Hunsur

T Narisipur

Virarajendrapet

Nanjangud

To Kannur

To Kozhikode   To Ooty

0   10   20 km

Assistant Director, Bandipur National Park, Bandipur
(☎ 21)
Chief Wildlife Warden, Aranya Bhavan, 18th Cross, Malleswaram, Bangalore (☎ 34-1993)
Forest Officer, Forest Dept, Woodyard, Ashokpuram, Mysore

Places to Stay There are huge deluxe *bungalows* at the park with bathrooms, mosquito nets, hot water and a big lounge for Rs 45 per night plus a one-time charge of Rs 25. The caretaker (or somebody) will fix excellent meals, and you can see chital (spotted deer) right from your windows. Films are shown at the centre each night.

Getting There & Away You can make a day trip to Bandipur by catching the 5.30 am bus from Mysore to Ooty. You'll arrive at the Bandipur office two or three hours later and can take a jeep trip or hire an elephant and guide. Doing both, you'll still be in time to catch the last bus back to Mysore around 5.30 pm.

Getting Around The Forestry Department has jeeps and trucks available for hire and, as in Mudumalai, you can go on an elephant-back safari. Jeeps are better than trucks, which tend to be crowded and noisy and so frighten away game. Boats are available for use on the river.

Brindavan Gardens

These ornamental gardens are laid out below the Krishnaraja Sagar across the Cauvery River, 19 km from Mysore. They're popular for picnics and pleasant enough, but probably not worth a special visit although they are colourfully lit for two hours each night – 'cosmic kitsch' is how somebody described the lighting – and there's a musical fountain! The lights are on from 7 to 9 pm, and the fountain from 7.30 to 7.40 pm.

Entry costs Rs 2 plus Rs 20 (!) if you have a camera.

Places to Stay The cheapest place to stay is the KSTDC's *Hotel Mayura Cauvery* (☎ Belgola 52) which is similar to that at Somnathpur but more expensive at Rs 85/100 for singles/doubles with attached bathroom.

More expensive is the *Hotel Krishnarajasagar* (☎ Belgola 22) which belongs to the Ritz chain of hotels. Rooms with attached bathroom and colour TV cost Rs 250/325, or Rs 325/450 with air-con. There's a range of services including a bar, barbecue and restaurant serving Indian, Chinese and Continental dishes.

Getting There & Away One of the tours operated by the KSTDC will bring you here, or there are buses (No 150) from the Mysore City bus stand every half-hour.

Bylakuppe

At Bylakuppe, 80 km to the west of Mysore, is a Tibetan refugee settlement called Rabgayling – which means Good Progress Place although nobody calls it that! There are 15 villages scattered over low, rolling hills in a grid pattern – lovely to see against the green cornfields. There are two monasteries, one of them a Tantric college, both involved in the village life.

The two carpet factories are glad to produce Tibetan carpets to your own design. Thankas are painted at the Tantric college.

There's no commercial accommodation in the area although two small cafes serve momos, noodles and curd.

BELUR & HALEBID

The temples at Belur and Halebid, along with that at Somnathpur east of Mysore, are the cream of what remains of one of the most artistically exuberant periods of Hindu cultural development. The sculptural decoration on these superb temples even rivals the temples of Khajuraho (Madhya Pradesh) and Konark (Orissa) or the best of European Gothic art.

The Hoysalas, who ruled this part of the Deccan between the 11th and 13th centuries, had their origins in the hill tribes of the Western Ghats and were for a long time feudatories of the Chalukyas. They did not become fully independent until about 1190 AD, though they first rose to prominence under their leader Tinayaditya (1047-78 AD), who took advantage of the waning power of the Gangas and Rashtrakutas. Under Bittiga (1110-52 AD), better known by his later name of Vishnuvardhana, they began to take off on a course of their own and it was during his reign that the temples of Belur and Halebid were built.

Vishnuvardhana's conversion to Vishnu worship was one of the main factors which led to a decline of Jainism, but it was not the only one. Corruption among the priesthood and the public defeat of the Jain texts by Ramanuja also undermined its influence, but it was by no means extinguished and at least one of Vishnuvardhana's wives and a daughter continued to practise that faith. Later Hoysala rulers also continued to patronise the religion. This normally easy coexistence between Shaivites, Vaishnavaites and Jains explains why you will find images of all these various sects' gods, their consorts and associated companions in Hoysala temples.

The early temples of this dynasty closely followed the style of those of their Chalukyan overlords, but by Bittiga's time they had developed a distinctive style of their own. Typically, the temple is a relatively small star-shaped structure set on a platform to give it some height, with most of the attention devoted to sculptural embellishment.

It's quickly apparent from a study of these sculptures that the arts of music and dancing reached a high point in grace and perfection during the Hoysala period. As with Kathakali dancing in Kerala, the arts were used to express religious fervour, the joy of a victory in battle, or simply to give domestic pleasure. It's obvious that these were times of a relatively high degree of sexual freedom and prominent female participation in public affairs. Most Indian books which describe these temples and the ones at Khajuraho bend over backwards to play down the sensuality of these sculptures. Perhaps this embarrassment reflects the repressed attitudes of the average urban Indian today regarding all matters physical. Of course a century ago our Victorian ancestors were also slightly shocked by some Indian temples!

The wealth of sculptural detail on the **Hoysaleswara Temple** at Halebid makes it easily the most outstanding example of Hoysala art. Every cm of the outside walls and much of the interior are covered with an endless variety of Hindu deities, sages, stylised animals and birds, and friezes depicting the life and times of the Hoysala rulers. No two are alike. Scenes which depict war, hunting, agriculture, music and dance, and some very sensual sculptures explicitly portraying the après-temple activities of the dancing girls, are all represented here, together with two huge Nandis (Siva's bull) and a monolithic Jain statue of the Lord Gomateshvara.

The Hoysala temples are squat and low, more human in scale than the soaring temples found elsewhere in India. What they lack in size they make up in the sheer intricacy of their sculptures. The Hoysaleswara Temple at Halebid was constructed about 10 years after the temple at Belur, but despite 80 years labour was never completed. There is also a smaller temple, the Kedareswara, at Halebid.

At Belur, the **Channekeshava Temple** is the only one at the three Hoysala sites still in daily use. Non-Hindus are allowed inside. It is very similar to the others in design but here much of the decoration has gone into the internal supporting pillars and lintels, and the larger but still very delicately carved images of deities and guardian beasts. As at Halebid, the external walls are covered in friezes. The other, lesser, Hoysala temples at Belur are the Channigaraya and the Viranarayana.

The Hoysala temples at Halebid and Belur are open every day. A spotlight is available inside to enable you to see the sculptural work (it's quite dark otherwise), but if it's not already turned on you'll be charged Rs 2 for the privilege. Entry to Halebid is free although, as at Belur, there is a Rs 0.20 charge for the shoe-minder. The Halebid temple is maintained by the Archaeological Survey of India, and there is a small **museum** adjacent to the temple, although it is of little interest.

Places to Stay

The following hotels are in Belur. If you don't want to stay in Belur then there's the option of using either Hassan or Arsikere as a base. Accommodation and transport facilities at both of these places are covered later in this chapter. There is no accommodation in Halebid.

Perhaps the best place to stay is the KSTDC's *Hotel Mayura Velapuri* (☎ 9) which is only 200 metres from the temple and five minutes walk from the bus stand. Rooms cost Rs 60/80 with attached bathroom and meals can be supplied with advance notice.

There's also the basic *Shri Praghavendra Tourist Home* just to the right of the temple entrance. Rooms have nothing more than a couple of mattresses on the floor and cost Rs 25 with bathroom.

The *New Gayatri Hotel* (☎ 55) and the *Hotel Vishnu Prasad* (☎ 63) are both on the main road through the town and charge around Rs 35 for a double. They also have restaurants and are a two-minute walk from the bus stand.

SRAVANABELAGOLA

Population: 3500

This is one of the oldest and most important Jain pilgrimage centres in India, and the site of the huge 17-metre-high statue of Lord Bahubali (Gomateshvara), said to be the world's tallest monolithic statue. It overlooks the small town of Sravanabelagola from the top of the rocky hill known as Indragiri and is visible from quite a distance. Its simplicity is in complete contrast to the complexity of the sculptural work at the temples of Belur and Halebid. The word Sravanabelagola means the Monk on the Top of the Hill.

History

Sravanabelagola has a long historical pedigree going back to the 3rd century BC when Chandragupta Maurya came here with his guru, Bhagwan Bhadrabahu Swami, after renouncing his kingdom. In the course of time Bhadrabahu's disciples spread his teachings all over the region and thus firmly established Jainism in the south. The religion found powerful patrons in the Gangas who ruled the southern part of what is now Karnataka between the 4th and 10th centuries, and it was during this time that Jainism reached the zenith of its influence.

Information

The tourist office is right by the entrance to the hill and is open from 10 am to 1 pm and 3 to 5.30 pm daily. It's staffed by a friendly and helpful man – a stark contrast to many tourist offices in India where monosyllabic grunts and general indolence are the order of the day.

Gomateshvara Statue

The statue of Lord Bahubali was created during the reign of the Ganga king, Rachamalla. It was commissioned by a military commander in the service of Rachamalla and built by the sculptor Aristanemi in 981 AD.

Entry to the site is Rs 2, and you have to leave your shoes at the entrance. This creates a real problem in the summer as you then have to scamper up the 614 rock-cut steps which become scalding hot. Coir mats are laid down but these don't cover the entire distance. Get there before the heat of the day to avoid this small bit of purgatory.

The statue is the subject of the spectacular Mahamastakabhisheka ceremony, which takes place once every 12 years when the small town of Sravanabelagola becomes a Mecca for thousands of pilgrims and tourists from all over India and abroad. The climax of the Mahamastakabhisheka involves the anointing of Lord Bahubali's head with thousands of pots of coconut milk, yoghurt, ghee, bananas, jaggery, dates, almonds, poppy seeds, milk, gold coins, saffron and sandalwood from the top of a scaffolding erected for the purpose. There must be a lot of work for cleaners after this event! The next one is in December 1993.

The rest of the time, Sravanabelagola reverts to a quiet little country town which is a very pleasant place to stay for a few days. The people are friendly, the pace is unhurried and the place is full of cosy little chai shops.

Other Temples

In addition to the statue of Lord Bahubali there are several very interesting Jain *bastis* (temples) and *mathas* (monasteries) both in the town and on Chandragiri Hill, the smaller of the two hills between which Sravanabelagola nestles.

Two of these, the **Bhandari Basti** and the **Akkana Basti**, are in the Hoysala style, and a third, the **Chandragupta Basti**, is believed to have been built by Emperor Ashoka the Great. The well-preserved paintings in one of the temples are like a 600-year-old comic strip of Jain stories.

Places to Stay & Eat

The only accommodation is the *Shriyans Prasad Guest House* pilgrims' quarters next to the bus station, at the foot of the hill. Double rooms cost Rs 50.

There is a very basic refreshment canteen in the bus station, and there are a couple of vegetarian restaurants in the street leading up to the entrance to the hill.

Getting There & Away

There are direct buses from Sravanabelagola to Arsikere, Hassan, Mysore and Bangalore. See the Hassan transport section for full details of buses in this area.

If your time is short and you have to see Belur, Halebid and Sravanabelagola in one day, your only choice is the very rushed KSTDC tours from Mysore.

HASSAN

Population: 108,000

Hassan is probably the most convenient base from which to explore Belur, Halebid and Sravanabelagola. It has little of interest, and is simply a place for accommodation and transport.

Information

The tourist office is a total waste of time, and the staff are not particularly helpful.

Places to Stay – bottom end

There are quite a few hotels in Hassan. Only a few minutes walk from the bus station is *Vaishnavi Lodging* (☎ 67-413). This relatively new lodge is excellent value at Rs 45/64, and all rooms have a bathroom, mosquito netting on the windows and are big, clean and airy.

About 10 minutes walk from the bus station in the centre of the town is the *Hotel Lakshmi Prasanna* (☎ 68-391). Rooms in this basic hotel are a good size and cost Rs 30/50. Right next door is the *Hotel Sanman* (☎ 68-024) which is one of the cheapest around at Rs 25/40. It's also quite OK for an overnight stay. In the same area, the *IJV Lodge* (☎ 68-574) is dirt cheap at Rs 18/28 but also very grubby.

The *Sathyaprakash Lodge* (☎ 68-521) almost next door to the bus station is also good at Rs 25/35 for rooms with bathroom. The *Hotel Dwaraka* next door is to be avoided at all costs. It has the dubious distinction of not only being uninhabitable (not altogether uncommon) but also of being the filthiest pit we saw in 10,000 km of travel in south India.

There's just one *retiring room* at the railway station.

Places to Stay – middle & top end

The relatively new *Hotel Amblee Palika* (☎ 67-145) is very clean and well maintained. The rooms are large and comfortable and have mosquito netting on the windows. Ordinary rooms are Rs 80 (single or double) plus there are deluxe rooms for Rs 130 if you want carpets and a few more light switches to play with.

The one-star *Hotel Hassan Ashok* (☎ 68-731) is the best hotel in town and one of the chain of ITDC hotels you will find all over India. Rooms with attached bathrooms cost Rs 350/650 or Rs 395/750 with air-con. Facilities include a bar and restaurant (Indian and Continental) and there's a colour TV in all the rooms.

Places to Eat

The *Hotel Sanman* has a very popular vegetarian restaurant which serves a good thali for Rs 8. They also have excellent dosas and idli. The restaurant at the *Hotel Lakshmi Prasanna* is much the same.

An old favourite for years has been the restaurant under the Sathyaprakash Lodge. It has undergone a few name changes over the years; in its present incarnation it's known as the *Shanthala Restaurant*. The thalis are still good although the waiters have the annoying habit of hovering for a tip.

For something a bit better, the Hotel Amblee Palika has the *Malanika Restaurant* and a bar. For non-vegetarian food, a good choice is the *Hotel New Star*. It is open quite late and does good mutton and beef curries. For north Indian and Chinese dishes, the *Abiruchi Restaurant* is not bad although it's a little expensive by local standards – a good meal costs about Rs 30.

On the city circle *Ruchi* does good fruit drinks and excellent ice creams and desserts.

Getting There & Away

Bus There are buses in either direction between Belur and Halebid, so if you plan to visit both of these sites in one day, there's no

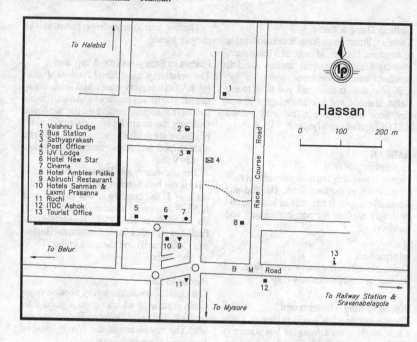

1 Vaishnu Lodge
2 Bus Station
3 Sathyaprakash
4 Post Office
5 IJV Lodge
6 Hotel New Star
7 Cinema
8 Hotel Amblee Palika
9 Abiruchi Restaurant
10 Hotels Sanman &
    Laxmi Prasanna
11 Ruchi
12 ITDC Ashok
13 Tourist Office

Hassan

To Halebid

To Belur

To Mysore

To Railway Station &
Sravanabelagola

Race Course Road

B M Road

need to return to Hassan after visiting one to reach the other. In addition to these bus services, there are at least 20 buses daily to Mysore and the same number to Bangalore

There are about 20 buses daily from Hassan to Belur; the first leaves at 6.15 am. The journey takes 1½ hours and costs Rs 6. Ignore the claim on the timetable about some of the buses being 'express'; it's a figment of the imagination.

From Belur there are infrequent buses to Halebid; ask at the bus stand in Belur. Once the bus arrives don't hang about – there is always a mad rush. This bus takes about half an hour and costs Rs 2. There are also small and crowded private minibuses operating on this route.

There are 10 buses daily from Hassan to Halebid. The journey takes one hour and costs Rs 4.50. The first bus departs at 8 am, and the last bus back to Hassan leaves Halebid at 6.15 pm. It's more convenient to visit Halebid first, as there are many more

buses from Belur to Hassan and they run until much later at night.

There are three buses daily from Hassan to Sravanabelagola; the 1½-hour journey costs Rs 6. The first bus is at 9 am. It's better to get an early start from Hassan and catch a bus first to Channarayapatna at 6.30 am (one hour, Rs 5), then take another to Sravanabelagola from there at 7.45 am (30 minutes, Rs 2). Late in the afternoon bus paranoia sets in and the usual chaos results.

There are also direct buses from Sravanabelagola to Mysore, Arsikere and Bangalore.

Train The station at Hassan is about two km from the centre of town, so either hire an auto-rickshaw (about Rs 5) or walk.

There are three passenger trains to and from Mysore daily. The 119-km journey takes 4½ hours and costs Rs 18 in 2nd class (no 1st class). These trains from Mysore also continue on to Arsikere, a further 1½ hours. There's also one passenger train daily to

Mangalore which takes eight hours to cover the 189 km. The daily *Mahalaxmi Express* is marginally quicker at 6½ hours. The cost is Rs 42/151 in 2nd/1st class (1st class available only on the express train). Both trains travel by night and arrive in the morning. This line may be closed during the monsoon season from June to September.

ARSIKERE
Population: 39,000

Like Hassan, this is a convenient base from which to explore the temples of Belur and Halebid and the Jain centre of Sravanabelagola, but unlike Hassan it has a Hoysala temple of its own. Unfortunately, much of the temple has been defaced and vandalised, and many contemporary structures have been added so it's no longer very representative. It's about a 15-minute walk down the road next to the Co-operative Bank on the main road just up from the bus station.

Arsikere is also a railway junction with express trains to Bangalore, Bombay, Jog Falls and Goa.

Places to Stay

Just outside the railway station is the clean, quiet and friendly *Geetha Lodge*. Rooms cost Rs 20/30 with bathroom.

The *Hotel Mayura* (☎ 358) is in the centre of town near the bus station. The staff are helpful and they have rooms for Rs 25/40. The *Janata Hotel* (☎ 471) opposite the bus station has rooms where you stand a sporting chance of surviving for a night without being eaten alive, and it's cheap at Rs 15/25.

There are also two *retiring rooms* at the railway station.

Places to Eat

The *Janata Hotel* has an excellent 'meals' dining hall on the ground floor – Rs 6 for all you can eat. In the non-veg department, the *Elite Hotel* is just up from the bus stand on the main road.

Getting There & Away

Bus Buses to Arsikere depart many times daily to Belur and Halebid but the exact times are hard to ascertain as the bus schedule is entirely in Kannada. The journey to Belur takes about 1½ hours along a good road and costs Rs 9.

If you intend heading for Goa after Arsikere then there's an interesting alternative to taking the train if you have a few days to spare. This route will take you through the hills and forests of the Western Ghats to Goa. It does involve quite a bit of bus travel but the buses are relatively uncrowded. Very few tourists see this area.

The first stage is to Sringeri (four hours), from where there are buses to Sagar (five hours) and on to Jog Falls (one hour). From Jog Falls, there are buses to Karwar (six hours) and others from there to Panaji (four hours). There is accommodation in Sringeri (at the temple), Jog Falls and Karwar.

Train Various expresses operate between Bangalore and Bombay which you can pick up at Arsikere *(Mahalaxmi Express, Brindavan Express, Sahyadri Express, Udyan Express* and *Bangalore Express)* but most require a change of train at Miraj. In addition, Arsikere station doesn't have a sleeping accommodation quota for any of these expresses. The nearest cities where you can arrange this in advance are Mysore and Bangalore so, if you are going all the way to Bombay from Arsikere after visiting Belur and Halebid, make sure you arrange this before leaving. The fastest train to take is the *Udyan Express*.

Arsikere to Bangalore is 156 km and the fare is Rs 38/130 in 2nd/1st. From Arsikere to Bombay is 1055 km and the fare is Rs 150/572 in 2nd/1st class.

For those heading to Goa, there is the daily *Vasco Mail* from Bangalore to Vasco da Gama which departs Arsikere at 9.10 pm and arrives in Vasco 16 hours later. Fares for the 534-km journey are Rs 94/349 in 2nd/1st class.

There are three passenger trains daily between Arsikere, Hassan and Mysore at 3.50 and 8 am and 2.15 pm which take 1½ hours to Hassan and six hours to Mysore.

The fare is Rs 40 in 2nd class (no 1st class) to Mysore.

Getting to Hospet (for Hampi/Vijayanagar) from Arsikere involves quite a bit of effort. By rail it involves a change at Hubli and possibly again at Gadag. An alternative is to take a train to Harihar and then a bus from there to Hospet. The bus station at Harihar is just opposite the railway station.

MANDYA DISTRICT

While the Hoysala temples of Somnathpur, Belur and Halebid and the Jain centre of Sravanabelagola are the most famous and visited of the rural sights in southern Karnataka, there are several other beautiful Hoysala temples in Mandya district which stretches north and east of Mysore.

Some 30 km north of Mysore via the town of Pandavapura, is the Cheluvarayaswami Temple at **Melkote** which was built in the 12th century and later came under the patronage of the Mysore maharajas and even of Tipu Sultan. It's an important religious centre and there's a festival (Vairamudi) each year during March/April when the image is adorned with jewels belonging to the maharajas of Mysore. Some six km away is the lake of Tirumalasagara where there are two other examples of Hoysala architecture.

North of Melkote is **Nagamangala** which was an important town even in the days of the Hoysalas. Its principal attraction is the Saumyakeshava Temple which was first built in the 12th century and later added to by the Vijayanagar kings.

West of Melkote is **Krishnarajpet** and some two km from here is the village of **Hosaholalu**. Here there is a superb example of 13th-century Hoysala temple architecture in the form of the Lakshminarayana Temple which rivals in artistry the temples at Belur and Halebid.

Some 25 km north of Mandya, the district administrative centre on the main Mysore-Bangalore road, stands the village of **Basaralu** where there is the exquisite 12th-century Mallikarjuna Temple executed in early Hoysala style. It's adorned with beautiful sculptures including a 16-armed Siva

dancing on Andhakasura's head and Ravana lifting Kailasa.

Getting to any of these towns involves the use of local buses and quite a few changes and you'll have to ask around to find the right ones as all the timetables are in Kannada. Mysore is your best base for all of them except Basaralu for which you might find Mandya town a better base. There's a range of modest accommodation in Mandya.

Coast & Western Ghats

MADIKERI (Mercara)
Population: 28,000
The small town of Madikeri, the capital of Coorg region, is 124 km west of Mysore. Until 1956, when it was included in Karnataka, Coorg (or Kodagu) was a mini-state in its own right. It is a mountainous area in the south-west of the state where the Western Ghats start to tumble down towards the sea, and is green, scenic and fertile. Coorg is an important coffee-growing area. The view from Raja's Seat, the local scenic lookout, is wonderful.

There is a fort here which has played an important part in Karnataka's tumultuous history, and there's also the Omareswara Temple. The temple is one km from the centre of town back towards Mysore. A small museum is housed in an old church within the walls of the fort, while the old palace itself is now used as the local municipal headquarters.

The town is well spread out along a series of ridges but the bus station and the bulk of the hotels and restaurants are in a compact area. There is very little to do in this quiet and unhurried hill station other than walk around and take in the cool air.

Information
There is a tourist office in the PWD Bungalow on the main road into town. Their handout is full of the usual convoluted English mumbo jumbo and speaks of the coffee plantations and 'orange grooves'.

Places to Stay

The quiet *Anchorage Guest House*, visible from the State bus stand, is on a large bare block of land. Double rooms cost Rs 40 with bathroom. Also very close to the bus station is the *Hotel Sri Venayaka Lodge* with dull but adequate rooms for Rs 30/50. There are a few other rock-bottom places in the main street but they're not very good.

The *Hotel Cauvery* (☎ 6292) is five minutes walk from the bus station and next to the cinema. Rooms in this clean and friendly place cost Rs 35/70 with bathroom, and there is hot water in the mornings.

The KSTDC's *Hotel Mayura Valley View* (☎ 6387) is on the edge of the ghats, half a km up behind the town hall. It's about Rs 5 by auto-rickshaw or 20 minutes on foot, and the views are excellent. Rooms cost Rs 75/110 in the high season (September to June) and Rs 65/85 for the rest of the year.

Places to Eat

The *Chitra Lodge* on the main street does a good standard 'meal' for Rs 6. Also on the main street is the *Popular Restaurant*, which in no way lives up to its name.

For something a bit more sophisticated, the *Hotel Capitol*, next to the Hotel Cauvery, is mainly a bar but also serves good food. The menu is limited and the service slow but there's not much choice in Madikeri. The vegetable fried rice is worth the wait.

Getting There & Away

The State bus stand is right in the centre of town and, as Madikeri is on the main Mysore to Mangalore road, there are plenty of buses running to both places. To Mysore buses take three hours and cost Rs 18; to Mangalore it's 3½ hours and Rs 21. There are 10 buses daily to Bangalore (six hours), and at least one bus each day to Hassan, Arsikere, Belur and Chikmagalur.

NAGARHOLE NATIONAL PARK

This 634-sq-km wildlife sanctuary is in the south-east of Coorg and was, until recently, one of the country's finest deciduous forests and home to tigers, elephants, panthers, sloth bears, bisons, barking deer and sambars. The animals here were also well protected from poaching by an enthusiastic bunch of Forest Department officials and research biologists.

Unfortunately, over the last couple of years, tensions developed between officials involved in anti-poaching activities and local graziers and farmers. It came to a head in March 1992 when forestry officials shot dead a local coffee planter who they claimed was poaching. Tensions boiled over and for the next 48 hours rampaging mobs swept through the park mindlessly sprinkling petrol on shrubs and setting them alight. Despite valiant efforts by some 500 officials and tribals to put out the blaze, by the time it was brought under control some 20,000 acres of forest was destroyed – and the bulk of it in the core. It will take many, many years for the forest to regenerate and for the animals to repopulate it. In the meantime, the national park was closed to visitors but it should open again once the monsoon has put leaves back on what remains and tempers have cooled.

The best time to visit the park is from October to May. In theory, the Forest Department has jeeps available for wildlife viewing from 6 to 9 am and 4 to 6.30 pm for a cost of Rs 15 per person for two hours but, until further notice, you should make enquiries locally or in Bangalore or Mysore.

The park entry fee is Rs 2 and there is a Rs 1 camera fee.

Places to Stay

There are three *government lodges* operating, with tariffs ranging from Rs 25 to Rs 50 for a double. The privately run *Kabini River Lodges* are somewhat more expensive at Rs 110 per person for full board.

The government lodges can be booked in advance from any of the following:

Range Forest Officer
    Nagarhole National Park, Kutta (☎ Kutta 21)
Chief Wildlife Warden
    Aranya Bhavan, 18th Cross, Malleswaram, Bangalore (☎ 34-1993)
Forests Officer
    Forest Dept, Woodyard, Ashokpuram, Mysore

MANGALORE
Population: 426,000
The west coast railway line through Kerala crosses the border into Karnataka and terminates at this port. At one time Mangalore was a port of great importance and the major seaport and shipbuilding centre of Hyder Ali's kingdom. Even today it is a major centre for the export of coffee and cashew nuts, but its attractions are very limited. If Mangalore is on your way it can make a convenient overnight stop, but otherwise you won't miss too much by passing it by.

The only remnant from the past is the Sultan's Battery on the headland to the old port. It really doesn't rate as one of the not-to-be-missed wonders of India. To get to it take a No 16 bus from the centre of the city. Alternatively, it costs about Rs 15 by auto-rickshaw for the round trip.

Orientation
Mangalore is a hilly place so the streets twist and wind all over the place. For this reason navigation can be difficult. Fortunately all the hotels and restaurants are in or around the hectic city centre, as is the railway station. The bus station is a few km to the north and you'll need to catch an auto-rickshaw (about Rs 10).

Information
There is a tourist office at the Hotel Indraprastha, in the centre of town, but the guy staffing it seems to be permanently out to lunch. In the same hotel is an office of KSRTC, the state bus company. The GPO is about 15 minutes walk downhill (south) from the centre, just past Chetty Circle.

Places to Stay – bottom end
Mangalore's hotels are concentrated along K S Rao Rd in the centre of the city. The huge *Hotel Vishnu Bhavan* (☎ 24-622) is extremely basic but passably clean and habitable. As is so often the case, the rooms at the front of the building are extremely noisy; those at the back are much better. Rooms here cost Rs 45 a double with bathroom.

Also on K S Rao Rd is the *Hotel Vasanth Mahal* (☎ 22-311) with single/double rooms for Rs 40/65. The *Hotel Roopa* (☎ 21-271), on the other side of Light House Hill Rd, has rooms without air-con for Rs 40/65 or there are air-con doubles for about twice the price.

If you want to stay near the bus station, the *Panchami Boarding & Lodging*, right opposite, is good for an overnight stop. Rooms are adequate and cheap at Rs 35/60. There are also railway *retiring rooms* and dormitory beds.

Places to Stay – middle & top end
For something better try the *Hotel Navaratna* (☎ 27-941) on K S Rao Rd. Rooms at this friendly hotel cost Rs 60/90, and Rs 150/170 with air-con. Next door is the brand new *Hotel Navaratna Palace* (☎ 33-781). It has spotless, well-furnished rooms for Rs 95/145 without air-con and Rs 225/250 with air-con.

Other hotels with room prices in the lower range of this category include the *Hotel Maurya* (☎ 32-316), K S Rao Rd; the KSTDC's *Hotel Mayura Nethravathi* (☎ 24-192), Light House Hill Rd, and the *Hotel Indraprastha* (☎ 33-756), Light House Hill Rd. At the Nethravathi, all rooms have phone and hot water, and those at the front have balconies with views out over the city and the ocean. The tariff is Rs 60/75 for singles/doubles and you get a paper under your door in the morning. The Indraprastha costs Rs 100 a double with attached bathroom and hot water but there are no views of the ocean from this place.

Up in price, there are two three-star hotels, the *Hotel Srinivas* (☎ 22-381), G H S Rd, and the *Hotel Moti Mahal* (☎ 22-211), Falnir Rd, both of which have a good range of facilities including a bar and restaurant. Rooms at the Srinivas are Rs 100/120 or Rs 150/175 with air-con. At the Moti Mahal, rooms are Rs 150/200 or Rs 200/250 with air-con, and there are more expensive suites. The Moti Mahal also has a swimming pool.

Also in this category is the *Hotel Poonja*

International (☎ 31-821), K S Rao Rd, which has rooms for Rs 200/250, or Rs 250/350 with air-con. The restaurant here serves Continental, Chinese, Indian and Mughlai dishes.

More expensive is the *Summer Sands Beach Resort* which consists of a number of bungalows each with two double rooms with attached bathroom, large living room, kitchen and porch. Doubles without air-con cost Rs 216 to Rs 282 or Rs 360 to Rs 468 with air-con. Top of the line is the *Welcomgroup Manjarun* (☎ 31-791), Old Port Rd, which is centrally air-conditioned and has rooms from Rs 500/790.

Places to Eat

The *Safa Dine* is a small non-veg restaurant in the lower level next to the Roopa Hotel. They serve excellent biryani and Sri Lankan paroda.

The Roopa Hotel itself has a couple of restaurants – the *Shin Min Chinese Restaurant* is acceptable, and there's also the *Vyshaki Non-Veg Corner*, the *Kamadhenu Veg Restaurant* and the *Big Daddy Ice Cream Parlour*.

In the arcade just below the Hotel Indraprastha is the *Panchali Restaurant*, which is a popular 'meals' place.

The *Hotel Maurya* has a lunchtime buffet on weekdays but at Rs 25 it's not fantastic value. The main attraction seems to be the cowboy movies on the video (at full volume of course), and the air-con.

More expensive is the friendly *Heera Panna* air-con veg and non-veg restaurant and bar at the Navaratna Complex on K S Rao Rd, where the food is excellent. It's open from 11 am to 3 pm and 7 to 11 pm. At the front of the same complex is the *Palimar*, a brand-new, air-con vegetarian restaurant where the food is very good and the staff very friendly.

Getting There & Away

Air The Indian Airlines and Air India offices (☎ 21-300) are in the Poonja Arcade of the Hotel Poonja International on K S Rao Rd in the centre of town. The office is open from 9 am to 1 pm and 1.45 to 4 pm daily. Indian Airlines flies Bombay to Mangalore twice daily in either direction (US$75) and four flights a week to Bangalore in either direction (US$35).

Bus The main bus station is fairly quiet and well organised. There are daily departures to Hassan, Hospet, Karwar, Goa, Madras, Bombay, Mysore and Bangalore.

Train The twice-weekly Bangalore to Mangalore fast passenger train takes about 16 hours for the 447-km trip. Fares are Rs 81/301 in 2nd/1st class. Thiruvananthapuram (Trivandrum) to Mangalore takes about 17 hours for the 921-km trip via Kozhikode (Calicut), Ernakulam and Kollam (Quilon). Fares are Rs 138/508 in 2nd/1st class.

On the Mangalore to Hassan run there are two trains daily, the *Mahalaxmi Express* at 11 pm, and the fast passenger at 6.10 pm which take 6½ hours to cover the 189 km up through the Western Ghats. The fare is Rs 42/151 in 2nd/1st class. Trains on this line are suspended during the monsoon season if the rain has been particularly heavy.

Getting Around

To/From the Airport The airport is 20 km from the town centre. The bus to the airport leaves from the Poonja Arcade of the Poonja International Hotel (Rs 29).

Bus & Auto-Rickshaw Mangalore's local buses are privately owned, and there's a confusing array of them. The only one you're likely to need is the No 16 out to Sultan's Battery.

As always, there are plenty of auto-rickshaws.

AROUND MANGALORE

If you liked Sravanabelagola (near Mysore) and would like to visit other famous Jain pilgrimage centres, there are several fairly close to Mangalore:

Dharmastala

A little south of the Mangalore to Belur road, about halfway between the two, there are a number of Jain bastis at Dharmastala, including the famous **Manjunatha Temple**. There is also a 14-metre-high statue of Lord Bahubali which was erected in 1973.

Venur

Midway between Mangalore and Dharmastala, 41 km from the latter, Venur has eight bastis and the ruins of a Mahadeva temple. An 11-metre-high **statue of Lord Bahubali** stands on the south bank of the Gurupur River, where it was installed in 1604.

Mudabidri

At this site, 22 km from Venur, there are 18 bastis, the oldest of which is the **Chandranatha Temple** with its 1000 richly carved pillars.

Karkal

A further 31 km north of Mudabidri are several important temples and a 13-metre-high **statue of Lord Bahubali**, which was completed in 1432.

SRINGERI

In the lush coffee-growing hills of Chikmagalur, near Harihar, Sringeri is the southern seat of the orthodox Hindu hierarchy. The other three centres founded by Shankaracharya are Joshimath in the Himalaya (north), Puri (east) and Dwarka (west). The very interesting **Vidyashankar Temple** has zodiac pillars and a huge paved courtyard. A beautifully clean second temple is dedicated to Sharada, the goddess of learning. The Tunga River flows past the old monastery in this charmingly unspoilt town.

Places to Stay & Eat

As this is a major pilgrimage centre, there is a range of pilgrim accommodation available in different buildings around the town. A charge of Rs 15 per person is made for spartan single or double rooms with bathroom. You must report to the small office at the temple entrance to be allocated a room.

There's a vegetarian restaurant in the bus station, which is in the centre of town.

Getting There & Away

There are plenty of buses from Sringeri to virtually all points in Karnataka, including Mysore, Hassan, Chikmagalur, Sagar and Bangalore.

JOG FALLS

Near the coast, 348 km north-west of Mysore and not far from the terminus of the Birur Junction railway line, Jog Falls are the highest in India. The Shiravati River drops 253 metres in four separate falls known as the Rani, the Rocket, the Raja and the Roarer.

During the dry season the falls are less impressive and in the wet they may be totally obscured by mist and fog. The best time to see them is just after the monsoon. The most exciting view is from the top of the Raja, where you can see it fall over the Roarer! Even in the dry season the ever-changing fans of rainbows over the falls are superb.

To get to the falls from the hotels, take the road towards Sirsi, cross the bridge, turn left and take the second path on your left. Don't fall off the cliff!

The view of the falls from in front of the Inspection Bungalow is also excellent, and there are steps leading down the side of the cliff.

By the Hotel Woodlands there's a swimming pool with diving platforms although the water is usually green and home to dozens of frogs.

Places to Stay & Eat

Accommodation possibilities in Jog Falls are very limited. The PWD Inspection Bungalow commands the best position but is almost always full. Instead, try the Tourist Home which has doubles for Rs 75.

The food options are even more limited. It's best to order meals in advance at the place you are staying; otherwise there are just a couple of decrepit stalls selling chai and bananas.

Getting There & Away

Bus There is a daily bus from Karwar (seven hours) which leaves in the early afternoon and returns from Jog Falls on the following morning.

There are plenty of local buses to Sagar, 30 km south-east of Jog Falls, from where you can head south through the forests and coffee plantations of the Western Ghats to Tirthahalli, Sringeri, Chikmagalur and Hassan. It's a pleasant two-day journey to Hassan, stopping overnight at the temple in Sringeri.

Train Talguppa Railway Station is a few km east of Jog Falls, and it's the end of the line. There's one express passenger train daily to Birur from where you can get connections to Arsikere and Bangalore. One carriage of this train continues on to Arsikere where it is attached to another train going to Mysore, so it can be a useful way of getting from Jog Falls to Hassan or Mysore. It's an unreserved carriage but it is usually not too full to start with.

UP THE COAST
Ankola

There's a little-used **beach** at this small village. Near the main road are the ruined walls of **King Sarpamalika's Fort**, and a **temple** (Shri Venkatraman) which dates back to the same period, about the 15th century. In an unmarked mud-brick garage near the temple are two giant wooden chariots, large enough to be pulled by elephants and carved all over with scenes from the *Ramayana*. Near Ankola is the village of Gokarna, an important pilgrimage place due to the **Mahabaleshwara Temple**.

Places to Stay & Eat The *Jai Hind Lodge* is a 'dingy, wretched pit' and the toilets smell. However, it's cheap. *Azab's Cold Drinks* is nice. There are no restaurants to speak of, just 'meals' places.

Karwar

Karwar, only a short distance south of Goa and 56 km north of Gokarna, has excellent beaches. However, the whole nature of the town is likely to change in the future as it has been chosen as the site of a major new naval base.

You can make trips up the Kali River from Karwar, or take a walk to see the spectacular bridge over the Kalinadi River north of town – it's about a 45-minute walk, or Rs 5 by rickshaw.

Places to Stay & Eat There's a range of budget places in Karwar. Close to the bus station is the *Hotel Ashok* (☎ 6418), or the *Tourist Home* (☎ 6380). Other hotels include the *Savan* (☎ 6481) and the *Govardhan* (☎ 6456). The *Anand Bhavan Lodge* (☎ 6356) is good value at Rs 35 for doubles with bathroom.

One km back along the coast road to Panaji is the very pleasant *Inspection Bungalow*.

Probably the best place in town to eat is the vegetarian restaurant in the bus station. The *Hotel Ashok* has non-veg food.

Getting There & Away The Karwar bus station, close to the centre of town, is total madness at times as hordes of people battle for limited seats.

There are Kadamba buses almost hourly for the 4½ hour journey to Panaji (Rs 12).

There are at least daily departures for Hubli, Bijapur, Belgaum, Mangalore, Bellary, Belur, Sringeri, Chikmagalur and Jog Falls (Kargal).

Central Karnataka

HAMPI
Population: 800

The Vijayanagar city ruins at Hampi are one of the most interesting and least visited historical sites in south India. It is set in a strange and beautiful landscape – hill country strewn with enormous, rounded boulders – with the Tungabhadra River running along the northern edge of it. It has a magic quality and the ruins are superb, though scattered over a large area.

It is possible to see all the main sites in one day on foot if you start early, but the best way of soaking up the atmosphere here is to spend several days and take your time. Signposting on the site is somewhat inadequate and a lot of the land between the ruins is planted out with sugar cane, bananas and other crops. All the same, even where the trail is indistinct, you can't really get lost and there's always someone around to point you in the right direction should you manage to do that.

History

Hampi (Vijayanagar) was once the capital of one of the largest Hindu empires in Indian history. Founded by the Telugu princes Harihara and Bukka in 1336, it reached the height of its power under Krishnadevaraya (1509-29), when it controlled the whole of the peninsula south of the Krishna and Tungabhadra rivers, except for a string of commercial principalities along the Malabar coast.

Comparable to Delhi in the 14th century, the city, which covered an area of 33 sq km, was surrounded by seven concentric lines of fortification and was reputed to have had a population of about half a million. It maintained a mercenary army of over one million according to the Persian ambassador, Abdul Razak, which included Muslim mounted archers to defend it from the Muslim states to the north.

Hampi's wealth was based on control of the spice trade to the south and the cotton industry of the south-east. Its busy bazaars, described by European travellers such as the Portuguese Nunez and Paes, were centres of international commerce. The religion was a hybrid of current Hinduism with the gods Vishnu and Siva being lavishly worshipped in the orthodox manner though, as in the Hoysala Kingdom, Jainism was also prominent. Brahmins were privileged; sati (the burning of widows on the funeral pyres of their husbands) was widely practised and temple prostitution was common. Brahmin inscriptions discovered on the site date the first Hampi settlement back to the 1st century AD and suggest that there was a Buddhist centre nearby.

If anywhere in India is comparable in mystique and romanticism to Macchu Picchu in the Peruvian Andes, then this is the place.

The empire came to a sudden end in 1565 after the disastrous battle of Talikota when the city was ransacked by the confederacy of Deccan sultans (Bidar, Bijapur, Golconda, Ahmednagar and Berar), thus opening up southern India for conquest by the Muslims.

Information

There are good Archaeological Survey of India maps of the area available in Hampi Bazaar. A publication entitled *Hampi* by D Devakunjari and published by the Archaeological Survey is on sale at the museum in Kamalapuram for Rs 4. It gives a history of the Vijayanagar Empire and a description and layout of the ruins. For a good overview of the site there is a large scale model in the courtyard of the museum at Kamalapuram. There's also a completely useless tourist office in Hampi Bazaar.

Things to See

The best plan for a visit to the ruins is to start and finish in Hampi Bazaar. From here it's possible to walk to all the main sites and down to the museum at Kamalapuram, from where there are buses back to Hospet, or you can walk back to Hampi along the road in 40 minutes. It's at least one full day's outing, and it's a good idea to bring some food and water along, although there are restaurants in both Hampi and Kamalapuram as well as a few soft drink stalls and the occasional chai shop.

The old **Hampi Bazaar** is now a bustling village, and the locals have inhabited the old bazaar buildings which line the main street. The town has become something of a travellers' Mecca and is a superb place to stay if you're not too concerned about minor luxuries, though the restaurants which cater for Westerners are almost as good as any

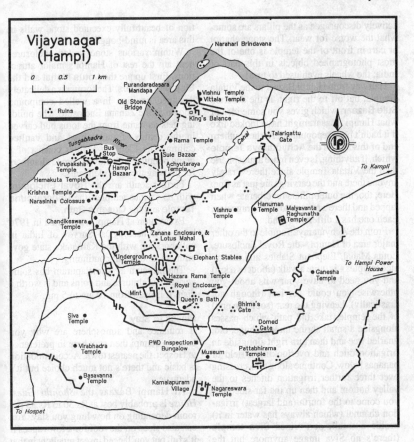

Vijayanagar (Hampi)

0   0.5   1 km

∴ Ruins

Narahari Brindavana

Purandaradasara Mandapa

Old Stone Bridge

Vishnu Temple
Vittala Temple

King's Balance

Tungabhadra River

Rama Temple

Canal

Talarigattu Gate

Bus Stop
Hampi Bazaar

Sule Bazaar
Achyutaraya Temple

Virupaksha Temple

Hemakuta Temple

Krishna Temple

Narasinha Colossus

To Kampli

Chandikeswara Temple

Vishnu Temple

Hanuman Temple

Malyavanta Raghunatha Temple

Zanana Enclosure & Lotus Mahal

Underground Temple

Elephant Stables

To Hampi Power House

Hazara Rama Temple

Royal Enclosure

Mint

Ganesha Temple

Queen's Bath

Bhima's Gate

Domed Gate

Siva Temple

Virabhadra Temple

PWD Inspection Bungalow

Museum

Pattabhirama Temple

Basavanna Temple

Kamalapuram Village

Nagareswara Temple

To Hospet

you'll find in Goa. There's also a good book-shop as well as a lot of soft drink stalls, trinket stalls and the like. The village is dominated by the **Virupaksha Temple** with its 52-metre-high gopuram. The temple dates back to the middle of the 15th century and is popular with Indian tourists. A sign in the temple courtyard reads: 'Please keep off the Plantains from the sight of the Monkeys', which translates to something like, 'Watch out or the monkeys will pinch your bananas'.

From the far end of the bazaar an obvious track leads left to the highlight of the ruins, the **Vittala Temple**, some two km away. This

temple is a World Heritage Monument (one of only three in south India, the others being at Thanjavur and Mahabalipuram in Tamil Nadu) and is in a good state of preservation, though purists may well have reservations about the cement-block columns which have been erected to keep the main structure from falling down. Although it was never finished or consecrated, the incredible sculptural work of the Vittala Temple is of the highest standard and is the pinnacle of Vijayanagar art. The outer pillars are known as the musical pillars as they reverberate when tapped, although this practice is being actively discouraged as the pillars are some-what the worse for wear. The stone chariot or cart in front of the temple is one of the most photographed objects in this part of India; the wheels even used to turn!

Halfway from Hampi Bazaar to the Vittala Temple, but off to the right, is the deserted **Sule Bazaar**, which gives you some idea of what Hampi Bazaar might have looked like if it hadn't been repopulated. At the southern end of this area is the **Achyutaraya Temple** which, if anything, is even more atmospheric than the Vittala Temple since there's rarely anyone there and the carvings are just as fine. Here, too, the outer pillars reverberate when tapped and there's no-one to discourage you. Each one has a different sound.

From the Achyutaraya Temple to the other major area of Hampi – the Royal Enclosure, Lotus Mahal, Elephant Stables and associated temples – is quite a walk (about two km) and you need to have your wits about you otherwise you could get lost (though not drastically). Leaving the rear (southern end) of the temple, take the path which passes alongside a small shrine under a huge, old, gnarled tree and then turn right alongside an irrigation ditch and overlooking a field of bananas below. Continue along this, crossing over three further irrigation ditches to the valley bottom and then up the far side until you come to the fourth (and largest) irrigation channel (which always has water in it) beside a small, part-ruined **Siva temple** (there's no Siva image anymore but the Nandi is still there).

Right opposite this temple is a stone bridge across the channel. Cross this and head to the right. This will take you past another (disused) temple after which you need to veer off to the right until you get to the palace walls. The entrance through the walls is off to the right close to where another banana plantation begins. Once through the walls, turn sharp left and follow the gravel road until you get to the Palace Enclosure.

This area of Hampi is quite different from the northern section in that there are nowhere near as many rounded boulders littering the site which is not surprising – the prolifera-

tion of beautifully executed stone walls in this area is mind-boggling.

Within various stone-walled enclosures here are the rest of Hampi's major attractions. First up are the **Lotus Mahal** and the **Elephant Stables**. The former is a delicately designed pavilion in a walled compound known as the Zanana Enclosure. The building gets its name from the lotus bud carved in the centre of the domed and vaulted ceiling. The Elephant Stables consist of a grand building with eleven domed chambers for housing the state elephants.

Further south are the **Royal Enclosure** with its various temples, the **Underground Temple** and the **Queen's Bath**.

Excavation at Hampi was started in 1976 by the Archaeological Survey of India in collaboration with the Karnataka state government, and is still continuing.

The museum at Kamalapuram has some very fine sculptures and coins and is worth a visit. It is open from 10 am to 5 pm.

Places to Stay

If romance and atmosphere are why you came to Hampi then stay here in preference to Hospet, the nearest town. Accommodation is basic and there's not much choice but it's adequate.

At Hampi Bazaar the *Shanthi Guest House* is probably best at Rs 30 to Rs 35 per room depending on how long you stay. You can also sleep on the roof for a few rupees if it's full but you'll need insect repellent in that case as the mosquitoes are voracious. To get to the Shanthi, walk up to the temple entrance, turn right, then first left and you'll see it as you walk along the temple tank in front of you.

The other place is the *Rahul Guest House* on the left hand side just before you enter Hampi Bazaar coming from Hospet. It costs the same. If both are full, ask around for a room with local people or enquire at the tourist office in Hampi Bazaar.

At the southern end of the ruins is the *PWD Inspection Bungalow*. It is actually an old temple which was converted to a residence by an early British governor. It's rarely

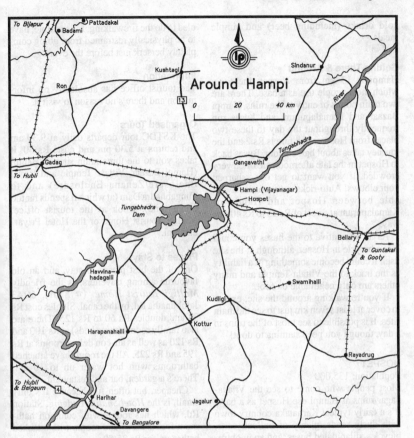

Around Hampi

To Bijapur
Badami
Pattadakal
Kushtagi
Ron
Gadag
To Hubli
Sindanur
Gangavathi
Tungabhadra
River
Hampi (Vijayanagar)
Hospet
Tungabhadra Dam
Bellary
To Guntakal & Gooty
Hawina-hadagalli
Swamihalli
Kudligi
Harapanahalli
Kottur
Rayadrug
To Hubli & Belgaum
Harihar
Davangere
Jagalur
To Bangalore

0   20   40 km

occupied and there are only a couple of rooms, which cost Rs 25. Meals are available if ordered in advance from the chowkidah. There are also a couple of basic eateries close by in Kamalapuram village.

The *Hotel Mayura Lotus Mahal Restaurant* has no accommodation.

Places to Eat

There are plenty of simple restaurants along Hampi Bazaar as well as soft-drink stalls. One of the most popular is the *Welcome Restaurant* which does very tasty Western-style meals (omelettes, chips, spaghetti,

vegetable stews, etc) at reasonable prices. Others do similar fare.

Halfway to the Vittala Temple and close to the northern end of Sule Bazaar is a cafe overlooking the river adjacent to a temple which offers simple rice dishes, lassi and chai. There's also a soft drink stall (no ice or coolers) outside the Vittala Temple.

Other than this there's only the KSTDC *Hotel Mayura Lotus Mahal Restaurant* between the Zanana Enclosure and the Royal Enclosure at the southern end of the ruins. It's a ridiculously sited blot on the landscape and totally out of character, but you can get cold drinks (including beer) and simple meals.

Getting There & Around
Hampi is 13 km from Hospet, the town which most people use as a base. There are two main points of entry to the ruins, Hampi Bazaar and Kamalapuram, and buses run frequently throughout the day to these two places from Hospet. The fare is Rs 2 and the journey takes about half an hour. Buses back to Hospet in the late afternoon are often very crowded. If you want to get on – sharpen your elbows! Auto-rickshaws are also available between Hospet and Hampi or Kamalapuram at a cost of Rs 35 to Rs 40 one way.

As an alternative to the buses you could hire a bicycle in Hospet, although at the site itself it could become something of a liability as the track to the Vittala Temple and many others are only negotiable on foot.

If you're walking around the site, expect to cover at least seven km just to see the main sites. It is possible to see most of the ruins in a day, though you need stamina to do it!

HOSPET
Population: 135,000
Most people who come to see the Vijayanagar ruins at Hampi use Hospet as a base. It's a fairly typical Karnataka country town with dusty roads, plenty of bullock carts, bicycles, dilapidated buses, and an unobtrusive industrial area near Tungabhadra Dam.

For much of the year Hospet is not a particularly interesting place in itself, but because it has a large Muslim population it comes alive during the festival of Muharram. If you're here at this time don't miss the firewalkers, who walk barefoot across the red-hot embers of a fire that's been going all day and night. Virtually the whole town turns out to watch or take part and the excitement reaches fever pitch around midnight. The preliminaries, which go on all day, appear to be a bewildering hybrid of Muslim and Hindu ritual, quite unlike any other Muslim festival I've ever seen. Those who are sched-uled to do the firewalking, for example, have to be physically restrained from going completely berserk just before the event.

Information
The tourist office has absolutely no information and there's no reason to visit it.

Organised Tours
The KSTDC tour departs daily at 9.30 am and returns at 5.30 pm and costs Rs 50. It takes you to the three main sites at Hampi (Hampi Bazaar, Vittala Temple and Royal Enclosure/Zenana Enclosure) and to Tungabhadra Dam (at which it spends far too much time). Book at the tourist office, Malligi Tourist Home or the Hotel Priyardarshini.

Places to Stay
One of the best places to stay, and an old favourite among travellers, is the friendly *Malligi Tourist Home* (☎ 8101), 6/143 Jambunatha Rd, by the canal. Singles cost Rs 38 and doubles Rs 60 to Rs 125. There are also family rooms (three beds) at Rs 100 and Rs 120 as well as air-con deluxe rooms at Rs 195 and Rs 225. All the rooms have attached bathrooms with hot water up to 10 am. There's a garden, bar and restaurant.

Cheaper, but often full because it's only small, is the *Hotel Shalini Lodging*, Station Rd, which has rooms with common bathroom for Rs 20/25 and rooms with attached bathroom for Rs 35/50.

Up the scale a little is the *Hotel Sandarshan* (☎ 8128), Station Rd, which has singles with common bathroom for Rs 25 and singles/doubles/triples with attached bathroom for Rs 30/52.50/73.50 including taxes. Checkout is 24 hours. Very similar in standard is the *Hotel Vishwa*, Station Rd, opposite the bus stand, which has large, clean rooms with attached bathroom which are very good value at Rs 38/74 and four-bed rooms at Rs 148 including taxes.

Top of the line is the *Hotel Priyardarshini* (☎ 8838), also on Station Rd and almost next door to the Sandarshan. Singles cost Rs 38 and Rs 45, doubles Rs 75, Rs 90 and Rs 135,

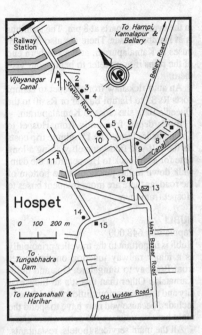

1	Hotel Shalini Lodging
2	Hotel Sandarshan
3	State Bank of India
4	Hotel Priyardarshini
5	Hotel Vishwa & Shanthi Restaurant
6	Prabhu Hotel
7	Malligi Tourist Home
8	Eagle Garden Restaurant
9	Petrol Station
10	Bus Stand
11	Tousist Office
12	Hotel Mayura
13	Post Office
14	Vegetable Market
15	MRK Lodge

Hospet

0   100   200 m

and triples Rs 99 and Rs 150. There are also air-con doubles for Rs 220. It's clean and comfortable, there's hot water and the rooms have a small balcony. There's an agency for KSTDC tours in the lobby. Checkout is 24 hours.

There are railway *retiring rooms* at the station but this is none too convenient as it is more than one km from the centre of town.

Outside Hospet at the Tungabhadra Dam is the KSTDC's *Hotel Mayura Vijayanagar* (☎ 8270) which has rooms for Rs 60/75. It's good value but far too inconvenient for anything other than T B Dam.

Places to Eat

The *Shanthi Restaurant* in the Hotel Vishwa does excellent vegetarian meals at lunchtime for Rs 8, and snacks the rest of the day. A similar place is the *Amruth Garden* at the Malligi Tourist Home, which offers good vegetarian food.

Very popular is the outdoor *Eagle Garden Restaurant* opposite the Malligi. The food is good and the service prompt, although it's a bit more expensive – count on about Rs 50 for two. They also have cold beers at normal prices. The menu here is amazing, with no fewer than 33 ways to have your chicken served, 28 ways for mutton and good biryanis, even chicken ones. There are some real howlers, too: everything from Chicken Skylob and Chicken Hens to Chicken Dry and Chicken Bullet! There's even a Chinese soup called Chicken Sings Poor. Or how about Egg Cycloned Parrots! It's open from 7 am to 11 pm daily.

Another good place to eat is the Hotel Priyardarshini which has the enclosed vegetarian *Chalukya Restaurant* and the non-veg open-air garden restaurant called the *Manasa Bar & Restaurant*. Prices at both are very reasonable and the food is tasty. The Manasa is a popular drinking and eating spot in the evenings. The Chalukya is open all day whereas the Manasa is open for lunch and dinner only (until 11 pm).

Getting There & Away

Bus The bus stand in Hospet is fairly well organised with the bays marked in both English and Kannada. On the other hand, the buses in this part of the state are pretty rough and ready, you must fight to get on, and they're crowded, though it often takes less time to get to a nearby town or city by bus than it does by train.

Ten express buses run daily between 7 am and 11.45 pm on the 358-km trip from Hospet to Bangalore.

Heading towards Goa, there are three buses daily for the 3½-hour trip to Hubli.

Hyderabad is 445 km away and there's one express bus daily. The daily bus from Hospet to Badami, 170 km away, takes six hours to do the trip. There's also one direct bus to Bijapur, and this gruelling 190-km trip takes eight hours.

Buses depart almost hourly to Bellary. Other services include Davanegere, Shimoga, Mangalore, Hassan and Karwar.

Train Hospet railway station has a healthy sleeper quota for the express trains between Hubli and Bangalore and they are rarely booked up more than one day in advance. There is one direct train daily between Hospet and Bangalore (on the broad-gauge system) at 8.30 pm. The 491-km journey takes about 11 hours and costs Rs 87/327 in 2nd/1st class. All other trains to Bangalore (most of which are passenger trains) require a change at either Gadag or Guntakal, depending on which route you take.

Heading to or from Goa, the best train to get is the *Guntakal-Vasco Express* which comes through Hospet at 5.30 am and does not involve a change at Hubli. All other trains involve a change at Gadag and/or Hubli.

For Badami and Bijapur, there's one direct train daily at 12.30 pm which does not involve a change at Gadag. It only has 2nd class and costs Rs 22 to Badami and Rs 57 to Bijapur. The 152-km trip to Badami takes about six hours.

Getting Around

Hospet railway station is a 20-minute walk or Rs 5 by cycle-rickshaw from the centre of town.

Buses run frequently to Hampi from stand No 10 at the bus station; the trip takes about half an hour and costs Rs 2. The first bus is at 6.30 am, and they depart almost hourly from then on. The last one back from Hampi

in the evening departs at 8 pm. The terminus is at Hampi Bazaar. There are also frequent buses to Kamalapuram, at the southern end of the ruins if you prefer to begin your visit there.

An auto-rickshaw from Hospet to Hampi costs Rs 35 to Hampi Bazaar or Rs 40 to the Queen's Bath site close to Kamalapuram.

Buses depart frequently from Hospet to Tungabhadra Dam. The 15-minute trip costs Rs 0.80. If you find yourself waiting a long time for a bus back to Hospet from the dam, walk down to the junction at the bottom of the road, as there are more frequent buses to Hospet from there.

HUBLI

Population: 648,000

Hubli is important to the traveller principally as a major railway junction on the routes from Bombay to Bangalore, Goa and north Karnataka. Other than this it's an industrial city and there's precious little to see. It's only included because you may have to spend the night here on your way to somewhere else.

All the main services (hotels, restaurants, etc) are conveniently close to the railway station. The bus station is at the far end of Lamington Rd, 15 minutes walk from the railway station.

Places to Stay

The highly recommended *Hotel Ajanta* (☎ 62-216) is a short distance off the main street and visible from the railway station. It's a huge place and you'll always be able to find accommodation here. Rooms with common bathroom cost Rs 35/50 or Rs 50/80 with attached bathroom. There are also triples with attached bathroom for Rs 99. On the ground floor there is a 'meals' cafe.

The *Modern Lodge* (☎ 62-664) is on the main street before you get to the Hotel Ajanta. This is a typical cheap hotel with basic facilities. Rooms cost Rs 20/30 without bathroom and Rs 30/45 with bathroom. There is a 'meals' cafe on the ground floor.

The *Ashok Hotel* (☎ 62-271) is on Lamington Rd, which is parallel to the railway line, 500 metres from the station.

Rooms with attached bathrooms are good value at Rs 58/110 plus there are deluxe doubles at Rs 209 and suites for Rs 450.

Up the scale and better still is the *Hotel Kailash* (☎ 52-235/6), Lamington Rd, five minutes walk from the bus station. It has good, clean rooms with hot water at Rs 88/99, deluxe doubles for Rs 175 and air-con doubles at Rs 300 including tax.

Opposite the Hotel Ajanta on Station Rd is the *Hotel Nataraj* (☎ 66-621) which has clean, spacious rooms for Rs 70/120 and deluxe doubles for Rs 200 plus tax.

There are also *retiring rooms* at the railway station which cost Rs 35 or there are dorm beds for Rs 20.

Places to Eat

Kamat's Wasant Bhavan Hotel, opposite the railway station, offers fairly good plate meals at lunchtime for Rs 10. There's also an air-con dining hall upstairs, and during the rest of the day coffee and tiffin are available.

Better is the *Hotel Vaishali*, a couple of doors down from the Modern Lodge. They have excellent biryanis for Rs 12 to Rs 17. Next to the Modern Lodge is the *Parag Bar & Restaurant* which has an open-air rooftop restaurant and is a good place to eat (vegetarian and non-veg Indian and Chinese cuisine). If there's no moon, it's often too dark to see what you're eating but the food is tasty and they have cold beers.

For dessert, ice cream or fruit juices, try the *Royal Femila* opposite the Parag.

Getting There & Away

Bus Hubli has a large and busy bus station. Buses to Panaji (Goa) take 11 hours and leave three times a day. These Goa government Kadamba buses are semi-luxe and should be booked in advance from 6.30 am to noon and 2 to 3.30 pm.

Other bus destinations from Hubli include Bangalore (four daily), Mysore (two daily), Mangalore (daily), Bijapur (four daily), Bombay (two daily) and Pune (two daily).

Opposite the bus station are plenty of private companies operating superdeluxe video coaches. These buses run to Bombay

and Bangalore, but don't expect any sleep with the confounded video blaring away all day and night.

Train Hubli is a major rail junction on the Bombay to Bangalore route and for trains to Bijapur and Hospet. If you're heading for Goa (either Vasco da Gama or Margao) the No 237 Gadag to Miraj *Link Express* at 8.30 pm has a 2nd-class three-tier sleeping coach and another combined 1st and 2nd-class two-tier sleeping coach attached to the train, and these go all the way to Vasco da Gama, thus avoiding the need to change at Londa. At Londa these coaches are detached from the 237 and added to the 7806 Miraj to Vasco *Gomantak Express* at about 3.30 am.

There's a quota for the three-tier sleeper, the two-tier sleeper and for 1st class at Hubli station. The full quota is rarely taken up even on the day of departure, but you may have to opt for 1st class, and booking closes at 5 pm. After this you have to apply for reservations at the ticket collector's office, but don't count on getting one at that time. The fare for the 302-km trip is Rs 63/224 in 2nd/1st class.

The railway reservation office is open from 8.30 am to noon and 2.30 to 5 pm.

Northern Karnataka

BELGAUM

Population: 402,000

In the north-west corner of the state and on the Bombay/Pune/Goa bus and rail route, Belgaum was a regional capital in the 12th and 13th centuries. Today there's an old town area, a more modern cantonment, and Sunset Point on the old racetrack road which offers fine views.

Fort

The old oval-shaped stone fort is near the bus station, but it's of no real interest unless you like malarial moats, although Gandhi was locked up here once. Outside the fort gate to the left is the local cattle market, which is colourful and aromatic.

Mosques, Temples & Other Buildings

The **Masjid-Sata** mosque dates from 1519. There are also two interesting **Jain temples**, one with an extremely intricate roof, while the other has some fine carvings of musicians. Belgaum's **watchtower** gives a nice panorama of the countryside.

Gokak Falls

A little north of Belgaum, eight km off the railway line from Gokak road, are Gokak Falls where the Ghataprabha River takes a 52-metre drop.

Places to Stay & Eat

The *Hotel Sheetal* (☎ 25-483) in Khade Bazaar is clean, bright, efficient and very comfortable. Ordinary rooms are Rs 35/50, deluxe ones Rs 50/75.

The *Hotel Tapuam* – turn right when you are outside the bus station and walk for 20 minutes – has singles with shower for Rs 25 and is good value. The railway *retiring rooms* cost Rs 20/30.

The bus station canteen has excellent and inexpensive snack foods. Belgaum also has lots of sweet shops.

CHALUKYAN CAVES & TEMPLES

Set in beautiful countryside amongst red sandstone hills, rock-hewn tanks (artificial lakes) and peaceful farmlands, the three small rural villages of Badami, Aihole and Pattadakal were once the capital cities of the Chalukyan Empire which ruled much of the central Deccan between the 4th and 8th centuries AD. Here you can see some of the earliest and finest examples of Dravidian temples and rock-cut caves. The forms and sculptural work at these sites provided inspiration for the later Hindu empires which rose and fell in the southern part of the peninsula before the arrival of the Muslims.

Though principally promoters of the Vedic culture, the Chalukyans were tolerant of all sects, and elements of Shaivism, Vaishnavism, Jainism and even Buddhism can be found in many of their temples, especially in the rock-cut caves at Badami.

Orientation & Information

Badami, Pattadakal and Aihole are fairly close to each other and can be visited from single base, either Badami or Aihole Badami is the more popular and has the better facilities; there are no accommodation facilities at Pattadakal.

Local buses connect Badami, Pattadakal and Aihole, and you can easily see the three sites in a day using these buses.

At the first cave temple in Badami you can occasionally buy a copy of *The Cave Temples of Badami* by A M Annigeri for Rs 4. It's worth buying if you'd like more detail about the cave temples or the other monuments at Badami, though it's written in typically verbose Indian English and peppered with nonsense like: 'This shows dwarfs dancing in different poses...Some of them have interesting hair-styles...They are also engaged in different activities...Visitors forget themselves at the sight of these delightful dwarfs' and 'These dwarfs are very amusing and create laughter...These arrest the attention of the visitors'.

Badami

Population: 16,000

Badami, the capital from about 540 until 757 AD when the Chalukyans were overthrown by the Rashtrakutas, is magnificently nestled in a canyon and is famous for its **rock-cut temples**. Cut into the cliff-face of the red sandstone hill and overlooking the picturesque tank of Agastyatirtha (itself constructed in the 5th century), these caves display the full range of religious sects which have grown up on Indian soil.

There are five caves altogether, four of them artificial and one natural, all connected by flights of steps. Of the rock-cut temples, two are dedicated to Vishnu, one to Siva and the fourth is a Jain temple. The natural cave is a Buddhist temple. There are excellent views over the town and surrounding plains from the caves.

The caves are only one of the many things

Top: Hampi, Karnataka (HF)
Bottom: Sadhus at Hampi, Karnataka (HF)

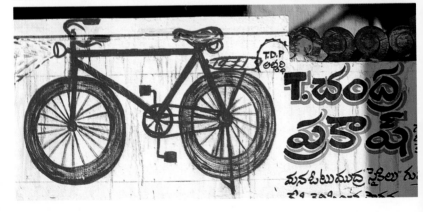

Top: Golconda Fort near Hyderabad, Andhra Pradesh (TW)
Middle: 'Thums Up!', Golconda Fort, Andhra Pradesh (TW)
Bottom: 'Vote Bicycle' – election campaign, Hyderabad, Andhra Pradesh (TW)

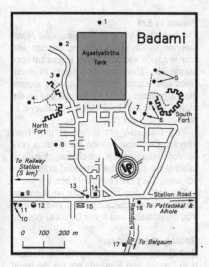

Badami

1	Bhutanatha Temples 1
2	Bhutanatha Temples 2
3	Archaeological Museum
4	Temple
5	Cave Temples
6	Cave Temples
7	Mosque
8	Tipu Sultan's Treasury & Malagitti Shivalaya Temple
9	Hotels Chalukya & Makambi
10	Hotel Sanman
11	State Bank of India & Canara Bank
12	Bus Stand
13	Tonga Stand
14	Shri Laxmi Vilas Hotel
15	Post Office
16	Archaeology Office
17	Hotel Mayura Chalukya

to be seen at Badami. All over the sides and tops of the hills, which enclose the tank on three sides, are temples, fortifications, carvings and inscriptions dating not just from the Chalukyan period but from other times when the site was occupied as a fortress. After it fell to the Rashtrakutas, Badami was occupied successively by the Chalukyans of Kalyan (a separate branch of the Western Chalukyans), the Kalachuryas, the Yadavas of Devagiri, the Vijayanagar Empire, the Adil Shahi kings of Bijapur and the Marathas.

All these various rulers have left their mark at Badami, and there's even a Pallava inscription dating back to 642 AD when their king, Narasimhavarman, briefly overwhelmed the Chalukyans and occupied Badami for 13 years before being driven out again. Of these other monuments, some of the most beautiful are the two groups of lakeside temples (known as the **Bhutanatha temples**). The **Archaeological Museum**, on the north side of the tank, is also well worth a visit. It houses superb examples of sculpture collected locally, as well as the remarkable Lajja-Gauri images of a fertility cult which flourished in the area.

Between the second and third cave is a stone staircase leading up to the south fort, although it seems that the steps were cut by someone with a grudge against anyone less than about three metres tall.

Badami is a small town, and off the main street it's full of narrow, winding lanes, old houses, the occasional Chalukyan ruin and tiny squares. It's a pleasant place and people are friendly, but the street kids can be incredibly persistent in hassling you for pens and money.

Aihole

At Aihole, the regional capital between the 4th and 6th centuries, you can see Hindu temple architecture in its embryonic stage, from the earliest **Ladkhan Temple** to the later and more complex structures like the **Kunligudi and Durgigudi temples**. The Durgigudi is particularly interesting, and probably unique in India, being circular in shape and surmounted by a primitive gopuram, those structures which typify the temples throughout Tamil Nadu.

There are over 70 structures in and around this village which are monuments to the vigorous experimentation in temple architecture undertaken by the Chalukyans. Most are in a good state of preservation.

Pattadakal

Pattadakal reached the height of its glory during the 7th and 8th centuries, when most of the temples here were built. It was not only the second capital of the Badami Chalukyans, but the place where all coronations took place.

The most important monument here, the Lokeshwari or **Virupaksha Temple**, is a huge structure with sculptures that narrate episodes from the Hindu epics, the *Ramayana* and *Mahabharata*, as well as throw light on the social life of the early Chalukyans. The other main temple, **Mallikarjuna**, has sculptures which tell a different story – this time from the *Bhagavad Gita*, the story of Lord Krishna. The old **Jain temple** with its two stone elephants, about a km from the centre, is also worth visiting.

Places to Stay

Badami There are several basic lodges along the main street of Badami, including the *Hotel Chalukya*, the *Hotel Makambi*, and the *Shri Laxmi Vilas Hotel* but they've all tuned in to the tourist trade and overcharge (Rs 60 a double is normal) so you might as well stay at the 'best' hotel in town.

This is the KSTDC's *Hotel Mayura Chalukya* (☎ 246), Ramdurg Rd, about half a km from the centre of town. It's in an advanced state of decay but the gardens are quiet and colourful, the beds clean, mosquito nets are provided and the plumbing, though vandalised, still works and there's hot water. Rooms cost Rs 65/80. Don't leave your room open unattended for too long as the resident monkeys are fond of pinching things.

Similar in price is the *Hotel Satkar* which is very clean and costs Rs 80 a double. Two sheets, a clean towel and hot water are provided.

Aihole Accommodation is available at the KSTDC *Tourist Bungalow* (☎ Aminagad 41), and rooms with bathroom cost Rs 35 to Rs 50. It's not as good as the Hotel Mayura Chalukya at Badami. The food is OK although you can grow old waiting for a meal to arrive.

Places to Eat

The best place to eat in Badami is the *Hotel Sanman* which offers tasty vegetarian and non-veg food and cold beers. Prices are very reasonable. There are also plenty of small cafes and 'meals' places especially around the tonga stand on the main road and on the road down to the Hotel Mayura Chalukya, as well as cold drink places.

You can also get meals at the *Hotel Mayura Chalukya* but the selection is very limited (tomato soup, omelettes, chips and salad is the limit) and you need to order in advance. They also have cold beers.

The arak (rice liquor) dens on the main street are worth checking out if you have an iron constitution and a yen for local gossip.

Getting There & Away

Bus The timetable at the bus stand in Badami is in English and Kannada but it's the usual rugby scrum to get on a bus when it arrives. Use the trains for anything other than local travel. To Bijapur there is one bus daily and the four-hour journey costs Rs 23. There are also daily buses to Bagalkot, Hospet, Hubli, Bangalore, Kolhapur and Gadag.

Train All the trains passing through Badami station are passenger trains and most are 2nd class only. There are six daily trains from Badami to Bijapur but three of these are at night. The most convenient ones are scheduled to come through at 11.15 am, 3.22 and 4.59 pm, though they're often late. The 3½-hour journey to Bijapur costs Rs 19 in 2nd class. Three of these six trains terminate at Bijapur but the others continue on to Sholapur, a major railway junction, where you can change onto the broad-gauge system for cities such as Bombay.

Heading south, there are passenger trains to the railway junctions of Gadag, Guntakal or Hubli (again, on the broad-gauge system) five times daily, the most convenient at 9.10 and 10.40 am and 3.09 pm (usually late).

For Hospet and the Vijayanagar ruins at Hampi, there is one passenger train daily via Gadag (no change necessary) but it's not listed on the timetable at the station so make enquiries. The six-hour trip costs Rs 22 (2nd class only).

Getting Around

Badami railway station is five km from the village itself and a tonga from outside the station costs Rs 25 shared between however many there are of you. This is clearly a ripoff and local people pay much less but it's virtually impossible to haggle down the price. If your budget doesn't stretch to that, walk out of the station and catch a local bus or minibus (which depart frequently).

The best way to explore the area is by local buses as they are fairly frequent and run pretty much to schedule. Take the 8.15 am bus from Badami to Aihole. It takes a tedious two hours and seems to go halfway around outback Karnataka. From Aihole there is a bus at 1 pm back to Pattadakal, from where there are frequent buses and minibuses back to Badami. As there's nowhere much to eat in Aihole, it's a good idea to bring some food along.

Taxi drivers in Badami quote Rs 500 for a day trip taking in Pattadakal and Aihole.

BIJAPUR

Population: 193,000

Bijapur is the Agra of the south, full of ruined and still-intact gems of 15th to 17th-century Muslim architecture – mosques, mausoleums, palaces and fortifications. Like Agra, it has its world-famous mausoleum, the Golgumbaz. This enormous structure with its vast hemispherical dome, said to be the world's second largest, dominates the landscape for miles around.

The austere grace of the monuments in this city is in complete contrast to the sculptural extravaganza of the Chalukyan and Hoysala temples further south. The Ibrahim Roza mausoleum, in particular, is one of the most beautiful and finely proportioned Islamic monuments anywhere.

Bijapur was the capital of the Adil Shahi kings (1489-1686), one of the five splinter states formed when the Bahmani Muslim kingdom broke up in 1482. The others, formed at roughly the same time, were Bidar,

Golconda, Ahmednagar and Gulbarga. Like Bijapur, all these places have their own collection of monuments dating from this period, though the ones at Bijapur are definitely more numerous and generally in a better state of preservation.

Bijapur is well worth a visit. It's a pleasant garden town, still strongly Muslim in character and small enough not to be overwhelming, although in some ways it is more like the cities of the north than those of the south. You will need at least a day to see the monuments in a fairly leisurely manner since they are spread out across the city.

Orientation

The two main tourist attractions, the Golgumbaz and the Ibrahim Roza, are at opposite ends of the town. Almost all the major hotels and restaurants are along the main street, Station Rd (M G Rd). The bus stand is a five-minute walk from Station Rd, near the citadel ruins, while the railway station is two km east of the centre.

Information

The tourist office is in the Hotel Sanman on Station Rd opposite the Golgumbaz.

The State Bank of India won't change travellers' cheques and will direct you to the Canara Bank where the clerks take forever to do the transaction.

Power cuts are frequent in Bijapur and often last for hours so have candles handy.

Golgumbaz

The largest and most famous monument, though not the most beautiful, is the Golgumbaz. Built in 1659, it is a simple building with four walls that enclose a majestic hall 1704 sq metres in area, buttressed by octagonal seven-storey towers at each of the corners. This basic structure is capped by an enormous dome said to be the world's second largest after St Peter's, Vatican City, Rome. The diameter of St Peter's dome is 42 metres, St Paul's in London is 33 metres, and the Golgumbaz is 38 metres.

Around the base of the dome at the top of the hall is a three-metre-wide gallery known

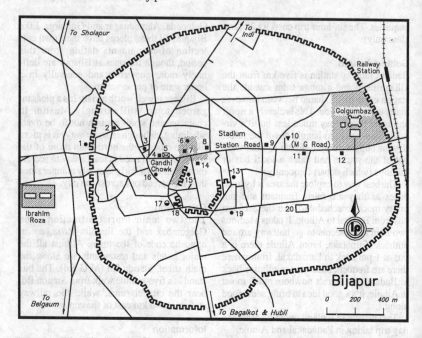

Bijapur

Scale: 0 200 400 m

1	Malik-e-Maidan Cannon
2	Upli Buruj
3	Market
4	Hotel Tourist
5	Post Office
6	Bara Kaman (Ali II Roza)
7	Midland Hotel & Mysore Lodge
8	Hotel Mayura Adhil Shahi Annexe
9	Hotel Megharaj
10	Chetan Bar & Restaurant
11	Hotel Samrat
12	Hotel Sanman & Tourist Office
13	Asar Mahal
14	Hotel Mayura Adhil Shahi
15	Citadel (Gagan Mahal, Sat Manzil Anand Mahal & Mecca Masjid)
16	State Bank of India
17	Bus Stand
18	Hotel Lalit Mahal & Hotel Santosh
19	Mehtar Mahal
20	Jami-e-Masjid

as the 'whispering gallery', since the acoustics here are such that any sound made is repeated 10 times over (some guidebooks claim it's repeated 12 times over). Fortunately, you won't have the chance to get embroiled in that controversy as the 'whispering gallery' is permanently full of children running amok and screaming at the top of their voices. 'Bedlam gallery' would be a more appropriate name. Access to the gallery is via a narrow staircase up one of the towers.

The views over Bijapur from the base of the dome are superb. You can see virtually every other monument and almost the whole of the city walls from here. The views are best in the early morning. The monument is set in well-manicured gardens which are stunningly green during and just after the monsoon season.

The Golgumbaz is the mausoleum of Mohammed Adil Shah (1626-56), his two wives, his mistress (Rambha), one of his daughters and a grandson. Their caskets stand on a raised platform in the centre of the hall, though their actual graves are in the crypt, accessible by a flight of steps under the western doorway.

It is open from 6 am to 6 pm and entrance costs Rs 0.50, except on Friday, when it's free. If you get there before 7 am you may actually be able to test the gallery acoustics too – the school groups don't start to arrive until then. Shoes have to be left at the entrance. An **archaeological museum** in the front opens at 10 am and is free.

Ibrahim Roza

The beautiful Ibrahim Roza was constructed at the height of Bijapur's prosperity by Ibrahim Adil Shah II (1580-1626) for his queen. Unlike the Golgumbaz, which is impressive only for its immensity, here the emphasis is on elegance and delicacy. Its minarets, which rise 24 metres from the ground, are said to have inspired those of the Taj Mahal. It's also one of the few monuments in Bijapur with substantial stone filigree and other sculpturally decorative work.

Buried here are Ibrahim Adil Shah, his queen, Taj Sultana, his daughter, two sons, and his mother Haji Badi Sahiba. There is no entrance charge, and shoes should be left on the steps up to the platform on which the mausoleum stands.

Jami-e-Masjid

This is another finely proportioned building with graceful arches, a fine dome and a large inner courtyard containing fountains and a reservoir. It's quite a large monument covering an area of 10,800 sq metres and has room for 2250 worshippers. Spaces for them are marked out in black on the polished floor of the mosque.

There's very little ornamentation here, the whole concept being one of simplicity. The flat roof is accessible by several flights of stairs. This mosque was constructed by Ali

Adil Shah I (1557-80), who was also responsible for erecting the fortified city walls and Gagan Mahal, and for installing a public water system.

Asar Mahal

To the east of the citadel, the Asar Mahal was built by Mohammed Adil Shah in about 1646 to serve as a Hall of Justice. The rooms on the upper storey are profusely decorated with fresco paintings, many of them using foliage and flower motifs, some portraying male and female figures in various poses. The latter have all been defaced. The building was also used to house two hairs from the Prophet's beard. The front of the building is graced with a square tank still fed by conduits from Begum Tank.

Women are not allowed inside the main structure.

Citadel

Surrounded by its own fortified walls and wide moat in the city centre, the citadel once contained the palaces, pleasure gardens and Durbar Hall of the Adil Shahi kings. Unfortunately, most of them are now in ruins although some superb fragments remain.

Of the important fragments, the **Gagan Mahal** probably gives the best impression of the scale on which things were built here. This monument was built by Ali Adil Shah I around 1561 to serve the dual purpose of a royal residence and a Durbar Hall. Essentially it's an enormous hall completely open to the north, so that an audience outside the hall had a full and unobstructed view of the proceedings on the raised platform inside. The hall was flanked by small chambers used to house the families of the royal household.

Nearby, the **Sat Manzil**, Mohammed Adil Shah's seven-storey palace, is now substantially in ruins and the remaining parts of it are used for public offices, but just across the road stands one of the most delicate pieces of architecture in Bijapur. This is the **Jala Manzil** or Jala Mandir, a water pavilion no doubt intended as a cool and pleasant place to relax in the days when it was surrounded by secluded courts and gardens within the palace precincts. Opposite the citadel on the other side of Station Rd are the graceful arches of **Bara Kaman**, the ruined mausoleum of Ali Roza.

Malik-e-Maidan

This huge cannon must be one of the largest medieval guns ever made. It measures over four metres long and almost 1½ metres in diameter, and is estimated to weigh 55 tonnes! It was cast in 1549 by Mohammed-bin-Hasan Rumi, a Turkish officer in the service of the King of Ahmednagar, from an alloy of copper, iron and tin. It was brought to Bijapur as a trophy of war and set up here with the help of 10 elephants, 400 oxen and hundreds of men. Its outer surface is polished dark green and adorned with inscriptions in Persian and Arabic. One of them attributed to the Moghul emperor, Aurangzeb, says that he subdued this gun. The name of the cannon, Malik-e-Maidan, means Monarch of the Plains.

Upli Buruj

This watchtower, 24 metres high and on high ground near the western walls of the city, was built by Hyder Khan, a general in the service of Ali Adil Shah I and Ibrahim II, in about 1584. The tower can be climbed by a flight of steps which winds around the outside of the building. The top commands a good view of the city and is well furnished with guns, powder chambers and water cisterns. The guns are much longer than the Malik-e-Maidan (nine metres and 8½ metres respectively), but of a much narrower bore – only 29 cm.

Other Monuments

There are a number of other monuments worth visiting in Bijapur, the most important being the **Anand Mahal** and the **Mecca Masjid**, both in the citadel, and the **Mehtar Mahal**. The much-photographed Mehtar Mahal is typical of the architecture of Bijapur and has been richly decorated with sculptural work. It serves as an ornamental gateway leading to a small mosque.

Places to Stay

One of the cheapest habitable places to stay is the *Midland Hotel* (☎ 299), Station Rd, which has rooms for Rs 32/45. Next door is the even cheaper *Mysore Lodge* but you'd have to be desperate to stay here.

Much better is the *Hotel Tourist*, also on Station Rd next to the post office, which is friendly and has ordinary rooms for Rs 34/63 or Rs 42/79 for the 'special' rooms, although there's nothing at all special about them. All the rooms have attached bathroom, and mosquito nets are provided.

Cheapest around the bus station is the *Hotel Lalit Mahal* (☎ 761) where the rooms are arranged around a central courtyard. Singles/doubles/triples with common bathroom cost Rs 25/40/50 or Rs 30/45/55 with attached bathroom. There's also a restaurant. Close by and equally basic is the *Hotel Hindustan*.

Better appointed rooms can be found at the *Hotel Santosh*, right opposite the bus station, though they're overpriced. Singles/doubles/triples with attached toilet and bucket water are Rs 43/63/94. There are also 'deluxe' singles/doubles with attached bathroom for Rs 45/75 but the showers didn't work in either of the rooms which I saw. It's a somewhat pretentious place.

The most popular place by far, and certainly the best in terms of setting and atmosphere, is the KSTDC's *Hotel Mayura Adhil Shahi* (☎ 20-943) at the junction of Station Rd and Anand Mahal Rd. The rooms here are set around a quiet, leafy and colourful garden courtyard which doubles as an open-air restaurant in the evenings. Clean, airy rooms with attached bathroom and hot water cost Rs 60/75. Mosquito nets are provided. There's a bar and restaurant with reasonably tasty food, though the choice is limited.

If the Mayura is full, there's the *Hotel Mayura Adhil Shahi Annexe* (☎ 20-401) close by on Station Rd which is also surrounded by its own gardens. The rooms here are Rs 100/120.

Further up the same road on the opposite side is the *Hotel Samrat* (☎ 21-620). This is also a fairly new place with good rooms at Rs 52/73. All rooms have attached bathroom, and mosquito nets are provided. The rooms at the front have a balcony. It's a good choice, and on the ground floor there are separate vegetarian and non-veg restaurants and a bar.

Finally, there are *retiring rooms* at the railway station where beds cost Rs 15 in double rooms.

Places to Eat

For just a snack, the *Prabhu Cafeteria* on the ground floor next to the Hotel Tourist is a popular place serving excellent dosas, bhelpuri, lassis and other snacks. On the first floor of the same building, the *Swapna Lodge Restaurant* has good veg and non-veg food as well as cold beers.

The *Hotel Mayura Adhil Shahi* has a restaurant in the middle of the courtyard, and it's a reasonable place to eat, although it's not somewhere you'd go to pick up a quick bite as the service is slow. Lunch is generally a standard thali but there's more choice in the evening.

For excellent vegetarian food, probably the best place is the *Prabhu Restaurant* at the Hotel Samrat which has both air-con and non-air-con sections. Prices are reasonable and it's a popular place to eat. Smoking is prohibited. In the same building is the veg and non-veg *Presidents Bar & Restaurant* where the food is very tasty and there's plenty of choice. The only drawback to eating here in the evening is that it's so dark you can hardly see what you're doing. Still, it's air-conditioned (after a fashion) and cold Kingfisher beers are available.

The cheapest bar in town is the *Chetan Bar & Restaurant* about 100 metres off Station Rd (signposted). This is an open-air bar/restaurant under a pergola and is definitely the best place for a cold beer in the afternoon or evening.

Getting There & Away

Bus The timetable at the bus station is entirely in Kannada. The only place you'll find a timetable in English is in the lobby of the Hotel Tourist. Buses run from Bijapur to Badami (two daily, one goes via Kerur), Bangalore (630 km, six daily in the evening only), Belgaum (12 buses daily), Bidar, Hubli (11 daily), Hyderabad (two daily), Hospet (daily), Pune (daily), Kolhapur (five daily) and Sholapur (12 daily; three hours).

Train Bijapur station has a healthy quota of sleeping berths allotted to it on all the main trains which pass through Sholapur (Solarpur) and Gadag. These are rarely taken up more than one day in advance. Going south, there are three daily trains to Hubli at 3.40, 6.55 and 11.30 and another only as far as Gadag which leaves at 5.50 pm. The 258-km trip to Hubli takes about seven hours and costs Rs 53/193 in 2nd/1st class.

To Bangalore, there's one express daily at 11.35 pm. You can use any of the above trains and the one to Guntakal at 6.15 am to get to either Badami (3½ hours, Rs 19/30 in 2nd class ordinary/express and Rs 107 in 1st) or Hospet (285 km, about nine hours, Rs 33/57 in 2nd class ordinary/express and Rs 210 in 1st).

Going north, there are trains daily to Sholapur at 3.35, 7.15 and 9.35 am and 3.06 and 8.05 pm. Fares are Rs 18/27 in 2nd class ordinary/express and Rs 104 in 1st. Sholapur is where you connect with the broad-gauge system for trains to Hyderabad and Vijayawada, and Pune and Bombay. The station has a computerised booking hall.

Getting Around

Bus There's a surprisingly uncrowded local bus system which has only one route: from the railway station, along Station Rd to the gate at the western end of town. Buses run approximately every 15 minutes and the standard fare is Rs 0.50.

Cycle-Rickshaw, Auto-Rickshaw & Tonga Bijapur has many cycle-rickshaws, but they must have been designed by an ergonomist who had his legs amputated at the knee! Expect to pay Rs 5 from the bus station to the Hotel Mayura Adhil Shahi (about two km). Auto-rickshaw drivers charge what they think you will pay and resolutely refuse to use the meters. Expect to pay around Rs 15 to the railway station after intense haggling.

The tonga drivers are eager for business and hassle you at every opportunity either to take you around the major sites or to the railway station. Rs 12 seems to be about the going rate from the station to the Hotel Mayura Adhil Shahi. Other trips you'll have to haggle over.

THE NORTH-EAST
Bidar

This little visited town in the extreme north-east corner of the state was the capital of the Bahmani Kingdom from 1428, and later the capital of the Barid Shahi dynasty. It's a pleasant town with a splendid old 15th-century **fort** containing the Ranjeenmahal, Chini Mahal and Turkish Mahal **palaces**. The impressive **Khwaja Mahmud Gawan Madrasa** and the **tombs** of the Bahmani and Barid kings are also worth seeing.

Places to Stay & Eat The best place to stay is the KSTDC's *Hotel Mayura Barid Shahi* (☎ 6571) on Yadgir Rd near the bus station which has rooms with attached bathroom from Rs 40/55. Otherwise, try the *Sri Venkateshwara Lodge* on the main street. The adjoining *Kalpana Hotel* has good food.

Gulbarga
Population: 310,000

This town was the Bahmani capital from 1347 until its transfer to Bidar in 1428. Later the kingdom broke up into a number of smaller kingdoms – Bijapur, Bidar, Berar, Ahmednagar and Golconda. The last of these, Golconda, finally fell to Aurangzeb in 1687. Gulbarga's old **fort** is in a much deteriorated state, but has a number of interesting buildings inside.

The **Jami Masjid**, inside the fort, is reputed to have been built by a Moorish architect during the late 14th or early 15th century who imitated the great mosque in Cordoba, Spain. The mosque is unique in India, with a huge dome covering the whole area, four smaller ones at the corners, and 75 smaller still all the way around. The fort itself has 15 towers.

Gulbarga also has a number of imposing tombs of Bahmani kings, a shrine to an important Muslim saint and the **temple of Sharana Basaveshwara**.

Places to Stay & Eat The best place to stay is the KSTDC's *Hotel Mayura Bahamani* (☎ 20-644), Public Garden, which has rooms for Rs 45/60. The hotel has its own bar and restaurant.

Andhra Pradesh

Population: 64 million
Area: 276,754 sq km
Capital: Hyderabad
People per sq km: 241
Main Language: Telugu
Literacy Rate: 45%

Andhra Pradesh was created by combining the old princely state of Hyderabad with the Telugu-speaking portions of the former state of Madras. Most of this large state stands on the high Deccan plateau, sloping down to the low-lying coastal region to the east where the mighty Godavari and Krishna rivers meet the Bay of Bengal in wide deltas.

Andhra Pradesh was once a major Buddhist centre and part of Ashoka's large empire until it broke apart. Traces of that early Buddhist influence still remain in several places, particularly at Amaravathi, the Sanchi of Andhra Pradesh. Later, in the 7th century, the Chalukyas held power but they, in turn, fell to the Chola Kingdom of the south around the 10th century.

The 13th century saw the rise of the Kakatiyas who ruled from Warangal but by this time Muslim power was beginning to assert itself in the form of the sultans of Delhi, who made many raids into the area. They were not able to establish themselves, however, until 1323. Even then, their hold was tenuous and they were soon displaced by the Hindu Vijayanagar Empire.

There followed two centuries of Hindu-Muslim power struggles until, in 1543, the Qutab Shahi dynasty was established at Hyderabad.

It was this dynasty which built the vast and almost impregnable stone fortress of Golconda – surely one of India's most impressive yet seldom visited monuments. Not only that but the nearby tombs of the rulers of this Muslim dynasty rival those of the Delhi sultans and the early Moghuls in size and splendour. None of the other central Deccan Muslim kingdoms ever left monu-

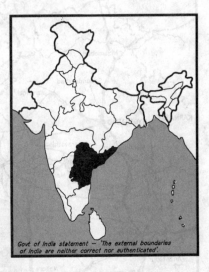

Govt of India statement — 'The external boundaries of India are neither correct nor authenticated'.

ments quite as grandiose as these – though Bijapur (Karnataka) came close. Their reign came to an end in 1687 when the kingdom was taken over by a general of the Moghul Emperor Aurangzeb. The general's successors, the nizams of Hyderabad, ruled the state right through to Independence.

The final nizam of Hyderabad was reputed to be one of the richest men in the world, but Andhra Pradesh itself is one of the poorest and least developed states in India. New dams and irrigation projects are improving the barren, scrubby land of the plateau, but much of the state remains economically backward.

Tourism is not well developed in Andhra Pradesh, although not because of the lack of worthwhile sights. The capital, Hyderabad, is naturally a magnet, not only in its own right for its Muslim heritage, famous museum and enormous Buddha statue, but also for the nearby Golconda Fort and Qutab Shahi tombs. Further afield, there are the

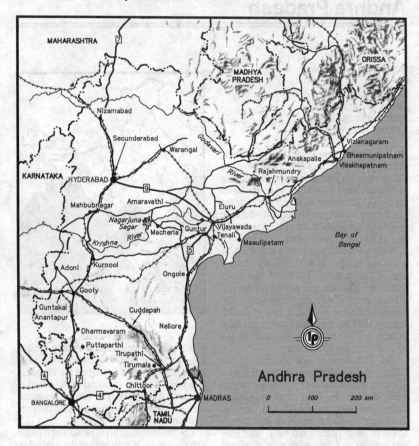

Andhra Pradesh

0   100   200 km

impressive ruins of the Kakatiya Kingdom at Warangal, which was commented on by Marco Polo, and the Buddhist sites of Nagarjuna Sagar and Amaravathi, as well as the beautiful Kanakadurga Temple at Vijayawada, and the famous temple complex of Tirumala in the state's extreme south-east.

HYDERABAD & SECUNDERABAD
Population: 4,300,000

Like Bijapur to the west in neighbouring Karnataka state, Hyderabad is an important centre of Islamic culture and central India's counterpart to the Moghul splendours of the northern cities of Delhi, Agra and Fatehpur Sikri. Consisting of the twin cities of Hyderabad and Secunderabad, it is the capital of Andhra Pradesh and is famous as the former seat of the fabulously wealthy nizams of Hyderabad.

Here, lively crowded bazaars surround huge and impressive Islamic monuments dating from the 16th and 17th centuries. The city, India's sixth largest, was founded in 1590 by Muhammad Quli, the fourth of the Qutab Shahi kings. They ruled this part of the Deccan from 1512 until 1687, when the last of their line was defeated by the Moghul emperor, Aurangzeb, following failure to pay the annual tribute to their nominal suzerain in Delhi.

Before the founding of Hyderabad, the Qutab Shahi kings ruled from the fortress city of Golconda, 11 km to the west. The extensive ruins of this fort, together with the nearby tombs of the Qutab Shahi kings, are the principal attractions of a visit to Hyderabad.

After Aurangzeb's death in 1707, Moghul control over this part of India rapidly waned and the Asaf Jahi viceroys who had been installed to look after the interests of the Moghul Empire broke away to establish their own independent state, taking first the title of subedar and, later, that of nizam. These new rulers, allied to the French, became embroiled in the Anglo-French rivalry for control of India during the latter half of the 18th century. However, the defeat of the French and subsequent Maratha raids seriously weakened their kingdom and they were forced to conclude a treaty with the British, relinquishing most of their power.

When Indian independence was declared in 1947, the nizam toyed with the idea of declaring an independent state and went so far as to allow an Islamic extremist group to seize control. However, this led to his downfall when the Indian government, mindful of Hyderabad's Hindu majority of around 85% and unwilling to see an independent and possibly hostile state created in the centre of the Deccan, used the insurrection as an excuse to occupy Hyderabad in 1948 and force its accession to the Indian union. The dusty city retains much of its 19th-century atmosphere, unlike cities further south. Hyderabad is also unique among southern cities in that Urdu is the major language spoken.

Orientation

The old city of Hyderabad straddles the Musi River while, to the north, the Hussain Sagar effectively separates Hyderabad from its twin city Secunderabad. Most of the historical monuments, the bulk of the hotels and restaurants used by travellers, the city bus station, Salar Jang Museum and the zoo are all in the old city. Budget hotels are mainly found in the area known as Abids, between the GPO and Hyderabad railway station. The main road to Abids from Secunderabad is Mahatma Gandhi Rd, which further south becomes Nehru Rd. This road is also often referred to as Abids Rd. The main APSRIC bus station is south-east of Abids, near the river in the Gowliguda area.

The ruins of Golconda Fort and the tombs of the Qutab Shahi kings lie about 11 km west of the city.

The newer city of Secunderabad is on the north side of Hussain Sagar and, if you arrive by train, it will probably terminate at Secunderabad railway station (the main station), though there are quite a few which continue on to Hyderabad station. The YMCA, YWCA and Youth Hostel are all in Secunderabad so get off there if that's where you want to stay. Hyderabad is about 20 minutes away by bus, auto-rickshaw or taxi across Hussain Sagar dam wall.

Information

Tourist Offices There are tourist information kiosks at both Secunderabad and Hyderabad railway stations but neither is very good. The ITDC tourist office (☎ 66-877) is in the Sendozi Building at 26 Himayatnagar Rd but they only have the usual range of coloured brochures. It's open Monday to Friday from 9.15 am to 5.45 pm and on Saturday from 9.15 am to 1 pm.

The Andhra Pradesh Travel & Tourist Development Corporation (APTTDC) (☎ 55-7531) is at 5th floor, Gangan Vihar, Mukarramjahi Rd, but, despite appearances, they're completely useless. They don't even have a list of the prices of their own lodges and guest houses, though they will fix you up with any of the tours which they operate. The office is open daily from 9 am to 7 pm.

Money There are a number of banks in the Abids Circle area, including the State Bank of India and the Bank of Baroda. Both are fast and efficient – if they have the current

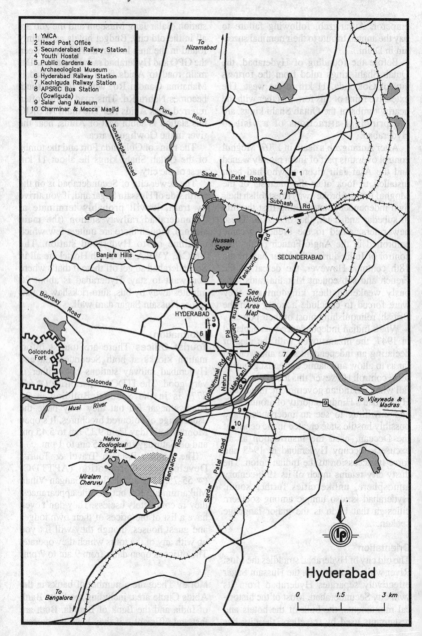

1 YMCA
2 Head Post Office
3 Secunderabad Railway Station
4 Youth Hostel
5 Public Gardens &
   Archaeological Museum
6 Hyderabad Railway Station
7 Kachiguda Railway Station
8 APSRTC Bus Station
   (Gowliguda)
9 Salar Jang Museum
10 Charminar & Mecca Masjid

To Nizamabad

Pune Road

Sanatnagar Road

Sadar Patel Road

Subhash Rd

Hussain
Sagar

Banjara Hills

Tankbund

SECUNDERABAD

Anand Rd

Mahatma Gandhi Rd

See Abids
Area Map

HYDERABAD

Bombay Road

Golconda
Fort

Golconda Road

Musi River

Goshamahal Rd

Nehru Rd

Mahatma Gandhi Rd

Jhansi Rd

To Vijaywada &
Madras

Nehru
Zoological
Park

Miralam
Cheruvu

Bangalore Road

Sardar Patel Road

To
Bangalore

Hyderabad

0   1.5   3 km

exchange rates (these often don't come through until early afternoon).

Post & Telecommunications

The head post office is just south of Sadar Patel Rd, Secunderabad. There is a GPO on Abids Circle, Hyderabad.

There are many long-distance/ISD outlets in the city, but the best place to make international calls from is Doorshanchar Bhavan, Station Rd, opposite the Annapurna Hotel. It's open 8 am to 8 pm daily. The telephone area code for Hyderabad is 0842.

Bookshops

Ashad Books is a good bookshop and can be found just off Mahatma Gandhi Rd, near the Hotel Emerald in Abids. Another is A A Hussain & Co, Abids Rd, on the left hand side as you walk uphill.

Charminar

Standing in the heart of the old walled city and surrounded by lively bazaars, this huge triumphal arch was built by Muhammad Quli Qutab Shah in 1591 to commemorate the end of a plague in Hyderabad. An image of this building graces every packet of Charminar cigarettes, one of India's most popular brands. The arch is illuminated daily from 7 to 9 pm.

Mecca Masjid

Next to the Charminar is the Mecca Masjid. This is one of the largest mosques in the world and is said to accommodate up to 10,000 worshippers. Construction began in 1614, during the reign of Muhammad Quli Qutab Shah, but was not finished until 1687, by which time the Moghul emperor, Aurangzeb, had annexed the Golconda Kingdom.

The colonnades and door arches are made from single slabs of granite. According to historical records, these massive stone blocks were quarried 11 km away and dragged to the site by a team of 1400 bullocks! The minarets were originally intended to be much higher, but the enormous cost of erecting the main part of the building appar-

ently forced the ruler to settle for something less grand.

Unfortunately, this beautiful and impressive building has been disfigured by huge chicken wire awnings, erected in an attempt to stop birds nesting in the ceiling and liming the floor. The birds still get in and the steel supports which have been carelessly cemented into the tiled and patterned floor to hold this netting are nothing short of vandalism.

To the left of the mosque is an enclosure containing the tombs of the nizams.

Birla Mandir (Naubat Prahad) Temple

This stunningly beautiful modern Hindu temple, built out of white marble, graces the rocky hill which overlooks the south end of Hussain Sagar. There are excellent views over the city from the summit, especially at sunset. The temple is a very popular Hindu pilgrimage centre, but non-Hindus are allowed inside.

It's open from 4 to 9 pm on weekdays, and from 7.30 to 11 am and 3 to 7.30 pm on weekends. There's no entry fee and the priests do not press you for contributions.

Nearby, the **Birla Planetarium** has presentations in English several times daily. Admission is Rs 5.

Buddha Statue

Hyderabad, in keeping with the state's history as one of the most important Buddhist centres of India, boasts one of the largest stone Buddhas in the world. The brainchild of Telugu Desam's president, N T Rama Rao, work on the project began in 1985 at Raigir, some 50 km from Hyderabad, and was completed in early 1990. From there, the 17½-metre-high, 350-tonne, monolithic statue was transported to Hyderabad and loaded onto a barge for transportation across Hussain Sagar where it was to be erected on the dam wall.

Unfortunately, disaster struck and the statue sank into the lake taking with it eight people. There it languished for another two years while ways of raising it were discussed. Finally, in April 1992, a Goan-based salvage company raised it once more – undamaged! – and took it to the dam wall where it was finally erected on the Buddha Purnima complex. Though its cost caused political ructions at the time, it promises to be a major tourist draw for the city.

Salar Jang Museum

This is India's answer to the Victoria & Albert Museum in London. The museum's collection was put together by Mir Yusaf Ali Khan (Salar Jang III), the prime minister of the nizam. It contains 35,000 exhibits from all corners of the world and includes sculptures, woodcarvings, religious objects, Persian miniature paintings, illuminated manuscripts, armour and weaponry. You'll also see the swords, daggers and clothing of the Moghul emperors and of Tipu Sultan, as well as many other objects. All this is housed in one of the ugliest buildings imaginable.

The museum is open daily, except Fridays, from 10 am to 5 pm, but avoid Sundays when it's bedlam. Entry is Rs 2. Bags and cameras must be deposited in the entrance hall.

Archaeological Museum

The Archaeological Museum is in the public gardens between Public Gardens Rd (Nampally High Rd) and the branch railway line which leads to Hyderabad railway station. It has a small collection of archaeological finds from the area, together with copies of the Ajanta frescoes. Opening hours are 10.30 am to 5 pm daily, except Mondays, and entry is Rs 0.50.

The gardens also feature an aquarium in the Jawahar Bal Bhavan. It's open from 10.30 am to 5 pm daily, except Friday.

Nehru Zoological Park

One of the largest zoos in India, the Nehru Zoological Park is spread out over 1.2 sq km of landscaped gardens with animals living in large, open enclosures. They don't look any less bored than animals in zoos anywhere else in the world, but at least an effort has been made here, which is more than can be said for most Indian zoos. There's also a prehistoric animal section, a toy train around

the zoo (Rs 1, every 15 minutes), and a lion safari trip (Rs 5, every 15 minutes).

The park is open daily from 8.30 am to 5 pm, except Mondays, and entry costs Rs 1.

Golconda Fort & Tombs of Qutab Shahi Kings

This is one of the most magnificent fortress complexes in India. The bulk of the ruins date from the time of the Qutab Shahi kings (16th to 17th centuries), though the origins of the fort have been traced to the earlier Hindu periods when the Yadavas and, later, the Kakatiyas ruled this part of India.

In 1512, Sultan Quli Qutab Shah, a Turko-man adventurer from Persia and Governor of Telangana under the Bahmani rulers, declared independence and made Golconda his capital.

Golconda remained the capital until 1590, when the court was moved to the new city of Hyderabad. The fort subsequently came into its own again when, on two separate occasions in the 17th century, Moghul armies from Delhi were sent against the kingdom to enforce payment of tribute. Abul Hasan, the last of the Qutab Shahi kings, held out here for seven months against a Moghul army commanded by Emperor Aurangzeb before losing the fort through treachery in 1687. Following Aurangzeb's death early in the next century, his viceroys (later the nizams) made Hyderabad their capital, abandoning Golconda.

The citadel itself is built on a granite hill 120 metres high and is surrounded by crenellated ramparts constructed of large masonry blocks, some of them weighing several tonnes. The massive gates are studded with large pointed iron spikes, intended to prevent elephants from battering them down, and are further protected by a cordon wall to check direct attack. Outside the citadel stands another crenellated rampart with a perimeter of 11 km. All these walls are in an excellent state of preservation.

Unfortunately, many of the structures inside the citadel – the palaces and harem of

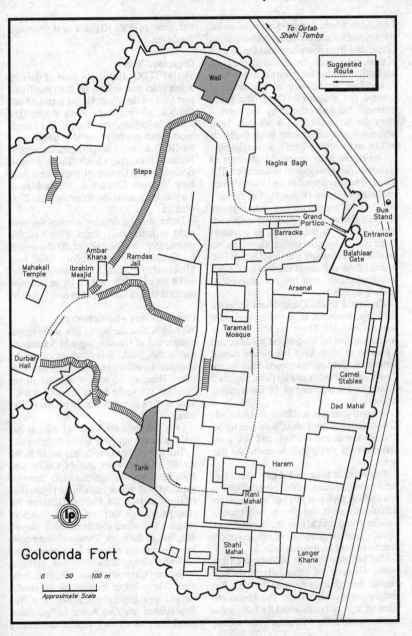

To Qutab
Shahi Tombs

Suggested
Route

Well

Nagina Bagh

Steps

Grand Portico

Barracks

Bus
Stand

Entrance

Balahisar
Gate

Ambar
Khana

Ramdas
Jail

Ibrahim
Masjid

Mahakali
Temple

Arsenal

Taramati
Mosque

Camel
Stables

Durbar
Hall

Dad Mahal

Tank

Harem

Rani
Mahal

Shahi Mahal

Langer
Khana

Golconda Fort

0   50   100 m

Approximate Scale

the Qutab Shahi kings, assembly halls, arsenal, stables and barracks – have suffered a great deal from past sieges and the ravages of time, but enough remains to give a good impression of what the place must once have looked like. Restoration of the buildings around the Balahisar Gate (the main entrance) has been underway for years – even the wrought iron work has been replaced – and it's looking good though it will be many years before it is completed.

One of the most remarkable features of Golconda Fort is its system of acoustics. The sound of hands clapped in the Grand Portico can be heard in the Durbar Hall at the very top of the hill – a fact not lost on tour guides (or their charges), who compete with each other to make as much noise as possible! There is also supposed to be a 'secret' underground tunnel leading from the Durbar Hall to one of the palaces at the foot of the hill but, predictably, you are not allowed to investigate this.

The tombs of the Qutab Shahi kings lie about one km north of the outer perimeter wall of Golconda. These graceful structures are surrounded by landscaped gardens, and a number of them have beautifully carved stonework. The tombs are open daily except Friday and entrance costs Rs 0.50, plus Rs 2 if you have a camera (Rs 10 for a movie camera).

A small guidebook, *Guide to Golconda Fort & Qutab Shahi Tombs*, is on sale for Rs 2 at the tombs and the fort, and is a good investment if you intend to spend the day here.

You need at least half a day to explore these extensive ruins, so the tourist office bus tours which give you just one hour here are ridiculously short. An hour is only enough time to climb quickly to the summit and, equally quickly, descend. A full day spent here would not be wasted.

City bus Nos 119 and 142 take you from Public Gardens Rd (Nampally High Rd), outside the public gardens, to the main fort entrance at Balahisar Gate. The 11-km trip takes an hour and costs about Rs 2. An autorickshaw costs Rs 55 return plus waiting time charges of Rs 10 per hour if you retain the driver.

Organised Tours

The APTTDC offers daily tours of the city. These tours start at 7.30 am from the Transport Unit on the Youth Hostel premises and finish at 5.30 pm at the Birla Mandir. The cost is Rs 45 plus entry charges, and a vegetarian lunch can be arranged in advance for Rs 10. The tours visit Osmania University, Buddha Purnima, Qutab Shahi Tombs, Golconda Fort, Gandipet (lunch stop), Salar Jang Museum, Charminar, Mecca Masjid, the zoo, the handicrafts emporium and Birla Mandir.

Unfortunately, the time allowed for each sight is ludicrously short. Five and 10-minute stops are the order of the day except for Golconda Fort (one hour), Salar Jang Museum (90 minutes) and the zoo (one hour) and a lot of time is wasted on an inconsequential visit to Gandipet Lake.

Places to Stay – bottom end

Way up behind the Boat Club at the northeastern end of Hussain Sagar in Secunderabad is the *Youth Hostel*, which offers the cheapest dormitory-type accommodation in town. There are 51 beds at only Rs 10 per night but it's so far out of the way that it's hard to think of another good reason to stay here.

Only Secunderabad railway station has *retiring rooms* but there are no dormitories.

The best of the cheap hotels are all in the Abids area between Abids Circle and Hyderabad railway station. Right opposite the short road which leads up to Hyderabad railway station on Public Gardens Rd (Nampally High Rd) is a whole clutch of lodges all of which call themselves 'Royal' this, that, or the other. There's nothing quite like this attempt to jump on a bandwagon anywhere else in India other than, perhaps, in Varanasi where it's 'Guru' this, that, or the other. These lodges include the (original?) *Royal Lodge, Royal Home, Royal Hotel, Neo Royal Hotel* and *Gee Royal Lodge*. Good grief! They're all very similar and there's

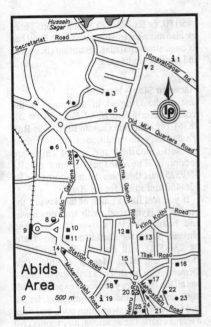

little to choose between them. Count on Rs 59/105 for singles/doubles with attached bathroom and fans. Hot water is usually only available in the mornings.

The *Hotel Rajmata* (☎ 20-1000) offers budget accommodation in the old wing for Rs 35/50 without own bathroom, Rs 50/70 with own bathroom and non-air-con 'deluxe' rooms with colour TV, hot water, towel and soap for Rs 180/230. There's also an attached restaurant.

Next door is the *Hotel Imperial* (☎ 23-5436), right on the corner of Station Rd and Public Gardens Rd (Nampally High Rd). It's similar to the Royals but the rooms on the roof are unbearably hot in summer. The hotel restaurant serves both non-vegetarian and vegetarian food.

Across the road from the above is the *New Asian Lodge* (☎ 20-1275) which is a typical, no-frills Indian boarding house but it's adequate at Rs 59/85 with attached bathroom and fan. Bucket hot water is available.

Further afield, the *Everest Lodge*, Tilak Rd off Mahatma Gandhi Rd (Abids Rd), is even cheaper but only for the desperate and, in any case, it's often full as it only has seven rooms.

Somewhat better is the large *Hotel Sri Brindavan* (☎ 20-3970), Station Rd, near the junction with Abids Circle. It offers singles/doubles with attached bathroom for Rs 100/130. Hot water is available from 4 to 7.30 am. There are vegetarian and very good non-vegetarian restaurants and a bar. The rooms are arranged around a quiet courtyard off Station Rd.

Also reasonable is the *Apsara Hotel*, Station Rd, which has rooms for Rs 90/110 with attached bathroom, fan and hot water in the mornings.

The *Hotel Suhail* (☎ 41-286) is clean,

quiet and good value at Rs 100/120, and there are deluxe doubles at Rs 160 and air-con doubles at Rs 185, as well as more expensive suites. All the rooms have attached bathroom with hot water and most have a balcony. The hotel is situated in an alleyway behind the GPO; the easiest way to find it is to walk through the car park between the Ramakrishna Cinema and the Hotel Aahwaanam and turn left. The hotel is up a little further, on the left.

Places to Stay – middle

The best value by far in this range is the brand new, spotlessly clean and friendly *Hotel Saptagiri* (☎ 44-601) just off Station Rd and round the corner from the Annapurna Hotel. The rooms here are superb value at Rs 95/135, and Rs 225 a double with air-con including taxes. All the rooms have a balcony and an attached bathroom with hot water, and the air-con rooms are carpeted and have a colour TV. There's a restaurant of sorts but it only serves snacks – fine for breakfast.

Also top value for money is the *Hotel Aahwaanam* (☎ 40-101), off J N Rd and right opposite the Ramakrishna Cinema. Like the Saptagiri, it's brand new, spotless and the staff are friendly. Rooms cost Rs 145/185 or Rs 240/270 with air-con. All the rooms have attached bathroom with hot water and the air-con rooms have a colour TV. There's no restaurant or bar.

Equally good value is the *Hotel Jaya International* (☎ 23-2929), off Bank St, which has rooms for Rs 130/165 or Rs 240/280 with air-con. Credit cards are accepted but there's no restaurant or bar.

The older *Taj Mahal Hotel* (☎ 23-7988), at the junction of Mahatma Gandhi Rd (Abids Rd) and King Kothi Rd, has been popular for years. It's a huge rambling place set in its own grounds, with car parking facilities and a restaurant. Rooms with attached bathroom, hot water and TV cost Rs 165/225, or Rs 230/300 with air-con.

Top of this range is the *Hotel Siddhartha* (☎ 55-7421), Bank St, which is a beautifully appointed and quiet place, yet costs only Rs 145/180, or Rs 225/275 with air-con. There are also more expensive suites. The hotel has its own, almost palatial, restaurant (licenced) and accepts credit cards.

Places to Stay – top end

One of the cheapest in this range is the recently refurbished *Hotel Emerald* (☎ 20-2836), off Mahatma Gandhi Rd (Abids Rd). It's centrally air-conditioned, all the rooms are self-contained and credit cards are accepted. The cheapest rooms are Rs 360/525 plus there are deluxe rooms for Rs 325/450 and suites for Rs 700.

If you feel like a touch of the days of the nizams of Hyderabad, with spacious lawns and beautiful views over the city and Hussain Sagar, then head for the *Ritz Hotel* (☎ 23-3571), Hill Fort St, Basheer Bagh, close to the Birla Mandir Temple. This former palace is rated as a four-star hotel and has all the facilities you would expect including a restaurant (Indian, Continental, Italian and Chinese), bar, swimming pool, and even a tennis court. The spacious, airy rooms cost Rs 299/575, and there are deluxe doubles for Rs 650 and suites for Rs 775. It's a very mellow place and the staff are friendly.

More expensive and much further from the city are the five-star *Krishna Oberoi* (☎ 22-2121), at US$60/65, and the *Gateway Hotel on Banjara Hill* (☎ 22-2222), at US$75/85, or US$95/105 in the 'superior' rooms. Both these hotels are on Road No 1, Banjara Hills, are centrally air-conditioned and have a full range of modern facilities.

Places to Eat

Good, cheap vegetarian meals can be found at any *Kamat Hotel*, where the standard fare costs Rs 10. There's one in Abids on Station Rd, near the junction with Public Gardens Rd (Nampally High Rd), and another near the Indian Airlines office. Almost opposite the Kamat on Station Rd is the small *Punjab Restaurant* which serves reasonable north Indian non-vegetarian food if you like things hot (chillies, that is). If you don't, avoid the place. It has a classic misspelt menu, the most notable item of which is 'Green Peace soup'!

The *Priya Hotel* is opposite the Hotel Sri Brindavan. It's air-con and has good vegetarian and non-vegetarian lunchtime meals from Rs 15. Food at the *Hotel Swagat* almost next door is also good. Meals cost Rs 12.

Nirala's Open House is a modern fast-food place on Himayatnagar Rd, near the corner of Basheerbagh Rd. It offers typical Western food such as chips, pizza, sandwiches, milk shakes and ice creams.

The *Grand Hotel*, just around from the Hyderabad GPO, is far from grand but has good cheap non-vegetarian food such as biryanis and mutton cutlets and is popular with local people. Also in the Abids Circle area, the *Liberty Restaurant* is another Western-style place and serves Chinese and Indian dishes.

Possibly the best place to eat without going for a splurge is the *Shalimar Bar & Restaurant*, part of the Hotel Sri Brindavan on Station Rd. The food here is excellent and tasty. Soups are Rs 10, curries Rs 25 to Rs 35 and vegetarian dishes Rs 15 to Rs 20. It's open from 11 am to 11 pm daily. Try their 'Mongolian' dishes!

Things to Buy

Hyderabad is famous for glass bangles and these can be bought in Lud Bazaar, the street running to the right of the Charminar (when coming from Abids). Prices range from as little as Rs 8 for a box of a dozen or so up to Rs 30 for one.

Getting There & Away

Air The Air India office (☎ 23-7890), near the public gardens, Vayudoot (☎ 23-2625) and Indian Airlines (☎ 72-051) offices are open Monday to Friday from 9.30 am to 1 pm and 2 to 5 pm, and on Saturday from 9.30 am to 1 pm; closed on Sunday.

To book flights on East West Airlines, call 52-6518.

There are Indian Airlines flights in either direction daily between Hyderabad and Bangalore (US$56), Bombay (US$74), Calcutta (US$134), Delhi (US$124), Madras (US$57), Bhubaneswar (US$95) via Nagpur (US$55), and to Vishakhapatnam (US$58).

Vayudoot operates services from Hyderabad to Tirupathi (US$120), Vijayawada (US$80), Rajahmundry (US$94) and Madras (US$160). East West Airlines has flights once daily to Bombay (US$74).

Bus Buses leave from the main APSRIC bus station, Gowliguda, for all parts of the state. The buses are well organised into separate bays, there's a timetable in English, and a computerised advance booking office which is open daily from 8 am to 9 pm.

A selection of superdeluxe and semideluxe buses (usually two seats on either side of the aisle) is as follows:

Amaravathi:	One daily at 9 pm
Aurangabad:	One daily at 4 pm, Rs 118
Bangalore:	10 daily (mostly in the evening), Rs 131
Bidar:	19 daily, Rs 25 (express only)
Bombay:	Eight times daily, Rs 203 (superdeluxe)
Gulbarga:	12 times daily, Rs 56
Kurnool:	Seven times daily, Rs 40/48
Madras:	One daily, Rs 138 (superdeluxe)
Nagpur:	Twice daily, Rs 106 (semideluxe), Rs 132 (superdeluxe)
Nizamabad:	32 times daily, Rs 33 (semideluxe), Rs 39 (superdeluxe)
Tirupathi:	11 times daily, Rs 99 (semideluxe), Rs 122 (superdeluxe)
Vijayawada:	24 times daily, Rs 51 (semideluxe), Rs 61 (superdeluxe)

There are also a number of private bus companies offering superdeluxe video buses to such cities as Bangalore, Bombay, Madras, Nagpur and Tirupathi. Most of their offices are on Public Gardens Rd (Nampally High Rd) close to the Hyderabad railway station entrance road. They include Asian Travels (☎ 20-2128), inside the Asian Lodge, and Noble Travels (☎ 20-1275), next to the New Asian Lodge. Most have one departure daily, usually in the late afternoon. To Bangalore it's Rs 150 and 12 hours; to Bombay Rs 190 and 14 hours, and to Nagpur Rs 150 and 12 hours.

Train The main railway station is at Secunderabad and this is the one where you catch through trains (ie, all trains other than those originating in Hyderabad; trains originating in Hyderabad can usually be boarded there). Trains can be booked, however, either at Hyderabad station or Secunderabad station. Both have a tourist quota and the booking offices are open Monday to Saturday from 8 am to 2 pm and 2.15 to 8 pm, and on Sunday from 8 am to 2 pm. As elsewhere, the fastest night express trains are booked up days in advance, so reserve your seat or sleeper as early as possible.

The 1675-km trip from New Delhi to Hyderabad on the *Nizamuddin-Hyderabad Express* takes 33½ hours and costs Rs 186/789 in 2nd/1st class. The quickest route from Calcutta is to take the daily *Coromandel Express* from Howrah Station and change at Vijayawada. The 1591-km journey takes about 32 hours and costs Rs 181/751 in 2nd/1st class.

From Hyderabad, the 862-km trip to Madras takes 13½ hours on the daily *Charminar Express*; the fare is Rs 132/487 in 2nd/1st class. The 790-km trip from Hyderabad to Bangalore takes 17 hours and costs Rs 124/472 in 2nd/1st class.

The line from Secunderabad to Aurangabad is metre gauge – the 517-km trip on the *Ajanta Express* takes 12½ hours at a cost of Rs 92/337 in 2nd/1st class. The express continues through Aurangabad to Manmad, on the Bombay to Delhi line. The Secunderabad to Ajmer line is also metre gauge. This 1138-km route passes through Khandwa, Mhow, Indore, Ratlam and Chittorgarh, a 39-hour journey which costs Rs 158/611 in 2nd/1st class.

Getting Around

To/From the Airport There is no airport bus, but an auto-rickshaw to or from Abids should cost about Rs 20 by the meter, though drivers usually refuse to use it if you're going to the airport, so you'll have to haggle.

Bus Getting on any city bus in Hyderabad, other than at the terminus, is (as one traveller put it) 'like staging a banzai charge on

Guadalcanal'. He wasn't exaggerating! Buses you might find useful include:

No 2 – Secunderabad railway station to Charminar
No 7 – Secunderabad railway station to Afzalganj and return (this is the one to catch if you're heading for Abids, as it goes down Tankbund Rd and Nehru Rd via the GPO)
No 8 – connects Secunderabad and Hyderabad railway stations
Nos 119 & 142 – Nampally High Rd to Golconda Fort.

Auto-Rickshaw & Taxi Flagfall on auto-rickshaws is Rs 3.70 plus Rs 0.55 for each additional km. Some drivers need no prompting to use the meter but others do. A return trip to Golconda Fort is Rs 55 by the meter plus waiting charges at Rs 10 per hour but they'll expect a tip on top of that.

Taxis tend to be expensive and you'll have to haggle over the price. For a return trip to Golconda, for example, including waiting time, they'll quote you Rs 200.

Car Typical hire rates are Rs 200 for four hours or 40 km, Rs 325 for eight hours or 80 km, and Rs 2.50 per km for journeys longer than a day with a minimum of 300 km per day. These rates include the driver. Try Ram Reddy (☎ 84-3931) next door to the ITDC office.

NAGARJUNAKONDA & NAGARJUNA SAGAR

Nagarjunakonda, 150 km south-east of Hyderabad on the Krishna River, was one of the largest and most important Buddhist centres in southern India from the 2nd century BC until the 3rd century AD. Known in those days as Vijayapur, Nagarjunakonda takes its present name from Nagarjuna, one of the most revered Buddhist monks, who governed the *sangha* for nearly 60 years around the turn of the 2nd century AD. The Madhyamika school he founded attracted students from as far afield as Sri Lanka and China.

The site was discovered in 1926. Subsequent excavations, particularly in the '50s and '60s, have unearthed the remains of stupas, viharas, chaityas and mandapas, as well as some outstanding examples of white marble carvings and sculptures depicting the life of the Buddha. These finds were taken to an island following the decision to flood this entire area to build the Nagarjuna Sagar. This dam is touted as one of the largest masonry constructions in the world and India claims that it will create the world's third-largest artificial lake.

Places to Stay

The choice of accommodation maintained by the APTTDC (☎ Hyderabad 55-7531) includes the *Vijay Vihar Complex* (☎ 3625), which has double air-con rooms and cottages, *Project House*, Hill Colony, and the *Konda Guest House* (☎ 2668). There's also a *Youth Hostel* in Hill Colony.

Getting There & Away

The easiest way to visit Nagarjunakonda and Nagarjuna Sagar is to take the deluxe tourist bus from Hyderabad organised by the APTTDC. It departs daily (if demand warrants it) at 6.30 am, returns at 10.30 pm and costs Rs 75. The tour includes visits to the Nagarjunakonda Museum (closed Fridays), Pylon (an engraved granite monolith from the Buddhist period), Nagarjuna Sagar, Ethiopothala Waterfalls and the working model of the dam.

If you'd prefer to make your own way there, regular buses link Hyderabad, Vijayawada and Guntur with Nagarjuna Sagar. The nearest railway station is at Macherla – a branch line running west from Guntur – and regular buses leave there for Nagarjuna Sagar.

Getting Around

Boat If you're not taking one of the local tours or those organised from Hyderabad, launches to Nagarjunakonda Museum depart at 9.30 am and 1.30 pm at a cost of Rs 15 per person.

WARANGAL

Population: 467,000

This was once the capital of the Kakatiya Kingdom, which spanned the greater part of present-day Andhra Pradesh from the latter half of the 12th century until it was conquered by the Tughlaqs of Delhi early in the 14th century. The Hindu Kakatiyas were great builders and patrons of the arts, and it was during their reign that the Chalukyan style of temple architecture and decoration reached the pinnacle of its development.

If you have an interest in the various branches of Hindu temple development and have either visited or intend to visit the early Chalukyan sites at Badami, Aihole and Pattadakal in neighbouring Karnataka state, then an outing to Warangal is worthwhile. Facilities are adequate for an overnight stopover, or it can be visited in a long day trip from Hyderabad.

There's a colourful **wool market** a couple of hundred metres past the bus stand.

Fort

Warangal's main attraction is the enormous, abandoned mud-brick fort, which has a terrific atmosphere and many interesting features. Carved stones from wrecked Chalukyan temples are set indiscriminately in the massive stone walls which form a distinct fortification almost a km inside the outer mud walls.

Chalukyan Temples

The most notable remaining Chalukyan temples are the **1000-Pillared Temple** on the slopes of Hanamkonda Hill (one shrine of which is still in use), the **Bhadrakali Temple** on a hillock between Warangal and Hanamkonda, and the Shambu Lingeswara or **Swayambhu Temple** (originally a Siva temple). Built in 1162, the 1000-Pillared Temple is, however, inferior to those found further south. It is in a sad state of disrepair, and looters have removed many of the best pieces and chiselled away the faces of statues.

Places to Stay & Eat

Accommodation facilities are modest. Most of the hotels are on Station Rd, which runs parallel to the railway line; turn left as you leave the station. The *Vijya Lodge* (☎ 5851) is excellent value at Rs 45/70, and has an attached restaurant serving both vegetarian and non-vegetarian food. Similar is the *Hotel Shanthi Krishna* (☎ 5305) which is behind the post office, also on Station Rd.

Up behind the bus station and near the huge market, the basic *Vikas Lodge* (☎ 5943) has rooms with bathroom for Rs 30/45.

There are also a couple of *retiring rooms* at the railway station.

Getting There & Away

Regular buses run between Warangal and Hyderabad, Nizamabad and other major centres. Local buses connect Warangal with Kazipet and Hanamkonda.

Warangal is a major railway junction in Andhra Pradesh and many expresses stop here. The 152-km journey to Hyderabad or Secunderabad takes about 3½ hours. Warangal to Vijayawada takes about the same time and costs Rs 36/129 in 2nd/1st class.

Getting Around

The bus station is directly opposite the entrance to the railway station but the time-table is entirely in Telugu so you'll have to make enquiries.

Bus No 28 will take you the five km to the fort at Mantukonda. Otherwise, it would be worth negotiating a fixed price for an auto-rickshaw to take you there and back and allow you sufficient time to see the ruins.

TIRUPATHI & TIRUMALA

The 'holy hill' of Tirumala, 20 km from its service town of Tirupathi in the extreme south of Andhra Pradesh, is one of the most important pilgrimage centres in all India because of the ancient Vaishnavaite temple of Lord Venkateshwara (Sri Balaji). This is the god whose picture graces the reception areas of most lodges and restaurants in southern India. He's the one with his eyes covered

(since his gaze would scorch the world) and garlanded in so many flowers that only his feet are visible.

Among the powers attributed to Lord Venkateshwara by his devotees is the granting of any wish made in front of the idol at Tirumala. On the basis of such a legend, pilgrims flock here from all over India. There are never less than 5000 here at any one time and, in a day, the total is often as high as 100,000, although the average is a mere 30,000. The temple staff alone number nearly 6000!

Such popularity makes the temple one of the richest in India, with an annual income of a staggering five billion rupees which is administered by a temple trust which ploughs the bulk of the money back into hundreds of choultries (pilgrims' accommodation) and charities such as homes for the poor, ophanages, craft training centres, schools, colleges and art academies.

It's considered auspicious to have your head shaved when visiting the temple, so if you see people with shaved heads in south India, you can be pretty sure they've recently been to Tirupathi – this applies to men, women and children. This practice is known as tonsuring.

In order to cope with the army of pilgrims, everything at Tirupathi and Tirumala is organised to keep the visitors fed, sheltered and moving. Most are housed in special pilgrim accommodation in both Tirupathi and Tirumala. However, the private hotels and lodges are in Tirupathi, so a whole fleet of buses constantly ferries pilgrims between Tirupathi and Tirumala from before dawn until well after dark.

The temple is one of the few in India which will allow non-Hindus into the sanctum sanctorum. After paying Rs 25 for 'special darshan', you're allowed into the temple. Special darshan means you can enter ahead of all those who have paid nothing for ordinary darshan and who have to queue up – often for 12 hours and more – in the claustrophobic wire cages which ring the outer wall of the temple. To find the start of the queue, follow the signs to 'Sarvadarshan', around to the left of the temple entrance. 'Special darshan' is supposed to get you to the front of the queue in two hours, but on weekends when the place is much busier it can take as long as five hours, and you still have to go through the cages. A signboard at the entrance tells you how long you can expect it to take.

As you face the entrance to the temple, there is a small **museum** at the top of the steps to the left. Among other things, it has a good collection of musical instruments, including a tabla-type drum called a Ubangam!

It's an engrossing place where you can easily spend a whole day just wandering around and, despite the huge numbers of pilgrims here, the place sees very few foreign visitors.

Organised Tours

The APTTDC runs weekend tours to Tirupathi from Hyderabad. The tours which leave at 4 pm on Friday and return at 7 am on Monday include accommodation and 'special darshan' and cost Rs 350. It's also possible to take the bus only, and this costs Rs 120 one way.

There are also daily tours to Tirupathi from Madras run by the Tamil Nadu Tourist Development Corporation and by the ITDC which cost Rs 200 including breakfast and lunch, but this is guided-tour madness at its very worst. The tour takes about 15 hours, at least 12 of which are spent on the bus to and from Madras. In addition, the schedule allows for a two-hour wait for 'special darshan' (included in the tour price), but if the wait is much longer (as it is on weekends), it's not uncommon for the bus to return to Madras at midnight and even as late as 3 am! See the Madras chapter for details.

Places to Stay

Tirupathi Tirupathi is the town at the bottom of the hill and the transport hub. It has plenty of hotels and lodges, so there's no problem finding somewhere to stay.

The popular *Bhimas Hotel* (☎ 20-766), 42 G Car St, is a good place to stay, with non-

air-con singles/doubles with bathroom for Rs 50/115 or doubles with air-con for Rs 250. The hotel has its own vegetarian restaurant.

Directly opposite the railway station, the noisy *Gopi Krishna Deluxe Lodge* has small rooms for Rs 55 with bathroom. The colour schemes in these rooms are really something else.

Almost next door to the Bhimas Hotel is the *Bhimas Deluxe Hotel* (☎ 20-121), 34-38 G Car St. This is a two-star hotel with rooms for Rs 110/140, and from Rs 175/200 with air-con. All the rooms have attached bathroom and the air-con rooms have TV. There's a range of other services including a restaurant with north and south Indian food.

There are also a whole group of hotels around the main bus station, 500 metres from the centre of town, as well as *retiring rooms* at the railway station.

Top of the line is the *Hotel Mayura* (☎ 20-901), T P Area, a three-star hotel close to the railway station which has rooms with attached bathroom for Rs 145/165, or Rs 250/300 with air-con. There's a restaurant serving Indian and Mughlai cuisine.

Tirumala Tirumala has only one hotel offering private rooms – most pilgrims stay in the vast *dormitories* which ring the temple. This pilgrim accommodation is open to anyone. If you want to stay there, check in at the accommodation reception in Tirumala and you'll be allocated a bed or a room. It's best to avoid weekends when the place becomes outrageously crowded.

The Tamil Nadu Tourist Development Corporation has *tourist cottages* for rent at Tirumala. These can be booked at their office in Madras, or ask at cottage No 304 near the bus station in Tirumala.

Places to Eat

Tirupathi The *Lakshmi Narayana Bhavan* is a good vegetarian restaurant opposite the main bus station. The *Bhimas Hotel* also has a good vegetarian restaurant, including an air-con dining hall. On the same street, you can get non-vegetarian north Indian food at the *Restaurant Peacock*.

Tirumala Huge dining halls serve more than 3000 free meals daily to keep the pilgrims happy. Other than that, there are a few no-frills 'meals' places.

Getting There & Away

Air The Indian Airlines office (☎ 2369) is in the Hotel Vishnupriya complex, opposite the main bus station in Tirupathi.

Vayudoot flies to Madras (US$40) and Hyderabad (US$120).

Bus It is possible to see Tirupathi on a long day trip from Madras if you make a very early start, but staying overnight makes it far less rushed.

Thiruvalluvar has express buses (route No 802) from the Thiruvalluvar bus station in Madras at 8.15 am, 3.30 and 8.30 pm. There are also many other ordinary buses, although these are not particularly recommended as they take circuitous routes. The express buses take about four hours and can be booked in advance in Madras. The expresses to Madras from Tirupathi leave at 9.30 am, 1.15 and 8.30 pm plus there are plenty of other normal buses.

A day trip from Hyderabad is not possible as the 570 km journey takes 14 hours. It's far better to do the trip by rail and plan on staying overnight in Tirupathi.

Train As a popular pilgrimage centre, Tirupathi is well served by express trains. The 147-km trip from Madras takes 3½ hours and costs Rs 33/127 in 2nd/1st class; there are three trains daily.

The daily *Rayala Seema Express* connects Hyderabad and Tirupathi. The trip takes 16 hours and costs Rs 73/268 in 2nd/1st class. There are three expresses to Vijayawada daily and one of these, the *Tirupathi Express*, goes on to Puri. The trip to Vijayawada is 389 km, takes eight hours and costs Rs 73/273 in 2nd/1st class. The 1207-km trip to Puri takes 18 hours and costs Rs 164/649 in 2nd/1st class.

Getting Around

Tirumala Link buses operate from both the main bus stand, and the Tirumala bus stand in the centre of Tirupathi. The 20-km trip takes 45 minutes and costs Rs 6 one way, or Rs 10.50 return. To get on a bus in either Tirupathi or Tirumala, you have to go through a system of crowd-control wire cages which are definitely not for the claustrophobic. At busy times (weekends and festivals), it can take up to two hours to file through the cages and get onto a bus. If you're staying in Tirupathi, it's worth buying a return ticket which saves you some queueing time in the cages at the top of the hill. There are no cages at the main bus station.

Finding the queue for the buses in Tirupathi can also be a task. The entrance to the choultry (through which you have to walk to reach the cages and ticket office) is opposite the bottom of the footbridge over the railway line – just follow the crowd. There's always a steady stream of people filing in.

The road to Tirumala winds precariously upwards and the bus drivers have perfected the art of maniacal driving. The road they drive down is the old one and is very narrow and winding. It has 57 hairpin bends, which means 57 adrenalin rushes for you as the buses hurtle down – total lunacy.

Taxi If you're in a hurry, or don't like the cages, there are share taxis running up and down the hill all the time. Seats cost around Rs 25, depending on demand.

PUTTAPARTHI

Prasanthi Nilayam, the ashram of Sri Sathya Sai Baba, is in Puttaparthi. Sai Baba's followers are predominantly Indian but he also has many Western followers. When he celebrated his 60th birthday in late 1985, 400,000 people came to his ashram. Known as the Abode of Highest Peace, it is spacious and beautiful with good food and accommodation – at least when the numbers aren't overwhelming. It does get very dry here in the hot season.

Getting There & Away

Puttaparthi is in Andhra Pradesh, but it is

most easily reached from Bangalore, 150 km away. Take a train or bus to Dharmavaram or Anantapur, the nearest railway station.

EAST COAST

Although the main Calcutta to Madras railway line runs along the east coast of Andhra Pradesh, few travellers stop south of Orissa. During the monsoon, the extensive deltas of the Godavari and Krishna rivers may flood, forcing trains between Calcutta and Madras to detour further inland through Raipur, Nagpur and Hyderabad.

Waltair & Visakhapatnam
Population: 1,051,000
These two towns have really merged into one and the local people do not recognise any distinction between them. The northern residential area can be thought of as Waltair and the booming southern business and industrial area towards the docks as Visakhapatnam (abbreviated as Vizag). The railway station, roughly in the centre, is called Visakhapatnam Junction.

Waltair, a popular seaside resort, boasts rocks and pools as well as several km of sand. There are two beaches: **Mission Beach**, about three km from the centre, and **Lawson Beach**, a distance of about six km. Simhachalam Hill, about 10 km north of Waltair, has an 11th-century **Vishnu temple** in fine Orissan style.

There is a tourist office in the railway station but it has precious little specific information.

Places to Stay – bottom end Vizag has plenty of hotels right up to five-star quality. The excellent bus station has *retiring rooms*. Cheap hotels include the *Hotel Poorna* (☎ 62-344) on Main Rd, where self-contained rooms with attached bathroom cost Rs 40/60. Very similar and on the same road is the *Hotel Prasanth* (☎ 65-282).

Places to Stay – middle & top end The two-star *Ocean View Inn* (☎ 54-828) is near the better (northern) end of the beach and is very comfortable, peaceful and friendly, with singles/doubles for Rs 100/250. Rooms with air-con cost Rs 175/200. All rooms have TV and in-house videos and the hotel has its own restaurant.

The three-star *Hotel Daspalla* (☎ 64-8250) is centrally located and has rooms for Rs 150/175, and Rs 220/250 with air-con. The hotel has a range of shops and facilities including a bar and two restaurants (Indian, Chinese, Continental, Mughlai and tandoori).

The *Hotel Apsara* (☎ 64-861) on Waltair Main Rd is another three-star hotel and is similarly priced; all the rooms are air-con. It offers much the same facilities as the Daspalla.

Up in price, the centrally located *Dolphin Hotels Ltd* (☎ 64-811), is a four-star hotel with a whole range of facilities including a swimming pool. Top of the line is the *Park Hotel* (☎ 54-181), Beach Rd, which has air-con rooms for Rs 390/600 and suites for Rs 780 to Rs 1500. Facilities include a swimming pool, bookshop and multi-cuisine restaurant.

Getting There & Away Indian Airlines flies from Hyderabad to Vishakhapatnam daily in either direction. The flight take one hour and costs US\$58.

Vizag is linked by broad-gauge railway line to Raipur. There's also a relatively new, well-organised bus station which is quite a change from the usual bus station confusion. Good services run to and from Puri and Vijayawada.

Around Waltair & Visakhapatnam
Twenty-four km north-east of Vizag is **Bheemunipatnam**, one of the safest beaches on this part of the coast. It is the site of the ruins of the oldest Dutch settlement on the east coast (17th century). A little way inland from here is **Hollanders Green**, the Dutch cemetery.

Some 90 km from Vizag are the million-year-old limestone **Borra Caves** which are filled with fascinating stalagmite and stalagtite formations.

Vijayawada

On the banks of the mighty Krishna River, only 149 km south of Rajahmundry and the Godavari River, Vijayawada is the junction for the railway line to Warangal and Hyderabad. Today it's a major industrial centre but it has a history going back some 2000 years when it was an important Buddhist centre – there's a colossal black granite Buddha housed in the city's Victoria Museum. It also has a number of important **Hindu temples** as well as two 1000-year-old **Jain temples**.

Only a few km from Vijayawada, but across the river, are the ancient Hindu cave temples of **Undavalil**.

Vijayawada is a fairly hectic town and few travellers stop here but it's the most convenient place from which to visit Amaravathi, the Sanchi of Andhra Pradesh.

Places to Stay & Eat The main hotel area in Vijayawada is quite a walk from both the bus and railway station. If you have any luggage you'll need a cycle-rickshaw. Best value is the *Hotel Swapna Lodge* (☎ 72-172) on Durgaiah St. It's friendly and clean, and rooms cost Rs 45/70, more with air-con. Also relatively cheap is the *Sree Lakshmi Vilas Modern Cafe* (☎ 62-525), Besant Rd, about one km from the railway station, which has rooms with attached bathroom for Rs 60/90. The hotel has its own vegetarian restaurant.

Going up in price, the *Hotel Raj Towers* (☎ 61-311), Congress Office Rd, has rooms with attached bathroom for Rs 140/180, and Rs 200/260 with air-con. It has a multicuisine restaurant. A similar place is the *Hotel Manorama* (☎ 77-221), 27-38-61 Bunder Rd, which has rooms with attached bathroom for Rs 125/165, or Rs 175/225 with air-con.

Top of the line is the *Hotel Kandhari International* (☎ 47-1311), M G Rd. This three-star hotel is fully air-con and has rooms for Rs 315/440.

Getting There & Away As Vijayawada is a major railway junction, there are frequent rail services. Air and bus services are also available.

Air Vayudoot flies from Hyderabad to Vijayawada Monday to Saturday. The one-hour flight costs US$80 one way.

Bus The bus station in Vijayawada is totally chaotic. From here, buses travel to all parts of Andhra Pradesh, and also to Madras.

Train Vijayawada is on the main Madras-Calcutta and Madras-Delhi lines and all the expresses stop here. The quickest train from Vijayawada to Madras is the Calcutta-Madras *Coromandel Express*, which does the 432-km journey nonstop in a shade under six hours. The fare is Rs 81/301 in 2nd/1st class. In the opposite direction, the same train takes just 27 hours for the 1236-km journey to Calcutta. The fare is Rs 164/649 in 2nd/1st class. There are slower expresses, such as the *Tirupathi Express*, which you can catch to Puri.

The 351-km trip to Hyderabad takes seven hours and costs Rs 70/253 in 2nd/1st class. The *Tamil Nadu Express* takes 50 hours to cover the 1761 km to New Delhi. The fare is Rs 191/823 in 2nd/1st class.

There are also direct trains to Kanyakumari, Thiruvananthapuram (Trivandrum), Bangalore and Varanasi.

Around Vijayawada

Masulipatam Masulipatam, 80 km southeast of Vijayawada on the coast, once had English, Dutch and French factories and was the subject of violent Anglo-French rivalry.

Amaravathi Some 60 km west of Vijayawada stands the ancient Buddhist centre of Amaravathi, the former capital of the Satvahanas, who were the successors to the Mauryas in this part of India. Here you can see the 2000-year-old **stupa** with its intricately carved pillars and marble-surfaced dome which itself is equally richly carved. The carvings depict the life of the Buddha as well as scenes from everyday life. It's not as large as that at Sanchi in Madhya Pradesh but it is worth a visit if you're interested in Buddhist relics of the Hinayana era. There's a **museum** on the site containing relics found in the area.

Buses run to Amaravathi from Vijayawada along a sealed road.

Kerala

Population: 29 million
Area: 38,864 sq km
Capital: Thiruvananthapuram (Trivandrum)
People per sq km: 747
Main Language: Malayalam
Literacy Rate: 91%

Kerala, the land of green magic, is a narrow, fertile strip on the south-west coast of India, sandwiched between the Lakshadweep Sea and the Western Ghats. The landscape is dominated by rice fields, mango and cashewnut trees and coconut palms. The Western Ghats, with their dense tropical forests, misty peaks, extensive ridges and ravines, have sheltered Kerala from invaders from the rest of India but, at the same time, have encouraged Keralans to welcome maritime contact with the outside world. In Kochi (Cochin), there is still a small community descended from Jewish settlers who fled Palestine 2000 years ago. Christianity has also been in Kerala for as long as it has been in Europe! When the Portuguese arrived here 500 years ago, they were more than a little surprised to find Christianity already established along the Malabar coast, and more than a little annoyed that these Christians had never heard of the Pope.

People from far-off lands have been coming to Kerala since ancient times. They came in search of spices, sandalwood and ivory. Long before Vasco da Gama led the Portuguese to India, the coast had been known to the Phoenicians, then the Romans and later the Arabs and Chinese. It was the Arabs who long controlled the shipment of spices to Europe and it was this, in turn, which motivated the Portuguese to find a sea route to India and break the Arab monopoly. In those days, Kerala was not only a spice centre in its own right, but a transhipment point from the Moluccas. It was also through Kerala that Chinese manufactures and ideas found their way to the West. Even today, local fishers still use Chinese fishing nets.

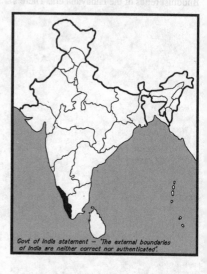

Govt of India statement – 'The external boundaries of India are neither correct nor authenticated'.

Such long contact with people from overseas has resulted in the blending of various cultures and given Keralans a cosmopolitan outlook. Unlike the Gujaratis and Tamils, who generally followed the fortunes of the British Empire in emigrating to such places as East Africa, South Africa, Fiji and Guyana, Keralans have had a tradition of independently seeking their fortunes overseas or throughout the rest of India. You can generally find a Keralan in any nook and cranny around the world and they make up a major component of the Indian labour force in the oil fields of the Persian Gulf.

The present-day state of Kerala was created in 1956 from Travancore, Kochi (Cochin) and Malabar. Malabar was formerly p'art of Madras State, while both Travancore and Cochin were princely states ruled by maharajas. Unlike some maharajas in other parts of India who exploited their people and squandered the proceeds on high and often frivolous living, the maharajas of

Travancore and Cochin paid considerable attention to the provision of basic services and education for their subjects. It was this early concern for public welfare which gave Keralans a head start and resulted in the post-Independence state being one of the most progressive, literate and highly educated of all the states in India.

One of Kerala's other distinctions is that it was the first place in the world to freely elect a communist government (in 1957). They have been in and out of office ever since and, although the princely state of Travancore had already implemented a far-sighted land ownership policy over a century ago, there is little doubt that the relatively equitable distribution of land and income found rarely to the same degree elsewhere in India is the direct result of successive communist governments. This policy of equity also applies to health and education. Infant mortality in Kerala is the lowest in India, and the literacy rate is the highest – claimed to be about 100% but closer to 90%, nearly double the all-India average. These results have been achieved without spending a higher proportion of state income on health or education than other states. It's also the only Indian state in which females outnumber males, though the main reason for that is the recent trend among males to seek a modest fortune in the Gulf oil fields before returning home to settle down.

For the visitor, Kerala offers an intriguing blend of cultures and some unusual ways of travelling around. Perhaps more than anywhere else in India, getting around can be half the fun, particularly on the backwater trips along the coastal lagoons. It also offers some of the best and most picturesque beaches in India, the one at Kovalam, a little south of Thiruvananthapuram, being the most popular. Best of all, Kerala has an easygoing, relaxed atmosphere unlike the bustle you find elsewhere in India. Even the capital sports the atmosphere of a country town.

Religion

The population of Kerala is roughly 60% Hindu, 20% Muslim and 20% Christian.

Christianity was established here earlier than almost anywhere else in the world. In 52 AD, St Thomas the Apostle, or 'Doubting Thomas', is said to have landed on the Malabar coast near Cranganore, where a church with carved Hindu-style columns supposedly dates from the 4th century AD.

Further south, there is the 9th-century Syrian church of Vallia Palli. Kerala's Syrian Christians were here by 190 AD – a visitor at that time reported seeing a Hebrew copy of the gospel of St Matthew. Kerala's main Christian area is in the central part of the state, around Kochi and Kottayam.

Hindus are mainly concentrated in southern Kerala, around Thiruvananthapuram, though Muslims are also a prominent and vocal component of the population as their reaction to the events in Ayodhya (Uttar Pradesh) have shown. The main Muslim area is in the northern part of the state, particularly around Kozhikode (Calicut).

The diminishing Jewish population of Kerala also made a very early appearance on the subcontinent. The 'black Jews' are said to have fled here in 587 BC when Jerusalem was occupied by Nebuchadnezzar. Their descendants have now intermarried with the Hindu population, but there is still a very small number of the later 'white Jews' in Kochi.

Name Changes

A number of towns and districts have been stripped of anglicised names and given new Malayam names, which can be confusing. The major places affected include:

Old Name	New Name
Alleppey	Alappuzha
Calicut	Kozhikode
Cannanore	Kannur
Changanacherry	Changanassery
Cochin	Kochi
Palghat	Palakkad
Quilon	Kollam
Sultan's Battery	Suthanbatheri
Tellicherry	Thalasseri
Trichur	Thrissur
Trivandrum	Thiruvananthapuram

MAHÉ

Mahé, 60 km north of Kozhikode (Calicut), was a small French dependency handed over to India at the same time as Pondicherry, and is still part of the Union Territory of Pondicherry. Like Karaikal and Yanam on the east coast of India, there's little French influence left here today and its main function seems to be supplying passing truck drivers with cheap Pondicherry beer.

The English factory established here in 1683 by the Surat presidency to purchase pepper and cardamom was the first permanent English factory on the Malabar coast. The East India Company also had a fort here in 1708.

Places to Stay & Eat

It's actually far more pleasant to stay at Thalasseri (Tellicherry), eight km north. However, if you want to stay in Mahé, the *Government Tourist Home*, near Tagore Park about one km from the bus stand, is one of the cheapest at Rs 12/20 for singles/doubles, although you'll have trouble getting a room if there is a government delegation in the area.

More expensive is the *Hotel Arena* (☎ 2421), Maidan Rd, which has ordinary singles/doubles for Rs 50/80 and air-con doubles for Rs 120. There's an attached restaurant serving south Indian, Chinese and Continental food. The *Rivera Tourist Home* by the river has also been recommended. The rooms overlooking the river are good, but others are by the road and they're noisy. The hotel's *Rainbow Restaurant* has passable food.

Getting There & Away

Mahé is too small to warrant a bus station. Instead, buses stop on the northern side of the bridge, outside the Rivera Tourist Home.

There are regular buses to Mangalore and Kozhikode (Calicut).

THALASSERI (Tellicherry)

Thalasseri is a typical Keralan fishing village (and smells like it) right off the tourist circuit. Perhaps its biggest claim to fame is as the home town of many Indian circus performers. It's certainly not worth a special detour but, if you are making your way along the coast, it's a pleasant, unhurried place to stop for a night. Tourists are definitely a rare breed here.

The town's fishing fleet returns in the late afternoon, and the beach becomes an animated impromptu fish market as people haggle over the catch.

Places to Stay & Eat

The cheapest places to stay are the *Chattanchal Tourist Home* (☎ 22-967), Convet Rd; *Brothers Tourist Home* (☎ 21-558), *Minerva Tourist Home* (☎ 21-731), Logans Rd; and the *Impala Tourist Home* (☎ 20-484), Narangapuram. All of these places offer singles/doubles for Rs 20/35 to Rs 35/50.

Avoid the *Mayflower Lodge* just outside the bus station. It's cheap but damp and dirty and the water supply is erratic.

Better is the *Hotel Pranam* (☎ 20-634), Narangapuram, which has ordinary singles/doubles for Rs 44/77 and air-con doubles at Rs 184. There's an attached restaurant serving South Indian, Chinese and Continental meals. Similar is the *Paris Lodging House* (☎ 20-666), Logan's Rd, which has ordinary singles/doubles at Rs 35/53 or Rs 120/150 with air-con. There's an attached restaurant serving south Indian food.

The *Hotel New West End* in the busy main shopping square has good non-vegetarian food – their fish curry is excellent. Also in the square, the *Lazza Ice Cream* shop has a variety of food, including delicious kulfi.

Getting There & Away

Frequent trains and buses head up the coast to Mangalore and south to Kozhikode and Kochi.

KOZHIKODE (Calicut)

Population: 801,000

Vasco da Gama landed at Calicut in 1498, becoming the first European to reach India via the sea route around the southern cape of Africa. His arrival heralded the period of Portuguese supremacy in India. The history of Calicut after 1498 was certainly dramatic. The Portuguese attempted to conquer the town, a centre of Malabar power under the Zamorins or Lords of the Sea, but their attacks in 1509 and 1510 were both repulsed, although the town was virtually destroyed in the latter assault. Tipu Sultan laid the whole region to waste in 1789, and British rule was established in 1792.

Despite its colourful past, there is little of interest for a noncommercial visitor, though it does have a not very attractive beach some two km from the centre of town. Five km from town at East Hill is the **Pazhassirajah Museum**, an archaeological museum with copies of ancient mural paintings, bronzes and old coins as well as models of temples and megalithic monuments. It's open daily except Monday from 10 am to 5 pm. Next door to it is the **Krishnamenon Museum**, which houses paintings of Raja Ravi Varma and Raja Raja Varma as well as memorabilia of a former president of India. It's open daily except Monday and Wednesday morning from 10 am to 5 pm.

Information

The State Bank of India is on Bank Rd.

Places to Stay – bottom end

There are well over a dozen budget hotels to choose from in Kozhikode. Among those closest to the bus station are the *Metro Tourist Home* (☎ 50-029), Mavoor Rd, which has ordinary singles/doubles at Rs 38/60 or doubles with air-con for Rs 172, and the *Hotel Sajina* (☎ 76-146), Mavoor Rd, which has ordinary singles/doubles for Rs 33/54 and doubles with air-con for Rs 132. The latter has an attached restaurant serving south Indian food.

Slightly more expensive is the *Laxmi Bhavan Tourist Home* (☎ 63-927), G H Rd, which has ordinary doubles at Rs 70 and air-con doubles at Rs 125. The Laxmi has an attached bar and restaurant with south Indian cuisine.

Further afield, about two km from the railway station and one km from the bus station, are the *Hotel Maharani* (☎ 76-161), Taluk Rd, which has singles/doubles for Rs 45/86 or Rs 200/250 with air-con, and the *Hotel Malabar Mansion* (☎ 76-101), S M St, which has singles/doubles from Rs 50/75 or suites with air-con for Rs 275. Both hotels have an attached restaurant with south Indian, Chinese and Continental food. The Maharani also has a bar.

Places to Stay – middle & top end
The *Kalpaka Tourist Home* (☎ 76-171), on Town Hall Rd close to the railway station and about two km from the bus station, is good value in this category. It has ordinary singles/doubles for Rs 83/138 and air-con doubles for Rs 248. There's an attached restaurant serving south Indian food and all major credit cards are accepted.

More expensive is the two-star *Paramount Tower* (☎ 62-731), Town Hall Rd, which has ordinary singles/doubles for Rs 90/150 or Rs 140/200 with air-con. There's an attached restaurant serving south Indian, Chinese and Continental food and credit cards are accepted. It's Muslim-owned and therefore 'dry' though the waiters will go out for beer and bring it back swathed in napkins so that it looks like soft drink.

Top of the line is the *Sea Queen Hotel* (☎ 58-504), Beach Rd, about one km from the railway and bus stations, which has singles/doubles at Rs 120/150 or Rs 180/235 with air-con. There's an attached bar and restaurant which serves some of the best seafood in town.

Places to Eat
If you're not eating in your hotel (where there's a restaurant), the *Ruchi Restaurant* in the Hotel Foura on Mavoor Rd does a terrific vegetarian thali for Rs 10 which includes a sweet, three vegetable curries, curd and papadams. Next door to the Foura, the *Hotel Sarovar* serves very mediocre non-veg food.

The *Hotel Sea Shell* is a small restaurant in the bazaar area, tucked away at the top of a stairway near the Cosmopolitan Lodge. It serves good non-vegetarian food, including an excellent fish korma.

On Bank Rd, opposite the tank, the pleasant open-air *Park Restaurant* is open in the evenings, when this area is lively with buskers and other footpath entertainers.

Getting There & Away
Air The Indian Airlines office (☎ 65-482) is in the Eroth Centre on Bank Rd, close to the junction with Mavoor Rd (also known as Indira Gandhi Rd). For flights on East West Airlines call 64-883.

Indian Airlines and East West Airlines fly to and from Bombay daily (US$98).

Bus The main bus station is on Mavoor Rd, a few minutes walk from Bank Rd. The timetable is in English and there are regular departures to Bangalore, Mangalore, Mysore, Ooty, Madurai, Coimbatore, Pondicherry, Thiruvananthapuram (Trivandrum), Alappuzha (Alleppey), Kochi (Cochin) and Kottayam.

The bus to Ooty or Mysore climbs up and over the Western Ghats. Sit on the left for the best views of this spectacular scenery. The trip to Mysore takes 5½ hours.

Train The railway station is not far from the town centre and within walking distance of the bazaar area. It costs about Rs 5 by auto-rickshaw from the bus station and the hotels in the Bank Rd area.

Regular trains go north to Mangalore. It's a 222-km journey which takes three hours and costs Rs 48/175 in 2nd/1st class. Heading south-east, there are trains via Palakkad (Palghat) to Coimbatore, Bangalore, Madras and Delhi. Following the coast due south, it's five hours and 200 km south to Ernakulam at a cost of Rs 42/156 in 2nd/1st class. The 414-km trip to Thiruvananthapuram (Trivandrum) takes 10 hours and costs Rs 80/289 in 2nd/1st class.

Getting Around
There's no shortage of auto-rickshaws in Kozhikode, but it is difficult to get the drivers to use the meters. It should only cost about Rs 5 from the railway station to the bus station or hotels on Bank Rd.

Left: Tikka powder seller, Devaraja market, Mysore, Karnataka (MH)
Right: Kovalam boy carrying his catch from boat to the beach, Kerala (MH)
Bottom: Hero bicycles, Mysore, Karnataka (MH)

Top: Kerala backwaters (HF)
Middle: Kovalam beach, Kerala (HF)
Bottom: Rockbusters, Kovalam, Kerala (HF)

THRISSUR (Trichur)

Thrissur, 74 km north of Ernakulam, has the old **Temple of Guruvayur** (Hindus only), a museum and a zoo with a notable collection of snakes. The annual **Pooram Festival**, held in April-May, is one of the biggest in the south, with fireworks and colourful processions, including brightly decorated elephants. This festival was first introduced by Sakthan Thampuram, the maharaja of the former state of Kochi (Cochin).

Places to Stay & Eat

Rock-bottom places close to the bus and railway stations include the *Jaya Lodge* (☎ 23-258), Kurrupam Rd, the *Shanti Tourist Home* (☎ 25-418), and *Chandy's Tourist Home* (☎ 21-167), Station Rd. All of these have singles/doubles for around Rs 25/45.

More expensive is the *Hotel Suria International* (☎ 24-774), Kokkalai, which has singles/doubles for Rs 40/75, or Rs 125/145 with air-con. The hotel has its own bar and restaurant. Similar is the *Hotel Luciya Palace* (☎ 24-731), Marar Rd, which has ordinary singles/doubles for Rs 60/100 and Rs 150/200 with air-con. There's a bar and restaurant.

Top of the line is the *Casino Hotel* (☎ 24-699), T B Rd close to the bus and railway stations, which has ordinary singles/doubles for Rs 150/175, and Rs 275/300 with air-con. There's a bar and restaurant, swimming pool and bookshop, and credit cards are accepted.

KOCHI (Cochin) & ERNAKULAM

Kochi population: 582,000
Ernakulam population: 200,000

With its wealth of historical associations and its beautiful setting on a cluster of islands and narrow peninsulas, the interesting city of Kochi reflects the eclecticism of Kerala perfectly. Here, you can see the oldest church in India, winding streets crammed with 500-year-old Portuguese houses, cantilevered Chinese fishing nets, a Jewish community whose roots go back to the Diaspora, a 16th-century synagogue, a palace built by the Portuguese and given to the Raja of Cochin (later renovated by the Dutch, it contains some of India's most beautiful murals) and several places where you can see a performance of the world-famous Kathakali dance-drama.

The older parts of Fort Cochin and Mattancherry are an unlikely blend of medieval Portugal, Holland and an English country village grafted onto the tropical Malabar coast – a radical contrast to the bright lights, bustle and big hotels of mainland Ernakulam.

Kochi is also one of India's largest ports and a major naval base. On any day of the year, the misty silhouettes of huge merchant ships can be seen anchored off the point of Fort Cochin, waiting for a berth in the docks of Ernakulam or Willingdon Island. This artificial island, created with material dredged up when the harbour was deepened, also provides a site for the airport.

Orientation

Kochi consists of mainland Ernakulam, the islands of Willingdon, Bolgatty and Gundu in the harbour, Fort Cochin and Mattancherry on the southern peninsula, and Vypeen Island north of Fort Cochin, all linked by ferry. In addition, there are bridges and a road connecting Ernakulam with Willingdon Island and the Fort Cochin/Mattancherry peninsula. The railway and bus stations, Tourist Reception Centre and most hotels and restaurants are in Ernakulam.

Almost all the historical sites are in Fort Cochin or Mattancherry, but the area's accommodation and restaurant facilities are limited to a few budget-type hotels. The airport is on Willingdon Island. At the tip of the island, opposite Fort Cochin, is the ITDC tourist office and Kochi's top hotels, the Malabar and the Casino.

Information

Tourist Offices The Tourist Reception Centre (☎ 35-3234) on Shanmugham Rd in Ernakulam has friendly, helpful staff but not much literature. They'll organise accommodation for you at the Bolgatty Palace Hotel

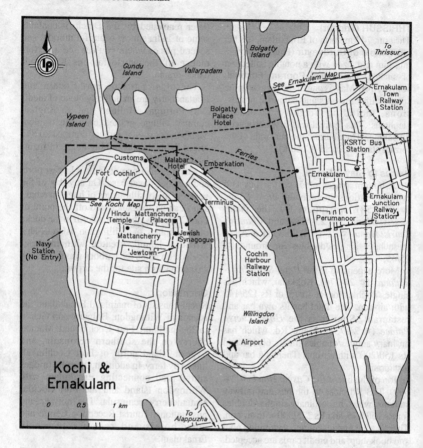

Kochi &
Ernakulam

and arrange conducted boat cruises around the harbour. The office is open from 8 am to 6 pm.

The Government of Kerala tourist information centre is in the old collectorate building on Park Rd. It has a useful booklet entitled *Kerala – Travel Facts*, compiled by the Department of Tourism.

The Government of India tourist office (ITDC) (☎ 34-0352) is next to the Malabar Hotel on Willingdon Island. The people here are friendly and helpful and offer a range of leaflets and maps.

Tourist Desk operates a free service counter at the main ferry station, Ernakulam, which is open daily from 9 am to 5 pm. They also have an information counter at the Junction Railway Station at Ernakulam, and publish a series of handbooks for tourists.

Post & Telecommunications The GPO (including poste restante) is at Fort Cochin but you can have mail sent to the main post office in Ernakulam, as long as it's specifically addressed to that office. The Ernakulam Telegraph Office is at the junction of Broadway and Canon Shed Rd. It's open 24 hours a day and international calls are connected fairly quickly.

Kochi's telephone area code is 0484.

Visa Extensions You can apply for these at the office of the Commissioner of Police, at the northern end of Shanmugham Rd, Ernakulam, but they can take up to 10 days to issue and you have to leave your passport at the office during that time.

Bookshop Bhavi Books on Convent Rd, Ernakulam, is an excellent bookshop.

Fort Cochin

St Francis Church This is India's oldest European-built church. Vasco da Gama, the first European to reach India by sailing around Africa, died in Cochin in 1524 and was buried here for 14 years before his remains were transferred to Lisbon in Portugal. His tombstone still stands.

The church was built in 1503 by Portuguese Franciscan friars who accompanied the expedition led by Pedro Alvarez Cabral. The original structure was wood, but the church was rebuilt in stone around the mid-16th century – the earliest Portuguese inscription found in the church is dated 1562. In 1663, the Protestant Dutch captured Kochi and restored the church in 1779. After the occupation of Kochi by the British in 1795, it became an Anglican church and, at present, it is used by the Church of South India.

Also in Fort Cochin is the much later **Santa Cruz Basilica**, which is worth a visit.

Chinese Fishing Nets Strung out along the tip of Fort Cochin opposite Vypeen Island, these cantilevered fishing nets were introduced by traders from the court of Kublai Khan. You can also see them along the backwaters between Kochi and Kottayam, and between Alappuzha (Alleppey) and Kollam (Quilon). They're mainly used at high tide.

Mattancherry

Mattancherry Palace The palace was built by the Portuguese in 1557 and presented to the Cochin raja, Veera Kerala Varma (1537-61), as a gesture of goodwill (and, probably, as a means of securing trading privileges). It was substantially renovated by the Dutch after 1663, hence its other name, the 'Dutch Palace'. The double-storey quadrangular building surrounds a courtyard containing a Hindu temple. The central hall on the first floor was the Coronation Hall of the rajas of Cochin; on display are their dresses, turbans and palanquins.

The most important feature of this palace, however, is the astonishing **murals** in the bedchambers and other rooms, which depict scenes from the *Ramayana, Mahabharata* and Puranic legends connected with Siva, Vishnu, Krishna, Kumara and Durga. These murals are undoubtedly some of the most beautiful and extensive to be seen anywhere in India. You can pick up numerous Indian tourist pamphlets containing breathless descriptions of the murals at Ajanta but never see a mention of these, although they are one of the wonders of India. The Siva temple in Ettumanur (a few km north of Kottayam) has similar murals.

The palace is open daily except Friday and national holidays from 10 am to 5 pm. Entrance is free. Flash photography is prohibited, effectively precluding photography altogether, which is a great pity as there are no books or postcards for sale. If you haven't got a tripod, the murals can be photographed quite well by holding your camera on the railing, wrote one visitor. There are three black-&-white photographs of the murals in the Archaeological Survey of India's booklet, *Monuments of Kerala* by H Sarkar (1978, Rs 3.25). Other books in which they're illustrated are *Cochin Murals* by V R Chitra & T N Srinivasan (Cochin, 1940), and *South Indian Paintings* by C Sivaramamurti (New Delhi, 1968).

Jewish Synagogue Constructed in 1568, this is the oldest synagogue in the Commonwealth. An earlier one, built at Kochangadi in 1344, has since disappeared, although a stone slab from this earlier building,

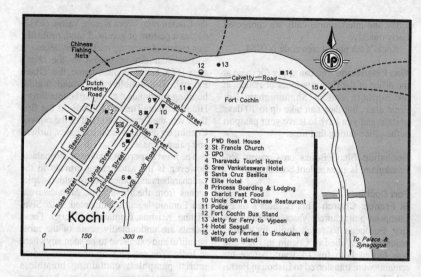

Chinese Fishing Nets

Dutch Cemetery Road

Beach Road

Quiros Street

Rose Street

Princess Street

KB Jacob Road

Bastian Street

Burgher Street

Calvetty Road

Fort Cochin

Kochi

0   150   300 m

1 PWD Rest House
2 St Francis Church
3 GPO
4 Tharavadu Tourist Home
5 Sree Venkateswara Hotel
6 Santa Cruz Basilica
7 Elite Hotel
8 Princess Boarding & Lodging
9 Chariot Fast Food
10 Uncle Sam's Chinese Restaurant
11 Police
12 Fort Cochin Bus Stand
13 Jetty for Ferry to Vypeen
14 Hotel Seagull
15 Jetty for Ferries to Ernakulam & Willingdon Island

To Palace & Synagogue

inscribed in Hebrew, can be found on the inner surface of the wall which surrounds the current synagogue.

The original building was destroyed by shelling during a Portuguese raid in 1662 and was rebuilt two years later when the Dutch took over Kochi. It's an interesting little place with hand-painted, willow-pattern floor tiles (no two alike) brought from Canton, China, in the mid-18th century by Ezekial Rahabi who had trading interests in that city. He was also responsible for the erection of the clock tower which tops the building.

The synagogue is open daily from 10 am to noon and from 3 to 5 pm, except Saturdays and Jewish holidays. Entrance is Rs 0.50. The synagogue guardian is very friendly and keen to tell you about the history of the place and the Jewish community here, and to talk about what's happening in the rest of the world. He speaks fluent English.

This unexpected and isolated Jewish community dates back to the time of St Thomas the Apostle's voyage to India in AD 52. The first Jewish settlement was at Kodungallur (Cranganore), north of Kochi (Cochin). Like the Syrian Orthodox Christians, the Jews

became involved in the trade and commerce of the Malabar coast. Preserved in the synagogue are a number of copper plates inscribed, in an ancient script, with the grant of the village of Anjuvannam (near Kodungallur) and its revenue to a Jewish merchant, Joseph Rabban, by King Bhaskara Ravi Varman I (962-1020). You may view these plates with the permission of the synagogue guardian.

The concessions given by Ravi Varman I included permission to use a palanquin and parasol – in those days the prerogative of rulers – and so, in effect, sanctioned the creation of a tiny Jewish kingdom. On Rabban's death, his sons fought each other for control of the 'kingdom' and this rivalry led to its break-up and the move to Mattancherry.

A lot of research has been done into this community. One particularly interesting study by an American professor of ethnomusicology found that the music of the Cochin Jews contained strong Babylonian influences and that their version of the Ten Commandments was almost identical to a Kurdish version housed in the Berlin Museum Archives. Naturally, there's also been much local influence and many of the hymns are similar to ragas.

The area around the synagogue is known as Jewtown and is one of the centres of the Kochi spice trade. Scores of small firms huddle together in old, dilapidated buildings and the air is filled with the pungent aromas of ginger, cardamom, cumin, tumeric and cloves. Many Jewish names are visible on business premises and houses, but the community has diminished rapidly since Indian independence and now numbers less than 30. As there has been no rabbi within living memory, all the elders are qualified to perform religious ceremonies and marriages. There are many interesting curio shops on the street leading up to the synagogue.

Ernakulam & Bolgatty Island

Kathakali Dancing The origins of India's most spectacular dance-drama go back some 500 years to a time when open-air performances were held in a temple courtyard or on the village green. There are over 100 different arrangements, all of them based on stories from the *Ramayana* and *Mahabharata*, those two epics of Indian mythology, and they were designed to continue well into the early hours of the morning. Since most visitors don't have the inclination to stay up all night, the centres which put on the dance in Ernakulam offer shortened versions lasting about 1½ hours.

Kathakali isn't simply another form of dancing – it incorporates elements of yoga and ayurvedic (traditional Indian) medicine. All the props are fashioned from natural materials – powdered minerals and the sap of certain trees for the bright facial make-up; the beaten bark of certain trees, dyed with fruits and spices, for wigs; coconut oil for mixing up the colours; burnt coconut oil for the black paint around the eyes; and eggplant flowers tucked under the eyelids to turn the whites of the eyes deep red. Usually, you're welcome to watch the make-up process before the dance – quite a show in its own right. The dancers are accompanied by two drummers and a harmonium player. A government-run school, near Palakkad (Palghat)

in northern Kerala, teaches Kathakali dancing.

All the places which put on performances start the evening with an explanation of the symbolism of the facial expressions, hand movements and ritualistic gestures involved in the dance-drama. This is followed by an actual dance-drama lasting about one hour. The centres offering Kathakali are:

Indian Performing Arts Centre, Shaunmughan Rd – Under the auspices of Kerala Kalabhavanam, a nightly Kathakali performance (Rs 50) is held from 6.30 pm. The Kerala Kalabhavanam society also conducts training in Kathakali and other classical Hindu arts. Enquiries can be made to the secretary, Jaya Prakash Narayanan, Northgate, Vaikom (☎ (0489) 2549).

Cochin Cultural Centre (☎ 35-4162, 36-7866), 'Souhardham', Manikath Rd – Entry to the daily performances, which run from 6.30 to 8 pm, is Rs 50. Make-up (which you are welcome to attend) starts at 4 pm. Advance booking is not required. The dance is held in a specially constructed theatre designed to resemble a temple courtyard and it's air-conditioned. They also offer ayurvedic oil massages between 8 am and 6 pm.

Devan Gurukalum, in Kalathiparambil Lane near the Piazza Lodge – This centre is at Mr Devan's home and he gives an amusing preshow chat on dance history and a somewhat simplistic explanation of Hinduism. The shows last from 7 to 8.30 pm but you should get there by 6 pm if you want to see the make-up routine. Entry costs Rs 25.

Parishath Thampuram Museum

This museum is housed in what was previously Durbar Hall on Durbar Hall Rd – an enormous building constructed in traditional Keralan style. Although it contains collections of 19th-century oil paintings, old coins, sculptures and Moghul paintings as well as exhibits from the Cochin royal family, it's hardly anything special. The museum is open daily, except Mondays and public holidays, from 9.30 am to 12.30 pm and 3 to 5.30 pm. Entry is free.

Gundu Island

The smallest island in Kochi harbour, Gundu Island is close to Vypeen Island. The only building on the island is a coir factory, where

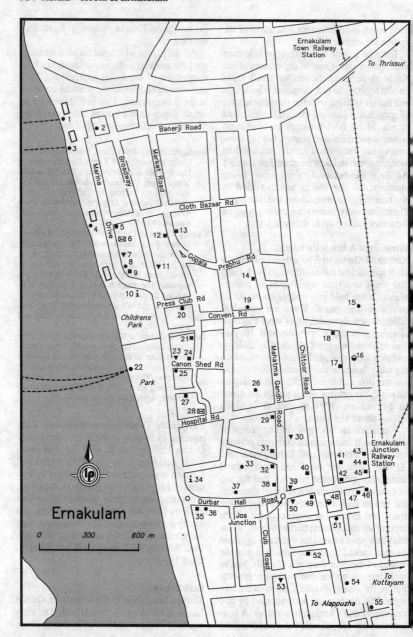

Ernakulam Town Railway Station

To Thrissur

Banerji Road

Market Road

Broadway

Marine Drive

Cloth Bazaar Rd

Gopala

Prabhu Rd

Press Club Rd

Childrens Park

Convent Rd

Canon Shed Rd

Park

Mahatma Gandhi Road

Chittoor Road

Hospital Rd

Ernakulam Junction Railway Station

Durbar Hall Road

Jos Junction

Club Road

To Kottayam

To Alappuzha

Ernakulam

0   300   600 m

PLACES TO STAY

5	Sealord Hotel
9	Hakoba Hotel
12	Blue Diamond Hotel
13	Modern Guest House
14	Hotel Abad Plaza & Regency Restaurant
17	Ninan's Tourist Lodge
18	Hotel Luciya
20	Basoto Lodge
21	Deepak Lodge
24	Biju's Tourist Home
27	Maple Tourist Home
29	Grand Hotel
31	Woodlands Hotel & Jaya Cafe
32	Geetha Lodge
35	Bharat Tourist Home
38	Anantha Bhavan Lodge
40	Hotel Sangeetha
41	Paulson Park Hotel
42	Shaziya Hotel
43	Ernakulam Tourist Bungalow
44	Hotel KK International
45	Premier Tourist Home
46	Central Lodge
47	Piazza Lodge
49	Hotel Joylands
52	Hotel Excellency

▼ PLACES TO EAT

7	Athul Jyoti Restaurant
11	Chick-Chow Restaurant
23	Indian Coffee House
30	Pandal Restaurant
39	Indian Coffee House
50	Bimbi's & Khyber Restaurant
53	Chinese Garden Restaurant

OTHER

1	High Court Jetty & Ferry to Bolgatty
2	Commissioner of Police
3	Vypeen Island Ferry Jetty
4	Sealord Jetty
6	Post Office
8	State Bank of India
10	KTDC Tourist Reception Centre
15	Stadium
16	State Bus Stand
19	Bhavi Books
22	Jetty for Ferries to Willingdon Island & Fort Cochin
25	Telegraph Office
26	Playing Fields
28	GPO
33	Shiva Temple
34	Kerala Tourist Information Centre
36	Indian Airlines
37	Parishath Thampuram Museum
48	Bus to Fort Cochin
51	Devan Gurukalum
54	Art Kerala
55	Cochin Cultural Centre

attractive doormats are made out of coconut fibre. You come across these mats all over Kochi. The only way to get there is on the Kerala Tourist Development Corporation boat tour.

Organised Tours

The Kerala Tourist Development Corporation's daily conducted boat cruises around Kochi harbour visit Willingdon Island, Mattancherry Palace, the Jewish Synagogue, Fort Cochin (including St Francis Church), Gundu Island, the Chinese fishing nets and Bolgatty Island. The first tour runs from 9 am to 12.30 pm, and the second from 2 to 5.30 pm. This very worthwhile 3½-hour tour costs Rs 30.

Also scheduled is a daily Kochi Sunset Cruise from 5.30 to 7 pm for Rs 25, but this is frequently cancelled so you need to check this out early in the day to avoid disappointment. If it is cancelled, try *Princy Tours*, in the GCDA Complex opposite the Sealord Hotel in Ernakulam, who operate the same tour, also for Rs 25.

For reservations on the KTDC cruises, contact either the Tourist Reception Centre (☎ 35-3234), Shaunmughan Rd, Ernakulam, or the manager, Bolgatty Palace Hotel (☎ 35-5003), Bolgatty Island. The tour starts and finishes at the Sealord boat jetty in front of the Sealord Hotel, Shanmugham Rd, Ernakulam. You can also board the boat at the tourist office jetty at Willingdon Island, 20 minutes after the start of each tour.

Places to Stay

The top-range hotels are in Ernakulam and

on Willingdon Island. You'll find mid-range hotels at Ernakulam and Bolgatty Island. Budget hotels can be found only in Ernakulam and Fort Cochin, although the choice is better in Ernakulam.

Places to Stay – bottom end

Fort Cochin This is definitely the most romantic place to stay and well worth the extra effort getting there. The choice of places to stay has improved considerably over the last few years but it's still almost exclusively budget accommodation.

By far the best place to stay is the recently opened *Tharavadu Tourist Home* (☎ 22-6897), Quiros St, behind the GPO. This airy and spacious hotel has been created by converting a traditional house and it's run by a very friendly local man. The top room (Rs 100 a double) is perhaps the best but involves sharing a bathroom. Other rooms here cost Rs 78/120 a single/double with own bathroom. It's very peaceful and there's a rooftop area with good views over the surrounding streets.

Almost all the other budget places to stay are on Princess St. The friendly *Elite Hotel* (☎ 25-733) is an old-time favourite and has singles/doubles with common bathroom for Rs 15/35 and doubles with own bathroom for Rs 45. The popular non-vegetarian cafe on the ground floor is excellent value. Even more basic than this place is the *Sree Venkateswara Hotel* at a similar price, though none of the rooms have their own bathroom. Diagonally opposite the Elite is the *Princess Boarding & Lodging* which is a little more upmarket but somewhat featureless, plus there's a sign saying 'No alcohol'. It costs Rs 40 for a double with common bathroom and Rs 80 a double with own bathroom.

There's also the shabby *PWD Rest House* but, although it's cheap, it's a dump and often full for some strange reason.

Ernakulam The *Basoto Lodge* (☎ 35-2140) on Press Club Rd is one of the best budget hotels in Ernakulam. This small, simple,

friendly place is popular with travellers, so get there early. Rooms with common bathroom cost Rs 20, and with own bathroom, Rs 50. Mosquito nets are provided. Another good cheapie is *Deepak Lodge* (☎ 35-3882) on Market Rd. Although the rooms are painted a sickly shade of green, they are large and quiet and cost Rs 25 a single with common bathroom or Rs 28/55 for singles/doubles with attached bathroom.

Close to the market area is the *Modern Guest House* (☎ 35-2130) on Market Rd. It has good singles/doubles for Rs 40/71 with bathroom. The *Hakoba Hotel* (☎ 35-3933) is conveniently located on the busy waterfront road, Shanmugham Rd. It's a good place to stay and not too big, although the views have been spoilt by a huge concrete monstrosity across the road. Rooms cost Rs 45/82 with attached bathroom plus there are more expensive air-con rooms. The hotel has a restaurant, bar and even a (not very reliable) lift.

Further afield and close to the railway station but almost always full is the *Shaziya Hotel* (☎ 36-9508), which is excellent value at Rs 45/85 for singles/doubles with attached bathroom. Right opposite the railway station are the *Premier Tourist Home* (☎ 36-8125) with single/doubles at Rs 32/54 with attached bathroom, the *Ernakulam Tourist Bungalow* (☎ 35-2412), which is clean and friendly and has singles/doubles with attached bathroom for Rs 38/68, and the *Hotel KK International* (☎ 36-6010), a large place with singles/doubles at Rs 50/90, plus air-con rooms at Rs 110/150. Mosquito coils are available at reception for Rs 2.

The only budget hotel close to the state bus stand is *Ninans Tourist Lodge* (☎ 35-1235), but it's a dreadful place, dirty and depressing and you'd have to be desperate to stay here. It's also outrageously priced at Rs 45 a double for what is essentially a pigsty.

Excellent value at the top end of this category is *Biju's Tourist Home* (☎ 36-9881) close to the junction of Canon Shed Rd and Market Rd. This is a very friendly place and has singles/doubles with attached bathroom at Rs 50/95 as well as air-con doubles at Rs

190. There's hot and cold running water and TVs can be rented.

Close by, only recently opened, and very good value is *Maple Tourist Home* (☎ 35-5156), XL/1271 Canon Shed Rd (actually between Canon Shed Rd and Hospital Rd), which has ordinary rooms for Rs 75/100, deluxe rooms for Rs 120/140, and air-con doubles for Rs 165. Mosquito nets are provided, long-distance/ISD facilities are available and there's a roof garden facing the main boat jetty.

Places to Stay – middle

Fort Cochin Right on the waterfront overlooking the harbour, the *Hotel Seagull* (☎ 22-8128), Calvetty Rd, is about halfway between the two ferry stops and the only mid-range hotel in this part of the city. The hotel has been created by converting a number of old houses and warehouses. Doubles (there are no singles) cost Rs 100, Rs 175 with air-con. The hotel has a bar and a restaurant from which you can watch the ships come and go.

Bolgatty Island Despite being somewhat run down, the *Bolgatty Palace Hotel* (☎ 35-5003) on Bolgatty Island is spacious and full of character though some of the rooms don't even have windows which look out onto the harbour and gardens (a ridiculous oversight on behalf of those who converted it into a hotel!). Formerly a palace built by the Dutch in 1744, and later a British Residency, the hotel is now run by the Kerala Tourist Development Corporation. It's set in six hectares of lush, green lawns with a golf course and bar, and a restaurant with enthusiastic staff but very slow service.

All 11 rooms are different and cost from Rs 165/220 for singles/doubles (Rs 220/275 for the suite rooms) to Rs 330/385 for an air-con cottage to Rs 385 for an air-con 'honeymoon' cottage and Rs 660 for a double air-con suite. The 'honeymoon' cottages are separate and right on the water's edge. Credit cards are accepted. Checkout time here is noon (which is unusual for Kerala).

If you want to stay here, make enquiries first at the Tourist Reception Centre, Shanmugham Rd, otherwise you'll waste a lot of time if it's full. A regular ferry (Rs 0.20) leaves the High Court Jetty every 20 minutes between 6 am and 10 pm but, if you want to get across at any other time, private launches are available for Rs 15 per person (or, sometimes, Rs 15 for the launch).

Ernakulam One of the cheapest places in this range is the *Blue Diamond Hotel* (☎ 35-3221), Market Rd, which is a pleasant place to stay and has singles/doubles at Rs 70/150, and air-con doubles at Rs 200. Similar is the *Hotel Sangeetha* (☎ 36-8736), Chittoor Rd, which has singles/doubles for Rs 65/120 and deluxe singles/doubles for Rs 120/180. The price includes breakfast. The hotel has its own vegetarian restaurant serving south Indian, tandoori and Chinese food.

Another hotel in this same range but further afield is the *Bharat Tourist Home* (☎ 35-3501) on Durbar Hall Rd.

Very close to the state bus stand is the *Hotel Luciya* (☎ 35-4433) which is very good value, pleasant and friendly. Singles/doubles cost just Rs 40/75 plus there are air-con singles/doubles for Rs 100/180. Facilities include a bar and restaurant, TV lounge and laundry service.

Going up in price but fantastic value is the brand new three-star *Hotel Excellency* (☎ 36-4520), Nettipadam Rd not far from Jos Junction. It has a superb range of facilities yet costs just Rs 85/110 for singles/doubles and Rs 190/230 for air-con rooms. The price includes bed tea. The hotel has its own restaurant serving Indian, tandoori and Chinese food and credit cards are accepted.

Also excellent value is the *Paulson Park Hotel* (☎ 35-4002), close to the railway station. This is another brand new hotel, and it offers singles/doubles at Rs 80/120, or Rs 190/300 with air-con. All the air-con rooms have a TV and fridge.

Down on M G Rd, the *Hotel Seaking* (☎ 35-5341) is a good choice with single/double/triple air-con suites at Rs 150/250/300. There are also less expensive non-air-con rooms. There are two restaurants, one serving Chinese food and the other south Indian food, and there's also a bar.

Somewhat cheaper is the older but well-appointed *Woodlands Hotel* (☎ 35-1372), M G Rd near Jos Junction. Facilities include a vegetarian restaurant and roof garden and all the rooms have a colour TV and hot water. Singles/doubles are Rs 110/165, or Rs 185/230 with air-con.

Places to Stay – top end
Willingdon Island Kochi's best hotel is the five-star *Malabar Hotel* (☎ 34-0010), part of the Taj Group of hotels. It's superbly located at the tip of Willingdon Island, overlooking the harbour and has the full range of facilities which you'd expect in this price range, including a swimming pool. Standard rooms cost US$75/85 for singles/doubles and US$90/95 for superior rooms plus there are more expensive suites.

Close by is the three-star *Casino Hotel* (☎ 34-0221) which also has an excellent range of facilities including a swimming pool and multi-cuisine restaurant, but is cheaper at Rs 575/775 for air-con singles/doubles.

Ernakulam Excellent value in this bracket is the *Sealord Hotel* (☎ 35-2682), Shanmugham Rd, although the views of the harbour which it used to enjoy have been blocked by the shopping complex across the road; the only clear view you'll get is from the rooftop restaurant. The rooms are very pleasantly furnished and the hotel is centrally air-conditioned. Ordinary singles/doubles cost Rs 220/300 and there are deluxe rooms for Rs 350/450. Other than the rooftop restaurant (Chinese cuisine), there's a bar and another restaurant (Indian and Continental dishes) with a resident live band. Credit cards are accepted and checkout time is noon.

The elegant and very spacious *Grand Hotel* (☎ 35-3211), M G Rd, has a similar range of services including what it describes as a 'fully illuminated lawn with fresh air'! Singles/doubles cost Rs 150/175, and stan-

dard air-con rooms, Rs 190/225. There are also more expensive suites at Rs 425 and 500. The hotel has two restaurants, credit cards are accepted and checkout time is 24 hours after check-in.

Lastly, there's the *Hotel Joyland* (☎ 36-7764), D H Rd, not far from the railway station. This is a brand new hotel and very well appointed. Singles/doubles are Rs 225/275, or Rs 300/350 with air-con. There are also more expensive deluxe rooms. The hotel has a rooftop restaurant serving Indian, Chinese and Continental food. Checkout is 24 hours.

Places to Eat
Fort Cochin The eating options in Fort Cochin are severely limited. One of the cheapest places is the restaurant in the *Elite Hotel*, Princess St, which offers good non-vegetarian meals including fish curries at around Rs 10.

At the end of this same street is the popular *Uncle Sam's Chinese Restaurant.* It's only open in the evenings and is a modest splurge. Right opposite Uncle Sam's is the open-air *Chariot Fast Food*. This is open all day and does a range of Indian and Western snacks (including breakfasts). It's a very pleasant place to sit around with a cold drink or two in the heat of the day and watch the world go by. The only bar in this area is that at the *Hotel Seagull* on Calvetty Rd. There's also a reasonable restaurant at this mid-range hotel.

In the Mattancherry Palace area, *Cool of Cools* serves great fresh fruit juices for just a few rupees.

Willingdon Island The plush *Rice Boats* restaurant in the Malabar Hotel has a lunchtime buffet from noon to 3 pm. You can pig out for Rs 100, but think twice before ordering a beer as they're expensive.

Ernakulam As is usual in Keralan towns, an *Indian Coffee House* offers good snacks and breakfasts. There are two in Ernakulam, one not far from the railway station and the other on the corner of Canon Shed Rd and Park Ave. They are popular with local people and always busy. The waiters are very quaint in their cummerbunds and shabby white uniforms.

Opposite the Indian Coffee House near M G Rd, the popular *Bimbi's* is a modern, self-serve, fast-food restaurant offering both Indian and Western dishes. It has a huge sweet store in the front, and the more expensive air-con *Khyber Restaurant* upstairs.

Towards the railway station, on the same street, the *Shaziya Hotel* does good vegetarian meals for Rs 10 and various non-vegetarian Indian dishes, including excellent fish curries, although the size of the piece of fish makes sardines look enormous. They also have Chinese dishes.

Another good 'meals' place is the *Jaya Cafe*, in the Woodlands Hotel on M G Rd. A vegetarian thali costs Rs 10 and their lassis are excellent. There's an air-con dining hall too. The *Chick-Chow Restaurant* on Broadway has good chicken dishes and also serves Western breakfasts.

For a Western escape, the *Pandal Restaurant* opposite the Grand Hotel on M G Rd gets the thumbs up from many travellers. It serves good pizza, hamburgers and banana splits, as well as absolutely superb north Indian food, although the portions are stingy. Also relatively expensive, the *Chinese Garden Restaurant* is just off M G Rd, south of Durbar Hall Rd. The service here is very attentive and the food is good. Expect to pay around Rs 40 to Rs 50 per person at either of these places.

For a good splurge, try the *Princess Room* restaurant in the Sealord Hotel on Shanmugham Rd. Their speciality is seafood dishes done in both Continental and Indian style plus there's a live band playing Western music in the evenings.

On the 2nd floor of the Abad Plaza Hotel, the classy but reasonably priced *Regency Restaurant* offers good Indian, Chinese and Western food.

Getting There & Away

Air The Indian Airlines office (☎ 35-3901) is in Durbar Hall Rd, next to the Bharat Tourist Home. Air India (☎ 35-1295) is on M G Rd,

a couple of blocks south of the Chinese Garden Restaurant. For flights on East West Airlines call 36-1632.

Indian Airlines has flights between Kochi and Bombay (US$109), Bangalore (US$40), Goa (US$68), Delhi (US$200), Madras (US$69) and Thiruvananthapuram (Trivandrum, US$23).

Vayudoot flies to Kozhikode (Calicut, US$40), Madras (US$160) and Agatti (US$134). East West Airlines flies once daily to and from Bombay (US$109).

Bus The bus stand is right by the railway tracks in Ernakulam, between the railway stations. Because it is almost in the middle of Kerala, the routes of many buses starting in places north and south of here pass through Ernakulam. It's often possible to get a seat on these buses, but you can't make advance reservations. You simply have to join the scrum when the bus turns up. All the buses listed in this section originate in Ernakulam.

You can make reservations up to five days in advance on many of the buses which start in Ernakulam. The timetable is in English as well as Malayalam and the station staff are usually quite helpful. The monthly booklet *Time Table* (Travel & Tourist Guide), published by Jaico, is helpful. It costs Rs 2.50 and is available at the bus station and at hotels and bookshops around town. It gives a complete rundown of the schedules, journey times and fares for all KSRTC bus routes, together with details of buses for which it's possible to make advance reservations. It also contains train and air schedules, and a list of the better hotels. Another similar publication is *Cochin – Tourist Information* published by Tourist Desk which costs Rs 5.

Going South More than a dozen buses a day go to Alappuzha (Alleppey), including a couple of limited-stop buses. You can also get to Alappuzha on any of the express buses heading south to Kollam (Quilon) and Thiruvananthapuram (Trivandrum). The fare is Rs 12 and the 62-km journey takes 1½ hours.

There are numerous fast passenger services to Kollam, 150 km away, the first at 9.40 am. The fare for the four-hour journey is Rs 27. You can reach Kollam at other times of the day by taking a Thiruvananthapuram bus via Alappuzha.

There are two routes to Thiruvananthapuram (221 km), one via Alappuzha and the other via Kottayam. About 15 buses take the Alappuzha route daily, another four the Kottayam route. The fare is Rs 35 by fast passenger (6½ hours) and Rs 42 by express (about five hours).

A bus leaves at 10 am each morning on the 302-km journey to Kanyakumari. It takes nine hours and costs Rs 59.

Going East Four buses a day make the 324-km trip to Madurai in Tamil Nadu (Rs 56.50, 9¼ hours). To Madras, there are two daily buses at 2.30 and 3.30 pm (Rs 102, 16 hours).

There are 14 buses a day to Kottayam (76 km). The fare is Rs 14 and the journey takes 2¼ hours. To Thekkady (Kumily), there are six buses daily from 5.40 am to 8.30 pm (Rs 37, 192 km, seven hours). All the buses to Madurai also pass through Thekkady.

Going North Interstate express buses make the 565-km trip to Bangalore daily at 5.30 and 7 am (Rs 100, 15 hours) plus there's a super-deluxe bus daily at 8 pm (Rs 140). All these buses go via Kozhikode and Mysore.

There are buses every half-hour throughout the day to Kozhikode. The 219-km trip takes five hours and the fare is Rs 39.

In addition to the state buses, there are a number of private bus companies, mostly along Shanmugham Rd and M G Rd, which have super-deluxe video buses daily to Bangalore, Bombay and Coimbatore. Check out Princy Tours (☎ 35-2751) in the GCDA Complex on Shanmugham Rd opposite the Sealord Hotel – there's a sign outside advertising their bus services. This particular company has daily buses to Coimbatore which leave at 7 am and 6 pm (Rs 40, five

hours), Bangalore at 6 pm (Rs 130), and Bombay at 6 pm (Rs 370).

Others to check out, all of them around Jos Junction (junction of M G Rd and the road leading to the railway station), include Indira Travels (☎ 36-0693), S B Travels (☎ 35-3080), Conti Travels (☎ 35-3080) and K R M S Travels.

Train Ernakulam has two stations, Ernakulam Junction and Ernakulam Town, but the one you're most likely to use is Junction as it's in the centre of town. None of the through trains on the main trunk routes go to the Cochin Harbour Station on Willingdon Island. The booking office at Ernakulam Junction station has no tourist quota and is usually busy. It is open from 7 am to 1 pm and 1.30 to 7.30 pm.

The weekly *Himasagar Express* connects Delhi and Ernakulam. The 2833-km trip takes 56 hours and costs Rs 245/1205 in 2nd/1st class. The 221-km trip to Thiruvananthapuram (Trivandrum) takes four hours on the *Vanchinad Express*. The train leaves at 6 am and costs Rs 48/175 in 2nd/1st class. In the opposite direction, it leaves Thiruvananthapuram at 5.15 pm. This is a very fast train, stopping only in Kottayam and Kollam (Quilon).

Ernakulam to Bangalore is a 629-km trip taking 14 hours. The fare is Rs 108/397 in 2nd/1st class. Bombay is 1841 km and 35 hours away on the three-times-weekly *Netravati Express*. The trip costs Rs 197/858 in 2nd/1st class. The daily *Cochin Express* to Madras takes 14 hours to cover the 708 km at Rs 116/434 in 2nd/1st class.

If you're heading to or from Udhagamandalam (Ooty), there are quite a few expresses which stop at Coimbatore. The 198-km trip takes about six hours and costs Rs 42/156 in 2nd/1st class.

The *Malabar Express* makes a daily run along the Kerala coast from Mangalore to Thiruvananthapuram, through Kozhikode, Trissur, Ernakulam, Kottayam and Kollam. Other trains follow part of this coastal route.

Getting Around

To/From the Airport A bus to the airport will cost Rs 0.50. A taxi from Ernakulam to the airport costs about Rs 40, and an auto-rickshaw should cost about Rs 20.

Bus & Auto-Rickshaw There are no convenient bus services between Fort Cochin and the Mattancherry Palace/Jewish Synagogue, but it's a pleasant half-hour walk through the busy warehouse area along the port-side road. Auto-rickshaws are available, though the drivers will need persuasion to use the meters – this is tourist territory.

In Ernakulam, auto-rickshaws are the most convenient mode of transport. The trip from the bus or train stations to the tourist reception centre on Shanmugham Rd should cost about Rs 8. The drivers have a strong aversion to using the meters and will usually quote around Rs 15.

The buses are fairly good and cheap – minimum fare is Rs 0.50 for a long journey, such as Shanmugham Rd to the airport.

If you have to get to Fort Cochin after the ferries stop running, catch a bus in Ernakulam on M G Rd, just south of Durbar Hall Rd. The fare is Rs 1.40. Auto-rickshaws will demand at least Rs 50 once the ferries stop.

Taxi Taxis charge round-trip fares between the islands, even though you only go in one direction.

Ferry This is the main form of transport between the various parts of Kochi. The ferry stops are all named, which helps to identify them on the timetable at Main Jetty in Ernakulam. The stop on the northern side of Willingdon Island near the Malabar Hotel is called Embarkation, the one around the corner opposite Mattancherry is Terminus. The main stop at Fort Cochin is known as Customs; the other one (for Vypeen Island) is unnamed.

Getting onto a ferry at Ernakulam can sometimes involve scrambling across several others to get to the one on the outside. If you have to do this, make sure you get onto

the right one or you may find yourself going to Vypeen instead of Fort Cochin, for instance (although this isn't really a major inconvenience).

Ernakulam to Mattancherry via Willingdon Island (Terminus) and Fort Cochin (Customs). This, the most useful ferry, runs 30 times daily from 6.30 am to 9.40 pm. The fare to both Fort Cochin and Mattancherry is Rs 0.80.

Ernakulam to Vypeen Island via Willingdon Island (Embarkation). Ferries run every 15 to 30 minutes between 5.30 am and 10.30 pm. The fare to Vypeen is Rs 0.80. There are also ferries to Vypeen (usually via Bolgatty Island) which leave from High Court Jetty on Shanmugham Rd.

Fort Cochin to Willingdon Island Ferries leave from the Customs stop approximately once every half-hour to the Malabar Hotel and the Tourist Office.

Fort Cochin to Vypeen Island Ferries cross this narrow gap virtually nonstop from 6 am until 10 pm and the fare is Rs 0.25. There is also a vehicular ferry every half-hour or so.

Hire Boats There are a number of motorised boats of various sizes for hire in the small dock adjacent to the Main Jetty in Ernakulam and there's also a booking office which deals with them. They're an excellent way of exploring Kochi harbour at your leisure in your own time and without the crowds. However, they are not cheap and you'll have to get a group together to share the cost if your budget is tight. You'll need to haggle over the cost.

KOTTAYAM

Population: 166,000

Kottayam was a centre for the Syrian Christians of Kerala and there are several of their churches, including Cheriyapalli and Valliapalli, about three km north-west of the heart of town. The former is famous for its beautiful murals and the latter for its Persian cross and Phalvi inscriptions. Today, Kottayam is also a centre for Indian rubber production. Its main street is busy and colourful.

As there are direct buses from here to Periyar Wildlife Sanctuary, as well as ferries to Alappuzha (Alleppey), you may well find yourself passing through. There is a regular ferry service (more than 10 boats a day) through the lagoons from Alappuzha to Kottayam – a fascinating alternative to the Kollam (Quilon) backwater trip. Many people think that this trip is actually more interesting because the scenery is more varied.

Places to Stay

The *Hotel Ambassador* (☎ 3293) is on K K Rd, 15 minutes walk from the bus station. It's good value for money at Rs 44/99 for singles/doubles with bathroom, Rs 120 a double with air-con. The hotel is set back off the road, so the driveway is easy to miss. There's a bar and restaurant attached.

Almost opposite the bus station on T B Rd, the basic *Anurag Lodge* is OK for an overnight stay. Rooms cost Rs 30/45. *Kaycees Lodge* (☎ 3440), on YMCA Rd near the central square, has good rooms with bathroom and telephone for Rs 40/65.

Going up in price are the *Hotel Nisha Continental* (☎ 56-3984), Shastri Rd, which has non-air-con singles/doubles at Rs 75/125 or doubles with air-con at Rs 200; and the *Hotel Aida* (☎ 61-391), M C Rd, which costs the same. Both hotels have their own restaurants (south Indian, Continental and Chinese food).

Top of the line is the two-star *Anjali Hotel* (☎ 56-3661), K K Rd, which has only air-con rooms at Rs 205/280. There's an attached bar and restaurant. Slightly cheaper is the *Hotel Green Park* (☎ 56-3311), Nagampadam, about 1½ km from the railway station and close to the bus station. Ordinary rooms here cost Rs 100/125 or Rs 200/225 with air-con. The hotel has a bar and restaurant.

Places to Eat

An *Indian Coffee House* a couple of doors along from the Anurag Lodge serves the usual snacks and breakfast. It's open from 8 am to 9 pm. A bit further along the street, the *Hotel Black Stone* has good vegetarian food.

The *Hotel Vysak* on K K Rd, just up from the Hotel Anjali, serves non-vegetarian meals. The railway station has vegetarian and non-vegetarian 'refreshment rooms', although the menus are a bit limited.

Getting There & Away

Bus The busy bus station is in the centre of town and, as at Kochi (Cochin), the timetable is in English. Most of the buses are coming through from somewhere else, so you may have to sharpen your elbows to get a seat.

There are plenty of buses to Thiruvananthapuram (Trivandrum) via Kollam (Quilon) and to Kochi, and seven daily to Thekkady (and Periyar, four hours). Buses to Madurai (seven hours), of which there are four daily, also go through Thekkady.

Train Kottayam is well served by express trains running between Thiruvananthapuram and Kochi.

Boat The ferry jetty is about three km from the railway station and about one km from the bus station. Eight boats daily make the 2½-hour trip to Alappuzha (Alleppey), the first at 7.30 am and the last at 8.30 pm. This interesting trip is good if you don't have the time or the inclination for the longer one between Kollam and Alappuzha.

Getting Around

The railway station, bus station and ferry jetty are well apart, so you need to catch an auto-rickshaw from one to another. An auto-rickshaw from the railway station to the ferry (ask for 'jetty') is Rs 10; it's Rs 5 from the bus station to the ferry.

The bus station is very central but, from either the ferry or train, you'll need to take an auto-rickshaw into the centre. A map on a signboard at the entrance to the GPO gives you a good idea of the town layout.

AROUND KOTTAYAM
Kumarakom
Sixteen km west of Kottayam is the bird sanctuary of Vembanad Lake. The area was formerly a rubber plantation. Domestic birds such as water fowl, cuckoo and wild duck can be seen in abundance here, as well as Siberian storks which migrate to this area each year. The sanctuary is open from 10 am to 6 pm daily.

If you'd like to stay here there's a KTDC *Tourist Complex* (☎ 58) on the lake which was formerly a British plantation family's old house. Rooms cost Rs 66/88. You can also rent boats here which take up to 10 people at Rs 50 per hour.

PERIYAR WILDLIFE SANCTUARY
This 777-sq-km sanctuary in the Thekkady district, on the Tamil Nadu border, is one of the most important in India. Once, you could reasonably expect to see elephants, bison, antelope, sambar, wild boar, monkeys and, if you were very lucky, those elusive tigers. These days, wildlife sightings are usually limited to a few elephants and bison, especially if you only take the sightseeing boat around the lake. One guide said he hasn't seen a tiger since 1976. Unless you are travelling between the Kerala coast and Madurai, it's hardly worth the long haul up from the coast just for this. On the other hand, if you intend to spend several days in the park and stay overnight in one of the observation towers well away from the main areas, you could be well rewarded.

The park is centred around a large artificial lake, and there's a choice of private or KTDC accommodation. Unfortunately, if this is as far as you get, you won't see much in the way of wildlife, as there's too much human activity and traffic noise around the lodges. Indeed, at weekends, they're inundated by day trippers and tourist coaches, and the only things you will hear are transistor radios and the ape-like noises of fellow human beings.

Elephants are the animals you're most likely to see although, as with any wildlife sanctuary, it's quite possible to see nothing at all. They're worth seeking at the right time of year.

If you don't have four or five days to spare, you'll have to take one of the launch trips down the lake. These are OK as far as they go, but you'll be lucky to see much in the way of game. 'As soon as a shy animal sticks its head up', reported one visitor, 'all aboard shout and scream until it goes again'.

It's advisable to bring warm clothes and waterproof clothing to Periyar. Kumily is the nearest place to buy supplies if you're going to stay in one of the forest observation towers/rest houses, although these are booked out weeks in advance.

The best time for a visit is between September and May.

Orientation & Information
Periyar means the whole park; Thekkady is used to refer to the area where Aranya Nivas and Periyar House are located. Kumily is a separate village with accommodation, restaurant facilities and a bus station. These three place names tend to be used synonymously and confusingly.

The buses stop at the station in Kumily and continue down to the lake, to the Aranya Nivas Hotel.

The tourist office at the Hotel Ambadi, between Kumily and the lake, is not a government office and is just an attempt by the hotel to attract custom. The staff member's local knowledge is strictly limited – he tried to convince me that the Mangaladevi Temple was 60 km away.

Mangaladevi Temple
A visit to this temple, 13 km from Kumily, is an interesting excursion. Although the temple is just a few ruins, the views are magnificent. You can hire a bicycle and ride there, but it's uphill all the way (coast back). Alternatively, rent a jeep (about Rs 150) for the trip – it's three to four hours with a lunch stop.

Places to Stay
Thekkady The Kerala Tourist Development Corporation runs three hotels in the park and,

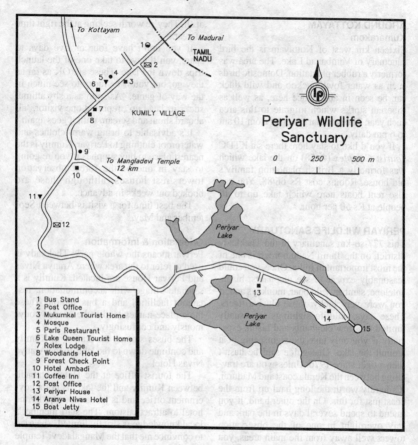

To Kottayam

To Madurai

TAMIL NADU

KUMILY VILLAGE

To Mangladevi Temple
12 km

Periyar Wildlife Sanctuary

0   250   500 m

Periyar Lake

Periyar Lake

1 Bus Stand
2 Post Office
3 Mukumkal Tourist Home
4 Mosque
5 Paris Restaurant
6 Lake Queen Tourist Home
7 Rolex Lodge
8 Woodlands Hotel
9 Forest Check Point
10 Hotel Ambadi
11 Coffee Inn
12 Post Office
13 Periyar House
14 Aranya Nivas Hotel
15 Boat Jetty

if you're visiting on a weekend, advance reservations are necessary. You can make these at any Keralan tourist office.

Periyar House (☎ Kumily 2026) is the cheapest of the three and is very popular so, unless you get there early or make advance reservations, it will almost certainly be full, although you can be lucky. Singles/doubles cost Rs 55/140. There's also a cheaper dormitory with 10 beds. The restaurant serves good vegetarian and non-vegetarian food and, considering you have no choice, the prices are reasonable.

Aranya Nivas (☎ Kumily 2023) is classi-

fied as two-star and is considerably more expensive. All the rooms have three beds and cost Rs 795 to Rs 865, and Rs 1195 to Rs 1300 with air-con. Full board (American plan) costs Rs 1015 to Rs 1165, and Rs 1525 to Rs 1750 with air-con. There's a restaurant, bar, postal and banking facilities and a handicrafts showroom. The Aranya Nivas is at the end of the road leading into the park from Kumily. Periyar House is about half a km back along the road.

The most expensive of the three hotels, the *Lake Palace* (☎ Kumily 2023), is on the lake shore, a long way into the park. If you can afford it, this is a delightful place to stay and you can actually see animals from your room. Deluxe doubles here are Rs 1750 and deluxe suites Rs 2500 with full board. There is a restaurant, bar, postal and banking facilities and a handicrafts showroom. To stay at the Lake Palace, you must be at the Aranya Nivas launch jetty by 4 pm at the latest. The ferry trip is included in the tariff.

In addition to the above KTDC places, there are *Rest Houses* inside the forest which are run by the Forest Department (reservations from the Chief Conservator, Forest Wildlife, Thiruvananthapuram (Trivandrum) or the Forest Information Centre in Thekkady). The rest houses can only be reached by boat and cost Rs 25 per person per night. They're located at Manakavala (8 km from Kumily), Mullakkudy (39 km from Kumily), and Edappalayam (five km from Kumily). There are also two watchtowers inside the forest and, although they're primitive and you must provide all your own food and bedding, you stand the best chance of seeing animals if you rent one. The charge for two people is Rs 5 per day.

Kumily If the government places are full, or you want something cheaper, stay in Kumily. The four km to the lake make a pleasant shady walk, or you can hire a bicycle or catch a share jeep.

There's a fair selection of cheap accommodation in Kumily. One of the better choices is the *Mukumkal Tourist Home* (☎ 2070) on the main street (it's virtually a one-street town), a couple of minutes walk from the bus station. The hotel has its own generator, which is a mixed blessing if you're in one of the back rooms as it makes an incredible racket when switched on. The ordinary doubles cost Rs 60 with bathroom and an air-con double is Rs 198. There's an attached restaurant.

The *Rolex Lodge* (☎ 2081), on the road to the park, has basic rooms with bathroom for Rs 30/40. Close by, the *Woodlands Hotel* (☎ 2077) is a bit gloomy but at Rs 35 a double with bathroom it's good value. Another cheapie is the *Karthika Tourist*

Home (☎ 2146), about one km from the bus station, which offers singles/doubles for Rs 30/60 and a dormitory for Rs 10 per person. It too has an attached vegetarian restaurant.

The *Lake Queen Tourist Home* (☎ 2084) is the largest building in town with 54 rooms. Although it's popular with Indian holidaymakers, you can usually find space here. Rooms cost Rs 37/75 with bathroom and there's an attached restaurant. Closer to the park, 500 metres from Kumily, the *Hotel Ambadi* (☎ 2192) is at the forest checkpost. The air-con cottages here are not all that old, but little time appears to be spent on maintenance. They cost Rs 140 a double or Rs 350 for a deluxe double. It has a coffee shop and restaurant.

Places to Eat

If you're staying in Thekkady, the government lodges have reasonable food. Halfway between Thekkady and Kumily, the outdoor *Coffee Inn* has a good selection of music and good travellers' food. In the evenings, they serve fabulous home-made brown bread with honey. It's open from 7 am to 10 pm and, in the tradition of popular Indian travellers' restaurants, the food takes a while to arrive. Take a torch (flashlight) if you eat here at night – it can be a dark walk back to Kumily or Thekkady.

The restaurant at the *Hotel Ambadi* is quite good and you can expect to pay about Rs 80 for a full meal for two.

For a vegetarian meal, the dining hall in the *Mukumkal Tourist Home* is OK.

Getting There & Away

Bus The bus station in Kumily is just a bit of spare land at the northern edge of town, near the barrier on the state border. It's chaotic when more than three buses are there at once.

All buses originating in Kumily start and finish at Aranya Nivas by the lake, but also stop at the bus station.

There are direct connections with Kottayam (six daily, four hours, Rs 20.50), Ernakulam (two daily, six hours), Thiruvananthapuram (Trivandrum; three daily, eight hours) and Kovalam (one daily, nine hours) in Kerala, as well as buses to Madurai (four daily, 3½ to four hours) and Kodaikanal (one daily at 6.30 am) in Tamil Nadu.

Getting Around

Car & Bicycle Jeeps down to the lake cost Rs 20 for the vehicle. If you pay on a Rs 2 per person basis, you have to wait for the jeep to fill up. It's also possible to walk or, better still, rent a bicycle in the main street of Kumily. There's not much traffic on this road.

Boat Both the Forest Department and the KTDC operate launches on the lake but, although there are five scheduled departures daily (at 7, 9.30 and 11.30 am, 2 and 4 pm) you sometimes have to wait up to an hour for the boat to fill up. The cost is Rs 7 per person and the trip lasts two hours. Buy tickets at the jetty. The KTDC also rents boats for two-hour cruises. These cost from Rs 150 (up to 15 people) to Rs 300 (up to 60 people). These will leave whenever the full fee has been paid so you don't have to wait until they're full if you're prepared to pay extra. Buy tickets at the Aranya Nivas Hotel.

Rides & Treks You can organise elephant rides into the sanctuary for Rs 30 for a group of four people for an hour or a guided trek on foot for three hours for Rs 5. Both these should be booked through the Forest Department.

OTHER SANCTUARIES
Thattekkad Bird Sanctuary

This sanctuary is 20 km from Kothamangalam, on the Ernakulam to Munnar road. It's home to such birds as the Malabar grey hornbill, woodpecker, parakeets and rarer species like the Sri Lankan frogmouth and rose-billed roller. Boat cruises are available from Boothathankettu to Thattekkad. The best time to visit is from 5 to 6 am. There's an *Inspection Bungalow* at Boothathankettu as well as a few mid-range hotels in Kothamangalam.

Parambikulam Wildlife Sanctuary

The Parambikulam Wildlife Sanctuary, 48 km south of Palakkad (Palghat), stretches around the Parambikulam, Thunakadavu and Peruvaripallam dams and covers an area of 285 sq km adjacent to the Anamalai Wildlife Sanctuary in Tamil Nadu. It sports elephant, bison, gaur, sloth bear, wild boar, sambur, chital and the occasional tiger and panther, as well as numerous crocodiles in the reservoirs. The sanctuary is open all year but is best avoided from June to August due to the monsoon. The sanctuary is open daily from 7 am to 6 pm and entry costs Rs 0.50 per person plus Rs 5 for a light vehicle. Motorcycles and bicycles are not allowed.

The sanctuary headquarters are at Thunakadavu where the Forestry Department has an *Inspection Bungalow* and a tree-top hut (book through the Range Officer). At Parambikulam there is a *PWD Rest House* and a Tamil Nadu Government *Inspection Bungalow* (book through the Junior Engineer, Tamil Nadu PWD, Parambikulam). There are also two watchtowers, one at Anappadi (eight km from Thunakadavu) and another at Zungam (five km from Thunakadavu).

The best access to the sanctuary is by bus from Pollachi (40 km from Coimbatore and 49 km from Palakkad Palghat). There are four buses in either direction between Pollachi and Parambikulam daily and the trip takes two hours.

Boating facilities are available at Parambikulam. A two-hour cruise costs Rs 50 shared by up to 15 people. Row boats can also be hired at Thunakadavu for Rs 2 per hour.

ALAPPUZHA (Alleppey)
Population: 265,000

Like Kollam (Quilon), this is a pleasant, easy-going market town surrounded by coconut-palm plantations and built on the canals which service the coir industry of the backwaters. While there's precious little to see in Alappuzha for most of the year, there is one event which you should not miss if you're anywhere in the vicinity on the second Saturday of August. This is the snakeboat race for the Nehru Cup.

The only reasons to pass through here on any other day of the year are, of course, to make the backwater trip to Kollam or, if you're coming from Kollam, to stay here overnight before heading further north. For full details of the unforgettable backwater boat trip, refer to the section on Kollam later in this chapter.

Alappuzha is infamous for its drinking water – dysentery is a speciality. Even if you normally drink the tap water in other places, it's advisable to give it a miss here.

Orientation

The bus station and boat jetty are conveniently close to each other on the canal, and there are plenty of hotels within walking distance.

Nehru Cup Snakeboat Race

This famous regatta takes place every year on 14 August (Independence Day). On that day, scores of long, low-slung dugouts with highly decorated sterns and up to 100 rowers shaded by gleaming silk umbrellas compete for the cup, watched from the banks by thousands of spectators. The annual event celebrates the seafaring and martial traditions of ancient Kerala.

Tickets for the race are available on the day from numerous ticket stands on the way to the lake where the race is held, and cost from Rs 15 to Rs 30. This entitles you to a seat on the bamboo terraces which are erected for the occasion and from which you'll get an excellent view over the lake. The only drawback to sitting on these terraces is that shortly into the race they get invaded by local (ticketless) youths seeking a better view. So far, the scaffolding hasn't collapsed but one day it just might! If you're not keen on testing fate, there are also Rs 100 tickets available which give you a place on the Rose Pavilion, a stand built in the middle of the lake.

It's advisable to take food and drink along with you as there's little available on the lake shore. You may also need an umbrella as the weather can alternate between driving rain and blistering sunshine – this is the monsoon season.

Places to Stay – bottom end

There are a few hotels worth trying just north of the canal. The cheap and habitable *Sheeba Lodge* (☎ 4871) has singles/doubles for Rs 25/40. The *Karthika Tourist Home* (☎ 2554) in the same area is good value and costs about the same.

Right opposite the boat jetty, the *Sree Krishna Bhavan Boarding & Lodging* (☎ 3453) has small, basic rooms around a

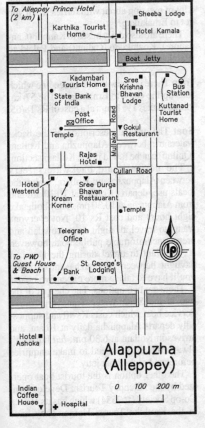

To Alleppey Prince Hotel (2 km)

Sheeba Lodge
Karthika Tourist Home
Hotel Kamala

Boat Jetty

Kadambari Tourist Home
Sree Krishna Bhavan Lodge
Bus Station

State Bank of India
Kuttanad Tourist Home

Post Office
Mullakal Road
Gokul Restaurant

Temple

Rajas Hotel

Cullan Road

Hotel Westend
Sree Durga Bhavan Restaurant
Kream Korner

Temple

Telegraph Office

To PWD Guest House & Beach

St George's Lodging
Bank

Hotel Ashoka

Alappuzha (Alleppey)

0   100   200 m

Indian Coffee House
Hospital

courtyard. It's OK (just) for a night's stay and costs Rs 20/30.

On the main street, right in the centre of town, the *Kadambari Tourist Home* (☎ 4210) is very dirty and the staff couldn't care less. Even at Rs 35/50 with attached bathroom, it's a rip-off.

St George's Lodging (☎ 3373), C C N B Rd, about half a km from the bus station and ferry jetty, is another place where standards have slipped. Singles/doubles cost from Rs 16/24 to Rs 23/42.

Places to Stay – middle

For something better, close to the bus station and ferry jetty, try the *Kuttanad Tourist Home* (☎ 4354) or the *Komala Hotel* (☎ 3631). Both of these have singles/doubles for Rs 40/50, and air-con singles/doubles for Rs 150/175, as well as their own bar and restaurant serving south Indian, Chinese and Continental food.

Further afield is the *Hotel Raiban* (☎ 3477), about one km from the bus station, which has singles/doubles for Rs 40/60, or Rs 150/200 with air-con.

Places to Stay – top end

Top of the line is the *Alleppey Prince Hotel* (☎ 3752), A S Rd, about three km from the bus station. This two-star hotel has air-con singles/doubles for Rs 315/385. Facilities include a bar and restaurant (south Indian, Chinese and Continental food) and a swimming pool.

Places to Eat

The *Indian Coffee House* is 15 minutes walk south of the southern canal, opposite the hospital. It's dirty, and huge cockroaches are an ever-present part of the clientele but it does serve very cheap food as well as excellent real coffee.

The *Arun Restaurant* in the Komala Hotel, on the other side of the canal bridge, is the best eatery in town. For cheap non-vegetarian food, the small *Kream Korner* restaurant on Cullan Rd does good chicken dishes. On the same road, the non-vegetarian *Rajas Hotel* is also cheap.

On the main street, the *Gokul Restaurant* serves good vegetarian meals and dosas.

Getting There & Away

Bus There are buses every half-hour throughout the day to Kollam (Quilon). Most of these buses continue on to Thiruvananthapuram (Trivandrum).

About 40 buses daily go to Ernakulam; the 1½ to two-hour trip costs Rs 12. If you are heading for Fort Cochin rather than Ernakulam, you can get off this bus just before the bridge which connects Kochi (Cochin) and Willingdon Island. Take a local bus or auto-rickshaw from there into either Mattancherry or Fort Cochin. This saves you a lot of messing about with ferries when you get to Ernakulam.

There are also daily buses to Kannur (Cannanore), Kozhikode (Calicut) and Palakkad (Palghat).

Train There is a new broad-gauge line which runs up the coast to Ernakulam. The 57-km journey takes 1½ hours at a cost of Rs 18/65.

Boat The general description of the backwaters trip between Alappuzha and Kollam (Quilon) can be found in the Kollam section.

The normal state backwaters ferry between Alappuzha and Kollam, which the locals use, departs Kollam at 10.30 am and from Alappuzha at 10.30 pm. They both take eight hours and cost Rs 10. Not everyone wants to travel all night on a crowded and pretty uncomfortable public boat, however. If you want to travel during the hours of daylight between Alappuzha and Kollam, you'll have to take a more expensive boat.

There are two options. The cheaper of the two is the State Water Transport Tourist Service boat which costs Rs 40 and supposedly departs Alappuzha daily at 10 am, and arrives in Kollam at 6.30 pm; *but* it doesn't always run, so you need to make enquiries beforehand at the boat jetty.

The other option is the tourist boat operated by the Alleppey Tourism Development Co-op Society (☎ 2554) which has its offices in the Karthika Tourist Home. They have departures from Alappuzha at 9.45 am on Monday, Wednesday and Friday during the season, arriving in Kollam at 5.45 pm. The fare is Rs 75.

If you don't want to do the full backwaters trip but prefer a shorter one, there are several options but they are all by normal state ferries. The first is to Kottayam for which there are 11 departures daily between 5 am and 9.30 pm. Ferries take two hours to cross Vembanad Lake and cost Rs 3. Another is to Changannur (Changanacherry), on the road and railway line 18 km south of Kottayam, 78 km north of Kollam. There are about 10 boats daily which take three hours and cost Rs 3.

There are also state ferries to Kochi (Cochin) on alternate days at noon, but make enquiries beforehand.

KOLLAM (Quilon)
Population: 362,000

Nestled amongst coconut palms and cashew tree plantations on the edge of Ashtamudi Lake, Kollam is a typical small Keralan market town, with old wooden houses whose red-tiled roofs overhang winding streets. If you're coming up from the south, it's also the gateway to the backwaters of Kerala. The trip by boat to Alappuzha (Alleppey) through these backwaters is a unique and fascinating experience.

Kollam dates back many centuries and, in fact, the Malayalam era is calculated from the founding of this town in the 9th century. Kollam's history is interwoven with the rivalry between the Portuguese, Dutch and English for control of commodities grown in this part of the subcontinent, and of the trade routes across the Indian Ocean.

At Thangasseri, only three km from the centre of town, stand the ruins of a fort originally constructed by the Portuguese and later taken over by the Dutch, as well as a number of churches constructed in the 18th century. In Ashtamudi Lake, there are many Chinese fishing nets of the type more usually associated with Kochi, further north.

Should you use the European name for

Kollam – Quilon – remember that it's pronounced 'koy-lon'.

Information
The main tourist office is some three km from the centre of town next to the Tourist Bungalow, but it's not worth visiting since it's hardly ever open. Better is the information kiosk on the railway station platform. This is currently staffed by an enthusiastic young woman who hands out a good map of the town.

The railway station and boat jetty are some three km apart so you'll need to take an auto-rickshaw between the two.

Things to See
Apart from the miserable ruins of the Portuguese/Dutch fort at **Thangasseri**, there are no 'sights' in Kollam. It's just a pleasant place to stroll around for a day or so, soaking up the atmosphere of a Keralan market town. Most travellers come here to take the boat through the backwaters or, if coming from Alappuzha, they are en route to Thiruvananthapuram (Trivandrum). As such, it's an overnight stop for most.

Places to Stay – bottom end
The most interesting place to stay is the *Tourist Bungalow* – a magnificent, spacious old British Residency which stands in its own colourful gardens by the water's edge about three km from the centre of town. Yet, despite its superb potential and proud tourist literature claims that 'Lord Curzon slept here', it's totally run down and neglected, though repairs to the roof were undertaken in mid-1992. If this were Rajasthan, it would have had funds lavished on it long ago and reopened as one of Kerala's tourist hotel gems. In the meantime, it's dirt cheap at Rs 50 a double, but it's usually full as there are only eight rooms. Breakfast is the only meal available. The only trouble with staying at this place is getting here. You'll need an auto-rickshaw from town. Getting back into town is an even greater hassle as it's not on any normal auto-rickshaw route.

In the centre of Kollam, one of the most

Astamudikayal (Lake)

Kollam

0   0.5   1 km

To Thangasseri

To Thiruvananthapuram

Main Road

Chinnakkada

Kollam Canal

Kollam Beach

ARABIAN
SEA

1 KTDC Tourist Bungalow
2 Jetty
3 KSRTC Bus Stand
4 Hotel Sea Bee
5 Hospital
6 Hotel Sudharsan
7 Telegraph Office
8 Hotel Shah International
9 Post Office
10 Fruit & Vegetable Market
11 Iswarya Lodge
12 Hotel Guru Prasad
13 Hotel Karthika
14 Suprabatham Restaurant
15 Clock Tower
16 Hotel Ravathi
17 Railway Station
18 State Bank of India

popular places to stay is the *Hotel Karthika* (☎ 76-240). It's a large place built around a central courtyard and, although there are some hideous sculptures in the courtyard, the rooms are not too bad. The ordinary rooms are Rs 33/60 plus there are air-con doubles at Rs 125 and suites at Rs 160. All the rooms have attached bathrooms and there's mosquito netting on the windows.

The *Iswarya Lodge* (☎ 75-384) in Main Rd is slightly cheaper at Rs 33/51/60/88 for singles/doubles/triples and rooms with four beds, including tax, but it's often full. Even cheaper, but a place with a strange, gloomy atmosphere, is the *Hotel Ravathi* which says it has singles/doubles with attached bathroom for Rs 20/25 but then won't let you have one! Its main function seems to be as a bar and restaurant.

Right opposite the bus station is the cheap but very basic *Mahalakshmi Lodge* (☎ 79-440). You get what you pay for here at Rs 18/30 for singles/doubles and all the rooms have common bathroom.

If you'd prefer to stay close to the railway station, there's the *Hotel Rail View* (☎ 76-981) right opposite. This has singles/doubles for Rs 25/40 plus there's an attached bar and restaurant, with south Indian and Chinese food.

Places to Stay – middle

Just up the road from the boat jetty and bus station is the large but soulless *Hotel Sea Bee* (☎ 75-371), Hospital Rd, which offers ordinary singles/doubles at Rs 50/80 and air-con rooms with TV for Rs 100/200. Though the staff are very friendly, the rooms are dirty and grubby and give the appearance of never having been cleaned. The restaurant here serves greasy, overcooked Chinese food and should be avoided. There's also a bar.

Slightly more expensive but more recently built and far more attractive is the *Hotel Shah International* (☎ 75-362), Tourist Bungalow Rd, which has singles/doubles for Rs 65/85 and the same with air-con for Rs 125/175. There's an attached restaurant offering south Indian, Chinese and Continental food.

The most expensive place (at least with air-con), but for no discernible reason as the rooms are no better than in the Shah International, is the *Hotel Sudharsan* (☎ 75-322), Parameswar Nagar, close to the Sea Bee, which has singles/doubles for Rs 50/70, or Rs 200/250 with air-con. All the rooms have attached bathrooms, there's a very dark but good bar and two restaurants. One of the restaurants is a cheap vegetarian 'meals' type place and the other is a more expensive non-vegetarian place with air-con and TV which the staff spend more time paying attention to than they do to the clientele.

Places to Eat

The restaurant on the ground floor of the *Iswarya Lodge* has good vegetarian food. The *Hotel Guru Prasad*, Main Rd, is another vegetarian place which serves excellent food. It does delicious banana shakes for Rs 4. The *Indian Coffee House* on Main Rd is, as usual, good value. Opposite, the *Azad Hotel* does good vegetarian meals.

The *Village Restaurant*, next to the Sika Lodge, is only open in the evenings. It serves excellent chicken dishes. If you are staying at the Karthika, the *Suprabatham Restaurant* near the clock tower is a convenient place to eat. This place is a typical south Indian 'meals' restaurant.

Kollam is a cashew-growing centre and many shops and hotels sell them roasted and salted, frequently in presentation packets. You won't find them cheaper anywhere else in Kerala.

Getting There & Away

Bus Many of the buses leaving the Kollam bus station are en route from somewhere else so it's the usual rugby scrum when one arrives. This is not the case with the express buses, which can be reserved in advance. Do yourself a favour and reserve one of those seats (or travel by train).

There are express buses going north (to Alappuzha and Kochi, for example) six times daily but only three during daylight hours. Going south to Thiruvananthapuram (Trivandrum), there are express buses 17 times daily, many of them during daylight hours. The trip to Thiruvananthapuram takes two hours and costs Rs 15.

Train Kollam is 156 km south of Kochi. The three or four-hour train trip costs Rs 38/130 in 2nd/1st class. The *Trivandrum Mail* from Madras goes through Kollam, as does the *Bombay to Kanyakumari Express* and the Mangalore to Thiruvananthapuram coastal service.

There are also trains between Kollam and Madras (Egmore) via Madurai (760 km, eight hours, Rs 121/454 in 2nd/1st class). The trip across the Western Ghats is a pure delight. Passenger trains between Kollam and Thiruvananthapuram are very slow, but there are plenty of expresses.

Backwater Boat Trip This trip to Alappuzha (Alleppey) is one of the highlights of a visit to Kerala. It takes you across shallow, palm-fringed lakes studded with cantilevered Chinese fishing nets, and along narrow shady canals where coir (coconut fibre), copra (dried coconut meat) and cashews are loaded onto dugouts. Along the way, you call at many small settlements.

It's interesting to see how people live on narrow spits of land only a few metres wide, practically surrounded by water, and still manage to keep cows, pigs, chickens and ducks and cultivate small vegetable gardens. On the more open stretches of canal, you'll see dugouts with huge sails and prows carved into the shape of dragons. The sight of three or four of these sailing towards you in the late afternoon sun is never to be forgotten. The boat crews are friendly – if you exchange a little conversation with them, they'll let you sit on the roof. It gets hot up there, though.

On some days during the winter season, almost half the boat passengers could be Western travellers. There are two 10-minute 'chai stops' along the way where snacks and tea can be bought. Beware of inflated prices for refreshments at these stops. You may decide it's worth bringing some food with you.

There is a normal state ferry from Kollam

to Alappuzha daily at 10.30 am which arrives at 6.30 pm and costs Rs 10. Also from the same jetty is a State Water Transport Tourist Service boat which leaves Kollam daily at the same time and costs Rs 40, but it may be cancelled so make enquiries beforehand.

If you don't want to take either of the boats operated by the state authorities and you prefer a bit of space on board, there's another option. This is the tourist boat operated by the Alleppey Tourism Development Co-op Society which has its office in the Hotel Sea Bee (☎ 75-371), just up the road from the jetty in Kollam. They have departures from Kollam to Alappuzha at 10.15 am on Tuesday, Thursday and Saturday. The trip takes eight hours and costs Rs 75.

If the full eight-hour backwaters trip is too long for you then try a shorter ride to either Guhanandapuram (eight boats daily, one hour) or Muthiraparam (four boats daily, 2½ hours).

Other options are to take a bus or train for the 78-km trip from Kollam to Changannur (Changanacherry) and from there to take one of the 10 daily boats to Alappuzha (three hours) or to go all the way to Kottayam by train or bus and take a boat from there to Alappuzha.

One point of interest on the backwater trip is the **Mata Amritanandamayi Mission** (☎ Vallickavu 78) at Amritapuri, which you are welcome to visit and where you can stay and eat on a donation basis. It's the residence and headquarters of Sri Sri Mata Amritanandamayi Devi, one of India's very few (but in this case very much revered) female gurus. Quite a few travellers call off here and stay for a few days, and have highly recommended the place.

Getting Around
The transport facilities are at opposite ends of the town, three km apart. This means that, if you arrive by rail and want to get to the bus station or the boat jetty, you'll need to take an auto-rickshaw. The drivers of these refuse to use the meters so you'll have to fix the fare beforehand – expect to pay Rs 10 to Rs 15.

VARKALA

Only 19 km south of Kollam and 55 km north of Thiruvananthapuram, the seaside resort of Varkala boasts a **mineral-water spring** on the beach and the **Janardhana Temple**. One of the earliest British East India Company trading posts was established at nearby **Anjengo** in 1684.

Places to Stay

There are very few places to stay. Try the *Babuji Lodge* (☎ 2243) which costs Rs 35/40 for singles/doubles or the *Anandan Tourist Home* (☎ 2135) which has the same for Rs 30/35. Both of these are in Varkala itself and the beach is two km distant. The only places to eat are in town.

THIRUVANANTHAPURAM (Trivandrum)
Population: 826,000

As you stroll around this friendly, relaxed city built over seven forested hills, it's hard to imagine that it is a state capital. The City of the Sacred Snake is unlike any other Indian state capital and has managed to retain the magic ambience so characteristic of Kerala in general – red-tiled roofs, narrow winding lanes, intimate corner cafes, dilapidated municipal buses and necessary business accomplished in a friendly manner with a relatively high degree of efficiency. The only real bustle you'll encounter here is during rush hours.

At least, this is how it is when political tensions between the various factions haven't reached the stage where they erupt into violence on the streets. Political slogans, emblems and flags, especially those of the communist and Muslim parties, are a notable feature of the urban landscape of Kerala. Luckily, even when there is violence, it rarely affects the visitor.

On the other hand, there isn't a great deal to see in Thiruvananthapuram itself, and non-Hindus aren't allowed into the famous Sri Padmanabhaswamy Temple. The main reason people come here is to stay at magnificent Kovalam Beach, 16 km south. You might also find yourself here for a day or so if you plan to fly to Sri Lanka, the Maldive Islands or the Persian Gulf.

Orientation

Thiruvananthapuram covers a large area, but most of the services and places of interest are on or very close to Mahatma Gandhi Rd – the main road running through the centre of the city from the museum and zoo to Sri Padmanabhaswamy Temple.

The long-distance bus station, railway station and tourist reception centre are all close to each other, as are many of the budget hotels. The municipal bus stand is 10 minutes walk from the railway station, opposite Sri Padmanabhaswamy Temple.

The museum, zoo and airline offices are all in the north of the city and you'll need an auto-rickshaw to reach them.

Information

Tourist Offices The Tourist Reception Centre (☎ 75-031) in front of the Chaithram Hotel, near the railway station and central bus station, has basic information but is essentially there to promote their guided tours to Thiruvananthapuram, Kanyakumari, Periyar Wildlife Sanctuary and Kodaikanal.

If you want more detailed information or any of the booklets that the KTDC produce you'll have to make a trip to the main office, the Tourist Information Centre (☎ 61-132), Museum Rd, opposite the museum/zoo at the north end of M G Rd. The people who staff this office are very enthusiastic indeed and they have a range of well-researched and informative booklets which include, *Kerala – Travel Facts* (free), *Fairs & Festivals of Kerala* (free), *Travel Information – Kerala, Tamil Nadu, Karnataka, Goa* (Rs 30), and *Hotels of Kerala* (Rs 30) plus many other free leaflets.

Post & Telecommunications The GPO is tucked away down a small side street off M G Rd, about 10 minutes walk from the

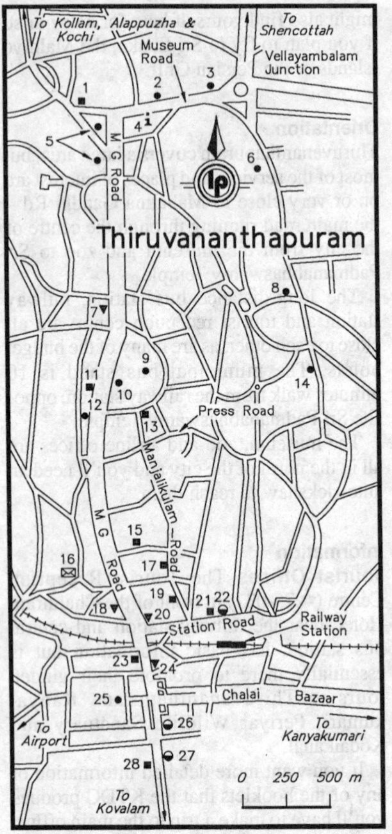
To Kollam, Alappuzha & Kochi
To Shencottah
Museum Road
Vellayambalam Junction
M G Road
Thiruvananthapuram
Press Road
Manjalikulam Road
M G Road
Station Road
Railway Station
Chalai Bazaar
To Airport
To Kanyakumari
To Kovalam
0 250 500 m

■ PLACES TO STAY

- 1 Mascot Hotel & Indian Airlines
- 11 Hotel Pankaj
- 15 Bhaskara Bhavan Tourist Paradise
- 17 Pravin Tourist Home
- 19 Hotel Highland & Manacaud Tourist Paradise
- 21 Tourist Reception Centre
- 23 Nalanda Tourist Home
- 28 Hotel Continental Luciya

▼ PLACES TO EAT

- 7 Indian Coffee House
- 18 Omkar Cafe & Safari Restaurant
- 20 Chicken Corner Restaurant
- 24 Indian Coffee House

OTHER

- 2 Museum, Zoo & Art Gallery
- 3 Air India
- 4 Tourist Office
- 5 Stadiums
- 6 Swimming Pool
- 8 Air Lanka
- 9 Stadium
- 10 Secretariat
- 12 Central Telegraph Office
- 13 British Library & YMCA
- 14 Commissioner of Police
- 16 GPO
- 22 Central Bus Station
- 25 Sri Padmanabhaswamy Temple
- 26 Fort Bus Station
- 27 Kovalam Buses & Taxis

Station Rd area. Most of the counters, including poste restante, are open Monday to Saturday from 8 am to 8 pm.

There's no packing service available here but there's a small tailor's shop opposite which will stitch up and seal parcels at a very reasonable rate.

The Central Telegraph Office is on M G Rd, midway between Station Rd and the museum and 20 minutes walk from either. It is open 24 hours a day. The telephone area code for Thiruvananthapuram is 0471.

Visa Extensions Apply for visa extensions at the office of the Commissioner of Police (☎ 60-555) on Residency Rd. Extensions take between four days and a week to issue but you don't have to leave your passport there. It speeds things up if you give the name of a Thiruvananthapuram hotel as your address rather than somewhere in Kovalam. Surprisingly, this office is open on Saturdays as well as weekdays, from 10 am to 5 pm.

Bookshops & Libraries The British Library (☎ 68-716), in the YMCA grounds near the Secretariat building, is supposedly only open to members, but they seem to welcome visitors. It has three-day-old British newspapers and a variety of magazines.

There's a branch of Higginbothams bookshop on M G Rd, just up from Station Rd.

Museum, Gallery & Zoo

These are all in the same area, in the park at the north end of the city. The zoo is open daily except Monday from 9 am to 5 pm and the other two daily except Monday between 10 am and 5 pm. Entry to the museum costs Rs 1, and it's Rs 2 to the others.

Housed in an attractive building, the **Napier Museum** has a good collection of bronzes, historical and contemporary ornaments, temple carts, ivory carvings and life-size figures of Kathakali dancers in full regalia. The Science & Industry Museum is not that interesting unless you are a high-school science student.

On display at the **Sri Chitra Art Gallery** are paintings of the Rajput, Mughal and Tanjore schools, together with works from China, Tibet, Japan and Bali. There are also many modern Indian paintings, especially those of Ravi Varma.

Although the **Zoological Gardens** are among the best laid-out zoos in Asia, set amongst woodland, lakes and very well-maintained lawns, some of the animal enclosures are still miserable. The zoo's botanical garden includes examples of almost every tropical tree.

Sri Padmanabhaswamy Temple

This temple, thought to be to the 'presiding deity' of Thiruvananthapuram, is dedicated to Vishnu. It was constructed in the Dravidian style by a maharaja of Travancore in 1733. Only Hindus are allowed inside, and even they have to wear a special dhoti which can be rented for Rs 1. The temple incorporates a tank in which the faithful bathe.

Organised Tours

City Tour The Thiruvananthapuram city tour leaves daily at 8 am, returning at 7 pm, and costs Rs 60 per person. It includes visits to Sri Padmanabhaswamy Temple (for Hindus only), the museum, art gallery, zoo, Veli Lagoon and Kovalam Beach. This tour is of little interest to travellers since the temple is off limits to non-Hindus and who wants to gawp at fellow travellers sunbathing on the beach at Kovalam in any case?

Kanyakumari The daily Kanyakumari (Cape Comorin) tour departs at 7.30 am, returns at 9 pm and costs Rs 100. It includes visits to Padmanabhapuram Palace (except on Monday) and Kanyakumari. This isn't bad value if you want to avoid the typical public bus system rugby scrums and aren't particularly interested in staying overnight in Kanyakumari.

Ponmudi There's a daily tour to this hill resort in southern Kerala which departs at 7.45 am, returns at 7 pm and costs Rs 85.

Periyar Wildlife Sanctuary The tour to this sanctuary, in the mountains of Kerala near the Tamil Nadu border, departs every Saturday at 6.30 am and returns the following evening at 9 pm. It costs Rs 185, excluding board and lodging. This must be one of the silliest tours in India, as there's no way you're going to have time to see any wildlife at all – even if it were that easy in the company of a busload of garrulous honeymooners.

Other Tours There are other tours to places further afield, such as Kodaikanal (three days), Bangalore (seven days), Tirupathi (five days), Goa (seven days) and even Bombay (15 days) but they're of little interest to most people.

Places to Stay – bottom end

There are many cheap lodging places along or close to the Station Rd area (near the railway station and bus stand), but many are very basic and this road is busy and noisy. The beach at Kovalam is so close and is a far more pleasant place to stay. It is possible, however, that you might have business to transact which might involve an overnight stay in Thiruvananthapuram. Assuming that's the case, the best hunting ground for a reasonable cheapie is along Manjalikulam Rd, a narrow road heading north off Station Rd. This road is lined with all manner of hotels, from bottom-end through mid-range to top end, for almost a km so you're guaranteed to find somewhere that suits your pocket and level of comfort. It's also quiet and just as convenient as Station Rd.

At the bottom end of this category, the friendly *Pravin Tourist Home* (☎ 75-343) has large rooms for Rs 40/70 and suites for Rs 90. Close by, the hopefully named *Bhaskara Bhavan Tourist Paradise* (☎ 79-662) is a bit gloomy but otherwise OK. The rooms are good value at Rs 26/45 and there are suites for Rs 63. Similar is the *Vijai Tourist Home* (☎ 79-727) with rooms for Rs 35/55 and suites for Rs 77. At the bottom of the scale is the *Sundar Tourist Home* (☎ 76-632). It is extremely basic but has rooms for Rs 20/35.

Up the scale a bit, the clean and well-kept *Sivada Tourist Home* (☎ 75-320) has rooms around a pleasant courtyard for Rs 38/65 and Rs 143 for a double with air-con.

Not far from Station Rd are the *Manacaud Tourist Paradise* (☎ 69-5001), a relatively new place, with large, clean rooms for Rs 38/65 with attached bathroom, and the *Hotel Ammu* (☎ 79-906) which has rooms for Rs 71/90, and Rs 175/225 with air-con.

All the above hotels are on or near Manjalikulam Rd.

South of the railway line is the *Nalanda Tourist Home* (☎ 71-864) on busy M G Rd, though the rooms at the back are not too noisy. It's cheap at Rs 25/40. There are also *retiring rooms* including a dormitory at the railway station.

Places to Stay – middle

The relatively new *Chaithram Hotel* (☎ 75-777), Station Rd next to the bus station, is run by the Kerala Tourist Development Corporation and is a relatively popular place to stay. Rooms cost Rs 175/250, or Rs 300/350 with air-con. There are also more expensive deluxe rooms in both categories. Facilities include a bookshop, coffee shop, one of south India's lightest and friendliest bars,

and a very mediocre restaurant with tasteless food and slow service. It's a large place, so rarely full.

Back on Manjalikulam Rd, the *Hotel Highland* (☎ 78-440) is one of the tallest buildings in the area and readily visible from Station Rd. The staff are friendly and rooms are Rs 80/110, or Rs 143 in a deluxe double. Air-con rooms are Rs 201/316. There's an attached restaurant.

Further up this road is the *Hotel Regency* (☎ 78-377), Manjalikulam Cross Rd, which has rooms for Rs 175/225, and Rs 225/325 with air-con. The hotel has its own restaurant.

Away from this area on M G Rd opposite the government Secretariat is the *Hotel Pankaj* (☎ 76-667). It has a bookshop, a bar and two restaurants, one on the roof overlooking the city, with a choice of south Indian, Chinese and Continental cuisine. Doubles are Rs 200 to Rs 290, and singles/doubles with air-con are Rs 350/490.

Places to Stay – top end

One of the cheapest in this bracket is the *Hotel Fort Manor* (☎ 70-002), Power House Junction, which has air-con rooms for Rs 350/550 and suites for Rs 950. There's a bookshop, rooftop restaurant and bar.

At East Fort, close to the Sri Padmanabhaswamy Temple, the three-star *Hotel Continental Luciya* (☎ 73-443) is a good choice. It has rooms for Rs 200/300, or Rs 395/790 with air-con. There's a bookshop, bar and restaurant.

Top of the line is the *Mascot Hotel* (☎ 68-990), Museum Rd, another three-star place and the only one with a swimming pool. All the rooms are air-con and doubles cost Rs 695 to Rs 795 plus there are suites for Rs 1195. Other facilities include a number of shops plus a bar and restaurant.

Places to Eat

An excellent place for a dirt cheap breakfast (omelette, toast and tea for about Rs 5) is the tiny cafe at the junction of Station Rd and

Manjalikulam Rd. It doesn't have a name but you can't miss it.

The *Athul Jyoti* on M G Rd, near the Secretariat, serves good vegetarian food, and a thali with a variety of vegetables, dhals and curd for only Rs 10. Despite the name, the *Sri Ram Sweet Stall* is actually a very good vegetarian restaurant. It's at the entrance to the Pankaj Hotel on M G Rd.

Also on M G Rd, but down near Station Rd, the small *Omkar Cafe* does an unusual thali with a tangy curd sauce for Rs 10. A couple of doors down, the *Safari Restaurant* is none too popular but a good place if you're just after a beer.

Almost opposite the Safari is the *Chicken Corner Restaurant*, specialising in chicken dishes at around Rs 15 to Rs 20. The *City Queen Restaurant* in the Highlands Hotel does good Chinese dishes and also serves Indian and Western food.

The *Indian Coffee House* is the usual good value. There are two in Thiruvananthapuram, both on M G Rd. One is just north of the Secretariat, the other south of the railway line near East Fort.

On Station Rd, you'll find a few vegetarian restaurants serving the usual 'meals' thalis for under Rs 10. There are also two pretty good restaurants on either side of the entrance to the Chaithram Hotel which specialise in chicken dishes and are relatively inexpensive.

Getting There & Away

Air The Air India office (☎ 64-837) is on Museum Rd, by Vellayambalam Circle. Indian Airlines (☎ 66-370) is on the same road, next to the Mascot Hotel. The Air Lanka office (☎ 68-767) is in the Geethanjali Building at 15/1289/1 Ganapathy Kovil Rd, east of the Secretariat building. The agent for Maldives Airways is the S&J Sales Corporation (☎ 66-105), in the Glass House Building north of the bus station. For flights on East West Airlines call 77-235.

Thiruvananthapuram is a popular place from which to fly to Colombo (Sri Lanka) and Malé (Maldives). To Colombo there's a choice of Air Lanka or Indian Airlines which,

between them, have four flights a week in either direction (on Monday and Thursday with Indian Airlines). To Malé there are flights with Indian Airlines on Monday, Tuesday, Thursday and Saturday in either direction which cost US$63 one way.

Domestically, there are flights with Indian Airlines to Bombay (US$124), Kochi (Cochin, US$23), Goa (US$84), Delhi (US$219) and Madras (US$65).

East West Airlines flies daily in either direction between Thiruvananthapuram and Bombay (US$124).

Bus The bus station, opposite the railway station, is total chaos. Although there is a timetable in English, it's largely a fiction and, as there are no bays, you have to join the scramble every time a bus arrives just in case it happens to be the one you want. The law of the jungle applies each time a battered old bus comes to a screeching halt in a cloud of dust. There are frequent buses to all the main cities in Kerala and to Kanyakumari. Also available are long-distance buses to Madras and Bangalore, but it's better to take a train if you're going that far.

There are buses every half-hour throughout the day to Kochi (Cochin, five hours) which also pass through Alappuzha (Alleppey, 3½ hours). Likewise, there are frequent buses throughout the day to Kollam (Quilon, 1½ hours). To Kanyakumari there are buses every hour (2½ hours). To Thekkady there are three buses daily at 3.30, 8.45 and 11.30 am (eight hours).

Most of the bus services to places in Tamil Nadu are operated by Thiruvalluvar (the Tamil Nadu state bus service) which has its office at the east end of the central bus station. It has services to Madras (four daily, the first at 9.45 am and the last at 7.30 pm, 17 hours), Madurai (10 daily between 4.30 am and 11 pm, seven hours), Pondicherry (once daily at 3.30 pm, 16 hours) and Coimbatore (once daily at 6.30 pm) as well as Nagercoil and Erode.

Train Although the buses are much faster than the trains, Kerala State Road Transport buses, like most others in southern India, make no concessions to comfort and the drivers are pretty reckless. If you prefer to keep your adrenalin levels down, the trains are a pleasant alternative.

The reservation office, on the first floor of the station building, is efficient and computerised and there are plenty of tourist quota tickets on most trains. On the other hand, you must book in advance as far ahead as possible as all trains out of Thiruvananthapuram are heavily susbscribed. Trains to Madras, Bangalore, Bombay and Delhi, for instance, are often fully booked out up to a month in advance. That doesn't always mean you have no chance of getting on but you must get waitlisted. The booking office is open Monday to Saturday from 8 am to 2 pm and 2.15 to 8 pm; on Sunday, it's open from 8 am to 2 pm. The foreign tourist booking 'cell' is at counter 8.

Going up the coast, you can take virtually any train you like as far as Kollam (Quilon) but, beyond that. the choice is restricted since the trains going east and north-east branch off at Kollam and head for Shencottah. Further north still, beyond Thrissur (Trichur), many others branch off east and go through Tamil Nadu via Palakkad (Palghat).

Trains which go all the way up the coast as far as Mangalore include the daily *Parasuram Express* and *Malabar Express*. There's also the daily *Vanchinad Express* which goes to Ernakulam and the *Cannanore Express* which goes to Kannur (Cannanore). It's 65 km from Thiruvananthapuram to Kollam (Rs 20/69 in 2nd/1st class); 201 km to Ernakulam (Rs 47/161); 414 km to Kozhikode (Calicut; Rs 80/289); and 634 km to Mangalore (16 hours, Rs 108/397).

For the long-haulers, there's the daily *Kerala Express* to Delhi which takes 52 hours to cover the 3054 km and costs Rs 255/1274 in 2nd/1st class. There's also the once-weekly (Friday) *Himsagar Express* to Jammu Tawi which goes via Delhi.

To Madras, there's the daily *Trivandrum-Madras Mail* which takes 16 hours to cover the 925 km and costs Rs 138/508 in 2nd/1st class. The daily *Nagercoil/Bangalore Express* from Thiruvananthapuram to Bangalore takes 18 hours and the fares for the 855-km trip are Rs 139/473 in 2nd/1st class. The 2062-km trip to Bombay on the *Kanyakumari Express* takes 45 hours and costs Rs 205/926 in 2nd/1st class. You can, of course, use this same train as it comes south to get to Kanyakumari. The 87-km trip costs Rs 21/90 in 2nd/1st class.

It's a nine-hour journey to Coimbatore (for Mettupalayam and Ooty) and there's a choice of express trains. The 427-km trip costs Rs 80/297 in 2nd/1st class.

Those wishing to go direct to Calcutta without a change must take the weekly (Thursday) *Gawahati Express*.

Getting Around

To/From the Airport The disorganised little airport is six km from the city centre. A No 14 local bus will take you there for around Rs 1. A taxi will cost around Rs 50 and an auto-rickshaw Rs 25 but you'll have to haggle for these prices.

Local Transport There are very crowded local state government buses, as well as auto-rickshaws and taxis. For transport around the city itself, auto-rickshaws are probably your best bet. The drivers are reluctant to use the meters, but flagfall is officially Rs 3 for the first km.

Bus No 111 for Kovalam Beach departs 25 times daily from stand 19 of the Fort Bus stand. This platform is actually on M G Rd, 100 metres south of the bus station, directly opposite the Hotel Luciya. The first bus leaves on the half-hour journey at 6.20 am and the last at 9 pm. The fare is Rs 2.50. Although the bus starts out ridiculously overcrowded, it rapidly empties.

A share taxi from this bus stand to Kovalam Beach costs Rs 20 per person and they leave when full (up to eight passengers is standard). An auto-rickshaw costs Rs 35 *if* the drivers are desperate to return to Kovalam but normally it's Rs 45 to Rs 50 – more if it's obvious you've just arrived (I met people who were hit for Rs 100!). This is the fare to the bus stand at Kovalam but, if you want to go to the lighthouse end of the beach (Vizhinjam) then the fare is Rs 60 as it's a longer trip. Be certain to agree on a price before setting out – some drivers get very aggressive.

AROUND THIRUVANANTHAPURAM
Padmanabhapuram Palace

Although actually in Tamil Nadu, this fine palace is easily visited from Thiruvananthapuram or Kanyakumari. It was once the seat of the rulers of Travancore, a princely state for over 400 years which included a large part of present-day Kerala and the western littoral of Tamil Nadu. The palace is superbly constructed of local teak and granite and stands within the massive stone town walls which kept Tipu Sultan at bay in the 18th century. The architecture is exquisite, with ceilings carved in floral patterns, windows laid with jewel-coloured mica, floors finished to a high polish with a special compound of crushed shells and coconuts, eggwhite and the juices of local plants. The 18th-century murals in the puja room on the upper floors are in an excellent state of preservation, surpassing even those at Mattancherry in Kochi – ask at the curator's office for special access.

With its banqueting halls, audience chamber, women's quarters, recruiting courtyard, cool, louvered galleries and many other features, the palace is a must for anyone visiting this part of the country. The palace is closed on Mondays.

To get there, you can either catch a local bus from Thiruvananthapuram (or Kovalam Beach) or take one of the Kanyakumari tours organised by the Kerala Tourist Development Corporation.

Vijnana Kala Vedi Centre

If you'd like to study Indian arts under expert supervision in a village setting, it's worth considering taking one of the courses offered at the Vijnana Kala Vedi Centre at Aranmula, a village 12 km from Changannur (which is about halfway between Thiruvananthapuram and Kochi). Main subjects include: Kathakali, Mohiniattam and Bharata Natyam (of Tamil Nadu) dancing, Karnatic vocal music, percussion instruments, woodcarving, mural painting, Keralan cooking, languages (Hindi, Malayalam, Sanskrit), *kaulams* (auspicious decorations), Kalaripayat (Keralan martial art), ayurvedic medicine, mythology, astrology and religion.

You can put your own course together and stay as long as you like, though they prefer people who will stay a minimum of one month. Fees, which include full board and lodging, and two subjects of study, are US$200 per week, reduced to US$160 per week if you stay for four weeks or US$700 per month, reduced to US$500 per month if you stay over four months.

For further details about this centre, contact Louba Schild (Director), Vijnan Kala Vedi Centre, Tarayil Mukku Junction, Aranmula 689533, Kerala, or Stages Kerala Ecole du Mouvement, 7 rue du Debarcadere, 75017 Paris (☎ 45-74-27-30).

KOVALAM

Kovalam, just south of Thiruvananthapuram, is one of India's best beaches and *the* favourite watering hole of travellers in southern India. The main beach consists of a two fairly small, palm-fringed coves which are separated from the beaches on either side by rocky headlands. There is good surf on most days but, if you're not a strong swimmer, you should approach the water cautiously until you're familiar with the rip – one or two people drown here every year. Lifeguards patrol the main two bays during daylight hours, and flags indicate where it's safe to swim.

There's a plethora of places to stay ranging from cheap, simple concrete boxes with shared showers and earth toilets to comfortable and well-positioned mid-range hotels and a five-star luxury hotel belonging to the Ashok Group. Likewise, there's a bewildering choice of beach-style restaurants, most right on the water's edge, all of which offer a variety of seafood as well as Western dishes and desserts.

Despite its popularity with Western travellers, the atmosphere at Kovalam is still fairly mellow. Back from the the two main coves, the local people continue to cultivate their rice, coconuts, bananas, pawpaws and vegetables, and the fishers still row their dugouts out to sea and pull in their nets by hand, though, these days, there's the inevitable outboard motor attached to the stern.

On the other hand, the beach's popularity has brought changes. It's certainly not anything vaguely resembling the archetypal 'deserted beach'. In the high season (November to February) it's awash with bronzed sun, sand and wave worshippers from all over the world and, at weekends, it attracts hordes of Indian tourists, many of whom seem to come here solely to gawp at the exposed flesh liberally distributed over the sand. If you're a woman, you may find this obtrusive attention, and the giggling and silly comments which accompany it, wearing and tedious. At such times you may have to seek sanctuary in one of the beach cafes which the day-trippers don't patronise (mainly because of the relatively high prices of anything other than tea). Late in the afternoon and at night (and throughout the low season), calm once again descends on the place.

Remember, however, Hinduism is the predominant religion in Kerala, and bold displays of naked flesh may be considered offensive. Be discreet and respect the local sensibilities.

Another of the changes which have been wrought is the appearance of numerous craft and carpet shops (usually of Tibetan, Kashmiri and Rajasthani origin), clothing stores (ready to wear and made to order), book exchanges (excellent choice in most European languages), general stores selling everything from toilet paper to sunscreen, travel agents, yoga schools and even massage parlours. And, just in case you thought you'd left home to immerse yourself in a different culture, Western videos are now firmly entrenched in a number of the restaurants with two shows a night. If you missed out on Pink Floyd's *The Wall* or the latest action-packed cliff-hanger – no problem – you can see it here.

None of this comes particularly cheaply since, wherever there's money floating around, everyone wants a piece of the action. If you're on a tight budget you're going to have to watch carefully what you eat, drink and otherwise do, and where you stay. You also need to be careful with valuables since wealth always attracts thieves.

Orientation

Kovalam is spread out and finding a place to stay which has a vacancy and suits your budget can involve quite a bit of walking. It's about 15 minutes on foot from the bus stop to the lighthouse end of the second cove and most of the hotels and restaurants.

The paths through the coconut palms and around the back of the paddy field are hard to negotiate at night without a full moon, unless you're familiar with them.

You can visit the lighthouse between 2 and 4 pm for Rs 1.

Information

Money The branch of the Central Bank of India at the Ashok Radisson Beach Resort changes travellers' cheques quickly, without fuss and in a friendly manner. It is only open from 10.30 am to 2 pm Monday to Friday, and 10.30 am to noon on Saturday.

Post The nearest post office is in Kovalam village.

Travel Agencies Try Aries Travel, who are based in Thiruvananthapuram and have an office in Kovalam. According to a traveller, they are very efficient and among other things offer trips to the Maldives for US$70 return from Thiruvananthapuram.

Warning Don't drink local well water at Kovalam. There are so many pit toilets almost adjacent to wells that you're guaranteed to get very sick if you do. Stick to bottled mineral water even if it does cost half the price of a bottle of beer.

Places to Stay

There is no shortage of accommodation at the bottom end of the market – the coconut groves behind the beach are littered with small lodges, houses for rent and blocks of recently constructed rooms. To a large extent, you get what you pay for, though you must shop around and not necessarily take the first place you are offered. You also need to avoid touts who wait for the arrival of the buses from Thiruvananthapuram. If you let any of these people take you to a hotel or house then you'll pay more.

In general, there are two main factors which affect how much you pay. These are proximity to the beach and the season. The nearer you are to the beach, the more you pay. In the high season (November to February), all the hotels jack-up their prices but some budget hotel owners do this with a vengeance which knows no bounds – up to four times the low-season price is not that unusual. Under these circumstances it often costs only slightly more to stay in a good mid-range hotel with the comfort, security and value for money which they offer even though it may involve a few minutes walk to the beach. It's amazing how many travellers will pay silly prices for a concrete box with just a bed and outside bucket shower just for the sake of being right on the beach.

If you intend to stay in a budget hotel, you need to be aware of theft. This has inevitably risen as the number of visitors to Kovalam increases each year. It certainly hasn't reached alarming proportions, but you definitely need to watch your gear. The most common trick is to hook stuff out of your room through the bars on the windows, even at night while you're in there! The options are to close the windows (not much fun on warm nights) or, more sensibly, stash your gear under the bed. Make sure the room has a decent bolt and windows which lock. Most mid-range hotels have safe deposit boxes.

Places to Stay – bottom end

To get a good deal in this category in the high season you need to shop around and you need to do this without a pack on your back.

If it's obvious you've just arrived, you'll pay whatever they think you can afford. Dump that pack in a restaurant, have a friend look after it, and then go looking. And have a good idea about how long you intend to stay as most places will offer a substantial discount if you're staying more than just a few days.

Kovalam is the sort of small, informal beach where travellers quickly develop a liking for particular lodges and restaurants, so it's hard to single out particular establishments for recommendation without being unfair to the others. Most, though not all, of the cheapest places are along or just at the back of the beachfront. There are others along the road in from Thiruvananthapuram and along 'lighthouse road'. Many of the beach restaurants also have a few basic rooms with shared bathroom and toilet facilities but other facilities are minimal. To get one of these rooms in the high season often involves leaving a deposit and waiting a few days for people to move on. Popular in this category is *Jeevan House*, right in the centre of the lighthouse cove.

Close by and just back from the beachfront is *Surya Tourist Home* run by the very friendly and helpful Surya. This is a no-frills place without mosquito nets but with fans and costs Rs 20/25 with common bathroom or Rs 30/40 with own bathroom in the low season and Rs 50/100 or Rs 60/125 respectively in the high season. Next door is the *White House* which has rooms for Rs 20/40 with attached bathroom in the low season and Rs 60/125 in the high season.

At the southern end of the lighthouse cove is the *Sea Flower Home*, next to the general store, which offers small concrete boxes with attached bathroom for Rs 60/80 in the low season but an outrageous Rs 300/400 in the high season. Further up 'lighthouse road', opposite the Varmas Beach Resort, the *Eden Seaside Resort* is good value at Rs 75 a double in the low season and Rs 150 in the high season. All the rooms have attached bathroom but there are no singles. Almost next door is the *Hotel Thiruvathira* (☎ 657) which has downstairs doubles at Rs 75 and upstairs doubles with balcony and bay views

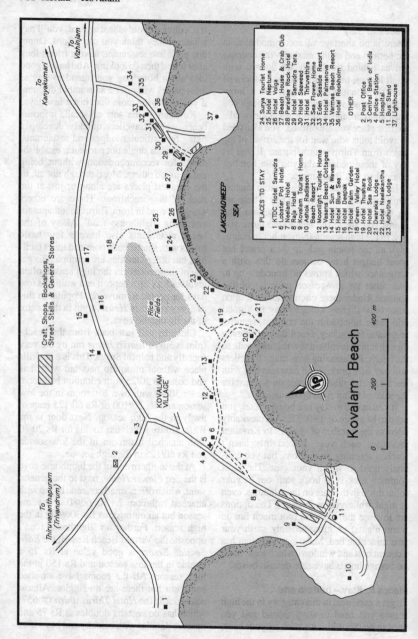

PLACES TO STAY

1   KTDC Hotel Samudra
6   Lobster Pot Hotel
7   Neelam Hotel
8   Raja Hotel
9   Kovalam Tourist Home
10 Ashok Radisson
    Beach Resort
12 Vasanta Seaface Tourist Home
13 Vasans Beach Cottages
14 Hotel Sun & Waves
15 Hotel Blue Sea
16 Hotel Deepak
17 Hotel Palm Garden
18 Green Valley Hotel
19 Hotel Thushara
20 Hotel Sea Rock
22 Hotel Neelakantha
23 Achutha Lodge
24 Surya Tourist Home
25 Hotel Neptune
26 Hotel Volga
27 Beach House & Crab Club
28 Paradise Rock Hotel
29 Hotel Samudra Tara
30 Hotel Seaweed
31 Hotel Thiruvathira
32 Sea Flower Home
33 Eden Resort
34 Seaside Resort
35 Varmas Beach Resort
36 Hotel Rockholm

OTHER

2   Post Office
3   Central Bank of India
4   Police Station
5   Helipad
11 Bus Stand
37 Lighthouse

for Rs 100. All rooms have attached bathroom and the manager assured me prices are the same throughout the year.

Back down 'lighthouse road' close to the beach is *Paradise Rock* (☎ 658), which has downstairs doubles at Rs 100 and upstairs doubles at Rs 150. High season rates are twice this amount (negotiable). An extension and restaurant should be completed in 1993.

Back from the beach on lighthouse cove is the relatively large *Beach House & Crab Club*. The management here are keen and offer doubles with attached bathroom for Rs 60 in the low season and Rs 150 in the high season. There's an attached restaurant with good seafood.

Up near the hospital below the road in from Thiruvananthapuram is the *Lobster Pot Hotel* which has singles/doubles in the low season for Rs 75/100 or Rs 150/200 in the high season. It's a little bit tatty but the staff are friendly and it has a restaurant. Not far from here and just back from the main road is the *Neelam Hotel*, a concrete structure with no character whatsoever and an air of neglect. It has doubles at Rs 50 in the low season and Rs 100 in the high season. There's a restaurant of sorts.

Right at the back of the paddy field is the *Green Valley/Silent Valley Hotel* (☎ 636), usually referred to as 'Sergeant's Place'. This, too, is popular and has rooms for Rs 50/75 in the low season and Rs 75/125 in the high season. They also have a number of very attractive stone-built cottages further up the hill which cost Rs 100 a double in the low season and Rs 200 in the high season. All rooms have attached bathroom and there's a restaurant.

Further afield, the *Kovalam Tourist Home* (☎ 441) has seven pleasant rooms, all with attached bathroom, for Rs 40/75 in the low season and Rs 50/100 in the high season as well as an air-con double for Rs 300. There's a bar and restaurant. The trouble with this place is that it's too far from the beach and involves a lot of walking. However, the staff are friendly.

There are at least a dozen other bottom-end lodges and new ones pop up all the time.

Places to Stay – middle

The best hunting ground for mid-range hotels is 'lighthouse road' though there are others elsewhere.

Just up from the beach on this road is the *Hotel Seaweed* (☎ 391). This is an excellent place, very friendly, secure and with sea breezes and bay views. It's been imaginatively built and has a range of rooms to suit all budgets and tastes from Rs 110 up to Rs 440 for a double with attached bathroom, plus there are more expensive but very spacious rooms with balconies. Prices in the low season are less. It's very clean, towels, soap and toilet paper are provided and there's a rooftop restaurant with views and good food but no beer.

Just below the Seaweed is the *Hotel Samudra Tara* (☎ 653) which is also pleasant but doesn't have the same range of rooms. Rooms with attached bathroom are Rs 110/165 in the low season; more in the high season. Don't confuse this hotel with the KTDC Hotel Samudra much further away on the beach beyond the Radisson Ashok.

Further up 'lighthouse road' is the *Hotel Rockholm* (☎ 406/7), another very good choice with great views over the small cove beyond the lighthouse. In the high season rooms cost Rs 475/500; in the low season there's a 25% discount. Avoid the rooms on the roof if possible as they get very hot during the day. The hotel has its own restaurant (Indian, Chinese and Continental cuisine).

Next up is *Varmas Beach Resort* (☎ 54-478), a new place, beautifully built and with great balconies overlooking the small cove. It's excellent value at Rs 200 for a small double or Rs 300 for a large double, and there are large air-con doubles at Rs 400 in the low season. In the high season prices are Rs 300, Rs 500 and Rs 600 respectively. There's no restaurant, but they have tea, coffee and fruit.

Last up on this same road is the *Hotel Palmanova* (☎ 494). This, too, is an excellent choice with a good range of facilities including a restaurant (Indian, Chinese and Continental) and private beach, and the staff are friendly. All the rooms have attached bathroom, their own private balcony and they all face the sea. In the cheapest season (May to September) singles/doubles cost Rs 150/200 or Rs 300/350 (October, November, March and April). Between 1 December and 20 December and between 6 January and 28/29 February they cost Rs 450/500; between 21 December and 5 January they cost Rs 725.

Back on the beach itself (lighthouse cove), there are two mid-range hotels adjacent to each other. First is the *Hotel Neptune* (☎ 222/622), set back from the beach, which has three types of room: standard, balcony and air-con. In the low season (May to September) singles/doubles are Rs 75/125, Rs 100/150 and Rs 275/350 respectively or, in the high season (October to April), Rs 175/250, Rs 225/275 and Rs 325/450. Prices between 21 December and 5 January are Rs 350, Rs 385 and Rs 600. Tax of 15% must be added to these rates. Kathakali dance performances can be arranged here. Similar to the Neptune is the *Hotel Volga* which stands at the back of the restaurant of the same name right on the beachfront.

Right on the beachfront at the beginning of the next cove is the *Hotel Sea Rock* (☎ 422), an older place which has been popular for a number of years. It is run by the friendly Saludin, who himself has done a lot of overseas travelling and brooks no nonsense from touts. In the low season, doubles (no singles) cost Rs 110/220 for rear/front rooms and Rs 150/440 in the high season. All rooms have attached bathroom. There's a restaurant which serves excellent, tasty food, safe deposit lockers, laundry service and motorcycle hire (Rs 350 per day).

Across the other side of the (usually dry) creek adjacent to the Sea Rock and into the coconut palms a little is the small *Hotel Thushara* (☎ 692). There's both an old part (cheaper) and a new part which consists of a number of superbly built, beautifully furnished self-contained cottages. These cost Rs 150 in the low season and Rs 460 in the high season including taxes. They're spotlessly clean and cool, and soap, towel and

toilet paper are provided. The owner is very friendly indeed plus there's a restaurant.

Up the track behind the Sea Rock is *Vasans Beach Cottages*, a small cluster of self-contained cottages which are very clean and pleasant and cost Rs 175 in the low season and Rs 400 in the high season. Up above here is the popular *Moonlight Tourist Home* (☎ 375) which offers spacious rooms with poster beds and mosquito nets and is squeaky clean. Some of the rooms have their own small balcony. Downstairs/upstairs doubles in the low season cost Rs 150/300 or Rs 350/600 in the high season. They also have one air-con double which costs Rs 650 regardless of the season.

On the hill, up above the main road into Kovalam, is the *Raja Hotel* (☎ 355/455) which rarely seems to attract travellers, but is good value at Rs 100/250 for singles/doubles in the low season and Rs 150/350 in the high season. All the rooms have attached bathroom and face the sea, there's a restaurant (Indian, Chinese and Continental) and a bar. They occasionally have live bands at weekends.

Lastly, there's the KTDC *Hotel Samudra* (☎ 54-242) but it's very inconveniently located about two km north-west of the main two coves. On the other hand, if you don't like crowded beaches, this could be an advantage. Facilities at this hotel include a bar and restaurant and foreign exchange. Doubles cost Rs 280 to Rs 490, or Rs 740 with air-con.

Places to Stay – top end

Top of the line is the five-star *Ashok Radisson Beach Resort* (☎ 68-010) superbly located on the headland at the north end of the second cove. Major extensions should have been completed by the time you read this. It has all the facilities which you'd expect of a hotel belonging to the Ashok chain including central air-conditioning, a bar and restaurant (south Indian and Continental), swimming pool, outdoor and indoor sports facilities, bank, bookshop and car rental. Rooms in the low season cost Rs 1300/1450, or Rs 1450/1600 in the high season. There are also suites at Rs 3000 to Rs 4500. All major credit cards are accepted.

Places to Eat

Lighthouse beach is literally wall-to-wall restaurants the whole way along plus there are others scattered among the coconut palms back from the beach as well as those which are part of the various hotels. Almost all of them cater to an international palate with Western-style breakfasts (porridge, muesli, eggs, toast, jam, pancakes), seafood with chips and salad, and a variety of fruit salads and desserts. There's even a 'Lonely Planet vegetarian restaurant' – no, it has nothing to do with us and we're not planning to open a franchised chain soon!

Everyone has their favourite and there's a lot of variety to choose from. Some are more intimate than others, some have music while others don't, and a few have videos with two shows per night. Quite a few of them put half their tables and chairs out on the beach at night so you can have dinner by candlelight. The majority have cold beers (and various spirits) but some don't carry stock without advance notice. A few stay open until the small hours (sometimes all night) but others are closed by 11 pm. You'll soon find out which they are.

It's probably true to say that they all try hard to please but some are definitely more successful at achieving this than others. In a fishing community such as this, various forms of seafood are obviously a favourite item with travellers but, unfortunately, the standard of preparation is generally only average. Fish, in particular, is too often dry, overcooked and almost tasteless even if you go to great pains to explain how you'd like it done. They can usually turn out good chips and reasonable salads, though, and it's difficult to ruin an omelette. Curried dishes tend to fare better. The volume of clientele which a restaurant gets *may* be an indication of the standard of its cuisine, though not always. One night it could be good; another only average.

The other factor about these beachside restaurants is the sheer cost of a seafood meal. While there may appear to be fish (or other seafood) on the menu at a reasonable price, what normally happens is that they'll bring the freshly caught items to show you and ask you to choose. Be sure to ask the price of what you choose as it will often bear no resemblance to what it says on the menu. A plate of king prawns, for example, can be well over Rs 100 and fish in the Rs 60 to Rs 70 bracket. When you add to this the cost of chips, salad, dessert and drinks, it can get very expensive. These are obviously Western prices – you won't see Indians eating at these places. Breakfast items are generally much more reasonably priced.

It would be unfair and, in many cases, misleading to recommend any of the beach-side restaurants to the exclusion of others since there's not a great deal to choose between them. Much of the time, where you eat will depend on the friends you make or what sort of ambience you're looking for. Videos certainly don't make for a lively conversation, for instance.

Again, given the sort of prices which the beachside restaurants charge for seafood and the quality of their product, it's worth considering eating occasionally in one or other of the restaurants in the mid-range hotels. By doing so, there's a fair chance they'll have reasonable equipment and properly trained staff capable of turning out something tasty and attractively presented.

In addition to the restaurants, a number of local women do the rounds of the sun worshippers on the beach, selling fruit. The ring of 'Hello, baba. Mango? Papaya? Banana? Coconut? Pineapple?' will soon become a familiar part of your day. Naturally, they'll sell you fruit at any price you're willing to pay so, on your first few encounters, establish what you think is fair for certain fruits. After that, they'll remember your face and you don't have to repeat the performance. They rarely have any change, but they're reliable about bringing it to you later. There are also guys on the beach selling batik lungis, beach mats and leaf paintings. Plenty of others offer cheap Kerala grass. Toddy (coconut beer) and feni (spirits made by distilling the fermented mash of either coconuts or cashew nuts – the two varieties taste quite different) are available from shops in Kovalam village.

Although cold beers are available at most of the beach restaurants, the only actual bars ('permit rooms') are at the Ashok Radisson Beach Resort, Hotel Raja, and the Kovalam Tourist Home.

Getting There & Away

Bus The local No 111 bus to Thiruvananthapuram runs 25 times daily, but the schedules are not too believable. The first bus leaves at 6.15 am, the last at 10 pm, from the stand outside the entrance to the Ashok Radisson Beach Resort. It costs Rs 2.50.

There are also direct services to Ernakulam and Kanyakumari (Cape Comorin), which are a good way of avoiding the crush at Thiruvananthapuram. Kanyakumari is two hours away and there are four departures daily. One bus leaves each morning for Thekkady in the Periyar Wildlife Sanctuary. Direct buses go to Kollam if you want to do the backwater trip.

Taxi & Auto-Rickshaw Share taxis are available to or from Thiruvananthapuram. They leave when full (up to eight passengers) and cost Rs 20 per person. Autorickshaws *may* be available for Rs 35 if the drivers are desperate to return to Thiruvananthapuram, but otherwise you're looking at Rs 45 to Rs 50 from the Ashok and Rs 60 from 'lighthouse road'. If you're coming into Kovalam from Thiruvananthapuram, it's best to arrive at the lighthouse end of the beach (Vizhinjam) as you're much closer to the hotels here and there usually aren't any touts around.

OTHER KERALAN BEACHES

If you're one of those seekers after almost-deserted and unspoiled beaches and you find Kovalam too blasé and crowded to handle, there may be good news. But, at present, you'll have to be satisfied with somewhat primitive accommodation and minimal facilities. It's been designated for development

by the state tourist organisation but that will obviously take some time to accomplish.

In the meantime, there's a superb, palm-fringed and extensive beach at **Bekal** in the extreme north of the state just south of Kasaragod just waiting for you. Give it a try, but take with you everything you wouldn't expect to find in a small coastal village.

LAKSHADWEEP

Population: 51,000

The Lakshadweep archipelago consists of 36 islands some 200 to 300 km off the Kerala coast and forms a northern extension of the Maldives chain. Ten of the islands are inhabited. They are Andrott, Amini, Agatti, Bitra, Chetlat, Kadmat, Kalpeni, Kavaratti (headquarters), Kiltan and Minicoy. The islands form the smallest of the Union Territories of India and are the country's only coral islands. The population stands at around 51,000, 93% of whom are Muslims of the Shafi school of the Sunni sect. Malayalam is the language spoken on all the islands except Minicoy where it is Mahl – also spoken in the Maldives. The main occupation of the people is fishing and the production of copra and coir. Tourism is an emerging industry.

Legend has it that the islands were first settled by sailors from Kodungallur (Cranganore) who were shipwrecked there after going in search of their king, Cheraman Perumal, who had secretly left on a pilgrimage to Mecca. The first historical records, however, date from the 7th century when a *marabout* (Muslim saint) was shipwrecked on the island of Amini. Despite initial opposition to his efforts to convert the inhabitants to Islam, he eventually succeeded and when he died was buried on Andrott. His grave is revered to this day as a sacred site.

Even after the conversion of the entire population to Islam, sovereignty remained in the hands of the Hindu Raja of Chirakkal. However, it eventually passed to the Muslim rulers of Kannur (Cannanore) in the 16th century and later, in 1783, to Tipu Sultan. Following the defeat of Tipu Sultan by the British at the battle of Srirangapatnam in 1799, the islands were annexed by the East

India Company. The Union Territory was constituted in 1956.

These palm-fringed coral islands with their beautiful lagoons are every bit as inviting as those in the Maldive archipelago but, due to the lack of infrastructure, they remained essentially off limits to foreign tourists until very recently. Only with a special permit was it possible to go there and, only then, to one of the islands. This is now changing with the opening up of four of the inhabited islands (Kavaratti, Kalpeni, Minicoy and Kadmat) to Indian tourists and the building of a resort complex on the uninhabited island of Bangaram, which is open to both Indian and foreign tourists.

Permits

All tourists need permission to visit Lakshadweep, except those booked on a package cruise, in which case permission is automatic. Permits are issued by the Secretary to the Administrator (☎ 69-131), Union Territory of Lakshadweep, Indira Gandhi Rd, Willingdon Island, Kochi (Cochin) 682 003; or the Liaison Officer (☎ 38-6807), Lakshadweep, 202 Kasturba Gandhi Marg, New Delhi 110001. Four passport photos are needed. Foreigners are only allowed to visit Bangaram island.

Places to Stay & Eat

Except on Bangaram, where there is a purpose-built tourist resort with limited recreational facilities, no tourist accommodation exists on the islands other than Government Guest Houses and the private huts of the package tour organisation, SPORTS (Society for the Promotion of Recreational Tourism & Sports), on Kavaratti and Kadmat. Likewise, there are no restaurants or snack bars other than those at the tourist complexes apart from the occasional 'meals' restaurants serving local food.

Package tourists are accommodated and fed on board ship except at Bangaram, Kavaratti and Kadmat.

On Bangaram island there is the *Bangaram Island Resort* which offers full board for US$75 to US$125 (twin share per person), US$140 to US$240 (single), or US$375 to US$625 (deluxe bungalow accommodating four people) depending on the season. Leisure activities (scuba diving, snorkelling, deep sea fishing and boat trips) are extra. Reservations should be made through the Manager, Bangaram Island Resort, Casino Hotel (☎ 34-0221), Willingdon Island, Kochi 682003.

Getting There & Away

Air Vayudoot flies to Agatti from Kochi (Cochin, US$134), Kozhikode (Calicut, US$120) and Madras (US$103). Transfer to Bangaram Island is by speedboat (US$30) or helicopter (US$75) during the monsoon season (May to September).

The islands are interconnected by helicopter flights.

Boat Package tours by luxury ship are arranged through SPORTS (☎ 34-0387), Lakshadweep Office, Indira Gandhi Rd, Willingdon Island, Kochi (Cochin) 682003. Foreign tourists should contact their representative at the Hotel Casino on Willingdon Island in the first instance.

These tours take place on the MV *Tipu Sultan* which plies regularly between Kochi and Lakshadweep between September and April. Both two-berth and four-berth air-con cabins are available with common bathrooms, and there are also 1st-class cabins with own bathrooms. Bed linen and towels are provided. Only Indian food is available on board. The prices of these tours are all-inclusive.

The other vessel which plies the same route as the *Tipu Sultan* on a regular basis is the MV *Bharat Seema*.

Bookings for the tours should be made in advance as the ships' programmes are subject to change at short notice. Four different package tours are available, one of them of five days duration and the rest of four days duration.

Madras

Population: 5.4 million
Main Language: Tamil

Madras, India's fourth-largest city, is the capital of Tamil Nadu state. It suffers far less from congestion and overcrowding than other big cities in India, but this is rapidly changing and it won't be long before it rivals the others for bustle, noise, fumes and the odours associated with untreated sewage. Catch it whilst it's still half-pleasant!

Madrassis are zealous guardians of Tamil culture which they regard as inherently superior to the hybridised cultures further north. They have, for instance, been among the most vociferous opponents of Hindi being made the national language, and Madras is the film centre for Tamil movies – even the State Chief Minister, Jayalalitha, is an ex-movie star. There is also a deep grassroots sympathy for the Tamil separatist movement in neighbouring Sri Lanka, though few would have expressed support for the assassination of Rajiv Gandhi at the hands of Tamil extremists.

On a culinary level, Tamil Nadu is India's vegetarian state *par excellence*. It was also, until just a few years ago, a 'dry' state and, although prohibition has been essentially abolished, drinking alcohol in a bar in this state can still leave you with the feeling that it's only barely tolerated.

On an organisational level, the state and the capital city has a remarkably efficient range of public services. Here it's possible to use public buses without undue discomfort and the urban commuter trains without a second thought. There are, it is true, slums and beggars but they are far less obtrusive and smaller in number than in other major cities. The state tourist corporation is also well organised as a rule and has created a chain of hotels which offer reasonable midrange accommodation in most centres of interest. Although the city has long been important for textile manufacturing, a great

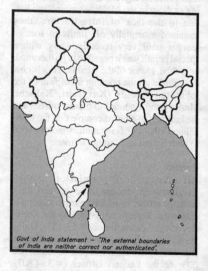
Govt of India statement – 'The external boundaries of India are neither correct nor authenticated'.

deal of industrial expansion, including car-assembly plants, railway coach and truck works, engineering plants, cigarette factories, film studios and educational institutes, has taken place in recent years.

As a tourist attraction, Madras is something of a nonevent compared to the real marvels elsewhere in the state. The main reason travellers come here is to transact business or to make a long-distance travel connection.

The city suffers from acute water shortages in the summer months, especially if the last monsoon season has been a poor one.

History

Madras was the site of the East India Company's first settlement – founded in 1639 on land given by the Raja of Chandragiri, the last representative of the Vijayanagar rulers of Hampi. A small fort was built on the settlement in 1644, and a town, which subsequently became known as George

Town, in the area of Fort St George, arose north of it. The settlement became independent of Banten, Java, in 1683 and was granted its first municipal charter in 1688 by James II. It thus has the oldest municipal corporation in India, a fact which Tamil Nadu state governors are only too keen to point out at every available opportunity.

During the 18th and early 19th centuries, when the British and French competed for supremacy in India, the city's fortunes waxed and waned; it was briefly occupied by the French on one occasion. It was also the base from which Clive of India set out on his military expeditions during the Wars of the Carnatic. During the 19th century it was the seat of the Madras presidency, one of the four divisions of British Imperial India.

Orientation

The city may be conveniently divided into two parts. The older section, known as George Town, is west of the dock area and north of Poonamallee High Rd. In these narrow, busy streets are the offices of shipping and forwarding agents, some cheaper hotels and restaurants, large office buildings, bazaars and the GPO. The area's main focal point is Parry's Corner – the intersection of Prakasam Rd (more commonly known as Popham's Broadway) and N S C Bose Rd. Many of the city buses terminate here; the Tamil Nadu State bus stand and the Thiruvalluvar bus stand (the two long-distance bus stations) are close by on the Esplanade.

The other main part of the city is south of Poonamallee High Rd. Through it runs Madras' main road, Anna Salai, which is still generally known as Mount Rd. Along it are most of the airline offices, theatres, banks, bookshops, craft centres, consulates, tourist offices and, close by, the bulk of the top-range hotels and restaurants.

Egmore and Central, Madras' two main railway stations, are close to Poonamallee High Rd. If you're arriving from anywhere other than Tamil Nadu or Kerala you'll come into Central Station. Egmore is the arrival point for most Tamil Nadu and Kerala trains.

Egmore also has the largest concentration of bottom and middle-range hotels, although these days it's difficult to get a cheap room after noon.

Information

Tourist Offices The Government of India tourist office (☎ 86-9685) at 154 Mount Rd is open Monday to Friday from 9.15 am to 5.45 pm and on Saturday and public holidays from 9 am to 1 pm. It's closed Sunday. This office is a good one; the staff are knowledgeable, friendly and helpful. A bus (No 11 or 18) from Parry's Corner or Central Station takes you there.

There are also information counters at the domestic and international airport terminals but they only have limited information.

The India Tourism Development Corporation (ITDC; ☎ 47-4216) is at 29 Victoria Crescent on the corner of Commander-in-Chief (C-in-C) Rd. It's open from 6 am to 8 pm Monday to Saturday, and 6 am to 2 pm Sundays. This is not a tourist office as such, but all the ITDC tours can be booked, and in fact start, here.

The Tamil Nadu Government tourist office (☎ 84-0752) is at 143 Mount Rd. It is open daily from 10 am to 5 pm Monday to Friday. You can book all Tamil Nadu Tourism Development Corporation (TTDC) tours from here as well as make bookings for any of their hotels and lodges. The Tamil Nadu government also maintains offices at Central Railway Station (☎ 56-3351) and the Thiruvalluvar bus station.

The Automobile Association of South India (☎ 58-6121) is at 187 Mount Rd. Apart from route information, the organisation offers accommodation for members of any foreign automobile association, and car-parking facilities on the premises.

Money The State Bank of India's main branch is at the beginning of North Beach Rd and, if you want to change travellers' cheques, this is where you should go. The branch on Mount Rd officially will not change them (though sometimes they will).

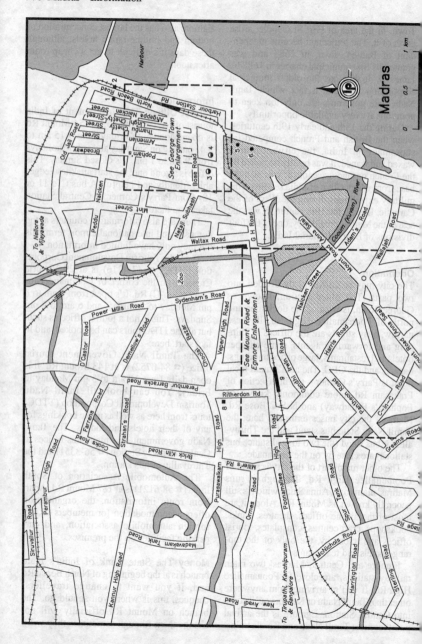

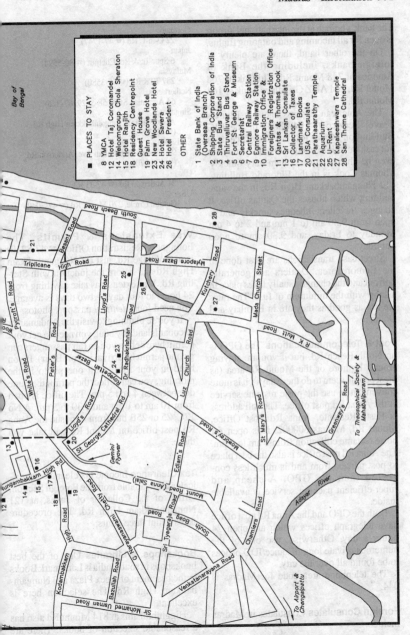

PLACES TO STAY

8 YMCA
12 Hotel Taj Coromandel
14 Welcomgroup Chola Sheraton
15 Hotel Ranjith
18 Residency Centrepoint
19 Guest House
19 Palm Grove Hotel
23 New Woodlands Hotel
24 Hotel Savera
26 Hotel President

OTHER

1 State Bank of India
   (Overseas Branch)
2 Shipping Corporation of India
3 State Bus Stand
4 Thiruvalluvar Bus Stand
5 Fort St George & Museum
6 Secretariat
7 Central Railway Station
9 Egmore Railway Station
10 Immigration Office &
   Foreigners' Registration Office
11 Qantas & Thomas Cook
13 Sri Lankan Consulate
16 Collector of Taxes
17 Landmark Books
20 USA Consulate
21 Parathasarathy Temple
22 Aquarium
25 U-Rent
27 Kapaleeshwara Temple
28 San Thome Cathedral

Bay of
Bengal

South Beach Road
Besant Road
Triplicane High Road
Mylapore Bazar Road
Kutchery Road
Mada Church Street
R K Mutt Road
Lloyd's Road
Pycroft's Road
Wood   Road
Peter's Road
White's Road
Rosapettah Bazar
Dr Radhakrishnan Rd
St George Cathedral Rd
Luz Church Road
Edlam's Road
St Mary's Road
Greenway's Road
Mowbray's Road
Cathedral Road
Chamiers Road
Mount Road (Anna Salai)
Gemini Flyover
Nungambakkam High Rd
South Boag Road
Sri Tyagaraja Road
G N Chetty Road
Kodambakkam
Sir Mohamed Usman Road
Bazullah Road
Venkatanarayana Road
Adyar River
To Theosophical Society &
Mahabalipuram
To Airport &
Chengalpattu

The bank's branch at the international airport is open for all incoming and outgoing flights.

On the other hand, there are plenty of foreign banks, including the Bank of America at 748 Mount Rd, Citibank at 768 Mount Rd, and ANZ Grindlays Bank at 164 Mount Rd.

The American Express agent is Binny's Travel Service (☎ 84-0803) in the LIC Building on Mount Rd, but this office does not cash travellers' cheques and they may not even be able to replace them very quickly. Thomas Cook is in the Eldorado Building, 112 Nungambakkam High Rd, in the same building which houses the Qantas office. It changes travellers' cheques quickly and is open from 9.30 am to 1 pm and 2 to 4 pm Monday to Friday, and 9.30 am to noon Saturday.

Street cash transactions are best done in the Egmore area. Dealers are generally upfront and the change usually takes place in a shop with the minimum of fuss. The rates are not as good as they are in Bombay and Delhi.

Post & Telecommunications The GPO is on North Beach Rd, but if you are staying around Egmore or the Mount Rd area (as most people seem to do these days), it is more convenient to use the poste restante service at the Anna Rd post office. The full address is Poste Restante, Anna Rd Post Office, Mount Rd, Madras 600002. It is open for poste restante collection from 8 am to 6 pm. The Anna Rd post office is also the best place to post parcels from and is much less congested than the GPO. A cheap and super-efficient packing service is available inside.

Both the GPO and the Anna Rd post office have telegraph offices which are open 24 hours a day. Otherwise, use one of the numerous private long-distance/IDD offices to be found all over the city.

The telephone area code for Madras is 044.

Foreign Consulates Consulates in Madras include:

Germany
    22 C-in-C Rd (☎ 47-1747)
Japan
    6 Spur Tank Rd, Chetput (☎ 86-5594)
Malaysia
    287 TTK Rd (☎ 45-3580)
Netherlands
    64 Armenian St (☎ 58-5829, 67-326)
Singapore
    Apex Plaza, 3 Nungambakkam High Rd (☎ 47-3795)
Sri Lanka
    9-D Nawab Habibullah Ave, Anderson Rd (☎ 47-2270)
UK
    24 Anderson Rd (☎ 47-3136)
USA
    Gemini Circle, 220 Mount Rd (☎ 47-3040)

Visa Extensions & Permits The Foreigners' Registration Office (☎ 47-8210) is at 9 Village Rd, just off Nungambakkam High Rd and before the junction with Sterling Rd. Visa extensions take anything from 24 hours to four days – two days is average. You need four *identical* passport photos.

If you're planning to visit the Andaman & Nicobar Islands by boat, you need to get your permit here before you go (air passengers can get the permit on arrival in Port Blair). If you hand in your form with one photo in the morning, you can collect the permit the same day between 4 and 5 pm. The office is open from 10 am to 1 pm and 2.30 to 5 pm. A No 17C, 25 or 25B bus from opposite the Anna Rd post office on Mount Rd will take you there.

Tax Clearance Income tax clearance certificates are available from the Foreign Section, Office of the Collector of Taxes, at 121 Nungambakkam High Rd. The procedure takes about three hours.

Bookshops & Libraries One of the best bookshops in south India is Landmark Books in the basement of Apex Plaza at 3 Nungambakkam High Rd. The selection here is excellent.

Higginbothams at 814 Mount Rd also has a reasonable selection of books. There are also good bookshops in the Hotel Connemara and the Hotel Taj Coromandel.

The British Council Library, 737 Mount Rd, is at the end of a small bumpy lane, next to the building with the big Phillips sign on the roof. It's open from 11 am to 7 pm, Tuesday to Saturday. Casual visitors are not actively encouraged but if you are going to be around for a while you can take out temporary membership for Rs 20 a month.

The American Center Library (☎ 47-7825) is attached to the US Consulate and is open from 9.30 am to 6 pm, Monday to Saturday. The Alliance Française de Madras (☎ 47-9803) is at 40 College Rd, Nungambakkam.

The Krishnamurti Foundation (☎ 41-6803) is at 64 Greenways Rd, Adyar, south of the river. Also in Adyar is the Adyar Library, which is attached to the Theosophical Society. There's a huge and comprehensive collection of books on religions of all types, philosophy and mysticism. Get there on bus No 5 along Mount Rd. In Mylapore, the Ramakrishna Mutt Library at 16 Ramakrishna Mutt Rd, not far from the Kapaleeshwara Temple, specialises in philosophy, mythology and Indian classics.

Fort St George & St Mary's Church

Built in 1653 by the British East India Company, but much altered from its original design, the fort presently houses the Secretariat and the Legislative Assembly. The 46-metre-high flagstaff out the front is actually a mast salvaged from a shipwreck in the 17th century.

The **Fort Museum**, open from 10 am to 5 pm but closed on Fridays, has a fascinating collection of memorabilia from the days of the East India Company and the British Raj. Entrance to the museum is free. Upstairs is the **banqueting hall**, built in 1802, around the walls of which hang many paintings of Fort St George's governors and other high officials of the British regime. Just south of the museum is the **pay accounts office**. It was formerly Clive's house, and one room, known as Clive's Corner, is open to the public.

St Mary's Church, built in 1678-80, was the first English church and the oldest surviving British construction in India. There are reminders in the church of Robert Clive, who was married here in 1753, and of Elihu Yale, the early governor of Madras who went on to found the famous university bearing his name in the USA.

North of the fort is the old 1844 **lighthouse**, superseded in 1971 by the ugly modern one on the Marina.

High Court Building

This red Indo-Saracenic monster at Parry's Corner is the main landmark in George Town. It was built in 1892. It's said to be the largest judicial building in the world after the Courts of London.

You can wander around, and sit in on one of the courtroom sessions. Court No 13 has the finest furniture and decor.

Government Museum & Art Gallery

The Government Museum & Art Gallery is on Pantheon Rd, near Egmore Station. The most interesting parts of the museum are the archaeological section and the bronze gallery.

The archaeological section has an excellent collection of pieces from all the major south Indian periods including Chola, Vijayanagar, Hoysala and Chalukya. There's also a good zoology section.

The bronze gallery has some fine examples of Chola bronze art. The museum and gallery are open daily, except on public holidays, between 8.30 am and 4.30 pm. Entrance is Rs 0.50, and the ticket includes entry to the bronze gallery, which the city tours omit.

The building originally belonged to a group of eminent British citizens, known as the Pantheon Committee, who were charged with improving the social life of the British in Madras.

Kapaleeshwara Temple

Off Kutchery Rd, in the southern part of the city, this ancient Siva temple has a typical Dravidian gopuram. It's worth a visit if your time is limited and you won't be visiting the more famous temple cities of Tamil Nadu. As with other functioning temples in this state, non-Hindus are only allowed into the outer courtyard.

San Thome Cathedral

Near Kapaleeshwara Temple at the southern end of South Beach Rd, close to the seafront, this Roman Catholic church is said to house the remains of St Thomas the Apostle (Doubting Thomas). It was originally built in 1504 but was rebuilt in 1893.

Parathasarathy Temple

On Triplicane High Rd, this temple is dedicated to Lord Krishna. Built in the 8th century during the reign of the Pallavas, it was subsequently renovated by the Vijayanagar kings in the 16th century.

Marina & Aquarium

The sandy stretch of beach known as the Marina extends for 13 km, as far south as the San Thome Cathedral. The tour guides on the city tour insist that this is the longest beach in the world!

The aquarium, on the seafront near the junction of Pycroft's Rd and South Beach Rd, is open daily between 2 and 8 pm, except on Sundays and holidays when it is open from 8 am. Entrance costs Rs 0.50 but it's a miserable place, worth missing just to discourage its continued existence.

Near the aquarium is the 'ice house'. This relic of the Raj era was used over 150 years ago to store enormous blocks of ice cut from the Great Lakes in the northern USA and sent to India by sailboat. If you wanted a cold drink, that was how you got it in the days before refrigeration.

Guindy Deer & Snake Parks

Close to Raj Bhavan at Guindy, on the southern outskirts of Madras, this is the only place in the world where it is still possible to see large numbers of the fast-dwindling species of Indian antelope (black buck). It also has small numbers of spotted deer, civet cats,

jackals, mongoose and various species of monkeys.

The reptile house is open daily between 9 am and 5.30 pm and entrance costs Rs 0.50. Probably the best way to get to Guindy is to take the urban commuter train from either Beach Railway Station, opposite the GPO, or from Egmore Station. There are also regular buses from the centre of Madras (No 21E from Parry's Corner, or Nos 5 and 5A from Mount Rd opposite the Anna Rd post office).

Organised Tours

Both the India Tourism Development Corporation (ITDC) and Tamil Nadu Tourism Development Corporation (TTDC) have tours of Madras, the nearby temple cities and further afield:

City Sightseeing Tour This includes visits to Fort St George, Madras Museum & Art Gallery, Valluvar Kottam, Gandhi Mandapam, Snake Park, Kapaleeshwara Temple and Marina Beach. The daily tours are fairly good value, although rushed as usual.

The morning tour is from 8.30 am to 1.30 pm, and the afternoon one from 2 to 6 pm; the cost is Rs 40. The TTDC tour commentary is a nightmare of tautologies and non-English gibberish, but the guides are helpful.

Kanchipuram, Tirukkalikundram & Mahabalipuram This tour includes visits to three of the four ancient temples at Kanchipuram, the famous hilltop temple of Tirukkalikundram and the .7th-century Pallavan antiquities at Mahabalipuram. A stop is also made at Fisherman's Cove (Covelong) and the Crocodile Farm between Madras and Mahabalipuram.

These tours include a breakfast and lunch halt. The daily tours start at 6.20 am and finish at 7 pm, and cost Rs 60 or Rs 90 (air-con bus). It's good value if you're strapped for time, but otherwise a breathless dash around too many places.

Tirupathi This all-day tour to the famous temple of Sri Balaji at Tirumala in southern Andhra Pradesh is good value if you don't have the time or inclination to do it yourself. It is, however, a hell of a long day, with at least 12 hours spent on the bus. The price includes 'special darshan' at Tirumala, and the tour allows two hours for this. That's usually fine on weekdays but on weekends and holidays it can take five hours or more, which means the bus doesn't get back to Madras until midnight or later.

The daily tours officially last from 6 am to 9 pm. The fare is Rs 150 (deluxe bus) and Rs 200 (air-con), and includes breakfast, lunch and the Rs 25 'special darshan' fee at Tirumala.

All these tours, operated by TTDC, can be booked at their office, 143 Mount Rd (☎ 84-9803), at the Thiruvalluvar bus stand on Esplanade Rd (☎ 56-1982) between 6 am and 9 pm, or at Central Railway Station (☎ 56-3351).

The ITDC tours can be booked at the Mount Rd (☎ 86-9685) or C-in-C Rd (☎ 47-8884) offices.

There are also a number of private travel agents around the Egmore Station area which offer similar tours for the same price. If you're staying in this area, they may be more convenient.

Festivals

From the end of November until the second week of January, Madras is host to a Carnatic classical dance and music festival. Performances are held at various music academies; contact the tourist office for details.

Places to Stay

There are three main areas for hotels in Madras. The top-range hotels are mainly along Mount Rd (Anna Salai) and the roads off this principal artery. Around Egmore Station and along the section of Poonamallee High Rd between Egmore and Central Station are mid-range places interspersed with a few budget places. The cheapest hotels are in George Town between Mint Rd, NSC Bose Rd (Parry's Corner/Popham's Broadway) and North Beach Rd.

Egmore Station is the most popular area for travellers these days, but places like Broadlands in the Mount Rd area and the Malaysia Lodge in George Town continue to be well patronised.

Places to Stay – bottom end

Mount Rd Area The very popular *Broadlands* (☎ 84-5573, 84-8131) is at 16 Vallabha Agraharam St, off Triplicane High Rd, opposite the Star Cinema. It's a beautiful, whitewashed old place with rooms around three interconnected leafy courtyards. The rooms, though simple, are spotless and have a table and chair, two wicker easy chairs, a coffee table, and beds, of course. There's also a good notice board and you can hire bicycles, but the best thing about Broadlands is the tranquil atmosphere and how well it's run. You can make international phone calls from here for a service charge of Rs 15.

No other hotel in this area compares *but*, as many travellers have commented, some of the staff are rabidly racist. If you're White, you're all right; if you're Indian, you're not even allowed in the place! Take an Indian friend in with you and see what happens.

Dorm beds here cost Rs 25, small single rooms with common bathroom Rs 50, and other singles/doubles/triples with attached bathroom are Rs 72/138/157, including taxes.

To get there take an auto-rickshaw – most of them know where it is – or bus No 30, 31 or 32 from Esplanade Rd outside the Thiruvalluvar bus stand in the centre of town. From Egmore Station take bus No 29D, 22 or 27B – even some of the bus conductors know where Broadlands is! It's about 20 minutes walk from the tourist office – see the map.

Conveniently close to Central Station is the *TTDC Youth Hostel* (☎ 58-9132) on Poonamallee High Rd. It's only a couple of minutes walk from the station, and although the road is incredibly busy, this place doesn't suffer too badly from the noise. Dorm beds are Rs 40 and doubles with attached bathroom are Rs 175. It's not a bad place if you're just in Madras overnight.

Places further down Poonamallee High Rd from Central Station are assaulted by horrendous noise and pollution from the road in front, the railway line and the 'river' behind. They include the *Devi Lodge*, which has singles/doubles with common bathroom for Rs 27/45 and the same with attached bathroom for Rs 45/77, and the *Everest Boarding & Lodging* (☎ 30-772), which has singles/doubles with attached bathroom for Rs 77/98 including taxes.

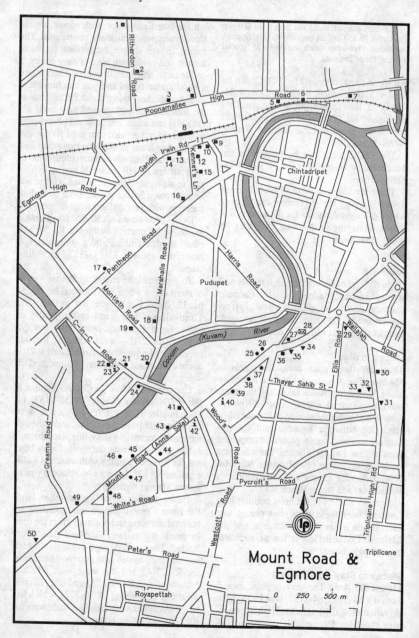

Mount Road &
Egmore

0   250   500 m

■ PLACES TO STAY

1 YMCA Vepery Youth Centre
2 Salvation Army Red Shield Guest House
3 YWCA International Guest House
4 Hotel Peacock
5 Everest Boarding & Lodging
6 Devi Lodge
7 TTDC Youth Hostel
9 Vaigai Hotel
10 People's Lodge
11 Hotel Imperial & Chandra International Hotel
12 Hotel New Victoria
13 Hotel Impala Continental
14 Tourist Home & Hotel Ramprasad
15 Hotel Pandian
16 Dayal-De Lodge
18 Hotel Guru
19 Hotel Ambassador Pallava
22 Hotel Kanchi
30 Wheat Hotel
36 Hotel Sangam & Buharis Restaurant
41 Hotel Connemara
49 Madras International Hotel & Yamuna Restaurant

▼ PLACES TO EAT

29 Coronation Durbar Restaurant
31 Ganga Restaurant
32 Maharaja Restaurant
34 Yadgaar Restaurant
35 Chungking Restaurant
50 Richy Rich Restaurant

OTHER

8 Egmore Railway Station
17 Government Museum & Art Gallery
20 Air India & Indian Airlines
21 Vayudoot
23 Indian Tourism Development Corporation (ITDC) Office
24 British Airways
25 Higginbothams
26 Poompuhar Handicrafts Emporium
27 Tarapore Tower
28 Anna Road Post Office
33 Broadlands
37 Southern Railways Booking Office
38 Binny's Travel Service (American Express)
39 State Bank of India
40 Tamil Nadu Tourist Office
42 Government of India Tourist Office
43 Spencer Plaza Shopping Complex
44 Singapore Airlines, Lufthansa & Grindlays Bank
45 Bank of America
46 British Council Library
47 Automobile Association of South India
48 Malaysian Airlines

George Town If you're in search of crowds and city centre bustle at its most extreme, this is the place to stay. The *Malaysia Lodge* (☎ 27-053), 104 Armenian St, off Popham's Broadway at the back of the GPO in George Town, has been a popular place for years. It was once a minor legend among travellers in the 1970s but not many people stay here any longer, preferring the Egmore area. On the other hand, it's still very cheap but equally basic.

If the Malaysia is too basic for your tastes, try the *Hotel Surat* (☎ 58-9236) at 138 Popham's Broadway, above the Madras Cafe. It's not bad value but the rooms at the front are incredibly noisy.

Egmore This is the real accommodation and travel hub of Madras, and competition for rooms can be fierce depending on the season. Quite a few places seem to be permanently full, and getting a room in the afternoon can be an exercise in persistence.

Cheapest of the lot, though 20 minutes walk from Egmore Station, is the popular *Salvation Army Red Shield Guest House* (☎ 33-148), 15 Ritherdon Rd, which takes both men and women. It's a clean, quiet place in leafy surroundings and the staff are very friendly. A dorm bed costs Rs 20 and doubles/triples are Rs 60/90. Clean sheets are provided and the rooms have a fan but all bathroom facilities are communal. Checkout time is 9 am.

A little further up this same road, but for men only, is the *YMCA Vepery Youth Centre* (☎ 32-831), 74 Ritherdon Rd, which has similarly priced dormitory beds as well as

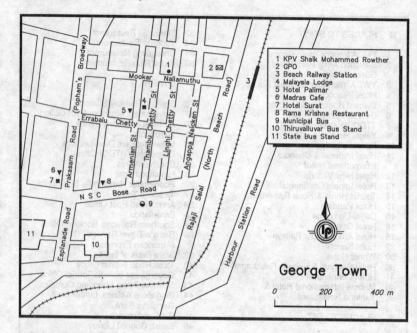

1 KPV Shaik Mohammed Rowther
2 GPO
3 Beach Railway Station
4 Malaysia Lodge
5 Hotel Palimar
6 Madras Cafe
7 Hotel Surat
8 Rama Krishna Restaurant
9 Municipal Bus
10 Thiruvalluvar Bus Stand
11 State Bus Stand

George Town

0   200   400 m

three double rooms with attached bathroom. Close to Egmore Station itself, the cheapest accommodation is to be found either at the *Alarmel Lodge*, 17-18 Gandhi Irwin Rd, right opposite the station, at Rs 40/60 for singles/doubles with communal bathroom, or at the *Hotel Majestic*, Kennet's Lane, which has singles/doubles with common bathroom for Rs 40/70 or Rs 49/99 with attached bathroom. The latter is an older place but reasonably well maintained.

Also in this league is the *Sri Lakshmi Lodge*, also on Kennet's Lane. It's a huge place (153 rooms), clean and quiet, and has singles/doubles with attached bathroom for Rs 66/99 including taxes. Similar is the *Hotel Sri Durga Prasad* (☎ 82-53883), at 10 Kennet's Lane, which has singles/doubles/triples for Rs 70/90/120. The hotel has its own restaurant.

The *People's Lodge* (☎ 56-6938), Whannels Rd, has been popular for years but is often full. It offers doubles with attached bathroom for Rs 75 including taxes.

Again in front of the station, and also relatively cheap but often full, is the *Chandra International Hotel* (☎ 56-8863), 6 Gandhi Irwin Rd. There's building work going on here at present so the occupancy situation may change.

A little further afield at the end of Kennet's Lane is the *Dayal-De Lodge* (☎ 56-8359), 486 Pantheon Rd, which is run by the very friendly and helpful Christopher. It is good value and has singles/doubles/triples for Rs 77/150/175, all with attached bathroom and hot water 24 hours a day.

The *Hotel Ramprasad* (☎ 56-7875), 22 Gandhi Irwin Rd, is also cheap but almost always full.

Somewhat more expensive but excellent value is the friendly and very popular *Tourist Home* (☎ 56-7079) at 21 Gandhi Irwin Rd. It's a large place and the rooms are spacious but you must get there early in the day if you want a room. Avoid the top floor in summer as those rooms get very hot. All the rooms have attached bathrooms.

There are also *retiring rooms* at Central and Egmore railway stations.

Places to Stay – middle

Most of the mid-range hotels are to be found in the Egmore area, though there are one or two elsewhere.

Good value in this range is the *Hotel Impala Continental* (☎ 825-0484), 12 Gandhi Irwin Rd, right opposite Egmore Station. Encircling a quiet courtyard, this hotel was completely rebuilt a couple of years ago and offers a range of rooms from singles/doubles at Rs 109/161 to deluxe doubles at Rs 195 and air-con doubles/triples at Rs 270/300 including tax. All the rooms have attached bathrooms and there's hot water 24 hours a day. A TV can be hired for Rs 35 a day. Credit cards are not accepted.

Close by, but not such good value if you get one of the older rooms where mosquitoes are a problem, is the *Hotel Imperial* (☎ 825-0376), 6 Gandhi Irwin Rd. Like the Impala, it's set around a courtyard with shops, massage parlours, a newsstand, travel agents and a long-distance/IDD telephone office. Ordinary singles/doubles are Rs 90/175, or Rs 245/275 with air-con. There are also air-con suites for Rs 350/395. The hotel has two restaurants (one open air, the other enclosed with a live band in the evenings), a nightclub and a popular bar.

Also excellent value in this area is the brand new *Hotel Pandian* (☎ 825-2901), 9 Kennet's Lane, which looks expensive but is surprisingly reasonable. Ordinary singles/doubles are Rs 190/240 and deluxe doubles are Rs 350. Air-con singles/doubles are Rs 270/320-895. The hotel has its own restaurant serving south Indian, tandoori, Chinese and Continental food and there's a bar. Credit cards are accepted.

Last in this immediate area is the *Hotel Vagai* (☎ 83-4959), 3 Gandhi Irwin Rd, a somewhat featureless modern-style, though older, hotel which has doubles at Rs 160 to Rs 210 and air-con doubles at Rs 290 to Rs 325. The hotel has its own vegetarian restaurant and credit cards are accepted.

Further afield, there is the *Hotel Peacock* (☎ 39-081), 1089 Poonamallee High Rd, which offers ordinary singles/doubles for Rs 160/240 and air-con singles/doubles for Rs 240/325 as well as deluxe suites at Rs 395. There's a restaurant similar to that at the Pandian, and a bar. If you decide to stay here then get a room at the back as Poonamallee High Rd is very busy and noisy.

Just up the road from the Peacock is the *YWCA International Guest House* (☎ 34-945), 1086 Poonamallee High Rd, which takes both men and women. Singles/doubles cost Rs 250/300, air-con doubles Rs 450, and family rooms (three beds) Rs 450. There's also a transient membership fee of Rs 10 valid for one month. The staff here are extremely friendly and helpful plus there's a restaurant serving both Indian and Western food.

Away from the Egmore area, check out the *Hotel Kanchi* (☎ 47-1100), 28 C-in-C Rd, which, like the Pandian, looks expensive but is actually excellent value at Rs 175/225 for singles/doubles or Rs 280/300 with air-con. There are also more expensive suites. There are two restaurants (one on the roof), a bar, and credit cards are accepted.

Out of this area entirely but convenient for consulates, airline offices, shopping centres and the Foreigners' Registration Office is the *Hotel Ranjith* (☎ 47-0521), 9 Nungambakkam High Rd, which is good value for this area of town. Singles/doubles are Rs 212/299, or Rs 312/357 with air-con including taxes. Cheaper is the *Hotel Palm Grove* (☎ 47-1881), 5 Kodambakkam High Rd, which has singles/doubles at Rs 200/225, or Rs 225/295 with air-con. There's a bar and restaurants but no swimming pool.

Places to Stay – top end

The majority of top-end hotels are situated in an arc which stretches from Nungambakkan High Rd to Dr Radhakrishnan Rd, south-west of Mount Rd, though there are a few along or just off Mount Rd itself.

Close to Egmore Station, the only top-end hotel is the *Hotel New Victoria* (☎ 825-3638), 3 Kennet's Lane, a relatively new place with standard singles/doubles at Rs

380/600 and deluxe rooms at Rs 395/700. It's centrally air-conditioned and there's a bar and restaurant serving Indian, Chinese and Continental dishes.

Closer to Mount Rd is the four-star *Hotel Ambassador Pallava* (☎ 86-8584), 53 Montieth Rd. This place has all the usual facilities including central air-conditioning, a swimming pool and multi-cuisine restaurants. Singles/doubles cost Rs 1050/1200.

Between there and Mount Rd is perhaps Madras' best known hotel, the old-fashioned but elegant *Hotel Connemara* (☎ 86-0123), Binny Rd, close to the tourist office on Mount Rd. It has all the facilities you would expect including a swimming pool, bar, bookshop and restaurants and costs US$70/80 for standard singles/doubles or US$90/100 for deluxe rooms.

On Mount Rd itself, the *Madras International Hotel* (☎ 86-1811) at No 693 is cheaper at Rs 390/600.There are the usual facilities but no swimming pool.

Further afield, one of the cheapest in this range is the *New Woodlands Hotel* (☎ 47-3111), 72/75 Dr Radhakrishnan Rd, Mylapore, which has good facilities including a swimming pool, billiard room and two restaurants. The majority of the rooms are air-conditioned. The vegetarian restaurant here gets rave reviews for its superb, crisp dosas, tandoori items and milk burfis. Close by is the more expensive *Hotel Savera* (☎ 47-4400), 69 Dr Radhakrishnan Rd, which has air-con singles/doubles for Rs 900/1000. Facilities include a swimming pool, bar and three restaurants. Further down this road is the *Hotel President* (☎ 83-2211), 16 Edward Elliots Rd, which has all the usual facilities and air-con singles/doubles at Rs 390/550. There's a discount of 10% from 1 April to 30 September.

Back up in Nungambakkam are two of Madras' most luxurious hotels. The first is the *Hotel Taj Coromandel* (☎ 47-4849), 17 Nungambakkam High Rd, approached through what could be the Hanging Gardens of Babylon. Like all Taj group hotels, it has the lot. Rooms range from US$85/95 to US$120/150 for singles/doubles. There are

also more expensive suites. Not far from here is the equally luxurious *Welcomgroup Chola Sheraton* (☎ 47-3347), 10 Cathedral Rd, which has singles/doubles from US$80/85 to US$160/275.

There's also *The Trident* (☎ 43-4747), 1/24 G S T Rd, much further out, which has singles/doubles at US$80/90. These last three hotels are all five-star.

Places to Eat

There are thousands of vegetarian restaurants in Madras ranging from the simple 'meals' restaurants where a thali lunch is served on a banana leaf for around Rs 10 to sumptuous spreads for 10 times that amount in the major hotels. Breakfast at the simpler restaurants, which open shortly after dawn, consists of such staples as masala dosa, idli, curd and the like followed by coffee. Some, though not all, of the simpler 'meals' restaurants also offer thalis similar to those served at lunchtime or in the evening.

Non-vegetarian restaurants are much thinner on the ground and Western-style breakfasts almost impossible to find outside mid-range and top-end hotels. If you're not a vegetarian or simply want a break from south Indian cuisine, it's probably best to go for lunch or dinner at a hotel which has a restaurant specialising in such things as tandoori, Mughlai, Chinese or Continental dishes. Obviously prices vary, but a meat or fish dish in a mid-range hotel should cost between Rs 30 and Rs 50. If you like a beer with your meal, it's good to remember that most non-vegetarian restaurants will have them while exclusively vegetarian restaurants will not.

Mount Rd Area There are several good eateries along Mount Rd and close to the Broadlands Hotel. Just around the corner from Broadlands on Triplicane High Rd, the *Maharaja Restaurant* has good toasted sandwiches and lassis, and does snacks right up until midnight. It's become something of a travellers' hangout as it's the best place in the vicinity of Broadlands. Close by, the *Ganga*

Restaurant in the Annapurna Hotel has good vegetarian snacks.

The *Coronation Durbar Restaurant* is on Wallajah Rd near the junction with Mount Rd. It has a good rooftop terrace which is pleasant in the evenings. The food is good, but even by Indian standards they are a little heavy-handed with the chilli.

On Mount Rd, the *Mathura Restaurant* on the 2nd floor of the Tarapore Tower is an upmarket vegetarian restaurant. Thalis here cost Rs 25 and are good value. Their business lunch from 11 am to 3 pm on weekdays for Rs 15 is also good value. Across the road the *Buharis Restaurant* has excellent chicken dishes, and there's an air-con dining hall and an open-air terrace upstairs.

Opposite Tarapore Tower, the *Hotel Gangothri* offers one of the best thalis in town for just Rs 17.

For Chinese food the *Chungking* restaurant almost opposite the Anna Rd post office can't be beaten. It's a very popular place and the food is excellent. Count on around Rs 45 to Rs 50 per person. Also on Mount Rd is the *Hotel Inland*, close to the Anna Rd post office. It has a rooftop section as well as an air-con room, and an excellent four-course meal costs around Rs 60. The *Manasa* restaurant next to Higginbothams on Mount Rd has also been recommended, as has the *Open House*, also on Mount Rd.

Only a few doors down from the tourist office on Mount Rd, *Aavin* is a stand-up milk bar where you can get lassis, ice cream and excellent cold milk, plain or flavoured.

The *Hotel Connemara* has a wonderful pastry shop, but for a real treat head for the Connemara's Rs 100 buffet. This is a long-running favourite, the food is fantastic and the pianist knows a few good numbers. Also in the Connemara is the *Raintree* restaurant. It's only open in the evening and is definitely upmarket, but the outdoor setting is superb, the service very attentive (you even get a mosquito coil under your table) and there's live classical dancing and music. It's not difficult to spend Rs 200 on a meal for two here. According to one waiter the drinking water is 'very much boiled'.

Further south along Mount Rd, the air-con *Yamuna Restaurant* does an excellent lassi, and the masala dosas and dahi vada are also worth trying.

George Town In the old part of the town there are many vegetarian restaurants. Few stand out, although the *Madras Cafe* on Popham's Broadway does excellent and cheap thalis. There's also a good stand-up vegetarian fast-food place at the junction of Mookar Nallamuthu St and Angappa Naicken St which is very popular with local office workers. It also specialises in fruit juices.

The *Hotel Palimar* on Armenian St is a good air-con vegetarian restaurant – convenient if you're staying at the Malaysia Lodge.

Egmore Most of the restaurants here are along Gandhi Irwin Rd, in front of Egmore Station. They include the vegetarian *Rajabhavan* at the entrance to the Hotel Imperial and the nearby *Vasanta Bhavan* which also has non-vegetarian food. Also good value is the very popular *Cleopatra* on the corner of Gandhi Irwin Rd and Kennet's Lane (owned by the Hotel Impala) with its army of cooks, waiters, cleaners and cashiers. Once your face gets known here, they really look after you. The stall at the front sells milk-based sweets.

Non-vegetarian food is good at both the *Omar Khayyam* restaurant in the Hotel Imperial and at the restaurant in the Hotel New Victoria. There's a live band in the Omar Khayyam in the evenings.

Entertainment

Night life in the Egmore area (or anywhere in Madras outside the top-end hotels) is pretty tame and even Maxim's, the nightclub at the Hotel Imperial, closes at 11 pm. This is a legacy of Tamil Nadu's days as a prohibition state when foreigners (or Indians) who wanted an alcoholic drink had to obtain a liquor permit from the tourist office before being allowed to buy a beer from a 'permit room' (bar). These were always a farce since, if you actually consumed as much as the permit allowed you to purchase, you would have ended up with cirrhosis of the liver! Prohibition has been abolished but the name 'permit room' survives.

The prohibition lobby, however, remains strong and there are draconian government taxes on alcohol which ensure that the price of a beer in Tamil Nadu is one of the highest in India (well over US$1 at the current rate of exchange). The lighting, too, in most bars is sufficiently nonexistent to impress on you that you're up to no good drinking alcohol.

One bar (sorry, 'permit room') which doesn't resemble purgatory is Sherry's at the Hotel Imperial. It's a popular place and attracts a bunch of lively locals who trade jokes and stories all day and night plus there's an enormous fan which will remind you of cyclones in the Bay of Bengal.

If you don't frequent bars, it's early to bed and up at sparrow's fart.

Things to Buy

The stalls which clutter the footpaths in both Mount Rd and around Parry's Corner are excellent places to pick up cheap 'export reject' clothes. You need to choose carefully, but good shirts for Rs 25 are not hard to find. There are similar stalls lining Gandhi Irwin Rd in front of Egmore Station but they specialise in T-shirts with logos. Most of the logos you'd be embarrassed to sport on your chest but there are some which might pass muster elsewhere in the world. There are also a lot of stalls selling watches and electronic goods in case you missed the duty free on the way into India.

For more conventional souvenirs, there's a whole range of craft shops and various government emporia along Mount Rd near the tourist office. The emporia, as elsewhere in India, have more-or-less fixed prices.

Getting There & Away

Air The Indian Airlines/Air India building is on Marshalls Rd, five minutes walk from the Hotel Connemara, across the Cooum River. Both offices are open daily except Sunday from 10 am to 1 pm, and 1.45 to 5 pm.

Air India
    19 Marshalls Rd, Egmore (☎ 47-4477)
Air Lanka
    142 Nungambakkam High Rd (☎ 47-1195)
British Airways
    26 C-in-C Rd (☎ 47-7388)
East West Airlines
    (☎ 47-7007)
Indian Airlines
    19 Marshalls Rd, Egmore (☎ 47-8333/7888)
Malaysian Airlines
    189 Mount Rd (☎ 86-8970)
Maldives Airways
    Crossworld Tours, Rosy Towers, 7 Nungambakkam High Rd (☎ 47-1497)
Singapore Airlines
    167 Mount Rd (☎ 86-2871)
Vayudoot
    Travel Express, Wellington Estate, C-in-C Rd (☎ 86-9901, Airport 43-5521)

Madras is an international arrival point for India as well as an important domestic airport. The relatively new international terminal is well organised and not too heavily used, making Madras a good entry or exit point. There's rarely more than one plane on the ground here at any given time.

There are flights from Singapore (Singapore Airlines, Air India and Indian Airlines), Penang and Kuala Lumpur (Malaysian Airlines), Colombo (Air Lanka and Indian Airlines), Malé (Indian Airlines) and London (British Airways).

The domestic terminal in Madras is also new and well organised. It's right next door to the international terminal, so walking between the two is quite easy.

Indian Airlines connects Madras with the following towns and cities in India: Bombay (at least twice daily, US$110), Delhi (twice daily, US$162), Calcutta (daily, US$137), Bangalore (five daily, US$33), Coimbatore (daily, US$53), Hyderabad (daily, US$57), Thiruvananthapuram (Trivandrum; daily, US$65), Trichy (daily, US$34), Madurai (daily, US$46), Kochi (Cochin; daily, US$69) and Port Blair (four times weekly, US$136).

Indian Airlines also operate on the international routes to Sri Lanka (Colombo), Maldives (Malé) and Singapore.

Vayudoot has flights from Madras to Bangalore (three days a week, US$80), Kochi (Cochin; three days a week, US$160), Hyderabad (once weekly, US$160), Pondicherry (three days a week, US$40) and Tirupathi (four days a week, US$40).

East West Airlines flies Madras to Bombay once daily (US$110).

Bus The Tamil Nadu state bus company is called Thiruvalluvar, and the bus station is on the Esplanade in George Town, around the back of the High Court building. This is also known as the Express bus stand, and all interstate buses leave from here.

The reservation office (☎ 56-1835) upstairs is computerised and there is advance booking on most routes. The office is open from 7 am to 9 pm daily. There's a Rs 2 reservation fee, and you have to pay Rs 0.10 for the form! It's worth picking up a copy of the *Bus Route Guide & Map*, for Rs 5, which is sporadically available from the enquiry office downstairs. It has a comprehensive list of all Thiruvalluvar bus routes, journey times and fares, and there's also an excellent map of Tamil Nadu.

See the table for details of destinations served.

The Tamil Nadu state bus stand is on the other side of Popham's Broadway. This station is fairly chaotic and there is nothing in English. However, this does not present

any real difficulties since an army of young boys attach themselves to every foreigner who enters the station and for Rs 1 or so they'll find your bus.

The main reason to use this station is for the buses to Mahabalipuram. There are a number of services, the quickest being No 188, 188A/B/D/K. The journey takes two hours and costs Rs 8.40. There are 17 of these daily. The other Mahabalipuram services are Nos 19C, 119A (via Covelong, 21 times daily) and No 108B (via Madras airport, nine times daily).

In addition to the state buses, there are also a number of private bus companies which have their offices mainly in the Egmore area. They all run superdeluxe video buses on a daily basis to major centres of population such as Bangalore (Rs 100), Coimbatore (Rs 100), Madurai (Rs 85) and Trichy (Rs 65). There's not much difference in price between these buses and those operated by Thiruvalluvar, but the private buses are far more comfortable.

Train The reservations office at Madras Central Station is on the 2nd floor of the building adjacent to the station itself (across the incredibly smelly drain which passes between the two buildings). It's all computerised and extremely well organised. There's even a computer display of the state

Madras Bus Routes

Destination	Route No	Frequency	Duration	km	Fare
Bangalore	831, 828	14 daily	8 hours	358	Rs 70.50
Chidambaram	300, 301	6 daily	12 hours	233	Rs 32
Kanyakumari	–	6 daily	14 hours	760	Rs 104
Kodaikanal	–	1 daily	12 hours	450	Rs 67
Madurai	137	4 daily	10 hours	447	Rs 58.50
Mysore	863	1 daily	11 hours	497	Rs 78.50
Ooty	465	1 daily	15 hours	565	Rs 81
Rameswaram	166	1 daily	13 hours	550	Rs 73.50
Thanjavur	323	13 daily	8 hours	321	Rs 42.50
Trichy	123	23 daily	8 hours	319	Rs 42.50
Thiruvanan-thapuram	894	4 daily	17 hours	752	Rs 112.50

of the booking on all metre and broad-gauge trains as well as for trains originating on other regional networks.

Also here is the 'Tourist Cell' which deals with Indrail Pass and tourist-quota bookings. This 'cell' is immensely useful for foreign visitors unfamiliar with the Indian Railways system, but remember that any bookings made here have to be paid for in foreign currency (in contrast to bookings made in the main hall where you can pay in rupees). In this same booking hall you can also make reservations for trains originating in Bombay, Ahmedabad, Pune, Calcutta, Patna, Delhi, Jaipur, Lucknow and many other places (at separate counters).

The reservation office is open from 7.30 am to 1 pm and 1.30 to 7.30 pm Monday to Saturday, 7.30 am to 1 pm on Sunday. At Egmore Station, the booking office is in the actual station and is open the same hours as at Central.

The rail journey to Delhi is 2194 km; it takes 40 hours on the *Tamil Nadu Express* and costs Rs 210/961 in 2nd/1st class. Calcutta is 1663 km away, and the *Coromandel Express* does it in the relatively quick time of 27 hours at a cost of Rs 186/789 in 2nd/1st class. The *Ganga Kaveri Express* connects Madras and Varanasi. The 2147-km journey takes 38½ hours at a cost of Rs 210/961 in 2nd/1st class.

The fastest train on the 1279-km trip to Bombay is the *Dadar to Madras Express*, which takes 24 hours at a cost of Rs 164/649 in 2nd/1st class. The Bombay, Calcutta and Delhi trains all depart from Madras Central Station.

The daily *Cochin Express* runs from Central to Ernakulam (Kochi) – a 708-km trip taking 14 hours and costing Rs 107/421 in 2nd/1st class. To Thiruvananthapuram (Trivandrum), the *Trivandrum Mail* is the quickest over the 925 km. It takes 16½ hours at Rs 138/508 in 2nd/1st class.

The overnight *Nilgiri Express* runs daily from Central, taking 10 hours to make the 530-km trip to Mettuppalayam, from where you continue by the rack train up to Ooty. Fares are Rs 94/349 in 2nd/1st class. Banga-

lore, 356 km away, is connected by frequent trains from Central. Both the *Brindavan Express* and the *Bangalore Express* take a little over six hours to do the journey and cost Rs 70/253 in 2nd/1st class. Booking is heavy on these two trains.

Also from Central the daily *Charminar Express* whisks you to Hyderabad, a 794-km journey, in 15 hours for Rs 124/472 in 2nd/1st class. The daily *Saptagiri Express* covers the 147 km to Tirupathi in 3½ hours at a cost of Rs 33/127 in 2nd/1st class.

From Egmore there are a number of daily trains to Trichy. The most convenient overnight train is the *Rameswaram Express* which covers the 401 km in 10 hours for Rs 75/282 in 2nd/1st class. This train continues on to Rameswaram but not via Madurai. If that's where you want to go, you need the *Quilon Mail*. This is another overnight train which takes 11½ hours to cover the 556 km journey at Rs 95/355 in 2nd/1st class.

The fast overnight *Sethu Express* to Rameswaram takes only 15½ hours for the 656-km trip. Fares are Rs 108/408 in 2nd/1st class. Otherwise, take the *Rameswaram Express* which takes a little over 16½ hours. There are also trains from Egmore to Chidambaram (244 km, six hours) and Thanjavur (351 km, nine hours).

Boat Shipping Agents in Madras include:

Binny & Co Ltd
    65 Armenian St (☎ 58-6894)
KPV Shaik Mohammed Rowther & Co Ltd
    202 Linghi Chetty St (☎ 51-0346)
Shipping Corporation of India
    Jawahar Bldg, North Beach Rd (☎ 51-4401)

The Shipping Corporation of India (SCI) used to operate a service to the Andaman and Nicobar Islands (see that section for details) but the service was suspended as of March 1992. The ship which used to do this run is being scrapped. Negotiations were underway at that time to acquire a replacement vessel but that might take some time. In the meantime, contact Mr K C Shiva Manohar (Assistant Manager) (☎ 51-4401 or 52-4964 direct) at the Shipping Corporation of India's offices.

If the Andaman & Nicobar island service is resumed, fares are Rs 1256 (Deluxe Cabin), Rs 1154 (1st class), Rs 874 (2nd class) and Rs 188 (Bunk class). Meals on board are Rs 88 per day in the cabin classes and Rs 44 per day in the bunk class.

There is still no service to Malaysia although there are mutterings from time to time that it will be recommenced. Check with the SCI, or with their agent K P V Shaik Mohammed Rowther & Co (☎ 51-1535), 202 Linghi Chetty St.

Getting Around

To/From the Airport The domestic and international terminals are adjacent to each other, 16 km south of the centre. The cheapest way out there is by suburban train from Egmore to Tirusulam, which is right across the road from the terminals. The trains run from 4 am until late at night, and the journey takes about 45 minutes.

Public buses go right by the airport entrance from Mount Rd, but trying to board a bus with a rucksack can be fun and games, especially during peak hour. The buses to use are Nos 18, 18J, 52, 52A/B/C/D and 55A. All buses start and finish at Parry's Corner, but if you want to get on or off at Mount Rd, only bus Nos 18 and 18J go along there.

There's also a minibus shuttle service between the airport and the major hotels which calls at the Air India/Indian Airlines offices but it's a slow way to get into the centre because of the number of stops it makes and it will only run if it's full or near full. It costs Rs 30 and there's a booking counter for it at the airport adjacent to the taxi counters.

An auto-rickshaw to the airport costs around Rs 70 or Rs 140 by taxi (most drivers refuse to use the meters). At the airport itself, you can buy a ticket for a taxi ride into the centre for a fixed Rs 110 at the prepaid taxi kiosk inside the terminal.

Bus The bus system in Madras is less over-burdened than in the other large cities and can be used fairly easily, although peak hour is best avoided. The seats on the left-hand side and the rear seat are reserved for women.

Some useful routes include:

Nos 23A & 27C – Egmore (opposite People's Lodge) to Mount Rd.
Nos 31, 32 & 32A – Triplicane High Rd (Broadlands) to Central Station and Parry's Corner. The No 31 continues on to North Beach Rd for the GPO and the Shipping Corporation of India.
Nos 22 & 27B – Egmore to Wallajah Rd (for Broadlands).
Nos 17C, 25 & 25B – Mount Rd (opposite Anna Rd post office) to Nungambakkam High Rd for Foreigners' Registration Office and Income Tax Office.
Nos 9, 10, 17D – Parry's Corner to Central and Egmore stations.
Nos 11, 11A, 11B, 11D, 17A, 18 & 18J – Parry's Corner to Mount Rd.

Taxi Taxis take up to five people and cost Rs 10 for the first 1.6 km and Rs 2 for each subsequent km. Most drivers will attempt to quote you a fixed price for any destination rather than use the meter so negotiation is usually the name of the game.

Auto-Rickshaw Auto-rickshaws cost Rs 4.40 for the first 1.6 km, and Rs 1.50 for each subsequent km. Again, persuasion may be required before they'll use the meter.

Moped If you are feeling like a bit of a daredevil (and have an international motor-cycle licence) you can hire mopeds or scooters. The cost is Rs 90 per day for a Kinetic Honda scooter, or Rs 50 for a TVS moped. Insurance is an additional Rs 7 and Rs 5 respectively, but the price does include use of a helmet (of sorts). The company which rents them is U-Rent (☎ 84-1345) at 119 Dr Radhakrishnan Rd in Mylapore, not far from the Hotel President.

Tamil Nadu

Population: 58 million
Area: 130,069 sq km
Capital: Madras
People per sq km: 428
Main Language: Tamil
Literacy Rate: 64%

The southern state of Tamil Nadu is the most 'Indian' part of India. The Aryans never brought their meat-eating influence to the extreme south, so this is the true home of Indian vegetarianism. The early Muslim invaders and, later, the Moghuls made only fleeting incursions into the region. As a result, Hindu architecture here is at its most vigorous while Muslim architecture is virtually nonexistent. Even the British influence was a minor one, despite the fact that Madras was their earliest real foothold on the subcontinent.

There were a number of early Dravidian kingdoms in the south. The Pallavas, with their capital at Kanchipuram, were the earliest and were superseded by the Cholas, centred at Thanjavur (Tanjore). Further south, the Pandyas ruled from Madurai, while in the neighbouring region of Karnataka, the Chalukyans were the main power.

Tamil Nadu is the home of Dravidian art and culture, characterised best by the amazingly ornate temples with their soaring towers known as gopurams. A trip through Tamil Nadu is very much a temple hop between such places as Kanchipuram, Chidambaram, Kumbakonam, Tiruchirappalli, Thanjavur, Madurai, Kanyakumari and Rameswaram. There are also earlier temples in Tamil Nadu, most notably the ancient shrines of Mahabalipuram. In addition, the state has an important group of wildlife reserves, some fine beaches and a number of pleasant hill stations, including the well-known Udhagamandalam (Ooty).

The people of Tamil Nadu, the Tamils, are familiar faces far from their home state,

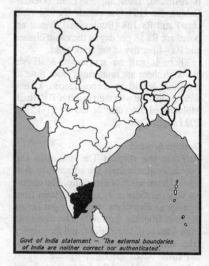

Govt of India statement – 'The external boundaries of India are neither correct nor authenticated'.

many having emigrated to Singapore, Malaysia and Sri Lanka. Despite their reputation as hard workers, Tamil Nadu is a relatively easy-going and relaxed state.

Tamil Nadu offers the traveller excellent value, particularly in accommodation. Prices are generally lower than they are further north and standards are often higher. There are many modern, low-priced hotels and the food is also good – you may get jaded with endless thalis while you're here, but they are consistently good value.

Architecture

The Dravidian temples of the south, found principally in Tamil Nadu, are unlike the classically designed temples found further north. The central shrine of a Dravidian temple is topped by a pyramidal tower of several storeys known as the *vimana*. One or more entrance porches, the *mandapams*, lead to this shrine. Around the central shrine, there is a series of courts, enclosures and

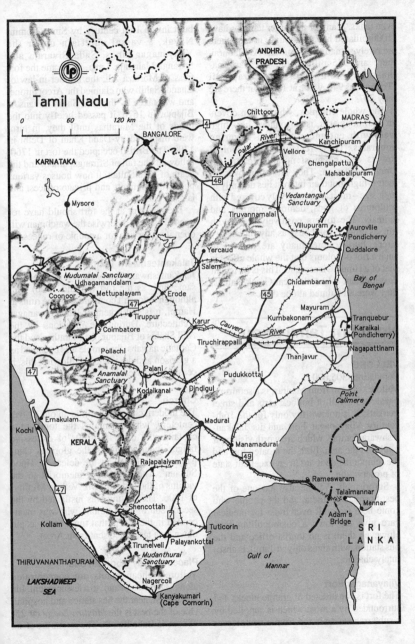

Tamil Nadu

0   60   120 km

even tanks. Many of the larger temples have '1000-pillared halls' although, in fact, there are rarely actually 1000 pillars. At Madurai, there are 985 pillars; the Sri Ranganathaswamy Temple in Tiruchirappalli (Trichy) has 940, while at Tiruvarur there are only 807.

The whole complex, which often covers an enormous area, is surrounded by a high wall with entrances through towering gopurams. These rectangular, pyramidal towers are the most notable feature of Dravidian design. They are often over 50 metres high, but their interest lies not only in their size – most are completely covered with sculptures of gods, demons, mortals and animals. The towers positively teem with life, as crowded and busy as any Indian city street. Furthermore, many are painted in such a riot of colours that the whole effect is that of a Hindu Disneyland. This is no recent development – like classical Greek statues, they were all painted at one time.

Northern Tamil Nadu

VELLORE
Population: 305,000

Vellore, 145 km from Madras, is a semirural bazaar town full of bullock carts and street markets. It is noteworthy only for the 16th-century Vijayanagar Fort and its Jalakanteshwara Temple, which are worth visiting if you're in the area. Both the moated fort and the temple inside it are in an excellent state of preservation.

Surprisingly, Vellore also has one of the best hospitals in India, and the people who come here from all over India for medical care give the town a cosmopolitan feel. However, there is no tourist office and the bus station, with signs only in Tamil, is absolutely chaotic.

Vijayanagar Fort
The fort is constructed of granite blocks and surrounded by a moat which is supplied by a subterranean drain fed from a tank. It was built in the 16th century by Sinna Bommi Nayak, a vassal chieftain under the Vijayanagar kings, Sada Sivaraja and Sriranga Maharaja. Later, it became the fortress of Mortaza Ali, the brother-in-law of Chanda Sahib who claimed the Arcot throne, and was taken by the Adil Shahi Sultans of Bijapur. In 1676, it passed briefly into the hands of the Marathas until they, in turn, were displaced by Daud Khan of Delhi in 1708. The British occupied the fort in 1760, following the fall of Srirangapatnam and the death of Tipu Sultan. It now houses various public departments and private offices, and is open daily.

The museum at the fort should have re-opened by now, otherwise the watchman will open it up for you for a couple of rupees.

Jalakanteshwara Temple
Jalakanteshwara Temple was built about the same time as the fort (around 1566) and, although it doesn't compare with the ruins at Hampi, it is still a gem of late Vijayanagar architecture. During the invasions by the Adil Shahis of Bijapur, the Marathas and the Carnatic nawabs, the temple was occupied as a garrison and desecrated. Following this, it ceased to be used.

Church
The modern church is built in an old British cemetery, which contains the tomb of a captain who died in 1799 'of excessive fatigue incurred during the glorious campaign which ended in the defeat of Tipoo Sultaun'. There is also a memorial to the victims of the little known 'Vellore Mutiny' of 1806. The mutiny was instigated by the second son of Tipu Sultan, who was incarcerated in the fort at that time, and was put down by a task force sent from Arcot.

Places to Stay – bottom end
Vellore's cheap hotels are concentrated along Babu Rao St and, to a lesser extent, Ida Scudder St, near the bus station and hospital. One of the best is the *Mayura Lodge* (☎ 25-488) at 85 Babu Rao St. The rooms are clean

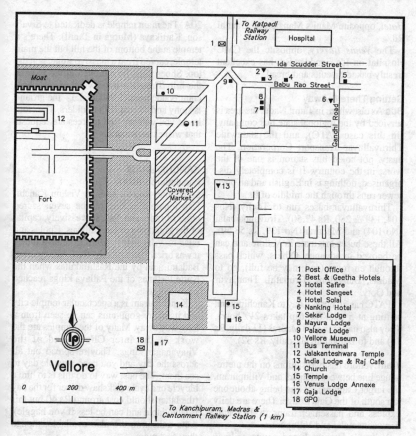

Vellore

1 Post Office
2 Best & Geetha Hotels
3 Hotel Safire
4 Hotel Sangeet
5 Hotel Solai
6 Nanking Hotel
7 Sekar Lodge
8 Mayura Lodge
9 Palace Lodge
10 Vellore Museum
11 Bus Terminal
12 Jalakanteshwara Temple
13 India Lodge & Raj Cafe
14 Church
15 Temple
16 Venus Lodge Annexe
17 Gaja Lodge
18 GPO

To Katpadi Railway Station

Hospital

Ida Scudder Street

Babu Rao Street

Gandhi Road

Moat

Fort

Covered Market

0   200   400 m

To Kanchipuram, Madras & Cantonment Railway Station (1 km)

and airy, and good value at Rs 35/60/80 for singles/doubles/triples. On the same street, the *Hotel Solai* (☎ 22-996) is more expensive at Rs 40/70, and the rooms have no windows.

Places to Stay – middle

One km north of Vellore on the Katpadi road is the *Hotel River View* (☎ 25-768). It is definitely misnamed as it's at least 500 metres from the river with views of nothing more exotic than a smelly drain. However, it's modern and clean. Rooms cost Rs 120 for a double with bathroom, Rs 200 with air-con, and there are three restaurants.

Places to Eat

In the India Lodge opposite the bazaar, the *Raj Cafe* has good vegetarian meals and excellent dahi vada.

Ida Scudder Rd is dotted with 'meals' restaurants. The *Hotel Geetha* is a good one with excellent masala dosas, while the *Hotel Best* next door serves non-vegetarian food and is a good place for an egg breakfast. For pseudo-Chinese food there's the *Nanking*

Hotel, opposite Mani's Mansion on Gandhi Rd.

The *Venus Bakery*, opposite the CMC Hospital on Ida Scudder Rd, has excellent freshly baked biscuits and bread.

Getting There & Away

Bus As elsewhere in Tamil Nadu, the area is serviced by the regional state bus company, (in this case PATC), and the statewide Thiruvalluvar Transport Corporation. The dusty, pot-holed bus station is one of the worst in the country. It is completely disorganised, nothing is in English and an open sewer runs through the middle of it.

Thiruvalluvar buses run to Trichy (Nos 104, 139 & 280, Rs 42.50), Tiruvannamalai (No 104) and Madurai (No 139, Rs 58.50). All these buses originate in Vellore and can be booked in advance. Others, which pass through en route (and may be full), go to Madras, Bangalore, Tirupathi, Thanjavur and Ooty.

PATC has 26 buses a day to Kanchipuram, starting at 5 am. The trip takes 2½ hours. They also have buses to Madras (11 daily, Rs 16) and to Bangalore (11 daily, Rs 32).

Train Vellore has two stations on the metre-gauge line between Katpadi and Villupuram, the larger Cantonment one being about one km south of the Gaja Lodge. There are daily express and passenger trains to Tirupathi, Tiruvannamalai and Villupuram.

Vellore's nearest broad-gauge railway station is at Katpadi, on the main Bangalore to Madras line. Buses wait outside the station for trains to arrive and the journey into Vellore takes anything from 10 to 30 minutes.

The 228-km trip from Katpadi to Bangalore takes four hours and costs Rs 49/175 in 2nd/1st class. It's 130 km from Katpadi to Madras, and the two-hour journey costs Rs 31/111 in 2nd/1st class.

AROUND VELLORE
Vellamalai

The temple of Vellamalai is only 25 km from Vellore, a one-hour trip on bus No 20M or 20A. The main temple is dedicated to Siva's son, Kartikaya (Murga in Tamil). There's a temple at the bottom of the hill but the main temple, carved from a massive stone, is at the top. Shoes must be removed at the base of the hill. There's a good view of the bleak countryside around Vellamalai – the ground is stony and strewn with boulders. The cloth knots you will see tied to trees are requests that wishes be granted.

KANCHIPURAM
Population: 170,000

Sometimes known as Siva Vishnu Kanchi, Kanchipuram is one of the seven sacred cities of India and was, successively, capital of the kingdoms of the Pallavas, Cholas and rajas of Vijayanagar. During Pallava times, it was briefly occupied by the Chalukyans of Badami, and by the Rashtrakutas when the battle fortunes of the Pallava kings reached a low ebb.

Kanchipuram is a spectacular temple city and its many gopurams can be seen from a long way away. Many of the temples are the work of the later Cholas and of the Vijayanagar kings. They're spread out all across the city and you need a whole day to see them. The best way to do this is to hire a bicycle or a cycle-rickshaw driver for the day (the latter should cost around Rs 40 but this is negotiable and can be less if you haggle). Auto-rickshaws are also available, though they cost more.

Have plenty of small change handy when visiting the temples to meet various demands for baksheesh from 'temple watchmen', 'shoe watchers', 'guides' and assorted priests. As it's a famous temple city visited by plenty of pilgrims and tourists, there is usually an army of hangers-on.

Kanchi is also famous for its hand-woven silk fabrics. This industry originated in Pallava times, when the weavers were employed to produce clothing and fabrics for the kings. The shops which sell silk fabrics are used to busloads of Indian tourists in a hurry and prices are consistently higher than in Madras. To get any sort of bargain you

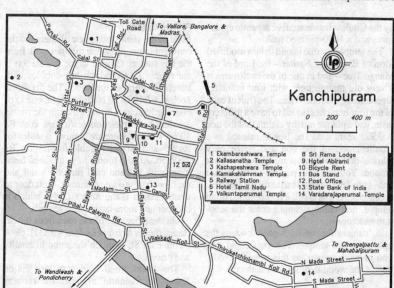

Kanchipuram

0   200   400 m

1 Ekambareshwara Temple	8	Sri Rama Lodge
2 Kailasanatha Temple	9	Hotel Abirami
3 Kachapeshwara Temple	10	Bicycle Rent
4 Kamakshlamman Temple	11	Bus Stand
5 Railway Station	12	Post Office
6 Hotel Tamil Nadu	13	State Bank of India
7 Valkuntaperumal Temple	14	Varadarajaperumal Temple

need to know your silk well and have done some legwork on prices in Madras.

Other than the temples, Kanchipuram is a dusty and fairly nondescript town and there's precious little to see or do except when the temple cart festivals take place.

Kailasanatha Temple

Dedicated to Siva, Kailasanatha is one of the earliest temples. It was built by the Pallava king, Rayasimha, in the late 7th century, though its front was added later by King Mahendra Varman III. It is the only temple at Kanchi which isn't cluttered with the more recent additions of the Cholas and Vijayanagar kings, and so reflects the freshness and simplicity of early Dravidian architecture, of which other examples can be seen at Mahabalipuram.

Fragments of the 8th-century murals which once graced the alcoves are a visible reminder of how magnificent the temple must have looked when it was first built.

The temple is run by the Archaeology Department and is very interesting. It's closed between 12.30 and 4 pm.

Vaikuntaperumal Temple

Parameshwara and Nandi Varman II built this temple between 674 and 800 AD, shortly after the Kailasanatha Temple. It is dedicated to Vishnu. The cloisters inside the outer wall consist of lion pillars and are representative of the first phase in the architectural evolution of the grand 1000-pillared halls of later temples.

Ekambareshwara Temple

The Ekambareshwara Temple is dedicated to Siva and is one of the largest temples in Kanchipuram, covering nine hectares. Its 59-metre-high gopuram and massive outer stone wall were constructed in 1509 by Krishna Devaraja of the Vijayanagar Empire, though construction was originally started by the Pallavas and the temple was later extended by the Cholas. Inside are five separate enclosures and a 1000-pillared hall.

The temple's name is said to be a modified form of Eka Amra Nathar – the Lord of the Mango Tree – and in one of the enclosures is a very old mango tree, with four branches representing the four Vedas. The fruit of each of the four branches is said to have a different taste, and a plaque nearby claims that the tree is 3500 years old. The tree is revered as a manifestation of the god and is the only 'shrine' that non-Hindus are allowed to walk around. You can also partake of the sacred ash (modest contributions gratefully accepted). As this is still a functioning Hindu temple, non-Hindus cannot enter the sanctum sanctorum.

A 'camera fee' of Rs 3 goes towards the upkeep of the temple. The visit could cost you more, however, as this is undoubtedly one of the worst temples for hustlers.

Kamakshiamman Temple

Dedicated to the goddess Parvati, this imposing temple is the site of the annual car festival, held on the 9th lunar day in February-March. When not in use, the ornately carved wooden car is kept partially covered in corrugated iron halfway up Gandhi Rd. The temple has a golden gopuram in the centre.

Varadarajaperumal Temple

Like the Ekambareshwara Temple, this is an enormous monument with massive outer walls and a 1000-pillared hall. One of its most notable sculptural features is a huge chain carved from a single piece of stone. The temple is dedicated to Vishnu and was built by the Vijayanagar kings. Entrance is Rs 1 and there is a 'camera fee' of Rs 3.

Other Temples

In addition to the more famous Kanchipuram temples described in this chapter there are many more, both in the city and outside it. Walk or cycle in any direction and you will come across others.

Places to Stay

Most of the cheap lodges are clustered in the centre of town, just a few minutes walk from the bus station. Closest to the bus station is the *Rajam Lodge* which has doubles with attached bathroom for Rs 55. The *Sri Rama Lodge* (☎ 3195), 20 Nellukkara St, boasts of offering 'gracious living', though the rooms are basic. Singles/doubles/triples cost Rs 40/60/100 plus there are 'deluxe' doubles for Rs 95 and air-con doubles/triples for Rs 220/250. All the rooms have attached bathroom with hot and cold running water and the hotel has its own restaurant. Next door to the Sri Rama is the *Raja's Lodge* which is cheaper and more basic but often full.

On the other side of the road from the Sri Rama, the *Sri Krishna Lodge* (☎ 2831), 68-A Nellukkara St, is much the same in quality and price.

The *Hotel Tamil Nadu* (☎ 2561) is on Kamatchi Sannathi St, near the railway station. It's the best place in town, is very clean and everything works. Standard double rooms cost Rs 90 plus there are air-con doubles for Rs 200 and Rs 250. All the rooms have attached bathrooms with hot and cold running water, and there's a bar and simple restaurant with a limited menu. Bicycles can also be rented here, although they cost more than elsewhere (Rs 25 per day negotiable).

Places to Eat

There are many small vegetarian places in the vicinity of the bus stand where you can buy a typical plate meal for around Rs 10. Try the *Hotel Abirami*, Kamaraj Rd. If you're tired of thalis – and there's not much else – you could try the non-vegetarian *Sri Muniyundi Restaurant* on Kossa St near Nellukkara St.

For a minor splurge, go for a meal at the *Babu Soorya* (☎ 3575), 85 East Raja St, where they serve excellent vegetarian meals. Go there hungry and come away bloated for around Rs 50.

Getting There & Away

Bus As elsewhere, the timetable here is in

Tamil, but there is no problem finding a bus in the direction you want to go. There are five direct buses daily to Mahabalipuram (No 212A, about two hours, Rs 8.40), the last at 7 pm. Alternatively, take one of the more frequent buses to Chengalpattu (Chingleput) and then catch another one from there to Mahabalipuram.

There are direct Thiruvalluvar buses to Trichy (No 122), Pondicherry (No 804), Madras (No 828) and Bangalore (No 828).

There are also plenty of PATC buses to Madras, Vellore and Tiruvannamalai.

Train Trains run from Madras Beach Station to Kanchipuram via Chengalpattu (Chingleput) at 5.33 and 6.15 pm and in the opposite direction at 6.05 and 6.40 am. The journey takes about three hours. It's also possible to get to Kanchipuram from Madras and vice versa via Arakkonam on the main Bangalore-Madras (Egmore) broad-gauge line but there are only two connections per day in either direction (at 7.50 am and 5.20 pm from Arakkonam to Kanchi and 9.25 am and 6.58 pm in the opposite direction).

MAHABALIPURAM (Mamallapuram)

World famous for its shore temples, Mahabalipuram was the second capital and sea port of the Pallava kings of Kanchipuram, the first Tamil dynasty of any real consequence to emerge after the fall of the Gupta Empire.

Though the dynasty's origins are lost in the mists of legend, it was at the height of its political power and artistic creativity between the 5th and 8th centuries AD, during which time the Pallava kings established themselves as the arbiters and patrons of early Tamil culture. Most of the temples and rock carvings here were completed during the reigns of Narasimha Varman I (630-668 AD) and Narasimha Varman II (700-728 AD). They are notable for the delightful freshness and simplicity of their folk-art origins, in contrast to the more grandiose monuments built by later larger empires such as the Cholas. The shore temples in particular strike a very romantic theme and are some

of the most photographed monuments in India.

The wealth of the Pallava Kingdom was based on the encouragement of agriculture, as opposed to pastoralism, and the increased taxation revenue and surplus produce which could be raised through this settled lifestyle. The early Pallava kings were followers of the Jain religion, but the conversion of Mahendra Varman I (600-630 AD) to Shaivism by the saint Appar was to have disastrous effects on the future of Jainism in Tamil Nadu, and explains why most temples at Mahabalipuram (and Kanchipuram) are dedicated to either Siva or Vishnu.

The sculpture here is particularly interesting because it shows scenes of day-to-day life – women milking buffaloes, pompous city dignitaries, young girls primping and posing at street corners or swinging their hips in artful come-ons. In contrast, other carvings throughout the state depict gods and goddesses, with images of ordinary folk conspicuous by their absence. Stone carving is still very much a living craft in Mahabalipuram, as a visit to any of the scores of sculpture workshops in and around town testifies.

Today, Mahabalipuram is a very pleasant and easy-going little village of essentially two streets. Positioned at the foot of the low-lying, boulder-strewn hill where most of the temples and rock carvings are to be found, it's very much a travellers' haunt. Like Puri, Kovalam and Goa, it's a place to hang around in, meet people and relax. After the noise, bustle, fumes and crowds of Madras and other large cities, Mahabalipuram is like another planet. Here you can find an excellent combination of cheap accommodation, plenty of mellow restaurants catering to Western tastes (especially in terms of seafood), a good beach, handicrafts *and* the fascinating remains of an ancient Indian kingdom.

Orientation & Information

The tourist office at the entrance to the village is staffed by helpful and enthusiastic people. They have a range of leaflets as well as a list of bus times and can direct you to an agency which will make railway bookings for trains out of Madras. It's open daily from 10 am to 5.45 pm.

You can change travellers' cheques at the Canara Bank.

Orient yourself by visiting the lighthouse, from where there are good views over the whole town. It's open from 2 to 4 pm and the entry fee is Rs 0.50. No photography is allowed for 'security reasons' – there's a nuclear power station visible on the coast, a few km south.

Mahabalipuram's telephone area code is 04113.

Arjuna's Penance

Carved in relief on the face of a huge rock, Arjuna's Penance is the mythical story of the River Ganges issuing from its source high in the Himalaya. The panel depicts animals, deities and other semidivine creatures, fables from the *Panchatantra*, and Arjuna doing a penance to obtain a boon from Lord Siva. It's one of the freshest, most realistic and unpretentious rock carvings in India.

Mandapams

In all, there are eight mandapams (shallow, rock-cut halls) scattered over the main hill, two of which have been left unfinished. They are mainly of interest for their internal figure sculptures.

Krishna Mandapam This is one of the earliest rock-cut temples. It features carvings of a pastoral scene showing Lord Krishna lifting up the Govardhana mountain to protect his kinfolk from the wrath of Indra.

Rathas

These are the architectural prototypes of all Dravidian temples, demonstrating the imposing gopurams and vimanas, multi-pillared halls and sculptured walls which dominate the landscape of Tamil Nadu. The Rathas are named after the Pandavas, the heroes of the *Mahabharata* epic, and are full-size models of different kinds of temples known to the Dravidian builders of the 7th

century AD. With one exception, the Rathas depict structural types which recall the earlier architecture of the Buddhist temples and monasteries. Though they are popularly known as the 'Five Rathas', there are actually eight of them.

Shore Temples

These beautiful and romantic temples, ravaged by wind and sea, represent the final phase of Pallava art and were built in the late 7th century during the reign of Rajasimha. The two spires of the temples, containing a shrine for Vishnu and one for Siva, were modelled after the Dharmaraja Ratha, but with considerable modification. Such is the significance of the shore temples that they were given World Heritage listing some years ago. Following that, a huge rock wall was constructed on the ocean side to minimise further erosion. It's hardly the most sensitive of structures but at least the temples are no longer in danger of being engulfed by the ocean.

The temples are approached through paved forecourts, with weathered perimeter walls supporting long lines of bulls, and entrances guarded by mythical deities. Although most of the detail of the carvings has disappeared over the centuries, a remarkable amount remains, especially inside the shrines themselves.

Tiger Cave

This shady and peaceful group of rathas is five km north of Mahabalipuram and signposted off to the right of the road. The carvings here are similar to those of the other rathas in town, but Tiger Cave is unspoilt by touts, souvenir junk stalls and busloads of rubbernecks. To get there, take any Madras bus or rent a bike.

Beach

The village itself is only a couple of hundred metres from the beach. The beach is very wide and, as there is no shade, it gets uncomfortably hot surprisingly early in the day.

North of the shore temples, the local fishers pull in their boats. The local toilet is also here, and a walk along the beach is an exercise in sidestepping the turds. You need to go south of the shore temples, or 500 metres or so north to the resorts to find a clean stretch of beach.

Festival

Mahabalipuram is the site of the annual **Mamallapuram Dance Festival** which runs from 15 January to 16 February. During the month-long festival, dances from all over India are staged here including Kathakali (Kerala), Kuchipudi (Andhra Pradesh) as well as tribal dances, puppet shows and classical/traditional music. Pick up a leaflet of events at the tourist office in Madras.

Places to Stay – bottom end

If you don't mind roughing it a bit, it's possible to stay with families in the area around the Five Rathas, a 15-minute walk from the bus stand. Rooms are generally nothing more than thatched huts, with electricity and fan if you're lucky, and basic washing facilities. Touts who hang around the bus station will find you accommodation in the village but, of course, you'll pay more if you use them. The usual cost is around Rs 150 per week; more if a tout takes you. *Mrs Rajalaxmi's* is the best in the village. The rooms have fan and electricity, and her back yard shrine is extremely well kept. Meals are available on request. She also does intricate rangolis (the white chalk designs put on the doorsteps of many houses) each morning and is happy to explain their meaning.

Very popular, but with only a few small rooms is the *Tina Blue View Restaurant & Lodge*, run by the friendly Xavier. Singles with common bathroom facilities cost Rs 35 and doubles with attached bathroom are Rs 75. The upstairs restaurant, which catches the sea breezes, is a great place to eat and/or linger over a cold beer. Close by is the equally popular *Uma Lodge* (☎ 322) which has large, clean doubles at Rs 60 with somewhat grim common facilities and Rs 75 with attached bathroom. Make sure you get an upstairs room.

A popular budget hotel right by the bus station is the *Mamalla Bhavan* (☎ 250) which has clean rooms with bathroom for Rs 45. There are no singles. Close by on the main street is the *Mamalla Lodge*, run by the same people. Singles/doubles here with common showers and toilets cost Rs 20/25 plus there are singles/doubles with attached bathroom for Rs 30/40.

Also popular is the TTDC *Hotel Tamil Nadu Unit II Camping Site* (☎ 287). Situated in its own shady grounds on the road down to the shore temples, it offers dorm beds at Rs 20 with lockers to put your gear in during the day. In addition, there are double cottages available at Rs 125 to Rs 170 depending on position and amenities. The cottages are basic but clean and have an attached bathroom and fan but no mosquito nets (which can make life unpleasant at certain times of year). The staff are friendly and facilities include a bar and restaurant serving south Indian and Continental dishes (open from 6 am to 10 pm).

Going up in price, the *SRP Lodge* (☎ 294), 50 Thirukkula St, is a good choice and offers very clean, attractive doubles at Rs 70 and Rs 130 with attached bathroom. Similar in price is the *Surya Hotel* situated in pleasant, shady surroundings overlooking a small lake. It offers a number of plain and air-con rooms and cottages with attached bathrooms, but they're overpriced, somewhat small and airless and there are no mosquito nets.

There are several other lodges in Mahaalipuram, including the *Kavitha Lodge*, *Suresh Lodge* and the *Sea View Lodge* which also offer budget accommodation, but they're overpriced and in an execrable state, their walls spattered with the desiccated spittle of generations of previous occupants. The beds have the appearance of tussocks of paspalum grass and the sheets (where they exist) bear the indelible stains of numberless actual or imagined nuptials. Give them a miss if you value your health and mental equilibrium. How much does a new sheet and a can of whitewash cost?

Just outside Mahabalipuram, close to the entrance to the Temple Bay Ashok Beach

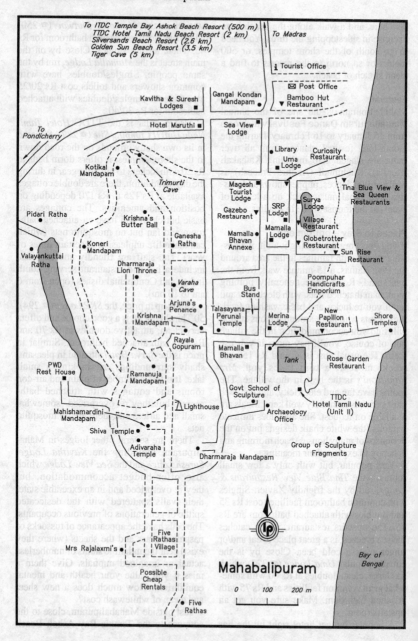

To ITDC Temple Bay Ashok Beach Resort (500 m)
TTDC Hotel Tamil Nadu Beach Resort (2 km)
Silversands Beach Resort (2.6 km)
Golden Sun Beach Resort (3.5 km)
Tiger Cave (5 km)

To Madras

i Tourist Office

⊠ Post Office

Bamboo Hut Restaurant

Gangai Kondan Mandapam

Kavitha & Suresh Lodges

To Pondicherry

Hotel Maruthi

Sea View Lodge

Library

Curiosity Restaurant

Uma Lodge

Kotikal Mandapam

Trimurti Cave

Magesh Tourist Lodge

Tina Blue View & Sea Queen Restaurants

Krishna's Butter Ball

Gazebo Restaurant

SRP Lodge

Surya Lodge

Village Restaurant

Ganesha Ratha

Mamalla Bhavan Annexe

Mamalla Lodge

Globetrotter Restaurant

Pidari Ratha

Koneri Mandapam

Dharmaraja Lion Throne

Sun Rise Restaurant

Valayankuttai Ratha

Varaha Cave

Poompuhar Handicrafts Emporium

Arjuna's Penance

Bus Stand

Krishna Mandapam

Talasayana Perunai Temple

Merina Lodge

New Papillon Restaurant

Shore Temples

Rayala Gopuram

PWD Rest House

Ramanuja Mandapam

Mamalla Bhavan

Tank

Rose Garden Restaurant

Govt School of Sculpture

TTDC Hotel Tamil Nadu (Unit II)

Mahishamardini Mandapam

Lighthouse

Archaeology Office

Shiva Temple

Adivaraha Temple

Group of Sculpture Fragments

Dharmaraja Mandapam

Mrs Rajalaxmi's

Five Rathas Village

Bay of Bengal

Possible Cheap Rentals

Mahabalipuram

Five Rathas

0   100   200 m

Resort, is the *Jawaharlal Nehru Rest House* (☎ 208) which offers dorm beds for Rs 10 per person or doubles with attached bathroom for Rs 20. It's very basic and I've never heard of or seen any foreigner staying there but it would have to be the cheapest place in the village.

Places to Stay – middle & top end

In the village itself, there's the brand new and spotlessly clean *Mamalla Bhavan Annexe* (☎ 260) on the main street. This is superb value at Rs 99 for a double with attached bathroom or Rs 175 for an air-con double. There are no singles. The hotel has its own vegetarian restaurant.

The cottages at the *TTDC Hotel Tamil Nadu Unit II*, mentioned earlier, also fall into this category but they're poor value by comparison.

The other mid-range and top-end hotels are scattered over several km along the road north to Madras. Most of them take the form of beach resorts with a range of facilities which usually include a swimming pool, bar, restaurant(s) catering to both Western and Indian tastes, games, children's playground and sometimes a disco. They vary a lot in terms of price, the quality and location of the rooms, and amenities but some of them are excellent value for money. The further north you go, however, the more inconvenient it becomes to get into Mahabalipuram without a bicycle or your own transport. Taxis and auto-rickshaws are usually available but they've got you over a barrel so prices are high.

Unlike the hotels in the village where checkout time is usually 24 hours, most of the beach resorts have noon as their checkout time.

Going north, 500 metres from Mahabalipuram, the first of the resorts is the *Temple Bay Ashok Beach Resort* (☎ 251). This is the most expensive of the lot. Air-con singles/doubles with attached bathroom, fridge, telephone and colour TV cost Rs 395/795 in either the main block or the detached cottages. There's a bar, restaurant, swimming pool, tennis court, and live entertainment. All major credit cards are accepted.

Next up, about two km from town, is the TTDC *Hotel Tamil Nadu Beach Resort Complex* (☎ 235, 268). This place is superb value and definitely has the best swimming pool of all the resort complexes. The rooms are in groups of double-storey cottages facing the sea, all of them with attached bathroom (hot and cold running water) and balcony. Doubles here cost Rs 250, or Rs 330 with air-con. Other amenities include a bar, restaurant (Indian and Chinese), exchange facilities and bicycle hire. Visa cards are accepted. This is definitely the place to stay if you have the money (though it's not the best place to eat).

A little further north are the *Mamalla Beach Cottages* (☎ 275). Doubles cost Rs 150/200 depending on whether you want a downstairs or upstairs room, and there are air-con upstairs doubles at Rs 250. All the rooms have attached bathrooms with hot and cold running water, and breakfast is available. There are no other facilities at present but a restaurant is under construction.

Next up is the *Silversands* (☎ (04113) 228). This is the largest of the resorts and has a plethora of different rooms and cottages but it's seen better days and is now overpriced for what it offers. Prices vary according to the season, ranging from Rs 200/250 to Rs 350/400 for single/doubles to Rs 300/400 to Rs 375/550 for an air-con single/double. There are also more expensive beachfront suites and villas with four beds. Credit cards are accepted and there's a shuttle bus to/from Mahabalipuram four times a day for Rs 15 one way. The atmosphere at this place is somewhat strange and the staff indifferent. It's perhaps not fully recovered from the days when it used to cater for the Soviet *nomenclatura* here on R&R at government expense.

Further north is the *Golden Sun Beach Resort* (☎ 245/6). This is another excellent choice if you don't mind the distance from Mahabalipuram. It's friendly and pleasant and singles/doubles cost Rs 260/300 (non-air-con), Rs 310/380 (air-con) and Rs

360/450 (air-con deluxe). All the rooms have attached bathrooms and facilities include a swimming pool, shady garden, and restaurants offering Continental, Indian and Chinese dishes.

Next up is the *Pearl Beach Resort*, a cluster of cottages on a rise overlooking the ocean. It has prices similar to the Mamalla Beach Cottages but facilities are limited.

The last of the resorts is the *Ideal Beach Resort* (☎ 240), 3½ km from town. This is also an excellent choice and small enough to retain the owner's intended warm and intimate atmosphere. Rooms/cottages cost Rs 275 to Rs 300 and air-con rooms/cottages Rs 350/400. Facilities include a restaurant (Indian, Sri Lankan, Chinese and Continental), barbecue and swimming pool. Credit cards are accepted.

Places to Eat

When travellers congregate on a beach, you can be pretty sure that, sooner or later, there will be good seafood restaurants. Mahabalipuram is no exception, with several places offering excellent, attractively presented seafood and desserts. They're popular, pleasantly relaxed (generally with a good selection of contemporary Western music) and they all try hard to please. Most of them will show you the fresh fish, prawns, crabs and squid before cooking them so you can make your choice. Be sure, however, to ask the price before giving them the go-ahead. Some items can be very expensive: a dish of king prawns, for example, is often priced at between Rs 100 and Rs 120 – hardly what you would call 'Indian' prices.

On the road down to the shore temples, the most popular place is the *New Papillon/Le Bistro* which stays open late and is run by an enthusiastic crew. Cold beers are available. Similar, but less popular, because the energy which used to sustain it is no longer there, is the *Rose Garden*. Better is *Swamis Fiesta Restaurant* on the same street, which you enter through a narrow alleyway (signposted). Here there are chairs and tables around a courtyard. It's an attractive place to eat and have a drink.

At the back of these two across the playing field and close to the ocean is the *Sun Rise Restaurant*.

Going north along the back road are the *Globetrotter* and the *Village Restaurant*. Both of them are good though the Village is the more popular of the two and also one of the oldest in town. It's also one of the few with fans. Get there early in the evening if you want a table. The Globetrotter stays open until early morning. Further along this road is the *Surya* restaurant which also has a good selection of food.

The *Tina Blue View Restaurant* in the north of town close to the beach is a good place especially in the heat of the day, as the shady upstairs area catches any breeze that might be around and there's a good view of the shore temples. The service is slow but the mellow atmosphere makes up for that. Cold beers are available. Next door is the *Sea Queen Restaurant*. It's a good place for seafood, and the desserts are also recommended.

Other restaurants worth trying are the *Curiosity Restaurant*, close to the Uma Lodge, and the *Gazebo Restaurant*, on the main street. Some travellers rate the seafood at the Gazebo as the best in town. Choosing one of these places over another is really just a matter of personal preference – they're all worth trying.

For south Indian vegetarian food, the place to go is *Mamalla Bhavan*, opposite the bus stand. You can eat well at standard Indian 'meals' prices here. Around the back of the main restaurant, the special thali section serves different thalis every day for Rs 10 – it's definitely above average, but at lunchtime only. The dining hall at the front does regular (but still tasty) thalis and other familiar south Indian snacks.

For a vegetarian splurge, try the *Golden Palate Restaurant* in the Mamalla Bhavan Annexe.

Things to Buy

Mahabalipuram has revived the ancient crafts of the Pallava stonemasons and sculptors, and the town wakes every day to the sound of chisels chipping away at pieces of granite. Some excellent work is turned out. The yards have contracts to supply images of deities and restoration pieces to many temples throughout India and Sri Lanka. Some even undertake contract work for the European market. You can buy examples of this work from the Poompuhar Handicrafts Emporium (fixed prices – in theory) or from the craft shops which line the roads down to the shore temples and to the Five Rathas (prices negotiable).

Also for sale in these shops are soapstone images of Hindu gods, woodcarvings, jewellery and bangles made from seashells and other similar products. This is one of the best places to buy soapstone work.

Another recent introduction is the leaf paintings of rural and family life more commonly found in Kerala.

Getting There & Away

The most direct route to/from Madras is on bus Nos 188, 188A/B/D/K of which there are 17 daily. The trip takes 2½ hours and costs Rs 8.40. Bus Nos 19C and 119A go to Madras via Covelong and there are 21 buses daily. To Madras via the airport you need to take No 108B of which there are nine daily.

To Pondicherry take bus Nos 188 or 188A of which there are eight daily. The journey takes 2½ hours and costs Rs 12. Get there early if you want a seat. There are 11 daily buses (Nos 157A/M or 212A/H) to Kanchipuram which take about two hours and cost Rs 8.40. These buses go via Tirukkalikundram and Chengalpattu (Chingleput). Alternatively, take a bus to Chengalpattu and then another from there to Kanchipuram.

Taxis are also available from the bus stand but long-distance trips require hours of haggling before the price gets anywhere near reasonable.

Getting Around

Bicycles are available for hire in the village if you want to visit Tirukkalikundram, the Crocodile Farm or Tiger Cave. There's a cycle shop about halfway between the Mamalla Lodge and the Mamalla Bhavan

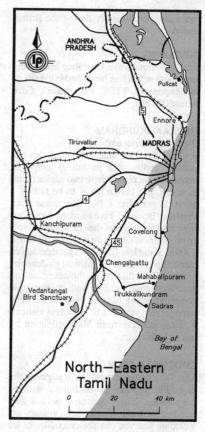

and another opposite the Rose Garden Restaurant. The usual price is Rs 15 per day. There's no deposit – just give your name and passport number.

Auto-rickshaws are also available but, since this is a tourist town, they won't use meters so negotiation is essential.

CHENGALPATTU (Chingleput)

Chingleput is on the road between Madras and Trichy and the junction of the rail spur to Kanchipuram. It is noteworthy for the ruins of an ancient Vijayanagar fort which had a chequered history during the British period.

COVELONG

Spelt in various ways, Covelong is a fishing settlement with a fine beach and is the site of the expensive TTDC *Fisherman's Cove Resort* (☎ 268).

TIRUKKALIKUNDRAM (Tirukazhukundram)

Fourteen km from Mahabalipuram, this pilgrimage centre with its hilltop temple is famous as the place where two eagles come each day, just before noon, to be fed by a priest. Legend has it that they come from Varanasi (Benares). Five hundred very steep steps lead to the top of the hill where the soft drink sellers at the top do a brisk trade when it's hot! Some less-fit visitors get themselves carried up in baskets. What most guidebooks ignore about this place, however, is the amazing temple complex with its enormous gopurams at the base of the hill. It's very impressive, yet seems to have few visitors. You can get here from Mahabalipuram by bus or by bicycle.

CROCODILE FARM

This farm breeds crocodiles to augment the crocodile populations of India's wildlife sanctuaries. There are now only a few hundred of these reptiles left. Visitors are welcome and you can see crocodiles of all sizes, from the newly hatched to adults. The farm is about 15 km from Mahabalipuram on the road to Madras, and is signposted. You can get there by bicycle or on any Madras bus from Mahabalipuram.

TIRUVANNAMALAI

Further south towards Pondicherry, a 66-km detour inland from Tindivanam will bring you to the temple town of Tiruvannamalai. There are over 100 temples here, and the Siva-Parvati Temple of Arunachaleswar is said to be the largest in India. The main gopuram is 66 metres and 13 storeys high, and there is a 1000-pillared hall. The splendid old fortress of Gingee can be visited between here and Pondicherry.

Places to Stay

Try either the *Park Hotel* or the *Modern Cafe,* both of which are clean.

GINGEE

Gingee (pronounced 'shingee') is about 150 km south-east of Madras, on the road to Tiruvannamalai. There is an interesting complex of forts here, constructed mainly around 1200 AD during the Vijayanagar Empire. The fort is built on three separate hills, joined by three km of fortified walls. The buildings – a granary, audience hall, Siva temple and a mosque in memory of a favourite general – are fairly ordinary, but the boulder-covered mountain landscape is impressive.

Gingee is pleasantly free of postcard sellers and the like; in fact it's deserted. You can easily spend a whole day here exploring. There's an uneven staircase of stone slabs up Krishnagiri Hill, but the route to Rajagiri Fort is much more difficult to follow. A rickshaw from the town to the hills and back, including waiting time at the site while you explore, costs about Rs 20.

PONDICHERRY

Population: 517,000

Formerly a French colony settled early in the 18th century, Pondicherry became part of the Indian Union in the early '50s when the French voluntarily relinquished control. Together with the other former French enclaves of Karaikal (also in Tamil Nadu), Mahé (Kerala) and Yanam (Andhra Pradesh), it now forms the Union Territory of Pondicherry.

A few years ago, the tourist literature used to project a somewhat false image that Pondicherry was an enduring pocket of French culture on the Indian subcontinent, when the only remaining visible French influences were the red *kepis* and belts worn by the local police, the French Consulate-General, the Hotel de Ville and a few streets around the central square which exuded a Mediterranean ambience. These days, such claims are substantially true as a result of extensive restoration work undertaken by the Aurobindo Ashram, the Alliance Française, and other bodies.

The houses and institutions in the streets between the waterfront and the canal are now very chic and gentrified, their gardens ablaze with flowering trees and bougainvillea, and their entrances adorned with shiny brass plates. There are still the occasional down-at-heel buildings but, for the most part, the prevailing impression is of gleamingly white-washed residences and a concern for maintaining standards rarely encountered elsewhere in India.

The transformation has been nothing short of miraculous yet, beyond the canal, Pondicherry is as Indian as anywhere else in India, although it is relatively well-lit, paved and laid out, and the signs are in English or Tamil, not French.

The main reason people visit Pondicherry is to visit the Sri Aurobindo Ashram and its offshoot, Auroville, 10 km outside town. The ashram, founded by Sri Aurobindo in 1926, is one of the most popular in India with Westerners, and is also one of the most affluent. Its spiritual tenets represent a synthesis of yoga and modern science. After Aurobindo's death, spiritual authority passed to one of his devotees, a French woman known as The Mother, who herself died in 1973, aged 97. These days, the ashram underwrites and promotes a lot of cultural and educational activities in Pondicherry, though there is a certain tension between it and the local people because it owns virtually everything worth owning in the union territory but is reluctant to allow local participation in the running of the society.

Orientation

Pondicherry is laid out on a grid plan surrounded by a congested semicircular boulevard, so it's easy to find your way around. A north-south canal divides the town into an eastern and a larger western part. In colonial days, the canal separated Pondi-

cherry's European and Indian sections. The French residential area was near the present-day harbour.

The Aurobindo Ashram, its offices, educational institutions and guest houses are clustered around the streets between the waterfront and the canal. The French Consulate-General is also in this area. The streets in this part of town are very attractive and strongly reflect their French origins.

Most of the hotels are on the west side of the canal, except the Ashram accommodation which is by far the best (although not the cheapest) in town. The railway station is at the southern edge of town, while the bus station is one km west along the main drag, Lal Bahabhur St.

Information

The tourist office is on Goubert Ave, the road along the waterfront, but it is of absolutely no use. The GPO is right by the canal in the centre of town, and the telegraph office (open 24 hours) is in the same building.

The Vak Bookshop on Rue Nehru is one of the best in the country for books on religion and philosophy. Equally good (if you read French) are the Kailash French Bookshop on Lal Bahabhur St and the French Bookshop on Suffren St next to the Alliance Française Library. There's a branch of Higginbothams on Gingy St, across the canal from the International Guest House.

Sri Aurobindo Ashram

The main ashram building is on Rue de la Marine and is surrounded by other buildings given over to the various educational and cultural activities of the Aurobindo Society. The ashram is open every day and you can be shown around on request. The room in which Aurobindo and The Mother used to meditate (Aurobindo's Samadhi) is open for viewing daily between 11.30 and 11.45 am, by appointment only. Personally, we found its air of self-conscious otherworldliness somewhat contrived.

Opposite the main building is the educational centre where you can sometimes catch a film, slide-show, play or lecture. These

PLACES TO STAY

1 GK Lodge
2 Victoria Lodge
5 Aristo Guest House
7 Amala Lodge
8 Hotel Ellora
9 Hotel Kanchi
18 International Guest House
21 Sea Side Guest House
23 Cottage Guest House
32 Ajantha Beach Guest House & Restaurant
36 Park Guest House

▼ PLACES TO EAT

4 Hotel Aristo
6 India Coffee House
10 Priya Restaurant (non-veg)
11 Priya Restaurant (veg)
14 Bliss Restaurant
20 Penguin Restaurant
26 Le Café
28 Bar Qualithé Hotel

33 Blue Dragon Chinese Restaurant
34 Le Club French Restaurant
37 Seagulls Restaurant
38 China Town Restaurant

OTHER

3 Market
12 Auroville Shop
13 Higginbothams Bookshop
15 Sri Aurobindo Ashram
16 French Consulate-General
17 Vak Bookshop
19 GPO
22 Romain Roland Library
24 Old Lighthouse
25 Gandhi Memorial
27 Museum
29 Foreigner's Registration Office
30 Government Tourist Office
31 Kailash French Bookshop
35 Alliance Française
39 Alliance Française Library
40 French Bookshop
41 Water Tower

very popular events are open to all and audiences are usually half-Western and half-Indian. There's usually no entry charge, but a donation is sometimes collected.

Daily (8.30 am) ashram tours cost Rs 6, but they basically consist of being shuffled around by taxi to all the ashram shops and getting the hard sell at each.

French Institute (Alliance Française)

The French Institute on Dumas St was established in 1955, primarily as a research centre for Indian culture. Its vegetation maps are universally acclaimed. Today, the scope of its activities is far broader and includes French classes, a French restaurant and library.

Pondicherry Museum

The museum has an interesting, eclectic and well-displayed variety of exhibits ranging from French furniture to a history of bead making. It is at 1 Romain Roland St, south of the main square, and is open between 9

am and 5 pm from Tuesday to Sunday. Entry is free.

Places to Stay – bottom end

The cheapest accommodation in Pondicherry is found at the typical Indian hotels west of the canal. The *Amala Lodge* (☎ 23-589), 36 Rangapillai St, and the *Hotel Raj Lodge* (☎ 27-346), 57 Rangapillai St, both offer singles/doubles with own shower and toilet for Rs 35/55. Better, and on the same street at No 33, is the *Hotel Ellora* (☎ 24-474) which has singles/doubles/triples for Rs 35/60/70, deluxe doubles for Rs 80, and air-con doubles for Rs 175. All the rooms have attached bathroom (cold water only) plus the hotel has its own bar and restaurant.

Excellent value in this range is the *Aristo Guest House* (☎ 26-728), 50-A Mission St, which is very clean and friendly and has singles/doubles for Rs 50/75 as well as air-con doubles for Rs 150. All the rooms have attached bathrooms. Similar in price is the *Victoria Lodge* (☎ 26-366), 79 Rue Nehru, which is shabby but clean enough, and has rooms for Rs 40/65 with own bathroom. Also, there's the *GK Lodge* (☎ 23-555) on the very noisy and congested Anna Salai (Pondy's ring road). Self-contained singles/doubles/triples cost Rs 40/70/125. At the top end of this range is the *Hotel Kanchi* (☎ 25-540), Mission St, the facade of which would suggest that it was a mid-range hotel – the facilities inside certainly don't match that description. It is, however, clean and quiet and some of the rooms have a balcony. Large, self-contained singles/doubles cost Rs 80/150.

There's a *Youth Hostel* on the beach, way out on the northern edge of town, but the inconvenience of the location outweighs any fiscal advantage of staying there. It costs Rs 12 per night, but there's nowhere to eat and no way of cooking anything. The easiest way to get there is by bicycle. Head north along M G Rd, and you'll eventually find black-and-yellow signs directing you to the hostel, though they're not very obvious.

Places to Stay – middle

The best places to stay by far in Pondy are the guest houses run by the Aurobindo Ashram. They're all immaculately maintained and in the most attractive part of town and, although classified here as mid-range, some offer rooms which are cheaper than those in the budget hotels mentioned above. The only drawback with ashram accommodation is that they all have a 10.30 pm curfew which can be a nuisance if you want to eat late and linger, though arrangements can usually be made with the doorkeeper to come back later. Smoking and alcoholic drinks are banned at all ashram guest houses.

The best of these guest houses is the *Park Guest House* (☎ 24-412) at the southern end of Goubert Ave. It's a large place and all the rooms on the front side face the sea and have a balcony. Ordinary singles/doubles are Rs 100/125 and deluxe singles/doubles are Rs 200/250. All the rooms are self-contained and the guest house has its own vegetarian restaurant.

If this is full (which is rare), try the *Inter-national Guest House* (☎ 26-699) on Gingy St which has a variety of rooms. The cheapest are in the old wing where singles/doubles on the ground floor are Rs 40/60 and doubles/triples on the upper floors are Rs 60/85. Doubles in the new wing cost Rs 85, and Rs 200 with air-con. All the rooms have attached bathrooms with hot water on request. There's a curious note on the board in reception here saying, 'Cleanliness is the first indispensable step towards the supramental manifestation. We cannot shelter hippies in our guest house', in gold-tinted pseudo-artistic scrawl. While it's a suitable comment on their attitude to room maintenance, someone should inform them that 'hippies' are on the endangered species list.

More homely and olde worlde than the above is the *Sea Side Guest House* (☎ 26-494) at 10 Goubert Ave. There are only eight rooms in this old house but they're very spacious, all self-contained and there's hot water in the showers. Doubles are Rs 85 to Rs 200 depending on size, while with air-con they cost Rs 220 and Rs 250. Breakfast is available without prior notice but other meals must be ordered in advance.

The last of the ashram guest houses is the *Cottage Guest House*, just across the canal from the International. It's usually full but, if you can get a room, it's the cheapest of the lot.

Apart from the ashram guest houses, there's the *Ajantha Beach Guest House* (☎ 28-898), Goubert Ave, very close to the Park Guest House. This is part of the Ajantha Restaurant & Bar complex. All the rooms here are on the ground floor so there are no ocean views. There are no singles, and doubles/triples at the back cost Rs 125/150 or doubles at the front Rs 150.

At the top of the range is the *Hotel Mass* (☎ 27-221), Maraimalai Adigal Salai (the continuation of Lal Bahabhur St), situated between the state bus stand and the Thiruvalluvar bus stand and thus inconvenient for the rest of town. Ordinary singles/doubles are Rs 250/340 and deluxe rooms Rs 395/430. All the rooms are air-con with colour TV and hot water 24 hours a day.

Facilities include veg and non-veg restaurants and a bar. Credit cards are accepted.

Places to Eat

Pondicherry has some excellent places to eat Indian, Chinese and French food.

The popular rooftop restaurant at the *Hotel Aristo* is the best Indian restaurant in town. It has a 207-item menu with everything made to order, so expect to have to wait at least 20 minutes for your food to arrive. A great deal of effort is put into preparation and presentation.

For Indian snacks or breakfast, the *Indian Coffee House* on Rue Nehru is good value. In the same street, the *Priya Restaurant* has good non-vegetarian Indian food. At the *Bliss Restaurant*, alongside the canal and close to the Aurobindo Ashram, straightforward thalis cost Rs 10. This restaurant is closed on Sundays.

On Dumas St, near the Park Guest House and the Alliance Française, the *Blue Dragon Chinese Restaurant* serves good Chinese food as does the *China Town Restaurant* on Suffren St, opposite the Alliance Française library.

Another very popular place, with moderate prices and an upstairs open-air balcony overlooking the ocean, is *Seagulls Restaurant*, right next door to the Park Guest House. The food (Continental and Indian) is tasty and there's plenty of it, and alcoholic drinks are available.

Right in the centre of town, on the south side of the main square, is the *Bar Qualithé Hotel (sic)*, an old unrenovated place with a lot of atmosphere. It's principally a bar but it offers very tasty food such as meat, fish, eggs and breakfasts which include bacon, sausage, etc at very reasonable prices (nothing over Rs 20). The management are very friendly. There are also rooms here but they're decidedly decrepit.

Going up in price, try the *Hotel Dhanalakshmi*, 39 Rangapillai St, for Indian, tandoori, Chinese and Continental food. It's open daily from 10 am to 11 pm and there's an attached bar.

For a full-on splurge, there are two places to go. The cheaper of the two is the rooftop *Ajantha Restaurant* on Goubert Ave near the Park Guest House. It's a very popular place and the food is usually good yet the prices are moderate. Get there early if you want a table with ocean views. On the ground floor is a bar which is popular with young professional people. Top of the line is *Le Club French Restaurant*, 33 Dumas St, which has the best food in town. The cuisine is French and the service immaculate. Wine and beer are available (naturally), both French and English are spoken, and it's open for breakfast (7 to 9 am), lunch (noon to 2 pm) and dinner (7 to 10 pm); closed Monday. No-one who's anyone in Pondy eats anywhere else and it's amazing how many budget travellers you'll encounter here some nights. Expect to pay between Rs 80 to Rs 100 per person for dinner, excluding wine or beer.

Entertainment

Other than the restaurants, there's not a great deal to do in Pondy in the evening. Beer drinkers, however, are in for a pleasant surprise after the high prices in Tamil Nadu. A bottle of Haywards costs just Rs 13, Kingfisher Rs 16 and Kalyani Black Label Rs 19. Try the Bar Qualithé Hotel mentioned previously, or the Ajantha Bar.

Getting There & Away

Air Vayudoot flies from Madras to Pondicherry (US$40) and vice versa on Monday, Wednesday and Friday.

Bus The Thiruvalluvar bus station is on Maraimalai Adigal Salai, the extension of Lal Bahabhur St, 500 metres west of the traffic circle at the junction with Anna Salai. It's quiet and well organised, in stark contrast to the state bus stand 500 metres further west.

The timetable at the Thiruvalluvar stand is in English, and there are buses to Madras at least once an hour, Chidambaram (seven daily), Tiruvannamalai, Bangalore (twice daily), Madurai (once daily) and Ooty (once daily). All these buses can be booked in advance on the computerised booking system.

From the chaotic State bus stand (time-table also in English), there are regular buses to Bangalore (twice daily), Kanchipuram (five times daily), Kumbakonem (three times daily), Madras (10 times daily), Mahabalipuram, Nagapattinam (three times daily), Tiruchirappalli (four times daily), Vellore (twice daily), and Villupuram.

Train Pondicherry does not have the busiest railway station you're likely to come across – most people go by bus. The two daily passenger trains run to Villupuram on the main Madras to Madurai line. From Villupuram, many expresses go in either direction. The 38-km trip between Pondicherry and Villupuram takes two hours and costs Rs 12/58 in 2nd/1st class.

Getting Around

Pondicherry's only public transport is a baffling system of three-wheelers which are a bit like overgrown auto-rickshaws and seem to go all over the place. As there are no signs indicating their destination, they're not much use. It's interesting to watch them on Gingy St – they are often so full that the driver is more out of the vehicle than in and the steering wheel is in front of a passenger. Perhaps it's just as well that it's too complicated to use them.

Although there are plenty of cycle and auto-rickshaws, many people hire a bicycle during their stay. This is also a good idea if you plan to visit Auroville. At many of the bike hire shops on M G Rd and Mission St, you will be asked for Rs 300 or your passport as a deposit. The only way around this is to have proof of which hotel you are staying in (they may check this, too). The usual rental is Rs 15 per day.

With an international driving licence, you can also rent a Honda Kinetic motorcycle from Vijay Arya (☎ 26-179), 7 Aurobindo St. Rates are Rs 60 per day or Rs 55 per day on a weekly basis. Your passport must be left as a deposit.

AUROVILLE

The brainchild of The Mother and designed by French architect Roger Anger, Auroville was conceived as 'an experiment in international living where men and women could live in peace and progressive harmony with each other above all creeds, politics and nationalities'. Its opening ceremony on 28 February 1968 was attended by the President of India and representatives of 121 countries, who poured the soil of their lands into an urn to symbolise universal oneness. For a time, idealism ran high and the project attracted many foreigners, particularly from France, Germany, the UK, Holland and Mexico. Construction of living quarters, schools, an enormous meditation hall (the Matri Mandir) and dams, and reafforestation, orchard and other agricultural projects were started. The amount of energy and effort invested in Auroville in those early days – and since – should be immediately obvious to anyone, and the idealism with which the place began is still tangible.

Unfortunately, the death in 1973 of The Mother, undisputed spiritual and administrative head of the Sri Aurobindo Society and Auroville, resulted in a power struggle for control of Auroville. In support of its case for control, the Society quoted The Mother as having said that 'the township with all its property will belong to the Sri Aurobindo Society', but the Aurovillians countered this with her statement that 'Auroville belongs to nobody in particular, (it) belongs to humanity as a whole'.

The struggle soon became acrimonious, with both sides making bitter accusations. On the one hand, the Aurovillians accused the Society of diverting and misusing funds meant for the project, and of making it difficult for the foreigners at Auroville to renew their visas. On the other hand, the Society accused the Aurovillians of corrupting The Mother's concept by indulging in free sex and using drugs. On two occasions in 1977 and 1978, violence led to police intervention.

Though the Aurovillians retained the sympathy of the Pondicherry administration, the odds were stacked against them, because all funds for the project were channelled through the Society.

The Society also had the benefit of powerful friends in the Indian Government, including three former cabinet ministers, who consistently sided with the ashram. In a demonstration of their hold over Auroville, the Society began to hold up funds. Construction work, particularly on the Matri Mandir, had to be temporarily abandoned.

The Aurovillians reacted resourcefully to this takeover bid, pooling their assets to take care of the food and financial needs of residents and setting up 'Auromitra', a friends-of-Auroville fund-raising organisation. Nevertheless, in early 1976, things became so serious that the ambassadors of France, Germany and the USA were forced to intervene with offers of help from their governments to prevent the residents from starving.

Finally, an Indian government committee recommended that the powers of the Aurobindo Society be transferred to a committee made up of representatives of the various interest groups, including the Aurovillians, with greater local participation. The news, in 1980, that the central government would take over the project was greeted with cautious optimism by the Aurovillians. However, despite this decision, Auroville remained independent of both the government and the Aurobindo Ashram.

In 1988, under the Auroville Foundation Act, the administration of Auroville was taken over by a body of nine eminent persons who act as intermediaries between the central government and the Aurovillians. The government has actually gone so far as to nationalise Auroville, but the long-term future of the place still seems unclear. What was definitely restarted and is now nearing completion is the Matri Mandir.

The project has over 30 settlements and about 800 resident foreigners, including children. The settlements include: Promesse, on the road to Madras; Forecomers, involved in alternative technology and agriculture; Certitude, working in sports; Aurelec,

devoted to computer research; Discipline, an agricultural project; Fertile, Nine Palms, Ermitage and Meadow, all engaged in tree planting and agriculture; Fraternity, a handicrafts community which works in close cooperation with local Tamil villagers; and Aspiration, an educational, health care and village industry project and, currently, the largest community.

The huge Matri Mandir, designed to be the spiritual and physical centre of Auroville, is clearly visible from many points. Its construction has been very much a stop-start affair because the flow of funds has been less than steady. However, the meditation chamber and the main structure are now complete leaving only a number of finishing touches (metal discs) to be added to the external skin. Likewise, the extensive landscaping associated with the project is well under way with the help of a small army of local labourers.

Yet, while the Matri Mandir is undoubtedly a remarkable edifice and certainly the focal point of the community, not all Aurovillians would agree that the vast sums spent on its construction were a wise use of the available funds. The more pragmatic among them would have preferred the money spent on community infrastructure and on projects of a more tangible nature. Both camps have their valid points, though it's perhaps well to remember that Auroville is a quasi-religious community (despite denials to the contrary) and that to have abandoned the Matri Mandir may have amounted to denying the community of a unifying focus. Without any such physical manifestation of Auroville's (and, therefore, The Mother's) spiritual ideal, the community may have splintered long ago, particularly in view of the financial and physical hardships endured by many of its less affluent members.

While that may be true, it's worth reflecting on whether the huge banyan tree adjacent to the Matri Mandir might have provided just as effective a meditation focus for the community as the one which has soaked up the lion's share of the funds. Some two thousand

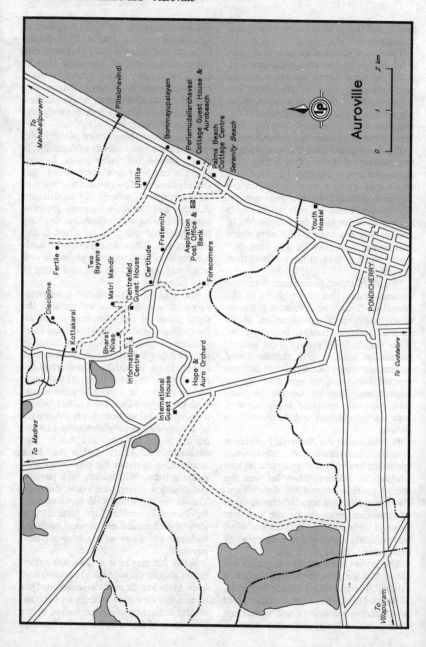

Auroville

To Mahabalipuram

Pillaichavindi

Bommayupalayam

Periamudallarchavaai

Cottage Guest House &
Aurobeach

Palms Beach
Cottage Centre

Serenity Beach

Utilite

Fraternity

Aspiration
Post Office &
Bank

Fertile

Two
Bayans

Certitude

Forecomers

Discipline

Matri Mandir

Centrefield
Guest House

Kottakarai

Bharat
Nivas

Information
Centre

Hope &
Auro Orchard

Youth
Hostel

International
Guest House

PONDICHERRY

To Madras

To Cuddalore

To Villapuram

0   1   2 km

years ago, a similar tree at Bodhgaya was apparently sufficient for the Buddha to reach enlightenment under. Perhaps it all comes down to whether you do or do not accept The Mother as your spiritual mentor and the subsequent interpretations of her visions by acolytes who survived her.

Information

The Auroville Shop has information and maps of Auroville. The main Auroville Information & Reception Centre is at Bharat Nivas in Auroville, together with their handicrafts shop. The shop is closed on Saturdays and Sundays. There's very little printed information about Auroville here – they mostly sell books on and by Sri Aurobindo and The Mother. Better is the information available from the Matri Mandir Information Centre outside the entrance to the building of the same name.

Places to Stay & Eat

On the road going north from Pondicherry towards Auroville in the village of Chinna Mudaliarchavadi and right by the roadside is the *Palms Beach Cottage Centre*. This is a very mellow little place in its own grounds and popular with travellers having their own transport. It consists of three circular thatched huts (the best if available) as well as a number of smaller rooms in a concrete block. Clean toilets and showers are shared, and there's an open-air, two-storey gazebo for eating and relaxing in. All meals are available and the food is good. Rooms here cost Rs 60 a double.

A little further on, down the lane on the left opposite the sign pointing to Auroville, is the *Cottage Guest House*. It offers basic rooms with mosquito nets in a semi-concrete block for Rs 30/60 a single/double with shared bathroom facilities. There's a thatched communal dining area and all meals are available.

There are also a number of travellers' huts and lodges just back from the beach but they're extremely rough and ready and really for the die-hards who want to stay maximum time for minimum cost. They include the

Sunshine Rest House, *Chez Mohan* and *Serenité Cottage*. Serenity Beach has one small restaurant, by the beach.

In Auroville itself, the usual place to stay is the *Centrefield Guest House* (☎ 2155), very close to the Matri Mandir Information Centre. This is run by members of the community and offers a range of cottages for between Rs 81 and Rs 150 per person per day. It's friendly and pleasant, and very tasty vegetarian meals are available for Rs 20 (advance notice not usually required). They also hire out bicycles and offer tours of Auroville for Rs 175 to Rs 200 including lunch.

You can also stay with virtually every one of the 33 community groups here. This is very well organised though conditions, facilities and costs vary a great deal. Some places are quite primitive with minimal facilities; others have the lot. Prices range from Rs 15 to Rs 160/200 though most are in the Rs 60 to Rs 80 range. They prefer people who are going to stay at least a week and, although work isn't obligatory, it's very much appreciated. You come here, after all, to get to know people involved in Auroville.

If you're interested in staying, a book is kept at the Matri Mandir Information Centre listing all the groups, their origins and composition, their interests and activities and even their likes and dislikes regarding visitors so it's easy to pick a group with interests approximating your own. Similar information can be found at the Centrefield Guest House. You should note that none of these community groups will offer free accommodation in exchange for work. For most groups, money is tight. On the other hand, if you stayed a long time, this might be negotiable depending on the contribution you were making.

Getting There & Away

There are several ways to enter Auroville but the best is from the coast road, at the village of Chinna Mudaliarchavadi. Here there's a signpost on the left-hand side indicating Auroville off to the left along a gravel track. It's also possible to enter from the main Madras to Pondicherry road at Promesse, though there's no signpost here. The best way to get around is by bicycle (rented in Pondicherry) since everything is so spread out and it's not practical on foot. Count on cycling at least 30 km to/from Pondicherry. There are some sections of tarmac road but, for the most part, it's good gravel tracks. Most of the community centres (eg Matri Mandir, Bharat Nivas, etc) are signposted but the individual settlements frequently are not. And, while most visitors attempt to see Auroville in a day, you will not get the feel of the place unless you spend several days here.

HOGENEKKAL

This beautiful, quiet **waterfall** is 25 km from Dharampuri and 80 km from Bangalore towards Salem. Here, the Cauvery River enters the plains and the river dashing against the rocks is a great sight. It's particularly impressive in July-August.

A huge weekly fair is held in the nearby village of **Pennagaram**.

Places to Stay

The *Hotel Tamil Nadu* (☎ 47) has double rooms for Rs 60, or Rs 125 with air-con. Dormitory beds in the attached *Youth Hostel* cost Rs 20.

YERCAUD

Yercaud is 33 km uphill from Salem. A quiet and low-priced hill town with many coffee plantations, this is a good place for trekking and boating.

Place to Stay

The *Hotel Tamil Nadu* (☎ 273) has rooms for Rs 60, and Rs 100 with air-con. Dormitory beds cost Rs 20, or Rs 35 in an air-con dorm.

Central Tamil Nadu

THANJAVUR (Tanjore)

Population: 200,000

Thanjavur was the ancient capital of the Chola kings whose origins, like those of the Pallavas, Pandyas and Cheras with whom they shared the tip of the Indian peninsula, go back to the beginning of the Christian era. Power struggles between these groups were a constant feature of their early history, with one or other gaining the ascendancy at various times. The Cholas' turn for empire-building came between 850 and 1270 AD and, at the height of their power, they controlled most of the Indian peninsula south of a line drawn between Bombay and Puri, including parts of Sri Lanka and, for a while, the Srivijaya Kingdom of the Malay peninsula and Sumatra.

Probably the greatest Chola emperors were Raja Raja (985-1014 AD), who was responsible for building the Brihadeshwara Temple (Thanjavur's main attraction), and his son Rajendra I (1014-44 AD), whose navies competed with the Arabs for control of the Indian Ocean trade routes and who was responsible for bringing Srivijaya under Chola control.

Thanjavur wasn't the only place to receive Chola patronage. Within easy reach of Thanjavur are numerous enormous Chola temples. The main ones are at Kumbakonam (40 km away), Thiruvaiyaru (13 km), Thirukandiyur (10 km) and Gangakonda-cholapuram (71 km). The Cholas also had a hand in building the enormous temple complex at Srirangam near Tiruchirappalli – probably India's largest.

Orientation

The enormous gopurams of the Brihadeshwara Temple dominate Thanjavur. The temple itself, between the Grand Anicut Canal and the old town, is surrounded by fortified walls and a moat. With its winding streets and alleys and the extensive ruins of the palace of the Nayaks of Madurai, the old town was once surrounded by a fortified wall and moat, although most of this has now disappeared.

Between the railway station and the bus stand at the edge of the old city runs Gandhiji Rd, along which are most of the hotels, a number of restaurants, the Poompuhar Arts & Crafts Emporium and the GPO.

Information

The tourist office is in front of the Hotel Tamil Nadu on Gandhiji Rd. It is open from Sunday to Tuesday between 8 am and 8 pm, and from Wednesday to Saturday from 8 to 11 am and 4 to 8 pm. The office has a hand-out map of the area but very little else.

The Canara Bank on South Main Rd is probably the best place to change travellers' cheques. The Hotel Parisutham will also do this, but at a lousy rate.

Brihadeshwara Temple & Fort

Built by Raja Raja (985-1014 AD), the Brihadeshwara Temple is the crowning glory of Chola temple architecture. This superb and fascinating monument is one of only a handful in India with World Heritage listing and is worth a couple of visits. On top of the apex of the 63-metre-high temple, a dome encloses an enormous Siva lingam (Hindus only). Constructed from a single piece of granite weighing an estimated 81 tonnes, the dome was hauled into place along a six-km earthwork ramp in a manner similar to that used for the Egyptian pyramids. It has been worshipped continuously for more than 1000 years.

The gateway to the inner courtyard is guarded by one of the largest Nandis (Siva's bull) in India, also fashioned from a single piece of rock. The carved stonework of the temple, gopurams and adjoining structures is rich in detail and reflects not only Saivite influences, but also Vaishnavaite and Buddhist themes. Recently discovered frescoes adorning the walls and ceilings of the inner courtyard surround have been dated to Chola times and were executed using techniques similar to those used in European fresco work.

Inside the inner courtyard, off to the left, the well-arranged **Archaeological Museum** has some interesting exhibits and photographs showing how the temple looked before much of the restoration work was done, as well as charts and maps detailing the history of the Chola Empire. The museum is open daily from 9 am to noon and 4 to 8 pm, and sells an interesting little booklet titled *Chola Temples* for Rs 2. Also on sale at the entrance is a small booklet called *Thanjavur & Big Temple*. It costs Rs 2.50.

The temple is open every day from 6 am to noon and 4 to 8.30 pm. There is no admittance charge but, as this is still a functioning Hindu temple, non-Hindus cannot enter the sanctum sanctorum.

Palace, Art Gallery & Saraswati Mahal Library

The huge corridors, spacious halls, observation towers and shady courtyards of this vast labyrinthine building in the centre of the old town were constructed partly by the Nayaks of Madurai around 1550, and partly by the Marathas. Some sections are now in ruins, but a substantial amount remains intact and houses various government offices.

The poorly marked entrance is a wide break in the eastern wall, which leads to a large tree on a traffic circle, and a police station. The palace entrance is off to the left, through the arched tunnel.

The **Art Gallery** has a superb collection of bronze statues from the 9th to 12th centuries, and the view from the tower on the far side of the courtyard is worth the climb. The gallery is open from 9 am to 1 pm and 2 to 5 pm. Entry costs Rs 1.

The **Saraswati Mahal Library** is next door to the gallery. Established around 1700 AD, the library contains a collection of over 30,000 palm-leaf and paper manuscripts in Indian and European languages, and has a set of prints of prisoners under Chinese torture on its walls! It is open from 10 am to 1 pm and 2 to 5 pm daily, except Wednesday. Don't miss the highly decorated Dharbar Hall off to the left of the library – follow the signs to Mahratta Palace Museum.

The **Tamil University Museum** contains a good coin collection, and a badly neglected collection of stringed instruments. No-one seems to mind if you pick something up and have a pluck – in fact, the custodian practically thrusts instruments at you.

Places to Stay – bottom end

Many of the hotels are either along Gandhiji

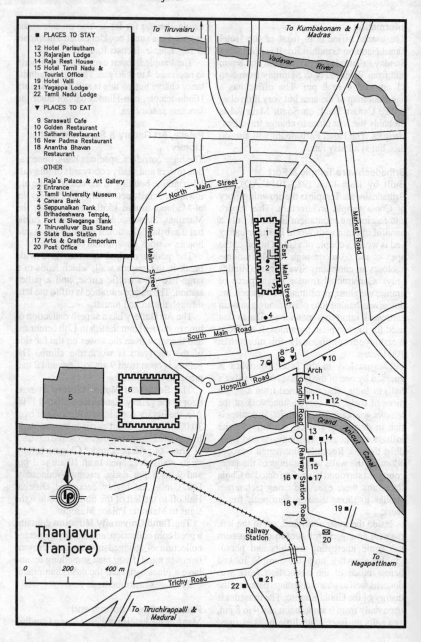

PLACES TO STAY
12 Hotel Parisutham
13 Rajarajan Lodge
14 Raja Rest House
15 Hotel Tamil Nadu &
   Tourist Office
19 Hotel Valli
21 Yagappa Lodge
22 Tamil Nadu Lodge

PLACES TO EAT
9 Saraswati Cafe
10 Golden Restaurant
11 Sathars Restaurant
16 New Padma Restaurant
18 Anantha Bhavan
   Restaurant

OTHER
1 Raja's Palace & Art Gallery
2 Entrance
3 Tamil University Museum
4 Canara Bank
5 Seppunalkan Tank
6 Brihadeshwara Temple,
   Fort & Sivaganga Tank
7 Thiruvalluvar Bus Stand
8 State Bus Station
17 Arts & Crafts Emporium
20 Post Office

Thanjavur
(Tanjore)

0   200   400 m

Rd between the bus and railway stations, or at the back of the railway station itself along Trichy Rd – otherwise known as Vallam Rd.

Best value in town is the quiet *Raja Rest House* at the back of the Hotel Tamil Nadu on Gandhiji Rd. The large rooms are arranged around three sides of a huge courtyard, and cost Rs 35/60 with bathroom and fan. The staff are very friendly. It's about 10 minutes walk from either the bus or railway station.

Next to the bridge which crosses the Anicut Canal is the *Rajarajan Lodge* (☎ 21-730) which is cheaper but noisier, with rooms for Rs 22/35 and doubles with two beds for Rs 50.

At the back of the railway station, just off Trichy Rd, is the *Tamil Nadu Lodge* (☎ 22-332) which has singles/doubles with attached bathroom for Rs 40/65 but it's somewhat inconvenient for the centre of town. Opposite is the *Yagappa Lodge* which has similar prices but is best avoided as it's decidedly run down.

There are also *retiring rooms* at the railway station.

Places to Stay – middle

For value in this bracket, you can't beat the *Hotel Tamil Nadu* (☎ 21-421) on Gandhiji Rd, run by the Tamil Nadu Tourism Development Corporation (TTDC). It's spacious, spotless, and very pleasantly decorated, and the rooms have curtains, fan, desk, wardrobe, comfortable beds, blankets and bathrooms with hot water in the mornings. The rooms surround a quiet leafy courtyard, and the staff are helpful. All this costs just Rs 55/77, or Rs 130 for a double with air-con. There is an attached restaurant, and a bar with cold beers. If you want to eat lunch or dinner here then order in advance. The hotel is an easy 10-minute walk from either the bus or railway station.

The other mid-range hotel is the relatively new *Hotel Valli* (☎ 21-584), 2948 M K M Rd, down an alleyway off to the left past the GPO. It offers self-contained singles/doubles without TV for Rs 55/88 or Rs 66/99

with TV, including taxes. There are also triple and four-bed rooms.

Places to Stay – top end

Thanjavur's best hotel is the relatively new *Hotel Parisutham* (☎ 21-466) on the canal at 55 Grand Anicut Canal Rd. It's very well appointed and has all the facilities you'd expect of a hotel in this range, including a bar, two restaurants and manicured lawns but no swimming pool. Singles/doubles cost Rs 225/325, or Rs 330/425 with air-con. There are also more expensive deluxe rooms and suites. All major credit cards are accepted.

Places to Eat

There are plenty of simple vegetarian restaurants around the bus stand and along Gandhiji Rd, with plate meals for Rs 10. The *Saraswati Cafe* on the corner of Hospital and Gandhiji roads is also good for snacks. If you arrive late and these restaurants are closed, there are a variety of street stalls along Gandhiji Rd which are open until very late where you can get a variety of snacks (omelette, fried eggs and various breads) for just a few rupees.

The *Golden Restaurant* on Hospital Rd does good vegetarian meals in its air-con upstairs dining hall. They cost Rs 14 and include a pan at the end. The rooftop is pleasant in the evenings. *Sathars* is a good non-vegetarian restaurant which is open until midnight.

For a splurge, the Hotel Parisutham has the best restaurants in town – the non-veg *Les Repas* serves Indian and Chinese dishes, and the *Geetham* offers vegetarian food. There's also a bar/permit room called the *Last Drop* in the basement which is a popular place for a late evening beer and complimentary snacks.

The restaurant at the *Hotel Tamil Nadu* is OK for breakfast but not the best place to eat lunch or dinner as there's usually only one item on the menu (chicken or simply vegetables without chicken).

For ice cream, lassi and milk shakes, the best place is *Sea Kings* on the road at the back of the Hotel Parisutham.

Getting There & Away

Air Although there is an airport at Thanjavur, Vayudoot, which used to service the city, no longer flies here. The nearest domestic airport is at Tiruchirappalli.

Bus The Thiruvalluvar bus station is fairly well organised but, as usual, there is no time-table in English. The computerised reservation office is open from 7 am to 9 pm. Buses, which can be booked in advance, depart for Madras 13 times daily (No 323, 8¼ hours, Rs 42.50), Pondicherry (No 331, twice daily) and Tirupathi (No 851, daily). There are also numerous buses passing through on their way to Tiruchirappalli and Madurai.

The State bus stand is chaotic, with no timetable in any language. Buses to Trichy leave from bays No 9 and 10; the 1½-hour journey costs Rs 9. Kumbakonam buses leave from bays No 7 and 8 on a trip that takes about an hour. There are departures for both destinations every 15 minutes or so.

Train It's nine hours and 351 km between Thanjavur and Egmore Station in Madras on the *Cholan Express*. The fare is Rs 70/253 in 2nd/1st class. The 50-km trip to Trichy takes two hours and costs Rs 12/63 in 2nd/1st class, less (and longer) on a passenger train but there are no convenient mail/express trains during the day (these come through very early in the morning or late in the evening). The trip to Kumbakonam takes one hour, and it's 2½ hours to Chidambaram. The 192-km trip to Villupuram (for Pondicherry) takes five hours at a cost of Rs 42/156 in 2nd/1st class.

AROUND THANJAVUR

Many of the smaller towns in the Thanjavur area are famous for their huge and impressive Chola temples. The distances of each from Thanjavur are in brackets.

Get a copy of *Chola Temples* by C Sivaramamurti, published by the Archaeological Survey of India. Costing just Rs 2, it describes the three temples in Thanjavur, Dharasuram and Gangakondacholapuram.

You can buy it at the Brihadeshwara Temple museum in Thanjavur or the Fort St George Museum in Madras.

Thirukandiyur (10 km)

The Thirukandiyur temples are dedicated to Brahma Sirakandeshwara and Harsaba Vimochana Perumal and are noted for their fine sculptural work.

Thiruvaiyaru (13 km)

The famous temple at Thiruvaiyaru is dedicated to Siva and is known as Panchanatheshwara. Accommodation is completely booked out every January, when an eight-day music festival is held in honour of the saint, Thiagaraja.

Tiruvarur (55 km)

The Siva temple at Tiruvarur, between Thanjavur and Nagapattinam, was gradually extended over the years. Its 1000-pillared hall actually has just 807 pillars.

Kumbakonam (40 km)

There are five temples in this typical south Indian town. The most important are Sarangapani, Kumbeshwara and Nageshwara, the largest of which is second in size only to the Meenakshi Temple at Madurai. The temples are noted for their colourful semi-erotic sculpture.

All the temples in Kumbakonam are closed between noon and 4.30 pm.

Thousands of devotees flock to a festival held at the **Mahamaham Tank** once every 12 years, when the waters of the Ganges are said to flow into the tank. According to legend, a kumbh (pitcher) came to rest here after a big flood (hence the town name). Siva broke the pot with his arrow, and its spilled contents gathered at what is now the sacred Mahamaham Tank.

The last such festival was held in early 1992 and was attended by the Chief Minister of Tamil Nadu, Jayalalitha. Unfortunately, things went seriously wrong at one point and there was a stampede in which a number of people were trampled to death and many more seriously injured. Just why this hap-

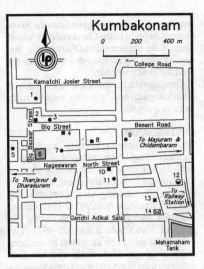

Kumbakonam

0   200   400 m

College Road

Kamatchi Josier Street

Big Street

Besant Road

To Mayuram &
Chidambaram

Nageswaran

North Street

To Thanjavur &
Dharasuram

To
Railway
Station

Gandhi Adikal Salai

Mahamaham
Tank

1 Chakkarapani
2 VPR Lodge & Hotel Siva
3 State Bank of India
4 Hotel AAR
5 Kumbeshwara Temple
6 Poothamari Tank
7 Sarangapani Temple
8 Pandiyan Lodge
9 Town Hall
10 New Diamond Lodge
11 Nageshwara Temple
12 Bus Stand
13 PRV Lodge
14 GPO & Clock Tower

pened isn't clear: some blamed the police for inadequate crowd supervision; others said it was caused by Jayalalitha's appearance on the scene.

Kumbakonam also makes an excellent base from which to visit the very interesting nearby towns of Dharasuram and Ganga-kondacholapuram.

Places to Stay & Eat The cheapest place to stay, and very good value considering its cleanliness, is the *New Diamond Lodge* (☎ 20-870), 93 Nageswaran North St, which has singles/doubles for Rs 17/35 with attached bathroom. Also excellent value and brand new is the *Pandiyan Lodge* (☎ 20-397), 52 Sarangapani East St, which offers singles/doubles with attached bathrooms for Rs 40/60. Similar in price is the *PRV Lodge*, 32 Head Post Office Rd, close to the GPO and the Mahamaham Tank.

Going up in price, the new *Hotel Raya's* (☎ 21-362), 28/29 Head Post Office Rd, next to the PRV Lodge, offers singles/doubles from Rs 80/100 and air-con singles/doubles from Rs 175/200. The rooms are well furnished with telephone and, in most cases, a colour TV, and there are separate vegetarian

and non-vegetarian restaurants. Similar is the *Hotel Siva/VPR Lodge* (☎ 21-045), 104/105 Big St. This is excellent value, spotless and offers doubles with attached bathrooms and hot water for Rs 100 (non-air-con) and Rs 200 (air-con).

Another good hotel in this range is the *Hotel ARR* (☎ 21-234), 21 Big St, which has singles/doubles for Rs 80/100 and Rs 150/200 with air-con. There are also more expensive air-con suites, as well as a dormitory at Rs 50 per person.

There are also railway *retiring rooms* at the station but this is somewhat inconvenient for the town centre.

Kumbakonam is hardly a gourmet's delight, but the *PRV Lodge* has a good vegetarian 'meals' restaurant and the vegetarian restaurant in the *Hotel ARR* does excellent vegetable biryani. Although the non-veg restaurant is not up to the same standard, it is about the only place in town where carnivores can indulge themselves.

Very good vegetarian meals can be found in the new, air-conditioned *Arul Restaurant* on Sarangapani East St opposite the Pandiyan Lodge.

Getting There & Away The bus station is just north of Mahamaham Tank. Once again, there's nothing in English, but there are frequent departures to Thanjavur.

Thiruvalluvar buses use the same station and four buses a day make the 7½-hour journey to Madras (No 305, Rs 27.50). Others pass through here on their way to Madurai, Coimbatore, Bangalore, Tiruvannamalai, Pondicherry and Chidambaram.

The railway station is 500 metres east of the Mahamaham Tank (about Rs 5 by cyclerickshaw from Big St). Trains depart for Madras, Chidambaram, Thanjavur and Trichy.

Dharasuram (44 km)

The small town of Dharasuram is four km west of Kumbakonam. Set behind the village, the Dharasuram or **Airatesvara Temple** is a superb example of 12th-century Chola architecture. This temple was built by Raja Raja II (1146-63) and is in a fine state of preservation.

The temple is fronted by columns with unique miniature sculptures. In the 14th century, the row of large statues around the temple was replaced with brick and concrete statues similar to those found at the Thanjavur temple. Many were taken to the art gallery in the Raja's Palace at Thanjavur, but have since been returned to Dharasuram. The remarkable sculptures depict Siva as Kankala-murti (the mendicant) and show a number of sages' wives standing by, dazzled by his beauty. The Archaeological Survey of India has done quite a bit of restoration here in recent years.

Although the temple is used very little at present, there is a helpful and knowledgeable priest who speaks good English. He is available from 8 am to 8 pm daily and, for a small consideration, will give you an excellent guided tour of the temple.

The best way to visit Dharasuram is to hire a bicycle in Kumbakonam.

Gangakondacholapuram (71 km)

The gopurams of this enormous temple dominate the surrounding landscape. It was built by the Chola emperor, Rajendra I (1012-44), in the style of the Brihadeshwara Temple at Thanjavur (built by his father), and is dedicated to Siva. Many beautiful sculptures adorn the walls of the temple and its enclosures. You'll also see a huge **tank** into which

were emptied vessels of water from the River Ganges, brought to the Chola court by vassal kings. Like the temple at Dharasuram, this one is visited by few tourists and is no longer used for Hindu worship.

Gangakondacholapuram is 35 km north of Kumbakonam and is easily visited from there as a day trip.

CHIDAMBARAM

South of Pondicherry, towards Thanjavur, is another of Tamil Nadu's Dravidian architectural highlights – the temple complex of Chidambaram with the great temple of Nataraja, the dancing Siva. Chidambaram was a Chola capital from 907 to 1310 and the **Nataraja Temple** was erected during the reign of Vira Chola Raja (927-997). The complex is said to be the oldest in southern India. It covers 13 hectares and has four gopurams, the north and south ones towering 49 metres high. Two of the gopurams are carved with the 108 classical postures of Nataraja, Siva in his role as the cosmic dancer.

Other notable features of the temple are the 1000-pillared hall, the Nritta Sabha court carved out like a gigantic chariot, and the image of Nataraja himself in the central sanctum. There are other lesser temples in the complex, including ones dedicated to Parvati, Subrahmanya and Ganesh, and a newer Vishnu temple.

The Nataraja Temple courtyard with its many shrines is open from 4 am to noon and 4.30 to 9 pm. The **puja ceremony**, held at 6 pm every Friday evening, is certainly spectacular with fire rituals and clashing of bells and drums. Although non-Hindus are not allowed right into the inner sanctum, there are usually priests around who will take you in – for a fee, of course.

There is a tourist office at the Hotel Tamil Nadu.

Places to Stay

The *Star Lodge* (☎ 2743) on South Car St, five minutes walk from the bus station, is the best of the cheap accommodation. Rooms cost Rs 35/45 and are very clean and habit-

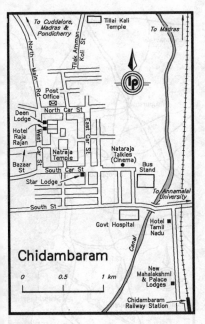

To Cuddalore, Madras & Pondicherry

Tillai Kali Temple

To Madras

North Main Rd

Tilak Amman Koil St

Post Office

North Car St

East Car St

Deen Lodge

Hotel Raja Rajan

West Car St

Nataraja Temple

Bazaar St

South Car St

Nataraja Talkies (Cinema)

Bus Stand

Star Lodge

South St

To Annamalai University

Chidambaram

0   0.5   1 km

Govt Hospital

Hotel Tamil Nadu

Canal

New Mahalakshmi & Palace Lodges

Chidambaram Railway Station

able, though the windows have only grills – no glass.

On West Car St, the *Hotel Raja Rajan* (☎ 2690) is more expensive at Rs 45/80 with bathroom. The friendly *Deen Lodge* (☎ 2602) close by has reasonable rooms for Rs 30/45.

The *Hotel Tamil Nadu* (☎ 2323) *may* be a good place to stay if they've laundered the sheets recently but they're not keen on doing this and the staff are apathetic. Rooms here cost Rs 40/75, or Rs 125 for an air-con double. Dormitory beds are occasionally available for Rs 20.

The *Hotel Saradharam* (☎ 2966), 19 V G P St, near the bus stand, has reasonable singles/doubles for Rs 99/115, or doubles with air-con for Rs 172, though the bedsheets are usually far from clean. The staff are helpful and there's a bar and two restaurants: vegetarian at the front and air-con non-veg at the back. Food in the non-veg restaurant is very good and prices are reasonable but get

there early for lunch or dinner as it's very popular.

There are a couple more basic lodges by the entrance to the railway station, and at the station itself there are two *retiring rooms*.

Places to Eat

The choice of restaurants in Chidambaram is extremely limited. The *Babu Restaurant*, on the ground floor of the Star Lodge, offers good vegetarian meals at rock-bottom prices.

The best place to eat for non-vegetarians is the restaurant at the *Hotel Saradha Ram*.

Avoid eating at the *Hotel Tamil Nadu* as the food there is very mediocre.

The *Milky Mist* cafe is opposite the Hotel Tamil Nadu and has excellent snacks and sweets.

Getting There & Away

The railway station is 20 minutes walk south of the temple, or Rs 5 by cycle-rickshaw. There are express and passenger trains to Madras, Kumbakonam, Thanjavur, Trichy and Rameswaram.

The bus station is more central and is used by both Thiruvalluvar and local buses. Thiruvalluvar buses leave for Pondicherry and Madras almost every hour (Nos 300 & 326), and others go to Nagapattinam (No 326) and Madurai (No 521).

PICHAVARAM

The sea resort of Pichavaram, with its back-waters and mangrove forest, is 15 km east of Chidambaram. A Marine Research Institute is at nearby Porto Novo, a former Portuguese and Dutch port.

Places to Stay

The TTDC *Youth Hostel* (☎ 32) charges Rs 20 for a dormitory bed.

TRANQUEBAR

Tranquebar, south of Poompuhar, was a Danish trading post in the 18th century and has a church built by the Lutherans. Later, it came under British rule. **Danesborg Fort** still looks out to sea, impressive and decaying, and there are some fine old colonial houses. Lots of children will pester you to buy Danish coins.

The town has been targetted as a possible beach resort/historical location to rival Mahabalipuram and the Danish government has expressed keen interest in developing the spot as a result of approaches made by the Indian ambassador to Denmark.

KARAIKAL

The former French enclave of Karaikal is part of the Union Territory of Pondicherry but those in search of lingering French influence will be disappointed, since precious little is left apart from the Catholic church of Our Lady of Angels which was originally built in 1740 and rebuilt in 1828. On the other hand, Karaikal is an important Hindu pilgrimage town with its Siva temple (Lord Darbaranyeswar Temple) and another dedicated to Punithavathi, a female Saivite saint subsequently elevated to the status of a goddess (Ammaiyar Temple).

Unless you're a pilgrim, there's little to attract you to Karaikal and tourist facilities are minimal. There is, however, an excellent and deserted, though windy, beach about one km from town and boating is available on the estuary alongside which Karaikal is built.

Orientation & Information

The tourist office (☎ 2596), telephone exchange, State Bank of India and most of the hotels and restaurants are along Bharathiar Rd, one of the town's main roads.

The telephone area code for Karaikal is 04368.

Places to Stay & Eat

Accommodation is very limited. The only reasonable places are the *City Plaza Hotel* and the *Government Tourist Motel*, both of which offer doubles with attached bathroom and fan for Rs 50. Both are on Bharathiar Rd but several hundred metres apart.

The *Hotel Nala*, next to the City Plaza Hotel, is the best place to eat. It offers tasty vegetarian 'special meals' at Rs 12. For vegetarian and non-vegetarian Chinese-style

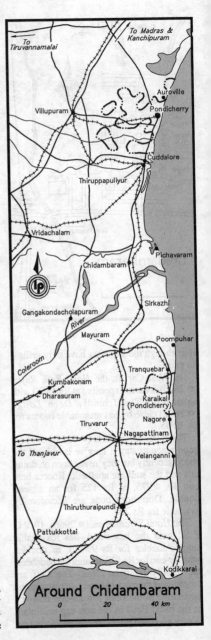

Around Chidambaram

0   20   40 km

meals, try the *Hotel Annapurna*, 117 Bharathiar Rd.

The tourist corporation operates *Le Café* at the start of the road which leads down to the lighthouse and beach alongside the estuary but it only serves meals in the evening. Rowboats can be hired from here.

Getting There & Away

The bus station in Karaikal is close to the mosque. Bus No 459 connects Kumbakonam with Karaikal.

NAGORE & VELANGANNI

The Nagore Andavar Dargah is an important Muslim pilgrimage centre at Nagore, 45 km from Thanjavur. Velanganni (90 km) is the site of the famous Roman Catholic Church of Our Lady of Good Health. People of all religions flock to the church, many donating gold or silver models of cured bodily parts! A major festival is held here on 8 September. There's a *PWD Rest House* at Ettukudi, six km away, or write to the vicar of St Mary's Church, Velanganni, about accommodation. The *St Joseph's Pilgrims Quarters* at Velanganni charges Rs 25 for a double with bathroom, and the *Matha* restaurant next door is good.

POOMPUHAR

Only a small village now stands at the mouth of the Cauvery River but it was here at Poompuhar that the rulers of the Chola Empire conducted trade with Rome and with centres to the east. The town has a fine beach, a good *Rest House* and some very cheap south Indian vegetarian restaurants. This Chola seaport has also given its name to the chain of craft emporia run by the TTDC.

TIRUCHIRAPPALLI

Population: 711,000

This city is usually known by its shortened names of Trichy or Tiruchy. Its most famous landmark is the Rock Fort Temple, a spectacular monument perched on a massive outcrop of rock which rises abruptly from the plain to tower over the old city. There are a few other such outcrops on the way to

Thanjavur, one of which has a temple built on it, but none are as large or as tall as the one at Trichy. The Rock Fort Temple is reached by a steep flight of steps cut into the rock, and the views from the summit are magnificent.

The other landmark at Trichy is much less well known, which is surprising because it's probably the largest and one of the most interesting temple complexes in India. This is the Sri Ranganathaswamy Temple (Srirangam), built on an island in the middle of the Cauvery River and covering a staggering 2½ sq km! There is also another huge temple complex nearby – the Sri Jambukeshwara Temple. Both are visible from the summit of the Rock Fort Temple, shrouded in coconut palms, and it's worth spending a day or two exploring them.

Trichy itself has a long history going back to the centuries before the Christian era when it was a Chola citadel. In the 1st millennium AD, it changed hands between the Pallavas and Pandyas many times before being taken by the Cholas in the 10th century AD. When the Chola Empire finally decayed, Trichy passed into the hands of the Vijayanagar kings of Hampi and remained with them until their defeat, in 1565 AD, by the forces of the Deccan sultans. The town and its fort, as it stands today, was built by the Nayaks of Madurai. It was one of the main centres around which the wars of the Carnatic were fought in the 18th century during the British-French struggle for supremacy in India.

Monuments aside, the city's good range of hotels and facilities makes it a pleasant place to stay. Though spread out, Trichy has an excellent local bus system which doesn't demand the strength of an ox and the skin of an elephant to use.

Orientation

Trichy is scattered over a considerable area. Although you will need transport to get from one part to another, most of the hotels and restaurants, the bus stand, railway station, tourist office, airline offices and GPO are within two or three minutes walk of each

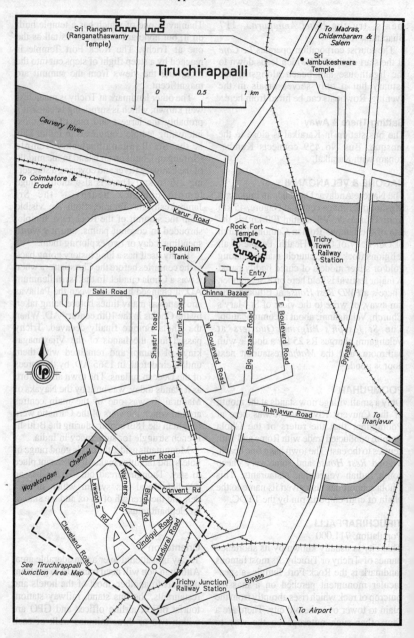

Tiruchirappalli

0   0.5   1 km

To Madras,
Chidambaram &
Salem

Sri
Jambukeshwara
Temple

Sri Rangam
(Ranganathaswamy
Temple)

Cauvery River

To Coimbatore &
Erode

Karur Road

Rock Fort
Temple

Trichy
Town Railway
Station

Teppakulam
Tank

Entry

Salai Road

Chinna Bazaar

Shastri Road

Madras Trunk Road

W. Boulevard Road

Big Bazaar Road

E. Boulevard Road

Bypass

Thanjavur Road

To
Thanjavur

Woyakondan Channel

Heber Road

Convent Rd

Cleveland Road

Lawson's Rd

Warners Rd

Birds Rd

Dindigul Road

Madurai Road

See Tiruchirappalli
Junction Area Map

Trichy Junction
Railway Station

Bypass

To Airport

other in what is known as the junction (or cantonment) area.

The Rock Fort Temple is 1½ km north of this area, near the banks of the Cauvery River. A further 1½ km north, on an island in the Cauvery, are Trichy's two main temples.

Information

The tourist office is at the front of the Hotel Tamil Nadu, within sight of the bus station. It's open daily, except Sundays and public holidays, between 10.30 am and 5.30 pm. You can buy a good map of the Trichy region here for Rs 3 – a good investment if you plan to explore.

Rock Fort Temple

The Rock Fort Temple tops a massive outcrop of rock, 83 metres high. The views from the top are well worth the stiff climb up 437 steps cut into the stone. Non-Hindus are not allowed into the sanctum sanctorum at the summit, or into the Sri Thayumanaswamy Temple dedicated to Siva, halfway up, so a visit here tends to be a brief affair.

The monument is open daily from 6 am until 8 pm. Entry is Rs 0.50, plus Rs 5 if you have a camera. (The only photographically interesting vista is the one to the north over the temples at Srirangam.) You must leave your shoes at the entrance, where you can amuse yourself by offering the temple elephant a coin. He takes this in the tip of his trunk, passes it to his keeper and rewards you by tapping you on the head with his trunk.

Srirangam (Sri Ranganathaswamy Temple)

Surrounded by seven concentric walls with 21 gopurams, this superb temple complex is probably the largest in India. Most of it dates from the 14th to 17th centuries, and many people have had a hand in its construction, including the Cheras, Pandyas, Cholas, Hoysalas and Vijayanagars. The largest gopuram in the first wall on the southern side (the main entrance) is as recent as 1980.

The temple is very well preserved, with excellent carvings throughout and numerous shrines to various gods, though the main temple is dedicated to Vishnu. Even the Muslims are said to have prayed here after the fall of the Vijayanagar Empire. Non-Hindus are, of course, not allowed into the sanctum sanctorum, but this is no major loss since the whole place is fascinating, and non-Hindus can go as far as the sixth wall. Bazaars and Brahmins' houses fill the space between the outer four walls, and you don't have to take your shoes off or deposit your bicycle until you get to the fourth wall (Rs 0.20). If you have a camera, you'll be charged Rs 10 at this point.

Opposite the shoe deposit is the 'Art Gallery', where you buy the Rs 2 ticket to climb the wall for a panoramic view of the entire complex. A guide will go with you to unlock the gates and tell you what's what. It's well worth engaging one of the temple priests as a guide as there is just so much to see. Expect to pay around Rs 20 for a couple of hours, although you could easily spend all day wandering around this complex. The inner temple is open daily from 6.15 am to 1 pm and from 3.15 to 8.45 pm.

An annual **car festival** is held here between 15 December and 25 December each year, drawing pilgrims from all over India. Make sure you see it if you're in the area at the time.

Guidebooks There is a book sold in certain shops in the temple complex called *Sri Ranga Kshetra Mahatmyam* by R Narasimhan Praveen, at Rs 1.50. The author probably intended to produce a guidebook and collection of legends about the temple, but it's full of the most incomprehensible nonsense you're ever likely to encounter. For this reason alone, it's worth buying. Some gems from it include:

Pavithrotsava is conducted to the Lord for nine days from the Sukla-Paksha 'bright fortnight' Ekadasi day. To the negligence committed during all these days in the years in the Pujas, remedy is being sought for otherwise Aparadakshanpana is being sought for.

Thondar-Adi – He is called as Vipra Narayana – He was born in a sacred place called Thirumadangudi. His Janma Nakashatra is Jyeshta in Margazhi month.

He was living in Srirangam and engaged himself in presenting Thiru Thuzhai or Thulasi to Sri Tanganatha and garlands of beautiful and scented flowers were daily offered by him to the Lord. He has sung the famous Thirumalai, which is especially in devotion to Lord Sri Ranganatha and no others. His another prabandha named Thiruppalli Yezhuchi is the most important part of the Thirumozhi group to wake up the Lord everyday. It is also spoken as Thirumalai Ariyar – Perumalai Ariyar – ie Those who do not know Lord Sri Ranganatha. Sri Vanamal of Lord Vishnu took the avatar of this Tondar Adi Podi Alwar.

Sri Jambukeshwara Temple

On the opposite side of the main Madras to Salem road to Sri Ranganathaswamy Temple, the Sri Jambukeshwara Temple is dedicated to Siva and has five concentric walls and seven gopurams. Its deity is a Siva lingam, submerged in water that comes from a spring in the sanctum sanctorum. Non-Hindus are not allowed in this part of the temple. The complex was built around the same time as the Sri Ranganathaswamy Temple and is equally interesting. It's open daily between 6 am and 1 pm and between 4 and 9.30 pm, and there's another Rs 5 camera fee.

St John's Church

Trichy also has some interesting Raj-era monuments. Built in 1812, St John's Church has louvered side doors which can be opened to turn the church into an airy pavilion. It's interesting for its setting and architecture and also for the surrounding cemetery. Rouse the doorkeeper to let you in.

Places to Stay – bottom end

Two of the cheapest hotels, right opposite the State bus stand, are the *Vijay Lodge*, 13-B Royal Rd, and the *Guru Hotel* (☎ 41-881), 13-A Royal Rd. Both of them are typical Indian lodging houses but are clean and pleasant enough. The Vijay has singles/doubles at Rs 49/77 with attached bathroom, and the Guru has the same at Rs 55/80 plus deluxe doubles at Rs 95. Also cheap but with better facilities is the *Hotel Lakshmi* (☎ 40-098), 3-A Alexandria Rd, which has

singles/doubles/triples with own bathrooms at Rs 45-55/70/120.

Slightly more expensive is the *Hotel Ajanta* (☎ 40-501), Junction Rd, which offers good singles/doubles/triples at Rs 60/95/130 and air-con singles/doubles at Rs 125/175, all plus luxury taxes. The hotel has a good vegetarian restaurant. Similar is the *Hotel Arun* (☎ 41-421), 24 State Bank Rd, with singles/doubles/triples at Rs 70/99/175 or Rs 140/175/225 with air-con, plus luxury taxes. All the rooms are self-contained.

The *Hotel Aanand*, 1 Racquet Court Lane, is probably the most attractive of the cheaper places, although it's a bit grubby. Rooms cost Rs 77/115 plus there are air-con doubles at Rs 240, all including taxes. There are no air-con singles. All rooms have bathrooms and there is a good restaurant.

Not far from the Aanand, the older *Hotel Aristo* (☎ 41-818), 2 Dindigul Rd, situated in its own leafy gardens, has singles/doubles at Rs 55/75 or Rs 110/140 with air-con. There are also air-con cottages at Rs 195/285 for single and double occupancy. There's a restaurant serving both Indian and Continental food and credit cards are accepted.

There are *retiring rooms* at the station which have dorm beds for Rs 15 per person plus doubles at Rs 60 and air-con doubles at Rs 100.

There's also the very basic *Modern Hindu Hotel* on Dindigul Rd, which, though one of the cheapest, is a strange and shabby place and there's frequently no-one around for hours in the afternoons. It also has some hilarious rules: 'Liquors and gambling are strictly prohibited. Like playing cards'; 'Brothel and bad character women are not allowed. During police raid management are not responsible for them. If any suspect is found, the management will inform police'.

Places to Stay – middle

Right outside the State bus stand are a whole bunch of relatively new and brand new mid-range hotels to choose from. At the bottom end of the scale is the *Hotel Tamil Nadu* (☎ 40-383), McDonald Rd, which is fairly

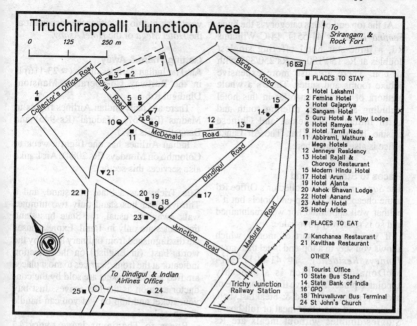

Tiruchirappalli Junction Area

0   125   250 m

To Srirangam & Rock Fort

■ PLACES TO STAY
1 Hotel Lakshmi
2 Femina Hotel
3 Hotel Gajapriya
4 Sangam Hotel
5 Guru Hotel & Vijay Lodge
6 Hotel Ramyas
9 Hotel Tamil Nadu
11 Abbirami, Mathura & Mega Hotels
12 Jenneys Residency
13 Hotel Rajali & Chorogo Restaurant
16 Modern Hindu Hotel
17 Hotel Arun
19 Hotel Ajanta
20 Ashok Bhavan Lodge
22 Hotel Aanand
23 Ashby Hotel
25 Hotel Aristo

▼ PLACES TO EAT
7 Kanchanaa Restaurant
21 Kavithaa Restaurant

OTHER
8 Tourist Office
10 State Bus Stand
15 State Bank of India
16 GPO
18 Thiruvalluvar Bus Terminal
24 St John's Church

pleasant though nowhere near as palatial as its sister establishment in Thanjavur. Singles/doubles are Rs 70/100 or Rs 130/245 with air-con. Towels and toilet paper are provided. The tourist office is in this hotel and there's a good restaurant and bar.

If you prefer olde-worlde atmosphere, touches of the Raj and spacious rooms, try the *Ashby Hotel* (☎ 40-652), 17-A Junction Rd, which has singles/doubles at Rs 60/80 or Rs 170/205 with air-con. All the rooms are self-contained plus there's a bar and restaurant which has both outdoor and air-con indoor sections. The indoor section is open for lunch (11 am to 3 pm) and dinner (7 to 11 pm) while the outdoor section is open from 6 pm to 1 am. The cuisine is south Indian, Chinese and Continental.

Of the modern hotels, the *Hotel Ramyas* is excellent value with spotlessly clean rooms, a balcony and superb bathrooms and it is remarkably reasonable in price. Singles/doubles cost Rs 90/140, or Rs 190/230 with

air-con and colour TV. Room service is good and most credit cards are accepted.

Very similar to the Ramyas is the *Hotel Abbirami* (☎ 40-001), 10 McDonald Rd, diagonally opposite. The price of rooms here is much the same, as are the facilities. There's a bar and both vegetarian and non-vegetarian food is available.

Adjacent to the Gajapriya are two other modern hotels, the *Hotel Mathura* (☎ 43-737), Rockins Rd, and the *Hotel Mega* (☎ 43-092), 8-B Rockins Rd. The Mathura has singles/doubles at Rs 75/100, or Rs 140/200 with air-con, and the Mega has much the same for Rs 85/130, or Rs 130/175 with air-con. Both hotels have vegetarian restaurants but no bar.

Not far from here, the equally modern *Hotel Gajapriya* (☎ 41-144), 2 Royal Rd, offers singles/doubles at Rs 110/140, or Rs 190/230 with air-con. There's a bar and restaurant offering both vegetarian and non-vegetarian dishes.

At the top end of this category is the huge *Femina Hotel* (☎ 41-551), 14-C Williams Rd, a three-star hotel offering singles/doubles at Rs 150/180, or Rs 250/320 with air-con. There are also more expensive deluxe rooms and suites. There's a whole plethora of services on offer in this hotel including a restaurant offering south and north Indian, Continental and Chinese cuisine, but there's no bar. The Air Lanka office is also situated here.

Places to Stay – top end

The *Sangam Hotel* on Collector's Office Rd is the cheapest of the top-end hotels but it's neither well appointed nor well maintained and so is relatively poor value.

If you have enough of money which allows you stay in a top-end hotel then go to *Jenneys Residency* (☎ 41-301), 3/14 McDonald Rd, which is a superbly appointed place. You have the option here of taking a room only, bed & breakfast, bed, breakfast and one other meal or full board. Singles/doubles without meals are Rs 160/320 or Rs 250/450 with air-con; full board costs Rs 360/720 or Rs 450/850 respectively. Taxes on all the above room rates (luxury, expenditure and sales taxes) amount to an additional 40%.

Places to Eat

There's little choice when it comes to eating. The Guru Hotel has the *New Kurunchi Restaurant* and, in the group of shops between it and the corner, the tiny *Maharaja Restaurant* offers good cheap non-vegetarian food from a limited menu.

The *Kanchanaa Restaurant* on Williams Rd, just along from the tourist office, is a popular vegetarian and non-vegetarian restaurant with both open-air and enclosed sections and is an agreeable place to sit outside and eat in the evenings. Also popular is the vegetarian *Kavithaa Restaurant* which does excellent, highly elaborate thalis for Rs 12, and has an air-con room.

Other than the above, it's down to eating at one or other of the hotel restaurants. Take your pick but do try either the restaurant at the *Hotel Mega* or the *Hotel Ashby*.

Getting There & Away

Air The Indian Airlines office (☎ 23-116) is in the Railway Co-operative Mansion, Dindigul Rd.

There are daily Indian Airlines flights to Madras (Rs 767), Madurai (Rs 945) and Bangalore (Rs 847).

Indian Airlines has one flight a week to Colombo on Mondays (Rs 2084). Air Lanka also services this sector.

Bus Trichy has a State bus stand, and a Thiruvalluvar bus stand only two minutes walk away. As usual, the State bus stand timetables are only in Tamil. Express buses are distinguished from ordinary buses by the word 'Fast' (in English) on the direction indicator at the front. Services to most places are frequent and tickets are sold by the conductor as soon as the bus arrives. Just buy your ticket and hop on – if you can handle the chaos.

Buses to Thanjavur leave every 15 minutes or so, and the one-hour journey costs Rs 9. There are also frequent buses to Madurai, which is a four-hour trip.

The Thiruvalluvar buses originating in Trichy can be computer-booked in advance. These buses include: Bangalore (three daily, Rs 49.50), Coimbatore (twice daily, Rs 28.50), Madras (23 daily, eight hours, Rs 42.50), Nagarcoil via Madurai (eight daily, Rs 47.50) and Tirupathy via Vellore (four daily, 9½ hours, Rs 56.50). In addition, there are many buses passing through and you can usually get a seat on these.

There are also superdeluxe buses to Madras from the Thiruvalluvar station four times daily for Rs 48.50.

In addition to the above buses, there are private super deluxe buses to Madras. They include AKM Travels, opposite the Hotel Tamil Nadu (four daily, six hours, Rs 68) and KPN/RR Travels, outside the Hotel Aanand (10 times daily, six hours, Rs 68).

Train Trichy is on the main Madras to

Top: Sri Menakshi Temple, Madurai, Tamil Nadu (HF)
Bottom: Detail of Sri Menakshi Temple, Madurai, Tamil Nadu (BT)

Top: Brihadeshwara Temple, Thanjavur, Tamil Nadu (PT)
Left: Krishna's Butterball, Mahabalipuram, Tamil Nadu (TW)
Right: Temple priest, Trichy, Tamil Nadu (HF)

Madurai railway line and some trains run directly from Madras. It's 337 km, takes five to eight hours, and costs Rs 65/241 in 2nd/1st class. Other trains go via Chidambaram and Thanjavur, 64 km further. The Madras to Madurai and Madras to Rameswaram trains also go through Trichy. It's about seven hours from Trichy to Rameswaram, and the 265-km trip costs Rs 54/199 in 2nd/1st class.

It's 155 km from Trichy to Madurai at a cost of Rs 38/129 in 2nd/1st class. The fastest train is the *Vaigai Express*, which covers the distance in 2½ hours. Slower trains take up to four hours.

Getting Around

Bus Trichy's excellent local bus service is uncrowded and comparatively easy to use. Take a No 7, 63, 63A, 122 or 128 bus to the airport, allowing about half an hour to get there.

The No 1 bus from the State bus stand goes to the Rock Fort Temple, the main entrance to Srirangam and close to the Sri Jambukeshwara Temple. The service is frequent and relatively uncrowded. It takes a full day to do the circuit.

Bicycle The town lends itself well to cycling as it's dead flat. There are a couple of places on Junction Rd where you can hire bicycles for Rs 15 per day.

Heading back from the Rock Fort, the incredibly busy Big Bazaar Rd is one-way traffic (heading north), so you have to get off your bicycle and walk or take a detour.

UDHAGAMANDALAM (Ootacamund, Ooty)

Population: 82,000

This famous hill station near the tri-junction of Tamil Nadu, Kerala and Karnataka is 2268 metres above sea level in the Nilgiri mountains. It was founded by the British in the early part of the 19th century to serve as the summer headquarters of the government of Madras. Before that time, the area was inhabited by the Todas. These tribal people still live there, but today, only 3000 remain. The Todas were polygamists and worshipped buffaloes, and you can see their animist shrines in various places.

Until about 10 years ago, the town resembled an unlikely combination of southern England and Australia, with single-storey stone cottages surrounded by bijou fenced flower gardens scattered along leafy, winding lanes with tall eucalypt stands covering the otherwise barren hilltops. Since their introduction back in the 19th century, the eucalypts have spawned a small oil-extraction industry in the area, and bottles of eucalyptus oil are sold in many of the town's shops.

The other main reminders of the British period are the stone churches, the private schools, various maharajas' summer palaces, and the terraced Botanical Gardens, in which Government House still stands on the lower slopes of Doddabetta (2623 metres), the highest peak in Tamil Nadu. From the top of Doddabetta you can see Coonoor, Wellington, Coimbatore, Mettupalayam and, on a clear day, as far as Mysore.

Although it quickly became the principal hill station in southern India during the Raj, Ooty was not the first in this area. As early as 1819, the British began to build houses at nearby Kotagiri. This much smaller town survives as a minor hill station, and has a climate midway between that of Ooty and Coonoor.

Parts of Ooty still exude this fading atmosphere of unhurried privilege, leafy seclusion and nostalgia for the 'green, green grass of home', especially on the western and southern margins of the lake, but elsewhere hoteliers and real estate developers and the influx of tourist hordes with their city habits, demands and expectations have totally transformed it.

These days, at least in the high season, it's a dreadful place full of vacuous yuppies, day trippers and the like playing at Daddy Cool with their ghetto blasters on overdrive, pushing and shoving their way into and onto everything, throwing litter everywhere and generally behaving like a bunch of pigs. You can no longer walk down the country lanes without being deafened by car horns or nearly run down by speeding buses and trucks. The sewage system, too, is clearly incapable of dealing with the demand placed on it as a glance at the town's central, open sewer will immediately demonstrate. It's also good to remember, should you be thinking of boating, that all this untreated filth flows directly into the lake.

All in all, Ooty is best avoided these days unless you can afford to stay in one of the ex-palaces. It's been totally screwed, there's precious little to do, unless you're fond of long walks and boating on the lake, and the only things it has going for it is the journey up there on the 'toy' train and the fact that it's cool when the plains down below are unbearably hot.

In the winter months and during the monsoon, the weather in Ooty can take you by surprise. At these times you will need warm clothing as the overnight temperature occasionally drops to 0°C.

Orientation

Ooty is spread over a large area amongst rolling hills and valleys. The most notable features are the lake and the racecourse. The railway station and bus stand are between the two while the bazaar, tourist office, restaurants and most of the hotels are north and east of the racecourse especially around Charing Cross (the junction of Coonoor, Kelso and Commercial roads).

Information

Tourist Office The tourist office on Commercial Rd, opposite the Hotel Nahar, is surely one of the worst in southern India. The only literature available here is a leaflet containing a poor map of Ooty and details of the current hotel prices. The office staff can add nothing to the information in the leaflet they hand you and care less.

Post & Telecommunications The GPO is at the traffic circle known as Town West Circle. The telegraph office is also here, and is open from 7 am to 10 pm Monday to Saturday, and 8 am to 4 pm Sunday.

Mudumalai Park Office If you intend to visit Mudumalai, it's wise to arrange accommodation in advance to be sure of a bed for the night. Book with the Range Officer (☎ 3114), at the Wildlife Warden's office in the APT Mahalingam Building on Coonoor Rd.

Bookshop Higginbothams, just across the road from Chellaram's Department Store in the Charing Cross area, is an excellent bookshop.

Things to See & Do

Ooty is a place for outdoor activities. There are any number of long walks and some superb views over Ooty and the Nilgiris – just head in any direction. If you'd prefer to go on horseback, hire a horse at the Tourist Cafe on the north side of the lake but haggle hard over the price as they'll quote whatever price they think you'll pay. You can ride on your own or hire one of the owners as a guide.

Rowboats and motor boats for use on the lake can be rented from the Tourist Cafe but, be warned, this is where the tourist hordes are at their worst. It's Holocaust Corner. You even have to pay Rs 0.50 for the privilege of getting to the boat jetty plus Rs 3 for a camera (or Rs 100 for a movie camera!). Rowboats (two seat) cost Rs 12 or Rs 18 per half-hour, depending on the season, and motor boats (eight seat) are Rs 55 or Rs 65 per half-hour. You can even get someone to row you around for Rs 5 extra.

Entry to the 'Lake Park', between the eastern end of the lake and the boat jetty, costs Rs 1 plus the same charges as the boat jetty for cameras. It's the ideal place for masochists.

Race meetings are held at the racetrack during the monsoon season. These are quite an event, although the betting is all very tame. Entry is Rs 5.

Organised Tours

Several private companies offer daily tours of Ooty (Rs 40), Ooty and Coonoor (Rs 60), Ooty and Kotagiri (Rs 65), and Ooty and

Mudumalai Wildlife Sanctuary (Rs 75). The first three may well be worth it if you don't mind being rushed from one point to another without a moment to spare. The Mudumalai tours are a complete waste of time and the chances of seeing anything more exotic than a tame elephant are exceedingly slim. Tour prices generally include a vegetarian lunch. Try Naveen Tours & Travels (☎ 3747) in the Nahar Shopping Complex at Charing Cross if interested.

Places to Stay

Since Ooty is a sellers' market in the high season (1 April to 15 June), hoteliers hike up their prices by a staggering 300% on what they are in the low season. This is clearly a blatant rip-off since prices don't necessarily equate with quality, but there are few options. It can also be very difficult to find a room in the high season due to advance booking so you may have to do a lot of walking around until you find something. Be careful to note the checkout time at any hotel. Unlike the rest of Tamil Nadu where checkout is generally 24 hours, in Ooty it's usually noon but can be as early as 9 am.

Places to Stay – bottom end

Many of the budget hotels in the bazaar area are very poor value and definitely only for the desperate. Two which are passable are the *Vishnu Lodge*, Main Bazaar, which is basic and offers singles/doubles at Rs 60/100; and the *Tourist Lodge*, Commercial Rd, which has similar rooms with common bathroom for Rs 45/66.

The cheapest place to stay, if you're content with dormitory accommodation, is the *Youth Hostel* at Charing Cross. This is a branch of the TTDC Hotel Tamil Nadu and offers beds at Rs 20 in the low season and Rs 35 in the high season.

The only bright spot in this otherwise gloomy picture is *Reflections Guest House* (☎ 3834), North Lake Rd, which is within walking distance of the railway station. This is a very pleasant place to stay with good views over the lake and offers doubles at Rs 150 in the high season (less in the low

season). It has only six rooms, but there is hot water and the atmosphere is homely. The friendly Anglo-Indian manager, Mrs Dique, is a good source of information on the region's history.

The *YWCA* (☎ 2218), Ettines Rd, on the south-east side of the racecourse, is also very good value but, because it's cheap it's often full. A dorm bed costs just Rs 15 (low season) or Rs 20 (high season) and doubles with attached bathrooms are Rs 43 and Rs 72 (low season) and Rs 160 and Rs 180 (high season). There are also double cottages at Rs 108 and Rs 210 in the low and high seasons respectively. Meals are available and, in the winter months, there is a lounge with an open fire.

Places to Stay – middle

A good place to stay in this range is the large and pleasant *Hotel Tamil Nadu* (☎ 2543) on the hill above the tourist office. Doubles with own bathroom here cost Rs 130 (low season) and Rs 250 (high season). There's a restaurant but no bar. The easiest way to get to it is to take the steps up the hill adjacent to the tourist office.

Also relatively cheap and fairly popular is the *Hotel Sanjay* (☎ 3160) at the junction of Coonoor Rd and Commercial Rd. Doubles with attached bathrooms cost Rs 200 or Rs 300 for a deluxe double in the high season. There's a good vegetarian restaurant on the first floor.

Up in standard, the *Hotel Nahar* (☎ 2173) at Charing Cross has reasonable doubles with attached bathrooms and TVs for Rs 250, Rs 350 and Rs 450 in the low season, rising to Rs 300, Rs 400 and Rs 500 in the high season. It's rarely full as there are 100 rooms. The hotel has two restaurants and a snack bar.

Not far from Charing Cross on Ettines Rd is a whole cluster of mid-range hotels. Some have been there for some time; others are brand new. At the beginning of the road is the *Hotel Durga* (☎ 3837) which has doubles with own bathrooms and TVs for Rs 140 to Rs 199 (low season) and Rs 300 to Rs 400 (high season). The hotel also has its own

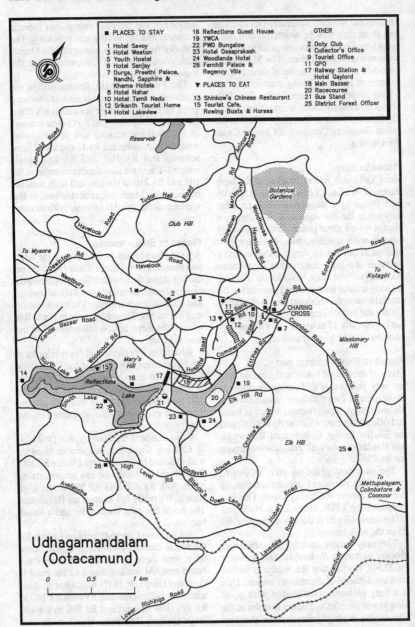

PLACES TO STAY

1 Hotel Savoy
3 Hotel Weston
5 Youth Hostel
6 Hotel Sanjay
7 Durga, Preethi Palace, Nandhi, Sapphire & Khems Hotels
8 Hotel Nahar
10 Hotel Tamil Nadu
12 Srikanth Tourist Home
14 Hotel Lakeview
16 Reflections Guest House
19 YWCA
22 PWD Bungalow
23 Hotel Dasaprakash
24 Woodlands Hotel
26 Fernhill Palace & Regency Villa

▼ PLACES TO EAT

13 Shinkow's Chinese Restaurant
15 Tourist Cafe, Rowing Boats & Horses

OTHER

2 Ooty Club
4 Collector's Office
9 Tourist Office
11 GPO
17 Railway Station & Hotel Gaylord
18 Main Bazaar
20 Racecourse
21 Bus Stand
25 District Forest Officer

Udhagamandalam
(Ootacamund)

0   0.5   1 km

vegetarian restaurant. Close by is the *Hotel Preethi Palace* (☎ 2789) which, in the high season, has deluxe doubles for Rs 400 and Rs 500.

Just round the corner from the above two on what is Shoreham Palace Rd are the *Hotel Nandhi*, *Hotel Sapphire* and the *Highland Lodge* which are similar in price. If you don't speak Tamil, you can expect the staff at the Highland to switch into Neanderthal mode.

Above these is the brand new and superbly appointed *Hotel Khems* (☎ 4188) whose tariff card claims that, 'Nobody gives you Ooty like we do'. It's certainly not a run-of-the-mill hotel but then neither are the prices. In the low season, standard/semideluxe/deluxe doubles are Rs 195/250/300; high-season prices are Rs 300/400/500. The staff are friendly and helpful and the hotel has its own restaurant.

Further west, on the south side of the racecourse, is the friendly and popular *Woodlands Hotel* (☎ 2551), an old, traditional-style hotel dating from colonial days, with rooms in the main building and a number of detached cottages. It's a very quiet and pleasant place with doubles with own bathroom at Rs 350 in the high season, cottages at Rs 500 and suites at Rs 750. Prices in the low season drop by around 25%.

At the western end of the lake is the *Hotel Lakeview* (☎ 3904), West Lake Rd, which is very popular with affluent Indians. The name is not very apt as most of the 'cottages' have a view of nothing more than the back of the 'cottage' in front. The charges in the low season range from Rs 190 to Rs 350, and in the high season from Rs 290 to Rs 450. There's a restaurant offering Indian, Chinese and Continental dishes and a bar. Credit cards are accepted.

On the hill overlooking the bus stand to the south is the *Hotel Dasaprakash* (☎ 2434), another long-established hotel. It's nothing special as the maintenance is not what it might be, and it's often full. Doubles with attached bathroom are Rs 400 in the high season; less in the low season. There's a vegetarian restaurant but no bar. It's somewhat overpriced.

Lastly in this range, out along Club Rd towards the Ooty Club, is the *Hotel Weston* (☎ 3500) which is similar to the Woodlands.

Places to Stay – top end

For a magnificent and palatial touch of the Raj you can't beat the *Fernhill Palace* (☎ 3910). Patronised by the Bombay film set and affluent Westerners, it's in a quiet forest setting 1½ km from the railway station and is the former palace of the Maharaja of Mysore. Built in the days when expense was of no concern and master artisans didn't command fortunes, it offers a range of doubles and suites from Rs 400 to Rs 750 (low season) and Rs 700 to Rs 1050 (high season) plus 40% taxes. Meals are served in the former ballroom and there's a bar with a range of old hunting photographs and other memorabilia (open to nonresidents).

Adjacent to the Fernhill Palace, but owned by the same people, is *Regency Villa* which is more rustic (and run down) but just as quiet and cheaper than the palace itself. The best rooms are spacious, with bay windows, fully tiled Victorian bathrooms (with hot water) and Raj-era memorabilia liberally distributed around the room. The staff are friendly and simple meals can be arranged if ordered in advance but there are no other facilities. You're looking at around Rs 70 per head in the smaller rooms and Rs 600 for the huge triple suite. Both the Fernhill Palace and Regency Villa are due to be taken over by the Taj Group and rehabilitated so prices are bound to rise.

If you want modern luxury, there's the *Hotel Savoy* (☎ 2572) which has prices similar to those at the Fernhill Palace.

Places to Eat

For standard south Indian food, the vegetarian restaurants in the *Hotel Nahar* and *Hotel Sanjay* are OK and relatively cheap.

There are plenty of other basic vegetarian 'meals' places further along Commercial Rd and Main Bazaar. In the vicinity of the bus stand are a gaggle of street stalls selling snacks and tea. However, if you're thinking of eating there, before ordering take a look at the open sewer around which they're clustered and the flies which migrate between them.

Back on Commercial Rd, the *Tandoori Mahal* looks expensive but isn't and the food is very tasty. Service is good and you can eat here for around Rs 30 to Rs 40.

Up on Town West Circle, *Shinkow's Chinese Restaurant* has some really good food. It's run by a Chinese family so the Chinese dishes are fairly authentic. The chips are excellent, as is the cassata ice cream. Expect to pay about Rs 30 per person.

Entertainment

There's virtually nothing to do in the evening in Ooty and the place closes down early. There are also very few bars where you might be able to meet other people and certainly none outside the top-end hotels. If this is what you're looking for then grab a taxi and go to the Fernhill Palace. The bar here is open to nonresidents and, despite the price of the rooms, the drinks are not expensive.

Getting There & Away

Bus The orderly bus station is fairly central at the western end of the racecourse. From there, it's only about 10 minutes walk to the centre of the bazaar and about 20 minutes to Charing Cross.

Local buses leave hourly on the Rs 5, 1¼-hour trip to Kotagiri. There are a dozen buses daily to Coonoor and the one-hour trip costs Rs 3.

Cheran Transport Corp, the regional bus company, operates buses to Bangalore, Coimbatore, Kodaikanal and Mysore. To Bangalore there are five semideluxe buses daily which take eight hours and cost Rs 54.50. To Coimbatore, buses leave every 20 to 30 minutes throughout the day, take three hours and cost Rs 12.90. To Mysore there are five semideluxe buses daily which take five hours and cost Rs 25. To Kodaikanal there's only one bus daily at 6.40 am which arrives at 3.30 pm.

If you're heading for the Mudumalai Wildlife Sanctuary, take one of the Mysore buses and get off at Theppakadu – the reception centre. The trip from Ooty takes about 2½ hours. An alternative route to Mudumalai involves taking one of the small buses which go via the narrow and twisting Sighur Ghat road. Most of these buses travel only as far as Masinagudi, but there are plenty of buses from there to Theppakadu.

The reservation office for Cheran buses is open from 9 am to 1 pm and 1.30 to 5.30 pm.

Thiruvalluvar buses also use the same station and their reservation office is open from 9 am to 5.30 pm (except from 12.30 to 1.30 pm). They have buses to Bangalore (via Mysore) which leave four times daily at Rs 56 and to Madras (via Erode and Salem) twice daily at Rs 72. They also have daily buses to Kanyakumari, Shenkottah, Thanjavur, Tirupathi and Thiruvananthapuram (Trivandrum).

In addition to the state and local bus lines, there are a number of private bus companies which offer daily services to Bangalore, Kodaikanal and Mysore. All of these are superdeluxe buses, often with videos, but they are comfortable, seats can be booked (no standing) and there's no hassle with a backpack (they go on the roof). Most of the companies are clustered around Charing Cross. They're a little more expensive than the state buses, but worth it. Ooty to Mysore takes about 4½ hours and costs Rs 65; Ooty to Kodaikanal costs around Rs 150.

From Coimbatore to Ooty there are Cheran departures daily every half-hour throughout the day, which take about 3½ hours and cost Rs 12.90.

Train Like Darjeeling and Matheran, Ooty has a miniature railway connecting it with the lowlands. The trains, with their quaint yellow-and-blue carriages, are not quite as small as the Darjeeling toy train, but they're still pretty tiny. The unique feature of this line is the toothed central rail onto which the locomotives lock on the steeper slopes. Also unusual is the little locomotive, which is at the back pushing rather than pulling from the front. Each of the four or five carriages has its own brakeman, who sits on a little platform on the front of the carriage. It's quite a circus when the train is about to pull out of a station and each brakeman in turn waves his green flag.

This is an excellent way of getting to Ooty and affords some spectacular views of the precipitous eastern slopes of the rainforest-covered Nilgiris. Views are best from the left on the way up and from the right on the way down.

The miniature railway starts at Mettupalayam, north of Coimbatore, and goes via Coonoor to Ooty. The departures and arrivals at Mettupalayam connect with the *Nilgiri Express*, which runs between Mettupalayam and Madras. If you're heading for Ooty, the *Nilgiri Express* departs Madras at 9.05 pm and arrives at Mettupalayam at 7.15 am. You can catch this train from Coimbatore at 6.20 am.

The miniature train leaves Mettupalayam for Ooty at 7.50 am and arrives in Ooty at 12.15 pm. On the downhill journey, there's a 2.50 pm departure from Ooty which arrives at Mettupalayam at 6.30 pm to connect with the *Nilgiri Express* which departs Mettupalayam at 7.15 pm. The 116-km journey takes about 4½ hours up to Ooty and about 3½ hours going down. During the high season, there is an extra departure in each direction daily, from Mettupalayam at 9.10 am and from Ooty at 2 pm. There are also trains which run only between Ooty and Coonoor, twice daily in either direction. The fares from Mettupalayam to Ooty are Rs 30/107 in 2nd/1st class.

Getting Around

There are plenty of auto-rickshaws in Ooty which have their base outside the bus stand but they have no meters and the drivers are rapacious. In the high season, they will quote you outrageous fares even between the bus stand and Charing Cross and especially if you have a rucksack on your back. Haggling might get you around 20% off the first price quoted but nothing more, so it's worth walking. In the low season, of course, they're virtually unemployed so you can almost

dictate the fare. Normal taxis are also available – at even higher rates.

Hiring a bicycle as soon as possible after arrival is the way to avoid this but many of the roads are steep so you'll end up pushing them uphill (great on the way down though!).

KOTAGIRI & COONOOR

Kotagiri and Coonoor are much smaller and quieter hill stations, especially the former, and are within easy reach of Ooty. From Kotagiri, the more pleasant of the two, about 28 km from Ooty, you can visit **Catherine Falls** (eight km away), **Elk Falls** (eight km) and **Kodanad View Point** (16 km), where there is a fine panoramic view over the plains and the eastern slopes of the Nilgiris.

Places to Stay & Eat

Kotagiri There are a few basic lodges in Kotagiri, such as the *Hotel Ram Vihar* where rooms start at Rs 40. The *Queenshill Christian Guest House* has beautifully furnished rooms for Rs 30 and serves excellent Western breakfasts.

Coonoor Perhaps the best place to stay here is the *YWCA* which is lost within greenery and is a handsome old house with views over Coonoor, two terraces, large, clean rooms, monkeys all around and an eccentric old hostess. Doubles cost Rs 140, there's hot water and good food available, plus, if your budget is tight, they also have dorm beds. The *Vivek Tourist Home* in the Bedford area is also worth checking out if the YWCA is full.

In Coonoor, the *Sri Lakshmi Tourist Home* (☎ 635) offers basic singles/doubles for Rs 40/75 (low season) and Rs 50/100 (high season). Better are the *Hampton Manor Hotel* (☎ 244), at Rs 125/225 (low season) and Rs 150/300 (high season) for singles/doubles, and the *Hotel Ritz* (☎ 242) on Orange Grove Rd where rooms cost Rs 175/200 (low season) and Rs 250/300 (high season).

One of the best restaurants in the area is

the *Blue Hill Restaurant* which will cost you around Rs 60 for a meal and drink.

COIMBATORE
Population: 1.1 million

Coimbatore is a large industrial city at the foot of the Nilgiri mountains, full of 'suitings and shirtings' shops. Its main interest for travellers is as a way station en route to Ootacamund (Ooty) and the other Nilgiri hill stations.

Orientation
The bus and railway stations are about two km apart, so you'll need an auto-rickshaw to get from one to the other. A number of mid-range and budget hotels are clustered around both the bus and railway stations.

Information
There's a tourist office at the railway station, but it's hard to think of a reason to visit it.

Places to Stay – bottom end
Bus Station Area The *Hotel Sree Shakti* (☎ 34-225) at 11/148 Sastri Rd is a large, modern hotel with friendly staff. Rooms are pleasantly decorated, reasonably clean, have a fan and bathroom and cost Rs 45/80/105 for singles/doubles/triples.

Also on Sastri Rd, the *Sri Ganapathy Lodge* (☎ 27-365) is behind the bus stand. It's much the same as the Sree Shakti and rooms cost Rs 45/80. Similar in price, the *Zakin Hotel*, Sastri Rd, is a few doors up from the Shakti and also close to the bus station.

One block further north, Nehru St is also lined with hotels. The *Hotel Blue Star* (☎ 37-117) offers good value at Rs 73/126 with bathroom. They also have more expensive air-con rooms.

Railway Station Area Opposite the railway station, the small Davey & Co Lane is a solid enclave of hotels. They are all fairly quiet as it's one block back from the main road. The *Hotel Sivakami* (☎ 26-669) is one of the best

in the area. It's well maintained and rooms are good value at Rs 45/80 with bathroom.

The *Hotel Anand Vihar* (☎ 26-584) is friendly and helpful and has rooms with bathroom for Rs 55/90. Up the range a bit, the *AP Lodge* (☎ 24-773) has large, well-furnished rooms with bathroom for Rs 65/105.

The noisy railway *retiring rooms* are relatively new and significantly more expensive than usual at Rs 50/100, or Rs 250 for an air-con double. The dormitory, in the older building on platform 1, has beds for Rs 20.

Places to Stay – middle
The *Hotel Tamil Nadu* (☎ 36-311) on Dr Nanjappa Rd is right opposite the state bus stand, and so is a convenient place to stay for the night if you're heading for Ooty. Rooms cost Rs 120/150 for singles/doubles and Rs 150/200 for air-con rooms, and there are deluxe doubles for Rs 250.

Next up in price is the *Hotel Alankar* (☎ 26-293), 10 Sivasamy Rd. This place is under-maintained and overpriced with singles/doubles from Rs 80/145 to Rs 175/225 and air-con singles/doubles from Rs 225/325 to Rs 250/350. There are also air-con cottages at Rs 395. The hotel has its own vegetarian restaurant and bar.

Opposite the Alankar is the *Hotel City Tower* (☎ 37-681), Coimbatore's best hotel, with a whole range of facilities including two restaurants (vegetarian and non-vegetarian) and an airport shuttle coach service. Compared with other similar hotels elsewhere, it's excellent value at Rs 210/280 for singles/doubles and Rs 320/370 in the air-con rooms. The staff are friendly and credit cards are accepted.

Places to Eat
In the railway station area, the small *Hotel Sunrise* restaurant serves reasonable non-vegetarian food and vegetarian meals on a banana leaf for Rs 5. The *Royal Hindu Restaurant* on the main road, just north of the station, is a huge place offering good vegetarian meals.

The *Hotel Top Form* on Nehru Rd serves

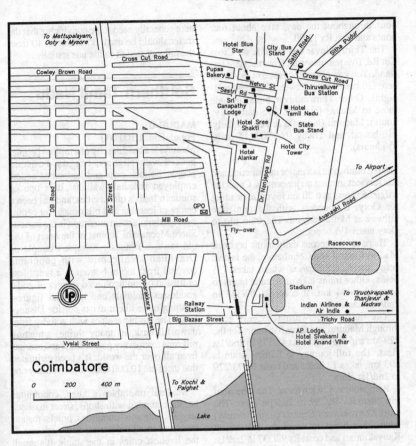

Coimbatore

0   200   400 m

interesting non-vegetarian food at reasonable prices.

For a splurge, eat at one of the two restaurants at the *Hotel City Towers*.

Getting There & Away
Air The Indian Airlines (☎ 22-743) and the Air India (☎ 23-933) offices are in Indian House on Trichy Rd.

There are Indian Airlines flights between Coimbatore and Bangalore (daily, US$28), Bombay (daily, US$94) and Madras (daily via Bangalore, US$53).

East West Airlines (☎ 21-7751) flies once daily to Bombay (US$94).

Bus The large and well-organised state bus station only has timetables in Tamil, except for buses to Bangalore and Mysore. There are four lines of bus bays. Buses to Bangalore (twice daily) and Mysore (three times daily) can be booked at the reservation office (on Bay 4, the furthest one from the main road) between 9 am and noon and 1 to 9.30 pm. The ordinary buses to Ooty leave from opposite the reservation office every half an hour throughout the day, take about four hours and cost Rs 12.90.

The Thiruvalluvar bus stand is on Cross Cut Rd, five minutes walk from the state bus stand. You can also get buses to Ooty from here (20 buses daily between 4 am and midnight). Other Thiruvalluvar buses include those to Madras (No 460, five daily, 11½ hours), Madurai (Nos 600 & 626, 19 daily, 5½ hours), and Trichy (No 700, 15 daily, 5¼ hours).

Train Coimbatore is a major rail junction and has services to most major centres. Catch the *Nilgiri Express* at 6.20 am if you're heading for Ooty; it connects with the miniature railway at Mettupalayam. The train trip to Ooty takes 4½ hours.

There are numerous daily trains between Madras Central and Coimbatore, the fastest being the *Kovai Express* which takes 7½ hours. Other trains take up to nine hours to cover the 494 km. It costs Rs 87/327 in 2nd/1st class.

The daily *Rameswaram Express* goes through Madurai and takes 5½ hours for the 229-km trip at a cost of Rs 48/175 in 2nd/1st class. The full journey to Rameswaram is 393 km, takes 12 hours and costs Rs 73/279 in 2nd/1st class.

Bangalore is 424 km away. The nine-hour trip costs Rs 80/289 in 2nd/1st class. The daily *Kanyakumari Express* (from Bombay) takes 13½ hours to travel the 510 km to Kanyakumari and costs Rs 92/337 in 2nd/1st class.

To the Kerala coast, the daily *West Coast Express* from Madras Central goes to Kozhikode (Calicut) (185 km, 4½ hours) and on to Bangalore (504 km, nine hours).

Getting Around

Bus Useful buses around Coimbatore include No 20 from the railway station to the airport, and No 12 from the railway station to the bus stations. There is also a shuttle bus from the Hotel City Tower in Coimbatore to the airport at noon and 4.05 pm daily.

Auto-Rickshaw The auto-rickshaw drivers here generally need some convincing that the meter should be used. It's about Rs 10 from the railway station to the bus stations.

Southern Tamil Nadu

MADURAI
Population: 1,100,000

Madurai is a bustling city of a million people, packed with pilgrims, beggars, businesspeople, bullock carts and legions of underemployed rickshaw-wallahs. It is one of southern India's oldest cities, and has been a centre of learning and pilgrimage for centuries. Madurai's main attraction is the famous Shree Meenakshi Temple in the heart of the old town, a riotously baroque example of Dravidian architecture with gopurams covered from top to bottom in a breathless profusion of multicoloured images of gods, goddesses, animals and mythical figures. Nothing quite like it exists outside Disneyland! The temple seethes with activity from dawn till dusk, its many shrines attracting pilgrims from every part of India and tourists from all over the world. It's been estimated that there are 10,000 visitors here on any one day!

Madurai resembles a huge, continuous bazaar crammed with shops, street markets, temples, pilgrims' choultries, hotels, restaurants and small industries. Although one of the liveliest cities in the south, it's small enough not to be overwhelming and is very popular with travellers. You'll love it!

History

Madurai's history can be divided into roughly four periods, beginning over 2000 years ago when it was the capital of the Pandyan kings. Then, in the 4th century BC, the city was known to the Greeks via Megasthenes, their ambassador to the court of Chandragupta Maurya. In the 10th century AD, Madurai was taken by the Chola emperors. It remained in their hands until the Pandyas briefly regained their independence in the 12th century, only to lose it again in the 14th century to Muslim invaders under Malik Kafur, a general in the service of the Delhi Sultanate. Here, Malik Kafur established his own dynasty which, in turn, was overthrown by the Hindu Vijayanagar kings of Hampi. After the fall of Vijayanagar in 1565, the Nayaks ruled Madurai until 1781 AD. During the reign of Tirumalai Nayak (1623-55), the bulk of the Meenakshi Temple was built, and Madurai became the cultural centre of the Tamil people, playing an important role in the development of the Tamil language.

Madurai then passed into the hands of the British East India Company, which took over the revenues of the area after the wars of the Carnatic in 1781. In 1840, the company razed the fort, which had previously surrounded the city, and filled in the moat. Four broad streets – the Veli streets – were constructed on top of this fill and define the limits of the old city to this day.

Orientation

The old town of Madurai, on the south bank of the Vaigai River, is bounded by the Veli streets (South Veli St, East Veli St, etc). In this rectangular area, you will find most of the main points of interest, transport services, mid-range and budget hotels, restaurants, the tourist office and the GPO.

Most hotels and restaurants used by travellers are west of the Meenakshi Temple between North and South Masi Sts, particularly along Town Hall Rd and West Masi St. Two of the three bus stations, the railway station and the GPO are on West Veli St. So is the tourist office, which is close to the Hotel Tamil Nadu, near the junction with South Veli St.

On the north bank of the Vaigai River in the cantonment area are top-end hotels, the Gandhi Museum and one bus station. The Mariamman Teppakkulam tank and temple stand on the south bank of the Vaigai, several km east of the old city.

Information

Tourist Offices The tourist office (☎ 22-957) at 180 West Veli St is close to the Hotel Tamil Nadu. The staff are friendly and helpful, and provide some information about the city as well as free maps of Madurai. The office is open Monday to Saturday from 10 am to 5.30 pm, and on Sunday between 10 am and 1 pm. There are also branch offices at Madurai railway station and the airport.

Post & Telecommunications The GPO is at the northern end of West Veli St, while the Central Telegraph Office is across the river in the north of town – you can see the telecommunications mast from some distance away.

Shree Meenakshi Temple

Every day, the Meenakshi Temple attracts pilgrims in their thousands from all over India. Its enormous gopurams, covered with gaily coloured statues, dominate the landscape and are visible from many of the rooftops in Madurai. The temple is named after the daughter of a Pandyan king who, according to legend, was born with three breasts. At the time of her birth, the king was told that the extra breast would disappear when she met the man she was to marry, and this duly happened when she met Lord Siva on Mt Kailas. Siva told her to return to Madurai and, eight days later, arrived there himself in the form of Lord Sundareshwara to marry her.

Designed in 1560 by Vishwanatha Nayak, the present temple was substantially built during the reign of Tirumalai Nayak (1623-55 AD), but its history goes back 2000 years to the time when Madurai was the capital of the Pandya kings. There are four entrances to the temple, which occupies six hectares. It has 12 towers, ranging in height from 45 to 50 metres, and four outer-rim nine-storey towers, the tallest of which is the 50-metre-high southern tower. The hall of 1000 columns actually has 985.

Depending on the time of day, you can bargain for bangles, spices or saris in the bazaar between the outer and inner eastern walls of the temple, watch pilgrims bathing in the tanks, listen to temple music in front of the Meenakshi Amman Shrine (the music

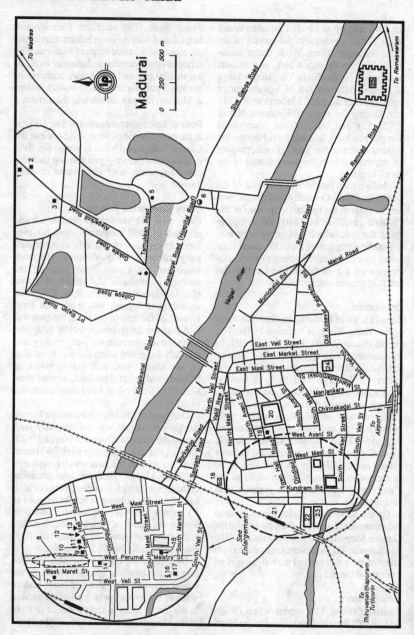

Madurai

0   250   500 m

To Madras

To Rameswaram

To Thiruvananthapuram & Tuticorin

To Airport

Sive Ganga Road

New Ramnad Road

Ramnad Road

Manal Road

Vaigai River

Alagarkoil Road

Tamukkan Road

Rangavel (Hospital Road)

Gokale Road

Minochi Road

College Road

Kodaikanal Road

Workshop Road

Sangam Road

Dindigul Road

Town Hall Road

North Avani St

North Masi Street

Yakil New St

West Veli Street

Municbali Rd

Old Kosavery Rd

Old Pandiga Rd

East Veli Street

East Market Street

East Masi Street

East Veli St

Manjiyadapokkil St

Manjankara

Chinnakadai St

South Nedevan St

South Masi St

South Market Street

South Veli St

West Avani St

West Masi St

Kundram Rd

See Enlargement

West Masi Street

West Perumal St

West Maret St

West Veli St

Town Hall Road

Dindigul Road

South Masi Street

South Market St

South Veli St

Malstry St

West Masi Street

7 8 9 10 11 12 13 14 15 16 17 18 19 20 21 22 23 24 25 1 2 3 4 5 6

is relayed through the whole complex on a PA system), or wander through the interesting though decidedly dilapidated museum.

The **museum**, called the Temple Art Gallery, is worth a visit. It contains some beautiful stone and brass images, examples of ancient south Indian scripts, friezes and various attempts to explain the Hindu pantheon and the many legends associated with it, as well as one of the best exhibits on Hindu deities anywhere. Unfortunately, many of the labels are missing. Entrance to the Art Gallery costs Rs 1, plus (officially) Rs 5 for a camera if you intend to use it.

On most evenings between 6 and 7.30 pm and 9 and 10 pm, temple music is played outside the Meenakshi Amman Shrine –

mantras, fiddle, squeeze box, tabla and bells. Among those who play are some excellent musicians.

The temple is usually open between 5 am and 12.30 pm and again between 4 and 10 pm. Photography inside is only allowed between 12.30 and 4 pm on payment of Rs 10. This is actually a good time to go in even if you don't want to take photographs, because it gives you a chance to wander around without the crowds, though it will cost you Rs 10. Leave your shoes at any of the four entrances, where 'Footwear Safe Custody' stalls will look after them for a small fee.

Many of the priests inside are very friendly and will take the trouble to show you around and explain what's happening. Licensed guides charge Rs 10 for an hour.

At 9.30 each evening, there's a closing ceremony in which an image of Siva is carried in procession to Parvati's bedroom. (It's taken back at about 6 o'clock the next morning.) The ceremony starts inside the temple, at the Sri Sudareswara Shrine near the east gopuram.

Tirumalai Nayak Palace
About a km from the Meenakshi Temple (Rs 2 by rickshaw), this Indo-Saracenic palace was built in 1636 by the ruler whose name it bears. Much of it has fallen into ruin, and the pleasure gardens and surrounding defensive wall have disappeared. Today, only the entrance gate, main hall and dance hall remain. The palace was partially restored by Lord Napier, the governor of Madras, in 1866-72, and further restoration work is currently in progress. It is open daily from 9 am to 1 pm and 2 to 5 pm. Entry costs Rs 1 and there's no photography charge. The entrance is on the far (eastern) side.

You can get there on a No 11, 11A or 17 bus from the Central bus stand, or take the 20-minute walk from the Meenakshi Temple through an interesting bazaar area. There is a Son et Lumiére in English, daily at 6.30 pm, telling the history of the city with sound and coloured lights on the temple carvings. The sophistication of both the soundtrack and the lighting is surprising. It's excellent entertainment. Tickets cost Rs 1 to Rs 3 and you should bring mosquito repellent.

Gandhi Museum

Housed in the old palace of the Rani Mangammal, this oddly moving museum provides some little-known facts about the Mahatma, although the only real piece of Gandhi memorabilia is the blood-stained dhoti from the assassination, displayed behind a bulletproof screen. Unfortunately, all the captions are in Tamil or Hindi.

The museum also has an excellent walk-through History of India display with some fine old photographs. The local government museum is in the same grounds, but you needn't waste your time.

To get there, take a No 1 or 2 bus from the State bus stand to the Central Telegraph Office (look for the telecommunications mast). From there, it's a walk of about 500 metres along a shady street.

Mariamman Teppakkulam Tank

This tank, several km east of the old city, covers an area almost equal to that of the Meenakshi Temple. It is the site of the Teppam Festival (Float Festival) in January and February, which attracts thousands of pilgrims from all over India. At other times of year, the empty tank is put to good use by the local kids for cricket games, but it's not really worth a visit then. The Mariamman Teppakkulam Tank was built by Tirumalai Nayak in 1646 and is connected to the Vaigai River by underground channels.

The No 4 bus from the State bus stand terminates at the tank.

Festivals

Teppam (Float) Festival This very popular festival attracts pilgrims from all over India. Images of Shree Meenakshi and Lord Sundareshwara (Siva) are mounted on floats and taken to the Mariamman Teppakkulam Tank where, for several days, they are pulled back and forth across the water to the island temple in the tank's centre, before being taken back to Madurai. The annual festival occurs in January or early February.

Chithirai Festival Held in late April-early May, the Chithirai Festival celebrates the marriage of Shree Meenakshi to Lord Sundareshwara.

Avanimoola Festival In late August-early September, temple cars are drawn round the streets of Madurai.

Places to Stay – bottom end

In a pilgrim city of Madurai's size and importance, lots of cheap hotels and lodges offer basic accommodation. Many are just flophouses which bear the scars of previous occupants' bad habits – OK for a night, but not for much longer. On the other hand, there are a few which are clean and very good value. These are mostly found along Town Hall Rd and Dindigul Rd.

The *New College House* (☎ 24-311) at 2 Town Hall Rd is a huge place where you'll almost certainly get accommodation at any hour of the day or night. The rooms are clean enough and cost Rs 48/88/99 for ordinary singles/doubles/triples plus there are more expensive deluxe and air-con rooms if you prefer.

Close by is the *Hotel Senthosh* (☎ 26-692), 7 Town Hall Rd, which has basic singles/doubles with attached bathroom for Rs 35/49 and deluxe doubles for Rs 66 including taxes. Next up is the *Krishna Lodge* but this only has singles with attached bathroom for Rs 30. It's essentially a choultry for pilgrims.

Also very good value on this street is the new *Hotel Times* (☎ 36-351), 15/16 Town Hall Rd, which has ordinary singles/doubles at Rs 60/90 plus air-con doubles at Rs 160 and air-con deluxe doubles with TV at Rs 230. Diagonally opposite here down a side street is the *Hotel Ramson* which looks expensive but isn't at Rs 35/45 for singles/doubles with attached bathroom.

If you want temple views, you can't beat the friendly *Hotel Devi* (☎ 36-388) at 20 West Avani St. It's about 15 minutes walk from the bus or train station, but only a minute or two from the temple. The view of the temple from the roof is the best you'll get in the whole city. Try to rouse yourself out of bed for the sunrise. The rooms are good too, and those on the upper two floors have more light. They cost Rs 75 for a double with bathroom and are reasonably clean.

The other good hunting ground for both budget and mid-range hotels is West Perumal Maistry St. One of the cheapest is the *Ruby Lodge* (☎ 32-059) at 92 West Perumal Maistry St which has small singles with common bathroom for Rs 20 and singles/doubles with attached bathrooms for Rs 25/40. The hotel has its own pleasant outdoor restaurant.

Further up this same road going north is another cluster of hotels which, from their outside appearance, would seem to be mid-range yet prices don't reflect this. The *TM Lodge* (☎ 37-481) at No 50 has singles/doubles with attached bathrooms at Rs 49/99 and air-con doubles with TV at Rs 149.50, all including taxes. Close by is the *Hotel Grand Central* (☎ 36-311) at No 47/48. Ordinary singles/doubles cost Rs 49/85, and there are air-con doubles for Rs 160. Almost next door is the *Hotel International* (☎ 31-552) at No 46. This modern hotel has self-contained singles/doubles at Rs 45/75 and deluxe doubles at Rs 90. Further up is the *Hotel Gangai* (☎ 36-211), opposite the Prem Nivas, which has singles/doubles at Rs 39/60.

At the railway station, the *retiring rooms* are noisy and cost Rs 25/40; dorm beds are Rs 10.

Places to Stay – middle

Very popular in this range is the relatively new *Hotel Aarathy* (☎ 31-571), 9 Perumal Kovil West Mada St, just a few minutes walk from the bus station. All rooms have bathrooms with hot water and cost Rs 75/98 for ordinary singles/doubles plus there are more expensive air-con rooms. It's comfortable and secure, towel, soap and toilet paper are provided and most of the rooms have a small balcony. There's a pleasant open-air restau-

rant (vegetarian) in the courtyard and, if you get up early enough, you can make friends with the temple elephant which is led through here each morning!

Diagonally opposite the bus station is the TTDC *Hotel Tamil Nadu* (☎ 37-470), West Veli St, with singles/doubles at Rs 75/130 or Rs 130/200 with air-con. It's fairly well run plus there's a restaurant and one of the few bars in town. There's another branch of this hotel chain (☎ 42-465) across the river opposite the Pandyan and Madurai Ashok hotels on Alagarkoil Rd, though it's somewhat more expensive. Ordinary singles/doubles here cost Rs 150/175 or Rs 180/225 with air-con. The bathrooms have hot and cold running water plus the hotel has its own bar and restaurant.

Back in town, two good choices in this range are the *Hotel Prem Nivas* (☎ 37-531), 102 West Perumal Maistry St, and, on the same street, the *Hotel Keerthi* (☎ 31-501) at No 40. Singles/doubles at the Prem Nivas are Rs 82/131 and there are air-con doubles at Rs 190. Facilities are excellent and the hotel has its own air-con vegetarian restaurant. The Keerthi has singles/doubles for Rs 75/99 and air-con doubles with TV at Rs 175 to Rs 240. There's a restaurant and Visa cards are accepted.

Also in the centre of town is the *Hotel Supreme* (☎ 36-331), 110 West Perumal Maistry St, which has doubles at Rs 180 plus a range of air-con doubles at Rs 285, Rs 335 and Rs 385 as well as a number of more expensive suites. The facilities are excellent and there's a rooftop restaurant.

Places to Stay – top end

Madurai's two best hotels are well out of the town centre across the Vaigai River, along Alagarkoil Rd. An auto-rickshaw should cost no more than Rs 20, although the price will at least double when they hear where you want to go! City buses No 2, 16 or 20 (among others) will get you there for about Rs 1.

The *Hotel Madurai Ashok* (☎ 42-531) and the *Pandyan Hotel* (☎ 42-470) are both centrally air-conditioned and the facilities are superb though only the Ashok has a swimming pool. The Pandyan costs Rs 395/700 plus 35% luxury and sales taxes. There's a bar and restaurant serving Indian, Chinese and Continental food. The Ashok costs US$20/38 for singles/doubles and there's a bar and restaurant similar to those at the Pandyan. Both hotels have a shopping arcade (including a good bookshop) and accept all major credit cards.

Places to Eat

There are many typical south Indian vegetarian restaurants around the Meenakshi Temple and along Town Hall Rd, Dindigul Rd and West Masi St. The dining hall in *New College House* is very popular and the thalis are good value.

The non-vegetarian *Taj Restaurant* on Town Hall Rd is not bad for breakfast. Just a few doors further along, the air-con *Mahal Restaurant* is very popular with travellers. It's a little more expensive but the food is very tasty and the staff friendly. It serves both vegetarian and non-vegetarian dishes.

The non-vegetarian *Subham Restaurant*, next to the Ruby Lodge on West Perumal Maistry St, is also good and much cheaper. It's an outdoor place which is only open in the evenings. The *Indo-Ceylon Restaurant* at 6 Town Hall Rd serves good non-vegetarian meals.

Also on Town Hall Rd is the *Amutham Restaurant*, near the corner of West Masi St. Again, the food is non-vegetarian. The stuffed parottas (their spelling) are excellent – try chicken & egg.

For a splurge, you need to go to one or other of the mid-range hotels on West Perumal Maistry St. The *Surya* restaurant, on the roof of the Hotel Supreme, serves Indian, Chinese and Continental vegetarian food. All credit cards are accepted.

Getting There & Away

Air The Indian Airlines office (☎ 26-795) is at the northern end of West Veli St. There are daily flights to Tiruchirappalli (US$16), Madras (US$46) and Bangalore (US$39).

Bus There are three bus stands in Madurai. Two are next to each other on West Veli St and the third is across the river, north of the centre. The State bus stand is for local city and short-distance buses. The Thiruvalluvar bus stand is for long-distance buses, such as those going to Madras or Kanyakumari. Across the river is the Anna bus stand. Buses leave here for Thanjavur, Trichy and Rameswaram. If your bus terminates at the Anna bus stand, bus No 3 will take you to the State bus stand, or you can catch an auto-rickshaw for Rs 10.

There are also two 'relief' bus stands; one for a combination of state buses and Thiruvalluvar buses across the road from the main stands, and another on West Perumal Maistry St near the junction of West Veli St for state buses. The latter is just a patch of dirt.

Seats on the Thiruvalluvar buses can be reserved in advance either at the main stand or at the relief stand and there's a timetable in English (see table below).

Buses to Madras (route No 137) leave every quarter to half an hour round the clock.

Thiruvalluvar Bus Routes from Madurai

Destination	Route No	Frequency	km	Hours	Fare
Bangalore	846	14 daily	550	15	Rs 62
Coimbatore	600	2 daily	350	10	Rs 29.50
Ernakulam	826	2 daily	324	10	Rs 56.50
Kanyakumari	101	3 daily	253	6	Rs 34
Pondicherry	847	2 daily	329	8	Rs 44.50
Thiruvananthapuram	820	6 daily	305	7	Rs 42
Tirupathi	–	5 daily	595	16	Rs 72.50

The 447-km journey takes 10 hours and costs Rs 67.50 on a superdeluxe bus, of which there are 13 daily.

Plenty of other Thiruvalluvar buses pass through, serving these and other destinations. As these can't be reserved in advance you take pot luck, but it's not usually a problem to get a seat. Thiruvalluvar does not run buses to Kodaikanal.

The main bus you are likely to catch from the State bus stand (or the relief stand) is the bus to Kodaikanal, operated by RMTC and PRC, the regional bus companies. There are eight departures daily and the four-hour trip costs Rs 16. During heavy monsoon rain, the road sometimes gets washed away and the buses have to go via Palani, adding an hour or two to the journey.

In addition to the state and Thiruvalluvar buses there are several private bus companies which offer more expensive superdeluxe video buses to such places as Madras and Bangalore. Tickets for these are sold by agencies which operate in the vicinity of the state bus stand. Beware of buying a ticket for any destination other than the above major cities, however. All of them will sell you a ticket to virtually anywhere (such as Kodaikanal or Rameswaram) but you'll find yourself dumped on a state bus and they'll have sold you a ticket for it at double the price you could have paid yourself, despite promises that the bus would be a superdeluxe. It's a blatant rip-off but a well established scam in Madurai.

Train The railway station is right on West Veli St, only a few minutes walk from the main hotel area.

The 492-km journey from Madras to Madurai takes eight hours via Trichy, longer via Chidambaram and Thanjavur. Fares are Rs 87/327 in 2nd/1st class. The all-2nd-class *Vagai Express* is particularly fast and comparatively luxurious.

It takes six hours to cover the 164 km to Rameswaram on the daily passenger train at 5.20 am but there's only 2nd class available. The fare is Rs 22.

If you're heading for Kerala, the best train to take is the morning *Madras-Quilon Mail*, as the line crosses the Western Ghats through some spectacular mountain terrain, and there are some superb gopurams to be seen at Srivilliputur (between Sivaksi and Rajapalaiyam) and Sankarankovil. This trip takes eight hours and the 268-km journey costs Rs 54/199 in 2nd/1st class. The train gets into Kollam (Quilon) in plenty of time for you to make it to Thiruvananthapuram (Trivandrum) or Kovalam Beach later in the afternoon.

Getting Around

To/From the Airport The airport is six km from the city centre and you need to take an auto-rickshaw or taxi but you'll have to haggle like crazy to get it for a reasonable price. Expect to pay around Rs 50.

Bus Some useful local buses include No 3 to the Anna bus stand, Nos 1 and 2 to the Hotel Tamil Nadu and the Gandhi Museum, No 4 to Mariammam Teppakkulam Tank, No 5 to the Tiruparankundram rock-cut temple (eight km outside Madurai) and No 44 to the Alagarkoil Vaishnavaite shrine (21 km from Madurai). All these buses depart from the State bus stand.

Auto-Rickshaw Drivers are extremely reluctant to use the meters and will quote whatever they think you will pay. If you can't agree, they won't go. This is particularly true if you want to go across the river to any of the expensive hotels there. The usual price first quoted for this journey is Rs 50! Obviously, if you're staying there, you must be rich so what's Rs 50?

KODAIKANAL

Population: 27,000

Of the three main hill stations of the south – Udhagamandalam (Ootacamund), Kodaikanal and Yercaud – Kodaikanal is undoubtedly the most beautiful and, unlike Ooty, the temperature here rarely drops to the point where you need to wear heavy clothing, even in winter. Kodaikanal is on the southern crest of the Palani Hills, about 120 km north-west of Madurai, surrounded by thickly wooded slopes, waterfalls and precipitous rocky outcrops. Some of the views to the south are spectacular, and the viewpoints are within easy walking distance of the centre of town – unlike Ooty, where you have to walk at least several km to find them or go on a tour bus.

Kodaikanal is not just for those who want to get away from the heat of the plains during the summer months, but also for those seeking a relaxing place to put their feet up for a while and do some occasional hiking. Like Ooty, Kodaikanal has its own landscaped, artificial lake with boating facilities but, unlike Ooty, it's not overrun with tourists intent on squeezing every bit of value out of the price they paid for their hard-earned break.

All in all, Kodaikanal is by far the best and most beautiful of Tamil Nadu's hill stations but, like Ooty, once you've rowed around the lake, admired the views and put in a few days hiking, there isn't a great deal more to do, especially if you're travelling alone.

Apart from one or two restaurants down Hospital Rd, there's really nowhere for people to gather in the evenings, so it's back to your hotel and early to bed. It's primarily a place to relax and get away from the heat of the plains. The journey up there and back down again is also spectacular, though there's no toy train and access is by bus or car.

Orientation

For a hill station, Kodai is remarkably compact. The main street is Bazaar Rd (Anna Salai), and the real bottom-end hotels (except the Greenlands Youth Hostel), the restaurants and the bus station are all in this area.

Most, though not all, of the better hotels are some distance from the bazaar, but usually not more than about 15 minutes walk.

Information

There is a tourist office close to the bus stand but they have little information except a poor

map of the town. The office is open from 10 am to 5 pm Monday to Friday. If you want literature about Kodai, try the CLS bookshop more or less opposite.

April to June or August to October are the best times to visit Kodaikanal. April to June is the main season, whereas the peak of the wet season is November-December. At an altitude of 2133 metres, temperatures here are mild, ranging between 11°C and 20°C in summer and 8°C and 17°C in winter.

There's a railway booking office in the side street off Bazaar Rd where you can book seats on most of the express trains which stop at Kodaikanal Road. It's open from 9.30 am to 12.30 pm and 2.30 to 4.30 pm, Monday to Saturday.

Kodai Walks

The main activity in Kodai is walking around enjoying the sights and views. The rolling lawns of the numerous stone and wood cottages from the British period are edged with flowering shrubs and trees.

The views from Coaker's Walk (entry Rs 0.50), where an observatory with telescope is available, and from Pillar Rocks, a seven-km hike, are two of the most spectacular in India. Bryant Park is also worth a visit, especially if you have an interest in botany. The park was laid out, landscaped and stocked over many years by the British colonial administrator after whom it is named.

Flora & Fauna Museum

Also worth a visit is the Flora & Fauna Museum at the Sacred Heart College at nearby Shembaganur. It's a six-km hike and all uphill on the way back. The museum is open from 10 to 11.30 am and 3.30 to 5 pm, and is closed on Sundays. There are numerous waterfalls in the area – you'll pass the main one, Silver Cascade, on the road up to Kodai.

Astrophysical Laboratory

The Astrophysical Laboratory is built on the highest point in the area, three km uphill from the lake. It houses a small **museum** which is only open from 10 am to noon on

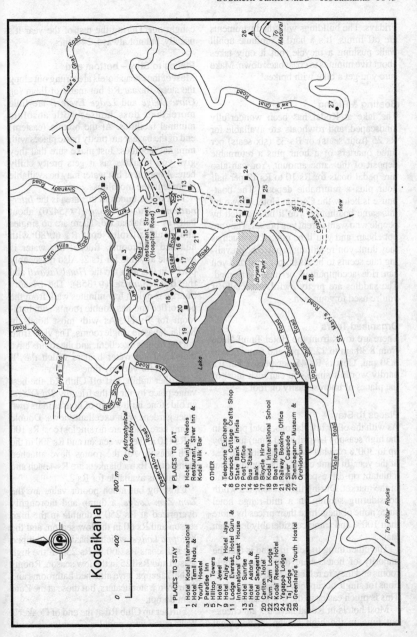

Kodaikanal

0   400   800 m

PLACES TO STAY

1 Hotel Kodai International
2 Hotel Tamil Nadu & Youth Hostel
3 Paradise Inn
5 Hilltop Towers
7 Hotel Jewel
9 Hotel Anjay & Hotel Jaya
11 Lodge Everest, Hotel Guru & International Guest House
13 Hotel Sunrise
15 Hotel Astoria & Hotel Sangeeth
20 Carlton Hotel
22 Zum Zum Lodge
23 Kodai Resort Hotel
24 Yagappa Lodge
25 Taj Lodge
28 Greenland's Youth Hostel

▼ PLACES TO EAT

6 Hotel Punjab, Nedos Restaurant, Silver Inn & Kodai Milk Bar

OTHER

4 Telephone Exchange
8 Cottage Crafts Shop
10 State Bank of India
12 Post Office
14 Bus Stand
16 Bank
17 Bicycle Hire
18 Kodai International School
19 Boat House
21 Railway Booking Office
26 Silver Cascade
27 Shembaganur Museum & Orchidorium

Fridays. The buildings with the instruments are off limits. It's a hard 45-minute uphill walk pushing a bicycle, but it only takes about five minutes to coast back down. Make sure you get a bike with brakes!

Boating & Riding

The lake at Kodai has been wonderfully landscaped, and rowboats are available for Rs 25 (four seats) or Rs 35 (six seats) per three quarters of a hour plus a returnable deposit of the same amount. You can also hire pedal boats for Rs 10 to Rs 12 per half hour plus a returnable deposit. The boathouse is below the Carlton Hotel. Down by this same boathouse, you'll be accosted by people who want to rent you horses. They are not cheap, and you'll be quoted as much as they think you're willing to pay. The prevailing rate seems to be Rs 35 per hour and you can ride accompanied or unaccompanied. The saddles are pretty awful, especially if you're used to your own.

Organised Tours

There are tours from the Hotel Tamil Nadu from 8.30 am to 12.30 pm and from 2.50 to 6.30 pm. Cost is Rs 45 per person but it's hardly worth it since you can visit most of the places of interest easily on foot.

Places to Stay

As with the other hill stations, hotel prices in the high season (1 April to 30 June) jump up to 300% of what they are during the rest of the year. In some cases, this is nothing but a blatant rip-off, especially at the lower end of the market. During this season, it's worth considering staying in a mid-range hotel since none of them hike their prices by more than 100% and some considerably less than that.

The other thing to bear in mind is that the majority of hotels here don't have single rooms and they're reluctant to discuss reductions for single occupancy in the high season. This is much easier in the low season.

Most hotels in Kodai have a 9 am checkout time in the high season so don't get caught out. During the rest of the year it's usually, but not always, 24 hours.

Places to Stay – bottom end

Most of the cheap hotels are strung out along the steep Bazaar Rd but many of them (eg *Guru Lodge* and *Lodge Everest)* are little more than doss houses with absolute minimal facilities. At the bottom (eastern) end of the bazaar are pretty basic places with minimal facilities. Just make sure that they give you blankets, as it gets pretty chilly here. A bucket of hot water may be available at some in the mornings.

Pick of the bunch in this area is the *International Guest House* (☎ 5420) about halfway up Bazaar Rd. There are no singles and doubles/triples cost Rs 60/80 with attached bathrooms. Bucket hot water is available anytime for Rs 2. Also reasonably priced in this area are the *Hotel Jayaraj* and the *Hotel Sunrise* (☎ 358). The friendly Sunrise is only a few minutes walk from the post office and has double rooms with bathroom for Rs 80. As with most hotels in Kodai, it has no single rooms. The view from out the front is excellent, and the rooms have individual hot water heaters which they'll switch on for you any time.

Further uphill, just off Club Rd, the best value place by far is the friendly *Taj Lodge*, an old stone-built group of houses in its own quiet gardens with excellent views. Double rooms here (there are no singles) cost Rs 100 to Rs 150 in the low season and Rs 300 in the high season. All the rooms have attached bathrooms. Extra blankets are Rs 4 each and hot water is available for Rs 2.

Close by but much poorer value are the *Zum Zum Lodge*, a dump and thoroughly overpriced at Rs 250 a double in the high season and Rs 60 in the low season, and the *Yagappa Lodge*, which is basic and cramped but still costs Rs 200 to Rs 250 in the high season and Rs 125 in the low season. Rooms at the Yagappa have attached bathrooms and their own water heaters, but those at the Zum Zum do not.

Further up Club Rd at the end of Coaker's Walk is the very popular *Greenlands Youth*

Hostel. This place has perhaps the best views of any hotel in town and it's where you'll find most of the budget travellers. A bed in the dorm costs Rs 25 plus there are a number of more expensive double rooms with attached bathrooms. There's also a *Youth Hostel* at the Hotel Tamil Nadu, but it's a long walk from the bus station and the centre of town. Beds cost Rs 25 in the off season and Rs 35 in season.

Places to Stay – middle

At the bottom end of this category, the *Hotel Anjay* (☎ 489), Bazaar Rd, isn't a bad choice though it's often full. Double rooms with attached bathrooms and hot and cold running water cost Rs 160 to Rs 190 in the high season and Rs 120 to Rs 150 in the low season. At the back of this hotel is the *Holiday Home* which has a strange atmosphere and isn't such good value at Rs 140/180 for ordinary and deluxe doubles.

Nearby, opposite the bus station, is the *Hotel Sangeeth* (☎ 608) which is good value at Rs 180 a double in the high season or Rs 100 in the low season. All the rooms have attached bathrooms with hot and cold running water.

One of the best places in this range is the *Kodai Resort Hotel* (☎ 605) near the start of Coaker's Walk. It's fairly new and caters mainly to tour groups, but the 50 cottages, each with a lounge room, bedroom, open deck and bathroom with constant hot water, are well designed and comfortable. Rates per cottage are Rs 390 in the high season, Rs 250 in the winter season (15 October to 14 January) and Rs 180 for the rest of the year. The resort has its own restaurant serving Indian, Chinese and Continental food and there's even a supervised children's playground.

At the top of Hospital Rd, opposite the Kodai International School, is the *Hotel Jewel* (☎ 629) which is excellent value at Rs 400/450 for ordinary/deluxe doubles in the high season and Rs 195/220 in the low season. All the rooms are well furnished with wall-to-wall carpeting and colour TV. Similar, but more expensive, is the *Paradise Inn* (☎ 774) at the bottom of Hospital Rd on Law's Ghat Rd. Well-appointed rooms here cost Rs 500/600 for semideluxe/deluxe doubles in the high season and Rs 250/350 in the low season.

Closer to the centre and right opposite the bus station is the *Hotel Astoria* (☎ 792) which has ordinary/deluxe doubles at Rs 325/350 in the high season and Rs 200/225 in the low season. The hotel has its own restaurant serving both north and south Indian dishes.

The older *Hotel Tamil Nadu* (☎ 481) on Fern Hill Rd is another option but it's a long walk from the centre and maintenance isn't what it should be. It has a restaurant and one of the very few bars in Kodaikanal.

Places to Stay – top end

The best place to stay at the lower end of this range is the brand new *Hilltop Towers* on Club Rd opposite the Kodai International School. The staff are keen and friendly and double rooms/suites cost Rs 400/550 in the high season or Rs 250/375 in the low season.

Judging from the way in which the *Hotel Kodai International* (☎ 767) is advertised all the way up the road from the plains, you'd think it was the best hotel in Kodai. It isn't. It's also the most inconvenient place of the lot to stay at. Basically a Novotel clone, the rooms are certainly comfortable with all the amenities you'd expect, but the staff are untogether and the food in the restaurant is decidedly average. Double rooms/suites cost Rs 495/595 in the high season or Rs 375/450 in the low season. There are also more expensive suites and cottages. The much touted bar may also be inexplicably closed.

Kodaikanal's most prestigious hotel is the *Carlton Hotel* (☎ 252), Lake Rd, which overlooks the lake. This hotel used to be a colonial-style wooden structure but was completely rebuilt recently and is simply magnificent. Singles/doubles with full board cost Rs 1125/1350 in the high season and Rs 875/1100 in the low season. There are also more expensive suites and cottages. Credit cards are accepted and the hotel has its own bar and restaurant.

Places to Eat

Hospital Rd is the best place for restaurants and it's here that most of the travellers and also students from the Kodai International School congregate. There's a whole range of different cuisines available in the restaurants here, ranging from Western fast food to tandoori, Mughlai, Chinese and Tibetan. At the top of the road is *JJ's Restaurant* and the *Tava Restaurant*, below the Hotel Jewel. The former offers Continental and Chinese fast food and is good for breakfast and snacks. The Tava offers vegetarian Indian food.

Going down the road further there are, in order of appearance, the *Hotel Punjab* (tandoori specialities), the *Apna Punjab* (vegetarian and tandoori specialities), the *Silver Inn Restaurant* (Continental food and very popular), the well-known and popular *Kodai Milk Bar*, the *Chefmaster* (Continental, Chinese and Keralan) and lastly *Lobsang's Restaurant* (Mughlai, Chinese and Continental). Which one you choose on any particular day is largely a question of personal choice and who you find yourself with. They're all pretty good.

If you're just looking for a cheap Indian vegetarian meal, the restaurant at the *Hotel Astoria* is a good bet.

For a splurge, go to one of the better mid-range hotels or, best of all, to the *Carlton Hotel*. Here, they put on an evening buffet from 7.30 to 10.30 pm which is excellent value for Rs 120. You can relax in the bar after eating – one of only two in Kodaikanal – though drinks are a little on the expensive side compared with elsewhere.

Things to Buy

The Cottage Crafts shop on Bazaar Rd opposite the post office has some excellent bits and pieces for sale. It is run by Corsock, the Co-ordinating Council for Social Concerns in Kodai. This organisation, staffed by volunteers, sells crafts on behalf of development groups, using the commission charged to help the needy.

Corsock also runs the Goodwill Centre on Hospital Rd. It sells clothing and rents books, with the proceeds again going to needy causes.

Above the junction of Bazaar Rd and Hospital Rd on a patch of lawn you'll find a number of stalls run by Tibetans selling clothing and other fabrics. Prices are very reasonable.

Getting There & Away

Bus The bus station in Kodai is basically a patch of dirt off Bazaar Rd and opposite the Hotel Astoria. Timetables, where they exist, are entirely in Tamil as are most of the direction indicators in the front of the buses. There are eight buses a day to Madurai (3½ hours, Rs 16), one daily to Tiruchirappalli, one daily to Coimbatore, one daily to Kanyakumari, and one daily to Madras. Other buses leave throughout the day for Palani, Dindigul and Kodai Road (for the train station). All these are ordinary state buses. There's also a KSRTC semideluxe bus daily to Bangalore which leaves at 6 pm and takes 12 hours.

Deluxe minibuses operate in the high season between Kodaikanal and Udhagamandalam (Ooty) but they are suspended in the monsoon. They cost around Rs 120 and take all day. Enquire at mid-range hotels for frequency of departure.

You'll also see quite a few superdeluxe buses arriving and departing from Kodaikanal but these are tour buses and they neither pick up nor put down passengers in the town.

Train The nearest railway stations are Palani to the north, and Kodai Road to the east.

There is a massive rebuilding and re-routing programme being undertaken on the rail line between Madurai and Dindigul so it may be that, in future, arrangements to get to Kodaikanal by rail and bus change.

Getting Around

You can hire bicycles at the main intersection at the top of the bazaar. The rate is Rs 15 per day (negotiable). The hills can present quite a problem but, as you'd be walking up them anyway, it's not that much extra hassle to push a bike and at least you can coast down!

Taxis in Kodaikanal are very expensive compared with elsewhere even though half of them stand idle most of the day. There's a notice at the bus stand which states that sightseeing tours (eight sights) by taxi cost Rs 15. How long it's been there is anyone's guess but taxi drivers will fall about laughing if you try to get one for that price. The usual first quoted price is Rs 50 regardless of distance.

AROUND KODAI
Palani
There are fine views of the plains and scattered rock outcrops on the bus ride from Kodaikanal to Palani. The hill temple is dedicated to Lord Maruga, and an electric winch takes pilgrims to the top.

RAMESWARAM
Population: 33,000
Rameswaram is the Varanasi of the south and a major pilgrimage centre for both Saivaites and Vaishnavaites. Ramanathaswamy Temple is one of the most important southern temples.

This is also the port from which the ferry to Talaimannar (Sri Lanka) used to depart before normal passenger services were suspended. It's now used to ferry refugees from Sri Lanka to India. As a result, there are now very few foreign visitors.

Orientation & Information
Rameswaram is an island in the Gulf of Mannar, connected to the mainland at Mandapam by rail, and by one of India's engineering wonders, the Indira Gandhi Bridge. The bridge took 14 years to build and was finally opened by Rajiv Gandhi late in 1988.

The town itself is small and dusty, with most of the hotels and restaurants, the ferry jetty, railway station and post office clustered around the Ramanathaswamy Temple. The bus stand is some two km west of the town centre and from here there are frequent shuttle buses to the town centre for Rs 0.60.

The Thiruvalluvar booking office is on North Car St, next to the Hotel Chola.

It can be difficult to get accommodation here if there's a festival on, especially if you arrive late in the day.

There's a tourist office in the railway station but it has only a map of the town and nothing else.

Ramanathaswamy Temple
The town's most famous monument is the Ramanathaswamy Temple, a fine example of late Dravidian architecture. Its most renowned feature is its magnificent corridors lined with massive sculptured pillars, noted for their elaborate design, style and rich carving. Legend has it that Rama (of the Indian epic the *Ramayana)* sanctified this place by worshipping Lord Siva here after the battle of Sri Lanka. Construction of the temple began in the 12th century AD and additions were made to the building over the succeeding centuries by various rulers, so that today its gopuram is 53.6 metres high. Only Hindus may enter the inner sanctum.

The temple is open from 4 am to 1 pm and 3 to 9 pm. Like Kanyakumari, excessively loud and distorted temple music is blasted out from the temple from about 4.30 am onwards – just in case you had any ideas about sleeping in. It's torture for anyone who is not totally deaf but, as usual, the locals seem to be totally oblivious to it.

Kothandaraswamy Temple
This is another famous temple, about three km from the extreme tip of the island. It was the only structure to survive the 1964 cyclone which washed the rest of the village away. Legend states that Vibishana, brother of Sita's kidnapper Ravana, surrendered to Rama at this spot.

Adam's Bridge
Adam's Bridge is the name given to the chain of reefs, sandbanks and islets that almost connects Sri Lanka with India. According to legend, this is the series of stepping stones used by Hanuman to follow Ravana, in his bid to rescue Sita.

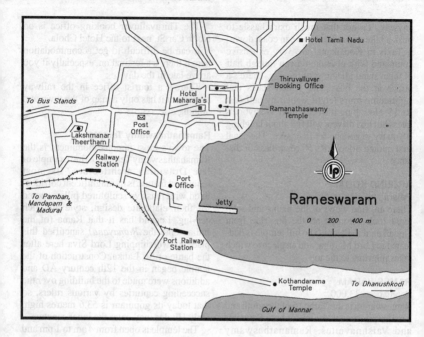

To Bus Stands

Lakshmanar
Theertham

Railway
Station

To Pamban,
Mandapam &
Madurai

Post
Office

Port
Office

Port Railway
Station

Hotel
Maharaja's

Jetty

Hotel Tamil Nadu

Thiruvalluvar
Booking Office

Ramanathaswamy
Temple

Rameswaram

0   200   400 m

Kothandarama
Temple

To Dhanushkodi

Gulf of Mannar

Other Attractions

There is a lovely bathing pool at **Dhanush-kodi** on the very tip of the peninsula, which is deserted except for friendly fisherfolk. The buses stop at Kothandaraswamy, about three km away, so you have to walk the rest of the way or flag down one of the Public Carrier vans delivering goods to the villagers.

For a good **beach** much closer to town, try the one in front of the Hotel Tamil Nadu. Most of the time you'll have it to yourself.

Places to Stay

There are some 19 basic lodges in town, all of them typical Indian boarding houses with the usual range of rooms, some with common and others with attached bathrooms. They're all very much of a similar standard with prices ranging from Rs 20/30 for singles/doubles with common bathroom and Rs 30/50 with attached bathroom. The best of the bunch are the *Santhana Lodge*, South Car St, the *Santhiya Lodge* (☎ 329),

West Car St, and the *Devasharma Lodge*. The last also has a few air-con doubles for Rs 120.

Also very good is the *Swami Ramanatha Tourist Home* (☎ 217) which has good, clean doubles with attached shower for Rs 50. The *Alankar Tourist Home*, West Car St, has also been recommended and there are a number of fairly cheap retiring rooms at the railway station, as well as dorm beds.

Going up in price, the best place to stay is the *Hotel Maharaja's* (☎ 271), 7 Middle St, the street heading west from the west gopuram of the temple. The hotel is conveniently situated and has clean, pleasant doubles/triples with attached bathroom and balcony for Rs 70/90 as well as air-con doubles with TV for Rs 220. Its only drawback is that it's right in the line of fire of the temple loudspeakers.

Also good is the *Hotel Venkatesh* (☎ 296), Sithi Vinayagar Kovil St, which has clean doubles with attached bathroom for Rs 60 and four-bed rooms for Rs 110. There are also a few air-con doubles for Rs 150.

Last up is the TTDC *Hotel Tamil Nadu* (☎ 277) on the beach at the north-east end of town. Here you can get a dorm bed for Rs 20 or an ordinary/deluxe double for Rs 115/140. There are also triple, five-bedded and six-bedded rooms as well as air-con doubles with TV for Rs 260. It's fairly good value and all the rooms face the sea. The hotel has its own vegetarian and non-vegetarian restaurants.

Places to Eat

A number of vegetarian restaurants along West Car St serve typical south Indian thalis, all of a pretty dismal standard.

Getting There & Away

Bus The bus station is two km west of town. Thiruvalluvar buses run to Madurai four times daily (four hours, Rs 23) and to Kanyakumari, Trichy and Madras. Local buses run to Madurai more frequently and take a little longer but are marginally cheaper. There are also a number of buses to Pondicherry, Trichy and Thanjavur via Madurai.

Train There are two expresses to/from Madras daily, the *Sethu Express* (No 6113/4), and the *Rameswaram Express* (No 6101/2). The 666-km trip takes 15 hours and costs Rs 109/417 in 2nd/1st class. Neither of these trains go through Madurai – they take the direct route from Manamadurai Junction to Trichy.

The only way to get from Rameswaram to Madurai or vice versa direct is on the daily *Rameswaram-Madurai Passenger* train. the trip takes 6½ hours to cover the 164 km and costs Rs 22 in 2nd class.

Getting Around

Bus Town buses run backwards and forwards between the temple and the bus station from early morning until late at night and cost Rs 0.60.

Auto-Rickshaw, Cycle-Rickshaw & Tonga These ply the streets at all hours. Count on paying around Rs 10.

Bicycle Riding a bicycle is a good way of getting around Rameswaram, and out to Dhanushkodi at the tip of the peninsula. You can rent them from around the temple or at the Hotel Tamil Nadu for about Rs 15 per day.

TIRUCHENDUR

South of Rameswaram and Tuticorin is this impressive temple. You may be able to enter the inner sanctums here and watch the enthusiastic proceedings. Just be careful if they offer you a gulp of the holy water. Pouring it over your hands and rubbing them together joyously is an acceptable substitute for drinking it!

Places to Stay

The *Hotel Tamil Nadu* (☎ 268) has singles/doubles with bathroom for Rs 40/60.

KANYAKUMARI (Cape Comorin)

Population: 17,500

Kanyakumari is the 'Land's End' of India. Here, the Bay of Bengal meets the Indian Ocean and, at full moon, it's possible to enjoy the unique experience of seeing the sun set and the moon rise over the ocean simultaneously. Kanyakumari is also a popular pilgrimage destination of great spiritual significance to Hindus. It is dedicated to the goddess Kanyakumari, Youthful Virgin, who is an incarnation of Devi, Siva's wife.

Otherwise, Kanyakumari is highly overrated, with its trinket stalls, a lousy beach and one of those places with megaphones at the end of each street which rip your eardrums apart between 4 am and 10 pm.

Most interesting are the pilgrims who come here from all over the country, representing a good cross section of India. You can safely give this place a miss if your time is limited but, if you want to stand on the very tip of the subcontinent, it's the place to do it – but watch where you tread: there's human

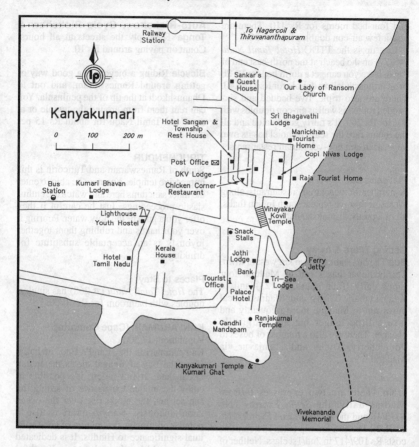

Kanyakumari

excrement everywhere on the rocks and the stench is dreadful on a hot day.

Orientation & Information

The town is fairly spread out and both transport centres are out of the way. The railway station is almost a km to the north, while the bus station is 500 metres west of the town centre.

There is a tourist office near the Gandhi Mandapam but it's of little interest.

Kanyakumari Temple

Picturesquely located overlooking the shore,

the Kumari Ghat attracts pilgrims from all over India to worship and to bathe. According to legend, Devi did penance here to secure Siva's hand in marriage. When she was unsuccessful, she vowed to remain a virgin (Kanya). The temple is open daily from 4.30 to 11.45 am and from 5.30 to 8.45 pm, but non-Hindus are not allowed into the inner sanctum. Men must remove their shirts, and everyone their shoes, on entering this temple.

Lighthouse

There are excellent views of the countryside

from the lighthouse. It is open from 3 to 7 pm and entry costs Rs 0.25. Unfortunately, photography is prohibited.

Vivekananda Memorial

The Vivekananda Memorial is on two rocky islands projecting from the sea about 500 metres offshore. The Indian philosopher Swami Vivekananda came here in 1892 and sat on the rock, meditating, before setting out as one of India's most important religious crusaders. The mandapam which stands here in his memory was built in 1970 and employs architectural styles from all over India. The ferry service to the island every half-hour costs Rs 3 per person, plus an entry fee of Rs 2 to the Rock Temple. The islands are open to visitors from 7 to 11 am and 2 to 5 pm.

Suchindram Temple

Dedicated to Indra, the Suchindram Temple is about 13 km from Kanyakumari (Rs 10 by auto-rickshaw) and can be visited by non-Hindus. It's worth joining the Friday sunset ceremonies. You have to hire a special dhoti and a guide will 'rush you around but will paste your forehead, chest and arms with white ash paste', according to one traveller.

Places to Stay – bottom end

Hotels can be heavily booked, which tends to push the prices up. At the bottom end of the market, there are a bunch of cheap hotels clustered just north of the Vinayakar Kovil Temple. Two of these are the *Raja Tourist Home* and *Gopi Nivas Lodge*, with rooms at Rs 25/40. Both are basic but adequate.

The very comfortable *DKV Lodge* is in the same area. Rooms 7 and 9 have excellent views of the town and Vivekananda Memorial, as well as a sea breeze. Double rooms cost Rs 70 with bathroom; there are no singles.

The *Township Rest House* on Main Rd also has only doubles, and these cost Rs 40. On the town's central street, the *Jothi Lodge* is grubby and gloomy. Rooms are Rs 25/40 with bathroom.

You can get a bed for Rs 20 in the *Youth Hostel* at the Hotel Tamil Nadu. Accommo-dation in the tidy dorm at the bus station *lodge* also costs Rs 20. You get a locker under the bed to stow your gear and there is hot water.

The railway *retiring rooms* cost Rs 20/30; a bed in the six-bed dorm is Rs 10.

Places to Stay – middle

The *Hotel Sangam* (☎ 351) on Main Rd is next door to the Township Rest House. Rooms (doubles only) cost Rs 110 with bathroom and hot water. The hotels along the waterfront west of the temple are very pleasant but, unfortunately, you're unlikely to get in without a booking. The *Hotel Tamil Nadu* (☎ 257) has doubles for Rs 100, or Rs 125 with air-con. *Kerala House* is run by the Kerala Tourism Development Corporation, but it seems to be monopolised by Kerala government officials.

The relatively new *Manickhan Tourist Home* has doubles for Rs 140 without sea view or Rs 160 with sea view. The hotel's restaurant is good and does excellent dosas.

The *lodge* at the bus station has large double rooms for Rs 95 with bathroom and hot water.

Places to Eat

The popular *Palace Hotel* in the main part of town serves good vegetarian meals on a banana leaf for Rs 8.

Non-vegetarian food is harder to find. The *Chicken Corner* has fish and mutton as well as chicken, and the *Manickhan Tourist Home* also has a non-vegetarian restaurant.

Snack stalls selling chicken, paratha and other dishes are set up on the main intersection in town in the evenings. This is the way to go if you're on a tight budget.

Getting There & Away

Bus The new bus station is an edifice which seems quite out of proportion to the size of the town. Everything here is well organised, with timetables in English, restaurants, waiting rooms and even a lodge upstairs. The reservation office is open from 7 am to 9 pm.

The station is a dusty 15-minute walk from the centre.

There are Thiruvalluvar buses to Madurai three times daily (No 101, six hours, Rs 34), to Madras six times daily (No 282, 16 hours, Rs 104), Thiruvananthapuram (Trivandrum; No 800, 2½ hours) and Rameswaram (No 520, 8½ hours).

Local buses go to Nagercoil, Thiruvananthapuram and Kovalam, among other places.

Train Grandiose transport centres are definitely the rage in Kanyakumari. The railway station is almost as over-the-top as the bus station and wouldn't look out of place in Delhi or Bombay.

The one daily passenger train to Thiruvananthapuram does the 87 km in a dazzling three hours at Rs 14 in 2nd class.

The *Kanyakumari Express* travels to Bombay daily in a shade under 48 hours, departing Kanyakumari at 5.15 am. The 2149-km trip costs Rs 210/961 in 2nd/1st class. This train will also take you to Thiruvananthapuram (2¼ hours) and Ernakulam (eight hours).

For the real long-haulers, the weekly *Himsagar Express* runs all the way to Jammu Tawi, a distance of 3676 km, taking 10 hours under four days. It's the longest single train ride in India, and leaves from Kanyakumari on Thursdays and from Jammu Tawi on Saturdays. This train also goes to Madras (952 km, 12 hours) and Delhi (3141 km, 72 hours) on the way.

Wildlife Sanctuaries

There are six wildlife sanctuaries in Tamil Nadu, three close to the east coast and the others in the richly forested mountains on the borders of Kerala and Karnataka. The Guindy Deer Park, within the metropolitan boundaries of Madras, is the smallest.

All sanctuaries except Guindy have accommodation and transport facilities. Although it's possible to turn up at any of them without making prior arrangements,

Wildlife Sanctuaries

it's advisable to book in advance. Rooms in sanctuary lodges and rest houses cannot be allocated to unannounced guests until very late in the afternoon, when there's no further possibility of anyone arriving with a booking.

Motorised transport can be arranged to the more remote parts of the sanctuaries, where you're far more likely to see animals, which don't often venture too close to main roads or areas of human settlement. Some of the sanctuaries offer elephant rides through the forest which usually don't need to be booked in advance. Although these are great fun, you're unlikely to see many of the animals which live in these sanctuaries from the back of an elephant.

At present, most of the sanctuaries are geared to groups who arrive with their own transport and who have prebooked at least a few days ahead. If you're alone and haven't booked, you could find that a lot of your time is taken up waiting for the arrival of a group to which you can attach yourself. Your choice of accommodation is also limited by a lack of transport, unless you can get a lift. It's time the Indian tourist organisation gave some thought to catering for visitors without their own transport and those who can't make bookings weeks in advance because of the way they travel. Nevertheless, visiting at least one of the sanctuaries can be a very rewarding experience.

MUDUMALAI WILDLIFE SANCTUARY
In the luxuriantly forested foothills of the Nilgiris, Mudumalai is part of a much larger sanctuary which includes Bandipur and Wynad in neighbouring Karnataka and Kerala. The main attractions here are the herds of chital (spotted deer), gaur (Indian bison), elephant, tiger, panther, wild boar, sloth, and the otters and crocodiles which live in the River Moyar. It's possible to see all these animals if you have made arrangements with the Forest Department for a vehicle to take you to the more remote parts of the sanctuary.

The main service area in this sanctuary, Theppakadu, is on the main road between Udhagamandalam (Ooty) and Mysore. The Wildlife Sanctuary Reception Centre, Sylvan Lodge, Youth Hostel and elephant camp are here. Even around Theppakadu, you can sometimes see spotted deer, elephant and wild boar.

It's advisable to book sanctuary accommodation and transport in advance, either with the Forest Officer in Ooty on Coonoor Rd, or at a Tamil Nadu tourist office. There are entry fees for visitors, vehicles and cameras. Jeeps and minibuses can be hired in the park, and elephant rides are available. The elephants go crashing through the bush over a four to five-km circuit and are great fun, but you'll be lucky to see anything other than spotted deer, wild boar, gaur and monkeys. The elephant rides must be booked in advance in Ooty.

The best time to visit the sanctuary is between February and May, though you can visit at any time of the year, except during the dry season when it may be closed. Heavy rain is common in October and November.

Places to Stay & Eat
Theppakadu The most convenient place to stay is the TTDC *Youth Hostel* (☎ Masinagudi 49), where dorm beds cost Rs 20 and basic meals are available. There's no need to book in advance.

The various rest houses cost Rs 40 for a double. The *Sylvan Lodge* is the best and looks out over the river.

The *Abhayaranyam Rest House* has rooms from Rs 25. There's also a dormitory at the *Range Office* a short way from the Rest House.

At the *Reception Centre*, there is an eight-bed dormitory (four per room) with toilet and shower but no catering facilities. If you're staying here, you can eat at the *Sylvan Lodge* or *Youth Hostel* as there are no other restaurants – Theppakadu is not really a village, just the park headquarters on the main road.

Masinagudi Masinagudi is a small village eight km east of Theppakadu. The privately run *Mountania Lodge* (☎ 37) has cabins with bathroom for Rs 180/200. Meals are available here, or you can try the couple of basic 'meals' places in the village.

Bamboo Banks (☎ 22) is more expensive again and is inaccessible without your own transport. The *Chital Walk (Jungle Trails) Lodge* (☎ Masinagudi 56), eight km east of Masinagudi, is a good place if you have a keen interest in wildlife. It offers double rooms at Rs 175 and dorm beds for Rs 30. Good meals are available. The Sighur Ghat buses to or from Ooty can drop you off on the road near the Valaitotam turnoff if you ask and, from there, it's a few hundred metres off the road.

Right opposite the police station in Masinagudi is a *Travellers Bungalow* with a couple of double rooms for Rs 80.

Getting There & Away
The buses from Ooty to Mysore, Bangalore

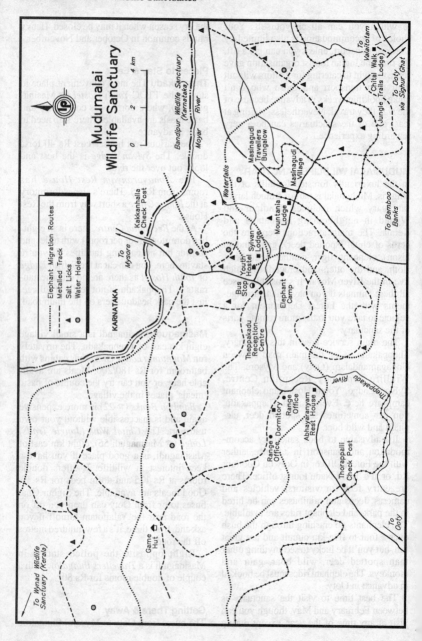

Mudumalai Wildlife Sanctuary

4 km

0   2   4 km

Bandipur Wildlife Sanctuary (Karnataka)

Moyar River

To Valaitotam

(Chital Walk)

(Jungle Trails Lodge)

To Ooty via Sigbur Ghat

To Bamboo Banks

Masinagudi Travellers Bungalow

Masinagudi Village

Mountania Lodge

Waterfalls

Sylvan Lodge

Kakkanhalla Check Post

To Mysore

Bus Stop

Youth Hostel

Elephant Camp

Theppakadu Reception Centre

Mappayadu River

Range Office, Dormitory

Range Office

Abhayaranyam Rest House

Thorappalli Check Post

To Ooty

KARNATAKA

Elephant Migration Routes

Metalled Track

Salt Licks

Water Holes

To Wynad Wildlife Sanctuary (Kerala)

Game Hut

and Hassan stop at Theppakadu, and it's not too difficult to wave them down.

The more interesting route to or from Ooty involves taking a bus to Masinagudi, then one of the small government buses which make the trip up (or down) the tortuous Sighur Ghat road. It's actually shorter than the main road, but the bends are so tight and the gradient so steep that large buses can't use it. In fact, there's a sign on the road leaving Masinagudi warning that 'you will have to strain your vehicle to reach Ooty'!

You can also visit the sanctuary on tours from Ooty, but you're unlikely to see anything other than tame elephants.

VEDANTANGAL WATER BIRDS SANCTUARY

This is one of the most spectacular breeding grounds in India. Water fowl gather here for about six months of the year from October/ November to March, depending on the monsoons, and their numbers peak in December and January. At the height of the breeding season, you can see up to 30,000 birds at once. The best times to visit are early morning and late afternoon.

Cormorants, egrets, herons, storks, ibises, spoonbills, grebes and pelicans come here to breed and nest, and many other species of migratory birds also visit the sanctuary.

The best way to get there is by bus from Madras to Chengalpattu (Chingleput), but you will have to hire transport to take you to the *Forest Rest House* – it's the only place to stay, with rooms from Rs 35.

CALIMERE WILDLIFE SANCTUARY

Point Calimere, on the east coast just south of the Pondicherry territory of Karaikal in Thanjavur district, is noted for its congregation of black buck, spotted deer and wild pig, and the vast flocks of migratory water fowl, especially flamingoes. Every winter, the tidal mud flats and marshes are covered with masses of birds – teals, shovellers, curlews, gulls, terns, plovers, sandpipers, shanks, herons and up to 3000 flamingoes at one time. In the spring, a different set of birds – koels, mynas and barbets – are drawn here by the profusion of wild berries.

Visit between November and January. There is very little activity from April to June, and the main rainy season is between October and December. You can get to Point Calimere either by rail on the Mayavaram to Thiruthuraipoondi section, or by regular bus from either Thanjavur or Mayavaram. A *Forest Rest House* has rooms from Rs 35, but facilities are very basic and no meals are available.

MUNDANTHURAI TIGER SANCTUARY

Mundanthurai is in the mountains near the border with Kerala. The closest railway station is at Amabasamudram, and regular buses run from there to the sanctuary. From Tirunelveli, buses go to Popanasam and, from there, you can catch another bus to the Forest Rest House.

As the name implies, this is principally a tiger sanctuary and the best time to visit is between January and September, though you can come at any time of year. The main rainy season is between October and December. Tiger sightings are apparently extremely infrequent and, in addition, the *Forest Rest House* is poorly maintained, food is not available and the staff are unhelpful.

ANAMALAI WILDLIFE SANCTUARY

This is the third of the wildlife sanctuaries in the mountains along the border between Tamil Nadu and Kerala. Anamalai is south of Coimbatore and can be reached by regular bus from Coimbatore, or by rail to Pollachi and then bus to the sanctuary. The Reception Centre is at Parambikulam Dam. Anamalai's major attractions are elephant, gaur, tiger, panther, spotted deer, wild boar, bear, porcupine and civet cat. The Nilgiri tahr, commonly known as ibex, can also be seen here. Transport within the sanctuary can be arranged through the Forest Department.

Accommodation is available at three places: the *Forest Rest House* at Topslip, with six rooms; *Varagaliar Rest House*, deep in the forest with basic accommodation (but you must take your own provisions as there are no catering facilities); and *Mount Stuart* *Rest House*, with two rooms and meals available. The sanctuary can be visited at any time of the year, and very early morning or late evening is the best time for wildlife viewing.

Top: Arjuna's Penance, Mahabalipuram, Tamil Nadu (TW)
Left: Boy on fishing boat, Kanyakumari, Tamil Nadu (HF)
Right: Kodaikanal, Tamil Nadu (HF)

Top: Jolly Buoy Island, Andaman Islands (BT)
Middle Left: Church on Ross Island, Andaman Islands (BT)
Middle Centre: Hermit Crab, Jolly Buoy Island, Andaman Islands (BT)
Middle Right: Overgrown doorway, Ross Island, Andaman Islands (BT)
Bottom: Cellular jail, Port Blair, Andaman Islands (HF)

Andaman & Nicobar Islands

Population: 278,000
Area: 8293 sq km on 319 islands
Capital: Port Blair
Main Languages: Hindi, Bengali, Tamil &
    various tribal languages

This string of over 300 richly forested tropical islands lies in the middle of the Bay of Bengal, two-thirds of the way between India and Myanmar (Burma), and stretches almost to the tip of Sumatra. Ethnically, the islands are not part of India and, until fairly recently, they were inhabited only by indigenous tribal people.

The majority of the Andaman & Nicobar Islands are still uninhabited, surrounded by coral reefs, white sandy beaches and incredibly clear water – the perfect tropical paradise. The Maldives must have been something like this before they were 'discovered' and developed. No doubt it's only a matter of time for the Andamans. For the moment, however, scuba divers must bring their own equipment as very little is available here. If you wish to go snorkelling it's better to bring a mask with you, although there are a few for hire from the various tour operators.

While Indian tourists may roam freely, foreigners are constrained by permits allowing only limited travel. The reasons given by the tourist office are that it is for our own protection ('some of the tribal people are very aggressive') but the naval base here may have something else to do with it. The government is certainly trying to promote the Andamans as a tourist destination and it's worth checking to see if the permit situation has been relaxed. There's even talk of a new air route between here and Bangkok (only 350 km from Port Blair) but that's likely to be several years away.

History

Very little of the early history of the Andaman & Nicobar Islands is known but

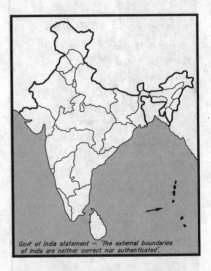

Govt of India statement – 'The external boundaries of India are neither correct nor authenticated'.

among the first Western visitors was Marco Polo. In the early 18th century, the islands were the base of the Maratha admiral, Kanhoji Angre, whose navy harassed and frequently captured British, Dutch and Portuguese merchant vessels. In 1713, Angre even managed to capture the yacht of the British governor of Bombay, releasing it only after delivery of a ransom of powder and shot. Though attacked by the British, and later, by a combined British/Portuguese naval task force, Angre remained undefeated right up to his death in 1729.

The islands were finally annexed by the British in the 19th century and used as a penal colony for Indian freedom fighters. In the notorious 'cellular jail' many of the inmates were executed, either judicially or clandestinely. Building started in the last decade of the 19th century and the jail was finished in 1908. During WW II, the islands were occupied for a time by the Japanese, but they were not welcomed as liberators and the

1057

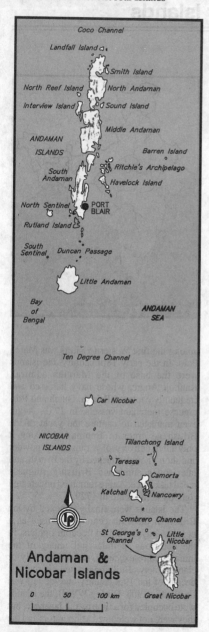

Andaman & Nicobar Islands

Coco Channel

Landfall Island

Smith Island

North Reef Island   North Andaman

Interview Island   Sound Island

ANDAMAN
ISLANDS

Middle Andaman

Barren Island

South
Andaman

Ritchie's Archipelago

Havelock Island

North Sentinel   PORT
BLAIR

Rutland Island

South
Sentinel   Duncan Passage

Little Andaman

Bay
of
Bengal

ANDAMAN
SEA

Ten Degree Channel

Car Nicobar

NICOBAR
ISLANDS

Tillanchong Island

Teressa

Camorta

Katchall   Nancowry

Sombrero Channel

St George's
Channel

Little
Nicobar

Great Nicobar

0   50   100 km

local tribes took up guerrilla activities against them. The islands were incorporated into the Indian Union when independence came to India in 1947.

The Indian government is fond of eulogising its efforts to bring 'civilisation' to these islands but, reading between the lines, it obviously regards the indigenous tribes here as stone-age people, and its attitude towards them is condescending.

In an effort to develop the islands economically, the government has completely disregarded the needs and land rights of the tribes and has encouraged massive transmigration from the mainland – mainly of Tamils who were expelled from Sri Lanka – which has pushed the population from 50,000 to 278,000 in just 18 years. The original islanders' culture is being swamped. It's not only the people who have been squashed in the path of 'development'. Vast tracts of forest were felled in the '60s and '70s. There has been some replanting of the land with 'economic' timber like teak, but much of it has been turned over to rubber plantations.

Climate

There is little seasonal variation in the climate. Continuous sea breezes keep temperatures within the 23°C to 31°C range and the humidity at around 80% all year. The south-west monsoons come to the islands between mid-May and October and the north-east monsoons between November and January. The best time to visit is between mid-November and April. December and the early part of January are the height of the season.

Tribal People

The indigenous tribal people are the victims of the government's continuing policy of colonisation and development. They now constitute a mere 11% of the present population and in most cases their numbers are falling. Of Negroid stock, the Onge, Sentinelese, Andamanese and Jarawa are all resident in the Andaman Islands. The second group, on the Nicobar Islands, is of Mongoloid descent and includes the Shompen and Nicobarese.

Nicobarese The 29,000 Nicobarese are the only indigenous people whose numbers are not decreasing. They are fair-complexioned horticulturalists who have been partly assimilated into contemporary Indian society. Living in village units led by a headman they cultivate coconuts, yams and bananas, and farm pigs.

Inhabiting a number of islands in the Nicobar group, centred on Car Nicobar, the majority of the Nicobarese are Christians.

Shompen Living in the forests on Great Nicobar, only about 200 Shompen remain. They are hunter-gatherers that have resisted integration, tending to shy away from areas occupied by Indian immigrants from the mainland.

Andamanese Numbering only 19 people, it seems impossible that the Andamanese can escape extinction. There were almost 5000 Andamanese when the British arrived in the mid-19th century. Their friendliness to the colonisers was their undoing and by the end of the century most of the population had been swept away by a series of epidemics: measles, syphilis and influenza. Their decline continues although they've now been resettled on tiny Strait Island.

Onge Unlike the Andamanese it is not disease that is wiping out the Onge. An anthropological study made in the 1970s suggested that they had become severely demoralised by loss of territory. Two-thirds of the Onges' island of Little Andaman has been taken over by the Forest Department and 'settled'. The 100 or so remaining members of the Onge tribe are confined to a 100 sq km reserve at Dugong Creek. In spite of the study, the government allowed further development including the building of roads, jetties and a match factory. They've even built a number of tin huts for these nomadic hunter-gathers to live in.

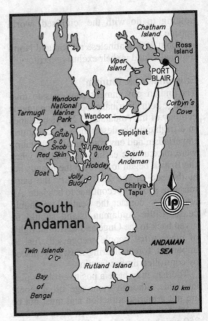

Jarawa The Jarawa are suffering from similar encroachment of territory but are at least putting up a fight, killing one or two Indian settlers each year. The 250 remaining Jarawa occupy the 750 sq km reserve on South and Middle Andaman Islands. Around them forest clearance continues at a horrific rate and the Andamans Grand Trunk Road, now under construction, runs through part of their designated territory.

Sentinelese The Sentinelese, unlike the other tribes in these islands, have consistently repulsed any attempts by outsiders to make friendly contact with them. Every few years, contact parties arrive on the beaches of North Sentinel Island, with gifts of coconuts, bananas, pigs and red plastic buckets only to be showered with arrows. It's as if the Sentinelese know that the only way they will be able to preserve their cultural identity and their physical and mental health is by having nothing to do with the 'civilised' world outside.

About 100 Sentinelese remain and North Sentinel Island is their exclusive territory.

Environment & Tourism

The Indian government continues to mismanage both the tribal people and the unique ecology of the Andaman & Nicobar Islands in a frighteningly destructive way. Cultural imperialism and environmental exploitation were inexcusable earlier this century when the British began to develop the islands but at the end of the 20th century the same mistakes should not continue to be made. All attempts to contact the Sentinelese should cease. Little Andaman Island should be given back to the Onge and territorial rights of other tribal people recognised. Just as important, forest clearing must be replaced by controlled timber farming.

Tourism may have a positive role to play in all this, although 'stone-age' tribal people are not a tourist attraction and must not be promoted as such. However, there are over 250 uninhabited islands in this area, most with superb beaches and coral reefs ideal for divers. Looking to the Maldives, where a few uninhabited islands have been developed exclusively for tourism, the Indian government is considering following the same example. This could compensate for the earnings lost from reduced tree-cutting and would place a value-tag on the preservation of the environment. Whilst there would inevitably be some environmental damage on these 'tourist islands' it would surely be preferable to the mass deforestation and destruction of tribal areas and the tribes themselves that is happening now.

Permits

Foreigners need a permit to visit the Andaman Islands. (The Nicobar Islands are completely off limits to non-Indian tourists.) The permit allows you to visit only the Port Blair area and the islands of Red Skin, Jolly Buoy, Cinque, Neil and Havelock. Certain other islands can be visited with an additional permit, obtainable from the District Commissioner of Police in Port Blair. Overnight stays are permitted only at Port Blair and on Havelock Island. The permit is valid for just 15 days. If you have a very good excuse you might be able to get a two or three day extension but nothing longer than that.

Permits are issued to visitors, without fuss, on arrival in Port Blair by air. Those arriving by ship are usually required to get their permit in advance (in a few hours from the Foreigners' Registration Office in either Madras or Calcutta) before the Shipping Corporation will issue tickets. Immediately on arrival by ship, you must visit the deputy superintendent of police (near the Annapurna Cafe in Aberdeen Bazaar) to register your arrival, or you could have problems on departure proving you've not been here longer than 15 days.

Having gone through the rigmarole of getting the permit, you have to be stamped out of the place when you leave as well. Indian red tape is alive and well in the Andamans!

PORT BLAIR

Port Blair, the administrative capital and only town of any size on the islands, has the lively air of any Indian market town. It's pleasantly situated on the main harbour and, as it's a hilly town, there are good views from quite a few vantage points.

Even though the Andamans are not far from mainland Myanmar (Burma), they still run on Indian time, which means that it is dark by 6 pm and light by 4 am.

Orientation

The town is spread out over a few hills, but most of the hotels, as well as the bus station, passenger dock, and Shipping Corporation of India office, are in the main bazaar area, known as Aberdeen Bazaar. The airport is a few km south of town over at least one steep hill. The nearest beach is at Corbyn's Cove, 10 km from Aberdeen Bazaar.

Information

Tourist Offices The helpful Andaman & Nicobar tourist office (☎ 20-933) is by the gate to the Secretariat, which is at the top of the hill overlooking the town. There's also a regional tourist counter at the Tourist Home (☎ 20-380) in Haddo, about 20 minutes walk from the centre. The Government of India tourist office (☎ 21-006), above Super Shoppe, has little of interest so don't waste your time.

For more information about the tribal people of these islands an interesting series of paperbacks, published for the Anthropological Survey of India, is available from Living Literature bookshop. The library, on the same road as the post office, is also a good place to find information about the islands.

Money Although Port Blair boasts no less than seven banks, foreign exchange facilities are available only at the State Bank of India and the larger hotels.

Post & Telecommunications The post office is not far from the centre, with the telegraph office in a wooden shack next door. You can make international calls from a number of places in Aberdeen Bazaar, including the New India Cafe.

Cellular Jail
Built by the British at the beginning of this century, the cellular jail is now a major tourist attraction, preserved as a shrine to India's freedom fighters. It originally consisted of six wings radiating out from a central tower, but only three remain today. It still gives a fair impression of the terrible conditions under which the detainees were incarcerated. It's open daily from 8 am to noon and 2 to 5 pm, and there's no entry charge. Don't miss the Sound & Light show, which is excellent. The English-language show is at 7 pm each night. A minimum of 10 people is required but since tickets cost only Rs 3 it would be worth buying a few extra tickets to make up the numbers if you can't get a group of 10 together.

Marine Museum
It's worth visiting this museum to identify some of the fish you may have seen while snorkelling. The Nicobarese curator is very friendly and informative about the 350 species on display here. It's open every day from 8.30 am to 12.30 pm and 1.30 to 5 pm.

Anthropological Museum
At this small museum there are displays of tools, dress and way of life of the indigenous tribes. It's open from 9 am to noon and 1 to 4 pm daily except Sunday, and there's no entry charge.

Mini Zoo & Forest Museum
Over 200 Andaman & Nicobar species are found nowhere else in the world. Some can be seen at the Mini Zoo, including the Nicobar pigeon and Andaman pig. The saltwater crocodile breeding programme has been very successful and many have been returned to the wild. Fortunately their natural habitat is dense mangrove swamps – there have been no reports of crocodiles attacking swimmers here. The zoo is open from 7 am to noon and 2 to 5 pm but is closed on Monday. Entry is Rs 0.50.

Nearby is the small Forest Museum with a display of the different types of woods that grow here including padauk, light and dark-coloured wood occurring in the same tree. Elephants are still used at some of the lumber camps. Entry is free and the museum is open from 9 am to noon and 3 to 5 pm (daily except Sunday).

Chatham Sawmill
The sawmill, seasoning chambers and furniture workshop in one of Asia's largest wood processors can be visited. As the government tourist literature enthuses, you'll see 'some of the rare species of tropical timber like padauk'. If they're acknowledged as rare you wonder what they're doing in a sawmill. It's open from 6.30 am to 2.30 pm. The nearby Wimco match-splint factory seems to have closed, one hopes permanently.

Organised Tours
A range of tours combining most sights or visits to islands are offered by the A&N

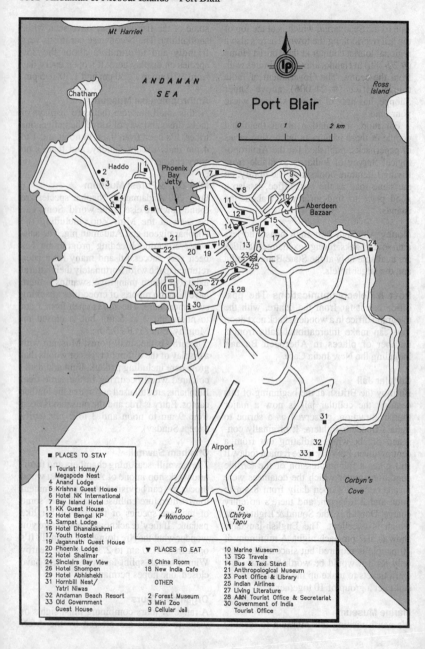

ANDAMAN SEA

Port Blair

Mt Harriet

Chatham

Haddo

Phoenix Bay Jetty

Aberdeen Bazaar

Ross Island

0   1   2 km

Airport

Corbyn's Cove

To Wandoor

To Chiriya Tapu

■ PLACES TO STAY
1 Tourist Home/
   Megapode Nest
4 Anand Lodge
5 Krishna Guest House
6 Hotel NK International
7 Bay Island Hotel
11 KK Guest House
12 Hotel Bengal KP
15 Sampat Lodge
16 Hotel Dhanalakshmi
17 Youth Hostel
19 Jagannath Guest House
20 Phoenix Lodge
22 Hotel Shalimar
24 Sinclairs Bay View
26 Hotel Shompen
29 Hotel Abhishekh
31 Hornbill Nest/
   Yatri Niwas
32 Andaman Beach Resort
33 Old Government
   Guest House

▼ PLACES TO EAT
8 China Room
18 New India Cafe

OTHER
2 Forest Museum
3 Mini Zoo
9 Cellular Jail
10 Marine Museum
13 TSG Travels
14 Bus & Taxi Stand
21 Anthropological Museum
23 Post Office & Library
25 Indian Airlines
27 Living Literature
28 A&N Tourist Office & Secretariat
30 Government of India
   Tourist Office

tourist office (☎ 20-380), Shompen Travels (☎ 20-425) in the Hotel Shompen, Island Travels (☎ 21-358) in Aberdeen Bazaar, and Andaman Beach Resort (☎ 20-599). Shompen Travels runs a trip (daily except Monday) to either Jolly Buoy or Red Skin for Rs 300.

Every afternoon at 3 pm, a 1½-hour harbour cruise leaves from the Phoenix Bay Jetty. The trip costs Rs 20 and the main point of 'interest' is the huge, floating dry-dock facility. The tour stops briefly at tiny Viper Island where the remains of the gallows tower built by the British still stand. However, the trip to Ross Island is much more interesting than the harbour cruise.

Places to Stay

Accommodation is geared to tourists who are the main visitors although, even in the season, it is possible to bargain prices down quite a bit.

If you want to be near a beach, the only place to go is Corbyn's Cove, where there's one expensive resort hotel and two cheap government places. Since all the accommodation is quite spread out, it's worth hiring a bicycle or moped to get around.

Places to Stay – bottom end

Best value at Corbyn's Cove is the old government *Guest House*, just above the beach. However, there are only four rooms here, all with attached bathrooms and balconies, at Rs 25/50. Reservations must be made at the A&N tourist office. Most travellers stay at the friendly *Hornbill Nest* (Yatri Niwas) which is about one km north of Corbyn's Cove, with views across the sea. It's a fairly new place with dorm beds at Rs 35 in four and six-bedded rooms and doubles for Rs 70, all with attached bathrooms. Mosquito nets are provided. There's a good restaurant but some dishes need to be ordered in advance.

The *Youth Hostel* is a reasonable place with dorm beds for Rs 10 (Rs 20 for non-members) and a few double rooms. There's a restaurant for residents with set lunches and dinners at Rs 8 for non-veg, Rs 6.50 for veg.

In Aberdeen Bazaar the *Sampat Lodge* is

basic but friendly with rooms for Rs 35/50. The *KK Guest House* is run down with tiny rooms for Rs 25/45. The nearby *Hotel Bengal KP* is much better with clean singles/doubles for Rs 40/60 with attached bathrooms. Also in Aberdeen Bazaar is *Ram Nivas Lodge* with singles with common bathroom at Rs 25, doubles with attached bathrooms for Rs 65.

Along the road to Haddo there's the excellent *Jagannath Guest House* with spotless singles/doubles/triples for Rs 50/100/150, all with attached bathrooms. Further along the same road the *Phoenix Lodge* is not so good with rooms for Rs 40/50 with common bathroom.

In Haddo there's the basic *Krishna Guest House*, a small friendly place with dorm beds for Rs 15, and singles/doubles for 25/40 with common bathroom. *Anand Lodge* nearby is better value with rooms for Rs 20/30 or Rs 30/50 with attached bathroom.

The *Central Lodge*, out past the Hotel Shompen at Middle Point, is a wooden lodge with a verandah, friendly management and rooms from Rs 25/50.

Places to Stay – middle

The *Tourist Home/Megapode Nest* (☎ 20-207), at Haddo on the hill above the bay, is a good place with a range of rooms although your own transport would be useful here. There are doubles for Rs 100 or Rs 250 with air-con, all with attached bathrooms. For upmarket air-con accommodation, the *Nicobari Cottages* represent excellent value at Rs 350 for a double and are part of this complex. There's a good restaurant and great views over the harbour.

The *Hotel Abhishekh* (☎ 21-565) is good value with clean singles/doubles/triples for Rs 80/120/160 or Rs 160/190/230 with air-con. All rooms have attached bathrooms and the hotel has its own restaurant. Only a few years old, it's well run by a friendly manager. Equally good value is the spotless *Hotel Shalimar* (☎ 21-963) which is on the road to Haddo. Rooms are Rs 80/125/180 with attached bathroom and air-con doubles are Rs 260.

The *Hotel Dhanalakshmi* (☎ 21-953) in Aberdeen Bazaar has good rooms for Rs 115/150 or Rs 205/240 with air-con. All rooms have attached bathrooms and there's a restaurant.

Rooms at the *Hotel Shompen* (☎ 20-360) are overpriced at their quoted rate of Rs 240/310 or Rs 320/390 with air-con. However, outside the peak of the high season you should be able to get discounts of 50% to 75%. There's a restaurant here and a travel agency that runs tours to some of the islands.

Near the Phoenix Bay jetty, the *Hotel NK International* (☎ 20-113) is nothing special with double rooms for Rs 200, or Rs 300 with air-con.

Places to Stay – top end

On the road to Corbyn's Cove is the *Sinclairs Bay View* (☎ 21-159). Only recently taken over by the Sinclairs group, rooms are still a bit tatty although renovations are under way. They cost Rs 365/550 or Rs 399/690 with air-con. There are good views over the sea but no beach. Tours can be organised from here.

Out at Corbyn's Cove, the *Andaman Beach Resort* (☎ 21-462) is excellently located in a very quiet part of the island, just across the road from the beach. Rooms in the main block are Rs 650/800, and in the very pleasant air-con cottages rooms cost Rs 830/1000. As with everywhere else discounts are negotiable outside the peak season. There's a bar, restaurant, foreign exchange facilities and a boat for hire.

With views over the sea, the Welcomgroup *Bay Island Hotel* (☎ 20-881) is the top hotel here. Beautifully designed by the well-known Indian architect Charles Correa, it's made almost entirely from local padauk wood. The staff are very friendly but rooms are rather overpriced, ranging from US$45/55 right up to US$120. Only the more expensive rooms have air-con. The hotel has a good restaurant and open-air bar – good for a quiet beer (Rs 66), although the wind usually gets up in the late afternoon. There's no beach nearby but the hotel has a sea-water swimming pool. Below the hill, a private pier extends into the bay with a 'human aquarium'. You climb down into a glass-windowed chamber to view the multicoloured fish that congregate here to be fed.

Places to Eat

Most of the hotels have restaurants but for fish, prawns and lobster you may have to order in advance.

There are a number of cheap places in Aberdeen Bazaar. The *Annapurna Cafe* is a recommended restaurant for veg and non-veg dishes. The *Manila Cafe* and *Anand Lodge* are also good for a snack. In the hotel of the same name, the *Dhanalakshmi* stays open late and main dishes are Rs 20 to Rs 25. Nearby is the tiny *Kattappamman Hotel* where masala dosas are Rs 4 and banana-leaf thalis cost Rs 8. You pay extra for meat (Rs 4) and have to clear your own leaf away.

Along the road to Haddo, the *New India Cafe* is a very popular place serving mainly south Indian dishes. Masala dosas are Rs 5, fried fish Rs 4 and chicken biryani Rs 15. Further along this road, near Hotel Shalimar is the *Royal Restaurant* with tandoori dishes for Rs 20 and fish for Rs 12.

On Corbyn's Cove *The Waves* has snacks and sandwiches, and fish dishes can be ordered in advance. It's said to be run by the police which might account for the good supplies of cheap beer (Rs 25) available here!

The *China Room*, run by a delightful Burmese couple, is the best place to eat in Port Blair. It's really just the front room of their house but the quality of the seafood they serve is nonetheless superb. Prices range from Rs 20 for basic dishes like veg noodles to Rs 95 for Szechuan-style lobster or Peking duck, though these require 24 hours notice. Their garlic prawns (Rs 35) are excellent and it's worth going there for lunch to discuss the menu for a slap up dinner for the following night.

Getting There & Away

Air Indian Airlines (☎ 21-108) has flights between Port Blair and Calcutta (US$134) on Monday, Tuesday, Thursday and Saturday. There are flights between Port Blair and Madras (US$136) on Tuesday, Wednesday, Friday and Sunday. The 25% youth discount is applicable on these fares. The flights can also be included on the US$400, three-week flight pass. They take two hours, leaving the mainland very early in the morning and returning the same day.

The Indian Airlines office is in the orange wooden shack round the corner from the post office. They're very friendly and have a computer link. Flights can be heavily booked and you need to have a confirmed ticket to be sure of a seat. Waitlisted passengers usually miss out. The office is open from 9 am to 4 pm every day.

Train There's a railways out-station booking office at the Secretariat.

Boat Schedules are rather erratic. There used to be more than four sailings a month between Port Blair and Madras or Calcutta on the vessels operated by the Shipping Corporation of India (SCI). There was even once a route between Visakhapatnam (Andhra Pradesh) and Port Blair. By 1992 most of them had been withdrawn for repairs and only one boat was operating on the Port Blair to Calcutta run, going twice a month. Contact SCI for the latest information and schedules since the Madras route may be recommenced. For tickets out of Port Blair, given the uncertain schedules, it's probably better to arrange these in Calcutta or Madras (if possible).

The trip takes three to four days and is never particularly comfortable as the sea can be rough. Foreigners usually have to travel 2nd class (four or six-berth), 1st (two or four-berth) or deluxe (two-berth) for Rs 874/1154/1256 per berth. If you can get a ticket for bunk class it'll cost just Rs 188. Prices are the same for both the Calcutta and Madras routes. Food costs Rs 88 per day and is usually nonstop thalis for breakfast, lunch and dinner, so you need to bring something to supplement this boring diet.

The SCI may insist that you have a permit before selling you a ticket. If they don't, you can get one in Port Blair. However, if you get your permit in advance, you must still register with the deputy superintendent of police on arrival in Port Blair or there may be problems when you leave, since they won't know how long you've been on the island.

The Port Blair SCI office (☎ 21-347) is in Aberdeen Bazaar. In Calcutta the SCI office (☎ 28-2354) is on the 1st floor at 13 Strand Rd. In Madras, the SCI (☎ 52-4964) is at Jawahar Building, Rajaji Salai (opposite the Customs House). In Visakhapatnam, the office where you can find out if this route is operating is Garuda Pattabhiramayya (☎ 65-584) opposite the main gate at the port. Two photos and a whole lot of form-filling are required, and bookings close four days before sailing.

Getting Around

There are no cycle-rickshaws or auto-rickshaws, just taxis buzzing around Port Blair. They have meters (and charts since the meters need recalibrating) but drivers need a bit of persuasion to use them. From the airport, the trip to Aberdeen Bazaar should cost Rs 20; a little less to Corbyn's Cove. A taxi between Corbyn's Cove and Aberdeen Bazaar would be around Rs 25.

There's a tourist bus which runs between the airport and the Andaman Beach Resort at Corbyn's Cove, which is free if you stay at the hotel. From the bus stand in Port Blair, there are regular departures to Wandoor (Rs 3, 1½ hours).

It's best to have your own transport to explore parts of the island. You can hire bicycles in Aberdeen Bazaar for Rs 15 per day. An even better way to get around is by moped or motorbike. Roads are not bad and very quiet. TSG Travels (☎ 20-894) rent motorbikes (Suzuki 100s), mopeds or scooters all for Rs 120 per day. Moped rental includes fuel.

Private boats can be hired from the tour operators but charges are high – around Rs 9000 to Rs 10,000 per day. Boats are restricted in the Wandoor National Park but from Chiriya Tapu you may be able to rent a boat from local people for a day trip to

Cinque Island for Rs 800 to Rs 1000. This would need to be arranged in advance.

AROUND PORT BLAIR
Mt Harriet

Permission is required from the Forest Department at the Secretariat for visits to this area, across the water north of Port Blair. There's a nature trail up to the top and if regulations are relaxed it may be possible to stay in the *Forest Department Guest House*.

Ross Island

Twenty minutes across the water from Port Blair is Ross Island, chosen by the British for their administrative headquarters. In the early part of this century, there would have been manicured lawns leading up to the ballroom, umbrellas round the swimming pool and daily services in the church. Deserted since the British left during WW II, the jungle has taken over and peacocks and spotted deer forage amongst the ruined buildings. On the top of the hill stand the remains of the church, its tower strangled by roots and vines.

Ross Island is a distinctly eerie and rather sad place but well worth a visit. There are ferries from Phoenix Bay jetty at 8.30 and 10.30 am, 12.15 and 2 pm daily except on Wednesday. From Ross Island there are departures at 9.15 and 11 am, and 12.30 and 4 pm. No permits are required but you must sign in on arrival, since the island is in the hands of the navy.

Corbyn's Cove

Corbyn's Cove is the nearest beach to Port Blair, 10 km from the town and four km beyond the airport. Out in the bay here is a small island surrounded by coral and you can sometimes get people to take you over in their fishing boats. Some people swim out to it but this is inadvisable as the current can be strong. There are a number of places to stay here and a snack bar by the beach.

It's a long, though pleasant, walk along the cliffs from Port Blair. Taxis cost about Rs 25 each way.

Sippighat

The government-run Sippighat Water Sports Complex is 11 km from Port Blair on the road to Wandoor National Park. Open daily (except Monday) from 8 am to 5 pm, it's more a boating rather than a swimming complex as it's inland on a river and there's no beach. However, you can rent kayaks for Rs 20 per hour or 10 horse-power motorboats for Rs 60 per hour.

On the same road, 15 km from Port Blair, is the government experimental farm, where tour groups often stop. New types of spices, such as cinnamon, pepper, nutmeg and cloves, are being tested here.

Wandoor National Park

This 280 sq km park comprises 15 islands and diverse scenery including mangrove creeks, tropical rainforest and reefs supporting 50 types of coral. Boats leave from Wandoor village, which is 29 km from Port Blair, at around 10 am (daily except Monday) for visits to Jolly Buoy or Red Skin Islands. Although it's worth going along to see the coral (they usually have a few snorkels for hire) only just over an hour is spent at the islands. It is very frustrating to get to such a stunningly beautiful place only to have to leave so soon. The trip costs Rs 100 for foreigners (Rs 35 for Indians). An entry permit (Rs 2) for the park must first be purchased at the kiosk by the jetty.

You can reach Wandoor by bus from Port Blair (Rs 3, 1½ hours) or by joining a tour. There are a number of good sandy beaches at Wandoor and a *Forest Guest House* with great views over the sea but it's supposedly for VIPs only.

Chiriya Tapu

Thirty km south of Port Blair is this small fishing village with beaches beside the mangroves. It's possible to arrange boats from here to Cinque Island.

Other Islands

Although the following islands are open for foreign visitors, it may still be necessary to get your permit endorsed at the Secretariat.

Apart from the red tape, most of the islands require quite a lot of travelling time to reach them, leaving little time on the islands themselves.

Cinque Island The coral and beaches here are reputedly even more impressive than at Red Skin and Jolly Buoy. It's two hours by boat from Chiriya Tapu or three hours from Phoenix Bay. This island has been targeted for future tourist development.

Neil Island Forty km east of Port Blair, this forested island is now inhabited by what the government euphemistically calls Bengali 'settlers'.

Havelock Island Fifty-four km north-east of Port Blair, Havelock covers 100 sq km and is also 'settled'. There are good beaches, coral reefs and basic government accommodation: a *Yatri Niwas* should now be open. At present this is the only other place in the Andamans where you're allowed to stay apart from Port Blair. Ferries depart from the Phoenix Bay jetty.

Glossary

Indian English is full of interesting little everyday expressions. Whereas in New York you might get robbed by a mugger, in India it will be a *dacoit* who relieves you of your goods. Politicians may employ strong-arm heavies known in India as *goondas*. There is a plethora of Indian terms for strikes, lock-outs and sit-ins – Indians can have *hartals, bandhs* and *gheraos* for example. And then there are all those Indian servants – children get looked after by *ayahs*, your house (and your *godown* if you have one) is guarded by a *chowkidah* (but they're reputed to be a lazy bunch much given to lying around on *char-poys*), and when the toilet needs cleaning there is no way your *bearer* is going to do it, that requires calling in a *sweeper*.

Then there are all the religious terms, the numerous Hindu gods, their attendants, consorts, vehicles and symbols. The multiplicity of religions in India also provides a whole series of terms for temples, shrines, tombs or memorials.

It's surprising how many Indian terms have crept into everyday English usage. We can sit out on a *verandah* and drink *chai* (hence char lady), wear *pyjamas* or *sandals* and *dungarees* (which may well be *khaki*), *shampoo* our hair, visit the *jungle*, worry about protecting our *loot* – they're all Indian words.

The glossary that follows is just a sample of words you may come across during your Indian wanderings. See Food in the Facts for the Visitor chapter for lots more.

Abhimani – Agni, eldest son of Brahma.
Abhimanyu – son of Arjuna.
acha – OK or 'I understand'.
acharya – revered teacher; originally a spiritual guide or preceptor.
adivasi – polite term for a tribal person.
agarbathi – incense.
Agasti – legendary rishi, highly revered in

the south as he is credited with bringing Hinduism as well as with developing the Tamil language.
Agni – fire, a major deity in the *Vedas*, mediator between men and the gods.
ahimsa – discipline of nonviolence.
amrita – immortality.
ananda – happiness.
Andhaka – 1000-headed demon, killed by Siva.
anikut – weir or dam.
anna – a 16th of a rupee; it's now extinct but still occasionally used in marketplace conversation, ie eight annas are Rs 0.50.
Annapurna – form of Durga, worshipped for her power to provide food.
arrak – distilled liquor made from coconut sap, potatoes or rice.
apsaras – heavenly nymphs who distracted rishis.
Aranyani – goddess of forests.
Ardhanari – Siva in half-male, half-female form.
Arishta – A *daitya* (giant) who, having taken the form of a bull, attacked Krishna and was killed by him.
Arjuna – *Mahabharata* hero and military commander who married Krishna's sister (Subhadra), took up arms against and overcame all manner of demons, had the *Bhagavad Gita* related to him by Krishna, led Krishna's funeral ceremony at Dwarka and finally retired to the Himalaya.
Aryan – Sanskrit word for 'noble'; used to refer to the people who settled in northern India from Persia.
ashram – spiritual college cum retreat.
astrology – far more than just a newspaper space filler; marriages are not arranged, flights not taken, elections not called without checking the astrological charts.
Avalokitesvara – one of the Buddha's most important disciples.
avatar – incarnation of a deity, usually Vishnu.
ayah – children's nurse or nanny.

yurvedic – Indian natural and herbal medine.

aba – religious master, father, and a term f respect.

abu – lower-level clerical worker (derogary).

agh – garden.

ahadur – brave or chivalrous; honorific tle.

aksheesh – tip, bribe or donation.

alarama – brother of Krishna and viewed y some as the seventh incarnation (avatar) f Vishnu.

ali – A daitya king, he was restrained by ishnu in his incarnation as a dwarf; his apital was Mahabalipuram.

anain – T-shirt or undervest.

andar – monkey.

andh – general strike.

aniya – moneylender.

anyan – Indian fig tree.

aoli – well, particularly a step-well with indings and galleries, found in Rajasthan nd Gujarat.

aradari – summer house.

azaar – market area. A market town is alled a bazaar.

earer – rather like a butler.

egum – Muslim woman of high rank.

etel – nut of the betel tree, chewed as a mild itoxicant.

hadrakali – another name for Durga.

hagavad Gita – Song of the Divine One; rishna's lessons to Arjuna, the main thrust f which was to emphasise the philosophy of hakti (faith); part of the Mahabharata.

hairava – the Terrible; refers to the eight icarnations of Siva in his demonic form.

hang – dried leaves and flowering shoots f the marijuana plant.

hang lassi – a blend of lassi with bhang, a rink with a kick.

harata – half-brother of Rama; ruled for ama while the latter was in exile.

havan – house, building.

hima – another Mahabharata hero, brother f Hanuman and renowned for his great trength.

histi (bheesti) – water carrier.

bhojnalya – basic eating house.

bidis (beedies) – small, hand-rolled cigarettes; really just a rolled-up leaf.

black money – undeclared, untaxed money. There's lots of it in India.

bo tree – ficus religiosa, the tree under which the Buddha attained enlightenment.

Bodhisattva – 'one whose essence is perfected wisdom'; one who has almost reached Nirvana, but who renounces it in order to help others attain it.

Brahma – source of all existence and also worshipped as the creator in the Hindu triad. Brahma is depicted as having four heads (a fifth was burnt by Siva's 'central eye' when he spoke disrespectfully). His vehicle is a swan or goose and his consort is Saraswati. Also the name of the highest Hindu caste, whose members can become priests.

Brahmanism – early form of Hinduism which evolved from Vedism; named after the Brahmin priests and the god Brahma.

Brahmin – a member of the priest caste, the highest Hindu caste.

Buddha – 'Awakened One'; originator of Buddhism who lived in the 5th century BC; regarded by Hindus as the ninth reincarnation of Vishnu.

bugyal – meadow.

bund – embankment or dyke.

burkha – one-piece garment which totally covers Muslim women.

bustee – slum areas of Calcutta.

cantonment – administrative and military area of a British Raj-era town.

caste – one's station in life.

chai – tea.

chaitya – Buddhist temple.

chakra – focus of one's spiritual power; disc-like weapon of Vishnu.

chalo, chalo, chalo – 'let's go, let's go, let's go'.

Chamunda – form of the goddess Durga. A real terror, armed with a scimitar, noose and mace, and clothed in elephant hide. Her mission was to kill the demons Chanda and Munda, from whence comes the name.

chance list – waitlist on Indian Airlines flights.

Chanda – another manifestation of the goddess Durga.

Chandra – the moon, or the moon as a god.

Chandragupta – important ruler of India in the 3rd century BC.

chang – Tibetan rice beer.

chapati – unleavened Indian bread.

chappals – sandals.

charas – resinous exudate of the marijuana plant, hashish.

charpoy – Indian rope bed.

chat – general term for small snacks, papris, etc.

chauri – fly whisk.

chela – pupil or follower, as George Harrison was to Ravi Shankar.

chhatri – tomb or mausoleum.

chikan – embroidered cloth.

chillum – pipe part of a hookah; commonly used to describe the small pipes for smoking ganja.

chinkara – gazelle.

choli – sari blouse.

chorten – Tibetan word for stupa.

choultrey – *dharamsala* (pilgrim accommodation) in the south.

chowk – courtyard or marketplace.

chowkidah – nightwatchman.

Cong (I) – Congress Party of India.

country liquor – locally produced liquor.

CPI – Communist Party of India.

CPI (M) – Communist Party of India (Marxist). It's the bigger, more powerful party and is currently in power in West Bengal (Calcutta).

crore – 10 million.

curd – yoghurt.

cutcherry – office or building for public business.

daba – boxed lunches, delivered by *dabawallahs* via an amazingly complex yet efficient system to office workers.

dacoit – robber, particularly armed robber.

dahi – yoghurt.

Daityas – demons and giants who fought against the gods.

Dalit – preferred term for India's casteless class; see Untouchable.

Damodara – another name for Krishna.

dargah – shrine or place of burial of a Muslim saint.

darshan – offering or audience with someone, usually a guru; viewing of a deity.

darwaza – gateway or door.

Dasaratha – father of Rama in the *Ramayana*.

Dattatreya – a Brahman saint in whom the Hindu triad were all present.

devadasi – temple dancer.

Devi – the Goddess; Siva's wife. She has a variety of other forms.

dhaba – hole-in-the-wall restaurant or snack bar.

dhal – lentil soup; what most of India lives on.

dharamsala – pilgrim accommodation.

dharma – Hindu/Buddhist moral code of behaviour.

dhobi – person who washes clothes.

dhobi ghat – the place where clothes are washed.

dholi – covered litter or stretcher. You may still see elderly tourists being carried around in a dholi.

dhoti – like a lungi, but the cloth is then pulled up between the legs.

dhurrie – rug.

digambara – 'sky-clad' Jain sect followers who extend their disdain for worldly goods to include not wearing clothes.

diwan – principal officer in a princely state royal court or council.

Diwan-i-Am – Hall of Public Audience.

Diwan-i-Khas – Hall of Private Audience.

dowry – money and goods given by bride's parents to son-in-law's family; it's illegal but no arranged marriage – and most marriages are arranged – can be made without it.

Draupadi – wife of the five Pandava princes in the *Mahabharata*.

Dravidian – a member of one of the aboriginal races of India, pushed south by the Indo-Europeans and now mixed with them. The Dravidian languages include Tamil, Malayalam, Telugu and Kannada.

dupatta – scarf worn by Punjabi women.

durbar – royal court; also used to describe government.

Durga – the Inaccessible; a form of Siva

wife Devi, a beautiful but fierce yellow woman riding a tiger; the major goddess of the Sakti cult.

dwarpal – doorkeeper; sculpture beside the doorways to Hindu or Buddhist shrines.

election symbols – identifying symbols for the various political parties, used since so many voters are illiterate.

Emergency – the period during which Indira Gandhi suspended many rights and many observers assumed she was intent on establishing a dictatorship.

eve-teasing – the Indian equivalent of Italian bottom-pinching.

export gurus – gurus whose following is principally from the West.

fakir – accurately a Muslim who has taken a vow of poverty, but also applied to Hindu ascetics such as sadhus.

feni – distilled liquor made from coconut milk or cashews, found in Goa.

firman – a royal order or grant.

freaks – Westerners wandering India. The '60s live!

gaddi – throne of a Hindu prince.

Ganesh – god of wisdom and prosperity, elephant-headed son of Siva and Parvati, probably the most popular god in the whole Hindu pantheon; also known as Ganapati, his vehicle is a rat. He is depicted as being four-handed: in one hand he holds a water lily, in another a club, in a third a shell and the fourth a discus.

Ganga – Ganges River, said to flow from the toe of Vishnu; also goddess representing the sacred Ganges River.

ganj – market.

ganja – dried flowering tips of marijuana plant.

garh – fort.

gari – vehicle; motor gari is a car and rail gari is a train.

Garuda – man-bird vehicle of Vishnu.

Gayatri – sacred verse of the *Rig-Veda*, repeated mentally by Brahmins twice a day.

ghat – steps or landing on a river.

ghazal – Urdu songs derived from poetry; sad love themes.

ghee – clarified butter.

gherao – lock-in, where the workers lock the management in!

giri – hill.

Gita Govinda – erotic poem by Jayadeva relating Krishna's early life as Govinda the cowherd.

godmen – commercially minded gurus; see export gurus.

godown – warehouse.

gompa – Tibetan-Buddhist monastery.

Gonds – aboriginal Indian race, now mainly found in the jungles in central India.

goondas – ruffians or toughs. Political parties often employ gangs of goondas.

gopis – cowherd girls. Krishna was very fond of them.

gopuram – soaring pyramidal gateway tower of a Dravidian temple.

Govinda – Cowkeeper; also Gopala, one of Krishna's names.

gurdwara – Sikh temple.

guru – teacher or holy person.

Haji – a Muslim who has made the pilgrimage *(haj)* to Mecca.

hammam – Turkish bath.

Hanuman – monkey god, prominent in the *Ramayana*, follower of Rama.

Hara – one of Siva's names.

Hari – another name for Vishnu.

Harijan – name given by Gandhi to India's Untouchables. This term is, however, no longer considered acceptable. See Dalit and Untouchable.

hartal – strike.

hathi – elephant.

haveli – traditional mansions with interior courtyards, particularly in Rajasthan and Gujarat.

havildar – army officer.

hindola – swing.

Hiranyakasipu – Daitya king killed by Vishnu in the man-lion (Narasimha) incarnation.

hookah – water pipe for smoking tobacco.

howdah – framework for carrying people on an elephant's back.

hypothecated – Indian equivalent of leased or mortgaged. You often see small signs on taxis or auto-rickshaws stating that the vehicle is 'hypothecated' to some bank or other.

idgah – open enclosure to the west of a town where prayers are offered during the Muslim festival of Id-ul-Zuhara.

imam – Muslim religious leader.

imambara – tomb of a Shi'ite Muslim holy man.

IMFL – Indian Made Foreign Liquor; beer or spirits produced in India.

Indra – the most important and prestigious of the Vedic gods of India; god of rain, thunder and lightning and war; his weapons are the *vajra* (thunderbolt), bow, net and *anka* (hook).

Ishwara – Lord; a name given to Siva.

Jagadhatri – Mother of the World, another name for Siva's wife.

Jagganath – Lord of the World; a form of Krishna. The centre of worship is at Puri (Orissa).

jaggery – hard, brown sugar-like sweetener made from kitul palm sap.

Jalasayin – Sleeping on the Waters; a name for Vishnu as he sleeps on his couch over the water during the monsoon.

Janaka – father of Sita (Rama's wife in the Ramayana).

janata – people, thus the Janata Party is the People's Party.

Jatakas – tales from the Buddha's various lives.

jauhar – ritual mass suicide by immolation, traditionally performed by Rajput women at times of military defeat to avoid being dishonoured by their captors.

jawan – soldier.

jheel – swampy area.

ji – honorific title that can be added to the end of almost anything; thus Babaji, Gandhiji.

juggernauts – huge, extravagantly decorated temple 'cars' dragged through the streets during Hindu festivals.

jumkahs – earrings.

jyoti linga – the most important Siva shrines in India, of which there are 12.

kachahri – see cutchery.

Kailasa – a mountain in the Himalaya, home of Siva.

Kali – the Black; a terrible form of Siva's wife Devi. Depicted with black skin, dripping with blood, surrounded by snakes and wearing a necklace of skulls.

Kalki – the White Horse and future (10th) incarnation of Vishnu which will appear at the end of Kali-Yuga when this world-history will come to an end. Kalki has been compared to Maitreya in Buddhist cosmology.

Kama – the god of love.

kameez – woman's shirt.

Kanishka – important king of the Kushana Empire who reigned in the early Christian era.

Kanyakumari – the Virgin Maiden; another name for Durga.

karma – fate.

karmachario – workers.

Kartikiya – god of war, Siva's son.

kata – Tibetan prayer shawl, traditionally given to a lama when pilgrims are brought into his presence.

Kedarnath – a name of Siva and one of the 12 important lingas.

khadi – homespun cloth; Mahatma Gandhi spent much energy in encouraging people to spin their own khadi cloth rather than buy imported English cloth.

Khalistan – Sikh secessionists' name for an independent Punjab.

khan – Muslim honorific title.

kibla – niche in the wall to which Muslims look when praying in order to face Mecca.

kot – fort.

kothi – residence, house or mansion.

kotwali – police station.

Krishna – Vishnu's eighth incarnation, often coloured blue; the most popular Indian deity, he revealed the *Bhagavad Gita* to Arjuna.

kumbh – pitcher.

kund – lake.

kurta – shirt.

Kusa – one of Rama's twin sons.

lakh – 100,000.

Lakshmana – half-brother and aide of Rama in the *Ramayana*.

Lakshmi (Laxmi) – Vishnu's consort, goddess of wealth; sprang forth from the ocean holding a lotus, a flower she is often associated with, and so is also called Padma (lotus).

lama – Tibetan-Buddhist priest or holy man.

lassi – very refreshing sweet yoghurt and iced-water drink.

lathi – baton; what Indian police hit you with if you get in the way of a lathi charge.

lenga – baggy cotton pants.

lingam – phallic symbol; symbol of Siva.

lok – people.

Lok Dal – political party, one of the components of the Janata party.

Lok Sabha – lower house in the Indian parliament, comparable to the House of Representatives or House of Commons.

lungi – like a sarong.

Mahabharata – Great Vedic epic of the Bharata Dynasty; an epic poem, containing around 10,000 verses, describing the battle between the Pandavas and the Kauravas.

Mahabodhi Society – founded in 1891 to encourage Buddhist studies in India and abroad.

Mahadeva – the Great God; a name of Siva.

Mahadevi – the Great Goddess; a name of Devi, Siva's wife.

Mahakala – Great Time; a name of Siva the destroyer, and one of the 12 sacred linga (at Ujjain in Madhya Pradesh).

mahal – house or palace.

maharaja, maharana, maharao – king.

maharani – wife of a princely ruler or a ruler in her own right.

mahatma – literally 'great soul'.

Mahayana – greater-vehicle Buddhism.

Mahayogi – the Great Ascetic; another name for Siva.

Maheshwara – Great Lord; Siva again.

mahout – elephant rider/master.

maidan – open place or square.

Makara – mythical sea creature, Varuna's vehicle and Capricorn in the Hindu zodiac; also a crocodile.

mali – gardener.

mandala – circle; symbol used in Hindu and Buddhist art to symbolise the universe.

mandapam – pillared pavilion in front of a temple.

mandi – market.

mandir – temple.

mani stone – stone carved with the Tibetan-Buddhist chant 'Om mani padme hum' or 'Hail to the jewel in the lotus'.

mantra – sacred word or chant used by Buddhists and Hindus to aid concentration; also the part of the *Vedas* consisting of hymns of praise.

mantra-shakti – priest power.

Mara – Buddhist god of death, has three eyes and holds the wheel of life.

Maratha (Mahratta) – warlike central Indian race who controlled much of India at various times and gave the Moghuls a lot of trouble.

marg – major road.

Maruts – the storm gods.

masjid – mosque; Jami Masjid is the Friday Mosque or main mosque.

mata – mother.

math – monastery.

maund – now largely superseded unit of weight (about 20 kg).

mela – a fair.

memsahib – married European lady, from 'madam-sahib'; still more widely used than you'd think.

mendi – ornate patterns painted on women's hands and feet for important festivals, particularly in Rajasthan. Beauty parlours and bazaar stalls will do it for you.

Meru – mythical mountain found in the centre of the earth; on it is Swarga, the heaven of Indra.

mihrab – see kibla.

Moghul – the Muslim dynasty of Indian emperors from Babur to Aurangzeb.

moksha – salvation.

monsoon – rainy season from around June to October, when it rains virtually every day.

morcha – mob march or protest march.

mudra – ritual hand movements used in Hindu religious dancing.

muezzin – one who calls Muslims to prayer from the minaret.

Mughal – alternative spelling for Moghul.
mullah – Muslim scholar, teacher or religious leader.
munshi – writer, secretary or teacher of languages.

nadi – river.
Naga – mythical snake having a human face and the tail of a serpent; also a person from Nagaland.
Nanda – the cowherd who raised Krishna.
Nandi – bull, vehicle of Siva and usually found at Siva temples.
Narasimha (Narsingh) – man-lion incarnation of Vishnu.
Narayan – an incarnation of Vishnu the creator.
Nataraja – Siva as the cosmic dancer.
nautch girls – dancing girls; a nautch is a dance.
nawab – Muslim ruling prince or powerful landowner.
Naxalites – ultra-leftist political movement, started in northern part of West Bengal where it appeared as a rebellion against landlords by peasants. Characterised by extreme violence, it originated in the village of Naxal and is now fairly subdued in West Bengal, but still exists in Uttar Pradesh, Bihar and Andhra Pradesh.
Nilakantha – form of Siva with blue throat from swallowing poison that would have destroyed the world.
nilgai – antelope.
nirvana – the ultimate aim of Buddhist existence, a state where one leaves the cycle of existence and does not have to suffer further rebirths.
nizam – hereditary title of the rulers of Hyderabad.
nullah – ditch or small stream.
numda – Rajasthani rug.

Om – sacred invocation representing the absolute essence of the divine principle. For Buddhists, if repeated often enough with conplete concentration, it should lead to a state of emptiness.

padyatra – 'foot journey' made by politicians to raise support at the village level.
pagoda – Buddhist religious monument composed of a solid hemisphere topped by a spire, containing relics of the Buddha; also known as a dagoba, stupa or chedi.
palanquin – box-like enclosure carried on poles on four men's shoulders; the occupant sits inside on a seat.
Pali – the original language in which the Buddhist scriptures were recorded. Scholars still look to the original Pali texts for the true interpretations.
palia – memorial stone.
palli – village.
pan – betel nut plus the chewing additives.
pandit – teacher or wise man. The word is often used in Kashmir where there are many of these. Sometimes used to mean a bookworm.
Parasurama – Rama with the Axe; the sixth incarnation of Vishnu.
Parsi – adherent of the Zoroastrian faith
Parvati – the Mountaineer; another form of Siva's wife.
peepul – fig tree, especially a bo tree.
peon – lowest grade clerical worker.
pice – a quarter of an anna.
pinjrapol – animal hospital maintained by Jains.
pradesh – state.
pranayama – study of breath control.
prasad – food offering.
puja – lit. 'respect'; offering or prayers.
pukkah – 'proper'; very much a Raj-era term.
punkah – cloth fan, swung by pulling a cord.
Puranas – set of 18 encyclopaedic Sanskrit stories, written in verse, relating to the three gods, dating from the period of the Guptas (5th century AD).
purdah – isolation in which some Muslim women are kept.

qila – fort.

Radha – the favourite mistress of Krishna when he lived as Govinda (or Gopala) the cowherd.
raga – any of several conventional patterns

of melody and rhythm that form the basis for freely interpreted compositions.

railhead – station or town at the end of a railway line; termination point.

raj – rule or sovereignty.

raja – king.

Rajput – Hindu warrior castes, royal rulers of Rajasthan.

rakhi – amulet.

Rama – seventh incarnation of Vishnu, his life story being the central theme of the *Ramayana*.

Ramayana – the story of Rama and Sita and their conflict with Ravana. One of India's most well-known legends, it is retold in various forms throughout almost all South-East Asia.

rangoli – design (chalk).

rasta roko – roadblock for protest purposes.

rath – temple chariot or car used in religious festivals.

rathas – rock-cut Dravidian temples at Mahabalipuram.

Ravana – demon king of Lanka; he abducted Sita, and the titanic battle between him and Rama is told in the *Ramayana*.

rawal – nobleman.

rickshaw – two-wheeled vehicle in which one or two passengers are pulled. Only in Calcutta and one or two hill stations do the old human-powered rickshaws still exist. In towns there are now generally bicycle-rickshaws.

Rig-Veda – the original and longest of the four main *Vedas*, or holy Sanskrit texts.

rishi – originally a sage who had the hymns of the *Vedas* revealed to them; these days any poet, philosopher or sage.

road – railway town which serves as a communication point to a larger town off the line, eg, Mt Abu and Abu Road; Kodaikanal and Kodai Road.

Rukmini – wife of Krishna; died on his funeral pyre.

sadar – main.

sadhu – ascetic, holy person, one who is trying to achieve enlightenment. They will usually be addressed as 'swamiji' or 'babaji'.

sagar – lake, reservoir.

sahib – 'lord', title applied to any gentleman and most Europeans.

Saivaite (Shaivaite) – follower of Lord Siva.

Saivism – the worship of Siva.

salwar – trousers worn by Punjabi women.

samadhi – an ecstatic state, sometimes defined as 'ecstasy, trance, communion with God' or 'ecstatic state of mystic consciousness'. Another definition is the place where a holy man was cremated, usually venerated as a shrine.

sangam – meeting of two rivers.

Sankara – Siva as the creator.

sanyasin – like a sadhu.

Saraswati – wife of Brahma, goddess of speech and learning; usually seated on a white swan, holding a veena.

Sati – wife of Siva, became a sati ('honourable woman') by destroying herself by fire. These days it applies to any woman who does this. Although banned a century or so ago, occasionally sati is still performed.

satsang – discourse by a swami or guru.

satyagraha – nonviolent protest involving a fast, popularised by Gandhi. From Sanskrit, literally 'insistence on truth'.

sepoy – private in the infantry.

serai – place for accommodation of travellers, specifically a caravanserai where camel caravans once stopped.

shakti – creative energies perceived as female deities; Shaktism is a cult which adheres to this notion.

shikar – hunting expedition, now virtually extinct.

shikara – gondola-like boat used on Dal Lake in Kashmir.

shirting – the material shirts are made out of.

sikhara – Hindu temple-spire or temple.

singh – lion, name of the Rajput caste; adopted by Sikhs as a surname.

sirdar (sardar) – leader or commander.

Sita – in the *Vedas* the goddess of agriculture, but more commonly associated with the *Ramayana*, where she is Rama's wife and was abducted by Ravana and carted off to Lanka.

sitar – Indian stringed instrument.

Siva – (Shiva) the destroyer; also the creator, in which form he is worshipped in the form of the *lingam* (a kind of phallic symbol).

Skanda – another name for Kartikiya, the god of war.

sof – aniseed seeds; comes with the bill after a meal and you chew a pinch of it as a digestive.

soma – intoxicating drink derived from a plant, features prominently in the *Rig-Veda*, raised to the status of a deity for its power to heal, provide wealth and impart immortality; in the *Puranas* it is taken to mean the moon.

sonam – karma built up in successive reincarnations.

sri (sree, shri, shree) – honorific prefix, but these days the Indian equivalent of Mr or Ms.

Subhadra – sister of Krishna as Jagganath; had an incestuous relationship with him.

Subrahmanya – another name for Kartikiya, god of war.

sudra – low Hindu caste.

sufi – ascetic Muslim mystic.

suiting – the material suits are made out of.

Surya – the sun, a major deity in the Vedas.

sutra – string; a set of rules expressed in verse. Many exist, the most famous being the Kama Sutra.

swami – title given to initiated monks; means 'lord of the self'.

swaraj – independence.

sweeper – lowest caste servant, who performs the most menial of tasks.

syce – groom.

tabla – a pair of kettle drums which are played with the fingers.

taluk – district.

tank – artificial water-storage lake.

Tantric Buddhism – Tibetan Buddhism with strong sexual and occult overtones.

tatty – woven grass screen which is wetted and hung outside windows in the hot season to provide a remarkably effective system of air-cooling.

tempo – noisy three-wheeler public transport vehicle.

thakur – Hindu caste.

thali – traditional south Indian and Gujarati 'all-you-can-eat' vegetarian meal; very widespread and an excellent, tasty meal.

thanka – rectangular Tibetan painting on cloth.

Theravada – small-vehicle Buddhism.

thirathyatara – a king of pilgrimage.

thug – follower of Thuggee, religious-inspired ritual murderers centred in Madhya Pradesh in the last century.

tiffin – snack, particularly around lunchtime.

tilak – the spot devout Hindus put on their foreheads with *tika* powder.

tirthankars – the 24 great Jain teachers.

toddy – alcoholic drink, tapped from the palm tree.

tonga – two-wheeled horse or pony carriage.

tope – grove of trees, usually mangoes.

topi – hat, much used by the British in the Raj era.

torana – architrave over temple entrance.

Trimurti – Triple Form; the Hindu triad – Brahma, Siva and Vishnu.

Tripitaka – the classical Theravada Buddhist scriptures, which are divided into three categories, hence its name the Three Baskets. The Mahayanists have other scriptures in addition to the Tripitaka.

tripolia – triple gateway.

Uma – Light; Siva's consort.

Untouchable – lowest caste or 'casteless' for whom the most menial tasks are reserved. The name derives from the belief that higher castes risk defilement if they touch one. Formerly known as *Harijan*, now *Dalit*.

Upanishads – Esoteric Doctrine; ancient texts forming part of the *Vedas* (although of a later date), they delve into weighty matters such as the nature of the universe and the soul.

Valmiki – author of the *Ramayana*.

Vamana – the fifth incarnation (avatar) of Vishnu, as the dwarf.

varna – the concept of caste.

Varuna – supreme Vedic god.

Vedas – the Hindu sacred books; a collection of hymns composed in pre-classical Sanskrit during the second millennium BC and divided into four books: *Rig-Veda*, *Yajur-Veda*, *Sama-Veda* and *Atharva-Veda*.

veena – Indian stringed drone instrument.
vihara – monastery.
vimana – principle part of a Hindu temple.
Vishnu – the third of the Hindu trinity of gods along with Brahma and Siva, the preserver and restorer, who so far has nine avatars; these, in order, are: the fish Matsya; the tortoise Kurma; the wild boar Naraha; the man-lion Narasimha; the dwarf Vamana; the Brahmin Parashu-Rama; Rama (of *Ramayana* fame); Krishna, and the Buddha.

wallah – person involved with a specific thing. Can be added onto almost anything:

thus dhobi-wallah (clothes washer), taxi-wallah etc.

wazir – prime minister.

yagna – religious self-mortification, such as a snake-yagna where you sit in a cage full of snakes trying to get yourself in the *Guinness Book of Records*. Being interred alive is another popular yagna feat.
yakshi – maiden.
yatra – pilgrimage.
yoni – vagina, female fertility symbol.

zamindar – landowner.
zenana – area of a high-class Muslim household where the women are secluded.

Index

TEXT

Map references are in **bold** type.

Thanks

Thanks to the many travellers who wrote in with helpful hints, useful advice, and interesting and funny stories.

Jens Aagaard-Hansen (Dk), Nick Abraham, RC Sharma Vyakul Acharya (I), Jan & Grada Achten (Nl), Linda Acton (UK), John Adair (C), Paul Adams (UK), Rachel Adams (UK), SL Adelson (C), Suyil Adesaxa (I), Maree de Adman (NZ), Chris Aertssen (B), Paul Affleck (Aus), Michael Agelasto, Peter Ager (Aus), Qamar Ahmed (I), Bill Aitken, Kathleen Akin (USA), Clement Alan (UK), Walter Albrecht (CH), Esther Alderson, Joseph Alexander (USA), Theo Alkemade (Nl), Hamish Allan, Kelly Allen (C), Duke & Edith Alley (Aus), John & Karen Alliott (UK), Ed Almstead (USA), Eric Alsruhe (F), Urs Altmann (Aus), Jean Charles Ambroise (F), Yoni Amir (Isr), Hadar Amrami (I), Anando (I), Dalia Anavian (Jap), Paul Anderjon (Aus), Helle Andersen (Dk), Katherine Andersen (Dk), Richardson Anderson (USA), Paul Anderton (Aus), Ayesha & Tariq Ansari, Zoe Apostolides (G), Michie Araki (I), Peter Arbenz (CH), Matti Ariel (Isr), Elizabeth Arndt (UK), Anne Arrowsmith (USA), Genevieve Arter (Aus), Eva & Casimir Arunbruster (A), Michael Ash, Kevin Ashton (UK), William Atkins (USA), Melina Auerbach (C), Simonetta Avigdor (It), Derek Aylen (C), S Aylward (IRE)

Brian & Sandra Bach (USA), Steen Bachmann (Dk), Norman Backhaus (CH), Peter Bailey (Sw), Philip Baker (UK), J Bakker (Aus), Alan Balchin (UK), Lizabeth Ball (C), Jane Bannister (UK), Monish Bansal (I), S Barclay (Aus), Freda Barfoot (UK), Rachel Barker (UK), Kim Barnhardt (C), Tim Barraclaigh (UK), Jean Bartam (Thai), Amanda Bartlett (UK), David Bashin (USA), Bonnie Baskin (USA), Kate Bassford (UK), Emma Batchelor (UK), Malcolm Bates (UK), Thomas Bator (C), Maarten Bax (Nl), Lucy Beaghen (UK), Agnes Beaton (Aus), Lynda Beck (Aus), Sarah Beck (UK), Esti Becker (Isr), Karin Beckers (Aus); Sally Beeston (UK), Mark Behan (USA), David Bell (Aus), Derek Bell (Aus), Georgina Benison (UK), Jonnie Benjiman (UK), Rolf Bennhagen (Sw), Cristina Bernat, Catherine Berset (CH), J & J Bertheau (C), Michael Berube (C), Kirthi Betai (I), Malcolm Betts (UK), Samir Bhagat (I), Meher J Bhandara (I), Pratap Bhandari (I), Mani Bhushan (I), Amardeep Bindra (I), Valerie Birt (UK), Gunther Bisges (D), Liz & Mike Bissett (UK), T & Y Bitan (ISR), Oliver Black (UK), Mark Blackburn (UK), Jeremy Blades (UK), Sebastien Blais-Ouellette (C), Trevor Blake (C), Mordechay Blau (Isr), A Block (B), H Blom (Nl), Anders Blomqvist (Sw), Diana Boaler (UK), Neil Bodman, Robert Bogucki (USA), Michael Boker (D), Stefan Boldt (D), Patrick Boman (Fr), Steve Bond (UK), Angelica Bonfanti (It), JM Bora (I), Lianne Bosch (Nl), Federica Boschetti (F),

Nirmal Bose (I), Jan Botman (Nl), Martin Bottenberg (Nl), Bound (UK), Daniel Bpksjoe (Sw), Manon Braam (NI), Fadhilla Bradley (USA), Sarah Bradshaw (UK), Susie Bradshaw, Diane Brady (C), Roger Bramble (UK), Lisa Brandt (USA), Francis Brannigan (UK), Rob & Laura Breen (Aus), Andrew Brem (UK), Anita Brennan (UK), Thomas Brennessel (D), Chris Brereton (UK), Maureen Brew (Aus), Sarah Brindle (UK), Margreet Brinkkemper (Nl), Michael Bromilow (Aus), Karen Brott (Aus), Nicola Brown (UK), Lance Jay Brown (USA), Sally Brown (UK), Henry Brownrigg (UK), Giampadlo Brunazzo (UK), Judith Bruno (USA), Emma Bryand (UK), Richard Buckland (UK), Edward Buckland (UK), Roberto Buizza (It), Sara Bunge (C), Rob Burford (Aus), Nieves Burgos (Sp), Catherine Burke (UK), Joanna Busvine (UK), Joyce & Len Butcher (UK), Pam Buthwell (UK), Jo Butler (UK), Candace Butler (USA), Daniel Butler (USA), Pam Buttwell (UK), Andreas Martin Butz (D), Lawrence Buytaert (F), Christine Byrne (NZ)

Nadia Cafritza (Aus), Judith Cahill (UK), Brad Cain (UK), Katie B Calhoun (USA), Jenny Calvert (UK), Thomas Camacho (USA), John Cambridge (NZ), Robert Campbell (UK), Lorraine Campbell (UK), Darianna Cardilli (UK), Donna Cariss (Aus), Linda & Russell Carling (Aus), Ruby Carmichael (UK), Jacob Caron (Nl), Stephen Cartwright (UK), Beatrice Carusiello (Arg), Louise Case (UK), Cipriana Casetti (It), Charles Casselman (C), Glenn Cassie (C), Alan Castle (UK), Diane Caulkett (UK), I Cem Kocak (USA), Ashok Chadha (I), Ashok Kumar Chadha (I), Arun Chadha (I), Subhash Chandra (I), Deirdre Chapman (UK), Rob Chapman (Aus), Martin Charlton (UK), Elaine Charteris (C), Lesley Charters (UK), SW Chastain, Tapan Chatterjee (I), Tapan Chatterjee (I), G M Chatterjee (I), Nicholas Chatzitsolis (G), A Cheema (I), Kati Chellew (UK), Oby J Cherian (I), Jane Chester (UK), Kate Childs (UK), Mark Chilvers (UK), Jeremy Chipperfield (UK), Andrew Chisholm (USA), Trina Cholewicki (C), Gong Yee Choon (Sin), S Roy Choudhury (I), Chowringhee Hotel (Ind), Mario Cittadini (It), Ruth Clapp (USA), Alex Clapson (I), Marg & Michael Clark (Aus), James Clausing (Aus), Mark Clayton (UK), Philip Clegg (UK), David Clennett (UK), Tim Clifton (UK), John & Joyce Clinch (Aus), Jem Cloot (D), Antonina Cloquell (Sp), Tim Coates (USA), Sandra Cock (Aus), Rachel Codd (Aus), Richard Codlin (D), Esther Coelho (I), Sue Coldridge (UK), Mike Collenette (UK), Mina Collins, George Collins (NZ), Glen Collis (Aus), Jim Conboy (UK), Sean Conneally (Ire), Maureen Connolly (UK), Jacqueline Connors (C), Ursula Connu (CH), Martin Cooke (UK), Jeannette Coppiens (Nl), Annette & Joe Coppola (Aus), Sean Corcoran, Pam Cordell (USA), Bob Corkyn (UK), Bernard Cornelissen (Nl), Denys Correll (Aus), Brendan Corrigan (Aus), Lucie Cote (C), Mandy Cotteleer (Nl), Frederique Coulan (F),

(UK), Ian Saunders (Aus), Andreas Sauner (D), DC Saxena (I), SS Saxena (I), Jane Scarriot (USA), Christian Schlaepfer (Mex), Karin Schlapbach (CH), Karin Schneider (Sw), Anja Schnell (D), CA Scholten (Nl), Dieter Scholz (A), WJ Schouten (Nl), Marilynn M Schroeder (USA), Georg Schwartzel (D), Daniel Schweid (USA), Benjamin Scrimgeour (UK), Anne Scruton (UK), Reed Searle (UK), Dawn Seguin (C), Olarn Seriniyom (Thai), Natasha Serventy (Aus), KK Seth (I), AJ Severs (NZ), Donald Sewell (USA), Patricia Seymour, Jina Shah (USA), Hotel Shahansh (I), Sigal Shalev (Isr), Chen & Yuval Shamir (Isr), Yogi Prakash Shankar Vyas (I), Anil Sharma (I), Rajesh Sharma (I), J Sharpe (UK), Barbara Shaw (USA), Evan Shaw, Helena Shaw (UK), G Shepherd (Aus), Joseph Sherman (Isr), Mirchoomal R Shroff (I), Daniel Shurman (USA), Jan Erik Sigdell (CH), BW Sigg, Siru Sihvonen (Fin), Colin Silove, Alan Sim (UK), Chris Sim (Aus), Simon & Keith (US), Eric Simonot, AJ Simpson (UK), Dorothy Simpson (UK), Kathi Simpson (USA), A Singh (I), Amrendra Singh (I), Asha Singh (I), Bhavna Singh (I), Chandrashekhar Singh (I), Digvijay Singh (I), Harpreet Singh (I), Iqbal Singh (I), Kishan Singh (I), Mahendra Singh (I), Ravindra Singh (I), RP Singh (I), Sidarth Singh (I), Th Sunder Singh (I), Carmine Sinno (It), Helen Sirkin (USA), June Skelley (UK), Susanne Slangen (D), Ken Slatter (UK), Carolyn Sleightholme (UK), Cliff Sloane (USA), Danielle Smaling (Nl), Andrew Smith (UK), DJD Smith (UK), EF Smith (I), Greg C Smith (C), Lisa Smith (UK), Pat Smith (UK), Ellen Snowball (UK), Elston Soares (I), Eliana Soares (Bra), Julia Sobolewska (CH), J Sommerville, Tony Sonet (USA), Sameer Sood (I), G Souriappan (I), Manuel de Sousa (P), Thomas Spang (D), Heather & Ian Spence (Aus), David Spence (UK), Hilary & Andrew Spenceley (UK), Emma Spencer (UK), Penny Spiller (UK), Aruce Spilman (UK), Peter Spilsbury (UK), Brian Spink (UK), Marie Spodeck (USA), Ann Spowart Taylor (UK), Devabhaktuni Srikrishna (I), Finn Stahl (Sw), Kim Stalidzans (Aus), Linda & James Stallone (USA), Debbie Stamp (USA), Sara Stanier (UK), Leona Starkey (Can), Dominic Stayne (UK), Michael Steenhart (NZ), Maggie Stephen (UK), David Stephens, Mary Sterling (USA), Anna Stern (USA), T & J Sternau (Isr), David Steuerman (C), David Stevens (UK), Ella & Erik Stevens (Nl), Kay Stevens (UK), Henry Stevenson (UK), Cathy Stewart (Aus), Tim Stickland (UK), Jan Stiebert (D), Sue & John Stillman, TG Stones (UK), Isabelle Storder (B), Thea Straathof (I), Olivier Streichenberger (F), Mark Strevett (UK), Petra Strombom (Sw), Berno Strootman (Nl), Debbie Stuart (UK), Donal Stuart (UK), Swallow & Mike Stuart (HK), Andreas Sturm (Aus), Ravi Subramanian (I), Shelley Sugarman (C), Ajit (Dicky) Sukhija (I), Hatty Sumption (UK), Mycall Sunanda (USA), Norman Sung (C), Jane Surita (Isr), Irving D Suss (USA), Susan Sutcliffe (UK), Rosalind Sutton (UK),

Melissa Sweet (Aus), Maxine Swensson (Aus), Sandor Szigethy (Sw)

Sabrina & Alain Tacot-Descombes (CH), Vesa Taiveaho (Fin), Francesca Tanca (I), Gavin Tanguay (UK), Dharmesh Tanna (UK), Claudia Taranto (Aus), Heidi Tarr (USA), Andrew Taylor (UK), A Tennant (UK), Hotel Sandegh (I), Maya Hotel (Indo), Ramu (I), Louise Theophanous (UK), C Thomas (I), Vincent G Thomas (USA), Claire Thompson (UK), Dave Thompson (UK), DJ Thomson (SA), Fiona Thompson (UK), Niobe Thompson (C), Peter Thorpe (UK), James Timms (UK), Christine Timson (UK), Barbel Tobler (CH), Arjen Tolsma (Nl), Mike Tonkin (UK), Caroline J Tosswill (UK), Christine Townsend (UK), Sajive Trehan (I), Thomas Trenatinaglia (D), Jenny Tribe (Aus), Myfawny Tristram (UK), Andrew Truslove (UK), Helen Tsoi (UK), Sharpa Tulku (I), Ellen Fisher Turk (USA), Richard Turner (UK), Michael Turton (USA), Fred Tustin (C), Kenneth Twyford (UK), Martin Tyneman (UK)

Kate & Ross Umbers (Aus)

Carmen Vallis (UK), Anne & Hein van Adrichen (Nl), Veronique van Bambeke (B), Annette van Citlers (Nl), LJ van Dam (Aus), Hans & Joke van der Louw (Nl), Werner van der Meer (Nl), Marie-Anne van der Plaetsh (B), Matthias van der Reyden (Nl), Maarten van der Sman (Nl), Marieke van Doorn (Nl), Rene van Gelder (Nl), Klaas van Giffen (Nl), Jan van Heiningen (Nl), Peter van Ooijen (Nl), Ch van Vigt (Nl), Ton van Wijk (Nl), Chris Vanderheyden (B), ST Varadarajan (I), Radhakrishna Varma (I), Klaus Vellguth (D), Frans Verdurman (Nl), Mariette & Eric Verheijen (Nl), Jacques Vigne (Fr), K Vijayakumar (I), Sabine Volchok (USA), Mirjam Vossen (Nl), Yogi PS Vyas (I), Jeanet Vyphuizen (Nl)

Ramakant C Wadkar (I), RC Wadkar (I), Carina Wagenaar (Nl), Michael Wakefield (UK), Ant Walker (UK), Frances Wall (C), Gary Wallach (USA), Clare Ward (UK), David Ward (USA), Michael Wardle (UK), E Waring (UK), Andrew Warnington (UK), Anne Warren (Aus), Naomi Waterman (Aus), Rachel Waters (Aus), Polly Watkins (Aus), Juliet Watkinson (UK), Neil Watts (UK), Aline Wauters (B), Vincent Weafer (Aus), Edwin Wecker (Aus), Rosaleen Weddle (USA), Charles Weilman (USA), Darna Weinstein (Nl), Geoff Welby (Aus), Peter Wells (UK), Harriet Wells (UK), C & H Wermuth (CH), Bob Whelan (Aus), James White (USA), Max White (Aus), Peter Whitehead (UK), Rose Whyte (NZ), Jez Wicken (UK), Kathleen Wigan (UK), Catherine Wigglesworth (UK), Jackie Wigh (Aus), C Wigram (HK), Cindy & Mark Wilcox (USA), Janice Wildbone (UK), Janet Wilkinson (NZ), Holger Wille (D), Carl & Katie Williams (Aus), Porscha Williams (USA), Randolph A Williams (UK), Simon Williams (Aus), Charlotte Willis (UK), Steve Willis, T Willis (UK), Derek Wilson (UK), Nick Wilson (UK), Tom Wilson (USA), Stephan Winkler (D), Jeremy Witherow (NZ), Ross Witherspoon (Aus), Kristel & Luc Wittourk (B),

Keep in touch!

We love hearing from you and think you'd like to hear from us.

The Lonely Planet Newsletter covers the when, where, how and what of travel. (AND it's free!)

When...is the right time to see reindeer in Finland?
Where...can you hear the best palm-wine music in Ghana?
How...do you get from Asunción to Areguá by steam train?
What...should you leave behind to avoid hassles with customs in Iran?

To join our mailing list just contact us at any of our offices. (details below)

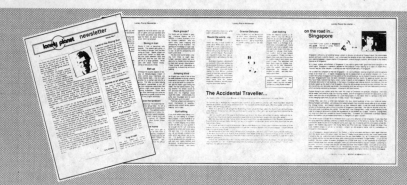

Every issue includes:

* *a letter from Lonely Planet founders Tony and Maureen Wheeler*
* *travel diary from a Lonely Planet author - find out what it's really like out on the road*
* *feature article on an important and topical travel issue*
* *a selection of recent letters from our readers*
* *the latest travel news from all over the world*
* *details on Lonely Planet's new and forthcoming releases*

Also available Lonely Planet T-shirts. 100% heavy weight cotton (S, M, L, XL)

LONELY PLANET PUBLICATIONS
Australia: PO Box 617, Hawthorn, 3122, Victoria (tel: 03-819 1877)
USA: Embarcadero West, 155 Filbert Street, Suite 251, Oakland, CA 94607 (tel: 510-893 8555)
UK: Devonshire House, 12 Barley Mow Passage, Chiswick, London W4 4PH (tel: 081-742 3161)

Guides to the Indian Subcontinent

Bangladesh – a travel survival kit
This practical guide – the only English-language guide to Bangladesh – encourages travellers to take another look at this often-neglected but beautiful land.

Karakoram Highway the high road to China – a travel survival kit
Travel in the footsteps of Alexander the Great and Marco Polo on the Karakoram Highway, following the ancient and fabled Silk Road. This comprehensive guide also covers villages and treks away from the highway.

Kashmir, Ladakh & Zanskar – a travel survival kit
Detailed information on three contrasting Himalayan regions in the Indian state of Jammu & Kashmir – the narrow valley of Zanskar, the isolated 'little Tibet' of Ladakh, and the stunningly beautiful Vale of Kashmir.

Nepal – a travel survival kit
Travel information on every road-accessible area in Nepal, including the Terai. This practical guidebook also includes introductions to trekking, white-water rafting and mountain biking.

Pakistan – a travel survival kit
Discover 'the unknown land of the Indus' with this informative guidebook – from bustling Karachi to ancient cities and tranquil mountain valleys.

Sri Lanka – a travel survival kit
Some parts of Sri Lanka are off limits to visitors, but this guidebook uses the restriction as an incentive to explore other areas more closely – making the most of friendly people, good food and pleasant places to stay – all at reasonable cost.

Tibet – a travel survival kit
The fabled mountain-land of Tibet was one of the last areas of the world to become accessible to travellers. This guide has full details on this remote and fascinating region, including the border crossing to Nepal.

Trekking in the Indian Himalaya
All the advice you'll need for planning and equipping a trek, including detailed route descriptions for some of the world's most exciting treks.

Trekking in the Nepal Himalaya
Complete trekking information for Nepal, including day-by-day route descriptions and detailed maps – a wealth of advice for both independent and group trekkers.

Also available:
Hindi/Urdu phrasebook, Nepal phrasebook and Sri Lanka phrasebook.

Lonely Planet Guidebooks

Lonely Planet guidebooks cover every accessible part of Asia as well as Australia, the Pacific, South America, Africa, the Middle East, Europe and parts of North America. There are five series: *travel survival kits*, covering a country for a range of budgets; *shoestring guides* with compact information for low-budget travel in a major region; *walking guides*; *city guides* and *phrasebooks*.

Australia & the Pacific
Australia
Bushwalking in Australia
Islands of Australia's Great Barrier Reef
Fiji
Melbourne city guide
Micronesia
New Caledonia
New Zealand
Tramping in New Zealand
Papua New Guinea
Bushwalking in Papua New Guinea
Papua New Guinea phrasebook
Rarotonga & the Cook Islands
Samoa
Solomon Islands
Sydney city guide
Tahiti & French Polynesia
Tonga
Vanuatu
Victoria

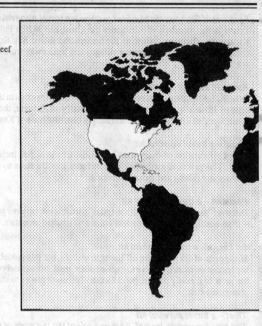

South-East Asia
Bali & Lombok
Bangkok city guide
Cambodia
Indonesia
Indonesia phrasebook
Laos
Malaysia, Singapore & Brunei
Myanmar (Burma)
Burmese phrasebook
Philippines
Pilipino phrasebook
Singapore city guide
South-East Asia on a shoestring
Thailand
Thai phrasebook
Vietnam
Vietnamese phrasebook

North-East Asia
China
Beijing city guide
Mandarin Chinese phrasebook
Hong Kong, Macau & Canton
Japan
Japanese phrasebook
Korea
Korean phrasebook
Mongolia
North-East Asia on a shoestring
Seoul city guide
Taiwan
Tibet
Tibet phrasebook
Tokyo city guide

West Asia
Trekking in Turkey
Turkey
Turkish phrasebook
West Asia on a shoestring

Middle East
Arab Gulf States
Egypt & the Sudan
Arabic (Egyptian) phrasebook
Iran
Israel
Jordan & Syria
Yemen

Indian Ocean
Madagascar & Comoros
Maldives & Islands of the East Indian Ocean
Mauritius, Réunion & Seychelles

Mail Order

Lonely Planet guidebooks are distributed worldwide. They are also available by mail order from Lonely Planet, so if you have difficulty finding a title please write to us. US and Canadian residents should write to Embarcadero West, 155 Filbert St, Suite 251, Oakland CA 94607, USA; European residents should write to Devonshire House, 12 Barley Mow Passage, Chiswick, London W4 4PH; and residents of other countries to PO Box 617, Hawthorn, Victoria 3122, Australia.

Indian Subcontinent
Bangladesh
India
Hindi/Urdu phrasebook
Trekking in the Indian Himalaya
Karakoram Highway
Kashmir, Ladakh & Zanskar
Nepal
Trekking in the Nepal Himalaya
Nepal phrasebook
Pakistan
Sri Lanka
Sri Lanka phrasebook

Africa
Africa on a shoestring
Central Africa
East Africa
Trekking in East Africa
Kenya
Swahili phrasebook
Morocco, Algeria & Tunisia
Arabic (Moroccan) phrasebook
South Africa, Lesotho & Swaziland
Zimbabwe, Botswana & Namibia
West Africa

Central America
Baja California
Central America on a shoestring
Costa Rica
La Ruta Maya
Mexico

Europe
Dublin city guide
Eastern Europe on a shoestring
Eastern Europe phrasebook
Finland
Hungary
Iceland, Greenland & the Faroe Islands
Ireland
Italy
Mediterranean Europe on a shoestring
Mediterranean Europe phrasebook
Poland
Scandinavian & Baltic Europe on a shoestring
Scandinavian Europe phrasebook
Switzerland
Trekking in Spain
Trekking in Greece
USSR
Russian phrasebook
Western Europe on a shoestring
Western Europe phrasebook

North America
Alaska
Canada
Hawaii

South America
Argentina, Uruguay & Paraguay
Bolivia
Brazil
Brazilian phrasebook
Chile & Easter Island
Colombia
Ecuador & the Galápagos Islands
Latin American Spanish phrasebook
Peru
Quechua phrasebook
South America on a shoestring
Trekking in the Patagonian Andes

The Lonely Planet Story

Lonely Planet published its first book in 1973 in response to the numerous 'How did you do it?' questions Maureen and Tony Wheeler were asked after driving, bussing, hitching, sailing and railing their way from England to Australia.

Written at a kitchen table and hand collated, trimmed and stapled, *Across Asia on the Cheap* became an instant local bestseller, inspiring thoughts of another book.

Eighteen months in South-East Asia resulted in their second guide, *South-East Asia on a shoestring*, which they put together in a backstreet Chinese hotel in Singapore in 1975. The 'yellow bible' as it quickly became known to backpackers around the world, soon became *the* guide to the region. It has sold well over half a million copies and is now in its 7th edition, still retaining its familiar yellow cover.

Today there are over 120 Lonely Planet titles in print – books that have that same adventurous approach to travel as those early guides; books that 'assume you know how to get your luggage off the carousel' as one reviewer put it.

Although Lonely Planet initially specialised in guides to Asia, they now cover most regions of the world, including the Pacific, South America, Africa, the Middle East and Europe. The list of *walking guides* and *phrasebooks* (for 'unusual' languages such as Quechua, Swahili, Nepalese and Egyptian Arabic) is also growing rapidly.

The emphasis continues to be on travel for independent travellers. Tony and Maureen still travel for several months of each year and play an active part in the writing, updating and quality control of Lonely Planet's guides.

They have been joined by over 50 authors, 54 staff – mainly editors, cartographers, & designers – at our office in Melbourne, Australia, 10 at our US office in Oakland, California and another three at our office in London to handle sales for Britain, Europe and Africa. In 1992 Lonely Planet opened an editorial office in Paris. Travellers themselves also make a valuable contribution to the guides through the feedback we receive in thousands of letters each year.

The people at Lonely Planet strongly believe that travellers can make a positive contribution to the countries they visit, both through their appreciation of the countries' culture, wildlife and natural features, and through the money they spend. In addition, the company makes a direct contribution to the countries and regions it covers. Since 1986 a percentage of the income from each book has been donated to ventures such as famine relief in Africa; aid projects in India; agricultural projects in Central America; Greenpeace's efforts to halt French nuclear testing in the Pacific and Amnesty International. In 1993 $100,000 was donated to such causes.

Lonely Planet's basic travel philosophy is summed up in Tony Wheeler's comment, 'Don't worry about whether your trip will work out. Just go!'